THE LETTERS OF
MRS GASKELL

THE LETTERS OF
MRS GASKELL

edited by
J. A. V. Chapple and Arthur Pollard

MANDOLIN

This edition published by MANDOLIN,
an imprint of Manchester University Press
Oxford Road, Manchester M13 9NR, UK
and Room 400, 175 Fifth Avenue, New York, NY 10010, USA

First published 1966 by Manchester University Press

Distributed exclusively in the USA
by St. Martin's Press, Inc., 175 Fifth Avenue, New York, NY 10010,USA

British Library Cataloguing-in-Publication Data
A catalogue record for this book is available from the British Library

Library of Congress Cataloging-in-Publication Data applied for

ISBN 1 901341 03 8 *paperback*

Printed in Great Britain
by Clays Ltd, St Ives Plc

To
OUR PARENTS

CONTENTS

ACKNOWLEDGEMENTS

It would be impossible to record every detail of the help and encouragement that we have received during the years spent in preparing this first edition of the letters of Mrs Elizabeth C. Gaskell. What follows is our attempt to acknowledge our major debts.

We are most grateful to Mrs Trevor Jones, Mrs Gaskell's oldest surviving descendant in the direct line, who has given her permission for the publication of these letters and to the private and institutional owners of them for allowing us free access to their texts. (Names and titles are separately recorded in Appendix B.)

We are deeply indebted to many generous helpers who have undertaken the often difficult task of examining original letters when we were unable to see them for ourselves: Mr John Alden of Boston Public Library, Mrs Helen Arnold, Mr John C. Broderick of the Library of Congress, Mr Rodney G. Dennis III of The Houghton Library (Harvard University), Mr D. W. Evans of Birmingham University Library, Ronald L. Fingerson of the State University of Iowa Libraries, Mrs Suzanne N. Griffiths of the University of Illinois Library, Mrs Christine D. Hathaway of Brown University Library, Mrs Alison K. Kerr of Cornell University Library, Mrs C. M. Lewis of McGill University Library, Jean Preston of the Henry E. Huntington Library and Art Gallery, Mr Richard E. Priest of the Pierpont Morgan Library, Mr J. S. Ritchie of the National Library of Scotland, a staff-member of Rutgers University Library, Mr J. G. Sharps, Mr William B. Todd of the University of Texas Library, Mr Alexander D. Wainwright of Princeton University Library, Mr Brooke Whiting of the University of California (Los Angeles) Library, Mr R. N. Williams and the Manuscript Department of The Historical Society of Pennsylvania, and Miss Marjorie G. Wynne of Yale University Library. We have, quite apart from this, invariably met with courtesy and ready assistance from the staffs of all libraries and institutions we were able to visit in person and to which we wrote. Manchester Central Library also allowed us the use of a special study carrel in which to keep our transcripts and files.

For making available financial help towards the costs of preparation of this edition we must thank the Vice-Chancellor of Manchester University, Sir William Mansfield Cooper, Professor Frank Kermode and Manchester University Press.

We are greatly indebted to the following for aid and advice of many kinds: Professor J. D. Barry, Mr B. S. Bloomfield, Mr J. L. Bolton, Mr George A. Carter, Mr Herbert Cahoon, Mrs D. Dandy, Mr Ronald Hall, Mr S. Horrocks, Mrs Madeline House, Mr K. W. Humphreys, Mr Arnold Hyde, Professor Frank Kermode, the Reverend R. D. Mallet, Mr D. I. Masson, Miss D. L. Minard, H. Hans von Mohl, Mr James M. Osborn, Mr S. Roberts, Professor C. R. Sandars, Mr F. W. Saunders, Mr J. G. Sharps, the Reverend A. Smith, Dr Moses Tyson, Miss Winifred Village, Professor D. Welland, Professor A. Stanton Whitfield, Dr Margaret Wright, Mr D. F. Cook and our colleagues at Manchester University.

Finally, we have to thank our respective wives and Miss Judith Burt, Mrs N. Chappell, Miss Frances Mawson and Mrs Lynne Wolfenden for constant help with the more tedious, though absolutely essential, tasks of getting material ready for the press.

INTRODUCTION

I

'Don't you like reading letters? I do, so much. Not grand formal letters; but such as Mme Mohl's, I mean' (195).[1] Mrs Gaskell knew the fascination of other people's letters. Writing to her sister-in-law, Mrs Charles Holland (née Elizabeth Gaskell), she wondered 'if odd bundles of old letters would amuse you in your confinement' (145). She also recognised the importance of letters written by famous people. Her own biography of Charlotte Brontë relies substantially upon its subject's correspondence. It does so, because Mrs Gaskell realised the supreme value of letting Charlotte speak for herself. In this way, she knew, her readers would gain a better idea of Charlotte Brontë than from anything she might herself say. The unique revelation which letters provide and the intrinsic attractiveness of Mrs Gaskell's own writings in this mode will serve, it is hoped, sufficiently to justify the publication of this work.

At the same time the editors are conscious of what might have been Mrs Gaskell's own feelings on the subject. She had set her face against any biography in her lifetime (570, 571) and two of her daughters sought assiduously to prevent any being written after her death. G. A. Payne, presumably repeating an oral tradition, ascribed this to a desire on Mrs Gaskell's part expressed after hearing that Thackeray had stated a similar wish to his daughters (*Mrs Gaskell, A Brief Biography*, 1929, p. 14). It may also be that Mrs Gaskell remembered the troubles that surround the writing of biography from her own unhappy experience with the *Life of Charlotte Brontë*: 'Oh! if once I have finished this biography, catch me writing another!' (318). She appears to have been opposed not only to a biography, but even to the preservation of some at least of her letters. She bade her eldest daughter Marianne to burn those she received (185), and she tried carefully to separate those to her publisher George Smith which he might keep from those she wanted destroyed: '*Don't* send them to the terrible warehouse where the 20,000 letters a year are kept' (324). Fortunately for posterity some of her correspondents did not take her at her word. Chief among these was Marianne, and it is

[1] References to letters will be given by the number assigned to them in the main text below.

through the very great kindness of Marianne's grand-daughter, Mrs Trevor Jones, that it has been possible to publish this work. Appropriately at Knutsford she showed to one of the editors, Mr Pollard, the substantial collection of letters in her possession and hitherto not known to scholars. This volume took its origin from that occasion, and the encouragement of Mrs Trevor Jones played an essential part in the inception of the task. Nevertheless, we still recognise that it is possible that this edition would not have pleased Mrs Gaskell herself. We also feel that a public figure by the very act of becoming so forfeits much of his or her right to privacy. When that public figure takes on historical importance, we think that later generations should feel even less inhibited in their investigations. It might be claimed that only those aspects of the subject's career which influenced the public role should be matter for enquiry. If that is admitted, there follows the immediate difficulty of deciding what is relevant and what is not. The case of the author is here most difficult of all, for out of the inmost thoughts and feelings and out of the intimate and even apparently insignificant experiences the stuff of the writings takes its birth. Whatever be the ultimate judgement of this question, the letters discovered and printed here have more than justified the belief with which the editors set out, namely, that they would be worth collecting and that together they would enhance the reputation which Mrs Gaskell already so deservedly enjoys as a woman of character and a considerable writer.

The six hundred and fifty odd letters in this edition are the fruits of a search which found a ready and heartening response from owners, both individuals and institutions, in this country and America. The principal collections are in the possession of Mrs Trevor Jones, Sir John Murray, the Universities of Leeds (Brotherton Collection), Harvard, Princeton and Yale, and the Pierpont Morgan Library. A complete list of owners and locations is set out in Appendix B, and the editors are grateful for the kindness and generosity they almost everywhere encountered. Mrs Gaskell's principal correspondents were Marianne, her friend Eliza ('Tottie') Fox, her publisher George Smith and the young American friend of her later years, Charles Eliot Norton. There are also smaller groups of letters to her sister-in-law Elizabeth Gaskell, later Mrs Charles Holland, to her first publisher Chapman, to Lady Kay-Shuttleworth and to Catherine Winkworth. It is difficult to believe that only those letters have survived which are here printed to a friend so close as Miss Winkworth. The doubt is accentuated by the fact that Elizabeth Haldane (*Mrs Gaskell and Her Friends*, 1931) knew of and had access to letters which have eluded our enquiries in spite of repeated attempts to find them. This is but one instance of our disappointment.[1] After what Mrs Gaskell said of Madame Mohl's letters, it is sad to have none of Mrs Gaskell's missives to that remarkable Englishwoman in Paris, with whom she shared such an intimate friendship. The search for these letters involved enquiries in Paris, Basle, Grenoble, Munich and Berlin, only for us to discover that it is presumed that any letters there may have been were destroyed in the bombing of the last-named city in 1944. On the same day as this information was received the editors were also told that any Gaskell papers which the family's solicitors in Manchester may have held (and there was reason for thinking there were some) must have perished when an incendiary bomb hit the office during the war. Besides the paucity of letters to Catherine Winkworth and the absence of those to Madame Mohl there is a still greater omission. There are no letters to Mrs Gaskell's husband, William, and only a few to the other daughters apart from Marianne. Mrs Gaskell was often away from home, and both she and her husband were given to journeying apart. She must have written to him often; and the intimacy of later years between herself and her second daughter Meta (Margaret Emily) must have produced its own considerable correspondence. The disappearance of these letters is explicable. It is quite unlikely that they would have been found among any family papers which survived. In the last months of her life, report has it that Meta (doubtless as she felt in pursuance of her mother's wish not to be written about) held a series of bonfires in which she systematically destroyed a large quantity of family papers. What and how much then perished we shall never know.

II

The letters in this volume cover the whole period of Mrs Gaskell's life, from just before her marriage to the last dated letter which was written in the week of her death and is appropriately concerned with business about the house she had bought for her husband's retirement. It is easy to argue, as Aina Rubenius has

[1] See, for example, the fragmentary letter 149 below. If the rest of the letter is as lively as the brief portion we print from Haldane, our failure to find the original is doubly disappointing.

done (*The Woman Question in Mrs. Gaskell's Life and Works*, 1950), that there was a strain between husband and wife, but it seems wrong to do so. William Gaskell went his own way, spent his holidays apart from his family, was active in the many pursuits in which his work as a Unitarian minister involved him (570); and altogether he seems to have been a singularly self-sufficient person. It is also evident from the letters that his wife occasionally became irritated by some of his ways. To this it is perhaps sufficient to remark that it would have been an unusual marriage indeed if she had not. Against any annoyance must be set her tireless efforts for his welfare. The purchase of the house at Alton is one instance; her negotiations to free him from his duties for a holiday in Italy are another (531). These examples come from the last years of Mrs Gaskell's life, but there is nothing to suggest that they represented a growing together after a growing apart. The marriage may not have had much of the nature of a passionate alliance, but it seems to have been firmly based upon deep mutual respect and affection. In any event, the evidence is by no means enough to be conclusive.

This is not the case with Mrs Gaskell's relationship with her daughters and especially with Marianne. Here there is plenty of evidence. There was a tremendous vitality of passion in her; this can be traced especially in the honeymoon letter (2). She was certainly attracted by and attractive to men (633), and William may have been rather remote and reserved. The result may, to some extent, have been to direct Mrs Gaskell's passion even more strongly than it would normally have been towards her children. The marriage took place in September 1832, and there were six children, of whom four survived. The first was still-born and a son, 'little Willie', died at the age of ten months. The loss of this child was a terrible blow (25a, 70). Marianne was born on 12 September 1834, Meta on 5 February 1837, Florence Elizabeth on 7 October 1842 and Julia Bradford on 3 September 1846. When Marianne was born, Mrs Gaskell began to write a Diary (privately published by Clement Shorter, 1923), the opening lines of which read: 'To my dear little Marianne I shall "dedicate" this book, which, if I should not live to give it to her myself, will I trust be reserved for her as a token of her mother's love and extreme anxiety in the formation of her little daughter's character.' There was extreme anxiety on more accounts than this. MA, as Marianne was called (she is also Polly and Minnie and even on one occasion Molly), was a delicate child; and Mrs Gaskell at times feared as well for her own survival. There is a moving letter (16) to her sister-in-law Nancy Robson, in which Mrs Gaskell begs her to care for the children in the event of her own death. But besides the anxiety there was also the intense joy of the young mother, as in the description she gave to her other sister-in-law Elizabeth Gaskell: 'Baby is at the very tip-top of bliss . . . oh! you would laugh to see her going about, with a great big nosegay in each hand, & wanting to be *bathed* in the golden bushes of wall-flowers' (4). Such was Mrs Gaskell's pride in and anxiety for Marianne. The intimacy of mother and eldest daughter remained throughout life, and the solicitude of early years is matched by that of the final months when Mrs Gaskell wrote to Marianne's future husband, Edward Thurstan Holland, about her daughter's state of health (581). There is no doubt that in an especial sense Marianne was, as her mother at the last addressed her, 'my own darling' (585, 588).

Mrs Gaskell knew her children. In a letter to Nancy Robson (101) who seems to have been her confidante in family affairs (see 570) she gives a shrewd analysis of the salient character-traits and attitudes of all four—Marianne, 'a "law unto herself" now, such a sense of duty, and *obeys* her sense . . . looks at nothing from an intellectual point of view; Meta is untidy, dreamy and absent; but so brimfull of . . . something deeper, & less showy than talent . . . Florence has no talents under the sun; and is very nervous, & anxious . . . Julia is witty, & wild, & clever'. It was this five-year-old youngest child that won the heart of Charlotte Brontë when she stayed with Mrs Gaskell, two months before the lines above were written (*The Shakespeare Head Brontë*, ed. T. J. Wise and J. A. Symington, Vol. III, pp. 269, 278). Even at this time Meta at fourteen was '*quite* able to appreciate any book I am reading', and not surprisingly it was with her that her mother found her closest intellectual companionship in later years. This bond was probably strengthened by Mrs Gaskell's increased care and their travels together after Meta's brief engagement in 1857 and 1858 was broken off.

We must return to Marianne, however, for an insight into Mrs Gaskell's close and sustained parental care. Marianne's 'law unto herself' comprised not only a sense of duty but also other and less attractive qualities including simultaneously both a too easy compliance and a perverse obstinacy. During her schooldays she received a sharp rebuke about her apparently facile espousal of

Free Trade views: 'Do not again give a decided opinion on a subject on which you can at present know nothing' (93). In later years her mother was worried about 'her proclivities to R.C.-ism' and of her being driven further towards it by her father's hostility to it (507): 'Marianne has all her life been influenced by people, *out of her own family*—& seldom by members of it, in anything like the same degree.'

It would be wrong, however, to conclude on this note and better to end on one less serious with some of the humorous 'Precepts for the guidance of a Daughter' (MS. in the possession of Mrs Trevor Jones):

2. Wash your hands.
3. *When* you have washed them, hold a book in them.
8. Talk German so fast that no one can ascertain whether you speak grammatically or not.
9. Don't gobble; it turns maidens and turkey-cocks purple.
11. Don't talk like Scott & Adsheads' about young men's dress.
14. Assume the power of reading if you have it not.
15. Hold your book right way up . . . .

Altogether to conduct yourself as becomes the daughter of

E. C. Gaskell.

The charm, vitality and good-humour here displayed had much to do with Mrs Gaskell's social success both as a hostess and as a guest. All three Manchester homes at Dover Street, Upper Rumford Street and especially Plymouth Grove were the resorts of innumerable friends, both famous and otherwise. There were such early acquaintances as the Bradfords, the glitter of whose wealth seems both to have dazzled and embarrassed Mrs Gaskell (9); there were the Darbishires, at one time so close and then as a result of a misunderstanding so distant; above all, among the Manchester friends there were the ever-welcome Winkworth sisters who seem—or Susanna at least—to have broken down even William Gaskell's reserve. There were also less interesting characters, people on whom the narrowness of provincial and nonconformist society had such an effect that Mrs Gaskell could not help satirising them. One such was another Unitarian minister's wife, Mrs J. J. Tayler, who objected to five minutes' talk that Mrs Gaskell had had with one or two girls about Scott's *Kenilworth*—on a Sunday! (32). When this lady 'got an impromptu baby at Blackpool', Mrs Gaskell could not avoid remarking that 'Bathing places do so much good. Susan & Mary went to Blackpool last year, but did not derive the same benefit' (9). Besides narrowness there was also vulgarity and pretentiousness in Manchester society of the early and mid-Victorian age, seen in parties such as that at the Ewarts 'large, vulgar & overdressed' (175) and in the taste which rejected a cameo as 'not "large" enough for them, & cutting & execution is nothing to size' (255).

Crude though in many ways it was, based upon first-generation wealth from rapidly expanding industry, Manchester society, nevertheless, was intellectually alive. It tended to lionise its heroes, but at any rate it knew how to identify, and in some measure to appreciate, them. Some of the intellectual and cultural interest of the city must undoubtedly be ascribed to the small German colony, members of which often subscribed to the Unitarian faith as being nearest to the views of men who came from a country in which biblical criticism had originated and made most ready progress. The Schwabes and the Schuncks, to name no others, are found among the Gaskells' friends. Nor should we forget another foreigner, Charles Hallé. His name is a reminder of what is probably Manchester's greatest claim to cultural importance. His concerts began in the Manchester of Mrs Gaskell's time. In that time also Owens College was founded, later to become the first and largest of the civic universities. Its professors were among the Gaskells' friends, and William lectured there from its inception for many years (see 570). In 1857 the city staged its great Art Exhibition; and the British Association for the Advancement of Science, of which William Gaskell was an active member, met in Manchester in 1842 and 1861, on the latter occasion under the presidency of the Gaskells' friend, Sir William Fairbairn. The Art Exhibition in special buildings at Old Trafford was guaranteed by a hundred subscribers to the extent of £74,000. It included 2,000 paintings by old and modern masters, nearly a thousand water-colours and some 13,000 examples of other arts ranging from sculptures through furniture and ceramics to ivories and enamels. In five and a half months it was visited by 1,300,000 people, and the daily concert was, in fact, the means of inaugurating the Hallé Orchestra.

Manchester was an exciting place to live in and to visit. Besides these musical and artistic activities there were lectures and meetings in plenty. Mrs Gaskell describes some of these such as the meeting in support of Florence Nightingale (279) and mentions others such as Thackeray's lectures (134) and the banquet of the Guild of Literature and Art (131). On this last occasion the Dickens were in Manchester and visited the Gaskells. 42 Plymouth Grove was a house of hospitality and culture, and over the years its visitors included, among others, Charlotte Brontë, Harriet Beecher Stowe, and Richard Monckton Milnes. In her turn Mrs Gaskell visited the homes of many of the famous. She stayed at Haworth; in the Lake District she lodged with the Kay-Shuttleworths, met the Arnolds and Mrs Wordsworth and narrowly missed meeting Tennyson; in London she took part in one of the last of Rogers' famous breakfasts, met the ageing Leigh Hunt, the Carlyles and many others. Trollope she did not know, but she met his brother in Italy, where she established friendships with the Americans, the sculptor William Wetmore Story and the young Charles Eliot Norton. Her genius for friendship enabled her to create close relationships with young people. Norton is one example, Charles Bosanquet was another, and John Addington Symonds was a third. Her genius seems to have failed with only one author, Thackeray, whom she does not appear to have liked overmuch. Of others it is perhaps sufficient to mention her friendship with Ruskin, about whose marital difficulties she has left an important letter (195). Non-literary friendships of interest and significance included those with the beautiful and cultured Mrs Davenport of Capesthorne (later Lady Hatherton of Teddesley) and the Nightingale family.

Mrs Gaskell's travels provided her with much material for her letters. Amongst the most interesting are those in which she describes an unexpected visit to Chatsworth and a German holiday in the Rhineland. At Chatsworth there was a tour of the estate concluding with a drive through the conservatory, a large dinner-party followed by a concert given by the duke's private band, during which the duke, partially paralysed and very deaf but 'he can hear talking whenever music is going on', sat next to Mrs Gaskell and 'talked pretty incessantly' (372). Reputation could not awe Mrs Gaskell into respect. She found the Rhine a disappointment and Cologne, she thought, smelt of the bones of the three thousand virgins. Heidelberg, on the other hand, she found surprisingly beautiful, 'splendid scenery, dark pine woods[,] rocks, & the picturesque town, and noble castle to complete it' (15). She cherished the recollection of the places she enjoyed. Her long correspondence with Norton is full of happy reminiscences of her visit to Rome in 1857. Paris, too, was a city of pleasant associations. She stayed there on a number of occasions with Madame Mohl at her house in the Rue du Bac. She showed Meta many of the important places in the city, she met various notable figures of the time, and a *soirée* was given in her honour (see 230).

It will by now be sufficiently evident that Mrs Gaskell's life impinged upon that of some of the most interesting people of the period. None, however, was more interesting than Florence Nightingale. Mrs Gaskell made her acquaintance a few months before the Crimean War. She was in close touch with the family at this most important period of Florence's life. She stayed with them at Lea Hurst near Matlock, and it was there that she wrote a considerable part of *North and South*. From there on 20 October 1854 she told Catherine Winkworth of the noble work which Florence was doing at the Middlesex Hospital, coping with the cholera epidemic then raging (211). In later letters she spoke of the popular heroine-worship of Florence during the Crimean War, of 'babies ad libitum. . . being christened Florence here; poor little factory-babies, whose grimed stunted parents brighten up at the name' (255) and of a workman's rebuke of '*you* benevolent ladies [who] play at benevolence—Look at Florence Nightingale— there's a woman for you' (279). It is such details as these that give Mrs Gaskell's letters an importance as social report and comment- ary. Another such sidelight may be mentioned in passing: she gives a touching account of the sad Christmas of 1861 with the deep national sorrow that affected all ranks of society following the death of the Prince Consort (496).

It is, however, for their comment upon literature and Mrs Gaskell's own work, in particular, that the letters possess an especial value. The letters to her publishers tell us much about the business negotiations connected with her writing, and the series to George Smith gives us an almost stage-by-stage account of the progress and problems of the *Life of Charlotte Brontë*. There are also a number of letters which quite vividly indicate her diffi- culties with *North and South* and especially her troubles with Dickens arising from the serial publication of this novel (220, 225).[1] It is interesting also to compare her attitude towards her work at different periods of her life, to note her increasing assurance about

---

[1] The former letter, hitherto unknown, is the only one surviving of Mrs Gaskell's side of the correspondence. (Cf. A. B. Hopkins, *Elizabeth Gaskell, Her Life and Work*, 1952, p. 135).

its worth whilst all the time remaining deeply conscious of its defects. She chose to ignore reviews whenever she could (38), but she nevertheless feared them (326, 344) and at least once, with the publication of the *Life of Charlotte Brontë*, public reaction caused her acute suffering: 'I have cried more since I came home than I ever did in the same space of time before' (352). The sense of injury was the greater in proportion to what she thought to be the nobility of the task and the extent of her achievement. The *Life* derives its greatness as biography not least from the passion with which its author regarded its subject. It was not the first time Mrs Gaskell had had to suffer. *Mary Barton* had quickly stirred up a storm of protest (35 et seq.), and *Ruth* provoked a similar reaction (148, 154). *Cranford*, however, one is happy to discover, was a constant source of joy, and Mrs. Gaskell once wrote in reply to an admiring letter from Ruskin that she could still pick it up when she was feeling low and 'laugh over it afresh' (562).

It is not only reactions to her work that the letters so vividly reveal. We are able also to see something of the process of composition. The research for the biography of Charlotte Brontë is particularly well documented. We read of her quest for letters and papers, of her visits to Haworth, to Birstall and even to Brussels, of her queries to George Smith about publication dates and of a host of other details, some of which can be quite startling: 'Do you mind the law of libel.—I have three people I want to libel...'! (314). Many of her novels are set in places she knew well. She relied much upon her own experience. The Ruskin letter contains a humorous tale of real life, 'a bit of "Cranford" that I did not dare to put in, because I thought people would say it was ridiculous, and yet which really happened in Knutsford' (562). Even in *Sylvia's Lovers* she used her ten-day visit to Whitby in 1859 to give her the setting for her work (537). With this book also, placed as it was in an earlier era than her own, she appears to have engaged in some minute historical research (457). Besides the preparatory work we read also of the progress of her writing. She seems to have been able to write swiftly and continuously, given the opportunity. There was the Lea Hurst visit when she was shut up alone with her manuscript (211) and the so-called holidays at Dumbleton and Boughton when she wrote so much on Charlotte Brontë (308). The first of the letters referred to in the last sentence also shows something of the author's problems with *North and South*. More than once we can see her pondering as to how she should proceed with events in her tale (211, 217). The progress of her last novel, *Wives and Daughters*, is illustrated in another and pathetic way as we read of her struggle to write, of the battle between the need to complete the story and the failing physical health and strength that constantly impeded the effort (570).

It may be apposite to mention one other way in which these letters are interesting from a literary point of view. It is to be regretted that only so small a portion of Mrs Gaskell's correspondence with her fellow-writers has survived, for there must have been much more than we have found; but even in what remains and especially in what she says to her publisher George Smith we notice her deep interest in and shrewd judgement of literature. There is, for instance, the succinct summary of the first two chapters of *Little Dorrit* read over someone else's shoulder! (273). There is the sensitive appraisal of *Villette*, based on her knowledge of the author (154). Again, there is her immediate recognition of the greatness of *Adam Bede*. It is worthy of note that, strive as she had to do, Mrs Gaskell did not allow herself to be led into condemning the book, even though she deplored the author's manner of life (438, 451). Indeed, she wrote to George Eliot in praise of the novel (449). Another novel to which she gave unstinting approbation was Trollope's *Framley Parsonage*; she wished that it would go on for ever (456).

Most interesting of all her comments, however, is a letter of advice which she gave about *The Three Paths*, a work submitted by a would-be author, 'Herbert Grey' (420). She insisted that a novel must be a novel and not an essay, that it must be more than a set of opinions, that there must be a good plot, that this is more likely to come from observation and experience than from introspection, that the plot is the necessary ground-structure of the whole, that the author must so imagine events as to see them happening, that not a character must appear who is other than essential, and that the expression must be as economical as possible. The whole letter is a model brief guide to novel-writing, although we must admit that explicit comments on more subtle literary matters are lacking in this letter to a beginner. Indeed, comments such as the one about *Mary Barton* as Mrs Gaskell's 'idea of a tragic poem' (37, 42) are comparatively rare in the surviving letters, considering the quality and maturity of her actual practice as a novelist.

More important than what these letters have to tell us of Mrs

Gaskell's views on either literature or anything else, more important than what they show of what she did is the evidence they reveal of what she was. They come from the pen of a ready writer, and thus in their spontaneity they give us a fine impression of the woman as she really was. She was not writing for effect. As a result, we are able to appreciate her supremely human qualities. Because she was so human, so aware of her own humanity, she was so interested in other people, in their humanity. One feels her regard for her reader; she is always writing *to* the particular correspondent she is addressing. This is one aspect of her general kindliness. The letters also appeal in their revelation of another aspect of this quality. She was the minister's wife and she ably seconded her husband in his work, but there was no hint of 'professionalism' about her benevolence. It sprang from her character, from what she was. In her work for the needy millworkers during the 'Cotton Famine' of the American Civil War years, in her efforts for factory girls and women prisoners, we notice a genuine human concern. This was surely an extension of that love and affection which she showed as a mother and so movingly in her young womanhood as a foster-daughter to Aunt Lumb.

Next of her great qualities we must note Mrs Gaskell's moral seriousness. Mrs Carlyle indeed thought her dull and strait-laced in a peculiarly Unitarian fashion. She may have seemed so in 1848 to one so much more sophisticated than herself, but if the evidence of the letters is any guide, it would be difficult to argue that this was the kind of impression she gave in subsequent years. She could not have appealed to so many as she did if Mrs Carlyle had accurately expressed her attitude. There is a serene assurance about Mrs Gaskell's moral position. She knew generally where she stood, but rarely felt that she had need explicitly to indicate her situation. When it was necessary, however, she did so. This is seen in the candour with which she showed what she thought of George Eliot's liaison with Lewes. Yet she was no walking exemplar. Indeed, some of the most endearing of her letters are those in which she confesses her frailties and occasional uncharitableness about people. She was not without a light, attractive malice, which she deployed effectively at times. Witness Mrs J. J. Tayler, or the Darbishire family hypnotised by Froude (49) or her repetition of the story about Martin Tupper's extravagant salutation to Nathaniel Hawthorne (292). On occasion, her sharpness sprang from concern for others, as when she wrote of Mrs Wordsworth, 'It is curious the loving reverence she retains for Coleridge, in spite of his rousing the house about one in the morning, after her confinement, when quiet was particularly enjoyned, to ask for eggs and bacon! and similar vagaries' (139)—a very slight echo of the note she struck so firmly in her 'social novels'.

Her impulsive reactions remind us of yet another of her endowments as a person—her vitality. At some times this expressed itself in a piquant humour at the expense of pretension; at others it showed in the vivacity which marked her participation in events and her appreciation of people. She was so interested in everything that was going on around her—her children's dress, the latest batch of eggs for sitting, the last Hallé concert, the most recent books; everything from a cook's illness to abstruse political economy engaged her full attention and considerable powers. She never knew when to stop, and often, especially with her literary work, she drove herself into headaches, breakdown and enforced rest. It is this sense of her vitality, of life lived to the full, that in retrospect gives to the last letters much of their pathos. She was so tired. She who had done so much, who yet felt that within her there remained so much still to do, was moving swiftly to that sad day when literally in a moment she was cut off in the fullness of her powers. Only a few days before her own death she was lamenting that she would never see Florence's father-in-law, Judge Crompton, again. The lament assumes an ironic tinge as we contemplate the fact that the day approached in which those around her—and many in a wider circle—would have yet greater cause for lamentation. Though she died with much apparently still to give, there was (and is) the consolation that the life she lived was such as to leave behind the memory of a noble woman and a distinguished novelist.

Her letters strengthen this impression. Only a few are long, deliberately composed epistles. Most are hastily written, *calamo currente*. All, however, show her to have been a woman of intelligence, integrity and grace, gifted with an insatiable curiosity about life, a ready understanding of things and people, a deep regard for truth and a boundless sympathy for others. It is not surprising that Mrs Gaskell had so many friends. The letters reveal what a privilege it must have been to have been counted amongst them.

III

The aim of this edition is simple: to bring together all the letters by Mrs Gaskell that we can find in any form, taking our text from the originals if they are still extant.[1] In practice this has not been an easy task, since there has been considerable dispersal of the holographs, and where they do not appear to have survived at all as a sure source for our text, we have discovered that any one letter could exist in several variant copies. The edition contains some undoubtedly trivial notes and fragmentary letters, but they form a very small proportion of the whole. Mrs Gaskell has not been quite famous enough for collectors to bother with her scraps. On the other hand, many collectors have thought it worthwhile to preserve her letters of any length and importance, to an extent which made us decide to restrict the edition to letters by her and ignore those to her that still exist.[2]

We began our collecting in 1960 with a search of books and articles; we wrote letters to newspapers and journals, individuals and institutions; we gave talks to interested groups and took every opportunity of making our activity public. Our thanks and acknowedgements for assistance are separately recorded above, but we must not fail to make special mention of Mr J. G. Sharps. As editors we count the day fortunate on which we first heard from him; his readiness to share his discoveries of unknown letters, both original and printed in obscure places, has been matched by the generous way in which he has made available the wealth of information he gathered in the course of his own research. This edition would have been immeasurably poorer without his help. Yet despite all the aid we have been given so willingly over several years, we cannot suppose that everything possible has been discovered; and we have made the decision to go to press at this point, partly in order to publish by the centenary of Mrs Gaskell's death on 12 November 1865 but, more important, because we realised that the early flood of letters had become a mere trickle. It might well continue for many years to come.

By far our greatest difficulty has been caused by the fact that

[1] We have transcribed the original manuscripts we found in this country; for America we have relied upon photographic copies efficiently provided by the various holders. There are a few exceptions. (See Appendix E.)

[2] See especially Ross D. Waller, 'Letters Addressed to Mrs Gaskell by Celebrated Contemporaries, Now in the Possession of the John Rylands Library', *Bulletin of the John Rylands Library*, XIX, 1935, pp. 3–70.

the great majority of Mrs Gaskell's letters are not fully dated. Indeed, 'Sunday morning before breakfast' is an altogether typical —and essentially human—date; only rarely did she give the year, even when she wrote down the day and month. Quite apart from the need to date individual letters, our discovery that they were written to many different correspondents, and that only four large groups to particular recipients (Marianne, George Smith, E. Fox and C. E. Norton)[1] appeared to exist today, encouraged us to plump for arrangements by date rather than under the various names. The main section is therefore ordered chronologically, although we have had to gather together the fifty or so letters, most of them short, that defied our efforts to date them to a single year in a second section under the names of various recipients, where these are known.[2] It is, in fact, possible to follow through letters to any one correspondent in the main chronological section without constant, tedious reference to an index, by using the subsidiary numbers flanking the main number assigned to each letter[3] in the edition. In this way, we hope, the reader is allowed the advantages of both methods. (See p. xxvi below.)

The actual business of dating has been a fascinating and complex task. All legible postmarks have been recorded, together with any significant annotations made by relatives, owners and dealers. Some letters contain internal evidence of a particularly obvious kind: in one letter to Marianne (132), dated 'Friday', Mrs Gaskell wished her daughter many happy returns of the day when she began, and closed with 'Goodbye my eighteen-year-old'. Not all references are as straightforward as this, so from the beginning we have kept indexes of the material in an attempt to keep control of the more elusive details, which we hope have been utilised to the fullest extent. Other letters have needed more than one line of attack, and more than one logical step, before we could date them. Letter 129, for example, is headed 'Plymouth Grove | Saturday, Augt 7', which means that it was written after early 1850, in which year the Gaskells moved to that address. Reference to a Perpetual

---

[1] The letters to and from Norton have been edited as a separate correspondence by Mrs Jane Whitehill (Harvard University Press, 1932), and those to George Smith have been extensively quoted in a special chapter of Miss A. B. Hopkins' *Elizabeth Gaskell, Her Life and Work*, 1952.

[2] The few letters to which we have not been able to assign any more than the year are collected at the end of that year in the main sequence.

[3] Numbers followed by a or b have been given where letters had to be inserted in an established sequence. Appendix A contains letters that turned up at the very last moment.

Calendar shows that August 7 fell on a Saturday in the years 1852 and 1858 (Mrs Gaskell died in 1865); the format, watermark and embossing of the paper on which this letter is written associate it with four others, all of which had been placed in the former year on other grounds. Even this falls short of absolute proof, although the tracing of the internal reference to a presentation might clinch the matter. In general, then, we have included in the main chronological section letters dated with widely varying degrees of probability, calling attention to those we are least confident about, rather than permitting them to languish in the limbo of the second section of undated letters.[1] No method or combination of methods, we have found from experience, is infallible, and the possibility of human error on our part cannot be discounted; but with these letters of Mrs Gaskell and their special problems we felt that every straw should be clutched at in the necessary task of ordering as significantly as possible the mass of heterogeneous material. However, insofar as this has involved the analysis of more technical kinds of evidence, we have relegated it to the Appendices where it may be consulted by those who are interested.[2]

We met with some complications when we turned to the text of the letters. With those taken from copies, usually printed or in typescript at the Brotherton Library, Leeds, we had the problem of deciding on emendations where the text was evidently corrupt or, on occasion, which of several variant readings available was the most authoritative. Our general principle with texts taken from secondary sources has been to emend them silently, providing no substantive change was involved. We could not fail to notice at times when an original manuscript was discovered for a text we had previously taken from another source how frequently Mrs Gaskell's words had been bowdlerised, cut without warning, or otherwise altered.[3] (It is for this reason that we write

[1] Letter 115, for example, is assigned to 1852 on relatively flimsy grounds.

[2] The treatment of letter 129 above shows how useful physical examination of manuscripts can be. It can help bring together portions of the same letter that have been separated, confirm speculative datings from vague allusions in the text, ensure that comments about paper can be properly exploited (e.g. in 216: 'I am ashamed of my paper, but this is my last piece'), and so on. Possibly the most convincing fact is that watermarks at this period sometimes include dates, and many of Mrs Gaskell's letters were written within a year or two of such dates in their paper.

[3] One may compare the texts printed below from the original manuscripts (211, 306) with those in *Letters and Memorials of Catherine Winkworth*, ed. [S. Winkworth], pr. pr., Clifton, 1883, I, pp. 464–8; *Anna Jameson. Letters and Friendships*, ed. Mrs Steuart Erskine, [1915], pp. 298–9.

a short note in the main text if the letter has been taken from a copy, even though sources are given in Appendix E.) In the case of letters 75 and 76 it appears that Mrs Gaskell herself ran together portions of two letters and quoted them in her *Life of Charlotte Brontë*, but fortunately the whole of one of the originals is extant.[1]

Our treatment of original letters written by Mrs Gaskell, or by her daughters on her behalf,[2] has been rather different: they have undergone the minimum of change. Our aim has been to preserve their easy, unaffected flow, the authentic record of her thoughts and feelings in their true tone and inflexion. We have made some slight changes, on the grounds that they make for the comfort of the reader and hardly affect our major purpose. Addresses and dates at the end have been moved to the heading, and obvious postscripts shifted to the end wherever they actually appear in the manuscript. Similarly, we have allowed the sense to dictate the order in those letters where Mrs Gaskell has saved paper by writing across earlier pages at right angles to the original lines. Intolerably long paragraphs have been broken down. Mrs Gaskell did not usually indent their openings and it is often quite impossible to be certain of her intentions in this respect, as it is also in her punctuation and use of capitals. We have tried to adopt the most helpful alternative in ambiguous cases.[3] Where some error or idiosyncrasy of Mrs Gaskell has caused real obscurity, we have either written a footnote or interposed in the usual editorial square brackets. Other signs found in the main text are angle brackets for lacunæ, braces for deletions and solidi for insertions.[4] They are far from frequent and, we feel, when the symbols become familiar they can positively intensify our appreciation of the letters themselves as spontaneous literature.

[1] In fact, the manuscript of the *Life* (in the Manchester University Library) shows that Mrs Gaskell marked the end of the first letter with quotation marks, but she did not use them at the beginning or end of her quotation of the second letter. A case of one letter being divided into two is provided by Letter 638: the beginning is at Princeton; the end at New Haven.

[2] Footnotes call attention to letters not in Mrs Gaskell's autograph. (See also Appendix F.) There is even a letter to Marianne asking her to write to an author for her mother, so long that Mrs Gaskell might as well have written in the first place (420).

[3] The diversity of forms of Mr, Mrs and Dr has forced us to normalise them throughout, and we have brought down any superscript letters in abbreviations, omitting the full stop or dash after contracted forms. We also read 'Brontë' throughout.

[4] Thus: ⟨ ⟩ { } \ /. We have tried to supply brief gaps and to read all cancellations.

We have, as far as footnotes are concerned, attempted to keep the pages as free as possible, writing none, for instance, where the reasons for dating a particular letter are fairly obvious.[1] Addresses, postmarks, important annotations and the few seals are described in a footnote where they exist, and it may be assumed that if no separate cover is mentioned, either it is not extant or such details were taken from a folded sheet of the letter. Again, to help the reader we have supplied explanatory notes when Mrs Gaskell was vague and allusive, or where the letter would be much clearer with some knowledge of the references. When Mrs Gaskell wrote to Parthenope Nightingale on 21 July [1855] that she was sorry to hear that there was still cause for anxiety concerning a lady being cared for by the Bracebridges, we naturally consulted the biographies of Florence Nightingale to help date the letter; and it therefore seemed doubly valuable to note that at this time in 1855 Florence was just convalescing from the Crimean Fever that had struck her down at Balaclava in the previous May (255). We may well have missed veiled references here and there, and we have certainly failed to run down every allusion amongst those we did see. One common kind has been surprisingly difficult: book-titles are not always to be found in the British Museum Catalogue or in the standard bibliographies of nineteenth-century literature. It was perhaps naïve of us to fancy that here was plain sailing, when all that we know of the situation with the two Short Title Catalogues of books printed up to 1700 should have warned us of squalls ahead. A minor surprise was to find that no scholarly reference work appears to notice the story of the old woman's pig that would not jump over the stile (436), although Mrs K. Chapple supplied a full text without hesitation and told us that she had seen a contemporary children's picture-book containing it!

The moral may be that an edition of this nature will be read by a widely varying public, which has legitimate demands to make of its editors; they will therefore have to make certain compromises in the interests of all, scholars and general readers alike. As editors, too, we wish to do justice to the individuality of Mrs Gaskell. Our practice, then, has been controlled by several factors; and our general solution has been to remove purely technical data to the Appendices, largely reduced to tabular form, and to make what-

---

[1] Frequent references to *Letters* and *Memorials*, ed. Winkworth, are not gratuitous. They are usually the evidence for dating, since these two volumes chronicle at length many of the same events.

ever alterations and annotations of the main text we thought strictly necessary, while at the same time trying to leave that main text relatively unimpeded. We hardly expect to find that our many particular answers to problems will meet all tastes. We only hope that readers who know the institution from which Manchester University has developed will not nod their heads in regretful agreement when they come to Mrs Gaskell's passing remark that Owens College, where her husband was also a lecturer in English literature, has fallen off lately (222).

POSTSCRIPT

A number of letters became available after this work had reached page-proof stage from a source till then inaccessible. These and some other very late discoveries form Appendix A. The appearance of a large asterisk * after a letter in the main sequence indicates that the next letter in chronological order will be found there. Such late letters have been given a number as if they were in the main sequence with the necessary addition of a, b or c. (In the few cases where late letters fall between the plain number and a successor already given an *a* number the symbols + or ++ have been used instead.) Some late letters we have not been able to date have been simply numbered on from the end of the undated section and printed in the beginning of Appendix A.

NOTES TO THE NEW EDITION

The remarkable resurgence of interest in Elizabeth Gaskell during the past thirty years has led to the discovery of well over two hundred more of her letters. These additional letters, which are still turning up in salerooms, present a time-consuming editorial task of some complexity. However, the first edition of 1966, long out of print, is extremely difficult to purchase. It has therefore seemed useful in the meantime to issue it in paperback form with notes calling attention to important corrections and amendments.

A lists textual corrections and solved problems of transcription. B contains a selection of notes about individual letters, mostly concerning new manuscript sources, dating or integrity. John Geoffrey Sharps, *Mrs Gaskell's Observation and Invention* (Fontwell, 1970), should also be consulted for his valuable notes on variant copies where autographs have not been found. Elizabeth Kemp, Angus Easson, Michael Wheeler and Philip Yarrow supplied helpful comments on the original edition.

A number of additional letters have been printed since 1966 (not always accurately): for references see the standard Gaskell bibliographies by R.L. Selig and Nancy S. Weyant. A supplementary edition now being prepared will contain amended versions, as well as the texts of many other newly discovered letters.

A

Page, line	
9,24	*For* Wm *read* H
15,14	*Read* musing, with
28,6 f.bottom	*Read* One is the custom, on
47,10	*For* [?Merg's] *read* Merz's
75,8	*Read* feeling
89, 2 f. bottom	*For* coute *perhaps read* crack *or* cank
91,13 f. bottom	*For* dame *read* dama
110,3	*Read* versa
124,14	*For* [?Fleet] *read* Tent
191, 16 f. bottom	*For* Howarth *read* Howorth
223, 8	*Read* S.D. *for* J.W.
233, 20	*Delete* she said
302, 17 f. bottom	*For* where *read* when
302, 7 f. bottom	*For* last; *read* last:

338, 13 and 14	*Read* taken *and* Jameson
353, 1	*Read* you that there
380, 2	*For* the [?], *read* them;
419, 4	*Read* indiscriminately
419, 8	*Read* doles
419, 9 f. bottom	*Read* long and
506, 14	*For* hear *read* bear
513, 17	*For* 105 *read* 150
539, 16	*For* Homrath *read* Hormuth
603, 13	*Read* fully
626, 4	*For* Furnival *read* Turnival
627, 5	*For* Furnivall *read* Turnivall
692, 1	*For* have *read* name
692, 6	*For* book *read* work
699, 4	*Photocopy unclear: perhaps* 1852
721, 16	*For* cleaning *read* clearing
797, 1	*Read* or been
809, 15	*Read* Yours very
810, 1	*Read* indeed to
830, 15	*Read* circumstance
830, 18	*For* if *read* it
839, 5	*For* supposing *read* suppose
870, 11	*For* very *read* most
880, 12 f. bottom	*For* Soison *scilicet* Toison
915, n. 1	*Read* J.B.G.
930, 3 f. bottom	*Read* why I
968, 9 f. bottom	*Read* her look
968, 7 f. bottom	*Read* I know, I know she

B

Page, line	
45	Letter 16 redated: [23 December 1840]
48, n.1	Julia Gaskell was baptized 17 March 1847
89	Letter 55 composite. See Jeanette Eve in *N&Q* for March 1987
141	Letter 88 perhaps to Revd. J.R. Beard
158	Letter 100 redated: [9 February 1851]
179	Letter 115 redated: February 24th [1851]
222	Letter 149 redated: [*c.* May 1853]
222	MS of Letter 150 in Pierpont Morgan Library, N.Y.
230	For first part of Letter 155, 3 May [1853], see

	Dorothy W. Collins in *Bulletin of the John Rylands Library* 69 (1986)
243	MS of incomplete Letter 166 in Brotherton Library
265	Letter 180 redated: February [1852]
379	Letter 277 to R. Monckton Milnes
522	MS of Letter 406 in Brotherton Library
555	Letter 429a redated: [25 March 1861]. See Angus Easson in *Notes & Queries* for February 1976
651	MS of letter 486 in New York University Library
674	Letter 498 redated: [post-February 1860]
714	Letter 535 redated: Octr 22nd [1863]
747	MS of Letter 562, 24 February [1865], in Harvard University Library
766-7	Letters 577 and 579 probably to Sampson Low
767	Letter 578 probably to R. Monckton Milnes
784	Letter 593 to Henry Arthur Bright [post-1858]
786	Letter 595 dated: April 10th [1860-65]
788	Letter 600 dated: [*c.* November 1860?]
793	Letter 608 dated: [*c.* 1854]
794	Letter 609 dated: Decr 4th [?1859]
796	Letter 614 dated: 13th February [1849]
797	Letter 616 dated: [May-August 1838]
798	Letter 617 dated: [18 August 1838?]
802	Delete Letter 624. See ECG, *Life of Charlotte Brontë*, 1857, II. 164
802	Letter 626 dated: [*c.* 1854]
809	Letter 636 in National Library of Scotland
825	Letter 17a dated: [April 1847?]
826, n. 4	Caroline ('Cousin Coo') and Gertrude were daughters of Dr Henry Holland. Cp. J.A.V. Chapple and Anita Wilson, *Private Voices*, Keele, 1996, pp. 88,95
839	MS of frag. Letter 97b on deposit in Brotherton Library, Leeds
914	MS of Letter 475c in Yale University Library
930	MS of Letter 519a in Knutsford Library

A smaller number on the left of any main letter number in heavy black type is that of the previous letter to the same correspondent; one on the right that of the next letter to the same person. Smaller numbers with asterisks refer to late letters printed in Appendix A.

DATED LETTERS

1

ELIZABETH GASKELL[1]

Tuesday Evening. Knutsford.
[20 March 1832]

You ought indeed, my dearest Eliza, to consider it a great proof of my love, that I can even meditate writing to you on William's last evening (See how impudent I've grown) but my conscience would reproach me for ever and a day if I let him go without my portion of thanks for your kind letter. He may finish his half at Ardwick, and as I shan't be there to see, he may say what scandal he likes of us all, and give me as bad a character as he chooses. N.B. I have been behaving very well, so don't believe a word to the contrary.

He has not seen half, no nor a quarter so much as I wished of my darling Aunt Lumb. I scarcely like to think of the cause now she is so much better, but the very morning after he came, she broke a small bloodvessel which alarmed us all very much indeed, and has confined her to bed ever since. William has, however, seen her several times, and though not nearly enough, yet I hope knows her a little bit. And you can't think what rude speeches she makes to me. To give you a slight specimen—'Why Elizabeth how could this man ever take a fancy to such a little giddy thoughtless thing as you' and many other equally pretty speeches.

And he's seen and properly admired his traveling [*sic*] companion from Leeds. But oh dear! I shall miss him sadly tomorrow, and I'm sure you will be very sorry for the reason when you hear it. He had a letter this morning from Mrs Robberds begging him to come home against Thursday morning to old Mrs Robberds funeral. She was not very well when we left, and on Monday her son was called up early in the morning—and before he could get to Mrs Alcock's she was dead.[2] I could not say a word on such an occasion to urge your brother's staying, and I must look forward to the *28th of March 1832*[3] when he has promised to come back again. Pray give my warmest thanks to your sister, for her kind addition to your letter—and do you, dearest, pray write again to

[1] Original MS. not seen.
[2] The *Manchester Guardian* of Saturday, 31 March 1832, contains a report of the death of Mrs Sarah Robberds.   [3] The source reads '1932'.

I

me, and that right speedily—tell me anything that interests you—
and oh! don't forget how to fight with pillows and 'farm yard
noises' when Edward heard you laughing so plainly. I can't write
a word more now, seeing I have 150 things to say to this disagreeable brother of yours—so believe me

Your very loving crony
E. C. Stevenson

₁ **2** ₃

ELIZABETH GASKELL[1]

[*c.* 17 Sept. 1832]

My dearest Eliza,
    That most wicked brother of yours & husband of mine, has
left me such a wee wee bit of time to write all *my* news, & thanks
having taken such a time to *his* eloquence that poor I must write
helter-skelter[.] And first and foremost thanks upon thanks from
the very bottom of my long heart, for yr letter which was *so*
welcome, as we had been longing for news from *our home*. It was
very nice of you writing to *me*, your new *sister* too. Kate ha⟨d⟩
sent us a long long letter a few days before—and among other
things mad⟨e⟩ us laugh exceedingly with telling us one *report* of
which I dare say neither you nor Sam were aware. Pray ask him
with my love whether \he/ knew that Sue put his shoulder out of
joint by pulling him to her at the altar, and that so much force was
required on *Susan*'s part, because Kate was pulling so at his other
arm. Since hearing this Wm & I have felt rather anxious to hear of
his health. As you justly conjecture I *have* a *great* deal of trouble, in
managing this obstreperous brother of yours, though I dare say he
will try and persuade you the trouble is all on his side. I find he has
been telling you I look very well, so I think that is a pretty broad
hint that I am to tell you he is looking *remarkably* well which he
really is. Mountain seems to agree with us & our appetites
admirably[.] You would be astonished to see our appetites, the
dragon of Wantley, 'who churches ate of a Sunday, Whole
dishes of people were to him, but a dish of Salmagunde'[2] was

---

[1] *Address* Miss Gaskell | 1 Dover Street | Oxford Road, Manchester. *Postmark*
CAERNARVON | SE 17 | 183[2]. *Annotations* for MA | Wedding Trip *and* Sep 17/32.
[2] Reference to a humorous ballad, possibly of the seventeenth century.

really a delicate appetite compared to ours. If you hear of the
principality of Wales being swallowed up by an earthquake, for
earthquake read Revd Wm Gaskell—How very good ⟨you⟩ are
to be staying at home by yourself while   here's post

Your most affect[ionate] Sister
E. C. Gaskell

₂ 3 ₄

ELIZABETH GASKELL[1]

[c. 16 December 1833]

My dearest Lizzie,

Many thanks to Dicky of Wigan for this frank, for I have been
longing to write and ask you my dear just how do you do, this
long time and more especially since we received the newspaper
\yester/day. I am very sorry my mother[2] does not make such
rapid progress as we could wish; but do not be disheartened dear
Lizzie—I know what it is to watch by a sick bed—in Aunt
Lumb's illness—and I found that it was the best way to reckon
from one day to that day *week*—from day to day I could see no
progress—but Aunt Lumb got up first on a Wednesday I remember well, and that day week every symptom of weakness was just
the same except that she could now *lift herself up* to be carried
from her bed to the sofa in the drawing room. Try this plan
dearest Lizzie, and try (which is the most difficult part) to help
thinking about it till that day week comes, & then you will find it
such a pleasant surprise to find how the imperceptible progress
each day has made a good piece at last[.] Dearest Anne! I am very
sorry to hear she is so delicate. You must both come and recruit
here when you can leave my mother. Aunt Lumb left me the
day that the hamper went to Warrington or I should certainly
have written, but I grudged every moment of time that last day.
Fanny (Kate's sister) has been spending a few days with me but has

<hr>

[1] *Address (not in Mrs Gaskell's hand)* 1833 | Manchester December | Sixteen |
Miss Gaskell | Revd E. R. Dimock | Warrington | Richd Potter. *Postmark* MAN-
CHESTER | De 16 | 18⟨3⟩3. *Square seal* Bird with branch.

[2] This is, of course, a reference to her mother-in-law. See *A History of the Family
of Holland*, ed. W. M. Irvine (coll. E. S. Holland), priv. pr., Edinburgh, 1902,
pp. 87–9, for further details.

left me now and is at Mrs Robberds. Agnes Robinson was
married the beginning of this month, and is in lodgings in Princes
St. Fanny went to call on *Mrs Carlisle*, and found her quite
orthodoxly happy. They wanted Kate to be bridesmaid but she
was not able to leave home. Mrs Edmund Potter is going to be
confined again. I had a letter from Aunt Lumb on Saturday
telling me that Mary Anne was brought to bed on Wednesday—
stay! Thursday of a noble little boy. She was taken ill at 1 on
Wednesday night, but was nothing to signify till 6 and before 8
little Master Dean was born—is it not short, & a very easy time
into the bargain. They say the young gentleman has red hair,
because Mama's was black & Papa's light. Aunt Lumb is going to
have Mr & Mrs Harrison on Friday next—and I am ordering cake
for her[.] Mrs Harrison is very ladylike—upper face handsome,
lower face plain. I think Mrs Holbrook will think I have written
her great nonsense. Sam (the wretch) has never been over, & I am
longing to hear all about the Thomsons. My little miss of a ½ sister
is to be married this Christmas—only 17 this 8th of December.
Susan has kept putting off & putting off and now says she will
come for a fortnight or so after Christmas. My love to Bob, and
tell him we are already getting the mince meat ready for the
mincepies he is to eat. We inte⟨n⟩d to waylay Sam & make him
sleep here the night of Mrs Marsden's party. William goes ⟨. . .⟩[1]
Mrs Worthington called the other day, & I shall see Anne this
week as she will be in Manchester. Tomorrow Mrs Clegg, and
Miss Taylor & Miss Crook (or as Betsy calls them) *Mrs* Taylor &
Miss *Cook* & the Robberds drink tea here. By the bye you are such
a favourite with little Betsy. 'Fanny and I often talk about Miss
Eliza Gaskell, and we always say there is not such another young
lady in the world' is only one of the numerous pretty speeches she
says about you. William called the other day on Mrs Smith—no
thanks to me though, as it seemed to me that he waited till I had
done asking him to go before he would. Oh the obstinacy of
husbands!—Tell me in a whisper when Betsy Gaskell is to be
married—and tell her with my kind love that William & I each
from our own particular experience of the married life warn her
against it. 'Silly girl', quoth Mr Willie. People here say he is
looking very well. Lucy is going to Newcastle upon Tyne at
Christmas & thence in May (or perhaps she comes home first I'm
sure I don't know—to London—Sue has refused every invitation

[1] Fragment of paper torn away.

but to me! there's a compliment—and she has had 5 to my certain
knowledge. Bessy is still in Gloucestershire. Anne (Kate's sister)
is coming to Mr Carson's at Everton in January. So the Fisher did
not irradiate the Wellington Rooms after all 'you know'—young
North was unkind or faithless, and the mind affects the body.
Report says Mr James Herford is going to marry Miss Emma
Ryland—there's a bit of scan-mog[1]—for the Bewsey St[2] girls.
Susan brings her guitar which is very charming[;] the darling[—]
how I do love that girl. Tell my dear dear mother how I did
enjoy her pears—only I was sorry she did not keep them herself.
My blessing (there are two senses to that word) to Mr Dimock.
That pretty little fair red-haired Miss Flack (that we met at the
Alexr Henrys in days of yore is going to be married to Mr George
Gardner. Addio carissima mea, vi bacio le mani—Kind love to the
Bewsy St family, Mrs Saml Gaskell—& kinder than kind to Anne.
Your affectionate and loving sister
E. C. Gaskell.

Oh Bob! What glorious games at whist you & I & Willie will
have when you come with an independent dummy who *shall*
play as he likes—Recommend Miss Mitchell's school through
thick & thin—Only 25 guineas a year for boarders.

3 **4** 5

ELIZABETH GASKELL[3]

Sandlebridge.[4] Thursday Mg
[12 May 1836]

My dearest Lizzy,
    I wish I could paint my present situation to you. Fancy me
sitting in an old fashioned parlour, 'doors & windows opened
wide', with casement window opening into a sunny court all
filled with flowers which scent the air with their fragrance—in the
very depth of the country—5 miles from the least approach to a
town—the song of birds, the hum of insects the lowing of cattle

[1] ? Scandal-mongering.   [2] In Warrington.
    [3] *Address* Miss E. Gaskell | Revd E. R. Dimock's | Warrington. *Postmark* KNUTS-
FORD | MY [?]13 | 1836. *Annotation* May 13./1836.
    [4] The home of the Hollands, Mrs Gaskell's mother's (and Aunt Lumb's) family.

the only sounds—and such pretty fields & woods all round—
Here are Baby[,] Betsy, Mama, & Bessy Holland—and indeed at
this present moment here is Sue, who has ridden over, to bring us
news of the civilized world—in the shape of letters &c &c[.] One
from Aunt Lumb enclosing yours, & so full of gratitude about the
rasberry wine, & so overflowing with thanks to you and your
mother, that I fear there is little chance of my coming in for any
of it. I shall try & put an *affront* into her head I can assure you, but I
fear she will 'swallow['] the affront. She begs her kind regards to
your mother, & that I will say how *very* kind she thought it of her,
& how much she shall enjoy getting tipsy—It *was* very kind of you
to think of it, & you are a nice creature, & every body has so liked
you, & I do so wish you were here to revel in flowers, & such
thorough country. We are up with the birds, and sitting out on the
old flag steps in the very middle of fragrance—'far from the busy
hum of men', but *not* far from the busy hum of bees. Here is a
sort of little standard library kept—Spenser, Shakspeare, Wordsworth, & a few foreign books, & we sit & read & dream our time
away—except at meals when we *don't* dream over cream that
your spoon stands upright in, & such sweet\(not sentimental but
literal)/oven-cakes, and fresh butter. Baby is at the very tip-top
of bliss; & gives a happy prospect of what she will be at your
Aunt Holbrook. There are chickens, & little childish pigs, & cows
& calves & horses, & *baby horses,* & fish in the pond, & ducks in the
lane, & the mill & the smithy, & sheep & baby-sheep, & flowers—
oh! you would laugh to see her going about, with a great big
nosegay in each hand, & wanting to be *bathed* in the golden
bushes of wall-flowers—she is absolutely fatter since she came
here, & is I'm sure stronger. I suspect I'm writing a queer medley,
for I have had a walk in the heat, & my hand trembles & I think
my brain trembles too—I ramble so. I was so sorry to miss you,
and for James going when there was no need whatever for you to
go. I rode above 18 miles that day, & lunched at Mr Davenport's
at Capesthorne—such a beautiful place, not the house which is
rather shabby; but the views from the Park—The next day Wm
and I had a ride, Mr Deane mounting & accompanying us both—
nearly to Boden [*sic*]. Saturday & Monday I rode again, & came
here on Tuesday, having my choice, between coming here, &
another 18 mile ride with Mr Deane—but I longed to see the old
familiar place. The house & walls are over-run with roses[,]
honeysuckles & vines—not quite in flower, *but all but*—Betsy is

quite in her element, and teaches baby to call the pigs, & grunt just like any old sow. I have brought Coleridge with me, & am *doing*[1] him & Wordsworth[—] *fit place for the latter*! I sat in a shady corner of a field gay with bright spring flowers—daisies, primroses, wild anenomes, & the 'lesser celandine,' & with lambs all around me—and the air so full of sweet sounds, & wrote my first chapr of W. yesterday in pencil—& today I'm going to finish him —and my heart feels so full of him I only don't know how to express my fullness without being too diffuse. If you were here, I think your advice, & listening, would do me so much good—but I have\to/do it all by myself alone, crunching up my paper, & scuttering my pencil away, when any one comes near. I have done all my *composition* of Ld B—, & done Crabbe outright since you left & got up Dryden & Pope—so now I'm all clear & straight before me. I shall dearly like seeing your book but I fear it will vex me by giving more beautiful quotations of people I can't go back to—but I want to see how many moderns he has done &c— If I don't get much writing done here, I get a{n} great many thoughts on the subject—for one can't think any thing but poetry & happiness. The worst is tomorrow evening—Mrs Robt Greg & her sisters are coming to see Bessy being her great cronies, & I don't care an atom for them, yet shall have to be tidy & civil. Oh! I wish you could have staid; it would have been so glorious this weather—& your not going to {Knutsford}\Liverpool/was the most provoking, because your being good seems so useless. I stay here till Saturday, when we go home, and next week Sue & Bessy come to stay here again, & William & I are to come over for a day.—Was it not provoking? if we had not been so delicate we might have had Benjie & gone over to Boden—he wants work—I am very sorry to hear of Jane having the smallpox—mind you tell me how she is when you write again—Pray thank your dear mother for Baby's biscuits. Poulton goes on sounding as cheap, & I think we shall go there in August. *I bought* Bessy's bonnet for 15s—(*Aunt Lumb* paying for it) and people say it suits me! It is ley-day, & cows & horses come by dozens down the Shady Lane— some from Manchester[,] only think. Bessy & I have our German novel here, but I shy it rather being very anxious to get on with my poets—I think I shall go home (to M[ancheste]r next Saturday week—or I may stay over the next week, as it will be M[ancheste]r

---

[1] A reference to the imitations of the poets which she and William Gaskell planned to do.

Race-week which I hate—Sue sends 'very big thanks' for the
song, and is so shocked at the length of the song but thinks it very
pretty—It is *11* just, & Sue thinks we are so *late dining*; she has 'no
idea of such fashionable hours *here*'[.] To comfort her I can tell her
here is a capital skull come in, since she stuck her head through the
window. Baby is gone into the wood to see the merry little Brook.
Can you fancy us—Bessy is persuading Sue to stay—and offering
her clothes—and Sue thinks if she does stay she must follow
Bessy's Welsh example & turn her riding habit into a night-gown.
Fancy the *comfort* of it this hot weather. Oh! that Life would make
a stand-still in this happy place? Uncle Holland saw Baby yesterday & took word home (Sue says that she looks better already.[)]
Now mind you write again, & none of your nimini-pimini notes,
but a sensible nonsensical crossed[1] letter as *I do*—Baby often talks
of Liz—and we keep you up in her mind[.] I am glad John is
going to Germany—very— & I know that Mr Perry & like him—
I'll take care about the basket, & now goodbye seeing the table is
wanted for dinner. Now *do* write love—

Your very affectionate   & sending love to
Anne & your mother   sister Elizabeth Gaskell . . .

₄ 5 ₇

ELIZABETH GASKELL[2]

Saturday afternoon
[18 March 1837]

My dearest Eliza,

I received your most kind and affectionate letter this morng
and though wearied with letter writing in answer to enquiries
from unknown friends of Aunt Lumb's in Yorkshire I must not
let such a dear letter remain unanswered. Those who love me are
indeed becoming precious. Wm's account of this dearest of aunts
wd of course only go to Wednesday when he left. That afternoon
she began to grow worse, and all Thursday she was in an agony of

---

[1] I.e. with the text of the latter part written vertically over the horizontal sec-
tions at the beginning. This happens with the first 2 pages of this letter, 'come over
for a day . . . ' to the end being written over the first part as far as ' . . . but the
views from'.

[2] *Address* Miss E. Gaskell- | Revd E. R. Dimock's | Sankey St | Warrington.
Postmark KNUTSFORD. *Annotation* Feb./37.

pain in her head & side—her right hand, convulsed, her whole frame trembling, yet never uttering a word—or groan except when directly asked how she was—when she merely said 'no better'—My Uncle durst not order any more leeches, as she only took little morsels of black currant jelly to moisten her mouth. All that night she continued the same—yesterday m[ornin]g at 7 my uncle ordered 4 more leeches to be applied—which did not relieve the pain while they reduced her to so feeble a state that she hardly spoke all yesterday—*see*, she cannot for she is completely blind, not even distinguishing light from darkness. Last night her sufferings were so very great that my uncle ordered an anodyne draught which sent her into a most gentle & easy sleep. When she wakens the pain is nearly as violent, catching her breath in deep gasps, & her head is dreadful—but this calm deep sleep *must*[,] I cannot help fancying[,] do her good. This morng she surprized us all by asking for a bit of what we call muffin & you pikelake.[1] I think she had tasted nothing but tea & bits of preserve & a *little* arrow-root since Wednesday week.[2] Lucy went out directly & searched the town over for one, and she eat about this much of the whole thickness of a penny one, [here a small diagram of a segment of a circle is inserted] which I can not help fancying a good sign. And yet the feeling is that this longing to have her still is selfish. Oh what a blessed change would it be to her! And if she did recover Uncle Wm says she would be blind & crippled on her left side for life. Oh Lizzy! is it not sad? When I see her almost intolerable sufferings, which are in no ways relieved by any efforts of those around her I almost feel as if I could give her up, so that she could 'enter upon her *rest*'—Then again, as now, when she is gently & calmly asleep I hope against hope that my uncle may be wrong & that we may yet have her once again among us with her gentle loving voice & deep tender interest in those around her— Oh there never will be one like her—She never never has said so much as Oh! or groaned though at times in such extremity of suffering. I believe my uncle says it is very unusual for a paralytic case to be accompanied with so much pain. Her faint broken voice is for ever thanking us for our kindness, as if *we* could ever repay her thousand kind thoughts & deeds to us. This morng I told her I had heard from you & that your mother was not

---

[1] Pikelet (NED).

[2] A diary Mrs Gaskell once kept gives Wednesday, March 8th, as the date of Mrs Lumb's paralytic stroke. See Hopkins, *Gaskell*, p. 61.

very well. She did not speak nor did I feel then that she heard me—
but nearly an hour after I saw her trying to speak, & bending over
her caught in her gasping breath with many pauses even in this
short sentence. 'I have been thinking I should like to send Mrs
Dimock something as she is poorly.' I thanked her—and after a
pause she said again 'I should like it exceedingly—some of this
scent I like so much—get a bottle' but the words I write—& you
read in a minute—took her five minutes, I am sure[,] & she was
quite faint with pain. The day before yesterday I was naming a
poor woman to one of my cousins as we stood in the room by the
fire thinking she was asleep—the poor woman had lost her baby
and was distressed with her milk not going—Some time after
Nurse (the nurse who was with me in my confinement) came in
& Aunt Lumb made a sign to her to come to the bedside & asked
her what was good to assuage the milk—and when she told her
Aunt L. said to me 'Elizabeth send word to Mrs Greenwood, be
sure'. But I shall have many particulars to tell you & Anne when I
see you that I know & (thank you for it, dear sisters) you will be
interested in hearing. All this time I have never thanked you for
your kind offer about dear little Marianne[.] Of course Wm told
you our plan. The next door but one I have lodgings where I
sleep leaving here at 10 and always back by 8 if not sooner. Betty
& the two children are there—so whenever Baby wants nursing I
am in in a minute—at the beginning of the week I shd have been
most thankful for your offer about MA, but now I have two reasons
against it. One is that she has a violent cold in her head & a slight
cough and the other is that Aunt L. has once or twice expressed a
strong wish to hear 'her dear little voice once again' and has had a
spunge biscuit behind her pillow this 4 days to give her. So I shd
not like her to be out of the way. Aunt L has seen her once since
she was taken ill. But every one says Aunt L's heart & soul for the
last 8 weeks have been with the child—never parting with her day
or night, & feeling the responsibility so deeply—*too* deeply. Give
my dear love to Anne & my mother & thank you once again for
all the expressions of affection. Do write again—You don't know
how hurriedly this is written or you would excuse it. Yours ever
affectionately & gratefully

                                                        E C Gaskell.

I fear the scent wd not be worth the carriage or I would get it.
Aunt L does not know we are in lodgings[.]

₀ **6** ₀

?HOLBROOK GASKELL

Knutsford, Wednesday,
[c. 1837][1]

My dear Holbrook,

I have been a long time in writing to you have not I? and now that I am taking up my pen it is such a bad one that I long to lay it down again. I am very sorry to say that old Betty declines coming to you. She has settled down in Warrington as a washerwoman, and as she has pretty good employment she feels unwilling to give it up. Now it is upon her you must lay the burden and the blame of my not having written sooner, for as she declined the situation she was unwilling to put Miss Mitchell to the expense of postage, —so sent it by a coalman who forgot to deliver it till yesterday. As soon as I heard of her refusal I went off to my second hope in the shape of a very respectable widow—about 35. She lost h⟨e⟩r husband about three months ago, and my cousins have known her long, and been much interested for her. She has only been married a short time and had previously been 16 years in service, as cook and as housemaid. She bears a most excellent character. I have sent for her, and been speaking again to her this morning. She is I think a person that would just suit you; but at present she can hardly decide as to whether she will take the place or go out as a nurse which some of her friends wish her to do. She has also some debts owing to her late husband which she wishes to collect —so that if she came it would hardly be under two months I am afraid. I said I would write to you and ask if you could wait as long, and I desired her to let me know in the course of next week if she will take the place, if you and she agree. Perhaps you will be kind enough to write, and tell me if you could wait for 2 months ⟨...⟩[2]
the carriage will come to fetch my cousins to their weekly duties at the Sunday School. I am afraid you will be disappointed at the uncertainty in which everything seems involved, but do not get into the dungeon of Giant Despair, nor yet into the Slough of Despond for there is no knowing what I may not *achi*eve, (or

---

[1] Dating very doubtful, but Mrs Gaskell's eldest daughter Marianne, born 12 September 1834, is the only one mentioned at the end of the letter.
[2] Rest is missing; what follows is crossed writing on page 1.

*atch*ieve?) yet. Besides you know Faint heart never won fair lady in the shape of a servant, and Nothing venture nothing have &c &c. I may hear of some one else through my cousins who know the ins & outs of every poor family in Knutsford. Marianne sends 'a kiss and a love, and wants to come & see you.' Goodbye my dear Holbrook.

Your affect[ionate] coz
E. C. Gaskell.

'Mrs. Gaskell
  P. Holland's Esqre
  Knutsford'

₅ 7 ₉

ELIZABETH GASKELL[1]

Wednesday wine time.
[30 March 1838]

My dearest Lizzy,

I ought to feel very grateful and I do feel very grateful to you for your coming to us in the 1st instance, and for writing to tell us of Mr & Mrs H G's promised visit,—you not being a housekeeper cannot tell the blessing it is to have a little announcement of visits, and our 'large dinner' shall be kept till Thursday. Moreover naturally tomorrow would have been a regular rummaging brushing, carpet taking up, cleaning day; and 10 to 1 we should have been caught in the middle of our hubbub as we have been aforetime. In short my gratitude for this has nearly knocked the other gratitude (for your coming) out of my head—but you cannot think how I rejoiced when I got yr letter saying you wd come—So did dear Marianne who told every body for the next day or two 'Aunt Lizzy is coming',—and we are to go and see that everything is comfortable in your little mousehole of a room. She is to be your little maid, and help you dress, (such dressing,) and run your errands,—and [at] least this she is to do, if she is well;— In order to prevent her reckoning too securely on your coming I said Aunt Lizzy will come if we are all well but who must we ask to keep us well— (MA.) God;— (after a pause), 'I shall ask God to keep Aunt Lizzy well too[']. Poor child; she had an attack of croup

---

[1] *Address* Miss E. Gaskell. *Annotation* March 30–/38.

on Friday night—about 8 o'clock. I heard a cough which though
I had never heard croup I felt sure must be croup, & so thought
Wm; he went for Sam, after giving her 24 drops Ipec wine—Wm
went to the Infirmary in 10 minutes—Sam was out, but William
sent a note after him, & by 11 he was here,—he sat quietly enough
till she coughed when he flew up stairs, & said we must send for
Mr Partington instantly; it was ½ p. 12. Mr P. came & he & Sam
got it under,—Sam & Wm sat up all night—& I was up till 2—She
has begun to come down stairs again muffled in a blanket, and is in
capital spirits, though she still coughs at night & has got a bad
tongue[.] I expect to hear of poor little Edward Deane's death by
every post—He was *so* well last week when Mrs Deane was here,
& had the croup so on Sunday that my cousins wrote word he was
given up. Since I began this note Charles (Liverpool) has been
here,—I have asked Anne (it was such a temptation) to come &
spend two days here in the Bazaar week—I knew I should & I
thought you would enjoy seeing her & enjoy hearing all about
Kate's wedding, though as Wm says where you are to put Anne is
a mystery to me—however I think you will put up with a few
scrambles for a night—won't you. Kate is to be married on the 10th
I think. I will send you Anne's letter—her wedding dress white
chip hat, orange flowers pale lavender satin pelisse trimmed with
swansdown—they ford across the Tratte, a most dangerous place
by the way full of quick sands[,] are married, breakfast at the
beautiful little inn near there, & the whole party accompany the
happy pair for a stage or two—they go to London to choose
carriage &c & then to Paris &c—By the way—we sell in bonnets
at the Bazaar—you said something about a cap, but here we sell in
bonnets—I have a beauty coming for the occasion,—& your pink
will be exquisite. I WISH you cd come before Saturday,—for I shall
have a deal for you to do in the way of folding up and arranging
for OUR stand—I have a good many things already and about 1
doz, which I myself would say thank you for—I have been so
anxious about MA that I am feeling most unfit for fatigue—I am
as weak & as thin,—but when I told Mrs Robberds I feared it
would be too much for me & that I had rather stay & take care of
MA she said they had had such difficulties in getting *standers*,
that I must[.] Wm says I look *miserable*—which remark he repeats
about 20 times a day—but I have not been out for a week.—We
stand from 10 till 5—But Oh what teas we must & will have.—
Dearest Lizzy ever since you were such a dear comforter last

summer I long for you in every grief & anxiety—and last week
when MA was so poorly I often wished for you—I quite look
forwards to seeing you,—Meta has a bad cold too—I expect you
will be delighted with her, bless her—My kind love to all—E C G.

0 **8** 12

WILLIAM and MARY HOWITT[1]

[14 Dover Street
Oxford Road
Manchester.
May 1838]

[She thanks them for the great pleasure two of their works had
given her 'by their charming descriptions of natural scenery and
the thoughts and feelings arising from the happy circumstances of
rural life'.]

I was brought up in a country town, and my lot is now to live in
or rather on the borders of a great manufacturing town, but when
spring days first come and the bursting leaves and sweet earthy
smells tell me that 'Somer is ycomen in,' I feel a stirring instinct
and long to be off into the deep grassy solitudes of the country,
just like a bird wakens up from its content at the change of the
seasons and tends its way to some well-known but till then forgotten land. But as I happen to be a woman instead of a bird, as I
have ties at home and duties to perform, and as, moreover, I have
no wings like a dove to fly away, but if I travel I must go by
coach and 'remember the coachman,' why I must stay at home
and content myself with recalling the happy scenes which your
books bring up before me.

The old solitary manor-houses, surrounded with trees, grey
with lichens, and with their painted windows, from which one
may in fancy catch a glimpse of the inhabitants of former days
walking through long dark avenues—with their solemn deserted
feeling reminding you of the merry laugh or of the burst of grief
that may never more be echoed by the old walls, of the love and
the life that touched up with warmth and beauty the stately
desolation around—oh! I am particularly glad you are thinking of
describing some of these solemnly poetical places.

[1] From a printed source.

Near the little, clean, kindly country town, where, as I said before, I was brought up there was an old house with a moat within a park called Old Tabley, formerly the dwelling-place of Sir Peter Leycester, the historian of Cheshire, and accounted a very fine specimen of the Elizabethan style. It is beautifully kept by its owner, who lives at a new house built about half a mile off, the velvet lawn up to the deep windows being mown and rolled most regularly, and the large laurels and the magnificent beeches trimmed with most excellent care. Here on summer mornings did we often come, a merry young party, on donkey, pony, or even in a cart with sacks swung across—each with our favourite book, some with sketch-books, and one or two baskets filled with eatables. Here we rambled, lounged and meditated: some stretched on the grass in indolent repose, half reading, half musing with a posy of musk-roses from the old-fashioned trim garden behind the house, lulled by the ripple of the waters against the grassy lawn; some in the old crazy boats, that would do nothing but float on the glassy water, singing, for one or two were of a most musical family and warbled like birds: 'Through the greenwood, through the greenwood,' or 'A boat, a boat unto the ferry,' or some such old catch or glee. And when the meal was spread beneath a beech tree of no ordinary size (did you ever notice the peculiar turf under beech shade?) one of us would mount up a ladder to the belfry of the old chapel and toll the bell to call the wanderers home. Then if it rained, what merry-making in the old hall. It was galleried, with oak settles and old armour hung up, and a painted window from ceiling to floor. The strange sound our voices had in that un-frequented stone hall! The last time I was there during the fall of rain from one of those heavy clouds which add to a summer day's beauty, when every drop of rain is sun-tinged and falls merrily amongst the leaves, one or two of Shakespeare's ballads: 'Blow, blow thou winter wind,' and 'Hark, hark the lark at Heaven's gate sings,' &c. were sung by the musical sisters in the gallery above, and by two other musical sisters (Mary and Ellen Need-ham from Lenton near Nottingham) standing in the hall below.

How I wish my dear husband and I could afford to ramble about the country this summer, the sun is shining so brightly. But we are not the richest of the rich (my husband is a Unitarian minister), and, moreover, I have two little girls to watch over.

ELIZABETH GASKELL[1]

Tuesday morning—14 Dover Street
[17 July 1838]

My very dearest Lizzy,

Here's a sheet of paper for you! I only hope it may come to you on a wet day. I shall put down every thing; not knowing whether you will care to hear it, or not, but I have not much time, and I must write straight forward whatever comes into my head. (In the first place I do thoroughly sympathize with you, leaving a large merry party in a house,—and I can quite fancy the sort of looks you send to the mountains, the other side of which look *towards* if not *to* a place where you have been very happy.) Beaumaris itself I remembered as a pretty watering place, as watering places go; but not wild or grand or anything in that line; and it is rather tantalizing to see mountains without being able to get at them, and it is a very long round {from}\by/the Bridge. Still I wish you could get to see Aber, (5 miles from Bangor on the Conway road & right opposite you by sea, only you can't get at it, coz of the shore being so bad) where Wm and I spent a fortnight of our wedding journey—and where I spent a very happy month with 17 aunts, cousins and such like, once before—and then Conway; a Saracenic town, built when folk had just been crusading it and thought of nothing but the 'Paynim Soldan Saladin', and —and—Oh how I should like to go sometime with you into Wales & show you all my favourite haunts. I am very sorry you could not go up Snowdon, and it is a great pity you could not join them again at P P[2]—if it were only for that. It is perhaps as well that you should come down gradually from mountains; not at once from Snowdonia to flat Lancashire. I remember when I first came from spending a very happy fortnight at Plâs Brereton (nr Caernarvon you know) to Liverpool I used to get on a sort of knoll from which I could see the Welsh hills, and think of the places beyond again. When I was at school I think I liked Harriet Twamley very much; Louisa was not so clever (but a better temper;) not that we reckoned Harriet anything particular in the

---

[1] *Address* Miss E. Gaskell. | Revd E. R. Dimock's | Mrs Cooper's | 7, The Green | Beaumaris | Single Sheet. *Postmark* MANCHESTER | JY 18 | 1838 [a Wednesday].
[2] Plas-yn-Penrhyn, Merionethshire, which belonged to Samuel Holland, Elizabeth Gaskell's future father-in-law.

clever line, but she was *very* painstaking, and I never saw two sisters that loved one another more dearly. Then when I saw her a year or two ago she struck me as very much gone off—I had heard of her being a great flirt in the mean time, and she seemed to me to have got a very commonplace sort of second rate cant; (such as calling Uncle Holland 'that dear sweet old gentleman' and that sort of very second-rate sweet sentimental affectation[)]. I was very sorry for her for she evidently could hardly bear to hear the Sharpes sing some of the duetts that she & Louisa used to sing. But you know I only saw her once or twice then, so I had no oppy of judging. I know Fanny thinks her very much improved. In one of your letters you mention Uncle Sam having his meals alone. That was a sign that he & Sam had had a tiff, ten to one about their mining speculations. Edward Holland allows Uncle S. 200£ a year as long as he does not speculate, and Sam is to mention if he does. Now Sam's notion of speculations and Uncle Sam's differ widely—so you may fancy the uncomfortable work that sometimes ensues. I know Cwm Morfyn Lake very well. Lucy & I walked there from Ffestiniog last autumn, and I could fancy that in dry weather it would be a very pleasant place for a picnic. When we were there it was as wet and boggy as heart could desire, and I sopped my feet completely, and went into one of those little cottages to take off my shoes & stockings and give them a thorough drying, and the woman cd not speak English or we Welsh, but we had merry laughs and some conversation, and a good piece of oat cake notwithstanding. How I shall enjoy talking over Wales with you—*When* shall we meet. I wish with all my heart you were coming here instead of going home to talk parle voo to little petticoats. Could not you manage it? *Do* if you possibly can; & bring Anne with you. Bob says she is gone to Beaumaris to join you, and we will so talk all three at once if you will. And why the d—(Honi soit qui mal y pense) should not you—it would save expense to come straight from Lpool—And now must I tell you something about ourselves—We are 'here today, & gone tomorrow', as the fat scullion maid said in some extract in Holland's Exercise book. I staid a week longer at Knutsford than I intended at Mrs Green's, and very pleasant it was; & very glad I was to get MA the oppy of being with such nice little girls as Annie & Ellen, who are charming little unselfish things. I saw a good deal of Mrs John Long whom I like,—and something of Mrs Henry Long but not much. She & I get on much as usual[,] that is to say[,] not at all. Mrs Green hardly sees anything of her[.] They have each called on one another twice, and two times out of the four have missed. I called her but they were out. Then I saw *the* Coronation gaieties in Knutsford which I enjoyed because I knew every body.—And the next morng I left by Ruffley with my children twain. That was on Friday—Monday we drank tea with the Miss Marslands, and went to see a night blowing Cereus at Dukinfield Darbishire's. Such a flower—a splendid white flower with a golden glory round it. Tuesday went to see the Collins in their new house—Mrs C—as large as life. Wednesday had an invitation to a Christening where we had never been before—at a Mr Bradford's an American, who married a Miss Taylor sister of that pretty Mrs W. Holland you saw here once on a call—both very nice looking people. So we set off earlyish 4 o'clock say & called on Sam on the way whom we found not looking well certainly though he said he was better than he had been. About six we arrived at a large handsome house far away on the left of Pendleton toll bar. Ushered in with much astonishment[,] heard scuttering away to dress—and found that the Christening had been in the morning, and that we were dreadfully too early. However when Mr & Mrs Bradford were dressed—(she in a *beautiful* worked white muslin over white satin[1] shoes, brussels lace, & flowers in her hair looking so very pretty,) I in the very gown I am now sitting in, great thick shoes, & Wm in boots & without gloves) they came in & very agreeable he was & very lovely she. He is a great friend of Bryant the poet, so W. & he had some pleasant confabulation—about 8 oclock full dressed people began pouring in, and we went into a large dancing room—windows open, hothouse plants, muslin curtains &c, & there we danced till supper at 12, & such a supper! I suppose the Bradfords are very rich,—for wine & grapes, & pines, & such cakes my mouth waters at the thought, & ducks & green peas, & new potatoes & asparagus & chickens without [e]nd, & savoury pies, & all sort of beautiful confectionery—and we wended our way home by day*light*— $\frac{1}{2}$ past 3 when we got home walking to be sure. You would have enjoyed it—waltzing, galloppes, &c &c—Mrs W. Holland looked so well, & on dit is going to be married again to a Mr Bischoff a german. Thursday a quiet day. Friday after breakfast D Darbishire called, and arranged that Marianne & I should go to Rivington (where Mrs D D. and all the little D D's are staying) that

---

[1] The words 'white satin' are repeated in the MS.

afternoon & Wm who has to preach at Cockey Moor on Sunday
should join us on Monday. So such a bustle, arranging for Mrs
Green & Annie & Ellen coming as today, to stay till Thursday;
a party on Thursday evening of Mr & Mrs ⟨?⟩ford, a school committee meeting here on Wednesday, & Mrs Clegg to meet
⟨? Mrs⟩ Green too for Wednesday; and at 5 MA & I were off in
the Bolton railway, & thence on in D D's gig to Rivington. A
walk and a heavy thunderstorm that night. The next morning a
most charming drive, in the evening up the Pike with MA and
all the children\and a couple of Miss Fletchers from Lpool/.
Poor MA was thoroughly wearied & wet,\in the bogs/which
was a drawback.\We were not home till ½ past 8 having been on
our legs since 4./Sunday to chapel in the morning two walks in
the afternoon—Oh Rivington is such a very pretty place, & so
thoroughly country. Yesterday morning I sketched & Wm came;
in the afternoon we both rode on horseback up & down the
country—then a walk after tea. This morning we were off at half
past 8 for Bolton, home per rail road—found your letter, & re-
fusals to every one of our invites to meet the Bradfords, so we are
in a comfortable dilemma as to who will come to meet them at so
short a notice. Carvers & Marsdens we ought to have & we shall
have a respectablish supper—but too short an invitation, & too
cardplaying, too old,—Worthingtons,—too young, wd come but
what must we do with 'em when we have got 'em—Not room
enough for dancing,—and people get tired of bagatelle else we
have got the Mason's bagatelle board—So what *are* we to do—
Well! that job will be jobbed before you get this letter. Next
Tuesday W, I, & MA, go to Mrs Alcocks of Gatley for a day or
two. I forgot to say Mrs Green had put off her coming which is
just the most provoking thing in the world, as I had engaged a
girl from Knutsford who is here to stay over this week to help in
all the extra work, & meant to get all sorts of things in.—Baby
really walks alone now & is getting a sweet little thing—MA's
cough is much better thank you. This Rivington air has done
wonders; and made me so strong & so hungry. Good air for ever!
Hurrah! I wonder if we ever can hit upon the same excursion at
the same time. I should so like to be at Beaumaris with you. Wm
is with Dr Bernstein or I would ask him your propriety questions.
Oh! who *must* we ask to meet the Bradfords—hang 'em. You
have been a precious sister in the writing line, and Mrs Purse is
not at all displeased with you. Did you see Mr Brown? did you

think my memory sketch of the house like? We staid rather longer
at Knutsford in the sweet thought that perhaps Aunt Ab might do
what she once talked of—ask us to keep house for her while she
went to Weston Point; but I thought she repented & cooled in her
invite and Susan said we should be more prudent to go, for Aunt
Ab would be sure to find fault with every thing we did in her
absence, and we shd only get into scrapes. *Perhaps* in August we
go to Rowsley Wm I & Susan—I don't go if Sue does not. W.
preaches at Buxton on the 17th[.] My love to Ann & ask her how
the Queen was when she last saw her? How's John—The Masons
are in Paris. Alcocks & Asplands in Scotland,—'Dance Merryman
dance Out of Scotland into France.' Charles called twice last
week; unlucky*ish*[,] for Eliz was gone home, & we looked a little
HUG-HER, MUG-HER? which I know ⟨he⟩ notices and abhors. I will
always send you any P Penrhyn news I hear; & you do d[itt]o. Dr
Bernstein is gone, so now we must attack the Bradford dilemma
in a solemn divan—Farewell sweet sister—Thank you for telling
me all about the [?Puffins;] don't you think\Criccaeth/a wild
pretty little fishing-town—The pleasure of sketching is the reminding you of the time you did it. You have been *very* good
about writing, and I'll ask for you to go another journey again.
Wednesday morning,—and our Bradford dilemma not solved.—
William is going to give a course of lectures on the poets & poetry
of humble life at the Mechanic's Institute (or Institution?) at Miles
Platting—a new subject, & if W had taken time to it he would have
done it capitally—as it is I fear his usual fault of procrastination
will prevent him doing justice to it. Mrs J J. Tayler has got an
impromptu baby at Blackpool;—went there and lo & behold a
little girl unexpectedly made her appearance, & clothes have had
to be sent in such a hurry. Bathing places do so much good.
Susan & Mary went to Blackpool last year, but did not derive the
same benefit. Mr J J Tayler came home\from London/on
Saturday hoping to find wife & children at home but had to post
off to Blackpool leaving Father Abraham to preach, & on Sunday
morning Mrs J J T presented him with the little lady—So ends
Mrs J J Tayler's '*delicate state of health, arising from some internal
complaint,*' as Mr Ransom called it. Now am I not writing you a
proper long letter? I consider it to *both* of you, for if I had known
Ann's address I should have written to her in London, to thank
her for a very nice letter she wrote me nearly six weeks ago. I
wonder what you are doing at Beaumaris—I wish you would go

to Priestholme or Puffin's Island—It is such a singular place & to a botanist (*like you* Ma'am) would be a great treat—Many ships returning from Foreign ports—used to make offerings at the monastery there,--and cast out their ballast, which often contained curious seeds which took root—The old monastery is in ruins—but there is a telegraph station[;] the man who kept it years & years ago in my youth, had fought in the Victory with Nelson—the Puffins too are queer uncanny looking animals. I *long* to be in those wild places again, with the fresh sea breeze round me, so thoroughly exhilarating. How does Mr Dimock like Beaumaris? What a pleasant change to Ann after hot horrible smoky wicked Babylon the Great—only I wish you were in a wilder more Welshy place. I cannot help *feeling* the *feelings* for you. I know [how] you must be *feeling* at the last happy six weeks over & gone, with the uncertainty when such another may come again.

You never mention Capn Barton. Is he 'to the fore' yet? Did you ever see Mr Greaves? Now do think of coming here from L-pool you & Anne—If you do not spend the 2 sovereigns *my* way, I'll spend it for you Miss, & never shall you set eyes on their bonny yellow faces—you & Anne—Anne said she would come & leave the little petticoats awhile in peace. How will you answer for it when you meet Coleridge in heaven, & he hears you have been teaching his abhorred language—Ten to one he gives you a box on your etherial ear.—Dearest Lizzy thank you for feeling sure of my sympathy—there is nothing that I like better than the trust in my *responding feeling*. Now for a grand Johnsonian sentence which I beg you will read aloud to elevate me in the Dimockian eyes. He who can wander by the melodious waters of the Menai and partake of the finny tribes that gambol in the translucent current, and can disport himself at pleasure in the lunar-governed tide; the man who can do this, I say, and return to the home of his progenitors neither more rotund, with the careless felicity of such a mode of {living}\existence/, nor more attenuated from the excess of laudable excitement, deserves not to be classed with the human species, but to take his station among the moluscar tribes—Find out my meaning if you can, for I can't —So ends my tale[.] Love to all[.] Write very soon to yr affect [ionate] sister

E C Gaskell

₉ **10** ₁₁

ELIZABETH GASKELL[1]

[7 August 1838]
Tuesday ½ past 12. What were we saying &
doing & feeling & thinking this time last
week?

My dearest dear Lizzy,
     You have no notion how overwhelmed with business I have
been since I came home, or you may depend upon it you wd have
heard sooner from me if only to tell you how very full my head
& heart have been in thinking of you. Lucy must have found me
desperately dull on Thursday & Friday, for I could not keep from
thinking of you & your affairs. Chas came & met Sam on Friday
as promised, & afterwards I had a confidential & *satisfactory* talk
with Sam, & urged him with all my eloquence to write & I hope
he has done before this. *He* thinks Chas like Wm in looks & manners, which is *funny*. I don't. Charles talked over you when we
got a private word or two after we had *packed* Lucy off into town;
and said pretty much the same things as before, about yr superi-
ority &c. He sent off his letter from here. I longed to tell MA
to call him *Uncle* Chas, but resisted the D—l. On Saty we (Lucy &
I) went to Patricroft, to call on Nasmyths & Mrs R. G. found
James Nasmyth gone to Sheffield to make an offer, so I suppose
being ⟨in⟩ love is an epidemic complaint just now. Lucy in raptures ⟨over⟩ the ⟨N⟩asmyths paintings—(Hurrah by the way! for
we've got our ⟨   ⟩ precious painting at this very moment glad-
dening Wm's eyes.) Asked Mrs R G & Miss Nasmyth to come &
dine here today & we're expecting them every instant (which
makes me too hurried to go into any expression of feeling for you
my darling Lizzy though my heart is full of {them}\it/).We came
home desperately tired, and found something to cheer me in the
shape of a letter about which I will tell you when I have more
time. Sunday I asked Sam to come which he never did, & Arthur
Boult to come to tea which he did. Yesterday settling accounts
for 3 weeks, & ordering two such pretty little Dunstable straw
bonnets lined with white (hatband), & white ribbon, thanks to

[1] *Address* Miss E. Gaskell | Revd E. R Dimocks | Sankey Street | Warrington.
Octagonal Seal Man's head facing left. *Annotations* Aug. 7/38 *and* Mother's Engagement.

dear Grandmama who must come & see them. In the eveng to a stupid dinner at the Darbishires. Horners, Alcock & Jas Turners. Wm went off to finish his lectures in the shape of one on Burns. He was famously clapped bless him, though for want of you to plague he plagues me. I say it is a godsend for me to have something to write about. Today Nasmyths & Gaskells. Funny it will be if Holbrook Gaskell & Chas meet, yet ten to one they will for Charles sends word he is coming to tea, & I begged Mrs R. G to bring Holbrook. Chas would tell you about Aunt's [*sic*] Ab's letter. I send you Annes nice letter to me which please take care of —but it will fill out mine, for writing expecting an interruption every instant is not a good time for telling all one thinks & feels. One is thankful to get in bare facts. By the way after all Susans declining to go with us any where at any time, on account of Saba, she is going to Scotland in a fortnight, which is one of the things I have to struggle against being hurt by. For you don't know how we urged her & wished her & offered to accomodate [*sic*] to her wishes. It seems selfish, & I do try against feeling it. The little girls are I think *so* improving. MA so much more obedient & Meta so very lively, walking here & there & every where bless them, the darlings. They wanted to know when you were coming & I do *so* look forward to it. As soon *as ever* W. comes back. You will see I have heard a vague account of proceedings in Annes letters but I want to know *all* Mr D said & did —Who told him when he was told. My dear dear love to my sweet Anne. I do so love her. I hope she has *quite* got over her attack. Did Fanny Brown spread any report? Oh how much you have too [*sic*] tell! I must end for people come—*Best* love to yr Mother & Bob—ask him to come over—tell him the children will quite forget him. Your own loving sister

E C Gaskell

10 **11** 13

ELIZABETH GASKELL[1]

Friday Evening 8 o'clock.
[17 August 1838]

My dearest Lizzie,

Have not I taken a sheet that will beat yours hollow? Not that I undertake to fill it seeing that I am very tired, having walked to the Fairbairn's and *not* found them at home, so have trudged back without rest & drunk tea at the Mason's &c—Still I have a great deal to tell you of—Anne's charming visit &c—and I know unless I write, you are not likely to write back again—and yours are much the most interesting letters of the two.—I have not written since Tuesday week.[2] Wednesday Chas went to you, and would tell you most of the occurrences of Tuesday afternoon—Miss Nasmyth & Mrs R Gaskell to dinner, James N. & Sam to tea, & Chas too—a pleasant eveng—every body talking at once, which every body likes. Wednesday—Lucy was off at skrike o'day, and I did—what did I do? went to pay some calls methinks—In the evening to the Sydney Potters to meet the Noah Jones I suppose. She is a lively agreeable person; but I do not like him; he sneers at every body & every thing; so I worked away like a tiger. There were the usual Potter set Edmund Potter &c &c—Thursday was a thoroughly wet day here but I did get out for about 20 minutes in the evening, during which time I was caught in a shower, and had the pleasure of seeing Chas Robberds, Mrs & Mr Henry, & Mr & Mrs Lea Birch all in the same misfortune. Friday I over slept myself or I was to have gone with Wm to breakfast with the Noah Jones at Mrs James Darbishire's—However *we* went to christen Mrs Woolley's (Miss Saxon before the Flood) child in the evening. It was but a small room & 21 people in it, doors & windows shut & oh! how close! and oh! how cross-feeling it made me. It was a noble child to make up for every thing else & was called *Edwin* by way of an ugly fine name. Saturday I thought surely *surely* Anne will come today, but Chas came & said Uncle Sam was come & she could not leave him &c. Poor Chas he was in great anxiety at first from the news Anne had brought him

---

[1] *Address* Miss Eliza Gaskell. | Revd E. R. Dimock's. | Favoured by John Allen Esqre. *Octagonal seal* Man's head facing left. *Annotations* Aug/38 *and* Mother's Engagement.   [2] A reference, we have assumed, to Letter 10.

from Warrington; about R. V. Y's letter, and your Uncle's comments thereon.—I sympathized, & William made light of it, & he proved the best comforter, & Chas went away a good deal lighterhearted I guess. I went to to [*sic*] tea to the Miss Marslands uninvited—Sunday to chapel as usual, walked back as *un*usual—consequently rather tired. Sam came in the evening as true as he always is, bless him. I asked him to come and see Anne thinking she would come on Monday as Chas half promised for her. But she never turned up all Monday—and in the eveng Mrs Robberds came, and Sam came but no Anne was there—I felt very poorly too—But Wm read his 2 first lectures on Poetry &c aloud which people seemed very much to like & I lay on the sofa & enjoyed myself in listening. Tuesday Mrs James (Bazaar) Tayler called, and in the middle of her call I heard a rustle in the spare room, and felt sure Anne was come, and so it was—the darling! Can not you fancy how I enjoyed her talking,—the only thing that distressed me was to hear her say she was going by the 5 o'clock train that evening, but after a little coaxing we arranged for her to stay till the next morng and accordingly Wm went down with a note to Chas, whom he met coming up, just for a minute or two—I was just reading your letter when he came in, & I suppose he knew the writing, for after some time he snatched it off my knee; I knew I could not get it by force, so I said very *dignifiedly*! if there is such a word 'Chas I trust to your honour &c',and he soon gave it me back again—and then jumped up & was off in a twinkling. William was sent for to christen the Collin's baby which was dying—not from any superstitious notion—and that kept him away the greater part of the eveng so Anne & I talked & talked—about you & Chas in every possible shape—His fears & wishes at Plas P—[,] his visit at Shottery between times—his scolding Kate for never having made you known before; his letter from the Nag's head *the* Tuesday night—his visit to you,—by the way he likes Mr Dimock better than he expected; Ann's visit to you;—*she* likes & admires our sister Ann so very much &c &c—nor was my tongue idle—in short as Anne says we talked up our talk—not separating till $\frac{1}{4}$ to 12. We agreed amongst other things that when people are come to *yr time of life*, there is no use having long engagements; and that it is a *great* pity, in which Wm fully agrees with us that you should have begun with the petticoats again or rather that you shd be thinking of it, for we do hope you will not really do so foolish a thing, begging your & Mr Dimock's pardon—it is

already nearly half through the $\frac{1}{4}$ & how can you do justice to
them with your mind full of other things? Besides your promise
of coming to us interferes—about this I have much to say, & I
must write to you again as soon as ever you write [?]me word
how affairs are getting on. I can not conceive how they are not
satisfied with R V Y's letter![1] it was much better than I expected!
However you must not be discouraged one bit my darling, but
feel confident in Chas as I'm sure you do—and remember in
trade there always are ups & downs, and you must make up
your mind to times of anxiety—still it will be with the person
you love, & moreover with one who is not of a very anxious
disposition, which is another great blessing—and even if you
should gratify your Aunt & Uncle with a failure you can bear a
little privation, in love & hope and trustfulness. And never mind
every bodys not liking him as well as you do all at once. It{s}
will come in time—nobody ever did like nobody all at once.—
and perhaps it is not desirable that every body should be in love
with Chas all at once.—Every one in his turn.—Well Anne went
early on Wednesday, but first we had Sam to breakfast & a very
pleasant breakfast it was—As soon as Anne was gone, Wm the
two ch⟨ic⟩ks Eliz & I set off to town, & on the road we met
Hunter Miss Nasmyth & Mrs ⟨   ⟩ They turned back with us
but had nothing particular to say. Then W⟨m⟩ saw us M.A.
M.E., Eliz. & I off into an Omnibus to go & spend the day with
Mrs Bradford at Seedly near or beyond Pendleton, & a very
pleasant day we had—but nothing particular in the way of events
—Yesterday afternoon Wm & I went to see Mrs Collins who had
lost her baby & drank tea there—today we have been as I said
before to Mr Fairbairns & back sans rest, sans any thing. Certainly! let Chas pay his postage—he will not write one bit sel-
domer, & its [sic] a very good use ({} I think) for him to put
money to.—Perhaps & prob⟨a⟩bly Holbrook goes with Wm &
S⟨am⟩ who are off on Tuesday—go to Grange the first day Anne!
Wm goes to Buxton to-morrow & comes back on Monday.
After all, and my dear Lizzy I have struggled with my touchy
temper about this, *Susan* & Lucy are going (for 10 days or a fortnight to Scotland), tomorrow—we offered Sue her choice of
time or place almost—to go with us! I do hope my dear Willie
will have fine weather—I shall be so lonely. He has had 2 deputa-

[1] Charles Holland had trading interests in South America. R V Y may be
Richard V. Yates of Liverpool.

tions today to ask him to repeat his lectures—one from the
Teachers of the Sunday School & Senior Scholars—the other
from the Salford Mechanic's institution. Neither of them pay,
whilk is a pity—but *if* the Manchester M. Institution come—
shan't they pay for all. In the mean time we look gracious &
affable as a new made Queen, and are 'most happy' &c—I am
sorry to say Baby is suffering a good deal from her teeth—her eye
teeth which I dread—They are the teeth MA was so ill with at
Prospect Hill—and here we have no boiler to keep water constantly ready. She has cried a good deal since going to bed, &
hardly eaten any supper. Her little mouth is so hot too. I am so
afraid of her being ill while Wm & Sam are away. *If* I show you
one of Wm's letters you must show me one of Chas. That but
fair. I can fancy what a comfort Anne must be to you. She wrote
me such a charming note. I love & admire her so much. I wish
she could come & stay with me while Wm is away, but I fear this
is selfish and I am sure I ought not\to/be selfish after seeing her.
It will be dreary at night, won't it? Now pray write very very
soon, for you cannot think with what interest I look for yr letters
& for your next one particularly—and pity my desolate condition. So you *don't* consider yourself engaged, don't you! What
cd you say about Chas coming over. Coming to buy pins to send
to the South American aboriginal? or what? You may have some
idea what Chas says of you, but for fear you should not have a
correct one he says you are a disagreeable creature—very plain,
very stupid, & the little love he had for y⟨o⟩u once is quite
we⟨a⟩ring away. Do you believe me? Wm has promised\or I
for him, {as we}/to marry you if it comes to a runaway match.
Lucy k⟨n⟩ows nothing from *me* but may guess for Chas said
before her he was going to Warrington the ne⟨x⟩t day—and
called you Eliza—I should like to tell Mrs Robberds *when* you
give me leave. Mr Robberds has been in Wales for a week or 10
days, the greater part of which I fancy he must have spent at
Bangor for Mrs Robberds had a letter from him dated the Pen-
rain arms, where he had been 3 wet days. Baby is crying so—
Poor little thing! I know she is going to have the same bout she
has always had before cutting any teeth, & probably worse as the
eye teeth are always worse. I must say good night in haste—*Do*
write often & soon—and tell me everything. Wm's kind love. My
most especial love to Anne   Yours most affec[tionate]ly
                                                           E C Gaskell

8 **12** 0

MARY HOWITT[1]

[18 August 1838]

I am very glad indeed Mr Howitt thinks of going to Clopton; and one of my reasons for wishing to write soon is that I may beg him thoroughly to explore the neighbourhood (that of Stratford-on-Avon). As a schoolgirl I could not see much, but I heard of many places that I longed to know more about; and yet I can only give you glimpses of what those places were. I know there was a mysterious old farmhouse near Clifford, which had been the family mansion of the Grevilles, and where Sir Fulke Greville, the servant of Queen Elizabeth, the counsellor of King James, and the friend of Sir Philip Sidney, was born and bred. A visit to this spot would not come inappropriately after Mr Howitt's visit to Penshurst.

Then there is an old curious seat of the Marquis of Northampton, who married Miss Clephane, Sir W. Scott's friend, Compton Winyates, near Edgehill, and someway connected with the history of the battle. Shottery, too, where Ann Hathaway (she hath a way) lived, is only a mile from Stratford. Charlecote, of course, is worthy of a visit, though it was not out of that park that Shakespeare stole the deer. I am giving but vague directions, but I am unwilling to leave even in thought the haunts of such happy days as my schooldays were.

And now to my country customs, by which I earn the privilege of again writing to you. Though a Londoner by birth, I was early motherless, and was taken when only a year old to my dear *adopted native* town, Knutsford, and some of the customs I shall mention are peculiar to the district around that little market town.

One of the customs, on any occasion of rejoicing, of strewing the ground before the houses of those who sympathise in the gladness with common red sand, and then taking a funnel filled with white sand, and sprinkling a pattern of flowers upon the red ground. This is always done for a wedding, and often accompanied by some verse of rural composition. When I was married,

[1] From a printed source, which gives the date above.

nearly all the houses in the town were sanded, and these were the
two favourite verses:

> 'Long may they live,
> Happy may they be,
> Blest with content,
> And from misfortune free.
>
> Long may they live
> Happy may they be,
> And blest with a numerous
> Pro-ge-ny.'[1]

Various and grand were the flourishes on the late coronation,
and there were one or two amusing distichs, but I do not remember them.

The tradition about this custom is that there was formerly a
well-dressing in the town,[2] and on the annual celebration of this
ceremony they strewed the flowers to the house of the latest
married bride; by degrees it became a common custom to strew
the houses of the bride and her friends, but as flowers were not
always to be procured, they adopted this easy substitute. Some
people choose to say that it originated in the old church being too
far out of town for the merry sound of bells to be heard on any
joyful occasion, so instead of an audible they put a visible sign.
But you cannot think how pretty our dear little town looks on
such occasions.

'Riding Stang' (I spell it as pronounced, but I wonder what it is
derived from, some old Saxon word?) is a custom all over
Cheshire. When any woman, a wife more particularly, has been
scolding, beating or otherwise abusing one of the other sex, and
it is publicly known, she is made to ride stang. A crowd of people
assemble towards evening after work hours, with an old, shabby,
broken down horse. They hunt out the delinquent from her rest-
ing-place and mount her on their Rozinante, but not in the legitimate fashion; for will she, will she not, she sits astride with her
face to the tail. So they parade her through the nearest village or

---

[1] The second verse is given in *Sylvia's Lovers*.
[2] This would be in the Rogation Days, when a portion of Scripture was
publicly read at each wayside well and a blessing invoked on the waters. They were
adorned with green boughs and flowers and acquired the name of 'Gospel Places.'
The custom still prevails in parts of Derbyshire.

town; drowning her scolding and clamour with the noise of fry-
ing pans, &c., just as you would scare a swarm of bees. And
though I have known this done in many instances, I never knew
the woman seek any redress, or the avengers proceed to any more
disorderly conduct after they had once made the guilty one 'ride
stang.'

Now perhaps to keep myself to some sort of order, I had better
begin at the beginning and go through the year with such of our
Cheshire customs as are, I fancy, unknown to you. While I call
them *Cheshire* customs, I believe them to extend into Lancashire
and Yorkshire.

About Knutsford we have Christmas carols, such a pretty
custom, calling one from dreamland to almost as mystic a state of
mind; half awake and half asleep, blending reality so strangely
with the fading visions; and children's voices too in the dead of
the night with their old words of bygone times!

Then on Mid-Lent Sunday, instead of furmenty we eat Simnel
cake: a cake made variously, but always with saffron for its principal ingredient. This I should fancy was a relic of Papistry, but I
wonder how it originated. Lambert *Simnel* the impostor in Henry
the Seventh's time was a baker's son, I think. The shop windows
are filled with them, high and low eat them.

Lifting Monday and Lifting Tuesday[1] are still kept up in their
full vigour. My husband has had to run hard to escape; and at my
Knutsford home the doors were kept barred on Easter Monday.

The next day of note is the first of May. I never heard of its
being kept as it is by the common people in Lancashire and
Cheshire. Early in the morning at daybreak, some one hangs up a
bush or a branch of a tree at every one's door; and that is a kind of
Langue des Arbres, for these branches bear reference to the character
of the principle female of the house. A branch of birch signifies a
pretty girl, an alder (or owler they call it) a scold, an oak a good
woman, a broom a good housewife. But I am sorry to say there
are many symbols hung up in spite, which have anything but a
good meaning. If gorse, nettles, sycamore or sawdust are placed at
the door, they cast the worst imputation on a woman's character,
and vary according as she be girl, wife, or widow. One of my

[1] From the ancient custom of 'lifting' or 'heaving' the master of the house or
the stranger under his roof. It is said that seven maids of honour burst into the
chamber of King Edward I, on Easter Monday, 1290, and kept lifting him in his
chair until he was glad to pay fourteen pounds to enjoy 'his own peace.'

servants, of whom I have just been making inquiries, says many a poor girl has had her character blasted by one of these bushes being hung up by some one who owed her a grudge. The early passers-by saw it, and the report was buzzed about, without the accusation being tangible enough for her to refute it.

I cannot at present remember any peculiar customs between May Day and All Souls' Day, when parties of children go from house to house singing:

> An apple, a pear, a plum or a cherry,
> Or any good thing to make us merry.
> One for Peter and one for Paul,
> And one for Him who saved us all.

This is sung over and over again to a very monotonous tune, till some trifle is sent to them.

Another of our customs now rather passing away is *Marling*. When marl was used for manure there were marl-pits up and down Cheshire, and if any one chanced upon the men while at work, they were expected to make them a present. In an evening they formed themselves into a ring in the market-place and called out, '*Oyez, oyez, oyez*, Mr So-and-so has given us the 2000th part (if it was a shilling) of a hundred pounds, a hundred pounds, largo, largo, largo.' Of course the part varied according to the amount of the donation.

There are many superstitions kept up about Cheshire and Lancashire. The servant-maids wear a bag containing a druggist's powder called Dragon's Blood upon their heart, which will make them beloved by the person they love. A pretty servant once told me: 'It always had the desired effect with her.' They make a curtsey to the new moon when first they see it, and turn the money in their pockets, which *ought* to be doubled before the moon is out.

Many poetical beliefs are vanishing with the passing generation. A shooting star is unlucky to see. I have so far a belief in this that I always have a chill in my heart when I see one, for I have often noticed them when watching over a sick-bed and very, very anxious. The dog-rose, that pretty libertine of the hedges with the floating sprays wooing the summer air, its delicate hue and its faint perfume, is unlucky. Never form any plan while sitting near one, for it will never answer.

I was once saying to an old, blind countrywoman how much I

admired the foxglove. She looked mysteriously solemn as she
told me they were not like other flowers; they had 'knowledge'
in them! Of course I inquired more particularly, and then she told
me that the foxglove knows when a spirit passes by and always
bows the head. Is not this poetical! and of the regal foxglove with
its tapering crimson bells. I have respected the flower ever
since.

Moreover, I know a man who has seen the Fairies and tells the
story in the prettiest possible way. And if you were on Alderley
Edge, the hill between Cheshire and Derbyshire, could not I point
out to you the very entrance to the cave where King Arthur and
his knights lie sleeping in their golden armour till the day when
England's peril shall summon them to her rescue.

To go back in rather a random manner to old halls and family
traditions. I have had very delicate health since I married, and
have not been able to ramble about much, so I do *not* know
Haughton Tower.[1] I wish I did. I like your expression of 'an un-
written tragedy.' It quite answers to the sadness which fills my
heart as I look on some of those deserted old halls. Do they not
remind you of Tennyson's 'Deserted House'—'Life and thought
are gone away,' &c.

I should like nothing better than to roam through the old nooks
of Lancashire, exploring more fully a place near Rivington which
I just glimpsed at lately, a country hall with the odd name of
Street, looking down a beautiful valley. It is falling to ruins now,
but in the reign of Queen Anne belonged to a Lord Willoughby,
the President of the Royal Society, and author of some book on
natural history. He left two daughters, and the estates were dis-
puted and passed away to the heir male by some law chicanery;
his descendants are cotters in a neighbouring village. Some friends
of mine walked to the Hall one evening; part of it was occupied
by little farmers, but they peeped into large wainscoted rooms
and wandered about fine, old-fashioned gardens, when one of the
party bethought himself of asking for admittance into the house
to explore the deserted rooms. The woman of the place looked
aghast at this proposal, for it was twilight, and said: They dare not
go to that part of the house, for Lord Willoughby walked, and
every evening was heard seeking for law-papers in the rooms
where all the tattered and torn writings were kept.

I have been a good deal in Northumberland, and have just

[1] Near Preston, Lancashire, the seat of the Hoghton family.

remembered a custom there. When a baby goes out for the first time, it is taken to the houses of the parents' friends, who each give it an egg and salt. There it is so general they carry a basket. Here my baby once came home with an egg and salt, so I suppose it was once a general custom. Oh! dear, I wonder whether you will be tired if I go on writing; and yet I must tell you one thing.

My husband has lately been giving four lectures to the very poorest of the weavers in the very poorest district of Manchester, Miles Platting, on 'The Poets and Poetry of Humble Life.' You cannot think how well they have been attended, or how interested people have seemed. And the day before yesterday two deputations of respectable-looking men waited on him to ask him to repeat those lectures in two different parts of the town.[1] He is going on with four more in the winter, and meanwhile we are *picking up* all the 'Poets of Humble Life' we can think of.

As for the Poetry of Humble Life, that, even in a town, is met with on every hand. We have such a district, and we constantly meet with examples of the beautiful truth in that passage of 'The Cumberland Beggar:'

> 'Man is dear to man; the poorest poor
> Long for some moments in a weary life
> When they can know and feel that they have been,
> Themselves, the fathers and the dealers out
> Of some small blessings; have been kind to such
> As needed kindness, for this simple cause,
> That we have all of us a human heart.'

In short, the beauty and poetry of many of the common things and daily events of life in its humblest aspect does not seem to me sufficiently appreciated.

We once thought of *trying* to write sketches among the poor, *rather* in the manner of Crabbe (now don't think this presumptuous), but in a more seeing-beauty spirit; and one—the only one— was published in *Blackwood*, January 1837. But I suppose we spoke of our plan near a dog-rose, for it never went any further.

[1] Cf. pp. 26–7 above. One of these long letters perhaps took two days to write.

11 **13** 14

ELIZABETH GASKELL[1]

Sunday Evening.
[19 August 1838]

My very dearest Lizzy,

When I had finished my last letter Willm looked at it, and said it was '*slip-shod*'—and seemed to wish me not to send it, but though I felt it was not a particularly nice letter I thought I wd send it, or you would wonder why I did not write. But I was feeling languid and anxious and tired, & have not been over-well this last week, and moreover the sort of consciousness that Wm may any time and does generally see my letters makes me not write so naturally & heartily as I think I should do. Don't begin that bad custom, my dear! and don't notice it in your answer. Still I chuckled when I got your letter today for I thought I can answer it with so much more comfort to myself when Wm is away which you know he is at Buxton. Baby has been very poorly since I wrote—very feverish, and fretful, and restless, but it has been with her teeth, and Sam has given her two doses of calomel which has done her good. These two last nights I have been up till one with her, which makes me feel weary and X and face-achy. Thank you dear Lizzy for telling me so nicely all about your feelings &c—you can not weary by so doing, for I take the greatest interest in every particular, and I heartily wish you were here, with your sweet comforting face, and I would listen, and talk, & talk, & listen. I feel lonely from comparing this absence of Willm's to those old absences when I had dear Aunt Lumb to care about, and open my heart to—Times that can never come again! However I hope I am not complaining, for I *am* very happy. Well but to answer your letter more especially—Sam gave it to me as I took refuge and dined with him at the Infirmary during a heavy shower coming from chapel—so I read bits out to him, and can give you 'counsels opinion' on various subjects. I believe I am more open with Sam than I dare to be with William, and I love Sam as a dear brother. And—now to business. I suppose

---

[1] *Address* Miss E. Gaskell. | Revd E. R. Dimock's | Sankey Street | Warrington | Single Sheet. *Postmark* MANCHESTER | AU 20 | 1838 | F. *Octagonal seal* Man's head facing left. *Annotations* Mothers engagement *and* Aug 20/38.

Chas said his say about you the first night down in the dark in
your dining-room, for he does not say much now about you
personally, though every word and thought seems absorbingly
full of love for you,—how to obviate difficulties—if I thought you
loved him? and repeated exclamations of 'Oh! she thinks too
highly of me,—how shall I be worthy of her?' &c. One day he
called you 'pure and innocent,' and he admired your eyes another
day; but this is all the *direct* speaking *of* you we have had. Anne
and I talked more about you—praising you from top to toe, inside
and out.—But by the way I must tell you Chas does not like
(Anne says) your *horrible* straw bonnet any more than I do, and
thinks you look much better in close shapes. Moreover it has
been agreed in full conclave that *white* and *pale* pink are yr colours,
and that you spoil yourself occasionally by wearing dark coarse
pinks or rose colours. So remember this about your wedding
clothes. And now to the important point of the *when*—which you
may be sure Anne and I discussed. In many cases I quite think it
desirable that the engagement should last some time—where the
parties are too young,—where the circumstances render it impru-
dent[.] Still even then I would not have the engagement much
prolonged. Better to suffer a little poverty than to have the *wearing*
anxiety of an engagement, for certainly one if not both of the
parties suffer. And what reason of *this kind* you have to wait for
I cannot tell. The circumstance⟨s⟩ are favourable, and you are
each arrived at years of discretion. (I am speaking Sam's opinion
as well as my own)! The reason you urge does not stand good—
wishing to know more of Chas. You have felt sufficient knowledge of him to love him, and sufficient confidence in him to
promise yourself to him. You may depend upon it when I say you
will gain more real knowledge of his tastes and habits in a week
living in the house with him, or in a day married to him, than by
years of these pop visits, where the joy of seeing you swallows up
as it were any individual peculiarity of character. In another
person's house too how could he express wishes or feelings or
tastes about many little things. You would not feel happy—
should you? if Charles could not come over often, often to see
you, and yet were this system continued long it would assuredly
injure his business, and perhaps bring on the failure so desired up
at Prospect Hill. I am urging *matter of fact* objections—\to your
pleas—/I am saying nothing of the anxiety which Chas would
naturally feel, and the loneliness which unless Anne neglected her

home-duties in the winter he would have to undergo. I do not think a long engagement a bit desirable for you either[,] easy and happy as you may feel it now. You will always (put it off for 20 years) have a month of nervousness at last to go through—a feeling of awe on entering on a new state of life, and quitting old habits and old places &c,—but you only put off the evil time by delaying your marriage. You *will* 'keep fancying something else will happen', till it is put beyond the reach of Fate[.] As to your visit to Preston! hang it! they have lived 26 years (pretty nearly/ without you), and may drag on another 26 surely—besides 'when a wedding is in the case, you know all other things give place.['] No! come here as soon as you can, and let us talk over your wedding clothes, and buy any that fall in our way,—Anne and I talked over the kind of visiting dresses you will principally require; and you know you can easily get any after you are married that you find you want. Then as to linen it is quite out of fashion to have a large stock—Kate has only just enough Anne said,—and remember you don't wear 2 shifts at a time because you are married. Come here and we will have merry sewings of your wedding shifts—you, I, and Eliz—you don't know what a good work-woman I am when I am put to it, and you have often helped me in worse things. Besides I have much to say to you on the score of wedding clothes. Has not our dear Willie empowered me to get you a wedding dress\as a present from him/including bonnet and collar, and how the deuce am I to do this unless we have a grand palaver. I have an idea in my own mind but I want to talk the business over with you. And I am quite serious in saying how much I wish to help you in making your wedding linen. Mrs Stuart who fits beautifully shall make you any thing you like, 'specially your wedding dress, for I would have them *well* made if I had all the fewer, for fashion & make is everything. I feel as if there were only one objection to *it's* being this autumn and that is your own feeling—but that reluctance to fix will always be—, and I am sure you are not so selfish as to merely think of yourself —Yet I do not mean to deny that you ought to consult your own feelings, for if you really and truly feel repugnant to it's taking place so soon I am sure Chas, however it might grieve him, would not urge it. As to your mother—finish yourself first, and then wonder if your mother would consent. An you love me don't have it in the winter—Fancy slip, slop, splash splash to the chapel, or going in pattens to the carriage—and red noses and blue cheeks, and a great red swelled finger to wriggle out of the glove, and present for the ring. William said the other night I had not said half enough to you about coming here—he says your mother pro⟨m⟩ised him, and he does not know who has a claim upon you at thi⟨s⟩ particular time if we have not. You only came over for the *gaiety* of the Bazaar⟨.⟩ *Now* come and see if you could enjoy a *quiet* visit with us—we saw nothing of you. [*sic*] then. Oh if you could but come over to me in my loneliness!—I did not mention a word to Lucy but she must have guessed something was 'up.'—I have today told my first person Mrs Robberds under a strict promise which you and I know she will keep, of secrecy; but I thought you would not mind her knowing as she loves you so dearly, and she had kept wondering what took me to Warrington and broke my engagement to her—I begged her even not to tell Wm she knew—she sends her dearest love & congratulations to you. Mr R was at Plas P[1] last week but they were all out except Sam—Pray write again soon, for you can hardly think how constantly I am thinking of you, and longing to be listening & talking to you—Do not make Charles unhappy—you will be glad you have consented when you are married. Marianne keeps wondering *when* Aunt Lizzy will come—It is two years since you were staying here—oh do come[!] MA is so strong—runs out without her things & has no symptoms of cold or cough—she is as rough as a boy—Sam sends 'superfine love'—he is gone to Woodbank to tea—, he is looking very well—Now write soon there's a darling—When you come you shall see William's letters to me if you like. Sam & W. go on Tuesday to the Lakes—Best love to {Anne} all specially to dear Anne—I shall probably write to her next unless I see her—oh how I *wish* she would come—

Your most affec[tionat]e sister

E. C. Gaskell—

[1] Plas-yn-Penrhyn. See p. 16, n. 2.

13 **14** 15

ELIZABETH HOLLAND[1]

Seedley. Sunday morning
before breakfast.
[2 December 1838]

I wish I could have given my dear dear Lizzie a welcome to her
new home by word of mouth rather than by word of pen, but as
that cannot be, you must take my very warmest wishes dearest
Lizzie for many many happy years, not exactly in that house, but
in your husband's home, 'his dear delight to make' wherever you
are. I do think you have every chance for happiness, but of course
there will be joys and sorrows to vary every life, (like the pretty
sunlight and shade which keep chasing each other over the lawn I
see as I write,) and you must try and make yourself as trustful as
possible, not that I don't think you are very trusting;—you must
trust in your husband, & even more trust that God from 'seeming
evil still educeth good.'[2] Oh it is such a beautiful morning;—I
hope it will be like this tomorrow when you are carried over the
threshold, alias up that long flight of steps. Thank you my dear
for yr letter which I had been watching for many a long day. It
was very particularly interesting, and you need never fear being
too particular; you can not give me too many minutiae. Tell Anne
Holland I am sitting in that room we were shown into—so sunny
and pleasant; *you* do not know where I am yet I guess. At my dear
Mrs Bradford whom with her husband I admire more than ever.
And it is getting so late, & we have not had breakfast, and I am
afraid we shall be late for chapel and yet I am anxious to catch
every minute to write to you my pet;—I came here on Friday
with Mari-Anne [*sic*] & have been so quiet & happy—long
working talking morng with Mrs Bradford—(breakfasting at
10m. to 10 my dear so other folk are as bad as we are.) Mr Bradford coming home to late dinner and so agreeable;—knowing
W. Irving[,] Bryant, Van Buren intimately in the American line.
Long acquainted with the Earl of Leicester, where he has met
nearly every distinguished statesman of that party when staying at

[1] Née Gaskell. *Address* Mrs Charles Holland | 27 Hope Street | Liverpool.
Postmarks MANCHESTER | DE 2 | 1838 | E *and* LIVERPOOL | DE 2 | 1838 | L. *Square seal*
Bird with branch. *Annotations* Mothers wedding *and* Dec 2-38.
[2] 'From seeming evil still educing good.' J. Thomson, *A Hymn*, l. 114.

Holkham,—full of agreeable conversation. After tea he writes—
(oh the autographs the man has.) I am to see his collection of
letters some day &c &c—we go on Tuesday—Wm comes to dinner
after the afternoon service today—oh what a hurry I am in. I have
asked A. Gaskell who is staying with Miss Sanderson to come to
me on Tuesday and go to a gay Book sale at the Dukinfield Darbishires on Wednesday. She leaves on Thursday—I wish you
could have seen Mrs Bradford—she & Mrs Wm Holland spent
Wednesday with us, & in the eveng Sam and Mr Bradford came.
Sam did so admire Mrs W H—said she was too pretty—he never
could take his eyes off her—that in walking the streets it must be
painful to her to excite the notice such beauty must. Here comes
Mrs Bradford—Perhaps I can fold up my letter & pocket it &
write some more to this worthless scratch when I go home after
chapel to see how affairs go on.—Mrs Bradford is clever & so
charming—Here comes breakfast in right good earnest. How did
you like Johanna your second time of seeing her. I am curious to
get her letter about you.—I only sigh in secret that you have not
one gown made high up—that green is murdered, though pretty
enough in the funereal line, but you have not one what I call
morning gown[.] This thought haunts me in my sleep. Pack
Charles up to Dover St some day that we may see *our brother*—
Private/I think Anne Holland would stay with you longer than
till Xmas *if you wished it*. I asked her once if she shd stay till
March—she said—I cannot tell at all—it will depend on how they
want me at home, & if they really seem to wish me to stay in
Hope St[.]½p1. 14 Dover St Here I am, after service waiting for
Mrs Bradford; and having just read Anne's (sister Anne's) very
nice & very kind letter. Thank her much for it. I meant to have
begged her when I wrote to keep 1£ out of Miss Mary Gaskell—
so that's all right—and I am sorry I did not write sooner to my dear
sister, but I feel as if I had been in a whirl ever since I came home[.]
Marianne is much better, indeed quite well, & highly enjoying her
visit at Mrs Bradford's, and Mrs B— and I are amusing ourselves
by teaching her the decencies of civilized life, how to use her nap-
kin at dinner; to make a piece of bread serve for fork &c—Mr
Bradford has been 20 years in & about Europe with good long
visits to America, so is rather toryish *I guess*, than American in
many little ways—I tried to get him to say he felt reverence for
titles but it would not come out, if it was in—It seems funny to
dine with a man who has dined with the Pope, who always seems

such a queer, unreal, faraway sort of personage—He has collected all sorts of beautiful things many of which lie packed up in boxes at L.pool—Dresden china—valuable paintings, cameos, mosaics, ivory sculpture,—and I should so like to see them. It is singular that to the best of his belief he is the 1st person who ever brought the likeness of Columbus into the United States. He wished to send something to his friend Van Buren, and was negotiating about some kind of snuff box when he saw in the Royal Museum at Naples such a glorious likeness of Columbus by an old Spanish Master, so he got it copied by a Roman Artist. I shall come home on or towards Tuesday.—There is an invite to the Alcocks (—) for the 12th[.] Meta looks 'bonnie bonnie' since she got up—Her hair is so very pretty—Thank Anne Holland much for her letter.—I shall write to the two Annes very soon but must conclude now. It is a *silly piece* of *bride-like affectation* my dear, not to sign yourself by your proper name. Kate signed herself right the day after her marriage, and all sensible people admired her—I among the rest. So goodbye my dear Mrs Elizabeth Holland.— My dear love to your family circle—and remember you're [?] this 1st week

Yours most affectionately
E. C. Gaskell—

Dear Lizzie I've only just time to send my love to you & Charles & Anne, which Lily in her hurry has forgotten—W. G.

14 15 •16a

ELIZABETH HOLLAND[1]

Monday morning, Knutsford—
[Late 1841]

My dearest Lizzy,
I shall be so outrageously busy when I get home (whither I am going tomorrow morning) that I shall employ this gap of spare time by writing to thank you for your kind letter received at Warrington. (I never received a letter I understand you sent to Heidelberg) I am very sorry your little lassie sounds so cranky; *I* do in my own mind think you ought to have a wet nurse if your

[1] Hopkins (*Gaskell*, p. 63) dates this letter 1841.

own milk fails. Disagreeable people *thoroughly I know* most of them are—still there are exceptions. And even supposing that they are disagreeable, I doubt if you are right in subjecting a baby to so much suffering as poor Charlie had.[1] You cannot be sure that the poor little things will come out of the fiery furnace so unscathed in temper as he appears to be, or so healthy as he now is. But even suppose all this[,] a year of suffering, to anyone, more especially to a helpless child, whose greatest\& only/happiness is in having a body free from pain, should be most carefully avoided.—However I dare say you have different feelings,—only *do* think about it. Bessy speaks of your poor little lassie as looking so very delicate. Bessy wrote an acct of her visit to Lucy— but does not mention the ⟨[small piece of letter cut out]⟩ any, only says 'Charles and Lizzie met us at the door',—and then says what you did with her &c. And now to some account of 'Germany & the Germans',—I know it's dull work talking about cathedrals, but I must just say, no human being who has not seen them can conceive the sublime beauty of the cathedrals in the grand old cities in Flanders. The architects, (so unknown by name to us) must have been the noblest poets, for I never saw such practical poetry—I enjoyed Bruges Ghent & Antwerp—more than I can tell.—While every bit was picturesque the whole was so solemn & sublime, appearing so deserted & lonely, as if the world had stood still with them since the 14th century.— If ever you go—don't miss these towns on any account. Aix la Chapelle too is another point of grandeur not to be missed—We got to the Rhine at Cologne which smells of the bones of the 3,000 virgins.[2] The Rhine (very sub rosa) was a disappointment. To be sure it rained cats & dogs— but the hills & rocks are round not pointed in their outline—just like Mrs Robberds['] engravings—do you remember 'em. We met some charming people,—had a splendid day for ascending the Drackenfels, & breakfasting among the vineyards at the top, with a party including some relations of Coleridge—one a son of Judge Coleridge, & all remembering & speaking with affection of the 'old man eloquent'. I should like to tell you of *our* conversation it was so high-toned & so superior,—not that we spoke much, we only listened and admired. You know don't you that

[1] Charles Menzies, b. 11 November 1839; Margaret Anne, b. 21 June 1841. Pedigree in *Holland Family*, ed. Irvine.
[2] St Ursula was reputedly killed, together with 11,000 virgins, by the Huns, whilst she was on a pilgrimage to Cologne.

Heidelberg is not on the Rhine,—about 20 miles from it in a valley far more beautiful, the valley of the Neckar. It's no use trying to describe, & I hate people who attempt it. You must fancy 'an union of all beauties', for Heidelberg,—splendid scenery, dark pine woods rocks, & the picturesque town, and noble castle to complete it. As for legends the place is haunted. There is an Ondine (the name of a genus as well as an individual,) who dwells in the secret spring of the sea green Neckar. The waters of the Neckar as like sea water exactly—rushing & foaming over red-sand-stone rocks, which make the most beautiful colouring you can imagine. All this is to relieve my own mind from the oppressive recollection of so much beauty—just the sort of scene of loveliness which made one sigh to look at it. All this has done me good like the word in 'The Doctor &c',[1] which relieved the author so much. So now to something that will interest you. We were invited to stay at a sister's of Mrs Schwabe, Frau von Pickford, englished into Mrs Pickford, though I found you can't slight a German noble more than by dropping the aristocratic *von*, though nearly every other person is noble. Nothing being required but a patent of nobility to enable any one to become a 'noble lady', & these patents being given on very slight occasions but never purchased. Then the descendants are *vons* for ever— Mrs Pickford is a widow with 3 daughters at home. Emma 29, very good & very plain,—sensible unselfish & the refuge of the whole family in any dilemma, Thekla 19, *very* lovely, and one of the most elegant people I ever saw, and Matilda sixteen—fine looking with pale red hair—the two youngest very full of fun, and all very ladylike. The house is out of Heidelberg, with a splendid view from the windows, gardens & fountains on each si⟨de, [small piece of letter cut out]⟩ g never ending, and most tiring walk up the wooded hill behind from which you have splendid views (don't be tired of '*splendid views*', I can't help it there were so many.) We got there the first evening at tea-time unexpected as to the day, though they were aware of our coming. Mrs P. told us they were all planning to go with Mrs & Miss Howitt to a festival at the Wolf's brunnen about 2 miles off—would we like to go. To be sure we were up to anything—and hardly staid to enquire what & where but flew to put on our things and on returning to the drawing room found Mrs & Miss H & every body ready. Our first glimpse at 'Mary' as we called her in joke to each

[1] By Robert Southey.

other till I was afraid we should slip it out before her was in the dusk, & I could only see instead of the simple Quaker I had pictured to myself, a lady in a gay-coloured satin, black satin scarf & leghorn bonnet with a plume of drooping white feathers. It was such a funny feeling of astonishment, and Miss Howitt was equally unquakerish—so we sallied forth with very dancing spirits along the picturesque road overhung with walnut trees and winding by the side of the Neckar[,] the moon rising over the hill-tops—Presently we left the road & began to follow a rougher path through a pine wood,—very mysterious & dark-looking.— We began to hear music—the most lively waltzes and presently came to a splashing fountain, set round with coloured lamps,—20 yards, and another turn and we were in an open space in the dark wood—boarded over, the grass, & about 20 people whirling to the most spirited band I ever heard—About 200 stood by ready to spin off when any one gave up. Most of the men were Heidelberg students, with their pointed beards mustachios, caps and blouses— the girls were peasant girls, in their picturesque dresses—the dark trees round were hung with lamps—The peasants don't learn dancing[,] it comes by instinct. A very fashionable waltz step came up while we were at Heidelberg the ecossaise,—and the little girls with their empty milk pails went dancing it along the road. To go back to our merry night scene. Mrs P. was afraid the students a most riotous race, might get too boisterous so we did not stay half so long as I should have liked but came home, & a merry supper ended our first eveng—we as intimate with the nice Pickford girls as if we had known them for years. I think I must tell you about our sitting-rooms they were so german, 3 opening one out of the other by folding doors as all rooms do in Germany, the Howitts had 6 rooms which were generally all thrown open in this way. No carpets of course on the floors of any rooms,—but worsted work chairs cushions & sofas without end—all furniture of walnut-tree wood (so pretty,) and looking glasses in every hole & corner. We breakfasted at ½ past seven—little rolls of exquisite white bread (made with *vinegar*-barm Mrs Housekeeper) butter without salt, & coffee. The Ps took a cup of coffee & 2 mouthfuls of bread without butter & their breakfast was done, while we used, hungry & ashamed, to keep stealing one roll after another. After breakfast we read, sauntered in the beautiful garden, called on the Howitts, shopped (so amusing) received callers listened to Thekla's magnificent playing—½ past 12 dinner which was a long affair, first soup, then boiled meat & potatoes (which last we never saw again, then sausages & pancakes (no bad mixture) then RAW pickled fish & kidney beans or peas stewed in oil, then pudding, then roast meat & salad, then apricot or cherry open flat tart about 1 yd ½ in circumference\& no joke/such immense things; then desert-cakes, apricots wild strawberries—then coffee —all this spun out till 2 o'clock when we generally went some excursion or at any rate some walk. We never drank tea alone I think. Sometimes some of the students when we had music dancing & all manner of games; sometimes the Howitts—when we all told the most frightening & wild stories we had ever heard, —some *such* fearful ones—all true—then we drank tea out at the Howitts,—looking over all the portfolios of splendid engravings, casts &c they had collected—(My word! authorship brings them in a pretty penny)—at the Webers—he a Dr of Philosophie— grave German & philosophical, to say nothing of politico-œco- nomical evenings—at the Schlosser's, & Nies's, two gay balls—of which (of the Schlosser's at any rate) I must give you an account. Mme Schlosser & Mme Nies are sisters—very wealthy—live in Frankfurt in the winter in grand old mansions one of which belonged to Charles Vth and in summer live near Heidelberg.— Mme Nies is a protestant-matter of fact person living in a new country-house, full of new elegances, with the most beautiful new paintings up & down—she is a widow. Mme Schlosser is a strict Catholic, lives in a house 450 years old, which till lately was a convent, has a picture-gallery filled with the oldest productions of art Van Eycks, Albert Durers &c.—She is a highly accomplished woman—has made some very fine published translations from the Spanish dramatists & is in correspondence with many foreign literati. Wordsworth has lately been staying there—James the novelist Mrs Jamieson &c. She is cousin of Goethe.—Her ball was not 'zu ehren Herrn, und Frauen Gaskell', but Mme Nies was. Notwithstanding this, I preferred Mme Schlosser's. We first went to call & present our letters—and were then taken over the old conventual house & grounds—terrace below terrace—walks trellised with vines—and farther away, a wilderness of wood, rock & waterfall—the house with noble old oak furniture polished floors, a library with 40,000 vols—room within room & recess beyond recess, with the fine painted glass arch windows throwing a 'dim religious' light over all. The chapel is magnificent though small, and in every nook—on the wide staircase, along the galleries were

orange trees, & oleanders in tubs,—in full flower.—Mme Schlossers
had the house full of company as it always is during summer, and
a gay party were assembled on the terraces where footmen were
handing them coffee in a very al-fresco style.—She wanted us
much to stay all day but we could not,—nor could we fulfil a half
promise we made of coming to spend a long evening with her
before the Ball. So to the ball one ⟨. . .⟩[1]

₀ **16** ₁₀₁

?ANNE ROBSON[2]

Wednesday Evening. 9 o'clock—
[23 December 1841]

My dearest Nancy,
    I am sitting all alone, and not feeling over & above well; and it
would be such a comfort to have you here to open my mind to—
but that not being among the possibilities, I am going to write you
a long private letter; unburdening my mind a bit. And yet it is
nothing, so don't prepare yourself for any wonderful mystery. In
the first place I got yr letter today and thank you very much for it
—I will send for the eggs on Saty. I am so glad to say MA is
better;—she has jelly & strengthening medicine each twice a day,
& is to have broth & eggs whenever she can particularly fancy
them, and seems much less languid—though still I fear she is not
strong.—I once did think of offering myself and her for a week or
so, to Sam as visitors, for I have such faith in him; & have fancied
that *if* there were any *latent* disease in her (which sometimes
haunts me fearing that there is some return of her old baby complaint in the head) *he* could detect it, and would take such
interest in her, & know so well how to prescribe for her. We have
Mr Partington of course & he was very encouraging this morning
and she certainly *is* better—but one can't help having 'Mother's
fears'; and Wm[,] I dare say kindly[,] won't allow me ever to
talk to him about anxieties, while it would be SUCH A RELIEF often.
So don't allude too much to what I've been saying in your
answer. William is at a minister's meeting tonight,—and tomorrow
dines with a world of professors and college people at Mark

---

[1] What appears to be the continuation and conclusion of this letter will be found
under **15** in Appx A.
[2] William Gaskell's sister.

Philips—and the next day Xmas day[1] it has been a sort of long promise that we all should spend at the Bradford's—by all, I mean Wm, myself, two children & Elizth and all stop all night— Yesterday this plan seemed quite given up—today Mr Partington seemed to think the little change might do MA good,—so it's *on* again—if all goes on well. I have of course had MA more with me during this delicacy of hers, and I am more and more anxious about her—not exactly her health; but I see hers is a peculiar character—*very* dependent on those around her—almost as much so as Meta is *in*dependent & in this point I look to Meta to strengthen her. But I am more & more convinced that love & sympathy are very *very* much required by MA. The want of them would make MA an unhappy character, probably sullen & deceitful—while the sunshine of love & tenderness would do everything for her. She is very conscientious, and very tender-hearted—Now Anne, will you remember this? It is difficult to have the right trust in God almost, when thinking about one's children—and you know I have no sister or near relation whom I could entreat to watch over any peculiarity in their disposition. Now you know that dear William feeling most kindly towards his children, is yet most reserved in *expressions* of either affection or sympathy—& in case of my death, we all know the probability of widowers marrying again,—would you promise, dearest Anne to remember MA's peculiarity of character, and as much as circumstances would permit, watch over her & cherish her. The feeling[,] the conviction that you were aware of my wishes and would act upon them would be *such* a comfort to me. Meta is remarkably independent, & will strengthen MA, if she is spared. Now don't go & fancy I am low-spirited &c &c. As for death I have I think remarkably little constitutional dread of it—I often fear I do not look forward to it with sufficient awe, considering the futurity which *must* follow—and I do often pray for trust in God, complete trust in him—with regard to what becomes of my children. Still let me open my heart sometimes to you dear Anne, with reliance on your sympathy\and secrecy/. And now I won't write any more about feelings but try & give you some news. I have just finished Miss Martineau's new romance.[2] Toussaint the hero is a magnificent character,—and all connected with his

---

[1] The reference below to Harriet Martineau's 'new romance' seems to place this letter in 1841, although in that year December 23rd was a Thursday.

[2] *The Hour and the Man*, 1841. *Deerbrook* was published in 1839.

personal private character is very interesting, & the conversations (where we may suppose she speaks herself) are just like those in Deerbrook very interesting. The *story* is too like reading a history —one knows all along how it must end,—& there's a map at the beginning *like* a history. William was flamingly indignant at Mr Briggs being too late—and will complain to the theological tutor —says it will get the students into disrepute &c &c. It *was* to have been Mr Smith, who is a very nice youth; the flower of the college flock—why Mr B went we don't know. Miss Mitchell has been here a week—only left today—came to see after Mr [?Merg's] situation which is not yet decided;—will be next week—I hope in her favour. Old Mr Robberds is very poorly. Oh how cold it is, and how I long for some of your elderberry wine—It's now past 10—don't expect Master Billy home till 12 or thereabouts— Everybody very eager about bazaar—to begin on Jany 11th. I should like to come to you of all things on Wm's Sunday, but these plaguy servants rather harass my plans.—I certainly hope to come soon. I am glad you are going to L.pool. I am sure you must want some change after all your riots and anxieties. We hear everywhere that Mr D. is going to settle at Rivington[,] some say in the capacity of minster[,] others as that of gentleman at large. We are invited to Mrs Cleggs on the 30th; dare say I told you before, but don't know. Saw Mrs Cobden once or twice lately; very pretty woman pearls & white lace, & jet black hair & eyes, & an exquisitely clear olive complexion without a particle of colour— Wm and I have rather taken to chess. At least when he has time, for oh! he is so busy. And Elizth has amused herself by having the nettle-rash, so we have had the children in the night and had to put off washing &c—& now I must end & go to bed all in a minute—so good bye—Ever yours most affec[tionate]ly.

E. C. Gaskell.

*

o **17** *17a*

MARIANNE and MARGARET EMILY GASKELL

[?1846]

My dearest girls,

I think we shall all gladly subscribe the shilling necessary (I believe,) to have the name of Lætitia altered. I don't think we should any of us like it, and I cannot think what made Papa think of it.[1] Florence has been so gay this week. On Tuesday she went to Formby with Mr Dukinfield Darbishire's family, and the Miss Marslands &c. On Wednesday she went to dine at Miss Marianne Marsland's and came back loaded with presents; Noah's ark; a box of pewter tea-things, an apple &c &c; Thursday—let me see—where did the little lady go? Oh, she and I went to drink tea at Mr D Darbishire's. She went earlier than I did, and I found them all at high-jinks when I went; Flossy not a bit shy. (I am writing while I eat my dinner, so I dare say it is not very legible.) Emily Darbishire made a puzzle which I send you; What is that monster with 10 legs, cased in armour; carnivorous, and piscivorous, and very good to eat? All the children were very kind to Florence, and made her paper boxes, and boats; and her poor little lips quivered when at last I said it was time to come away, but she *man*fully choked down her crys and came away like a very good dear little girl. The next day *we* had Louy, Emily, Agnes, Francis and Charlie (only 2 years old;) they came at three o'clock, and Florence displayed all her playthings, and we did very well, and they were very unwilling to go at $\frac{1}{2}$ past 6[.] Their brother Robert came for them and brought a *bat* he had caught and was going to tame; it was going to sleep for the winter; it has a sort of hand-claw at the end of it's wings, by which it hangs itself up very tidily. However that night it ate very hungrily of bread and milk, fed with a round candle-lighter. I dare say you may see it sometime. It had been found in a turf-stack. Saturday Florence dined at *our* Miss Marsland's and had a funny dinner. 1 Fowl, 1 Partridge 7 snipes, and 4 plovers. We are all looking forward to Thursday with great pleasure; we leave here a $\frac{1}{4}$ before ten; by Miles' coach. The Miles with whom we lodged last time you know. Mrs J. B. Smith and her children are here; and Mrs Allen, & Marianne and Arthur. And now it's full post-time, so goodbye darlings. Give the enclosed slip of paper to Anne, & ever believe me to be your affect[ionate] Mother

E C Gaskell

My best love to Papa & Daddy

*

[1] This, we assume, could refer to the youngest daughter, who was born on 3 September 1846, when her sisters were eleven, nine and three.

*17a **18** 19

MARIANNE and MARGARET EMILY GASKELL

Clapton, before breakfast.
Thursday. [December ?1847][1]

My dearest girls,

Here we are, safe and sound so far! And very anxiously looking forward to a letter from you, darlings, at Crix. I want to hear how you, Marianne are; don't over-tire yourself, & be wise & ready to go to bed at night in good time, for on Monday night I thought you looked rather pale. Well! We had time to get a comfortable breakfast, and sit a while with the little ones, (who are still confined to the nursery with colds,) before setting off to go to the Station. We left Manchester at 26 minutes to 10, and from that time till we got here last night, we never stirred out of the Railway carriage. For we went by the Trent Valley, which does not pass through Birmingham or stop any where, so we were very glad of some sandwiches (put up in Mrs Darbishire's bag,) that Papa had scouted at first. Then when we got to London we took a cab & went driving through wide lighted streets—Papa said very much like Oldham Road in Manchester, but I thought much handsomer. They sell geese here with their necks hanging down at full length, instead of being tidily tucked up like Lancashire geese,—and the shops are full of them against Xmas, & you can't think how funny they look. Well after a five miles drive we got to Mr Howitts— Aunt Anne can describe the house having been here, but I don't think she can describe the room we had,—such a blazing fire— such a crimson carpet—such an easy chair—such white dimity curtains—such a pretty vase of winter flowers before the looking glass. Then we came down into an equally comfortable dining-room, where was a dinner-tea to which we did ample justice I can assure you. Then Mr & Mrs & Miss & Master Howitt, and we went on talking till 12 o'clock[.] What do you think of *that*? And now I am sitting writing in such a pretty dining room, looking into a garden with a rockery, and a green-house, & all sorts of pretty plants, arbutus, and ever-greens—There are so many

---

[1] References to 'little ones' in the nursery and to Grandmama date this letter between 3 September 1846 (birth of Julia Bradford Gaskell) and 12 January 1850 (death of Mrs Margaret Dimock). In the Decembers of 1848 and 1849 Mrs Gaskell was probably in Manchester.

pretty casts here that you would like so much to see. The Isis out of a flower that Selina Winkworth copied is on the stair-case—And a Venus picking up a shell, that is so beautiful—I wish you could see it. We dine here today, & then go on to Crix, & shall be there about six; Tell Aunt Anne to send a message *by the electric tele-graph*, if you are both drowned, or burnt, &c—My best love to her & Grandmama[;] to you two darlings—write very soon to yr very affec[tionat]e

E C Gaskell

18 19 21

MARIANNE and MARGARET EMILY GASKELL

Sunday. [December ?1847][1]
Crix.

My dearest Girls,

I am very very glad to have heard from you today; only in future direct your letters (*be sure*) to *Crix Chelmsford Essex*, they reach me a whole day sooner; *don't* put in either Hatfield or Witham. Well! Crix is far more beautiful than I expected, not the house, that is only a great large red brick house. But I never saw such beautiful grounds and I keep constantly longing for you two. Fancy a row of six oaks much about the same size in the garden, the largest measuring 22 feet round. There are so many ever-greens that one might fancy it summer, for *that*. We have quite a summer nosegay in our room that Annie gathered for us before coming. She is as nice as ever,[2] indeed nicer, for I like to see her going about her home duties so regularly and quietly and above all so good temperedly; though she as keeper of the keys, has often to leave her book or music to go and give something out of the store room. Mrs Shaen is kindness itself and Miss Shaen (Louy) is so very very pretty. Mr Ben Shaen is here. Mr Bradford has sent Annie 'Evangeline'[3] like mine you know. Papa has had a very bad cold almost ever since coming here; but it is now better. We have

---

[1] Letter from a typed source, which dates it '1853, 4, 5 or ?.' However, this appears to be the first visit to Crix and is probably to be associated with Letter 18.
[2] Catherine Winkworth writes in a letter of 16 November 1847 of a visit by Miss Annie Shaen to the Gaskells. *Letters and Memorials*, ed. Winkworth, I, p. 132.
[3] Longfellow, *Evangeline*, 1847.

had very good account of the little girls too today; but we did not hear until today (owing to the mistake in the direction which made me rather uneasy). We arrived here about ½ past six (or nearer to seven) the other night and to our surprise found dinner just ready. Annie came out in the hall to meet us and brought us into this great large drawing room which looked dazzling after the darkness and full of people; only there really was only Mr and Mrs and Mr Sam Shaen, Louy, Annie and Emma. Then Annie took us upstairs to our bed room where there was a cheerful fire which however we had not time to stay and enjoy; but tidied ourselves and hurried down to dinner. After dinner tea almost directly, a little music from Louy and Emma, and then to bed where I was very glad to go on many accounts, principally for Papa's cold which was very bad. He had some gruel, however, thanks to Annie. The next morning you may be sure we were curious enough to see what sort of a place it was we had got to for it was dark when we came here. Our window looked out upon a lawn with beautiful ever greens and beyond that only separated by a wire fence, a large parklike field with sheep in it and beyond that woods. No hills are any where to be seen. All morng we sat with books in our hands but not reading much, only talking. After lunch (at 12) I went out with the girls—round the grounds— a good long walk; and then into the lane up to the village, which is very pretty. Then home, read loitered and talked till dinner time (6 o'clock) and all evening they kept expecting their brothers Will and Ben. The former came before we went to bed the other did not come until yesterday. You should have seen the sirloin of beef (more than 40 lb.) we had at the bottom of the table and *2 turkeys* at the top yesterday—but then we were 10 in the parlour and 32 in the servants hall. I never saw such an immense piece of beef, as I have been telling Flossy she might have hidden herself behind it. Last night we had talking, laughing and singing (Oh! I forgot! yesterday for a walk I went to the farm and round the kitchen garden and saw all the peach trees—but no peaches alas!!) Today Mr Shaen has been reading a sermon to us; Papa is not going out of doors but I am as soon as I have finished these letters—and so dears good bye. Give my very best love to Aunt Anne, Grandmama Uncle Bob and I am so glad to hear you are so diligent and mend all your things—and I am your very affec[tionate] mama

E. C. Gaskell

₀ **20** ₀

MRS MONTAGU

[c. 1847]

⟨. . .⟩ see anything of dear Miss Jane. When I was very ill of the measles last spring, I received a letter from her, which was mislaid, and consequently, when I recovered I was unable to write, not knowing her address.

Do you ever see Kate Thomson? or any of our old schoolfellows. It is 20 years since I have been at dear Avonbank.[1]

My dear Mrs Montagu I have sometimes caught glimpses of you, (through Miss Noble &c,) but don't let me quite lose sight of you; I know you must often be very busy; but if every holidays, if not oftener, you would just send me a few lines I should be very glad indeed.

May I send my thanks through you to Mrs Montagu for her kind message? And will you always remember, that as far as my power extends, you have a kind and affec[tionat]e friend in me.

E. C. Gaskell

₁₉ **21** ₂₇[2]

MARIANNE and MARGARET EMILY GASKELL

[Bollington, near Macclesfield]
[?1847][3]

My dearest girls,

I have got up early in order to write, and beg you to write back to me as soon as ever you receive this, and tell me exactly how Papa is. I begged him yesterday to promise to write and tell me how he was this morning, but he would not; so you must be my correspondents, and tell me every particular. Now don't forget, dears! I have not much to tell you but I think you will like to hear what I have to say. Mr & Mrs Hervey were in the same carriage as I dare say Papa told you; they asked me how long I was going to

---

[1] See Hopkins, *Gaskell*, pp. 31, 343, for Mrs Gaskell's schooldays at Avonbank, Stratford-upon-Avon.
[2] To Marianne; to Meta also, 47.
[3] Julia Gaskell is seemingly still very young.

stay; I told them about Papa; but said if you would write and send a good account, I shd stay till Thursday at any rate; so they said then, if they heard nothing to the contrary they should send over for Florence and me on Thursday Morng, & send us down to the same railway train we came by on Thursday night. I went on to Macclesfield,—about five minutes beyond Prestbury; where Mr Greg's man got me a 'fly', a word which puzzled Florence extremely; and which she talked about, for an hour I think. It was three miles here all in mist and darkness; when we got here Mrs Greg was busy & Mr Greg resting so we were shown into a charming bedroom with a fire in it; and Mrs Greg came very soon to us with her little boy; she said tea was just ready; so I began to unpack as quickly as I could, but when Florence came to button her shoes, one of the buttons came off. I had desired Hearn particularly to see after them, and in the hurry, and desire to be punctual on first arriving it was very provoking. I wanted Florence to be content to wear her slippers at tea, but I found she did not like the idea so I rang for some black thread, & at last we made our appearance downstairs, Florence had tea with us, the two eldest little things at home playing about. The eldest is not five; and the three above her are from home. They have regretted very much that Baby is not here, and I do think she would have enjoyed it. There was a cot by my bed all ready for her; and such famous nurseries. Florence did not like the nurses to put her to bed last night, so I did, and she would sleep in the cot prepared for Baby. However I took her into bed when I went. I worked till bed-time; and sometimes Mr Greg was in the room, and sometimes he went into another. To-day we are going to lunch with Mrs Davenport—it is 7 miles to Capesthorne, and we set off at 11, and that's all I know about anything. Florence made friends with the little ones last night, and wanted to be dressed so early this morng—long before it was light that she might be ready to see the garden, which delights her. When the nurse came, she chose to go to the nursery to be dressed and has been playing about ever since with them. I hope breakfast is nearly ready. Yes! I have had my breakfast, and so has Florence, who looks as bright as the morning. The country is so beautiful, golden coloured all over! I find the post does not go out till $\frac{1}{2}$ past 5, (but we set off very soon for Capesthorne) I am afraid you won't get this till tomorrow morng, & then I can't hear till Thursday morning[;] letters have just come at breakfast time for Mr & Mrs Greg; so I suppose that's

the time they come in. Kiss Baby many times for me; be sure &
write *directly* at any rate, & send it down to the *town* post & I am
                    Your affect[ionat]e old mother E C G.

                        Turn over.

I have just heard what Florence is to do today; and it is so
pleasant I must tell you. She is now putting on her things to go
down with Alice, Herbert, Katie (2 years old today) & the Baby
to the Farm to get some cream; which then they are to come back
& churn *themselves*; then they dine and then have little tea in the
nursery, with their *own* butter. Flossy is in high glee, and
thoroughly at home.

                    0 **22** 23

                EDWARD CHAPMAN

                            121, Upper Rumford St
                            Manchester.
                            March 21. [1848]

Dear Sir,
    When I had the pleasure of being introduced to you at the
beginning of the year, I think you led me to understand that my
work was to follow Miss Jewsbury's[1] in the publication of your
Series. I am naturally a little anxious to know when you are
going to press.
    I can not help fancying that the tenor of my tale is such as to
excite attention at the present time of struggle on the part of work
people to obtain what they esteem their rights; on the other side
it is very possible that people are now so much absorbed by
public work as to have very little time or interest to bestow on
works of fiction.
    As you have the MS in your hands I am trusting to you to see
that it is set up so as to make the right quantity. Perhaps you will
favour this with an answer at your convenience.
    Believe me to remain dear Sir
                            Yours truly
                            E. C. Gaskell
Mr Chapman
    Strand
        London

                    [1] *Half Sisters.*

EDWARD CHAPMAN

121, Upper Rumford St
Manchester
April 2nd [1848]

Dear Sir,

I begin to think it probable that you never received a letter, which I addressed to you about 10 days ago; and in which I made an enquiry as to the probable time, when my MS, (a Manchester Love Story,) would be published.

I am led to make this enquiry by the statement you made when I had the pleasure of being introduced to you in January; that my story would succeed Miss Jewsburys; and would be published in two or three months from that time; and I hope you will not think me impatient in expressing my natural wish to learn when you are going to press, as I think the present state of public events may be not unfavourable to a tale, founded in some measure on the presen⟨t⟩ relations between Masters and work people. Requesting an immediate answer, I remain dear Sir

Yours very truly
E. C. Gaskell

— Chapman Esqre

EDWARD CHAPMAN

121 Upper Rumford St
Manchester
April 13th [1848]

Dear Sir,

Allow me to remind you of the promise you kindly made of letting me know what decision you came to, with regard to the publication of my novel.

I fear from your delay in writing, you have thought it desirable to defer the appearance of my work until a volume of a different character has appeared; and I must confess this will be a disappointment to me; as both from Mr Howitt's report of the agreement you came to with him on my behalf, and from your own statement to me, I believed there was no doubt it would have been published by this time. However I am, (above every other consideration,) desirous that it should be *read*; and if you think there would be a better chance of a large circulation by deferring it's appearance, of course I defer to your superior knowledge, only repeating my own belief that the tale would bear directly upon the present circumstances.

I remain dear Sir

Yours very truly
E. C. Gaskell.

E Chapman Esqre

24 **25** 26

EDWARD CHAPMAN

121 Upper Rumford St
April 17, 1848

Dear Sir,

Thank you for your suggestions; you will see that I have adopted the additional title of '*Mary Barton*', a Manchester Love Story.

It is so difficult living in Lancashire to decide upon words likely to be unintelligible in another county; but my husband has put notes to those we believe to require them. The three verses of the Oldham Weaver are enclosed. You will see that I have decided on mottoes.

Believe me, dear Sir,

Ever yours truly
E. C. Gaskell.

E Chapman Esqre

0 **25a** 60

?ANNE SHAEN[1]

Home.
[?24 April 1848]

Knowing Crix ways and customs I felt pretty sure I should have a budget this evening: we were sitting at tea in the

---

[1] From a printed source, where it is dated 'April 24, 1851' and addressed to Miss Shaen. Cf. also Hopkins, *Gaskell*, p. 66.

drawing room when Hannah entered. Wm seized the letters saying he was sure they were for *him*; but perceiving that yours and Mrs Shaen's were for me, he said *this* is Louey's and this I *know* is for me. You see he thought all that sitting by her at the piano had not been without due effect. ⟨. . .⟩

I have just been up to our room. There is a fire in it, and a smell of baking, and oddly enough the feelings and recollections of 3 years ago came over me so strongly—when I used to sit up in the room so often in the evenings reading by the fire, and watching my darling *darling* Willie, who now sleeps sounder still in the dull, dreary chapel-yard at Warrington. That wound will never heal on earth, although hardly any one knows how it has changed me. I wish you had seen my little fellow, dearest dear Annie. I can give you no idea what a darling he was—so affectionate and *reasonable* a baby I never saw. ⟨. . .⟩ Read 'Jane Eyre', it is an uncommon book. I don't know if I like or dislike it. I take the opposite side to the person I am talking with always in order to hear some convincing arguments to clear up my opinions. Tell me what Crix thinks—everybody's opinions. Mary Holland has just received 'Notes from Books'[1] from her friend Henry Taylor and said she liked them as well as 'Friends in Council.' I have copied Lizzie Lindsay—such a pretty old Irish air with words by Lady Balfour which must be sung very *naïvely*; it is pathetic and must not be made fun of, only you can't keep from smiling, on the making a compliment and spoiling it (??)⟨. . .⟩ Lizzie Lindsay is a glorious specimen of man monarchy? The poor Glasgow burgher's daughter is wooed by an unknown suitor and naturally asks who he is, whereupon he makes answer 'Oh Leezie lass! ye maun ken little—Sin that ye dinna ken me,' and tells her he is Lord Ronald Macdonald; whereupon she drops a curtsey and says 'thank ye Sir';—never mind! it is a very pretty *naïve* little thing, and we can't always be high flown and moral in our stories. If you like you may adopt a sentence out of Mary Wolstonecraft to this air.

[1] *Notes from Books, in Four Essays*, 1848.

25 **26** 28

EDWARD CHAPMAN[1]

[?]Gale Cottage
Tuesday, July 10th [1848]

Dear Sir,

I would rather leave the decision regarding the time of publication to you; as your experience must lead you to judge better than I can do on the subject. What is the opinion of the gentleman to whom you once before referred as the Editor of the Series? Perhaps you will let me know what you fix upon.

I hardly know what you mean by an 'explanatory preface'. The only thing I should like to make clear is that it is no catch-penny run up since the events on the Continent have directed public attention to the consideration of the state of affairs between the Employers, & their work-people.

If you think the book requires such a preface I will try to concoct it; but at present, I have no idea what to say.

I remain, dear Sir

Yours truly
E. C. Gaskell.

21 **27** 47

MARIANNE GASKELL

1 Waterloo Terrace
Southport, Monday
[?Early October 1848][2]

My dearest Marianne,

I was glad to hear from dear Meta's letter of your enjoyment on Saturday; it was most kind of Papa to think of dearest Flossy; what a charming kitchen she must have got at last; it sounds quite complete, and as if a dinner could be cooked out of it at once. You will just have ended your German lesson; I do hope it has gone off well. I have very little news to tell you, my dearest

[1] *Address* E. Chapman Esqre.
[2] Mrs Gaskell made several visits to Southport to see Catherine Winkworth between October 1848 and January 1849. (*Letters and Memorials*, ed. Winkworth, I, pp. 138, 155.) This, we think, reads like an early letter describing a new place.

lassies. Mrs Leisler lives next door but two; there is a fellow lodger here, called Mr Peplow Ward; but Emily has christened him Mr Pepper and Water; he smokes in his bedroom, and orders dinner in such a loud voice we hear all his receipts. It has rained all morning; so I have never been out. Kate is lying down and Emily is gone to put on her things to take these letters to the post. I met such a droll man in the omnibus. He gave me a receipt for making 'sun pictures' as he called them[.]

> Take of bi-chloride of potash
> > An ounce to a gill,
> Mix them as you like to stand as
> > long as you will,
> Expose them to the light where
> > the sun doth forth shine,
> And you may have a picture
> before that you dine.

He meant it for poetry but it's not very like it I think. However he was a very kind old man and spoke nicely to every one. I often wish for you here to run up and down these steep stairs for me; they are very tiring. I shall write to Meta tomorrow; and tell her of Emily and my walks this afternoon, for I mean to go out I am so tired of staying indoors. Now goodbye darling. Kiss Meta Florence & Baby for me, and tell me how Hearn's mother is.

Your ever affect[ionate] Mother
E C Gaskell.

Mind the address
1 Waterloo Terrace.

26 28 31

EDWARD CHAPMAN

S. Holland's Esqre
Plas Penrhyn, near
Port-Madoc
Caernarvon.
Oct. 19th [1848]

Dear Sir,

Shall you have any objection to the name of 'Stephen Berwick' as that of the author of 'Mary Barton' which I have just seen advertised in the new Edinburgh. Can you put me in the way of getting articles inserted in any magazine?

You were so good as to say you would allow me to have another copy; would you be so kind as to send it to me *here*, through Pritchard—Bookseller Caernarvon. When you answer this note will you address it to me *here*, as I shall not return to Manchester for many weeks.

Yours truly
E. C. Gaskell

0 **29** 30

CATHERINE WINKWORTH[1]

Plas Penrhyn, Port Madoc, North Wales.
Nov. 2nd, 1848.

My dearest Katie,

I wonder if I can slip in a letter between Emily's to thank you for writing to me; I was so glad to receive your letter, which was very interesting in many ways. ⟨. . .⟩ I do so like hearing from you, and if I never asked, it was from a feeling that perhaps writing might not be good for you. Do you know, not seventy but a great many horses went to Rumford, in Essex, the very Tuesday before Emily came, so now the estate is rather bare of horses, having black cattle upon it instead for winter grazing. I have not yet offered Emily a ride on an ox, but mean to do it before she leaves ⟨. . .⟩ I don't think one does *admire* (it is far too good a word to be used on the subject) 'Susan Hopley'[2]; it is a series of most unnatural adventures, naturally told, in a common-place way; but some people can't even be common-place natur-ally. They just interest one in certain states of the mind in which one is too lazy for thought or any high feeling, and only *up* to being a bit occupied by scenes passed before you without much connexion, like those unrolling views we show children. Oh dear! I envy you the *Times*;—it's very unprincipled and all that, but the most satisfactory newspaper going. Now is not that sentence un-becoming in a minister's wife? I never can ascertain what I am in politics; and veer about from extreme Right,—no, I don't think

---

[1] From a printed source.
[2] By Mrs Catherine Crowe (?1800–1876), 3 vols., 1841.

I ever go as far as the extreme Left. ⟨. . .⟩ I don't know how it is our days go away in doing so little. We breakfast nominally at half-past 8, only it is always 9; sit an hour over it talking; come into the drawing-room, and stand over the fire talking, and looking at the lovely view through the window over the fireplace; suddenly remember the post comes in and whisks out again any time between 12 and 2, so hurry away to write letters for the bag; are urged to go out and not lose the beautiful weather by Fanny, but do contrive to hang about, much to her righteous reprobation and indignation and all the others that end in *ation*, till the bag comes in; tumble over each other in our haste to get our letters; speak crossly to anyone who speaks to us till we've read, and if possible answered, our letters—then comes a calm in which we can draw deep breaths, for the event of the day is over—the bag is gone off again. Then walk till dinner (4 to 5). Uncle Sam always comes in to dinner and we talk to him; he is charmed with Emily and they carry on a regular flirtation. After dinner, slip-slop sleepy talk; a little music; a good deal of lounging on sofas and easy chairs; a great longing for tea, which comes in about 8, lasts till 9, and then when we are all thoroughly wakened up, it is our duty to go to bed—so run our days. ⟨. . .⟩ Emily will come back brimful of Welsh stories I think; for Sam pours them into her not unwilling ears. Give my best love to Süschen, the prettiest abbreviation I have seen of Susanna yet. And believe me, dearest Kate-Bettina[1] (for somehow you two are inextricably blended, with a touch of Selina over both), your very affectionate E. C. G.

29 **30** 32

CATHERINE WINKWORTH[2]

Novr 11th, 1848. Manchester.

My dearest Katie,

At last I have a minute or two, which I may devote to Emily and you. You don't see me, but I often am sitting in the rocking-chair unbeknow*nst* to you. So 'don't talk scandal about Queen

---

[1] A reference to Bettina von Arnim's book, *Goethe's Correspondence with a Child* (Susanna Winkworth's note).   [2] From a printed source.

Elizabeth', my dear! Do call me Lily, and never mind respect to your elders. *Ils sont passés ces beaux jours là*, when old people were looked upon as people who could do no wrong; and were to have all outward and inward respect paid to them; so let me for one of the body, have affection instead of respect. I wish I had five sisters, who were bound to love me by their parents' marriage certificate; but as I have not, I mean to take you for sisters and daughters at once. ⟨. . .⟩ By the way, Emily was curious to know the name of the person who wrote 'Mary Barton' (a book she saw at Plas Penrhyn), and I am happy in being able to satisfy her Eve-like craving. Marianne Darbishire told me it was ascertained to be the production of a Mrs Wheeler, a clergyman's wife, who once upon a time was a Miss Stone, and wrote a book called 'The Cotton-Lord'.[1] Marianne gave me many proofs which I don't think worth repeating, but I think were quite convincing.

I have had a busy week arranging lessons and children's winter things; both of which are now satisfactorily in progress. I am writing while I am eating my lunch, which must be an excuse for my letter if it has more of the body than the mind in it. There is three-quarters of a pig awaiting me in the kitchen; and work of all kinds in the nursery; and the girls should go out before callers 'come down like a wolf on the fold'. ⟨. . .⟩ The Darbishires' house is in a most upside-down state; not an atom of furniture in either of the drawing-rooms, and we are to go there to a very large party (according to Mrs D.) on Wednesday next. I suppose we are to sit in white-washers' pails, and on steps of ladders, which will be original. ⟨. . .⟩ I don't hear anything of the Schwabes; nor who is lion now in the interregnum between Mr A. J. Scott and Jenny Lind, who is coming to them again in December for two Concerts for the Infirmary; one in the Concert Hall, supported by the Liedertafel, price £1 1s. (*one guinea*, my dear!), the other in the Free Trade Hall, supported by the Madrigal Society. Chevalier Neukomm has been couched, and can see to a certain degree, but has great pain in his eyes. ⟨. . .⟩ The weather here is the perfection of dreariness; grey black fog close to the house; clinging to everything and penetrating to one's very soul. I think of your room at Southport as a nest of warm comfort; and shall love the very name of Bettina as reminding me of you and Southport.

---

[1] Mrs Elizabeth Stone wrote *William Langshawe, the Cotton Lord*, 1842. Mrs Gaskell's *Mary Barton* had just been published anonymously on 25 October 1848. Hopkins, *Gaskell*, p. 70.

Don't forget we left Mdme de Stael at the bed of Venus. My dearest love to my girls Emily and Selina, and ever believe me (now lunch is done) your very affectionate Lily.

₂₈ **31** ₃₃

EDWARD CHAPMAN

121, Upper Rumford St   Novr 13. [1848]

Dear Sir,

May I trouble you to post the accompanying letter to Mr Carlyle. I don't know if the address he has put on will be sufficient, but it is all the date he gives in his note, which I have just had forwarded to me. I am only just returned from Wales; I find every one here has most convinving proofs that the authorship of Mary Barton should be attributed to a Mrs Wheeler, née Miss Stone, and authoress of some book called the 'Cotton Lord'. I am only afraid lest you also should be convinced and transact that part of the business which yet remains unaccomplished with her. I do assure you that I am the author, and so remain

Yours very truly

E. C. Gaskell

₃₀ **32** ₃₅

CATHERINE WINKWORTH[1]

Nov. 29th, 1848. Manchester.

⟨. . .⟩We are having a domestic to-do to-night, and I sadly want Slee[2] to come; only she thinks it a step-filial duty to stay at home with Mrs W. I had the Sunday School girls here last Sunday, and Susanna came to help me, and I thought we went off gloriously, only—(everything has its *only*)—in repeating our subjects of conversation, I named an accidental five minutes conversation with one or two of the girls about Sir Walter Scott's novels (*apropos* of a picture of Queen Elizabeth, *via* 'Kenilworth', &c.) and Mrs J. J. Tayler is shocked at such a subject of conversation on a

---

[1] From a printed source.   [2] Selina Winkworth.

Sunday,—so there I am in a scrape,—well! it can't be helped, I am myself and nobody else, and can't be bound by another's rules. The Darbishires are coming tonight with 'Zoe',[1] Dr Hodgson, Mr Green (shan't we be intellectual, that's all?) and a few others. I wish myself well thro' it.⟨...⟩

₃₁ **33** ₃₄

EDWARD CHAPMAN

121, Upper Rumford St
Decr[2] 5th 1848.

Dear Sir,

I wish you could know how *very* much I dislike writing this note; and yet we are really beginning to think you have forgotten that you have never completed your part of the agreement respecting M Barton. I do not know how it is selling of course, but I understood that it was to be paid for on publication, independently of the success, or otherwise, of the sale. Hitherto the whole affair of publication has been one of extreme annoyance to me, from the impertinent and unjustifiable curiosity of people, who have tried to force me either into an absolute denial, or an acknowledgement of what they must have seen the writer wished to keep concealed.

In looking over the book I see numerous errors regarding the part written in the Lancashire dialect; 'gotten' should always be 'getten'; &c.—In the midst of all my deep & great annoyance, Mr Carlyle's letter has been most valuable; and has given me almost the only\unmixed/pleasure I have yet received from the publication of MB.

I remain, Sir,

Yours truly
E. C. Gaskell

---

[1] Geraldine Jewsbury, *Zoe* being the title of her first novel. (Susanna Winkworth's note.) [2] Alteration from 'Novr'.

33 **34** 37

EDWARD CHAPMAN

Friday morning
Decr 7th 1848.

My dear Sir,

I acknowledge, with many thanks, the first half of the 100£, due to me for the MS of 'Mary Barton'. I am very much obliged to you for your note; and for the friendly and just manner in which you write about my annoyance respecting my name being known. I certainly did not expect that so much curiosity would be manifested; and I can scarcely yet understand how people can reconcile it to their consciences to try and discover what it is evident the writer wishes to conceal. I have been made very unhappy by my own self-reproaches for the deceit I have practised, and into which I have almost been forced by impertinent enquiry; and these last few days I have thought it better simply to acknowledge the truth, in order to put a stop to all these unpleasant manifestations of curiosity.

I know that my cousin Dr Holland and Lady Coltman *conjectured* very early that I was the writer, and as they were not bound by honour, they told their idea to several people; Mrs Marsh (Dr Holland's sister in law) M. Guizot, Mr Hensleigh Wedgwood &c, so if Mr Carlyle thought it worth enquiring about, he might easily hear of it from some of them as a *conjecture*. Who writes the literary reviews in the Examiner? I hoped Mr Forster, because I was so much delighted with Oliver Goldsmith's life, and (long ago,) with the Lives of the Statesmen &c; but people say he no longer writes the literary articles.

I do indeed value Mr Carlyle's note, and for the precise reason you mention; it bears the stamp of honesty and truth; in the discriminate praise; and\shows that he/thinks me worthy of being told of my faults. I half thought of sending you a copy, but I don't know if you would care to see it. I have seen enough of the way in which authors in general *flummery* each other up with insincere and overdone praise to be disgusted with flattery for ever. Neither Mr Dickens nor Mrs Davenport have ever acknowledged their copies; but I sent them more to satisfy my own feelings, than to receive thanks.

I will send you a corrected copy either today or tomorrow or Monday, by railway.

Once more thank you for your friendly note, and ever believe me to remain

Yours truly

E. C. Gaskell

32 **35** 49

CATHERINE WINKWORTH[1]

Manchester. Decr 23rd [1848]

Now, dearest Kate, I've just got your letter. I've not read it yet, but I shall answer as I read.⟨. . .⟩ We expected Mr W. Shaen to breakfast *here*, and were all ready, but my lord dashed in, hat in hand, and, despising cold pheasant, ham, and what not, said he was 'going to the Winkworths' to breakfast'; and on my accompanying him out of the children's presence into the hall, he said, 'Congratulate me, congratulate me!!'[2] whereupon he shook my hand till I winced with pain.⟨. . .⟩ Now I'm going to read a bit more of your letter, which is *out-and-out* welcome. I am so queer and desolate today, everybody being gone, and I not yet understanding solitude and husbandless independence!⟨. . .⟩ I mean to come and see you this day fortnight,—and then you and I and Süschen will be so jolly. I should like so much to talk to Mr Winkworth about the master and workman part of 'Mary Barton'. Some say the masters are very sore, but I'm sure I *believe* I wrote truth. I shall want to hear what Mr J. W. says much, and I sadly want to have a talk with you and Süschen about it altogether. Mr Edmund Potter thinks it so true he is going to buy it for his men. Thank you, thank you, for all you say about it (—you'll see I write this as I read). I like you to *understand* it. It is a painful subject and *must* be painful, and I felt it all so deeply myself I could hardly be light-hearted any part of the time I was writing it. ⟨. . .⟩

[1] From a printed source.
[2] He had become engaged to Emily Winkworth.

₀ **36** ₀

MARY EWART[1]

[?Late 1848]

My dear Miss Ewart,

I cannot tell you what a surprise your letter was to me last night; but I will throw myself on your honour and confess that the surprise was simply occasioned by the intelligence that 'Mary Barton' was so much read, and that you had guessed (*I cannot imagine how?*) that I had written it.

I did write it, but how did you find it out? I *do* want it to be concealed if possible, and I don't think anybody here has the least idea who is the author.⟨...⟩ I am almost frightened at my own action in writing it. I wonder how far the 'fanciful and fastidious' (they are your own epithets, and I have no other means of designating him) gentleman is right. If you were here I should very much like to talk to you about it, but as you are there[2] I can only say I wanted to represent the subject in the light in which some of the workmen certainly consider to be *true*, not that I dare to say it is the abstract absolute truth.

That some of the men do view the subject in the way I have tried to represent, I have personal evidence; and I think somewhere in the first volume you may find a sentence stating that my intention was simply to represent the view many of the work-people take. But independently of any explicit statement of my intention, I do think that we must all acknowlededge that there are duties connected with the manufacturing system not fully understood as yet, and evils existing in relation to it which may be remedied in some degree, although we as yet do not see how; but surely there is no harm in directing the attention to the existence of such evils. No one can feel more deeply than I how *wicked* it is to do anything to excite class against class; and the sin has been most unconscious if I have done so.⟨...⟩ I could only repeat that no praise could compensate me for the self-reproach I shall feel, if I have written unjustly.⟨...⟩ I am highly amused at the French ladies puzzling out the Lancashire.⟨...⟩ I am sorry to have taken up so much of my letter with egotism.⟨...⟩ Remember that you

[1] Original MS. not seen.
[2] 'Miss Ewart was in London on a visit to Lady Coltman.' (Note in source.) See Letter 34, above.

M.G.L.—D

are an accomplice after the fact, and bound to help in concealing it.⟨...⟩

34 **37** 38

EDWARD CHAPMAN

121, Upper Rumford St
Janry 1st [1849]

Dear Sir,

I want another copy of Mary Barton for a cousin of mine; now I don't like buying it at a bookseller's, and I don't like being under further obligation to you, so will you let me have one at the trade price whatever that is, and send it addressed to

The Honble Mrs Holland
8, Upper Wimpole St
London—

Half the masters here are bitterly angry with me—half (and the best half) are buying it to give to their work-people's libraries. One party say it shall be well abused in the British Quarterly, the other say it shall be praised in the Westminster;[1] I had no idea it would have proved such a fire brand; meanwhile no one seems to see my idea of a tragic poem; so I, in reality, mourn over my failure.—Mr Carlyle's letter remains my real true gain.

Yours very truly
E C Gaskell.

37 **38** 41

EDWARD CHAPMAN

121, Upper Rumford St
Wednesday [?3 January 1849]

Dear Sir,

I have heard this morning from Mrs Holland who wants me to write her name in the copy of Mary B. I don't know how to manage this; unless you can gum, or otherwise fasten in the

[1] *The British Quarterly Review*'s article (February 1849, IX, pp. 117–136) was very critical. *The Westminster Review* (April 1849, II, pp. 48–63) was appreciative, especially of Mrs Gaskell's exposition of the industrial situation.

enclosed slip of paper. If the copy be already gone, of course it does not signify.

Thank you for yr letter. I do not say this as words of course, but because one or two of your letters have really done me good, (this among the others;) and put things in a right point of view, at which I was looking a little morbidly. I have not troubled myself about the reviews, except the one or two which I respect because I know something of the *character* of the writers; what I felt was the angry feeling induced towards me personally among some of those I live amongst; and the expressions of belief from some of those whom in many ways I respect that the book wd do harm. I am sure in the long run it will not; I have faith that what I wrote so earnestly & from the fulness of my hear⟨t⟩ must be right, but meanwhile & when I am not quite well this\angry talking/ troubles me in spite of myself. Thank you for knowing I shd care to see Mr Carlyle's letter. I should like to know which part is 'the water'; I fix first on one & then on the other till sometimes it all melts into water. I wish people wd tell authors privately & *fully* what are their real faults. I, for one should be thankful. I try and find out the places where Mr Forster said I strained after common-place materials for effect, till the whole book dances before my eyes as a commonplace piece of effect. The best way is to put it on one side altogether, and to try & 'do silently good actions which is far more indispensable'.[1] Not the least agreeable part of yr letter is that in which you speak of the book 'being a source of profit to the publisher⟨'.⟩ I am truly glad to hear of it. I hope you don't think I am taking too great a liberty with you in writing such long notes; this shall be the last.

Yours truly
E. C. Gaskell.

₀ 39 ₀

Miss Lamont

121, Upper Rumford St,
Manchester—
Jan—5th [1849]

On my return home from a visit of a few days near Rochdale I found your note my dear Miss Lamont. You can not think how it

---

[1] See next letter.

pleased me; I don't know what other people feel, but I am so glad when any body will take the kind trouble of *expressing* satisfaction at Mary B. I should like much to have a long talk with you about it, but there you are far away in Ireland. 'John Barton' was the original name, as being the central figure to my mind; indeed I had so long felt that the bewildered life of an ignorant thoughtful man of strong power of sympathy, dwelling in a town so full of striking contrasts as this is, was a tragic poem, that in writing he was [?]my 'hero'; and it was a London thought coming through the publisher that it must be called *Mary* B. So many people over-look John B or see him merely to misunderstand him, that if you were a stranger and had only said that one thing (that the book shd have been called *John* B) I should have had pleasure in feeling that my own idea was recognized; how much more am I pleased then when the whole letter comes from one whom I so much liked and admired in our few & far between glimpses as I did you. Some people here are very angry and say the book will do harm; and for a time I have been shaken and sorry; but I have such firm faith that the earnest expression of any one's feeling can only do good in the long run,—that God will cause the errors to be temporary[,] the truth to be eternal, that I try not to mind too much what people say either in blame or praise. I had a letter from Carlyle, and when I am over-filled with thoughts arising from this book, I put it all aside, (or *try* to put it aside,) and think of his last sentence—'May you live long to write good books, or *do silently good actions which in my sight is far more indispensable.*'

Did you read a little piece of Carlyles on the death of Charles Buller, that appeared about a month ago in the London Examiner?[1] I never heard of Chas Buller before; but was struck with the beautiful testimonial after his death; I think I can remember the exact words of one part—

'And in his patience with the much that he could not do, let us grant there was something very beautiful too'. So dear Miss Lamont though your plans have failed partially and though your struggles have not met with the reward you desired of having a home of your own wherein to care for yr mother your patience with what you can not do will have something beautiful in it.

I remember Mrs Roberts very well, and dear little Dora, have I ever seen Mr Roberts?—and Miss Roberts? Not long to be Miss

---

[1] Buller, Chief Poor Law Commissioner, died on 29 November 1848. Carlyle's appreciation was published on 2 December.

Roberts I hear; and I wish her all happiness—Mr Gaskell is in
Essex; he will come home tomorrow morning, and will I am
sure be glad to know I have heard from you. If Mrs Darbishire
lives near you, will you give my kind love to her? And believe me
dear Miss Lamont ever yours affectionately

E C Gaskell

*

₀ 40 ₀

UNKNOWN

Thursday morning.
[?8 March 1849]

Dear Sir,

I write by return of post to thank you, not merely or principally
for your kindness and trouble in procuring us orders; but for the
'plain speaking', and really friendly warning against being
'lionized'. I am truly grateful to you for it. I hardly understand
what is meant by the term; nor do I *think* anything could alter me
from my own self; but I will be on my guard. If such a man as
the Rajah Brooke, such a noble fellow as he, suffered in character,
it would ill become me to say I might not be materially altered for
the worse by this mysterious process of 'lionizing'. How am I to
help it? There are people I really want to see as well as things. I
do think praise to one's face is a greater impertinence than blame;
and either, with reference to a book published anonymously, a
most under-bred thing. I shall however remember yr warning,
with many internal thanks to you. Luckily for me Miss Holland
possesses excellent sense, and a very fair proportion of satirical
power, which she is not at all unwilling to exert; and I shall tell
her not to spare me in the least.

Oh dear! I wish poor Mary Barton could be annihilated this
next month; and I then might go where I liked, & do & see what
I liked naturally & simply. I shd not like to go to Leslie's lectures
unless they were commonly attended by ladies; so if there be any
doubt about it, that is at once shut up. I did not know orders were
ever given for theatres, nor do I quite understand *how*; what I
meant by my indefinite request for 'orders' were [*sic*] for things
which I understood money cd not purchase, but which were

privileges accorded to acquaintanceship or friendship. But if
orders to theatres & Concerts do not involve any money obligation, and are to be easily procured without any great trouble to
yourself, I believe we should like them. But pray understand that
what I meant to ask for were simply for sights not to be seen
without such orders.

We still hope to go up on the 14th;[1] that is to say if the landlady of the lodgings will ever answer a letter written 3 weeks ago.

Yours gratefully & faithfully

E C. Gaskell

33 41 44

EDWARD CHAPMAN[2]

[9 March 1849]

My dear Sir,
Thank you for the two copies of Mary B, safely received
through Simms and Dinham yesterday. I am not thinking of
writing any thing else; le jeu ne vaut pas la chandelle. And I have
nothing else to say. I shall be amused to read the manufacturing
novel you tell me is forth-coming; I suppose the writer's name is
a secret, but I wish her every success. It is a large subject, & I think
it ought to be written upon.

I fear Mr Lewes' lectures did not succeed, at any rate as regards
number of audience, so well as you heard they did; the cause of
their non-success did not lie in the mustachios, but in the quantity
of evening engagements there are in Manr at this time of the year.
It is the very worst a lecturer cd fix upon. I did not like Mr Lewes
at first, but I have liked him better every time I have seen him.
He is to appear in Shylock tomorrow evng, but I am afraid I
cannot go to see it.[3] Can you put me in the way of obtaining
employment for a friend as a translator from either french,
german, or latin? She writes a good english style, and is conscien-

---

[1] Mrs Gaskell seems to have gone up to London in March. See Hopkins, *Gaskell*,
p. 85.
[2] *Annotation* From Forster's Life of Dickens.
[3] G. H. Lewes lectured on Speculative Philosophy at the Athenaeum. He also
appeared as Shylock at the Theatre Royal on 10 March 1849 (*The Annals of
Manchester*, ed. W. E. A. Axon, 1886, p. 250).

tious in doing her best⟨,⟩ with great general knowledge, whh might be brought to bear on all solid & thoughtful subjects. She has been educated abroad. You would be doing me a favour if you can tell me how these powers might be made available.

Yours truly
E C. Gaskell

₀ 42 ₀

MRS GREG[1]

[?Early 1849]

My dear Mrs Greg,

May I write in the first person to you, as I have many things I should like to say to the writer of the remarks on 'Mary Barton' which Miss Mitchell has sent me, and which I conjecture were written by your husband? Those remarks and the note which accompanied have given me great and real pleasure. I have heard much about the disapproval which Mr Greg's family have felt with regard to 'M. B.,' and have heard of it with so much regret that I am particularly glad that Mr Sam Greg does not participate in it. I regretted the disapprobation, not one whit on account of the testimony of such disapproval which I heard was to arise out of it,[2] but because I knew that such a feeling would be conscientiously and thoughtfully entertained by men who are acquainted by long experience with the life, a portion of which I had endeavoured to represent; and whose actions during a long course of years have proved that the interests of their work-people are as dear to them as their own. Such disapproval, I was sure, would not be given if the writing which called it forth were merely a free expression of ideas; but it would be given if I had misrepresented, or so represented, a part as the whole, as that people at a distance should be misled and prejudiced against the masters, and that class be estranged from class.

I value the remarks exceedingly, because the writer has exactly entered into my own state of mind, and perceived the weakness

---

[1] An 'uncompleted draft' from a printed source.
[2] W. R. Greg's review appeared in the *Edinburgh Review* (April 1849, LXXXIX, pp. 402–35). See Letters 85 and 186.

of which I was conscious. The whole tale grew up in my mind as imperceptibly as a seed germinates in the earth, so I cannot trace back now why or how such a thing was written, or such a character or circumstance introduced. (There is one exception to this which I will name afterwards.) I can remember now that the prevailing thought in my mind at the time when the tale was silently forming itself and impressing me with the force of a reality, was the seeming injustice of the inequalities of fortune. Now, if they occasionally appeared unjust to the more fortunate, they must bewilder an ignorant man full of rude, illogical thought, and full also of sympathy for suffering which appealed to him through his senses. I fancied I saw how all this might lead to a course of action which might appear right for a time to the bewildered mind of such a one, but that this course of action, violating the eternal laws of God, would bring with it its own punishment of an avenging conscience far more difficult to bear than any worldly privation. Such thoughts I now believe, on looking back, to have been the origin of the book. 'John Barton' was the original title of the book. Round the character of John Barton all the others formed themselves; he was my hero, *the* person with whom all my sympathies went, with whom I tried to identify myself at the time, because I believed from personal observation that such men were not uncommon, and would well reward such sympathy and love as should throw light down upon their groping search after the causes of suffering, and the reason why suffering is sent, and what they can do to lighten it. Mr Greg has exactly described, and in clearer language than I could have used, the very treatment which I am convinced is needed to bring such bewildered thinkers round into an acknowledgment of the universality of some kind of suffering, and the consequent necessity of its existence for some good end. If Mary Barton has no other result than the expression of the thoroughly just, wise, kind thoughts which Mr Greg has written down with regard to characters like John Barton, I am fully satisfied. There are many such whose lives are magic [?tragic][1] poems which cannot take formal language. The tale was formed, and the greater part of the first volume was written when I was obliged to lie down constantly on the sofa, and when I took refuge in the invention to exclude the memory of painful scenes which would force themselves upon my remembrance.

[1] Dr J. M. S. Tompkins has also independently suggested this emendation. See also Letter 39.

It is no wonder then that the whole book seems to be written in the minor key; indeed, the very design seems to me to require this treatment. I acknowledge the fault of there being too heavy a shadow over the book; but I doubt if the story could have been deeply realized without these shadows. The cause of the fault must be looked for in the design; and yet the design was one worthy to be brought into consideration. Perhaps after all it may be true that I, in my state of feelings at that time, was not fitted to introduce the glimpses of light and happiness which might have relieved the gloom. And now I return to the part I named before, where I can trace and remember how unwillingly and from what force of outside pressure (which is, I am convinced, a wrong motive for writing and sure only to produce a failure) it was written. The tale was originally complete without the part which intervenes between John Barton's death and Esther's; about 3 pages, I fancy, including that conversation between Job Legh, and Mr Carson, and Jem Wilson. The MS. had been in the hands of the publisher above 14 months, and was nearly all printed when the publisher sent me word that it would fall short of the requisite number of pages, and that I must send up some more as soon as possible. I remonstrated over and over again—I even said I would rather relinquish some of the payment than interpolate anything; that the work ⟨. . .⟩

o **43** 207

GERALDINE JEWSBURY

April 2. [1849]

Dear Miss Jewsbury,

I send you back 'Ambarvalia'[1] with many thanks; I am also much obliged to you for sending me Mr Espinasse's prospectus, which had before excited my attention. I should like particularly to have heard the lecture tonight; Robert Clive was a great friend of my mother's family, and at the old house in Cheshire which was their home there are two pillars at the gate way into the court, (a flight of stone steps leading up to the said gateway,)

[1] *Ambarvalia*, a collection of poems by A. H. Clough and Thomas Burbidge, 1849.

which were surmounted by great stone balls about 6 or 7 feet
apart. Young Clive used to put my great-grandmother into a
terrible fright by jumping from one of them to the other{s}; and
when I was a child his exploits were traditional in the neighbourhood, & spoken of under the breath as something too daring to be
told aloud.[1]—Of course all this made him into a hero before
I knew there was such a place as India;— but however much I shd
have liked to have gone\to hear this lecture,/my travels, for today
at least, are confined to a 'voyage autour de ma chambre', as one
of my little girls is only recovering from an illness; as for next
Monday I shall try and go, if I can induce Mr Gaskell. I am writing
in a darkened room, with only light enough to see that I ought to
make an apology for my writing. My copy of 'Margaret' is in such
demand since the review in the Athenæum;[2] it is pledged 3 deep.

Yours very truly
E. C. Gaskell

41 44 66

?EDWARD CHAPMAN[3]

11 Panton Sq.
Thursday [?26 April 1849]

My dear Sir,
    I return you the Athenæum tickets with many thanks for the
pleasure we have derived from the use of them. I remain, dear Sir,

Yours very truly
E. C. Gaskell

---

[1] See E. Haldane, *Mrs Gaskell and Her Friends*, 1931, p. 20.
[2] A review of *Margaret, a Tale of the Real and the Ideal* appeared in *The
Athenaeum*, No. 1116, 17 March 1849. It spoke of the book's showing 'the
redeeming influence of sorrow . . . leaving no poisoned incurable wound, but
bringing forth the peaceable fruits of well-doing from its harsh teaching'.
[3] *Postmark* AP 27 | 1849. *Annotation* E. Cha[pman?] | 186⟨⟩ [Mrs Gaskell is
perhaps using an old cover.]

₀ **44a** ₄₆

ELIZA FOX[1]

27 Woburn Square,
Saturday Evening.
½ p. II
[?5 May 1849]

My dear Miss Fox,

I think I have behaved most abominably in never taking any notice of your great kindness in sending me David Copperfield,[2] *and* your note. Oh, dear! I have been so whirled about {against} since I saw you last that I hardly know what I write. I do so like D. Copperfield; and it was a charming liberty you took in sending it. I don't know if you did *finally* ask us to dinner at five on Wednesday; but the Fates (in the shape of Mr Forster,) seem to have determined it for us, whether you will or no, my dear! And we mean to Sadlers-Wells it afterwards, a⟨s⟩ you proposed. May we?

We are staying here now,—i.e. going to Windsor tomorrow for the day, to Mr Chorley's for the evening; we shall just sleep here on Sunday night, and off again. I have letters from home that make me quite happy, in the good accounts I receive. I shall send o⟨r⟩ bring your Examiners & David Copperfield back tomorrow. I remain yours *affectionately*

E. C. Gaskell.

I am intoxicated with sparkling conversation heard tonight at Mrs Procter's. I keep smiling to myself and trying to remember things —all to no purpose,—the foam has faded from the Champagne.

[1] *Address* Miss Fox | 5 Charlotte Street. *Seal, broken and illegible.*
[2] *David Copperfield* was issued in 20 monthly parts beginning on 1 May 1849, and in book-form late in 1850. Other visits in this letter appear to relate it to E. Winkworth's of 8 May 1849. See *Letters and Memorials*, ed. Winkworth, I, p. 179.

₀ **45** ₁₅₃

ANNA JAMESON[1]

27, Woburn Square,
Saturday morning.
[12 May 1849]

My dear Mrs Jameson,

Thank you *very* much for the gracious and kind manner in which you have acceded to my (half impudent) request. *I* shall value your note to me in a higher and better way than as an autograph. I will tell you what I plan to do on Monday. I plan to go as early as I can, after breakfast, to bid the Carlyles goodbye.[2] I really want to see them, so I shall go to Chelsea very early, say at ½ past 9, and come back to town via Montpelier Square in Brompton, where an old lady lives whom I wish to see. Do you think this could be done before 12? I should much like to see you again, but the great distances of London are such a bewilderment to me, that I hardly know how long this expedition will take me. At any rate believe me, dear Mrs Jameson,

Yours very faithfully,
E. C. Gaskell

*

₄₄ₐ **46** ₄₈

ELIZA FOX[3]

[?London]
[?Early May] 1849.

My dear Eliza,

(I sha'nt Miss Fox you any more, I wish you were here I am so lonely, for Emily[4] is gone to the Opera, that's all a parenthesis at the beginning, and now I'm going to begin.)

---

[1] From a printed source.
[2] An Emily Winkworth letter (11 May 1849) mentions a final visit planned for Monday, 14 May, *Letters and Memorials*, ed. Winkworth, I, p. 183.
[3] Original MS. not seen.
[4] We assume that Emily was Miss Winkworth.

My dear *Eliza*,

You are very [?] and dear to think of my little girls, and they
shall learn to love you now and some day I hope personally. 〈...〉

21 *and* 27 **47** 90[1]

MARIANNE and MARGARET EMILY GASKELL

Shottery, near Stratford on-Avon
Thursday [17 May 1849][2]

My dearest girls,

I was so glad to get your letter, dearest Meta, waiting for me here
last night; and again this morning, another telling me about your
visit to Sandle-bridge, and your different weights. I got here last
night just at the same time as cousin Bessy; and you can not
think what a pretty place it is; last night we threw open the windows, and smelt the scent of the sweet-briar, and the wall-
flowers; and heard the nightingales singing away so deliciously,
it was such a pleasant contrast to our little dusty noisy lodgings in
Panton Square, where nevertheless we had been very happy &
merry indeed. I forget when I wrote last to you, but I know it is
several days since I told you anything. I wrote a letter to Annie
Green on Sunday which would I thought perhaps interest her;
telling her about the Dickens dinner. On Sunday we went to
breakfast with the Howitt's; to church to hear Mr Maurice, whom
I like very much indeed, and who wrote the preface to the Saint's
tragedy[3] I like so much. {We} I dined at Mr Hensleigh Wedge-
woods; with whom I hope you will be acquainted sometime, and
went with them to hear Mr Scott. On Monday Emily & I went
once more to the Exhibition of paintings; and then on to Chelsea
to see the old place once more, and bid the Carlyles goodbye, as
they had asked us to do. Then we came home, & went out to
dinner, meeting Mr & Mrs Dickens, and Mr Frank Stone who
painted that picture of which there is an engraving in Papa's study.
He used to go to Cross Street chapel when he was a little boy.
On Tuesday Emily & I went to call on Mr Rogers to bid him

---

[1] To Marianne; to Meta, *118a.

[2] Dated by comparison with Emily Winkworth's letters from this period, some
of which are not accurately dated. However, the extended similarities in the
sequence of visits described make the month and year certain.

[3] By Charles Kingsley, 1848.

goodbye; and he was very kind and showed us many beautiful things; and asked us to breakfast the next day with him. Then we went to Tot-hill fields prison to see the silent associated system, of which our dear Mr Wright thinks so highly[—]home and wrote many letters & notes. Yesterday we went to breakfast with Rogers!, poor old man; he looks so very old, and feeble, and yesterday morning he was sadly put out, by some people coming very late indeed; so that altogether I did not enjoy it so much as our call the day before, though he again showed us some beautiful things —ornaments for the head, ears, neck dug out of Etruscan, Pompeian, & Egyptian tombs; some were as elegant as anything that is made now. Then I came on here; and arrived about 9; finding cousin Bessy just arrived. And now we are going to dinner; after which we shall go to Warwick, see the Castle, and drink tea with Mrs Marshall, who used to live in Manchester, and whose son is the Minister at Warwick. On Saturday, we go to see a curious old place called Compton Wingates;[1] on Monday to dine at Mr Greaves at Radford, the father of Mr R. Greaves; and on Tuesday, I hope, home to my darlings, whom I am longing to see. Ever my dear girls your affec[tionat]e mother

E C Gaskell

46 **48** 51

ELIZA FOX[2]

121 Upper Rumford St.
Monday,[3] May 29, 1849

⟨...⟩I did not come home straight as you thought I did. Your mesmeric clairvoyance ought to have carried you that same Wednesday night, to a very pretty, really old fashioned cottage, at Shottery, the village where Shakespeare's wife lived in her maiden days, near S. on Avon; a cottage where one's head was literally in danger of being bumped by the low doors, and where the windows were casements: where the rooms were all entered by a step up, or a step down: where the scents through the open hall door were all of sweet briar and lilac and lilies of the valley:

---

[1] Compton Winyates.   [2] Original MS. not seen.
[3] Tuesday. See text below also.

where we slept with our windows open to hear the nightingales' jug-jug, and where the very shadows in the drawing room had a green tinge from the leafy trees which over hung the windows. Cd. there be a greater contrast to dear charming, dingy dirty Panton Square? Anne Holland had preceded me a day as you know, and did not we pour out the treasures of our London campaign to the rural inhabitants staying in the house, who believed in ghosts, and told some capital stories thereupon; and another cousin; and we had rainy days for rest; when we sat with open windows, revelling in the sound of the raindrops pattering among the trees; and we had brilliantly fine days when we went long drives; in one of which (to a place where I believed the Sleeping Beauty lived, it was so over-grown and hidden up by woods) I SAW a ghost! Yes I did; though in such a matter of fact place as Charlotte St I should not wonder if you are sceptical; and had my fortune told by a gypsy; curiously true as to the past, at any rate, and I did my duty as a meek submissive lion, fresh imported from the desert (i.e. London), at a party; and then I rushed home; turning regularly home sick, all on a sudden; leaving Anne at Shottery, so it was on Tuesday evening last, this day week you should have been clair-voyant to the extent of seeing me arrive at the Manchester station, Mr Gaskell meeting me; (I wonder what yr notion of him is,—he *is* 6 feet tall, thin hair inclined to grey as far as outward man goes, does that accord with clair-voyance?) We joggled home; our home is a mile and a half from the *very* middle of Manchester; the last house countrywards of an interminably long street, the other end of which touches the town, while we look into fields from some of our windows; not very pretty or rural fields it must be owned, but in which the children can see cows milked and hay made in summer time. The four girls rushed upon me, and almost smothered me; (the second is Margaret, always called Meta) and to the best of my recollection, we all six husband wife and children four, talked at once, upon different subjects, incessantly till bed-time for the younger ones; when the elder two had a little peace, and did really talk. The next day my husband left home on business; and Susanna Winkworth came to spend the day; my ancles ached with talking at the end of the day; its a *true* and not a figurative expression; they did ache, and I had (not) walked a step only talked. The next day I fairly settled down to home life, lessons till 12—lunch walk, etc; and so we've gone on ever since. The Winkworths are at Alderley;

(18 miles off) for the summer which is a great loss to me; Selina came over yesterday, and we had a charming long piece of enjoyment of each other; and abuse of Emily for never writing.⟨...⟩ I do think our home *is* very bright. The little ones were delighted with the gutta perch-heads;[1] and I duly ins(?) them that it was not Mama who sent them but '*Eliza*' so you see you are beginning to be the name of a shade in our house, and I hope some day you will be something more. Yes! I got some words of wisdom, *very* kindly and nicely given; and I could have done with more, but there was no opportunity for speaking to him in the quiet wood again. Nobody and nothing was real (I am sorry for you, but I must tell the truth) in M. Barton, but the character of John Barton; the circumstances are different, but the character and some of the speeches, are exactly a poor man I know. I am glad you like Mary, I do: but people are angry with her just because she is not perfect. I told the story according to a fancy of my own; to really SEE the scenes I tried to describe, (and they WERE as real as my own life at the time) and then to tell them as nearly as I could, as if I were speaking to a friend over the fire on a winter's night and describing real occurrences. I am at the end of my paper, and the girls are waiting with lessons to say. If you can see Blackwood's Magazine for Jan: 1837 you will see a poem of mine,[2] the germ of 'Alice.'

Yours affectionately,
E. C. Gaskell.

35 49 57

CATHERINE WINKWORTH[3]

Drawing-room, Sunday afternoon, Aug. 21. [1849]

My dearest Katie,

You've no notion how cold it is in these northern regions; be thankful you're in the South. If you want an agreeable book, read 'Lives of the Lindsays'.[4] Do you know what an American 'Bee' is? You know it's the sort of pic-nic they get up in the back-woods, when they want to build a house or a bridge, &c., in a hurry.

---

[1] *Sic*; perhaps 'gutta-percha heads' is meant.
[2] 'Sketches Among the Poor', No. 1.
[3] From a printed source. 21 August 1849 was in fact a Tuesday.
[4] By Lord Lindsay; published in June 1849.

Well; I'm going to have a 'Bee' here next week, and I wish you
and Emily could come to it. There are 192 tucks to be run in my
children's garments all at once! so I am going to have a 'Bee'.
Agnes and Eliza Paterson and Susanna are coming, and if Selina and
Emma Shaen are get-at-able from Alderley, I shall have them too.
I am afraid Marianne Darbishire and Emily Tagart would think it
a very dull piece of gaiety, or I would ask them. The refreshments
are a puzzle to me. I find that in America, toasted cheese spread
with honey is *the* thing at 'Bees'; but I am afraid my guests would
not appreciate it. What do you suggest?

You sound very comfortable in the Isle of Wight. How big is
it? I never yet could understand its size. Is it not slightly cockney?
Have you to dress finely? What *are* the Needles, people always
talk about so much? Have you seen Mr White[1] of that Ilk yet?
or my fat friend, Mr Forster, who would have found you out if
he could (*i.e. Emily*) I've a notion. What sort of rooms have you?
Grand proper rooms, I dare say, as dull as dust, with no amusing
warming-pans, nor crockery, nor spurs, nor dresser, as Selina and
we had at the Lakes; our dear charming farm-kitchen at Skelwith
was worth a dozen respectable properly-furnished rooms. However, we're all at home now, and settled down into soberness. The
Darbishires are all at Rivington today. They've got into a very
helter-skelter way of spending Sundays ever since they read the
'Nemesis';[2] tomorrow they've a dance; we're asked but I'm going
to have a headache, and Sukey is going to 'quite accidentally'
come in on her way from her District and sit with me.⟨...⟩
Dearest Katie, I have so much to tell you; about the Lakes, and
the people we met there, and I wonder when I shall see you? Next
winter but one, if we are all alive, I mean you to be very strong,
and to come and stay with us for a long piece of time, when I can
talk up my talk to you. Meanwhile, if Emily had any proper feeling,
she'd break it off with Will Shaen, and want me to comfort her;
and then it would be my *duty* to go and see the Isle of Wight.

Mr Froude is domesticated at the Darbishires' till October, when
he is to be married and go to the Satterfields' old house in Green
Heys. If any one under the sun has a magical, magnetic, glamour-
like influence, that man has. He's '*aut Mephistophiles aut nihil*',
that's what he is. The D. D.'s all bend and bow to his will, like

---

[1] Mrs Gaskell had written a letter of introduction to the Rev. James White.
Letters and Memorials, ed. Winkworth, I, p. 193.

[2] J. A. Froude's *The Nemesis of Faith*, 2nd ed., July 1849.

reeds before the wind, blow whichever way it listeth. He smokes cigars constantly; Père, Robert, Arthur, Vernon (nay, once even little Francis), smoke constantly. He disbelieves, they disbelieve; he wears shabby garments, they wear shabby garments; in short, it's the most complete taking away their own wills and informing them[1] with his own that ever was.⟨...⟩ I stand just without the circle of his influence; resisting with all my might, but feeling and seeing the attraction. It's queer!⟨...⟩ I've scarcely seen anyone yet; but then I've made four flannel petticoats, and I don't know how many preserves and pickles, which are so good and successful I am sure it is my vocation to be a house-keeper; not an economical one, but a jolly extravagant one.⟨...⟩

₀ **50** ₅₆

JOHN FORSTER[2]

[*c.* 8 Oct. 1849]

My dear Sir,

Now I want to ask for your kind offices, and I don't know how to begin. I think I must commit a plagiarism on a 'Tea and Coffee' circular lying before me. 'Emboldened by past favours Mrs Gaskell ventures to solicit a continuation of future kind attention to the'—the next word is merits, and I am not sure if that would quite do. So you must suppose the prettiest apology in the world made, and also the most earnest *real* request made that you won't scruple to say No, plump *No*, if you would rather have nothing to do with the matter. And now to begin. You know Tennyson, don't you? (Miss Fox said you did,) and you know who Samuel Bamford is, don't you? A great, gaunt, stalwart Lancashire man, formerly hand-loom weaver, author of 'Life of a Radical' &c,— age nearly 70, and living in that state which is exactly 'decent poverty', with his neat, little apple-faced wife; they have lost their only child. Bamford is *the* most hearty, (and it's saying a good deal) admirer of Tennyson I know. I dislike recitations exceedingly, but he repeats some of Tennyson's poems, in so rapt, and yet so simple a manner, utterly forgetting that any one is bye, in the delight in the music and the exquisite thoughts, that one can't

---

[1] Source reads 'him'.

[2] *Address* John Forster Esq | 58 Lincolns Inn Fields | London —. *Postmarks* MANCHESTER | OC 8 | 1849 | G *and* H [crown] Z | OC 9 | 1849.

help liking to hear him. *He* does not care one jot whether people like hearing him or not, in his\own/intense enjoyment. Then once I saw him blaze up when some one in an argumentative moral & utilitarian spirit 'wondered what Tennyson had done for his pension'. He had been 'minding his manners' till then, but this was too much; so he first choked, & then broke out into beautiful broad Lancashire, and then as that hardly served to carry him high enough, he took to Bible language till his adversary fairly stood rebuked. One more thing—he says when he lies awake at night, as in his old age he often does, and gets sadly thinking of the days that are gone when his child was alive, he soothes himself by repeating T's poems. I asked him the other day if he had got them of his own;—'No' he said, rather mournfully;—'he had been long looking out for a second hand copy,—but somehow they had not got into the old book-shops, and 14s (or 18. Which are they?) was too much for a poor man like him to give'—and then he brightened up, & said 'Thank God, he had a good memory, and whenever he got into a house where there were Tennyson's poems he learnt as many as he could of[f] by heart; & he thought he knew better than twelve',—& he began Œnone, & then the Sleeping Beauty. Now I wonder if you catch a glimpse of what I want. I thought at first of giving him the Poems this Xmas; but then I remembered with what beautiful composure and boldness you asked Mr Stone for those two engravings, and I thought you were not likely, (at all, at all,) to have grown either shy, or ill-natured,—and so I thought you would perhaps ask Tennyson if he would give Bamford a copy *from himself*; which would be glorious for the old man.—Dear! how he would triumph. He would set off, I dare say next Christmas, wrapped in his plaid, and tramp away to the hidden nook where Tennyson abides, and come looming down upon him to thank him some foggy Jany morning. If you would rather not do it, pray never mind, and take no notice of my request. I do so dislike refusing myself, that I would much rather spare you the pain, as I know you would do it, if you thought it right or proper.

Yours very truly
E Gaskell.

His address is,
    Samuel Bamford
        Middleton near
            Manchester.

₄₈ **51** ₅₂
ELIZA FOX[1]

[?Early November] 1849.

My dear Eliza,

We dined at the Darbishire's last night, and talked so much
about you my dear—(⟨...⟩) that I am seized with a crave to
write to you today; although you don't write to me. I don't
exactly know anything I have to say, but I am looking forward
to your coming with great pleasure and you are to be so good as
not to cheat me. I wonder if you ever see Mr Newman's papers
on Hungary[2] or if you care to;—Kossuth is coming here to visit a
friend of ours, so I mean to see him by hook or by crook ⟨...⟩ We
are all just now in a state of great curiosity about the Mrs Froude
Mr F. is bringing home on Saturday; it is a very romantic story;
she was going into a convent when he went[3] away from Oxford,
took refuge at her brother\s?/-in-law's (where should the 's' come?)
Mr Kingsleys; but instead of a nunnery she has chosen a marriage,
—still she is a strict Puseyite, confesses to a priest etc: etc:⟨...⟩ It
always seems of no use beginning on long subjects in a letter; but
we will have some famous 'coutes'[4] when you come. I don't think
you know what a coute is, do you now?⟨...⟩ I always feel very
full of something to the exclusion of almost everything else; and
just now houses haunt me.⟨...⟩ Are you prepared for a garret,
rather like Campbell's rainbow, 'a happy spirit to delight mid
way twixt earth and heaven;'[5] with *no* fireplace, only a great
cistern, which however we lock up for fear of our friends com-
mitting suicide. Are you prepared for a cold clammy atmosphere,
a town with no grace or beauty in it, a house full of cold draughts,
and mysterious puffs of icy air? Are you prepared for four girls in
and out continually, interrupting the most interesting conversation
with enquiries respecting lessons work, etc:—If these delights thy

[1] Original MS. not seen.
[2] Stephen Winkworth writes on 11 November 1849 of an article on Hungary
by F. W. Newman in the November *Prospective* [?*Review*, xx, pp. 369-408].
Letters and Memorials, ed. Winkworth, I, p. 214.
[3] Source reads 'sent'.   [4] See Letter 55.
[5] Still seem as to my childhood's sight
    A midway station given
  For happy spirits to delight
    Betwixt the earth and heaven.
      'To A Rainbow', ll. 5-8.

mind can move, come live with me and be my love. I like the
house very much, though I acknowledge we have out grown it;
you shall have a bottle of hot water in bed, and blankets ad libitum,
and we keep glorious fires. The girls *are* very nice ones though I
say it that should not say it, and I do think that you will like them
all in their separate ways, so please write soon and fix you[r] time
for coming.

⟨. . .⟩ My dear Eliza I am your affec[tionate]

E. C. Gaskell.

₅₁ **52** ₅₃

ELIZA FOX[1]

[?November 1849]

My dear Eliza,

On coming home from spending a day or two in the country
last night, I found your note. I am very sorry, so indeed are we all;
and I am doubly sorry because I did so want you to see Plas
Penrhyn in all its autumn glory. I can hardly fancy your not
coming today. I had so completely planned it in my own mind.
Tomorrow I meant to have dragged you through mills and
manufacturies without end, by way of getting one's duty done
to Manchester.⟨. . .⟩ Oldham. If you fill that up with an oath
Hony soit qui mal y pense. *I* did not write it. However I look
forward to December, the Darbishires and Winkworths will be
at home then:[2] and will be very jolly in spite of wind and weather,
and there being no fire in our spare room—'and what will poor
Robin do then, poor thing!' Yes I *do* know my dear Mr Newman,
we all here reverence him with true reverence as you would if you
knew him. He is so holy! You may often if not always see him at
Mr Scott's lectures. He sits in one regular place. I think I see him
now stealing in rather late to his usual place on the back benches
to the right hand Mr Scott. His life, his spiritual and religious life
is very interesting. I heard it from Mr Price (Dr Arnold's correspondent), just lately at the Lakes.[3] We first knew Mr Newman

[1] Original MS. not seen.
[2] Catherine and Emily returned about 8 December 1849. *Letters and Memorials*,
ed. Winkworth, I, 193.
[3] Mrs Gaskell had been at Skelwith in the summer. *Ibid.*, p. 192.

from his coming here to be a professor at the Manchester College —and the face and voice at first sight told 'He had been with Christ'. I never during a 6 years pretty intimate acquaintance heard or saw anything which took off that first conviction. Oh dear! I long for the days back again when he came dropping in in the dusk and lost no time in pouring out what his heart was full of, (thats the secret of eloquence) whether it was a derivation of a word, a joke or a burst of indignation or a holy thought. I can't go into his life just now, it's too interesting to be compressed, (oh you provoking creature! why don't you come here to be talked to, instead of written to.) Suffice it to say that its who can revere Mr Newman most with Mr Darbishire, the Winkworths and myself, the book is absolutely simply the utterance of the man.

₅₂ **53** ₅₅

?ELIZA FOX[1]

Sunday evening.
[25 November 1849]

⟨...⟩ You have heard Mr Newman speak 'I guess.' His voice and pronunciation are perfect; I do like that rich melodious accent which Oxford men have, though it is called 'bumptious', but Mr Newman's self is not bumptious. He dresses so shabbily you would not see his full beauty,—he used to wear detestable bottle green coats, wh. never show off a man. Mrs Newman is a Plymouth Brother which is a sort of community-of-goods-and-equality-of-rank-on-religious-principles association and *very* cal-vinistic. Will you get to know for me what tragedies Mr Wright has written: 'I am asked' and can't tell, and want you to, through the Macreadys or somebody. By the bye I saw Mr Macready, and wish I'd seen more of him. I saw him in King Lear and out of King Lear. I never saw him but once before, and that was in King Lear. I had a little bit of talk with him and liked him *extremely* as soon as the little bit of stiff stateliness has gone off. I only grudged the evening being so short.⟨...⟩ I hope I shall remember all the things I want to say when you come. I suppose you've read

[1] Original MS. not seen. The Macready reference seems to connect this with Letter 55. (Cf. Letter 54.)

Ruskins 7 Lamps from what you say. I long to, but find it difficult
to get books. I've seen Mrs Froude, she's not a heroine of romance-
looking woman.

Ever yrs affec[tionately]

E. Gaskell.

₀ **54** ₀

Unknown[1]

Sunday evening,

Nov. 26th,[2] 1849

⟨. . .⟩ I am sure the more you know the more you will like Mr
Newman—he is so high, and noble, and child-like.⟨. . .⟩ I must
tell you about some of the Sunday school girls, one of the teachers
has been teaching them what dancing mistresses call calisthenic
exercises, thinking that as they worked so much in factories, this
exercise (which she called doing their arms), would be good for
them; but one day two or three refused to do it, looking grave and
conscientious, but very resolute; so she asked why, and they said
it was forbidden in the Bible,—She asked where, and they showed
her 'Do not thy alms before men,' thats truth and happened this
week.⟨. . .⟩

Mrs Froude is not worthy in appearance and manner to be a
heroine; she is kind hearted and hearty though, and that's a great
deal in this cold world. But I don't know what age she is—and
that was a blow.⟨. . .⟩

₅₃ **55** ₆₃

Eliza Fox[3]

[Monday] Nov. 26, 1849.

You must bring me details when we have our coute; a coute is
—a coute—two or three people,—sitting by firelight, in a very

---

[1] Original MS. not seen. If Letter 53 was sent to Eliza Fox, it seems unlikely
that this one was also, despite its source (see Appx E).

[2] Sunday fell on 25 November 1849.   [3] Original MS. not seen.

confidential open-hearted mood, talking of everything that comes uppermost,—a conversation is a coute. What language the word belongs to I don't know. I don't think its Lancashire, probably Northumberland, or Scotch, I picked up quantities of charming expressive words in canny Newcastle 'and I suspect' coute's parish is there, only I don't mean to pass it back again. I wish you would remember me very kindly to Mrs Macready. I liked her tone of conversation so much one morning at Rogers that I don't want her to forget me.⟨...⟩ I long to see Macready, I see him advertised, and wish to see him. One comfort is they all seem to say his King Lear is the best, I did like him *very* much and think with great regret of the easy way in which I left my place thinking I should hear him talk again, and I never did; and I wonder if you are puzzled about the shaking-hands ceremony as I am, never knowing when, (in what stage of intimacy) it begins, so Macready and I backwards and forwards our hands, and ended by not shaking at all⟨...⟩ Have you read Southey's memoir?[1] but of course you have, happy creature—and do you know Dr Epps— I think you do—ask him to tell you who wrote Jane Eyre and Shirley,—⟨...⟩ Do tell me who wrote Jane Eyre.

Tuesday.⟨...⟩ Oh! I am so sorry about Miss Macready, I can not think how she came to be consumptive. I am sure she ought not. And why in the world had Mr Forster to go with her? Is her father away? or her mother had her confinement[?] Do tell me all you know about them for I did so like Mrs Macready. Now don't forget. Secondly, you interest and amuse me about George. It is so exactly Meta over again, she is *growling* like thunder at me all day for having 'forced' her to go to the Froude's last night.⟨...⟩ I mean to copy you out some lines of my *hero*, Mr Kingsley; and I want to ask you and Mr Fox if you know anything of a co-operative tailor's shop established by Prof. Maurice, Archdeacon Hare, Mr Ludlow[2] &c., &c., &c., & Kingsley (many *clergymen*) on Louis Blanc's principle, Jules Chevalier for a guide, in the New Road, or Tottenham Court Road (they're the same thing aren't they—and Mrs Schwabe has been here since I began. She has been staying in London (Cobdens) and has been to see Mr Watts the artist, and is charmed with him, &c &c., and is full of Mr Nash's Ragged School, and of $\frac{1}{2}$ hundred people besides, poor poor Mrs Macready among the number; she (Mrs S.) says the account of

---

[1] *Life and Correspondence of Robert Southey,* ed. C. C. Southey, 6 vols., 1849–50.
[2] Established at the beginning of 1850.

Nina is better since she went to Hastings, is it so? do tell me. She says poor Mrs Macready is wretched oh dear! it makes my heart sore—do tell me the latest account. Mrs S. saw Nina with her hair cut short so pale and worn and changed and when consumption begins in a family—! We are going to the Ss. on Friday to go and call on the Bishop and Mrs Lee, who took the decided step of calling upon us, (Units) the other day. Don't congratulate us too soon my dear! The house is as far off as ever. The nurseries were not healthy in the otherwise perfect house at Cheetham Hill, windows looked into a dry well in the middle of the house; so that's thrown up sky-high, and we're still hovering and quavering and wavering. Our girl (yours and mine sails in the Royal Albert on March 4, and her outfit is ready all except the sheets, which I must see about today; but except that[,] all is ready and right; and I like the girl much, poor creature. I have been to see her twice a week, and Agnes Ewart says she does so brighten up at the sight of me and seems so affectionate to everyone. Well I suppose it won't do to pull this world to pieces, and make up a better, but sometimes it seems the only way of effectually puryfying it. M. Darbishire is in London at the Hummuns (I don't know which should be u/s and which n/s and which m/s—Covent Garden—Now am not I good to write when I ought to be doing 50 other things. Next week, Monday I go to Mrs Davenports Capesthorne—a place and person for an artist to be in—old hall, galleries, old paintings, &c. and such a *dame* of a lady to grace them: you would long to sketch her, it and them perpetually, and would be hiding up a corner with yr little sketch-book. I mean to get strong and revel for a day or two. We drank tea at the Froudes last night. *Is* Miss Jewsbury's review shallow? It looked to me very deep, but then I know I'm easily imposed upon in the metaphysical line, and could no more attempt to write such an article than fly—⟨. . .⟩ Meanwhile Marianne is practising gorgeous Litanies to the Virgin with Mrs Froude which she has brought from Rome; and I am going through a course of John Henry Newman's Sermons. *Our* own Mr Newman is just going to publish something on public worship[1] and Mr Froude's Life of Tacitus gets on grandly (in imagination his wife says)[2] And now

[1] F. W. Newman: *Phases of Faith* was published in May 1850. This may be the book to which Mrs Gaskell is referring.

[2] See letter to Mrs Wm Long, 30 November 1849, where Froude speaks of his work on ' "The Era of Tacitus".' W. H. Dunn, *James Anthony Froude* 1961, Vol. I, p. 166.

I must copy Mr Kingsley's lines—as far as I did copy them: and tell me if you don't like them and write soon, you little good for nothing and tell me about Mrs Macready and with all our love I am ever yrs affect[ionate]ly,

E. C. Gaskell.

Re Miss Martineau⟨. . .⟩ Your ears ought to have tingled last Saty week when Miss Martineau and I spoke about you, a l'envoie l'une de l'autre.

50 **56** 59

JOHN FORSTER[1]

121, Upper Rumford St
Monday morning
[26 November 1849]

My dear Sir,
   'Tennyson' has arrived safe, without a shadow of damage and thanks without end for it. I have been half-opening the pretty golden leaves, and peeping here and there at old favourites ever since it came. But I have shut it up close again, that it may all properly stick together like a newly-bound book, before I take it to Bamford; and please to remember he lives six miles off; however *two* friends have offered to take me there; and if, at the end of this week, I find I have slipped between my two stools, I shall set off on a walking-expedition, as I am very impatient to see him receive it. I wish I could tell you how happy, and pleased it has made me. Now I am going to copy you an extract of a letter from Lady (North-Pole) Richardson. 'If you know any MPs whose hearts are made of penetrable stuff bid them read, (at page 107,) an account, given by the Bishop of Cape Town[2] in his Missionary Tour, of the treatment of captive negroes taken by our ships to St Helena. Sir John is trying to get in [*sic*] brought before parliament. It is published for 1s. by the Society for promoting Xn Knowledge. The Bishop's brother sent it to us with reference to

___

[1] *Annotation* (*pencil*) Nov 28/49 [*Wednesday*].
[2] Robert Grey (1809–72).

that page. We are writing about to different people of influence.'
So the ball being thrown to me, I throw it to you, and if you will
catch it I will pass on Ly Richardson's very pretty compliment

> '*You*, who fill your odorous lamp
> With deeds of light'.

Most undeserved compliment in my case! for my last 'deed' was,
I fear, one of mischief, in being so wrong & foolish as to repeat
what Mr White had said. My annoyances are always over directly,
and I should not have annoyed you, or done any thing to cause the
very slightest feeling of estrangement between friends. Will you
'forgive & forget' in consideration of Mr White's *great* kindness
to my friends.[1] When I saw you calling it '*impertinence*' you
cannot think how much I felt I had been to blame. *So please never
allude to it again.* I have seen Miss Jewsbury this morng and she
has been talking about you in a way to make me feel as 'awe
stricken' as she professes to be before you; 'I never dare to say
anything that is not profound sense before him', she says; so I
(in private) wince and shrink up at the idea of all I have said that
is not sensible.   Yours very truly
                                        E C Gaskell.

₄₉ **57** ₇₅

?CATHERINE WINKWORTH[2]

[?Late November 1849]

Currer Bell (aha! what will you give me for a secret?) She's
a she—that I will tell you—who has sent me 'Shirley.'[3]

---

[1] See page 83, n. 1.
[2] From a printed source, which identifies the recipient as Miss Winkworth.
[3] Published 26 October 1849. Catherine Winkworth knew of Charlotte
Brontë's identity by 5 December. See *Letters and Memorials*, ed. Winkworth, I,
p. 215.

₀ **58** ₇₈

CHARLOTTE FROUDE

121, Upper Rumford Street,
Thursday, Decr 6th [1849]

My dear Mrs Froude,
I was very glad to hear that you were better yesterday, and I
hope that this fine day will help you forwards grandly. It will give
Mr Gaskell and myself much pleasure if you and Mr Froude will
come and drink tea with us next Friday but one, (tomorrow week.)
Pray get well, and come; though we have nothing to offer you
but a very quiet evening.

Yours very truly
E. C. Gaskell

₅₆ **59** ₁₃₉

JOHN FORSTER[1]

Friday [7 December 1849]

My dear Sir,
I have not yet taken my bonnet off after hunting up Bamford.
First of all we went to Blakeley, to his little whitewashed cottage
at the end of a row, bordered round, close under the windows
with wall-flowers, some of which were yet in bloom. His pretty
wife, (don't fancy her young because she's *not*, but she is so
womanly, sweet & pretty she makes one think of hawthorn blossom,) was cleaning, and our visit would have been ill-timed to
any one but a lady, as she is; but she put away pail, & dusters and
all, & welcomed us heartily in her gentle way only regretting 'her
master' was not at home; 'he had gone into Manchester,' where
she did not know. She showed us a present they had had of two
birch-wood rocking chairs, with 'Mima' & 'Sam' carved in old
English on the back of each. They were evidently her pride; and
made the only ornament of the little whitewashed room, with the
exception of a pair of stag's horns. She gave us bread and butter,
and many kind gentle words. Then we bade her goodbye, and set

[1] *Annotation (pencil)* Dec 7/49.

off to find 'her master' in Manchester, which was like finding a
needle in a bottle of hay. But I shan't go into the details of the
'hunting of this day' but at last we pounced upon the great grey
stalwart man coming out of a little old-fashioned public house,
where Blakeley people put up. When he came up I kept my book
back, (like a child eating the paste before the preserve), till we had
got through all the common-place crust of our conversation.
Then I produced it; and he said 'This is grand'! I said 'Look at the
title page', for I saw he was fairly caught by something he liked in
the middle of the book, & was standing reading it there in the
street. 'Well! I am a proud man this day,' he exclaimed,—then he
turned it up and down, & read a bit, (it was a very crowded street),
and his grey face went quite brown-red with pleasure. Suddenly
he stopped—

'What mun I do for him back again?' 'Oh you must write to
him, and thank him.' 'I'd rather walk 20 mile than write a letter
any day.' 'Well then! Mr Bamford, suppose you do set off this
Xmas and walk and thank Tennyson'—He looked up from his
book right in my face, quite indignant—'Lord, woman! Walking
won't reach him! We're on the earth, d'ye see, but he's there, up
above—I can no more reach him by walking than if he were an
eagle or a skylark high above my head!'

(I think that almost comes up to the coal-heaver's compt to the
Duchess of Devonshire,) especially as it came fresh warm straight
from the heart, with\out/a notion of making a figurative speech,
but as if it were literal truth & I were a goose for not being aware
of it.

Then he dipped down into his book, and began reading aloud
the Sleeping beauty, and in the middle stopped to look at the
writing again, and we left him in a sort of sleep[-]walking state,
& only trust he will not be run over.

Thank you for the *great* pleasure I have had.

Yours very truly

E C Gaskell

25a **60** 0

ANNE SHAEN[1]

[?20 Dec. 1849]

My dearest little Annie, here's news of the bride, nice tender news,
so I send it on to you.[2] I do so often want to *speak* to you for I
don't think one can shade off one's meaning in writing half so
well. I wish I cd see you. When shall you be coming this-wards.
Here's a heart & a home ready for you & Emma at any time. I
have often meant to write to Emma, especially about Shirley, but
oh dear! this crowded bustling jostling world! Well! if health
lasts, & our present ideas-of-castles-in-the-air-plans hold, I shall
have a peaceful 3 months next summer. I hardly dare tell you how
it seems so visionary, but *if* we build in Victoria Park, ie, *if* Mr D
Darbishire, builds *for* us, we shall be turned out of this house at
Midsummer and have no new house until September, so that
3 months we have a vision of spending at Silverdale. Do you
know I don't think {how} I ever told you how very fond I grew
of Emma. I always *did* like her but I used to think she did not like
me, but she said such a pretty thing and I know she *means* her
pretty things, that I did away with all doubts about her not caring
for me, & I only wish she had stayed longer, for every day made
me love her better & better, & I never got to the end of my talks
that I meant to have had with her. I shall write to her next. Have
you heard that Harriet Martineau has sworn an eternal friendship
with the authoress of Shirley[;] if not I'll tell you. She sent Shirley
to Harriet Martineau. H M. acknowledged it in a note directed
to Currer Bell *Esq*—but inside written to a *lady*. Then came an
answer requesting a personal interview. This was towards or
about last Saturday week, and the time appointed was 6 o'clock
on Sunday Eveng; and the place appointed was at Mr Richard
Martineau's, (married a Miss Needham,) in Hyde Park Square.
So Mr & Mrs R. Martineau and Harriet M. sat with early tea
before them, awaiting six o'clock, & their mysterious visitor,
when lo! and behold, as the clock struck, in walked a little, very
little, bright haired sprite, looking not above 15, very unsophisti-
cated, neat & tidy. She sat down & had tea with them; her name

---

[1] *Address* Miss A. A. Shaen | Crix | Chelmsford. *Postmarks* MANCHESTER | DE ⟨ ⟩ |
18⟨49⟩ *and* CHELMSFORD | DE 21 | 1849 *and* 21 DE 21 | 49.
[2] Louisa Shaen had married Dr G. J. Allman on 3 December 1849.

being still unknown; she said to H M, 'What did you really think
of "Jane Eyre"?' H M. I thought it a first rate book, whereupon
the little sprite went red all over with pleasure. After tea Mr & Mrs
R M. withdrew and left sprite to a 2 hours tête-a-tête with H M,
to whom she revealed her name & the history of her life. Her
father a Yorkshire clergymen who has never slept out of his house
for 26 years; she has lived a most retired life;—her first visit to
London, never been in society, and many other particulars which
H M. is not at liberty to divulge any more than her name, which
she keeps a profound secret; but Thackeray does *not*. H M. is
charmed with her; she is full of life and power &c &c, & H M hopes
to be of great use to her. There! that's all I know, but I think it's a
pretty good deal, it's something to have seen somebody who has
seen nominis umbra. We are all deep in preparations for Xmas, &
blindness & deafness are in great fashion. We dine at the D D's. I
am puzzled about MA how far to let her accept the 1001 invitations to dances thronging in—I have attempted to draw a rule
that she may go where I go, and no where else, but I am not
sure if it will do. Meanwhile she is having the debauchery of a
white tarlatane frock, which will be very pretty. I am writing
abominably but Katie & Emily are coming to dinner & I must
walk my girls first, & am not strong, & want sorely to send off
this letter to assure you my dearest Annie, you have not been forgotten at this time which I know has been one of trial to you.
Don't suppose I *don't* know it because I don't speak of it my
dearest. Best love & thanks for the wedding cake. I was very glad
to see you kept up the good old-fashioned custom. Thanks to Mrs
Shaen, whose handwriting I was quite glad to recognize outside of
Louy's cards. My kind love to you all, Mr Mrs Emma & last not
least in affection although in person little Miss Annie. Ever your
very aff[ectionate] E C Gaskell.

₀ **61** ₆₂

CHARLES DICKENS

121, Upper Rumford Street
Manchester
Janry 8 . [1850]

My dear Sir,

In the first place I am going to give you some trouble, and I must make an apology for it; for I am very sorry to intrude upon you in your busy life. But I want some help, and I cannot think of any one who can give it to me so well as you. Some years since I asked Mr Burnett to apply to you for a prospectus of Miss Coutt's refuge for Female prisoners, and the answer I received was something to the effect that you did not think such an establishment could be carried out successfully anywhere, *unless connected with a scheme of emigration, as Miss Coutts was.* (as I have written it it seems like a cross question & crooked answer, but I believe Mr Burnett told you the report was required by people desirous of establishing a similar refuge in Manchester.)

I am just now very much interested in a young girl, who is in our New Bayley prison. She is the daughter of an Irish clergyman who died when she was two years old; but even before that her mother had shown most complete indifference to her; and soon after the husband's death, she married again, keeping her child out at nurse. The girl's uncle had her placed at 6 years old in the Dublin school for orphan daughters of the clergy; and when she was about 14, she was apprenticed to an Irish dress-maker here, of very great reputation for fashion. Last September but one this dress-maker failed, and had to dismiss all her apprentices; she placed this girl with a woman who occasionally worked for her, and who has since succeeded to her business; this woman was very profligate and connived at the girl's seduction by a surgeon in the neighbourhood who was called in when the poor creature was ill. Then she was in despair, & wrote to her mother, (*who had never corresponded with her all the time she was at school and an apprentice;*) and while awaiting the answer went into the penitentiary; she wrote 3 times but no answer came, and in desperation she listened to a woman, who had obtained admittance\to the penitentiary/ solely as it turned out to decoy girls into her mode of life, and left with her; & for four months she has led the most miserable life!

in the hopes, as she tells me, of killing herself, for 'no one had ever cared for her in this world,'—she drank, 'wishing it might be poison', pawned every article of clothing—and at last stole. I have been to see her in prison at Mr Wright's request, and she looks quite a young child (she is but 16,) with a wild wistful look in her eyes, as if searching for the kindness she has never known,—and she pines to redeem herself; her uncle (who won't see her, but confirms fully the account of the mother's cruel hardness,) says he has 30£ of her father's money in his hands; and she agrees to emigrate to Australia, for which her expenses would be paid. But the account of common emigrant ships is so bad one would not like to expose her to such chances of corruption; and what I want you to tell me is, how Miss Coutts sends out *her* protegees? under the charge of a matron? and might she be included among them? I want her to go out with as free and unbranded a character as she can; if possible, the very fact of having been in prison &c to be unknown on her landing. I will try and procure her friends when she arrives; only how am I to manage about the voyage? and how soon will a *creditable* ship sail; for she comes out of prison on Wednesday, & there are two of the worst women in the town who have been in prison with her, intending to way-lay her, and I want to keep her out of all temptation, and even chance of recognition. Please, will you help me? I think you know Miss Coutts. I can manage all except the voyage. She is a good reader[,] writer, and a beautiful needlewoman; and we can pay all her expenses &c.

Pray don't say you can't help me for I don't know any one else to ask, and you see the message you sent about emigration some years ago has been the mother of all this mischief. Will you give my love to Mrs Dickens & Miss Hogarth & believe me.

Yours very truly
E C Gaskell

Turn over

I have not told you one incident about the poor girl. Her seducer was lately appointed assistant surgeon to the New Bayley Prison; and as Pasley was not quite well she was sent for for him to see her. The matron told me when they came thus suddenly face to face, the girl just fainted dead away, and he was so affected he had to sit down,—he said 'Good God how did you come here.' He has been dismissed from his post in consequence. The chaplain will guarantee the truth of all I have said. She is such a pretty sweet looking girl. I am sure she will do well if we can but get her out in a *good* ship.

₆₁ **62** ₂₂₀

CHARLES DICKENS

121, Upper Rumford Street
Saturday, Jany 12th [1850]

My dear Sir,
   I am exceedingly obliged to you for what you have done about my poor girl. I return you Miss Coutts' letter, (which I only received late last night). It is really and truly kind, for she has taken the trouble to think of several plans, and her suggestions are very valuable. As she is out of town, I have written off at once to the fore-woman at Silvers', choosing out the plan which seemed to me the most desirable,—i.e. placing the girl under the charge of some respectable family, (of the working-class if possible). If Miss Kaye should not know of any one, then, if you will allow me, I will write again to ask Miss Coutts, through you, if she will kindly write to the Plymouth Ladies, of whom I never heard before—I have already received kind offices from Mrs Chisholm in helping out a family of emigrants, but I thought she required those whom she assisted to be of unblemished character. —Miss Coutts is very, very kind—for she evidently thinks as she writes, of what can be done.—
   My head & eyes ache so, with crying over the loss of three dear little cousins, who have died of S. Fever since I last wrote, leaving a childless mother, that I hardly know how or what I write, but will you thank Miss Coutts as you know she will like best. Of course I never named her name at Silvers'.
   The girl herself is in a Refuge—a literal refuge, for any destitute female without enquiry as to her past life being made,—all are received, and not classified. So it is a bad place, but what can we do? I am going to see her today to keep up & nurse her hopes & good resolutions.
   My best love to Mrs Dickens & Miss Hogarth.
                                        Yours truly
                                        E C Gaskell

₅₅ **63** ₆₄

?Eliza Fox[1]

Tuesday, Jan. 24 [?22], 1850

⟨. . .⟩such a tragedy here yesterday,[2] which you will see in the papers. We knew Mrs Novelli! She was a madonna-like person with a face (and character I believe) full of thought and gentle love, Miss Maistaids faithful servant and friend. Joseph has broken a blood vessel, and we are going to see him or them as soon as I have written this. My and your girl is going on well *as yet* in the Refuge where Agnes Ewart and I go to see her, and my letter to Dickens induced a very wise suggestion one from Miss Coutts to him, on which I acted, and have found a man and his wife going to the Cape, who will take loving charge of her; and sail in February. I have got Mr Nash the ragged school master to take care of her up to London when the ship is ready to sail and have found out a whole *nest* of good ladies in London, who say they will at any time help me in similar cases. On Saturday I heard from Mr Tom Taylor to this effect. A Mr Watts (*who is he*, answer me *that* Master Brook) an artist inspired by the record of Mr Wright's (whom Mr Taylor will call Mr *Hill*) good deeds, has painted a picture for the Academy Exhibition of the Good Samaritan,[3] under which is to be an inscription relating to Mr Wright,—now Mr T. Taylor says some people in London desirous of honouring Mr W. and encouraging the application of art to such high purposes are desirous of purchasing this picture and presenting it to some Manchester charity and he wants some detailed acct of Mr W. and to know if there would be any response in Manchester to this plan. I have got Mr Schwabe, the Bishop, and Dr Bell all pretty well interested, and have copied out prison reports, by way of statistical information as to Mr Wright. Then Miss Maggie Bell has sent me MS. novel to look over,—she is a nice person, and I know I once wanted help sorely, or else I am *so* busy what with making mourning etc:⟨. . .⟩ I must write again soon to you darling, for this is not satisfactory, and tell me all about Mr Watts, no one

---

[1] Original MS. not seen.
[2] Mrs Novelli was murdered on [Sunday] 20 January 1850. (*Annals*, ed. Axon, p. 252). Since 22 January was a Tuesday, Mrs Gaskell may here refer to the newspaper reports of Monday.   [3] Exhibited in R.A. Exhibition, 1850.

here knows either him or Mr Tom Taylor even by name, I think Mr Schwabe confused the latter up with Jeremy Taylor. Now write and tell me about Mr Watts. Mr Cobden will be here the end of this week, and I want to work him up, but must know about Mr Watts. William's best love. We long for you back, the little ones ask after you—Children dear was it yesterday—(call once more,) that she went away.

Yrs truly affe[ctionatel]y,
E. C. Gaskell.

63 64 68

ELIZA FOX[1]

Tuesday [?Thursday], January 24th, 1850

My dearest Tottie,

Last night came your charming parcels, and this morning your most kind, tender, and sympathising note. The week before last did seem crowded up with death, and death-ful associations. Mrs Dimdle[2] died full of years, surrounded by loving children, whom she had brought up to fill their places well in the world; but the poor little Knutsford children! and the desolate nursery swept bare. That is indeed mysterious—their sweet *childless* mother is full of faith, and stills her heart by saying God's will be done, and is a comfort and support to all around—but I know how long her heart will bleed with an unhealed wound.

Now to your parcel '*Dearie*' how good of you to think of us all. Wm. had particularly wished to see the Hymn Book, Marianne is glorious over her music, and I revel in the thoughts of reading Vivia, and enjoy having your sketches of your father and Miss Flower; and more I am pleased and peaceful in the kind thoughts that sent them. Oh dear! how much has happened since you were here! In every way. Do you know I thought you were very 'pretty behaved' to me, but I had no idea it was poor Mary Barton's fault. I wish you had said the things you wanted to say very much; but do write to me, love, if you ever would like it:

---

[1] Original MS. not seen.
[2] Faulty transcription of 'Dimock'? See p. 49, n. 1.

for it would give me great pleasure—my address is 121, Upper
Rumford St. Manchester. Once more, and once again Goodbye.
My kind regards to Mr Fox.

Yrs. really affectionately

E. C. Gaskell.

Thank you dear.

₀ 65 ₁₈₀

JAMES CROSSLEY[1]

121, Upper Rumford Street
January 25. [1850]

Dear Sir,

I hope you will not consider that I am taking {a}\too great a/
liberty in\complying with the request contained in these letters/
calling your attention to the subject of them. You are probably
acquainted with Mr Tom Taylor, (the late Professor of Eng. Lit.
in University College, and the writer of Punch's Spanish Ballads
&c,) and if so, you will know that his opinion of any artist is not
that of an ignorant enthusiast, but of one who has devoted much
earnest study to the subject, and believes that it may be the means
of doing a great work in the world. It is perhaps rather unbusiness-
like to with-hold the price of the picture; but apropos of that, I
will quote a passage from a letter which I do not forward.
'Remember we do not want *subscriptions* in the common sense of
the word. We would rather have a man's interest and appreciation
of our plan than his money; indeed we should despise the latter
unless his hearty feeling went with it.'

Will it be too much to ask for your 'hearty feeling', and will
you evince this by looking at the painting in Mr Watt's studio,
30, Charles Street, Berkeley Sqr. Perhaps you will be so kind as to
call Mr Schwabe's attention to this address; and also to the PS
at the beginning of the last note in which Mr Taylor says 'he
knows Chevalier Bunsen, & is sure of his co-operation.'? My last

---

[1] Identified by J. A. Green, who prints this letter in his *Catalogue of an Exhibition of Books and Autographs Illustrating the Life and Work of Mrs E. C. Gaskell*,
Manchester, 1914, pp. 2–3.

request is that you will excuse the liberty I have taken in writing
to you, and believe me, dear Sir,

with the truest respect

Yours sincerely

E C Gaskell.

44 **66** 87

?Edward Chapman

121, Upper Rumford St
Saturday [?Early 1850][1]

Dear Sir,

I have just received your judgement on my tale and quite
acquiesce in your decision that I cannot write a Xmas book.[2]
I am very glad that we have both arrived at this conclusion, so
soon, for I shall be so much occupied this summer, that I should
have found it extremely difficult to find time for any other
engagements.[3] I remain

Dear Sir
Yours very truly
E. C. Gaskell

0 **67** 0

William Robson[4]

121, Upper Rumford St
Manchester
[c. 20 February 1850]

Dear Sir,

I hope you will not think I have taken too great a liberty in
having requested a pamphlet and two papers, (which will explain

---

[1] Placed with Letter 65, also written on mourning paper.

[2] Possibly *The Moorland Cottage*, though we have to assume that this decision
was later changed. (Cf. Letters 79 and 81.)

[3] Dickens had invited Mrs Gaskell to contribute to his new periodical, *Household Words*, on 31 January 1850. Hopkins, *Gaskell*, p. 88.

[4] *Address (on envelope)* Mr William Robson | Bath Buildings | Warrington.
Postmarks MANCHESTER | FE 20 | 1850 | L *and* WARRINGTON | FE 21 | 1850 | A.

themselves,) to be forwarded to you. The pamphlet is the first of a series 'on Christian Socialism' proposed to be issued by the writers of 'Politics for the People': those writers were as you probably know, the revd Frederick Maurice, the author of No 1, of the Present tracts; the revd Charles Kingsley, (who will soon publish No 2, of tracts on Christian Socialism,) Mr Ludlow, a barrister writing under the pseudonym of 'John Townsend', Mr Scott the Prof. of English literature at the University College, &c. They are anxious to obtain a circulation among the working-classes for these tracts, and it is they who have instituted the Co-operative Tailors Society; and who hope to form a similar Society for Needlewomen. Even if you differ considerably from them, by helping them to circulate their views, and have their plans discussed, you will be helping them in their earnest loving search after the Kingdom of God, which they hold far above any plans of their own. (If you will allow me I will just copy a sentence out of a note of Mr Kingsley's.) 'But['], like Dicken's [*sic*] barber, 'most folks draw the line somewhere, we does at coal-heavers';— and we, at 'household suffrage and free-trade', and we at 'the triumph of intellect', and we, further going, at barricades,—but all stop somewhere, and begin to curse the poor enthusiast, who run right ahead into the infinite unknown possible, and will stop at nothing short of 'God's kingdom *come*'. Now, my dear Mr Robson—I have written thus far, for you to read aloud, (& save me the trouble of writing) to Philip Carpenter; to whom I am also sending tracts &c & what I want you both to do is to get them circulated among working men,—they\the editors/want their advice, & thoughts, & practical sense. Can you help in circulating them by getting some sellers of working men's papers to put them in their shops? Mr Solly of Cheltenham,—Oh I don't know what I was going to say I have been so interrupted—and now I must end—I am so much obliged to you for the autographs—many are just what I wanted. My dearest love to Nancy, & a kiss to the bairn, whom Baby will call '*my* baby'.

Yours most truly

E C Gaskell

₆₄ **68** ₆₉

ELIZA FOX[1]

Tuesday, a week ago.
[*c.* February 1850]

My dearest Tottie,

Here is Mr Broinett[2] giving his lesson, and I am playing
Dragon; so while I dragonize, (I wish you could hear O Salutaris
Hostia they are now singing,) I shall write to you. I have a great
deal to say; only I don't know if I can ever get the leisure to think
and say it out. One thing I must say is that your letters do give
me so much pleasure, I look them over and wonder what it is
that pleases me so much, and I can't make out.⟨. . .⟩ And now I
could say so much about the Munich plan; and what follows in
your letter about home duties and individual life; it is just my
puzzle; and I don't think I can get nearer to a solution than you
have done. But if you were here we cd talk about it so well. Oh!
that you were here! I don't like the idea of your being a whole six
months away from call; but that is selfish and not to be taken into
consideration. One thing is pretty clear, *Women*, must give up
living an artist's life, if home duties are to be paramount. It is
different with men, whose home duties are so small a part of their
life. However we are talking of women. I am sure it is healthy for
them to have the refuge of the hidden world of Art to shelter
themselves in when too much pressed upon by daily small Lilli-
putian arrows of peddling cares; it keeps them from being morbid
as you say; and takes them into the land where King Arthur lies
hidden, and soothes them with its peace. I have felt this in writing,
I see others feel it in music, you in painting, so assuredly a blending
of the two is desirable. (Home duties and the development of the
Individual I mean), which you will say it takes no Solomon to
tell you but the difficulty is where and when to make one set of
duties subserve and give place to the other. I have no doubt that
the cultivation of each tends to keep the other in a healthy
state,—my grammar is all at sixes and sevens I have no doubt but
never mind if you can pick out my meaning. I think a great deal
of what you have said.

---

[1] Original MS. not seen. Dated by comparison with Letter 69.

[2] Henry Burnett? Dickens's brother-in-law taught music in Manchester. See
Annals, ed. Axon, p. 246.

Thursday.

I've been reading over yr note, and believe I've only been repeating in different language what you said. If Self is to be the end of exertions, those exertions are unholy, there is no doubt of *that*—and that is part of the danger in cultivating the Individual Life; but I do believe we have all some appointed work to do, whh no one else can do so well; Wh. is *our* work; what *we* have to do in advancing the Kingdom of God; and that first we must find out what we are sent into the world to do, and define it and make it clear to ourselves, (that's *the* hard part) and then forget ourselves in our work, and our work in the End we ought to strive to bring about. I never can either talk or write clearly so I'll ee'n leave it alone. Hearn has been been nearly 3 weeks away nursing her mother who is dying, so we are rather at sixes and sevens upstairs. The little ones come down upon us like the Goths on Rome; making inroads and onslaughts into all our plans. I was very nearly going to the Cobden's for 6 days or so last week—but did not. I have sent such a number of charming people to see Mr Watts, he must think I have a glorious circle of friends.

G . . .[1]

68 **69** 70

ELIZA FOX[2]

[?April 1850]

My dearest Tottie,

I was going to have written a letter to myself, and sent it to you to fill up, only your most welcome letter this morning put a stop to that. I am so glad always to hear from you, and should be more gladder to see you, dear little lady. And we've got a house. Yes! we *really* have. And if I had neither conscience nor prudence I should be delighted, for it certainly *is* a beauty. It is not very far from here, in Plymouth Grove—do you remember our plodding

[1] Letter 118 should have been inserted here. See p. 182, n. 2.
[2] Original MS. not seen.

out *that* last Saty in snow to go and see houses? and looking at 2, one inhabited by a Jewish Mrs Abram *and* old clothes. Well, its nearly opposite to the *first* we looked at (*not* the old clothes one) I shall make Meta draw you a plan. You *must* come and see us in it, dearest Tottie, and try and make me see 'the wrong the better cause,' and that it is right to spend so much ourselves on *so* purely selfish a thing as a house is, while so many are wanting— thats the haunting thought to me; at least to one of my 'Mes,' for I have a great number, and that's the plague. One of my mes is, I do believe, a true Christian—(only people call her socialist and communist), another of my mes is a wife and mother, and highly delighted at the delight of everyone else in the house, Meta and William most especially who are in full extasy. Now that's my 'social' self I suppose. Then again I've another self with a full taste[1] for beauty and convenience whh is pleased on its own account. How am I to reconcile all these warring members? I try to drown myself (my *first* self,) by saying it's Wm who is to decide on all these things, and his feeling it right ought to be my rule, And so it is—only that does not quite do. Well! I must try and make the house give as much pleasure to others as I can and make it as little a selfish thing as I can. My dear! its 150 a year, and I dare say we shall be ruined; and I've already asked after the ventilation of the new Borough Gaol,[2] and bespoken Mr Wright to visit us— The said good Mr Wright drank tea here last night, and said '*By Jingo*' with great unction, when very much animated, much to William's amusement, not to say delight. (We have a greenhouse at the new house—to be; which delights the girls; we shall remove in about 6 weeks.) I long to see the pictures going this year; your account makes my mouth water for those Lees and Creswicks and red [?] mountain chieftains. Mr Schwabe goes up to the Cobdens again next Tuesday; then to Paris in 10 days, a fortnight hence back to London, tour in Devonshire.[3] Mr W. Darbishire goes to my dear old dreamy Panton Square very often. Schuncks are gone to the Gallengas;[4] where Miss Jewsbury joins them,—[?] gone abroad. Ewarts probably going to Switzerland— there is a most extraordinary clearing off of Manchester this summer—no! I have not read that poem of R. Brownings. I saw

[1] Source reads 'task'.

[2] In Hyde Road; completed 1850. *Annals*, ed. Axon, p. 255.

[3] Catherine Winkworth wrote in February 1850 that Mr Schwabe was going to London to call on Mr Watts. *Letters and Memorials*, ed. Winkworth, I, p. 219.

[4] 'Schwenks' and 'Galliezas' in source.

the review in the Examiner, (no end of thanks to you for the said,)
but I don't think I've fairly read it yet![1] You see I've been very
poorly; and yet we've been dining out at a great rate, bidding
good bye to people in the unsentimental way of eating their
dinners; and old friends have been about in Manchester too,—
dear Mr Newman and Lady Murray, and we wanted to see
them; Oh Mr Newman is more delightful than ever. His life
seems to have got into harmony with his idea whh it was *not*,
here; and he seems so happy and peaceful! Meta is better than she
was with her iodide of iron, but my darling Baby has been ailing
for the last week or so and is being doctored and medicinized.
Hearn is still away; but her mother died yesterday, so I suppose she
will return before long; only I think she is so knocked up with
sorrow and nursing that we shall have to send her into the country
to recruit a little. Mr T. Taylor told me last year of the Gardiner's
Daughter—to-be but I don't think I like taking so *complete* a
picture in words and transferring it to canvas. George and Meta *do*
sound so alike. William has just been pleased to observe that it is
not often I make such a 'sensible' friendship as the one with you,
which I rather resent; for I am sure all my friends *are* sensible.
Emily Winkworth is I think the very essence of good sense. Yes
that discovery of one's exact work in the world is the puzzle: I
never meant to say it was not. I long (weakly) for the old times
where right and wrong did not seem such complicated matters;
and I am sometimes coward enough to wish that we were back in
the darkness where obedience was the only seen duty of women.
Only even then I don't believe William would ever have *commanded* me. I can understand your nervous headache so well,
having just worried myself into a similar state. Only I've had no
Mary to put me to right. Marianne is coming on grandly with her
music, and we're going to get her a new piano.—Sometimes her
singing and (less seldom) sometimes her playing seem to put me
into harmony. I wish I had the opportunity of hearing more
grand sacred music[;] you have great things in London for calming
yourself—grand pictures—holy music seem so to take the fretting
pain out of one's heart—I wonder if R. Browning's poem would
do the same. But here we have no great external beauty either of
nature or art the contemplation of which can put calm into one;
and take one out of one's little self—and shame the demon (I beg

---

[1] 'Christmas-Eve and Easter-Day', published 1 April 1850; reviewed 6 April.
W. C. DeVane, *A Browning Handbook*, 2nd ed., 1955, pp. 194, 204.

its pardon) Conscience away; or to sleep. My idea of Heaven just
now is, a place where we shan't have any consciences,—and Hell
vice versa,. Thats a rough notion of our house; only it's a very
puzzling one to draw. *When* will you come and see us—in
August if you don't go to Munich.

[Here a large space is left.]

Your room will be over the drawing-room, our's over the dining-
room—the girls over their schoolroom, Nursery over Hearn's
bedroom—What's your opinion about gas? Healthy or not—do
you burn it? William sends his love to you—Mrs Fletcher, Mrs
Davy were to have come here this week with a maid; and we
should have gone into your room leaving ours for Mrs Fletcher,
Dear old lady! I wish she had come under our roof; but she was ill
and could not. Where are the Brownings. Dearest little Tottie, we
all send love and shall want you to 'handsel'[1] our house. Poor
Madge is ill at Norwich. Tell me about Cissy.

> Yours very affec[tionately],
> E. C. Gaskell.

₆₉ **70** ₇₃

ELIZA FOX[2]

April 26, 1850

Dearest little Tottie,

   This piece of paper tempts me to write to you. Are not you a
wicked woman not to say the old serpent herself to try and
decoy me up to your Babylon. Oh for shame! but oh dear how I
should like to come and see the Exhibitions—(you did not think I
had so much of the artist about me Missie—now did you?) and
you (poor Macready—I never think of him without a sigh.) But
my dear, don't you see there are beds to be taken down, and
curtains dyed and carpets cleaned, and cornices chosen and carpets
selected, and cabbages planted in *our* garden,—and that I am the
factotum della città—and its Figaro quà, Figaro la,—all day long.
No my dear little lassie,—if I have a peep at you in November I
shall be thankful—I mean in your own big place,—I've half a

---

[1] To be a first visitor to.   [2] Original MS. not seen.

notion, and have made a whole promise of going to Crix,[1] (the Shaens[2] in Essex) in October,—and perhaps—perhaps—; Mrs Hensleigh Wedgwood has written to invite me, also naming the Exhibitions, (you see what comes of my knowing way of talking about the 'aerial distances,') but alas! and the Shaens[2] begged me to come in rose-time to them. All idea of leaving home till the removal is complete must be given up; and it won't be complete till we go to Silverdale that's clear. Do come to us soon! I want to get associations about that house; *here* there is the precious per-fume lingering of my darling's short presence in this life—I wish I were with him in that 'light, where we shall all see light,' for I am often sorely puzzled here—but however I must not waste my strength or my time about the never ending sorrow; but which hallows this house. I think that is one evil of this bustling life that one has never time calmly and bravely to face a great grief, and to view it on every side as to bring the harmony out of it.—Well! I meant to write a merry letter. My dear—I am very much inter-ested about George. Do you know I have a good piece of comfort to give you. Miss Mitchell told me yesterday (apropos of Meta) that she had noticed that children accustomed to tidiness and cleanli-ness from their babyhood, even if that tidiness and cleanliness was produced by the exertions of others entirely without any thought or contrivance of their own, when withdrawn from this situation where everything is done for them, had acquired such a taste for order that they will exert themselves ever so much to procure it. Now George seems to have been accustomed to moral order and purity and so very likely he never thought about it when it was present, yet now he is deprived of it he is likely to struggle after it. Oh! I really am very wise, but I can't express myself very clearly: ⟨. . .⟩ It is a great trial for a boy, and mine is spared the trial and the temptation! Do you know I believe the garden will be a great delight in our new house. Clay soil it *will* be, and there is no help for it, but it will be gay and bright with common flowers; and is quite shut in,—and one may get out without bonnet, which is a blessing, I always want my head cool, and stray about in the odd five minutes. You should see Baby and Florence! their delight is most pretty to see every day they go there; and every new flower (plant) that peeps up is a treasure. Hearn is back and the idea and thought about the removal com-forts her for her mother's death in[3] a gentle natural kind of way.

[1] 'Aix' in source.   [2] 'Marns' in source.   [3] Source reads 'is'

That meteor Mr Wm[1] Taylor has darted across my firmament
again. I could make you laugh with an account of our correspondence; but I do like and admire him in spite of his whirlwind-
ness.—Meanwhile I work at the Bishop,—who is I think taking it
(Mr Watt's picture) up in a hard measured superior kind of way—
(Oh I must tell you about the Bishop's pet picture, but not now)
and I'm getting money subscribed for it, and could get more if
Mr W.[2] T. would be a fixed star for a moment, and condescend
to give me a little light about prices etc; which Manchester people
will know, before they will se[3] laisser aller into enthusiasm. And
now I'll tell you a bit about our call on the Bishop. As luck would
have it it was a visitation or a something-ation, and upwards of 20
clergymen were there. Such fun! we were tumbled into the
drawing room to them; arch-deacons and all (Florence stay'd in
the carriage). Mrs Lee is a little timid woman—*I* should make a
better Bishop's wife if the Unitarians ever come uppermost in my
day: and she thinks me 'satirical' and is afraid of me Mrs Schwabe
says. So you may imagine the mal aproposness of the whole
affair. Mr Stowell was there and all the cursing Evangelicals.
Luckily we know Canon Clifton and one or two of the better
sort, so we talked pretty well till the Bishop came in. I thought I
would watch him and see how he took the affair; if he skirted
Unitarianism as a subject, as he generally talks about it to William,
but no! he pounced on the subject at once; and it was funny to
watch the clergymen of the Evangelical set, who looked as if a
bombshell was going off amongst them. Well! when the call was
ended the Bishop took us into his library and that brings me to the
picture. Over the door being an exquisitely painted picture of a
dead child perhaps Baby's age,—deathly livid, and with the most
woeful expression of pain on its little wan face,—it looked too
deeply stamped to be lost even in Heaven. He made us look at it
and then told me the history. It was painted by some friend or
pupil [of] Maclises and was so true to the life that an anatomist of
that sort of thing on seeing it said 'that child has lost its life by an
accident which has produced intense pain'—and it was true,—it
had been the child of the people with whom the artist lived, and
had been *burnt*, had lingered 2 days in the greatest agony, poor
darling—and then died! I would not send my child to be educated
by the man who could hang up such a picture as that for an object

---

[1] Probably 'Tom'. See Letter 65, above.   [2] Probably 'T'.
[3] Source reads 'so'.

of contemplation; for it was not the quiet lovely expression of angelic rest, but the look of despairing agony. Not all his kind pleasant tat[t]le with Florence set him right with me. He's got something wrong with his heart. ⟨...⟩ Then to complete the grotesque oddity of the whole call, picture and all, Florence (who had been in the carriage all the time) said to me, 'Mama the footman was so kind he told me all the churches we could see—(it is on a hill,) but I thought it very odd he should speak to me as we had never been introduced.' Well may her sisters call Florence the little lady! I shall ask you how much you'll give me a sheet I think, for really this is a volume. Do you know they sent me 20£ for Lizzie Leigh? I stared, and wondered if I was swindling them but I suppose I am not; and Wm has composedly buttoned it up in his pocket. He has promised I may have some for the Refuge. W. Connington was telling me that Emerson refers to Mr Froude when he speaks of the 'languid gentleman at Oxford', who says 'nothing is new,'[1] 'nothing is true,' and 'it does not signify'. Mr C. stammers and twitches awfully and he had got into this story before Mr Froude was aware, but when he heard what he was saying he tried to check him by nods and winks and anything but wreathed smiles. Mr C. however was not to be stopped, especially as he had puckered up his eyes for a good stammer, he twitched and made grimaces, and at length he jerked it out with the air of a man who has done a great action, and opened his eyes to Mr Froude's angry face. ⟨...⟩ Perhaps I may come in for a sight of Macready if he is not to act till next winter. I never saw him but in King Lear. Goodbye again and for the 3rd time why don't you go,—you keep me talking all night. Yrs affect[ionate]ly,
Lily.

⟨...⟩ That Mr Tom Taylor is born to get me into scrapes I verily believe! Did I tell you of his wishing to be introduced to Mr Schwabe to plan about Manchester's having the Good S[amaritan] (which Manchester somewhat contemptuously declines) so I wrote a very proper note of introduction: and the trouble it is to me to write a *proper* note no one can tell save those who have seen my improper ones ⟨...⟩ and Mr Schwabe, (staying at the Cobdens) wrote to say he would call on Mr Taylor at Gwydir House on such a day;—went and called—Mr Taylor ill—'not able to leave home and come to his office'—Mr Schwabe drove to the

[1] Source reads 'now'.

Temple,—Mr Taylor *well*, [']had gone to some rehearsal'!! Remember Mr Schwabe is *punctuality* personified. Well Mr T. had the grace to send an apology,—and appoint Tuesday next as the day when he should be at Gwydir House all day etc: Mr Schwabe went on Tuesday,—Mr Taylor was again nobody knows where. So of course Mr Schwabe looks upon him as not a good person to conduct any business affair, and draws out of the whole, and thinks it [']a pity Mr Watts has such injudicious friends'—and such a quantity of persuasion and talking as I have wasted! So now Mr T. T. has written to propose a portrait by Mr Watts to Mr Schwabe,—and Mr S. declines having anything more to do with it—(he was sadly put out by Mr T. T.'s never being where he ought to be) and I have had to write to the *Wases* (t.t.s.) there! that's not bad for me. I hope you've performed the duties of a friend and laughed. ⟨. . .⟩ Why is the Emperor of Russia like a beggar at Xmas? Because he's confounded Hungary and wants a slice of Turkey. I thinks that's old ⟨. . .⟩ How can we prove that Time flies fast? Because we no sooner get up in the morning than we enter on the close (clothes) of the day. Why are stars the best astronomers? Because they've studded (studied) the heavens for thousands of years. What's the difference between forms and ceremonies? We *sit* upon forms and stand upon ceremonies. Why is a lame beggar an inconsistent man? Because he asks for alms when he wants legs. How could a house be built of a pocket handkerchief? If it became brick. (These are none of them bad enough to be good) ⟨. . .⟩ Why is the letter g the most fatal of all letters? Because it turns hosts into ghosts.

₀ **71** ₀

JOHN SEELY HART

Upper Rumford Street
Manchester
April 28th 1850.

Dear Sir,

It is only an hour since I received your 'Essay on the Fairy Queen'[1] &c; but I will not lose any more time before thanking

---

[1] *An Essay on the Life and Writings of Edmund Spenser, with a Special Exposition of the Fairy Queen*, New York and London, 1847. Hart also produced *The Female Prose Writers of America* (1852) and *A Manual of English Literature*, 1872.

you for the pleasure which I promise myself in reading your book, and still more for the kind feeling towards me, which induced you to send it. I received a note from you, containing an expression of this feeling which gratified me exceedingly, although I am ashamed to think how long a time has elapsed without my answering it. But, owing to some mischance, the book, (the Essay,) was not to be found. Mrs Howitt had sent it to my publishers, who had mislaid it, and forgotten the very fact of its receipt. I have written often to try if I, at this distance, could find out where it was in London; and I did not like writing to you before I could acknowledge it's safe arrival. Will you forgive me?

The pamphlets you name are not to be heard of anywhere, but the fact of your sending them remains the same, and it gives me great pleasure to think of it. The writing of 'Mary Barton' was a great pleasure to me; and I became so deeply, sometimes painfully, interested in it, that I don't think I cared at the time of it's publication what reception it met with. I was sure a great deal of it was truth, and I knew that I had realized all my people to myself so vividly that parting with them was like parting with friends. But the reception it met with was a great surprize to me. I neither expected the friends nor the enemies which it has made me. But the latter I am thankful to say are disappearing while the former are (some of them,) friends for life. A good deal of it's success I believe was owing to the time of it's publication,—the great revolutions in Europe had directed people's attention to the social evils, and the strange contrasts which exist in old nations. However I must not intrude upon your time, which sounds to be most valuable, and to be devoted to the highest purposes. I have not told you though how I have liked to receive an expression of approval from an *American*.

Yours very truly
E. C. Gaskell[1]

0 **72** 72a
LADY KAY-SHUTTLEWORTH[2]

Knutsford, May 14. [1850]

My dear Lady Kaye Shuttleworth,

Your letter has interested me much in so many ways, that I can't resist the impulse to write 'on the rebound', just as if I were

[1] See Letter 88 and note.   [2] *Annotation* 1850.

talking to you. Perhaps a little bit of my great desire to write to you this morning may arise from the very fact of your saying you do not expect an answer; but I don't think it *does*; I think it is because some of the things you say exactly fall in with my own puzzles in life; and I want to know more exactly and fully what you think on the subject. I am almost glad you did not call on Friday, as I was, (and am still,) from home for a very few days as I am not very strong just now; but I am sorry to hear the reason you allege in yr husband's suffering from head-ache. No! I never heard of Miss Brontë's visit; and I should like to hear a great deal more about her, as I have been so much interested in what she has written. I don't mean merely in the story and mode of narration, wonderful as that is, but in the glimpses one gets of *her*, and her modes of thought, and, all unconsciously to herself, of the way in wh she has suffered. I wonder if she suffers *now*. Soon after I saw you at Capesthorne I heard such a nice account of her, from a gentleman who went over to see her father, & staid at the inn, where he was told of her doings as well as her sayings & writings. I should like very much indeed to know her: I was going to write to 'see' her, but that is not it. I think I told you that I disliked a good deal in the plot of Shirley, but the expression of her own thoughts in it is so true and brave, that I greatly admire her. I am half amused to find you think I could do her good, (I don't know if you exactly word it so, but I think it is what you mean,) I *never* feel as if I could do any one good—I never yet was conscious of strengthening any one, and I do so feel to want strength, and to want faith. I suppose we all *do* strengthen each other by clashing together, and earnestly talking our own thoughts, and ideas. The very disturbance we thus are to each other rouses us up, and makes us more healthy. I fancy you have some individual case in your mind which you allude to, or which has suggested the thoughts in the latter part of your letter, which was particularly interesting to me, as falling in with my own perplexities. I am so much inclined to admire Miss Sellon's[1] conduct in many things, (if she can but persevere in the simplicity which I have heard that she possesses,) that I do not think you can allude to her; indeed you exclude some 'sisterhoods' from your condemnation; but do you not think many single women would be happier if, when the ties of God's appointment were absolved by death, they found them-

[1] Miss Priscilla Lydia Sellon's community of Sisters of Mercy was established in 1848.

selves some work like the Sisters of Mercy? I feel sure you do—I do not think they need to be banded together, or even to take any name, unless indeed such forms strengthened their usefulness; but I think I see every day how women, deprived of their natural duties as wives & mothers, must look out for other duties if they wish to be at peace. Do you mean that girls, having all {these} the home-duties of parents dependent upon them, brothers & sisters relying on them for companionship & comfort, are joining any institution which should make them desert the post where God has placed them? Do you know a little book written by a daughter of Sir Jas Stephens, called 'Passages in the life of a Daughter at Home'?[1] It is very painful, and from the impression of pain, which, in despite its happy ending, it leaves upon one I think it must want some element of peace, but still it is very true, and *very* suggestive; and a description to the life of the trials of many single women, who waken up some morning to the sudden feeling of the *purposelessness* (is there such a word) of their life. Do read it if it comes in yr way. But I think you are probably seeing more of what has never fallen in my way exactly, but of what I read of in that striking and curious sermon of Mr Maurice's, en-titled 'Religion versus God'. In which he spoke of the falseness of that religious spirit which led people to disregard those nearest to them, to wound or leave those whom God had placed around and about and dependent on them, in search of some new sphere of action. What you say of the restlessness of the age, of the 'search after the ideal in some, and morbid dread of the ideal in others', strikes me as very true; and it is difficult to steer clear of these two extremes, between which characters seem thrown backwards & forwards like shuttlecocks. I never cd enter into Sartor Resartus, but I brought away one sentence which does capitally for a reference when I get perplexed sometimes. 'Do the duty that lies nearest to thee.' It is so difficult to test the difference between the love of excitement which made the French ladies of a certain age turn dévote formerly, & which certainly is widely diffused in England just now, and the real earnest Christianity which seeks to do as much and as extensive good as it can. It seems hardly fair even to propose the performance of home-duties *first*, as a test, when one remembers such a man as Howard, whose good works and true religion one cannot doubt, although I suppose he did neglect that poor son of his sadly. I fancy you see things much

[1] By Caroline Emelia Stephen (1834-1909).

more clearly than I do. I often feel in such a mist; and then I yearn
so for the time when in 'His light we shall all see light'. I am
always glad and thankful to Him that I am a wife and a mother
and that I am so happy in the performance of those clear and
defined duties; for I think there must be a few years of great
difficulty in the life of every woman who foresees and calmly
accepts single life. Oh I wonder if you care to read all my bewildered thoughts; which however are called out by your own
letter, which falling on a leisure time, has produced all this. To
return to Miss Brontë; I should like to know her very much.
Does she ever come to Manchester, can you tell? Bradford is not
so far away but what she might. I am glad you give so good an
acct of the Establishment for Gentlewoman during illness; and
that you are satisfied with Miss Woolley. I saw the account of Mrs
Strutt's sister's death, and I was very sorry for her, {at} simply as
losing what I fancy must be so charming a species of relation;
and from your account of her character she must indeed be a loss.
If you see Mrs Strutt will you give her my kind regards; and now
I am going to end: and I think I will copy yr concluding sentence
and say 'Of course you will not think for one moment of answering this long letter'; I hope you found your children well. I hear
almost daily from mine; but yours I think have not got to the age
when letter-writing is a pleasure.

Yours very sincerely Elizabeth Gaskell.

*

72 72a *74a

LADY KAY-SHUTTLEWORTH[1]

Silverdale, near Lancaster
July 16. [?1850]

My dear Lady,
    I am feeling very guilty in that I have never answered two of
your letters; for though in both you were kind enough to say that
you did not expect an answer, yet at the time of reading them, I
intended to write back directly, and reply to them; and my

---

[1] *Annotation* 1851. [However, the reference to the removal to Plymouth Grove
and the fairly detailed account of Mrs Gaskell's movements in July 1851 (see p. 160)
make 1850 more probable.]

reasons for not having done so consist in the quantity of time and thought which were taken up by a removal to a new house, (*Plymouth Grove*, Manchester) and then by our annual migration to the sea-side. Silverdale can hardly be called the sea-side, as it is a little dale running down to Morecambe Bay, with grey limestone rocks on all sides, which in the sun or moonlight, glisten like silver. And we are keeping holiday in most rural farm-house lodgings, so that our children learn country interests, and ways of living and thinking. I wonder where you are: I can hardly fancy a greater contrast in the mode of\thoughtful English/existence than what yours, if in London, must present to ours. Now I am going to answer your letters; and I shall take the last first. I cannot think that you could for a moment imagine that I should be 'offended' by, or 'think you impertinent' for evincing such kind interest in the direction and object of any future writing of mine. Several people whose opinion I have very much respected have suggested the same subject as that which you did; but after a good deal of thought I feel that if it is to be done, it must be by someone else. I think so, for several reasons, which I will tell you if it will not weary you. In the first place whatever power there was in Mary Barton was caused by my feeling strongly on the side which I took; now as I don't feel as strongly (and as it is impossible I ever should,) on the other side, the forced effort of writing on that side would{be}\end in/a weak failure. I know, and have always owned, that I have represented *but one* side of the question, and no one would welcome more than I should, a true and earnest representation of the other side. I believe what I have said in Mary Barton to be perfectly true, but by no means the whole truth; and I have always felt deeply annoyed at anyone, or any set of people who chose to consider that I had manifested the whole truth; I do not think it is possible to do this in any *one* work of fiction. You say 'I think there are good mill-owners; I think the factory system might be made a great engine for good'; and in this no one can more earnestly and heartily agree with you than I do. I can not imagine a nobler scope for a thoughtful energetic man, desirous of doing good to his kind, than that presented to his powers as the master of a factory. But I believe that there is much to be discovered yet as to the right position and mutual duties of employer, and employed; and the utmost I hoped from Mary Barton has been that it would give a spur to inactive thought, and languid conscience in this direction. (Am I tiring you?) I think the best and most benevolent employers would say how difficult they, with all their experience, found it to unite theory and practice. I am sure Mr Sam Greg would. How could I suggest or even depict modes of proceeding, (the details of which I never saw,) and which from some error, undetected even by anxious and conscientious witnesses, seems so often to result in disappointment? It would require a wise man, practical and full of experience,\one/ able to calculate consequences, to choose out the best among the many systems which are being tried by the benevolent millowners. If I, in my ignorance, chose out one which appeared to me good, but which was known to business men to be a failure, I should be doing an injury instead of a service. For instance Mr Sam Greg's plans have been accompanied with great want of success in a money point of view. This has been a stinging grief to him, as he was most anxious to show that his benevolent theories, which were so beautiful in their origin, might be carried into effect with good and *just* practical results of benefit to both master and man. He knew that he was watched in all his proceedings by no friendly eyes, who would be glad to set down failure in business to what they considered his Utopian schemes.[1] I think he, or such as he, might almost be made the hero of a fiction on the other side of the question[—]the trials of the conscientious rich man, in his dealings with the poor. And I should like some *man*, who had a man's correct knowledge, to write on this subject, and make the poor intelligent workpeople understand the infinite anxiety as to right and wrongdoing which I believe that riches bring to many.

I acknowledge,—no one feels more keenly than I do, the great fault of the gloominess of M B. It is the fault of the choice of the subject; which yet I did not *choose*, but which was as it were impressed upon me. Some time or other I should like to show you some letters I have had on the subject, if you cared to see them; and are not already wearied by what I have now written. I hardly dare begin, after having written so much, on the subject of your former letter, which yet interested me so much. I was very much obliged to you for your little pamphlet on the Institution of the Diaconesses in Paris. I have hardly ever had it at home, for it has interested people so much, that it has always been on its

[1] Greg's efforts at industrial welfare and his energetic proselytising caused a breakdown of health and compelled his retirement. See *Letters and Memorials*, ed. Winkworth, I, p. 338 n.

travels, and is just now gone to pay a visit to an old lady whom I think your husband may know, Mrs Fletcher, formerly of Edinburgh, who has\lately/had a poor friend undergoing an operation at the Asylum for Invalid Gentlewomen, and who is in consequence, full of gratitude to the originators of such an institution, and interested to learn all that suggested it. I had no idea of the existence of the sisterhoods you describe. They quite startled me. It seems strange that such things can be going on in England. I cd write much more, but I must end. My dear lady, I am

Yours very faithfully, E. C. Gaskell.

Has Miss Brontë been with you in town? And will you sometime send me her address, please.

₇₀ **73** ₇₉

?ELIZA FOX[1]

[?July 1850]

⟨. . .⟩ is going to buy an annuity!!! think of that. May his shadow never be less! And I've caught an innocent young man and 'honoured' him by borrowing In Memoriam—but it is a book to brood over—oh *how* perfect some of them are—I can't leave them to go on to others, and yet I must send it back tomorrow. By dint of coaxing however, I've got Wm to promise he'll *give* it me, so I sing Te Deum. Do you know I've a great fancy for asking Barbara Smith to come and pay us a visit. *Do* you think she'd come? Do you know Miss Tennyson[2] (Arthur Hallam's Miss) is just going to be married to a poor lieutenant,— and she wrote to Hallam to give up her annuity but he would not let her. You are a little plague about autographs—How do I know now but what A. Howitt has manufactured all you have sent? Oh! I've a favour to ask—only don't do it if you'd rather not dear. There are two middleaged people going up from a retired Cumberland farmhouse—(they are educated women) for a *week's* first and only visit to London. *If* I sent you their address are there any 'orders' to be procured—they have but a small sum to spend—

---

[1] Original MS. not seen.

[2] Emily Tennyson received a pension of £300 per year from Henry Hallam. She married Richard Jesse, a naval lieutenant, in January 1852, but by August 1850 (see Letter 79) Mrs Gaskell had her own copy of *In Memoriam*.

and would not be particular—considering dullness in London equal to pleasure in the country. Don't give yourself any trouble. Only they are two charmingly original people.

₀ **74** ₁₂₇

MARY COWDEN CLARKE

> Plymouth Grove,
> Manchester. Saturday
> Augt 17. [1850]

My dear Mrs Clarke,

I am so glad you liked the Sextons hero well enough to want a copy of your own; and I only hope this will reach you before you go to Nice. I have been hunting up your address, and have only just received it from Helen Tagart, or I would have sent it sooner. I am almost afraid now that it will not reach you in time; as I have to send this to some booksellers, and ask them to get the books which are rather difficult to be procured, from having been privately published.[1] 'Libbie Marsh' I send too; one of my cousins liked it so much that I gave it to her, and she published it on her own behalf.[2] Do you remember our lunch at Mr Tagart's, and how we waited for Leigh Hunt—and how he never came; and now I shall never see him I am afraid. If I could I would gladly have written your name in the books, but it would cause a day's detention; however you must imagine that in them is written to Mary Cowden Clarke, in pleasant recollection of a few hours spent in her company from E. C. Gaskell. If ever you come to Manchester again you will come and see me and mine, won't you?

> Yours very truly
> E. C. Gaskell.

You don't know what a favourite tale 'Perseverance' is with my children. I remembered it myself with such pleasure when it was first published (in the London Journal was not it?) and I was quite glad to get it again for them.

*

[1] In 1850. See A. S. Whitfield, *Mrs Gaskell, Her Life and Work*, 1929, pp. 29, 221.
[2] See Letter 108a.

57 **75** 149

CATHERINE WINKWORTH

Plymouth Grove,
Sunday Evng [25 August 1850]

My dearest Katie,

If I don't write now I shall never. A fortnight ago I was in despair, because I had so much to say to you I thought I shd never get through it, and now, as you may suppose, I shall find I have more to do. Only I'll let you know I'm alive. And that on Thursday last I was as near as possible drinking tea with the Tennysons,—and that I *have* been spending the week in the same house with Miss Brontë,—now is not this enough material for one letter, let alone my home events,—& fortnight-ago, richness of material. Oh how I wish you were here. I have so much to say I don't know where to begin. Wm is in Birmingham preaching to-day. He stays over tomorrow. The two Greens are here; and Fanny Holland expected any day. That's all *here* I think. {[3½ lines deleted]} Last Monday came a note from Lady Kay Shuttleworth, asking Wm & me to go to see them at a house called Briery Close, they have taken just above Low-wood; and meet Miss Brontë who was going to stay with them for 3 or 4 days.[1] Wm hesitated, but his Birmingham sermons kept him at home; & I went on Tuesday afternoon. Dark when I got to Windermere station; a drive along the level road to Low-wood, then a regular clamber up a steep lane; then a stoppage at a pretty house, and then a pretty drawing room much like the South End one, in which were Sir James and Lady K S, and a little lady in black silk gown, whom I could not see at first for the dazzle in the room; she came up & shook hands with me at once—I went up to unbonnet &c, came down to tea, the little lady worked away and hardly spoke; but I had time for a good look at her. She is, (as she calls herself) *un-developed*; thin and more than ½ a head shorter than I, soft brown hair not so dark as mine; eyes (very good and expressive looking straight & open at you) of the same colour, a reddish face; large mouth & many teeth gone; altogether *plain*; the forehead square, broad, and *rather* overhanging. She has a very sweet voice, rather hesitates in choosing her expressions, but when chosen they seem without an effort, *admirable* and *just* befitting the occasion. There is

[1] See *The Brontës: Their Lives, Friendships and Correspondence*, ed. T. J. Wise and J. A. Symington, Oxford, 1932, III, p. 139.

nothing overstrained but perfectly simple. Well of course we
went to bed; & of course we got up again. (I had the most lovely
view from my bedroom over Windermere on to Esthwaite
Langdale &c.) Lady K S. was ill, so I made breakfast all the time I
staid; and an old jolly Mr Moseley Inspector of Schools came to
breakfast, who abused our Mr Newman soundly for having tried
\to acquire/various branches of knowledge which 'savoured of
vanity, & was a temptation of the D' 'literal.' After breakfast we
\4/went on the Lake; and Miss B and I agreed in thinking Mr
Moseley a good goose; in liking Mr Newman's soul,—in liking
Modern Painters, and the idea of the Seven Lamps, and she told
me about Father Newman's lectures in a very quiet concise
graphic way. After dinner we went a drive to Coniston to call on
the Tennysons who are staying at Mr Marshall's [?Fleet] Lodge—
Sir James on the box, Miss B & I inside very cozy; but alas it
began to rain so we had to turn back without our call being paid,
which grieved me sorely & made me cross. I'm not going to
worry you with as particular an account of every day; simply to
tell you bits about Miss Brontë. She is more like Miss Fox in
character & ways than anyone, if you can fancy Miss Fox to have
gone through suffering enough to have taken out every spark of
merriment, and shy & silent from the habit of extreme intense
solitude. Such a life as Miss B's I never heard of before Lady K S
described her home to me as in a village of a few grey stone
houses perched up on the north side of a bleak moor—looking
over sweeps of bleak moors. There is a court of turf & a stone wall,
—(no flowers or shrubs will grow there) a straight walk, & you
come to the parsonage door with a window on each side of it.
The parsonage has never had a touch of paint, or an article of new
furniture for 30 years; never since Miss B's mother died. She was a
'pretty young creature' brought from Penzance in Cornwall by
the Irish Curate, who got this moorland living. Her friends dis-
owned her at her marriage. She had 6 children as fast as could be;
& what with that, & the climate, & the strange half mad husband
she had chosen she died at the end of 9 years. An old woman at
Burnley who nursed her at last, says she used to lie crying in bed,
and saying 'Oh God my poor children—oh God my poor
children!' continually. Mr Brontë vented his anger against *things*
not persons; for instance once in one of his wife's confinements
something went wrong, so he got a saw, and went and sawed up
all the chairs in her bedroom, never answering her remonstrances

or minding her tears. Another time he was vexed and took the hearth-rug & tied it in a tight bundle & set it on fire in the grate; & sat before it with a leg on each hob, heaping on more colds [*sic*] till it was burnt, no one else being able to endure in the room because of the stifling smoke. All this Lady K S told me. The sitting room at the Parsonage looks into the Church-yard filled with graves. Mr B has never taken a meal with his children since his wife's death, unless he invites them to tea,—*never* to dinner. And he has only once left home since to come to Manchester to be operated upon by Mr Wilson for Cataract; at which time they lodged in Boundary St. Well! these 5 daughters and one son grew older, their father never taught the girls anything—only the servant taught them to read & write. But I suppose they laid their heads together, for at 12 Charlotte (this one) presented a request to the father that they might go to school; so they were sent to Cowan-Bridge (the place where the daughters of the Clergy were before they were removed to Casterton. There the 2 elder died in that fever. Miss B says the pain she suffered from hunger was not to be told & her two younger sisters laid the foundation of the consumption of which they are now dead. They all came home ill. But the poverty of home was very great ('At 19 I should have been thankful for an allowance of 1d a week. I asked my father, but he said What did women want with money'). So at 19 she advertised & got a teacher's place in a school,—(where she did not say, only said it was preferable to the governess's place she got afterwards but she saved up enough to pay for her journey to a school in Brussels. She had never been out of Yorkshire before; & was so frightened when she got to London—she took a cab, it was night and drove down to the Tower Stairs, & got a boat & went to the Ostend packet, and they refused to take her in; but at last they did. She was in this school at Brussels two years without a holiday except one week with one of her Belgian schoolfellows. Then she came home & her sisters were ill, & her father going blind—so she thought she ought to stay at home. She tried to teach herself drawing & to be an artist but she cd not—and yet her own health independently of the home calls upon her wd not allow of her going out again as a governess. She had always wished to write & believed that she could; at 16 she had sent some of her poems to Southey, & had 'kind, stringent' answers from him. So she & her sisters tried. They kept their initials and took names that would do either for a man or a woman. They used to read to each other when they had written so much. Their father never knew a word about it. He had never heard of Jane Eyre when 3 months after its publication she promised her sisters one day at dinner she would tell him before tea. So she marched into his study with a copy wrapped up & the reviews. She said (I think I can remember the exact words[)]— 'Papa I've been writing a book.' 'Have you my dear?' and he went on reading. 'But Papa I want you to look at it.' 'I can't be troubled to read MS.' 'But it is printed.' 'I hope you have not been involving yourself in any such silly expense.' 'I think I shall gain some money by it. May I read you some reviews.' So she read them; and then she asked him if he would read the book. He said she might leave it, and he would see. But he sent them an invitation to tea that night, and towards the end of tea he said, 'Children, Charlotte has been writing a book—and I think it is a better one than I expected.' He never spoke about it again till about a month ago, & they never dared to tell him of the books her sisters wrote. Just in the success of Jane Eyre, her sisters died of \rapid/consumption—*unattended by any doctor*, why I don't know. But she says she will have none and that her death will be quite lonely; having no friend or relation in the world to nurse her, & her father dreading a sick room above all places. There seems little doubt she herself is already tainted with consumption. Now I shan't write any more till you write again, & tell me how to get a letter to Annie\Shaen/kind of paper to be used &c—& how you & Emma are, & a quantity more I want to know. Love to dr Emma. Emily is at Crix? Kind love to Selina[.] I went to Arnolds \met some Bunsens, & were to have met Tennyson/—Davy's Mr Prestons

Yours very affect[ionately,]
E C Gaskell

₀ 76 ₀

UNKNOWN[1]

[c. 25 August 1850]

⟨. . .⟩ We were only three days together; the greater part of which was spent in driving about, in order to show Miss Brontë

---

[1] From the MS. *Life of Charlotte Brontë*, vol. 2; but perhaps *not* a letter. See Introduction, p. xxiii.

the Westmoreland scenery, as she had never been[1] {it}\there/be-
fore. We were both included in an invitation to\drink tea quietly/
at Fox How; and I then saw how severely {Miss Brontë's}\her/
nerves were taxed by the effort of going amongst strangers. We
knew beforehand that the number of the party would not exceed
twelve; but she suffered the whole day from an acute headache
brought on by apprehension of the evening.

Briery Close was situated high above Low-wood, and of
course commanded an extensive view and wide horizon. I was
struck by Miss Brontë's careful examination of the shape of the
clouds, and the signs of the heavens, in which she read, as from a
book, what the coming weather would be. I told her that I saw
she must have a view equal in extent at her own home. She said
that I was right, but that the character of the prospect from
Haworth was very different; that I had no idea what a companion
the sky became to anyone living in solitude—more than any
inanimate object on earth—more than the moors themselves.

₀ 77 ₀

UNKNOWN[2]

[c. 25 August 1850]

I arrived late at the house of a mutual friend, tea was on the
table, and behind it sat a little wee dark person, dressed in black,
who scarcely spoke, so that I had time for a good look at her. She
had soft lightish brown hair, eyes of the same tint, looking
straight at you, and very good and expressive; a reddish complexion, a wide mouth—altogether plain; the forehead square,
broad, and rather overhanging. Her hands are like birds' claws,
and she is so shortsighted that she cannot see your face unless you
are close to her. She is said to be frightfully shy, and almost cries
at the thought of going amongst strangers.

[1] Originally written 'seen'. This is the first of several alterations to the first
draft, some of which involved heavy cancellations. They have been ignored in
our text if we could not read them.

[2] This passage is prefaced in the article from which it comes with the words 'A
lady, who afterwards became intimate with Miss Brontë, thus describes her first
introduction to her'. The verbal echoes of other passages in which Mrs Gaskell
describes Charlotte Brontë are strong enough for us to agree with Mr J. G. Sharps,
who brought them to our attention, that these lines are Mrs Gaskell's. See also
TLS, 28 June 1963, p. 477.

CHARLOTTE FROUDE

[*c. 25* August 1850]

⟨. . .⟩ And now I have given you a bulletin of all our mutual
acquaintances I shall tell you about ourselves. In the first place I
must make an apology for Marianne, who has found out that she
has got your Agnus Dei in her portfolio. Unless I hear to the
contrary I shall send it by the first oppy to my cousins near Tre-
Madoc, who can easily forward it to Plâs Gwynant. We went at
the end of June to our farm-house in Silverdale; where we stayed
about five weeks. Since we came home, we have all{ways} been
'picking up our dropped stiches' of work in various ways. Our
only interruption has been my going from home for three days to
stay at Lady Kay Shuttleworth's to meet Miss Brontë. It was at a
very pretty place near Low Wood on Windermere; and I went to
see all our old friends at Skelwith and elsewhere. Miss Bronte I
like. Her faults are the faults of the very peculiar circumstances in
which she has been placed; and she possesses a charming union of
simplicity and power; and a strong feeling of responsibility for the
Gift, which she has given her. She is very little & very plain. Her
stunted person she ascribes to the scanty supply of food she had as
a growing girl, when at that school of the Daughters of the Clergy.
Two of her sisters died there, of the low fever she speaks about in
Jane Eyre. She is the last of six; lives in a wild out of the way
village\in the Yorkshire Moors/with a wayward eccentric wild
father,—their parsonage facing the North—no flowers or shrub or
tree can grow in the plot of ground, on acct of the biting winds.
The sitting room looks into the church-yard. Her father & she
each dine and sit alone. She scrambled into what education she
has had. Indeed I never heard of so hard, and dreary a life,—
extreme poverty is added to their trials,—it (poverty) was no trial
till her sisters had long lingering illnesses. She is truth itself—and
of a very noble sterling nature,—which has never been called out
by anything kind or genial. She was a teacher in a school, & a
governess for 4 or 5 years; till her health gave way; but with her
savings she put herself (between the two situations) to school at
Brussels, where she was 2 years. Then, when she was too ill to
leave home, she tried to train herself for an artist;—but though

she found she could express her own thoughts by drawing, she could make nothing grand or beautiful to other eyes. She is very silent & very shy; and when she speaks chiefly remarkable for the admirable use she makes of simple words, & the way in which she makes language express her ideas. She and I quarrelled & differed about almost every thing,—she calls me a democrat, & can not bear Tennyson—but we like each other heartily\I think/& I hope we shall ripen into friends. God keep you my dear Mrs Froude! Mr Gaskell desires his kind remembrances to you and Mr Froude. Marianne & Meta tell me to send their 'loves'[?]. Mr Gaskell regretted afterwards that he had not called to say goodbye that last Tuesday. But he was very busy, & thought you would be even more so. In great haste (be sure you thank Mr & Mrs Kingsley heartily for me.) I am Yours very truly

E. C. Gaskell

73 79 85

ELIZA FOX[1]

Tuesday [27] Aug: 1850

My dearest Tottie,

So you are come home again I conclude by the speed with which I received my i.e. *your* Examiner. Some charming angel took a fancy for some time to send me the Athenaeum; *always round by Silverdale*, but this week said anonymous angel has dropped it; mores the pity,—I am obliged to lie down on the sofa constantly which I think addles my brains for I feel very stupid; but I did too much last week in the way of motion. Thank you dearest for your last letter. What *is* the matter with Anna and Fanny? It is most mysterious to me: each writes to me begging me to write and cheer up the other, and what is the matter with either or both I cannot conceive. I hear that Fanny is at Susan Deanes at Knutsford, 'looking wretchedly ill;' and I suppose she will come on here soon. Wm is at Birmingham; he was preaching there last Sunday; and is staying for some days. It is funny how we *never* go from home together. He is so anxious about the children; he says he is never easy if we are both away; it takes away all his

---

[1] Original MS. not seen.

pleasure, so first he went to Edinburgh scientific association, and prowled about Scotland, then last week quite unexpectedly Lady Kay Shuttleworth wanted us to come and meet Miss Brontë, and William could not go,—and then the people he is with at Birmingham wanted us to go; and he said he shd not be happy if I went; so we are like Adam and Eve in the weather glass. I wish my dear, you were here. It would be a charming beguiling of my sofa imprisonment. I am very happy nevertheless making flannel petticoats; and reading Modern painters. Miss Brontë *is* a nice person. Like you, Tottie, without your merriment: poor thing she can hardly smile she has led such a hard cruel (if one may dare to say so,) life. She is quiet sensible unaffected with high noble aims. Lady K. S. was confined to one room so she and I had much of our day to ourselves (with the exception of some lectures on art, and 'bringing ourselves down to a lower level,' and 'the beauty of expediency,' from that eminently practical man Sir James, who has never indulged in the exercise of any talent which could not bring him a tangible and speedy return. However he was very kind; and really took trouble in giving us, Miss Brontë especially, good advice; which she received with calm resignation. She is sterling and true; and if she is a little bitter she checks herself, and speaks kindly and hopefully of things and people directly; the wonder to me is how she can have kept heart and power alive in her life of desolation. I made her give me an account of the 'Editorial party,'—Do you know who Annie and Ellen Green' are! two country friends of our girls aged 14 and 15. They are come here for a month's music-mastering; and the air is redolent of DO RE MI &c. I have been writing a story for Xmas;[1] a *very foolish* engagment of mine—which I am angry with myself for doing, but I promised it and have done it. I have got an In Memoriam of my own, it is a pleasure to me to have what I like so earnestly of *my own*. Do you know I was as near as possible seeing Tennyson. He and Mrs are staying at Coniston, and Sir James, Miss B. and I were on the Lake there, when we heard it; and Sir James knows him, and said he would go and call; and then looked up at the sky and thought it was going to rain, so he didn't. I held my peace, and bit my lips. All the world at the Lakes was full of the 'Prelude', have you read it. Miss Brontë has promised that Mr Smith (& Elder) shall lend it to me. Certainly Manchester is a behindhand place for books. Hearn is going out

---

1 *The Moorland Cottage.* See Letter 66 and Hopkins, *Gaskell*, pp. 99-100.

and is come for my letter. Susanne Winkworth is going to BONN not Rome. She is to live in the house of Professor Brandis at C. Bunsens recommendation and study German life for her [ ].[1] She makes me write and ask questions of Mr Forster, to which he answers by changing the words of my remarks on the question and passing them off as his own; so we don't get on; and yet I am astonished at my own wisdom, when it comes back to me dressed up grand. Now do write to me. The post coming is the great event of my day

Yours very affect[ionate]ly,
E. C. Gaskell.

₀ **80** ₀

Leigh Hunt[2]

Plymouth Grove, Sep. 13. [?1850]

I think that, if I were you, and had felt as you say you did, 'loth to make an objection' I should be glad to hear how thankfully my truth-speaking had been received; and so I write to you, just one little short note, to tell you that I value the kindness that will take the trouble and pains to point out errors or faults far more than any indiscriminate praise,—I had almost said more than any praise at all; and I think that wd have been the truth after all; for if I may ever hope to improve, and to make my standard high and higher still it must be by being a grateful listener to any one who will tell me where I am low or wrong. You make me *think*; I am not quite convinced that, as it is the custom here to keep birds, I might not, in trying to draw from the life introduce the circumstance; but yet I see that the introduction without one word of disapproval seems to lend a sanction to the custom; so tell your grandchildren that I own I was wrong, and thank you both for your note and your fable. I saw the mention of the cause of your sorrow in the newspaper, and I was sorry for you.

Yours, with true respect
E. C. Gaskell.

Leigh Hunt, Esq.

[1] Probably Niebuhr. The source also reads 'Brand' and 'Bunseirs' in this sentence, but cf. *Letters and Memorials*, ed. Winkworth, I, p. 231.

[2] A reply to a note about 'Jupiter', a caged canary, in *Libbie Marsh's Three Eras* (1847). See Whitfield, *Gaskell*, pp. 29–30.

*74a **81** 82a

LADY KAY-SHUTTLEWORTH[1]

Poulton-le-Sands, near
Lancaster
Sep. 25. [1850]

My dear Lady,

Your letter was forwarded to me here; where I am staying for
my health for three weeks or a month. I was very much obliged
to you for it; and I thought it very kind of you so readily to give
yourself the trouble of sending me on Ld Stanley's, and Mr
Thorold's praise of 'Mary Barton'. I am forbidden to write much
as I am suffering from what the doctors call spinal irritation; so I
shall reserve my long answer to your long letter, (the last but one,
which I have brought here with me, in order to answer it *sometime*,) and only tell you one or two things. I parted with the copyright of Mary Barton I believe; but I was then so unknowing, and
so little expected that it would ever come to a second edition, that
I did not sufficiently make myself acquainted with the nature of
the parchment document sent to me to sign. I received 100£ for
it; and as I had offered the MS for nothing, I was very thankful
as you may suppose. Only I wish I had retained some little power
over the succeeding editions. I only know from the public papers,
when a new edition is {to be} published; I am never consulted.
Now, from an accidental copy of the Leader I learn that a fourth
edition is just coming out; and I heartily wish it were a 5s. one as
Mr Thorold suggests. It *may* be too, but I have never heard a word
about it from the publisher in any way. I am almost sorry you
know I am going to publish another because I don't think you
will like it. Mr Chapman asked me to write a Xmas Story,
'recommending benevolence, charity, etc', to which I agreed,
why I cannot think now, for it was very foolish indeed. However
I could not write about virtues to order, so it is simply a little
country love-story called Rosemary,[2] which will I suppose be
published somewhere in November, and not be worth reading
then; it is bad to make a bargain beforehand as to time or subject,
though the latter I have rejected. I am glad you like Mrs Arnold. I
hope you will like Mrs Davy too, if you happen to see her. I must

[1] *Annotation* 1850.
[2] Chapman and Hall published *The Moorland Cottage* in December 1850.

stop, or I shall receive a scolding from my nice doctor. I have not forgotten my note that I owe to Ughtred.

Yours most truly

E. Ċ. Gaskell.

₀ **82** ₁₀₈

?LOUISA BELL

42 Plymouth Grove,

Octr 5th [?1850][1]

My dear Miss Bell

May we hope for the pleasure of seeing you & your sisters & Dr Bell to tea on the evening of the 25th? It sounds a long invitation for a quiet party, but if we put it off till nearer the time, the friends we want to see are sure to be engaged. With very kind regards, I remain

Yours very truly

E. C. Gaskell

₈₁ **82a** ₈₃

LADY KAY-SHUTTLEWORTH

Plymouth Grove,

Monday [?October 1850]

My dear Lady,

May I ask you to forward the enclosed note to Mr Kay if he has left you? I have been very ill for the last week, and unable to write any letters; or you may be sure I should have thanked both you and Ughtred for your letters. There is a great deal in yours I should like to answer at some length; and I mean to do so soon. I am very much obliged to Ughty for his nice little note, and remembrance of me, and I shall send him an answer some day very soon.

[1] The Bells left Manchester in July 1855. (See Letter 259.) If this is accepted as a terminal date, the only other possible years for a letter headed Plymouth Grove are 1850 and 1853. (Late information about the paper makes 1853 the more likely year.)

Mrs Hollond is I believe coming here very soon, to try and interest people about the nurseries;[1] and many seem to be taking up the subject with interest; if I did not know how averse working people are to anything new, I should be disheartened by the vast number of objections they raise. However I remember your liking for 'good objectors'; and perhaps as ladies are so fond of novelty it is a very good check upon us to have such cold water thrown upon the scheme by the working people.

I *must* not write more; my husband is crying out as it is; but in a few days I shall write you a long letter, for I have a great deal I want to say to you. It is so cold here; I hope you are taking care of yourself. Ever my dear Lady

Yours most truly
E C Gaskell

82a 83 86

LADY KAY-SHUTTLEWORTH[2]

The Cliff, near Warwick,
November 12, [1850]

My dear Lady,

I received your *very* kind letter before I left home; but I was so busy that I was unable to answer it then; and I believe it had been kept for a short time at Gargrave before they could ascertain my address; so I dare not look at the date for fear of being convicted of great negligence in not sooner writing to thank you for your real true kindness in wishing me to come to the Briery; and be nursed. Before your letter reached me I had found out that Manchester was undoing all the good I had received in the country, so my dear husband determined that I should again set off on my travels and spend these two months, (usually so damp in Manchester,) in a warmer and drier place. Accordingly my eldest girl and I are again exiles from home; and *if we were not*, I should be enjoying very much this opportunity of seeing dear cousins from whom I have been separated nearly eighteen years, but with whom are associated some of the happiest recollections of my childhood. The weather here is so different from Man-

---

[1] See Letter 83.   [2] *Annotation* 1850.

chester, owing I suppose to the soil being limestone instead of clay, that we have sunshine here, and leaves on the trees while last week at Manchester the trees were bare, and there was thick fog till ten or eleven, beginning again at four. The worst is my husband's duties prevent his joining me, (even for a few days,) at present. I wanted to tell you and Miss Paplouska more particularly, that there will be a little story of mine in the next No of Household Words,[1] which she is most welcome to translate if she thinks it worth while. *I think* it will be called Pen-Morfa. Of course in all this I should be quite sorry if Miss Paplouska thought herself obliged to do anything of mine, because I sent it or named it to her; pray don't let her suppose I should not fully understand; and perhaps enter into, her preference of another writer's productions. I only name my little story because I should be very glad to feel of use to her. I always feel as if I had more to say to you than I had any chance of getting into a letter; but one thing I must ask you, if you are at all interested about, or acquainted with the want of a children's hospital in London, and if you will sometime look over the accompanying papers; sent me by Dr West.[2] You will [be] glad to hear that before Christmas a trial-public nursery will be established in Manchester; the subject is taken up very warmly. I hope they will make it as nearly self-supporting as they can, and as little of a charity as possible; but I am afraid the latter is the error they are likely to fall into. Before very long I shall be obliged to go up to London for a few days, for we have determined to place my eldest girl at school there for a year; and I want to see for myself the various school-mistresses that have been recommended to us; and I have thought if I could I would go to the nursery in Nassau St. That is all the address I know about; but I suppose there would be no difficulty in finding it out from a directory. Both Mr Gaskell and I are very anxious about the school to which we send our dear girl. She has hitherto been brought up at home entirely, but my husband thinks she has some faults of \mental/ indolence which may be cured by associating with other girls for a year or so; and we want to obtain good music and singing lessons for her, because her only talent seems to be for music, and we want her to view this gift rightly and use it well. Ughtred's letter

---

[1] 'The Well of Pen-Morfa' appeared in *Household Words*, II, pp. 182–6, 205–10, on 16 and 23 November 1850.
[2] The Children's Hospital in Great Ormond Street was established in Richard Mead's house in 1852 by Dr Charles West (1816–98).

was begun at Poulton. Pray thank Sir James for his kindness in wishing that I should come to the Briery; which I should have liked very much, if another plan had not been arranged previously.

What is this new book of Miss Brontë's,[1] do you know? It will be very interesting to hear more of her sisters; but rather difficult for her to do it well and discreetly.

Dear Lady Shuttleworth, I am[2]

Yours most truly and gratefully,

E. C. Gaskell.

₀ 84 ₀

UNKNOWN[3]

[*c.* November–December 1850]

['Regarding a school for her eldest girl she deprecated one which was'] so common—the very worst style of dogmatic hard Unitarianism, utilitarian to the backbone.

79 85 99

ELIZA FOX[4]

[?Late 1850]

My very dear Tottie,

Wm Greg (my old friend, of Edin: Review,) has been here till past post-time for to-day; so this letter can't go till to-morrow. Wm is almost as grateful as I am about your thought for MA— but says exactly what I thought he would,—viz that he should not like her to be without me for so long a time *just now*, when we want to examine into the real state of her feelings—(not much touched I fancy,)—and besides you know Wm's anxiety about his

---

[1] This is no doubt a reference to the new edition of *Wuthering Heights* and *Agnes Grey* which contained Charlotte Brontë's memoir of her sisters.

[2] The subscription has been cut away from this point, but the words are inserted in another hand lower down the page.

[3] From a printed source.

[4] Original MS. not seen. Source reads 'Reirus' for 'Review' in first line.

girls, and I believe he is afraid of her going to London for the first time without me to take care of her. *We* are very much obliged to you and Mr Fox, dearest Tottie, and if you'll offer *me* $\frac{1}{2}$ your bed for a few nights in about 3 weeks or a month I won't despise it.[1] We are very much taken with your opinion of Mr Lalors .⟨. . .⟩

83 **86** 154

LADY KAY-SHUTTLEWORTH[2]

Boughton-House near
Worcester. Dec 12 [1850]

My dear Lady Kay-Shuttleworth,
(This is such very bad paper I am very much afraid my writing may be illegible on the other side, and yet I have no other.) I have owed you thanks for a long long time for a very kind letter received from you, in which you express interest about my plans for Marianne, and give me some very useful advice. I\we are— i.e. Marianne & I/am going to London next Tuesday to stay with Mrs Wedgewood one of the visitors at the Queen's College; and I am rather dismayed to find from a letter which I have received from her this morning that Mr S. Bennett gives his last lesson on Harmony for this term on Monday next; just a day too soon, for I *cannot*, with the best will in the world, go up before Tuesday. I am very sorry that I did not enquire earlier. I have fixed as far as in me lies that, if it is possible, Marianne shall learn from him, and divide the hour between harmony & the performance of music, for I quite agree with you about the superficialness, if there is such a word, of learning the practice of music, without understanding the science. Besides in this instance it will I hope be of material service to her mental character by enabling her to concentrate her attention on a train of thought. We have very nearly decided on a school for her, and a personal interview with the lady next week will decide me. She is a Mrs Lalor of Hampstead. I am warned against her brusque unprepossessing manners; but told by her old pupils that her power of forming conscientious, thoughtful, earnest, independent characters is very great, and that her manners are very soft and tender towards her pupils, whatever they may be

---

[1] Miss Fox lived at 3 Sussex Place.   [2] *Annotation* 1850.

to comparative strangers. Now I like a dark cloud with a silver lining, far better than one that turns out all it's silver to inspection; and besides in our correspondence on the subject of Marianne when I named her fondness for music as her prevailing taste, and a certain degree of indolence of mind, which made her unwilling to think hard and long about anything as her great foible, Mrs Lalor said in reply 'Can we not make her taste available to the correction of the mental fault to which you allude['] and went on to speak of the lessons on Harmony\which I had never named/as the very thing to be recommended. I think I have rather made this one thing a test, at least I am accused of having done so; but I was struck with the difference in Miss Lewis. I *named* Harmony to her as one of the things I wished MA to learn; and in reply she said that they never recommended any pupil to study harmony unless she was to be a professional teacher of music; indeed that unless that were the case it was rather waste of time. I am inclined to think that Miss Lewis' school is admirable for sweet gentle manners, ladylike deportment and dress, and good regulation of the temper; all excellent things as far as they go; but the number of girls is too great, *30* I believe. I find at all the schools where I have made the enquiry that it is against all their rules and plans to allow any of their girls to come in to the lectures at the Queen's College. They say that the difficulty of sending them under proper escort to and fro is very great and loses a great deal of time. Miss Lewis goes farther, and disapproves of the Queen's College altogether. I mean to try Mrs Lalor once more for this one class; if not the hour's lesson must be divided. Mr S. Bennett does teach at some schools at Hampstead though not at Mrs Lalor's, but she said she would do everything she could to obtain his lessons for Marianne. Am I wearying you with my details? I think not because I know your power of sympathy. I shall go and see the Nursery. And will you tell me how I can see and hear about the Governesses Home, about which I am much interested. Or perhaps Mrs Wedgwood may know all about it. Then I am in great hopes that my husband may be able to come up in Xmas week, as I am yet forbidden to return to Manchester—and it would be very desolate to be thrown on the wide world,—even a wide world of friends,— without anything of home about one, that very week so sacred to homes & families and made so by the Birth of a Child. From thence I go to a friend's in Essex,[1] in whose warm sheltered

[1] Probably the Shaens at Crix near Chelmsford.

house I spend January; and then I leave Marianne at school, and return home{wards}. And I must try and make up by hard work for all this laziness. My husband may be detained in Manchester by his co-pastor's indisposition,—that is all I am afraid of; but if he comes, he will bring our second girl with him, and as the two sisters have never been separated so long before, and have neither of them ever been in London I fancy they will have a very merry pleasant Christmas week, if—they come.

I was very sorry to receive a note forwarded from home, from Miss Brontë, in which she says that in order to 'avoid settled depression of spirits' (poor poor creature!) she is going to break through her rule of keeping house all winter, and go to Miss Martineau's at Ambleside on the 16 for a few days; she writes to offer us a visit, which both my husband and I are most sorry to be unable to accept just now. I hope it is only deferred for a time; I long to have her quietly in our family, settled down for a visit; not the bustle of a few days only; and I would try and prevent her being worried by curiosity. I hope you will see her; but that you are sure to do. I wrote her a long letter of almost impertinent advice, (at least it would have been impertinent if it had come simply from the head, and not warm from the heart which ached for her loneliness,) and she replied by return of post, so very nicely and warmly, thanking me for all I had said.[1] I have been staying at my cousin's this last three weeks; and they tell me they asked a dear friend of theirs, who is also they think a great friend of yours, to be here at the same time, Mrs Greathed.

I am summoned, and I must go away while I had yet a great deal to say. I want you to thank Sir James for me for all his kind advice about my health; advice which I feel to be good, and yet which I cannot follow; for the work appointed both for my husband & me lies in Manchester. I would fain be in the country, —& this last experience of country air has done me so much good —I am a different creature to what I am in Manchester. However I have written enough about myself, and my own concerns. And now when you write will you tell me what you hear of Miss Paplouska, and if there seems any chance of her return. Poor little darlings—that dreaming of a lost one, & imagining the lost found, & back in the home once more makes the tears come into my eyes. Give my love to them if you please. I am ashamed of this letter; but unless I write in a hurry I never seem to find time to

[1] See *The Brontës*, ed. Wise and Symington, III, p. 187.

write at all. Will you remember me *thankfully* to Sir James, & ever believe me, dear Lady Shuttleworth,

Yours very truly
E. C. Gaskell.

Is there any chance of Mrs Strutt being in London? She asked me to call if ever I was there when she was.

66 **87** 89

?EDWARD CHAPMAN

3 Sussex Place
Regts Park
[?December 1850]

My dear Sir,

I do not at all like the title you have chosen, & I cannot think why I did not tell you so the other day, for I fully intended to do so.—May it, please, be December Days,[1] which is much more suggestive of the quiet tone of the story.

I had an exceedingly kind offer made me last night, which I pass on to you. The gentleman at whose house I was staying said if I would send him an early copy he would get it noticed in the Examiner. But your publications never are noticed in that paper I think?, and besides one should exceedingly dislike any notice arising out of private friendship. However if you think it worth while to avail yourself of this offer, (*not on my account,*) you must send a copy to G R. Porter Esq, Board of Trade, Whitehall.

I could not tell you yesterday because Mr Shaen was there, but Simms had no right whatever to say that he had been told by any friend of mine that I was writing again. *No one* in Manchester, (except my husband of course) knows of it or can do more than suspect it; but I know more than one who would try, and fish out from Simms if he knew anything about it, by stating it as a fact, and expecting him then either to contradict or confirm it, as he

---

[1] Probably the work eventually entitled *The Moorland Cottage*, published by Chapman and Hall, December 1850. See Mrs Gaskell's remark in Letter 382 to Smith: 'A poor title, pretty—I thought'.

was the person to fix suspicion on me before. I will disown that book if you call it The Fagot;—the name of *my* book is December Days—

Yours very truly
E C Gaskell

₀ 88 ₀

UNKNOWN[1]

121, Upper Rumford Street
Tuesday [?Early 1850]

My dear Sir,

May I take you into confidence about a plan I should exceedingly like for my husband, and which I am sure he would like for himself, if all difficulties were smoothed away? I do so want him to accompany you to Palestine; I see many recommendations to the plan; but until a few arrangements are made I don't want him to know anything about it. Will you tell me how long you are likely to be away? When you are going, and (if it be not too impertinent a question to obtain an answer,) what you imagine the expense of such a journey to be?

I can see that my husband is fagged with the monotonous exertions of so many years; and he received so much benefit from his continental journey nine or ten years ago,[2] that I imagine this Eastern journey would be the very thing to renovate health & spirits. Besides it is such a glorious thing to do in a lifetime, and if he puts it off, he will never have an opp[ortunit]y of so consonant a companion. The college & the congregation are *the* great difficulties; but surely some plan may be devised by which these may be set aside. He completely requires a change. Do not name the plan to him, please, just yet, except to urge his accompanying you if you feel so inclined.

Yours very truly
E. C. Gaskell

[1] After printing had begun it was noted that this letter might more appropriately have appeared after No. 71 in view of its address.

[2] Presumably the trip to Heidelberg in 1841.

87 **89** 235

EDWARD CHAPMAN

Crix,\nr/Chelmsford
Tuesday [14 Jan. 1851]

My dear Sir,
Mr Gaskell sends me word that he has received the 50£ quite safely; now I don't know if he is to acknowledge it or if I am; but I fancy you will like a double acknowledgement better than none at all; so I enclose one,[1] which seems to me very knowing, and business-like. Thank you for the Atlas. The Guardian (Puseyite) has been very busy praising M[oorland] C[ottage] too.[2] I hope the Times will be so kind as to leave it alone; for I think it would be a disgrace to be praised by the man who wrote that review of Mr Thackeray. Dr Whewell wrote that review in Fraser[3] I believe; and I have received a very complimentary note from him as well.
How is the Scarlet letter going on? Pray ease my mind by sending me the account *as soon as ever* it is rebound, and dispatched to it's destination. I send you some very sweet-scented flowers, & am

Yours very truly
E C Gaskell

47 **90** *91a

MARIANNE GASKELL

Monday, morning.
Plymouth Grove
[?17 February 1851]

My dearest Polly,
Papa is gone to breakfast with the High Sheriff, about which we have been laughing a great deal at him, and telling him he would be expected in a helmet and white cravat; as he and some other

---

[1] A receipt dated 14 January 1851 accompanies this letter.
[2] In its issue of 24 December 1850.
[3] Vol. XLIII (January 1851), p. 42.

gentlemen are to take the High Sheriff, (Mr Percival Heywood) to meet the judge. Flossy and Meta are going with Mrs Shuttleworth to see the show at 11, so that is the state of commotion our house is in. I was sorry that I could not write, as I intended yesterday; but Emily Winkworth came to spend the afternoon and evening. She is now staying in Dundas Place. I must try and tell you things a little more in order. I don't know how it is, but we all seem to have got it into our heads that *we* might only write *once* a week to *you*; which is a mistake is it not? but owing to it you had no letter last week, which shan't occur again, dear. Your yesterday's letter was a charming one; full of detail, and very satisfactory. I fancy this plan of only writing once a week is a very good one for you; it makes you think of all you want to say, and not write such good-for-nothing hurried letters as you used to do. Pray take pains about Pergetti. I have promised Papa such nice singing at Midsummer. I don't mean only take pains when he is there; but remember all his advice &c when you are practising; for you must either practise well or ill; and practising ill & carelessly only *confirms* you in *bad* habits. You ought to try and imagine the expression with which songs ought to be sung, according to their *words*, and meaning, and not be dependent upon pencil marks and accents; which is a very mechanical way of getting expression. The accident we had in coming down was simply this, the pilot-engine, (sent before to clear the way for an express train) got broken, and stopped up the *down*-line; so we had to wait 2 hours and a half in a very dull place, not at a station, and with a great white chalk bank on each side, waiting till all the *up*-trains had gone by that we might go back to the last station and go on the *up*-line without fear of an accident; it was only dull not dangerous. I sent your comb by Papa who went to call on Mr Fox, who would send it to Mr Ormsby, who would take it to you. I do not suppose you can get to see Mr Macready for 10s. I heard before I left London that all the tickets were to be a guinea; and I don't think it is worth *more* than 10s. at any rate. I did not see the Queen. Our box was right over her head. She is to be 'in state' at the benefit. No notice was taken of her that night any farther than that all eyes were directed towards the royal box, because she did *not* come in state. I am glad you seem to like Mr Ormsby. Emily Winkworth heard your letter. She said though the Sonata Pathetique was not one of the most difficult of Beethoven's, yet that you must practise *well*, to learn to play all the 19 pages in one week, with expression as they ought to be played. Will any one accompany you in the Concert-Stück? E W. says it is nothing but hard practice, without the accompaniment which gives it all the beauty. Will he give you Bach's Fugues, or are you not 'up' to them. Now I shall tell you a bit about last week. I had of course many callers. Miss Marslands, Mrs Robberds, Miss Mitchell, Mrs Leisler, Mrs Mason are some of those I remember just now—At Mrs Wolff's fancy-ball Miss Marsland & Mrs Sydney Potter went as the Merry Wives of Windsor, which was a capital idea was it not? Mr Robberds is going from home somewhere—to Southport or Lytham they speak about. Pretty Mrs William Booth is dead. The Leislers are leaving with the Darbishires from Mr Hatton. Mrs Mason is fast losing her eyesight I am afraid; and her niece has left her to go and live in Liverpool, and keep a milliner's shop there; but she has that cheerful good lame sister with her, who reads a great deal aloud to her. On Wednesday Papa married Stanley Darbishire to Ellen Carver; poor Wm Carver is very ill, they hardly thought he wd live over the wedding, but I believe he is alive yet. Mrs James Darbishire was there. Stanley has taken Mr Russell Taylor's old house just opposite to Mr Carver's. I heard that Emily Winkworth was to come to Dundas Place on Tuesday; so I called and left a message asking her and Stephen to come to tea. *She* staid at Alderley as it happened till Thursday, (as Selina was coming home from the Froude's on Wednesday)[1] so Ste came alone to tea on Tuesday Eveng, and Mr Ben Shaen popped in, just come from America with his wife and child; and in lodgings in Oxford Road, till they could meet with a house. I went to call on her on Wednesday, but found her at dinner, so I did not see her, but I asked her, nurse and baby, to dinner on Friday. Thursday Annie Austin came, and Papa went to Mr Shuttleworth's to dinner; where he met Mrs Darbishire, Mr Armstrong (the Recorder,) Sir James Kay-Shuttleworth, Mr and Mrs Scott, and Mr and Mrs Leisler, and Miss Noble of Silverdale, who is staying there. She & I had exchanged calls before; and I had asked her to dinner on Saturday. Friday Emily and Mrs Ben Shaen &c came to dinner; the latter looks good-tempered, and good; but not lady like. Bessy & Eliza Patterson came to tea, & Hannah Tayler too. Who do you think called that morning? Mr Sewell! Papa was at the College which I was very sorry for indeed.

---

[1] She was recently home from Plas Gwynant by Monday, 17 February 1851. *Letters and Memorials*, ed. Winkworth, I, p. 273.

Mr Sewell lunched with us; he was on his way back to Gargrave from Brighton, where he had been seeing Mrs Sewell. He thought he might be a month longer at Gargrave and after that their plans were uncertain, between Nova Scotea and Ireland, (Bantry Bay.) He half promised to come in the eveng but did not, so I suppose had left Manchester. Mrs Tagart is very kind in asking you; but I think I had rather *you did not go there*. If you go to one place there are many who would ask you, & with whom we are quite as intimate as with the Tagarts. Of course if you and Mrs Lalor have made an *engagement* for next Saturday, it is quite another thing, and it must be kept to *this once*; but not again, my dear girl; as I think you and I agreed before your going to school. I do not like the *tone* in the Tagart's family *at all*, though I feel all their kindness; now do not tell this last Item to any one, but remember I wish you *not* to visit anywhere, unless Mrs Lalor is kind enough to take you with her in the Easter holidays to any of her friends; perhaps you will give this as a message from me to Mrs Lalor\ with my kind regards/. I *particularly* wish this to be kept to. I know Mrs Lalor does not wish you to go; and I know (in your wise days) you did not wish to go; and I know I have a decided and explicit objection to it *anywhere*; and I make *no exception in favour* of the Tagarts. In case Mr and Mrs Austin come up with Annie I will write a note, requesting Mrs Lalor to allow you to see *them*; which perhaps she will allow. Miss Ewarts are going up to Mrs Henry Enfield's, sometime this spring, and if you go to one place, you must go to all; indeed there are *many* places I should prefer to Mrs Tagart's, as I dislike the rude quarrelsome tone there. Helen, Emily & Mrs Tagart are all very kind separately, but as a family there is something so decidedly wrong that I should indeed be grieved if you fell into their mode of thinking and speaking. On Saturday Miss Noble came to dinner, Mr & Mrs Shuttleworth, Miss Jane Noble, Mr & Mrs Charles Booth, & Miss Marsland's to tea. We turned the dining room into a drawing room, by sending the great table out, and bringing in the table out of Papa's study with the very gay table cover. I think every one was very merry; but both Papa & I were shocked and grieved by what we had heard of Mr Hodgett's sudden death, caused by an explosion in the naptha works, just when he had succeeded in his experiment ⟨. . .⟩[1]

[1] See below, Letter 116 and note.

₀ 91 ₀

W. C. BENNETT[1]

[c. 7 March 1851]

My dear Sir,

I have been from home for some time, and have only just heard from thence of your kindness in sending me the lately published vol. of your Poems, which I anticipate great pleasure in reading, and for which I beg to return you my best thanks, with some apology for my delay in acknowledging them.

I remain, dear Sir,

Yours very truly
E. C. Gaskell.

*   *

*91b 92 93

MARIANNE GASKELL

Plymouth Grove. Monday
[c. 28 March 1851]

My dearest Polly,

Do you know we were all so much disappointed not to hear from you yesterday; the servants and all looked out for your letter, and when none came we were all first so puzzled, and so certain the post-man 'must have forgotten the {lecture} letter &c &c.['] If you are in a very great bustle on Saturday, still try and write one line, love[,] to say you are well, & *why* you don't write; this week I am less uneasy because Uncle Sam is coming on Friday; and he says he will go and see you first.[2] Dr Carpenter is staying here; he lectures on Fridays & Mondays; [3] and between Mondays and Fridays he goes to Hale to lecture there. He is going to Warrington for next Sunday. Since I began this note Mrs Austin has been, and promised Annie that she might stay here till Wednesday. I have asked Mrs Austin to come any evening. They leave on Friday, according to the present plan. I will enclose a

[1] *Address (envelope)* W. C. Bennett Esq | Croom's Hill Grove | Greenwich. *Postmarks* MANCHESTER | MR 7 | 1851 | L *and* H [crown] Z | 8 MR 8 | 1851. *Annotation* Mrs E. C. Gaskell | March 7/51.

[2] Presumably at school in Hampstead.

[3] W. B. Carpenter, M.D., began to lecture on 'Microscopic Research' in the Royal Institution on 28 March 1851. *Annals*, ed. Axon, p. 256.

letter received this morning from your Aunt Anne, to make weight with this letter\mind you *burn it*/,which otherwise I fear won't be worth much. Dr Carpenter is dining out. Tottie ditto at the Shuttleworth's; Meta, Flossy and Annie at the Leislers. They were here, at least Agatha was last Thursday; the two Harrops, and the two Potters. The D Ds were asked but never answered till the eveng—& then could not come. It is curious how *all* intercourse has ceased between our two families; once so intimate!\I do believe it all dated from that *untrue* conversation at Miss Marslands[.]/There were some capital words on Thursday, which Annie, Meta and Tottie got up. They acted in the outer lobby, under the gas; and we stood on the stair-case,\in the inner hall[,]/and the folding doors were thrown open. The first word word was Author. Awe—a nun brought before the Inquisition. Tottie (nun) rushed in from the back stair-case door, was caught by Annie and the doors flew open, and displayed the three judges dressed in black with blk masks on (your 3 sisters.) Thor the Scandinavian god,—a piece of his life &c. Author a scene or tableau of Hogarth's Distressed Author,—Farewell & Breakfast were the two other words; but I won't go through them all. Mrs Davenport comes on the 14th. Baby has *had* a cold, Meta has a little but not enough to prevent her going to the lecture (Dr Carpenters). Papa is quite well again now; it was lumbago. The house the Austins have taken is in Chester Terrace (4 I *think*, near the gate nearest to Albany Street. Goodbye my darling[.] I have got a new silk gown, quaker-brown coloured,—Miss Daniels making it. If you want a new bonnet which I think you will, a white LINEN one, (like white *chip*) is both pretty and cheap. And have as little trimming put on as possible, but let that trimming be {cheap} *good*[.]

Your affect[ionate] Mother E C Gaskell

92 **93** 94

MARIANNE GASKELL

Monday.
[7 April 1851]

My dearest Polly,

I have no paper but this and too bad a cold to go out; so I shall write as far as it will go; and wait for the remainder. Pray *why* do you wish a Protectionist Ministry not to come in? Papa and I want terribly to know. Before you fully make up your mind, read a paper in the Quarterly on the subject of Free Trade, (written by Mr George Taylor) in (I think) the year 1839;[1] and then when you come home I will read with you Mr Cobden's speeches[.] But first I think we should read together Adam Smith on the Wealth of Nations. Not confining ourselves as we read to the limited meaning which he affixes to the word 'wealth'. Seriously, dear, you must not become a *partizan* in politics or in anything else,— you must have a 'reason for the faith that is in you',—and not in three weeks suppose you can know enough to form an opinion about measures of state. That is one reason why so many people dislike that women should meddle with politics; they say it is a subject requiring long patient study of many branches of science; and a logical training which few women have had,—that women are apt to take up a thing without being even able to state their reasons clearly, and yet on that insufficient knowledge they take a more violent and bigoted stand than thoughtful *men* dare to do. Have as many and as large and varied interests as you can; but do not again give a decided opinion on a subject on which you can at present know nothing. About yr bonnet get it *large*, and trimmed with (—*or*) white ⟨.⟩ ARE your shoulders lower? If not, and dancing or exercises will bring them down have another quarter & welcome. Papa will send you compasses by somebody and per-haps Shakspeare. Be sure you take care of MY *cameo* brooch. I find you have got it; now I only lent it you and I value it extremely, and would not have it lost on any account. We had some friends last Friday. Uncle Sam (who was only just arrived,) the Owens' professors, and appurtenances in the way of sisters & wives, Mrs Schunck and the two Miss Brookes, one of whom is to be Mrs Edward Schunck, Mr & Mrs Moule, Dr Hodgson &c. I had a dreadful cold, and could hardly speak; Indeed I am as hoarse as a raven still. Uncle Sam leaves us tomorrow. D. W. C. went to Hull this morning, and comes back on Friday, when your Aunt & Uncle Robert come to meet him, & stop all night. Cousin Anne Holland is come to live with Mrs Hodgetts: and I am going with Tottie to see her this afternoon, so I am writing as fast as I can to you my darling About [one word deleted] seeds I will see what I can do, but we are sowing very few annuals this year; striking

[1] This may refer to an anti-Free Trade article which appeared in Vol. 68 (June 1841), pp. 239–80.

plants in the frames, & relying on putting out the greenhouse things for a summer show. Annie Austin went to London last Saturday, but they had as yet no house. I had a long letter from Mrs Wedgwood—they are all going to Paris for Easter. Susanna Winkworth comes through London the first week in May back from Bonn.[1] Mrs Davenport comes to us on the 14 to stay till 16.[2] Mrs Davy & Mrs Fletcher very soon—goodbye darling

Yours very affec[tionate]ly
E C Gaskell

93 94 95

MARIANNE GASKELL

Plymouth Grove.
Thursday [17 April 1851]

My dearest Polly,

I was so busy with Mrs Davenport all Monday and Tuesday, and so very much tired yesterday that I could not write being quite worn out, as you will guess when I tell you the programme of our proceedings; in the first place Dr Carpenter was here; Tottie and I went down to the Station at $\frac{1}{2}$ past 12 on Monday, picked up Mrs Davenport, and Mr Crewe, (a clergyman on the estate and interested about schools,) I gave them a basket-full of lunch, & we joggled in a coach to Swinton; and a long time we were in getting there. It was *very* interesting. Mrs Davenport understood so much of what questions to ask &c. that she called out the best part both of teachers and scholars; she was so sweet in many ways that I am sure you would have been more charmed with her than ever[:] for instance, at 4 o'clock the children dispersed; and a band-master came to teach those who have any taste for music, so we went to hear the band, in a little small room, a great deal less than our schoolroom—20 boys, playing on trumpets &c every kind of brass wind instruments, a double-drum and *four* common drums. You may fancy the noise, as none played piano,—Mr Losh the Chaplain stopped 2 of the common drums on account of the noise, which was almost deafening; but Mrs D noticed that the two

[1] In 1851. See *Letters and Memorials*, ed. Winkworth, I, p. 289. Easter Day was on 20 April.

[2] In Letter 94 Mrs Gaskell writes of a visit starting on Monday; therefore, 14 *April.*

dumb drummers looked disappointed, so she said 'Oh do let us hear all the band.' so the 4 boys drummed away with all their hearts. We staid at Swinton till 5, stopped at the Peel Park, walked round it, made Mr Crewe too late for the train, so asked him to dinner; and Mr and Mrs Morell came to tea; Mr Morell is an inspector of schools, and Mrs Davenport and he had a great deal of talk about education &c; but we were all sadly tired, and not sorry to go to bed. The next morning Mrs Davenport and I set out to the Deaf & Dumb Asylum, and saw it—Tottie joined us there; and Mrs Mason's carriage came for us. I found in talking to one of the boys, aged about 16, that he was being brought up for a calico {printer}; or designer, but had never seen calico printing, so as we were going to see the Schwabe's print-works—and had a place in [the] carriage I offered to take him, and you can't think what a commotion of talking on the fingers there was directly among all the children. He was very soon ready, and we set off. We found Mrs Schwabe going off that eveng to London, as Mrs Cobden was very poorly. However we all went off to the works; and Tottie explained all to the boy; then we went & lunched at the Schwabes, and there was a great deal for the boy to see in that amazingly *smart* house; he is to write an account of his visit to Mrs D, & she is to send it to us. Then on our return Mrs D bought cricket bats & balls &c for the boys at Swinton, skipping-ropes for the girls—and soft balls for the infants. Home to dinner —In the evening Mr and Mrs Fairbairn, Mr & Mrs Shuttle-worth, & Mr Wright. and yesterday morning she went away promising Meta a whole quantity of plants, verbenas, heaths &c &c &c.—Last week your Uncle and Aunt Robert & Willie Carpenter, (Dr Carpenter's son, aged 10) came for Friday and Saturday. I asked Anne Holland to meet them. I am afraid she is very poorly still. And I do wish it was not so far off to Mrs Hodgetts. It is 5 miles there. Mrs Davenport asked us to Capes-thorne next week to meet Lord Ebrington, and Mr Monckton Milnes; but we seem to have too many engagements to be able to accept of it. Mrs Langshaw has written to say she will come for a day or two, on her way back from Knutsford, where she goes for a little Merriman's Christening. Mrs Procter has written to ask us if we would allow Agnes P to stay here a day or two on the way home from Lancaster, or wherever her Uncle lives,—so we cannot go to Capesthorne. Papa wants to know what was the object of the Hampstead Chapel Tea-party. Last night Tottie &

Papa went to the Shuttleworths to dinner, meeting Robert Greg, and rather a dull set; today Papa dines at Mr Fairbairn's, and afterwards goes with Tottie to the Schunck's. Tomorrow Mr Wicksteed preaches here for the\Sunday/schools. We almost think Flossy has got the hooping-cough; and don't regret if it be so at this time of the year. Meta cried sadly last Sunday because you did not write to her; suppose you write to her, instead of to me. I shall see the letters you know, & shall understand if you have not time to write both letters. Meta is improving so much in her music. We have heard from Annie that you are going there on Monday. The Wedgwoods are in Paris, or else you *ought* to call on them, being so near. *May* you have a cake, you great Baby? And if we send you a cake, you must have a box, & if you have a box, do you want anything besides compasses, & Shakespeares, & seeds. Send me word about the cake. We are going to Agnes Patterson's marriage on Tuesday next.[1] Think of her. The Amateur actors are going to act the new Play written by Sir Edward Lytton, in Devonshire House, (the D. of Devonshire's in Piccadilly) before the Queen for the 1st time.[2] Mrs Dickens is at Malvern, very poorly[.] Lady K S has been very poorly ever since she went to town or you would have seen her—but she is almost forbidden to stir, as she expects to be confined in the autumn. We shall expect many letters this Easter holidays. Can you tell us when the Midsummer holidays begin? We want to know about going from home.—Have you got your new bonnet? Ever dearest Polly your very affect[ionate] mother E. C. Gaskell.

94 **95** 96

MARIANNE GASKELL

[Late April 1851]

⟨. . .⟩ liberty; and Tottie and I staid in-doors by ourselves all day. Pretty much the same on Saturday I think. On Sunday Tottie went back with the Hodgetts' from chapel to spend the day with cousin Anne, and came home in the evening to supper. Monday I

---

[1] Easter Tuesday, 22 April 1851. *Letters and Memorials*, ed. Winkworth, I, pp. 278–9.

[2] *Not So Bad As We Seem* (published by Chapman and Hall, May 1850). The performance referred to took place on 14 May 1851.

began early in the morning to expect Mrs Langshaw, (who was coming from Knutsford, where she had been standing God-mother to a little Merriman;) but she had brought Emmy and Maggie & Arthur to Manchester to buy a present for their Aunt Fanny (who is to be married *early in May*) (*have you done the cushion? if so send it* CARRIAGE PAID.) They had bought a breakfast service for her; a very pretty one Mrs Langshaw said. Miss Yates gives her a dessert service. So Mrs Langshaw did not come until tea; and then seemed very tired. She had not brought any music with her; but we rummaged up the musical library: and made her sing out of that; and very good-natured she was, trying every one she thought she could manage, not minding her own stumbling so that she could give us pleasure. I had a great puzzle if I should go to Agnes Paterson's wedding on the Tuesday morng or not,—as I did not like leaving Emily Langshaw, who comes so seldom, and yet I knew the Patersons wished us very much to come; so we decided it in this way. E L. was to rest very late in bed, and as the breakfast was to be at $\frac{1}{2}$ past 8, we thought we should be back again before E L had done breakfasting with Tottie. Hearn, Maria & the two little ones, set out to call for Meta at Mrs S's, and to go on to Birch church to see the marriage, while Papa and I walked to the house. Agnes saw the little ones peeping through the fence and sent for them in, but they took fright and set off home, as soon as they saw the smart messenger, but it was very kind of her to think of them at such a time, was it not? Mr Edward Birch married them. All the Winkworths, & Mr W Shaen were there. Agnes is gone to Neuwied, crosses the Channel to-day [—] they are to live near Coventry. Flossy made her a scarlet kettle-holder, with A. H. S. worked on it in white floss silk; Meta a flower-stand, worked in white lilies, and set by Doveston in bird's eye maple. Emily W. is to be married in August; so you must set to work for her, for I am sure you would like to do her something. Katie went to London on her way to Crix. She will only be about 3 weeks away, and will return with Susanna. Then Selina goes to Crix & London—Everybody seems going up to see the Exhibi-tion. Mary Robberds, J. J. Taylers, Miss Boyce and those Taylors, &c &c &c &c. Emily Langshaw staid till Tuesday afternoon. I took her into town, and saw her off to Lancaster. Yesterday Selina & Hannah Tayler came to tea, & Tottie & Papa went to Dr Bell's to a very agreeable evening party. Your letter to Meta has come in, since I began this letter. One thing we want to know is *exactly* what you want in your box. *What* plays of Shakspere,—for it is of no use sending you the whole set of volumes. Papa says [it] is out of the question. Ogden shall come. So,—*Shakspere, Ogden, compasses &c, some seeds,*—What else, love, would you like? Answer this—Have you been to Windsor Castle? Eliza Paterson comes to spend the day with us today; she & Mr Satterfield & Miss\S/are going up to 4, Euston Square on the 29, and then I think to Switzerland for the summer. Marianne Rigby[1] has been down here and is now travelling with Mr & Mrs D D in Yorkshire,—the D Ds are said to be going to take Hornby Hall near Hornby Castle up in the valley of the Lune. There I think I have told you all the news I can think of. Let poor Flossy have the next letter—poor little woman! I intend to give you a famous stock of plain-work next year to school. Aunt Lizzie is going up to Uncle Sam's the 2nd week in May,—her children have all had the measles, and got well through them.   Ever your very affect[ionate]

E C Gaskell

95 96 *96a

MARIANNE GASKELL

Tuesday [?May 1851]

My dearest Polly,

Tottie has just left us; for London. She is coming to see you on Saturday\next/, and will report more of {you},\us/than I can tell in a letter. Your letter wanting a new gown came just before she left, so I have sent you my green merino one, which I have not worn since the beginning of winter, and which you may as well wear out. I have no time to spare Hearn for gown-making; it did very well while we were away and all the servants had comparatively little to do; but now I must have Miss Daniels for your gowns, and her charge is somewhere about 25s a dress. If you have any gowns made in London *have them well made*; I would rather put the expense into the make than the material; *form* is always higher than *colour* &c. I don't mean that I would ever have you get a *poor* silk instead of a good one; but I had rather you had a brown Holland, or a print gown made by a *good* dress maker, than a silk made by a clumsy, inelegant badly-fitting one. I don't

---

[1] Née Darbishire.

suppose the green merino will fit you particularly well though my
gowns do fit you; but for the small space of time remaining before
the warm weather comes it will do. I had a letter from Mrs
Isaac this week; she wants your address to go and see you. I will
enclose her letter. Aunt Lizzie & Uncle Charles are at Berners'
Hotel (wherever that is,) and then Aunt Lizzie goes to Uncle
Sam's. I fancy you will get yourself well laughed at amongst the
doctors, if you go about complaining of every little ache or pain;
as I told you before[,] Uncle Sam was very much amused at being
sent for to you; and 'wished he were half as well'. Mr and Mrs
Greaves are at our\old/lodgings in Panton Square. I *think* Papa
will fetch you, and take you to the Exhibition, so unless you wish
particularly to go before then, you need not. If you do, I will pay
for you. Meta is astonished at your indifference. I half hope Papa
will take her up for a week when he fetches you; *but we don't talk
much about it yet*; especially as we want to know *very* much if Mrs
Lalor's holidays will interfere with the\Papa's attending the/
British association at Ipswich the 1st of July. In short every
possible plan is in a whirl; and nothing is settled. Yes! one thing is.
Margaret is leaving this day month. She told me some days ago
she was obliged to leave, as her sister (the only one at home with a
widowed father, and 3 brothers) was going to be married. I am
sorry on some accounts; not upon others. I would rather part
with her than with Mary; Maria is going home for a fortnight
next week; and we are hoping we can do without fires before
then. Hearn and the two little ones are very full of a plan of
going to Lytham, as soon as ⟨. . .⟩

*

*96a 97 *97+

MARIANNE GASKELL

Thursday [?May 1851]

My dearest Polly,
    Nobody writes if I don't; so I shall try and send a line today,
though I am obliged to write lying down in {my}\the spare
room/dressing room. I am much better but have been very ill.
We want sadly to know when your holidays begin. Pray remind
Mrs Lalor of her promise to let us know as soon as they are fixed.
Papa's going to the Association at Ipswich &c—*so many* things

depend upon it, and at Mme de Wahl's they have been fixed this long time. You have *13 collars* down on your list. I can hardly fancy you want more as several were new; besides 10 pairs of sleeves, & materials for 3 more. I was a little bit sorry to hear you were wearing your *merino* in an *evening* that night when Tottie drank tea with you. Either you are getting into the dirty slovenly habit of not changing your gown in the day-time, or you are short of gowns to wear a *merino* to *tea*? Which is it, love? I hope you enjoyed yourself at the Austin's. Meta & I often thought of you on Saturday Evng. Uncle Sam is going to lodge out at Putney. I do hope you will be sufficiently advanced for Mr Bennett next half-year. We have never heard from Canobie yet, and are inclined to despair. Meta is planting out her greenhouse, and hot-bed plants. I tell Frank he must wait till I get out before I can let him do mine, for I dare not trust them to any one else. The two little ones are going with Hearn to lodge at Bowden in a farmhouse on Saturday. Florence is *very* delicate; so thin, and pale and weak; she wants to be nursed on the knee a great deal, and has no appetite; but the cough is nearly gone. You must bring home your green silk, because it matches Meta's; but you may leave your old merino, {and your black} if you like. Perhaps there is some servant, or Mrs Lalor may know of some poor person who would be glad of it. I think Papa enjoys the garden more than ever this year. He and Meta are constantly out of doors. Will you tell me if you want a low-bodied gown this next half-year. You will have your new silk, an embroidered brown Carmelite that Miss Daniels is making for you now, and your new muslin. Shall you want any more? The reason why I must ask all these questions is that we shan't be at home during the holidays, and I want to have all *ready* that you will require. I have seen no one all week of course, and had very few letters, so I have very little news. The Shuttleworths are gone up to the G. R. Porter's at Putney. Cousin Mary is very poorly indeed, I am afraid. This is a shabby note; it is only to show you you are not forgotten, darling, but I am so weak, I am tired out with writing it. *Do* find out about the holidays. We have so much to fix, & I am afraid of Papa's having to give up Ipswich unless we begin fixing in time.\if we know in time whenever the holidays begin we can arrange it./Dearest goodbye—   Your very affect[ionate] Mother

                                                    E C Gaskell

                                    *

*97+ **97a** *97b

MARIANNE GASKELL

Sunday afternoon
[June 1851][1]

My dearest Polly,

Hearn, Mary, Margaret, Meta, Flossy, & Baby are all at
Bowden: and Papa at chapel: He took Meta yesterday; the little
ones met him at the rail-road Station, and he went with them all
into the Park; a good long walk he says; and that Flossy was not
much tired with it; only a good deal frightened by the deer; in a
way which he does not think she would have been if she had been
strong. However, Hearn gives a very good report of her; appetite
& cough better &c. They stay there all this week and I do hope I
may get over to see them. Hitherto I have not been beyond the
garden except in Mrs Mason's carriage. I hope Miss Banks is
better. Susanna Winkworth is in Dundas Place,\for the Sunday/
and came to see me this morning. Why have we had no letter
from you this morning? We *always* expect one on Sundays. I
was half afraid yr bonnet would be too large for you; but Miss
Daniels said not. It was 22 shillings[.] What wd it have been in
London?

After the 20, Mr & Mrs Winkworth Emily, Alice, & Ste go up
to London and are joined by Selina from Crix. Miss Marslands
are gone for a week; only think of that! And Mrs Shuttleworth
means to call and see you, (kind creature! Give her a welcome;)
but when I don't know. Canobie seems all at an end. The house is
being repaired, and they have only 3 beds to offer us &c &c. I am
VERY sorry. I wanted to see Carlisle, & Scotland again, and I
dread being thrown upon Silverdale, which knocked me up so
thoroughly last year. There is no news here. Maria is come back.
Cousin Anne is I fear very poorly indeed. The garden is very
pretty; and every day makes it prettier; to say nothing of the
strawberry-blossom, Papa goes to dine at the Robert Worthington's on Wednesday. That is I think the only engagement in the
family. Ever your very affec[tionate]   E C Gaskell.

*   *

[1] See *Letters and Memorials*, ed. Winkworth, I, pp. 290–3.

*97c **98** 0

Mrs Booth

11 Panton Square,
Wednesday [9 July 1851]

My dear Mrs Booth,
I am very sorry that anything prevented your coming yester-
day, as I was at home all day, and should have been delighted to
see you. Now I am afraid I must not anticipate this pleasure as we
return home on Saturday next; to go north to a place called
Holborn Hill at the foot of Black Comb in Cumberland, next
Wednesday.[1] I must hope to see you in Manchester in the autumn.
Yours very truly
E. C. Gaskell

85 **99** 108a

Eliza Fox[2]

[?10 July ?1851][3]

My dearest Tottie,
It's *not* the Poet Laureate, but it *is* a cousin, not seen for years,
and who has been round the world since, who has volunteered to
come up 15 miles to see me and dine at the Wedgwoods at 6, so I
dine there and appear at your house (as soon as Charles Darwin is
off) to *tea*.
E. C. Gaskell.
Some Institution, name not known, lighted by gas, so I conclude its past 5, sitting all alone by myself with a lady who seems
to be treasurer and secretary, and I believe its Friday, but am so
'*dazed*' I don't exactly know.

[1] Cf. Letter 101.
[2] Original MS. not seen.
[3] Dating very uncertain. We connect it, perhaps arbitrarily, with Letter 100.

*97b **100** *100a

?MARIANNE GASKELL[1]

[13 July 1851]

⟨. . .⟩ people that I knew and many that I did not know. Mr and
Mrs Ruskin among the number. Wednesday I did not go to
Richmond, it was too bad a day for him to draw but I went with
Mrs Wedgwood and Miss Doyle to Bermondsey to see the Con-
vent of Sisters of Mercy.[2] Bermondsey is a very bad part of
London; and these Sisters have been established about 11 years,
and have done a good deal of good and established a great large
school. We went all over the Convent heard all their plans and
altogether I think I liked it even better than the Convent of the
Good Shepherd. I rested all evening. Tuesday[3] a long piece of
Richmond again. I think it is like me; I hope Papa will think so but
I am almost doubtful. In the afternoon I shopped and got presents
for all the home people and went to dine at Mrs Wedgwood to
keep Snow's birthday—Mr Darwin his two sisters all the children
Mr Furnival and Mr Clough, Lady Alderson and 2 of the girls
made a great large party and very pleasant it was. The Bunsens
had asked me to dine there but I had planned to go and breakfast
with them the next day. (Friday) which I accordingly did; and
very agreeable it was. Chevalier Bunsen gave me his book of
devotions with a long writing *in German character* at the beginning
to 'his well beloved friend' etc. Then I went to wish Mrs Chorley
goodbye, and she spoke much in praise of your kindness dear that
day when Miss Chorley was so ill[,] and both desired their love to
you. In the evening with Mrs Wedgwood. Yesterday Tottie and I
came home; we had an accident (of no consequence) which kept
us till very late. Frank was there waiting for us. The house looked
very nice; but ⟨. . .⟩

*

[1] Original MS. not seen. The source is dated '[Early summer 1851]', so we
associate this letter with Letters 98–101.
[2] Established under the encouragement of Pusey in the early 1840s.
[3] Thursday? Mrs Gaskell's portrait was painted by George Richmond. Hopkins,
Gaskell, p. 115 and opp. p. 161.

ANNE ROBSON

Plymouth Grove,
Monday. [1 September 1851]

My dearest Nancy,

Now I'll write off instanter, and answer yr letter which I was *so* glad to get this morning. We are in a commotion today because Wm is to marry Emily Winkworth to Wm Shaen tomorrow,[1] at Dean Row Chapel, and all the Shaens are afloat in Manchester to-day; Annie staying here, and the rest coming in & out; and we (Wm & I, not poor Meta, to her sad disappointment,) are going to Lea Hall (Mrs Hervey's) at 2 o'clock, to sleep there, & be in readiness for tomorrow morning. So the whole household is in a sort of unsettled state, which is not the best time to choose to write a letter quietly, only I *was* so glad to hear from you, that I want to write on the rebound. Always tell me of Lizzie & her affairs. I never hear of them but through you; and I always want to know. Also if *you* ever hear of Anne Holland? *I* never do since she left Manchester & went to Cheltenham, & I want to know very much. Your boys sound grand. I can't fancy Willie such a grown-up young man, nor the younger one at all. I wish I could come & see you for a day, & I shall make an effort when you're settled in your new house. I don't know it. I dare say Wm does. *Our* house is proving rather too expensive for us,—MA's schooling taken into account; we aren't going to furnish drawing room, & mean\to be/, and are very œconomical because it seems such an addition to children's health & happiness to have plenty of room, & above all a garden to play in. Well! now I shall tell you a bit about ourselves, trusting you can read my writing, though I am going as fast as I can move my pen. We went *about* June 30 to London, W. Meta & I, to our old Panton Sq lodgings. Marianne joined us the next Friday, looking very pale chilly & ill, and with no appetite; but in every other way as happy & improved as heart could desire. Of course we did the Exhibition. I went 3 times, & should never care to go again; but then I'm *not* scientific nor mechanical. Meta and Wm went often, but not enough they say. That's difference of opinion. We came home the Saturday week *after* going to London. On the Tuesday\July 14 I think/we set off

[1] 2 September 1851. *Letters and Memorials*, ed. Winkworth, I, p. 294.

for a place near Broughton in Furness, at the mouth of the
Duddon Sands—called Holborn Hill; we stayed at a clean nice
little inn, Hearn with us, & paid 5£ a week for all & everything;
had plenty to eat, & the house very comfortable, but it was an
ugly place; 2 miles along a dull road to the sea, & not near any
pretty walks; so at the end of 10 days we went to our old lodgings
in that nice farm house at Skelwith at the entrance to the Langdales (near Ambleside, &c) There we staid till the 16 Aug; when
we came home, & busy work Hearn & I had then to get MA
ready for school; to which place she went back on the 21st Hearn
taking her, to have a week's pleasure in London, which we thought
she deserved after her long faithful service. Then ever since we
came home we have had Winkworths & Shaens backwards &
forwards making preparations for this wedding. The young
couple will be *very* poor, and helping them to plan has been a
great interest; and I like their way of bravely facing poverty in
order to be together, instead of waiting till they can set off in style.
Now about the children. It is delightful to see what good it had
done MA, sending her to school; & is a proof of how evil works
out good. She is such a 'law unto herself' now, such a sense of
duty, and *obeys* her sense. For instance she invariably gave the
little ones 2 hours of patient steady teaching in the holidays. If
there was to be any long excursion for the day she got up earlier[,]
that was all; & *they* did too, influenced by her example. She also
fixed on 9 o'clock for her own bed-time, & kept to it through all
temptations. These are but small instances but you will understand their force. She grew strong, & fat, & ruddy in the holidays,
& I could not find out any reason for the paleness &c on first
coming home. She seemed well, had plenty and good food to eat;
plenty of rest & exercise, and was evidently very happy at school,
& with reason, for Meta (who staid one night with her while we
were in London, & was strongly prejudiced against the school
before going,) said every one was so kind, such good dinners, such
a pretty garden, & a bathroom to every bed-room, all which
things took my second little lady's fancy very much. I wish you
could hear MA sing. It is something *really* fine; only at present she
sings little but Italian & Latin Mass Music. It is so difficult to meet
with *good* English songs; and then they all say so difficult to pronounce our close sounds clearly & well. Now to turn to Meta,
who is a great darling in another way. MA looks at nothing {in}
\from/ an intellectual point of view; & will never care for reading,

—teaching music, & domestic activity, especially about children will be her forte. Meta is untidy, dreamy, and absent; but so brim-full of I don't know what to call it, for it is something deeper, & less showy than talent. Music she is getting so fond of, which we never expected; and I'll tell you a remark of hers the other day, whh will explain a little of what I mean. She had a piece by Mendelsohn to learn called The Rivulet. When she was playing it to me she said towards the end 'Now Mama I transpose this into the minor key, for I think the rivulet is wandering away and lost in the distance, & then you know brooks have such a sad wailing sound'. Now it's a great deal of trouble to transpose a piece, but she had done it perfectly & played it so. Then her drawings are equally thoughtful & good. She has no lessons, for Miss Fox said lessons from any drawing master *here* would spoil her, but she reads on the principles of composition &c, & does so well. She is *quite* able to appreciate any book I am reading. Ruskin's Seven Lamps of Architecture for the last instance. She talks very little except to people she knows well; is inclined to be *over*-critical & fastidious with everybody & everything, so that I have to clutch up her drawings before she burns them, & she *would* be *angry* if she could read this note, praising her. Then she loses time terribly,— and *wants* MA's sense of duty, for she gets so absorbed in her own thoughts &c that she forgets everything. Florence has no talents under the sun; and is very nervous, & anxious; she will require so much strength to hold her up through life; everything is a terror to her; but Marianne at any rate is aware of this, and is a capital confidante for all Florence's anxieties; which are often on *other* people's behalf, not her own. Julia is witty, & wild, & clever and droll[,] the pet of the house; and I often admire Florence's utter absence of jealousy, & pride in Julia's doings & sayings. These are my 4 children; for you must go on knowing them as they are, not their mere outsides, which are all you can see in pops. I wish we lived in the same town. Now I must go—My love to your husband & kisses to your bairns

Yours very affectionately
Elizabeth C. Gaskell.

As if I had not been asked for my autograph this many a time, & I generally write it in this way. I *do*, really,

[Ornate signature]

They think it *so* grand.

*

*101a **102** *102a

MARIANNE GASKELL

Friday [September 1851]

My dearest Polly,

This has been such a busy week; I wrote last on Thursday I think. Well! Maria and Hearn were both taken ill about then, and to add to the complication, Mr Carlyle offered to come to us for a night or two on his way from Scotland,[1] and Helen & Emily Tagart wrote to know if I could receive them a week sooner than I had asked them for, making it altogether a regular dilemma. Then Frank came to ask if he might go to Southport by some cheap train, on Monday to stay the week. Altogether you can fancy, but I can't describe, the household commotion. Eliza Thornborrow came on Monday; Hearn grew worse, and we had Mr Mellor to her, and she is only *just* coming round into strength; Maria is now quite well again, & Frank is come back from Southport today, and the Tagarts are staying at the Darbishires till Monday. Mr Carlyle came on {Wednes} Tuesday and Mrs Carlyle came to breakfast on Wednesday; and they both left about 12. Papa dined at Mr Shuttleworth's on Tuesday; and Annis Smith is coming today. So you may pick out of this confusion what has been done every day if you can. I know I have been pretty well knocked up by it; for by way of making the nights as busy as the days, poor little Flossy has taken to have terrible pains in the night, and I have had to be up with her a great deal, now however I have got the smaller bed out of your room, moved to ours and she sleeps in it, close by me; so that I can soothe & comfort her without getting out of bed. And who do you think is going to be married? Why our cook Mary. And her lover is coming on a visit today. He is a widower, a neighbour of hers in the country; pretty well off, and very suitable in age &c— so I must look out for a cook, and meanwhile we are dining early ($\frac{1}{2}$ past 12) today, altogether, so as to make less work while the gentleman is here. You have left your 'Amor del mio penar' behind you, do you want it? I am glad you have been to the Opera,—and glad you heard Soutay. I fancy Cruvelli is not *by far*

[1] See Waller, 'Letters Addressed to Mrs Gaskell', pp. 12–13, for possibly related letters by Jane Carlyle.

so good a singer, though I don't wonder at your crying over Fidelio. Mary Ewart says you can't POSSIBLY have a good singing lesson in the evening, and so does Selina. I see they think Pergetti is not a very scrupulous master, if he is going to give you lessons then,[1] as they say you can't profit as you should by them. I am sorry for it, but you must try and do your best. Papa won't hear Annie Shaen sing, he says it is so incorrect & slovenly it gives no pleasure; so do take pains to be *very* correct, and careful. I hope you *never* sing any of your old badly-learnt songs, such as Masaniello,—or those. You may come to them again, if you only get out of the habit of your present way of singing them. The little ones are all agog to see the Queen[.] She comes somewhere about the 10th of Octr,[2] but I don't know where I must arrange for them to go. Your jackets are of course much thrown back by Hearn's illness. We are going to drink tea with Susanna tomorrow evng, which will be quite a new thing I think. Selina goes back to Alderley on Wednesday. Owing to Hearn & Maria's illness I put off the Sunday school girls from last Sunday to this. Mary's 'husband' as the children will call him is arrived, & meets with Flossy & Baby's approbation. Papa is to marry her,\from here of course/& there is some talk of Flossy & Baby being bridesmaids!!! Presents too are a great subject of conversation. Emily & Helen Tagart come on Monday. Ever darling thy affectionate mother E C Gaskell.

*

*102a **103** 104

MARIANNE GASKELL

Uncle Holland's, Thursday
[23 October 1851]

My dearest Marianne,
    You must not expect a very long letter for I have a great deal to do and arrange. I am going to Capesthorne for a couple of days, and meanwhile I have to meet Mrs Green, and if she does not come here I must go there, & I have to pack up, & borrow a night

---

[1] In the new school session? Cf. Letter 90 above.
[2] She visited Manchester on 10 and 11 October 1851. *Annals*, ed. Axon, pp. 258–9.

gown, and night caps that will fit me, for I only came for a week, and do the same kind office for Meta who is to stay here till Saturday when I return from Capesthorne, and then we two stay on here till Tuesday, (in order to let Lucy stay at Sandlebridge till then,) and then we go for a week to Mrs Green's, returning home on Novr 4th, so your two next letters if written to us, must be directed\the first/one to Uncle Hollands, the second to Mr Green's. Meanwhile I hear that a new housemaid whom I have engaged is coming (*from Stamford in Lincolnshire*) the day after tomorrow, and I must write untold of directions home about things, as the servants don't expect her, and mayn't give her a welcome. It is quite possible that Miss Bremer may be at Capesthorne when I get there today; Mrs Davenport told me she would be; but I have had a letter from Miss Bremer this morng in which she says nothing about it,[1] so I don't know whether she will. Cousin Susan goes with me to call there. That's all about our plans, which I dare say told in this hurry sound very confused, but they are not so in reality my dear. I am going to take May's class at the Sunday school, & read to Uncle Hollands. Meta is making out a list of roses which we should so like to have for the greenhouse. They are getting some here, and ours would come to 12s. 3d, and we are wondering what the carriage would be from Berkhampstead wherever that is. Meta is making such beautiful plaits to my hair to compensate I suppose for my not having a night gown. I have many letters to write. We do so want to know *what* are the names of the pieces you are learning with Mr Bennett—& what songs with Pergetti, & will send you back yr next letter *unpaid* if you don't tell us. I shall leave this letter for Meta to tell you about the concert last night. *What sort of frills do you want to your jacket.* We could do them quite well, if you will tell us *what kind*, exactly

E. C. Gaskell

[1] Waller ('Letters Addressed to Mrs Gaskell', pp. 66–7) quotes one postmarked 19 October 1851.

MARIANNE GASKELL

Heathfield. Wednesday
[29 October 1851]

My dearest Polly,

Here we came yesterday, for a week *exactly*; and here we are
{going t} sitting in the study, just 12 o'clock[,] Emily Annie &
Ellen just come in from lessons; Mrs Green and I working till just
this minute. I wrote last on Thursday I think; and in the afternoon
{Uncle Holland} Cousin Susan & I went to Mrs Davenport's; she
to call, I to stay till Saty. There were many people staying in the
house. Mrs Stanley the Bishop's widow was perhaps the most
agreeable; good simple and earnest; I liked her very much. The
others were Miss Shuttleworth (Mrs Davenport's Aunt) Bishop
Spencer[,] Mr Weigall, Mr John Norris, Lady Langdale, and her
only daughter Miss Bickersteth, a girl about Meta's age, but
much larger in person, Mr & Miss Crackenthorpe, an old lady &
gentleman from somewhere near Penrith; *he* is guardian to young
Mr Davenport. They were a very nice pair; he so attentive to his
sister; she so kind to every body, and so pleasant. They both knew
the Davy's—indeed so did Lady Langdale, who was very much
taken with DR Davy. She is going to live near Bowness, so I think
she will be partly undeceived, as to some of the good temper she is
attributing to him—a very intelligent well-informed man there is
no doubt he is. We were, as you see[,] a very large party; and yet
the life was very independent, and everybody might be as much
alone as they liked. Breakfast at 9, lunch at one, dinner at $\frac{1}{2}$ past 6,
bed at ten. I went a long drive with Mrs Davenport one day. You
know Miss Bremer was expected at Capesthorne, but she has put
it off twice, so I think it will be very doubtful if she will come at
all. Mrs D. asked Meta & me to go again this week, when Sir
David Brewster &c are to be there; but we were previously
engaged to the Green's. Uncle Holland & Meta fetched me back
on Saturday. Mrs Green, John Philip [Green] and Mr Steinthal
came to tea in the evening. I was so glad of your letter my darling
on Sunday. Do you think Pergetti is thinking that you are
practising enough for him? or *carefully* enough. It seems so
strange his only having given you one song since you went back,
—as if you had not prepared *up* to his expectation, which I hope

you *have*, my dear love, by being very careful conscientious working up in your practising for him. What is the name of the song Miss Banks lent you,—tell me, dear[,] when you write. We go on copying music for you, when we can pick up anything we like. And tell me WHAT SORT OF FRILLS you want for your jacket; I asked you once before; and we might as well set to to do it; if you have not time. Well! to return to Sunday, only *don't forget to answer me these questions.* Mr Steinthal preached on Sunday morning and as we were coming home Mr Green proposed that I should join Emily & Annie, who were going with him to preach (not all three, *to preach*) at Styall, (Mr Colston's congregation—) so I came home here, dined here, and at one we set off in a fly through Mobberley, & a variety of lanes, jolting and jogging for 2 hours when we came to Styall, a pretty place. After service we went home with Mr Robert Greg to Norcliffe, walked about the grounds there, which are beautiful. Mrs Robert Greg was too ill to come in but Caroline & Sophy were there, and very pleasant indeed. We came home at ½ past six, and it *was* so dark along the lanes. However by a little past 8, I was safely lodged at Uncle Holland's, when I found Mr & Mrs Charles\Aikin/Holland, Mr & Mrs John Long there. I was *very* tired, and went to bed before long. Monday I went to pay calls &c. & in the evening Susan Deane & Emmy & Maggie came. Yesterday afternoon we came here. *Next Sunday* we shall be here. I sent you Papa's note,—burn it, but I fancy you will like to hear what we are doing in Manchester. Ever darling your very affectionate Mother E. C. Gaskell.

_o **105** _o

MARIA JAMES

Knutsford. Oct. 29. [1851]

My dear Mrs James,

I must write, and congratulate you firstly and principally on the birth of another little {sister}\girl/, which Mrs Davenport told me of; and which I fancy must be now about three weeks old, is it not? I am so glad to hear that you went on all properly and according to rule. How does the elder little girl take to her new sister? Very much I should think to judge from my own children; who have always been delighted at the coming of every fresh baby; and is it not pretty to see the patronizing ways the little things assume towards the new-comer? Then again Mr Gaskell and I want to congratulate you and Mr James on his appointment as Master in Chancery; though what that mysterious office may be, and what the duties he will have to fulfil\are/I know about as much of as I know of the Grand Llama; but every body speaks of the appointment as a testimony to Mr James character and talents; and as such I know you will have a glad heart about it; and I hope it may give him a little more leisure at home, instead of the busy life which you described him as leading. Last week I spent two days with Mrs Davenport at Capesthorne, and there heard from Lady Langdale that it was Mr William James who was appointed. It was an unexpected pleasure my going to Capesthorne. I left home to stay with a blind uncle, whose daughter was gone away for a little relaxation; and I was surprized by an invitation from Mrs Davenport, who, I believed was in London; I found my uncle could manage without me, with the assistance of friends for two nights, so off I went. Miss Bremer was to have been at Capesthorne at the same time, but, as she intended to take that visit 'on her journey from London to Harrow' she discovered that it would be rather out of her way. She is a quaint droll little lady of 60—(I am guessing her age,) very plain, and rather untidy; but very kind and genial in her manners. She had annoyed Mrs Davenport and Mrs Stanley a little by her habit of—how shall I express it—*spitting* right and left, in the Exhibition, and not entirely sparing private houses.

What novel did you choose (in default of one from me,) for your confinement reading. I am afraid you did not get hold of the Young Protector;[1] it is too old a book to be met with easily. I see that Mr Thackeray is bringing out a three-volume novel;[2] and our nice little friend Miss Mulock is advertizing another.[3] I wish she had some other means of support besides writing; I think it bad in it's effect upon her writing, which must be pumped up instead of bubbling out; and very bad for her health, poor girl. I heard of your kind way of occasionally taking her a drive, and I

[1] The Young Protector, or Santo Sebastiano. See 'Morton Hall' (Works, ed. Ward, II, p. 478).

[2] This presumably refers to Henry Esmond, which appeared in 1852.

[3] Probably The Head of the Family.

silently thanked you for it. But I think that Miss Brontë had hold of the true idea, when she said to me last summer, 'If I had to earn my living, I would go out as a governess again, much as I dislike the life; but I think one should only write out of the fulness of one's heart, spontaneously.' How is your nurse going on? I hope she is still with you, and as satisfactory and good as she was, when you told me about her. Do you know Mrs Stanley? I suppose you do; I never saw her before the other day at Capesthorne, and I liked her very much indeed. It is pleasant to like the 'belongings' of such a man as Bishop Stanley. But most of all I admire Mrs Davenport more the more I see of her. She is such a queenly woman, is not she; and so good and beautiful to look at too; though it was not that quality which I was referring to as the ground of my admiration. I hope the wintry weather is bringing back the wanderers, and that you are getting surrounded with sisters. Goodbye my dear Mrs James, ever believe me

Yours most truly
E. C. Gaskell

60 106 0

ANNE SHAEN[1]

[?Early November 1851]

I am so much better for Knutsford—partly air, partly quiet and partly being by myself a good piece of every day which is I am sure so essential to my health that I am going to persevere and enforce it here. I don't mean to have odd poppers-in, in an evening unless I have visitors in the house. I mean to be out all calling time with the children, and I mean to get all my society duties done by great large parties where many people always entertain each other. Then I am going to confine my letter writing to Thursdays, when I always write to MA in singing lesson time— no—now he's coming on Monday—and scrabble in as many letters as I can after that one is done. So don't you approve of these rules for my life;—I don't mean with regard to writing anything like a book, but solely for my own health and mind.

[1] From a printed source.

Strange is it not that people's lives apparently suit them so little. Here is a note from Miss Brontë oppressed by the monotony and solitude of her life.[1] She has seen *no one* but her Father since 3rd of July last. Here is Mary Holland and Louy at Knutsford absolutely *ill* for want of being more by themselves—each wishing that she could be alone in the evenings. Well!—the world's a puzzle. ⟨...⟩

She—Susanna—has sent over to-day to ask if she may sit with me, but I, possessed with my love of solitude—or rather my sense of its *necessity*, savagely declined.

₁₀₄ **107** ₁₀₉

MARIANNE GASKELL

[Early November 1851]
Sunday afternoon.

Yes my dearest Polly, I have been a lazy mother about writing to you—the beginning of the week I expected *your* letter, and then came a great deal else to do; though what I am sure I don't remember. And now Mr Ed. Holland (of Dumbleton) and Sophy (Harriet you know,) are coming to us on {Frida} Tuesday to stay till Wednesday on their way from Scotland; so there is what we are likely to do on Tuesday & Wednesday. Mr Gunton did not come this last week to give Meta her music lesson, he had so bad a cold. She has been very gay the beginning of this week. She & I went with the Shuttleworths (who gave us our tickets,) on Monday to the concert—a bad one,—a bad selection, & Miss Birch, & Mr Phillips for singers who sing as if they had never felt anything in their lives. (I am so glad Miss Banks is going to be so kind as to ask Signor Pergetti for *better* music for you; more thoroughly good and classical.) Then on Tuesday Papa Meta Florence & I went to a child's dance at the Leislers. A great many Papas & Mamas were there & a very pretty thing it was[.] Maggie was *so* attentive to every one, never dancing herself in order that she might attend to every one else—Wednesday Meta went through

---

[1] Not in *The Brontës*, ed. Wise and Symington, but Mrs Gaskell told Catherine Winkworth of it on 7 November 1851. *Letters and Memorials*, ed. Winkworth, I, p. 299.

the snow to dine with Miss Marslands, who had Louy Bill (do you remember her?[)] staying with them. And last night she & Florence went with the Darbishires to the Schwabe's, so I think they have been pretty gay. Have you heard that as soon as there is a thaw we are to have a pig stye built near the frames; and *I* am intending to have a cow,—James our new man, understands both cows & pigs, and he & I plan it together, and plan to take the field joining our garden for the cow, and the Bellhouses will sell us their cow things, i.e. milking stool, cans &c &c &c. What say you to that? And then I have got 10 new roses for my greenhouse, from Lanes in Hertfordshire a famous place for roses, so we intend to excel in cream & roses[.] Thank you dear for your pleasant & interesting acct of your visit to Dr Carpenter's. I like him for asking Tottie and I wish you had told us something more about her, it is so long since she has written. Mrs Schwabe & Harriet have been here; how *good* she is! She had been seeing '*sorrowful*' people ever since 10 o'clock, & it was then past 4—Mrs Fletcher asks us to go to Lancrigg sometime before next May.[1] I have written to Mrs Austin to ask Annie here soon after Xmas, during your holidays; and I want the Deans to come too, poor girls—Xmas is such a sad anniversary for them. I am sadly afraid of Florence finding that I have forgotten this letter of hers (written *last* Sunday, & never sent) and Baby *wails* sadly over your never answering her pencil letter, the 'very *very* first I ever wrote'—Meta must have told you nearly all the news I think in this long letter of hers. We want sadly to know when you are coming down,—and please to enquire out at *your* end for some one who is coming about that time with whom you can travel. I hope you approve of the cow-place. I have engaged a new cook in Mary's place, Isabella Postle-thwaite of Legberthwaite near Keswick. She is to come some time before Mary leaves to learn our ways—Do make S. Pergetti give you GOOD music, not trumpery pièces de Societè; I suppose you are not 'up' to Mozart yet. Ask however. Have you ever written to Mrs Isaa*c*—now do*n't* go & spell it Isaa*c*s. Goodbye my darling

Yours very affec[tionate]ly
E C Gaskell

[1] She visited Mrs Gaskell about this time. See *Autobiography of Mrs Fletcher*, 2nd ed., Edinburgh 1875, p. 292.

82 **108** 0

?LOUISA BELL

Tuesday night
[?Early November 1851][1]

My dear Miss Bell,

I only learn tonight that Edward and Sophy Holland go on tomorrow to Knutsford by the one o'clock train; which will, I am sorry to say, prevent several of our plans being executed, amongst others that of lunching with you; which we all regret. Mr & Miss Holland *intend* to call if they can manage to accomplis⟨h⟩ it in the middle of a sight seei⟨ng⟩ morning; but pray do not stay in for them, if you were plann⟨ing⟩ to go out. With very kind regar⟨ds⟩ to your sisters, I am, dear Miss Bell

Yours very truly
E C. Gaskell

99 **108a** 110

?ELIZA FOX[2]

Monday [?17 November 1851]

I ought not to write to you, wherefore I do, you naughty, lazy abominable woman! you bid *me* write directly and I do, as directly as man can do and then please, *when* do you answer me? I am so glad you are returned to a Christian country,—I wish Sir John Franklin[3] were—your whereabouts of late days have been so much unknown to me as his. *Dear* and I have such a deal to say! Do you know I think we're going to keep a cow, and I'm sure we're going to keep a pig, because our pig stye is building and I find my proper vocation is farming; and Frank is gone poor fellow! and so going to live at Southport and we've got a new man James by name; and I've got a new cook instead of Mary,

[1] Possibly associated with Letter 107.
[2] Original MS. not seen.
[3] Sir John Franklin (1786–1847), Arctic explorer, disappeared whilst searching for the North West Passage. The search for him and his crew continued at various times until 1859 when Captain McClintock found remains and records, showing that Franklin himself had died on 11 June 1847.

who is to be married 'by Master' in February and said new cook
is coming in January, and her name is Isabella Postlethwaite of
Legberthwaite in Tilburthwaite, you may guess her habitat from
that; and we have got a Bessy instead of Maria, and a Margaret
instead of Margaret, all changes against my will at the time, but
improvements I think. What do you think of Kossuth[;] is he not
a WONDERFUL man for cleverness. His speech[1] was real eloquence,
I never heard anyone speak before that I could analyze as it went
along, and *think* what caused the effect but when he spoke I could
only feel;—and yet I am not quite *sure* about him, that's to
say I am *quite* sure about his end being a noble one, but I think
it has so possessed him that I am not quite *out and out* sure that
he would stick at *any* means, it's not for me to be poking into
and judging him.⟨...⟩ I wish you could see Lucy Holland's
water colour drawings; I wonder if you would think them *good*.
They are *very* pretty at any rate and Meta has been copying
some.⟨...⟩ And oh! Fanny and I have had a split about Libbie
Marsh, which that wretched man at Liverpool was going on republishing ad infinitum and I stepped in and objected as gently
as I cd, and I am afraid Fanny is hurt. I am *very* sorry; but I
showed my letter to Wm, and he says it was quite a gentle
proper letter. Do *you* hear any of her plans from any one? Susanna
W. keeps Wm busy at work correcting her proofs, for my dear!
Niebuhr is on the point of appearing before the public! and poor
Mary Barton gets more snubbed than ever as a 'light and transitory'
work. I have offered myself to the 'Critic' as a writer. I did it in a
state of rage at that Marples man at Liverpool, and Chapman[;]
and I swore I would penny-a-line and have nothing to do with
publishers never no more; so my critics generously offered me 7s.
a column. (I never saw the paper but I heard it was a respectable
dullard) and I counted up and think its about 3d a line, so I think I
shall do well,—Wm is very mad about it, and calls me names
which are not pretty for a husband to call a wife 'great goose' etc.
⟨...⟩ Tell me some literary gossip, for though I've turned
farmer, I've a little sympathy yet left for 'book sellers hacks'.
⟨...⟩ How are the Dickens? wretch that he is to go and write MY
story of the lady haunted by the face;[2] I shall have nothing to talk
about now at dull parties.⟨...⟩ Our cow is such a pet. Half

[1] He spoke in Manchester on Tuesday, 11 November 1851. *Annals*, ed. Axon,
p. 259.
[2] See A. J. C. Hare, *The Story of My Life*, 1896–1900, III, pp. 117–23.

Alderney, quarter Ayrshire quarter Holderness.[1]⟨. . .⟩ We've got
a mangle and we're washing at home, and we do it so beautifully.

*

107 **109** 114

MARIANNE GASKELL

Thursday [Late 1851]

Thank you, dearest Polly for sending on Helena's letter; it is a
very nice kind and affec[tionate] one: but do you know, dear, we
think you must decline it; for many reasons,—one is that we have
already promised *probable* visits to the Deanes, & Greens at Knutsford, and to the Winkworths at Alderley, & to Aunt Anne, *if
possible*; but she came in last with her invitation so I told her I
didn't know if we could spare you even for another couple of
days; and there are Annie, Emmy & Maggie Deane coming here;
and Miss Banks too, whom we shall be most happy to see, whenever it suits her, as I dare say we can arrange for the Deanes to
come at the other piece of time. I have your *one* reason love, but
there are many why we do not wish you to go to grown-up
dances &c this winter holidays,—I have hardly time left to speak
about your staying till the 23; but unless there is some *very* strong
reason we had better keep to the plan already arranged with Mrs
Wildes, & Annie Austin, viz that you & A. A. are to join Mr
Wildes & Lily on the Saturday. Papa is even going to ask Mr D
Darbishire if he is not coming down on the Friday;—I suppose
you want to see as much as you can of Miss Gully, and I don't
wonder at it, but remember how the little ones\& big ones too/
have been looking for you. Still, if you wish it VERY much,
darling let me know, & I will try & manage it,—but Mrs Souchay
& Mrs Benecke {know} think you *are*\NOT/coming with Adel-
heid,—(you would have liked nursing her baby should not you?)
If you could plan beds—*Annie Austin being here*\in the grey room/,
could you ask Miss Gully to join Miss Banks at Birmingham, and
come & see you during the holidays. The sleeping-room is *rather*
the puzzle in this plan; but think about it, if you like, dear. Baby
is very poorly, she ate a too hearty dinner yesterday, romped
violently in the drawing-room too soon after,—grew very tired

---

[1] This contradicts what Mrs Gaskell wrote above. Was the letter written at
different dates, or does the source represent fragments of more than one letter?

& hot & complained of headache, had a very restless night, and all day long has dozed either in Hearn's arms, or mine, whh is the reason why I have driven my letter so late. Papa has her her [*sic*] now. We *think* she is better,—and *always* remember no news is good news. Travers Madge is coming to tea at 5. We dined out Monday & Tuesday\& very dull it was/. The pig stye is finished— no time for more, love. Write a *nice long* letter to Helena on Saturday, even if we come short. If we can manage all our people at Xmas, I will ask her to come for a night or two.

> Ever your very affect[ionate] Mother
> E. C. Gaskell

108a 110 112

ELIZA FOX[1]

Dec[ember]: 1851

My dearest Tottie,

I've a deal to say more than mortal can get through in the $\frac{1}{4}$ of an hour I have before me, and now it's Sunday and I've the comfort of sitting down to write to you in a new gown, and blue ribbons all spick and span for Xmas—and cheap in the bargain, 'Elegant economy' as *we* say in Cranford—There now I dare say you think I've gone crazy but I'm not; but I've written a couple of tales about Cranford in Household Words, so you must allow me to quote from myself.⟨. . .⟩

₀ 111 ₀

EMILY ?TAGART

[? & 30 December 1851]

My dearest Emily,

There! now you know you have spoilt my dreams! I dream and dream again of Robert Darbishire as a Bloomer a daughter of mine with a 'pig peard under her muffler', & striding along in his pettiloons; and you can't think what an uncomfortable dream it is. Seriously—and very seriously I like him just in the venerating way you do.—I don't know any other young man at all like him; and I am consequently—

---

[1] Original MS. not seen.

Decr. 30——This beginning was written long [before] Marianne came home,—and I have forgotten my 'consequently' and all about it. And I have had a number of little notes given me for Helen, of which I can only collect one at present to send her, but Julia wrote one, which she and I together have lost, and as it was her first production in the writing way, her passionate grief is great, and we *must* find it. Marianne and Meta went to join A Austin yesterday at Alderley, and thence on to Knutsford today for a week; and the house sounds so quiet without them. Next week they return with Emily & Maggie Deane & Annie Austin; so then I suspect we shall have noise enough; more especially as we've hired a grand piano for the holidays, & got it in the dining-drawing room; and put the old one in the unfurnished drawing room. Who do you think we have staying with us? Mrs Preston from Skelwith; who has never been in a town larger than Kendal before. Kendal reminds me of Lancaster; and Helen's ungenerous suggestion, (knowing my attachment to that dear old town,) that my informant about the splendour of Mr Dickens' house came from Lancaster. Tell Helen my informant, who lives in *London* I beg to say, and in a capital circle in London too, writes me word that the Dickens have bought a dinner-service of *gold* plate. My informant dined with the Dickens the very day when he wrote to me, and told me this; so after *that*, let Helen doubt me as she will, and accuse my informant of being 'out of the world' and 'living at Lancaster' if she dares. My dear old Lancaster! I was *really* and *gravely* sorry for what I said in a letter to you about two months ago about Harriet Cobb. I might have thought how unhappy she must have been; and I was wrong to say what I did about her. You see I was very 'fidgetty' about that call! Miss Lloyd told me to do it, and I dare not disobey her if she told me to eat my grand-father, so I went, fearfully and trembling, having lectured William into the propriety of accompanying me. When we came to the door my heart misgave me, and I was very much inclined to make it a run-away ring; but I did not; still I was so uncomfortable that I dare say I was cross, and repelling, as people often tell me I am, where I know in my heart that I have been feeling frightened & miserable. But Robert *is* a noble person; and well worth Harriet's deep trembling anxiety; & I *will* get to know her for his sake. We are in a *very* uncomfortable state with the D Ds, and shall be all our lives long I suspect; we speak, but ice would be warmer than our manners; & yet I don't think it can ever get right and it would have been much *easier* to go on the dead-cut principle; if not quite so Christian,—& yet I am sure we have neither of us *any* smallest morsel of angry feeling, only a conviction that she is not to be trusted\& that from her nature, not her inclination/, which of itself puts a wet blanket on all freedom of intercourse. I wonder if we shall see MA Rigby. Emily Shaen sent such a *pretty* account of her delight in her baby, it made my heart quite warm to her. The gaiety on foot, which is not very much, is a party at the Sydney Potters on the 7th, which clashes with a party at the Reiss's the same night; and a party at the Schwabes\Liedertafel to sing/on Friday, which clashes with another to which we were previously engaged, which vexes me so much that I'm going to stop at home altogether. And we ourselves are going to do something wonderful on the 14th, though what we do not yet know. And today I'm going to take Mrs Preston to the Exhibition of pictures, (which is come down to twopence a head, so it won't ruin me,) and to see the Exchange; and to chaperone Katie Winkworth to the Concert tonight. I know I meant to write you a merry letter; but somehow it has turned itself round into a sort of confession of wickedness, which perhaps may be quite as amusing. Meta is very likely returning with MA— not to school; but to pay a visit at the Austins; and as Annie will {be at}\have to attend/her lessons I rather want to plan for Meta to have some drawing-lessons—(practising\for a music master/ might annoy the Austins, or else I would choose that,) and am in a puzzle how to manage;—she is taking a drawing fit just now. I'm going to write to Helen very soon; but I'm over-powered by my letters—that I owe I mean;—

Yours very affec[tionatel]y

E C Gaskell.

110 **112** 124

ELIZA FOX[1]

[?Early January 1852]

My dearest Tottie,

Your nice long comfortable letter deserves a longer answer than its likely to get. Annie Austin Emmy and Maggie Deanes in the

---

[1] Original MS. not seen.

house &c. R. E. and M. D. go on Monday. Then comes another friend, Mary Harvey, a distant cousin of the girls on the Gaskell side, and altogether we are in a whirl rather.⟨. . .⟩ This note is not a *letter* as you will perceive, only a small sort of how d'ye do— Mr Martineau called here on Wednesday. I had said I was engaged, having to write upon the very last day for the S. S. Magazine;[1] but Margaret with infinite discretion, and not knowing a bit *who* Mr M. was told me she thought it was a gentleman I shd like to see. Mary is to be married and we shall be nearly forty to break-fast I believe.⟨. . .⟩

0 **113** 122

GRACE SCHWABE

Capesthorne near
Congleton
Sunday [February 1852]

My dear Mrs Schwabe,
    Mrs Davenport is to be married on the 11th[2] and goes to Paris for three weeks; (thence to Amboise to see Abdel Kadr)[.] I have strengthened her in her wish to make M. Argents acquaintance, and see all that he has done for the poor English girls; but she has given her paper away & I can not remember *where* he lives. Would you send me another\printed/paper[,] my dear Mrs Schwabe, telling about him? if you *can* by return of post to me *here*, if before the 10th to Mrs Davenport, Capesthorne {Cheshire}, near Congleton. It is dark & I write to catch the post. Believe me
                            Yours affectionately
                                    E C Gaskell

You know that Sir Geo Grey has privately desired a memorial respecting Mr Wright to be sent to Government. *Our* Mrs Fletcher named the whole affair to Lady Grey, & sent me part of Sir George's letter, desiring that such a step might be taken. Mr Bagshawe is doing what he can—

[1] 'Bessy's Troubles at Home', *Sunday School Penny Magazine*, January 1852.
[2] She married Lord Hatherton on 11 February 1852.

109 **114** *114a

M<small>ARIANNE</small> G<small>ASKELL</small>

Bollington
Macclesfield
Saty [?*c*. February ?1852][1]

My dearest Polly,

I am sure you deserve a letter for your goodness in writing to me; and I think you will like to hear that Meta and Florence have arrived here quite safely, though I have hardly seen them; for I went with Mrs Greg and all the children, and a pony to meet them; and Meta mounted the pony, and rode home, and Florence disappeared among the group of children there were; and when Mrs Greg and I had come home, every one had disappeared on another long walk. Mrs Davenport sent me here about twelve o'clock today; Miss Watson came with me as far as Macclesfield; Mr Greg looks much worse than when I saw him last. They are *talking* of emigrating to New Zealand; that is to say Mr Greg is most anxious to do so; Mrs Greg not quite so willing; but they are reading and receiving letters about it daily. Florence seems as happy as happy can be with Alice[.] I think they are come in, & I must go & see them; Sunday afternoon.—I heard yesterday as soon as they came in that you had gone to Bowden, dearest Polly; I wish I had known before, for I had meant this note to do for Papa as well as you; and it was then just post-time, and too late to write another to him, and no post goes today to Macclesfield, so I can not send this until tomorrow. However I think Papa will know that they went quite safely and arrived here very well. Miss Malcham the 4 eldest Gregs, Meta Florence and I walked to chapel to Macclesfield this morning, 3 miles,—up hills and down hills, wind and dust too; and the little chapel itself was so very hot that it has made me very sleepy ever since; and we are all pretty well tired. Meta seems to be enjoying herself however. We shall come home early on Wednesday morning, so that Meta may not miss another of her drawing lessons, so be prepared with a welcome, there's a good lassie. And now goodbye, only very likely I may add⟨...⟩

*

[1] Mrs Gaskell may have gone over to Bollington from Capesthorne after previous visits to Mrs Davenport, but we cannot find firm evidence.

ₒ **115** ₒ

?GEORGE RICHMOND

Plymouth Grove
Manchester,
Febry 24th [?1852]

Dear Sir,
I must plead indisposition as an excuse for not sooner having
written to tell you that some time ago my husband placed £31–
10s to your account at Masterman's; he say[s] you will know
where that bank is, so I dare say my having forgotten the more
exact address will not signify. With many pleasant recollections
of the time I passed in your studio,[1] believe me to remain
Yours very truly
E. C. Gaskell

*114a **116** *116a

MARIANNE GASKELL

[?February 1852][2]

⟨...⟩to read it. Hannah seems to think it has been a great deal of
money for not *very* much. Kate says Annie Shaen's singing used to
give her positive pain like a slate-pencil on slate it was in so bad a
style; so do take care & profit by these lessons of yours, so as not
to give any one pain by singing out of tune or in a bad style.
Remember your error always is repeating people's *praises* of you,
and *omitting*, (I really think you *forget*) their blame or fault-finding.
Meta & Flossy are having pretty regular drawing lessons, and I
do think the latter has some taste that way. Annie Austin was too
ill, (Influenza again!) to come on Thursday. Meta began but I
popped her into a warm bath at once, & that cured her I think.
We are not going to have many\out of door/annuals sown this
year; but greenhouse annuals—which we are going to raise on the
hot-*hearth* in the kitchen. Frank has sown peas; and Uncle Robert

[1] We have assumed that this could be a reference to Mrs Gaskell's 1851 visit to
London. See Letter 100.
[2] Probably misdated. Catherine Winkworth (?Katie, below) was on a visit to
the Gaskells on 17 February 1851. *Letters and Memorials*, ed. Winkworth, I, p. 273.

has sent us some rhubarb, and I hope soon we can go on pretty straightly out of doors, without much check from the weather. Katie stays here till Thursday next. The Tuesday afterwards *perhaps* Mrs. Hodgetts & Emily come to stay here; I am afraid they are very badly off; and we want them to come & visit us till they can fix what to do, & where to set up a school. There is the teabell. Is Helen Tagart come home? I am not visiting in an evening; but the rest go tomorrow I believe, to Mr J J. Tayler's open evening. Adey Souchay (that was) has got a baby, a little girl. Now I must go, but I shall try to write again this week. Learn dancing if Mrs Lalor thinks it would bring your *naughty* shoulders down. I have brought home one of your shifts. You had better *alter your list*; & tell me how many silk stockings you have, both *black* & *white*. Goodbye my own dear girl.

Your very affect[ionate] Mammy
E C Gaskell

*

116a **117** 120

MARIANNE GASKELL

Tuesday morng
[2 March 1852]

My dearest Polly,

I only got yr letter last night, on our return from drinking tea at Mrs Mason's or I should have written immediately on receipt of it as you seem rather longing to hear from home. And now it is after breakfast, & before post-time, and after the post comes in I shall go down to the School. Hearn's love, & the receipt you want is ½ an oz of camphor, *chopped into small pieces*, 1 oz of Borax, and a quart of boiling water poured on it, and to stand in a warm place till all is dissolved, then to be bottled. It is a very cleansing thing *for the skin* of the head; nothing but brushing cleans the hair. Hearn holds up her hands over yr green frock, and proposes you should be dressed in leather. Can't you wear your *blk* jacket to your *green* skirt. I am very much obliged to Mrs Lalor for thinking of asking Meta for a day or two; and *I shall be* MOST happy for her to {come} accept the invitation. I wish you wd tell me in yr next if you thought she was well and happy last Sunday. *Can't* you go to Mr. Bennett's concert? If *you* cant,

I think it will be a very nice plan to offer your ticket to Emily Shaen, though I don't know that she can go. Oh! Emily Shaen means to ask you and Meta to spend a Saty & Sunday at her house; and if it is convenient & agreeable to Mrs Lalor &c to let you go when E. Shaen fixes the time, I hope you *will* go. Papa & I wish you to ask Mrs Lalor if she can tell us what *week* her holidays are likely to begin; for last year owing to the long delay in hearing, we were thrown out in our summer places. Of course the day cannot be fixed till much nearer the time. I suppose you would like to stay longer than Midsummer would not you, dear? till next Christmas? I don't mean that we should go entirely by what you *like*; only we should take that into consideration. Answer as many of these questions as you can when you write, will you? I am glad you like yr french lessons. I know that Voyage en lOrient, and I like it as much as I do anything of Lamartine's. Will you thank Mr Lalor for speaking to the Edit Inquirer about Mr Wright. We have got up to 2236£, and have more in hand. And I have had a letter from Mr Walpole (brother to the Home Secy) saying his brother will help on the Government pension, and the Hornbys (cousins of Lord Derby⟨⟩⟩ are stirring *him* up; so we are in good hopes. I should think any air of Mendelsohn's must be beautiful. *Don't* call Shifts Chemises. Take the pretty simple *English* word whenever you can. As Mrs Davenport said the other day 'It is only washerwomen who call Shifts "*chemises*" now.' But independently of the word we shall be most glad of the *thing*. Flossie is at her last shifts in two senses of the word. The old red Camellia has seven flowers all out on it. Meta's that A A gave her, has two—variegated *single*. I don't think there is much home news. Last week was very quiet; and very busy with writing. I heard from Uncle Sam who desired me to tell you he had very often to go & see poor Cousin Anne on Sundays at Notting Hill, which prevented his coming out to *you* so much. The Darbishires go today to their new house in Wales.[1] They have never called here to wish goodbye. The two little ones met Miss Fergusson the other day in the street. Flossy knew *her* but she did not know F E. till she spoke. Then she gave her some violets, asked after us all and said she was coming to see us very soon. I wish I had gone there when you were at home. All our new servants do very nicely. To be sure we are a very small family, and there is proportionably very little work to be done.

[1] 'Somewhere near Conway' (*Letters and Memorials*, ed. Winkworth, I, p. 332).

We have got peas, onions, beans down in the garden, tomatas, mignionette [both words—*sic*] &c &c in the greenhouse. Miss Lloyd has my blue-moiré antique to make. The two engagements we have are a party of *ladies*. Miss Noble, Marslands, Humphreys, Mrs J. Potter to tea on Friday, and to this dance at Mr Philips of the Park on the *26*[.] Here come the letters. Mrs Davy, Meta, & Emily Green. I'll enclose the latter to you; it will tell you the Knutsford news a little. And now I must write to Tottie, and ask her if it would be convenient for her to receive Meta,\the *early* middle part of next week/as I want her to go *there* from the Austin's, and then to the Tagart's. Goodbye, my darling girl. I will try & write again this week; but I have a *great deal* to do.

Yours ever most affec[tionate]ly

E. C. G.

₀ 118 ₀

MRS GRANVILLE[1]

Plymouth Grove,
March 2 [?1852][2]

My dear Mrs Granville,

I have not forgotten you, I assure you; I hoped before this to have been able to send you some intelligence of the decision of the Literary Fund about you; but the gentleman to whom I entrusted your case, (and a better advocate you could not have), wrote to me on Sunday last, and said that there had been no meeting of the Committee as yet, since I sent in your name; as soon as there was he would let me know the result. I have written to him by today's post, enclosing your letter as a 'reminder', and also to ask him for the name and address of the Secretary; two things I had quite forgotten. As soon as I hear I will write to you again. I only thought I would send you these few lines to show you that you were not forgotten. I sincerely sympathize with you in the grief you must feel at Mr Davenport's behaviour, and at the anxiety you experience in your daughters' illness, and remain Dear Madam,

Yours very truly

E. C. Gaskell.

*

[1] Mrs Richard Davenport. See Letter 180.
[2] The date of Letter 72 + in Appx A necessitates the correction of this year to 1850.

₀ **119** ₀

UNKNOWN

Plymouth Grove,
Manchester.
Tuesday Ap: 14 [?1852][1]

Dear Sir,

I received a letter yesterday from Mrs John Curtis (formerly Miss Crossley) at Heidelberg, in great anxiety as to the fate of three or four little orphan children of her cousin, Mr Robert Salter, who was drowned in the Mersey near Cheadle about a fortnight ago. She begs me to consult with you as to what can be done with these poor little things, as she is very anxious that they should *not* go to the Bolton workhouse, the only place to which she says they have any claim. I have been able to make some enquiry here respecting the family circumstances; and the only plan I see in any way open is for some one to make an earnest appeal to the relations, who, it seems, are very justly incensed with Mr Robert Salter's conduct; and are also struggling for a livelihood; but if they *could* take the children, it seems both the natural and the happiest way of providing for them, even if their bringing up be yet harder & more of a struggle than they would have to undergo in the poor-house. Of course there are numerous Orphan Houses; but I had occasion to make application to one of the most wealthy 2 years ago, & learnt that they had upwards of a *thousand* names on their books. So unless the grandmother & Aunts residing at Bolton,—or the uncle;—living on his means at Cheetham Hill & a member of Dr Beard's congregation,—will do some thing for them, I fear the poor-house must be their fate. I go from home on Friday; but if in the meantime I can do any thing will you suggest it to me.

Yours respectfully,
E C. Gaskell

[1] This could be 1863.

117 **120** *122a

MARIANNE GASKELL

Thursday morning.
[?Late April 1852][1]

My dearest Polly,

I was in hopes I should have had something decided to have
told you about our summer plans, and have been waiting day after
day to hear from Mr Jackson,—but no letter came—till this morning when it is unsatisfactory I am sorry to say: that is *our* house is
engaged till July 16th. We may have the *tower-house* at any time,
but there it was so close! Whether it was the full unhealthy
packing or what I don't know;—and we must remember one
object of our summer change is *health.* So we are all at sea again.
You shall [have] your winter gown made[,] dear; and your white
one I had already planned as *one* of your wants. You never say
what songs you are learning, and I often want to know. We are in
glory with our rain to-day. Our pretty white ducks quack about
with delight. Mr Coates is worrying us about our naughty poultry,
which *will* go up & down where they have no business to, & we
sadly want you for our poultry maid. Baby has had two teeth
taken out. Mrs Davy sends me word of a charming book with
such an unpromising title, that she & the Arnolds are so full of,
viz 'Report made by the Directors to the Proprietors of {Pral}
Palmer's patent Candle Company.' I am all curiosity I can't fancy
what it can be about. Grace & Eliz are in Edinburgh. Would you
like a Manchester Guardian now and then, for since Mrs Mason
is gone we are taking them in, all of ourselves? *Answer this.* Hearn
& the 2 little ones went to Bowden on Saty for the day. E Shaen
& S Winkworth came here to tea. I have seen a good deal of
E Shaen but she is now gone back to Alderley; she & Selina go to
London on the 6th, Selina to the Tagart's. Are you going to any
Concerts now? I hope you are, for we want you to be hearing
good music. Emily asked us if you were and said she hoped you
were going occa[sionally] to the Opera, now in ⟨London⟩, so as
to get to know the difference between different styles and different
masters &c &c &c, so as to understand what each had to express

[1] Not a firm date. The information below about Emily Shaen and Selina Winkworth, combined with the physical evidence of format, watermark and blind
stamp, make it a possible one.

and how they did it. Alice Winkworth seems a very nice girl. You know I have had a strong prejudice against her, but now it is being overcome. Papa is so much pleased with her as a pupil. I have had a long letter from Louisa Holland which I will enclose to make this worth postage. Goodbye my darling. Ever your affec[tionate] Mother

E. C. Gaskell.

Susan did not bring her baby. She only staid one night; but was very nice and sweet as she always is. She wishes you would learn a few *good* English songs. Captain Holland has bought Ashbourne Hall in Derbyshire, and is going to add to it considerably.

₀ 121 ₀

SALIS SCHWABE[1]

Plymouth Grove
April 29. [1852]

My dear Sir,
Mme Avril sent me her designs for Calicos on the 16th; instead of the 15th, as I had asked her. I sent and went with them four times to the warehouse in hopes of catching you, as you passed through from Huddersfield, and I finally left them there, in a sealed packet with a note from me to you, along with M. Avril's letter to me, on Monday the 19th as the clerk told me he could forward {them} it to you in Wales the next day. But on Tuesday last the packet was returned to me, the seals broken, and my letter inside. We were very much puzzled to know if you had ever seen it, but the messenger could tell nothing about it. However Mr Gaskell wrapped it up afresh in a brown-paper cover, and directed & sealed\it/asking them to forward to you or give it you, if, as the man said, you were likely to be in Manchester in a few days. But I think perhaps this letter may not come amiss to tell you the real state of the case; only I hope you will not think I am troubling you unnecessarily by sending it.
Will you tell Mrs Schwabe with my kind love, that I have had a letter from Mr Dickens saying he will see {& help} Dr Solger

[1] *Annotation 1852.*

with the greatest pleasure. So I trust Dr Solger will receive the assistance he desires from him.

In great haste, believe me eve⟨r⟩ dear Sir—Yours most truly
E. C. Gaskell

GRACE SCHWABE[1]

Plymouth Grove
Friday. [30 April 1852]

My dearest Mrs Schwabe,

I had a letter from Mrs *Davy* (at *Ambleside*) yesterday saying Mrs Fletcher and Lady Richardson were expected on the day on which she wrote at their *own home in Westmorland*. So there is no chance of your seeing the dear old lady just now. I don't know if Lady Hatherton will *expect* you to call; but I am *sure* she will be *very* glad to see you. Her address (as I think I told you,) is 40 Berkeley Sq. Thank you for even *thinking* of calling on my girls. But I know too well how much people have to do in London to wish you to carry your kindness into action, unless you are near them. Marianne as being the longer exile from home, would I know be *particularly* glad to see you if *any other business* takes you to Hampstead. She is at Mrs Lalor's, Holly Hill, Hampstead. Meta returns to us under charge of Mr John James Tayler on the 11th. She is at present staying with Miss Fox, 3 Sussex Place, Regent's Park.

I wrote to Mr Schwabe yesterday, directing to Glyn-Garth *near Beaumaris*; which I see is a mistake, & I am afraid he will not receive my letter; it was abou⟨t⟩ the patterns for Calico designing which Mme Avril sent the *day after*\16th/I told her\15th April/, & which I have made many fruitless efforts to get to Mr Schwabe, until, at last, last Monday, they (at the warehouse,) told me they would forw⟨ard.⟩ Thank you for your kind offer⟨.⟩ My sole want in the world in the dress line is a leghorn bonnet, and that I fear is not likely to be cheaper at London or Paris than here. Give my compliments to Paris, & say I hope to see it *sometime*[.] Mr Dickens wrote to me most kindly about Dr Solger. I must end; if I begin a good long *talk* I don't know where I should stop, but it is just post-time, so—

[1] *Annotation* 1852; (*pencil*) April 30th 1852.

I shall look what you send ⟨to⟩ Mr Gaskell, and send the same back to Mr Schwabe, attending to the proprieties, or who knows but what I might call Mr Schwabe 'dear—' remember me to good Mr Schwabe, (I must say a little more.) remember *me most kindly* to Mr Schwabe & ever believe with best wishes for your happy going out, and happy return,

Yours affectionately
E. C. Gaskell.

*

*122a 123 126

MARIANNE GASKELL

Thursday [13 May 1852][1]

My dearest Polly

We have got Meta at home at last safe and sound. She came very punctually at half past 10, & Papa who had gone to meet her brought her up here at 11; tired but well. We had the little ones up to see her: they having had an hour or two's sleep in the afternoon. Yesterday we talked our talk; today we are settling. I believe I never knew the feeling of being 'lonely' yet, but I am *very* happy to have Meta at home again. Hearn is going to see Mary on Saturday or Monday. Will Preston is coming to be our servant, & to {live}\sleep/over the stable, & to live with us. James was so drunken, poor fellow. Frank is here now and will be till we return from Silverdale. Margaret Preston goes home *about* June 9th & joins us at Silverdale, where she & Hearn and a girl, who *is to be* hired at Lancaster, are to be our servants. Miss Noble (of Manchester) is coming to dinner to-day; Mrs Shuttleworth being gone to Mrs James Booth's in London, to await Mr S's return from Paris. *About* next week she will be at the Rowland Hill's at Hampstead, & then means to call on you, my darling. Well! to return to tonight. I mean to ask Susanna, & Miss Acton, & so to have a party of unprotected females. My dear! your poor Papa lives in dread of that British Association, in W. Week!! If he does *not* go to London it will be because he's frightened away by it. Speechmaking, public-meetings and such noisy obtrusive ways of 'doing good' are his dislike, as you know; but oh! he is so good

[1] The news below, especially about Meta Gaskell and Selina Winkworth, places this letter in early May 1852. Cf. *Letters and Memorials*, ed. Winkworth, I, pp. 341, 346.

really in his own quiet way, beginning at home and working outwards without noise or hubbub—I am more & more convinced *be* good, & *doing* good comes naturally, & need not be fussed and spoken about. It is so funny, Papa's fright of that great *form* of the British Association. Yes! you may go and see Selina if you can manage it with Mrs Lalor's full consent. Mrs Lalor wrote to me about some Pughs, who have never made their appearance, & I hope never will, {but} for they must be impertinent people to think that *I*, at anybody's request, am going to show myself to gratify any body's curiosity. I'll show them my sick duck, if they come, cured by blue pill; for there it is going quacking about like a respectable, well-behaved fowl. You shall have yr clothes,—white muslin frock, winter do, & petticoat bodies made *for* you,—you must make hanging sleeves for yourself, my lady—*Do* remind Pergetti of his songs. I am sorry to hear of his forgetting 'em[.] Last week we had the farm-work thrown amongst us women; and I *carried the cow*, taking her under my care, & avoiding the pigs. Oh! it was such a commotion! past description, only very provoking & very funny at the time. About those hats for the children would they do for *best* bonnets? They have got every day ones. I had rather you & Meta had none. I hope you will go & see the\Academy/Exhibition; for even without knowing much of painting there must be something to be seen. My darling! Do*n't* particularly hope or expect to see much of me at Hampton darling [?]. I could not do with Mrs Lalor I believe, & She would 'testify' a la Mause Headrigg against me, which you would dislike, & 10 to 1 I should flame up against her. Ever your most affec[tionate]

E C Gaskell

112 124 137

Eliza Fox[1]

Wed. evening.
[c. May 1852]

My dearest Tottie

All day long I've been talking to Meta and spudding up dandelions, and now I've half a hundred letters to write, having sent the girl to bed. Oh dear! My dear little Tottie your note gave

---

[1] Original MS. not seen.

me a heartache going to bed the last thing at night, and when I wakened this morning I *knew* there was some bad news, though I could not remember *what*. My dearest Tottie I *was* so tired and ill last week I dare say I wrote roughly and 'nakedly'—and I did not tell you *half* what pleasure we should *all* have in your visit with us at Silverdale, or you *would* have come. When I gave up Bonn with many sighs because W. was so against it, I made a paction 'twixt us twa that you *should* come to Silverdale and now, love, *do* come the—my [*sic*] could not be spent in any way to give us *all* more pleasure, we have perhaps been foolish in talking of your coming as a certainty and the little ones, but they too talk so of your coming. I would paint a picture of the Corn Law League (do you remember my indignation against Herbert over the schoolroom fire?) to get you to come; *can* man say more? Oh! Mrs Fox will settle herself, and if it is a little later it does not signify,—and Charlotte will I know be on our side. Do let me help you to clear away difficulties. Leave it open if you like, but try. I'm afraid I burnt your note about F. H. and Mr Fox only yesterday morning—clearing off before Meta came. How well the lassie looks! and so full of politics and water colours. Such a pleasure to have her again. She has flown out upon us laughing at *her acct* of the Corsican brothers, which was irresistible though it was meant to be solemn—She has been *very* happy with you and has been *very* gay compared to what she will be here, but I did not want *gaiety* for her at all; only 'enlargement of ideas', as Mr Lalor wd say whh I think she has got in this absence from home. She shocks me by saying you told her Mrs Ruskin was separated from her husband—is it true?[1] Dear Tottie I return to the burden. *Do* come with us to Silverdale. As for our going up it is all in the clouds, may be, may not be,—x x x I am turning such a farmer— I bodily, carry the cow and carry her pail of licking. '*You* don't know what licking is?' not you. And with a ?spud under my arm I reckon I represent the agricultural interest[.] Tottie! you don't know how *beautiful* Silverdale is and a tower of our own! think of that! its a sort of country you never saw before. I'll answer for it. I dare say we shall never go there again—and I for one, don't expect to live till another summer, when you so coolly talk of coming—*Do* come,—think of it! difficulties vanish in thinking with me; or perhaps the thinking is the greater difficulty. I am not

[1] Cf. p.287, below. However, this year saw Miss Fox's visit to Silverdale. *Letters and Memorials*, ed. Winkworth, I, pp. 352–3.

half thanking you enough for all your kindness to Meta—but I *do* thank you. I have so much to say too, that can never come in in writing, an employment I hate more and more. Now I can't write more tonight I am sorely tired, not being strong. Thursday. I wish you could see S.W. she is so funny and cock a hoop about Niebuhr,[1] she snubs me so, and makes such love to William he says 'my life is the only protection he has—else he *knows* she would marry him'. I wish you could hear him speaking thus in a meek fatalist kind of way, and I believe she *would* too. *Can't* you marry her to Mr Forster; then I *cd* die in peace feeling that my husband was in safety. *Do* go darling Tottie do go to Silverdale with us.

Yours very affec[tionately],

E. C. G.

₀ 125 ₃₈₀

LORD HATHERTON

Plymouth Grove,

Friday, May 21 [1852][2]

My dear Lord Hatherton,

I am very much obliged to you for the kind trouble you have taken in writing down the particulars of how you obtained that Cornish ballad; which Mr Forster so justly called 'noble'. One of our servants, who comes from Cornwall, tells me it was a much longer song when she used to hear it from the miners in her youth. She lived near Penryn, which is the Trelawney country, and where this ballad was often sung, or rather chanted by old people. She has tried to obtain a copy of the longer song for me but without success; and the only difference between your Lordship's version and one sent me by an old miner, is that he repeats,

'But Forty thousand Cornish boys
Will know the reason why?'

as a sort of refrain or burden at the end of each verse.

Believe me, to remain, my dear Lord Hatherton

Yours very sincerely

E. C. Gaskell

[1] It was printed by 29 December 1851. *Letters and Memorials*, ed. Winkworth, I, p. 321.   [2] *Annotation* 1852.

MARIANNE GASKELL

Plymouth Grove.
Wednesday, 19 [May 1852]

My dearest Polly,

Mr Gunton is here. He is going to give Meta two lessons a week till the holidays to work her well up ('putting her in a hot-bed' *he* calls it.) Two afternoons she is to draw; & she is reading Alfieri (pretty difficult Italian[)] with Rosa, & beginning mathematics with Papa so she is pretty busy. Hearn is gone to spend a week with Mary Coup in Derbyshire; went last Monday—so we have the children on our hands,—very good they are. Yesterday we went to Mary Robberds' marriage. On Monday Miss Brandreth had come over from Knutsford to see Meta's drawings, & I had asked her to stay all night; we went in to the Domestic (i.e. Ministry to the Poor[)] Annual Meeting,—so she, Meta Florence Julia & I went to Brook St Chapel; and then I came home, & went to the breakfast; only, fearing from the number of people whom I knew were there to have one of my bad headaches, I did not go in to breakfast but sat in a room by myself, till the bride came down to go, when I had a little talk with her, & engaged her to come here on the *25 of June*, if all was well; so remember *that*, will you, Missy? Our Margaret Preston waited & looked so nice. Wm Turners (of Halifax) Sarah Howarth (bridesmaid) Kate Holland (do) Miss Herford (do) Chas Robberds Mr & Mrs John & Mr & Mrs Harry Robberds, Mr & Mrs Swanwick (of Alderley) a Mr Ivan Brook, & Vernon Herfords—old Mr Turner Mr & Mrs Alcock, Mr J J Tay⟨ler⟩ Papa Mr & Mrs Edward Herford—I think that was all,—but I considered myself well out of the room when Papa told me that there was *no* window open till just the last. I found Mrs Robberds ('Come with me and let us wander' by Henry Smart—Mr Gunton has just told me of this song, quite new he says, & will just suit your voice) did not [seem] to know what to do with her young people, who were to have gone to Dunham, but it rained so I (boldly) asked them all to come here which they did, & Arthur and Vernon & Mr Darbishire, and Robert Jones & Alice Winkworth & Stephen, so we had an impromptu *little-go* last night. You would hear from E. Shaen on Saturday that Papa & I are coming to her next Monday week[1] for three or 4 days; Papa must return on the Saturday. I *may* possibly stay to bring you home, but I am not sure—Mr Gunton is praising Meta's playing so much. She is rather wanting to go to Miss Martineau's school. I will send or bring you the measure of the little one's heads. Meta wants your *Octave* exercises sometime. Alice Winkworth staid all night with us. We all like her. Miss Mitchell came home yesterday from Bollington, & (you may tell Mrs Henry Enfield) she brings a very nice account of the Sam Gregs. No! Mrs Pugh has never turned {out} up—& I don't break my heart. *Do* work away at your singing. Louy Darbishire is in London (M A Rigby's) having lessons from Caradon Allan— Is S. Pergetti getting forgetful about your songs? We have found Ciocola-Chocolate—The two little ones were at Mrs Smith's yes-terday, & Annis comes here tomorrow.

Your very affect[ionate] mother
E. C. Gaskell

74 127 0

MARY COWDEN CLARKE

Sunday. [?23 May 1852]

My dear Mrs Clarke,

I think I *do* quite understand YOU, but I don't think *you* quite understand *me*! There's conceit for you! What I mean is you don't understand how in Manchester when you\or I/want a little good hearty personal individual exertion from any one they are apt to say in deeds if not in words 'Spare my time, but take my money'—a sort of 'leave me, leave me to repose' way, handing you their purse in order to be spared any trouble themselves, although by taking a little trouble they may benefit any person in a far more wholesome & durable way than by lazy handing over the money they don't want. It is the fault *of the place*; and our dear good Mr Darbishire has caught a little of it, dear friend, & noble fellow as he is. I have once or twice said to him 'when I want money, I will come and ask for it straightforwardly for any one', & I did *not* want money for Miss Elton—I wanted her to have as large a sphere as she could for the exercise of the gifts God has given her,—& I knew Mr Darbishire from his position knew

---

[1] Whit Monday 1852 (i.e. 31 May). See *Letters and Memorials*, ed. Winkworth, I, p. 346.

nearly every one of influence in Manchester; now, *many a one* (I don't\say/HE will, he is one of a thousand,) would just put all recollection of her on one side, feeling satisfied that they had done their duty in one act,—and if every one did so, think of the effect on her, or any one's character! As I felt vexed, & told Mr Darbishire just what I have told you, I felt justified in saying\to him/I would have nothing to do with it, but would forward it to you, (representing to me Miss Elton's guardians.) Mr Darbishire laughs at me, & calls me gruff, but if you knew and saw as I do how freedom of opinion & action are bought & sold, you would feel sorry that men can not find a better way of evincing their good feeling than by giving money. I say over & over again, Mr Darbishire is a person from whom it is a pleasure to receive; only for his own sake, I wish he would not take so lazy a way of doing good. I myself had so little to do with it in any way—(my 'eloquence' being a fabulous & mythical attribute,) that I willingly give full leave to have my small part in the whole business made known to Miss Elton. Your reason too has great weight with me, namely the 'injurious effect which the receipt of presents accompanied by the slightest mystery as to their source' may produce. Mr Darbishire is at his place in Wales,—near Conway; whether he will return or not before we leave for London, on Friday next, I don't know.[1] But I almost think I may give you leave to send Miss Elton his note. Believe me it was from no feeling of self-consciousness, as to the {[?]} very small part I had in the affair that made me not wish to be known; but because I do feel money-giving as a lazy\way of serving others/, often impertinent, and most often injurious to character.

The numbers of people who steadily refuse Mr Gaskell's entreaties that they will give their time to anything, but will give him or me tens & hundreds. that don't do half the good that individual intercourse, & earnest conscientious thought for others would do! I dare say you think I am going off on a rhapsody, but I have real cases in view, both of this kind, & of the kind where, having given money largely & from a really generous feeling at the time, a most bitter sense of ingratitude has been felt & expressed by the donor, if any difference of opinion, or resistance to what the donee thought wrong afterwards occurred.

[1] An attached letter from [? J] D. Darbishire, dated 25 May 1852, refers to his return on 24 May & to the gift. See also M. & C. C. Clarke, *Recollections of Writers*, 1878, p. 93.

Perhaps you had better just wait till I have heard from Mr Darbishire[.] I will let you know as soon as ever I do. Miss Elton was here on Friday, & comes to tea here on Tuesday. I beg your pardon for such writing. I don't usually write so badly, but I am very⟨...⟩

Miss Elton,
  Mrs Rogers'
   {16}186, Exmouth Terrace
    Oxford Road,
     Manchester.

₁₂₂ **128** ₁₆₂

GRACE SCHWABE

Plymouth Grove
Tuesday [*c.* May 1852]

My dearest Mrs Schwabe,
 Only two lines!—one to thank you *very much* not only for seeing my girls, but for finding time in your London bustle for writing to me about them. The second 'line' is this—Mme de Mery has just called; and I have persuaded her to let me *try* Her Hungarian Legend at Household Words.[1] I think they will take it. So if you have *not* sent it off anywhere else, would you please to send it to W. H. Wills Esq

   Household Words Office
    11 Wellington Street North
     Strand

With Mrs Gaskell's compliments just that they may know which MS to open, when I write to them about it. I *dare* not put in Mr Gaskell's very affectionate message to you, unless I may send the same to Mr Schwabe; but my husband is so grateful for your kindness in calling on his girls.
 May God have [you] in His holy keeping both in your going out, and in your coming in.
     Yours very affectionately
       E. C. Gaskell.

[1] There is no article of this title, but one on 'The Golden Age of Hungary' appeared in *Household Words* No. 144, 25 December 1852, pp. 342 ff.

ₒ 129 ₒ

UNKNOWN

Plymouth Grove
Saturday, Augt 7 [1852][1]

My dear Sir,

I am very sorry indeed to hear of this dishonest Manager. I have not got my bill, having sent it to Mrs Wedgwood, with the P.O order for the payment. The amount was 4£,—16 yards at 5s a yard,—I forget the 'trade' description of the gown; but the effect is polished steel colour, and I *think* it is a shot of French Black (blue black) and white.

Mrs Wedgwood's address is Sunny Beach House, Strone Point, Kilman, Argyleshire, N.B.

I believe I have to thank you for a 'Star of Freedom' containing a very interesting account of the Co-operative Conference, and of the Presentation of the Inkstand to Mr Maurice.[2]

I do hope those poor fellows the Silk Weavers, won't be losers by this Manager; but I am afraid from what you say they will.

Yours very truly
E. C. Gaskell

ₒ 130 ₒ

SIR JOHN POTTER[3]

Plymouth Grove
Monday Aug. 16, [1852]

Dear Sir,

I wish to give 'Mary Barton' and another little book to the Free Library. But before I do so I should like to make a *private* enquiry of you, (with whom the Institution has become so honorably [*sic*] identified,) as to how far my giving\the former of/these books would be distasteful to you. Of course I cannot be unaware of the opinions which you and your brother have so frequently &

---

[1] Only 1852 and 1858 are possible with a letter headed as above. The format, watermark and blind stamp combined make the former more probable.

[2] F. D. Maurice published *Reasons for Co-operation, A Lecture* in 1851.

[3] *Address (on envelope)* Sir John Potter | Brick Hill | Pendleton. *Postmark* MANCHESTER | AU 16 | 1852 *and* HIGHER ARDWICK.

openly expressed with regard to Mary Barton; and, as I feel great respect for all your exertions in behalf of the Library, it appeared to me as if it would be an impertinence on my part to send the obnoxious book to any collection in which you took an interest without previously asking you to tell me honestly if you would really rather that it was not included in the Catalogue?

May I add one word?

Of course I had heard of young Mr Ashton's murder[1] at the time when it took place; but I knew none of the details, nothing about the family, never read the trial (if trial there were, which I do not to this day know;) and {that} if the circumstance were present to my mind at the time of my writing Mary Barton it was so unconsciously; although it's occurrence, and that of one or two similar cases at Glasgow at the time of a strike, were, I have no doubt, suggestive of the plot, as having shown me to what lengths the animosity of irritated workmen would go. I have been exceedingly grieved to find how much pain I have un-intentionally given to a family of whom I know nothing but that they have suffered a great sorrow; I can hardly wonder that they, not knowing me, & believing what they did, should have been angry; but I would infinitely rather never have written the book, than have been guilty of the want of all common feeling, and respect for misfortune, which I should have shown if I had made Mr Ashton's death into a mere subject for a story. May I request you to consider this note, as private? I shall not name either it, or the purport of your answer to any one, except my husband, who is at present ignorant of my writing to you.

Yours truly

E. C. Gaskell

*

[1] In an explanatory note attached to this letter (dated 1 July 1914) Arthur B. Potter referred to the murder of Thomas Ashton of Pole Bank, Werneth, on the night of 3 January 1831 in consequence of a dispute with the Trades Union. The last person to speak to him was his 12-year-old sister Mary, who in 1847 married Thomas Bayley Potter, father of Arthur B. Potter and brother of Mrs Gaskell's correspondent (Sir John Potter) and a member of Cross Street Chapel. Mrs Potter fainted on coming to the account of the murder in *Mary Barton*, and the family felt that Mrs Gaskell had deliberately revived memories of the deed. An account of the murder will be found in Thomas Middleton's *Annals of Hyde and District*, 1899, pp. 85–94.

*130a **131** 132

MARIANNE GASKELL

Saty schoolroom
Question-time
[4 September 1852]

My dearest Polly,

There are so many odd things to tell you I don't know where to begin. George Fox came last Sunday, and Papa went to dine at the Shuttleworths. George F gave Meta & me a lesson in architecture. On Monday afternoon I went to the Schwabe's—Mrs was out, so I went to early tea at the Scott's, and then returned to the Schwabe's, meeting Mr & Mrs Adolf Schwabe who came to dinner. I staid all evening being kept by the rain. Tuesday was a very quiet day, and just as we were planning a Tourneyfication after dinner, Papa had a ticket sent him for the Banquet to the Guild of Literature & Art[1] to which he went at 10 minutes' notice. On Wednesday Morng Mr & Mrs Dickens & Miss Hogarth came to call *before 10*. Meta was out rather unluckily, & just came in as they were going out. Papa & I went behind the scenes to see the play[2] and had tea *there*, which was a very luxurious mode of seeing it. The Dickens asked me to go with them to the seats reserved for them by the Mayor at the Free Library, so I put in a word for Meta, & she & I went down to the Royal Hotel & joined the Dickens, Mr Charles Knight, Mr Mark Lemon, and then went to the Free Library where we had capital places, close to the speakers. But oh! my usual complaint! The room, in spite of it's immense size & heigth [*sic*] was *so close*, & the speeches were so long I could not attend & wished myself at home many & many a time[,] my only comfort being seeing the caricatures Thackeray was drawing which were very funny. He & Mr Monckton Milnes made plenty of fun, till poor Thackeray was called on to speak & broke down utterly, after which he drew no more caricatures[.] We went at ½ p. 9, & did not get out till ¼ to 4, which was too much of a good thing. Canon Clifton gave me a concert ticket, & as Meta had one we came home, had dinner, & went to the Concert. It was awkward for the singers did not expect the concert to begin till 8, & so did not come, & Mr Hallé had to play to

[1] On 31 August 1852. *Annals*, ed. Axon, p. 262.
[2] *Used Up* and *Charles XII*. *Letters and Memorials*, ed. Winkworth, I, p. 360.

fill up the time. (Madame Halle has called on me.) Yesterday Mr
Monckton Milnes came here; and we had a birthday party for
Julia, who was very outrageous at not having heard from you.
Meta Papa & I went with Tommy to see Mr Cropper of Stand
and his poultry. He gave Meta such a pretty hen, a silver pheasant,
black & white. I shall leave Meta to tell you all about the concert.
Agnes Sandars comes here on Tuesday, & I have asked Eliza to
come too. I *think* they go on Thursday. Cousin Susan has written
to ask Meta & me to go over there,\to Knutsford/but of course
I can't with Agnes coming; *and* I can't hear of a servant to take
Margaret's place, (she goes into the kitchen to take Isabella's.)
Old Mr & Mrs Shaen come{s} to the Ben Shaen's next week
sometime. I hope the Tagarts will come here *last* of all, because
of this dilemma & change of servants &c—Julia seems *very* well
just now

        Ever darling Polly
          Yours very affec[tionat]ely
                E C Gaskell

Oh! we *are* so angry if you went to the opera on Tuesday. *Bad*
music; bad singers!

         131 **132** 133

MARIANNE GASKELL

                Friday [10 September 1852]

My dearest Marianne,
    We have had a series of callers so I am afraid I shall have hardly
any time to write & wish you very many happy returns, my
darling of your birthday.[1] You see we have not forgotten your
wish that we should write to you that you might get your letters
on {Friday} Saturday. Agnes Sandars & Eliza Patterson have been
staying here till to-day, since Tuesday, when they came from
Alderley. We have been quite quiet ever since they came, until
to-day when there seems to have been an influx of callers, Miss
Walker to begin with, to ask us all to go to an Examination of the
Swinton schools on the 21st, and afterwards to tea at Worsley,—
then Mrs Leisler to ask if Papa would take Maggie Leisler as a

    [1] On Sunday, 12 September.

pupil when she comes back from Paris towards the end of Octr. (Agatha is going to Mrs Turner's.) then Agnes & Eliza went, we dined and Mrs Shuttleworth has been since to tell us all about poor Mr Porter, who is dead. The house is being painted *outside*, which makes so bad a smell inside, that Papa is planning where we can all go to forthwith—and we can't make out,—especially as he *must* be left behind because Mr Robberds is away, & he seems to suffer just as much as any of us. I have not heard of a servant yet, {yes} but we have bought a new cow; an Alderney, a very pretty young creature. My darling I seem to be saying very little about your birthday, but I only wish you were here to see how joyfully we would keep it. You know I said *my* birthday presents would be trying to furnish your dressing room as nicely as ever I could for you. Papa is gone into town. Before he went we turned over the capabilities & œconomies of Mrs Preston's, Silverdale, Southport, Bowden, New Brighton without deciding on any,—and thought of Meta's accepting Agnes Sandars' invitation for a fortnight, but nothing was decided on.\owing to Mrs Shuttleworth's coming/Don't be surprized to hear of the family being sprinkled abroad next week. And I am so wanting to stay settled at home! I got the garden so beautifully done up last week, & now it is all over ladders & paint-pots! so, as you may perceive we are all in a very bad temper; & very much 'set' against cleanliness & new-paint. Goodbye my eighteen-year-old—and dearly beloved!

Thy affect[ionate] mammy
E. C. Gaskell

Thanks for the book for Julia—Flossy has written this note to Evelene in such a hurry!

132 133 134

MARIANNE GASKELL

Tuesday morng—
[21 September 1852]

My dearest Polly,

Get your Carmelite gown, & get *quit of your other*. I think it will be a good trial how far Miss Alcock will do for you, & you can give her this to make. I hope you will be able to have lessons from Mrs Groom, but I am not *sure* if I have\from you/the right address; & Caroline Holland my informant is at Geneva;—Dr Holland *has* been at Moscow since you saw him, & *is* at Knutsford on his way to Algeria. To return to Mrs Groom, I should like you to go on with S. Pergetti *as well*; & if you can't do both, (whh *I shall be very sorry for.*) to go on with him, because as Emily Shaen said, it would be doing him great injustice to leave off now when you have only begun to get real benefit from him. Mrs Groom's terms are a guinea a lesson *at her own house.* She was companion to Mrs Siddons, so teaches English pronunciation most clearly & beautifully. I am glad, darling, to hear that about your harmony. There is no very particular news. The children & I went to the Park on Thursday, & had a beautiful day for it,—came home by ½ past 6 pretty well tired; met Bessy Howorth & Sarah there. Sarah to be married tomorrow. They go to the Lakes. She has a beautiful set of pearls, value I don't know how much, given her. That was all *that*, I think. Friday we left Miss Mitchell's, & came home. The house is painted & looks very clean & nice. Papa & I went to tea at Miss Marslands in the evening; I was so tired I could enjoy nothing. Saturday I dragged Meta out in the rain to Miss Mitchell's, when we heard that Father Newman was going to preach the next day, so Selina, Stephen, J. P. Green & I went to hear him. J. P. G came back here to dinner, and staid nearly all the afternoon. Papa had 3 services & came home very tired. Yesterday *I*, in my turn, had a headache, & could not go to the Examination of the Schools at Swinton.[1] Papa went, & did not come back till late at night. Meanwhile Cousin Lucy called, & staid two or 3 hours, & Selina came to tea. I worked away at flannels, (have you got your flannels, as you complain of cold? If not get them *at once*, dear. I am sure it is a great saving of illness, being warmly dressed early in autumn. The new cow's name is Daisy (so called by the children) Hannah has brought us a little white Bantam cock & hen.

Yours ever very affec[tionate]ly,

E C G.

My love to Miss Banks.

[1] Presumably the date given on p. 198 above should have been 20 September.

133 **134** *134a*

MARIANNE GASKELL

Saturday, Schoolroom
question time
[25 September 1852]

My dearest Polly,

It is not that I have got so very much to say, for I haven't, but
I want to keep to my regular day, though I have written before
this week. Moreover I never feel as if I deserved a letter from you
on Sunday, unless my {answer}\letter to you/is then on the road.
Mr J. Ewart*1 is engaged to be married to a Miss Molineaux,
daughter of a banker at Lewes; I suppose it will take place sometime this winter; & meanwhile Agnes & Mary and 'the Johns' are
looking out for a house near us; either in Hyde Grove—(the
small square near us) or in the street (I forget it's name just now),
leading up from Nelson St to the Park. *It is no* SECRET. Uncle Sam
is here; he came last night, and talks of going tonight, but will I
think stay longer, perhaps till tomorrow night. Annie & Ellen
Green are coming on Monday or Tuesday to go to Thackeray's
lectures (Tuesdays & Thursdays.) 6 of them. Your Aunt Lizzie
and your Aunt Robert are both expecting babies before Xmas;
& little cousins are pouring in upon the world. I don't think we
have done anything particular this week, except making 5 lb of
very good butter. We have had two drives with Tommy. And
Selina has been in a good deal. On Monday she joins the other
Winkworth's at Aberystwith, where they remain about a fortnight longer.[2] I have had no letters either. Oh! we drank tea with
Mr and Mrs Charles Herford's on Wednesday,—rather dull.
Florence has had a foreign letter from Annes, & Meta a long one
from A A. They\the A's/come home next Wednesday. Mr
Robberds comes home on Monday to marry Eliza Pilkington to
Mr Harland on Tuesday. He (Mr R has been staying at Llandudno
with the Alcocks, & the Isaacs are there too. I mean to give you
the charge of the green-house when you come home; as Meta has
assumed that of the poultry yard. I wonder if you would mind
copying me out the first sentence (about 4 lines *ending* with

---

[1] [Note in Meta's hand] *(What fibs you have been telling me of Miss Nare
M. E. G.) How arithmetical she will be!

[2] 27 September 1852. *Letters and Memorials*, ed. Winkworth, I, p. 363.

'*cheerful occupation*', in the review of 'Lena' in the last week's Inquirer, will you? I think I shall leave this sheet to be filled up by Meta.[1] I want to know what Mrs Groom says or said[.]

Ever thy very affect[ionate] mother

E C Gaskell.

*

*134a 135 136

MARIANNE GASKELL

Saturday morning

½ *past 8* [2 October 1852]

My dearest Polly,

Mr Gunton has taken to coming at this time; so here am I writing in the dining room with Meta; Annie & Ellen Green & the two little ones & Papa breakfasting (lucky people) comfortably in the school-room. We have been having the Influenza this week, & very poorly in consequence & a peculiar number of coming engagements as well. Thackeray's lectures on Tuesday & Thursday:[2] (we dined with him at the Scott's on Thursday before the lecture,) my birthday on Wednesday. Thank you, darling, for your note of wishes. I had a note from Mrs Fletcher on that day, (about which I will tell you soon,) and one from Helen Tagart, & a box of bon-bons from Annie Shaen (not a line with it but plenty of lemon-verbena;) the way my birthday was kept was by a holiday in the first place. I went with my *6* girls into town. I showed them some pictures at Agnew's, & at Grundy's; came home[,] had dinner, (which Julia had ordered much to her glory,) were all very tired. I had Johnson's lives of the people Thackeray was going to lecture about. Mrs Chadwick called; I sat a long time, then Jane Norris (a Capesthorne friend,) came & sat a long time—Then Miss Mitchell came by invitation to tea, & I began with my Influenza, & Papa & I sat groaning over the fire much like last Xmas day. Mrs Fletcher wrote to ask me there \Lancrigg/any day after the 15th & after some consideration of possibilities, (on account of her advanced age 83, I wish to go,) I

---

[1] Meta writes a few lines mentioning in particular Mr Gunton's present to her of Beethoven's Sonata, Op. 10, No. 3.

[2] Thackeray lectured in Manchester on the English Humorists at the end of September 1852.

wrote to say I would come somewhere about the 18, if I might bring Meta with me, (for sketching, & a little change of air, which Uncle Sam says she wants for her eyes, which are very sore just now.[)]] Uncle Sam staid till Monday morning; taking us by surprize by going off suddenly to Liverpool (Liscard) on Sunday morning. He brought a good account of Aunt Lizzie & her 8. The \old/house looks only like a little piece by the side of the additions; which themselves are only the beginning of a very large new house. They have built a large drawing-room with a boudoir opening out of it, & six bedrooms above. [Here is inserted a rough plan of the house] I have left out a very handsome hall with flight of front stairs *between* old & new; the *old* front door forming now the door of communication between the two parts. I had a note from Miss Paplowska, the Kay Shuttleworths very nice governess, about Lady K S whh I think Mr & Mrs Lalor may like to see, so I shall enclose it & then you may burn it. I am afraid she is still very poorly. Annie & E. Green came on Tuesday morng. I took 'em to Thackerays (at the Athenæum) on Tuesday Evening Papa being engaged; & Agnes & Mary took them down to meet us\from the Scott's/on Thursday[.] The lectures are delightful. Thackeray sails for America Octr 30. I think Agnes & Mary *will* take that house in Hyde Grove, but it a little depends on Major & Mrs Ewart, who have not yet seen it. Perhaps they 4 are coming here to tea tonight, & Jane Norris (he a school-inspector,) & Mrs Shuttleworth⟨...⟩

135 **136** 140

?MARIANNE GASKELL

[?October 1852]

⟨...⟩ of course I was coming here;[1] & so Papa undertook a small piece of Mr Vernon, & Major Ewart the rest, & we put off the Hathertons, & gave up Capesthorne. *That* occasioned writing, & before my letters were done came William Beamont of Warrington, & a Mr Westlake—both Fellows of Trinity, & two of the finest young men I have seen this long time. Mrs Wedgewood & I were both charmed with their spirit & intelligence, & we lost

---

[1] Lesketh How. For this series of visits see *Letters and Memorials*, ed. Winkworth, I, p. 369 n.

no time but plunged over head into the most interesting subjects at once. They staid to lunch when Papa was in, & they won his heart, just as they had done ours—Mr Westlake is a Xn Socialist, & a hearer of Mr Maurice, &c &c. By the time they went (their call lasted 3 hours.) Katie came to go to the Free Library, which we did, & just got back in time to dress for dinner at the Schwabes; just ourselves, nobody else. Sunday Papa preached at Rochdale. Mr & Mrs W. stayed in all day. The children & I went to the charity sermon at X Street; & in the evening Mr & Hannah Tayler came to tea. Monday morning we came off here at the same time that the Ws left us. It was a long journey, owing to delays at Kendal. Mrs Davy met us at the Station at Windermere. When we got here we had that delightful thing a bedroom tea, while we dressed for dinner; Mrs Arnold, Susan Arnold, Mrs Twining came to tea, & we were very lazy. (Dr Davy is from home.) Tuesday—we drove to Skelwith, & saw Mrs Preston as charming as ever. Then we went to Fox How, the Quillinan's, Mr Crewdson of Elleray, & were to have called on Mrs Wordsworth but had no time before dinner. Yesterday Meta[,] Grace & I went up to Stock Ghyll Force which I had never seen; home to lunch which was {Gr} Lizzie & Meta's dinner; then Mrs Arnold came, & she Mrs Davy[,] Grace & I went to dinner at Lancrigg,—Mr William Greg, & Dr Gibson Mr & Mrs Waterhouse,—quiet pleasant evening. The Gregs want us to go to Bowness but I can't, unless for a day,—as I have promised Mrs Arnold all my spare time, & I must go to Mill-Brow. We are receiving *no* letters, & rather getting to hunger after them. I have written to Papa every day, & have had no sign whatever from home. We lunch at 2, dine $\frac{1}{2}$ past 5—walk before lunch, drive after. The Lancrigg party are coming tonight & Mr Angus Fletcher is to arrange tableaux for the young people. That's all I think. Tomorrow we go to Lady Langdale's, whom we met at Capesthorne, & whose daughter (Miss Bickersteth) Meta admired so much. I want to call on Mrs Wordsworth, & Miss Martineau. Meta & Lizzie draw indefatigably, & are great friends.

                     Your very affect[ionate] mother

                                                    E C G.

About my book. I will certainly give a copy of it, dear, where you wish it. Only I dislike its being published so much, I shd not wonder if I put it off another year.

124 **137** 146

?ELIZA FOX[1]

Dr Davy's,
    Lesketh How,
        Near Ambleside.
            Friday. [?October 1852]

⟨. . .⟩ Well I'm here! *How* I came, I don't seem to know for of all the weary, killing wearing out bustles in this life that of the last week passed all belief. Thackeray's lectures, two dinners, one concert card party at home, killing a pig, *my* week at the school which took me into town from 9 till 12 every morning—company in the house, Isabella leaving, Wm too busy to be agreeable to my unfortunate visitors, (Mr and Mrs Wedgwood, Dot and Jane, their servant, Annie and Ellen Green, closely packed!) so I had to do double duty and talk æsthetically (I dare say) all the time I was thinking of pickle for pork, and with a Ruskian face and tongue I talked away with a heart like Martha's. And at last when Meta's and my cab came to take us to the station not before the house cleared, they smashed into Ruth in grand style. I have not much hope of her now this year, now I've been frightened off my nest again. Mr Chapman wrote a polite invitation to me to come and see the Duke's [Wellington's] funeral from his shop window (a sight I should dearly have liked,) *and*, also, that civility being furnished, informed me that Mr Forster had given him the MS. of Ruth and that the first 2 vols. *were printed*; all complete news to me! But I set to on the trumpet sound thereof, and was writing away vigorously at Ruth when the Wedgwoods, Etc. came: and I was sorry, *very* sorry to give it up my heart being so full of it, in a way which I can't bring back. That's *that*⟨. . .⟩

[1] Original MS. not seen.

₀ 138 ₀

MARY CARPENTER

Lancrigg
Grasmere
Oct 25 [1852]

My dear Miss Carpenter,
Thank you for writing so kindly and promptly, and for sending
me the circulars. Although you will but have one clear day, I do
hope, as my dear friend Mrs Davy lives so close to Miss Martineau's you will call upon her; and I think her mother Mrs Fletcher
(the same, who was your Father's friend,) will go over to Ambleside to have the chance of meeting you\at Mrs Davy's, Lesketh
How./. Mrs Fletcher (with whom we are now staying,) was for
17 years actively engaged in a somewhat similar work to yours in
Edinburgh; i.e—she went for some hours most days of the year
to{see}\visit/an Institution for friendless boys, most of whom
came out of prison. She says they were usually apprenticed to the
Master of the Institution, who had previously been a shoemaker;
as in Edinburgh they could get no *land* to employ their industry
upon. That\6 of/these poor boys were one day desired by their
master to wait for him at the corner of the street, and the police
spying out this gathering of suspicious characters, & imagining
that some mischief was in hand, went to them; whereupon they
cried out 'Oh! Sir we're not thieves the noo, we're Mistress
Fletcher's laddies.'
She & her daughter\Mrs Davy/would, *I feel sure*, delight you,
& are most anxious to make yr acquaintance. You will wonder
why, if Mrs Davy's house is so near, she can not call upon *you*,
instead of wishing to trouble you to call on her. I don't quite
understand the domestic politics of these vallies; but, both Mrs
Fletcher & Mrs Davy have thought it right to decline intercourse
with Miss Martineau, (except for causes of humanity,) since the
publication of her book.[1] *I* think this course is mistaken, but I am
sure they act conscientiously. At any rate so it is; and Mrs Davy

[1] No doubt *Letters on the Laws of Man's Nature and Development*, 1851, written in
collaboration with Henry Atkinson. Charlotte Brontë considered it 'avowed
Atheism and Materialism' and the Winkworth sisters found in it 'a strong sense of
relief and freedom at escaping from belief in God and a future life'. See Vera
Wheatley, *Life and Work of Harriet Martineau*, 1957, pp. 299, 303.

says she could not then justify to herself the calling on any one, whose acquaintance she wished to make, at Miss M's house. I saw your future assistant[1] the other day, & a very nice-looking person she is: and her brother, Miss Martineau's gardener seems very much pleased at the prospect of her marriage. 'Jane' as perhaps you know leaves Ambleside today for Australia, to which place she is going in something of a missionary spirit, and well stocked with tracts by *both* Mrs Davy & Miss Martineau.

Yours most respectfully & sincerely

E. C. Gaskell.

59 139 155

JOHN FORSTER[2]

Ambleside, Oct. 28, 1852

⟨...⟩ We dined quietly and early with Mrs Wordsworth on Monday. She is charming. She told us some homely tender details of her early married days, how Miss Wordsworth made the bread, and got dinner ready, and Mrs W. nursed all the morning, and, leaving the servant to wash up after dinner, the three set out on their long walks, carrying all the babes amongst them; and certain spots are memorial places to Mrs W. in her old age, because there she sat, and nursed this or that darling. The walks they took were something surprising to our degenerate minds. To get news of the French Revolution they used to walk up the Raise[3] for miles, in stormy winter evenings to meet the mail. One day when they were living at Grasmere (no post-office there) Wordsworth walked over to Ambleside (more than four miles) to post some poem that was to be included in a volume just being printed. After dinner as he sat meditating, he became dissatisfied with one line, and grew so restless over the thought that towards bedtime he declared he must go to Ambleside and alter it; for 'in those days postage was very heavy, and we were obliged to be very prudent.'

---

[1] Probably Martha, Harriet Martineau's servant, who married the master of Bristol Ragged School, which was Miss Carpenter's 'special care'. Jane was another of H. M.'s servants. See Wheatley, *Martineau*, pp. 317, 323–4.

[2] From a printed source, itself taken from an 1894 transcript of the original letter made by Whitwell Elwin.

[3] Dunmail.

So he and Miss Wordsworth set off after nine o'clock, walked to
Ambleside, knocked up the post-office people, asked for a candle,
got the letter out of the box, sent the good people to bed again,
and sat in the little parlour, 'puzzling and puzzling till they got
the line right'; when they replaced the letter, put out the candle,
and softly stole forth, and walked home in the winter midnight.

It is curious the loving reverence she retains for Coleridge, in
spite of his rousing the house about one in the morning, after her
confinement, when quiet was particularly enjoined, to ask for
eggs and bacon! and similar vagaries.⟨. . .⟩

136 140 141

MARIANNE GASKELL

Plymouth Grove   Monday eveng
½ past 8 question time
[15 November 1852]

My dearest Polly,
    You did not read my last letter carefully I conclude, or else your
letter was a long time on the way, I don't know which, for it had
to be forwarded to me from Fox-How, & reached here yesterday.
About the night gowns, they are at Knutsford, *being* made by
poor old Mrs Granville, whom it won't do to hurry; if I had
know [*sic*] here at Midsummer how very much you wanted them,
I would have had them put in hand sooner,—as it is, and what
with carriage &c they would come to as much as ready-made; so,
if you really are *dead*-pressed,\& can't wait till Xmas,/get {three}
two ready made (calico) from Silvers' Corn-Hill. Oh yes! We'll
send a P-order for your cloak, when you've got it & will send
word what it is. Get a *good* cut, a handsome, useful, *quiet* material
and *then take care of it.* Do you want a winter bonnet? You can get
them so much better in London, if you do? And I would send you
a P.O order*altogether*/: but there again get a *thoroughly good* one
of it's kind, no make-shifts or pretences—I don't want any finery[.]
E. Shaen wd be the best to help you in your choice*not* the
Tagart's on any acct/. I suspect I shall want your *felt* at Xmas for
one of the little ones. There I think that's all about dress,—except

2 gowns at Miss Alcock's which wo*n't* be included in the P.O
order,—and I want you to get a dozen of gloves at Shoolbred's,—
Mrs Wedgwood sent her maid there one day for me, & she
bought me a pair of *long* white gloves for 2-6, which here at
Satts I give 3-9 for,—and some of the dozen (*6* white (4 long
\white/2 short\white/)) might be for Meta you & me. Moreover Hearn wants you to be spying out & seeing if you cannot
see 2 little rough-bear coats or paletots for F E. & Julia,—like mine
which Mrs Carlyle got me last winter price 14s-6d at a shop at
Chelsea & which is *so* warm. Meta has taken to it desperately for
sketching &c. &c. You don't say a word, which rather perplexes
me, about my writing to Mrs Lalor about your going to the
Chapman's on Wednesday. However as I suppose you don't
think it necessary I shan't do it. Be gracious, civil,\& handsome to
servants/& write me a particular account, *not* so much of the
Duke's funeral, as of Mr Mrs Chapman & their ménage &
children. Every body here is going into mourning. I wish you
& I could get into my blk silk at once. However I must make my
grey look mourning. About Ruth! I don't think I shall give away
a single copy. I mean to take my copies out in somebody else's
books. I see no great use\in having my own/. However I sha*n't*
give one to Mrs Lalor for many reasons, & think it very doubtful
if I shall give one to Miss Banks,—though I would gladly show
her any attention both for {you} *her* sake, & yours, darling.
When Ruth will be published whether this year, next, or 10 years
hence I don't know. It is not *written* yet—although Agnes
Sanders was told at a Leamington library that it was coming
down next day. I have never asked for any copies for myself. But,
as I say again, *when* or *if ever* I shall finish it I don't know. I hate
publishing because of the talk people make, which I always feel as
a great impertinence, *if they address their remarks to me* in any way.

  Mrs Rich & Snow Wedgwood come here tomorrow[1] (to go off
from Ruth, the very thought of which makes me X, & the dress
& P order subjects) and I have asked Katie W to come here, &
{My dear Mrs}[2] help me to entertain them.\A letter since I began
this from her; and she comes;/ as I am going to the school 2
mornings, & to the night school on Wednesday, besides having
Margaret, who is very much frightened at 'company' to ins[?]
as to her cook-duties, & the two Ambleside girls, (Miss Mitchell's

[1] Visit cancelled. *Letters and Memorials*, ed. Winkworth, I, p. 368.
[2] Probably the beginning of another letter not proceeded with.

servant & mine) to receive on Thursday & take care of & see after. Besides we are going to have the flower-garden done up, & I want my roses &c all transplanted and must be in the garden at all odd hours, & besides I want to go & see one of the S.S. girls who is ill, & we must go to Miss Marslands who are come home from Southport, &c &c &c &c &c &c. I have seen, (we came home on Friday) the Scotts, when I drove all in the rain on Saturday to fix about Mrs Rich & Snow; they, the Scotts, where [sic] in a state of delight about Esmond, which Thackeray had given them. Then Mrs Shuttleworth came to call & she & I had a long sit,—& last night I had the S. S girls, & Miss Mitchell came in. She is very much pleased with the Italian singing master who is lodging there. Oh! before you come down here you *must* call at the dear Price's—tho' how you're to do it I've no notion. They live {at} in Prince's Terrace, Hyde Park, just close to the Prince's gate we used to go in{to} to the Exhibition—where Mr Hudson lives. I think if Mrs Wedgwood asks you that will be the best time for you to do it, as she will be sure to know the exact number—1, I think it is, and so did Mrs Arnold. Mrs Arnold wants you to go & stay at Fox How sometime. We did so enjoy our few days there; though it was very quiet,—as quiet as could be,—but we saw all the more of my dear Mrs Arnold, Mrs Twining & Fan, who were all that were at home. And Mrs Arnold nursed me out of my indisposition, which was *very* bad while it lasted, but cleared off the day of the Earth-quake,[1] of which we never heard, so I fancy I was sympathizing with my mother Earth; I always do feel thunder &c very much you know. Meta went to see the Ewarts on Saturday & saw your letter, which seems to have pleased them very much. They have taken the Nelson St house, (near S. Winkworths, who has been staying at Chevalier Bunsen's this last month,) *Of course* Meta made Mary sing to her, & Mrs Ewart play: and coaxed little Harry who, she says, is growing more & more charming. I wish you could have gone to Mr Chapman's shop 193 Piccadilly to save Mrs Chapman coming out for you,— whh is giving trouble I don't like,—especially if she has not a carriage of her own—but I am afraid it is now too late to make any other arrangement, & it must stand {by itself} now. Tell us about Mrs Groom's lessons? Meta & I are greedy of news of them. Mr Gunton & Meta are grumbling about the piano,—which *is*

---

[1] 'A severe shock of earthquake was felt in Manchester and neighbourhood.' *Annals*, ed. Axon, p. 262.

wretchedly bad. And that's all at present from your very affec[tionat]e mother

E Gaskell.

Yes! they were *very* nice little notes from Eveleen. Florence has set up a correspondence with Dot Wedgwood. The delectable Annis comes home on the 21st. When do yr holidays begin? Will Miss Banks & Eveleen be able to come *with* you?

140 **141** 142

MARIANNE GASKELL

Monday morning [22 November 1852]

My dearest Polly,

Thank you much for your letter, darling,—we were all craving to hear. Don't fidget yourself about my gown. It's all right. Miss Alcock wrote to *dis*commend glacé silk, & *re*commend what you've got, so I took it in preference, & forgot to tell you; indeed forgot all about it till I got your note. Poor child you sound tired! I suppose that makes you so utilitarian & Joseph Humy as you are about the Funeral. You are the only person among all those from whom we have heard, who have not felt that the solemn & impressive feelings of admiration excited in so many thousands is worth the money expended, even suppose it had not (as those well acquainted with the dead state of trade &c in London at this time of the year say it has,) given employment to thousands & thousands[.] As far as I can hear it was a far better way of expressing a nation's feeling than spending money on that great humbug of an Exhibition—a thing [from] which Manchester has not recovered yet,—but which I suppose will do good in time. I am sorry the funeral car was so ugly as every one says it was. However *that's* done & gone—And now about your letter to me, love. Rosa leaves us because she has a very good offer from Miss Macnicol—, and possibly a dim idea of succeeding to her in the school,—which Miss M. *wishes* her to do eventually,—but this\ *last*/is all a secret; only the present fact is that by being entirely at Miss M's she can earn far more than she does now, & that we ought not to stand in her way,—so that although she is desirous to stay on till Easter (indeed very sorry (she cried sadly,) to leave us at all,) we think she ought to go at Xmas;—we have been so taken by surprize, &

so full of business & company ever since it was told to us (this day
week,) that we have not been able to decide on any plan. We did
think of a very first rate German governess, whom Madame
Bunsen wanted to recommend to us—who could teach music &
singing, German, french Italian & what not,—but we dislike
having a governess in the house to break our privacy as a family,
—so I *think* that plan is at an end. In short we are all at sea.—I am
very much tempted by your offer, darling, because I do so like
your *moral* management of them,—and I think we shall accept it
for 3 months at any rate. The only thing is the difficulty about
regularity, *and* that you must not allow yourself to be fretted into
headaches if Florence *is* a little perverse. The difficulty about
regularity will be very great I am afraid. Though I should be sorry
for you to visit\unreasonably/often[,] yet of course you will be
free to go out with us when you are invited,—& equally of course
it will keep you up beyond your usual time—(& in close rooms
sometimes only *you* don't care for that as I do.) And then you will
feel tired in the morng,—and may be more liable to have headaches if Florence *is* tiresome. Besides some one coming *into* the
house *makes* us regular. There are the difficulties! However the
plan sounds at any rate the best thing we can adopt at present, so
I think we shall try it;—and thank you love! I have had long
interruptions owing to Eliza Patterson calling, & since then the
Miss Kerrs & Judy Scott, bringing a very bad account of Snow
Wedgwood, who is ill at the Scott's—Mrs Wedgwood came
down on Friday night, & yesterday Dr Holland & Mr Wedgwood
telegraphed for.—They hope she is better this morning,—but she
is still very ill—Mrs Rich was here last week; she & Snow were to
have come here on Tuesday, but Mrs Rich put it off till Wednesday
because Snow was not well, & then came alone. She staid here till
Saturday, charming us all. We were to have gone out to meet the
Kinkels, & Mr & Mrs Theodore Martin that Wednesday, but
were thankful to stop at home with Mrs Rich who was tired.
Thursday evng the Shuttleworths came. Friday J J Taylers, Miss
Jewsbury to dinner, & Mary[,] Agnes & Mrs Major. Mrs Rich had
never-ending accounts of her life to tell the children; how she had
been with Queen Hortense in 1815 when Napoleon reviewed his
troops before going out to Waterloo, right under their windows—
& the ceaseless tramp of troops out of Paris for 3 days & 3 nights—
the Emperor of Austria's return with the Austrian Army into
Vienna after that battle.—Her visit\with her father/to the Duke

of Wellington when he was English Ambassador at Paris,—her intimacy with Mme de Stael, her riding across Asia Minor as a Turkish horse*man*, turban pistols & all,—her life at Bagdad &c &c &c. She is a charming person, & Katie W (who was with us & staying here still)[1] thoroughly enjoyed her company. We are going to get a piano at Broadwood's. *Who are we to get to choose it?* Helen Tagart, & perhaps Ed. Bache with her? (I've not asked anybody)—or Emily Shaen, whom I *have* asked, & will do it *if I like*, only must have you to choose it with her as it is too great a responsibility &c. Then she might choose your bonnet too,—we all, Meta[,] Katie, Eliza & myself exclaim *against* dark blue silk,— 'very common', 'very old fashioned', 'sadly too old for Marianne', 'don't let it be like the Tagart's frightful bonnets', but we don't get any nearer to fixing what you *should* have[;] only if Emily chose it, it would be sure to be right, & I don't think you *can* fix before seeing. That's that. Then we are subscribing to Hallé's concerts this winter. There's for you! Only two subscriptions. Tonight Papa goes to Miss Marsland's. Tomorrow Katie goes\home/,& Papa goes in the evening to Lity & Philosophical. Wednesday Cousin Jane dines with us, Papa goes down to the night-school, & afterwards he & I go to the Sydney Potters to meet Silverdale Miss Noble. Thursday Mr & Mrs Winkworth come here to dine, & stay all night, & go with Papa & Meta to Hallé. Friday dinner party at the Shuttleworth's. Saturday S. S. girls here. Monday Papa dines out. Tuesday he & I dine at the Leislers,—so you see we seem very full of engagements of one kind or another. Susanna W. comes home to-day she has been staying at Chevalier Bunsen's till now. [One and a half lines cut away.]

That's all I *think*. Ever darling your very affec[tionate] mother

E C Gaskell.

Oh dear! we are expecting such wonders from Mrs Groom.— Mind you work away *very* hard at your singing. Papa wishes Mr Bennett wd choose our piano, but as your Uncle Langshaw is to have the trade reduction of price, I'm afraid he might not like to do it. Thank you for all yr details about the Chappys. Who are Mr & Mrs *William* Chapman?

Yours very affect[ionate]ly

E. C. Gaskell.

again

[1] See her letter of 22 November, especially her comments on Mrs Gaskell's revisal of *Ruth. Letters and Memorials*, ed. Winkworth, I, p. 369.

MARIANNE GASKELL

[*c.* 27 November 1852]

⟨. . .⟩ as the Tagarts was. You don't say when this dance is? You
had better go to Emily's some day to choose piano—& get yourself a bonnet under her taste; & if Mrs Lalor disapproves of your
going out so often you might perhaps do it by appointment with
Emily after a singing lesson; only remember *Emily's* time must
be THE time, because of her baby &c &c &c[.] About the time of
your coming home, my darling, it must depend on the opportunity we can find, but I will bear in mind your wish to accept
Mrs Lalor's kind invitation. Miss Banks I hope knows how glad
we shall be to see her *whenever* she can come. I hope Eveleen will
come too. Have you money enough of your own for your
bonnet? Not more than *35 shillings* for it? Send word about it.
Now I've a great piece of news for you. Meta is going to school,
to Miss Martineau's on the 20th of Jany[.] It is all fixed suddenly on hearing that Miss M. had a vacancy, as I always felt that
hers was the only school that would do for Meta, but until the
sudden leaving of Rosa I had given up all thoughts of her going.
She has been *so good* of late. Up early as soon after six as she cd, at
her practising at 7 &c—. But Rosa doubted if you could teach the
little ones if Meta were here, she said she occasioned such interruptions, & altogether it has been settled in a minute, & Miss
Martineau seems very much pleased, for it seems she took a
great fancy to Meta. I can tell you little more of the plan, except
that it makes me busy about her clothes, & that she is to learn
dancing, Italian, German, & music from Herman. And that she
rather likes the idea, only wishes she could 'take all her family with
her'. A Austin was to have come in Spring; but we have written
to ask her to come as soon as possible, so she will, perhaps, next
week, & Harriet Schwabe comes here on a visit after Xmas,—out
of friendship to Mr & Mrs Schwabe, who wish her to be kept out
of the stream of gaiety they have in their house,—or else, privately
speaking, I shall be rather afraid of her having a bad influence on
Flossy[.] She is so vulgar in her mind; & you must help me to keep
watch that this is not the case. How I am to pack all I don't
exactly know! Miss Banks & Eveleen in the Spare-room; Meta &

Annie *for that week* in the grey, & then Harriet *must* be in your room, & *you*, dear, must keep double watch over our little sweet Flossy. It is a real kindness to the Schwabes or I should never have asked her, poor girl! I shall write to Emily today to get the piano, —for I shall want it as soon as we can have it, if A A comes & then E. will write to you about the time. I am sorry for Mr Groom's death[.] Will you ask Mrs Groom if she will give you a lesson or two, if you should ever come up to London? I have not heard of Snow Wedgwood! except that they telegraphed to Mr W. & D. Holland last Sunday; but she was better on Monday. I ought to go & see how she is, but I am utterly lame, & have had to give up all this week's engagements,—and I have had some deliciously quiet evenings. Mr & Mrs Winkworth dined here on Thursday, & went to Hallé afterwards, Papa & Meta with them; then the W's slept here.[1] On Friday I had a levee, *nine* sets of callers running!—so close one on the other that I had never time to put on my stocking after Mr Mellor bandaged my leg—⟨. . .⟩

₁₄₂ **143** ₁₄₄

MARIANNE GASKELL

[?November 1852]

About you, love,—we think you must have music lessons once a fortnight when you come home, but this we must talk over— and we are hesitating whether we ought not to have Mr Gunton for Flossy,—not that she plays well, but to save you that worry. However one can't fix everything in a minute. Yes! love[,] get those books if you like them. Only remember they must do *hard* & *correct* as well as interesting work—I mean such things as French verbs, & geography for Flossy; the dry bones of know- ledge.[2] *Oh! poor baby sobbed so because she had no letter from you this morning.* Do write to her next, although I want to hear a great deal. She has had a bad cold & sore throat & been indoors all week. Our camelias are very forward this year. Here is a stupid pink card come, requesting the favour of '*my company* at *Exeter Hall*['] on the 1st of December. The Schwabes, the Wilmots, the Sam Gregs, have all asked me to go & see them. I shall put the Fearon *decision* in after I have spoken to Papa.

---

[1] See p. 213 above.   [2] See p. 212 above for Marianne's offer to teach.

Yes! you may go, & we hope you'll enjoy it, tho' Papa has just the same feeling I have about it. See about your gown (silk)

E C G

143 **144** *144a

MARIANNE GASKELL

Hulme Walfield
Congleton.
Decr 7 [1852]

My dearest Polly,

I left word yesterday that they were to write to you, but I dare say they haven't, so I shall just send you a line. I am here with the Wilmot's (where V. D. is,) came yesterday, go to Lady Hatherton at Capesthorne tomorrow, home on Thursday. This house is a large one & full of people; it stands just above Congleton and must be very pretty in fine weather. I am sorry dear, that you showed my letter to Miss Brooks I should certainly not have written so, if I had thought it was to be passed on, & another time I would rather you would take my permission to do a thing,—as I never say *half* things, or one thing while I mean another; and though I saw many objections to your going to Mrs. Fearon's yet as these were all based on matters of taste (not principle) I thought that your wish\to go/quite overbalanced them. And having been applied to for a decision and having given it, (although I certainly gave my reasons for personally disliking your mixing in any society of which I knew so little,) I hoped & expected you would have gone. Another time take me at my word dear! However I am sure you did what you think right; and I only hope[,] love, you will find pleasure in setting the others off. I have sent 10£ to Emily ready for you on Thursday. Be sure that you pay for your cabs out of that, & *don't let her tire herself* on your behalf. If you can get your bonnet, cloak & piano on Thursday I shall say you do well; if your silk gown besides I think you will do *better*. The Tagarts would help you to choose your gowns, but they have frightful bonnets &c—& Emily is the best for all I think. The—I forget what I was going to say.—Annie Austin is *hoped* for at home today[.] At any rate we asked Mr Richard Martineau to bring

her. And we have 3 Hallé tickets for Thursday so Papa Meta &
Annie can go all together which they will like[.] I am lame still,
& have to keep very still. My darling[,] I hope you don't mind
much not going to Mrs Fearon's. This is a short bad note, but I
write with no end of people in the room, all talking about things
that interest me,—I shall write when I get home. I gave up going
out last week, but Papa was out almost every night. Friday we dine
at Mr Henry's—Monday & Wednesday have people at home.
We are asking out for convoys for you home, my darling.

Ever your very affect[ionate] mother
E. C Gaskell

*   *

*16a 145 424

ELIZABETH HOLLAND

[After 8 December 1852]

⟨. . .⟩ Not having a tree. Our Xmas days are always very quiet,
principally a jollification for the servants. This long wet weather
makes every one poorly & depressed I think. Meta is going to Miss
Martineau's (have you heard?) after Xmas. (20 January) Miss
Rosa Mitchell who has taught the girls in the mornings has a better
engagement offered to her,—and to make a long story short,
Marianne wrote the prettiest sweetest letter begging to be
allowed to teach her\little/sisters & promising to be very regular,
and speaking very humbly & distrustfully of her own powers, but
saying she would do her best. So, then, we thought Meta had
better go to School, for a year or so, & hearing of a vacancy at
Miss Martineau's we wrote; & it was all settled. I am busy with
her clothes, having kept her on short allowance while she was
growing. Annie Austin (her great friend) is staying with us at
present so Marianne is to teach the two little ones 3 hours every
morng—Florence is to have a music master to relieve MA of *that*
piece. MA is to read with William twice a week, & also to have
music lessons from Mr Hallé. Can you fancy our household now
from these details. Poor darling Polly! I trust she is going on well,
but it is a sad blank not to have her coming home when we
expected; and the little ones had worked mats, & gathered
flowers &c &c for her dressing-room. I have been making this said

room as nice as I could for her,—bookshelves, table, inkstand &c,
engraving of that beautiful Madonna della Sedia. I am going to
make myself very busy today by way of passing the time away till
tonight's post, & have planned a long tramp to the work-house,
by way of working off fidgettiness. Your house sounded as if it
would be very pretty indeed from Sam's account in August.
When do you expect your 9th[?] I thought it was to have come
before Xmas![1] *And* I am wanting a waiter. Do you know of one?
I wonder if odd bundles of old letters would amuse you in your
confinement? I dare say you would not care for them; but you
might. Last week—no the week before, Wm brought me Bernard
Palissy,[2] but it so happened I had not a moment of time for reading
except one day, when I got very much interested in four or 5
chapters, & then the book had to go back. We are buying a new
piano which is a grand event in the family[,] semi-grand Broadwood,—not come yet. And I am turned farmer, do you know?
and particularly poultry farmer; & Wm will insist my bantams
are neither so small nor so pretty as yours. What sort *are* yours. I
wish I could shake off the feeling that something sad hangs over us
all this Xmas. I believe its the weather that makes one's heart
heavy. Wm looks so pale, and worn—very like your mother
about the cheeks the last time I saw her. *Don't do too much,* dear!
Take care of yourself

Yours ever very affe[ctionately]   E C Gaskell

137 **146** 150

ELIZA FOX[3]

Tuesday, Dec. 20th, 1852.

⟨. . .⟩ And Ruth is done—utterly off my mind and gone up to the
printers,—that's all I know about it. ⟨. . .⟩ ('you'll get a Ruth
one of these days from the author.') ⟨. . .⟩ Rosa Mitchell had
suddenly a better offer in the money line—a situation she cd not
refuse and we had to change our plans; and we wondered if it
would be fair to a girl of MA's age to ask her to teach little ones,

[1] Emily Lucy Holland (b. 1853). *Holland Family,* ed. Irvine, p. 87.
[2] ?H. Morley, *Palissy the Potter,* 1852.
[3] Original MS. not seen.

and to tie her; and we were doubting about it, when she wrote and offered, *in the nicest way*; humbly distrustfully, yet full of grave steady resolution. Meanwhile Katie was here and heard thro' Alice of a vacancy at Miss Martineau's which we grasped at for Meta, and in a week all these changes in our plans were made. ⟨. . .⟩ Miss Brontë has been ill—*very* ill I'm afraid, but I only heard of it yesterday morning thro' the Shaens, who had asked her there, and she gave that as her excuse or rather reason for not coming to them. I wrote to her directly—though I don't know that *that* did much good—only one felt how lonely and out of the world she must be, poor creature. I've a great mind to go and see her uninvited some day. I cd (that's to say if I'd the money stay at the Inn so as not to be in Mr Brontë's road) However I don't mean to stir from home this long time when I get back, but write, write, write, I really do mean to do something good and virtuous. Florence did not do well in the temper line during the holidays, she always wants to be one of [the] older girl[s] but when I left she was angelic. ⟨. . .⟩

*144b **147** *147a

MARIANNE GASKELL

Friday [?24 Dec. 1852]

My dearest Marianne,

A merry Christmas to you, and plenty of them, my darling. I wish you were at home, tho' it will be exceedingly quiet here. No one coming, nor going out except to Chapel. Flossy & Julia send their very very very best loves; we are not going to keep Xmas day till New Years day, partly because you won't be here, partly because the presents are not ready. A. Austin is gone to Alderley. Mrs Shuttleworth has been here today also the Ewarts to know when you are coming home—Mary Ewart brought word that you had been acting Louis Napoleon *last Saturday*, and made us rather wonder how you could do that, and yet not be well enough to come home on Tuesday. The Hallé last night was most beautiful they say: the Liedertafel sang in spite of my scepticism, & we had two tickets in addition to our own offered to us, one of

whh I took for Selina. All the Ws are gone to Alderley today.
E Shaen wants to know if you can go & choose one of two pianos
she has chosen as the best at Broadwood's. If not, the one *she* liked
best is to be sent. There is a great concoction of mince-meat &
plum-pudding going on. Huddlestone has never tasted either[.]
Hester must leave us, she is so very 'shapeless'[1] as Papa calls her;
we have been a long drive today and Meta was up late last night.
Be sure you write tomorrow & let us know how you are on
Sunday, & *be sure* that it is put in in good time, so as to reach here
on Sunday. My love to Miss Banks. Her room & her welcome is
ready for her; and for Evelene too. Do write. Once more God
bless you darling. Papa wishes you a merry Xmas, and wishes
you were here to enjoy it. Little Harry Ewart is much better. Mrs
Ewart has given Meta such a beautiful purse. Ever darling

Your affect[ionate] mother
E. C. Gaskell.

*

101 148 414

ANNE ROBSON

[Before 27 January 1853]

My dearest Nancy,
  A rebound of letters is the thing! I have a spare $\frac{1}{2}$ hour to write
now off at once to say how glad I am to begin our writing again;
my fault it was dropped &c. I sent Ruth of course. You are
mistaken about either letter or congratulations. As yet I have had
hardly any of the former: indeed I anticipate so much pain from
them that in several instances I have *forbidden* people to write,
for their expressions of disapproval, (although I have known that
the feeling would exist in them,) would be very painful & stinging
at the time. 'An unfit subject for fiction' is *the* thing to say about
it; I knew all\this/before; but I determined notwithstanding to
speak my mind out about it; only how I shrink with more pain
than I can tell you from what people are saying, though I wd do
every jot of it over again to-morrow. 'Deep regret' is what my
friends here (such as Miss Mitchell) feel & express. In short the
only comparison I can find for myself is to St Sebastian tied to a

---

[1] Wanting in energy and ability.

tree to be shot at with arrows; but I knew it before so it comes upon me as no surprize,—as what must be endured with as much quiet *seeming*, & as little inward pain as I can. Of course it is a prohibited book in *this*, as in many other households; not a book for young people, unless read with someone older (I mean to read it with MA some quiet time or other;) but I have spoken out my mind in the best way I can, and I have no doubt that what was meant so earnestly *must* do some good, though perhaps not all the good, or not the *very* good I meant. I am in a quiver of pain about it. I can't tell you how much I need strength. I could have put out much more power, but that I wanted to keep it quiet in tone, lest by the slightest exaggeration, or over-strained sentiment I might weaken the force of what I had to say. But I won't worry you any more about it. I had a terrible fit of crying all Saty night at the unkind things people were saying; but I have now promised Wm I will think of it as little as ever I can help. Only don't fancy me 'overwhelmed with letters & congratulations'[.] I have not had one as yet; and all the fruit thereof has hitherto been bitter. I am so glad to hear Eddie is better—I wanted to have got to see you before Ruth was published. I have taken leave of my *'respectable* friends' up & down the country; *you*, I don't call respectable, but you are surrounded by respectabilities, & I can't encounter their 'shock'. Meta goes to Miss Martineau on the 27th I take her to Liverpool. I wish, dearest Nancy, you would bring your boys & servant, & Mr. Robson[1] and come and see us. Seeing you would be a great comfort and pleasure to me and I want you to see both my girls. Say you came next Saturday. *Friday Evg* we are engaged, and I shd grudge losing your company, or else Friday would be better. I have ½ a large bed (with Flossy or Hearn) could share it with her, and your nurse could sleep with one of our servants,) and a small bedroom opening out of our large spare room, said spare room and all at your service. Do come on Saturday. Willie might have the little room out of yours; (doors left open) your nurse is provided for—and the large spare room for you and Eddie and Mr Robson if he came, or we could arrange it differently at your pleasure only do come dearest Nancy and you would have a quiet little time with us and see your 4 nieces &c., &c., &c., &c., don't you see the charms of the place?

[1] The letter in the possession of Mrs Trevor Jones ends here, but the final section is found on p. 108 of Jane Coolidge's typescript Life of Mrs Gaskell in the Brotherton Collection, University of Leeds.

The Tagarts come in February when we should not be so quiet a family. Do write and say you will and Mr Robson! do *make* her.

Yours very affec[tionate]ly,

E. C. G.

I myself, don't see how Mary B. and Ruth can be compared. They are so different in subject, style, number of characters &c.—everything, and made different partly that people might *not* compare them, but take each for the good that was in them.

Do come on Saturday; if not for your own pleasure, for the great comfort it would be to me, (*who need it*), to see you again.

75 149 211

CATHERINE WINKWORTH[1]

[*c.* January 1853]

〈. . .〉 The *North British Review* had a *delicious* review of 'Ruth' in it. Who the deuce could have written it? It is so truly religious, it makes me swear with delight. I think it is one of the Christian Socialists, but I can't make out which. I must make Will find out.

146 150 151

ELIZA FOX[2]

Monday, [?Early February] 1853.

My dearest Tottie,

I *have* been *so* ill; I do believe it has been a 'Ruth' fever. The beginning of last week my own private opinion was that I should never get better. I was so utterly weak after it but I have picked up, and this cold weather braces me—I suppose you abominate it. I should never have left your last letter unanswered so long if it was not for that—but oh! I was so poorly! and cd not get over the hard things people said of Ruth. I mean I was just in that feverish way when I could not get them out of my head by thinking of

---

[1] From a printed source.   [2] Original MS. not seen.

anything else but dreamt about them and all that. I think I must be an improper woman without knowing it, I do so manage to shock people. Now *should* you have burnt the 1st vol. of Ruth as so *very* bad? even if you had been a very anxious father of a family? Yet *two* men have; and a third has forbidden his wife to read it; they sit next to us in Chapel and you can't think how 'improper' I feel under their eyes. However some people like it— Mr J. W. Darbishire for one. However I won't bother you or myself any more about it. ⟨. . .⟩ We have capital accounts from Meta and Marianne *does* famously with the children; especially as her only two dances as yet have come on a *Friday* allowing her a good long sleep on Saturday morning when the children have no lessons. ⟨. . .⟩ Send me some London news—the world here is very flat, and my heart is very flat. Good bye my own dear Tottie, Yrs ever affe[ctionatel]y

[E. C. G.]

150 **151** 169

ELIZA FOX[1]

[?Early February] 1853.

My dear Tottie,

I have been so poorly and am so still[2]—influenza I suppose it is, but I bark like a dog, and am as weak as a cat; but I may as well vent some of the consequent inanity upon you as upon any one else, promising that you won't find me sensible or wise or amiable or agreeable or amusing—at least I am not to myself. About Ruth one of your London librarians (Bell I believe) has had to withdraw it from circulation on account of 'its being unfit for family reading' and Spectator, Lity Gazette, Sharp's Mag; Colborn have all abused it as roundly as may be. Litery Gazette in every form of abuse 'insufferably dull' 'style offensive from affectation' 'deep regret that we and all admirers of Mary Barton must feel at the author's loss of reputation' 'Thoroughly commonplace' etc., etc. I don't know of a newspaper which has praised it but the Examiner, wh. was bound to for Chapman's sake—and that's *that*, and be hanged to it.—No! I had not heard of Frankie coming home: was it on account of his bad health?

---

[1] Original MS. not seen.   [2] Source reads 'till'.

Anyhow the Mediterranean sounds much pleasanter as a station—
oh how I should like to be wafted out of this England full of
literal and metaphorical nipping east wind to Constantinople for a
month—a long sail along the Mediterranean, slowly and lazily
floating;—however I shall never get that, you may yet some [of]
these days. I am glad to hear about Charlotte; it is a nice bit of
news, and MA tells me that she has heard that hands do grow
bigger from practising. No! stick to it *not* to begin with one
parent and then go to another; not to begin in one place and then
go to another. Schools are such fickle things that often such little
changes as that affect them more when once established, how
much more when only just beginning. I should like to be at
school with Mrs Ellis in that charming house, else I fancy her an
almighty humbug. Poor little wee child—that Knatchbull child I
mean—I can hardly fancy any more trying scene. Unusually for
me I had noticed the death in the newspaper. To be sure dear you
shall have Williams's portrait, *tell us where to direct it to, and when
you would like it to come.* About MA it was *my* doing and not Mrs
Lalors. MA wrote to me about it a month before she left: but I
thought in the first place that she might have misunderstood you,
but the principal reason was that I thought that if you were
thinking of beginning your school at Xmas which you know you
did talk about that time, you might in all your thought and occupation have forgotten all about the offer you made in the summer,
and feel yourself rather bound, while in reality you were very busy
and full of other things. So I told MA to say nothing about it
unless she heard from you, and I don't know that ever she named
it [to] Mrs Lalor—MA is at home so good never reads a word; but
is patience sweetness etc: personified with the little ones, docile
and gentle to us, and altogether a treasure. We have capital
accounts of Meta; she and Miss Martineau mutually each.[1] Helen
and Emily Tagart are staying here;[2] ditto Selina W. for a day or
two. Helen is engaged to be married to a second cousin of hers and
Mr Gaskell's called E. Harvey a solicitor living in Liverpool, fair
haired 6 feet 2, aged 27 and thats nearly all I know of him, seeing I
hardly ever saw him till he came over last Saturday to see Helen.
MA is going to have music lessons from Hallé, and practises singing
every day with Mary Ewart. The Ewarts are come to live at

[1] Source has comma after 'each'.
[2] See Catherine Winkworth letter of 14 February 1853. *Letters and Memorials*, ed.
Winkworth, I, p. 384.

20 Nelson St.—near Susanna, who is wiser than ever since the Times said she was no average woman. The S. D.Ds and we are *really* I think becoming thick again, at least *they* would be if *we* would, but we hold off, on occasion of the uncertainty of her sayings and doings. I don't see any chance of my coming up to London this winter spring, or summer, though I should like very well to,—I must go to lie down; I am so tired with writing this. But I mean to write again soon: I am, dearest Tottie, now and always your own very affect[ionate] friend

E. C. G.

All (?) about George. We have three blk Spanish chicks out, and a Cochin sitting on her own eggs. How is poor Mr Forster?

0 152 156

R. MONCKTON MILNES[1]

Plymouth Grove,
Feb. 10th. [1853]

My dear Sir,—

I have been told that I ought to have too much 'self-respect' to care for people's opinions on what I wrote; but though in some instances this said stoical self-respect would have saved me pain, I am sure I would not purchase it by the loss of the zest with which I have enjoyed your approval. I am so glad you liked 'Ruth'. I was so anxious about her, and took so much pains over writing it, that I lost my own power of judging, and could not tell whether I had done it well or ill. I only knew how very close to my heart it had come from. I tried to make both the story and the writing as quiet as I could, in order that 'people' (my great bugbear) might not say that they could not see what the writer felt to be a very plain and earnest truth, for romantic incidents or exaggerated writing. But I have no right to presume upon your leisure, so I will only say, once more, thank you for taking the trouble of writing to express what you felt.

I do not know that I am likely to be in town soon; but if I am, I shall certainly have great pleasure in letting you know.

Yours truly, and also 'obliged,'
E. C. Gaskell

[1] From a printed source.

45 **153** 219

ANNA JAMESON[1]

Plymouth Grove
March 7th [1853]

My dear Mrs Jameson,

I meant, and I meant to thank you for your letter, and if I could, without telling you what had become of it; for every day I have been hoping it would be restored to me. Oh dear! Do you know it is lost! along with several other valued & comforting letters about Ruth; while every letter of reprobation and blame comes to me, straight as an arrow, the precious little packet I sent to a dear friend in London for her pleasure and sympathy was lost at the Post Office. We have made enquiries at both ends, and they give us hopes that it may be restored[,] but meanwhile I can not any longer delay writing my thanks for the kind words (that told of kind thoughts,) in your letter. I should have often found it a comfort and a pleasure to read it again,—a comfort and a pleasure because I am sure you understood what I aimed at,—from anyone who sympathizes in that aim I can bear a great deal of personal fault-finding. Not that you did anything of the kind[, dear][2] Mrs Jameson. I never spoke[3] much on the subject of the book before; and I am surprized to find how very many people—good kind people—and *women* infinitely more than men, really & earnestly disapprove of what I have said & express that disapproval at considerable pain to themselves, rather than allow a 'demoralizing laxity' to go unchecked. Three or four *men* have written to approve,—some—one or two at least high in literature,—and two, with testimony as valuable as fathers of families,—grave thoughtful practical men. I think I have put the small edge of the wedge in, if only I have made people talk & discuss the subject a little more than they did.

Goodbye my dear Mrs Jameson. The Scotts were quite well on Friday when we met the Leonard Homers[4] there.

Yours most truly
E. C. Gaskell

[1] Original MS. not seen. Transcript made by the then owner of Mrs Gaskell's letter.
[2] Supplied from *Anna Jameson*, ed. Erskine, p. 294.
[3] *Anna Jameson* reads 'I have spoken'.   [4] Horners.

86 **154** 181

LADY KAY-SHUTTLEWORTH[1]

Plymouth Grove
April 7. [1853]

My dear Lady Kay-Shuttleworth,

I think I may quote the beginning of your letter, and say '*I* have been intending to write to *you* &c', for it would be very true, and I am rather ashamed to find you have put your intention in practice first. I have had it in my mind to write ever since Mr Gaskell Meta and I came along the high-road from Colne to Burnley, and I made out we could see Gawthorp on the right hand-side just after coming through Padiham? Did we? That was in last August. I should like to see you to talk over Ruth with you; (that is to say if you were well enough,) for I know you have thought a great deal on the subject, and I should like to tell you why I did so & so and did *not* do so and so in writing it. Of course I knew of the great difference of opinion there would be about the book before it was published. I don't mean as to it's merely literary merits, but as to whether my subject was a fit one for fiction; and those, who thought it was not, were very likely to be disgusted at the plainness with which in one or two places I have spoken out\a small part of/what was in my mind. I think the extremes of opinion that I have met with have even gone farther than yours; for I have known of the book being *burnt*. But from the very warmth with which people have discussed the tale I take heart of grace; it has made them talk and think a little on a subject which is so painful that it requires all one's bravery not to hide one's head like an ostrich and try by doing so to forget that the evil exists. Yes! I did read that letter of a 'First Hand';—those letters indeed, and I liked the whole tone and mode of expression so much that I was thoroughly glad to see how people came forwards to set her up in her scheme. Do you know that little poem of Hood's called [']the Lady's Dream'; because it is so true what he says about evil being done by *want of thought*.[2] I can't help fancying the long credit

---

[1] *Annotation* 1853.
[2] See, e.g., the penultimate stanza:
'The wounds I might have heal'd! | The human sorrow and smart! | And yet it never was in my heart | To play so ill a part: | But evil is wrought by want of Thought, | As well as want of Heart!' |

some of those London dressmakers allow, and the consequent
risk of bad debts, must lessen their profits very considerably, and I
wish the First Hand would go on the ready money principle. I
never give anything to any Bazaar and never go to one, just for
the same reasons that you allege, and I feel that so many people,
here at least, are of the same mind that I fancy they are dying
away.

I will most gladly be a 'corresponding member' of the Establishment for Invalid Gentlewomen if the duties are not very onerous.
I am sure I can and will do all in my power to make it known; and
I can serve as a reference, having been over the house &c. I am
not a good beggar for subscriptions for anything; but I will name
your, i.e. the Committee's want of them to anyone who is
likely\to subscribe/; and I shall like having the information to
distribute, because I am sure the whole Establishment is of so
valuable a character. Shall I do for a corresponding member?
with the drawback of not being a good and efficient beggar?—I
ought to thank Miss Paplouska for her kindness in writing twice
to me last autumn to tell me how you were; will you give her my
very kind regards and best *true* thanks. I like what she said about
Ruth, and what she did about it too, Sunday as it was. The
difference between Miss Brontë and me is that she puts all her
naughtiness into her books, and I put all my goodness. I am sure
she works off a great deal that is morbid *into* her writing, and *out*
of her life; and my books are so far better than I am that I often
feel ashamed of having written them and as if I were a hypocrite.
However I was not going to write of myself but of Villette. I
don't agree with you that {it is} one cannot forget that it is a
'written book'. My interpretation of it is this. I believe it to be a
very correct account of one part of her life; which is very vivid &
distinct in her remembrance, with all the feelings that were called
out at that period, forcibly present in her mind whenever she
recurs to the recollection of it. I imagine she *could* not describe it
{with} in the manner in which she would pass through it *now*, as
her present self; but in looking back upon it all the passions &
suffering, & deep despondency of that old time come back upon
her. Some of this notion of mine is founded entirely on imagination; but some of it rests on the fact that many times over I
recognized incidents of which she had told me as connected with
that visit to Brussels. Whatever truth there may be in this conjecture of mine there can be no doubt that the book is wonderfully

clever; that it reveals depths in her mind, aye, and in her *heart* too
which I doubt if ever any one has fathomed. What would have
been her transcendent grandeur if she had been brought up in a
healthy & happy atmosphere no one can tell; but her life sounds
like the fulfilment of duties to her father, to the poor around her,
to the old servants (I have heard incidentally of such delicate
kindness\of her's/towards them) that I can not help hoping that
in time she may work round to peace,—if she can but give up her
craving for keen enjoyment of life—which after all comes only in
drams to anyone, leaving the spaces between most dreary &
depressing. Still it is easy to talk & arrange another person's life
for them; and I am sure I could not have borne, (even with my
inferior vehemence of power & nature) her life of monotony and
privation of any one to love. I hope she is coming here soon; and
when she comes and I get little viva voce glimpses into her daily
life I know I shall look up to her strength and (outward if you will)
patience with wonder & admiration.

Mr Gaskell desires his kind regards. I can't help hoping that you
may by some happy possibility be made acquainted this year.
Possibly—between a Possibly & a Probably he & I will go up to
town at Whitsuntide. Shall you be gone to Homburg [*sic*] then?
the 15th of May is Whitsunday. We don't know where we shall
be yet.

April 10th. Since writing my last sentence it is become 'between
a possibly and a probably' that we may go to Paris on May 12 or
13th! I have never been there; and we plan to take Marianne, our
eldest girl, who is a most gentle and patient teacher of her two
little sisters; Meta having taken her place at school. If so we shall
remain at Paris till the 23rd, and I *may* remain a little in London on
{my}\our/return; but Mr Gaskell must come home straight on
account of his congregational duties, and Marianne must not miss
any more of the music lessons she is having from Hallé. I don't
know if she or I are the most delighted with this sudden plan;
which after all can hardly be called a plan after all [*sic*], only an
idea.

I do not know Mr Joseph Kay's address or I should have
written to thank him for his valuable and most interesting pamphlet
on the Condition and Education of English children as compared with Germans;[1] I believe his address was signed at the end
of the preface, but this book was borrowed from me as soon

[1] *Condition of Poor Children in English and German Towns*, Longmans, 1853.

as I had read it, & has not yet been returned. Mr Gaskell is wanting it very much as he says it would give him some very valuable facts for a report on the better regulation of the places of public amusement which he is drawing up; it makes one feel very much ashamed of our boasted civilization as compared with that of other countries. I had no idea that there {was}\were/so many children uneducated here in proportion to the educated. Will you thank Mr Kay very much for me for so kindly remembering me. —And pray give my very kind regards to Miss Paplowska,—(I may beg your patience in reading this letter I think.) How are the children? Ughtred and Janet are all who will I think remember me.

     Ever my dear Lady Kay Shuttleworth your attached friend

                                  E. C. Gaskell

139 155 166

?JOHN FORSTER

[?Late April 1853]

⟨. . .⟩ More—she is so true, she wins respect, deep respect, from the very first,—and then comes hearty liking,—and last of all comes love. I thoroughly loved her before she left,[1]—and I was so sorry for her! She has had so little kindness & affection shown to her; she said that she was afraid of loving me as much as she could, because she had never been able to inspire the kind of love she felt.—She has had an uncomfortable kind of coolness with Miss Martineau, on account of some *very* disagreeable remarks Miss M. made on Villette, and this had been preying on Miss Brontë's mind as she says everything does prey on it, in the solitude in which she lives. She gave Mr Thackeray the benefit of some of her piercingly keen observation. My word! he had reason when he said he was afraid of her. But she was very angry indeed with that part of the Examiner review of Esmond (I had forgotten it) which said his works would not live; and asked me if I knew if you had written it. I wish you could have heard how I backed away

---

[1] Charlotte Brontë visited Mrs. Gaskell 'at the close of April', 1853. E. C. Gaskell, *Life of Charlotte Brontë*, 1857, II, p. 288.

from the veiled prophet, and how vehemently I disclaimed ever even having conjectured anything about any article in the Examiner. Thackeray has promised not to write a book about the Americans. He says they are foolish to have exacted such a promise; that if he had written at first, with the remembrance of their hospitality fresh in his mind he would have given them only kindly words, and gentle satire. As it is they are sure to appear in some of his works of fiction by & bye, and will be less mercifully treated. She seems to have a great idea of Thackeray as a worshipper of 'Dutchesses & Countesses', and to have disliked the tone of some of his lectures (that on Steele) exceedingly. She is not going to write again for some time. She is thoroughly good; only made bitter by some deep mortifications,—and feeling her plainness as 'something almost repulsive'. I am going to see her at Haworth, at her father's particular desire. Mr Smith has got her 100£, for a\French/translation of Villette (500£ for the copyright,)—) but Tauchnitz, or his agent Williams, have never applied to her about Leipsic re-publication. I thought you would be at the Academy dinner. Is not Millais's picture this year very beautiful.[1] I am very glad indeed to hear that you are so much better. I have written amid the distraction of children, all full of garden seeds, & coming for my advice at every moment, so this letter ought to have many apologies made for it,—only I must go out, & have no time for them. Ever yours most truly

E C Gaskell

152 **156** 168

R. MONCKTON MILNES

8 Hyde Park Gardens
[Before 31 May 1853][2]

Dear Sir,

I am more than half ashamed of my delay in answering your note, containing a kind invitation to dinner on Tuesday next; but, indeed, until today I hardly knew if I should be in town at that

---

[1] Millais was exhibiting 'The Proscribed Royalist' and 'The Order of Release'.
[2] Dating depends upon Letters 157 and 158.

time. Now however I am happy to say that I believe I shall be able to avail myself of the pleasure you offer me.

Yours very truly

E. C. Gaskell

*

0 **157** 217

EMILY SHAEN[1]

[?27 May 1853][2]

⟨...⟩ I should so like to come, and above all things to know a little of Mazzini, but there is a great dinner-party here, made for me—Macaulay, Hallam, Sir Francis Palgrave, and Lord Campbell —I don't *think* I can get away *before* 10, and then it is 3 miles to go —but I'll leave it a little open, please, for all that. ⟨...⟩ Another great dinner to-night, dinners being Lady C's visiting; she declines all evening parties. ['Lady C. would not hear of her going into lodgings'.] ⟨...⟩ I go to dine at the Monckton Milnes on Tuesday, to the Dukeries on Thursday, and must get in a day for Mr Carlyle.

*156a **158** 160

MARIANNE GASKELL

Crix—Sunday Eveng

[29 May 1853]

My dearest Polly,

I mean to write to all my daughters tonight, and have just accomplished a letter 3 sheets long to Meta, giving an account of my proceedings up to this time.

You have heard a good deal; I wrote a great long letter to Papa on Thursday; in the evening Ly Coltman—oh! first of all she & I, & Mrs Price & Rose set off at 4 o'clock to go & see Mr Nash's reformatory school in Westminster; & our party gathered like a snow-ball the Dean of Hereford, a Mr Vivian, Lady Bell, Lady Herschel, Bonham Carters &c—And *well* worth seeing it was.—

[1] From a printed source.   [2] 1858 (source). Our dating depends on Letter 158.

Only I have not time to tell you much about it: besides I think I
told Papa. Then we came back & dressed for a quiet party at the
Wm Duckworth's (dinner) no one but ourselves; but great plan-
ning about our coming there (Beechwood you Meta Papa & I) in
July.—(Think what we can best do with the little ones, to give
them pleasure, & yet keep them well during that hot month.
\Bowden too warm/Our own house would be the coolest,—&
Mr Mellor near,—) Friday I went with Ly Coltman to Covent
Garden Market, & to pay my bill to Mrs Dove, our landlady in
Bloomsbury Sq—home; dressed for dinner. Sir Charles & Lady
Trevelyan, Monckton Milneses, Milnes Gaskells, Dean of St Pauls
& Mrs Milman\Wm Duckworths/—Lady Coltman thought the
party flat—but I did not, though several of the people did not talk,
which made her very angry. Tomorrow however I expect she
will have too many talkers if Hallam, Macaulay, Vaughan,
(Regius Professor of History at Oxford) Sir Francis Palgrave &c
come. Saty I first walked with Ly Coltman all round Kensington
Gardens, & then went all by myself to call on Mrs James Booths,—
she was out, but Miss (Silverdale) Noble was there, and very
funny,—she sent her love to 'all my family' which she said she
said she meant for a delicate way of wrapping up her love for
Mr Gaskell. Mrs James Booth has written notes & called & I
don't-know-whated to beg I will go there if only for a day or two,
—according to a promise made last year (she says) that Papa & I
would make their house our home when we went; & meanwhile
& previously I had promised Mrs James to go to *her* on Wednesday
—oh! *she is* such a charming person. Don't forget Mr James[']
address *47 Wimpole Street*,—& Ly Coltman is vexed (in her pretty
way) that I don't stay *there*, and I have so many calls to pay: &
shall *utterly* offend the Carlyles, if I don't give them a day, they
have said so much about it. I really think if you don't want me at
home, darling I must stay on to Tuesday or Wednesday week (7 or
8) & then go straight to Miss Brontë's[1] by the Great Northern
railway, *leaving King* [sic] *Cross Station at ½ past 10, gets to Leeds at
4-50PM (Fare 33s) Leave Leeds at 5PM Arrive at Keighley at 5-56,
Fare 2s-10d* and then return home on Friday or Saturday[.] Any
how & most particularly *I must* ⟨. . .⟩

[1] Mrs Gaskell had been invited for Thursday, 9 June 1853, and had written to
accept by 6 June. (*The Brontës*, ed. Wise & Symington, IV, p. 70.) This visit fell
through.

₀ **159** ₁₆₄

F. J. FURNIVALL[1]

[?1 June ?1853]

My dear Sir
 I seize a little scrap of paper, (being on the immediate wing for
47 Wimpole Street,) to say I am half afraid of compromising
\myself the pleasure/for Thursday eveng at all,—I am so uncertain if I shan't be in Manchester; I can't say anything till I have seen
my new hostess Mrs James,—and IF I do go to Mr Ruskin's class,
I shan't have a minute to spare for anything else I'm afraid—I
EXTREMELY want to go. But this week is in a mist. I fear I shan't be
near Carlton Gardens; but I should like to see Ly Goderich—47
Wimpole St

Yours very truly
E C Gaskell

If I go, I shd be glad if you could call *here*, for I shall come that
aft. here to wish goodbye.[2]

₁₅₈ **160** ₁₆₃

MARIANNE GASKELL

Thursday Morng
[?June 1853][3]

Just off to St Pauls; we lunch at Deanery, & dine at Ly Coltman's
today; & after that, *if* we feel inclined, go to the Schwabes. My
darling, I'm *afraid* your Paris gown is not at all fit for an evening
party—you'd better come & look at it if you can, as it will crush
sadly in sending,—& may not do to wear. Meta is *sure* it won't; it is
not so 'dress' as your green silk. Please thank *very* much for the
concert recitals tomorrow—it was *very* kind of Mme Hallé. But it
is Julia's first night, & I doubt if it will please her if we leave her;

---

[1] *Address (on envelope)* F J Furnivall Esq | Old Square.
[2] Note inside flap of envelope.
[3] Dating doubtful. We assume that the lunch at the Deanery could have been
the Thursday visit to the Milmans of Letter 161.

besides which, as a rule, I am declining all *eveng* engagements. Still we may come, but it is not very likely. But please thank a great deal[.] In greatest haste.

Your most loving E C G.

Papa goes back on Saturday. Mr Vernon Lushington brought his sister Alice to tea last night, promiscuous, i.e. uninvited.

₀ **161** ₀

UNKNOWN

[?June 1853]

⟨...⟩ double acrostics,—our mutual passion—hoisted me. Mr Thackeray dined here on Friday, & I saw him at the Milmans the day before. You can't think how gentle & kind & happy he is— he won't hear a word, or a joke against the Americans: he says they never asked him an impertinent question,—& are far less censorious & unkind than the English,—he hopes to return there before long.[1]—and—and—arn't you tired?—and yet I have really 'a great many things to say to you' yet, besides the one great staring fact, that I am now as ever yours most truly

E C Gaskell

Do you really mean to say you can see Rotterdam,—if so, I don't know what's to hinder you from seeing the Ural mountains in Siberia.

₁₂₈ **162** ₀

GRACE SCHWABE

Plymouth Grove,
Sunday
[19 June ?1853]

My dearest Mrs Schwabe,
    I have such a great deal to say, a great deal more than you will have time to read I am afraid. In the first place thank you for so

---

[1] Charlotte Brontë probably refers to these meetings between Mrs Gaskell & Thackeray. See *The Brontës*, ed. Wise & Symington, IV, p. 78; G. N. Ray, *Thackeray. The Age of Wisdom*, 1958, p. 223.

kindly entertaining and speaking about the petition I sent you; I sent it partly because Mrs Davy and Mrs Fletcher, not knowing if it had been heard of here, wished me to make it known; I hardly expected or thought of your giving anything; I was glad to find you did know all about it, and did not think me impertinent for calling your attention to it. I find 400£ has been already raised, whh seems to me a great deal, though perhaps little in comparison with 1500. Then I wanted to tell you I have still got your two guineas. I should have sent or given them to Lieutenant Blackmore, but for two or three things which I heard and which I thought it would be right for you to know\before giving the money/. I met a Mr Allen at dinner at Mr Wedgwood's one Sunday; he is a relation of her's, and a *very* good active energetic young man; visiting at hospitals, and much among the very class whom Lieut Blackmore had tried to aid. We talked (apropos of Ruth) a good deal about the difficulty of reclaiming this class, *after they had once taken to the street life*, and as he knew Lieutenant Blackmore's place pretty well, I asked him about it, as I had before heard, through Lady Buxton, of things going on at it that were very far from right—he said there might be some exaggeration in what I had heard—(of men being concealed in the house,) but that Lieutenant Blackmore although sincere in desiring the attainment of a good object was neither scrupulous nor wise in his means; that he was the best 'touter' in all London, & that some of 'his statements were a tissue of lies.' I give the exact words. I believe 'touter' means a beggar for his particular object,—which is not wrong, if people only tell the truth in 'touting'. But altogether— hearing that visits were discouraged—although there might be good reasons for that in keeping the place private & not making it into a show,—and from what Lady Buxton & Mr Allen said, I did not feel that it would be right to give {the}\your/money, without your knowing more fully about it; especially as it could go any time by a Post Office order. Then I heard of another institution of the same kind only conducted by\a few/ladies⟨,⟩ Mrs Lancaster (do you know her) at the hea⟨d⟩, but this did not require money, & wishe⟨d⟩ to be very quiet & unnamed. Then I trie⟨d⟩ to gain information from Mr Dickens res⟨pecting⟩ one named in Household Words, about two months ago,[1]—this too did not require money, as it only wanted to try the powers of

[1] This may refer to an article appearing in *Household Words*, No. 161, 23 April 1853, pp. 169 ff.

reformation on *two* or *three* poor creatures, the conductors thinking that if a *number* are collected together they have not so good a chance; Mr Di⟨ckens⟩ said he would *tell* me more about this when he saw me; but he was ill, and I never saw him again. Please don't think me a very unsatisfactory agent, for I did take pains to learn what was right about it.

Oh! and I saw Mrs Stowe after all; I saw her twice; but only once to have a good long talk to her; then I was 4 or 5 hours with her, and liked her very much indeed. She is short and American in her manner, but very true & simple & thoroughly unspoiled & unspoilable. She promised (almost *offered*) to stay with us the two days she is allowing herself in Manchester; early in September; but I don't know if she will, for she is not famous for keeping her engagements, as we know. Then I went to see my friend Mr Wilson (Price's Candle Company,) and your friend Mr Nash; who is delightful. I also made acquaintance with two Mr Spottiswoode's; two young men much distinguished at Cambridge & well known to Chevalier Bunsen; they are printers (blue books, acts of parliament &c,) succeeding to a business which has been long in their family of King's Printer. They live in a great large house in Farringdon Street, and here they have all the 'printers devils' & apprentices &c to live with them. They have a room fitted up as a chapel at the top of the house, in which prayers are read; & hymns sung to an organ played by one of the Mr Spottiswoodes every morning & night. They take their meals, their work, their walks & pleasures all under the guidance of this Mr S. as if he were their elder brother. They have good engravings from all the great religious pictures (Christus Consolator. Christus Remunerator), &c. &c hung round their clean & cheerful eating room; they have a Xmas tree at Christmas,—in short they are like a large & happy family—and it seems such a beautiful life for this Mr Spottiswoode to be leading— He & Mr Wilson are great friends. Mr W gives his printing to Mr Spottiswoode to do,—& it is to be hoped that Mr Spottiswoode returns the compliment by burning Price's candles.

Thank you for asking us so kindly to come to you. If you will allow me to bring Hearn (our nurse, Mrs Curtis's sister) and my two youngest little girls, Florence & Julia, on *Saturday* week, the 2nd of July, Mr Gaskell will join us on *Monday* the 4th) He does not like leaving Mr Robberds to all the services of a first Sunday\in the month/,) and we will remain with you until the following

Thursday, the seventh; when Mr Gaskell & I must go on to pick up Marianne & Meta\who will be staying with friends in the neighbourhood of London—/, and fulfil our plan of making a little tour in Normandy during Meta's holidays. If this time does not suit you my dear Mrs Schwabe, I shall hope to be allowed to come to Glyn Garth after your return from Germany. Mr Gaskell desires his kind love to you, and joins with me in mine to Mr Schwabe. Meta came home on Thursday,—very much grown, & we also think improved in many ways; on Monday week she goes to spend 10 days with her friend Annie Austin, & Marianne goes to revisit her old schoolmistress & dearly loved friend, Miss Banks. I heard of Harriet very pleasantly the other day, as having said some very kind as well as very wise little things. Your loving friend E C Gaskell

160 **163** 165

MARIANNE GASKELL

Glyn Garth Tuesday
[5 July 1853][1]

My darling Polly[,]

I write in a great hurry, as if it is fine we are to go to see the South Stack lighthouse at Holyhead in less than an hour; and I have many letters to write previously. Perhaps I had better put my business in *first. Unless you hear to the contrary from me* you must be at 36 Bloomsbury *Sq. on Saturday morning next at* {11} ½ *past 11 o'clock*, with your boxes *directed Gaskell, W. Duckworth's Esq, Beechwood, near Southampton.* I have written to tell Meta this too, but there may be some alteration in the plan yet, as I can hardly get Papa to make any decision. I must leave it to you to settle if you had better go round & pick up Meta (I don't know distances or directions) *in which case you would have to make a previous arrangement with her*, or to come separately, & you must make some arrangement with Mrs Knight about *that* box. So there's *that* for you to think about, and plan, darling. I have little enough of news. We got here about seven on Saturday evening[.] It is a splendid place,—far more striking inside than Crumpsall; fitted

[1] See p. 237 above.

up by Grace, & all the arrangement of colours perfect. They say a
great deal about your coming here in the autumn, so I shan't go on
describing. Hearn & the little ones have an immense nursery;
only too far away from my room, that's the worst; Sunday Mr
Schwabe read the Brook St service & a sermon in the morning, &
in the afternoon some of us got into a little boat to go across the
Straits to service in Bangor Cathedral, but the waves were 'raging
white' & Miss Brendon & Florence were so much frightened we
put back. Yesterday morning Mr Schwabe went to Manchester;
he comes back today. Last night Papa & Mr Wright came; and
today it is planned that we should go to Holyhead if it will but be
fine, which it is not now I am sorry to say. It has rained almost
ever since we came here; and there are very few books, or other
readable things. Papa has brought me the Westminster Review,
which must go back to the Gregs. If you *cd* call on the Prices 11
Princes Terrace[,] Hyde Park South, I should be glad; but I am
afraid it will be quite out of your power. You were *quite* right
not to go to the Exhibition without Mrs Austin; I *guess* it was no
great loss to you, my lady. Florence *likes* being here now; for the
first day or two she *professed* not to like it; I wish it could be fine
for them to go out. All the James Martineaus come tomorrow.
They are at Pendyffryn; I wish they weren't coming.—I like to
range about ad libitum, & sit out looking at views &c; not talking
sense by the yard. Yes! I *am* sorry to hear there will be more
visitors at Beechwood, only those Ewarts are nice quiet girls, who
know how to be silent[.] We heard just the same account of MA
Rigby yesterday; also from Louy. Mrs Tagart's letter has been
forwarded here. I shall *try* to answer it today, only of course we
can't accept her kindness. Yes[,] you may ask Anne Norton—I
don't know Emily Palmer a bit, nor her belongings,—& you
know when (if) Mrs Stowe[1] comes we shall be full & busy[.]
Farewell! my 'Swan-necked Edith'. It is to be hoped you are not
looking for the body of Harold all this time—My love to Miss
Banks, & kind regards to Mr & Mrs Lalor. Kind love to Evelene.

Your own affec[tionate]
Mammy.

[1] She came in this year. See Mrs E. H. Chadwick, *Mrs Gaskell Haunts, Homes, and Stories*, rev. ed., 1913, pp. 198–9.

F. J. FURNIVALL[1]

> Beechwood
> near Southampton
> July 18 [?1853]

My dear Sir,

I have only just received your letter, forwarded to me from home; and as I am on the point of leaving for Normandy I am afraid I can do but little, personally; but I have written two letters to two people, Mr Herford & Mr Winkworth from whom I think you will receive thoroughly trustworthy replies. It is so difficult to conjecture\any/numbers who will or will not do this or that. Have you heard from Mr Scott? I am afraid he too is away. August is a bad month for people being away who might help in the arrangements. The Free Trade Hall, if not pulled down, is our largest building; too large for your purpose I fancy. Then comes the Corn Exchange in the very heart of the town (so far, so good!) holding about 2500 people,—used for political & literary lectures to which the Mayor does not choose to give his sanction, or lend his Town Hall. Cardinal Wiseman lectured there just lately.[2] Then the Mechanics Institute, the best I shd think—holding about 1200,—Then the Socialist & Secularist (Holyoake's &c) place of gathering the Carpenters Hall, where you would get the greatest number of working men, I believe, but which is often used for very disreputable dances &c, & so has justly earned itself an ill name, which you would have to struggle against. There is a great prejudice against Lord Goderich—fomented by a certain John Walker a basket maker, who has said a great deal about his bribing at Hull, & Lady Goderich's orders of dresses bonnets &c. I have heard a good deal said about this, whether true or not I don't know; but it has made our Manchester people believe Lord Goderich takes up anything, not from principle but to get into parliament for a good place. I write in a terrible hurry. I hope you can read it. Oh dear! *Does* Alexander Smith squint? Or is it only the 'poet's eye' [?]

> Yours truly
> E. C. Gaskell

I have snatched at *any* paper. Please excuse it.

[1] *Address (on envelope)* F J. Furnivall Esq | 11 New Square | Lincoln's Inn | London. *Postmarks* LYNDHURST | JU 17 | 1853 *and* 18 JY 18 | 1853.

[2] This may refer to a lecture on art which he gave on 27 April 1853.

₁₆₃ **165** ₁₇₃

MARIANNE GASKELL

[?Summer 1853]
Friday

My dear MA,

I was glad to get your letter today, love, & I do hope you will
try not quite so readily to say things that may serve as an excuse
& save you from blame, without ascertaining a little more if they
are correct, before stating them as *facts*. However we won't say
anything more about it now. I was so glad to get your letter. I am
very anxious about the children, & not feeling very light-hearted
myself, which is, I think owing to the weather. I called at Armitt's
on my way home, & saw the best collection of Parian figures yet—
a very pretty Flora, & the Ruth & Naomi group, but all very dear,
compared to what they can be got for at Minton's; but I have
written to your Uncle Langshawe today about them. I found Papa
copying out his sermon when I got home. He and Cousin Mary
had lunched together very cosily then Charles *Aikin* Holland came
and we had another lunch got up for him. Then Mr Spottiswoode
a friend of the Duckworths & Coltmans the King's Printer, &
nephew to that Mr Eyre, whose grounds we drove to see at
Beechwood, came to call; very agreeable & nice; and he stayed
till Mrs\G W/Wood came to dinner, & after dinner Mrs Robberds
came & stayed to tea; & the chickens were being hatched, tell the
children,—2 of Mr Armstrong's eggs, & 4 Dorkings, are already
out, & more coming. So it was a busy day, & I went to bed dead
tired. This morning came a box for you—I took out, but did not
read, enclosed note. And I send you a note of Miss Thornborrow's.
If you can call on her, & look at bureau sometime I shall be glad.
Papa goes to Dumbleton on Monday. Meanwhile he *is* here, &
thinks he is at Bowden. He slept here last night, & says he shan't
get off to Bowden till this evening,—copying sermon &c &c.
Whitewashers, Marshall taking down your beds, scouring cleaning, knocking, thumping, going on everywhere. Cousin Mary &
I are going to see after Miss Mitchell, who is said to have a heart-
complaint & to be very anxious about it.[1] Mrs Robberds is our
informant, so I hope there may be some mistake. I shall ask her to
come to tea tonight[.] I enclose a scrap from Meta if you can read it.

---

[1] An arrangement to help her was made about September 1853. See Letter 280.

Write often if only 2 lines. My next will be to *Florence*. My dearest love to her & Julia. Thank F. E. for her letter *very* much. Kind love to Hearn.

Yours very affec[tionatel]y

E C G

Be out of doors as much as you *possibly* can; but don't tire yourself with too much walking. As soon as ever it is warm enough, sit out.

155 **166** 191

?JOHN FORSTER[1]

[September 1853]

⟨. . .⟩We turned up a narrow bye-lane near the church—past the curate's, the schools and skirting the pestiferous churchyard we arrived at the door into the Parsonage yard. In I went,—half blown back by the wild vehemence of the wind which swept along the narrow gravel walk—round the corner of the house into a small plot of grass enclosed within a low stone wall, over which the more ambitious grave-stones towered all round. There are two windows on each side the door and steps up to it. On these steps I encountered a ruddy tired-looking man of no great refinement,—but I had no time to think of him; in at the door into an exquisitely clean passage, to the left into a square parlour looking out on the grass plot, the tall headstones beyond, the tower end of the church, the village houses and the brown moors.

Miss Brontë gave me the kindest welcome, and the room looked the perfection of warmth, snugness and comfort, crimson predominating in the furniture, which did well with the bleak cold colours without. Every thing in her department has been new within the last few years; and every thing, furniture, appointments, &c. is admirable for its consistency. All simple, good, sufficient for every possible reasonable want, and of the most delicate and scrupulous cleanliness. She is so neat herself I got quite ashamed of any touches of untidiness—a chair out of its place,—work left on the table were all of them, I could see,

---

[1] From a printed source; '*to a* Friend'.

annoyances to her habitual sense of order; not annoyances to her temper in the least; you understand the difference. There was her likeness by Richmond, given to her father by Messrs Smith & Elder, the later print of Thackeray, and a good likeness of the Duke of Wellington, hanging up. My room was above this parlour, and looking on the same view, which was really beautiful in certain lights, moon-light especially. Mr Brontë lives almost entirely in the room opposite (right hand side) of the front door; behind his room is the kitchen, behind the parlour a store room kind of pantry. Mr Brontë's bedroom is over his sitting-room, Miss Brontë's over the kitchen. The servants over the pantry. Where the rest of the household slept when they were all one large family, I can't imagine. The wind goes piping and wailing and sobbing round the square unsheltered house in a very strange unearthly way.

We dined—she and I together—Mr Brontë having his dinner sent to him in his sitting-room according to his invariable custom, (fancy it! and only they two left,) and then she told me that the man whom I met on the steps was a Mr Francis Bennock, something Park, Black Heath, who had written the previous day to say he was coming to call on her on his way from Hull where he had been reading a paper on currency. His claim for coming to call on Miss Brontë was 'that he was a patron of Authors and literature.' I hope he belongs to your Guild; Miss Brontë sent to the address he gave to say she had rather not see him, but he came all the same, captivated Mr Brontë, who would make his daughter come in; and abused us both for 'a couple of proud minxes' when we said we would rather be without individual patronage if it was to subject us to individual impertinence. (Oh, please burn this letter as soon as you have read it.) This Mr Bennock produced a MS dedication of some forthcoming work of Miss Mitford's to himself, as a sort of portable certificate of his merits and it sounded altogether very funny—but still a good natured person evidently, and really doing a good deal of kindness I have no doubt. Mrs Toulmin or Crosland, and Mr Charles Swain of our town were two authors to whom he hoped to introduce Miss Brontë at some future time.

Mr Brontë came in to tea—an honour to me I believe. Before tea we had a long delicious walk right against the wind on Penistone Moor which stretches directly behind the Parsonage going over the hill in brown and purple sweeps and falling softly down

into a little upland valley through which a 'beck' ran, and beyond
again was another great waving hill—and the dip of that might be
seen another yet more distant, and beyond that the said Lancashire
came; but the sinuous hills seemed to girdle the world like the
great Norse serpent, and for my part I don't know if they don't
stretch up to the North Pole. On the Moors we met no one.
Here and there in the gloom of the distant hollows she pointed
out a dark grey dwelling—with Scotch firs growing near them
often,—and told me such wild tales of the ungovernable families
who lived or had lived therein that Wuthering Heights even
seemed tame comparatively. Such dare-devil people,—men
especially,—and women so stony and cruel in some of their feelings and so passionately fond in others. They are a queer people
up there. Small landed proprietors, dwelling on one spot since
Q. Eliz.—and lately adding marvellously to their incomes by
using the water power of the becks in the woollen manufacture
which had sprung up during the last 50 years:—uneducated—
unrestrained by public opinion—for their equals in position are as
bad as themselves, and the poor, besides being densely ignorant
are all dependent on their employers. Miss Brontë does not what
we should call 'visit' with any of them. She goes to see the poor—
teaches at the Schools most gently and constantly—but the richer
sort of people despise her for her poverty,—and they would have
nothing in common if they did meet. These people build grand
houses, and live in the kitchens, own hundreds of thousands of
pounds and yet bring up their sons with only just enough learning
to qualify them for over-lookers during their father's lifetime and
greedy grasping money-hunters after his death. Here and there
from the high moorland summit we saw newly built churches,—
which her Irish curates see after—every one of those being literal
copies of different curates in the neighbourhood, whose amusement has been ever since to call each other by the names she gave
them in Shirley.

   In the evening Mr Brontë went to his room and smoked a
pipe,—a regular clay,—and we sat over the fire and talked—
talked of long ago when that very same room was full of children
and how one by one they had dropped off into the churchyard
close to the windows. At ½ past 8 we went in to prayers,—soon
after nine every one was in bed but we two;—in general there she
sits quite alone thinking over the past; for her eyesight prevents
her reading or writing by candle-light, and knitting is but very

mechanical and does not keep the thoughts from wandering. Each day—I was 4 there—was the same in outward arrangement— breakfast at 9, in Mr Brontë's room—which we left immediately after. What he does with himself through the day I cannot imagine! He is a tall fine looking old man, with silver bristles all over his head; nearly blind; speaking with a strong Scotch accent (he comes from the North of Ireland), raised himself from the ranks of a poor farmer's son—and was rather intimate with Lord Palmerston at Cambridge, a pleasant soothing reflection now, in his shut-out life. There was not a sign of engraving, map, writing materials, beyond a desk, &c. no books but those contained on two hanging shelves between the windows—his two pipes, &c. a spittoon, if you know what that is. He was very polite and agree-able to me, paying rather elaborate old-fashioned compliments, but I was sadly afraid of him in my inmost soul; for I caught a glare of his stern eyes over his spectacles at Miss Brontë once or twice which made me know my man; and he talked at her some-times; he is very fearless; has taken the part of the men against the masters,—and vice versa just as he thought fit and right; and is consequently much respected and to be respected. But he ought never to have married. He did not like children; and they had six in six years, and the consequent pinching and family disorder— (which can't be helped), and noise &c. made him shut himself up and want no companionship—nay be positively annoyed by it. He won't let Miss Brontë accompany him on his walks, although he is so nearly blind; goes out in defiance of her gentle attempts to restrain him, speaking as if she thought him in his second child-hood; and comes home moaning and tired:—having lost his way. 'Where is my strength gone?' is his cry then. 'I used to walk 40 miles a day,' &c. There are little bits of picturesque affection about him—for his old dogs for instance—when very ill some years ago in Manchester, whither he had come to be operated upon for cataract, his wail was, 'I shall never feel Keeper's paws on my knees again!' Moreover to account for my fear—rather an admiring fear after all—of Mr Brontë, please to take into account that though I like the beautiful glittering of bright flashing steel I don't fancy firearms at all, at all—and Miss Brontë never remem-bers her father dressing himself in the morning without putting a loaded pistol in his pocket, just as regularly as he puts on his watch. There was this little deadly pistol sitting down to breakfast with us, kneeling down to prayers at night to say nothing of a loaded gun hanging up on high, ready to pop off on the slightest emergency. Mr Brontë has a great fancy for arms of all kinds. He begged Miss Brontë (Oh, I can't condense it more than I do, and yet here's my fourth sheet!) to go and see Prince's Albert's armoury at Windsor; and when he is unusually out of spirits she tells him over and over again of the different weapons &c. there. But all this time I wander from the course of our day, which is the course of her usual days. Breakfast over, the letters come; not many, sometimes for days none at all. About 12 we went out to walk. At 2 we dined, about 4 we went out again; at 6 we had tea; by nine every one was in bed but ourselves. Monotonous enough in sound, but not a bit in reality. There are some people whose stock of facts and anecdotes are soon exhausted; but Miss B. is none of these. She has the wild, strange facts of her own and her sisters' lives,—and beyond and above these she has most original and suggestive thoughts of her own; so that, like the moors, I felt on the last day as if our talk might be extended in any direction without getting to the end of any subject. There are 2 servants; one Tabby, aged upwards of 90; sitting in an armchair by the kitchen fire,—and Martha, the real active serving maiden, who has lived with them 10 years. I asked this last one day to take me into the Church and show me the Brontë graves: so when Miss Brontë was engaged we stole out. There is a tablet put up in the communion railing—Maria Brontë, wife of the Revd Patrick B. died 1821 aged 39. Maria Brontë—May 1825 aged 12 (the original of Helen Burns in 'Jane Eyre.' She and the next sister died of the fever at the Clergy School). Elizabeth Brontë died June, 1825, aged 11. Patrick Branwell Brontë died Sept. 24, 1848, aged 30. Emily Jane Brontë died Decr 18, 1848, aged 29—Anne Brontë May 28, 1849, aged 27. 'Yes!' said Martha. 'They were all well when Mr Branwell was buried; but Miss Emily broke down the next week. We saw she was ill, but she would never own it, never would have a doctor near her, never would breakfast in bed—the last morning she got up, and she dying all the time—the rattle in her throat while she would dress herself; and neither Miss Brontë nor I dared offer to help her. She died just before Xmas—you'll see the date there— and we all went to her funeral. Master and Keeper, her dog, walking first side by side, and then Miss Brontë and Miss Anne, and then Tabby and me. Next day Miss Anne took ill just in the same way—and it was 'Oh, if it was but Spring and I could go to the sea,'—'Oh, if it was but Spring.' And at last Spring came and Miss

Brontë took her to Scarborough—they got there on the Saturday
and on the Monday she died. She is buried in the old church at
Scarboro'. 'For as long as I can remember—Tabby says since they
were little bairns—Miss Brontë and Miss Emily and Miss Anne
used to put away their sewing after prayers and walk all three one
after the other round the table in the parlour till near eleven
o'clock. Miss Emily walked as long as she could, and when she
died Miss Anne and Miss Brontë took it up—and now my heart
aches to hear Miss Brontë walking, walking, on alone.' And on
enquiring I found that after Miss Brontë had seen me to my room
she did come down every night, and begin that slow monotonous
incessant walk in which I am sure I should fancy I heard the steps
of the dead following me. She says she could not sleep without
it—that she and her sisters talked over the plans and projects of
their whole lives at such times.

   About Mr Branwell Brontë the less said the better—poor fellow. He never knew 'Jane Eyre' was written although he lived a
year afterwards; but that year passed in the shadow of the coming
death, with the consciousness of his wasted life. But Emily—poor
Emily—the pangs of disappointment as review after review came
out about 'Wuthering Heights' were terrible. Miss B. said she had
no recollection of pleasure or gladness about 'Jane Eyre,' every
such feeling was lost in seeing Emily's resolute endurance, yet
knowing what she felt.⟨. . .⟩

₀ **167** ₀

UNKNOWN[1]

[End of September 1853]

⟨. . .⟩ It was a dull, drizzly, Indian-inky day, \all the way on the/
railroad to Keighley, which is a rising wool manufacturing town,
lying in a hollow between hills—not a pretty hollow, but more
what the Yorkshire people call a 'bottom' or 'botham.' I left
Keighley in a car for Haworth, four miles off—four tough, steep,
scrambling miles, the road winding between the wave-like hills,
that rose and fell on every side of the horizon, with a long

   [1] From the MS. *Life*; 'parts of a letter I wrote at the time'. A few deletions
we could not read have been ignored.

illimitable sinuous look, as if they were a part of the line of the Great Serpent, which the\Norse/legend says, girdles the world. The day was lead-coloured; the road had stone factories alongside of it,—grey, dull-coloured rows of stone cottages belonging to these factories;—and then we came to poor, hungry-looking fields, —stone-fences everywhere, and trees nowhere. Haworth is a long straggling village: one steep narrow street—so steep that the flagstones with which it is paved are placed end-ways that the horses' feet may have something to cling to, and not slip down backwards; which if they did, they would soon reach Keighley. But if the horses had cats' feet and claws, they would do all the better. Well, we (the man, horse, car, and I,) clambered up this street, and reached the Church dedicated to St Autest[1] (who was he?); then we turned off into a lane on the left, past the curate's lodging at the Sexton's, past the School-house, up to the Parsonage yard-door. I went round the house to the front door, looking to the church; moors everywhere beyond and above. The crowded grave-yard surrounds the house, and small grass enclosure for drying clothes.

I don't know that I ever saw a spot more exquisitely clean; the most dainty place for that I ever saw. To be sure, the life is like clock-work. No one comes to the house; nothing disturbs the deep repose; hardly a voice is heard; you catch the ticking of the clock in the kitchen, or the buzzing of a fly in the parlour, all over the house. Miss Brontë sits alone in her parlour; breakfasting with her father in his study at nine o'clock. She helps in the housework; for one of their servants, Tabby, is nearly ninety, and the other only a girl. Then I accompanied her in her walks on the sweeping moors: the heather-bloom had been blighted by a thunder-storm a day or two before, and was all of a livid brown colour, instead of the blaze of purple glory it ought to have been. Oh! those high, wild, desolate moors, up above the whole world, and the very realms of silence! Home to dinner at two. Mr Brontë has his dinner sent into him. All the small table arrangements had the same dainty simplicity about them. Then we rested, and talked, over the clear bright fire; it is a cold country, and the fires were a pretty warm dancing light all over the house. The parlour has been evidently refurnished within the last few years, since Miss Brontë's success has enabled her to have a little more money to spend. Everything fits into, and is in harmony with the idea of a

[1] Haworth Church is dedicated to St Michael. For a possible explanation of Mrs Gaskell's error, see *The Brontës*, ed. Wise & Symington, IV, p. 86 n.

country parsonage, possessed by people of very moderate means. The prevailing colour of the room is crimson, to make a warm setting for the cold grey landscape without. There is her likeness by Richmond; and an engraving from Lawrence's picture of Thackeray; and two recesses, on each side of the high, narrow, old-fashioned mantel-piece, filled with books,—books given to her, books she has bought, and which tell of her individual pursuits and tastes; *not* standard books.

She cannot see well, and does little beside knitting. The way she weakened her eyesight was this: when she was 16 or 17, she wanted much to draw; and she copied niminipimini copper-plate engravings out of annuals, ('stippling,' don't the artists call it?) every little point put in, till at the end of six months she had produced an exquisitely faithful copy of the engraving. She wanted to learn to express her ideas by drawing. After she had tried to *draw* stories, and not succeeded, she took the better mode of writing; but in so small a hand that it is almost impossible to decipher what she wrote at this time.

But now to return to our quiet hour of rest after dinner. I soon observed that her habits of order were such that she could not go on with the conversation, if a chair was out of its place; everything was arranged with delicate regularity. We talked over the old times of her childhood; of her elder sister's (Maria's)\death—/ just like that of Helen Burns in 'Jane Eyre;' of those strange starved days at school; of the desire (almost amounting to illness) of expressing herself in some way,—writing or drawing; of her weakened eyesight, which prevented her doing anything for two years, from the age of 17 to 19; of her being a governess; of her going to Brussels; whereupon I said I disliked Lucy Snowe, and we discussed M. Paul Emanuel; and I told her of ——'s admiration of 'Shirley,' which pleased her, for the character of Shirley was meant for her sister Emily, about whom she is never tired of talking, nor I of listening. Emily must have been a remnant of the Titans,—great grand-daughter of the giants, who used to inhabit earth. One day, Miss Brontë brought down a rough, common-looking oil-painting, done by her brother, of herself,—a little, rather prim-looking girl of eighteen,—and the two other sisters, girls of 16 and 14, with cropped hair, and sad, dreamy-looking eyes.⟨. . .⟩ Emily had a great dog,—half mastiff, half bull-dog— so savage, &c.⟨. . .⟩ This dog went to her funeral, walking side-by-side with her father, and then, to the day of its death, it slept at her room door, snuffing under it, and whining every morning.

We have generally had another walk before tea, which is at six; at half past eight, prayers, and by nine all the household are in bed, except ourselves. We sit up together till ten, or past; and after I go, I hear Miss Brontë come down and walk up and down the room for an hour or so.⟨. . .⟩

₀ **167a** ₁₆₇ᵦ

BENTLEY

> Plymouth Grove
> Manchester—
> Sepr 29. [1853][1]

Sir,

Miss Mulock has sent me on a note of yours addressed to Mr Dobell, in which you say you would be 'glad of an opportunity of treating with Mrs Gaskell for her next work.' I have not a line written of anything whatever; I do not at present look forward to ever writing again for publication, having literally nothing to write about. And if I did write, I do not think I should be justified in leaving Messrs Chapman & Hall, against whom I have no complaint to make; & who took the risk of Mary Barton, when Mr Moxon refused it as a *gift*. So probably you wonder why I write at all to you, whom I do not know. It is that your PS. gives me a fellow-feeling; you there say you are suffering from tic & neuralgia; from which I have suffered most acutely for years; & have only lately i.e. within the last 12 months, found a remedy; namely rubbing the part where the agonized nerve shoots up to, with *viratria* ointment. I don't know if I spell the word rightly, but {it}\viratria/is the essential part of aconite; and though a new & very expensive drug, it is well known to all good chemists, who pronounce it, as I have written it. It was recommended to me by my cousin Sir Henry Holland, a physician of some repute. It was rubbed on *for* me; for I was convulsed with pain—a small (pins' head) quantity was put on flannel; and the rubbing was continued until a stinging pain was produced in the skin; a bad pain enough

[1] Dated from next letter.

of it's kind. The next day the tic made an effort to return at the usual time; the rubbing was repeated (on the temple to which the nerve shot with keen agony,) the tic went away, & I have never had it since. I have named it to two sufferers,—in both the tic has disappeared; but one had to rub oftener than I had.

Do you publish 'Christie Johnstone'. If you do, & I fancy you do, please put the price in\to the next advertisements/. Libraries will not order it without knowing the price, whh has hitherto been omitted in all advertisements.

Yours truly   E. C. Gaskell

167a 167b 0

BENTLEY

Plymouth Grove
Manchester
October 5 [1853]

Sir,

Are you inclined to see the MS of a translation from the German done by my friend Miss Winkworth ('Life of Niebuhr') and her sister? They have together translated all that is yet published of the autobiographical life of Perthes;[1] no, I see it is not *all* translated— they have stopped, when we novelists do—at the end of the adventures, & when Perthes is re-instated in his business, & in a fair way of doing well for himself. You probably know enough of his history &c to enable you in some measure to judge for yourself of the kind of book it is. A young German bourgeois, who makes his own way from nothing to a station of great wealth & influence both commercial & political: (he was a bookseller, &c) the personal story is very interesting & includes an account of the French occupation of Hamburgh &c.

Will you be so kind as to put the price in the advertisements of 'Christie Johnstone?' I can't get it till you do: and I am sure it would be for your interest to do so; as here, at any rate, no library will order a book in without knowing it's price.

---

[1] A letter of 14 Oct. 1853 states that every publisher has refused to accept this work. *Letters and Memorials*, ed. Winkworth, I, p. 410.

I hope the viratria is doing you some good.—I am going today to S. Greg's Esq

Bollington

Macclesfield   till Saturday,—on Monday to The
Lord Hatherton's
Teddesley
Penkridge—

but if you like to communicate straight with Miss Winkworth her address is

Dundas Place
Nelson Street
Manchester.

I need hardly say that the translation is well done, for you know how well she did Niebuhr.

Yours truly
E. C. Gaskell[1]

156 168 189

R. MONCKTON MILNES

Plymouth Grove
Manchester.
Octr 29. [1853][2]

My dear Sir,

With skilful diplomacy, for which I admire myself extremely, I have obtained the address we want.

The revd A. B. Nicholls
Kirksmeaton near
Pontefract,
Yorkshire

The only word I am uncertain about is Kirksmeaton, 4 letters of which are rather illegible in the Haworth postmaster's handwriting.

I felt sure you would keep the story secret,—if my well-meant treachery becomes known to her I shall lose her friendship, which I prize most highly. I have been thinking over little bits of the conversation we had relating to a pension. I do not think she

<hr>

[1] Letter 82 should perhaps follow on here.

[2] Dating depends upon Letter 189. W. Reid (*Milnes*, I, p. 476) dates it 1852, but Nicholls did not propose to Charlotte Brontë until the December of that year.

would take it; and I am quite sure that *one* hundred a year given
as acknowledgement of his merits, as a good faithful clergyman
would give her ten times the pleasure that *two* hundred a year
would do, if bestowed upon her in {a}\her/capacity as a writer.
I am sure he is a thoroughly good hard-working, self-denying
curate[.] Dr Hook has unluckily just filled up his staff of curates.
(Excuse me, if, being a dissenter, I use wrong words; 'staff' does
look military.) Her father's only reason for his violent & virulent
opposition is Mr Nicholls's utter want of money, or friends to
help him to any professional advancement. And now I won't
weary you any more. May I send my kind regards to Mrs Milnes?

Yours very truly
E. C. Gaskell

151 169 206

ELIZA FOX[1]

Wednesday, [9 November] 1853
Lord Mayor's day to be intelligible to
a cockney.

My dearest Tottie,

These Dorkings—what colour? How many toes? What age?
What price? They are very tempting, but I must hear (specially if
they've 5 toes,) before I invest. I won't have you for 2 weeks *only*,
you shabby creature! I am writing in desperate haste, but I am so
glad to get your letters always, oh! how delicious that ride
sounded! and how very nice George seems to be! I'm always
vexed he did not come that last day. He did so well with us; I
know it was only his delicacy that prevented him. I don't think
Willm will think Mr Florence and MA 'compatible elements' in
the same house or MA should willingly go and stay with you, if
she'd time. Have you seen Mr Browning's letters[2] to me? I forget
if I sent 'em or not, and they're worth reading. Florence is turned
so sweet and good she quite frightens me. Did you ever hear of
people being 'fey'—MA's influence is capital for her. I don't
know (or care) a straw about *lessons*; but temper &c. is so much

---

[1] Original MS. not seen.
[2] R. D. Waller prints letters of 1853 from *Mrs* Browning. 'Letters Addressed
to Mrs Gaskell', pp. 42–6.

improved. The carriage will *never* be painted poor thing. Mind the Dorking's toes—its an important point their heels ought to be double—[here follows tiny sketch] something like that. What did Mr Fox lecture on about the census[;] I mean what could he find to say. I can't imagine.

Yrs very affec[tionately]

E. C. G.

164 **170** 172

F. J. Furnivall[1]

Plymouth Grove

Monday [21 November 1853]

My dear Sir,

You can't think how greedily your letters &c are welcomed. There are so many people here anxious for every scrap of news about Mr Maurice, and yet not feeling near enough to him to venture to ask, or to express their deep sympathy——I do think Mr Maurice did quite *right* about the Queen's College, & feeling so, one dare not doubt about the end,—besides surely just now his movements are public enough to be known in all their details, & there is no chance of any misrepresentation of the kind you seem to dread,—viz, that it may be said that he was dismissed,—not that he offered to resign,—long obtaining currency. Then set against that Mr Arthur Stanley's taking up the question! I don't know him at all, but I have great faith in his clear-headedness (admire my English!) boldness, and bright sincerity. I won't take up your time—but I wish so I might do something, for Mr Maurice—If I could & might, even by merely writing a note to Mrs Maurice, will you tell me? The Scotts are full of interest as you will know,— so is my husband[,] so are we all. Surely you people at Lincoln's Inn won't let him go! I don't know the tenure of the Readership, —does it depend on bishops, or benchers or what? Yes! I will call & make acquaintance with Mr Dyson the next time I go into that part of the town.

Yours very truly

E. C. Gaskell

[1] *Address (on envelope)* F. J. Furnivall Esq | No 11 New Square | Lincolns Inn. *Postmarks* 5 EV 5 | NO 21 | 1853 | D *and* Greek St.

172 **171** 176

F. J. FURNIVALL[1]

Tuesday Evng [6 December 1853]

My dear Sir,

I should not 'quarrel with you' if I had time; but I should say you had mistaken my meaning in two or three things; but perhaps that was my fault, I am feeling so stupid just now. In the first place *I am as sorry as I can be* about Mr Maurice, & Lincoln's Inn; I separate that case quite & entirely from Q. College, which was so intimately connected with K. College,—whereas L. I[.] has nothing in the world to do with it. Moreover I knew that one or two of the more 'cautious' lady visitors,[2]—committee-women, or whatever they call themselves *were* going to raise the question as to whether Mr M. should not be asked to resign; for the very plausible reason that one of them alleged to me—'if our governesses have any suspicion of heterodoxy thrown on them we shall never get them situations, & we must look after their interests.' She had the grace to ask me if I thought her worldly. Now you know the lady, so I shan't tell you whh it was; but I knew that another lady was of her opinion & as they were two who are rather looked up [to], & might innocently do a good deal of mischief—I mean *not intending* to do harm,—I did feel that Mr Maurice took the brave bold step,[3] which seemed in fact necessary, towards an institution so connected with K. C. Then you might abuse any one I honoured & loved before many people; and you could make me cry,—or what do you think of an absolute box on the ears? Any sudden explosion of that kind I believe would come naturally to me, & any amount of evil & wrong feeling towards the person who outraged the name of any one I honoured; but I could not—physically *could* not, I believe, speak out more than a blurting sentence of abuse, tantamount to the box on the ear,—a 'That's a downright falsehood,' I might say, —or even *worse*, not *more*.—It is different when speaking as the character in a{s} story—or even as the author of a book. Do you think I cd say or write in a letter (except one that I was sure wd

---

[1] *Address (on envelope)* F. J. Furnivall Esq | New Square | Lincolns Inn | London. *Postmarks* MANCHESTER | DE 9 | 1853 | P *and* ⟨ ⟩ | 9 ⟨DE 9⟩ | 1853. [*Late information. This letter should follow* 172.]

[2] See p. 137 above.

[3] His letter of resignation is dated 15 November 1853. *Life of F. D. Maurice*, ed. F. M. Maurice, 1884, II, pp. 215–16.

be regarded as private by some dear friend) what I have said both
in M B & Ruth? It may seem strange & I can't myself account for
it,—but it *is* so.—

Yours very truly

E C Gaskell

170 **172** 171

F. J. FURNIVALL

Plymouth Grove

Saturday Decr 3. [1853]

My dear Sir,
   I have been very ill with influenza for the last ten days; and I
find it a most 'knocking-down' complaint. This is the second
letter that I have written since I received your last; and I hope also
to write to Mr Maurice by this post; but I do not at all agree to
your idea of printing that, or any other letter to that most valued
friend of many persons, in a newspaper, if they only contain
expressions of affectionate & respectful feeling. It seems to me very
different from the case of an argumentative letter, which might
have an effect upon many unknown individuals in the great
'public' to whom a newspaper is addressed, and who might find
help in forming their judgments by a good reasoning on the subject about which they are perplexed[.] On the contrary as regards
myself I hope nobody but Mr and Mrs Maurice will see what I
write, for the very same reason that would make you not talk
about your feelings before many people.
   Mr Dickens is in Italy,—I don't know when he returns, but as
soon as he does I will take care he is made aware of every circumstance relating to Mr Maurice's dismissal\&c/, & I am sure he will
feel hearty interest in it all. And I do talk & lend my pamphlets to
every body I meet with; because it is one of the subjects uppermost in my mind, and I am constantly hearing, & consequently
often repeating instances of people who have owed more than
they can well speak of without breaking down to Mr Maurice's
writings or Mr Maurice's self.—'Influence' is such a difficult thing
to trace and define; the most powerful is so like the great powers
of nature, so imperceptible in its working that it almost seems to
me as if too much talking about it vulgarized it. There is no doubt
whatever it seems to me of the *fact*—that Mr Maurice has more

influence over the more thoughtful portion of the English people than any one else I know of,—but almost the deeper the influence is the less people can put it into a clear cold expression, so as to logically convince those who have never felt what it is. But I learn what people think about Mr Maurice—those who know either him or his writings I mean, by a light in their eyes when his name is mentioned,

> (So turn & look back when thou hearest
> The sound of my name——)

and the warm way in which they press forward to hear the last piece of news about him. I sent Mr Scott word how much you thought Mr Maurice would like to hear from him,—& I know he wrote directly. I don't know any Editor but one, and he would not write or withhold a line at my request; simply because he chooses, I suppose, to do what he thinks right without any one's interference. But I *do* make people most interested in the whole case—most anxious to testify their respect & regard by signing the memorial if their signatures may be admitted. I hope you won't show this letter, please, because I have a great dislike to writing letters to be either shown, or spoken about. If I could write a grand logical reasoning argumentative letter—why then——

Yours truly

.E. C. Gaskell.

165 **173** 174

MARIANNE GASKELL[1]

[*c.* 13 December 1853]

	When I come	
Ivy Leaves	home *on Saty*	Price\of/leather
Blue silk.	M de Mery's cap	cover. Card-plate

Which being interpreted, dearest Polly, means that I jotted all this down last night; to remind you, please dear to buy me some ivy leaves to *match* those I have (3 sprays I think I want—I got those at Mrs Fuller's) to get Hearn, or ask yourself at the trunk shop,

---

[1] *Address* Miss Gaskell | Revd W. Gaskell's | Plymouth Grove | Manchester. *Postmarks* KNUTSFORD | DE 13 | 1853 | B *and* MANCHESTER | DE 14 | 185⟨3⟩ | A. *Octagonal seal* Man's head facing left.

what would be the price of a leather cover for a box of which Hearn will give you the dimensions; to call at James Wroe's Oxford Street—(not far from Duncombe's and Fosters,) & order your card plate & 100 cards, IF you like their patterns of engraving, &c—you must choose your own kind & size; you know it's to be part of my present to you, & is to cost, according to his advertisement 5s., to send a small pattern (Hearn will give it you,) of your light blue silk dress to Satts with a note saying it was got last year at some shop in the city, & asking if they can find out where, *so as to match it*; I don't want to *get* it *before* Xmas. To think what Flossy & Julia would like for Xmas presents. I do so want to hear that they did not catch cold yesterday, & how successful it was. To give Agnes the enclosed Clothing-Tickets, which are to be signed *Esther Mason*; I begged them from Mrs Mason yesterday; & if Agnes would kindly when giving the others take the trouble of seeing if Scattergood (widow living in a clean cellar in Stopford's Court,) *could* pay even 2d a week, because if so I should like her to have one. Now[,] love[,] I am afraid all these are rather troublesome commissions but I shall be very much obliged to you to get them done for me. Also to remind Margaret to order this next Friday pieces of Beef for our poor people Mary Moore (2 lb) Fanny Hindley (3 lb) Mrs Piercy (3 lb) Old Wm's wife (2 lb) Mrs Mack (2 lb) the widow Mr Curtis named to Hearn on Sunday (3 lb); and if you have a Sunday scholar or *two* you thought wanted a Xmas dinner you might put their names down in addition. I don't remember any more myself just now; but perhaps Hearn may. Have you finished covering your white satin shoes? because if you *have*, I've something to tell you. In my gown there is a pocket, in my pocket there is a purse, in my purse there is a paper —well! we won't go on with what is in *that*; but it is something you've to thank Mrs Mason for; & I have promised her (she cried sadly at our having been so long in coming to see her, & *especially* wanted to see you,) that you will come over by (return ticket) on Friday next, and stay an hour or two with her; & Peter is to take you down to the train (5 o clock?) that meets the afternoon Knutsford 'bus, where I shall be, & we will come home together. So mind you keep to this plan, or she will be sadly disappointed. Aren't you amused at Mrs Martineau[']s 'most affectionately'? I really do stride after her, but I can't get up to *that*. I send Examiner & Inquirer by this post; *try* & see that they are sent *on* tomorrow afternoon. It was that patient good lame Miss

Jane Mason who is dead; died quite suddenly of exhaustion produced by influenza. Mrs Mason was alone & sadly upset about it.
I came on here by the omnibus, which drank at every public
house on the road; & it was past ½ past 7 when I got here & tea
just done. I have seen no one yet but I am going to cousin Susan's
as soon as I think she will be up. I have cut you out a good deal
of work, darling[.] Will you fi⟨x⟩ with Hearn on Friday what
gown I'm to wear blue or lilac, &\tell her to/have it all out, for it
will be a bustle when we come in. Not *much* of one, for we shall
be in by half past 5. Ever yours 'most affectionately' E C Gaskell.

My dear love to the little ones. I have had no letters but the
enclosed. None from Mrs V. Smith, or from Meta; but they may
have written home, in which case send them. Write to M D about
worsted work pattern[.]

173 174 175

MARIANNE GASKELL

[?December ?1853]

My dearest Polly,
    I am rather vexed with Meta for being so extravagant & careless
—that carmelite frock had not a hole in it, I will answer for, when
it was sent only last Monday\week/. Helen puts her up to it all I
think; for Helen asked if she might have her\new/silk frock *to
wear* THERE,\at the Harvey's/& she\Helen/would keep it at her
house; so I don't think she could have felt her other things untidy.
I am sure she must have been very careless about her Carmelite;
& she ought to mend it. Her bonnet I do think she wants; and I
think your plan, love, a very good one about *fitting it & materials*
&c on Monday & trimming it & it could go on Tuesday. I cannot
trust Meta with her new silk at school especially after the usage
she must have given the Carmelite one; if it is in the unmendable
untidy state, she describes after only a week's wear. Helen asked
for it for her to wear at their house. Now I don't care what she
wears at Liverpool, provided only it is clean and whole. Except
Helen & Miss Martineau I had rather (from what I have seen of
Liverpool people) that she knew as few as possible in after-life;
and I always regret when I hear of Helen having taken her out or
introduced her to any of their acquaintances, such as the Benson

Rathbones &c. I had always rather have her *left* quietly at Helen's if they have an engagement for the evening; and then & there if she is neat & not in rags it is all she need mind about; no great stock of dress is required for this in winter[.]¹ Will you send this letter on to Meta or tell her what is necessary out of it. The bonnet she shall have as soon as we can send it—(thank you, love, about the trimming, I mean the offer *to*.[)] It is before breakfast, and a dingy rainy day. I got here about ½ past 5 last night, & had tea directly afterwards. I suppose from your dash under *if* you have not yet heard of a ticket. I heartily wish you could have mine that Mrs Sidney Potter offers me, but you see she does in some degree limit it to me. Papa goes to preach at Rawstenstall\near Bury/on Sunday next,—so I shall be alone in the house. I must write to Florence today. I think, if you will let me know by what train you come on Monday, I had better send down St Malo in the pony carriage for you to match shape &c &c as well as possible. I think if you go to London to have singing lessons you must plan to go *as early* as possible—*before* January as soon after Xmas day as you can; & Mrs Groom does *not* give lessons out of the house as I thought you knew; or else why was there such a difficulty about your going there before.² You might ask her if she could have you at the end of December (January is very vague), for you will have to be at home at the end of it, & if she ever *does* give lessons out of the house, without naming her coming to H[olly?] Hill, which I am afraid *would* be terribly expensive. It is *dead* quiet here, but the place so pretty. I write before breakfast. I will write to Meta myself.

Yours very affect[ionately]
E C Gaskell

174 175 183

MARIANNE GASKELL

Wednesday [Late December ?1853]

Dearest Polly,

Oh! only think what I've gone & done! opened a note from Cousin Susan to you, thinking that it might be something to be

¹ Meta had started school in Liverpool in January 1853. (See Letter 148.)
² See pp. 200, 202, 215 above.

done in a hurry &c & found it marked Private. However here it is, and two more notes besides, one in the child's handwriting, came by last night's post; the other, supposed to be from Mrs Groom with your note to Julia this morning. Lunch is just going in[.] There's the 2nd bell! After lunch! I ought to be out. Katie is in bed with a bad cold;[1] Selina gone out. Papa taking the little ones to walk with him in the Park, & make snow-balls. Do you wish to hear Mr James McConnell's explicit & elegant remark when told you were gone to London, & not likely to be at any dances &c 'Oh! bother!' From which you will gather that the Ewarts have been here this morng—I fancy their dance last night was large, vulgar & overdressed, they did not get home till ½ past 2. Yesterday K. & S. did not come till after lunch; so I did not get out. And we went at 8 to Mrs J's[,] Meta stopping at home, tired & going to bed. A large, dull party—Vaughans & Greenwoods, Sydney Potters (Tom & Jim inclusive\Mr Childs of course/) Marslands, Schuncks, Taylers Bowmans &c. Some singing\duets, Vaughan & Greenwood/every body out of tune with each other & with the piano. Home at 11. A note from Emily Green this morning which I enclose. Awkward, although I wrote yesterday to Mr! Mrs Shuttleworth can't go to the Concert tonight, so has sent me ticket,—and I don't like Meta to be disappointed, yet don't like leaving & missing the Winkworth's[.] There I think that's all! Write soon—

Yours very affec[tionate]ly
E C Gaskell.

171 176 188

F. J. FURNIVALL[2]

[c. 9 January 1854]

My dear Sir,

You will have thought me very ungrateful; and yet I am not a bit so in my heart. I have thanked you, silently, many a post-time of late. Not least this morning when I received the Chronicle. Miss [Susanna] Winkworth is too busy to be a good correspondent; & it seems through you alone that I hear what I hear.

---

[1] See *Letters and Memorials*, ed. Winkworth, I, pp. 423, 425.

[2] *Address (on envelope)* F. J. Furnivall Esq | New Square | Lincoln's Inn | London. *Postmarks* MANCHESTER | JA 9 | 1854 | P *and* ⟨ ⟩ | 10 JA 1⟨0⟩ | 185⟨4⟩. [*Late information.*]

I like the address of The Clergy & the working-people; thoroughly. Not so the address or proposal on the part of the Dissenters; though I doubt my power of clearly[1] explaining why.[2] It seems to me impertinent. The idea of a testimonial is (to me) *vulgar.* Yes! that is the only word. I am not——

Now here this letter has had to be put away for a week, and I can't exactly tell what I was going to say when I was interrupted; but I believe it was—I am not sure that I like testimonials when presented in acknowledgement of actions & courses of life,—but I am sure I do not like them if given {in acknowledgment of}\out of sympathy with/opinions; and I am sure that treatment such as Mr Maurice has received in consequence of his expression of the opinions he held places him in too sacred an aspect as a sufferer to be treated in so common & irreverent a way. Of course 'to my idea' is to be understood all along; & with\a feeling of/respect to the others who think differently from me. Tennyson is in the Isle of Wight—Black Gang Chine near Ventnor is I think his address, if a '*Chine*' is ever anybody's address[.] I have never made you understand how I had *no right* to do anything but stand afar off & reverence Mr Maurice,—and at last venture to write to him—, purely & simply *I* to *him*. If I had written any thing to appear before the public of Mr Maurice it would have been either con-ceited (*very* in me I think) or insincere; either way disrespectful to one whom I most deeply respect. If I had devoted intellect enough (always supposing I had it to devote) to the subject to make my *opinion* on it, & the feelings founded on that opinion worth any thing to the public[,] then it might be my business to write to the public. But I have not. I could give nothing to the public but my personal feeling towards Mr Maurice; and that from me to him would have been too impertinent—too absurdly patronizing at any time; & most of all now when he deserves such tender reverence.

Thank you for your letter of today with it's enclosure. To that I will willingly, heartily try & get signatures,—but I am off to Paris for a fortnight, so it won't be directly. No! I have not seen Mr Trench's letter, (there is a man who has a right to write—) I

---

[1] MS reads 'clearing'.

[2] These addresses are probably those referred to in letters by Susanna Wink-worth (20 December 1853) and by Emily Shaen (23 December 1853), both of whom were in London at the time. *Letters and Memorials*, ed. Winkworth, I, pp. 421, 423.

did enjoy the snow,[1] but this thaw has brought an accumulation of letters—

Ever yours truly & much obliged

E. C. Gaskell

*118a **177** 273

?MARGARET EMILY GASKELL

Between 12 & 1 Tuesday
morning [?January ?1854]

My dearest love,

I only found your letter when I came home from Emily's at past 10,\it was *not* here at 5/& I've had to pack up since, only I must write a line to thank you for your long nice letter,—I liked extremely to hear all about the Broadbent's dance, though I was sorry John was there, for I do *not* like anything I have heard of him. Tell Papa that Charlie B. is coming on Friday & that I think, if he comes at a meal–time he had better be asked to take pot-luck, for as they've been so kind & hospitable to you I shd not like any of that household to be slighted[.] I get so hot myself when I hear the clatter of plates that I know what it is. No success yet about Miss M's things, though I've tried hard again today,—& as I only saw Miss Banks for a moment I could not speak about little Cameron; indeed I *dont think it would do at all,* & the school Miss Acton named at Altringham would be *far* better in many ways. Will you tell that to Miss A. & thanks for\her/letter. I *must* go to bed. I like hearing details but miss[,] like the children[,] not having the dinner specified[.] My first letter from Paris will be to you darling.[2] Now goodnight[.]

Best love to you all.

Your affec[tionate] Mammy

---

[1] See *ibid*, I, p. 426 and n.

[2] Marianne was with her mother on this Paris trip (see p. 269), but the letter could be to Marianne if it relates to a later visit. See p. 329 below and Appx E.

0 **178** 179

WILLIAMS & NORGATE

46 Plymouth Grove,
Feb. 12th [?1854]

Mrs Gaskell presents her compliments to Messrs Williams and
Norgate, and having heard today from Baron Tauchnitz[1] that he
has not yet received the {volume}\copy/of 'Cranford' which she
desired Messrs Chapman and Hall to send through them to him
some time ago, she would feel extremely obliged to Messrs
Williams and Norgate if they would *at once* forward it to Leipzig
in case it has already reached them. If the negligence should have
been on the part of Messrs Chapman and Hall, Mrs Gaskell
believes that it will be remedied in the course of tomorrow, as
she has written to them to beg them in that case *immediately* to
send a copy to Messrs Norgate & Williams's care for Baron
Tauchnitz.

Mrs Gaskell would esteem it a favour if Messrs Williams and
Norgate would let her know, when the book has fairly been
sent off—

178 **179** 0

WILLIAMS & NORGATE

46, Plymouth Grove,
Feb. 25th [?1854]

Mrs Gaskell presents her compliments to Messrs Williams and
Norgate, and never having heard whether Cranford has reached
them or not, she would be extremely obliged if they would favour
her with a line to tell her. If it has *not*, she begs that they will send
up to Piccadilly for it, presenting the enclosed card to Mr
Frederick Chapman, to whom she does not like to write again, as
he may have already sent the copy. Mrs Gaskell is very sorry to
give so much trouble about it.

[1] Tauchnitz published *Chapters of Cranford* in *Household Words*, Leipzig in 1852
and 1853. Chapman & Hall published it in book form *c.* July 1853.

65 **180** 395

JAMES CROSSLEY

Plymouth Grove
February [?1854]

Sir,

In looking over the bound vol. of 'Notes and Queries' for the first half of 1851, I find a paper by you entitled 'Edmund Burke and the Annual Register'.[1] I hardly know if the vague information I am now going to send you will be of any use in 'assisting to define the limits of Burke's participation' in the Annual Register; it can certainly only be used as a means to obtain such a definition. About two years ago when I was at Knutsford my attention was directed to an old lady in very reduced circumstances, bearing the name of Granville. Her maiden name, she told me, had been Wheler, (one of the Whelers of Otterden Place, Kent,) she was a descendant of Sir George Wheler the traveller;[2] and her father's second\or it might be, his *first*, but not Mrs Granville's mother/ wife was a daughter of that kidnapped Earl of Annesley, who figures away in the Romance of the Peerage.[3] Mrs Granville was described to me as a widow; she was in great poverty, the sole dependence of herself and two widowed daughters being an annual 10£ sent her by the present possessor of Otterden Place, which had descended in the male line to a distant cousin. She was very ladylike, and simple in her manners, spoke well and with a pure accent, and, (although she was 74, and had had no fire except for cooking *dinner* in the house during the greater part of the previous winter,) she maintained a sort of dignity among her neighbours. She had been a great friend of the Miss Porters (Jane & Anna Maria)[4] in girlhood; and it was perhaps owing to their example that she had taken up the business of writing novels (at 10£ each) for the Minerva Press. I saw some of her tales, which were harmless enough, a weak dilution of Miss Porters in style and plot. In consequence of my knowledge of her extreme (though hidden) distress I resolved to apply to the Literary Fund for some

---

[1] By James Crossley, 7 June 1851, pp. 441–2.
[2] (1650–1723). Travelled in Greece, bringing back marbles and other antiquities.
[3] G. L. Craik, *Romance of the Peerage, or Curiosities of Family History*, 1848.
[4] Jane Porter (1786–1850)—principal works: *Thaddeus of Warsaw* (1803), *The Scottish Chiefs* (1810), *The Pastor's Fireside* (1815). Anna Maria Porter's (1780–1832) chief novels were *The Hungarian Brothers* (1807) and *Don Sebastian* (1809).

relief for her; but first I took the precaution of causing some enquiries to be made of a valued friend since dead (Mr George Taylor of Witton-le-Wear, father of Henry Taylor,) who was acquainted with some members of the Wheler family in the County of Durham. He confirmed the truth of her story. (You will think I am long in coming to the pith of *mine*.) I then applied through Mr Hallam, & Mr Forster for one of the Lit. Fund papers; and when it came I took it to her to fill up. It came out then that she was *not* a widow; that her real name was Davenport; that she had married\very young/to disoblige her family a certain\Mr/Davenport[1] who had acted as\a kind of/private Secretary to Burke; and who had had a good deal to do with the historical part of the Annual Register. He had proved a very bad husband, and she had for years lived separate from him. *All this I put down on my application*\(not on the printed paper but in a letter/, and I conclude it was correct (as all her other statements have been proved;) for Mr Forster (the Editr of the Examiner) sent me word that Davenport was the oldest pensioner on the Lity fund; a very old man; living in *Camberwell* I *think*. Mrs Granville spoke afterwards to me of her husband, as having been a protegée [*sic*] of Burke's, and introduced into literary employment by him; and she said {he}\Davenport/used to be a great deal at Beaconsfield, and wrote the historical portion of the Annual Register *under Burke's supervision* at the time of {his} \Burke's/death, & for some years later— If Davenport is still alive (and he seemed to be one of those disreputable persons living on the bounty of others who never die off,) he would probably be able to give you the information you require. His address could easily be obtained from Mr Blewitt, the Secy to the Literary Fund. His wife lives at Knutsford still under the name of Mrs Granville, by which alone she wishes to be known.

Begging you to excuse the length of this note, I remain, Sir,

Yours obediently

E. C. Gaskell

I think it quite possible from what I heard of Davenport that he might have one or two 'aliases'.

---

[1] Richard A. Davenport (?1777–1852), miscellaneous writer, translator and editor. Contributed historical, biographical, geographical and critical notices to *The Annual Register* for many years. Addicted to laudanum. Was found dying by a policeman in a house where he lived alone with a large collection of manuscripts, books, pictures, coins, etc.

₁₅₄ **181** ₂₃₁

LADY KAY-SHUTTLEWORTH[1]

Plymouth Grove
Manchester.
March 4th [1854]

My dear Lady Kay-Shuttleworth,

As I dare say Mrs Schwabe told you I had left Paris before your answer to my letter came; however Mrs Schwabe has kindly done all, or more, than I could have done. I went to see her yesterday; she only returned from London on March 1st; and she then told me many particulars of Miss Harvey, which we settled I was to send on to you. Mrs Schwabe has given me your letter to read in which you say that the friends of her mother will contribute 40£ per annum to having her educated, so as to fit her to become a governess; and you propose that she should be *thoroughly* instructed in French, but go on living with the kind & good Mme Leray (*5, Faubourg St Honoré.*) Mrs Schwabe has consulted Pasteur Vermeil about this plan, and they seem both to think that, if she is to make education her principal object, and have time to study she must live in some other place than at Mme Leray's, as she could not there have the requisite quiet &c for pursuing her lessons; and that the time which should be appropriated to hard work would naturally be broken in upon by the desire she would, (or ought to) have to go on assisting Mme Leray in keeping her books, & receiving customers when she is from home. *They say* also that she has been at a good French school, & is well acquainted with the language. I have my own doubts however if she knows French '*thoroughly*' as you would understand the word, and as it ought to be understood by any one professing to teach it. I remember your advice about Marianne's not learning music without at least as much instruction in thorough-bass, & what an awful person I thought you were when you told me you enjoyed *reading* Bach's Fugues, as much as reading any book. But whether Miss Harvey understands French\thoroughly/or no,\at present/ would be a question of little consequence if Pasteur Vermeil's advice were taken, which is that she should be placed *for a year* in a French school under his superintendance—(the Maison

[1] *Annotation* 1853. [But the autumn visit to Haworth was in 1853.]

Evangelique, I think;) where she might receive the religious instruction, of which poor girl, she sounds to stand in need; and be afterwards confirmed, say next Easter but one (1855.) Meanwhile she might well be trained in the French language, be examined, and receive her diploma, as one qualified to teach it or to open a school. By this time she would be 17; and then, if you & her mother's friends thought it desirable, she might go for a year or two to a German School, to learn German &c. It is more than probable that you or Miss Paplouska know of some place in Germany, in which, if this plan was carried out, you might like to place her; but, if not, Mrs Schwabe knows of a good school, Mrs Henning's, Altona near Hambourg, where they especially train girls in the art of teaching. I have a friend, who was there for a year or two in order to be prepared for a governess, and she speaks *most* highly of the benefit she received there. Mrs Schwabe did not distinctly say so, but I imagine this three years course would involve greater expense than you contemplated in planning that she should remain with Mme Leray.

Then there is another plan which has been suggested, which is that the girl should remain with Mme Leray, and learn from her, her business of dress maker, so as to be able to assist her, and ultimately succeed her. To this the girl herself inclines; Mme Leray says it was, what to a certain degree, she contemplated for her; but in an admirable manner {says}\adds/that she will most gladly forward any plan which may be for the best for the girl herself. I, personally, rather incline to this plan. It seems to me so very desirable to surround an *orphan* with something of the love & duties of a home, to place her as nearly as possible in the relation of a daughter, and to secure for her the nearest approach to the domestic relationships of which she has been deprived, that I think I should consider this education of the affections, and the domestic duties that arise out of them, as more than an equivalent for the accomplishments & languages which she would learn by the other plan, and the superior station in society which a governess may assume. Besides Mme Leray is, according to Mrs Schwabe, a woman of a certain degree of education; and of her generous & warm-hearted feelings & unselfish principles there seems little doubt. She has only been a dress-maker for three or four years; and it might be desirable to get Miss Harvey some first-rate finishing lessons from the *best* dress-maker in Paris; and of course it would always be open to her mother's friends to assist her when she was ready to begin business. She is at present not remarkably tidy in her habits; and having been tossed about from Protestants to Catholics, not very settled in her religious opinions. I will give you once more Mme Leray's address. *5 Faubourg St Honoré*.

I was so glad to see your dear little scrap of signature to my note; that is to say the note you wrote to me, first. I wish I had a chance of seeing you before 'many months' that you say you will be a fixture in Germany, and that I *know* I must be a fixture here. Mrs Schwabe wishes this note to go to-day; or else I have a great deal to say to you; about nothing particular, but only to put you au courant of my husband, myself, my girls & our goings on. Marianne was with me in Paris, and is now staying with Mrs James, a friend whom I owe to you. The other three are at home; well and happy. I hear often from Miss Brontë, and I have been to stay a few days with her at Haworth; this last autumn. I hope she will come & stay with us soon. I just did see Mr Joe Kay in London; once at the Chas Buxton's, when I did not speak to him, and once at Mrs Stanley's, when I asked him if he would send me word where I could get your little pamphlets on the Maison des Diaconesses; but I have not yet heard from him. Everyone here is speaking of the opening of the schools at Gawthrop, as trying such a new and admirable experiment. I have not heard from Ly Hatherton for more than two months. They had then given up their Sicilian plan, & had been spending Xmas at Capesthorne, on Mr Davenport's account; but of course you will have heard since. We spent a few days at Teddesley in the autumn, and I was amused to see how Lord Hatherton had learnt to acknowledge her wisdom & better judgment. This is not *the* long letter I promised you, but it is coming sometime soon. My love to Ughtred, Janet and Miss Paplouska; the other little people won't remember me. Mr Lalor (the husband of the lady with whom Marianne was at school, and your old acquaintance) is wintering at Nice on account of his health. Here is a letter full of crumbs of disjointed intelligence.

Ever dear Lady Kay Shuttleworth
Yours affectionately
E C Gaskell

In reading over my letter I forgot to say that Miss Harvey's wardrobe would need replenishing if she had to leave Mme

Leray. At present she is dressed in Mme Leray's old gowns &c.
That is the only expense which would have to be incurred at first,
as far as Mrs Schwabe knows.

o **182** 184

MISS KAY[1]

> Plymouth Grove
> Tuesday
> March 7. [1854]

My dear Miss Kay,

I cannot tell you how much obliged to you I am for your note.
It made me most completely share in your anxiety, for all the
Prestons have been friends of ours ever since we first went to
lodge there five years ago. We have *two* sisters and a brother of
Eleanor's living here; the elder Margaret is our Cook. I thought
a good deal about it before I spoke to her; and then, (never saying
{why}\from whom/it was that I heard, so your maid may be
quite at ease,) I read her parts out of your letter{s}; and I told her
that I thought it was the duty of one of the family to go up and see
Eleanor and *if possible* bring her down; indeed that it must be
done, if she was to be saved from shame. I told Margaret that
partly on account of her mother's failing health & partly for other
reasons that I thought this devolved upon either her, or the
brother, & that I advised her to go; as the brother is what they call
'an easy temper' easily persuaded, imposed upon or even intimi-
dated by a person of passionate wilfulness as they represent
Eleanor to be. Margaret cried sadly; said Eleanor never would be
guided,—that she had arranged with her present mistress to
accompany her from Kendal to London, without even naming it
to her parents till the day before she left; and that now they
thought something was wrong, for they had only heard from her
twice during the last 8 months, & that she had never answered the
letter asking her to come straight home after her present mistress
went into Wales; which Margaret thinks she is to do *about the
25th of March*. With this glimpse at Eleanor's imperious temper
Margaret & I planned that she\Margaret/should write proposing

---

[1] *Address (on envelope)* Miss Kay | 38 Gloucester Square | Hyde Park | London
—. *Postmarks* MANCHESTER | MR 7 | 1854 | P *and* [?]D[crown]C | MR | 1854 *and*
GREENHEYS.

a week's visit to London, (Eleanor's mistress had formerly asked her) before they leave & she loses the opportunity; & *arrange to come the next day after her writing*, so that Eleanor would have no time to put her off, if the lover took the alarm, & urged her to do so. Then Margaret, once with her, must not leave her till she brings her down. Perhaps Eleanor, who is an affectionate girl may *tell* her sister all when she sees her; but at any rate Margaret will not leave her in London come what may. Margaret is sensible, & spirited, not a very good temper, & I am *afraid* of her & Eleanor falling out; but I have given & will give her many warnings about this, & about the hidden influence that will be pulling on the other side. I write now not merely to thank you, which I do most heartily,—but to ask you if you can tell me exactly *when* Eleanor's mistress is likely to leave,—the 25 Margaret says; but so often people move before the day,—and as she is going into Wales she might be doing so too. I want Margaret to have a full week to influence Eleanor before she is left to herself by the breaking up of the house &c,—but it is not very convenient to part with Margaret and I don't want her to go *before* she is wanted; though of course a day or two too soon would be far better than an hour too late. Margaret has never been in London & her going even makes me a little anxious; as I fear this bad man. However it is the best I can do, or think of on the sudden spur of the moment, & if you can suggest anything to the security of success to the plan—I am sure you will do so. I write all sorts of grammar, & all sorts of spelling, & all sorts of paper, for I am in a great hurry. I can not tell you how much obliged we all are. I should be glad to hear again as to the *time* & any further glimpses as to Eleanor's plans. I find her mistress has been from home ever since last June.—

Yours ever most truly

E. C. Gaskell

175 **183** 185

MARIANNE GASKELL

[Before 15 March ?1854]

My dearest Polly—

(Oh —— the pen & my want of a penknife.) Your plans seem perfectly nice & satisfactory, *except* that I can't make out why you shd incur the expense of going up to Hampstead again, when you've once come down. Try to learn at Euston Sq if they would not take charge of your *heavy* rattletraps, so as only to have *one* cab down when you go to the Price's on Thursday; if you wanted to go back you might then go in the omnibus. Perhaps this plan won't do on enquiry; but you can but try, dear. If you don't come back with Mr M. on next Wednesday fortnight—March 22,[1] I make it out,—you might stay a few days longer if you liked it, only I wanted you to *finish out* yr visits at Hampstead, & then leave\there/for good & all. I shall be particularly glad, & so will Mary Ewart to hear you've done with Hampstead. So please arrange for this. I shall be in hot water till I hear you have left it altogether. Pray arrange for this, if possible. It is not merely the expense, though that is something; but we shall not feel comfortable till you are come down into another part of the town. I am *sure* you will do all that is right, dearest, but still disagreeable things may happen to annoy you at Hampstead, & on the road there. {Pray} You can go to Mrs Groom's I think, dear, the only thing is your being in a strange cab alone at night. Perhaps you cd go from Mrs James' who would send a servant for you. The plan of the list of names of good old music sounds very nice indeed. If Lady Holland asks you—and you can manage it—*not alone in a cab*, at night; *go*. Oh! & dear will you call on a first cousin of mine, (Marianne Stevenson, daughter of my uncle, Dr Stevenson of Berwick,) at 55 Gordon Sq. She is now a Mrs Mannisty, wife of a Queen's Counsel, who comes the Northern Circuit. She is sister to Mrs Church, the wife of the clergyman who died within 2 months at Torquay, & of Joseph Stevenson the clergyman at Leighton-Buzzard. {Her c} Stay! I will send you a letter which will put you a little au fait as to the family. They are my only relations on my father's ⟨. . .⟩

[1] March 22 fell on a Wednesday in 1854 and 1865.

₁₈₂ **184** ₀

Miss Kay[1]

Plymouth Grove
Wednesday. March 14.[2] [1854]

My dear Miss Kay,

I only write now to say that Margaret goes up tomorrow, Thursday, by the Parliamentary train, which stops at Kilburn I find; arriving there at 20 m. past 6. I told her yesterday through whom I had obtained my information, and she seemed very grateful to you. I also told her of your kind offer respecting Hird; and she shook her head, and said she should hardly dare to leave Eleanor. Only I think Eleanor sounds as if she would be busy in the day time, & as if Margaret's supervision wd be more needed in the evenings. Margaret{s} seems to think such decided opposition as Miss Bramorll's now is, {was} likely to do harm to one of Eleanor's temper; so I gave her every possible warning as to her own conduct to Eleanor. I feel very anxious on Margaret's account as well as Eleanor's. Her only friends to whom she can apply for advice &c, will be yourself, and Mr Joseph Kay; and I have also put up a little basket & asked her to take it to Mrs Shaen, a friend of mine, who was a Miss Winkworth and as such was known to Margaret formerly. She lives at 8 Bedford Row, and her husband is a solicitor, and agent for some protection Society which Mrs Shaen says makes him well acquainted with what snares to avoid in London &c. If you *can* conveniently write to me, & give me any information respecting the two sisters, while M. is away I shall be very much obliged to you, as I shall feel very anxious, & M. is not a good writer. My nurse is ill and every moment I have seems to have three separate calls upon it; or else I would write less rough & unfinished letters. But at any rate believe me ever,

Yours very truly & obliged
E C Gaskell.

I do hope that Margaret may manage to see a little of London. She has a friend who is maid to a Miss Stirling living with a Major

---

[1] *Address (on envelope)* Miss Kay | 38 Gloucester Square | Hyde Park | London —. *Postmarks* MANCHESTER | MR 15 | 1854 | P *and* [?]FJ | ⟨ ⟩ MR 16 | 1854.

[2] Wednesday was 15 March in 1854.

Stirling South Place (or Terrace) Knightsbridge just close to the Barracks, on the opposite side of the road; a house with a long covered {gate} way from the gate to the door. If she comes to see Hird, perhaps you would allow Hird to go across the Park with her to Major Stirling's. She won't know that she is in the direction of Knightsbridge[.]

183 **185** 187

MARIANNE GASKELL[1]

Friday [?Early March ?1854]

My dearest Polly,

This won't be an elegant letter but I will write on any scrap of paper to set you at ease. I wish I could have afforded to let you go to Portsmouth but you see I can't. You may get those songs Papa says, as I told you yesterday. Your note this morning was *very* nice, darling. Remember Miss Chorley's hours, *after* 12 *before* 2— The man came (M. Hallé's man Hinxman[]) to tune the piano yesterday—it was more than $\frac{1}{2}$ a note *flat*, besides being altogether out of tune—and he says it is all but ruined by being so shockingly tuned. It will take 4 tunings this next month, & cost *two guineas*,— something about the frame &c,—and so I must scrubble up money for that. *Pray* burn any letters. I am always afraid of writing much to you, you are so careless about letters. No news. Meta is going to Alderley at 4 this afternoon. Papa to dine with Mrs Schwabe. I can't go, have had & have one of my atrocious head-aches. As far as I know Susanna is gone to London today.[2] You & she might come back together if times fit. A letter directed to her, *Prussia House* would at any time find her as the Bunsens would know where she was. Remember you *are* to have the songs from Mrs G; & send word what money you want. Emily Tagart is coming to the Darbishire's. I am glad you have seen Jane Stewart. 'Scripture readers' are men, sent & paid by a London society to any clergyman who applies for them to help him to read the bible in his parish. There was one at Boughton you may

---

[1] A Lancaster transcript gives the address: 'Miss Gaskell | T. B. Price's Esq | 11 Princes Terrace | Princes Gate, | Hyde Park, London.'

[2] See *Letters and Memorials*, ed. Winkworth, I, p. 428, although the dates of the Bunsen and Winkworth letters there printed seem incompatible.

remember. They read & act under the clergyman's directions. The black kitten is lost. *The children have never missed her, so you must take no notice.* I have no time for more. Only be happy love & enjoy yourself. I wish you'd say if you've been to Mr Bowman again.

Ever your very affect[ionate],

E C G.

Burn this.

₀ **186** ₀

EMIL SOUVESTRE[1]

Plymouth Grove
Manchester.
Samedi, Mars 18th [1854]

Dear Sir,

As I know you can not read English, and as I am sorry to say I can not write good and grammatical French I send you a letter to the address of Madame Chapman {to beg you to excuse} to forewarn you of a liberty which I have taken, and to beg you to excuse it. Presuming upon the recollection of my agreeable conversation with you at the house of Madame Mohl, and remembering the kindness with which Madame Souvestre listened to my imperfect French at Madame Chapman's, I have given a letter of introduction to a gentleman, an old friend of mine, who is going to Paris in a few days, and is most anxious to make your acquaintance. The sole address I could give him was M. Emil Souvestre, Faubourg Poissoniere but with this he undertakes to find you, and I pray you to give him a little welcome for my sake. But for his own, he is, to a certain degree, worthy of knowing you. He is a distinguished writer in our 'Edinburgh Review'; choosing subjects relating to politics, or political œconomy in general, but sometimes reviewing 'belles lettres'. For instance he reviewed and abused 'Mary Barton'; and we are none the less friends. Just now he has been reviewing your 'Philosophe sous les toits', and it

---

[1] *Address (on envelope)* M. Emil Souvestre, | aux soins de Madame Chapman | No 5 Rue de Monsieur | Paris. | Affranchié. *Postmarks* MANCHESTER | MR 20 | [?]1854 *and* ⟨ ⟩ | MR 21 | 1854 *and* ⟨ ⟩ PARIS 2 ⟨ ⟩ | 22 | MARS | 54 *and* 2 ANGL. 2 | 22 | MARS | ⟨ ⟩.

is from admiration for this, and other works of yours, that he is led to wish to become acquainted with you. Pardon my vanity in saying that I knew you, and would venture to give him an introduction to you. And now you see I am turned coward, and fear, that on the presentation of my letter, you may turn it over and say 'Madame Gaskell! Madame Gaskell! mais, Monsieur, je ne connais pas cette dame.' Je vous prie, cher Monsieur Souvestre de vous souvenir de moi, car je me souviens tres bien de vous; et veuillez bien accueillir Monsieur *William Greg*, car je vous assure qu'il est homme d'esprit, et digne de votre connaissance. Assurez vous Monsieur de mes sentimens de respect; et croyez que je suis

Yours truly
Elizabeth Gaskell

185 187 193

MARIANNE GASKELL

Tuesday. [?21 March 1854]

My dearest Meta, no! I'll use it up for my dearest Polly.—*If* Mr Bowman does not want to see you again\after Friday/*come home as soon as possible,*—we all want you,—only having begun with him, *do go on, and get your poor eyes right,* if possible; *if he wants to see you again,*\stop; if not come home as soon as you can./ Susanna is at, or about Bedford Row, and perhaps it's the safest address for her; she depends so much on C. Bunsen that perhaps that's the reason she can't answer you off at once. I know she does not come back this week; & I think Annie & Mrs Shaen are at Emily's. I have sent on to Mrs. Green what you say Mr James says of J. Philip [Green]. Your gown &c sound very nice. I have no time for more. We shall want much to hear your plans. If S. W. still continues uncertain, *and Mr Bowman does not want to see you again* you had better come off home by yourself by the early morning express, that that gets in here at ½ past 4 in the aftn or thereabouts. We are all well, except Hearn, who is very languid & poorly. Margaret in London, coming down on Thursday with Eleanor Preston—No news.

Ever your very affec[tionate]
E C Gaskell.

176 **188** 198

?F. J. FURNIVALL[1]

Plymouth Grove
Thursday [?23 March 1854]

My dear Sir,

I am ashamed to thank you for the last of a series of kindnesses because the beginning is lost in the darkness of ungrateful unacknowledgment. Yes! I have gone on hearing what I wanted to hear—and seeing what I wanted to see, all through you, and I have never had the grace to say thankyou. I will say it in capital letters now to make up.

THANK YOU.

I did mean to thank you personally, only you were not to be seen, when twice I came out of Lincoln's Inn Chapel. I had a great deal to say, which I have no time to write. I thank you for Mr Ludlow's pamphlet today—I have thanked you (mentally) very much for Folious Appearances,[2] the humour, strength— and even affectation of which I like exceedingly. What is the name of the man, again?—

Yours very truly, and *not* ungratefully,
E. C. Gaskell.

168 **189** 204

R. MONCKTON MILNES

Plymouth Grove
Manchester—
April 20. [1854]

My dear Sir,

I have grateful remembrance of your kind exertions; and I think that the enclosed letter will give you true pleasure.[3] May I beg you to consider it as confidential as all our previous communications

---

[1] *Annotation* (March 28—54) [*a Tuesday*].

[2] A pencil note in another hand on the MS. reads '(by young John Tupling, bookseller).' *Folius Appearances, a Consideration of the Way of Lettering our Books* was published by J. R. Smith in 1854.

[3] See *The Brontës*, ed. Wise and Symington, IV, p. 116.

on this subject, and to return it to me as soon as ever you can. I can't help fancying your kind words may have made him feel that he was not so friendless as he represented {himself} & believed himself to be at first; and might rouse his despondency up to a fresh effort. I like her letter; don't you? Thank you. Will you accept our kind regards, and give them to Mrs Milnes, who is, I hope, stronger?

Yours very truly
E. C. Gaskell.

₀ 190 ₀

H. F. CHORLEY

[21 April 1854]

My dear Sir,

I am thoroughly obliged to you. I wanted to see the Duchess Eleanour[1] ever since I read that review—criticism—whatever you call it in the Times, long before I had the slightest suspicion it was yours; & more than suspicion I have not had till now. I looked for it among the announcements and could not,—and can not understand why it was——

So far had I got this Friday when my husband came in to tell me of the sudden death of the oldest friend we have in Manchester;[2] & I have been all day long with his widow—now I can but catch the post with this bare & brief acknowledgement, but tomorrow or Sunday I will write again if you will allow me; for, as usual, your note suggests many things I should like, & meant to say—

Don't speak of gratitude,—I *love* Miss Chorley, & am only too glad to do anything that may give her a moment's pleasure— only I'm afraid my letters must be dull.

Yours most truly
E. C. Gaskell

[1] *The Duchess Eleanour* by H. F. Chorley is recorded as having been first performed on 13 March 1854.

[2] William Gaskell's co-pastor, the Rev. John Gooch Robberds, died on Friday, 21 April 1854. *Annals*, ed. Axon, p. 266.

₁₆₆ **191** ₁₉₂

JOHN FORSTER

Sunday—[23 April 1854]

My dear Mr Forster,
     Thank you. That is capital. I was only afraid of Mr Chapman; I
believe that fear was put into me by Mr Gaskell, who said (when
your note came yesterday) that 'he did not like Mr Chapman to
be put to any expense on his account.' That has been his sole
objection. As to preface or appendix I don't think Mr Gaskell
cares one straw; whichever you wise London people think best,
we, provincials, must submit to. Mr Gaskell would not help me at
all in getting those reports for you; so I had to go off myself on
Friday to the Guardian office, & one copy was so excessively dirty
I objected to it; but they told me they were 'out of print' & were
the 'last copies they had'; and we don't take the Guardian, & I
don't know where to get any other copies. Mr Gaskell writes
short hand, & I can't read it, or I would copy it out for Mr
Chapman, as {he}\Mr Gaskell/is too busy to do it himself,—so,
please would it be better to send the copies you have (those
columns I cut out for you, I mean) to Bradbury & Evans, or
whoever is printing M. B;[1] or to\first/return those copies to Mr
Gaskell,\who/would correct {fr} them, & then send them up to
be printed from? If you think this last plan best Mr Gaskell says 'it
would save Mr Chapman expense', & he evidently looks upon Mr
Chapman as a poor victim to you & me) will you return them
directly, & they shall go back on Wednesday afternoon at the
latest. *If* the Guardian reports had better go *straight* to Bradbury &
Evans—will you give directions to omit all the little newspaper
falsification, at first, about the 'lecturer', 'numerous audience', &
plunge off into the lecture itself—*giving a separate paragraph to each
word.* Then I think—you may know my thoughts from Mr
Gaskell's because his are over-modest, & mine perhaps over-bold
—*I* think that Mr Chapman might strike off a few copies of the
lecture alone & give them to Mr Gaskell,—what do you think? I
think you are *very* kind about it. That *first* lecture was corrected by
Mr Gaskell himself, so perhaps if the separate paragraphs were

---

[1] This refers to the fifth edition of *Mary Barton* (1854), to which William
Gaskell's two lectures on the Lancashire dialect were appended. The reports
appeared in the *Manchester Guardian*.

attended to it would be pretty safe to print that off, & only return
the copy of the second, my unlucky correction. I will do anything
I can to save time, but that is not much, & Mr Gaskell is peculiarly
busy just now owing to the sudden death of his colleague Mr
Robberds on Friday morng.—But you may depend upon no time
being lost. Ah! did you not cheat me with your ('now don't tell')
at the bottom of the page! I turned over thinking you really had
guessed, & for that & previous misconduct on the same affair I
have half a mind not to tell you—Yes! she is going to be married!
to Mr Nicholls, who has returned to Haworth. He made some
kind of renewed application to her father {was} to be allow [sic] to
see them from time to time as an acquaintance, in *January*,—in
Feb.—he again spoke to her; & she says she can not tell me all the
details in a letter, but 'events have so flowed out of each other that
now she finds herself\what people call—/engaged'. Mr Nicholls
returns to Haworth to be curate to her father (himself only a
perpetual curate under the vicar of Bradford, with 250£ a year
pour tout potage, out of which he pays Mr Nicholls' salary. They
are\all three father daughter & husband/to live together; she says
her father seems now anxious to make up for former injustice, &
is so kind that at times she 'could cry that she has not been able
more to gratify his natural pride.' The 'old, the poor, the very
young' among the Haworth people are delighted; which speaks
well for Mr Nicholls, I'm sure. I am terribly afraid he won't let her
go on being as intimate with us, heretics. I see she is, too, a little.
However she is coming to us in May, & I must make the most of
her then, & hope for the future. I fancy him very good, but *very*
stern & bigoted; but I dare say that is partly fancy. Still it arises
from what she has told me. He sounds vehemently in love with
her. And I like his having known her dead sisters & dead brother &
all she has gone through of home trials, & being no person who
has {b} just fancied himself in love with her, because he was
dazzled by her genius. Mr N. never knew, till long after Shirley
was published, that she wrote books; and came in, cold & dis-
approving one day, to ask her if the report he had heard at
Keighley was true &c. Fancy him, an Irish curate, loving her even
then, reading that beginning of Shirley! However, with all his
bigotry & sternness it must be charming to be loved with all the
strength of his heart as she sounds to be. Mr Shaen accuses me
always of being 'too much of a woman' in always wanting to obey
somebody—but I am sure that Miss Brontë could never have

borne\not to be well-ruled & ordered/—well! I think I have got into a 'fiasco' and I have hardly any right to go on discussing what she could or she could not do—but I mean that she would never have been happy but with an exacting, rigid, law-giving, passionate man—only you see, I'm afraid one of his laws will be to shut us out, & so I am making a sort of selfish moan over it & have got out of temper I suppose with the very thing I have been wanting for her this six months past.

Oh! I wrote to Mr Dickens, & he says he is not going to have a strike,[1]—altogether his answer sets me at ease. I have half wondered whether another character might not be introduced into Margaret,[2]—Mrs Thornton, the mother, to have taken as a sort of humble companion & young housekeeper the\orphan/daughter of an old friend in humble, retired country life on the borders of Lancashire,—& this girl to be in love with Mr Thornton in a kind of passionate despairing way,—but both jealous of Margaret, & yet angry that she gives Mr Thornton pain—I know the kind of wild wayward character that grows up in lonesome places, which has a sort of Southern capacity of hating & loving. She shd not be what people call *educated*, but with strong sense.

I did so like your good long handsome note four or five days ago. I do so thank you for all your kindness. There! there are 2 sentences with 'so' in them not followed by 'as' as Mr Gaskell says they ought to be. I will make one grammatical sentence, & have done.

I am *so* much obliged to you *as* to be incapable of expressing my obligation but by saying that I am always

Yours most truly
E. C. Gaskell.

P.S. Do you know what 'petticoat-tails' are? because it is rather a pretty derivation. Petticoat-tails are a sort of little cake they sell in Edinburgh, the receipt for which was said to have been brought to Scotland by one of Mary Stewart's french servants, *petits gâtelles*—

Mr Gaskell is pleased about the lectures I am sure, though he does not say anything, except pitying Mr Chapman. I will do my best to make things smooth & rapid at this end.

[1] A reference to *Hard Times*.
[2] Published with the title *North and South*.

JOHN FORSTER

[?8–14 May 1854]

⟨. . .⟩ I troubled you with my groans, my dear Mr Forster, so now you see I am going to send you my reliefs—Selfish the first is. I don't believe Miss Brontë will *ever* become bigoted, or *ever* lose her true love for me,—but I do fear a *little* for her\happiness/just because he is narrow, and she is not.—good, true, pure, & affectionate he is, but he is also narrow, and she can never be so. That's gladness the first.

Secondly I have worried Mr Gaskell, by assuring him he shall have no peace or comfort at home, into going away. He has fixed to go away next Monday,[1] & looks better already with the prospects of a change, in which he now indulges himself. He will form no plans, but bachelorize off comfortably guided by the wind of his own daily will; but he faintly purposes to be in London,—& at the opening of the Crystal Palace. *You cannot think what a relief this is to me.* All last week I was *stupid* with anxiety, & the utter want of power to influence him. Now, if, as I said, we were not a full household till the 20th, and longer—(I could fly & I could run,) and I could write M. Hale, whh Mrs Shaen has put me into spirits by liking, much to my surprize; and she, trained in German criticism is a far severer judge than you,—grunting & groaning when she does not like.[2] She says it is good—but out of proportion to the length of the planned story,\written or published/—& so cramfull of possible interest that she thinks another character would make it too much—she finds faults, but not disheartening ones,—only still I feel it to be flat & grey with[3] no bright clear foreground as yet—Oh dear! I can't get Mr Gaskell to look at it, & it is no use writing much longer,—only I don't like showing it to you till I have got in something more distinct & telling. Miss Brontë has been telling me of a complete Mr Gradgrind,—a young man,—a young father—who set a trap to catch a sparrow, & caught a robin, which he did not intend. He said to

[1] See p. 285 below.
[2] She met Charlotte Brontë at Mrs Gaskell's on Tuesday, 2 May 1854. See *Letters and Memorials*, ed. Winkworth, I, p. 437.
[3] At this point a Brit. Mus. MS. ends & the letter is continued by a Nat. Lib. of Scotland MS.

Miss Brontë [']Now you shall see that cruelty is natural, & calls out glee in a child, till affectation calls out false sentiment &c[.'] So he took the dead bird & showed it to his little girl aged 2. The{n} child looked at it; realized {he} something strange & still, & began to cry—[']Oh nonsense' said he, quick⟨ly;⟩ [']this is a little chuckie; we will pluck the feathers off it, & Emily shall see it's head cut off, and it's inside taken out, and it shall be roasted for her dinner, & it will be so good!' This said Emily*his only child*/is delicate; and one day after dinner—he said to some strange gentleman, his wife an invalid sitting at the head of the table 'My child will die, that's very clear; and I shall be glad of it—Nay my dear! why do you look so miserable; her life would be only a prolonged trouble to herself & to us, while even she is spared much if &c.—' Yet in a way he is a decent kind of man.

Yours most truly
E. C. Gaskell.

I took heart of grace, & asked for a 'revise' of Mr Gaskell's lectures. Jacob Grimm wants one copy[.]

187 193 *198a

MARIANNE GASKELL

[14 May 1854]

My dearest Marianne,

I am very sorry I did not reply yesterday, by return; but the bare *writing*-time was not to be found,—callers all day long, which was doubly provoking as Emily Shaen was here for a solitary day,[1] & I had to leave her (and my lunch) perpetually. But I really don't know how to fix. I should *like* to come to Poulton, but I don't see any *chance* of it till far on in next week. *If* your bedroom is *airy* enough you had better keep to it at present, & let me decide a little more first about things. Cousin Mary stops till Saturday; because Mr Harry Holland is coming down to Manchester about a 'reference-case' Friday & Saturday, & I have asked him to come & sleep here, so as to see as much of his Aunt as possible. And Arthur Darbishire has this morning written to ask if he may have a bed on Friday night, perhaps afterwards, as Mr. & Mrs D—& Vernon

[1] See p. 290 below.

are coming to Manchester—& there is fever in his York Place
lodgings & he can't go there because the lady is not to be moved.
Of course I have sent him word he can come & for as long as he
likes: but *I* can't leave till he goes, even other things permitting,
whh I don't think they would. I enclose a note from Mrs Scott,
asking me to dinner to-day; and beside Mr Satterfield and Eliza
Patterson called to ask me for tomorrow, & the Bells asked us all
including Meta for Saturday to the evening. *I* shall go there. I
can't go to the Satterfields because of my visitors which I am
rather sorry for. Mrs Schwabe is going to have a sale at Crumpsall next Tuesday week. I enclose a note from Papa to make this
hurried letter fit for something. I hope you enjoyed last night; I
thought of you often. The Tagarts are going to have a large
party on Tuesday; Clara Potter going up to it, & 2 Miss Scotts. I
hope Papa won't tumble into the middle of the confusion. I hope
he will call at the James'. If you write to her, give his address as at
2 St James' Place. No letters this morning from any of you
absentees. Meta sounds very gay, does not she? I was so sorry to
part from Emily last night. Oh! Mrs Ed. Potter called yesterday
to ask Mrs Lalor's school for Polly. I recommended it, & I think
she will go. Write soon there's a darling. Can you tell what the
week's expenses have been—*about* I mean?

Yours very affec[tionatel]y
E C Gaskell

I shall write to Flossy next. Love to all.

0 **194** 199

JULIA BRADFORD GASKELL

Plymouth Grove
Monday morng
[?15 May 1854]

Madame! My dearest Julia,—this is the beginning of a french letter
to some lady, but I am sure I don't know to whom; only you see it
is going off to a little English girl at last, is it not? Do you know
we are going to have a little kitten sent us from Paris, with long
hair, and a very pretty face, and is called Cranford, can you guess

why? It is called an Angola or a Persian cat; and Minnie has seen it's mother! Yesterday seemed a great bustle. First came letters[—] one from Mme Mohl, and one from dear Florence & you. After reading those came cousin Mary's coach, to take us to Brook St. We sat in Mr Ewart's seat as we knew no one would be there, & all the rest of the chapel was crowded. Mrs Schwabe brought us to the end of Nelson St, & told us that Chevalier Bunsen was going to live at Heidelberg, & sell his museum. Then I found a note from Susanna, who had come over for Sunday, and asked me to go there to speak to her;[1] which I did, scuttered down my dinner, and drove off to the Sunday School; 13 in class[,] tell MA—I read the little Mountaineers to them after they had done their chapter, walked home, wrote a letter; Eustace Greg and Arthur Darbishire came to tea. Susanna Winkworth, and Mary Ewart afterwards. Mary brought a letter from Agnes, who had seen Meta, on Thursday Evening at a party at the Duckworth's, dinner first, & Meta came afterwards, and played Les Cloches very well, & the next day she had gone with Agnes to see Minna at Lady Coltmans, and lunched there. Miss Leonora Horner is to be married to Dr Perry by Mr Tayler on the 18th, Papa had to sit up till 12 o'clock correcting the proofs of his sermon. This morning he went by the $\frac{1}{2}$ past nine train, & will reach Evesham by 10 minutes to 4, & then he will have six miles to go in the carriage to Dumbleton.[2] I think it would be very nice for him to stay there till Saturday[,] then, by Oxford, and staying there a day to see the place to London, and then back by Ashbourne-Hall, Capn Holland's, who wrote yesterday to invite him to go there. But we must find out how long the Chapel will take to paint first I think. Tell Hearn the Town's water is to be laid on tomorrow, but I can *not* understand about the Gutta Percha pipes. I am going a drive with Mrs Shuttleworth today, while Cousin Mary stays at home to receive Mrs Kennedy, who is coming to sit with her. We are all very angry with Mrs Davis, who has broken her promise to us, & gone off to Alderley with 'Shaw's people'. Margaret went to tell her this morning that if she did not come to us on Thursday at the latest we must give her up altogether; and she said we must then. Tommy is very well, & took Papa to the station today. The cow is giving more milk than ever now she goes out into the field. The

---

[1] 'His sudden change of plans . . . naturally affected me, too, very painfully.' Susanna Winkworth, ed. *Letters and Memorials*, I, p. 442 n.

[2] See p. 290 below.

little chickens are doing very well indeed. Mary Ewart says Marianne has some message to me from Mrs Jenkin, and now goodbye my darling—Tell Flossy to take great care of her cold. It is both cold & close here today.

Your very affect[ionate] mother

E C Gaskell.

192 **195** 408

JOHN FORSTER[1]

Wednesday night—[17 May 1854]

My dear Mr Forster,

There is every chance you will have a long letter; but I'm afraid it will be a very dull one. For in the first place it is what ought to be sleepy bed-time, only I am not a bit sleepy; only so *very* sorry, that I could cry with a good grace, that Mrs Shaen's visit has come & gone all in the brief space of one day,—what I look forward to all through a long year cut short by this bad fever that is all about. Do you know 'Jess Macfarlane'? You ought to know it, it is so pretty; and the\some of the/words have run in my head all evening

> When first she came to town
> > They ca'éd her Jess Macfarlane
> But now she's come and gane
> > They ca' her the *wandering darling*.

And then don't you remember the naïve verse

> I writ my luve a letter
> But alas! she canna read—
> And I like her a' the better.

I am rather afraid I've heard somebody say it is not a proper song; but I don't know why it should not be for all I know of it, and I am sure my two verses are charming & innocent.

Oh! I am afraid this letter is going to be what Dr Holland once called a letter of mine 'a heterogeneous mass of nonsense.' But that was before I wrote Mary B—he would not *say* so now.

Oh! Mr Forster don't you think Mr Chapman has behaved

---

[1] *Annotation* May 18/54.

shabbily to me. Not *one* copy has he sent me, though I made it an
express stipulation that I should have some to give away, partly
because of Mr Gaskell's lectures. Mr Chapman agreed to it; and
now I have had to buy those to send off where Mr Gaskell told
me! After all you are not coming up to a certain Mr Hibbert who
is now reading Mary Barton for the *fourteenth* time. You once took
it down—(or *said* you did) to the Isle of Wight, & told me you
would read it & tell me what you thought of it, just as you do
now,—but the Fates dispersed your plan to empty air. But I *will*
flatter myself, & think you *are* reading it over your breakfast{s}. I
keep going on—and on—& not coming to what is on my mind, &
in my heart to say,—which is simply this[.] I don't believe one
word of what you say about Mr Ruskin. It has given me *great* pain
to have the idea[,] the diabolical idea[,] suggested,—but I think I
do know enough of them to assure myself it is not true. I never
spoke to him. All I had heard when I wrote was first—from Emily
Buxton who knows them pretty well. She said you will be sorry
to hear that Mrs R[uskin] has gone home to her father; they have
had a violent quarrel; but there are shocking & groundless
rumours in circulation. We (herself & her husband) were with
them at Denmark Hill on the very day, but of course knew
nothing of it.' Now I was asked by the Ruskins this very same
day to go with the C. Buxtons & Wm Cowpers to see the
Turners. Of course I should have liked to have gone but I was here
in Manchester; & the message that came afterwards from Mr
Ruskin was that if I came up to town *soon* after Easter I was to see
them; if not, he & his wife would be abroad in Switzerland till
August. You will wonder how he came to ask me—I have known
Mrs Ruskin for some time,—she was at the same school as I was—
though of course\she was/much younger. Still we had the bond
of many mutual schoolfellows. Now don't think me hard upon
her if I tell you what I have *known* of her. She is very pretty very
clever,—and very vain. As a girl when she was staying in Manchester her delight was to add to the list of her offers (27 I think
she was *at*, then;) but she never cared for any one of them. It was
her boast to add to this list in every town she visited just like
somebody in the Arabian Nights, who was making up her list of
1000 lovers. *Effie Grey was engaged at the very time she accepted Mr
Ruskin*\he did not know of it till after their marriage/. I don't
think she has any more serious faults that [*sic*] vanity & cold-
heartedness\not to her own people, nor her father's house/, but

you know how much suffering they may cause. Four years ago her old schoolmistress prophecied [*sic*] to me the precise end of it all;—just what *I* believe it to have been; that she, with her high temper & love of admiration would not submit to the rather strict rules he insisted upon as to hours &c. This very same lady has been staying with the Ruskins this Xmas, and after spending *a week or 10 days in their house* said that Mr Ruskin was spoiling Effie because he could not bear to thwart her, yet disapproved of all her excess of visiting &c. She said he had a bad temper, & Mrs Ruskin had been spoilt from her childhood—(her next youngest brothers & sisters were swept off by scarlet fever & she was left the only one for some time &c &c)—and that some day she (the schoolmistress) was afraid there wd be an outbreak—Don't you see all the elements for just such an event as that which has taken place? Mrs Wedgwood I know had just the same ideas & the same fears. All I heard till your letter came, was the fact of her having left him & gone to her parents—bad & sad enough, but not *so* terribly bad. I don't mean to say she was ever wrong, but I *know* that he forgave her many scrapes at Venice, and so many stories were told falsely about them—One was that when abroad\2 years ago/they travelled in separate carriages[.] Well! and the reason was this, for I saw some of the letters. He had to write a great deal, & had his carriage fitted up with desk &c, and he told her he should be but a dull companion, so if she liked, he would take another carriage, & she should choose whom she liked to go with her & he would pay all expenses. So she chose a Miss Kerr\a poor Scotch girl/, the niece of some friends of mine; who speaks of Mr Ruskin's kindness & tenderness & generosity (of course allowing for his bad temper which every body knows.) & how Mrs Ruskin & she used to enjoy the evngs when they all scrambled into one carriage &c. Now I *know* all this. And while I seem to be throwing blame on Mrs Ruskin I remember her unusually trying position,—so very lovely,—no children, not caring very particularly for any one but her home-people in Perthshire, & amused as well as flattered by the rapturous admiration she created. But she is gone to her father's I suppose? I can not bear to think of the dreadful hypocrisy if the man who wrote those books is a bad man. I almost hoped you might have contradicted the rumour of the quarrel & her having left him at all.

There! I am afraid I have not been very courteous in my contradiction of what you have said; but at any rate I have given

you my grounds at some length. Any how I am very very sorry
for both of them; & all these rumours make it so difficult for the
simple & natural reconciliation to take place; each conscious of
past faults, & each going to do better. She really is very close to a
charming character; if she had had the small pox she would have
been so. I'm sure you will not repeat what I have said of her. To
make up for my dull letter I enclose you Miss Brontë's announcement of her marriage-to-be—It is quiet, quaint, & a little formal;
but like herself, & meaning the full force of every word she uses.
She told me of Mr Milnes interview with Mr Nicholls,—& of the
latter's puzzle to account for Mr Milnes interest in him. He never
for an instant suspected anything; or my head would not have
been safe on my shoulders. To hear her description of the conversation with her father when she quietly insisted on her right to see
something more of Mr Nicholls was really fine. Her father thought
that she had a chance of some body higher or at least farther
removed from poverty. She said 'Father I am not a young girl,
not a young woman even—I never was pretty. I now am ugly. At
your death I shall have 300£ besides the little I have earned myself
—do you think there are many men who would serve seven years
for me?' And again when he renewed the conversation and asked
her if she would marry a curate?—'Yes I must marry a curate if I
marry at all; not merely a curate but *your* curate; not merely *your*
curate but he must live in the house with you, for I cannot leave
you.' The sightless old man stood up & said solemnly 'Never. I
will never have another man in this house', and stalked out of the
room. For a week he never spoke to her. She had not made up her
mind to accept Mr Nicholls & the worry on both sides made her
ill—then the old servant interfered, and asked him, sitting blind &
alone, 'if he wished to kill his daughter?;' and went up to her and
abused Mr Nicholls for not having 'more brass.' And so it has
ended where it has done. Since I have seen her I am more content
than this letter made me at first. You will return it to me, please. I
think by way of making my 3 sheets with your one,—which was
very 'nice' (ah! you see I have got to that word quite unconsciously
again,) very interesting, & very kind I must pop in 2 *clever* letters
from an old Parisian friend of mine\Madame Mohl/; an Orleanist
to the back-bone as you will see,—a friend of Mme Récamier's in
days gone by. The 'Emma' she alludes to is a very charming
American lady—& that I think is the only allusion that requires
explanation. Don't you like reading letters? I do, so much. Not

grand formal letters; but such as Mme Mohl's I mean. Is it not clever about Mr Senior & his way of reading books? Please to read my letters instead of Mary Barton one morning at breakfast, & then return all three to me. Oh! Mr Forster if you don't burn my \own/letters as you read them I will never forgive you! I am vexed with myself for having said that bad about Mrs Ruskin, but I wanted you to understand their position a little more than I thought you did. I have letters from my children daily; all brilliantly well. The panic among the servants still goes on, & will do I suppose till the fever has left the neighbourhood,—and {one} \I/feel{s} almost selfish to have got the children away, &\to be/ keeping the servants here. Shall I tell you a Cranfordism. An old lady a Mrs Frances Wright said to one of my cousins 'I have never been able to spell since I lost my teeth'. Mr Gaskell is at Dumbleton; going by Oxford to London next week. Mrs Shaen wanted me to return with her on Saturday[1] & give him a surprize; but I am not very sure that he would like it; and besides there's Margaret Hale! I have sent 76 pages to you by Mrs Shaen; all I have written except a very few lines. It is dull; & I have never had time to prune it. I have got the people well on,—but I think in too lengthy a way. But I can still make it good I am sure. I should like to see that French collection of pictures. I shd like to see the Francesca,—& M. Plassan, because you like them—& Rosa Bonheur's because I know her & like her. She is a spirited woman excessively fond of animals & out-door life. One of her pictures,— a\man following a/plough turning up rich brown ridges under a a [sic] full shadowless noonday sun is in the Luxembourg,—another still more famous is of horses,—a gathering of wild horses—she thinks that all animals have separate *countenances*, as well as separate ways of expressing passion—& to paint this famous horse picture, she dressed herself as a young man, & went & painted it in the greatest livery stables in Paris. I should think it was one or two o'clock in the morning but one clock is dissolutely wrong, another gone to be cleaned, my watch ditto and I only know I promised you a long letter, & here it is! The house seems so lonely & empty without any of my girls. I am literally alone in it —not even a book to beguile the time—five fathoms deep they lie beneath dust-sheets &c—safe from me & the white washers. Have compassion upon me, sometime; but not to trouble yourself

---

[1] This does not appear to be the visit referred to in Letter 192 above. See pp. 282, n. 2 and 283.

while you are writing about Lord Nugent, & be sure you tell us
all you can about his mother. I have done at last.

Yours most truly (I don't like
'sincerely')
E C Gaskell

₀ **196** ₁₉₇

WALTER SAVAGE LANDOR

42 Plymouth Grove
Manchester.
May 20th 1854

May I venture to send you a copy of my husband's Lectures on
The Lancashire Dialect? I am not sure if his modesty would
sanction this act of mine if he were at home: but, once done, I
know that he would feel gratified by the thought that you had
read them. With great admiration and respect, I remain, Sir

Yours truly,
Elizabeth Gaskell[1]

₁₉₆ **197** ₀

WALTER SAVAGE LANDOR

Plymouth Grove
May 22, 1854

Dear Sir,
   I have sent your letter on to my husband by this post; but I must
just say a very hearty thank you for the pleasure I know it will
give him. It will come to him at the same time as my little confession of having thought his lectures worthy of your reading. I
have been very much interested by your remarks which {are}\will
be/of course still more interesting to one capable of entering into
their full value. I fancy that many of the words in full use here to
this day, are also used, or have been very lately used in both
Cheshire, Staffordshire (Cannock Chase,—about Wednesday &c)

---

[1] The reply to this letter is printed in Waller, 'Letters Addressed to Mrs Gaskell',
pp. 30-1.

and Warwickshire. But Mr Gaskell, who is proud of his county, likes to consider these remnants of the old strong language as peculiar to Lancashire and the Yorkshire Dales. Do you know (I ask you the question because it has come as a natural form of sentence to the end of my pen,—not expecting any answer,) 'crying her *notchel*' for the form of advertisement that 'I so & so won't pay my wife's debts &c' And as you quote Warwickshire (where I was 5 years at school) you will remember the country people's use of the word 'unked.'[1] I can't find any other word to express the exact feeling of strange unusual desolate discomfort, and I sometimes 'potter' and 'mither' people by using it. I am sure I was taught and firmly believed till your letter came that Hannibal did dissolve mountains with vinegar. I never reasoned, only believed. There is the pretty old Carol that I used to hear in Warwickshire 'He neither was born, In housen nor in ha*ll*'—but hall was singular to rhyme with stall. In some country parts of Gloucestershire they use 'chick*en*' as we do poultry, and call the singular, *hen*, whatever its age may be; reserving Chicken for the Plural. In the little country-town in Cheshire, in which I lived till I was married, there were one or two peculiar customs, now slowly dying out. One was that all the friends of bride or bridegroom sanded before their doors on a wedding day.[2] It was done with tin funnels filled with different coloured sand in a sort of rude pattern [sketch follows] with a border round it and a doggrel verse in the centre

> Long may they live
> Happy may they be
> And blessed with a numerous
> Progeny.

We none of us knew why we did it, but a wedding would have been as incomplete without it as without ringing of bells. Then again on May morning there was a branch of a tree hung up before every person's door, implying their popular character. Each tree had {their} it's meaning. It was not always the householder who had to appropriate the character. If there was a pretty girl in the house there was a branch of birch hung-up, and so on. We, of the genteeler sort, rather chose to ignore some of the

[1] See *Wives and Daughters*, c. xv—'On Tuesday afternoon, Molly returned home—to the home which was already strange, and what Warwickshire people would call "unked" to her.'

[2] For details, see Henry Green's *Knutsford*, 1859, pp. 86-7.

meanings which I am sorry for now; I should like to have known more of this language of trees. I know that a bunch of nettles was an insult; but not equal to a little heap of saw-dust, which was the worst affront of all. But of the exact nature of the insult I have not a notion. I am ashamed of writing so much. Dear Sir, I remain

Yours respectfully and truly

E. C. Gaskell.

I thank you for your kind knowledge of how much I should like to have the Death of Blake.[1]

188 **198** 237

F. J. FURNIVALL[2]

[*c.* 27 May 1854]

Great Bear   Who's been sending me Goddard-v-Gee?
Middle Bear Who's been sending me Goddard-v-Gee?
Little Bear Who's been sending me Goddard-v-Gee?

*   *

194 **199** 203

JULIA BRADFORD GASKELL

[?May 1854]

My dearest Julia,

Do you know Fairy has been poorly, and has been to pay the doctor a visit, and has come home quite well, only very thin; and she was so pleased she came scampering upstairs. And do you know we are to have a kitten all the way from Paris, called Cranford; with very very long hair, and soft pretty eyes? I wonder if it will understand our English *Pussy*. I am getting my lunch (or rather dinner) while I write. Ham sandwiches and beer if you wish to know; and it is 12 o'clock. Then I shall go and dress, and go with Mrs Shuttleworth to pay calls; and go to a

[1] See Landor's letter, Waller, 'Letters to Mrs Gaskell', p. 32.

[2] *Address (on envelope)* F. J. Furnivall Esq | 3 Old Square | Lincoln's Inn | London. *Postmarks* MANCHESTER | MY 25 | 1854 *and* Y [crown] T | 27 MY 27 | 185⟨4⟩. *Annotations* The sale of the Cranford property was in the cause Goddard *v* Gee. . . . F. J. F. *and* Mrs Gaskell—enclosing note &c for G. Tupling—& in answer to [?] of Sale, of prop. at *Cranford.* When she wrote her *Cranford,* she didn't know there was such a place.

School Committee at five o'clock, on my way back, and then come home to a *thick* tea. I wonder how your cold is, my darling? No one tells me, so I hope it is better. Tell Minnie I am going to try to trim a bonnet for myself. My *mourning* bonnet has gone to be lined with double tarlatane at Miss Ogden's; and then I am going to set to work. They have got down in their cleaning to the study, and a pretty piece of work they are making of it. All dust, and soot, and pother! The cow does give such good milk, and such a quantity of it, now she has gone out to grass. Flossy's cuckoo-red sits very well; and it is supposed the eldest Dorking wants to sit, so I am going to write to Mrs Edmund Potter for eggs. It is raining very much, and I doubt if we shall go out in Mrs Shuttleworth's carriage. Last night Mr Charles Herford came; his little children are very well tell Flossy, who enquires after them. Then Stephen Winkworth came; Susanna had gone to tea at the Nicholls', so I fancy he was very glad to come here. He asked a great deal about *Meta*; and I understood his questions, and answered him accordingly. This morning there has been a letter from Minnie, & Emily Shaen, & Cousin Mary, and Miss Tollett, a lady whom Papa and I met at Teddesley last year, and who wants us now to go and see her (and 300 Cochin China fowls) at her father's house, Betley-Hall near Newcastle in Staffordshire, on June 13th[.]¹ I have sent the letter on to Papa; but I think I must write to her to explain my delay in answering her letter—or rather accepting her invitation. Will is mowing the grass. It is raining so hard. I shall send to Mrs S's to know if she is going. Goodbye my darling. I enclose Cousin Mary's letter for *Minnie to read, & burn* directly. Your very affec[tionat]e mother

E. C. Gaskell

My dearest love to Flossie, & kind love to Hearn.

₀ **200** ₀

UNKNOWN²

[?June 1854]

⟨. . .⟩ I have not written one line of 'Margaret' for three weeks for headaches and dizziness.

¹ A Tuesday, according to Letter 202. Also, Mrs Gaskell's stock of Letter 199's paper seems to finish on 25 October [1854] (see Letter 216).
² From a printed source.

₀ **201** ?447

FLORENCE ELIZABETH GASKELL

8 Bedford Row
Thursday [1 June 1854]

My darling Flossy,

I shall enclose a letter from Meta to me to make up for what I think will prove a dull note. Just after I had finished my letter to Minnie yesterday Mr Gaskell came,—Papa I mean,—He looks better I think; but did not know what to do with himself; how long to stay?—where to go to—how to get back at night to the Tagarts &c.—However he staid & had lunch here, he, Mr Shaen, & I. Then he went to see if there were any notes for him at St James Place; there were none. Meanwhile I lay down, for oh! I was so tired! The fatigue of the whole last fortnight or three weeks seemed to come upon me; & I fell asleep in the dining-room.

Suddenly I was wakened up,—Mrs Henry Jolly—who sate a very long time—till it was time to go & dress for Mr Fox's. I dressed, & Papa joined me here, & we went in a cab, & thought ourselves late, but had to wait $\frac{1}{2}$ an hour for Mr Forster, who came *very* late. There were six at dinner besides Mr & Miss Fox—firstly Papa & me, secondly Mr Willm & Katie Macready,—thirdly Miss Herrman, & fourthly Mr Forster. He & papa talked almost all through dinner & all the evening together about some secret plan of Mr Forsters—what I don't know, as Papa said he told him 'in confidence'. After dinner another Miss Herrman 2 Miss Whiteheads, Mr Dickenson (a bearded artist) & lastly Meta came. I ran out to meet her on the staircase—& she said Mama! are you *really* Mama?' and was rather stunned by the surprize I think; or dull or something, for she was very quiet and silent. Mr Shaen came too to take me back; he went & talked to Meta, & they got on very well; Papa & Mr Forster talked together; and Mr & Miss Fox were amusing the remainder of their visitors, so I was not sorry to come away which I did with Papa & Mr Shaen \walking/; but the former soon went off towards Hampstead—& Mr Shaen & I walked here, finding Emily sitting up for us; but very tired. This morning is very hot. I have been out, to buy some more blue Berlin wool to finish *somebody's* slipper, & to see a bureau; such a beauty! I long for it! I can't quite draw it; but it is

something like this [Here a sketch is inserted] looking glass doors
—escritoire, & three drawers, all *beautiful* marquetrie or like our
little round walnut-wood table. It is so hot, that I am come in,
tired & going to set to, sewing. Selina (who wonders why MA
does not send her love to her, & wishes she would do it)—& Katie
are gone to see Annie Shaen at Kennington,[1] over the river, &
don't come home till late at night. Tomorrow Meta comes here at
11 in the morning, & *perhaps* Papa comes too to see Mr Holford's
pictures. Dearest love to Julia & Marianne, & kind love to Hearn.

Your affect[ionate] Mammy
E. C. Gaskell.

*198b 202 205

MARIANNE GASKELL

Monday morng—
[5 June 1854]

My dearest Polly,

I wish you would write a 'Dear Sir' note to Thomas Baker Esq
Brazenose St Manchester as soon as you get this to say you made a
mistake about the address; that 2 St James' Place is the address of
your Uncle's chambers where letters were to be sent to be forwarded to your 'father'; but that the{se} people at the chambers
have been very careless in doing so, & that {you} he is staying at
Revd E. T's Wildwood Hampstead &c. Oh! stay I will write myself to him—no! I won't, because he will think it strange; do *you* do
it, love, & *directly too*; for if Mr Baker (who is the acting person
about the chapel) wished to write to Papa to tell him to stay
longer it would be provoking to have his letter lost. Besides I
should like {Papa}\the people/to know that he was regaining his
health at *Hampstead*, they have all such an idea of the unhealthiness
of London &c. You did quite right in sending on those letters;
some of which, about the Lancashire dialect, will please Papa.
British Association of\Art/Science meeting at Liverpool this
year, want him to write a paper for them,—&c[.] I must write to
Julia today, so you will find the letter with *news* in it at Poulton.
Only I have no news. I have seen no one as yet. I shall pay some
calls just before leaving, which I *must* do next Tuesday, 13th, to

[1] See *Letters and Memorials*, ed. Winkworth, I, p. 443, for this and subsequent
activities.

go to the Tollets, Betley Hall near Crewe. Meanwhile I write every spare moment in the little room beyond the dining-room. My only relaxation, as yet, has been going to see the French Play[1] (*pit*-places) on Saturday night about which I shall tell Julia— Papa seems better than when I came; every day now is doing him good; but *he* will never apply for longer leave of absence. If they offered it him he would take it; that's all. You certainly won't stop \at Poulton/beyond your six weeks—I don't know beyond five; but I hear through Susanna a famous account of your improved looks; & I am sure a good long spell of sea must be good for you. Keep on with your steel; and I hope you will not have overtired yourself in Manchester—I am rather afraid from what I hear of your doing on Sunday. I wish the Ewarts knew how to rest & be quiet, for it will be rather provoking if all the months good at Poulton is {over}done\away with/by bustling so in Manchester. Who preached yesterday[?] You don't say, & Papa will particularly want to know I am sure. Give my kindest love to Aunt & Uncle Langshaw[.] My pretty good love to Mrs Paley. See Julia's letter for news. I have literally been *no*-where, & never meant to go to Hampstead because it would be loss of a precious day, as I must go to the Tagarts as well if I went—But perhaps, if you wish me very much love, I could manage it. I don't mean to go *any*where that I can help, & no one knows of my being here, but Tottie, to whom I have been, & the Tagarts where I have refused to go. It may sound ridiculous but I did come here for *rest*!

Ever your very affect[ionate]   E C Gaskell

I shall see Meta soon & will tell her you want a letter.

199 **203** 208

JULIA BRADFORD GASKELL

Monday Afternoon [5 June 1854]

My dearest Julia,

I don't know that I have very much to say, only I promised you my next letter, and I must try and tell you all I have done since I

---

[1] 'La Joie Fait Peur.' (See next letter.)

wrote last. On Friday I hardly went out at all; Mr Crisp came in the evening; he has been two months away, & has been to the Madeira Islands, to Spain and Africa, and was very full of his travels, and all the curious things he had seen and done. He had seen a wedding in Africa, where the bridegroom rode very slowly along the streets of the town the night before he was married, and every unmarried person had a right to pelt him with stones, eggs, &c for leaving the number of the unmarried people; and the next day he rides on a very gay horse, with a large box carried after him, and what do you think is in this box? Why! the bride! She has holes to breathe through though. On Saturday I was busy all morning; and after dinner I went with Selina & Katie to see some french pictures; some of which were very beautiful. Then we came home, swallowed scalding tea, and went to the French Play to see a little play called La joie fait peur. (Minnie must tell you what that means.) It is a very small theatre and we saw the Queen & Prince Albert and the Prince of Wales, and Prince Alfred quite well. The two boys have coarse features, but look healthy and rosy. The Prince of Wales has a long-tailed coat on, which makes him look very funny he is so young. Prince Alfred has long soft shiny hair like Maggie's here. I must tell you all about the Play when I come home for it was such a pretty story. Yesterday I found that Mr Shaen was going to see his sister Annie, so I went with him. She is staying about 5 miles off, and is very poorly indeed. She has to lie down constantly. I found that she would be sadly disappointed if I did not stay with her, but came back to hear Mr Maurice as I had planned; so I staid all day, and came home here at night,—here I found Papa who had come to dinner, & taken Selina to Westminster Abbey, & had a walk with her, & had tea &c. He went away soon after I came home; and then John Philip Green came; but I barely saw him. This morning I wrote to Minnie, & was just going upstairs to put on my things to go & meet Meta & Annie & Papa at {the} Mr Holford's pictures in Russell Square, when Mrs James came in; had heard I was here; wanted Papa & me to go & stay there,—and to fix a day when we would go & dine to meet the Romileys & Dean of Hereford. I could not fix till I had seen Papa; he says Wednesday,—or Tuesday, or Thursday, so Katie wrote a note in my name to Mrs James to tell her so, as Papa & I went on to Mrs Shuttleworth's lodgings (near Uncle Sam's) to lunch after seeing the pictures. Tell Minnie to keep me the Times that have come since I left Manchr dating

from Tuesday 30. I am writing in a great hurry to catch the post:
and am always

Yours very affectionately
E. C. Gaskell

Love to Flossy & Hearn; there is a dog here called Floss.

189 204 275

R. MONCKTON MILNES

[?Early June 1854]

⟨. . .⟩ were, as we were 'hungry' to know; but we felt unwilling
to intrude upon you when you were certain to have so many
enquiries to answer, and contented ourselves with what we could
hear from Lady Hatherton.

Pray give my kind regards to Mrs Milnes. My husband is gone
home, and I am following early next week; but I hope before that
time to call in Brook Street, only I could not wait, and run the
chance of seeing you before thanking you most truly about Mr
Nicholls. I am sure you will keep the secret; and if you want a
steam-engine or 1000 yards of calico pray employ me in Manchester.

Yours very truly
E. C. Gaskell

202 205 *205+

MARIANNE GASKELL

Wednesday [?7 June ?1854]

My dearest Polly,

Every scrap of time seems pre-engaged,—now till I leave—I
have written too long, & not left myself time for seeing friends,
who will really be *hurt* if I don't see them. I can not think how my
strength is to hold out[.] Tomorrow I plan to take Meta into the
city & see St Paul's &c &c &c,—& last night I found that the
Whitmore Isaacs were in town, & that Louisa was there, & they
want Met⟨a⟩ & me to go there *first*; i.e. to Brook St ⟨ ⟩ the

City, & Mrs James wants me to ⟨ ⟩ breakfast *there* & I'm engaged out to dinner at ½ past 7. Mr Sam Shaen is going to take
Meta & me. You are quite right, love, about going to Lancaster.
Only don't *walk* back to Poulton. *Send Mme Mohl's letter to Papa.* I
thought he would never send it to *you*, if it went to him *first*. I
should excessively like to go to Lancaster, *but*, don't you see with
Leighton Buzzard & Betley, it is as much as I can manage. The
Froudes want me to go to Devonshire, & the Isaacs to Boughton
but home I must be by the end of next week. I saw your faithful
friend Sir Alexander Gordon last night at the M Milnes. He never
forgets your kindness to his little girl that night when she was
poorly at Dickens' long ago. No! Mr James is not *Sir*, & Mrs
James is very much annoyed at the Manchester Mayor's blunder.
On the contrary he goes out of office because of Mr Strutt's
resignation. Meta goes with Mrs James to a concert on Friday.
Friday we\Selina[,] Kate & I/plan to go to the Chrystal Palace. I
do not think I shall be able to squeeze in another letter to you
before next Tuesday from Leighton Buzzard, every moment seems
so taken up[.] ⟨I h⟩ave not seen or heard anything of that account
of Capn Gifford's death.[1] Was it in the Times? If so I rely upon
seeing it some how or another when I get home. My darling, this
is written in such a hurry, but if it only tells you a little bit how
dearly I love you that will do for the present, won't it? Your own
affec[tionat]e Mother   E C G.

Give my dearest love to the children & kind love to Hearn.

*

₀ **205a** ₂₇₈ᵇ

HENRY MORLEY

Plymouth Grove,
Monday.
[?June 1854]

My dear Sir,
    I have a friend who was educated at Neuwied,[2]—& who is just
crazy about 'Brother Mieth'.[3] First she made me write to Mr

---

[1] Henry Wells Gifford (1810–54) was in command of the *Tiger* which was
attacked by Russian field batteries as it lay off Sebastopol. Gifford died from
wounds received in the attack.
[2] The Patterson sisters were at Neuwied.
[3] 'Brother Mieth and His Brothers', *Household Words*, 27 May 1854.

Wills, and ask who wrote it; and now, as much would ever have more, she wants me to ask you if Brother Mieth was not Brother Andrup—(Anthrup?) and if you were there at the time of his death; and if you, like her, got a piece of \wood/shaving out of the bed on which he lay and kept it for a relic? and if you heard his Leben read?—and—and—I don't know how many more questions, all hinging on the one supposition that Brother Mieth was Brother Andrup—It is a charming\paper/, I, the exoteric may say. But she will hardly allow that I *can* recognize it's merits, and has gone off upon Neuwied ever since, taking the bit between her teeth. Would you be so kind as to stop her with a hair of the dog that bit her, & give us all another paper on Neuwied in some shape.

That reading the Diary & the Confession of sins over the coffin must have been most striking. I don't know half enough about the Moravians. You [will] be glad to hear what a very nice character I hear (quite indirectly but none the less truthfully,) of Arthur and Willie Holland, from their present schoolmaster & schoolfellows.

I remain

Yours very truly

E. C. Gaskell.

I hope Mrs Morley, and the 'little one' are well?

₁₆₉ **206** ₂₂₂

?Eliza Fox

[?Summer 1854][1]

IF you don't send me those Dorkings by some of the Gaskells! Ugh ugh ugh ugh.

Nature intended me for a gypsy-bachelor; that *I* am sure of. Not an old maid for they are particular & fidgetty, and tidy, and punctual,—but a gypsy-bachelor. I get up early. I breakfast with a book in my hand. I go out and feed all the animals, especially Tommy who is getting fatter than ever; and Fairy, who has had her eye bitten out, poor little mortal, and lives in a state of perpetual

[1] Dating not certain, but the references to Poulton can be associated with others in Letters 202 and 205. Also, Mrs Gaskell states later (see p. 315 below) that she is using her last sheet of this particular type of paper.

{winl} wink. I have set 2 hens on 27 eggs this morning, at the which I am very proud. I go out and plant cabbages,—Cincinnatus did something to turnips, didn't he, Mrs[1] Fox? but mine are cabbages. Some great man dibbled about them, I think. Well! I am like that great man! 2 feet apart is the right distance. Then the post comes and I have to write to every body; and feel like an ass between a great number of bundles of hay, with so many invitations, here, there, & everywhere.

Margaret comes in to know what time I would like, & what I will have for, dinner; but that fixes me too much; so I despise dinners, and eat when & where I like, like Sancho Panza & the birds. Not the fish, for mackerel come up regularly every 4 hours to {be} feed; I have been out a long day in Cardigan Bay, mackerel-fishing. Then I think of Poulton, & the sea,—and the children there—apropos of fish, d'ye see. And I long to be with them. Then on the other side come letters from Emily & Mr Gaskell,—Emily wanting me there, & Meta ditto. So between the two I go nowhere. But I have told every body I am going away, so they all think I am gone. And every morning in bed; I think I will go; and then I find too much to do, & the time slips by. I wonder where you *would* write, oh wretched woman, if I didn't—

Send me my Dorkings. Not if they're *above* 7s 6d a piece on any account. I am very poor; which eases my cares wonderfully, see somethingth satire of Juvenal. I don't know where the plate is. Nobody can find it, now Hearn (trusty guardian) is away. And I have 4 shillings in silver & some odd coppers. So I sleep with my windows wide open, listening to thrushes & defying burglars. We've got a thrush that sings in it's sleep, I'm sure. I bade farewell to a Capn Campbell, bound for the East, last week—he told me there {was}\would/not [be] a soldier left in Manchester on Saturday last; whereupon somebody observed that we were on the verge of a precipice! I don't know what they meant; but don't be surprized if you hear of a rising of the weavers, headed by a modern Boadicea. I am thinking of fastening Will's scythe to *one* of the wheels of the poney carriage and defending my country if the Russians do land at Liverpool.—Your affec[tionate] bachelor

E C Gaskell

---

[1] Doubtful reading, but perhaps jocular.

₄₃ **207** ₀

GERALDINE E. JEWSBURY[1]

21 July 1854

⟨. . .⟩ Miss Brontë is married, and I ought to write to her, but I've a panic about the husband seeing my letters. Bridegrooms are always curious; husbands are not.

₂₀₃ **208** ₀

JULIA BRADFORD GASKELL

Saturday [2 September 1854]

My dearest Julia,

Many happy returns of your birthday, dear little lady! I wonder what you will do on it. I hope it won't be a 'stoopid' day; but that it will be pleasant, though very quiet. We must keep it when we come home again. You can't think how quiet we are! Meta has picked up some friends who give her grapes, and tell her about battles in India, and all sorts of agreeable things of that kind—But *I* have no grapes given me; Not even a sour apple! And Meta won't have any dinners, and goes out and sketches instead. So if my birthday happened now I could not have a birthday pudding, which would be a pity! There are such a squealing, squeaking, wauling, wailing, whining set of little children in this house; they have come here since we did, and yowl like little puppy-dogs. We have seen two Manx cats without tails and uncommonly ugly they are. But some people like them, and give great prices for them. I would far rather have our own dear little Mimi. I have had a letter from [drawing of Manx cat] Flossy today. I suppose Aunt Lizzy is come back from what Florence says? Do you know they get even their *cabbages* from Liverpool? And yet all sorts of flowers grow almost wild here.[2] There is not a dirty little cottage by the road-side but what has it's fuschsia growing as high as the roof. Do you know that Isabella Ham is coming to live

[1] From a printed source.
[2] Mrs Gaskell had returned from the Isle of Man by 13 September 1854. *Letters and Memorials*, ed. Winkworth, I, p. 456.

in Manchester? I think we must keep your birthday till she comes. Ask Papa when that will be? My love to Hearn. Your affectionate Mama

E. C. Gaskell

*205+ **209** *209a

MARIANNE GASKELL

[?Early September 1854]

My dearest Polly,

I am not half dry yet, after two days drying. I want sadly to hear from you. There is the scarlet fever at Ballaugh, which was the place Meta set her heart upon 8 miles from here. *Do* write. Only think! it will be *Tuesday* before we can even hear from home; and certainly Thursday before we can hear from you, darling. But do write us a long letter, we seem so very far away from you; & I shan't begin to enjoy myself till I hear from you. My kind love to Ann Norton, & kind regards to Mrs Norton. We got your letter from Ely on Tuesday Evening[.]

Your very affect[ionate] mother
E C Gaskell

*

*209a **210** 212

MARIANNE GASKELL[1]

Tuesday. [26 Sept. 1854]

My dearest Polly,

Only a moments time to write. We are putting off Meta's visit to Boughton till {Sept}\Octr 7th/Papa goes to Birmingham to preach on the 8th; and would take her that far on the Saty & see her into a Worcester carriage. In this way she would see you without your hurrying. I got a letter from Woodgate today, saying the Bureau was sent off,—but it has never come. The packing case is to be *returned*. 5s charged for trouble of packing, canvas &c. Mrs Jameson comes tomorrow between 1-3. Dinner at $\frac{1}{2}$ p. 4. Un-

---

[1] *Address (on envelope)* Miss Gaskell | Mrs Lalor's | Holly Hill | Hampstead | | London. *Postmark* MANCHESTER |SP 26 | 1854 | D.

dress Concert with Mozart's Requiem in the evening. We've an order ready for you, if you turn up. A *small* party on Thursday evening. Ewarts, Major & Mrs & A. & M. Mr Satterfield & Eliza. Mr Gregan. No one else. Meta Selina & Katie gone to dine at the Scott's.

Your very affect[ionate] Mother
E C G

149 211 223

CATHERINE WINKWORTH[1]

Wednesday Evening   [11 to 14 Oct. 1854]
½ p. 5   Lea-Hurst, Matlock
Privatish

My dearest Katie,

I am going to begin a letter to you, which {I shall}\you must/ forward to Emily please, for there are things here & there I want to go to her. In the first place both an Ewart, & all the people who write about poor George Duckworth's death say that Cholera is *not* infectious i.e. does not pass from one person to another. Mr Sam Gaskell says so too; and last authority Miss Florence Nightingale, who went on the 31st of August to take superintendance of the Cholera patients in the Middlesex Hospital (where they were obliged to send out their usual patients to take in the patients brought every half hour from the Soho district, Broad St especially,) says that only two nurses had it, one of whom died, the other recovered; that none of the porters &c had it, she herself was up day & night from Friday\Sep 1/afternoon to Sunday afternoon, receiving the poor prostitutes, as they came in, (they had it the worst, & were brought in from their 'beat' along Oxford St—all through that Friday night,) undressing them—& awfully filthy they were, & putting on turpentine *stupes* &c all herself to as many as she could manage—never had a touch even of diarrhea. She says moreover that one week the chances of recovery seemed as 1 to 10, but that since the chances of recovery are as 20 to 1. Oh! Katie I wish you could *see* her\outsidely only—/. She is

---

[1] *Address (on envelope)* Miss Katie Winkworth | Alderley Edge near | Manchester. *Postmarks* MATLOCK BATH | OC 15 | 1854 *and* MANCHESTER | OC 16 | 1854. *Seal, octagonal, man's head facing left.*

tall; very slight & willowy in figure; thick shortish rich brown hair very delicate pretty complexion, rather like Florence's, only more delicate colouring,\grey/eyes which are generally\pensive &/drooping, but when they choose can be the merriest eyes I ever saw; and perfect teeth making her smile the sweetest I ever saw. Put a long piece of soft net—say 1½ yd half long, & ½ yd wide, and tie it round this beautiful shaped head, so as to form a soft white frame-work for the full oval of her face—[drawing] (for she had the toothache, & so wore this little piece of drapery,) and dress her up in black glace silk up to the long round white throat—and a black shawl on,—& you may get *near* an idea of her perfect grace & lovely appearance. She is like a saint. Mrs N. tells me that when a girl of 15 or so she was often missing in the evening, & Mrs N. would take a lantern & go up into the village to find her, sitting by the bedside of someone who was ill, & saying she cd not sit down to a grand 7 o'clock dinner while &c.—Then Mr & Mrs N. took their two daughters to Italy, & they lived there till it was time for them to be presented. In London she was excessively admired, & had (I have heard from other people) no end of offers,—but she studied hard with her father & is a perfect Greek & Latin scholar; so perfect that when she went to travel a few years later with Mr & Mrs Bracebridge & they were in Transylvania she was always chosen to address the old abbots &c at the Convents in Latin to state their wants. She travelled for a year & a half going to Athens, & all sorts of classical Greek places, up the Nile to the second Cataract with these Bracebridges. Mrs N. says they equipped her en princesse and when she came back she had little besides the clothes she wore; she had given away her linen &c right & left to those who wanted it. Then she said that life was too serious a thing to be wasted in pleasure seeking; & she went to Kaiser-werth & was there for three months, taking her turn as a Deaconess, scouring rooms &c. Then to Paris where she studied nursing at the Hospitals in the dress of {an}\a nun or/Abbess & was besides a month serving at a bureau in an arrondisement in order to learn from the Sisters of Charity their Mode of visiting the poor. And now she is at the head of the Establishment for invalid gentle-women; nursing continually, & *present at every operation*. She has a great deal of fun, and is carried along by that I think. She mimics most capitally the way of talking of some of the poor governesses in the Establishment, with their delight at having a man servant and at having *Lady* Canning & *Lady* Monteagle to do this & that for them. And then at this Cholera time she went off,—leaving word where she could be sent for; for she considered her 'gentle-women' to have a prior claim on her services—to the Middlesex Hospital &c! I came in here for the end of her fortnight of holiday in the year. Is it not like St Elizabeth of Hungary? The efforts of her family to interest her in other occupations by allowing her to travel &c,—but the clinging to one object! Now I must go & dress for dinner. We dine at 7.

Friday. Do you know Katie that I should not like what I say in this letter about Miss F. N. to go out of your family, hardly beyond Emily. I have been listening to her letters from Egypt this morning, yet not attending to them, I was all along so anxious to remember enough out of them to tell you & Emily,—expres-sions—thoughts—& you know *I* don't care for travels—I never cared for Egypt *much* before. But at last I heard they were to be printed, & I might have a copy—only 'not to circulate—not to be talked about'. So I mean to lend it or send it to E. to read after her confinement, if she can bear it, & it comes before then. She must be a creature of another race so high & mighty & angelic, doing things by impulse—or some divine inspiration & not by effort & struggle of will. But she sounds almost too holy to be talked about as a mere wonder. Miss [*sic*] Nightingale says—with tears in her eyes*alluding to Andersen*/that they are ducks & have hatched a wild swan—& she seems as completely led by God as Joan of Arc. Now don't name all this. But I never heard of any one like her—it makes one feel the livingness of God more than ever to think how straight He is sending his spirit down into her, as into the prophets & saints of old. I dare say all this sounds rather like 'bosh'—but indeed if you had heard all about her that I have you would feel as I do. You must take a good deal upon trust. *Saturday Evening* And now the house is cleared; and I am established high up, in two rooms opening one out of the other; the old nurseries; the inner one—very barely furnished—is my bedroom now; but usually Miss N's. It is curious how simple it is compared even to that of our girls. The carpet does not cover the floor, is far from new. The furniture is painted wood; no easy chair, no sofa, a little curtainless bed; a small glass not so large as mine at home. One of the windows opens out upon a battlement from which, high as Lea Hurst is, one can see the clouds careering round one; one seems on the Devil's pinnacle of the Earth. It is curious to see how simply these 2 young women have been brought up. *This* place

has nothing of the magnificence of Embley, their house in
Hampshire, yet is a stately enough kind of abode,—yet here is the
eldest daughter's room. In the outer room—the former day
nursery—Miss *F* N's room when she is at home every thing is as
simple; now of course the bed is *reconverted* into a sofa[,] two
small tables, a few empty bookshelves a *drab* carpet only partially
covering the clean boards, and\stone/coloured walls—as cold in
colouring as need to be, but with one low window on one side
trellised over with Virginia Creeper as gorgeous as can be; and
the opposite one, by which I am writing looking over such
country! First a garden with stone terraces and flights of steps,
and old stone columns with globes at the top of them in every
direction—the planes of these terraces being perfectly gorgeous
with masses of hollyhocks, dahlias, nasturtiums, geraniums &c—
Then a sloping meadow losing itself in a steep wooded—(such
tints!) descent to the river Derwent, the rocks on the other side of
which form the first distance & are of a\red colour streaked with/
misty purple. Beyond interlacing hills forming three ranges of
distance—the first dun brown with decaying heather[,] the next
in some mysterious purple shadow, & the last catching some
pale watery sun-light. I don't know where it comes from! In
every direction the walks are most beautiful[.] Old English Sir
Roger de Coverley kind of villages are hidden in the moorland
hills about here. *Dethick*, where Anthony Babington Mary Q of
Scotts' conspirator lived—his old Hall is still standing,—the
empty tomb he prepared for himself in the Church still there,—
empty—unoccupied by the poor 'head & four quarters of a
traitor', and all done round with a punning border of squat
barrels, with children's heads peeping out of them—*Babe-in-Tun*.
It is getting dark. I am to have my tea, up in my turret—at 6.—
And after that I shall lock my outer door & write. I am stocked
with coals, and have candles up here; for I am a quarter of a mile
of staircase & odd intricate passage away from every one else in
the house. Could solitude be more complete! The house is in a
wild park, along which I hardly yet know my way, so as to get to
the different gates. I went to lunch at the Arkwrights at Willersley
(we met them at Teddesley last year) on Thursday, and they asked
me to go often there; & wanted me to go with their large party
in the house and make excursions in the county, but I declined
manfully. They are the only people who can rout me out. Lady
Coltman has a house 7 miles off, & has begged me to go there; but

I have refused, & she goes to Brighton on Tuesday. So *ought* not
M. Hale to stand a good chance. I do think she is going on well. I
am satisfied. Not that I have written so much, but so *well*. There's
modesty for you. I have not half told you about Miss F. N. It must
keep. But she is thinking (don't name it because she has not
named it to the Committee of her present institution) of becoming
the Matron of one of the great London Hospitals as soon as she
has got this small Establishment into training. All this time I have
never thanked you dearest Katie for your letter & the pains you
have taken to get me that information about failures. I feel it's
value though I have not yet fully mastered it. And now I'm going
to tell you bits of fun &c. They have had Mr Hallam[,] Lord
Monteagle, Sir F. Doyle & several others staying here, & all the
talk was about Whewell's book the Plurality of Worlds[1] or
whatever it is. Lord Ellesmere said 'Well! Nature has but been
able to produce *one* Whewell. I think it a great evidence of the
benevolence of the Almighty.' Sir Francis Doyle (he, who said
last year when a very clever satirical Mrs\Milnes/Gaskell said she
wished people would not look at her, as if she were the author of
Ruth &c—said 'Can't you tell them, my dear, that you're Ruth-
less?') made this epigram on Whewell.

> {Should a man\{men}/to all space}
> Shd a man through all space to far galaxies travel
> And of nebulous films the remotest unravel
> He will find, shd he venture to fathom Infinity
> That the great work of God is the Master of Trinity

Ask Selina what's the difference between {an old wom} a *young*
woman and an *old* one? I must take another piece of paper.

> A young woman is careless and happy,
> An old woman is hairless and cappy.

I expect that will charm Selina. It is by Sir E. Landseer. The
Nightingales knew the Ruskins—were staying at some castle in
the Highlands with them last year, with them & Millais. She used
to say about 11 am. 'Everett[,] come & walk with me', & they
were out till dinner time 7 o'clock, Ruskin very uneasy all the

[1] Published anonymously in 1853. Whewell argued that there were no grounds
for believing in other inhabited worlds.

time.[1] She used to come down to *breakfast* with natural flowers in her hair, which he also objected to but she continued the practice. I must go to my *real* writing now; but I hope I have earned a letter from you. Post-coming in will be the event of my day. When I see the little bed in the inner room I long for a child; but I am afraid any one but poor little Meta would find it dull. She would sketch & dream to her heart's desire. I am afraid her life at Boughton is terribly against the grain. I have had a more dreary letter since this which I enclose. It is hard upon a girl like her to be treated so entirely like a child\as to companionship/. Just before she left I had a letter from Mrs Dacy asking her to go there in Novr and charmingly suggesting all sorts of places of pictorial or historic interest in the neighbourhood of Worcester, which she hoped they would take M. to see. But they don't seem to think of such a thing! It was *right* for her to go as I had promised—& that's the only comfort. Do write. What do you think of a fire burning down Mr Thornton's mills *and house* as a *help* to failure? Then Margaret would rebuild them larger & better & need not go & live there when she's married. Tell me what you think: M H has just told the lie, & is gathering herself up after her dead faint; very meek & stunned & humble. One companion I have got—an *owl*.[2] Miss Florence N. picked it up—thrown out of the nest in the Parthenon,—nursed the little round puff-ball, (just like the owls by Minerva & on Greek drachmas,) & here he is, a regular mischievous intelligent pet.

                              Your very affec[tionate] Lily.

210 **212** 226

MARIANNE GASKELL

Lea–Hurst
Friday [?13 October 1854]

My dearest Polly,

I should have tried to write you a very long letter to-day, but poor Miss Meta, as you will perceive from the enclosed letter,

---

[1] The Ruskin marriage was annulled in June 1854, and Mrs Ruskin later married Millais. See Letter 195.

[2] Found at Athens in the spring of 1850. (See E. T. Cook, *The Life of Florence Nightingale*, 1914, I, pp. 89, 160, 369.) Lady Verney wrote a short *Life and Death of Athena, an Owlet from the Parthenon* in 1855.

required a little comfort & strengthening, & so I have taken up more time than I intended in writing to her. But I must write to you, my good darling—if only to earn another letter. Papa is even worse than you about Mrs Ham; but is cruel enough to say 'Well! but tastes differ—perhaps *you* may like her.' Mr & Mrs & Miss N. leave here tomorrow. I shall feel very queer in this large house by myself. At first the servants will be here, packing up things; but after that the gardener & his wife come into the house; they will live in one part, far far away, & I have *all* the rest of the large place to myself, i.e; two rooms downstairs, & a room & a balcony high up at the top away from everybody & everything, all to myself. It will be very queer. I shall wish for you or Meta. Papa says he is going to-day to Mr Colstons, so there's no use sending a message to him; or else he would care to know that his friend, Mrs Arkwright sent him a very kind message of remembrance. They were sorry that I had not spoken to them on Sunday at Church, & sent to ask me to lunch there yesterday, & were very friendly & agreeable. Mr Arkwright said they were constantly going excursions to see the beauties of the county, & had plenty of room for me in the carriages; but I was obliged to decline because of my writing. Then they begged me to go there whenever I felt lonely without waiting for special invitations; but I don't know if I shall. It is nearly 3 miles off. I wish by the bye that you would send me some postage stamps. Mine are done; & none to be got nearer than Matlock, nearly 4 miles off; & I shall have nobody to send. Lady Errol, Mrs Daubeny, & Mrs Galton the 3 officer's wives who are with the Camp in the Crimea, dress as Vivandieres & wash their husbands' shirts, cook {each other's} \their/dinners &c, & say 'they never were so happy in their lives'. I have heard something of the truth of the Bekker[1] & Madame Mohl quarrel.

    Riddle   What is the difference between an {old}\young/and

        a {young}\old/woman?
        The young woman is *c*areless and *h*appy
        The old woman is *h*airless and *c*appy

I have sent it to Meta. I thought it would help to enliven her, & remind her of Ch. Ch. I have done little but write all day & it is now near 5, & I must go out. I have very little news to tell any one;

[1] Possibly Immanuel Bekker (1785-1871), classical scholar.

& my letters must needs be dull. Only give my dearest love to
Flossy & Julia. Write soon—Postage Stamps

Your very affect[ionate] Mother

E. C. Gaskell

₀ **213** ₂₁₆

ANNE HOLLAND[1]

Lea Hurst

near

Matlock

[*c.* 16 October 1854]

My dear Annie,

I shall be only too glad to come to you for a couple of days,
when I leave this place; which will be towards the end of next
week; by which time I hope dear Fred will be at home again,
though I should rather enjoy (no disrespect to my dear cousin)
having a tête à-tête visit with you. *I think* I shall have a daughter
with me; but all our plans are rather unsettled just now; and
perhaps you will let me write again when I can name the exact
day. Mr & Mrs Nightingale were speaking of you only the
other day, and would I am sure have been gratified by your
remembrances, but they are gone to London, and have left me &
mine in possession of this house; at least such rooms of it as are
not packed up. I never saw such beautiful country. I did not know
Derbyshire before. It is beautiful as distinct from wild or grand.
I have just received some letters which Mrs Duckworth has kindly
sent me, about poor Captain Duckworth's death. We were so
very sorry to hear of it, & these letters make us feel even more
sorry for the poor family who have lost such a son & brother.

My kind love to Fred.

Your very affect[ionate] cousin

E. C. Gaskell.

---

[1] Hon. Mrs Frederick Holland (née Denman).

₀ **214** ₂₁₅

PARTHENOPE NIGHTINGALE

Tuesday [17 October 1854]

My dear Miss Nightingale,

You can't think how generous I feel myself in giving you a whole sheet of paper, when I have but two left; exclusive of foolscap, all ready paged. But I want to send you your fern, and I want to tell you that Mr Sam Gaskell *is* at No 2 St James Place, and will be glad at any time & in any way to give Miss Florence Nightingale any information in his power.[1] *Also*, (as they tag banns of marriage on together without much connexion,) to say that I have never heard from the Glovers, to whom I wrote on the day I heard from Miss F. Nightingale; but then I desired them to consider with, & consult their medical man before they came to any decision. Don't let her think me ungrateful, because I don't bore her with a grateful letter before I can tell her what they settle to do. I went to see 'Widow' Littlewood on Saty. She was out, gone to Mrs Smedley's; but the daughter was in, with whom I sate some time. Then I went down to the river, *our* old walk; and coming back I gathered ever so many mushrooms, of which I generously made a present to Mrs Littlewood, whom I met in the meadow. She was so very much obliged to me for giving her what was not mine to give, that I felt ashamed of myself, and had to confess to Mr Nightingale. Sunday I meant to go to Church; but it rained and I did not, so my good intention went to pave the place where the thermometer stands high. Yesterday—Oh! how I wrote! and in the middle, to clear my brains which were becoming addled, I went with Soyer to the pig and Glass: made Mrs Radford's acquaintance; then went on and saw 'Jane', who was downstairs & considerably better, though obliged to give up nursing on one side, & feeding her baby on *sago*, which I disapproved of, rather to the old lady's annoyance. The old lady burst in (as a test of my right to judge of baby's food I believe) with 'Did I know *Lady Adeliga*?' Surname not given. And I think she looked upon me & my advice contemptuously when she heard I did not. Today I am going to see Mrs Buxton & to gather the ferns. I have thought of so many things I shd like to have said

[1] She left London on 21 October 1854. C. Woodham-Smith, *Florence Nightingale*, 1950, p. 146.

to you, & asked of you. I wish you would care to come to Manchester sometime; but unless you have a very strong desire for useful information and all that sort of thing I[1] am afraid it is not a tempting place. Never mind, we won't forget each other[,] will we? And it is possible that some day you may take to wishing to improve your mind à la Harry and Lucy by seeing the manufactures of your country; in which case I hope you know where to come to. Will you tell Mrs Nightingale that I am so comfortable and cosy, and undisturbed up here? and thank her for all her kindness[.]

Don't frame my letter though it is a rarity. How long is it since you had a crossed letter before?

Yours affectionately
E C Gaskell.

214 215 218

PARTHENOPE NIGHTINGALE

[?20 October 1854]

My dear Miss Nightingale

All I can say is that the light *is* shining bright on the Cross this morning that I receive your letter, and that God, whose angel has led her hitherto, will have her in His holy keeping. I, not having my eyes dimmed with the anxieties of affection, *see* this as if it were a visible march to heaven; but I can understand how you tremble in the midst of all your thankfulness *for* her, and *in* her. The poor poor little Owl is dead.[2] Last night about five, in came Mrs Watson almost in tears. 'Oh dear! Mrs Gaskell[,] whatever shall we do?' (She had it in her hands.) [']It was quite well at dinner time, and hopping about my room; and just now I found it on it's back quite stiff and cold.' I took it in my hands. I fancied I could just feel a fluttering, and I held it between my warm hands near the fire. But it was but a fancy; it must have died in some fit, I imagine. Mrs Watson was in terrible distress at thinking how sorry you, and especially 'Mistress' would be. She & I agreed that you would want to have it stuffed; and she is planning to leave it in Cavendish Sq. tomorrow as she goes through London. I went

---

[1] 'I' repeated in MS.   [2] See Letter 211 and note 2.

to Crich yesterday; & called on Mrs *Diarrhea* (for I don't know her other name,) who is much better, and sent her 'love', & the 'medecine [*sic*] did her a power of good.' Then to Mrs Storer's where I sate some time, making her husband's acquaintance, & hearing a deal about the lead mines. Mrs Storer seemed better, but complained of the pain in her side; was she not to have a belladonna plaster? Mrs Watson said she knew nothing of it,— should I order one at the polite & insinuating Cromford druggist? I wait your directions. All these things will come to you when you will be thinking them very 'small', in comparison with the great event of tomorrow. I should like to see Mr S. Herbert's letter,[1] & will return it immediately after reading it. God bless you all. I am in doubts about Mrs Glover: especially as it is after some deliberation that they send her. But—oh no! I'm afraid you can't thank Miss F N when you get this letter.

Yours affectionately

E. C. Gaskell

213 **216** 221

ANNE HOLLAND

Lea Hurst
near
Matlock
Wednesday Octr 25 [1854]

My dear Annie,

Thank you much for your kind proposal of sending for me; I shall be alone, and I shall gladly avail myself of it; on either Friday or Saturday, whichever day may suit your convenience; or Monday if that would do better? Will you let me know the exact railroads by which I had better send my trunk to Ashbourne? There is a railway, not far from here, that goes from Rowsley (near Bakewell) on one side to Derby on the other. Lea Hurst is on the Cromford side of Matlock; I am ashamed of my paper; but this is my last piece; & I must send it, blots, and all. I was in hopes I should have had a daughter to bring with me, but they have

---

[1] The Secretary-at-War wrote a private letter on 15 October 1854; the *Daily News* printed it on 28 October. Cook, *Florence Nightingale*, I, pp. 151, 154 n.

been staying with some little friends near Manchester, and Mr Gaskell does not think it desirable that they should leave home again. Meta is still at Boughton, & Louisa kindly writes to invite her to Dumbleton. I hope dear Frederick has got his troublesome journey over by this time.

Ever my dear Annie

Your very affect[ionate] cousin

E. C. Gaskell.

I am very much ashamed of my paper; but I am 3 miles from any kind of shop.

157 **217** 308

EMILY SHAEN[1]

Lea Hurst,
Oct. 27th, 1854.

Well! I vow I won't write letters; but it is no use, and I must answer you. You *have* done me so much good, dearest Nem; more than anyone else in my life—(that I am aware of) except my own darling Aunt Lumb and Miss Mitchell. I always feel raised higher when I am near you, and *held up* in a calmer and truer atmosphere than my usual anxious, poor, impatient one. One person may act on some and not on others—it's no cause for despair because, darling, you can't work on everybody; very few *can*—only such people as F. N. I'll enclose you two pieces of Mr S. Gaskell to show how *he's* carried off his feet. When I *told* him of Miss F. N. before he saw her, he called her my enthusiastic young lady and irritated me by speaking very contemptuously of her; as well-meaning, etc. Now here's his first piece and his second piece, and *you need not return 'em.* Oh! I wish I were with you, my dear E., to nurse you a bit, and pour into you. But I'll do the best I can tomorrow answering your questions. By the way, I've written in such a hurry to Katie that she has misunderstood me. The Egyptian letters *are* to be *printed*; only not some bits, which I thought specially beautiful and touching, and telling of individual character.⟨. . .⟩ Mrs Nightingale says she was a 'dreamy' child.

[1] From a printed source.

Did I tell you of her 18 dolls *all* ill in rows in bed, when she was quite a little thing? These two girls had a governess for two and a half years—from 7 to 9½ with F. N. Then she married, and they'd another whom they did not like, so then Mr N. took his girls in hand, and taught them himself. He is a *very* superior man; full of great interests; took high honours at college—and worked away at classics and metaphysics, and mathematics with them; especially F. N., who, he said, had quite a man's mind. She does not seem to have been wayward—only carried away by a sense of the 'Father's Work' that she ought to be about. She was early struck by all sorts of Catholic legends—(not that she's a bit Catholic, except as feeling that *that* is a living faith). One day she said (I can't remember many of her sayings, but I'll try and recollect all I can, and then remember they're private bits). 'There are two churches in Europe that are dead, the Anglican and the Greek—and two that are alive, the Roman Catholic and the Lutheran. The two former can be galvanised into action, but the actual living soul has departed out of them.' I used to ask Parthe N. a great deal about F. N. Parthe is plain, clever and *apparently* nothing out of the common way as to character; but she *is* for all that. She is devoted—her sense of existence is lost in Florence's. I never saw such adoring love. To set F. at liberty to do her great work, Parthe has annihilated herself, her own tastes, her own wishes in order to take up all the little duties of home, to parents, to poor, to society, to servants—all the small things that fritter away time and life, *all* these Parthe does, for fear if anything was neglected people might blame F. as well as from feeling these duties imperative as if they were grand things. Well! but to return[,] I was asking Parthe about F. and I never saw such intense affection as that with which she spoke of her. She said that she never saw anyone like Florence for the natural intense love of God—as a personal being. She says F. does not care for *individuals*—(which is curiously true)—but for the whole race as being God's creatures. One little speech of Florence's Parthe told me—'I look to 30 as the age when Our Saviour took up his work. I am trying to prepare myself to follow his steps when I am as old as He is.' Now she is 33 Florence takes up one thing at a time and bends her whole soul to that. Music was it once. When they were 17 and 18 Mr and Mrs N. took them to Italy before they were presented. And F. worked at music; the scientific part; and for the time cared for nothing but music. She has never cared in the least for art.

Then again the study of the truth as disguised in the myths and hieroglyphics of the Egyptian religion as the root of other religions, took hold of her; (you will see the exquisite beauty of her ideas on this head when you get her letters)—and for a year and a half in Egypt and in Athens she was absorbed in this. Now all this is swept away. They were correcting the proofs of her Egyptian letters when she was here—and had to refer to her about the myth about Thotte. She could remember nothing about it. She did not even care to try and remember. She never reads any book now. She has not time for it, to begin with; and secondly she says life is so vivid that books seem poor. The latter volumes of Bunsen are the only books that she even looked into here. She used to sit with her head bent a little forwards, one hand lying in repose over the other on her knees looking in that steady way which means that people are not seeing the real actual before them. The only thing she talked much about that I knew was suggested by Bunsen, who stated something like this—that among the Japhetic races *individuals* had not so much influence as among the Shemetic. Mr Nightingale said that that was a finer state of society when individuals were not so much ahead of those about them, etc., and she took up the other side very warmly, and said that her admiration of the heroic was of itself so fine a quality, and was lost—along with epic poetry, etc., where heroes were none, etc. etc. etc. It was *very* interesting, but I make a mess of it in repeating. I'll tell you one or two more of her speeches—only mind! I felt that I heard them as being received into the family, not as addressed to myself, so they are rather private. Speaking of the cholera in the Middlesex Hospital, she said, 'The prostitutes come in perpetually—poor creatures staggering off their beat! It took worse hold of them than any. One poor girl, loathsomely filthy, came in, and was dead in four hours. I held her in my arms and I heard her saying something. I bent down to hear. "Pray God, that you may never be in the despair I am in at this time." I said, "Oh, my girl, are you not now more merciful than the God you think you are going to? Yet the real God is far more merciful than any human creature ever was, or can ever imagine." ' Then, again, I never heard such capital mimicry as she gave of a poor woman, who was brought in one night, when F. N. and a porter were the only people up—every other nurse worn out for the time. Three medical students came up, smoking cigars, and went away. F. N. undressed the woman, who was half tipsy but kept saying, 'You would not think it, ma'am, but a week ago I was in silk and satins; in silk and satins, dancing at Woolwich. Yes! ma'am, for all I am so dirty I am draped in silks and satins sometimes. Real French silks and satins.' This woman was a nurse earning her five guineas a week with nursing ladies. She got better. F. N. has very seldom told her family of her plans till they were pretty well matured; then they remembered back for years little speeches (like that about our Saviour at 30), which show that the thoughts have been in her mind for years. I saw a little instance of this while she was here. She had the toothache, and an abscess in her mouth, and Mrs N. was *very* anxious about her, as she was evidently not strong. On Monday she said, 'I am going to-morrow.' This took them quite by surprise as she evidently was still very poorly; and Mrs N. remonstrated. But it turned out she had written and made so many arrangements depending on her presence, before she had even spoken about it to her family, that they had nothing to do but to yield; and it struck me that, considering how decidedly this step of hers was against their judgment as well as against their wishes, it was very beautiful to see how silently and diligently they all tried 'to speed the parting guest.' Indeed, Parthe one day said, 'She seems led by something higher than I can see, and all I can do is to move every obstacle in my power out of her path'; and so it is with them all. That text always jarred against me, that 'Who is my mother and my brethren?'—and there is just that jar in F. N. to me. She has no friend—and she wants none. She stands perfectly alone, half-way between God and His creatures. She used to go a great deal among the villagers here, who dote upon her. One poor woman lost a boy seven years ago of white swelling in his knee, and F. N. went twice a day to dress it. The boy shrank from death; F. N. took an engraving from some Italian master, a figure of Christ as the Good Shepherd carrying a little lamb in His arms, and told the boy that so tenderly would Christ carry him, etc. The mother speaks of F. N.—did to me only yesterday— as of a heavenly angel. Yet the father of this dead child—the husband of this poor woman—died last 5th of September, and I was witness to the extreme difficulty with which Parthe induced Florence to go and see this childless widow *once* while she was here; and though the woman entreated her to come again she never did. She will not go among the villagers now because her heart and soul are absorbed by her hospital plans, and as she says

she can only attend to one thing at once. She is so excessively soft
and gentle in voice, manner, and movement that one never feels
the unbendableness of her character when one is near her. Her
powers are astonishing. In one way you will see that in the
Egyptian letters. In another way in what she has done in the
Ladies' Hospital in Harley Street. She has been night-nurse and
day-nurse—housekeeper (and reduced the household expenses
one-third from the previous housekeeper who had been accustomed to economy all her life), mixer-up of medicine, secretary, attended all the operations—and rubbed cold feet perpetually at night—which last I name because they found that one lady
jumped out of bed when F. N. was coming round and stood with
her feet on the hearthstone in order to have them rubbed. To go
back to F. N.'s previous life, I believe there is no end to the offers
she has had—for nine years Mr M. Milnes was at her feet; but
Parthe says she never knew her care for one man more than
another in any way at any time. Mr and Mrs Bracebridge (named
in S. G.'s letter) went with her into Egypt. I long for those
Egyptian letters. They *must* come out before your confinement.
She and I had a grand quarrel one day. She is, I think, too much
for institutions, sisterhoods and associations, and she said if she had
influence enough not a mother should bring up a child herself;
there should be crêches for the rich as well as the poor. If she had
twenty children she would send them all to a crêche, seeing, of
course, that it was a well-managed crêche. That exactly tells of
what seems to me *the* want—but then this want of love for individuals becomes a gift and a very rare one, if one takes it in conjunction with her intense love for the *race*; her utter unselfishness
in serving and ministering. I think I have told you all—even to
impressions—but she is really so extraordinary a creature that
impressions may be erroneous, and anything like a judgment of
her must be presumptuous, and what a letter I have written! Only
if you are on the sofa it won't tire you as it might do if you were
busy.

    I have told Meta she may begin to prepare herself for enter-
ing upon a nurse's life of devotion when she is thirty or so, by
going about among sick now, and that all the help I can give in
letting her see hospitals, etc., if she wishes she may have. I doubt
if she has purpose enough to do all this; but I have taken great
care not to damp her—and if she has purpose, I will help her, as I
propose, to lead such a life; tho' it is not everyone who can be

Miss N. I wish, my darling, you were here for a day only. It is so lovely; so very lovely, and still, and out of the world; to say nothing of air more pure than I ever yet felt.⟨. . .⟩

I've got to (with Margaret—I'm off at her now following your letter) when they've quarrelled, silently, after the lie and she knows she loves him, and he is trying not to love her; and Frederick is gone back to Spain and Mrs Hale is dead and Mr Bell has come to stay with the Hales, and Mr Thornton ought to be developing himself—and Mr Hale ought to die—and if I could get over this next piece I could swim through the London life beautifully into the sunset glory of the last scene. But hitherto Thornton is good; and I'm afraid of a touch marring him; and I want to keep his character consistent with itself, and large and strong and tender, and *yet a master*. That's my next puzzle. I am enough on not to hurry; and yet I don't know if waiting and thinking will bring any new ideas about him. I wish you'd give me some. I go to Captain Holland's, Ashbourne Hall, Derbyshire, to-morrow and home on Tuesday next.

Your own grateful and affectionate,

Lily.

215 218 236

PARTHENOPE NIGHTINGALE

Ashbourn-Hall
Monday [30 October 1854]

My *dear* Miss Nightingale,

I do so want to hear about you all. I know I have no right from recent acquaintanceship to expect to hear at such a time as this; so I don't come as a claimant, but only as a beggar; but some-time,—in some odd leisure $\frac{1}{4}$ of an hour would you mind writing a little about what I am so greedy to know. I pick up all the scraps I can out of newspapers; but I think they only whet my hunger; and they tell me nothing, of course, about you and Mr & Mrs Nightingale, and I do so want to know about you all! The more I think about it the more it seems that all these steps in her life seem to have been 'leading her on' to this last great work. I have heard a good deal in a hurried fragmentary way from Mr Sam Gaskell. Don't think I should have written to you, solely to worry you for a letter when you must have so much to do, & to think of—(dear Miss Nightingale if it had not been for your careful performance of the quiet home duties, she would not have been at liberty for what she is now free to do—) but I wanted to return you the formal thanks I render, not the less truly than formally for my happy happy 'pause of life' at Lea-Hurst! I left it on Friday, the Hollands sending for me. I went the day before to see all our friends. Mrs Storer still complains of the pain in her side. The daughter at Mrs Littlewoods wanted a little doctoring in the Gregory line; which I gave her, as I had some by me. Mrs Diarrhea was quite well, only distressed about the price of flour, which had just risen, & was troubling Mrs Buxton also. I shall send you 'Margaret' as soon as I get home. Dear kind friends! may I send my love to you all. Don't forget me, & throw a crumb of correspondence sometimes to yours affectionately

E C Gaskell.

153 **219** 225

ANNA JAMESON

Plymouth Grove
Manchester
November 15 [?1854]

My dear Mrs Jameson,

Here is the beautiful Commonplace book[1] awaiting me on my return home! And I give it a great welcome you may be sure; and turn it over, & peep in, and read a sentence and shut it up to think over it's graceful suggestive wisdom in something of the 'gourmet' spirit of a child with an eatable dainty; which child, if it have the proper artistic sensuality of childhood, first looks it's cake over to appreciate the full promise of it's appearance,—next, snuffs up it's fragrance,—and gets to a fair & complete mouth-watering before it plunges into the first *bite*. I do like your book. I liked it before,— I like it better now—it is like looking into deep clear water,— down below at every instant of prolonged gaze, one sees some

[1] *A Commonplace Book of Thoughts*, 1854.

fresh beauty or treasure of clear white pebble, or little shady nooks for fish to lurk in, or delicate water weeds. Thank you for it. I do value it

I wonder where you are now; & if there is a chance of your coming this-wards. I heard of you from the Wilsons of Glasgow as being at Edinburgh; but I must direct this to Ealing. Do come to us if you can on your return.

Ever yours affectionately
E C Gaskell

62 220 0

? CHARLES DICKENS

Sunday [?17 December 1854]

My dear Sir,

I was very much gratified by your note the other day; *very* much indeed. I dare say I shall like my story, when I am a little further from it; at present I can only feel depressed about it, I meant it to have been so much better.[1] I send what I am afraid you will think too large a batch {o} of it by this post. What Mr Wills has got already *fills up* the No for January 13, leaving me only two\more/numbers, Janry 20, & Janry 27th so what I send today is meant to be crammed & stuffed into Janry 20th; & I'm afraid I've nearly as much more for Jany 27.

It is 33 pages of my writing that I send today. I have tried to shorten & compress it, both because it was a dull piece, & to get it into reasonable length, but there were [sic] a whole catalogue of events to be got over: and what I want to tell you now is this,— Mr Gaskell has looked this piece well over, so I don't think there will be any carelessnesses left in it, & so there ought not to be any misprints; therefore I never wish to see it's face again; but, *if you will keep the MS for me, & shorten it as you think best for H W.* I shall be very glad. Shortened I see it must be.

---

[1] 'She is writing furiously, thirty pages a week; expects to finish [*North and South*] in ten days. Mr Dickens writes to her praisingly, but he does not please me, and I hope she won't be "wiled by his fause flattering tongue" into thinking him true and trustworthy, like Mr Forster.' Catherine Winkworth on 17 December 1854, in *Letters and Memorials*, ed. Winkworth, I, p. 472.

I think a better title than N. & S. would have been 'Death & Variations'. There are 5 deaths, each beautifully suited to the character of the individual.

I was exceedingly interested & touched by that Soldier's Story. It is very 'war-music'al, & comes in beautifully just at this time. I must tell you 2 things. 1st Some fine-spinners in a mill at Bolton, earning their 36 shillings a week, threw up their work and enlisted last week, on hearing of the sufferings in the Crimea, for they said they could neither sleep nor eat for thinking how the soldiers there wanted help.

Some Bury men,\some very poor/seeing James Nasmyth's letter in the Times, subscribed a thousand pounds to enable him to try & make one of his guns; meanwhile Government had given {hi} him carte blanche. So he wrote back to thank them, & say so much had he felt their ready kindness that the first gun he made should be called 'The Voice of Lancashire.'

Yours most truly
E C Gaskell

I shall direct the batch of MS to the Office. Don't consult me as to the shortenings[;] only please yrself.

216 **221** 224

ANNE HOLLAND

Plymouth Grove
Monday morning
[?18 December ?1854]

My dearest Annie,

I wonder how Fred is? and if he is sufficiently well for me to propose a visit from my husband to Ashbourn next week. He is at liberty to leave home, which is an unusual thing with him; and, if you & Fred liked it—I don't mean liked it, but rather if it suited you, he would come to you for a few days after Xmas day. Now you see I am relying on your sincerity about the convenience of this proposal of mine; only somehow the plan of his coming to Ashbourn in the Spring[1] fell through, so both he & I thought that

---

[1] We assume that this refers to the projected visit mentioned in Letter 194.

it would be very pleasant if he could go and make your acquaintance now; but the fulfilment of this plan could easily be deferred
dearest Annie if it would suit you better, & he could go to some
other friends' house for he sadly wants a little rest & quiet, things
impossible to be procured in our busy busy place.

I am afraid E. Robinson fell through? Did she not? At least I
heard a rumour of her being engaged somewhere else; but if I
can make any further enquiries for you, I shall be very glad to do
so. With kind love to Fred, I remain

Your very affec[tionate] cousin

E. C. Gaskell.

206 222 240

ELIZA FOX[1]

P. Grove.

Monday, Dec. 24[?25], 1854

My dearest Tottie,

Oh what a shameful time it is since I've written to you! and
what a shame of me not to write, for yr last letter was such a nice
one, though its been stinging me with reproaches this two months
past, but I believe I've been as nearly dazed and crazed with this
c—, d— be h— to it, story as can be. I've been sick of writing, and
everything connected with literature or improvement of the
mind; to say nothing of deep hatred to my species about whom I
was obliged to write as if I loved 'em. Moreover I have had to
write so hard that I have spoilt my hand, and forgotten all my
spelling. Seriously it has been a terrible weight on me and has
made me have some of the most felling headaches I ever had in my
life, so having growled my growl I'll go on to something else. We
are all well that's the first unspeakable comfort.⟨. . .⟩ Altogether
everything looks very sad this Xmas. The war accounts make one's
blood run cold at the rotting away of those noble glorious men.
What *is* Mr Fox about to allow it? Mr Macready has been here;
yes! actually *staying* here from Saty noon, about 2 o'clock, to
Monday morning. It was very pleasant after I had got over my
fear of him: but it was Mr Gaskell's busy days, and so I had him

<hr>

[1] Original MS. not seen.

to myself, and I was afraid, at first, I confess, more especially as we could not muster up anybody worthy of meeting him. Mr Fairbairn away, Mr Scott came to dinner on Monday and that was nice! Said Mr Scott has been very ill almost ever since, diarrhea and those sort of things and Owen's College is falling off on account of the badness of the times. I expect *rather* to go to Paris with Meta in February; i.e. last year a Madame Mohl (English in spite of her name) whom I have known a little for many years asked us to go three times: and three times it had to be given up. Now she peremptorily commands us to come in February; so if all goes on well and my wretched story is done, I think we shall go and escape the reviews, hang 'em. Now my vision is this— what do you think of coming back with me when I come back— say 1st half of March—but I'm not sure of dates. We do so want to have you here a bit; and Manchester is not damp (because its east-windy) in the Spring,—& & we should so like it! all seems so uncertain I don't like to plan decidedly for even a month beforehand,—but will you try and turn events towards the fulfilment of this plan. About Wm Arnold? yes! I *just* know him. First he and his wife, out of their lieutenant's pay in India sent me £10 for the poor of Manchester,—I wrote to thank: and we corresponded once or twice till he came to England on acct of ill health. I fancy Oakfield[1] is a very literal piece of his own life, except that he recovered instead of dying on returning home. This year I just met his sister in the street, leaning on the arm of such a handsome beautiful elegant young man,—quite different to an Arnold; but this was Wm Arnold, as his sister told me. He did not catch my name, and I was in a hurry; and I don't think I even heard him speak. He was then afraid of having to return to India at the end of his 3 years absence, as no employment in England had turned up, but the very next week, I believe, Lady Byron employed him to be tutor to one of Lady Lovelace's boys; and so there he is dear[2] leading this young king at Bonn. How is Amelia Green getting on with her music? I wrote and ordered a Dorking cock,—lo behold! they sent me a pen, a cock and two hens, price 3. 12. 6. I cried my eyes out, for I had been so trying to be saving (given up the Times just at the most interesting time) and they would not take them back.⟨ . . . ⟩

[1] *Oakfield, or Fellowship in the East*, Longmans, 1854.
[2] ? bear.

211 **223** *509b

CATHERINE WINKWORTH[1]

Plymouth Grove. January 1st, 1855.

Dearest Katie,

Thanks for your note; and best and kindest wishes for you at the New Year; 'best' wishes leave *happiness* in the hands of God, to come or not at His good pleasure. I think 'best wishes' mean to me a deeper sense of His being above all in His great peace and wisdom, and yet loving me with an individual love tenderer than any mother's. Oh, Katie, that fall has made me ill! ⟨...⟩ a constant feeling of coming faintness which never comes, and has done with it. I hope, notwithstanding, to come to Alderley next week. I want to come so much ⟨...⟩ My dearest love to Sleeky. William wants her to come here *exceedingly*.⟨...⟩

How *pretty* about the Christmas tree!⟨...⟩ Miss Bronte's letter *is* very nice; I wish she'd write to me,—should I to her? Last time I wrote, it was a sort of explanation of my way of looking at her Church (the Establishment) and religion; intended for her husband's benefit. She has never answered it. I'm glad she likes 'North and South'. I did not think Margaret *was* so *over* good. What would Miss B. say to Florence Nightingale? I can't imagine! for *there* is intellect such as I never came in contact with before in woman!—only two in men—great beauty, and of her holy goodness, who is fit to speak?⟨...⟩[2]

221 **224** 0

ANNE HOLLAND

Plymouth Grove
Friday. [?Early January 1855]

My dearest Annie,

I ought to have written to you before, as Mr Gaskell told me to do,—but I have been very busy indeed. He wished me to write,

[1] From a printed source.
[2] This is followed in the source by a substantial extract from a letter of Florence Nightingale's, describing conditions in the hospital at Scutari.

and tell you for him how much he had enjoyed his visit, poorly as he was; and how he still intended to write to Fred, as soon as he was a little better. But I am sorry to say that he came back so ill, that for two days I was in great anxiety about him; and even yet he is very weak with this tiresome influenza. Only now that the ailment has departed I hope he will get strong again speedily. He says that packet must contain proofs of an address which he delivered to some 'Home-Mission' students;[1] and that, as he has since received duplicate proofs, those may be either destroyed, or if Fred cares to read it, it may be opened for that purpose. From Wm's account of the improvement he saw in Fred's looks during his stay at Ashbourne I can not help hoping that he really has now met with the means of some permanent improvement; and that the new treatment will afford relief to his general health. In haste, (as I think I am always in at home,)

I remain, dear Annie

Your very affect[ionate] coz

E. C. Gaskell

219 **225** 227

ANNA JAMESON

Plymouth Grove
Sunday Evening [January 1855]

My dear Mrs Jameson,

You can't think what pleasure your kind note of appreciation gave, and gives me. I made a half-promise (as perhaps I told you,) to Mr Dickens, which he understood as a whole one; and though I had the plot and characters in my head long ago, I have often been in despair about the working of them out; because of course, in this way of publishing it, I had to write pretty hard without waiting for the happy leisure hours. And then 20 numbers was, I found my allowance; instead of the too scant 22, which I had fancied were included in 'five months'; and at last the story is huddled & hurried up; especially in the rapidity with which the sudden death of Mr Bell, succeeds to the sudden death of Mr Hale. But what could I do? Every page was grudged me, just at last, when I did certainly infringe all the bounds & limits they set

[1] Given at Cross St Chapel on 4 December 1854.

me as to quantity. Just at the very last I was compelled to desperate compression. But now I am not sure if, when\the barrier gives way between/2 such characters as Mr Thornton and Margaret it would not go all smash in a moment,—and I don't feel quite certain that I dislike the end as it now stands. But, it is being re-published as a whole, in two vols;—and the question is shall I alter & enlarge what is already written, bad & hurried-up though it be? I can not insert small pieces here & there—I feel as if I must throw myself back a certain distance in the story, & re-write it from there; retaining the present incidents, but filling up intervals of time &c &c. Would you give me your *very* valuable opinion as to this? If I have taken to a book, or poem (Laodamia for instance,) the first time of reading I am like a child, and angry at every alteration even though it may be an improvement. I am going to follow your plan and run away from reviewers. (Now don't say it is not your plan because I have told Mr Gaskell it *is*.) Meta & I are going to Paris about the 13th for a fortnight or so; and I shall be sorry to think, in passing through London that I have not a chance of seeing you. I shall send you a copy of N. & S. if you will kindly accept it. And I really shall be grateful to you for an answer to my question about the alterations.

Yours ever most truly
E. C. Gaskell

210 226 229

MARIANNE GASKELL

Thursday [January ?1855]

My dearest Polly,

No news whatever, only a line to say How d'ye do. Here's a note from Meta, to explain her proceedings. One pig is sold. I've not a notion—oh! yes I have, what I did yesterday morning. Mrs Robberds came, & I had a long talk with her. She had been to call on Mrs Wm Turner the bride, & liked her much. I think Papa will go. Moreover she had been dining at the Hams', impromptu after calling at the Healds. (Oh! their concert-tickets—How am I to get them back?) And Mr Ham had consulted her on the desirability of taking his children to the Pantomime! Funny under the present circumstances of the Purse. *Don't name that however.*

After dinner, pheasant for Papa, beefsteak for us,—I left Papa asleep & went to Mrs Diggles, & talked her over to being on the Committee, &c &c, & then went on with the Concert Orders to the Mitchells; who didn't want 'em, & had orders from the Ransoms that they weren't going to use. I suspect orders were a drug last night. However I saw all over the house; and sate some time. *Our* Miss Mitchell was coming to tea, or I shd have gone on then about the lace; but I thought I should miss her, so left a message. Home to tea; & then [? Buzz] & names, till Papa fell asleep. Julia to bed. I looking over proofs, & arranging bits of business with Hearn. Mary Piercy's little boy much better, & ravenously hungry; *remember they don't want while I'm away*, but give in food or clothes rather than money. Hearn is going home. Schoolroom & nursery going to be cleaned; tomorrow & Saturday. Julia going to have Jessy Potter, at her own request, this afternoon. The 'young gentlemen' were very nice yesterday about Papa's cold; & offered to come *here* today; which they're to do, & have their 'lesson' in the *dining* room at 2; we dining at *one*. So I take myself out to Mme de Mery's. Sarah has utterly spoilt Meta's two *new* flannel petticoats, whh I was so busy making,—so I must go & buy more flannel this aft: All the Folkestone tides bad for our days, 12, or 13, or 14, or 15th, getting in to Boulogne at 6, 7, 8, 9, at night. I am puzzled. What with a new end to my book,[1] new flannel petticoats, & bad tides I'm altogether in a maze. My dear love to Flossy. I shall write to her next. Write often Kind love to Aunt Ann, Willie & Mr Robson. Your affec[tionate] Mother

                                                              E C G

225 **227** 234

ANNA JAMESON

                                                      Plymouth Grove—
                                                 Tuesday, Jan 30. [1855]

My dear Mrs Jameson

   No! indeed, you have not been a bit too abrupt. I wanted just what you tell me,—even more decidedly if need were; & truth is too precious & valuable a thing to need drapery,—you tell me just what I wanted to know. If the story had been poured just warm out of the mind, it would have taken a much larger mould.

---

[1] We assume she refers to *North and South*. See Hopkins, p. 151.

It was the cruel necessity of compressing it that hampered me. And now I can't do much; I may not even succeed when I try, but I will try for my own satisfaction even if it does not answer, & I have to cancel what I am now meaning to write, and all before the end of next week! So I have sent today since receiving your letter, to stop the press——

I shall be in a lodging at\the house where Steele lived, i.e. the *number*/36, Bloomsbury Square; out of your more direct way I fear; but on Monday morning, the 12, I will hold myself in readiness either to go to, or to receive, you. And I will not forget your sister. She deserves not to be forgotten. I don't know what I can do, but what I can, I will.

Ever dear Mrs Jameson

Yours most truly

E. C. Gaskell

₀ 228 ₀

FRANCES NIGHTINGALE

[*c.* 12 February 1855][1]

Mrs Nightingale
Only passing thro' London very sorry not to see you

₂₂₆ 229 ₂₃₀

MARIANNE GASKELL[2]

Friday noon
[February 1855]

My darling Marianne—

Mamma says you are to write *by return of post* a long & full account of how Papa is. You are to give every particular, and above all to send your letter off *by return* of post. We are just going out to see about your gown. We shall *possibly* send you

---

[1] Evidence is very slight for this date, but most of the letters in the Verney Collection (see Appx B) come from 1854–56 and this note picks up a phrase from Letter 225.

[2] This is a joint letter from Meta and Mrs Gaskell. See p. 263, n. 2 above.

patterns of some, for you to choose from. There is going to be a
dance here tonight—everything is in confusion—the great red
cushions of the salon being beaten & shaken till the room is
clouded with dust[.] They have been polishing the dining-room-
floor, till I anticipate a *fall* in every waltz. It is so funny the way in
wh. Mme Mohl has asked people to come in my name—Mrs
Hollond (whom I have never seen) was invited 'because it wd
give Miss Gaskell so much pleasure'—and Mlle Gaskell has a
prominent part in most of the invitation-notes. By the same post
as yours came—there was a letter from Annie—very full of
charades—: I wish I'd time to write to her. Tomorrow we dine at
the Scheffers', to meet Mme Viardot, & Mrs Holld—& afterward
go on to the Geoffroi St. Hilaires'—where I am afraid we shall
have to talk zoologically—&[1] be kissed.

E C G

Last night we went to Mr Thierrys[2]—very political indeed. Such
a commotion about a pamphlet, published in Brussels, giving a
real terrible acct of French army, as bad if not worse than Eng.
which the French government have stopped, & investigated to
find out author—M. Emile Girardin, instructed by Prince Louis
Jerome Buonaparte, the Prince at any rate who was in Crimea.[3]
We went to a magnificent party on Tuesday for grandeurs,
titles & dresses; but except for eyes, it was very dull, & prevented
one going to Mme Hollond's to dinner to meet V. Cousin. Mrs
Hollond goes back to England on Monday. I mean her to carry
my MS. tell Papa—*up to just* before Mr Bell's death. But I can
finish it up in no time if desired. I want to leave Paris, to have
some little time for London—only Meta's atelier is such a swal-
lower-up of time; I am in a great fidget about Papa too. I shan't
have any comfort till I hear again from you; & I'm writing,
standing, with my things on, just after reading yr letter because I
do so want to hear. It is so *puthery*[4] here, I can hardly walk. I do
hope you are getting it there. At present Meta has seen very little
of Paris[—]*Not* Hotel Cluny, Invalides, Sainte Chapelle, Pere la

---

[1] Mrs Gaskell's contribution begins here.
[2] Probably Amédée S-D. Thierry (1797–1873), brother of Augustin Thierry.
He held various official posts under both Louis-Philippe and Napoleon III.
[3] It was Napoleon Joseph Charles Buonaparte (1822–91), son of Jerome (1784–
1860), who led the French 3rd Division at Alma and Inkermann.
[4] A Northern dialectal word signifying hot, close atmospheric conditions.

Chaise, Place Royale[,] not properly Notre Dame. We *want so much to hear again*. I must go. Dear love to all. This is *no* letter. I'll write next to you.

Your very affec[tionate]

E C Gaskell

Take care your answer is in time.

229 230 234a

?MARIANNE GASKELL

[February 1855]

⟨...⟩ not let Meta do much because of the dancing in the evening. Great preparations were made; ices, & a man to wait, & galette ad lib: much to Meta's joy. She danced all evening; the rooms were crowded, & I can't tell you half the people. No Tourghieneffs. No end of Americans. Mrs Chapman & M. & Mme Laufel. A cotillion at the end. Quite new tours & some very pretty but too long to describe. Remember *mirror, kneeling*, and *gentleman's* chain. Saturday Atelier & then a short walk along the Quai's; then to dinner at the Scheffers' (such a good dinner!), Hollands, Pasteur Vermeil, Mrs Schwabe &c &c. Thence to the Jardin des Plantes, a great soiree got up in my honour (no kissing) but cups of rich chocolate & cream cakes, which made Meta wish she could have kept either her good dinner, or her good tea to another day, for she is perpetually hungry. We hardly ever have more than twice to eat in the day. Breakfast, tea & bread & butter. *Then* 6 o'clock dinner, & *nothing* whatever after, not even when we go to theatre. To return. There was a concert on Sunday to which the Scheffers had given us tickets. Not so good as the Conservatoire but of the same character, (& as it was not Conservatoire Sunday many of the same performers.) When we came home we found Mr Senior had been sitting here all the time we were away. Miss Carter at dinner. Monday I had to go to Mme Scheffer's to see her about business[;] back to meet a M. Hachette on the same business & then to see all Mme Mohl's callers, as it is her day for receiving. In the evening to Lady Elgin's. Tuesday morning came the great

relief of your letter, saying Papa was better. Meta went to her atelier after it came. In the evening Bertha Smith Hilary Carter, & two members of the Institute to dinner. Wednesday by appointment to Scheffer's Studio, to see his paintings &c. We met there M. de Circourt, Lady Mary Fielding, & two or three other people to all of whom Scheffer displayed & explained his pictures. It is a tremendous distance off, or else they ask us there so often, & it is such a pleasant house to go to! In the evening to the play; which Meta enjoys; but it is very little pleasure to me because of the air. Yesterday we picked Meta up at her atelier, & went to the Hotel Cluny, where we staid as long as we could, then to call on the de Circourts. Oh! one day Mrs Rich wrote to ask if I would go & call on Mme de Stael, who wanted &c. So I went; saw her brother-in law the Duc de Broglie, & his daughter, *said* to be very like her grandmother *the* Mme de Stael, who had the same dark red hair, dark red fiery eyes &c. Mme de Stael is coming here on Saturday to see me. Not that I want her. For M. Battel has written to ask me to see over the Hotel Dieu, & another hospital; & I wished particularly to get *both* done at once; & now I shall have to leave one undone. Tonight is Mme Mohl's open evening. Next Friday she 'gives dance' again. We have fixed to leave on Monday the 26th (I think.) It is the first day for a fortnight on which we can get through all in a day. But we don't know where to go that first night in London, and we shall be dog-tired; & not want to separate. Do you think Papa wants me? If so, I shd like to come home straight. If not, I should like to pay the promised visits in London; let me know particularly, & how he is. I think you had better *not* ask A. W. and I wonder at her asking you knowing how you are engaged. When Meta comes back you can go to Latch-ford, or to London—which you prefer; or both if you like it, for I am sure she will be glad to take her share. And as M. B is coming
⟨. . .⟩

181 **231** 494a

LADY KAY-SHUTTLEWORTH

19 Rue d'Angoulême
St Honoré
Paris
[?February ?1855]

My dear Lady Kay-Shuttleworth,
Will you write, (or cause to be written,) to me as soon as possible the address of that lady friend of yours whom you named to me last May, as being well known to you & the Duchess of Roxburghe, and as having had to go upon the stage, was it not? in Paris. You then wished me to go & see her, and find out quietly if I could, what her circumstances were. I am now very unexpectedly in Paris, and only for a very few days; but I will gladly do what you wish if you will tell me name & address.

I have been to the Maison des Diaconesses, seen the Pasteur Vermeil, met Mrs Hollond, once at Ary Scheffers, and once at her own house; and—in short I will write you a long letter if you will let me know if this reaches you safely, for I don't know your exact address, and feel rather as if I was sending a letter into the wilderness. I do *so* want to hear of you, too; of your health, and doings. My kind regards to Miss Paplouska and love to Janet & Ughtred; the others I fear will not remember me.

Yours affectionately
E. C. Gaskell.

0 **232** 233

JOHN GREENWOOD[1]

17 Cumberland Terrace
Regent's Park
London
Wednesday, April 4 [1855]

My dear Sir,
I can not tell you how VERY sad your note has made me. My dear dear friend that I shall never see again on earth! I did not

[1] *Address (on envelope)* Mr J. Greenwood | 224, Haworth, | Keighley | Yorkshire. *Postmarks* E.C. | AP 4 | 1855 *and* KEIGHLEY | AP 5 | 1855.

even know she was ill. I had heard nothing of her since the beginning of December when she wrote to a mutual friend saying that
she was well, and happy. I was meaning to write to her this very
day, to tell her of the appearance of a copy of my new book, whh
I was sending to her. You may well say you have lost your best
friend; strangers might know her by her great fame, but we loved
her dearly for her goodness, truth, and kindness, & those lovely
qualities she carried with her where she is gone.

I want to know EVERY particular. Has she been long ill? What
was her illness? You would oblige me *extremely* if you would,
at your earliest leisure, send me every detail. I am writing by this
post to Mr Brontë. You do not name Mr Nicholls. Pray let me
hear again from you, dear Sir. I loved her dearly, more than I
think she knew. I shall never cease to be thankful that I knew her:
or to mourn her loss.

Yours truly & obliged

E. C. Gaskell

Will you direct the letter I hope to receive from you to

T. B. Price's Esq.

11 Princes Terrace

Princes Gate

Hyde Park

London.

232 **233** 238

JOHN GREENWOOD[1]

11 Princes Terrace

Hyde Park

London

Thursday [12 April 1855]

My dear Sir,

Your letter had been awaiting me at the friend's house where I
am now staying for some days; which must be my apology for
being so long in thanking you for it. I am *extremely*—more than I

---

[1] *Address (on envelope)* Mr Greenwood | Haworth | Keighley | Yorkshire.
Postmarks 1855 | 12 AP 12 L L *and* KEIGHLEY | AP 13 | 1855 | A.

can put into words—obliged to you for it, most drearily, and painfully sad as it is. How I wish I had known! I do not wonder at your reluctance to write, when you feared it might be construed into 'meddling', and it is no use regretting what is past; but I do fancy that if I had come, I could have induced her,—even though they had all felt angry with me at first,—to do what was so absolutely necessary, for her very life. Poor poor creature! I can not understand it all. Her not seeing you more frequently for instance! It is nearly a year since she was with us; but I remember as if it were yesterday her turning to me & saying 'You will send some message to Mr Greenwood, won't you,' and then speaking about you to my husband with such true, warm regard & appreciation; saying you were the one *friend* she had in Haworth. All this —and more that I don't repeat makes me think that Mr Brontë *must* have concealed his portrait from her. He might have hung it up while they were away on their wedding-tour, and taken it down before their return from a sort of shy feeling at having had his portrait taken, however unconsciously, when he so often said that he would not. It is so unlike her not to be ready to acknowledge a kindness, even though her thanks came more through her eyes and the grasp of her hand than her tongue. Dear dear Miss Brontë. I wish I could do anything in my power for those whom she has loved, and left behind her! I shall be very much obliged to you, dear Sir, if from time to time you will let me know how Mr Brontë & Mr Nicholls go on & are in health; and I shall also always take a great interest in all your own personal concerns; and if I can do anything to forward any of your wishes, you must be sure, and let me know, for *her* sake. I almost think I shall try and come over for a day to Haworth this summer, & see Mr Brontë; but, as I know he would not like the idea of it, beforehand you had better not mention it. Did you see the notice of her in the 'Daily News'? If you did not, & will let me know, I will send you a copy. I, and most others believe it to have been written by Miss Martineau[.] I need hardly say how completely confidential I consider your most interesting letter. *Anything* else you can ever remember to tell me about her will be most valuable. Remember me kindly to Mrs Greenwood, and believe me to remain, dear Sir,

Yours most truly

E. C. Gaskell

On Monday next I return to Plymouth Grove, Manchester.

227 **234** 306

ANNA JAMESON[1]

11, Princes Terrace,
Thursday. [?April ?1855]

My dear Mrs Jameson,—

⟨...⟩ I have got out two used catalogues of the Louvre for you,
1854, both. I shall leave them with Mrs James, if I am *not* so
fortunate as to see you. Mr Gaskell sends me word of your kindness about that lecture, respecting which I took a warm interest,
and which is now amplified, is it not? I am truly obliged to you
for giving it to me and so imparting a double value to it. I read
(not my copy, it is at Mrs Wedgwood's) the day after it came
out, and I particularly thanked you for the broad basis you had
Jaken for your noble and true ideas. Believe me ever, dear Mrs
tameson,

Yours very truly and gratefully
E. C. Gaskell

You don't know the good you have done me in your life-time,
so I have a right to honour myself by signing 'gratefully.'

230 **234a** •242a

MARIANNE GASKELL

11 Princes Terrace
H Park
Tuesday [? April 1855]
Private.

My dearest Polly,

*Has Papa got a library table for his study? because if not, I have
found a very handsome oblong, second-hand one at the Baker-Street
Bazaar (where Tottie got E. Shaen's Davenport for us when she was
married,) mahogany, 3 large drawers on each side,\dark/green leather
top, five feet six inches in length, price 6£, and I would get it for him if
he has NOT got one; it is in first rate condition as good as new. Will you
& Hearn measure the size & see if it would do for the study; be large
enough, yet not too large, & let me have an answer here, if possible
by Thursday morng. I am writing in a terrible hurry, & I want if*

---

[1] From a printed source.

possible to write to Papa before going to the Duckworth's, where at last I have resolved to call, & to meet Meta, by way of fixing myself down to doing what is a very awkward miserable thing. So very soon I shall cross the Park to Bryanstone Square. Mrs Price comes & picks us up, & takes us on in *her* carriage to see Millais's Pictures[.] This is the week for the private view before going to the Exhibition[.] About Miss Banks, I am afraid it is no use trying to fix on any place at which she is to call on me. The Prices want me to stay here till Friday; but I think I shall go to Emily's on Thursday & if so Meta & I plan going out to Denmark Hill to call on Mrs Ruskin which would take up the whole day. Friday I ought to go with Mrs Wedgwood to the Huttons of Putney Park, but I shan't if I am tired. Saturday I have to come to Piccadilly to see Mr Chapman by appointment about business. Monday I planned coming home but Meta begs to stay over 'Lady Crompton's ball' on the Tuesday, 17th, so whether to leave her to come down alone on Wednesday, or to wait for her till then,—and if so, where? I don't know. I must fix however soon. I am so glad it is a cow-calf. Will you describe it? Beg Barbara & Will to take great care of it. I wish you would give me some notion of what the children would like to have in the present line. I brought them one or two *little* things from Paris. Tell Papa—no don't! I hope to write mys⟨elf. I⟩ want to come home on Monday, but as Meta has been disappointed about the Richmond ball, to whh Lady Crompton wanted to take her, only I wd not let her go to public ball without me,—I am sorry to cut her off from Ly C's *private* ball,— I almost think I shall let her travel *alone* next Wednesday. You are quite right about sending Miss M. rhubarb I am glad we have plenty. *What* earl is Mabel Barnes going to marry. Here is Mrs Price, & *no* silence[.] I must write to Papa. Oh & on Saty I am going to Mr Frank Stone's to get advice about Miss Mitchell's dresses.

Goodbye darling
Your very affe[ctionate]
E C G

89 **235** 305

EDWARD CHAPMAN[1]

Plymouth Grove
April 25 [1855]

Dear Sir,

We have taken your proposals into consideration, (and pray don't imagine that your kind promptitude in making them was lost upon me. I received the letter directed to Princes Terrace early on Saty morning, and I was *very* much obliged to you for the dispatch you had made.) Mr Gaskell consents to a trial of the cheap plan of publication\of Cranford, & the other smaller tales/for such a time\or such a number/as may be agreed upon; though with regard to Cranford it goes rather against the grain. What he wishes to know is what number you would propose to publish in the first instance?, and how soon you think the returns on that number are likely to be made? In order to save time, perhaps it might be as well if you were to send such form of agreement as may be requisite. I shall write by this post to Mr Dickens to ask for his formal consent for the republication of the H[ousehold] W[ords] Tales. Must I do the same with 'Mr Harrison's confessions'?[2] or should\you/not think them worth re-printing? You have a Libbie Marsh have you not? The others shall come when you want them. There is a piece in 'North & South' printed *twice* over. *16* lines. Page 262, & Page 312. Mr Gaskell, in returning one of the proofs, requested you to ask the printer to look whether there was not a repetition.

Yours ever very truly
E C Gaskell.

[1] The Pierpont Morgan library holds associated MSS, including a Wm Gaskell letter of 17 April 1855 on the cheap edition of *Cranford*.
[2] Originally published in *The Ladies' Companion*, February–April 1851.

218 **236** 255

PARTHENOPE NIGHTINGALE

Plymouth Grove—

May 3. [?1855]

Only best wishes & kindest regards. I have time for no more.
But I often think of you & her,[1] & you all. You'll let me have *one*
line to say how she is, when you return Mme Mohl—

Yours very truly

E C Gaskell

198 **237** 386

?F. J. FURNIVALL

[?May ?1855][2]

My dear Sir,

I am very much obliged to you, and Mr Macmillan, only you
see I am in the predicament of the M.P. to whom Punch offered
such good advice, & having 'nothing to say,' I think I had better
say it. I doubt if I shall ever write again for publication; but
nobody knows; not I, certainly, whether I shall keep to this idea,
or write a Dictionary, or some other good sensible voluminous
work.

But I will bear your kindness, & Mr Macmillan's proposal in
mind against the future days. I am sorry Mr Ruskin is not well. I
suppose I ought to be sorry that Mrs Marshall did not obtain her
wish of coming to see the W. Man's College. But I am not.

Yours very truly

E C Gaskell.

[1] Presumably Florence Nightingale.
[2] Dating very doubtful. The London Working Man's College began in late
1854 (W. G. Collingwood, *Life and Work of John Ruskin*, 1893, I, p. 184), and the
paper of this letter is like that of Letter 236.

JOHN GREENWOOD

Plymouth Grove,
Manchester
Saturday, May 5th [1855]

My dear Mr Greenwood,

I have thought a good deal about all that you have said, since
receiving your two last very interesting letters, and I must confess
that a great deal of it remains still incomprehensible to me. It is so
extremely unlike her, whom we both mourn so truly, not to welcome and meet even more than half way any little kindness and
attention that might be offered. So much so that I incline to think
that it must have been the extreme and growing languor of ill
health which made her perpetually delay thanking you for your
picture of her father. Are you not on sufficiently intimate terms
with Mr Nicholls to ask him, at some future time, what she
thought of it? It is possible that for some reason she did not
approve of your becoming too much interested in something that
might distract you from your business, (mind! I know nothing
about this,—) but I judge of you by myself when I say that I think
you would rather know the truth, than keep puzzling & puzzling
about it. Of course you could not ask Mr Nicholls just yet, & from
what you say I am afraid it may be some time before you have the
opportunity. I should like to know how he and Mr Brontë are.
Do you know if Mr Thackeray has ever written to Mr Brontë.
I am curious to know, for he had heard of her death, & was much
shocked by it. I can hardly believe it myself! I often find myself
thinking of things that I will tell her, or of subjects that we will
talk over when next we meet. There are some lines by Mr
Matthew Arnold in this month's Fraser's Magazine called Haworth
Churchyard,—falling into the same mistake Miss Martineau did. I
have not seen them, but I hear they are very striking. He inspected
the Dissenter's schools in Yorkshire, for some short time, &
told me some time ago that he had been at Haworth on that
business.

About the Marble Tablet—I see this great difficulty. I do not
quite think we have the right to take any plan of this sort out of
the hands of Mr Nicholls, who may have wishes of his own that
ought to be attended to in the matter. If I could ever get to know

him I should find out. But I bear your suggestion in mind, & let us have patience, & not forget our dear friend, & the time may come when we may do her some little tribute of honour & love. *Every* [thing] you can tell me about her & her sisters—of *her* especially is most valuable.

I wish they would allow her portrait to be daguerrotyped for her friends. But I am sure it is too soon to name or propose it to them as yet. Was there a new study built at Haworth Parsonage last summer? One of the newspapers says there was. When did *you* first know of '*Currer Bell?*'

I hope, dear Sir, you are feeling better. I know how great a trial her loss must be to you in some measure. But remember how brave *she* was, all through her many sorrows; and to whom she always looked as the Sender both of Sunshine & of Storm. She was a wonderful creature, & her life was wonderfully appointed; full of suffering as it was. Remember me to your wife, & believe me ever, dear Sir

Yours most truly
E. C. Gaskell

238 239 258

JOHN GREENWOOD

Plymouth Grove
Saturday [After 5 May 1855]

My dear Mr Greenwood

You can not think how your letter interests me. You may depend upon it that any thing you wish me to keep secret, shall not be revealed; but I could never be tired of hearing about my dear friend, and her early days; indeed all about her. Will you tell me what you know about that first visit to London as 'Currer Bell', when you have leisure for a little more writing. I have looked for Mr Macarthey's character in Shirley, and I find it exactly corresponds with what you have told me of Mr Nicholls, & also with what she herself has said to me before now. Yet it shows something fine in him to have been able to appreciate her. And I know of better curacies being offered to him, & one living indeed, {which}\the refusal of which/also seems to prove that he is not a worldly man, so that I can not understand how he should slight any one for another, inferior in character & attainments, but superior in fortune. A man who could do that would have snatched at opportunities of improving his own worldly condition. I don't like to believe him guilty of meanness because I could not then respect him as I like to respect *her* husband. Now I can respect {bigotry}\a bigoted person/although I may suffer from their bigotry. The one is an error of head, the other a fault of heart.

I am surprized at Mr Thackerays never writing to Mr Brontë. I wrote myself to tell him of her death; I have never heard from him in acknowledgment, & I thought that he might not have received my note. But he must have learnt of her death through the public papers.

Will you remember me to your wife; and with Mr Gaskell's respects to you,

Believe me to remain

Yours most truly

E C Gaskell

222 **240** 250

Eliza Fox

Tuesday, May 15th, 1855.

⟨. . .⟩ Here all is bustle and confusion, and I've to settle everybody's plans for 'em, having none of my own at this present time, I am in an unusual state of *busy-ness* for Hearn has gone to Cornwall for a holiday for the first time for 12 or 13 years; and the 'house' comes to me in every dilemma, and the children will do everything, (put coals on fire, light it, etc, etc) by way of being useful and womanly till I'm in a continual Panic. Fairy is dead too, and we've got a puppy, Lion, who is very charming, but up to all sorts of mischief. Mr Gaskell is so full of invitations for Whitsun tide, that I'm afraid he'll accept none of them, he wavers so much as to wh. would be the most charming. MA is setting off on her rounds too. It is very pretty to see Flossy turning out thoughtful and *fearless* in her desire to take care of Julia; running about in the dark in the middle of the night, because she thought Julia was ill. ⟨. . .⟩ Ask Mr Fox what is most like a hen stealing?

(a cock-robin.) Also why Pharaoh's daughter is like a basket maker—because they both get a little prophet (profit) out of rushes.

Yours very affec[tionatel]y,

E. C. G.

0 **241** 242

GEORGE SMITH

Plymouth Grove
Manchester
May 31st [1855]

Dear Sir,

I believe you have a copy of Richmond's portrait of Miss Brontë. I want to know if there is any probability of its ever being engraved; or if you would ever object to a daguerrotype being taken from it at some future time for my own self. I can not tell you how I honoured & loved her. I did not know of her illness, or I would have gone straight to her. It seems to me that her death was as sad as her life. Sometime, it may be years hence—but if I live long enough, and no one is living whom such a publication would hurt, I will publish what I know of her, and make the world (if I am but strong enough in expression,) honour the woman as much as they have admired the writer. I should like to know about the portrait at your convenience.

Yours truly
E. C. Gaskell

241 **242** 243

GEORGE SMITH

Plymouth Grove
Manchester
June 4. [1855]

Dear Sir,

I believe you will be much interested by the accompanying letter; but I must beg you to consider it as sent to you for your own private perusal, as you see what the poor man says at the end; and if I had not known of Miss Brontë's regard for you, & yours for her, I should not have thought myself justified in letting it pass out of my hands. But is it not sad? and does it not altogether seem inexplicable and strange? The writer, poor fellow, is a kind of genius in his way; & I know that Miss Brontë was a little afraid of his being too much of a Jack-of-all-trades to succeed in any. He is part mason, part gardener, plaisterer painter and what not, besides having a little stationer's shop, the only place where paper can be bought nearer than Keighley. In one of his letters (for he seems to have adopted me as his correspondent since Miss Brontë's death,) he says 'I had not much acquaintance with the family till 1843, when I began to do a little in the stationery line [.] Nothing of that kind could be had nearer than Keighley when I began. They used to buy a great deal of writing paper, and I used to wonder whatever they did with so much. When I was out of stock I was always afraid of them coming they seemed always so distressed if I had none. I have walked to Halifax (a distance of 10 miles) many a time for half a ream of paper, for fear of being without when they came. I could not buy more at once for want of capital; I was always short of that. I did so like them to come when I had anything for them; they were so much different to any one else, so gentle, & kind and so very quiet. They never talked much; but Charlotte would sometimes sit, and enquire about my family so feelingly.'

Miss Brontë took me several times to see this poor man when I stayed with her at Haworth; & the last time she was here (the last time I saw her,) she turned back out of the carriage when she was going away to say 'Do send a message to John Greenwood; he will so like it.' I think they are very unusual letters for a man in his station. He is a little deformed man, upwards of 50 years of age. I had never heard of her being ill; or I would have gone to her at once; she would have disliked my doing so, as I am fully aware, but I think I could have overcome that, and perhaps saved her life. I wrote to her last in October; and she had never replied to that letter, but as she knew I was very busy in completing a task which I extremely disliked, I fancied that her silence arose partly from the sensitive delicacy which always made her hold aloof from even the semblance of interruption or intrusion. Moreover in my last letter I had spoken a good deal of my views of the Church of England, which she knew well enough before, & sympathized in, but which I thought might probably annoy her husband, (Mr Macarthey in the 3rd vol of Shirley,) but I had promised her I would be very patient, and trustfully await her bringing him round to tolerate dissenters. And so,—half busy,—half trying to be patient, I never wrote to her again after that October letter; and I do so regret it now! I think it is from finding that you are suffering from a somewhat similar regret (that of not having cultivated her intimacy more assiduously,) that makes me write so openly & so much at length to you. I wish you *would* ask for permission to have a copy of the portrait, & that without much delay. I know so little of Mr Nicholls that I may have received a wrong impression of him; but my idea is that he will be less likely to consent to a copy being taken than Mr Brontë, in whose possession it is at present; but he is 80 years of age! He wrote to me once, and named your letter to him with a kind of touching satisfaction in what you had said.

She often asked me (after her marriage last year) to go over & see her; I never went, partly because it required a little courage to face Mr Nicholls, as she had told me he did not like her intimacy with us as dissenters, but that she knew he *would* like us when he had seen us. Now I intend to go over for one day to see Mr Brontë, and also to see her husband, & where she is laid. I am sure she would have liked to think of my doing so. I have tried\but I have failed,/to get a copy of the Belfast Mercury [April 1855], quoted in the Athenæum about three weeks, since, with reference to her family in Ireland; Mr Brontë says he was more pleased by a 'notice of her in an Irish paper than by any other that he has seen': and I fancy it must be this Belfast Mercury. It gave a similar account of her relations on her father's side, as she had given to me, in the long talks we had during my happy visit to Haworth.

It was from finding how much names and dates which she then gave me in speaking of her past life had passed out of my memory, that I determined that in our country-leisure this summer I would put down every thing I remembered about this dear friend and noble woman, before its vividness had faded from my mind: but I *know* that Mr Brontë, and I *fear* that Mr Nicholls, would not like this made public, even though the more she was known the more people would honour her as a woman, separate from her character of authoress. Still my children, who all loved her would like to have what I could write about her; and the time may come when her wild sad life, and the beautiful character that grew out of it may be made public. I thought that I would simply write down my own personal recollections of her, from the time we first met at Sir J. K. Shuttleworth's, telling {all}\what was right & fitting of what/she told me of her past life, and here & there copying out characteristic extracts from her letters. {describing} \I could describe/the wild bleakness of Haworth & speaking of the love & honour in which she was held there. But (from the tenor of Mr Greenwood's first letter.) you will see that this sort of record of her could not be made public at present without giving pain. I shall be glad if you will return me Mr Greenwood's letters, and with many apologies for the length of this,—⟨. . .⟩

*

242 243 244

GEORGE SMITH[1]

Plymouth Grove.
June 12th [1855]

Dear Sir,

I am beginning to be a little anxious respecting the fate of some letters (containing the particulars of Mrs Nicholls' last illness,) which I sent to you, for your private perusal,) on Monday the 4th instant. I am in no immediate hurry to have them returned, only I should like to be assured of their safety, as I have once or twice lost letters containing enclosures, through the post.

Yours very truly
E. C. Gaskell

243 244 245

GEORGE SMITH

Plymouth Grove—
Thursday [After 12 June 1855]

My dear Sir,

I have received your letter &c quite safely & I am now ashamed of having written to enquire after it; only having lost things by the post, I was needlessly afraid this time[.]

[1] *Address* George Smith Esq | Messrs Smith & Elder | Corn Hill | London.

But the reason why I write is this—I think you are right in feeling reluctant to act upon my hasty suggestion that you should write to Mr Brontë about the portrait; and I want now to prevent your doing so. It was my great anxiety to have a daguerrotype &c; & great fear that Mr Nicholls would object when it came into his exclusive possession, that made me too carelessly forget that Mr Brontë would naturally dislike parting with the original just now. All that you say of her is most true; & I think the word 'adroit' just describes her delicate neat way of giving advice.

One can see that poor John Greenwood takes things according to the impulse of the moment, from the contradictory accounts of Mr Nicholls that he sends—I enclose you two more of his letters. I will write again after I have been at Haworth; when I shall be able to go I don't know.

Yours very truly

E. C. Gaskell

244 **245** 256

GEORGE SMITH

Plymouth Grove

June 18. [1855]

My dear Sir,

I have received (most unexpectedly) the enclosed letter from Mr Brontë;[1] I have taken some time to consider the request made in it, but I have consented to write it, *as well as I can.* Of course it becomes a more serious task than the one which, as you know, I was proposing to myself, to put down my personal recollections &c, with no intention of immediate publication,—if indeed of publication at all. I shall have now to omit a good deal of detail as to her home, and the circumstances, which must have had so much to do in forming her character. All these can be merely indicated during the life-time of her father, and to a certain degree in the lifetime of her husband—Still I am very anxious to perform this grave duty laid upon me well and fully. Of course it strengthens my determination to go over to Haworth as now I

---

[1] Letter of 16 June 1855, now in the Christie Library of Manchester University. (It has been misdated 16 *July* 1855 in standard works.)

must see Mr Brontë; and you will extremely oblige me by confiding to me any information respecting her which you may possess, and not be unwilling to impart. Do you think that either you or I might venture to ask for a daguerrotype of the Richmond now. I think my wish to have a copy of it gains strength. I am so afraid of forgetting her face; and that was such a beautiful likeness.

In great haste, I remain, dear Sir,

Yours very truly

E. C. Gaskell

*242a 246 247

MARIANNE GASKELL

Tuesday. [?19 June 1855]

My dearest Polly,

Meta and I are going into town directly after a one o'clock dinner, at which Papa will not be at home, as he is going to Mr Kendall's examination. Have you got *Flossy*'s striped French muslin sleeves? You have left *your own* behind, known by their double button-holes, & we hope you have got Flossy's by mistake, as we can't find them anywhere. I do not think we shall go to Silverdale till the 7th; but nothing is fixed. Nothing more ever *will* be fixed, I believe. Emily S. comes here on Monday July 2 till the 16th. *Name the time you think of leaving & going to the Tagart's as early as ever you can to Mrs James*, for she *may* have some plan for which she may wish you to stay longer. But you are quite right in sticking to not going anywhere from her. I know how inconvenient that sometimes is to a family. Did I tell you that Mr Brontë had asked me to write a life of his daughter, & that I have consented? It makes me have to write to Mme Mohl to-day to get an address. Did you take your *lilac* ribbons that went with your LILAC MUSLIN DRESS *to London with you?* answer by return—Yes! I think you may go to the Price's. The 51st don't leave Manchester till the end of next month; & even then uncertain. Capn Agg stays with the depôt companies[.] Meta goes with me, as soon as Papa comes back from Cleator, (whither he goes on Friday from Miss Yates, whither he goes tomorrow after Mr Kendall's examination,) to Miss Tollets,—next Tuesday I expect[.] Betley-Hall Newcastle, Staffordshire is the address although the Hall is in Cheshire, & the grounds in Shropshire. Meta does not particularly like the idea of an Indian grass silk; & I don't *think* I do. Julia's is dirty *directly*; & never looked *very* nice. Meta says if she has one it must be trimmed with 'brun dorée,'— but think well about it, darling. Julia was sadly disappointed at having no letter from you to-day. We have comforted up as well as we could but the next letter *must* be to her. She has written you a letter which I hope you can read

Ever your very affect[ionate]
E C Gaskell

246 247 248

MARIANNE GASKELL

[?c. 19 June 1855]

My dearest Polly,

I am not well at all so you must not expect a long letter, but I have had a great deal to make me very anxious this past week or fortnight, to which *don't allude in reply*, as I shall tell it you, my darling when you return, & we can *talk* things over. All is ended now, as far as I can tell, & doubtless for the best; but I have had to see a great deal of honest suffering, which has oppressed me extremely. *Be sure & say nothing in answer*, as it is but to be patient a little, & you shall know all. Only I can not go into all the little details I used to do, partly because my back aches so much, too much to sit up for anything, and partly because my thoughts have been so much occupied otherways. I promised to write to you, more faithfully & often, did I not, love? We (Meta & I go to the Tollet's *Betley-Hall, Newcastle, Staffordshire*, on Tuesday to stay till Saturday. Write to us there. Tell us what people in London say about this terrible news about the war; *every scrap you hear*. Hearn comes back on Tuesday or Wednesday. I shall be very glad, as it will just save me from fairly giving way, & being beaten by over-fatigue & care. Goodbye, my dearest Polly. Every *thing*, & every *body* is quite right; so don't think anything is going wrong; only I have gone *through* an affair, which has doubtless ended for the best, only with a good deal of pain which I have had to see.

Not in our own family though[,] which is a blessing. Once more goodbye.

Your ever affect[ionate] mother
E C Gaskell

247 248 251

MARIANNE GASKELL

Tuesday Eveng [?26 June 1855)

Dearest MA

Acknowledge both to *me*, Betley, Newcastle Staffordshire & to Papa[.] Call upon Miss Emma Weston (Mme Van der Weyer's, Portland Place) & *on Mme Mohl* BE SURE

Your ever aff[ectionate] E C G

0 249 358

WILLIAM FAIRBAIRN[1]

Plymouth Grove.
[?Summer 1855]

My dear Mr Fairbairn,—I am ashamed that I have been so long in acknowledging your kind friendly note, and very just criticisms on 'North and South'. Do you know I have half begun to expect a note from you after the publication of every story of mine, and I was beginning to feel a little disappointed that none arrived on this occasion. You see how unreasonable authors (as well as other people) become if they have once been indulged.

Your kind and racy critiques both give me pleasure and do me good; that is to say, your praise gives me pleasure because it is so sincere and judicious that I value it; and your fault-finding does me good, because it always makes me *think*, and very often it convinces me that I am in error. This time I believe you have hit upon a capital blunder⟨. . .⟩ I don't think a second edition will be called for; but if it should be, you may depend upon it I shall gladly and thoughtfully make use of your suggestion.

[1] From a printed source.

I agree with you there are a certain set of characters in 'North and South', of no particular interest to any one in the tale, any more than such people would be in real life; but they were wanted to fill up unimportant places in the story, when otherwise there would have been unsightly gaps. ⟨. . .⟩

Mr Hale is not a 'sceptic'; he has *doubts*, and can resolve greatly about great things, and is capable of self-sacrifice in theory; but in the details of practice he is weak and vacillating. I know a character just like his, a clergyman who has left the Church from principle, and in that did finely; but his daily life is a constant unspoken regret that he did so, although he would do it again if need be.

But I am afraid I am taking up your time with what you will not care to read. Thank you again, dear Mr Fairbairn, for your note, which I shall always value, and believe me,

I am yours most truly,

E. C. Gaskell.

240 **250** 276

Eliza Fox[1]

July 8th, 1855

⟨. . .⟩ We are deep in military affairs in one way, having a regular stationed here, who *will* know us, and will call, and will be civil, and ask us to presentation of colours, and balls (to which I own we go) more than I like, as Miss Meta and one of the officers are a little too thick in the dancing line, 8 times in one evng being rather too strong, and drawing down upon the young lady a parental rebuke.—They are an Indian regiment, and ordered off to Crimea; have distinguished themselves in Burmah, or some out of the way place. ⟨. . .⟩ I am *very* sorry to hear your account of Barbara T. Is consumption in the family? I *too* distrust and dread that sweetness. Make me of any use about Paris. I can do something; I know, if I've time to think what. But I could *cry* with fatigue just now. My love to Charlotte.

Yrs very affec[tionatel]y,

E. C. G.

---

[1] Original MS. not seen.

MARIANNE GASKELL

Plymouth Grove
Sunday [8 July 1855]

My dearest Polly,

Julia & I are going to Brook St as Papa has advised us, being both much overdone with the heat, and as we are ready in good time I shall write a line or two to you. You will have heard before this that Meta stopped behind me at Teddesley. I left on Thursday and I have heard from her once since; she is very much enjoying herself, in a very quiet way, only Lady H, & Mrs Wellesley (the latter an insufferable bore of the sentimental incoherent Mrs Nickleby style.) I don't exactly know when Meta will come back; some day this week I fancy; & towards the *end* most probably. Next week she will go about the 18 or 19 to Mrs Davy's, who has asked her for 'ten days' only,—time very distinctly specified *not* to be longer; & it suits us better for her to go, & to join us at Silverdale. Papa is going to Switzerland on the 30th, & he has said he wants to hear of our safe arrival at Silverdale before he goes. But it would have suited me (as far as I myself goes [*sic*]) rather better to have had the house partly cleaned before I went. However for both Meta's & Papa's\& Julia's/sake I think we shall go to Silverdale on either the 27th or 28th (Friday or Saturday)[1] taking Elliott; to go home when the house is cleaned & Sarah to come & take her place. We are to stay there after Julia's birthday. Otherwise all our plans are in the usual confusion. Whether you & I go to Glasgow I don't know,—but ought to write & fix. Whether Papa & I go to Sir James Kay Shuttleworths at Gawthrop [*sic*] next week, I don't know. (*Don't name this invitation to any body on any account*). Let me see darling! You speak of coming home on the 25th Wednesday. *If* we go to Glasgow, you must let me know what things will want seeing after of yours in the two days before we go to Silverdale. And I want you to buy yourself & Meta two brown-straw hats, (I'll *give* you yours) of PRETTY SHAPE & *not* SMELLING *straw*. I can't get them here; & we could trim them at home. Mme de Merey is dead—Bring home your things *clean* if you can. Here is a letter from Emily

[1] July 1855: the Perpetual Calendar shows that this is a possible month. Also, it is consistent with the Letters immediately following.

Deane for you. *Where is Cousin Mary?* I want to write to her about Silverdale. Julia & I have sat in Robert Darbishire's pew. He & his wife were there. I *do* think they are the coldest people I know— However I have asked them to come here on Wednesday or Thursday to meet Emily.[1] Tomorrow we go to the Shuttleworths a very quiet party to meet Miss Hill, of happy memory. On Tuesday to the Schuncks to meet the Gallengas; equally quiet. I think our drawing-room never was so hot in it's life; it is like a stove. We *could* put off going to Silverdale a little later, but if you wish this you must write by return of post. Anyhow it need not limit you as to the length of your stay in London; for you could follow us. *When are the Ewarts coming home?*

Ever your very affect[ionate] mother

E C G.

251 252 252a

MARIANNE GASKELL

Thursday [12 July 1855]

My dearest Polly,

Agnes Sandars & her children are coming soon, & I may be interrupted any moment, but I write to say Papa has asked Uncle Sam to pay you 2£, which he owes Papa, which you must make *do* for your allowance at present. I don't see how you will get your *cap* to Papa. I *think* he will leave here on Monday 30th, he & Selina through London; and from your account, as far as I can make it out, you will be at Crix then. Perhaps Uncle Sam may be from home & so not receive Papa's letter; so not know where to find you. I think you had better write him a little note to No 2 St James' Place. The post has come in & brought no letters from you or Meta, or any one but the enclosed note from Cousin Mary. I am sorry she can not come to Silverdale. I think it is very likely that Selina may accompany Papa as far as Boulogne;[2] she is going to join the J. J. Taylers in Normandy where they are going to spend the summer & autumn. Emily & her bairns leave on Monday,[3] & I must try & get the children out of the house[,] the

---

[1] See p. 350 above.
[2] See *Letters and Memorials*, ed. Winkworth, I, p. 497.
[3] 16 July. See p. 350 above.

paint affects Julia so much. She is as white & weak as possible.
Mrs Shuttleworth has asked them & Hearn to go there on Monday, (when Miss Hill leaves her,) till we can get them lodgings
at Silverdale. I want very much to hear from you, darling.
Mrs R. D. Darbishire is walking in the garden with Emily &
Maggie, Godfrey D. holding Maggie's hand. Last night we had a
small party. Leislers, Schuncks, Gallengas, Shuttleworths, Miss
Hill, Maggie Leisler, & Arthur Darbishire forming our 'young
people[']. As they only came at 8 & went away at 10, they did
pretty well together, & we think that our party went off brisker
& better than the two other previous nights at the Schuncks &
Shuttleworths. Julia is gone into town to have a great deal of her
hair cut off, truly against her will, little woman. Flossy went off
hoping for a letter from you. I don't know if she met the post,
but if not none came from either you or Meta today. I want to
write to Madame Mohl very much. So I dare say I shall end this
now. Only understand about Uncle Sam having 2£ to give you,
whenever you can catch him. 2£ advanced on yr allowance.
Ever your very affec[tionate]

E C Gaskell

I almost think we might get Cousin Mary for a week before
leaving S. you know (*if the Silverdale people agree to it*) that we
have put off going there till August 3, 4, or 6th.

252 252a 253

MARIANNE GASKELL[1]

Sat [14 July 1855]

My dearest Polly,
    Meta comes home on Monday, when I will get the measure of
her head; I kept this note unanswered yesterday expecting you
today to say something about going to Crix. Emily does not think
it will be convenient to them at the time you planned & if not I
suppose you would have liked this Lancaster Yeomanry gaiety—
But ⟨. . .⟩

---

[1] Written on a letter of 11 July from Eliza Thornborrow, referring to Mrs
Gaskell's coming visit on Tuesday, 31 July, or week following. ('The Yeomanry
come in on the 27th and there is generally a little visiting while they stay'.) 31 July
was a Tuesday in 1855.

252a **253** 259

MARIANNE GASKELL

[July 1855]

⟨...⟩ you say nothing about it, so I {believe you} have thought
it better to write to Miss T, & say that unless she hears from you
to the contrary in the next 3 or 4 days, we can not come till the
week beginning Augt 6th if that suits her. The children will not
like it I'm afraid *as you must join Meta & me* at Carnforth on
Augt 3 or 4th) to save carriages, & so they will have seen little or
nothing of you. Meta goes to Mrs Davy[']s on the 20th & Hearn
& children with her as far as Carnforth; we have taken lodgings
for them at Silverdale. Send us measure of *length* of new shifts, &
how many breadths in each, & *how wide* the linen or calico *in* the
breadth. I enclose 2 bills come for you. I have heard from Mrs
Jenkin, Fleeming is not coming back to Manchester.[1]

Ever your very affec[tionate] mother

E C Gaskell

Write soon with a regular bulletin of plans—\days, hours, dates./
Gay dress *is* required, as an element of Science.

0 **254** 0

UNKNOWN COUSIN

Plymouth Grove
Tuesday [?17 July ?1855][2]

My dear Jane,

I am so complicated full of engagements that I don't see any
chance whatever of accepting your very tempting invitation. Today, tomorrow, Thursday & Friday are all quite full\with engagements here/, & on Monday I go into Yorkshire on business,[3]—
come back, send Mr Gaskell off to Switzerland, go to Fox How,
back to Lancaster, thence to Silverdale, thence to Glasgow.[4] The

[1] See p. 363 below.
[2] Various hands have added dates and altered them on this letter. We agree
with the year 1855 only.
[3] The visit to Haworth on 23 July 1855, we assume.   [4] See Letters 251 and *267.

absolute *business* arrangements of these movements perplex me extremely, & are very difficult to settle. At Glasgow I go to see a step-mother & step-sister whom I have not seen for 25 years & more. Altogether I feel very full of travelling that *must* be done, and quite unable at present to arrange for any extra days, much as I should like it. Emily Shaen &c left yesterday, & Meta came home; but our house is abominable with paint and smells so badly that we have gladly accepted Mrs Shuttleworth's offer to let the children sleep there. I should like extremely to see Helen & her boy, & if her time wd fit mine,—which I fear it would not, I would try to see her on my way back from Glasgow, which I fancy must be by sea, on account of the expense. Thank you very much for asking me.

Ever dear Jane
Your affect[ionat]e cousin
E. C. Gaskell

My kindest love to Helen.

236 255 262

PARTHENOPE NIGHTINGALE

Plymouth Grove
Saturday. July 21 [1855]

My dear Miss Nightingale,
 I have been so sorry to see by your letter to Ly Hatherton that you have still such cause for anxiety.[1] I can not tell you how much I think of you, & of her. Of you more than of her, as is perhaps natural, for suspense is *so* difficult to bear. There is but one way of getting through it. The Bracebridges[2] are still with her, are not they? But however I don't ask any questions, which, if you knew how I should like to have some answered, is very good of me.

---

[1] Florence had been suffering from a 'compound fracture of the intellects' (*sc.* Crimean fever!). See *Correspondence of Arthur Hugh Clough*, ed. F. L.Mulhauser, 1956, II, p. 504.
 [2] Charles Holte Bracebridge and his wife Selina of Atherstone Hall (near Coventry) met Florence Nightingale in 1847. A strong friendship grew up between Selina and Florence, and the Bracebridges accompanied Florence to the Crimea. They left the Crimea on 28 July 1855. For details, see Woodham-Smith, *Florence Nightingale*, 1951.

I have tried at many places to get that 'Ratchda' man's visit to th' Great Exhibition', for Mr Nightingale; but it is out of print they tell me. If, however I can pick up an odd old copy I'll send it to you. Moreover I have been trying to sell Miss Stuart Mackenzie's Cameo to some of our rich Manchesterians but, thank you, it is not 'large' enough for them, & cutting & execution is nothing to size, so on Monday I am going to send it by *registered parcel post*, to the Charter House Square address. The other day I saw an engraving in a shop window across a Street, & knew it at once. I crossed over & saw the poor little bird of wisdom & saw it was your drawing by the initials in the corner. Babies ad libitum are being christened Florence here; poor little factory babies, whose grimed stunted parents brighten up at the name, although you'd think their lives & thoughts were bound up in fluffy mills. But it's the old story 'for we have all of us one human heart', & these poor unromantic fellows are made, somehow, of the same stuff as *her* heroes of the East, who turned their faces to the wall, & cried at her illness. I am vexed with myself for writing you so long a note. I only meant to tell you about the brooch.

Yours affectionately
E C Gaskell

245 256 261

GEORGE SMITH

Plymouth Grove
Thursday Eveng
[?July 1855]

My dear Sir,

Can you furnish me with the address of a Mr Taylor, a friend of Miss Brontë's, (one of the 'Yorke' family, in Shirley;) I thought I had it, but I can not find it. He lives somewhere near Leeds; and his sisters were at school at Brussels with Miss Brontë, & her sister Emily. One of these Miss Taylors died abroad; the other, Yorke like, on receiving her portion of her father's property, said she did not see why she was to be debarred from entering into trade because she was a woman, so, although she had a very fair income, she emigrated to Melbourne, I think; and there set up a large shop, which is doing very well indeed. I name these circumstances, which are probably known to you, in order to identify *the* Mr Taylor, whose address I want.

    I should be most glad of any recollections or account of Miss Brontë which your mother could furnish me with. I am en train for applying to Miss 'Temple'[1] of Jane Eyre, who is married to a clergyman holding a living on the estate of a friend of mine; I think that she may give me some particulars of that terrible Cowan-Bridge time, & possibly some explanations whh may modify that account of the school in Jane Eyre, which took such strong hold on the public mind, that it absolutely affected the health of Mr Carus Wilson[.] Great errors, there were no doubt; but I have heard dear Miss Brontë herself regret that her account had, as it were, so bitten into people's thoughts & recollections. Then for the Brussels time I wanted, if I could, to have either seen or corresponded with this Mr Taylor. Can you suggest any more people to whom I can apply, always exclusive of the information to obtain which I must question Mr Brontë, & hear what he has to say. I will take care, as she would have wished me to be, and be be [*sic*] very moderate & discreet in the use of any materials I may obtain. But until I can form some idea of the amount of information &c to be obtained I can not make any plan about her Life. I am very much afraid of not doing it as it ought to be done; distinct and delicate and thoroughly well. But I will do my very best. You know a great deal of her, at one time as a friend; can you suggest any further steps that I can take at present?

Yours very truly
E. C. Gaskell

o 257 *259a

ELLEN NUSSEY

Plymouth Grove
Manchester
[24] July [1855]

My dear Madam
    I don't know if you have heard of Mr Brontë's request to me that I would write the life of his daughter Mrs Nicholls, who was,

[1] Based on Miss Jane Thompson who taught English, Reading and Poetry.

I am well aware your dear and long-tried friend. But if you have been informed of this wish of Mr Brontë's you will not be surprized to hear that I went over to Haworth yesterday to see {Mr Brontë}\him/, and make the acquaintance of Mr Nicholls. I told Mr Brontë how much I felt the difficulty of the task I had undertaken, yet how much I wished to do it well, and make his daughter's most unusual character (as taken separately from her genius,) known to those who from their deep interest and admiration of her writings would naturally, if her life was to be written, expect to be informed as to the circumstances which made her what she was. Both he and Mr Nicholls agreed to this; Mr Brontë not perceiving the full extent of the great interest in her personal history felt by strangers, but desirous above all things that her life should be written, and written by me. (His last words were 'No quailing Mrs Gaskell! no drawing back!') Mr Nicholls was far more aware of the kind of particulars which people would look for; and saw how they had snatched at every gossiping account of her, and how desirable it was to have a full and authorized {account}\history/of her life if it were done at all. His feeling was against it's being written; but he yielded to Mr Brontë's impetuous wish; and brought me down all the materials he could furnish me with, in the shape of about a dozen letters addressed principally to her sister Emily; one or two to her father & her brother; and one to her aunt. The dates extend from 1839 to 1843. But Mr Nicholls said that he thought that you were the person of all others to apply to; that you had been a friend of his wife's ever since she was 15; and that he would write to you today, to ask if you would allow me to see as much of her correspondence with you as you might feel inclined to trust me with. But recalling since, how often she has spoken of you to me, I should like very much to make your personal acquaintance if you will allow me: and, if agreeable to you I would come over from Manchester on either Friday\July 27th/or Saturday\July 28/next\whichever was most convenient to you?/by the train that arrives at Birstall at $\frac{1}{4}$ past 10 in the morning. I do not know if your old schoolmistress Miss Wooler is yet alive and living in Birstall, but if so, I shall endeavour to see her, and Mr and Mrs Taylor. Believe me, dear Madam,

Yours very sincerely

E. C. Gaskell

239 **258** 264

JOHN GREENWOOD[1]

Plymouth Grove
Wednesday, July 25th [1855]

My dear Sir,

I was so extremely sorry that my plan of going to see you was baulked by a variety of unforeseen circumstances on Monday. We thought that we could have gone on to your house from the Church, to which we had asked Martha to take us; imagining that perhaps it might be too painful to Mr Nicholls to take us there; but he expressed a wish to go with us. Then we planned to call, as we were passing in the car on our way back to Keighley but just at last there was some necessary and unexpected business to be done, as Mr Nicholls brought me a few old letters of his wife's to see, and that kept us from starting when we expected to do. As it was we were too late, & had to sleep at Skipton that night.

I believe however that, as Mr Brontë has asked me to write his daughter's life that I shall soon have occasion to go over to Haworth again; probably from Sir James Kay-Shuttleworth's in August; when I shall make a point of coming to see you, at *first*, and not wait for an opportunity which it may be difficult to find at last. I am sure I may trust to you not to name *to any one*, the request that Mr Brontë has made to me of writing his daughter's life. I saw your likeness of Mr Brontë hanging in his study, opposite to the windows, and both the lady who was with me, & I were very much struck by the likeness. Believe me to remain dear Mr Greenwood ever yours very truly

E C. Gaskell.

[1] *Address (on envelope)* Mr J. Greenwood | 224 Haworth | near Keighley | Yorkshire. *Postmarks* MANCHESTER | JY 25 | 1855 *and* LEEDS | JY 26 | 1855 *and* KEIGHLEY | ⟨...⟩

253 **259** 273

MARIANNE GASKELL

[27 July 1855]
Friday Evening.

My dearest Polly,

These last few days have been so very busy in settling things
that I have not written anything but absolute business letters,—
which are after all accumulating very much; partly on account of
my having undertaken to write Miss Brontë's life. I am now
writing (past 6) & expecting the three Miss Bells, whom I met
yesterday in Collins' paper Shop, to tea every instant. They have
been staying for three weeks at Dr Bell's old house in Mosley St;
the doctor having removed to Northampton, & the furniture being
the Miss Bell's, they have come to pack it up. Maggie Bell is, they
say, very poorly—she was not with them yesterday. Are *you*
SURE, *before I forget, that Mrs James can take you in? because* Lady
Hatherton writes Meta word that Lady Kay-Shuttleworth is staying at the James's. I am very sorry to hear that Annie has got such
a cold; give my dear love to her; & to Louy & Emma & tell Louy
how glad I was to see Dr Allman's election. Papa said, a day or two
ago, that he was going to write and thank you for the Cap; has he
not done so? He was very much pleased with it; the band round
it was a little too tight, but Marianne Ross made it all right very
soon. He finished up his Home Mission with an address to the
Students in the Chapel on Tuesday Evening. On Saturday last, in
the *morning* Fleeming turned up. He has got a situation at Penn's,
Greenwich; some place as known near London, he says, as Fairbairn's here. He came down for three days to wind up his Manchester affairs entirely, & was very much disappointed that neither
you nor Meta were here to be wished goodbye to. I asked him to
tea on Sunday,—which I thought was a bold stroke, but however
he agreed to come. Papa went in the evening to dine with Uncle
Sam, Bobby Milnes & his Papa at the Albion. Remind me of
Bobby calling Mr Darbishire 'a good kind of fellow!' Sunday
both Uncle Sam & Mr Green came to dinner; Mr Green having
got a supply[,] came over to hear Papa preach; he was very jolly[.]
They were going to Derbyshire the next day for three or four

days, making Rowsley their head-quarters. 'They' being Mr &
Mrs Green, Emily & Ellen. We sent for Katie in [*sic*] Tommy.
(Poor Tommy! we have parted with him to Mr Lawson,—he is
gone this afternoon. I could not bear to wish him goodbye. The
children don't know.) Fleeming, Katie, Papa, & I made our party
at tea. For a wonder Papa & Fleeming talked to each other a good
deal. After tea we sauntered out in the garden, Fleeming saying
how he had counted on his Saturday Aft: calls for nearly 4 years,
& I saying how hot I used to feel when the tea-bell rang, & owing
to it's being Papa's busy day, I could not ask him to stay. He
praised up you & Meta. Capt. Madden is engaged to Miss Hornby.
He staid to supper, & then bid us goodbye,—really, fairly, finally
gone! His mother is abroad for 6 months. He himself means to
stay at Penn's for 9 months or a year, & then get some engagement {at} in Canada or Australia. On Monday Katie & I set out
in that broiling heat for Haworth, & got there about 1 o'clock.
It was a most painful visit. Both Mr Brontë & Mr Nicholls cried
sadly. I like Mr Nicholls. We left very late & got to Skipton that
night, dead tired. Slept there, & *overslept* ourselves there, for we
missed the first train & consequently did not get home till past 8,
wet, tired, cold, & hungry. Papa was out down at Chapel. I have
given him a water-proof over-coat. He has bought himself a grey
suit of clothes, a là Brigstocke, & looks uncommonly nice in them.
He goes to London (Euston Sq hotel on Monday, & stays there till
Wednesday, on account of his Foreign Office Passport. *Will you
get me Dr Perry's address.* Wednesday Katie left, and it rained all
day. I wrote to Miss Nussey a friend of Miss Brontë's from childhood, who has all her correspondence since she was 15, offering
to come & see her near Leeds, *today*; and I did not go out. Yesterday I shopped final shoppings all afternoon. I bought your linen
13 yds 2s—4d a yard (1-9-4, is it not?) but durst not venture on
the edging work—none were *less* than 15d a yard, & none of them
pretty. We all think a band of *insertion* without any edging so
much the prettiest. However Sarah is washing the linen today, &
when you see it you can fix, & at any rate there will be as good
a choice at Lancaster as here, I do believe. I enclose a nice note
from Mrs Wilson, which you may destroy. Miss Nussey is from
home,[1] so my going to Leeds is put off. I left Mrs Hensleigh
Wedgwood's card with mine at the Carpenter's, which Mrs W.

---

[1] On 26 July 1855 she wrote to Mrs Gaskell offering an appointment in early
August. See *The Brontës*, ed. Wise & Symington, IV, p. 193.

said was the proper thing—Miss Wilken is a poor cousin; companion & housekeeper. Now goodbye. Your ever affec[tionate]

E C Gaskell

*

₀ **260** ₀

UNKNOWN

Plymouth Grove
Manchester
July 27 [1855]

Dear Sir,

Thank you for your note; it is very pleasant to hear how much you have liked my books. Libbie Marsh is going to be published in a 2s. vol, which Chapman & Hall are making of my stories in Household Words, & other places. I drummed away at them to get this done, for so many friends asked me to have them collected. Moreover I asked them (Chapman & Hall are my present 'thems') to publish L. M. the Sexton's H. & 'Xmas Storms & Sunshine', 'Hand & Heart' (I hope you will like that) & 'Bessy's troubles' (rather good for nothing) in separate little penny or 2d pamphlets.[1] For these stories are all moral & sensible,—and one or two of the H W. stories might not so well do for young people. One is an unexplained ghost story for instance. I am glad to hear that these stories are liked by working-men & women in your parts; I sometimes get *here* the pleasantest little glimpses of their being liked; but I did not know how far Southrons would care for them. Why don't you come to Mr Maurice's then? And where do you preach? & (generally) who are you? a friend of Mr Maurice's, & of Charles Buxtons, you ought to be something. However I shall hear all about you from my cousin Miss Holland, & meanwhile I am

Yours truly
E C Gaskell.

[1] *Hand and Heart* and *Bessy's Troubles at Home* was published in paper covers in 1855.

₂₅₆ **261** ₂₆₉

GEORGE SMITH

Fox-How[1]
Ambleside
Wednesday [?1 August 1855]

My dear Sir,
    Only one line to thank you for your letter, & to remind you that the address for the letters you are going to send me, will be *from now to September 6th*   Lindeth Tower
Silverdale
near
Lancaster.
    Pray don't lose sight of any clue to her Brussels life,—Madame Hezer's [*sic*] Rue d' Isabelle.
    I hear Mme Hezer has lost all her pupils since the publication of Villette. In greatest haste,
Yours very truly
E C Gaskell.

₂₅₅ **262** ₂₆₃

PARTHENOPE NIGHTINGALE

Fox-How—Friday [?3 August 1855]

My dear Miss Nightingale,
    Thanks many for the letters forwarded here this morning,—& read aloud, (I might? might not I?) to a set of eager Arnold listeners. Every scrap & crumb is more than welcome—We are on our way to our summer holiday-keeping at Lindeth Tower, Silverdale, near Lancaster, where we go to-day, & where, if you will send the further details, I will take precious care of them, and send them back to you right speedily. I had not heard of the meeting in Switzerland place. I saw Miss Clough[2] the other day. She said she had heard a rumour of Mr & Mrs Sam Smith[3] going

---

[1] See arrangement forecast in Letter 254. The paper also supports an 1855 dating.
[2] Anne J. Clough (1820–92), sister of Arthur Hugh Clough, who married Sam Smith's daughter.
[3] Sam Smith was Florence's mother's brother. He married Mai, sister to Florence's father. They arrived at Scutari on 16 September 1855.

out? is it {not}\so/? The Bracebridges will stay, won't they? My kindest regards to Mr & Mrs Nightingale.

Yours most truly
E. C Gaskell

262 263 268

PARTHENOPE NIGHTINGALE

[?Summer 1855][1]

⟨. . .⟩ *have* you seen these\enclosed/lines? They have taken my fancy greatly; I think them very noble, & I have not a notion who wrote them; but I have copied them for you, because I thought I should like to make sure that you saw them. And that's the reason why I write this letter. And pray remember me most kindly to Mr & Mrs Nightingale—& believe me ever

Yours very affectionately
E. C. Gaskell

258 264 291

JOHN GREENWOOD[2]

Lindeth Tower
Silverdale, near
Lancaster
[c. 5 August 1855]

My dear Sir,

I was very glad indeed to receive your letter, & to find that you understood how the difficulty at the last moment had prevented my calling to see you. The lady with me was a Miss Catherine Winkworth, who has long been a great friend of mine, and who made our dear Miss Brontë's acquaintance at our house.

---

[1] Sir Edward Cook describes the exceptional popular reactions after Florence Nightingale's near fatal illness (May & August 1855) in his *Florence Nightingale*, I, pp. 264–75.

[2] *Address (on envelope)* Mr Greenwood | 224 Haworth | Keighley | Yorkshire. *Postmark* LANCASTER | AU 5 | 1855 | C.

Now I should be very much obliged to you if you will do me a favour, which is to copy for me that Tablet over the Communion table, exactly. I meant to have done it myself, but I could not well, with Mr Nicholls with me; and I fancy some of the dates Mr Brontë has given me (of Maria & Elizabeth's deaths,) are incorrect. I dare say I shall have many another kindness to ask from you; but just now I can only write in the greatest hurry. Pray remember me to Mrs Greenwood; whose forgiveness I can easily fancy will be more difficult than yours to gain for any fancied slight to her husband; and ever believe me

Yours very truly
E. C. Gaskell

*　　*

₀ 265 ₀

Mrs Alcock

Plymouth Grove,
August 13th 1855.

My dear Mrs Alcock,

Will it suit you if I come to you on next Saturday by the train that arrives (*from Skipton*) at Hornby at 3.42?

I should then hope to spend Sunday with you, & return to Silverdale, (which place I left this morning,) on Monday next, by either Lancaster or Milnthorpe according to your convenience in sending me to either Hornby, or Milnthorpe. Perhaps you would kindly let me know which arrangement would suit you best, as I should have to write to be met at either place, & unluckily we have no post on Sundays at Carnforth.

Until Thursday morning I shall be here; after then at Sir J. P. K. Shuttleworth's

Gawthorpe Hall
Burnley

\One of/My girls would have enjoyed accompanying me but they are engaged with young friends from the Lakes at Silverdale. With very kind regards to Mr Alcock, believe me dear Mrs Alcock,

Yours affectionately
E. C. Gaskell

₀ **266** ₀

UNKNOWN

We remain here till Sepr 4th

> Lindeth Tower
> Silverdale near
> Lancaster
> 23rd August [1855]

My dear Sir,

You once said you knew, or had heard, or had the means of hearing a good deal about Miss Brontë (Currer Bell.) Her father has requested me to write her life; and I want *every particular* I can collect,[1] not necessarily for publication, but to trust to my honour and discretion, and to enable me to form a picture of her character, & a drama of her life in my own mind. I want to know all I can respecting the character of the population she lived amongst,—the character of the individuals amongst whom she was known. (Taylors of Gomersall, the 'Yorkes' of Shirley, for instance. I want to know where Gomersall,\Birstall/Mirfield, Dewsbury Heckmondwike &c are, in relation to each others position. I want to know who were the Sedgewicks of Stonegappe near Bradford, the Whites near Leeds with whom she was governess. Who were the Robinsons (she now Lady Scott) near York? &c. You will think these vague wild enquiries; but the{y}\answers/are of consequence to me, & I think it possible you may in your kindness put them [*sic*] in the way of getting some of them answered. Are there any local publications giving an idea of the peculiar\customs &c-/character of the population towards Keighley, Haworth &c. I have got the life of Mr Grimshaw clergyman 100 years ago at Haworth.

You will *exceedingly* oblige me if you can assist me in this research. I am ashamed of giving you so much trouble but I throw myself on your kindness, & remain dear Sir

> Yours very truly
> E. C. Gaskell

[1] See *Letters and Memorials*, ed. Winkworth, I, p. 501, for a contemporary reference to Mrs Gaskell's success in this respect.

*264b **267** *267

ELLEN NUSSEY[1]

September 6th, 1855.

My dear Miss Nussey,—I have read *once* over all the letters you so kindly entrusted me with, and I don't think even you, her most cherished friend, could wish the impression on me to be different from what it is, that she was one to study the path of duty well, and, having ascertained what it was right to do, to follow out her idea strictly. They gave me a very beautiful idea of her character. I like the one you sent to-day much. I shall be glad to see any others you will allow me to see. I am sure the more fully she— Charlotte Brontë—the *friend*, the *daughter*, the *sister*, the *wife*, is known, and known where need be in her own words, the more highly will she be appreciated.—Yours faithfully,

E. C. Gaskell.

*

263 **268** 279

PARTHENOPE NIGHTINGALE

Plymouth Grove, Oct. 3. [1855]

My dear Miss Nightingale,

    I am so sorry—so *very* sorry to decline coming, but I ought not to leave home again so soon. It is a very great temptation on many scores, and I should dearly like it, only I must not, & it is a shame even to feel temptation so strongly in opposition to duty, when writing to a Nightingale.

    Please ask me again, sometime to Lea-Hurst. I wrote a long letter to Mme Mohl last night, & have re-directed it this morning. Do urge her to come to us; she would tell us all about you and yours, as well as being herself.

---

[1] From a typescript source. However, a fuller text of this letter is now printed in Appendix A.

I do think I am so good. I should like to put a mark of admiration after my name. I will. I am

Yours affectionately
E. C. Gaskell!

My kind regards to Mr & Mrs Nightingale[.] Please thank them for me. And when you have time a crumb from Scutari[.]

*

261 **269** 270

GEORGE SMITH

Plymouth Grove.
October 10th [1855]

Dear Sir,

I am becoming very anxious to receive any materials you find you can furnish me with for my memoir of Miss Brontë. I want to know what I have to build up my life upon, before I begin upon the Sketch which I have prepared.

Yours very truly
E. C. Gaskell.

269 **270** 271

GEORGE SMITH

42 Plymouth Grove.
October 20th '55

Dear Sir,

Relying on your promise of putting at my disposal any papers or letters in your possession which might assist me in writing my Memoir of Miss Brontë, I wrote to you *ten days* ago to claim its fulfillment; and I have been both surprised & disappointed that so long a time has elapsed without your forwarding me the promised materials.

Believe me, dear Sir,
Yours truly
E. C. Gaskell.

*

270 **271** 284

GEORGE SMITH

Plymouth Grove—
Sunday. [?Late October ?1855]

Dear Sir,

I write a hasty line to acknowledge the receipt of the packet of
Miss Brontë's letters, with many thanks for the loan of them.

I have a series of 350 to one friend,[1] the earliest being written
in 1832, & continued up to a few days before her death.

Yours truly
E. C. Gaskell

P.S. I almost fancy that I have material enough, or nearly enough,
gathered together to enable me to make a vol: about the size of
Carlyle's Life of Sterling: but of course I can not tell at present.—
I *think* that what I have already got ready would be too long for
any prefatory notice to any of her works; and 'the Professor' Mr
Nicholls would not allow me to see, saying that whole pages of it
had been embodied in Villette. She had 50 pages or so of a new
tale written at the time of her death.[2] Will you let me know when
your mother returns? I should like to see her.

*

₀ **272** ₀

MARGARET WOOLER

Plymouth Grove
Manchester,
Monday Novr 12th [?1855]

My dear Miss Wooler,

I am sure you will be glad to hear that your valuable parcel
of letters was received in safety, and that I promise that the utmost
care shall be taken of them, and that they shall be returned to you
before very long. I hardly know how it is, but I like them better
than any other series of letters of hers that I have seen; (a few to
'Emily' those to Miss Nussey, and some to Mr Smith;) I am sure

[1] Ellen Nussey.   [2] *Emma.*

you will allow me to apply to you with any questions that may suggest themselves to me in the course of my work, which is getting on but slowly, owing to the pressure of business of other kinds that has been weighing upon me.

I hope you and your hostess continue as well satisfied with each other, as you spoke of being when I had the pleasure of seeing you at Brookroyd.

Believe me ever to remain dear Madam,

Yours respectfully & truly

E. C. Gaskell.

177 *and* 259 **273** 278*a*[1]

MARIANNE and MARGARET EMILY GASKELL

Church House
Saturday morning [?Late 1855]

My dearest girls,

I am very sorry I did not write yesterday, but I was so much tired, & people were here, Mary Worthington (staying) & Miss Brandreth calling &c,—so it slipped through. I got SAFELY! to Altringham, then in the 'bus I sate next to somebody, whose face I thought I knew, & then I made out it was only that he was very like Mr Hensleigh Wedgwood; however he read 'Little-Dorrit' & I read it over his shoulder. Oh *Polly*! he was such a slow reader, *you*'ll sympathize, Meta won't, my impatience at his *never* getting to the bottom of the page so we only got to the end of the page. *We* only read the first two chapters, so I never found out who 'Little Dorrit' is, only the story opens in a prison at Marseilles, a Swiss & an Italian prisoner getting their dinners. 2nd chap. English characters introduced in quarantine at Marseilles[,] heroine's name Pet Meagles, had a little dead twin sister, the remembrance of whom is always pricking her relations up to virtue, & who, I suspect, is 'little Dorrit'. By this time we got to Knutsford, & my friend got out, & now that I saw him no longer in profile but full-faced I recognized Mr Seymour, & was sorry I had not moved. Cousin Susan came to meet me, & Jackson, & then we came home & had lunch (hot coffee, so good!) & found Mr Worthington staying here, but going at 4. Then Susan read

[1] To Marianne; to Meta, see Letter 487.

us a letter from Maggie, giving an account of their evening at Mrs Stanleys. *They* were the 'Cologne singers', not the real true people who are in Cologne. The 4 girls sang their quartet, without accompaniment, & were complimented by Jenny Lind & Benedict, who told them he had written trios for 3 female voices which he recommended them to get, & Jenny Lind said, '& if you do, I will come & hear you sing, & sing to you again.' *She* sang 'John Anderson my jo, & some Swedish air which seems to have charmed them. They are going to the Creation, & to the Haymarket & to Jullien; Cousin Susan goes to London next week, to the C Buxtons first, where Arthur joins her, & they all come back just before Xmas. From Cousin Susan's account Mrs H. Long has behaved *very* shabbily about taking the evening the Deans wished to have, & I'm glad you're not going to her house. But by the way the Greens have altered their day to '*one a week later*' to use Miss Brandreth's expression, (I've seen none of them as yet,) because of Mr Arthur Darbishire's note, which was 'very pretty indeed' (says Miss B.) & because the Thornleys & Holts can't come, on account of family gatherings. Miss Brandreth was quite clear about all this much, but the exact day she did not seem to know. Cousin Mary *thought* Mr Green had said the 7th or 8th. We had a great deal of laughing at Cousin Susan for having called on Mrs Erskine, who lives in one of the\newish/houses on the Heath. It seems she was a Miss Spode, pottery-makers, friends (I believe⟨⟩) & *rivals* of the Wedgwoods in Staffordshire, *but* she drinks like a fish; the Clowes brought her here, & had a school-feast to which people round about were asked, & Mrs E. was seen sitting with her children grouped about her, & Mrs Clowes said she 'was the wife of a distinguished officer, now fighting his country's battles in the C.' Susan went to call on her, soon after, & had heard that the 51 were at Malta; 'You must be very thankful, Mrs E. that they were not in that fearful attack on Sebastopol Sepr 8!' 'Oh! but think of the chances of promotion the Major has missed'. Then Susan recommended another house to her, Mrs E. said 'Yes! but they won't let it for less than a year, & I can't take a house for more than 3 months, because you know the Major may very likely be killed before the end of that time.' She has a baby; and 3 or 4 little boys, & a little girl or two, eldest about 13. The Clowes are 'desperate intimate' with her, although nearly everybody else has dropped her, her character is so notorious. Curious enough there is a Lady Erskine, wife of Lord E, her husband's eldest brother living at Bollington, who tipples & 'gets squiffy' just like *this* Mrs E. Yours was the only note I got this morng—& I know no more news. My love to Minnie. Write & tell me *all* about your visit. I will keep this note open to see if I hear of the exact fixing of the day. Ever your very affect[ionate] mammy

E C G

Mary has a class of her\school/children teaching them singing downstairs. I don't know what *words* they are singing, but the *tune* is The Ratcatcher's Daughter. The tune came from Mary Harvey who sang the 'Ratcatcher's daughter at all the Knutsford parties.' 'it was encored two or three times every evening.'

Now they're singing 'Pop goes the Weasel' to the concertina. 'The Ratcatcher's daughter' is made into a Quadrille[.] Now it's 'Tinkle Tankle Titmouse'[.]

₀ 274 ∗314ₐ

W. S. WILLIAMS[1]

Plymouth Grove,
Decr. 15th [1855]

Dear Sir,

I am extremely obliged to you for the pacquet of Miss Brontë's letters which I found here on my return home, too late for Friday's post for me to acknowledge them. I have read them hastily over and I like the tone of them very much; it is curious how much the spirit in which she wrote varies according to the correspondent whom she was addressing, I imagine. I like the series of letters which you have sent better than any other excepting one that I have seen. The subjects too are very interesting; how beautifully she speaks (for instance) of her wanderings on the moors after her sister's death. I am extremely obliged to you, sir, for your kindness in sending them to me, and I will take great care of them as long as they are in my keeping.

I can fancy from the way in which you speak that your son's career in Australia has not been so prosperous as at one time perhaps both you and he hoped it might have been; but if you lived

---

[1] Original MS. not seen.

in such a town as this you would see how terribly injurious to young men mere worldly prosperity too often becomes. Still, Australia is a long way off, and his prolonged absence from you and his mother must, I am sure, be a trial to both you and him. Will you remember me to him when you write? Mr Gaskell thought he recognised him again in another Mr Williams whom he met with at Chamounix this summer; he still thinks it must have been Mr Frank Williams' brother to whom he spoke, the likeness was so great. Believe me to remain,

Yours truly and obliged,
E. C. Gaskell.

204 275 278

R. MONCKTON MILNES

Plymouth Grove
Sunday, Decr 16. [1855]

My dear Sir,

Though I have not yet got all the information about Mr French which I hope to obtain, yet I don't like to put off answering your note any longer. Mr French[1] has published the pamphlet for private circulation only; it is in substance the expansion of a communication made by Mr French some time since to the Gentleman's Magazine—A paper,—embodying the same facts, if not identically the same,—appeared in Chambers' Journal, March 6th 1841; and some late controversy in Notes & Queries has led to it's appearance in it's present form.

Mr French was a protegè{e} of Pugin's, and is I think an ecclesiastical architect, as well as a manufacturer of articles of Church furniture 'See advertisement'; in which branch of trade he has obtained so great a reputation that the Bolton cotton manufactures have lately assumed an oddly mediæval (all the letters *are* in,) character. Mr French has written 6 or 8 pamphlets on the

---

[1] Gilbert French (1804–66) communicated to *The Gentleman's Magazine* (July 1840) a sketch of the story of James Annesley, showing the resemblances between this and the history of Henry Bertram in *Guy Mannering*. This was reprinted in *Chambers' Journal* as stated above and then published in an expanded form separately in 1855 as 'Parallel Passages from Two Tales elucidating the Origin of the Plot of "Guy Mannering" '. See p. 379 below.

Archæology of Church Furniture. We don't know him personally, and hear various accounts of his judgement or folly according
to the High, Low or Broad Church or Dissenting tendencies of
our informants. I myself believe him to be a very ingenious man,
with a good deal of imagination\strongly excited on ecclesiastical
subjects/which has directed his powers into a very narrow channel;
but I believe him to be a conscientious authority.

'So much for Buckingham
Off with his head.'[1]

And now to the little mite of a Florence Milnes. I hope her
name may bring her a deep blessing. I suppose she ought to have
been a boy, and therefore has failed in her duty in the first instance; but I think you have done your best to remedy this first
defect of hers by giving her such a name. I wish I could tell you
that I saw much chance of *present* contributions to the Nightingale
fund; there is a great deal of latent enthusiasm, which came to the
surface at first, and exists still; but there is so very much distress
of all kinds close around just now,—and will be, till the preparations for the Spring trade gives [*sic*] business a fillip,—so that just
now would be a bad time to propose any subscriptions, not
immediately relating to this district. At any period I think one or
two people who have been directly acquainted with the details of
her conduct, (Mr Bracebridge for instance,) would bring out all
the gratitude which I am sure is felt towards her if they would
come & speak at a public meeting. I should like to hear the rounds
of applause which I believe our Lancashire work-people would
give to any one,—Mr Bracebridge Mr Stafford or S. G. O[sborne]
—who would come & tell them what they themselves saw &
heard, & what *she* did,—but no one has come here—as they have
done to other places—to tell the living truth as it stamped itself
upon their hearts—When people talk of the coldness of Manchester people, they should remember they have never had the
advantage of seeing any one, face to face, who has witnessed her
doings. We have many plebeian 'Florences'; and only this week I
have been spoken to by a poor pale stunted workman with almost
a fine indignation because, being of the same race, & holding the
same form as Florence Nightingale I & other women were what we
were, while she is what she is. I have a great deal more I shd like
to say to you,—about Miss Brontë, & 2 other sets of letters—about
Lord and Lady Ellesmere,—but it is getting dark, & I am afraid

[1] 'Off with his head! So much for Buckingham!'—C. Cibber, *Richard III*, IV, iii.

besides of taking up too much of your time. May I send my kind
regards to Mrs Milnes? Mr Gaskell desires his to you.

Yours very truly

E. C. Gaskell

*

•275+ **275a** •275a

ELLEN NUSSEY[1]

[*c.* 20 December 1855]

['To Miss Nussey a few days later[2] she wrote that she was most
anxious to see her. She had been very busy lately as there had been
a succession of callers at the house, and one of the maids had been
taken ill. She had not heard a word from Haworth since the
previous August but was hoping to get over to see Mr Brontë and
Mr Nicholls before Spring. Then she speaks of Charlotte Brontë's
letters to Mr Williams as being'] very fine and genial. She seems
heartily at her ease with him, which I don't think she does in those
I have seen to Mr Smith. ⟨. . .⟩ good[3] for nothing, or I would
have written sooner. My kind love to your sister. Your help and
sympathy do me a great deal of good in my perplexing search for
materials. How is Miss Wooler?

Yours most truly,

E. C. Gaskell

Any chance of borrowing Scatcherd's History of Birstall etc?
Are not *you* Caroline Helstone?

---

[1] This letter has been made up from two sources: J. Coolidge's typescript *Life
and Letters* (Brotherton Library) and a typed copy of a letter in the Brotherton
Library Shorter Collection. This admittedly tenuous connexion proved to be no
connexion at all when letters now appearing in Appx A became available. The
first passage forms part of Letter 275a and the second the end of 271a, both of
which will be found in Appx A.

[2] After 15 December 1855 letter to Williams.

[3] Shorter Collection fragment begins.

250 **276** 370a

ELIZA FOX[1]

Plymouth Grove,
Monday. [*c.* 1 Jan. 1856]

My dearest Tottie,

You ask for the petition back again without loss of time, so I send it you although today certainly I shan't be able to write a long letter, I don't think it is very definite, and *pointed*; or that it will do much good,—for the Turnkey's objection (vide Little Dorrit)[2] 'but if they wish to come over her, how then can you legally tie it up' &c. will be a stronger difficulty than they can legislate for[;] a husband can coax, wheedle, beat or tyrannize his wife out of something and no law whatever will help this that I see. (Mr Gaskell begs Mr Fox to draw up a bill for the protection of *husbands* against wives who will spend all their earnings) However our sex is badly enough used and legislated *against*, there's no doubt of *that*—so though I don't see the definite end proposed by these petitions I'll sign. I could say a great deal more, but have my own heart chock full of private troubles and sorrows just now,—a very little more and this letter would go to you wet with my tears. However its no use maundering,—and *perhaps* some day long hence, if you'll remind me of Xmas and New Year 1856 I may tell you a sad little story which only concerns me indirectly. I *will* write you a very long letter soon.

Yours very affect[tionately]
E. Gaskell.

*   *

0 **277** 0

MR RICHIES[3]

Plymouth Grove,
January 9th [1856]

Dear Mr Richies,

I wonder if you received the Gilbert French intelligence, and the copy of the Guy Mannering pamphlet I sent you about three

[1] Original MS. not seen.   [2] See Book I, c. VII.
[3] Original MS. not seen.

weeks ago? For I find from Mr Scott that I put quite a wrong address upon the [?], namely, *Grosvenor* instead of *Brook* Street.

Yours very truly,

E. C. Gaskell

275 **278** 287

R. MONCKTON MILNES

Plymouth Grove—
Sunday. [13 January 1856]

My dear Sir,

The Meeting[1] is held at the Town-Hall, on Thursday next, at 11 o'clock a.m. I *believe* the Mayor, 'James Watts' is to be Chairman. He is a new man, and new Mayor, unknown to most people here, as most of our Mayors are; they, being principally risen men, who are willing to give two or three thousand £ for the privilege of being Mayor, & the power which it gives them of getting into society. This Mr Watts has made a large fortune by manufacturing old pictures for the American Market,—& has built a splendid house—called *Abney* House, out of gratitude to Lady Abney who befriended his ancestor the Hymn Dr Watts. He is either an Independent or Methodist, I am not sure which, but he belongs to some rather Strict Dissenting body; still he must have wit in him, for the story goes that, on rummaging up a crest just lately, he was asked for a motto, & gave '*What's* in a name?'

Mr Sydney Herbert is to be his guest, & on Wednesday the solemn Magnates of the Corporation are asked to meet him at dinner at Abney House.

In the notice placarded about & in the advertisement there is no mention of *who* is to be Chairman at the Meeting; but Mr Gaskell thinks it is certain to be the Mayor. He has never spoken before in public, and the strings of most Mayors' opinions are pulled by Mr Heron the Town Clerk.[2]

I don't know if the offer of your old bed-room will be any accomodation [*sic*] (I *hope* you will come,) but if it will be, Mr

[1] The Manchester Nightingale Fund Meeting on 17 January 1856. *Annals*, ed. Axon, p. 269.

[2] Joseph Heron, first Town Clerk of Manchester, appointed in 1838, became consulting Town Clerk, 1885.

Gaskell begs me to make it, and to tell you how glad we shall be to have you once more as our guest.

Will you thank Mrs Milnes for her kind little note?

Yours truly

E. C. Gaskell.

273 278a 283

MARIANNE GASKELL[1]

Wednesday [?16 January 1856]

My dearest Polly,

I am disappointed not to have heard from you; but I write to say I shall come back {before} by the train *leaving here* at ½ past 9, tomorrow, & you must please send Will down to meet it & take charge of my box,\it comes in at 10, or a *very* few minutes later[;] if I am gone from the Station tell him to ask for my box/as I shall go straight to Satterfield's from the Station; where you & Meta must come to meet me, if you want to go to the Meeting. We are going at 12 to the Old Church at Alderley. The notes Hearn forwarded were from Miss Jewsbury, Eliza Thornborrow, & Cousin Susan, with the enclosed pieces for you. None from Mr M Milnes; so I suppose he is not coming, though if I were you & housekeeper\at home/for today, I should light a fire in the spare-room to have it ready for all chances.

Your very affect[ionate]

E C G

205a 278b 502a

HENRY MORLEY

Alderley,

Janry 16 [1856]

My dear Mr Morley,

Using my travelling writing case, (which I do not often do excepting when I am from home,) I come upon a letter of yours, received, when I was in Scotland in Sepr,[2] recommending a Miss

---

[1] Associated with Letter 278, we believe.   [2] See Letter *267.

Helen Clarke. I kept expecting her to call upon me after my return home, as I heard that she had never been during my absence; and so it has gone on till this morning, when on re-reading your letter I find you give me her address (7 Pleasant Sq) in a little nook of the crossing. Now if I had seen this before I should have either written to her, or made an attempt to see her; as it is, I have just kept on making a few enquiries in likely quarters for such a situation as I thought would suit her, and if I had heard of such a one I should have written to you. Is she still in Manchester? (I shall be at home tomorrow); does she still want a situation—not that I know of one, I am sorry to say; only I might perhaps be of some comfort to her, if I managed to see her, & if she is still in Manchester.

Did you ever hear how Mrs Wedgwood & I toiled & broiled in search of the very mysterious place where you live; (Mr Furnivall having given us your address)—last April,—and just as we must have been in sight of the New Hampstead Road, had to turn back for our time was up, & people were awaiting us at home?

Has Miss Vi got a brother or a sister?

Yours very truly

E C Gaskell.

268 **279** 300

PARTHENOPE NIGHTINGALE

Thursday [Friday, 18 January 1856]

My dear Miss Nightingale

I don't know where you are, but I suppose the Post will be able to find you and I am sending you a Manchester newspaper and just a few lines to say *how* well the Meeting went off yesterday! We had been afraid, for all sorts of small disheartening reports had been spread; threats of Low Church opposition[1] &c,—but all went off splendidly—the ladies (stupid creatures) did not fill the space alloted to them; but the men more than did,—& at 12, when some of the mills 'loose' their workpeople, plenty of grimy hands came in, all ready to cheer and applaud *their* heroine—for they feel her as theirs, their brother's nurse, their dead friend's friend,—in a

---

[1] For religious differences about F. N.'s work, see Woodham Smith, *Florence Nightingale*, pp. 143–4.

way which they don't know how to express. '*You* benevolent
ladies! Why you women all play at benevolence—Look at
Florence Nightingale—there's a woman for you.' That was a
speech made to me not long ago; and it was so true I could say
nothing, but keep humble silence. It is now Saturday, so much
have I been interrupted,—& you will have had the newspaper
before this, I hope. Mr Sydney Herbert spoke well, though he
was so anxious, in compliance with the practical nature of the
Manchester people I suppose,—to confine himself to facts, that
there was not the laisser aller, which I had anticipated, and which
must be there, to distinguish eloquence from argument or logic.
Lord Stanley speaks with difficulty, and mouths a great deal to
make his articulation distinct; but it was a noble and grave speech.
Dear Mr Milnes! his speech warmed my heart the most. He evidently forgot us all, in bringing up before himself *pictures* of former
days; of Florence Nightingale as a girl in her father's house,—of
his early knowledge of her, &c. His face grew quite pale, & you
forgot the fat in the features—the eyes fixed on bye-gone scenes,
not on all our poor upturned faces,—eyes, & nostrils quite dilated,
when he spoke of God's holy Providence calling the great heroes
& heroines of the world out of private life, out of deep self-
unconsciousness to do His service.

Well! all words are poor in speaking of her acts. I can only say
once more God bless her and you. There was a poor lady by me,
who bowed her head down on her hands, and shook all over with
her sobs. I don't know who she was,—or why she sobbed, unless
it was in very fervency of blessing.

Yours truly & affectionately

E C Gaskell—

₀ **280** ₀

UNKNOWN

42 Plymouth Grove
Manchester
Feb. 9 [1856]

Dear Sir

In a letter which my husband received from you, dated
September 23 1853, you very kindly expressed your willingness
to contribute 5£ annually towards the sum (50£) which we

hoped to raise each year for Miss Mitchell. May I be allowed to remind you that your subscription for 1856 is due? When the arrangements were all made Miss Mitchell's state of health was such (owing to a heart complaint,) that the doctor attending her desired that every cause for anxiety that could be removed, might be obviated; and accordingly, in compliance with the advice of my cousin Miss Holland & Mrs Sam Greg I told her of the sum which some friends of hers hoped to raise annually; I was almost afraid to see the tearful emotion of gratitude which succeeded; and she begged me earnestly to express her thanks to those, whose names she guessed, although we had agreed that they should be withheld from her.

Mr Gaskell thought it better to place the whole matter at once on a business footing, & to pay her 12£,-10s, quarterly; which he has done. And I do believe if you could all know how much you have done to smooth away a very natural care & anxiety from the last years of as good and as Christian a woman as ever was, you would be very much touched & gratified. Her health is better, though it can never be strong. She lives in a small house where her only lodgers are old Mr Turner (aged 94,) and his companion Miss Howarth. When Mr Turner dies the sum she receives with him will cease of course, and unless she can meet with another lodger, paying equally well, her only dependence will be on the 50£. I told her plainly out the wish which we all felt, that no one else should benefit by our contributions; and she very seriously promised that our desire on this head should be attended to. She keeps one servant; does all the cooking herself; I am sure, Sir, you will excuse this long letter. I thought you ought to know all the particulars I could give you of our dear old friend.

Yours truly
E C Gaskell

*

o 281 o

ELIZABETH BARRETT BROWNING

Plymouth Grove
March 8th [1856]

My dear Mrs Browning,

The bearer of this note is a Mr Darbishire a great friend of ours, who is stopping for a few days in Paris on his way to Italy, where he will reside for a few months. I have told him that I think it probable that you & Mr Browning, from your long residence in Italy, may be able to give him a little advice as to his proceedings there; and I should also be very much obliged to you if you would give him a few letters of introduction, which may procure him admission into the atéliers of artists. It is so very awkward to make a young man the bearer of his own praises that I shall only add that I do not think that any one who makes our friend's acquaintance will have cause to regret it—and that I only wish Mr Story had been at Rome, as I think that he and Mr Darbishire would have found pleasure in each other's society.

Believe me to remain, dear Mrs Browning,

Yours most truly

E. C. Gaskell.

I have written (a week ago) to Mrs Jameson to ask for letters of introduction for Mr Darbishire, but I suppose she is not at Ealing: as I have had no reply.[1]

₀ 282 ₀

TICKNOR & FIELDS[2]

Plymouth Grove

Manchester

March 14th 1856

Messrs Ticknor & Fields

Gentlemen—

I must sincerely apologize for my negligence in\not/replying to your first communication, received some weeks ago, but unfortunately I mislaid the letter and therefore was unable to answer it—

I have promised the early sheets of the life of Miss Charlotte Brontë to Messrs Appleton & Co New York who offered me £75 for it.

Their proposal I received before your first communication reached me—

I have the honour to be

Gentlemen

Yours sincerely

E. C. Gaskell—[3]

[1] See p. 407 below.   [2] Written in (?Mrs Gaskell's) formal hand.
[3] See Letter 386 and notes.

278a **283** *286a

MARIANNE GASKELL

Tuesday [?29 April 1856]

Dearest MA,

Only a line to say yesterday was very successful. You are to
write to Cousin Louisa 18 Clifford St when you come back to
London & she will ask Caroline Holland to dine with you. *No
letter either from Papa or E. Thornborrow* today which puts me sadly
out. I can arrange *nothing*, & Mrs Haydon (Brussels) is wanting an
answer all this time.[1] Oh! how I wish people wd write! I have
written to Papa every day; I don't even know if he will let Meta
go. What *I should like* would be to accept Ly C's invitation for
self Hearn & children—(I don't quite like putting Meta in although
(or rather *as*) Ly C is so hospitable & I shd have half a bed,) on
Friday; I to stay there till Antwerp packet sails at *12* Sunday noon,
& Hearn & children till Monday, so as to hear Kensington Garden
band which they missed last Sunday—then we could go to
Windsor on Friday, & to Duckworths to lunch on Saty[.]
Minna has sent to beg we will go there some day. But all is
un[c]ertain till I hear from Papa, E T & *when Meta comes*, she
must be here to go to debate on Thursday ¼ {to}\past/4 Westminster Hall. I have never heard from Mr Heywood about
Drawing-room Corridor, and we have waited in all morning, it
is today[—]hoping for the tickets. As it is[,] I must take children
to Uncle Sam's lodgings, afterwards to Panorama, then\send
them/to the Wedgwoods, & Tottie to tea with me. Tomorrow
Hampton Court. Thursday Meta & I & they to lunch-dinner at
18 Clifford St. Think & plan for me for I am utterly worn out &
perplexed. Thanks many for your note to E T darling. I shall use
it, when I can fix—I mayn't be able to write tomorrow for I want
to go off *early* to Hampton Court, & yet if Papa's & E. T's letters
come I shall have to write many letters, E. T, Brussels &c.

I heard the 'pretty' Miss Gaskell, & my 'beautiful daughter'
(rather *stumpy* it must be owned) twice enquired about yesterday.
Once by Mrs Gleig whom I rummaged out in Cousin Louisa's

---

[1] On two pages of this MS. is a note from Ma[rianne] Leisler, dated 22 April
1886 [1856], concerning Mrs Gaskell's projected visit to Brussels.

carriage—the Maxwells are in town for Ly Matilda's health—&
by Mrs Rich, where Miss Tollet is staying, & where I also went to
see her. I do *so* like her, E T I mean. She was engaged with Mrs
A. Clive when I got there, who wants to know *me*, so I'm going
with Mrs Rich on return from Brussels. Any number of offers of
'Studios' for Meta—*Wrapper never come.* Such a plague.

Ever your most affect[ionate]

E C G

Any letter *in reply* to this will reach on Thursday morning\break-
fast time/

271 284 286

GEORGE SMITH

Tuesday [?29 April 1856]

Dear Sir,

I am extremely obliged to you for your note which has caught
me just before I am going out, & which has 'heartened me' as we
say in the North, extremely, for I was & am very anxious to do
it thoroughly *well*, as anything about her ought to be done. I
don't mind how much I labour at it, only I am vexed to find on
reading it over, that my English is so bad. But it *shall* be good
before I have done.

I am sorry to decline seeing you at present. It was for that
reason that I did not give you my address. I am in London, i.e.
Chelsea, to show my two little girls London—in the true Country
cousin sense of the expression,—and every day is planned cramfull,—we have only been found in this morning because we have
been waiting for tickets for the Drawing-room Corridor. Tomorrow we are off very early to Windsor Hampton Court &
Kew. On Friday they either go home (most probable,) or we all
adjourn to Ly Coltman's till Monday,—when I go to Brussels *at
the latest*—I may go on Friday. I am declining *all* invitations till
my return, as I do not wish to separate myself from my children,—
& consequently however great the temptation I could not accept
your kind proposal to meet Mrs Smith. Moreover I have warned
all my friends, who know my address, off the premises,—for my
time just now is occupied with Gog & Magog, Cunningham's

Handbook,[1] and I am putting all business & pleasure on one side.

I have been hunting up & down Brussels, vicariously, in search of these very Wheelwrights,—do you think I may call on them when I come back—or had I better MAKE time to go *before* Friday? I should be glad if you wd answer this qustion. I am very much obliged to you for the pamphlet—It looks most interesting. —I shall, now I think of it—certainly be at Ly Coltman's, if only to wish her goodbye, before I leave, though I can't tell when,— and is not that\Hyde Park Gardens/near Kensington & the Wheelwrights?—

I am so ignorant of locality hereabouts that perhaps I am mistaken—or is it near the Tom Taylor's, Hereford Sq; or near Princes Terrace, to both of which places I must make my way on Thursday or Friday.

You now know quite as much about the uncertainty & whirl of my movements as I do myself. I have just sent you off a parcel by the Delivery Company.

Yours truly
E C Gaskell.

o **285** ₂₉₀

LAETITIA and — WHEELWRIGHT

3 Parham Place
King's Road
Chelsea
Wednesday morning [?30 April 1856]

Mrs Gaskell presents her compliments to the Miss Wheelwrights, and requests permission to call upon them about 10 o'clock tomorrow morning, with a view to making some enquiries from them, before proceeding to Brussels, whither she is going early in next week, to ascertain all the particulars she can, relating to Miss Brontë's residence there. She will feel *extremely* obliged to the Miss Wheelwrights if they will suggest any clues to information there.

*

[1] Peter Cunningham, *A Handbook for London, Past and Present*, 2 vols., 1849.

284 **286** 289

GEORGE SMITH

Monday morning
8 Hyde Park Gardens
[?5 May 1856]

Dear Sir,

I am extremely obliged to you for your note, although it suggests a long discussion about Mr Brontë, which I should like to have with you on my return.

I have seen Miss Wheelwright. I am very much obliged to you for your kind present of Mr Rawdon Brown's[1] book, and for the Chevr Bunsen's[2] both of which I shall much value. The latter work was sent me by the author, but in the original language, which unfortunately I can not read. In greatest haste, I remain

Yours very truly
E. C. Gaskell

*

278 **287** 388

R. MONCKTON MILNES

17 Cumberland Terrace
Regts Park
May 31st [?1856]

Dear Mr Milnes,

May I bring Meta some morning to look at your Blakes?[3] You once said that I might; and that you would let us come, as you once allowed me to do before,—without thinking it necessary that either you or Mrs Milnes should give up your time to me;—but letting me be turned loose into a room by myself.

Yours very truly
E C Gaskell.

---

[1] The book nearest in date by Rawdon Brown would appear to be his translation of *Five Years at the Court of Henry VIII . . . 1515–19* by Sebastian Giustinian, 1854.

[2] Bunsen, *Signs of the Times: Letters on Religious Liberty*, Smith & Elder. Susanna Winkworth received an early copy on [Monday,] 5 May 1856. *Letters and Memorials*, ed. Winkworth, II, p. 26. [3] See p. 398 below.

₀ **288** ₀

Mrs Milman

17 Cumberland Terrace
Friday, June 6th [?1856]¹

My dear Mrs Milman,
I am very sorry indeed to be obliged to decline your very kind invitation to breakfast on Thursday next,—I should have been delighted to avail myself of it, but I engaged myself this morning for breakfast on that day at Lord Stanhope's
Believe me to remain, dear Mrs Milman.
Yours very truly
E. C. Gaskell

₂₈₆ **289** ₂₉₃

George Smith

17 Cumberland Terrace
Regt Park
Friday June 13. [1856]

My dear Sir—
I am going to breakfast at 10 o'clock next Tuesday morning with the Milmans, at the Deanery St Paul's,—I suppose the breakfast will be over about 12,—if I came to you, *Cornhill*—could you go with me to the Chapter Coffee house² then?
In greatest haste
Yours very truly
E C Gaskell

¹ Mrs Gaskell did not appear to know the Milmans before 1853, so the possible years are 1856 and 1862. The address makes the former probable.
² See p. 394 below and *Life of Charlotte Brontë*, 1st edition, II, pp. 71–3.

285 **290** 304

LAETITIA WHEELWRIGHT

17 Cumberland Terrace
Regt's Park
Friday
[?13 June ?1856][1]

Dear Miss Wheelwright,

I am sorry I have so long delayed answering your kind note,
and acknowledging the valuable pencil enclosure, of which, you
may depend, I will take great care. But I wanted to see if either
my daughter or myself could remember Miss Carr's address. I
could find my way to it,—but I have forgotten the name of the
Street (out of the Rue des Paroissiens.) But Mr Jenkins, son of the
late Chaplain, took us to the door {of it}\where she lived/,—and
his mother would know the exact address. Her direction is

        Mrs Jenkins,
           Champs Elyssées
             Chaussée d'Ixelles.

I wish I could have given you more help.

                Yours very truly
                  E C Gaskell

264 **291** 356

JOHN GREENWOOD[2]

Plymouth Grove,
June 21st 1856.

Dear Sir,

I received your letter several days since, but I have really not
had time to write before to-day—I have been so extremely busy.
I still am so, what with working at Miss Brontë's Memoirs, &

---

[1] Dating not certain, but probably within the period when the *Life of Charlotte
Brontë* was being prepared.

[2] *Address (on envelope)* Mr John Greenwood | 225 Haworth—| Keighley |
Yorkshire. *Postmarks* MANCHESTER | JU 21 | 1856 | S and KEIGHLEY | JU 22 | 1856
| A and LEEDS | JU 22 1856 and BURLINGTON.

other unceasing occupation. My health does not give way however, thank you—I am unable to write any letters, but those of
business, and I have several lying by me, which I have never even
read.

I hope very much that the improvement in Mr Brontë's health
will continue.

Yours very truly
E. C. Gaskell

₀ **292** ₀

UNKNOWN

[?June–July 1856]

⟨. . .⟩ anyhow I shall get Susanna to help me; but pray come home
on Friday. Apropos of your friend, M. F. Tupper—he said he
(M F T) had got hold of Hawthorne when he was in London, &
invited him down to Albury,—where he met him & greeted him
All Hail Great Scarlet Letter! Mr H was dreadfully puzzled how to
answer,—but at last settled down on Good morning Mr Tupper.[1]
And now about my own plans; do you know I am thinking of
giving all the August visits up as far as I am concerned. You see
the new gardener comes on the 28th, and I should like to be here
to put him in our ways at first. Then I have an immense deal of
writing to do,—My letters to absent daughters at present taking
up nearly all my spare time, & other letters going almost unanswered—let alone Miss Brontë. Then Lewis and Allonby's bill
is a good deal,—& last not least *by far* is the uncomfortable state of
things between Flossy & Julia which ought to be remedied, in
some sort of way. However I must go now. My kind love to the
Prices.—

Yours most affe[ctionate]ly
E C G

[1] In early April 1856. For N. Hawthorne's version, see his *English Notebooks*, ed.
R. Stewart, New York, 1962, pp. 298–9.

289 **293** 297

GEORGE SMITH

Plymouth Grove—
Wednesday [?9 July 1856]

My dear Sir,

I am *very* much disappointed in Mr Nicholls' refusal to let you have his wife's portrait, with a view to getting it copied.[1] However I won't say any thing more about it; as you say, 'perhaps I have no right to complain.'

But now you see something of the doggedness which will I fear make any further application of mine for papers letters &c unavailing.

The portrait is by no means so sacred or private a thing as her papers; and you are a greater favourite than I.

I like Mr Brontë's note. But I am vexed with Mr Nicholls.

I did not acknowledge the valuable parcel, which I received, just after your letter, on Saturday. You would conclude from my *not* writing that I received them safely. Thank you very much for trusting them to me.

May I keep Mr Brontë's note a day longer, to show my husband, who is absent from home, but will return, I expect tomorrow?

Yours very truly
E. C. Gaskell

*280a **294** *294a

ELLEN NUSSEY[2]

Plymouth Grove,
Manchester, *July 9th*, '56.

My dear Miss Nussey,

You must excuse any kind of writing, for my girls are all from home, and I suppose I have between thirty and forty notes and

---

[1] This is referred to below, p. 399. See also *The Brontës*, ed. Wise & Symington, IV, p. 205, for Ellen Nussey's comments.   [2] From a printed source.

letters to answer this morning, *if possible* (which it is *not*), and yet I want to write you a long letter, and tell you all my adventures. Brussels, where Mme Héger, understanding that I was a friend of Miss Brontë"s, refused to see me; but I made M. Héger's acquaintance, and very much indeed I both like and respect him. Mr and Mrs Smith, junr., and Mrs Smith, senr. (*exactly* like Mrs Bretton). Mr Smith said (half suspiciously, having an eye to Dr. John, I *fancied*), 'Do you know, I sometimes think Miss Brontë had my mother in her mind when she wrote Mrs Bretton in *Villette*?' As I had not then seen Mrs Smith I could only answer, 'Do you?' a very safe reply. I went with Mr Smith to see the Chapter Coffee-House in Paternoster Row, where she and Anne Brontë took up their abode that first hurried rush up to London. In fact, I now think I have been everywhere where she ever lived, except of course her two little pieces of private governess-ship. I still want one or two things to complete my materials, and I am very doubtful if I can get them—at any rate, I think they will necessitate my going to Haworth again, and I am literally *afraid* of that. I will tell you the things I should *like* to have, and shall be glad if, knowing the parties, you could give me advice. First of all, I promised M. Héger to ask to see his letters to her; he is sure she would keep them, as they contained advice about her character, studies, mode of life. I doubt much if Mr Nicholls has not destroyed them. Then again, Mr Smith suggests—and I think with great justice—that if I might see the MS. of *The Professor* (which Mr Nicholls told me last July that he had in his possession), I might read it, and express my opinion as to its merits and demerits as a first work. He says that much of it—whole pieces of it, as far as he remembers—are so interwoven with *Villette* that it could never be published, nor would it be worth while to give extracts even if Mr N. would allow it; but if I might read it, I could give the kind of criticism and opinion upon it that Mr Brontë was anxious I should give on those published works of hers, on which (I told him) public opinion had already pronounced her fiat, and set her seal. So much for *The Professor* and M. Héger's letters. Now another of Mr Smith's suggestions is this: Might I, do you think, see the beginning (fifty pages, Mr Nicholls said) of the new story she had commenced? Reasons why desirable. Her happy state of mind during her married life would probably give a different character of greater hope and serenity to the fragment.

One thing more. Mr Smith says that her letters to her father from London, giving an account of places and persons she saw, were long, constant, and minute; they would not refer to any private affairs, but to the impressions celebrated strangers made upon her, etc.

I agree with Mr Smith that it would be a great advantage to me, as her biographer, and to her memory also, for I am convinced the more her character and talents are known the more thoroughly will both be admired and reverenced. But I doubt much if Mr Nicholls won't object to granting me the sight of these things; and all the remains, etc., appear to be in his hands. Read (and return, please) this note of Mr Brontë's to Mr Smith in reply to his application to be allowed to have a copy *for himself* (he thought it best to ask for this *only, which he had promised him*) at first. It seems as if Mr Brontë's own consent or opinion on these matters had very little weight with Mr Nicholls. I found Mr Smith an agreeable, genial-mannered man, with a keen eye to business; he is rather too stout to be handsome, but has a very pretty, Paulina-like little wife, and a little girl of eighteen months old. Mr Williams dined there when I did; grey-haired, silent, and refined.

Now for questions I should be much obliged to you if you would answer—I am afraid to say by return of post, but I should *like* that. Did *Emily* accompany C. B. as a pupil when the latter went as teacher to Roe Head? This was evidently the *plan*; yet afterwards it seems as if it were *Anne* that went. Why did not Branwell go to the Royal Academy in London to learn painting? Did Emily ever go out as a governess? I know Anne and Charlotte did.

I wrote twenty pages yesterday because it rained perpetually, and I was uninterrupted; such a good day for writing may not come again for months. All August I shall be away. But I am thoroughly interested in my subject, and Mr Smith, who looks at the affair from the experienced man of business point of view, says, 'There is no hurry; there would be a great cry of indelicacy if it were published too soon. Do it well, and never fear that the public interest in her will die away.' But a note of his (written after reading as much of my MS. which was then written, which you remember, I read to you), and which I enclose for your own *private* reading, makes me rather uncomfortable. See the passage I have marked at the side. Now I thought that I carefully preserved the reader's respect for Mr Brontë, while truth and the desire of doing justice to her compelled me to state the domestic peculiarities of her childhood, which (as in all cases) contributed so much to make her what she was; yet you see what Mr Smith says, and what reviews, in their desire for smartness and carelessness for scrupulous consideration, would be sure to say, even yet more plainly. May I call you simply 'Ellen' in the book? Initials give so little personality—they are so like a mathematical proposition. I should not even put an initial to your surname.

I have written you a terribly long letter, because, as somebody says, 'I have not time to write you a short one,' but I both wanted answers to my questions, and also wanted you to know how I am going on. We look forward to seeing you in the autumn. Mr Gaskell desires his kind regards; every one else is from home. Your sister must not forget me, for I do not forget her and her kind reception of me.—Yours faithfully,

E. C. Gaskell.

*

0 295 0

HOWARD RYLAND[1]

Plymouth Grove
Saturday July 19th 1856

My dear Sir,
I am sending by the same post as this letter, the book on Yorkshire, you were so very kind as to lend me. I cannot tell you how much use it has been to me; my paper marks, which I found had not been taken out of the book, before it was packed up, will, in a small degree, show you how much I have had to refer to in it.

Believe me to remain
Yours truly obliged
E. C. Gaskell

The Revd Howard Ryland.

[1] *Address (on envelope)* The | Revd Howard Ryland | Bradford | Yorkshire.
Postmarks MANCHESTER | JY 19 | 1856 | S *and* BRADFORD · YORKS | JY 20 | 1856 | B.

*286a **296** 330

M<small>ARIANNE</small> G<small>ASKELL</small>

Tuesday morning
[?22 July 1856]

My dearest MA,

I was glad to get a letter at breakfast time when every body else
had one but sorry to hear about my ribbon. I throw myself on
your taste; the white—(Oh! that there were enough!) & the
lavender edge—did you look after black, (imitation,—Cambray,
or Maltese) lace, for I want you to choose it.—And *do brush* up
Miss Booth WELL.—She is very careless about time, for, if {she}
\I/had taken the trouble to come at all yesterday\aft:/I *would* have
been in time. Make her come to Meta *tomorrow*\Wednesday/, &
be *very* particular about both your own dress & Meta's—fitting
I mean.—

Little has happened since last night. We *don't* go today to
Haworth;[1] but tomorrow at *10*, coming back at ½ p. *5*, too late to
get home tomorrow night, & I forgot to look for trains. However
I mean to come by the first I can on Thursday morning; so you
may safely enforce on Miss Booth coming to try on on Thursday
afternoon—I shall be at home by our ½ p. 1 dinner time. Will you
see Miss Mitchell? talk with Hearn\about F E/—write to Mrs
Isaac putting off till Saturday. I wish you'd told me how the
Ewarts were, but perhaps you had not asked. Mr Langton did not
go till after breakfast this morning, and asked me if I would allow
Mrs Langton & *his* 'young people' to call on my young people at
Silverdale—of course as they\ours/were returning they could not,
—but he did it very prettily. I want much to see the children,—
my dearest love to them. Capt North mistook our question of
who was the President *at Cheltenham* last night for who was the
U: States Prest, and moreover I am grateful to him for his great
attention in handing me bread & butter this morning when I was
rather late, & every body else was talking too busily to mind me.

---

[1] See following letters for dating, especially Letter 297.

293 **297** 298

GEORGE SMITH

Plymouth Grove
Friday [?25 July 1856]

Dear Sir,
I have had a very successful visit to Haworth.—I went from
Gawthrop, accompanied by Sir J P. K Shuttleworth, to whom it
is evident that both Mr Brontë & Mr Nicholls look up.—& who
is not prevented by the fear of giving pain from asking in a
peremptory manner for whatever he thinks desirable. He was
extremely kind in forwarding all my objects; and coolly took
actual possession of many things while Mr Nicholls was saying he
could not possibly part with them. I came away with the 'Professor' the beginning of her new tale 'Emma'[1]—about 10 pages
written in the finest pencil writing,—& by far the most extraordinary of all, a packet about the size of a lady's travelling writing
case, full of paper books of different sizes, from the one I enclose
upwards to the full ½ sheet size, but all in this\indescribably/fine
writing.—Mr Gaskell says they would make more than 50 vols of
print,—but they are the wildest & most incoherent things, as far
as we have examined them, *all* purporting to be written, or
addressed to some member of the Wellesley family. They give one
the idea of creative power carried to the verge of insanity. Just
lately Mr M Milnes gave me some MS. of Blake's, the painter's to
read,—& the two MSS (his & C. B's) are curiously alike. But
what I want to know is if a photograph could be taken to give
some idea of the fineness of writing,—for no words of mine could
explain it—I write in *great* haste.—I am just going to pay, along
with my husband & children, a series of visits to relations, & our
house will be almost shut up till the beginning of Sepr,—so I will
give you my addresses
J. Whitmore Isaac's Esq
Boughton
near
Worcester

[1] See p. 409 n. below.

TILL August 5. Then
> Edward Holland's Esq. M.P.
> Dumbleton
> near
> Evesham

& about August 14 or 15
> Wm Ewart's Esq M.P.
> Broad Leas
> near
> Devizes—

Will you return me the little book to 'BOUGHTON' *next week*—as I must return them to Mr Nicholls 'in a week or ten days.' Sir J. P K S. coolly introduced the subject of the portrait, as if he had known nothing of Mr Nicholls' reluctance, asked Mr Brontë's leave to have it photographed, whh was readily granted with a reference to Mr Nicholls for an ultimate decision, so then Sir James said 'Oh! I know Mr Nicholls will grant it—and we will trust to Mrs Gaskell to send over a photographer from Manchester, for I dare say he would not like to part with the portrait,—' & he so completely took it for granted that Mr Nicholls had no time to object. But I can not feel quite comfortable in absolutely wresting things from him by mere force of words. You have no idea what extraordinary things are in this packet of MS, written while she was between 13 & 18!

I hope you understand this letter; the real object of which is to see if you cd get one of these pages photographed for the Memoir. I don't understand the difficulties that may possibly be in the way; so if it is asking you to do a very difficult thing, you must put it down to my ignorance.

> Yours very truly
> E C Gaskell

Mr Nicholls could not find the reply to the Quarterly[1] and both he & Mr Brontë declared that all her letters were destroyed—

*

---

[1] C. Brontë, *A Word to the Quarterly*, in reply to Lady Eastlake's review of *Jane Eyre*. See p. 404 n. below.

297 **298** 299

GEORGE SMITH

Wednesday
Boughton near
Worcester.
[30 July 1856]

My dear Sir,
 I am very much obliged to you—very much indeed for the
lithograph. I *can* read it with the naked eye, but it hurts my sight,
—I am now so much satisfied with the lithograph, that I do not see
the necessity I did for the photograph; but I thought lithographing
always thickened the strokes, and I thought it would make it
illegible; but it does not in the least. Thank you very much.
 I enclose you this letter from Sir J. P. K. Shuttleworth,—for it is
meant for you and not for me. It has been sent round by Manchester & consequently delayed so I should like to have your
answer as soon as is convenient to you.
 I have only to suggest that Mr Nicholls (who entrusted the MSS
of the Professor to me, certainly at Sir J. K. Shuttleworth's
authoritative request,) ought to be consulted, as to whether it is
desirable or not to publish it. This Sir James seems entirely to lose
sight of.
 In haste, with many thanks, & hoping to hear from you soon—
(I go to E. Hollands Esq. M.P. Dumbleton, Evesham on Tuesday
\Aug 5/next.)

Yours very truly
E C Gaskell

Will you return Sir James' letter?

298 **299** 301

GEORGE SMITH

Friday [1 August 1856]
Boughton, Worcester

My dear Sir,
 I think I ought to send you a copy of my letter, (accompanying
yours,) to Sir James. I can not tell you how I should deprecate

anything leading to the publication of those letters\of M. Hégers/.
I have not seen the 'Professor' as yet, you must remember, so
perhaps all my alarm as to the subject of it may be idle and groundless; but I am afraid it relates to M: Héger, even more distinctly &
exclusively than Villette does. I have no doubt as to it's genius, &
the immense sale it would command. As to its genius she hardly
writes 2 lines on the commonest subject, in the most hasty
manner, but what there is a felicity of expression, or a deep insight into the very heart of things quite separate & apart from any
body else.

I foresee, if Sir James has set his will upon it, *it is* to be published
whatever may be the consequences. He over-rides all wishes,
feelings, and delicacy. I saw that in his way of carrying everything
before him at Haworth, deaf to remonstrance and entreaty. But
after all, it may not have so much reference to M. Héger as I dread;
yet ever so little, falling on a 'raw' in his, & his wife's mind will
be esteemed by them & their friends as such.

I am sure from numerous passages in her private letters that she
would not have wished Sir James to edit it. I should not in the
least mind saying so to him, if the publication is resolved upon.
But also, I could not undertake the editing (which would to a
certain degree seem like my sanctioning it,) after receiving M.
Hègers confidence, & hearing her letter if, as I fear,—it relates to
him.

My own feeling as to any revision would be that Mr Williams
should undertake it. I believe also from her opinions expressed in
her letters—that he would have been the person she would have
chosen. She continually speaks of him in the highest terms,—of
his admirable taste in literature &c &c,—for my own part I think,
as she had prepared it for the press, the editor should be careful &
very scrupulous in making any alteration.

Yours ever very truly
E. C. Gaskell

You will perhaps wonder why\I/did not say all this when I first
sent you Sir James' letter,—but we were on the point of starting
off for a review when his letter came, having been already
delayed, & I could not do more than enclose it—besides these
reasons against the publications have gathered force from consideration. I am very glad you have fished up the waiter,—I
wish I were at your lunch to ask questions.

279 **300** 0

PARTHENOPE NIGHTINGALE

Wednesday, Aug 6th [1856]
Dumbleton, Evesham.—

My dear Miss Nightingale,

Your letter has been forwarded to me here, and I learn that a 'roll' has arrived for me by Matlock post at home. Thank you exceedingly for both; also for the horseback sketch which I received quite safely {yes} from Meta when she returned home after rather a long stay in the South. I should have not merely acknowledged that, but written to you many times over, if I had not felt almost as if I had no right to do so 'in time of war', and war's consequences when I knew you must have head heart and hands full, and even the\merest/forms of every day life must be troubles to be avoided, unless absolutely necessary. Or else I *have* so much wanted to ask you a favour; might I have a copy of a letter from her to Mr Bracebridge, (I *think*) that Ly Augusta Bruce showed me, just after she had been to Embley in May? She, very rightly, said she could not give me a copy, but that if I wrote to you she thought I might have one, as I was one of those to whom your sister refers saying 'I don't wish this letter to be made public, but any one may see it who really feels interested'— or something like that. Now please, I *am* very very much interested,—but as soon as I found that I must apply to you for a copy, I did not like doing it for reasons afore-said. Just a day or two after I had seen it I met Lord Stanley, and as he began to talk about hoping they would not urge her to do things in a hurry I told him what I cd remember out of the letter, but I said it was a shame to say it in any other words than her own, and that if I could get a copy I would show it to him. May I? I asked Miss Ellen Tollet to find a good time to ask for it; but, you see, your letter has given me heart of grace and on the principle of 'him that has much would ever have more' I do want that letter very much. We are all here staying with my cousin Edward Holland for our summer holiday, till the 16th.

I did so like your letter. I was so glad to get it, you can not think, dear Miss Nightingale. Every scrap you can ever tell me about her is most valuable to my heart. God bless you both.

Yours affec[tionate]ly & truly
E C Gaskell

₂₉₉ **301** ₃₀₂

GEORGE SMITH

Dumbleton-Hall
Evesham.
Augt 13 [1856]

My dear Sir,

I think you will naturally like to know something about the Professor, and moreover I ought to have acknowledged the receipt of the Photograph (will you tell me what I owe you for that—) only I have been writing hard almost every day from breakfast till 5 o'clock; & am then so tired, that I have had neither heart, strength or fingers for anything of correspondence. I have read the Professor,—I don't see the objections to its publication that I apprehended,—or at least only such, as the omissions of three or four short passages not altogether amounting to a page,—would do away with. I don't agree with Sir James that 'the publication of this book would add to her literary fame'—I think it inferior to all her published works—but I think it a very curious link in her literary history, as showing the *promise* of much that was after-wards realized. Altogether I decline taking any responsibility as to advising for or against it's publication. I think, as I have told Sir James, that the decision\as to that/must entirely rest with Mr Nicholls. Sir James has written to him by this day's post urging its publication.—I have also written to Mr N., saying pretty much what I have said to you above,—but rather expressing my opinion that Miss B. would not have liked Sir J. P K Shuttleworth to revise it—if indeed she would have liked any one to do so. I have also enclosed to Mr N. the copy which I took of your note to me, *that you* ⟨. . .⟩

₃₀₁ **302** ₃₀₃

GEORGE SMITH

Dumbleton Hall
Evesham
August 15th 1856.

My dear Sir,

According to my promise, I send you Mr Nicholls' decision, \which/I think he is quite right in all that he says. As far as I can judge the rest of the negotiation will lie between you and him, as it ought to do, and I have only to say that if I can give any assistance of whatever kind, I hope both you, and he know how glad I shall be to render it.

I do not myself see that there is any occasion to regulate the appearance of the 'Professor' by the appearance of the memoir; it seems to me as if each would possess a strong independent interest. Perhaps you will let me know what you think.

Believe me to remain
Very truly yours
E C Gaskell.

₃₀₂ **303** ₃₀₉

GEORGE SMITH

Dumbleton-Hall
Tuesday. Aug. 19 [1856]

My dear Sir,

I have heard again from Mr Nicholls, simply to the effect that I am to send him the 'Professor' as soon as we reach home (the 27th) when he will look it over, & write to you on the subject. I *hope* he will expunge some expressions & phrases; but that must be left to him. I should like to know that they are expunged, before I write my tirade against Lady Eastlake;[1]—still whatever Miss Brontë wrote Lady E. had no right to make such offensive conjectures as she did. I suppose I am about ½ way through the Life— but the remainder will consist so very much of letters, involving

---

[1] See *Life of Charlotte Brontë*, 1st edition, II, pp. 87–9.

merely copying, that I do not fancy it will take me very long. I
do not wish the letters to assume a prominent form in the title or
printing; as Mr Nicholls has a strong objection to letters being
printed at all; and wished to have all her letters (to Miss Nussey &
every one else) burned. Now I am very careful what extracts I
make; but still her language, where it can be used, is so powerful
& living, that it would be a shame not to express everything tha[t]
can be, in her own words. And yet I don't want to alarm Mr
Nicholls' prejudices.

The Life will, I think, be ready by Xmas,—240 (of my pages)
are ready now.

The number of Miss Brontë's pages in the 'Professor' is 340.
Her writing is so beautifully even & regular that, from this, I
think you could make a good calculation.

Sir James, I fancy, will write pretty strongly to Mr Nicholls on
the desirableness of taking out one or two passages; but he and I
rather differed which.

We go to Wm Ewart's Esq M P
    Broad Leas
        Devizes
tomorrow[.]

Yours very truly
E C Gaskell

The Chapter Coffee house Waiter?   turn over

Have you ever been able to see Mr Lewes (*not from me*) about
the letter she wrote to Mr Empson, in reply to the article in the
Edin? Mrs Empson says it was forwarded to Mr Lewes as the
author.

290 **304** 340

LAETITIA WHEELWRIGHT

Wm Ewart's Esq. M.P. Broadleas,
Devizes, Wilts.
Augt 22nd [1856]

My dear Miss Wheelright [*sic*],
    I am going to avail myself of your kind permission to ask you
any\further/questions about Miss Brontë. I am just come in her

life to the part she spent at Brussels. If I remember rightly you went to Mme Hégér's at the beginning of the quarter that succeeded to the first September hol{l}idays {she spent} of her stay there. I forget whether you told me about those holidays, or how much you remembered. You would greatly oblige me if you \wd/have the kindness to write & tell me if she spent them entirely in the rue d'Isabelle, or if she had invitations from any friends during the vacation. It must have been before Mrs Wheelright's arrival in Brussels, so that she cannot have experienced her kindness as on future occasions in taking her away from the school in the holidays. I want to know where & how they were spent. And if you could give me any details about Charlotte & Emily's school life—their exact position in the school—their duties & occupations—If they had a bedroom to themselves—even the school-hours—all these details would be invaluable—as any others you might remember.

I distinctly recollect your account of Emily's appearance & manners—but I forget what you said was the first impression made by Charlotte on any casual observer. I suppose she was *extremely* shy—?

I shall be very much obliged to you if you will answer all my questions, & can only regret that some of them are repetitions of those whose answers I have forgotten.

With kind remembrances to Mrs Wheelright & your sister from my daughter & myself, I remain yrs truly,

E. C. Gaskell.

My address after Wedy will be

Plymouth Grove, Manchester

till then the present.

₂₃₅ **305** ₄₂₇

?EDWARD CHAPMAN

Plymouth Grove
Augt 27. [?1856]

Dear Sir,

Please to remember that August is drawing very near to a close, and that you have confessed yourself 'very much ashamed of the small amount you had to hand over &c' the last time;[1] so that *this* time I am hoping for some improvement in either you or the undiscerning public, which, if they won't buy, should be made to buy CRANFORD & LIZZIE LEIGH. Will you also kindly let me know what is due to me for any {increased} copies that may have been sold of the Moorland Cottage? It is nearly four years since I have heard anything of that unfortunate tale; & you know that after the sale of 2000 copies, (which had *then* been passed) I was to have half profits. Anxiously expecting your answer & 100£ note, & regretting the day I was ever deluded into a 'royalty' I remain dear Sir

Yours very truly
E C Gaskell

Tell me some news of Mr Forster please[.]

234 306 0

ANNA JAMESON[2]

Plymouth Grove
September 8th 1856

My dear Mrs Jameson

Your letter found me at home, many thanks for it, and for proposing to send me your second lecture. I shall like very much indeed to have it and shall be at home to receive it for a long time to come. You ask about my life of Miss Brontë. It is progressing, but very slowly. It is a most difficult undertaking. I have constantly to rewrite parts in consequence of gaining some fresh intelligence, which intelligence ought to have found place at some earlier period than the time I am then writing about.

I wrote to you this Spring,[3] but I think you must have been from home, asking for some introductions for a young friend of mine who was going to spend some months in Italy, and for whom I was very anxious to obtain as many as I could. I directed to Ealing Middlesex which you once told me would always find you[.] I have been from home for some weeks and only came

---

[1] The Pierpont Morgan Library holds a receipt of 26 February 1856 for royalties on *Cranford* and *Lizzie Leigh*.

[2] Perhaps a dictated letter.   [3] See p. 385 above.

home last Wednesday, and mean to work desperately hard at Miss Brontë and then hope some time to get it done.

Believe me to remain
Very truly yours
E C Gaskell

386 **307** 398

?F. J. FURNIVALL

Plymouth Grove
Septr 8. 1856.

My dear Sir,
I return you these verses, (of which I have taken a copy) with many thanks. I am always glad of your scraps of intelligence, which come in, with their pleasant *London-taste*, most acceptably into my Manchester life. These verses in particular are extremely humorous & characteristic.

Ever yours truly,
E. C. Gaskell

217 **308** 564

EMILY SHAEN[1]

P. Grove,
Sunday morning
[7 and 8 September 1856]

My dearest Emily,
I was so sorry when I got your note last night darling, that I had not written the day after I got home; that is not {tha n} I could not have written, but I *could* have made one of the girls do it,— but I wanted so very much to write to you myself, & that literally was impossible till I did. I am writing my *last* letters to-day; tomorrow I set to & fag away at Miss Brontë again. You see in general you

---

[1] *Address (on envelope)* Mrs William Shaen | Crix | Chelmsford. *Postmarks* MAN-CHESTER | SP 8 | 1856 | S *and* STOCKPORT | ⟨ ⟩ *and* CHELMSFORD | SP 9 | 1856.

hear, (& I like to feel you do,) all sorts of things about me & us
from Katie or Susanna so that I always feel you are au courant,—
and now it seems as if I had such a great deal to say to you. I
think I had better begin about Miss B. You would hear before {I}
\you/left Alderley that I had been to Haworth, with Sir J P. K. S.
He had not the slightest delicacy or scruple: and asked for an
immense number of things, literally taking no refusal. Hence we
carried away with us a whole *heap* of those minute writings of
which Willm showed you one or two at Alderley: the beginning
(only about 20 pages) of a new novel[1] which she had written at the
end of 1854, *before* marriage; & I dare say when she was anxious
enough. This fragment was excessively interesting; a child left at a
school by a rich flashy man, who pretended to be her father; the
school-mistresses' deference to the rich child—her mysterious
reserved character evidently painfully conscious of the imposition
practised; the non-payment of bills; the enquiry—no such person
to be found, & just when the child implores mercy & confesses her
complicity to the worldly & indignant schoolmistress the story
stops—for ever. Besides these things we carried off the Professor—
that *first* novel, rejected by all the publishers. This Sir James took
away with him intending to read it first & then forward to me.
He wrote to me before he forwarded it, praising it extremely—
saying it would add to her reputation,—objecting to 'certain
coarse & objectionable phrases'—but offering to *revise* it,—[']and
expunge & make the necessary alterations,'—& begging me to
forward his letter to Mr Smith. I dreaded lest the Prof: should
involve anything with M. Heger—I had heard her say it related to
her Brussels life,—& I thought if he were again brought before the
public, what would he think of me? I believed him to be too good
to publish those letters—but I felt that his friends might really
with some justice urge him to do so,—so I awaited the arrival of
the Prof. (by Mr Gaskell at Dumbleton,) with great anxiety. It
does relate to the School; but not to M. Heger, and Mme, or
Madame Beck, is only slightly introduced; so on *that* ground there
would be no objection to publishing it. I don't think it will *add* to
her reputation,—the interest will arise from its being the work of
so remarkable a mind. It is an autobiography—of a *man* the
English Professor at a Brussels school,—there are one or two

---

[1] *Emma* (see p. 398 above) published in the *Cornhill Magazine*, I, pp. 485–98, 1860,
with an introduction by Thackeray entitled *The Last Sketch*. See also *Brontë Society
Transactions*, Vol. II, Part X.

remarkable portraits—the most charming *woman* she ever drew, and a glimpse of that woman as a mother—very lovely; otherwise little or no story; & disfigured by more coarseness,—& profanity in quoting texts of Scripture disagreeably than in any of her other works. However I had nothing to do except to be a medium,—so I sent Sir J. P K S.'s letter on to Mr Nicholls, & told him I was going to send a copy of it to Mr Smith, if he had no objection; that I did not think so highly of the book as Sir J P K S; although I thought that great public interest would be felt in it,—that I thought that she herself having prepared it for the press Sir J. P K S ought not to interfere with it—as, although to my mind there certainly were several things that had better be expunged; yet that he (Mr N) was, it seemed to me, the right person to do it. I did not know what Mr N. might say to this, as he certainly is under obligation to Sir James for the offer of a living-&c, but I don't know if you remember some of the passages I copied out in her letters relating to Sir J. & there were others I did *not*[,] all making me feel she would have especially disliked *him* to meddle with her writings. However Mr N. quite agreed with me, & wrote to Sir James declining his proposal, saying privately to me that he feared Sir J. would be hurt (he,\Sir J./evidently wants to appear to the world in intimate connexion with her,) but that 'knowing his wife's opinion on the subject, he could not allow any such revisal,' but that he would himself look over the Professor, and judge as well as he could with relation to the passages Sir J. & I had objected to. So there it rests with Mr Nicholls, to whom the MS of the Prof: was returned a fortnight ago. With regard to Mr Smith of course he jumped at the idea; whatever sum *I* fixed on as the price should be cheerfully paid—(I declined the responsibility—but said I thought it ought to be paid for like her other works in proportion to the length.) Would I edit it? (No! for several reasons.) When would the Life be ready. Michaelmas? The time of publishing the Prof: would have to be guided by that. All I could say in reply was that I would make haste, but that it could not be ready by Michaelmas *possibly*. Since then (about 10 days ago) I have heard nothing either from Mr Smith, or from Mr Nicholls. Now as to the Life. Among that mass of minute writing I found quantities of fragments very short but very graphic written when she was about 12, giving glimpses of her life at that time, all of which I had to decipher, & interweave with what I had already written,—in fact I had to *re*-write about 40 pages. They give a much pleasanter though hardly less *queer* notion of the old father—moreover Mrs Wordsworth sent me a letter of Branwells to Mr W. & altogether it was dreary work, looking over, correct-ing, interweaving, &c &c &c and besides that I *wrote* 120 *new* pages while we were absent on our holiday, which was no holiday to me. I used to go up at Dumbleton & Boughton to my own room, directly after 9 o'clock breakfast; and came down to lunch at ½ p 1, up again, & write without allowing any temptation to carry me off till 5—or past; having just a run of a walk before 7 o'clock dinner. I got through an immense deal; but I found head & health suffering—I could not sleep for thinking of it. So at Broad-Leas (the Ewarts) I only wrote till lunch; and since then, not at all. I have been too busy since I came home. I enjoyed Broad Leas far the most of my visit, perhaps owing to my not having the sick wearied feeling of being over-worked; & Mr Gaskell being very jolly; & delicious downs (Salisbury Plain), get at able in our afternoon drives great sweeps of green turf, like emerald billows stretching off into the blue sky miles & miles away,—with here & there a 'barrow' of some ancient Briton, & Wansdyke, & Silbury Hill, and the great circle of Avebury all to be seen, while the horses went noisily over the thick soft velvety grass high up over blue misty plains, and villages in nests of trees, & church spires which did not reach nearly up to where we were in our beautiful free air, & primitive world.—At Dumbleton we heard nothing of the Aggs, only had Hewletts pointed out to us, *by mistake* one day, a great large house, larger than Crix; a Mr Owen lives there now; how, when, where &c all unknown. We are expecting a pretty considerable number of people this autumn as usual, but doubtless some will fall through. Louy Jackson (Meta's friend) Mrs Isaac (of Boughton) her daughter & maid, on their return from Scotland; Mrs Wedgwood & Mr Darwin in October,—Margaret Price in Novr; and I think a good sprinkling more. Mr Gaskell is going off with Mr James (Unit: minister of Bristol, his last year's Swiss travelling companion,) to the Lakes on Friday next for 10 days. It is now Monday morng—this letter has been written under all sorts of difficulties, & now I'm trenching on my precious Brontë time,—I got such a nice letter from my darling little Annie Shaen t'other day,—& a letter from Katie; that dear friend,—and *I should* like to answer both at length, only what *can* I do? The interruptions of home life are never ending; & I want to read &c with the girls. Margaret Preston (now married,

Mrs Knowles) came unexpectedly yesterday, & that made a long talk &c. I don't feel as if I had told you *half*—Oh will you send me word what my black silk mantle got at Lewis & Allonbys & put down in your bill, came to? I *must* go to duty writing. Ever your most affec[tionate] E C G.

I know no one at Rome but E. Weston. I had a letter from Arthur; he comes home this month, perhaps he could give some.

303 **309** 311

GEORGE SMITH

42 Plymouth Grove,
Manchester.
Septr 10th 1856.

My dear Sir,
   I am returned home, as you will see by the above date, and I have heard from Mr Nicholls about a fortnight ago of the safe receipt of the M.S. of the 'Professor'.
   I am extremely anxious to hear how affairs are proceeding between you & him, chiefly with a view to knowing the time of its publication.
   I rather fancy the wiser plan would be to defer the publication of the Memoir until I find out what the reviews say about the Professor; as I could then, without appearing to take any notice of them, reply to any objections they might raise. I am also anxious to know, as\soon as/you can find leisure to tell me, how the interview with the waiter of the Chapter Coffee House went off, & whether the 'admirable' luncheon was successful. Have you ever, *quite on your own hook*, made any inquiries from Mr Lewes, respecting the correspondence which I *know* he held at one time with both Emily & Charlotte Brontë, or of the existence of the letter which Currer Bell sent to him, in her public character of author, addressing the {writing}\writer of/the article in the Edinh Review on Shirley? You see I am sending you plenty of questions to answer, but if you knew the amount of writing I am getting through, you would think I deserved a few replies.

Yours very truly
E. C. Gaskell

₀ **310** ₄₂₃

ROBERT CHAMBERS[1]

> 42, Plymouth Grove,
> September 10th, 1856.

My dear Sir,—In the preface to the revised edition of 'Wuthering Heights and Agnes Grey' by Ellis, and Acton Bell, Miss Brontë says speaking of the difficulty of obtaining answers from Publishers:

'Being greatly harassed by this obstacle, I ventured to apply to the Messrs Chambers of Edinburgh, *they* may have forgotten the circumstances but *I* have not, for from them I received a brief and business-like, but civil and sensible reply, on which we acted, and at last made way.' This was in the autumn of 1845, or beginning of the following year. I mentioned this to you at Cheltenham, and you kindly promised me to look through your papers for the desired letters.

If you could forward me the correspondence, as soon as convenient to you, I should esteem it a very great favour and would return the letters immediately after copying them.—I remain,

> Yours very truly,
> E. C. Gaskell

*

₃₀₉ **311** ₃₁₂

GEORGE SMITH

> Wednesday. [?September 1856]

My dear Sir,

I am very sorry indeed to hear that Mrs Smith has been so ill. Your two letters came *together* this morning, so that I heard that she was out of danger at the same time that I heard of her illness. Pray tell her of an old saying we have in Lancashire, which monthly nurses here often comfort mothers with, who are disappointed in the sex of their children

Your son is yr son, till he gets him a wife,

Your daughter's your daughter to the end of her life—

[1] Wise and Symington (in *The Brontës*, IV, p. 210) head it 'To George Smith', but cf. *Life of Charlotte Bronte*, 1st ed., 1856, I, p. 336.

The letter to the Editor of the Edinburgh Review *was* written & sent. Mr Empson showed it to Mr W R. Greg, a friend of mine & contributor to the Review, who told me 'it was a *pungent* note'. Since I have been engaged in writing this Memoir, I asked Mr Greg to ask Mrs Empson to look through Mr Empson's papers for this letter. She did so, & it was not to be found, & we all consequently conjectured that it had been sent to Mr Lewes. But the 'I can defend myself from my enemies; God protect me from my friends' is as good, 'pungent' & characteristic as anything, thank you. Pray thank Mr Lewes kindly for sending those letters. I think it was very frank & pleasant of him. (Only I don't wish to have anything direct or personal to do with him.) I have no particular wish to have anything to do with Mr Dobell,[1] for I never could swallow a page of his poetry, begging your, his publisher's, pardon. But I know Miss Brontë corresponded with him, apropos of his review of Wuthering Heights in the Palladium, till he suggested some bosh about her and Miss Mulock's being 'kindred stars reflecting each other's light' when she began to laugh at him and leave him alone. Do you think those letters would be get-at-able? I should be obliged to you if you could discover the No of the Athenaeum containing the review of the *Poems*.[2] I should think it must be somewhere in the year 1846 that it appeared.

Thank you much for your kind offer of sending me the Working Man's Way in the World.[3] I should like much to see it. Please to tell me if 'Holme Lee'[4] is a man or a woman. I don't want real names; but I am always curious to know if my guesses about sex are right.

I hope in some way to hear a good account of Mrs Smith. After such an illness as hers you must expect her to be weak in spirits for a long time; but you look a cheerful person,—and as such will do her good.—

Yours very truly
E C Gaskell

What description of publisher is *Aylott*[5] Paternoster Row?

---

[1] Sydney Dobell (1824–74). The poem Mrs Gaskell disliked was probably *Balder* (1854), which has been described as a species of protest against the worship of the intellect.   [2] 4 July 1846.

[3] New edition, Cash, 1857. Its author was Charles Manby Smith.

[4] Harriet Parr (1828–1900), minor novelist.

[5] Published the Brontës' *Poems*.

311 **312** 314

GEORGE SMITH

Plymouth Grove. Tuesday.
Sepr 30 [1856]

My dear Sir,

You will wonder, & so will Mr Williams at my ungrateful non-
acknowledgement of your letters. I wrote too hard & long (I
suppose—) had a long fainting-fit one day ('quite promiscuous' as
servants say,) consequent doctor, *consequent* illness, consequent
ordering to sea side & prohibition of reading or writing, receiving
or answering letters—I was to do nothing but eat & sleep &
breathe fresh air—Now I'm at home, not quite strong but pretty
well; and I find I don't know how great an accumulation of
letters. Will you thank Mr Williams very much for his very
interesting letter? I shall write to him myself in a day or two. I
looked in last week's Examiner thinking there *might* be an
advertisement of the Professor. When do you think it will be
out?[1] It will not be a long book to print? If the publication of the
Professor takes place soon, when would you want the Life to
appear? And please am not I right in saying that 'Talbot Gwynne'
is a *lady*? Nobody will believe me, and yet I am almost certain
Miss Brontë told me this.[2] Will you remember me kindly to your
mother and to Mrs Smith? I have most pleasant recollections of
both.

I shall want to know very much about the Professor,—if Mr
Nicholls has made many alterations or omissions? when it is to
be published &c. I have not yet had time to read over Mr Lewes's
letters; thank you much for getting them for me. And thank you
especially for your capital account of the man merged into the
waiter,—I am only sorry you did not obtain a better dinner. The
laughing I had over that letter of yours was as good as a bottle of
medecine[.]

Yours very truly
E C Gaskell

[1] It was announced as 'just published' and reviewed in *The Athenaeum* of 13 June
1857.
[2] Charlotte Brontë wrote a critique of *The School for Fathers* in a letter of 3 April
1852. Wise and Symington (in *The Brontës*, II, p. 327 n.) identify the pseudo-
nymous author as Josepha Gulston.

₀ **313** ₃₂₉

?EMELYN STORY

[Autumn 1856]

['Mrs Gaskell . . . takes up, from Manchester, in the autumn of
1856, an acquaintance made, or rather, apparently, renewed, in
Paris in 1855.'[1]]
⟨. . .⟩ I like to think of *our* Sunday breakfasts in Paris, and your
Sunday bunches of violets, and the dear little girl, and the magnificent baby, and the Italian nurse, and the Etruscan bracelets, and
the American fish-rissoles; and then of Mr Story, high and far
above all, with his — Island ghost-story and his puns. Oh,
weren't we happy! ['She inquires as to the identity of'] a very
agreeable American Kennedy, whom I met a good deal in London
this year, and a very charming Mrs Edward Twisleton and a Miss
Dwight, her sister. ['Mrs Gaskell's letter of 1856 mentions as'] the
vaguest idea in the world ['the possibility of her going to Rome
with two of her daughters at the winter's end.'] I hope to have
finished my Life of Miss Brontë by the end of February, and then
I should like to be off and away out of the reach of reviews, which
in this case will have a double power to wound, for if they say
anything disparaging of *her* I know I shall not have done her and
the circumstances in which she was placed justice; that is to say
that in her case more visibly than in most her circumstances made
her faults, while her virtues were her own.

₃₁₂ **314** ₃₁₇

GEORGE SMITH

Plymouth Grove
Oct. 2nd [1856]

My dear Sir,
    Your letter has done me good. The doctor said I was to have my
mind at ease. How could I be easy thinking of that 'very indifferent
dinner' you ate in my behalf? But now I picture you to myself
with a haunch of venison before you, tender juicy and good, and

---

[1] From a printed source.

not even Mrs Smith to interrupt your enjoyment of your first mouthful by an ill-timed question, she being occupied upstairs with the 'finest baby that ever was seen'. I am content to know that I am right, and that Talbot Gwynne is a lady.

Now as to the Memoir &c. I perfectly agree with you. I had more than half come round to your opinion before you sent me your arguments in favour of it—which are very convincing. I believe, if Sir J. P K S had not suggested the publication I should not have done so. {It}\The Professor/is curious as indicating strong character & rare faculties on the part of the author; but not interesting as a story. And yet there are parts one would not lose—a lovely female character—& glimpses of home & family life in the latter portion of the tale.—But oh! I wish Mr Nicholls wd have altered more! I fear from what you say he has left many little things *you* would & I would have taken out, as {both not} \neither/essential to the characters or the story, & as likely to make her misunderstood. For I would not, if I could help it, have another syllable that could be called coarse to be associated with her name. Yet another *woman* of her drawing—still more a *nice* one still more a *married* one, ought to be widely interesting.

I think that,—placing myself in the position of a reader—instead of a *writer*—of her life,—I should feel my knowledge of her incomplete without seeing the 'Professor'. I suppose biographers always grow to fancy everything about their subject of importance, but I *really* think that such is the case about her; that leaving all authorship on one side, her character as a woman was unusual to the point of being unique. I never heard or read of anyone who was for an instant, or in any respect, to be compared to her. And everything she did, and every{thing}\word/she said & wrote bore the impress of this remarkable character. I\as my own reader/ should not be satisfied after reading the Memoir—(of which I may speak plainly enough for so much of it will consist of extracts from her own letters,) if I did not read her first work,—looking upon it as a phsychological [*sic*] curiosity. So again I think you are right, & that the Memoir must come first. I have written upwards of 300 of *my* (foolscap) pages, and I am just ending the year 1845. The next nine or ten years will be very interesting I have got such good materials. But I have now many threads of correspondence to interweave, and I want to look at several reviews,—(such as Athenms for her Poems; Athen & Examiners for Jane Eyre, as to how the appearance of so remarkable an

author was hailed &c—) and I shall have some difficulty in
rummaging them up—Still I look forward to all being ready by
Febry (*DV* to use her own pious expression,). I *think* it will be
nearly 600 pages in all. I have a vision in my mind. I am very sore
about reviews; I know it is a weakness, but unfavourable ones
depress me very much; I don't mean purely *severe* ones, when the
faultfinding is done in a friendly spirit; but supercilious, or personal ones, or impertinently flattering ones,—and I know I shall
be doubly sore about this. More than doubly, for I shall feel as if I
had done her an injury. So I plan getting out of England at the
time of publication &, if possible,\for us/to go to Rome for a
month ending up with the Holy Week—Easter being April 12th[.]

So you now see when I aim to have it finished. Will that time
suit you? I suppose it is not 'the season' is it? I can't write more
to-day—I have barely begun to read Mr Lewes' letters. I like, and
am obliged to him much for, his kindly way of sending them, &
the trouble he took to explain the occasions of their being written
—I know him a little; but I have not seen him for a long time; and
I did not like a certain familiarity of manner he assumed towards
me then; therefore I did not wish to have any direct intercourse
with him, & am obliged to you for managing the affair for me.

Do you mind the law of libel.—I have three people I want to
libel—Lady Scott (that bad woman who corrupted Branwell
Brontë) Mr Newby, & Lady Eastlake, the {two} first\& last/not
to be named by name, the mean publisher to be gibbetted.

Yours very truly
E C Gaskell—

*

*314a 315 335

?W. S. WILLIAMS[1]

Thursday [?October 1856]

My Dear Sir,

I am very much obliged to you for your letter, it gives me much
of the information I wanted. How stupid of the reviewers not to
find out its merit[2]—cautious dunces! I had no idea they were so

---

[1] Original MS. not seen.
[2] Probably *Jane Eyre*. Cf. the very similar comments in Chapter 16 of the *Life o,
Charlotte Brontë* (1st edition, II, p. 30).

long about it— Yes! I *should* be very much obliged to you indeed, if you would send me copies of the Athenaeum and Examiner notices. The Examiner is always a generous paper, if it does sometimes praise too much and too indiscriminatingly and from private personal motives; it never would let an unknown work of genius go without a hearty good word, whoever was the author or the publisher, or whatever newspapers had been niggardly in their dole. I suppose I may put in Mr Thackeray's little sentence about crying, it is far too good to be lost. I beg your pardon for writing as untidily as I do—(such a contrast to her neat delicate clear firm handwriting!) but somehow I am always in a hurry!

Yours very truly,
E. C. Gaskell.

₀ 316 ₀

UNKNOWN[1]

Plymouth Grove,
October 31, 1856.

I am tussling away at Miss Brontë's life and well understand your feeling of intense weariness after good hard absorption into a subject out of oneself. ⟨. . .⟩ I would not trust a mouse to a woman if a man's judgment was to be had. Women have no judgement. They've tact, and sensitiveness and genius, and hundreds of fine and lovely qualities, but are at best angelic geese as to matter requiring serious and long scientific consideration. I'm *not* a friend of Female Medical Education.[2]

₃₁₄ 317 ₃₁₈

GEORGE SMITH

Saturday [?Early November ?1856]

My dear Sir,

I have more gratitude in my heart than leisure on my hands to express it, so you must please take for granted my 'sense of past favours'.

---

[1] From a printed source.

[2] Mrs Gaskell refers above (p. 380) to a Manchester meeting to inaugurate the Nightingale Fund, which in 1860 supported the establishment of a Training School for Nurses at St Thomas's.

M.G.L.—P

I am very glad to hear a better account of Mrs Smith. It is fine weather for her recovery.

Aylott & Co sent a good bundle of characteristic letters.

Now to business. Will you read the enclosed, & send me word *by return of post, what size the Photograph must be, if it is to be engraved for the Memoir*; and also, *if you wish to have it engraved*. The first enquiry should have come last, but I believe I took it for granted that you *would* like to have a likeness. Mr Stewart[1] is a first rate amateur Photographer; gone out to Iceland by Danish Governments' request to take boiling springs & those sort of things,—has had to go & show his photographs to the Queen, as the 'crackest' things of the kind in the Kingdom, so I think he'll do it well,—& should he not take the view of house & village & moors beyond? I know a good view [drawing] very characteristic. Please write by *return*, & tell me exactly what you would like.

Yours very truly
E C Gaskell

P.S. To save time, and chances of fine days would you mind writing straight away to Mr Stewart & telling him the size &c required. The address is at the top of the copy of his letter

The Old Terrace
Poulton le Sands
Lancaster

317 318 319

GEORGE SMITH

[*c.* 15 November 1856][2]

My dear Sir,

I have just received a blow,—contained in a letter from Mr Chorley, in which he says, apropos to what he has heard relating to the letters which have been put into my hands as material for Miss Brontë's Life. 'Remember correspondent's permission to

---

1 Dating. This letter appears to contain the first mention of Mr Stewart.
2 *Annotation* recd. Saturday Nov: 15th 1856.

publish goes for nothing; the legal power over any deceased person's papers lies with the executors; this having been settled in the case of Dallas and Lord Byron, by Lord Byron's executors; and thus Mr Nicholls *may*, if he likes turn sharp round on you, and not merely protest, but *prohibit.*' Now I did *not* know all this; and Mr Nicholls is a terribly tickle person to have to do with; if I asked him for leave\to make large extracts from her letters as I am doing/, he would, ten to one, refuse it,—if I did not ask him, but went on, as I am doing, I *think* he would sigh & submit; but I could not feel sure. I was getting on so beautifully, & feeling or fancying, the interest growing with every page. I foresaw some difficulties certainly, as Miss Nussey evidently expects to see the extracts I have made from Miss B's correspondence with her,— interwoven as those extracts were into the Life,—while Mr Brontë & Mr Nicholls write to desire I will let *no one* but Mr Gaskell see the MS before it is given up into your hands. But the letters are the great perplexity—I will copy you out a piece of one of Mrs Nicholls' letters to Miss Nussey. I have not time to copy it, so I send you *my* copy which please *return.* I am *most* careful to put nothing in from Miss Brontë's letters that can in any way im- plicate others. I conceal in some cases the names of the persons she is writing to. But what shall I do if Mr N were to prohibit all I have written from appearing. I have received the Photograph from Mr Stuart. It is evidently a beauty, but it has got smashed in the post; and as he has two more, I am to return the smashed one, as he took *three*, under a solemn promise to Mr Nicholls, that *two should be returned*\to him/as soon as I had made my choice, and Mr N. wishes to have the smashed one back; and this although he knows it is to be engraved, & consequently numerous copies circulated. I name this to show how 'inconséquent' a man he is, with all his warm affections & amiable qualities. Sir J. P. Kay- Shuttleworth manages him the best, though in not a pleasant way. Oh! if once I have finished this biography, catch me writing another! I shall be heaved overboard at last, like the ass belonging to the old man in the fable.

Yours very truly
E. C. Gaskell

GEORGE SMITH

Pendyffryn, Novr 22nd [1856]

My dear Sir,

I have taken some days to consider which of the two plans you proposed is the most to be preferred; and I think on the whole the best mode of dealing with Mr Nicholls will be for you to send him the business form of application you spoke of; and I hope this will save any further trouble. Of course, if he refuses I shall have to re-write a considerable portion of the memoir, in which I have; (with the permission of the correspondents in whose possession the letters were,) been interweaving extracts from some of her letters. However we must hope for the best. I date from North Wales; but I shall be at home by the time you have any answer to send me.

I am glad to hear so good an account of Mrs Smith, and the young lady.

Ever yours

very truly

E. C. Gaskell

GEORGE SMITH

Saturday Decr 6th [1856]

My dear Sir,

Will you be so kind as to forward the enclosed note to Mr Thackeray as soon as ever you can? And if you would 'back' it by one from yourself, I should be very glad. The Mr Stewart, who is kindly photographing the likeness of Miss Brontë, and has already been twice to Haworth for that purpose—is most anxious to have an introduction to Mr Thackeray, and has applied to me to give him one. He wants it in a hurry, or would have obtained it through a much better channel, his cousin Miss Stewart-Macken-zie, who is a great favourite with Mr Thackeray. But Mr Stewart does not know her present address so writes\to/me in haste. And he has been so kind to me about the Photograph, that I don't like to refuse him, or else I am afraid Mr Thackeray will think I have no right to be introducing people to him; and the enclosed is a little private note apologizing for the liberty &c; and I want it to reach him, if possible, before the other. So will you speed it on its way to him, please?

I am very much obliged to you for the permission from Mr Nicholls. It is a great deal more than I hoped for. I have got a very good photograph of Richmond's picture, that Mr Stewart sent me yesterday; how long will it take to engrave it? Had I better send it you as soon as I can, or when? Mr Stewart is going again to take a view of Haworth village,—and I think I shall ask him, if he will also take the view of the Church Church Yard &c, that she had always present before her, as seen from the Parsonage windows.

Thank you much for Mr Dobells & Mr Taylors letters,—I have been too ill to read them; but I know they must be of value.

Yours very truly
E C Gaskell

₀ 321 ₀

?EDWARD COWARD

42 Plymouth Grove
Decr 10th [?1856][1]

Dear Sir,

If you are still in Manchester (as I hope you are) you will be amused at the round-about way in which I am obliged to send this letter; but I can only find your London address and I believe I neglected to ask where you were staying in Manr when you were so good as to call. Since then I have been very ill or I should sooner have conveyed the expression of Mr Gaskell's hope that you would come and drink tea with us quietly some evening. Will next{Tuesday}\Thursday but one/(18th I think) or\the day before/Wednesday (17th) suit you best? We should prefer the latter (Wednesday.) because we shall have an agreeable friend

[1] The possible years are 1851, 1856 and 1862. Letter 320 of 6 December with its reference to illness, persuades us to choose 1856.

then staying with us; but we are disengaged on both days—and
shall be most happy to see you on either, and may I remind you of
your kind promise to show me the likenesses of Leigh Hunt and
Miss Kavanagh?

Yours truly
E. C. Gaskell

I find, on consulting Mr Gaskell, that he will be obliged to attend a
long committee on Thursday so may I beg you to come on
Wednesday 17th? We drink tea at seven.

320 322 323

GEORGE SMITH

Decr 11th [1856]

My dear Sir,
    Business first and pleasure afterwards. Questions.
    When, *exactly*, was Jane Eyre published? Can you tell? It was in
Sepr 1847. Beginning, middle or end? Which was the first
review, giving note as it were of it's signal success? (Your correspondence with Miss Brontë stops at *Aug 24, 1847* and makes a
jump to Sepr 22nd 1849. There is a letter to Mr Williams November 10th 1847, but by that time the success of Jane Eyre is *assured*.[)]
Any recollections of how the extraordinary effect produced by
the book was first communicated to her, & especially *how
received* by her would be very valuable, & fill up a gap. For, to no
other correspondent\of her own friends/did she mention the
publication. Her sisters are dead; & her father both did not know
of it till much later (though he does not want to have this said.)
and dresses up facts in such clouds of vague writing, that it is of no
use to apply to him. I am writing in a terrible hurry as usual:
breaking off in the middle of my Biography-writing to ask
these questions, & to say how glad I shall be of a speedy reply.
Now to gossip, which of course, is a woman's pleasure. Mr
Thackeray has not come to Manchester, as yet, in consequence of
an attack of illness,—said to be spasms in the stomach,—which
seized him at Bradford. (I wonder if he has ever bethought him of
the neighbourhood of Haworth, & gone over there; it *would*
gratify poor old Mr Brontë if he did!) So where the various

letters of introduction to Mr Stewart are gone to, I can't tell. I am so glad that it was you, and not I, that had 'the fierce correspondence' with Mr Nicholls. I shd have been daunted at once. My next difficulty is this. There is some little jealousy (the nearest word, but not the right one) of Miss Nussey on Mr Brontë's part, and he especially forbids my showing the MS of my biography to her. Now she is about the only person who would care to see it in M S, because she wants to know what extracts I have taken from all her letters; and she has a right to know this, if she wishes. So, after some consideration, I find I must *read* it to her,—all where her letters are quoted from at any rate; & today I have written to ask her to come here, & be read to about January 10th[.]

I hope you will have it by about the end of January. I can't help thinking it will be good, just because I am so much interested in it; but I suppose all biographers get interested in their subject to an extraordinary degree, even when there was no personal knowledge & regard to bind the parties together.

I will send the Photograph either today or tomorrow. Will you let me know what Mr Richmond says about the Photo Copyright? I don't fancy he will make any difficulty.

Yours ever very truly
E C Gaskell.[1]

*   *

322 323 324

GEORGE SMITH

[?December 1856]

My dear Sir,
Please, the date of the 2nd edit of Jane Eyre (that with the Thackeray Dedication.) I want it as a proof of the rapid demand for the book,—the 3rd & 4th edit: following more slowly, don't so much signify.

Yours very truly
E C Gaskell

[1] Two envelopes survive without enclosures. (1) In New York University Libraries; *address* Mrs Ames | 5 Abercrombie Terrace | Liverpool; *postmarks* MANCHESTER | DE 11 | 1856 | S *and* LIVERPOOL | DE 12 | 1856 | A. (2) In collection of Sir John Murray; *addressed to* G. Smith; *postmarks* MANCHESTER | DE 12 | 1856 | S *and* STOCKPORT RD *and* ⟨ ⟩ | DE 13 | 1856; *annotation* Wanted. Date of publication of W:H: | 1 or 2 Reviews of do. (1st edi⟨tion⟩).

323 **324** 325

GEORGE SMITH

Thursday Morng—
[?December 1856]

My dear Sir,

Your *note* (received last night,) was a great relief to me, for I had been fancying that Mrs Smith was worse. Not that I was in any hurry about the letters relating to Jane Eyre, for, once having determined to go back to that time in the Life, I could easily afford to wait,—much longer than I have had to do,—but yr account of Mrs Smith being too weak to undertake the journey from Brighton made me feel about as anxious as I *could* be for a person whom I had only seen once. Do tell her my matronly experience. I *never* felt under her circumstances ever to *begin* to regain strength till 3 or 4 months after my confinement. But then, when I was once strong I was in better health than ever.

Now to business; only please when I write a letter beginning with a *star* like this on its front [drawing of a star], you may treasure up my letter; otherwise *please burn them*, & *don't* send them to the terrible warehouse where the 20000 letters a year are kept. It is like a nightmare to think of it—Can you begin to print before you have the whole of the MS. That is a question I want much to have answered, & I'll tell you why. I have 100 pages quite ready,—only with so many erasures, insertions at the *back* of the leaves &c (owing to the unchronological way in which I obtained information) that I should much like to correct all I can myself,—and I hope to get out of England by Febry 8th or 9th? I don't hear from Miss Nussey, & can't think why she has not answered my invitation,—I don't mind if she does not come; only I promised to let her know when it was nearly completed &c. Mr Stewart wrote to thank me for sending the introduction to Mr Thackeray, but had not seen him, so I am doubtful of his reception. Mr Procter rather curtly, declined 'giving me an introduction for a gentleman whom he had never seen', though I had told him all the circumstances of the case. Mr Thackeray is here lecturing.[1] I have longed to go & hear him, but Virtue

---

[1] Thackeray lectured on *The Four Georges* at various places in England and Scotland in November and December 1856.

conquered, & I have stopped at home like a heroine to work away at my Memoir. People say his Lectures are delightful, but he himself diabolically cross! I hope Mr Stewart (good & kind as he is!) won't get a {ref} rebuff. Mr Stewart is going to take many photographic views of Haworth—he says it is such an unique place—steep street,—view *of* Church & Church yard from Parsonage windows—he says we may have any to engrave from we like—

Yours very truly
E C Gaskell

324 **325** 326

GEORGE SMITH

Plymouth Grove
Decr 20. [1856]

My dear Sir,

Thank you for your letter; I wish you were able to give a better account of Mrs Smith. Is she come home from Brighton yet?

I am no judge of type &c—and I find it difficult to say how far the MS will extend; I can scarcely tell what space it will occupy, but my impression is that it could not be got into 2 vols of the ordinary novel size without smaller type than is desirable. Is there not something between this, and the large Octavo? With regard \to/the business question I should esteem it a favour if you would give me an idea of what you think would be a proper remuneration? You must know that *I*\am/inclined to part with the copyright; and that I am also inclined to put a very high value upon it, because, naturally I value it according\to the/anxiety thought & trouble it has cost me. But I remember that the man who carves a carriage & four, one wigged coachman & two footmen, out of a cherry-stone, may not find much demand for his long & tiresome labour,—now *you* are the best judge of what demand there will be for my work. I have said that I am inclined to part with the copyright. My husband on the contrary has always preferred my retaining the copyright of my works. Only I should not like the \specified/number of copies of an {spec} edition to be changed, on any pretext, after it had once been agreed upon. I name this because I hear from Miss Winkworth that *S & Co* did this with Tauler.[1] So on the whole I believe I shall prefer parting with the copyright, as a manner of doing business less liable to misunderstanding than the other; and 'short (agreements) make long friends.'

Believe me to remain
Yours very truly
E. C. Gaskell

325 **326** 328

GEORGE SMITH

Decr 26. [1856]

My dear Sir,

First of all to the first objection you raise. It is possible that it would be wiser not to 'indicate so clearly' (I was not aware that I had done so,) the lady concerned in Branwell's misdoing. I will see how this can be altered. What & where did you think pointed her out too distinctly. I wished to show the contrast between her present life, & the life which others had led through her guilt; and for that reason I named the circumstances by which she is surrounded at present. The part where I point her out most clearly seems to me to be 'Lady — in May-Fair.'[2] I thought when I wrote this that she lived in May-Fair,—I have since learnt that she does not,—but certainly there are plenty of 'Lady —',s in May Fair, though we will hope not so many as bad as she is. I put that in as I have said, to point the contrast of her life, & Branwell's death. However it may be better to alter it if that is *where* you thought it disagreeable to indicate her so clearly. Only will you tell me (if you can remember, after so hasty a reading) *where* you were particularly struck with it. About Newby I was quite aware that, as you saw the MS, my expressions were actionable; but I *think* you said that when this part was formally submitted to you, you would see that I steered clear within the law. This, however was to have been altered either by you, or by me. I should like to warn others off

[1] Susanna Winkworth's *Life of Tauler with Sermons*, Smith & Elder, December 1856.
[2] See *Life of Charlotte Brontë*, 1st edition, I, p. 328; II, p. 78.

trusting to him as much as I cd, because I really think it is only right,—but, of course, I don't want any action to be brought against either you or me. Had I better consult some of my lawyer friends, as to what words I *may* use.\or *will* you undertake to take out what you wd rather not have in./

I *do* think you were good and showed a fine discrimination in taking the parcel &c with all the directions on it—& I should like to have expressed my opinion on this subject—(just as I should like to express it when I think you have\not/done equally well—) only if you would rather not have that passage in I will take it out, —only you submitted to a good piece of just praise in the Biographical notice, remember![1] However *that* goes out, & voilà fini! Now as to Miss Brontë's letter—I am vexed about this,—I am indeed vexed I let you see the MS at all in so unfinished a state {bu} for I had often to trust long pieces of copying letters to one of my daughters, & I told her just to write straight on, and I should take out what it was undesirable to have published when I read it over with Mr Gaskell. There is a good deal in that letter that is very graphic,—but I should have thought you might have felt quite sure that I was going to take\out/all that ought to be considered as private or personal {out} before it was published. I suppose Mr Williams thought that I was going to print that part relating to his being like a 'faded Tom Dixon'. If I had no delicacy of feeling, I have at least a consciousness of what would\or ought to/interest readers, and I should have certainly scored out, so that no one could have read it through my marks all that related to any one's appearance, style of living &c, in whose character as indicated by these things the public were not directly interested. There is very little indeed in her letters of this kind,—and almost the only place where I thought of retaining what she says\on these points/is about her visit to Miss Martineau,—which is all pleasant & graphic & what has been said by many before, only not so well. I forget—there was one thing I meant to have inserted about her\first/visit to you in Westbourne Place;—it was this— that she names as an unusual attention and as {ind} showing a style of living to which she was not accustomed that she had a fire & candles in her bedroom—& also in the same letter—she says that your mother (I planned to have a blank for the name, 'watched {her}\me/very narrowly when surrounded by strangers; she never took her eye from me. I liked the surveillance; it

[1] See *Life of Charlotte Brontë*, 1st edition, II, pp. 22–3.

seemed to keep guard over me.' The first of these pieces shows how simply she & those few friends at whose houses she had visited, lived—The next showed a nice feminine sense of confidence & pleasure in protection—chaperonage—whatever you like to call it; which is a piece of womanliness (as opposed to the common ideas of her being a 'strong-minded emancipated' woman) which I should like to bring out. Of course there are other references to you & your mother up & down—such as 'If Mrs Smith were not kind I should sometimes be miserable' (from shyness &c[) ']but her attentions never flag'—or 'whenever I flagged\I cd see/Mr Smith became disturbed[;] he seemed to think something had occurred to annoy me, which never once happened, for I met with perfect good-breeding even from antagonists,' &c[.] I do not promise—for I am quoting much from memory that there shall be no\more/references to you or to your mother,—but they are of this incidental kind,—bringing out something of *her* character, & not in any ways referring to your private employments habits or circumstances—far less to your appearance. It has been a *very* great disadvantage to me that in order {to}\to give you an opportunity of/arriv{e}ing at some idea of length & quality I had to submit my MS to you in so great a hurry. And now to the money business. I have a great dislike to bargaining, & I should not like to be (what the Lancashire people call) 'having'; but if I must deal frankly with you, as I wish, the terms proposed for the Biography are below what I thought I might reasonably expect. My way of reckoning was this—For 'North & South' I received 600£ (from H. W. & Mr Chapman together,) retaining the copyright, having the Tauchnitz profit,—and only losing the American profit by my own carelessness in forgetting to answer the note, until some other \American/publisher had begun to reprint.

Now the amount of labour bestowed on the Biography, (to say nothing of anxiety in various ways,) has been more than double at least what the novel cost me; and I think that the Biography is likely to interest a wider class of readers, and to be in more permanent demand. I have also to take into account the expense which I have been at in journies to Brussels &c—and in collecting materials, which I can not set down at less than 100£. I suppose however that you would allow me to retain the profits arising from the American & Tauchnitz edit: which would probably amount to nearly this much.

I look forward also with a feeling of dread to the expressions of opinion, both public & private, which will cut me in two ways {of} on the appearance of the book, and am extremely anxious to be out of the country at the time of its publication.—I was therefore, as I think you know, planning to go on the Continent in February and was working at the top of my speed with this object in view, as it wd be absolutely necessary (owing to the number of friends we expect during the opening of our Art Exhibition that I should be at home for 6 months from the beginning of May,—and thus the publication of the work wd be deferred till the beginning of next Novr as the very soonest time at which I could go abroad. I have put these points before you, in order that you may judge whether I am unreasonable or not in expecting some advance on your present offer. I shall be glad to hear from you at once as if I am to give up my journey there will be no necessity for my tasking myself as I have been doing.

Yours very truly
E. C. Gaskell

*

*326a 327 352

ELLEN NUSSEY

[?December 1856]

My dear Miss Nussey,
  I shall be delighted to see you. I was sadly afraid you were ill, or not hearing, after the day had passed over on which we had thought we might have heard from you if you were in the South.

Yours affectionately
E C Gaskell

326 328 331

GEORGE SMITH

Plymouth Grove
December 29th 1856.

My dear Sir,
  Many thanks for your letter. I am much obliged to you for the alteration of the figure {8} 6 to *8*; the sum you now propose *fully*

satisfies me, and I do hope you won't have reason to repent of it. *Do* let me abuse Mr Newby as much as I dare, *within the law*. Your legal adviser will I trust keep me from a libel; but short of that I know there are a good many things that may be said.

Private

About Lady — (did I tell you the name?) I see you think me merciless,—but details of her life (past & present) which I heard from her own cousin when I was staying at Sir C Trevelyans & which were confirmed by Lady Trevelyan (also a connection) showed her to have been a bad heartless woman for long & long, —& to think of her going about calling, & dining out &c &c—(her own relations have been obliged to drop her acquaintance,) while those poor Brontës suffered so—for bad as Branwell was,—he was not absolutely ruined for ever, till she got hold of him, & he was not the first, nor the last. However it is a horrid story, & I should not have told it but to show the life of prolonged suffering those Brontë girls had to endure; & what doubtless familiarized them to a certain degree with coarse expressions, such as have been complained of in W. H & the Tenant of Wildfell Hall. However I will not name that she was a clergyman's wife—nor that she is a *Lady* any body. But you see *why* I wanted to contrast the two lives, don't you? Tell me, (if you see the proofs) if there is any thing you would like taken out—I ask you this, as you were a friend of Miss Brontë's, & must be as anxious as I am to place her where she ought to be. I don't *promise* to alter what you do not like. I only promise to consider of it. Miss Nussey comes here on the 12th to be read to. I shall be glad if you will begin to print as soon as you can. When I was at Oatlands Mr J. E. Taylor was introduced to me by Mr Rose the Vicar of Weybridge (also a cousin of my Lady —,) and Mr J. Edward Taylor has since written to me to ask if I would ask you if he might print this biography. I told him in my reply that I never had asked such a favour before, and did not know how great a one it was; but that, as he wished it, I would gladly name it to you, & say that if you had no other plans about the printing perhaps you would take his wish into consideration. That is all; and I am sure you will do what you think right.

About the American edition. When the advertisement or paragraph first went the round of the papers that I was writing Miss Brontë's Life,—I had three letters from three American publishers, making three 'bids'. One bid 10£, and another 35£, and another 75£. The one who bid (& all their letters must have come by the same mail, & they are curiously different values to affix upon the same thing—) was Messrs Appleton and Co. New York. I wrote to the American partner at Baring's, Mr Russell Sturgis who is a friend of mine to ask if he knew if this Appleton was an honourable man, for it seemed such a great deal more than 10£, that he offered; Mr Sturgis said that he was, he believed; and made enquiries for me. I then wrote to accept this offer, saying that I did not yet\this was in September 1855/know if the money was to be paid to you or to me; but that he should have two copies a fortnight before (some time I forget what—) for his 75£. He has an agent, a man in Little Britain, who writes to me about once a month to ask if I am not ready; and I believe—but I am afraid I have burnt all the recent notes, that he is the man to whom the copies are to be sent. Charles Layton, (Agent for Messrs Appleton & Co New York) 16 Little Britain London is his address. I hope I have not done wrong? I thought I was very wise in writing to Mr Sturgis, but I never heard of any Appletons, publishers? I am pledged by a French law-deed (such a long one!) to put on my works that I reserve the right of translation; and to send a copy of each of them as it is published to M — Hachette, 14 Rue Pierre-Sarragin. He sees if he cares to translate them within a certain time; if he does he pays me a franc & a half a page; if not done within a twelve month, they become my own property again. I think this must be a pretty good agreement—because through some back-stairs influence through M — de Morny Hachette has a queer sort of illegal power of stopping other translations, even when the author has not reserved the right, or on\works/published before the international Law. For instance neither Mary Barton nor Ruth were protected; but he has translated them, paid me ½ a franc per page; and stopped one or two other translations. I name all this to you, because M. Hachette constantly writes to me to ask me to tell him of good English novels, &, if I can, procure him personal introductions to their authors, to whom he has offered the same terms.—Now perhaps some of the ladies who write for you might be glad to know of this; and if I could conscientiously say their works were good, I would be so glad to help them; if it is help. Possibly you can manage all these things better than I can; only I never had any one to help me, & found them all out by accident {and}\as/it were; & I think other women may be like me. And about Tauchnitz I know nothing. Only for the sake of the great name in Germany of the Author of Jane Eyre he might possibly wish for the book. And now you know all. If there should be any offer from Tauchnitz perhaps you will tell me what it ought to be,—or manage it for me if you will. I {want}\mean/ to send 100£ to Mr Nicholls for the parish of Haworth—I shd like a village pump[;] they are terribly off for water—

Yours very truly E C Gaskell

313 329 342

W. W. or EMELYN STORY[1]

[Early January 1857]

⟨. . .⟩ I want just, if I can, to leave England on the day of publication of my book: this will be, I expect, one day in the first half of February; and I believe it will take us eight days to reach Rome—somewhere about Feb. 20th at the earliest. It might even be a fortnight later. I have still 200 pages to write, but they begin to print to-morrow. I shall bring you a copy with me, if it is out, in memory of our happy Paris Sundays. I think you'll be interested in it—I am so much so.

296 330 372

MARIANNE GASKELL

[?Early January 1857]

My own darling Marianne,

Nothing *could* be nicer, my own dear one than your note. Meta is bitterly penitent for having named her unhappiness & *so* caused the letters which made you unhappy. But I am *sure* it is best to speak about such things, *in the beginning* to the people themselves. Especially love, when they take it in such a right & *holy* spirit as you have done. It *is* holy to be humble in acknowledging the possibility of faults; & I am afraid I have too often set you a bad

---

[1] From a printed source.

example by being much hurt, as I sometimes am, when people I love dearly, find fault with me. I have no doubt as you say, dear that a good deal of what Meta has felt has been manner—only just *say* 'I am tired' when not inclined to talk &c. I know how a bad cold makes one languid & undemonstrative,—only remember people don't, at the *first* seeing one, know *exactly* what one's state of health is, so as to make allowances &c, and are consequently hurt; and that it is *better* to force oneself to a little exertion than to hurt them. So many of the 'coolnesses' of life,—not to say *quarrels* of life originate in *manner* that it is well to be on one's guard as to what gives pain, & what does not. But we will have faith in you, my darling after that letter, if you are as grumpy and sulky as any body you like,—only please love, *don't* be—I am *sure* this explanation, painful as it has been, will have done good. I could not bear my life if you & Meta did not love each other most dearly, and it is little *unspoken-of* grievances rankling in the mind that weaken affection, & it is so dreary to see sisters grow old, (as one sometimes does,) not caring for each other, & forgetting all early home-times. So now no more about this love.

Will you look after Julia's two ends, i.e. hair, & *bowels*? Hearn came home too late last night to curl former, & Meta has been writing almost day & night for me, & putting children to bed &c, & has not done it. She wanted *to*, but I said she had better not. The late omnibus will do for you, love,—& we shall look for our darling at 6 o'clock tomorrow eveng. The children must, I suppose, leave on Saturday morning by the *early* one to Bowden, —at least much will depend on what Mrs S says today to Hearn at Bowden, (Hearn goes home again till Monday.) It *now* seems a pity {they}\I/did not\it/[sic] arrange them to come with you, either to Mrs S's or home tomorrow night. I am obliged to give up my lodgings, tell cousin Susan,—in the first place 20th (Children's party) 22nd, & 23rd are engagements,—and in the week before (next week) I don't know when Miss Nussey will *go*, she comes on 12th—& altogether I am so behind-hand with my writing.—I *should* so have enjoyed a bit of quiet at Knutsford. I did plan once to ask Mrs Green to take *me* (alone) in from Saty 17th to Tuesday 20, then to Miss Marshalls to hear Rome,—till 22nd but I see I can't in any way. I am *so* tired of this writing, & so is poor Meta— it makes her out of spirits,—& she has strained her back so with lifting children's bath. She is going to Concert Hallé with Ewarts —and I am going with Papa to dine at Turners (& get a headache) tonight. Goodbye, my dearest dear child,—you don't know how fagged we both are,—and how truly I am

Your good for nothing mother
E C Gaskell

Wrap children *well* up on coming out of Woodlands tonight, & don't let them stay {too} late. E. Marsland will be here tomorrow for night—{yo} Julia's two ends. Love to Cousin Susan—

328 331 332

GEORGE SMITH

[Early January 1857]

My dear Sir,

I have received no proofs by this morning's post, at which I was a little surprized; but I suppose printing does not really proceed as quickly as one imagines.

Should you have any objection to telling me whether you mean to have the Memoir out by the 8th of February or not? as in the latter case I shall not overwork myself at it, there being no need that it should then appear till November.

I am anxious to know, as some plans of ours depend upon it, which I should like to arrange as soon as possible.

Believe me yours very truly

E. C. Gaskell.

331 332 333

GEORGE SMITH

Plymouth Grove,
January 7th [1857]

My dear Sir,

I have been much surprized and disappointed at receiving no proof-sheets by yesterday's or today's post. I shall be ready to correct them as soon as they are sent, which I should be very much obliged to you if you would allow them to be as soon as they are ready. Do you remember one of Miss Brontë's letters to you dated Jany 9th 1851? The beginning, (being {some}\a/rather far-fetched and satirical picture of two altars raised in a church by Mr Thackeray to St Bacon & St Bungay, &c &c.) I am going to omit;—indeed I only intend to quote the criticisms it contains further on about the 'Stones of Venice', *unless* you will give me leave to put in that piece about Mr Newby. It is so extremely amusing & characteristic, that I shall hardly be able to resist copying it into the Memoir; but still I shall, as in regard to the other passages on the same subject, be guided by your opinion as to the desirability of omitting it.

Believe me, dear Sir,
Yours very truly
E. C. Gaskell.

332 **333** 334

GEORGE SMITH

Plymouth Grove.
9th Jany [1857]

My dear Sir,
  I received your letter this morning a short time before the parcel came by the Railway delivery. I was extremely surprised at your saying in the former that {that} part of the M.S. was coming \back/, and my astonishment was not lessened on opening the parcel—for I have looked through it in vain, in hopes of discovering what alteration you think it requires. Will you be so kind as to let me know? I dare say new type is a very good thing, and that I shall be very glad you have used it, when my present impatience to receive the proof-sheets is gratified; but just now I care more how *soon* they come than anything else.
  Believe me in the greatest haste

Yours very truly
E. C. Gaskell.

GEORGE SMITH

Plymouth Grove—
January 12th [1857]

My dear Sir,

Thank you. Please will you put headings to right-hand pages?
Will you continue to send MS with the proofs?

(I hope Mr Stewart is photographing Haworth this fine day.)
Will you kindly send *two* sets of sheets to Messrs Appleton's
agent 'Charles Layton' 'Little Britain', London.

His exact number was given in an Athenæum or two back.

Again thank you. 50£ is more than I expected from Messrs
Williams & Norgate. I only hope you will get it. I don't *think* my
agreement with M. Hachette interferes with any German republication, as it only referred to a *french translation*, not to circulation
of English republication on the Continent. Messrs Harpers were
one of the three American publishers who wrote by one packet to
offer,—their offer was 35£.

I will send a batch more MSS tomorrow, by rail. You did quite
right to send it back. Miss Nussey comes today.

Yours very truly
E C Gaskell

?W. S. WILLIAMS[1]

Plymouth Grove
Monday. [?19 January 1857]

My Dear Sir,

I suspect I see your writing on the heading of the pages—
would it be giving you much trouble?—and would it *not* be
saving trouble to the printers, if, instead of waiting to insert the
accompanying extract in the proof I requested you to place it in

---

[1] Original MS. not seen. Wise & Symington (in *The Brontës*, IV, p. 210) identify
the recipient as George Smith. However, the opening words seem unusual on this
assumption.

the MS. It relates to the period when Miss Brontë went as *teacher* to Miss Wooler's school (1836 & '37) and her sister Emily accompanied her at her first going as a *pupil*. I found out from the letters that she did not remain long, by the substitution of *Anne's* name in Miss Brontë's letters for that of *Emily*; but I could not quite satisfactorily account for it, when I was writing the MS. In looking over the second notice of Emily (prefixed to one or two of her poems) at the end of 2nd edition of Wuthering Heights,—I found this extract; which exactly fills up a little blank and accounts for what wanted accounting for.

I will give you the date of the change of the sisters,—I am sorry I cannot refer you to the exact page of MS. (in looking over the letters I am sorry I cannot find the date, but I think you will easily see when it is to be inserted) Miss Nussey was here last week reading the MS. I was gratified to hear her repeatedly say how completely the life at the Parsonage appeared to her reproduced. Much of this was owing to the remarkable extracts from letters; but she said several times how exactly and accurately I had written about the life and characters.

Yours very truly,
E. C. Gaskell

*

334 **336** 338

GEORGE SMITH

[?January 1857][1]

My dear Mr Smith,
I am quite satisfied with all the past divisions, chapters, and headings,—& I only want to interfere (as I said in my last—) just in the two divisions I named—and I don't much care about them. I am 'quite better' as dear little Georgie says—except where I keep my dear tickle valuable brains too *persistently* at work,—I wish Meta was going on as satisfactorily as I am. However I don't write about family details of health; but because I fancy I know your '*man*', i.e Miss Courtenay. You want a clever woman, up in authentic fashionable gossip, yet not too— —? to put it into a

[1] Misdated: Monckton Milnes became 'Lord Houghton' in August 1863. In this case, the book referred to at the beginning may be *Cousin Phillis*. See Letters 545 and 553, especially the description in the latter of Meta's ill health.

marketable shape is it not so? I think Miss Courtenay is all this. She is the daughter of a man of very good family, {wh} a barrister—who did not practise much,—but who lived a good deal in the old witty godless Sheridan-Regency set—& was noted amongst them for his bon-mots & epicurism,—a sort of *poor* Rogers, or Luttrell or Conversation Sharpe. Well! he died,—& good go with him! leaving a son who had much the same kind of character, Frank Courtenay who was private secretary to Lord Dalhousie in India,—& afterwards something else there,—which ought to have made his fortune but did not. Miss Courtenay is *wonderfully* clever—I once went over Whitworth's (gun) works with her & Mr W. Her knowledge of machinery *he* said—he being cynical enough,—surpassed most men's. She writes what University men say are some of the most classical & witty Latin doggrel-verses embodying things of the day,—little events that happen in country houses where she is staying. She is said to have a first rate acquaintance with music, & knows & speaks well most European languages. What with her wit[,] her music, her capability of talking to clever men &c &c—she is much in society,—asked to make great houses amusing &c,—is very intimate at Lord Warwick's at the old Dss of Somerset's—& is, better judges that [*sic*] I am say—thoroughly up in 'on dits'.

She lives, or did live in lodgings in S. Audley St when at home. (By the way she is great in china & lace &c—) But I have sent for her exact address. For the society she keeps she is poor—(she is niece to a very different person—Dr Moberley Head Master of Winchester,—) and I FANCY would not be sorry to be put in the way of earning a little *quietly* and *genteelly*. I don't know how you can open negotiations however; but I will gladly give you a note saying you would like to speak to her on a little matter of business —I have been trying to find a little MSS of hers, but I believe I lent it to the present Bp of Lincoln who never returned it—It was the 'Naughty boys alphabet' a sort of parody on the old copybook moral sentences such as Procrastination is the Thief of Time &c—I can only remember *one* at this moment the letter Z Zeal and Teal should not be overdone—but they were all equally droll—some more so.—I know her pendant in Paris—a Mme la Csse de Peyronnet—(ask Lord Houghton about her) if you want such a person\in Paris[.]/She is pretty into the bargain. She is West Indian—brought up & married in Paris to the secretary of Prince Polignac,—who has come to grief because of his politics—*she* has

[?lost] her W. Indian property—is witty in either English, French *or Latin*—poor, highly connected—came over to London with her still prettier daughters in the last Exhibition,—& was quite fêted by the Houghtons Palmerstons, Henry Reeves, Nassau Seniors &c &c—. A year ago she wrote to me to ask if I wd let her translate my works &c—One of her daughters was engaged to M. Prévost Paradol,—& she was very intimate with the Guizots—& at the other end of respectability with Alfred de Musset &c &c— \She wrote two or three little comedies for the varieties[./] I know you will excuse my bad writing. I *am* in such a hurry.—

E. C. Gaskell

Thank you very much for the Life of Michael Angelo[1]—not read yet.

₀ **337** ₀

[Early February 1857]

⟨. . .⟩ and if in the latter, had you your meals sent in from a restaurant, or how? & what would be the charges? Did you engage attendance? or was it found you? & could you recommend your lodgings? (I am jotting my questions down in the most unceremonious way; but I hope you will excuse me).

How much knowledge of Italian did you find necessary, or did french pass current? Especially *in society* in Rome, was Italian necessary? or can the Roman ladies speak french or English in general? I suppose in hotels french is all that is required—? We are in most blissful ignorance of everything, & should be grateful for the smallest facts. Most of our friends give us poetical generalities, about Roman sunshine & ruins, instead of useful particulars as to the price of dinners, & the choice of lodgings.

I suppose the prices of lodgings & in fact\of/everything are much raised in the Holy Week? Was that when you were there? I really feel very guilty after having written down nearly two pages of questions, and shall wind up with apologies on the last.

Trusting you will excuse the trouble I am giving you, I remain yours very truly

E. C. Gaskell.

[1] Harford, *Life and Poems of Michael Angelo*, 2 vols., Longman, 1857.

GEORGE SMITH

Wednesday, Febry 4th [1857]

My dear Sir,

I am perplexed by the non-receipt of any proofs. Neither the 1st nor the 2nd volume seem to be getting on just now.

I wished very much to set out for Rome next week: but I hardly know when you are intending to publish the Life, and if you meant to defer it long I would rather give up going abroad now, and go nearer to the time of publication. I suppose I have no right to expect any portion of the payment of the Memoir before the day of publication; but *if it were to take place so soon as to enable me to go to Rome on the 14th* (Febry) at the latest—it would be a very great convenience if you would kindly let me have 250£.

It would also be an additional favour if you would obtain 150£ of this for me in Coutts Circular Notes, and send them to await me at Mr W Shaen's 8 Bedford Row, (who will give you a receipt for them) *before the 14th* of February. The notes I believe can be had of 5£ each, and if so, I should be glad to have them all of that amount.

I hope you understand that I shall only require to know in the first instance, when you expect to publish the Life, as every thing depends on that. I have today sent you by railroad the three Photographs Mr Stewart sent me last night along with the accompanying note.

The views disappoint me a little; but he is very good to have taken so much pains about them. They give an idea of wildness and desolation; but not of heigth [*sic*] & steepness, & of the sweeping line of moors beyond. The parsonage is that square house by itself to the\behind/left of the Church—very faint in all, owing to the distance.

Yours very truly
E C Gaskell

338 **339** 341

GEORGE SMITH

Plymouth Grove
Febry 6th 1857.

My dear Sir,
I send you a sepia drawing from a sketch of mine of Haworth Parsonage, Sexton's Shed, School-house, Sexton's (tall) House (where the Curate lodged,[)] & the Church.

I should like an engraving of the wild old place, & I think perhaps this would be better than the Photograph.

Will you be so kind as to make yr suggestions, & name the alterations you wish to have in writing?

If I go, we go, through London, from Manchester to Calais in one day.

Yours very truly
E C Gaskell.

304 **340** 0

LAETITIA WHEELWRIGHT

Plymouth Grove
Manchester
Saturday, Febry 7 [1857]

My dear Miss Wheelright [sic],
I have today finished my Life of Miss Brontë; and next week we set out for Rome. Before I go however I must return you your precious letters, with my best thanks, not merely for the loan of them, although their value has been great, but for the kind readiness with which you all, (especially you and your mother,) met my wishes about giving me information.

I hope sometime or other to be able to call upon you, and express all this personally, if you will allow me.

Meanwhile I trust you will accept a copy of the Memoir, which will be forwarded to you on publication; and with kind compliments,

Ever believe me, dear Miss Wheelright

Yours most truly
E C Gaskell

GEORGE SMITH

Plymouth Grove
Feby 8th [1857]

My dear Sir,

I am glad that the sketch of Haworth will do for the engraver. Would it save time if it were lithographed? on tinted paper—with white light{s}, perhaps. I am inclined to think this would give more the character of the place than engraving. But of that you can judge better than I can.

I hope you may receive a little more copy tomorrow-morning, and the conclusion on Tuesday morning, but of this I am not quite sure.

Before concluding any money arrangements with you I think I ought to mention how large a number of copies I shall wish to have at my private disposal, so that you may deduct the value of the extra {number of} copies from what I should receive. I enclose two lists of people to whom I wish them sent. One is of those to whom I owe copies, from their having assisted me in my work with lending me letters, or giving me drawings, information &c—the other is of friends to whom I habitually give copies of my works, and not as in the other case people to whom I offer them as marks of gratitude. By tomorrow I hope to have decided a little more, so as to be able to ask you how to dispose of the money. Mr Gaskell thinks that Circular Notes can be got through his bankers here, in which case we need not trouble you to procure them in London. I have also made up all the letters which have been lent me into separate packets, and have enclosed them to you along with the Edinburgh and Quarterly Review, in one parcel, while I put up the M.S.S. of Miss Brontë's works that you so kindly lent me in another. Both parcels shall be sent in the course of a few days.

Believe me yours truly

E. C. Gaskell.

329 **342** 345

EMELYN STORY[1]

Plymouth Grove, Manchester
Monday, February 8th [i.e. 9th], 1857

My dear Mrs Story,

We are really truly coming to Rome!!!!!! We are starting off on Friday next—the 13th—and if you don't want to have us on Saturday the 21st, will you write to us either to Paris, where we shall be on the 15th, 16th and 17th at the Hotel des Missions Etrangères, Rue de Bac, or to the Hotel de l'Orient, Marseilles, which we hope to reach on the afternoon of Wednesday 18th, and to leave by the direct (Thursday 19th) boat for Civita Vecchia— arriving there according to *promise* on 7 o'clock on Saturday morning, in time for the 10 o'clock diligence to Rome.

Will you really receive us for a few days? And are we really coming—and shall we truly see Rome? I don't believe it. It is a dream! I shall never believe it, and shall have to keep pinching myself!

Yours ever, dear Mr & Mrs Story, affectionately
E. C. Gaskell

341 **343** 344

GEORGE SMITH

42 Plymouth Grove
Manchester
Monday, Febry 8. [*i.e.* 9 February 1857]

My dear Sir,

The gravestones in the Haworth Church Yard, are FLAT, not many head-stones; and not a tuft of grass between. Will you be so kind as to pay 50£\on my account/to the Agent of *Macbean and Co* at Rome; I was told that '*Mackrakan*' or some such name was his London Correspondent, but I can't find any such name in the list of London Bankers.

[1] From a printed source, which notes that it was, *c.* 1930, in the possession of Mrs Waldo Story. We have been unable to find its present owner.

Perhaps you will kindly pay the remainder of the money (deducting *besides* the list sent yesterday, a copy for Mr Forster, former Editor of the Examiner, I don't know where he lives now he is married)—through Masterman's to my husband's account with Sir Benjamin Heywood & Co, Manchester. I won't trouble you about the Circular notes as I find they can be got here. We go on *Friday,* 13th.

Yours very truly
E. C. Gaskell.

343 **344** 348

GEORGE SMITH

Plymouth Grove
Wednesday. [?11 February 1857]

My dear Sir

Mr Gaskell says he will complete all arrangements with you: only as I have five minutes I just write to thank you for all your kindness and obligingness. We are going to friends, who are long resident at Rome, and who have often urged us to come and take up our abode with them there. So I do not *think* we shall want any rooms; but still I am much obliged to you for naming Mrs Smith, and will thankfully apply to her, if need be, for some advice &c—

Mr Richmond says he will do his part speedily,—and I am sure he will,—not merely for my & your sakes but for the friends through whom I can urge him to speed. I *do hope* it will be published soon. And please to remember I am just the reverse of Miss Brontë; I never want to see or hear of any reviews; when I have done with a book I want to shake off the recollection thereof forever. Besides I do not like reviewing, as it is carried on in England. I hope it will sell well for your sake,—for I think you have behaved very liberally about it.

I ought to send a copy to Miss Mary Taylor, Wellington, New Zealand.\please will you send one of my 20./She says in a letter to Miss Nussey. Does Mrs Gaskell know 'what a nest of hornets she is pulling about her ears?'[1]

---

[1] See *The Brontës*, ed. Wise & Symington, IV, p. 198. Letter to Ellen Nussey, 19 April 1856.

You will receive the formal receipt by this post. I give you my best thanks.

Yours truly E C Gaskell

₃₄₂ **345** ₃₇₅

W. W. and/or EMELYN STORY[1]

[?February 1857]

⟨. . .⟩ I must first of all thank you for all the kind help you have given us, and then accept most gladly your charming invitation to spend our first few days with you while we choose our lodgings and get a little initiated into Roman ways.

₀ **346** ₃₄₇

CHARLES ELIOT NORTON[2]

[Rome. Spring 1857]

Dear Sir,

My headache is quite gone, and we shall like a drive very much indeed. I am afraid from what I saw of Miss [Catherine] Winkworth yesterday that she will not be well enough to accompany us—so pray don't trouble yourself to send her word. We are going to beg that François[3] may take this note. Will you forgive me for taking the liberty? It is on the principle of 'Give an inch &c.'

Yours truly ever

E C G

[1] From a printed source, which dates 'apparently in March'. Something in the original gave Henry James the impression that there had been 'a delay in starting'. It was probably an obscure reference to the troubles experienced on the actual journey, including a boiler explosion on the ship out of Marseilles. See *Letters and Memorials*, ed. Winkworth, II, pp. 96, 108.

[2] *Annotation*: This is, I think, the first note I received from Mrs Gaskell. Rome, 1856. C. E. N. [His date is a year out.]

[3] Boggia, Norton's courier.

CHARLES ELIOT NORTON[1]

43 Via di San Isidoro
Tuesday March 30 [1857]

My dear Mr Norton,
Will you allow me to introduce Mr Norris to you? I think your acquaintance with him will prove a mutual pleasure to both. It is his first visit to Rome, and he takes interest in most of the things which have interested you. He is leaving Rome in a very short time so you must make the most of your few days.
Believe me to remain,
Yours very truly
E. C. Gaskell

REV. R. S. OLDHAM

Plymouth Grove
Manchester —
June 1 [1857]

My dear Mr Oldham,
We only returned from Italy on Thursday night last. Our letters had not been forwarded, which has led to much annoyance; more than I can speak of here.
I found above a hundred awaiting me, for my own personal share. Among others yours, which I value extremely; I think you rightly understand the characters of the three sisters. Emily impresses me as something terrific. Much could not be told of small details which wd have made them understood. I was under a solemn promise to write the Life,—although I shrank from the task; against which I was warned by one who knew all the circumstances well, as 'certain to pull a hornet's nest about my ears.' But it did not seem to me right to shrink from {a duty}\the work/

---

[1] *Address (on envelope)* Favoured by the revd Pilkington Norris | Charles. E. Norton Esq | 3 Piazza di Spagna | Ultimo Piano.

as soon as it appeared to me in the light of a duty. To do it at all it was necessary to tell painful truths. Like all pieces of human life, faithfully told there must be some great lesson to be learnt. May we try to learn in a humble spirit!

Marianne too found Mrs Oldham's most kind note. She would extremely like to accept the invitation contained in it, sometime later on. At present, after a long absence from home, she must take up her duties of various kinds. If you & Mrs Oldham are in our neighbourhood, pray let us know, that if possible we may arrange for you to come to us.

In greatest haste,—and with kindest regards to Mrs Oldham, believe me ever,

Yours most truly
E C Gaskell.

344 **348** 350

GEORGE SMITH

42 Plymouth Grove
Manchester
June 3 [1857]

Dear Sir,

I am at home, once more, & ready to do anything you may wish {fo} towards preparing the 3rd edition for the Press. Of course you are aware that several passages are to be taken out. Mr Shaen advises as little alteration of the paging as possible. Another omission, I wish for in the 1st vol. in compliance with the nicely & kindly expressed wish of some survivors.

To make up for these omissions I have several things to insert,— more characteristics of Haworth, volunteered by the gentleman who asks for the omission above,—corrections as to the power of presentation, & details respecting Mr Brontë's obtaining the living, an anecdote furnished by Miss Martineau, & many details sent me in a fresh letter from Miss Mary Taylor.

I have much information sent me about Cowan's bridge & Casterton Schools; but I have written to ask Mr Shaen whether I can make use of it.

I hate the whole affair, & every thing connected with it. I am very sorry indeed you have had so much annoyance. I will make up for it to you, as far as I can, by taking all possible pains with the third edition.

Mr Gaskell desires his best compliments.

Yours very truly
E C Gaskell

347 **349** 354

CHARLES ELIOT NORTON

Home!

42 Plymouth Grove
Manchester
June 3rd 1857.

My dear Mr Norton,

Only three lines to say we arrived safely at home last Thursday night, & found all well, and your letter of welcome awaiting us, for which *many* thanks. It took us *so* back to dear happy Venice. I found trouble enough awaiting me from the publication of my Life of C. B. or rather not 'awaiting' me, but settled without me; settled for the best, all things considered, I am sure. Well! we won't speak any more of that.

The girls are quite well & send kindest regards, & beg that you won't let François forget them. When will you come to us? I have not yet been to the Manchester Exhibition, having had too much to do in other ways, but Meta says it is charming, & exceeds her expectations. Mrs Stowe comes to us today for one night, & tomorrow I shall go for the first time with her. Tomorrow our house fills. Oh! the delicious quiet & dolce far niente of Italy! We stopped at Verona, one night, Milan one night, Como, one— Bellagio one, Como one, Arona two,\going to Orta from Arona/ Genoa three,—three on the Cornice (we were all ill, & slightly out of spirits in consequence, so the Cornice was a failure—) Nice (owing to mistake about steamer, our first mistake) 4—which we grudged. Marseilles one—Paris two—that is our dull dry outline, —but it was very happy—I found upwards of a hundred letters awaiting me, all wanting answers.—But I write just these hurried lines to you kind friend, to tell you we are once more safe here. I wish Mr Gaskell *looked* stronger,—he never complains, or will allow anything is the matter with him. I long for him to have the complete change of going from home. *I wish you could persuade him to go to America with you.* The congregation would gladly give him leave of absence—& I cd soon earn the passage & travelling money. He wants change, & yet hates leaving home. His flesh wants it, but his spirit abhors it, do you understand?

Yours most truly ever
E. C. Gaskell

348 **350** 353

GEORGE SMITH

June 5th [1857]

My dear Sir,

How had omissions better be made; *and additional material put in? in notes* or how?

And how had I better send you the corrections—will making them on a sheet of paper and referring to pages & lines, do?

I have heard no encomiums of the book, nor anything about it indeed, (as I had begged Mr Gaskell not to name it to me),—till on Monday *night*, (25th May) in Paris I met my letters—which, being 3 weeks old, were very vague; and only sufficed to make me anxiously hurry home, where I arrived on Thursday night, 28th & there heard all.

Since then Mr Carus Wilson is threatening an action, & printing a pamphlet; in 'refutation of the Charges against C. Bridge School,'—and the many who are now offering me testimony in proof of my correctness are poor people,—I mean governesses, struggling surgeons' wives, schoolmistresses &c.—who say I *may* make use of their names, if absolutely necessary—but that it may seriously injure them if I do. And of course I must do anything rather than bring them into trouble. I have sent some of the things to Mr Shaen,—and I won't bring you or any one else into any more scrapes, if I can help it.

Will you send me an *East Indian* Army-List, if there is such a thing? I don't know if there be. And have you a copy of Jane

M.G.L.—Q

Eyre, *with the preface & dedication to Thackeray*. I don't know which edition it is.

Mr Gaskell joins with me in hoping that you & Mrs Smith will come & pay us a visit before our beautiful Exhibition is closed. It really is beautiful,—even after Italy. Indeed I think Italy makes us enjoy seeing the pictures of our old friends, the great Masters, all the more.

But this is wandering off from the subject, which is to tell you that it is your bounden *duty* to come & see our Art-Treasures, and to bring Mrs Smith with you. You will never see such a collection again; and if you will only tell me about what time it would suit you best to come to us, I think we could soon arrange what I hope would be a mutual pleasure to {both}\all/of us.

Yours very truly

E. C. Gaskell.

Mr Gaskell desires his best compliments to you.

₀ **351** ₀

CHARLES KINGSLEY

Plymouth Grove

Manchester

June 6th [1857]

My dear Sir,

I came home from Italy last Thursday night but one,—May 28th.

Owing to some mistake on the part of the person to whom we entrusted our letters for the English post, while travelling in the North of Italy, I had received no letters from England for nearly five weeks, before I met those that had been lying for me for some time in Paris; which I received late on the night of the 26th. At home I found many letters, as none had been forwarded. Among others, yours. I valued it and value it now, more than perhaps you would like to have me tell you.

I can only say Respect & value the memory of Charlotte Brontë as she deserves. *No one* can know all she had to go through, but those who knew her well, and have seen her most intimate and confidential letters. The merciful judgment of all connected with that terrible life lies with God; and we may all be thankful that it does.

I tried hard to write the truth. Now Mr W. W. Carus Wilson threatens me with an action. I think I can stand it all patiently. Only do think of her, on, through all. *You do not know what she had to bear; and what she had to hear.*

Dear Mr Kingsley, will you give my kind regards to Mrs Kingsley and ever believe me, with truest respect,

Yours very truly
E. C. Gaskell

327 352 •353a

ELLEN NUSSEY

Tuesday, June 16th [1857]

My dearest Miss Nussey

I am in the Hornet's nest with a vengeance. I only hope you dear good little lady that {y} nobody is worrying you in any way. We came home on *May 28th* and I never heard of the Letters in the Times till my return. I have much much [*sic*] to tell you on this subject; but I am warned not to *write*; and must keep it till we meet.

Mr Carus Wilson threatens an action about the Cowan's Bridge School.

Mr Redhead's son-in-law writes to deny {that}\my/account of the Haworth commotions, & gives another as true, in which I don't see any great difference.

Miss Martineau has written sheet upon sheet regarding the quarrel? misunderstanding? between her & Miss Brontë[.][1]

Two separate householders in London *each* declare that the *first* interview between Miss Brontë and Miss Martineau took place at *her* house.

I am preparing a third edition, & must, I think, go over to Gawthorp for a night next week, (if they can have me,) to see some people there. But Marianne & Mr Gaskell would be at home.

---

[1] The passages objected against will be found in the first edition of the *Life*, I, pp. 63–78; pp. 30–3; and II, pp. 282–3 respectively.

Can you, dear Miss Nussey come to us any day *this* week the sooner the better for us, and stay till the end of next week. We do not go to the Queen's reception\on the 29/, but I *believe* we shall have our house full that week of friends, who do.

I want to show you many letters,—most praising the character of our dear friend as she deserves,—and from people whose opinion she would have cared for, such as the Duke of Argyll, Kingsley, Gleig &c &c. Many abusing me; I should think seven or eight of this kind from the Carus Wilson clique.

I am writing as if I were in famous spirits, and I think I *am* so *angry* that I am almost merry in my bitterness, if you know that state of feeling; but I have cried more since I came home that [*sic*] I ever did in the same space of time before; and never needed kind words so much,—& no one gives me them. I *did so try* to *tell the truth*, & I believe *now* I hit as near the truth as any one *could* do. And I weighed every line with all my whole power & heart, so that every line should go to it's great purpose of making *her* known & valued, as one who had gone through such a terrible life with a brave & faithful heart.

But I think you know & knew all this. One comfort is too that God knows the truth.

Do come if you can. Mere *seeing* you would do me good. My kindest regards to your sister.

Yours ever affectionately
E C Gaskell

You shall go to the Exhibition every day. It is lovely; only I have hardly had time to look at it[.]

350 **353** 363

GEORGE SMITH

June 17. [1857]

My dear Sir,

I am exceedingly obliged to you for the books—(you must please keep an acct against me for the India List & Jane Eyre. The Professor I gladly accept as a present.) May I have an Appendix to the 3rd edition, if I want it; *or*, in prohibiting Notes do you wish me strictly to confine myself to the regular narrative in pages, without any notice of Mr Carus Wilson (who threatens an action for 'spiritual pride', *and* heading a page 'Character of the revd Carus-Wilson &c'—) The anecdotes Mr Nicholls desires me to omit were heard of by me (and others) from eyewitnesses, or his own wife. However I submit. May I put in this Preface sent me from Paris.

'If anybody is displeased with any statement or words in the following pages I beg leave to with-draw it, and to express my deep regret for having offered so expensive an article as truth to the Public.'

It is clever, is it not?

Yours very truly & in great haste,
E. C. Gaskell

*

349 354 360

CHARLES ELIOT NORTON

Plymouth Grove
June 21 Sunday [1857]

My dear Mr Norton,

Many, many thanks for your letter. You can't think how kindness touches me just now; almost *painfully*. No! Neither Mr Gaskell nor I can possibly go with you on the 25th. He says it is quite out of the question on many accounts: he 'could as soon go to the Moon.' I WISH he could have such an entire change, very much. As for my going,—say Mr Gaskell was going,—and that the girls were 'seen after,' and that our law expences &c left us money,—still *I* could not go. I must stay here with as calm a face, and as brave a heart as I can, at any rate for the present.

But you *can* come to us—and now I'll tell you when[—]only I can't tell you. We have *two*\spare/bed-rooms till the 2nd of July —Thursday week—when Julia & Flossy & Hearn go to the Lakes for a month's change of air; and we shall consequently have *four* spare bedrooms during their absence. *But* I want you to see them—& you won't unless you come before July 2.

Now a friend (Miss Nussey the 'Ellen' of C. Brontë's Life[)] comes here on Tuesday next—till the 'end of this week'—a Mr

Wilson an extremely intelligent Scotch artist, married to a cousin of mine, comes on *Friday 26th* for a few days,—Mr Bonamy Price\Dr Arnold's friend/ comes 'some day in the week, beginning June 28th.' Now you see some of these 3 *might* overlap; but if you wd not mind being turned out *for the night only* if they did why you could come & see all 4[1] Miss Gaskells & their Papa & Mama before July 2nd, & as much after as ever you like—Queen comes on Monday 29th & Tuesday 30th is a shut day at the Exhibition except for 2 guinea ticket holders.

Any time in July we shall be most glad to see you. In greatest haste, but with kindest remembrances from all your fellow travellers,

Yours ever most truly
E. C. Gaskell

₀ 355 ₀

?WILLIAM SHAEN[2]

42 Plymouth Grove,
June 21st 1857.

Dear Sir,

Just as so often happens when one {has} puts by something in a particularly safe hiding-place, have I carefully secreted and consequently lost the report of the Casterton Schools for 1845. I am so extremely sorry to keep you waiting for it; but meanwhile I send you the one for the previous year—and you shall have its successor as soon as it reaches me from the hands of those\friends who live near C.,/whom I have set to work to procure me another.

Yours truly
E. C. Gaskell.

[1] From here to the end is a copy, with annotation: '(original ½ sheet & signature given away for Shawn bazaar) May 1905'.

[2] Cf. Letter 350 above.

₂₉₁ **356** ₃₆₂

JOHN GREENWOOD[1]

Plymouth Grove
June 23rd 1857

Dear Sir,

I must apologise very much for not {[?]} having answered your letter and for not returning you the document you were so kind as to send me. My time really has been so fully occupied that I have not been able to answer half my letters.

Would you kindly see for me if on the monument to the Brontë family in Haworth Church Anne Brontë died when she was only 27.

Believe me to remain
Yours very truly
E C Gaskell

₀ **357** ₀

UNKNOWN

Plymouth Grove
Tuesday June 23 [1857?]

Madam,

I must apologise very much for not sooner having answered your letter, but I was abroad when it came and ever since my return I & my daughters have been busily employed in answering letters we found waiting and those that have come every day. I am very sorry that I have no scrap of Miss Brontë's writing, all that I have it is of importance to keep, otherwise I should have had great pleasure in sending you some. I am always so pleased when my works have in any way helped to wile away any weary hours, and you say that I have been able to do that for you.

Mr Bronte still officiates at Haworth occasionally but he is very much helped by his son-in-law Mr Nichols. Again apologising for not sooner having answered your letter.

Believe me to remain
Yours faithfully
E C Gaskell

[1] *Address (on envelope)* Mr John Greenwood | 224 Haworth | Keighley | Yorkshire. *Postmarks* MANCHESTER | 2 S | JU 24 | 57 *and* LEEDS | JU 25 | 1857 *and* KEIGHLEY | JU 25 | 1857 | A *and* HAWORTH | JU 25 | 1857 | A *and* PLYMOUTH GROVE. The letter could be in M. E. Gaskell's hand.

249 **358** 0

WILLIAM FAIRBAIRN[1]

[June 1857]

Mr dear Mr Fairbairn,

I don't think you know how much good your letter did me. In the first place I was really afraid that you did not like my book, because I had never received your usual letter of criticism; and in the second, it was the one sweet little drop of honey that the postman had brought me for some time, as, on the average, I had been receiving three letters a day for above a fortnight, finding great fault with me (to use a *mild* expression for the tone of their compliments) for my chapter about the Cowan Bridge school.

So I gave your letter a great welcome, my dear Mr Fairbairn, and I should have replied to it sooner, but that it has seemed very difficult to catch you. No sooner did I hear you were in Manchester than you wrote to Mary Holland, saying that you were leaving; and, really, unless I had directed to 'Wm. Fairbairn, Esq., Railway Carriage,' I don't know where I could have found you.

I have had a preface to my (forthcoming) third edition sent to me, which I dare not insert there; but it is too good to be lost, therefore I shall copy it out for you:

'If anybody is displeased with any statement in this book, they are requested to believe it withdrawn, and my deep regret expressed for its insertion, as truth is too expensive an article to be laid before the British public.'

But for the future I intend to confine myself to lies (*i.e.* fiction). It is safer.

We did so enjoy Rome. We often thought of you, and half considered if you would not turn up in the Holy Week, which you hinted at as possible when we left. We came home by Florence, Venice, Milan, Genoa, and Nice. I wonder if you are at home, and if we could tempt you to come in to our 8 o'clock tea to-morrow night. We have Miss Brontë's faithful friend E. staying with us.[2]

Yours ever most truly and gratefully,

E. C. Gaskell.

[1] From a printed source ('probably June 1857').
[2] See p. 455 above.

₀ **359** ₀

UNKNOWN

42 Plymouth Grove
Saturday, June 27. [1857]

Dear Sir,

I believe some letters about my statements relating to Cowan Bridge School have appeared in some numbers of the Examiner & Times.

I am afraid it is giving you a great deal of trouble but will you be so kind as to order those numbers to be looked out & sent to me. I *particularly* want any letters of the revd H Shepheard.[1]—

With many apologies, believe me to remain,

Yours very truly
E. C. Gaskell

₃₅₄ **360** ₃₇₄

CHARLES ELIOT NORTON

Wednesday
July 1st [1857]

My dear Mr Norton,

We *are* so sorry—all of us, and each of us separately,—sorry for your not coming, & sorry for the cause. No! now you won't see Flossy & Julia, nor Hearn,—that is to say *if* you really do sail on the 25. Captain Hill is here too—and was, along with us, hoping to see you—when first of all came your telegraph, & secondly this morning comes your letter,—we had so many little plans for you, you naughty man to go and fall ill—just when Miss Ewarts had made first one, & then another arrangement for making your acquaintance,—which they *particularly* wanted to do.—

However you must come to us as soon as you are well; even if we have to find a\night/lodging for you—which I hope won't be the case. Ruskin lectures here on the 10 & 13th—*on* our Exhibition. It will be worth hearing—

Ever yours most truly in greatest haste
E. C. Gaskell

*

[1] A letter from Shepheard was published in *The Times* on 27 March 1857.

₀ **361** ₃₇₁

MARTHA BROWN

Plymouth Grove
Saturday July 11th [1857][1]

My dear Martha,
    I should be very much obliged to you indeed if you would be
so kind as to lend me the letters you speak of. I will take great
care of them and return them to you quite safely. I am very glad
you thought of it.

Yours truly
E. C. Gaskell

₃₅₆ **362** ₀

JOHN GREENWOOD[2]

Plymouth Grove
[c. 16 July 1857]

My dear Mr Greenwood,
    Thank you very much indeed for your kind note of sympathy
with me in my difficulties. I feel I have tried my utmost to write
the Life as truthfully as it has been in my power to do, if I have
failed I only regret it very much. Thank you also for the flowers
you sent me.

Believe me to remain
Yours sincerely
E C Gaskell.

*

[1] See Letter 371 for date.
[2] *Address (on envelope)* Mr John Greenwood | Haworth | Keighley | Yorkshire.
Postmarks MAN⟨CHESTER⟩ | ⟨ ⟩ *and* LEEDS | JY 17 | 1857 | B *and* KEIGHLEY | JY 17 |
1857 | A *and* HAWORTH | JY 17 | 1857.

359 **363** 364

GEORGE SMITH

> Mill-Brow,
> Skelwith Bridge
> nr
> Ambleside.
> July 28 [1857]

My dear Sir,

You must have thought me very neglectful, and I must hurry over my apologies.

Besides the Exhibition commotion this year which has absorbed all my spare time, about a month ago my second daughter became engaged to an Indian officer, whose furlough was almost immediately recalled—Under the circumstances an immediate marriage has been in contemplation, but after many preparations were made in a tremendous hurry, absorbing *all* my time, & making me very very anxious & unhappy this plan has been given up; & she does not go till next year, when he meets her in Egypt if all goes well.

Under this pressure of care & anxiety I commissioned Mr Shaen, on last *Monday fortnight*, to see you directly on his return to town, & beg you to get some one else to edit the 3rd edition—I sending all papers letters &c.—Daily have I expected to hear from Mr Shaen or you what you said to this proposal; but I have never had a word. On Friday I wrote, saying that as I was ill,—& coming here to recruit,—& my daughter's marriage put off—I could do the 3rd edition if some arrangement with you had not been already made, & the affair in the hands of some one else. Today I receive this note,—so I set hard to work on my weary & oppressive task —& only write this just to tell you how things have been—I am here till the end of this week—

> Yours very truly
> E C Gaskell

₃₆₃ **364** ₃₆₅

GEORGE SMITH

Mill-Brow, Skelwith nr Ambleside.
July 31. [?1857]

My dear Sir,
 Can you get the corrections *without* the 'high privilege['] of an
introduction to Mrs Gaskell. If you can't, why—I *must* have the
corrections, or rather you must. Just try a little agreeable coaxing.
Thank you for telling me about the Indian news. I have never had
a notion in my mind about India in any way,—I did not know
there were three presidencies till about two months ago; and as
for whether the natives are white green or blue I know nothing,
so that we are now going to read and learn as much as we can;
and are delighted to meet with any one who has been in India, &
can tell us something about it. Capt Hill belongs to the *Madras*
Engineers. We only hear rumours here, & return to Manchester
on Monday next at the *latest*,—but I suppose Madras is quiet. Do
you know India? How is it you publish an *Indian* newspaper?
                         Yours very truly   E C Gaskell

₃₆₄ **365** ₃₆₆

GEORGE SMITH

Plymouth Grove
                    Saturday. [?Early August 1857]

My dear Sir,
 Would you be so kind as to see that the alterations and omissions suggested by Mr Shaen in his letter (which I enclose) are
made?
 With respect to the contradiction\Page 66/involved in the 3£
entrance\for clothes/on the one page, and the 1£ entrance for
clothes on the next—I can only find out that it has been so printed
in the 1st edition, and has not been found fault with by any of
the Casterton critics. I don't understand it myself; but I know I
copied this from a Casterton Report; which I had to return. And
as Mr Shepheard declines letting me now see *any* Reports, & as

I don't know to whom else to apply for one, it must either stand as it does, or*one* statement/be omitted. Page 70, is quite a right & wise correction.

Page 73

Page 81. Insert Mr Shaen's alteration. I am only too glad to have his consent for the omission.

Page 82. Quite right. Only 'daily' *is* true.

All Mr Shaen's alterations on this page are good, & to be adopted.

My daughter had a letter from Captain Hill this morning, in which he speaks of the kindness you showed him yesterday. Believe me I am truly obliged to you for this. To return to the Life[.] Every one who has been harmed in this unlucky book complains of some thing. The two servants[1] named in page 49, make a doleful complaint, & have even been over to see Mr Brontë \\from Bradford to Haworth,/about my saying 1st line 'there was plenty & *even waste* in the house' &c.

If these three offensive words can be left out, please let them.

May I have two copies of the 3rd edition—one to be sent to the Secretary of the Mechanic's Institution, Haworth,\\Keighley &c/ who has written to ask for it—and another for an old friend & governess of mine here.—Do you know who Sir George Saville of Yorkshire (dead 60 or 70 years ago) was? Some of his friends have written to ask me to write his Life—and I have not a notion who he was—I *fancy* a great Yorkshire Sq: with political, & social opinions in advance of his age, & yet maintaining the state of an old English gentleman, & the head of a large 'gathering'. This I make out from their letters, which I have not answered.

Thank you very much for every word, every sign of sympathy about India. From the depths of ignorance I am roused up to the most vivid & intense interest. This daughter of mine is a most dear friend, more like a sister to me than anything else; and I like Capt Hill extremely; but the engagement is a most anxious one. Has Miss Martineau written to you about *her* Indian book[2]—

Yours most truly   E C Gaskell.

[1] Nancy and Sarah Garrs.

[2] *British Rule in India*, Smith & Elder, 1857. Originally appeared as articles in *The Daily News*.

GEORGE SMITH

Plymouth Grove—
Augt 13. [1857]

My dear Sir,

Your letter brings us the first intelligence about India; and I am very sorry to learn that the news is bad. Capt Hill, who came down here by the evening ex[press] last night, is very much disheartened by your brief account of the telegraphic message.

However thank you *much* for sending it. I return the proofs, having corrected them as well as I can. Will you ask the printers to leave out the 's in Cowan{'s} bridge? And will you kindly thank Mr Williams for his plan about Paternoster Row. I am very stupid with repeated headaches just now; and not quite sure if my corrections (or *absence* of corrections) are to be relied upon. I should be glad if some one would look over the French dévoirs, please.

Sir George Saville is buried in York Minster, with 'a very fine epitaph upon him.' I enclose another long letter respecting my imputations of waste. If not too late can you take out 'rough' and 'wasteful' at page 46. Vol 1. It is 'anything for a quiet life' with me just now; so if anybody objects to anything I am ready to take it out, and leave the Memoir as 'wersh[1] and fusionless', as need be.

Now I learn that Mrs Smith is still at Scarborough I have double & treble hopes of seeing you both here.

Yours very truly
E. C. Gaskell

GEORGE SMITH

Wednesday.
[Mid-August 1857]

My dear Sir,

I am not going to write a preface; if I did, it would involve so much *personal* appearance, as it were before the public, and so

[1] Tasteless, insipid. See 'Mr Harrison's Confessions', c. VIII (*Works*, ed. Ward, V, p. 438).

many consequent explanations that I am just going to say nothing at all. Or else I could insert such droll varieties of complaints. Every one writes to me, whose name has been named I think; or whose grandmother's great uncle once removed has been alluded to. Today I receive a letter from Ohio from some Hamilton J. S. Hill, who says I have alluded to his mother in the character of Miss 'Scatcherd',[1]—Now as I don't know who his mother was, I can't possibly say; but [as] he sends me three sheets of angry abuse I can only see that I have made some one very angry. However, I have, fortunately?, anxieties of another kind, which make me very indifferent to all this. Captain Hill again speaks of your 'kindness'; and again I heartily thank you. Sometime I may come upon you, for the practical advice which I fancy you can procure for me, when the day draws nearer for my daughter to join him. You, I fancy, know ladies who have been in India, and can give me practical advice about the 'outfit,' and journey. I do not require all this wisdom for some months, however.

I received your books last night quite safely, and plunged into 'Lutfullah'[2] with great interest, being prepared to like it from the notice in the Athenæum. The Bombay Q. Review looks good too, and I hit upon a lively paper describing the Overland journey, which fell in well with the direction of my curiosity.

Madame Mohl is a great friend of mine, and also a very old friend of Sir James Stephen's. I think, that partly owing to some very plain-speaking on her part he is trying to 'make friends' as the children say; and as she is also a relation of the Carus Wilsons, (though pretty bitter against them for reasons connected with property), I wished to accede to her desire of seeing the proofs relating to the C. W. & Lady Scott part. But unless you hear soon\in two days/from her, or from me, relating to her opinion, pray do not stop the printing.

Mr Gaskell is from home at the Lakes, so I have looked over these proofs, which I return by this post, myself; but I have not such a quick eye as Mr Gaskell for typographical errors, and very possibly some remain in.

I wish you would let us know if you and Mrs Smith intend

[1] In the Cowan Bridge prospectus Miss Finch was named as Scourge Mistress at 'a very trifling annual remuneration'.

[2] *Autobiography of Lutfullah, a Mohammedan Gentleman*, ed. E. B. Eastwick, Smith & Elder, 1857.

going to Liverpool; that we might see if we were not able to tempt you here for two or three days at that time. Our days are becoming fast filled up, but we have some 'gaps' between our different visitors and should be extremely glad if your time of coming to Liverpool, fell in with any of our 'gaps'. For instance the 24, 25, 26, and 27th of this month we should be delighted to welcome you & Mrs Smith; on either the 28th or 29th M. & Mme Mohl with their niece come here, after the Worcester Festival,— and will I hope remain a fortnight, after which I believe we should again be able to receive you. And would not we question you about India, that's all.

Yours very truly
E. C. Gaskell.

o 368 381

MARIA MARTINEAU

Sunday. [23 August 1857]

My dear Miss Martineau,

Thank you *very* much for writing, and thank your Aunt too very heartily & truly for thinking of me when she was so ill & feeble herself. I am in despair about 'the public'. For some reason they seem to say such bitter & hard things about me, & one never comes to an end of them. I do not know what to do; but if Miss [Harriet] Martineau advises me strongly to do any thing, I have such reliance on her strong sense & warm heart that I believe I should do it; even if I had to appear; how much more when she herself most kindly offers to be the medium of offering some explanation to the public. But the fact is I am so ill with a bad headache—(Captain Hill leaves us for India, in a few hours;[1] & we heard yesterday of the death of two *dear* dear friends massacred at Cawnpore,[2]) that I seem as if I could not think or act. Only would you be so good as to read these letters. Mr Rylands explains the 'animus' of Nancy Garr;[3] {one does} I have taken out 'plenty & even waste'[,][4] the words she first complained of & which {she} I inserted (they being the very words used by my informant,)

---

[1] Cf. below, p. 468 and n. But Sunday was 23 August.   [2] See Letter 369.
[3] See above, p. 463.   [4] 1st edition, I, p. 49.

to show that it was from no *stingy* motive that Mr Brontë refused his children (aged from 4 to 8) meat, but from the same kind of reason or fancy that made us confine our eldest child to vegetable diet till she was 6.

Mr Nicholls has sent me a list of omissions which Mr Brontë wishes to have made in this third edition; (refusal of animal food, sawing up chairs, burning hearth rug—(all told me on the authority of uneducated Haworth people) & the cutting up of the silk gown, an anecdote so strongly resembling the others in character as to be confirmatory to a certain degree, & told me by C. B. herself; & not only to me, but to Miss Nussey & Miss Wooler, both of whom believe it, I *think* to this day.

I enclose copy of Mr B's first letter; an intermediate letter about the mistakes, dated July 30, & one received *today* by the same post as yours, evidently meaning *very* kindly; and he really has been so steady in his way to me all along, that I would rather let them all go on attacking me, than drag him into any squabble either with me, or the public or any one.

All Mr Nicholls' list of omissions have been attended to,—he does not include the pistol-shooting, among the things he\as Mr Brontë's secy/wishes to have taken out.

As I said I am so in despair, in consequence of all this, that I don't feel as if any one would ever get me to rights; but I am only too thankful to any one who will judge for me. Only I must save Mr Brontë from worry as much as ever I can.

Yours most truly
E C Gaskell.

Do thank Mrs Martineau VERY much.

367 369 370

GEORGE SMITH

[23 August 1857]

My dear Sir,

Thank you for yr letter yesterday. Fortunately Mr Shaen was here, so I consulted him.

He said he would not take out the pistol shooting, as it was \not/included in Mr Nicholls list of omissions; but I am willing to 'do anything for a quiet life,—' so if you can, please take it out.

The Mr Dearden who 'gets up the case against me', in the Bradford paper, is employed by the servant who is indignant at being accused of wastefulness.

Miss Martineau has written to say she will reply in her own name (having seen Mr Brontë's first letter which I enclose for you to see) in the Daily News. But I imagine people will abuse me to the end of the chapter. I only hope Mr Brontë won't be over-worried. Hitherto he has acted like a 'brick'. (I hope you understand slang?) Capt Hill goes today; and we are dreadfully in the dumps. Somebody is crying in every room. Moreover Col. Ewart & his wife (he in command 1st Native Infantry at Cawnpore,) were our *very* dear friends, our only friends in India, & that horrid telegraph yesterday! Oh! I don't care what the people say of me. I am a great deal better than they give me credit for,—& don't mind about anything but India. Can you make head or tail of this letter—

Yours very truly   E C Gaskell

P.S. Return Mr Nicholls list of omissions & Mr Brontë's letter to me.

₃₆₉ **370** ₃₈₂

GEORGE SMITH

42 Plymouth Grove
Manchester.
Wednesday
[26 August 1857]

My dear Sir,
    I received the half of the 10£ note (from Capt Hill) quite safely yesterday, but only just as I was going out of town to a friend's wedding[1] so I was unable to acknowledge it, in proper business like fashion.

    Captain Hill told us to send any letters for him that might arrive after his departure to you. Some have already come,—but is there

[1] Selina Winkworth married John Collie on 25 August 1857. *Letters and Memorials*, ed. Winkworth, II, pp. 96, 155.

any use in sending them before the departure of the next mail, by which time more may have arrived? And when *exactly*, please must letters for Madras be posted,—what weight—what pre-payment? I fear I ask you troublesome questions, but I do not know who else to apply to; and in the hurry of Capt Hill's departure we forgot to ask him.

Thank you *much* for what you say about Cawnpore. We are most anxious about that *one* place, and had given our poor friends up for lost. Now there seems a faint {sha} glimmer of hope.

I find that the Exhibition here may close on the 15th of October; though it may be kept open till the end of that month. All will depend on the weather as the Executive Committee fear that damp may injure the pictures particularly the water-colours. But please bear this in mind, as if Mrs Smith should be strong enough to bear coming round by Manchester, she might return from Scarborough this way. We would take every care of her, & there are Bath chairs in the Exhibition, which are a wonderful relief to the weary. At any rate we do hope that we shall see you & Mrs Smith here, when you go to Liverpool.

Yours very truly
E. C. Gaskell.

P.S. I am very much obliged to you for the trouble you have taken about Sir George Saville. I am afraid he would require a greater knowledge of politics than I either have or care to have. I like to write about character, & the manners of a particular period—for the life of a great Yorkshire Squire of the last century, I think I could have done pretty well; but I cannot manage politics. Thank you very much, though.

276 370a 404

ELIZA FOX[1]

[c. 26 August 1857]

My dearest Tottie,

We have two rooms and 19 people coming to occupy them before the Exhibition closes, most of them relations—as soon as they will fix when each set *goes*, (a most difficult thing to get them

---

[1] Original MS. not seen. Source dates '1858'.

to do,) I will write to you. I do hope we shall have a spare bit[1] for
you: but I am shocked to find the X closes on the 15th instead of
end of Oct. We are worn out with hospitality—but I should
make no stranger of you dear, but gape in your face if I chose.
Oh I *am* so tired of it. X I mean,—I shd like it dearly if I weren't
a hostess.

Yours very affect[ionate]ly.,

E. C. G.

361 **371** 0

MARTHA BROWN

Plymouth Grove
Sepr 3rd [1857]

My dear Martha,
    I am very much obliged to you indeed for letting me see these
letters of your dear mistress. I am sending you a copy of the third
edition of her life; and you will find that in that book I have made
use of two or three of these valuable letters.
    I was very sorry indeed that I was out when you called here, for
I should like to have seen you very much.
    I altered the word 'seduced' to 'betrayed' in this edition, which
I hope will satisfy the poor young woman's friends.
    With kindest regards to Mr Brontë, believe me to remain,

Your sincere friend
E. C. Gaskell.

330 **372** *376a

MARIANNE GASKELL

Chatsworth Sunday, morng
[13 and 14 September 1857]

My dearest Polly,
    Such a delicious pen! it is quite a pity I have not a book to
write instead of a letter! You will be surprized at the date of this;
and so indeed am I? I feel more like Cinderella, than any one else
you can imagine. I am writing before breakfast; waiting for Meta,

[1] ? bed.

who I heartily wish was ready; for I do not {roo} know what room we are to breakfast in or how to find it out in this wilderness of a palace of a house. All yesterday we were driving and going about, so that it was impossible to write a line to any of you; but I thought of *you* often my darling, and of twenty three years ago, when you lay by my side such a pretty wee baby,[1] and I was always uncovering you to look at you, and always getting scolded for giving you cold by the nurse.—After Church time. You will wonder how we come to be here (with no clothes at all, in particular to start with,—Meta's brown silk, & brown muslin; my grey carmelite, & black moiré, high, & next to no collars p[?] hands &c—) Hearn packed us up a box for Rowsley in a great hurry on Friday morning [.] We went to the end of Shakspeare St in pouring rain, Joseph carrying our box, and found to our dismay that there was [*sic*] no inside places. However we got tilted up to the top of the coach behind by the eager & impatient coachman and were whirled off, hoping every moment that it would clear, but it would not & came down heavier & heavier to the great detriment of our clothes—(which however are all right again now.) I had no idea it was so long a journey,— it was $\frac{1}{4}$ to 4 before we left Buxton, where we *did* get inside,—and six before we got to Rowsley. We had a snug little sitting room with a fire and tea, and settled ourselves with that day's Times till bed-time. Yesterday directly after breakfast we took a little pony carriage, and came on here to see the house with our green card; as I expected I had soon a message from the Duke, who was not yet up—he is paralytic, & unable to move except in a bath chair, but quite clear in his mind &c—so a nice looking housekeeper took us over the house; and the duke's gentleman came to tell us that 'luncheon would be at two, and that rooms were prepared for us.' You may fancy how Meta and I looked at each other remembering our wardrobe,—which moreover was at Rowsley. I asked the housekeeper what ladies\or visitors,/were in the house —we had heard *none* at Rowsley[.] 'Mr & Lady Louisa Cavendish, and the two Miss Cavendishes, and Mrs Norton'—Mr Cavendish is brother to the Lord Burlington who will succeed the Duke— Well! we thought it was a pity to miss seeing & doing many agreeable things for the sake of no gowns.—so we bravely consented to stay, after sending an apologetic message to the Duke, and saying we were only in our travelling-dresses. So a maid was

[1] Marianne was born on 12 September 1834. This day fell on a Saturday in 1857.

sent back to Rowsley for what scanty clothes we had, and here we are established in two grand rooms (& a private W.C.) the curtains to my bed being of thick white satin stamped with silken rosebuds. Meta proposed that we should dress ourselves up in them. Presently the Duke came to us wheeled in his bath chair. He is very deaf; Meta made him hear better than I did. Then we went into the Sketch Gallery (not usually shown—) until luncheon time. At luncheon we were only ladies till Sir Joseph Paxton came in; he is quite the master of the place as it were; and was deputed by the Duke to arrange drives &c for the afternoon,—there were carriages and riding horses ad libitum. Meta, Mrs Norton, Sir Joseph & I went in a little low poney carriage, and four lovely (circus-like) ponies, postillions &c and felt like Cinderella. We went first to call on Lady Paxton, who lives in the grounds; a sort of fat pleasant looking Mrs Fairbairn,—then we drove through the kitchen gardens &c up to a point where the Duke & Lady Louisa were awaiting us,—there we talked and admired things, & then drove off again, up & down seeing views and improvements, & all the fountains playing, and all the waterworks going, and ending by driving *through* the conservatory home, to *dress* for dinner. Poor Meta & me! However Meta was done up in one of Mrs Norton's gowns, and I in my black silk,—and we thought we did very well, until we went down, to the library, where I should think there were half the clergy in the County of Derby with their wives, Oh! so fine; and the County Member & his wife, —I took a mortal panic lest there should be any Gisbornes or Scott relations among them; however if there were I did not find them out. Sir Joseph & Lady Paxton & a Miss Paxton were there; he almost like the host. After dinner the Statue Gallery and Orangery were lighted up, and then the Duke's private band (of 7 performers) played a collection of pieces, for which we had programmes given us; and then the County Member & his wife departed, Lady Louisa complaining that they had stayed so late. I sate next the Duke all the time of the Concert, as he can hear talking whenever music is going on, so he talked pretty incessantly. It was twelve o'clock before we came up to bed,—and we were to breakfast at ¼ p. 9; and, my dear, there is not a bell in the house because you are expected to have your own servants waiting in the antechamber, & I had forgotten to ask to be called, so I was afraid we should oversleep ourselves. However we did not; got up, had breakfast, went to Church—and are just come back. We have not seen the Duke this morning as yet. Meta likes Miss Cavendish very much; they are both pupils of Leitch, which helps on wonderfully. And now you know all our sayings & doings. I will add a little to this note by & bye.

Monday Rowsley, 1 o'clock. We came here to meet the coach, which is full from the railroad, so we must wait till tomorrow. Will you see that the rooms are got ready for Mr & Mrs Isaac, and their maid who MAY come (from Scotland) at ½ past 10 on *Tuesday* (tomorrow) night, & will want tea, *cold roast* fowls, & a tongue, which I gave orders to have boiled. In greatest haste

Yours most affe[ctionate]ly

E C G.

₀ **373** ₀

Mᴿ Dᴇᴀɴᴇ

42 Plymouth Grove
Saturday September 26th [1857]

Mrs Gaskell presents her compliments to Mr Deane and begs to inform him that Miss Meta Gaskell has received permission to copy any of Mr Stirlings pictures that she wishes. She therefore begs to remind him of his kind promise to admit her and the friends staying in her house who come from a distance tomorrow (Sunday), and as it would be pleasanter for Miss Gaskell to copy before the Exhibition is opened to the Public, Mrs Gaskell would be extremely obliged to Mr Deane if he would allow her daughter to have permission to enter at 8 o'clock.

₃₆₀ **374** ₃₈₄

Cʜᴀʀʟᴇs Eʟɪᴏᴛ Nᴏʀᴛᴏɴ

Monday, Sepr 28th
1857

42, Plymouth Grove, Manchester England, do you remember where that is? My dear Mr Norton, I am waiting for the girls, who are out, to come in, and so I have taken up any kind of a pen

and am sitting at the writing table in the drawing-room to write
to you. Only I feel as if one ought to have great events to write
about before beginning a letter into another continent; and I don't
know if this is the right kind of paper, or how many sheets of it
may go &c &c; so that altogether I feel very much as if I was talking Greek. I shall try to bring myself (& you too,) down to
homely details. It is nearly one o'clock, when Julia dines (Flossy
stays all day at school) and we lunch. Julia has burst in, & has
hunted for Minnie & Meta high and low, and not finding them
at home, has suddenly found out that the day is very hot, and she
is very tired, and, by my advice, has taken a book & gone
{down} to lie down upon her bed, till her sister's return and her
dinner has made her 'all right' again. Meta really did get up this
morning to a seven o'clock breakfast, and went, before I was
down, to the Exhibition to try and make a water-colour sketch of
that Murillo Study—a woman drinking,—for Lady Hatherton,
who asked Meta to do it for her. Marianne is gone into town; to
try on a pink barége dress, to see some poor people, & about
Flossy's boots, and to buy some pears for dessert,—for we have
company coming today: Mr Gaskell's sister married to my cousin,
and their daughter. Oh! I wish we could get good fruit. We have
tried here, & we have tried there for pears this year: paid 3d
a piece for them, & they are like turnips at the best! Mr Gaskell is
from home, gone to preach at Cleator (yesterday was Sunday in
Europe—I don't know what it was in America,—) a village in
Cumberland. By my contrivance (a letter written unknown to
him) he had an invitation to stay at Cleator as long as he possibly
could; for he perpetually *wants* change, and as perpetually rebels
against taking it; I do believe he does like Manchester better than
any other place in the world; and his study the best place in Manchester. He is better, however, a great deal than when you saw
him; a month's holidays did much to set him up. He spent it
partly at the Lakes, and partly at the Ewarts *in Wiltshire*. Our poor
Ewarts have been and are in terrible sorrow. Their brother
Colonel Ewart, his wife & little girl were in Cawnpore; and you
know all that garrison was massacred, under most horrible circumstances, and though they have never seen their brother's
name named, yet they have no hope; no more has anyone for
them. It is very very sad. One great comfort, as far as we selfishly
are concerned, is that Capt Hill's presidency, Madras, is as yet
quiet. Otherwise one's heart aches to think of India. We have

heard from Capt Hill from Suez, where he was on the 10th of Septr, waiting for a steamer, as the whole service of steamers had been disturbed. Of course he had no news to tell, except the gloomy accounts which he had received from the homeward bound passengers; and these he only alluded to.

Were Meta's plans fixed when you were here?—It is now settled that 'unless some unforeseen obstacle occurs' either her Papa or I are to take her out in Oct. Nov. Decr. 1858, to Alexandria where Capt Hill meets her and they are married, and return to his appointment {at}\in/Madras Presidency—(in the Mysore he *hopes* to have it—we have a great map of India, and study it and learn geography.—) There they remain until his time of service\May/1862 entitles him to a retiring pension, of 200£ a year; when, if we or he can in any way obtain an appointment at home,—Manager of railways, inspector of railroads &c &c &c they would come home & live at home; and oh! no one knows how much I wish this may be done,—and, if possible, that we might have a *promise* of it before Meta goes; as a thing to look forward to. He left us on August 24th and Meta is very bright & cheerful, much less anxious, indeed, I think than any of us.

Wednesday, Sepr 30. I dislike keeping letters by me, so I am going to send this off today, however little worth it may be. Mr Gaskell is come home again much better. He desires me to thank you much for the hymn books, duly received, and which will be of great use to him. I thank you too for C. E. and A. Bell's poems (my copy has never turned up—) & all the other books, especially your own, which you left behind you, some of which you are to reclaim when you come back again here; and that, you know, is not to be delayed for ever & ever. How far apart we, breakfast-party at Venice,\4 months ago/have drifted! One is in Asia,—one in America,—and we\Gaskells/all now so stationary at home that Italy & everything seems like a dream! Last night the Indian telegraph came in; Lucknow *not* relieved, & one shrinks & prays when one thinks of the news the next mail may bring of the poor people there; and a *Madras* Regiment has refused to march and has consequently been disarmed; otherwise *people say*, the Times leading the van, that the news is quite as good as can be expected &c &c &c.—I think I am very much tired today, for it seems depressing news to me.—There comes a ring—there comes a caller!—Our house has been fuller than full, day & night ever since you left, and this last fortnight it will be fuller than ever, as every one will want to see the Exhibition before it closes. I am *very* fond of all the people who are coming; but so worn-out that it is hard word [*sic*] to lash myself up into properly hospitable feelings. Marianne said yesterday 'Oh! are not you tired of being agreeable! I do so want leisure to sulk and be silent in;' and really after long hard hot days at the Exhibition showing the same great pictures over & over again to visitors, who have only time to look superficially at the whole collection, one *does* want 'to sulk & be silent' in the evenings. As for reading that is out of the question. IF I send a boy over to you three years hence or so, can he earn his livilehood [*sic*]? That is a comprehensive question, but I mean here is a stout strong good intelligent friendless boy, knowing (from the circumstances of his parentage) both French & English, & learning a good solid homely quantity of arithmetic &c,—and could he at 14 *do* in America?—earn enough to keep him,—and get on, if he deserved it? If he came, I know you would have an eye upon him,—so I don't ask *that*—but could such a one get on in the world? I have not heard from the Storys for a very long time; but it has been my fault; I really have been too busy to write. I despair of this letter ever reaching you; but then I always despair of every letter reaching its destination, if I begin to think about it. Only last week a letter to a little dressmaker, living not a mile off on our side of Manchester was returned to me by the Post Office,—& will this ever live to go over the great broad Atlantic—My kind regards to your dear Mother, & to 'Jane' & 'Grace'—Don't think I am cross; *I* think I am only tired;

Your affectionate friend

E C Gaskell

François & I have set up a correspondence. What nice letters he writes, poor fellow—What is Mr Child's address?

345 375 402

W. W. and/or EMELYN STORY[1]

[September 1857]

['We have her testimony, from the'] cold dim grey Manchester[:] ⟨. . .⟩ It was in those charming Roman days that my life, at any

---

[1] From a printed source, which tells us that the letter gave 'a full and interesting account' of the trouble over the Charlotte Brontë biography.

rate, culminated. I shall never be so happy again. I don't think I
was ever so happy before. My eyes fill with tears when I think of
those days, and it is the same with all of us. They were the tip-top
point of our lives. The girls may see happier ones—I never shall.

₀ 376 ₀

?Mrs Archer Clive

42 Plymouth Grove
Thursday Oct 1. [1857]

My dear Mrs Clive,
Thank you very much for proposing to call here; can you come
& have a 'preliminary' cup of tea at five? or can you come before
11 in the morning,—I am afraid that the rest of the day, i.e. from
12 to 4 I shall be pledged to be at the Exhibition. But I will come
at ½ past 1, & ½ past 2 to the green seat in the transept *outside* the
Hertford Gallery, & will wear a lilac plaided silk; & a white
bonnet,—just like a young lady answering a matrimonial advertisement—

Yours very truly
E. C. Gaskell

*

₀ 377 ₀

?Samuel Holland[1]

46 Plymouth Grove
Manchester
Saturday, Oct 10th [?1857][2]

⟨. . .⟩ tell us when there is a chance of you & Annie coming to
see us. Would any time in November do for you? We shall have
some good concerts in that month. Mr Gaskell's love,—& mine,

[1] *Annotation* Given by Mr Holland, Caerdeon (Mrs Gaskell's cousin) [My
mother—⟨[?]⟩ A E. S.
[2] Only two years are possible with this heading: 1857 and 1863. Later information about the watermark indicates that we should have chosen 1863.

& Marianne's & Meta's both to you and to Annie—whom Mr Gaskell knows tho' I don't. Now mind you both *try* & come soon to us.

Your very affec[tionate] coz

E. C. Gaskell

₀ 378 ₀

Unknown

Wrottesley Hall.

Novr 8th 1857.

Dear Sir,

I am not aware of '*North and South*''s having been translated into German, but I think before Mrs Taylor undertakes the task, some further inquiries had better be made, from some one more competent to give you certain information on the point.

Certainly I will gladly give my consent to Mrs Taylor's translating it.

Yours very truly

E. C. Gaskell.

My Manchester address
is *42*, Plymouth Grove.

₀ 379 ·₄₄₄b

Harriet Martineau

Wrottesley

Wolverhampton

Monday, Novr 9 [1857]

Dear Miss Martineau,

I am, (as you will see by the above date) from home, but I have all my letters forwarded to me. I have not received any letter from any Haworth person, since *about* the beginning of September when Mr Nicholls wrote in the authoritative style {commo} usual to him saying that the quotations I had given in the 3rd edition (as what you believed you had said in yr letter to C B about Villette) were incorrect; that {she did} you {and she} had said so & so, giving

me extracts with marks as of quotation; and that he {w} desired I
would correct this in the next edition. I must say I did not compare
the passages as *he* gave them in his letter, with the 3rd edition of
the Memoir for the very good reason that I had not (& have not)
any copy of that 3rd edition; but as far as I could judge they did
not appear to me to differ materially from what you had sent me.
I had however determined that should any future editions be
required—(a *most* unlikely thing, as the success of this 3rd edition
was problematical at the time of publication,—and it has sold
very slowly indeed in fact) that I would have nothing more to do
with preparing another edition for the press; nor was the tone of
Mr Nicholls' letter at all such as to make me wish to inform him
of this resolution otherwise than in the briefest manner consistent
with courtesy, which I accordingly did; saying at the same time
that I had done my best, and should now put the subject on one
side, referring all future letters to my solicitor. This is the last I
have heard of him—Mr Brontë, or any one at Haworth.

I gathered from Mr Greenwood's letter to you (just after C B's
death,) that your letters to her had been burnt. If you have the
letter\from J Greenwood/(I returned it) and will refer to it, you
will see the passage I mean. Moreover Mr Nicholls told me in
the first instance\when I first began to write the Life/that he had
destroyed all his wife's papers.

Yet he certainly seemed in this last letter to me to quote from a
letter before him,—I mean he gave certain passages with marks of
quotation '—'. But this is all I know. I destroyed his letter to me;
and have no copy of mine back again to him.

It seems to me that you allude to a recent correspondence on
the subject of which I am entirely ignorant; I can only extremely
regret it, as occurring when you are far from well, and I am *very*
sorry that your kindness to me\ever since I knew you,/(which
has been great, & is gratefully remembered,) shd have brought on
any vexation or extra trouble.

My address will be

> Wm Ewarts Esq M.P
> Broad Leas
> Devizes
> Wilts—

for the next ten days.

Our kindest regards to Miss M Martineau

> Yours most truly   E C Gaskell

125 **380** 383

LORD HATHERTON

Broadleas,
Devizes.
Novr 13 [1857]

Dear Lord Hatherton,

I hope you are at leisure to listen to a pretty long story, for I want so much to tell you of our happy and successful visit to Oxford, so much of the pleasure of which was owing to you.[1]

We arrived there soon after twelve on Tuedsay, and went straight to the 'Star' and ordered a fly. While it was being made ready Dr Wellesley came; most kind and courteous, with a proposal that we should go and lunch at his house, after which his daughter would accompany us to the lecture. He accordingly took us round by Jesus and Exeter into the Square with the Radcliffe Library,—on into High St and to see All Souls, (as being a Staffordshire College,) and thence to New Inn Hall. All the way he talked so agreeably, and his conversation was so interesting that I kept wishing that I might do nothing but listen, instead of feeling it my duty to devote half my brains to the service of my eyes. Mrs Mackenzie was confined to her room with a very bad cold, but Miss Wellesley received us most kindly, gave us some luncheon (in reality our dinner,) and let us walk round the room, and examine pictures as greedily as we liked. Then we all set off for the Theatre. I must tell you that at Dr Wellesley's I found a note˙of invitation from Mr{s} Stanley, also to lunch; and that a letter from Mrs Stanley has, since I arrived here, been forwarded to me from Wrottesley, viâ Manchester. Mr Stanley's lecture was very interesting; Meta thought it exceedingly so; but I felt rather tantalized by his giving us the heads of subjects that he meant to dilate upon in future lectures, and wanted to know a great deal more than there was any chance of my ever knowing. The lecture lasted about an hour, so it was a little past three when we came out of the theatre. I spoke to Mrs Stanley, and Miss Louisa Stanley, and a sister of hers,—Mr Matthew Arnold, the new professor of poetry, and was introduced to Dr & Mrs Cradock, who invited us to a party at Brazennose that evening. Dr Wellesley, being just

---

[1] See p. 490 below.

released from convocation, came to meet us, and he and his daughter accompanied us to the Radcliffe Library, and then through New College Gardens to Magdalen Chapel, where we went in and heard so beautiful a service that we must needs go and attend the evening-service (an hour later) in New College Chapel, after which Dr and Miss Wellesley took us to our inn, and went home to prepare for some evening engagement. We found Mr Arthur Stanley's card lying on our table, with an invitation to breakfast the following morning at his rooms. We had tea; & then found ourselves so miserably cold and tired, that, although we were longing to go to a College party at Brazenose, we decided that it would be wiser to go to bed, and accordingly I wrote and told Mrs Cradock of our pitiful state of fatigue, and we went to bed at half past eight!

The next morning we had a very agreeable breakfast at Mr{s} Stanley's rooms in High Street, meeting Dr and Mrs Ackland, Mr Conington (Latin Professor) and Mr and Mrs Brodie, he a son of Sir Benjamin's, and Professor of Chemistry. I had met Mr Brodie before in London, and he and Mrs Brodie had come, most kindly prepared with an invitation to us to move our quarters from the 'Star' to their house. But this was impossible, as we had to leave Oxford at half past eleven that very morning. So then they transferred their invitation to the time of our return homewards through Oxford; and accordingly we hope towards the end of next week to find ourselves under their roof, for a couple of nights, and to see something more of that most beautiful and stately of all the cities I have ever seen.

Mr Stanley walked down with us to Christ Church, and into the meadows up to the Bridge at one end of High St. Any thing more lovely than that morning cannot be conceived,—the beech-leaves lay golden brown on the broad pathway; the leaves on the elms were quite still, except when one yellower than the rest came floating softly down. The Colleges were marked out clearly against the blue sky, and beautiful broad shadows made the lighter portions of the buildings stand out clear in the sunshine. Oh! I shall never forget Oxford, and thank you and Lady Hatherton very much indeed for giving us the first impetus Oxford-wards, and then for all your help afterwards to make our visit agreeable.

I have more to thank you for[,] my dear lord; a favour for which I was always wishing to express my gratitude, and yet I never seemed to find the right opportunity, while we were at

Teddesley. I mean the trouble you took in writing to Lord Harris about Captain Hill, for which we all were *very very* much obliged to you.

We have been to call at Bowood today, as our friends are acquainted with Lord Lansdowne, and we wanted much to see so famous a house. But unfortunately he is just gone to Brighton to try and ward off an attack of gout; and only an old woman came to open the door of the deserted house.

With kind love to Lady Hatherton believe me to remain,

Yours sincerely,
E. C. Gaskell

368 381 *446+

Maria Martineau

Plymouth Grove

Wednesday[1] November 24th. [1857]

Dear Miss Martineau,

Thank you very much for letting me know that the correspondence is ended, and I hope it is quite satisfactory to your Aunt. It has begun with me[.] I have received a letter from Mr Nicholls, accusing me of stating quite falsely that I told Miss Martineau that he had destroyed all his wife's papers, and that he never said anything of the kind—I meant that he had destroyed all the papers excepting those he had shown me, which I know I mentioned to Miss Martineau in conversation. However I have written to him and explained to him that it is a mistake and that I am very sorry for it and I hope he will understand.

Believe me to remain

Very sincerely yrs
E C Gaskell.

*

[1] Wednesday fell on 25 November in 1857. Letter 382 seems to confirm 1857, however.

370 **382** 387

GEORGE SMITH

Plymouth Grove
Novr 26th [1857]

My dear Sir,

I received your letter at Oxford; we made a little détour in coming home from Wiltshire, as we had an invitation to pay Mr Brodie, (the Professor of Chemistry there,) a visit. I did not reply to it, because I wanted to acknowledge the books you were so kind as to promise me, and which I have duly received. I am very much obliged to you for them; and I intend to study Miss Martineau deeply. Indeed we, as a family, are going through a whole course of Indian literature—Kaye & Malcolm[1] to wit; but I am afraid I read it for duty's sake, without taking as much interest as I ought to do, in all the out-of-the-way names & places, none of which give me any distinct idea.

Do you know that Miss Martineau and Mr Nicholls have been having a warlike correspondence; *very* warlike, I imagine; and I must confess I should like to have seen it; only I thought it was better to mix myself up as little as possible with it. Each have written to me very angrily; I don't mean about me, myself—but about the other side. I don't think there ever was such an apple of discord as that unlucky book. Just lately we went to stay at Lord Hatherton's; and before we had been ¼ of an hour in the house we were told that Mr & Mrs Reeve (Edin Review) were among the other visitors. Remembering how Sir James Stephen had sent that message about the sentences which Mr Reeve would insert in Mr Fitz James Stephen's article, I thought this would prove rather an awkward rencontre; and so Lady Hatherton had evidently thought, for she said, they had all been abusing Mr Reeve for *admitting* those sentences—However I did not show that I minded meeting him, for the host & hostess's sake,—He eyed me askance for 24 hours; and the second day to every body's surprize marched across the room to take me in to dinner,—& began by saying how *charmed* he was to think there was going to be a family connexion between us; that 'Charlie Hill' was his wife's first

---

[1] Their works included *The Administration of the East India Company*, 1853 and *The Life and Times of Sir John Malcolm*, 1856, both by Sir John W. Kaye, and *The Government of India*, 1833, and *Instructions to Young Officers*, 1851, by Malcolm.

M.G.L.—R

cousin & a very great friend of his'; & altogether he evidently tried to make amende by an over-dose of civility,—asking us all to come and see them in London &c &c &c,—& writing a letter of delight at having made my acquaintance. I had the advantage over him all along, for I had never read what he had written, whereas he was fully conscious of it, as I could see, in every word he said.

Now about my copyrights. I should be very glad to dispose of any, if I had them, in my power. But I am afraid I have not. 'Mary Barton' & 'Ruth' were, I know, sold out & out. 'North & South' was sold by the *edition*. A second edition was called for 3 months after the first was published; and Mr Chapman purchased the right of printing a certain number for a certain sum; both number & sum forgotten just now. I am afraid this second edition hangs fire; for I saw 'North & South, 2nd edit', advertised the last in Chapman & Hall's list, about a week ago. Should I enquire as to the number remaining? or would you? or would it be worth while? Of course I should be glad to redispose of it.—As for Cranford, & Lizzie Leigh &c—he made a bargain with me before republishing them in his Railway Library. He was to have the sale of them for three years (expiring next May,) paying me a royalty of 3d on each copy sold.—About the Moorland Cottage (a poor little, pretty—I thought) Christmas tale, published 1850 he gave me a sum for 2000 copies, & half profits on any sold after that number—& I am afraid *that* has been a loss to him.

There are a few Household Words Tales, unpublished in any separate form of which I retain the copy right,—but I am afraid they are not half enough to form a volume.

I hope Mrs Smith is better. Please name her in your next letter.

Yours very truly
E C Gaskell.

I am very *very* much obliged to you for sending us the Homeward Mail. We read it from end to end; title-page, & printer's name.

₃₈₀ **383** ₀

LORD HATHERTON[1]

[*c.* 3 December 1857]

Dear Lord Hatherton,

I was very much obliged to you, indeed, for sending me Lord Harris's note. Through your, and his kindness, and we will hope a little through Capt Hill's own merits, he is appointed to the command of the regiment of Sappers and Miners, at Head Quarters; which are at present at Dowlaisheram, near the great Godavery Irrigation works; but I believe that Capt: Hill is in hopes that Lord Elgin may require their services in China, where the Madras Sappers and Miners were stationed during the last war.

Meta has heard today from Lady Hatherton, who does not give a much better account of your cold, and speaks of having one herself. All Manchester sympathizes with you; for I am sorry to say the bad times bring on a very low state of health; and the prevalent influenza is too often passing into a kind of typhoid fever here, making the town authorities very anxious.

We extremely regretted that our stay in Oxford was obliged to be so short. We remained until Tuesday Afternoon, (arriving late on Saturday.) But I think we made good use of our time. On Saturday the Brodies had a dinner party, to which Mr Jowett, the Master\Provost?/of Queens and Mrs Thomson, Max Müller, Saffi &c came. The next morning we heard Mr Temple, the newly-elected Master of Rugby, in St Mary's. He is a very striking preacher; I kept thinking of Dr Arnold, and of his school sermons all the time that I heard Mr Temple. Many of the customs in Church struck me as curious. The Vice Chancellor bowing to the Preacher,\and the latter returning the courtesy,/at the entrance of the nave,—the *thanks* for the dead,—so proper and Protestant a modification of the old Catholic *Prayer* for the dead, Founders, and benefactors &c. After dinner we went all over New College with one of the Fellows, a nephew of Dr Moberley, of Winchester. First into the kitchen, where I was relieved to see,—that if the Founders attended to the *mental* wants, there were Cooks and Scullions at least equally attentive to the Corporal wants of William of Wykeham's 'poor scholars'. Such good luncheons as

[1] *Annotation* 3 Decr 1857.

were going up into Collegiate cells! A certain Mr Holland was having,—all to himself,—stewed eels, minced chicken, beef steak with oyster-sauce, and College Puddings! I am afraid he requires one of the colds, of which you say 'they are sent to teach us temperance'. Then we went into the College cellar, and tasted the Ale; we were warned *only* to taste it, as our heads not being sufficiently strengthened by learning, might not be able to stand it. Then into the Buttery, to see the Plate; the Hall, with a grand piano in it, the Fellows being musical, the Muniment rooms, where we saw the old deeds; one, conveying lands from the second wife of Henry 1st, to certain monks, in order that they might sing masses for her husband's soul; supposed to be the earliest deed in existence. We heard how the system of College leases was so bad, that the immense property bequeathed to New College at various times only brought in 30,000£, which was reduced to 8,000£ per ann.; by the necessary expenses. In the secret places among the great deed Chests, we came upon a precious dozen of port,—each bottle with a paper-necklace, ticketing it as 'very precious'. In short it was very interesting, and not a little amusing. In the afternoon to Ch. Ch. to the service, and afterwards one of the Canon's ladies showed us the magnificent building,—which by the half light of the evening lamps, looked perhaps better and more impressive than it would have done by day. Dr Jeune came to dinner, and talked much of you and of Lady Hatherton, & of Teddesley. He was extremely agreeable, and *wonderfully* learned. I struggled after him to understand his historical allusions, but after\all my endeavours/I felt like 'Panting Time toiled after him in vain.'[1] He asked us to go there (i.e. to Pembroke—saying he should be 'delighted to receive us',) at Commemoration Time; and I gladly accepted,—for I should be delighted to go; but I am afraid he will forget it[.] You will think *I* have forgotten to end this letter; or perhaps say like the Irishman, that 'the other end must be cut off'. No! dear Lord Hatherton it is not; and here it is. Thank you & Lady Hatherton once more for helping us to all our Oxford pleasure; & believe me,

Yours very truly
E C Gaskell.

[1] Johnson, 'Prologue spoken by Mr Garrick at the opening of the Theatre-Royal, Drury-Lane, 1747', l. 6.

CHARLES ELIOT NORTON

Plymouth Grove—[1857]
Monday, Decr[7] (1st Monday
in December at any rate, because Mr Gaskell has a dozen
committees (be the same more or less,) to attend to, every first
Monday in the month, and he is going to them today.[)]

My dear Mr Norton,
Your letter to Polly (Novr 24) is just come. Breakfast is still
on the table; waiting for Mr Gaskell, who was very much tired
last night, and so is late this morning. I am sitting at the round
writing table in the dining-room,—Marianne is mending me a
pen, over the fire place, in order that the bits may drop into the
fender; Meta is gone into the garden, to tell Joseph about perennials for next year (new pen—Thank you Polly,) the said Meta's
last words being 'Dear good Mr Norton!' as she left the room,
after hearing Polly read yr *note*—your *letter* to me came 10 days
ago.—So here we all are, placed, ready to your imagination. Flossy
& Julia have been spending Sunday with a Schoolfellow in the
country four miles off,—and we have not seen them since Saturday. It is not exactly wintry weather here;—but a *grey* sky all over,
with a line of watery pale light in the west,—no snow though[.]
Why don't you send us over some Thanksgiving pies,—or at least
pie receipts. I remember Mrs Story telling us of unheard-of pies,—
When was Thanksgiving instituted?—you did not take it over
from England, I think for we have no relic of any such custom. If
you will send *me* over a pie-receipt, I'll answer for it I'll beat it, by
an equally original one,—namely a 'Cheshire-fitchet-pie'; which
is excessively good though no one will ever believe it. But I am
hanging on the edges of my letter, X—and since that cross, I have
been called off by ever so many people; that it makes me afraid
that if I don't plunge into the middle of my real subjects I may
never get my letter written at all. *When does the American post leave
England?* It sounds odd to ask *you*, but at the Post Office here,
they say it is sometimes on Saturdays, & sometimes on different
days of the month; in short they are so very vague about it, that
I suspect they know nothing at all. And now to the purport of this

letter, which is to thank you for your kindness about my story,[1] *very* much, and will you thank Mr Curtis too? The story, per se, is an old rubbishy one,—begun when Marianne was a baby,— the only merit whereof is that it is founded on fact. But at Mr Sampson Lowe's earnest entreaty I promised it to Messrs Harpers more than a year ago;—and, of course I relied a little on payment; (though what that is to be, I have not a notion;) and when Mr Lowe, (whom I have found out in other things to be rather a 'tricky man',) took such care not to acknowledge the receipt of the story in London, *until* he had sent it off to America,—coupled with rumours of Messrs Harpers' insolvency, I became suspicious, and determined to outwit the sleek old gentleman, & have my tale back, if it could not be paid for. Very worldly, is it not? But really I had relied on the money; and this will be an expensive winter to us, for we are, thanks to you Americans, surrounded with poor people out of work, and are beating our wits to pieces to know how best to relieve their present wants, without injuring them permanently. So don't give me up as a mercenary tricky woman, though I acknowledge I *should* like to out-dodge Mr Sampson Lowe if ever our wits came in contact. Are you never as wicked as this? I am sure if I were a servant, & suspected and things locked up from me &c, I should not only be dishonest, but a very clever thief. Oh! I have so much to say,—not of any thing particular but quantities of bits and crumbs, and people *will* come from the N & S, & E & W, wanting to speak to me this morning. I like Mr Lowell's marriage,—(Don't think I'm gone crazy if this letter is very much without method.) And you don't understand what are our 'aristocratical feelings' when you make a sort of apology to Marianne about his marrying a governess. That does not hurt us in the least,—it would if he married an uneducated girl, a daughter of a rich *trades*person.—My dearest friends, all through my life, have been governesses, either past, present or future. Is Mr Child married? I am always wanting to write & thank him for his Ballads, which I delight in,—only it is so hard to me to write a proper letter; with Dear Sir in the right place, & verbs agreeing with their nominatives, & {agreeing with} governing— their accusatives; and it is letters of that kind I dread receiving, because of the knowledge of grammar, & good pens required to answer them; those letters, & worse still, the abusive letters that I have been receiving all these last few months. Those are the

---

[1] *The Doom of the Griffiths.*

letters that make me dread the post; and not such as yours, dear
Mr Norton, so please don't go & suppose so,—for you will not
mind grammar or spelling or penmanship in my answers, will
you, so I shan't dread having to reply to them, all the time I am
having the *great* pleasure of reading them. Now you know I tell
truth; (unless such men as Mr Sampson Lowe are in question—)
so you must believe these words '*great* pleasure'. I sate down to
write this morning just five minutes after hearing your letter
because I like writing on the rebound; indeed if I don't do that, I
often don't write for a long time. But never think because I don't
write that I either forget you, or value yr friendship less. We
sadly want you to come over & see *us*. I wish you would, for I
don't see exactly what you do in America. You indigest, all of you,
and some of you make money at a great rate; and others lose it
just as fast. But I really am going to write a proper stately letter;
full of news; only I have not any news, and have a very runaway
kind of mind. Thank you for telling us about your library. It
sounds very pretty & pleasant,—and the views out of the windows
make me have a kind of a Heimweh,—as if I had seen them once,
& yearned to see them again,—instead of dear old dull ugly
smoky grim grey Manchester. And your views of Torcello—
where DID *you get that Photograph*, & the other Venetian one; and
why did not we get them? Oh! that exquisite dreamy Torcello
Sunday,—that still, sunny, sleepy canal,—something like the Lady
of Shalott,—tho' how, why, & wherefore I can't tell. If I had a
library like yours, all undisturbed for hours, how I would write!
Mrs Chapone's[1] letters should be nothing to mine! I would outdo
Rasselas in fiction. But you see every body comes to me perpetually. Now in this hour since breakfast I have had to decide on the
following variety of important questions. Boiled beef—how long
to boil? What perennials will do in Manchester smoke, & what
colours our garden wants? Length of skirt for a gown? Salary of a
nursery governess, & stipulations for a certain quantity of time to
be left to herself.—Read letters on the state of Indian army—lent
me by a very agreeable neighbour & return them, with a proper
note, & as many wise remarks as would come in a hurry. Settle
20 questions of dress for the girls, who are going out for the day;
& want to look nice & yet not spoil their gowns with the mud &c
&c—See a lady about an MS story of hers, & give her disheartening but very good advice. Arrange about selling two poor cows

[1] Mrs H. Chapone, *Letters on the Improvement of the Mind*, Groombridge, 1859.

for one good one,— see purchasers, & show myself up to cattle questions, keep, & prices,—and it's not ½ past 10 yet! Now I'm going to begin my real proper letter. For now I think of it I've got a real proper grand subject. Yes I have! You know we were dreadfully worn out with our Exhibition. So we, MA Meta & I, went off one Saturday once upon a time, in Octr and went to Teddesley, Lord Hatherton's,—or rather to my mind *Lady* H's. There we met Mr Sumner, your American friend. I respected him much; but I don't think we 'got on' together much, in our three days of being under the same roof. I can hardly tell why. To be sure we only talked over 'stock' questions,—condition-of working-classes (which *he* chose in compliment to author of M. B.) which is too great a subject, & too much of a problem to be talked over with a stranger except as the vaguest philanthropic generality of a subject, & *then* one is apt to talk Cant, i.e. used-up forms of speech, with the life withered out of them. Then he talked Anti-Slavery,—of the ins & out of which I know nothing,— so all I could say was that Slavery was a very bad thing, & the sooner it was done away with, & the better. So—don't you see,— we 'esteemed' each other exceedingly, and don't care if we never see each other again. Now remember this is nothing disparaging if Mr Sumner is your great friend—it is simply negative. Then we were inspired by Lady H. (& partly you, & partly Mr Ruskin in the back ground,) with a great desire to see Oxford. We *were* going into Wiltshire,—to Broadleas,—and were passing on a line of which Oxford was one of the stations,—and both Ld and Lady H. finding we had never been at Oxford wrote letters, almost before we were aware, right & left, facilitating every pleasant arrange- ment for our going there for one night; and hearing Arthur Stanley's lecture on the Eastern Churches,—said lecture being one of his course on Eccles: Histy of which he is Prof; & expected to be peculiarly interesting because he has just been spending the 'Long' at Moscow. So we went. (Star Hotel.) (We travelled 2nd class train to squeeze in Hotel expences [*sic*],—it was like Old China in the Essays of Elia,) as soon as we had arrived there came Dr Wellesley, Principal New-Inn Hall, & owner of those beauti- ful drawings from the old Masters in our Exhibition,— prodded up to civility by a letter from his brother-in-law Lord Hatherton, & he took us a race up past X where Ridley & Latimer were burnt,—{past}\thro'/the Radcliffe Quad into All Souls Quads, into High St—back to his own house to lunch; donned a scarlet robe himself, having to attend convocation, & rushed off (with scarlet wings flying all abroad,) with me on his arm, to deposit us at the Theatre to hear A. Stanley's lecture. The lecture was not (to me) so *very* interesting, being a sort of recapitulation of what he was *going* to say (if that's not Irish.) I saw Matt Arnold—who was in Oxford, getting ready for his inaugural poetry lecture, which came off the next Saturday,—and we were invited by the Cradocks to Brazennose in the evening, & by A Stanley to breakfast with him the next morng. Then Dr Wellesley picked us up again, rushed us up to the roof of the Radcliffe—(what a splendid view of towers & pinnacles)—to Maudlin [*sic*] to Chapel, & New College Ante Chapel, & up & down & round about so that I got quite bewildered. When we got back to our inn, I had one of my bad headaches, so we went to bed, instead of going to the Cradocks— Breakfast at A Stanleys was *very* pleasant. Your friends,—whom we do so like—Dr & Mrs Acland—(or are they Mr Ruskin's friends—& was it *he* that was speaking to us so much about them?) Mr & Mrs Brodie (known to us before)—Mr Conington, (another old friend, Prof. of Latin,) Matt Arnold. We were so jolly & happy. I do so like A. Stanley. He told me something I liked to hear, & so I shall tell it you. In Moscow he had seen a good deal of a priest of the Greek Church,—a pure Muscovite—but a very intelligent man. Speaking of forms of religion in England this priest was so well acquainted with the position of dissenting ministers with regard to their congregations that A S was sur- prized, & enquired where & how he got his knowledge. 'From an English novel. Ruth.' (Now I must put away my letter for today.) After breakfast was over we had 3 hours to spare before our train, to carry us on into Wiltshire, came; so we went in a merry procession thro' Ch. Ch. Peckwater Quad, Tom Quad,—up the broad walk in the meadows, talking, laughing &c in most un- academic fashion. It ended in every body voting we had not half seen Oxford, & must come back on our way home, & Mr and Mrs Brodie volunteered to be host & hostess. So we promised— and in 10 days we performed, going to Cowley House, across Maudlin bridge. It gave us a sort of 'homey' feeling to hear that you had breakfasted there. We got there on Saturday Evng— Thomsons (of Queens—Provost & Mrs Thomson) Jowett, Pattie- son[*sic*], Saffi, Max Muller, &c &c came to dinner; and it was *almost*—mind I don't say quite—as pleasant as A Stanley's break- fast. It was not *quite*, because A Stanley & Matt Arnold had gone

\away from Oxford/, and we never saw Mr Conington, & Dr and Mrs Acland were never asked to the Brodies &c—

Sunday—to hear Mr Temple, the newly elected Master of Rugby, preach in St Marys,—no prayers at all, save a curious (& I thought noble [)]—thanks for the dead founders—'We thank thee O Lord for the righteous who are living,—and in like manner we thank thee for the righteous dead, in that Thou sawest fit to send them among us, and in especial we are bound to thank thee[']—(& then came the names of the founders of the colleges—among them 'Mr Peter Blundell'—whose name hit my fancy, & made me wonder who Mr Peter Blundell was.[)]] I liked the sermon much, & augured well for Rugby School. It was on 'faith & good works', which he interpreted Grace & Discipline[.] I did not in the least agree with his interpretation,—but I extremely liked the sermon—I, a sermon hater. After that we picked up,—or were picked up by—a fellow of New College, & went over that building, from kitchen, cellar & buttery to the muniment chambers—Again that Sunday Evening people came in to dinner & tea,—none special. Monday to the Bodleian,—lunch with Mr Jowett. Bodleian again. Mr Cox showing us illuminated MSS. To the Union,—trying to understand the meaning of the paintings,—& in a little measure understanding; to call on the Aclands & Wellesleys—to see the Museum, home. I saw so much, I have hardly yet arranged it in my mind. But I like dearly to call up pictures,—& thoughts suggested by so utterly different a life to Manchester. I believe I *am* Mediæval,—and *un* Manchester, and un American. I do like associations—they are like fragrance, which I value so in a flower. None of your American flowers smell sweetly (do they?) any more than your birds sing,—now I like a smelling and singing world. Yes I do. I can't help it. I like Kings & Queens, & nightingales and mignionettes [*sic*] & roses. There!

Then we came home; and have been desperately busy ever since. Looking over stores, and clothes, & house-linen, & preserves &c &c &c &c &c[.] For all household affairs seem to have got into a helter-skelter state during the Exn: I mean to read the Atlantic soon; I find 2 numbers, one from you with names of authors, for the which *thank you*; the second no. has no such names,—& I'll tell you what I've read & liked. Your paper on India,—but then that was not fair, because I knew it was yours,—Floyd Ireson's ride VERY much. Turkey tracts,—yes, I did, & I just defy you, if you said you didn't; and Florentine Mosaics. I cd not read the other story,—and I did not care for Carlyle. I liked yr paper in the first no. on our Exhibition—only there *was* one Duccio da Siena, & you say there was not.—

Now about Capt Hill. We (*i.e.*) Meta get very nice letters from him—always remembering—& several times remembering—to send nice little presents to Hearn. He is appointed to the command of his regiment of sappers & miners at Dowlaisheram where they are busily employed on Godavery Irrigation. Meta is very well. Marianne accuses her of {the} two of the seven deadly sins, sloth & gluttony, for she sleeps like a top and is always hungry. We want to know something of Mr de Vere,—except thro' you we have never heard a word since we left Rome. Only we saw his lines on Shelley, dedicated to ['|J W Field Esq' (dear Mr Field!) in Fraser, & read them & liked them as well for their own sakes, as for that of the writer & Dedicatee, if there be such a word.—Are you going to be married? A little bird says you are, to somebody you have been engaged to ever so long? I like you so much I shd like to know if this is true; so don't think it impertinent. I am writing on regardless of postage—and it is clear that either you or I will be ruined. Read 'Scenes from Clerical Life', published in Blackwood,—\for/*this* year,—I shd think they began as early as Janry or February—They are a discovery of my own, & I am so proud of them. *Do* read them. I have not a notion who wrote them. Shall you get this before Christmas day—25th of December,—your poor dear Americans have Thanksgivings, but I suspect you have not Christmasses—& perhaps you won't know what I mean when I wish you & yours a merry & happy Christmas. However I *do*,—and I wish it to Mr Child too, and I believe he likes old things & customs enough to understand me. Is he married yet? Remember he & you are to have a children's party, comfit dress & all, when I go over to America. Mr Nicholls wrote for yr address a week or two ago. He *is* a nice fellow, so I hope you will see him. And now I have done my time,—if not all my news. Give my kindest regards to Mrs Norton & yr sisters,—and ever believe me your affectionate friend E C Gaskell.

MA & Meta are gone out, or wd send their own messages. MA will write soon, I doubt not, for the sake of the dear old Piazza di Spagna.

We were so sorry not to see Mrs & Miss Cleveland,—& so sorry to hear of the cause of their never coming—

₀ **385** ₀

?MR ANDERSON

Plymouth Grove.
Decr 9th 1857.

My dear Sir,
Your kind letter gave me much pleasure, and I must not
longer delay sending you my best thanks for it—
I think you will appreciate the characters of the poor Brontës,
though I cannot say I agree with you in preferring 'Wuthering
Heights' to their other works—notwithstanding its wonderfully
fine opening—Pray offer my compliments to Mrs & Miss Ander-
son, in which my daughters beg to join—
Believe me yours sincerely
E. C. Gaskell.

*

237 **386** 307

F. J. FURNIVALL[1]

Plymouth Grove
Tuesday [?March 1858][2]

My dear Sir,
Thank you very much indeed for your note full of news 'as an
egg is full of meat', & thank you too very much indeed for all the
trouble I have given you about the 'Germ'.[3] I knew all along that
it was Mr Lowes Dickenson, who lent them me. And I have not
LOST the 1st No, only I don't know where to find it,—do you
understand? I put it somewhere so dreadfully secure & safe, that I
can't remember in what hiding-place it is; some day I shall find it
& be able to claim it as my own own[*sic*]. We only came home
last night from Liverpool or I should have written to you to beg
& intreat that I might slip Meta into the place you so kindly offer
me for seeing Holman Hunt's pictures. I wish I could have seen

---

[1] *Address (on envelope)* F J. Furnivall Esq | 3 Old Square | Lincoln's Inn | London.
Postmarks MANCHESTER | AP 8 | 1856 | S *and* ⟨ ⟩ | AP 9 | ⟨ ⟩ [*Late information*].
[2] Misdated. This letter should follow 282.
[3] The short-lived journal edited by W. M. Rossetti, which appeared for four
issues only in 1850.

them—that I do! In all *chances* of any future admission to pictures may I send you her present address—

Alfred Austin's Esq

13 Sussex Place

Regents Pk

Believe me ever

Yours very truly

E C Gaskell

382 **387** 407

GEORGE SMITH

42 Plymouth Grove

Manchester

March 17th [1858]

My dear Sir,

I do not think I was ever more surprized than by the contents of your letter this morning. I had always felt that you had behaved to me most liberally in the first instance, and that in some respects, the book must have been a great source of annoyance and vexation to you; it was only the other day that I expressed my sense of your good & kind behaviour, under mortification & disappointment caused by me, to Mrs Clive; and now to receive a cheque for 200£! I am most sincerely & heartily obliged to you for it. As *money* it is very acceptable, just now, but I am even more touched by the kindness & liberality, which will always make me feel beholden to you.

I wish I could add something to this cheap edition to make the book more attractive, & likely to sell. Mr Brontë's letters are, as you know characteristic,—but I don't like to ask him to let me publish them. I had a letter from Miss Taylor, in New Zealand,—but it contained little more than a sort of accusation that I had softened the peculiarities and faults of the male portion of the family too much; & a pretty good bit about the portrait, saying it was too much flattered, and describing the real face.

This last, 3rd edition,—if it has been read at all by those who cared to correct mistakes,—has only elicited\expressions of/ approval; even Mr Carus Wilson has written to approve. I have had curious proofs of the great interest felt in her,—a letter from a young Russian lady, born & bred in a district on the South East of Moscow; odd Australiasian [*sic*] islands,—Americans by the dozen, all full of her; and these latter Yankees coolly describing her character at four or five sheets length to me, as if I had never heard of her, & giving me an abstract of the events of her life! I don't know how far it would answer your purpose,—or how far you could obtain Mr Nicholls consent,—to add as an *appendix*— (that's where I fear he would not give his consent,) *to the life*\whh he does not like/, the fragment of a tale she left. It was a very good beginning,—a child, left at a lady's school in England by a very dashing kind of man, appearing very rich, and calling himself her father. He pays down a years charges; and in consequence of his name & address & appearance the child is very much petted by the worldly sister schoolmistresses, but withdraws herself from their caresses, in a sad & timid way, puzzling them, and a middle aged gentleman friend, to whom they are in the habit of referring for advice. Sometime after the end of the year,—hearing nothing more of the father, & receiving no answers to their letters, they induce their friend to go to Something Park, where he is said to live,—but of course he is not there,—nor to be heard of, & the schoolmistresses begin to ill-treat the little girl, who has evidently known of, & been oppressed by the deceit all along,—when their bachelor friend takes her part—& there the story breaks off— it was begun a year or so before her marriage & Mr Nicholls always *groaned literally*—when she talked of continuing it. I read it, & liked it very much—it was about 50 pages long,—not an autobiography, but as if written by a spectator, who was after- wards to be worked into the story. One does so want to know who the child really was, & what was her connexion with the dissimilar flashy man.

If you can think of any way by which I could add to the interest of the cheap edition I am sure you will be kind enough to tell me.

I have got—to my shame be it said,—two Roman Photographs for Leigh Hunt. I meant to have sent them by Meta, but I forgot. Can you give me his address?

Yours most truly & obliged
E C Gaskell.

R. MONCKTON MILNES

Plymouth Grove
Manchester
April 5. [1858]

My dear Mr Milnes,

Can you give me any particulars about M. Meyer? Do you remember? You introduced him to me, & said that 'he had obliged to leave Paris from very painful circumstances, *which he would explain*'[.] This he never did.

I introduced him up & down and he gave a 'séance', by way of opening his course; and meanwhile paid many calls, staying a long time, & hearing much during these calls, some of which were made on French residents in Manchester. He began his classes a fortnight ago, my daughter attending one of them. Suddenly he left last week, returning all books, paying all debts &c &c; but his pupils were all in the lurch, & bewildered by his disappearance, although with some of the parents (myself among the number,) he left notes, saying that Mme Meyer was ill &c which necessitated his return. *Now* the report is spread that he is a spy of the Emperors; that he has wormed himself into people's confidence,—has heard much from French residents that may be seriously injurious to them,—nay, he is accused of having examined private letters left about. I do not believe all this; but as I recommended him I should like to be able to refute these charges by a more distinct statement than I have yet been able to give, both as to whom [*sic*] he is, & why he left Paris. (He was certainly in intimate correspondence with M. de la Gueronnière.) You will say that my desire for information on these points comes rather late in the day; and that it is locking the stable door after the horse is stolen.

But if M Meyer is a 'true man' I can do away with prejudices against him, which may seriously tell against his success, should he return to Manchester as he said he intended to do.

I should not have ventured upon my next request if I had not been already writing to you; indeed it has only come into my head in the last two minutes,—it is—I have a young cousin, Edward Thurstan Holland, who has just taken honours at Cambridge,—& who is going before settling down to the study of law, to travel in the United States.[1] He goes in the middle of this month, & has asked me for letters of introduction. Now I know many Americans; but where they live, N. S. E or W. I don't know. Would you mind giving me a few for him? He is *very* good, very intelligent, very gentlemanly, & very full of fun; aged 22, Eton & Trin. Coll. Cam. You would be doing me a kindness, if you thought it right to introduce him to any of your American friends.

    Believe me to remain ever

Yours most truly

E C Gaskell

384 **389** 394

CHARLES ELIOT NORTON

42 Plymouth Grove

Manchester.

April 7th

My dear Mr Norton,

    The bearer of this note will be my dear young cousin, Thurstan Holland. He is so good and intelligent that I am sure you will like him at once; and forward his views, for his own sake, as well as for mine,—in every way in your power. He is going to stay in America until next November. I am sure he will do credit to any introductions you may be kind enough to give him. And if it is possible that any one in America would care for him the more for the knowledge that his father is my very dear cousin, and that he inherits—as well as individually owns—a great piece of my regard, & that any kindness my distant unknown friends may show him I shall consider as done to me,—pray my dear Mr Norton,—name this.

    I want him to go directly to you; and fall into good hands at once—

    You have allowed Mr Nicholls to come back a PRO-slavery man. Fie! for shame!

Yours affectionately & truly

E. C. Gaskell

---

[1] See Letter 389.

₀ **390** ₀

N. Sherman[1]

42 Plymouth Grove
April 15th [1858]

My dear Sir,

Are your recollections of our acquaintanceship in Rome and Venice sufficiently strong for you to allow me to introduce to you, my cousin Mr Holland, who is sailing in a couple of days for America where he hopes to spend the next six months.

I at any rate remember so much of your kindness to another young friend of mine, Mr Bache, that I am tempted to beg you to forward Mr Holland's views of becoming acquainted with all that is peculiarly American during the period that will intervene between his leaving Cambridge, and his entering on the study of the English law. I do this with the more confidence as I think you will like Mr Holland for his own sake, if once you are kind enough to allow him to make your acquaintance. And, en révanche, I can only say how most gratefully I shall acknowledge any kindness done to my cousin, as if it were to myself.

With kindest regards to Mrs Sherman, believe me ever, dear Sir,

Yours very truly
E. C. Gaskell

₃₈₈ **391** ₀

R. Monckton Milnes

Plymouth Grove.
April 20. [1858]

My dear Sir,

Thanks for your letters. I am keeping that of M. {de} Remusat to show to one or two friends, in hopes of undoing something of the prejudice against M. Meyer.

But it arises—not unjustly—from such conduct as this— Yesterday I met M. Hallé (the pianist) here. M. Meyer had been introduced to him by Mme Roche: and the Hallés had shown

[1] *Address* N. Sherman Esq | New York | Favoured by Thurstan Holland.

him great kindness on her account. Their\house/door opens from
the outside, and to the left hand of the hall is M. Hallé's private
study. He had been writing letters (to friends in Paris among the
number,) and left them open in his portfolio when he was summoned to a pupil. No one except Mme Hallé goes into this room
in a general way. When the hour of lesson giving was over M.
Hallé returned to his letters and his room, & found M. Meyer
sitting there writing; having opened the\house/door himself,
walked in, without a person in the house knowing that he was
there, turned M. Hallé's letters out of the portfolio—(M. Hallé
fears he had read them, but of this there is no proof whatever
beyond the general unscrupulousness of the whole action;) and
written several letters himself, while waiting for the chance of
M. Hallé's return.

Now this is only one instance—I heard it almost in the words I
have given it from M. Hallé himself—of similar conduct. No one
here knew why he had left Paris, any more than we now know
why he returned. He told me that the physicians had recommended
change of air for his wife: which was the sole approach to a reason
for his coming here that he gave.

But with that we have nothing to do. Only his conduct in other
people's houses has been of a character to make some not un-
naturally afraid of the use he may make of knowledge un-
scrupulously obtained.

Thanks for telling me about the articles. I always like to read
anything of your writing, even when it is not of such supreme
interest as 'Lucknow' because your style (may I say it?) has such a
great charm for me. It is such pure beautiful English. I had heard
of the forthcoming article on Buckle, without knowing whom it
was by. Thank you for telling me.

Mr Gaskell & my girls desire to be most kindly remembered to
you.⟨...⟩

o 392 o

MR SHADWELL

Wednesday Evening
[?Early May 1858][1]

My dear Mr Shadwell,

I am very much obliged to Mr Coleridge for thinking of me and of my autographs; please thank him, & give him my best regards.

I have Sir Robert Walpole's *signature* (to an Exchequer bond) but nothing further and I should be very glad indeed of the 'top rare ones', if Mr Coleridge will bestow them upon me.

Believe me to remain

Yours very truly
E. C. Gaskell.

o 393 o

MR COLERIDGE

42 Plymouth Grove
Manchester
Monday May 10th. [1858]

My dear Sir,

May I begin in this way, please? Partly because of our kind and agreeable neighbour Mrs Shadwell;[2] and partly because I *am* very much obliged to you for all your autograph kindness; though I have seemed so negligent in acknowledging it. But I have been ill in bed for many days since Mrs Shadwell's return; and besides I wanted to obtain a portrait of Miss Brontë for you, to accompany the letter I am going to send of hers. Would you like a photograph of her father; very queer and characteristic, & photographs of the old parsonage at Haworth. I am vexed to find how short and poor my list of duplicates is compared to yours; but

[1] Associated with Letter 393 seemingly.

[2] Née Coleridge; a great-niece of S. T. Coleridge. She came to Manchester about 1856/7 and left in 1861 (see p. 672 below) which makes 1858 the only year which 10 May fell on a Monday.

please, if you want any *disreputable* autographs apply to me. You soar grandly among the Bishops but—should you wish for Louis Blanc, Ledru Rollin, or anything in the highly radical, or red Republican line—(I don't go down to assassins—) ask me, will you? And moreover if you have been long in search of any particular autograph will you put me on the scent? There is no knowing what I may be able to do,—having kind friends in America, Paris, Rome & Heidelburg; and I do feel so much indebted to you for the rich set you hav⟨e⟩ sent me, some of which are what I most particularly prize; such as the Duke of Wellington, and S. T. Coleridge⟨.⟩ I cannot tell you how I feasted on the consciousness of the possession of these, even when I was quite too much blinded by head-ache to read them. *Pray*, ask me to get you some; I shall so like doing something for you.

I have copied S. T. Coleridge's letter; and only wait for your reply to send any or all the duplicates on the list. I sincerely hope that Mrs Coleridge is recovering well from the effects of her very serious accident, of which we were very sorry to hear.

If my daughter & I go up to town for a few days in June, I have promised to take her over to see Windsor, when we shall do ourselves the pleasure of calling upon you.

Believe me to remain dear Sir,

Yours very truly
E. C. Gaskell

389 394 401

CHARLES ELIOT NORTON

Plymouth Grove
Monday, May 10th [and 14th 1858]

My dear Mr Norton,

Your letter, half begun on Sunday Eveng—April 26th, and finished the next day, has just come in. Just after our early dinner, Meta & her Papa being the first set of people to whom it was read, —Marianne reading it now, even while I answer, on the rebound (as it is always so much easier to answer—) Oh! if you were here how much we should have to say! And do you suppose *we* forgot the Torcello Sunday? No! not to the material fact of our hunger

& cold when we came in! *Our* sky *here* was so like the sky over the Lagoons on that day, and the lovely Stars of Bethlehem, and the stones, all carved, & square cut below the water level of the Canal Banks; & the Cathedral—oh happy lovely day,—I wish you could come over again. And the Campagna 'bits' in your letters always give one a sort of heimweh,—'Give our love to Mr Field; he won't like it the less for coming through you. But don't forget it. I do *love* him; it is no form of words. How I wish we could see our 'Romans' again, including François[.] Be sure you tell us about him. Yes, to be sure I like hearing about Mr Calvert just as you liked hearing about Hearn & Lion[1] in the lovely old Torre de' Schiavi days. And give my kind regards to Mr Child, & tell him we bargain for *two* days, one in *going*, that he may get to feel us as old friends, against the day in return when he brings *Mrs* Child to let us all get to know each other. (Oh how much I have to say! that comes in like a burden of an old song,—I feel to *want* to write of the old Roman days, and yet I must earn that pleasure by working through business.) First, because most disagreeable about Mr Underwood. I want (as I know you will see my letter to him,) to put you up to what made me feel it necessary to give up writing for the Atlantic in his. So I shall just give you an extract premising that I *quite* understand an *Editor's* desire to please his readers, but that I *can* not (it is not *will* not) write at all if I ever think of my readers, & what impression I am making on them. 'If they don't like me, they must *lump* me' to use a Lancashire proverb. It is from no despising my readers. I am sure I don't do that, but if I ever let the thought or consciousness of them come between me & my subject I *could* not write at all.

Now for Mr Underwood.

'I will not disguise from you, however, that I should feel considerable solicitude about the wide-spread success of any novel from an English author, on account of the *colouring* which your habits of life and thought must give to all your literature.' (This is very true E. G.) 'Only the greatest of English novelists are fully appreciated in America: the novelists of the second rank are by no means so much thought of as in England. Yr own experience with regard to French and German authors will furnish you with a parallel. It requires the force of genius to overcome the difficulties which arise from a difference in manners culture & institutions. And though we speak the same language, it is yet true that in a

---

[1] The Gaskells' dog.

certain sense England is a foreign country to the mass of our people. You can easily see that a novel might hold the attention of an English reader by its descriptions of scenery, or local customs, while here the same thing would be appreciated only by the more cultivated readers. I think, furthermore that we are now a more mercurial people than the English, and that readers here demand that the action of a story should always be moving.' (This is all perfectly true & sensible; don't think I don't see the full reasonableness of it all. To return—) 'As I look back on what I have written I am afraid you will think it rather presumptuous in me to make the suggestions I have,' (not at all,—it is not Mr Underwood's fault, if I CAN not write, if I think of my readers, & whether they are English or American,—) 'But believe me I entertain the highest opinion of your abilities, and *only mention such things [as] are proper to be considered in writing primarily for the American public.*' Now you will understand why I decline to write, don't you, dear Mr Norton. Thank you very much for your list of authors. You may think how we *savoured* the papers on the Catacombs. Marianne & Meta always write the names opposite to the articles in the Atlantic. I have had neither health nor spirits, nor strength to write, hitherto, for any thing or any body. I see my way to daylight at last, I think, if I were but feeling bodily stronger, and I suppose that will come in time. On June 17th we are all going, (except Mr Gaskell, who will I think go a pedestrian tour with his brother) to Silverdale, (near Lancaster—you *must* have heard us speak of it, —) close to Lancaster *Sands*, & Morecambe Bay, & Annie Austin comes to stay with us,—and there we shall remain for six weeks, and all get as strong as horses, it is to be hoped. We live in a queer pretty crampy house, at the back of a great farm house. *Our* house is built round a square court,—Stay. We have all that is shaded,[1] the rectangular piece is *two* stories high, the little bit by the lane one story, said little bit being kitchen & servants' bed rooms; the houses [*sic*] is covered with roses, and great white virgin-sceptred lilies, & sweetbriar bushes grow in the small flagged square court, across whch we merrily call for 'hot water,' 'more potatoes' &c in very primitive fashion to the kitchen. It is well for our dinner when it does not rain, otherwise what is meant to be hot has to be carried carefully under an umbrella, if our visitors are *very* particular people. The soil about the place is all sandy and heathery, and you know what delicate little plants

---

[1] Mrs Gaskell is referring to a plan she drew here.

grow in it; and hedgehogs, and glow-worms abound. In the garden, half flower half kitchen is an old Square Tower, or 'Peel' —a remnant of the Border towers. Think of the perils our legs of mutton undergo! First they are kept in the Larder, or lower story of the Tower. Rain or fair they have to be carried to the kitchen to be cooked. Rain or fair they have to be carried *hot* across the court. And to begin with Silverdale is so wild a place we may be happy to get a leg of mutton at all. I have had to dine 15 people, as hungry as hounds, on shrimps & bread & butter,—& when they asked for more had to tell them there was no bread nearer than Milnthorpe 6 miles off, and they had to come down to oat-cake, & be thankful! Then at the very end of the garden is a high terrace at the top of the broad stone wall, looking down on the Bay with it's slow moving train of crossers led over the treacherous sands by the Guide, a square man sitting stern on his *white* horse, (the better to be seen when daylight ebbs). The said Guide Carter by name is descended lineally from he who guided Ed. 1st over on his march to Scotland, & was by him given a coat of arms, & a grant of land. On foggy nights the guide, (who has let people drown before now, who could not pay him his fee, but who writes 'gentleman' after his name, thanks to Ed. 1st) may be heard blowing an old ram's horn trumpet, to guide by the sound,—

But I dare say you are tired of all this—*only write to us there*, for it will seem like introducing Newport and Silverdale together. We shall be there from June 17 for 6 weeks; and our address will be

Lindeth Tower
Silverdale, near
Lancaster.

It is a long hot walk to the post office and it is so disappointing to find no letters there when we get there.

Before now you will have received MA's letter about Thurstan Holland—I *hope* he has found you out, and I hope you like him, for he is worthy of being liked for himself, and the son of a very dear cousin of mine. I hope you Americans will all reckon him as a piece of me.

Well now! to direct home news. I am going to tell you something, which has been going on for a long time, and which is not yet *formally* decided upon; only as I hope & trust it is *really* decided upon I shall tell it to you, only don't name it please, as, as soon as I have any right to name it, I shall tell it to the Storys myself. I

believe it is certain that Meta will break off her engagement to
Capt Hill. She has heard some things which have made her have
a very different opinion of his character to what she had at first.
These come from so good authority (in fact from his own sisters)
that Meta's mind is quite made up, only she thought it right to
write to him, and to ask if he could give any explanation. It does
not seem to her *possible*; but you will see why, until his answer
comes, she nor I feel justified in speaking of the engagement as
definitively broken off. Nor shall we say more at any time, than
that it *is* broken off. Those who wish or care to know the reasons
must apply to him for them. Meta is *far* from well,—more from
deep disappointment in character, I think than from wounded
affection; for she says 'he is not in the least what she fancied he
was'. All I do, is to wait to help her to hear much 'public-talking'—
& possibly upbraiding from him; and to give her what strength &
sympathy I can. I am sure she has done right, & with a pure &
simple mind. It has been a most terrible anxiety to me. But the
little loophole of blue sky, & sunny heavens is widening daily.
Neither she nor I are well or strong,—we are each ordered 'tonics'
& 'change of air & scene,' but we do not like to separate. Marianne's good sense & merry ways make us cheerful whenever she
is with us. If I can muster up money (but you see I am very poor,
what with doctor's bills, half-got Indian outfit, inability to write,
for want of health—) I would try & persuade Mr Gaskell, to take
us three abroad, after we come back from Silverdale, and leave
us (when the children would be settled at school) for a few weeks
somewhere,—Rhine, Avranches in Normandy—&c &c. But Mr
Gaskell dreads foreign diet like poison. *He* is so much better you
would not know him! My own belief is that he had some internal
digestive complaint which had been coming on for years; came to
a crisis last autumn, & he has been gaining flesh, colour, strength
ever since. Now I shall put my letter away, till nearer Saturday,
post day. Tuesday. I am so far from strong that my only piece of
work yesterday, (writing this letter) utterly knocked me up, & I
have been quite unable to sleep. Whereupon, as events travel in
circles, I have been thinking during the night of no end of things
I want to say to you. First. (uncomplimentary.) I don't like
American biographies. Dr Kane's life is *murdered*,—and why do
you give us all those speeches & obsequy things at the end? It is
very ungrateful of me to say this, for Mr Elder sent it me. Next—
who is Mr Parton who writes biographies on your side of the

water? Barnum, & Aaron Burr—the first I literally *could not* read, just for the want of any moral feeling at all in it,—the last I have just read, because I wanted to get some knowledge of American \society/in the last centy & beginning of this,—and to know who Aaron Burr was? There is just the same, or worse, want of any idea of simply [*sic*] right or wrong,—but I don't come out clear as to what *could* have been Aaron B's *real* character—was he not *always* acting a part,—writing to Theodosia not as he really felt & thought, but as he wanted to persuade the world, & himself that he did think & feel. And after all did he not (in the Mexican affair,) only forestall 'vous autres' by fifty years. But it is strange to see the whole world rising up against him as against Cain,— who was a far finer fellow, because *he* humbled himself before God, & dared to be true, & to cry aloud,—you may depend upon it Cain was human & loveable compared to Aaron Burr. I must go back to the March Atlantic (I see by the May number,) for the review of this A B's life. Do tell me something *distinct* of the man's character. Next—our Venice seeds,—do you remember giving them to us,—have been sown this spring, and are coming up famously. Our Academy Exhibition this year is minus the Pre Raphaelites. Meta, who was in London in March, saw through the favour of Mr Ruskin Holman{'s} Hunt's new picture of Christ disputing with the Doctors,—which is not finished, & won't be this three months. Meta did *so* admire it—& him himself. And a sculptor of the name of Munro to whom Ruskin introduced her, as well. There! that's as much as I am going to write today.

May 14

Friday. This is the last day for posting a letter to America this week. So I shall send this off. *Did* I say I was going to London, to the Wedgwoods—because I am *not*. Meta is not strong, though in good spirits, and I don't like leaving her. Marianne is going to London, to a dentist! poor child! My kind regards to Mrs Norton & your sisters

Yours ever most truly

E C Gaskell

180 **395** 0

?JAMES CROSSLEY[1]

42 Plymouth Grove
May 13. [?1858]

Dear Sir,

May I recall myself to your recollection, as having had a very pleasant conversation with you at Sir James Watts, last February but one, as an excuse for making an enquiry or two from you. Can you tell me anything of a book, published or rather printed, by the late Earl of Bridgewater at his press in Paris. It was in the French language—& contained all the Egerton traditions, and papers relating to the Lord Chancellor Egerton.[2] The Egertons of *Tatton* know nothing of it. I do not know the present Lord Ellesmere well enough to ask him. 2ndly

Who was the lady, traditionally known as the '*Bold*' (or '*Noble*' according to some—) Dame of Cheshire[3]— She was a Cholmondeley, & lived *sometime* at Holford Hall near Northwich; and the story goes that she was knighted. A friend of mine is amplifying some lectures he delivered at Knutsford during this last winter in the History of that dear little town, and a circle of country about 20 miles round. He has discovered very curious family traditions and old facts; and he wants to make his book as perfect as possible, and I would gladly do what I can to help him, remembering what Southey says of how good & well it would be if every Parish priest would write down what he hears and learns about his own Parish, as traits of customs & manners & character might thus be preserved as Memoires pour servir. Pray excuse me; and believe me to be yours respectfully

E. C. Gaskell

[1] Identified by J. A. Green, *Catalogue*, p. 6 (Author's copy in Manchester Central Library).

[2] Francis Henry Egerton, 8th Earl of Bridgewater, *Aperçu Historique et Genealogique*, 1807. Quoted by H. Green, *Knutsford*, 1859, p. 102 n.

[3] Mary Holford, heiress to the Holford estates, married Sir Hugh Cholmondeley. James I on a visit to Vale Royal in 1617 called her 'The Bold Ladie of Cheshire'. There was also a tradition of her arguing with Queen Elizabeth. Green considers it probably a mere fancy that a Cheshire woman had been knighted and won spurs, deriving from the stories about this lady. See Green, *Knutsford*, pp. 73-4.

₀ **396** ₀

MR PARKER[1]

42 Plymouth Grove
Manchester.
May 20th [?1858]

Mrs Gaskell presents her compliments to Mr Parker, and, (in compliance with the request of Mr Underwood, of Boston U.S.) begs to inform him that it is out of her power to begin any serial in the Atlantic Magazine; & that therefore she begs he will make all arrangements without reference to her.

₀ **397** ₀

HENRY ARTHUR BRIGHT[2]

42 Plymouth Grove,
Thursday [May 1858]

My dear Mr Bright

I am very glad indeed to encourage any such good intentions as you propose; and I enclose you a note to Mr Rossetti; I only wish I were going too. Now don't give it up if he is not at home the first time you call,—It is the *last* house either on the right or on the left, before you come to Blackfriars' Bridge.

He goes a great deal to Oxford, as he is painting two compartments in the Mort d'Arthur frescoes on the 'Union' walls,[3] but he often returns to London; so please don't be disheartened.

Yours very truly
E. C. Gaskell

[1] *Annotation* [1857] (*cf. Letter 351*). We associate this letter with Letter 394.
[2] *Annotation* May 1858. See Waller, 'Letters Addressed to Mrs Gaskell', p. 53, for a Rossetti letter of 1858 referring to Bright's visit.
[3] Rossetti began the frescoes in 1857.

307 **398** 399

F. J. FURNIVALL[1]

42, Plymouth Grove.
June the twelfth. [1858]

My dear Sir,

I feel quite ashamed when I think Mr Gaskell has left your letter about {the}\his/Working-Men's-College-Class so long unanswered; but, as I feel sure that you would more easily forgive the neglect if you knew how it arose, I am going to explain to you that it\is/not in the least from any unwillingness—but simply from his having his time so completely occupied—that Mr Gaskell has let your inquiries remain without a reply. He has had so much to say to you on the subject that he felt he could never attempt to say it all in any but a long letter; and for that he has literally not had the time. He is, however, going to London next Saturday to stay till the 26th, and if you would let him know at what hour *your* class at the College is, I feel sure that he will if possible attend it, and afterwards give you any little assistance that he can. I know he means, if he can find time, to visit the Working Men's College; and as your class is in the Evening he will probably find that more convenient than at an earlier hour—

His address will be

care of the Revd J. J. Tayler—
22, Woburn Square—

If you would have the kindness to direct one line to him there \(mentioning the day & hour of yr class)/after next Friday, he would—I feel sure—be extremely obliged to you—

Believe me, my dear Sir,
Yours very truly
E. C. Gaskell.

<hr />

[1] See Letter 399.

398 **399** 425

F. J. FURNIVALL

42 Plymouth Grove
{17} 17th June [1858]

My dear Mr Furnivall,
Please send Mr Gaskell (*at Mr Tayler's*) the address of the
W. M. C. *Ormond St* is it not? *but what No?* Until he gets to Mr
Tayler's on Saturday he can't tell what his London engagements
may be,—but fully *means* to come & hear your class,—if he but
knew No—Thanks many for your letter—I have my *things on,*
going into a charming primitive desert[1] (butcher 15 miles off &c,—)
Lindeth Tower,
Silverdale

near

Lancaster
where any gossipy, newsy letters, or news of any kind, will be
most thankfully accepted[.] We shall be there 6 weeks.
Yours very truly
E C Gaskell.

I shd like to write, *along with those others,* for that Quarterly. No
time for more[.]

₀ **400** ₀

UNKNOWN

Lindeth Tower,
Silverdale

near

Lancaster.
June 29 [?1858]

Sir,
I see in an advertisement of the contents of a Magazine (the
Psychological,) of which I believe you are the Editor, a paper on
Charlotte Brontë.

[1] See p. 504 above.

Having a very strong interest in the subject I should particularly wish to see that number and if you would kindly direct it to be forwarded to me, I would return the publisher the amount in postage stamps.

I remain, Sir

Your obedient servant
E. C. Gaskell.

394 **401** 403

CHARLES ELIOT NORTON

Silverdale   July 25 [1858]

My dear Mr Norton,
The time here is slipping away so fast,—(next Thursday we go home—) that if I mean to keep my promise to you I must seize on today,—when I have been stopping at home with a headache, and all the others are out. My headache has cleared off, and I am in that sort of weak happy state of easy exhaustion, which follows on the cessation of extreme pain, so you must not expect a very *bright* letter. The greatest event in our family is this. Hearn is going to—je vous donne en un, je vous donne en deux &c—to *Venice*. Yes! our own old dear English Hearn! I'll tell you all about it. She has had a good number of distressing events in her family, & lost all her savings during this past year,—& she had been but in languid spirits, which we have been afraid were almost affecting her health. A week or two ago Meta was going sketching, & took Hearn to sit with her; not as chaperone, for we are too primitive here to require such articles,—but by way of giving Hearn a little fresh air, & merry talk. Meta came in, & said 'Do you know Mama the summit of Hearn's ambition is to go to Paris!!' Of course we began to wonder if we ever could take her &c,—& so it lay dormant in our minds, until last Sunday,—when there came a letter from a *very* good kind, & also very wealthy lady in Manchester, asking me if I could recommend her a respectable lady's maid for travelling,\as/she, her brother, father & niece were going abroad this autumn. (I understood from the 1st of Augt for 6 weeks.) I thought at once here was the opportunity for the change of scene &c &[c] Hearn wanted; and, as they were

going to take a courier with them, I thought she could do all they required; but I did not like to propose it (for fear of hurting Hearn, by *our* seeming willing to part with her &c—) till I had asked her. She quite jumped at the idea,—'if we could but spare her for the time' & has been so full of it ever since that I have been only afraid lest the *lady* should not agree to it, & so our poor Hearn be disappointed. However last night the lady (Miss Behrens) came to stay a day or two with us; & after some discussion it all got settled, —with this drawback only—that the Behrens don't go till the 11th of Augt, & stay two months *at least*, and it may be longer. And until Hearn comes back I fear I cannot leave to give Meta any necessary change, such as we had planned for this autumn; for we had made a lovely little plan of Belgian & Rhine towns, a month at Heidelberg for sketching & home; and will not the end of October be too late for anywhere on the Continent, short of regular winter-*residences* in towns in the far South? Please, you who are experienced, answer this question for me. Given *105£ & two months*—(I am republishing my Household Words Stories, under the title of Round the Sofa,—to get this money—) and 3 people,—& where can they go at the middle or end of October? Now do try & answer this. Then again the Behrens think they have missed engaging their usual courier; so we have put them up to writing to poor François, (François Boggia, No. 3, rue 29 Juillet, Paris, is it not?). Oh! we are getting so sorry to leave Silverdale. We know all the people here, & they know us, and all the duties of life seem so easy & simple compared to those of a great large town. However I won't grumble. Last Tuesday we had a party of boys & birds & girls. Mr Childs [*sic*] should have been here! We had a tame magpie, and a tame jack-daw (\the latter/belonging to a sweet little dwarf-child we picked up on a wild common one night—) said dwarf—and three children of a drowned fisherman &c—The birds fought for precedence but the children were very good & nice,—not flippantly clever like town children, but solidly-thinking with slow dignity. The birds sate at tea on the heads of their respective owners, occasionally giving a plug or a dig with their beaks into the thick curly hair, in a manner which *I* should not have liked, but it did not seem to disturb the appetites of the owners. It was very funny, & picturesque in the old quaint kitchen here. We have had but cold & wet weather on the whole; only it was free & sweet blowing, pattering rain, making merry music among the leaves, not sullen down falling inky drops like—Well! I won't now! Did I tell you of my charming dear Roman box,—every bit of wrapping paper thereof is treasured up, *because* it came from Rome. It came by Miss Carey, *I believe*—contained a long long letter from Mrs Story, an exquisite note from Mr Wild's [*sic*] (more like Charles Lambs for playfulness & tenderness,) and a letter from Mr Field, which I loved because it came from *him*. Then there was a paper-knife (angel poised on globe) from Miss Carey, and a pretty pen-wiper from Mrs Field, & a Roman scarf for my neck from Edie,[1] & last, very far from least—a number of what Mr Wild called caricatures—but I call very graceful likenesses of our Roman friends, as they appeared at the Story's bal costumé this Spring. By the way as I write here in Silverdale, under my very nose, is a pretty rough kind of basket Mrs Field gave me, full of flowers, in Rome. We want to write (I do *particularly*,) to Mr Wild & the Fields,—but can't make out what address to put? Will *Alhambra Spain* find them? {By the way,} I do so like receiving a box of that kind, full of little parcels & kind thoughts from distant friends whom I love. Every parcel is a separate pleasure, & wonder & surprize just as it used to be to me when I was a child. Speaking of letters to distant places I am receiving *such* nice letters *in English*— from a Russian girl with an unpronounceable name, living many leagues South East of Odessa,—she wrote to me about Miss Brontë's life, but we go on very pleasantly, as harmonious *strangers* can do after all, more confidentially than ɪɴharmonious acquaintances. And how are Lowell & Longfellow & all the Cambridge people; and are you ever going back from Newport to Shady Hill, and have you seen Thurstan Holland yet,—and how I should like to go to that grand old house in the South you describe!

I think,—and it is pleasant to think,—that one never is dis-appointed in coming back to Silverdale. The secret is I think in the expanse of view,—something like what gives it's charm to the Campagna—such wide plains of golden sands with purple hill shadows,—or fainter wandering filmy cloud-shadows, & the great dome of sky.—(We have not sate up all night\on our tower this time/, partly because there have been no *tranquil* nights, & partly because Julia (who is like Meta in her love of experiences & adventures) has been promised to sit up with us, the *next* time, & she is growing tall, & not quite strong enough for experiments.[)]

When will you come to England, & see us dear Mr Norton?

[1] Edith Story, daughter of William Wetmore Story.

We should be VERY proud, (too proud, quite cock-a-hoop,) if you came over & gave us a visit all to ourselves; but *that* can't be expected or thought of. But I wish very much indeed that you would come back to Europe. I don't believe from what I hear of your looks, that a Republic agrees with your health; do try a little aristocracy, and as a step to it, try a visit to us, who are admirers of that 'effete institution'. By the way to prove how Americanly I bring my children up fancy *Marianne* asking the other day, if a *baronet* was not the eldest son of a *Duke*? Meta came down upon her immediately with historical knowledge respecting the peerage, & showed herself a 'true Britisher.' But seriously dear Mr Norton, if you are not well, would it not be wise & right to try a few years more of travelling,—disagreeable as such a wandering & apparently purposeless life may be. And if so, won't you come to us as to an English *home* for the first step? My kindest regards to your Mother & Jane & Grace (you see I don't 'Miss' them.) (They are come back, raging hungry.)

Your affec[tionate] friend
E C Gaskell

375 402 450

W. W. and EMELYN STORY[1]

[? July 1858]

⟨...⟩ Oh, I so long for Italy and Albano that it makes me ill! ⟨...⟩ I am glad Domenico is with you. It is bad enough your having changed your house;[2] I don't like to think of your changing a single servant. Have you still Serafino? Our remembrances to Luigi and Clarke. Speak of us to Amante and Domenico. Have you still little birds for dinner, and the good 'dolci,' the creams of which it was necessary to be forewarned, lest we should eat too much previously?

[1] From a printed source ('apparently of 1858'). Perhaps in response to the Rome letter (see p. 514 above).
[2] 'To Palazzo Barberini' (Henry James note).

CHARLES ELIOT NORTON

42 Plymouth Grove
Manchester—
September 3d—[1858]

My dear Mr Norton

We, (Marianne, Meta Flossy & I) go to Heidelberg viâ Tournay, setting off from here, on Tuesday next. Letters will find us at Poste Restante Heidelberg, until Octr 15—to 20th.

Now as to the piece of business you were so kind as to undertake for me about Messrs Ticknor & Field's [sic] offer,—I have passed it on to Sampson Lowe & Co. (*Harpers Agents here,*) who made me the offer for the vol: of Household Words Stories,—*which also includes 'The Doom of the Griffiths,'* published in Harper's Magazine last Novr Decr or January,—& the reply I today receive from Sampson Lowe is as follows

'We would recommend you to {the} accept the offer of Messrs Ticknor & Field, especially as they are willing to take the risk of Messrs Harper's reprinting;—but we cannot undertake to give all the sheets four weeks before publication; it is more that [sic] Messrs Harpers ever expect for such works. You must engage for the delivery two weeks in advance of publication. We know this to be fair and ample time.'

I give you their very words that you may lay them before Messrs Field &c. I *have not full confidence* in their entire straightforwardness of meaning, though I can hardly say why. But it is for Messrs Ticknor & Field to judge. Only please don't let me be implicated in any transaction which may be likely to involve loss to them. Write to me at Heidelberg what their decision is, & I will do my best to carry it out.

Yours affec[tionate]ly & truly
E. C. Gaskell

Hearn did *not* go.

370a **404** 421

Eliza Fox[1]

Saturday, Sep: 4, 1858

My dearest Tottie,
  Address Poste Restante Heidelberg, from Sep: 20 for 3 weeks.
Then care of Monsieur Bernhard Tauchnitz, Leipzig. I'll do what
I can—I don't know Edward Frere. Mme Mohl is in England, and
she can do nothing for Paul. I think I can give you some nice
introductions in Rome, and to George too,—but not to Mon-
signors (I only know one)[2] or Cardinals—But you and George
should know our[3] dear Mr Story (sculptor) who would know
what you should do, and Mr Page American artist etc.:—
  We're just off, so no more. I'll send you letters for George to
any address in Paris or elsewhere from Heidelberg.
                          Yours very affec[tionately],
                                                    E. C. G.

                              *

*404a **405** 420

Marianne Gaskell

                          106 Haupt Strasse, *Tuesday*
                                    Oct 19 [1858]

My dearest Polly,
  It seems to be always me to write; but the thing is that the
others, Meta especially, do work pretty hard at their German; and
that we have more people popping in & out than we expected;
especially since we are nearer Ida and Anna. Please don't go on
hoping that 'Flossy enjoyed her birthday', for excepting a bunch
of grapes she had *no* present, and she *had* a German lesson; so
altogether she feels it a day manqué, *as* a birthday. I wrote last this
day week. On Wednesday we were as you may fancy very busy
packing up and removing here. Meta asked to have the packing up
left entirely to herself, and as many of the clothes were at the
wash I felt as if it would not be very much, and so Flossy and I
went about the town, payed bills, bought in things for our new

---

[1] Original MS. not seen.
[2] Mons. Talbot? See *Letters and Memorials*, ed. Winkworth, II, pp. 111, 129.
[3] Source reads 'one'.

method of housekeeping &c. But when Meta & her carriage
load full of things arrived here she was quite knocked up, and had a
fit of hysterical crying; I put her to lie down on the sofa; & she
said she felt so 'very weak she did not know what to do.' You may
fancy how anxious I was. Franz V. Schmidt had arrived the day
before, and Anna had been in to ask us to go to tea there & be
introduced to him; but I did not know if it would do for Meta or
not. However I got her some sal volatile; & gave her a private tea,
while she lay on the sofa; & towards nine we went in to the
Mohls; & I think it did her good, though they were struck with
her looking ill. They were very kind indeed. F. v. S. is a very little
man, without beard or moustache (both forbidden in Austria to
any but the military,) fair complexion rather pretty boyish
features. He speaks English pretty well having taught himself; but
is rather insignificant looking. However he seems to have a very
energetic character, & very strong will of his own, and to be
doing a great deal of good in his district in Hungary. He praised
Ida extremely to Meta in very funny broken English. I made
Meta take an aloetic pill on our coming home and she has taken
one every other night since, & it has done her so very much good
in relieving the sensation of extreme fatigue that I begin to think
her symptoms must have been something like Julia's, & arising
from the same cause. She is now both looking & feeling remarkably well. Something may be owing to the superior comfort of
these lodgings which charm us more every day; sunny pleasant
rooms, cheerful attendance, *most* comfortable beds, and plenty of
hot water, an article unknown at Zimmer's, where there was only
a fire in the whole house for half-an-hour at meal times, & having
no sun into the bargain, the house always felt damp & *welly*.—
However Meta is better, indeed quite well, & that is the grand
comfort. And as for Flossy I never saw so blooming a creature;
rosy, merry, hungry, strong. She *says* she is growing, and sadly
wants to have her frocks lengthened. Thursday I tried to keep
Meta out of doors without fatigue as much as possible; so I took
her Flossy & {Ida}\Anna/Mohl, out in a carriage by the hour, &
we bought grapes at a peasant's vineyard, & eat away at them;
then I made Meta lie down; and in the evening just as I was beginning to read Boswell aloud, & they to work M. Plarr came in. Oh
he *is* so tiresome & egotistical. We did nothing but talk of his
plan for the 'Triangulization of the Holy Land', whatever that may
mean,—and staid till past 10, talking of nothing but that, & the

geography of the Bible; to me too who know nothing about
geography. Friday morning before we were dressed came a note
from Ida; they were all going for the day to Spire, to see the
Cathedral, & had a place in their carriage for {Ida}\Meta/, if she
would go; she was not dressed, but I got her breakfast, & read
Murray to her while she was dressing, and got her off in time; &
then there was Flossy to soothe; left to her lesson with M. Plarr,
and a dull day with me. However she soon became good, and I
took her to her lesson, & then we lunched on bread & cheese, (we
saw no use in having our dinner as Meta was away, so ordered a
cold fowl at Sulzers instead for tea;) and we set off 2 class railway
to Mannheim, $\frac{1}{2}$ an hour off. We walked about the town, &
looked at shops, and saw the palace (rooms inside[)] & the Rhine
—& altogether Flossy was highly pleased; but the heat & sun gave
me a headache; and our first train back to Heidelberg was not till
7; so at 6, we went into a confectioner's shop and I gave Flossy her
choice of a cake & asked myself for tea or coffee; neither were to
be had. I said I had a [']migraine affreuse', and the girl brightened
up, & said she had something good for the migraine, poured something into a liqueur glass, gave it me, I drank it,—and lo! if it was
not *rum* pure, it was *rum* & *peppermint*!! However it *was* wonderful
for the headache, but Flossy backed away from me, saying it was
such a horrid smell. However my headache was better, and
Flossy said she could keep away from me but that 'I was like a
mixture of a public house & an apothecary's shop; she was *sure* it
was *rum*, for it was what all the cakes and puddings Minnie disliked smelt of.' We went to the Railway waiting-room, which
was all quiet and nicely-lighted up; so Flossy began to read a
book she had brought with her; and I got Hendschel's Telegraph
(the German Bradshaw) off the table, and began to puzzle out my
train to Strasbourg to meet Louy,—when lo & behold, Flossy
whispered to me, me, smelling of rum—that Mr Bosanquet had
come in! I tucked my head down over my book, & told F E. to
take no notice; but he drew nearer & nearer, pretending to look at
the affiches on the walls, till at last he came close, & said 'Mrs G.
can I assist you in making out yr train'—so I had to look up, & be
civil, & let him take my (second) class tickets (whereupon he said
it was thoroughly sensible, & I said nothing, because of the rum,—)
& he went with us, & managed everything for us. He said he had
just returned from Spire Cathedral,—he had been an Archeologi-
cal Nibelungen-Lied tour as Bunsen had directed him) & I asked if

he had seen Meta,—he gave an ambiguous answer, but when we got home it turned out they had seen each other in the Cathedral, but she had cut him. He is going to study *Law*, at his father's wish; & Bunsen is recommending him to stay *here* to study the Anglo-Saxon basis of our language & laws: so he wrote to his father to know how far he might stay, & was (on Sunday) in suspense awaiting his answer. He remained with us all evening, discussing Mainz Worms & Spire Cathedral with us—He did not admire the Canon von B. as much as Meta & I did, in Mainz Cathedral; but had heard that the real Canon had gone to Palestine & had died there; & that this effigy or tombstone had been cut in sand stone & *sent* home after death. Saturday I don't remember what we did; nothing particular I think. We were tired & rested & bought grapes; & went and called on Mme de Sternberg (she was a Miss Bunsen & had called on us—) & heard that the Baron had {call} gone to Berlin that day for a fortnight accompanied by Mr Carl Bunsen,—came home & went to bed early. Sunday went to Church; both morning & afternoon. Mr Bosanquet (in spite of rum) walked with us & Anna & Ida Mohl (Franz V. S had gone that day,) to the Wolf's brunnen. He talked to Meta a great deal about the sermon, which was taken from the Hymn in the Xn year, 'In quietness & in confidence shall be thy strength', so Meta asked me to tell him we were Unitarians,—which I accordingly did, and found it did not shock him so much as we had expected; though he & I had a long talk, about the Three Witnesses,[1] which he gave up as spurious, & the non mention of the Trinity in the Bible &c. He said 'any one who seeks in the Bible for their religion, & finds it there, I feel in communion with,'—so I said 'So do I[,] all but the Calvinists', whereupon he said there ought to be no exclusion,—that any one who took man for the interpreter of what we ought to find in the Bible, & prevented our looking for ourselves &c. In short we had a long theological talk which ended in his offering to accompany me to Carlsruhe & to get my passport vised for me (to go for a night to Strasbourg, *French* town[.] Yesterday we walked about & read & worked and did nothing; but Ida & Anna came to tea, & M. Mohl to fetch them, after an University Examination for *L.L.D*, accompanied by a supper. We received your Wednesday letter—English letters, arriving in the afternoon, are not distributed {then} on *Sunday* afternoon,—not till *Monday* morng—so avoid sending letters that come on a

[1] Cf. 1 John v. 7.

Sunday. One from L. V. J to say she will be at Strasbourg to-morrow night; I meet her there, & bring her back on *Thursday.* We are leaving off lessons with M. Plarr, & taking up another German master after every body's advice—M. Plarr only talks of his *own* plans—and in *French*, during all the lesson time. We want to know heaps of home things. We like all you say about the Jardin. What did the Shadwells give you for dinner? What did Miss Lloyd talk about.

Ever your most affect[ionate] mother

E C Gaskell

The girls will write home while I am away. My dearest love to Julia & Papa. I am engaging a German maid, unless I hear to the contrary—

₀ **405*a*** _{424*a*}

CHARLES BOSANQUET[1]

Plymouth Grove,
Decr 23. [1858]

My dear Mr Bosanquet,

In the first place a merry Christmas & a happy new year to you —it is a long way to send it to that mysterious 'Rock', far farther off than the Prinz Carl. In the second place here is the translation of Paul Gerhards hymn (by *John* Wesley)[2] that I promised you. You recollect the story of it's being addressed to his wife who was despondent as to their position during the 30 years' war? And the supper? And the man who brought the news of Gerhard's being appointed Court-preacher before supper was ended? In the third place you will receive a Lyra Germanica from me the day after you get this letter,—I always wanted you to have it, & wished for your appreciation of Kate Winkworth's translation when we were at Heidelberg; & now you must please accept it as a Christmas gift. In the next place I have remembered the text Meta spoke about as over the drawing-room door at Pollok,—it was 'Let your light so shine &c. We still cannot recollect Mrs Stowe's negress's name. But that will come in time. I am writing in a great hurry I

---

[1] *Address (on envelope)* Chas B. P. Bosanquet Esq | Rock | Alnwick | Northumberland. *Postmarks* MANCHESTER | 8X | DE 23 | 58; A | ALNWICK | DE 24 | 58 *and* RUSHOLME.

[2] The translation is attached. It is the hymn 'Commit thou all thy ways'.

have so much to do. We received yr letter in Paris, & were very glad to have some news of you, but since then you have vanished from our sight. Did you go to Oxford[?] Did you see Mrs Campbell[?]

Believe me ever yours very truly

E. C. Gaskell.

₀ **406** ₀

FLORENCE NIGHTINGALE[1]

[31 December 1858]

⟨. . .⟩ I read the *Subsidiary Notes*[2] first. It was so interesting I could not leave it. I finished it at one long morning sitting— hardly stirring between breakfast and dinner. I cannot tell you how much I like it, and for such numbers of reasons. First, because you know of a varnish which is as good or better than black-lead for grates (only I wonder what it is). Next, because of the little sentences of real deep wisdom which from their depth and true foundation may be real helps in every direction and to every person; and for the quiet continual devout references to God which make the book a holy one.

387 **407** 410

GEORGE SMITH

Plymouth Grove
[?1858]

My dear Sir,

A gentleman, who is rather more than an acquaintance & less than a friend has asked me for an introduction to you, with a view of submitting a MS, (nature unknown,) to you. I have ventured to give it, & I shall be much obliged to you if you will 'honour' it.

His name is Hamilton Aidé.[3] His mother was a rich Scottish

[1] From a printed source, which dates it.

[2] The second volume of *Notes on Matters affecting the Health, Efficiency, and Hospital Administration of the British Army*, priv. pr., 1858.

[3] Presumably the first mention by Mrs Gaskell. The paper of this letter is watermarked 1857 and several other references to Aidé occur in letters to Smith of February 1859. (We spell 'Aidé' throughout.)

heiress, his father a Greek exile, of *good* character; Mr Aidé, pere, is dead; the son lives with his mother now, has been a captain in some rather crack regiment, but is now living in Hampshire.

All that I know of him is that he & his mother have shown us great kindness in Paris & Rome; that he acts beautifully in either French or English private theatricals, sings enchantingly (you could not transact your business with him in a duett, could you? Without any disparagement to your possible musical talents I think you would be a gainer by any mode of hearing him sing,) draws passably—and is altogether full of *tastes*—about the *talents* I am not so sure. He is a great friend of Mrs Archer Clive's (Paul Ferroll,) the Nightingales, Bracebridges Mrs Norton\&c/; he is very amiable & kind, has lovely eyes, and neat little moustachios & favori. He is altogether graceful & gentlemanly.

Pray make him sing. The passers by, even in Corn Hill would stop to listen, and think it was Wordsworth's sky lark at the corner of Wood St.

My daughter desires to be very kindly remembered to you. I tell her it is an Irish message. I hope Mrs Smith is better?—

Yours very truly
E C Gaskell

195 **408** 0

?JOHN FORSTER

42 Plymouth Grove
Sunday, Janry 9 [?1859][1]

My dear Sir,

Will you kindly send an Examiner containing the Report of the speeches of the Working Men's College people—at the Corn Exchange on\last/Wednesday night to

Lt-Colonel Shadwell
Exbury House
Fawley
Hants.

Yours very truly
E C Gaskell

[1] Two years are possible, 1853 and 1859, but the Manchester Working Men's College was not founded till 1858. Hopkins, *Gaskell*, p. 45.

₀ **409** ₄₁₁

EDWARD THURSTAN HOLLAND

Plymouth Grove.

Janry [?]19 [1859]

My dear Thurstan,

This is your Sudeley day, and we are going to the Dugdale's this eveng where we have not been since you were with us last year—so don't you see how naturally it comes to me to sit down and write and thank you for your letter, received I don't know how many weeks ago, and for all the agreeable pieces of news about American friends you have sent in your letters to Marianne from time to time. Only I want to know much more; little details which it is 'beneath the dignity of man' to put on paper, though you are about as good a specimen of masculine letter-writing as I know in condescending to particulars. I wish you would come and be questioned before your American freshness goes off. Could not you find out that Manchester is half way between Dumbleton and London? It IS, if you look at geography in the right way. Please do take this into consideration. Thank you much for the Mocassins, and for North & South. They are great rascals (your dear Americans) to go and pirate 'Lady Ludlow';[1] but I am afraid their morality is rather slack in several ways. And you have brought me a portrait of the good charming Mr Field! Thank you very much for that. And what is *Mrs* Longfellow like,—and the new Mrs Lowell, and Mr Child? Oh! you *must* come & be gossipy in Plymouth Grove, before the outline of your ideas & recollections has got blurred & indistinct in the London world. I never fancy I should like Mrs & Miss Nortons as much as our own Mr Norton. But I don't know why, unless it is from a 'Doctor Fell' feeling. Did not you like Mrs Shaw? I don't know him; but he is descended from one of the Puritan Martyrs in Q. Elizth's days. I don't know Mr Curtis. Anna Curtis was a great friend of Meta's in Paris years ago. I don't know the Sturgises of Boston, but I know Mr Sturgis in London who is such a fine good man. Mrs Sturgis is very 'good to look at' as the Lancashire people say, but he is good in every way. We are a very small family this morning, but both Mr Gaskell and Minnie come home in the course of the day. We are all well and busy; but excepting this

---

[1] Published by Harpers in their Library of Select Novels, 1858.

piece of gaiety tonight we have none in prospect. So if you will kindly come you will have to come for ourselves alone; but we are (said to be) very agreeable people, and we will give you a hearty welcome.

I was very glad indeed to hear that dear little Jessy was better. There has been a great deal of illness here but we are all looking to today,—bright & sunny, as the beginning of better weather, which will bring a more healthy winter Season. Ever dear Thurstan, with much love to your family party, your affectionate cousin

Elizabeth C Gaskell
T.O.

Please give my (Meta's) love to Sophy & everybody.[1]

407 410 412

GEORGE SMITH

[c. 4 February 1859][2]

My dear Sir,

We were so very glad to receive the news of the birth of your little son. Don't you feel proud? How many times have you spoken of 'my son'. I hope a great many already, because, if so I should conjecture from that that Mrs Smith was going on being well. But if I remember rightly you had not your alarm the last time until two or three days after her confinement; and I should be very much obliged to you if you would not mind writing a couple of words towards the end of this week to say that all was going on well and prosperously with both Mrs Smith and the little boy.

We received, (that is to say I received,) Mr Aidés letter with a confession about Rita[3] along with yours. But as both Meta and I conjectured the kind of news yours was likely to contain, I opened & read it aloud to her first; so Mr Aidé's intelligence came too late to be a surprize. I have not seen Rita; but he wants me to read it, and say if my 'judgment agrees with that of Mr

---

[1] This sentence is in Meta's hand on the next page.
[2] This date has been pencilled on the letter.
[3] *Rita, an Autobiography* appeared in Bentley's Popular Novels Series in 1858.

Smith', adding that although most of the reviews speak well of it, yet that he has been much blamed for it's publication by private friends. He *is* a nice person, though I suspect I shall agree with the private friends rather than with the public reviews. Is there no chance of your ever coming to see us here? It would give us all such great pleasure; & I think there are things in Manchester you would care to see, and that in fact you ought to know about in order to teach your boy to know more than a young friend who has been staying with us this week, & who proposed to me this question 'Mrs Gaskell[,] is there any difference between cotton and linen?' Only think if young Master Smith should ask such a question and his Papa not be able to answer him!

Yours ever very truly

E C Gaskell

Pray give my very kind regards to Mrs Smith.

409 **411** 426

EDWARD THURSTAN HOLLAND

Plymouth Grove,
Saturday, Febry 5th [1859]

My dear Thurstan,

Just one line to say that I think it is very probable Mr (Charles) Bosanquet[1] may call upon you on Monday; he has left us this morning asking me for a message that might entitle him to call upon you. Upon the spur of the moment I could give him none beyond 'love to you'; but I think you may be prepared for a very tall young man with a stiff outside & manners à la Sir Charles Grandison, but with a very strong desire to know you, hidden under ice & snow, calling upon you, ostensibly to enquire with whom you are reading law &c,—he goes on Tuesday to Oxford, to be a month there for his master's degree (or something else equally unintelligible,) & then is going to enter at Lincoln's Inn, for the Chancery Bar. Parents live at Rock, Alnwick, Northumberland. His father is a clergyman. And I think he is a very fine fellow, religiously & morally, perhaps more than strikingly clever; but as you multiply velocity by weight to ascertain momentum,

---

[1] See Letter 485 below.

so multiply intellectual qualities by moral force of character to ascertain the real power for good. With which profound observation I shall end my letter, first thanking you heartily for yr last, & saying how glad we shall be to see you whenever you can come— the sooner the better. Write two lines sometime to say if Mr Bosanquet does turn up on Monday, and if he is your Eton friend.

Your affectionate cousin
E C Gaskell

410 **412** 413

GEORGE SMITH

42 Plymouth Grove
Manchester
Febry 10. [1859]

My dear Sir,

An acquaintance of ours, (the daughter of an officer in the army, & the wife of one in the R.N—& who has been much in the West Indies in consequence of these two connexions—) has written a novel,—the scenery of whh is laid partly in the W. Indies. It is not her first work of fiction—she wrote 'Violet Bank',[1] about a year ago,—which Messrs Hurst & Blackett published, & which was well-reviewed. She thinks however that Messrs H & B—behaved shabbily to her,—(and from her statement I quite agree with her—) and is anxious to have an introduction to you, for this second West Indian novel; which I have not seen, but of which Signor Ruffini ('Doctor Antonio,') thinks very highly. So an introduction from me to you is coming round in due form, viâ Conway where Mrs Jenkin is at present staying. And now having finished business let me say how glad Meta and I are to hear from your letters this morning how well Mrs Smith, and the young hero are going on. I shall not give you the compliment you fish for in asking me if it is not very satisfactory to say that the Baby is *not* like his Papa; nor shall I let Meta express her opinion on the subject, as I disapprove of gratifying such barefaced anglers. I hope all danger of illness is over now to Mrs Smith; and that she

[1] Mrs Henrietta Camilla Jenkin (? 1807–1885): *Violet Bank and Its Inmates*, 1856. Her next work was *Cousin Stella*. See Letter 434.

will regain her strength thoroughly this time; &, as a consequence, be able to come & see us at Manchester some time not so very far off. I cannot at present meet with Rita. I really do believe we Manchesterians are too English to have such a French novel in our circulating libraries. Nor am I in any hurry to express what I know will be my opinion to Mr Aidé; for I like the little gentleman,—although I think he has too many tastes ever to excel in any one pursuit—He is writing\& composing/an Opera now. Next he will be painting for the Exhibition. But he *is* to be liked, and I think respected by those, who know his life.

Is there any news in London. No one speaks of anything here but war & the chances of war. Is Thackeray going on with his lawsuit about the Garrick Club?[1] What was the anonymous letter that the Miss Thackerays told Meta of in Paris, as if it had been written by Dickens. In short I am ignorant & open to any amount of literary gossip, if any charitable person, au courant, will take pity upon me. Our kind regards to Mrs Smith.

Ever yours very truly

E C Gaskell

412 **413** 430

GEORGE SMITH

Plymouth Grove—

Febry 14th [1859]

My dear Mr Smith,

My opinion of you is that you are very wicked and naughty; depriving me—by an action which appears on the surface most kind and generous, till I begin to examine into the motives that prompted it,—of all excuse to Mr Aidé for not sending him word what I think of 'Rita'. You are quite aware that I must agree with you. I tell him my 'honest opinion' of his *first* volume at any rate: It introduces one just exactly into the kind of disrepuble [*sic*] society one keeps clear of with such scrupulous care in real life,—it is not merely *one* character that is none of the best,—but every one we get a glimpse of is the same description of person. I don't think it is 'corrupting', but it is disagreeable,—a sort of dragging one's petticoats through mud. I wish the little gentleman,—who really

---

[1] See Ray, *Age of Wisdom*, pp. 278–90.

seems more than commonly good (for a man,—begging your &
your son's pardon,) had not written this book; because it gives one
a sort of distrust of his previous life. However his present energies
are devoted to the composition of an Opera. I wish you could hear
him sing; some of the country airs he picked up at Naples '*Santa
Lucia*' for instance. Mind you ask for that if ever you come
across him again,—even in Cheapside; seize him by the button,
and say 'Santa Lucia, if you please'. It will be worth while.

I hope Mrs Smith is going on bravely and well. How does
'Dolly' like the little brother,—it is generally so pretty to see the
maternal ways of a little girl of three or four towards the new
baby; and to hear the morality they talk to it, and the good advice
they give it.

Did you ever hear the proverb of 'Much would have more'—or
'give him (her) an inch & he (she) will take an ell.' Because if you
did not I will explain these pieces of wisdom of our forefathers by
an illustration. Having sent me Rita, & I don't know how many
books beside—will you let me have a copy of Charlotte Brontë's
Memoirs,—the prohibited 1st edition will do, as it is to be sent
immediately into Hungary, to a young friend (of Sir James
Stephen's as well as mine,) who is just marrying an Austrian in
command of some utterly unpronounceable place,—where neither
the Times nor my name nor Lady Anybody's has ever penetrated.

Meta is gone to the School at which she visits weekly, like a
good girl as she is—or she would join with me in kind messages to
Mrs Smith.

Yours very truly
E. C. Gaskell

I hope for a letter of gossip some day[.]

148 414 558

ANNE ROBSON

[February 1859]

My dearest Nancy,

We have been so busy all week that we have not had a scrap of
time to thank you much for all your pretty presents to the girls;
which are at last equitably divided amongst them. Meta was

extremely pleased by Willie's kind remembrance of her birthday,
& means to write to him herself some day soon. Today she is
down at the Sunday School taking double work, as MA has hit
her head (temple) a severe blow against the woodwork of her bed
in getting up this morning, & has a bad headache in consequence.
Wm is off to Bury for the day. Perhaps you know that Flossy is
gone to school at the Green's at Knutsford.[1] I took her part way on
Tuesday last; and today we get very happy & settled letters from
her, which I must answer before long, as for the present we have
made a kind of rule to write to her every day. Bob would I fear be
vexed by my letter about Miss Remond, but with the greatest
respect for *her* herself, (*from all your accounts of her*) I disapprove of
her object in coming to England, and can only anticipate for her
failure in it, (even did I think success desirable.) All the Anti
Slavery people will attend her lectures to *be* convinced of what
they are already convinced, & to have their feelings stirred up
without the natural & right outlet of stirred up feelings, the power
of simple & energetic *action*,—I know they can use any amount of
words in reprobation of the conduct of American slave holders, but
I don't call the use of words *action*: unless there is some definite,
distinct, practical *course of action* logically proposed by those
words. Wm is even more vehement against the false course he
thinks they are adopting (by stirring up English opinion as an
agent,) than I am; so please don't send Miss Remond *here*: it will
only end in discomfort both to her & to me. We are being very
quiet as to any Manchester gaieties, as the girls don't particularly
care for it; but we are having a succession of their friends staying
in the house; & they are hard at work at many lessons & things
into the bargain. They now write nearly all either my or William's
private notes or letters, which is a great saving on mornings when
like this 15 came,—nine to Wm, alone, the remaining 6 amongst
the girls & me. Julia is very much grown; nearly 5 *inches* since last
September; she is almost as tall as Flossy; who will be a little
woman, I think, less & slighter than Polly. I think we shall be
busy with painters this spring, as all the upstairs rooms, passages
&c, are to be painted & Hearn is going to her friends in Cornwall
for a long two or three months holiday. She & Elliott talk of
going over to see A Cheshire someday soon; if they can find a
gap of time between pig-killing, painting, & visitors, *this* week
towards the *end* possibly. You will be seeing a book of mine

[1] See p. 537 below.

advertized; but don't be diddled about it; it is only a REpublication of H W Stories;[1] I have a rascally publisher this time (Sampson Low, who publishes Mrs Stowe's books,) & he is trying to pass it off as new. I sold the right of republication to him in a hurry to get 100£ to take Meta abroad out of the clatter of tongues consequent on her breaking off her engagement. And now goodbye, dearest Nancy. My love to the two Williams

Your ever affec[tionate] sister
E C G.

The last thing I had heard about Lizzie was her children all being ill; but I conclude they are well again now, as some of them were over at a dance. Our girls wish often they could see something of Maggie here; but she did not seem to be happy with us the last time, & we are afraid of asking her. We are sending Flossy's share of the presents to her tomorrow.

₀ 415 ₄₁₆

JOHN BLACKWOOD

Private.

42 Plymouth Grove
Manchester.
March 5th 1859

I am going to make a request to you, Sir, which is of a slightly impudent nature. It is, that you will be so good as to give me a copy of 'Adam Bede,'—and I advance three pretexts for asking this favour from you.

Firstly my delight in the book; and in the 'Stories from Clerical Life', ever since the first part of 'Amos Barton' in Blackwood. It almost seems presumptuous in me to express all the admiration I feel; you might be tempted to quote Dr Johnson.

Secondly. You and yours have of old time been very kind to me and mine. My father was one of the earliest contributors to

---

[1] *Round the Sofa*, 1859, which contained 'My Lady Ludlow', 'An Accursed Race'. 'The Doom of the Griffiths', 'Half A Lifetime Ago', 'The Poor Clare' and 'The Half-Brothers'. The last was new, and 'The Doom of the Griffiths' had appeared in *Harper's New Monthly Magazine*. All the rest had appeared in *Household Words*.

Blackwood's Magazine; & some Mr Blackwood was\for auld acquaintance sake/extremely kind in assisting in the education of a half-brother of mine, since dead. And the first time I ever saw anything of mine in print was in Blackwood's Mag:[1] So far for the claim which kindness previously received is generally supposed (by the recipient) to confer of asking for more—'Much would have more'—& 'give him an inch & he'll take an ell.'

But if you deny that your having been kind & generous should be any reason for your continuing to be so, I'll change my tactics, and say you owe me compensation for an article, {of}\under/ which if the wit had been a tithe equal to the wish to abuse I might have winced with pain. As it was I only felt indignant at the bad spirit in which the review of my Life of Charlotte Brontë[2] was written, & half inclined to offer my services to Mr Aytoun the next time he wished to have an article written which should point out with something like keen and bitter perception the short-comings of my books. Please see that my reviewers are clever men for the future, capable of discerning true faults, & then let them lash away.

Will you acknowledge that any of my three pretexts are good for anything? If you will I shall think that you are very good to me.

Yours truly
E. C. Gaskell.

415 **416** 417

JOHN BLACKWOOD

42 Plymouth Grove,
Manchester—
March 8th [1859]

Sir,

Pray receive my best thanks for so kindly complying with my request for a copy of 'Adam Bede'. I value it very much: & am grateful for your kindness.

Yours truly
E. C. Gaskell

[1] Sketches of the Poor, No 1, *Blackwood's Magazine*, January 1837.
[2] *Blackwood's Magazine*, July 1857, contained a savage attack on the *Life*.

416 **417** 0

J OHN B LACKWOOD

Plymouth Grove—
March 9th [1859]

Dear Sir,

As you would learn from my letter yesterday I received the copy of 'Adam Bede' which you were so kind as to send me quite safely; and I am very much obliged to you for it.—I thoroughly admire this writer's works—(I do not call him Mr Elliott, because I know that such is not his real name.) I was brought up in Warwickshire, and recognize the county in every description of natural scenery. I am thoroughly obliged to you for giving it me; it is a book that it is a real pleasure to have, and if for every article in your Magazine, abusive of me, you will only be so kind as to give me one of the works of the author of 'Scenes from Clerical Life', I shall consider myself your debtor. You must have been mistaken, or I must have explained myself badly, if you thought I believed that Mr Aytoun wrote the review of C Brontë. I know the author's name perfectly well.

I do not remember the {name}\title/of the article I wrote, & whh you published long ago, in 1835 or '36 I think. It was in the days of a very kind friend of mine who was then Editor,— Professor Wilson. My article was a poem on a character whom I subsequently introduced into 'Mary Barton'; and I remember it began

In childhood days I do remember me
Of a dark house behind an old elm tree
By gloomy streets surrounded &c &c

It was worth very little; but I was very much pleased, and very proud to see it in print. I sent some articles, in prose, afterwards to Blackwood,—but they were, as I now feel, both poor & exaggerated in tone; & they were never inserted.

Once more let me thank you for your kindness. One of Mrs Poyser's speeches is as good as a fresh blow of sea-air; and yet {it} she is a true person, and no caricature,—But I could go on pointing out touches that delight me till you might think it an impertinence.

Yours very truly
E C Gaskell.

CHARLES ELIOT NORTON

Plymouth Grove, Manchester.
March 9th [1859]

My dear Mr Norton,

Somehow it always seems in vain trying to do anything with America, it is so far off to get explanations; but I am going into a longish story today, with a very weak vain little hope that an answer *may* come in time. Meta is full of blame for herself for she thought that her last letter did not sufficiently explain what I wanted to know; and I dare say it did not, for I know, *I* told her, and *she* wrote, in a hurry. You know about our going abroad; and that I got money for it &c, by selling Lady Ludlow &c; but when at Heidelberg we wished to go on to Dresden (alas! we never went,—for the weather became so *intensely* cold, I was afraid to venture the girls' health in travelling,—) but I wrote two stories for Household Words, & asked for immediate payment, in order to obtain money to gratify this wish. And they,\Household Words,/(very kindly) sent me 40£, saying that it was more than the stories would come to they believed, but I could wait my own time for sending them a *third* story, which would make all straight. So I *fancy* (I cannot get them to *tell* me), that I am indebted to them about 18£.

But I was extremely annoyed & hurt by their conduct in Janry— They published a 'Chip', called '*Character-Murder*' alluding to & quoting from a paper of mine called 'Disappearances'—published long ago in H W, & since\with my [?leave]/republished along with Lizzie Leigh &c. They quoted *from it* up to a certain point; but then added more of their own *as a quotation*, which made the '*Character-Murder*', & went on to regret that the aspersion (of which I had never even heard,) had appeared in their pages. I thought that it was a mistake of theirs; & wrote to Mr Wills (the manager) sending him my paper 'Disappearances', & begging him to read Character Murder over again, to see how little I had said, in comparison with what I was there made to say by implication. He only returned for answer that 'he was sorry I fancied that I had any reason for annoyance.' And you know I have particular reasons for shrinking from any accusation of Character Murder. So I did feel both sorry and hurt. All this time I was writing my third story,—to pay off my debt to them,—whatever it is;—but instead of it's stopping itself, as it ought to have done at about 40 pages\of MS/, which I suppose would have brought in about 18£ in H W, & so set me clear, I very soon saw that I could not compress it into less than 200 pages,—upwards of 100 of which are already written.[1] *Now Mr Dickens objected (in the* case of North & South) *to any sending sheets in advance to America.* He said the end of the story would come back to England before it was all published here, & in fact he quite refused to allow me to do {Nort} so with regard to North & South; nor should I like to ask him now. But I wanted to revert to the old proposal of publishing *entire* in America. I don't *think* my present story would bear weekly splitting up into numbers. I am sure it would do much better published as a whole. But it is not very good; too melodramatic a plot; only I have grown interested in it, and cannot put it aside. I should much *much* prefer it's being published in America, either as a whole or by the Atlantic. (Mind it is not really good. I am quite aware of that. The fault is in the plot.) But now comes in the complication. I have within this week received an additional motive for wishing it *not* to be published in H. W. in the fact that last Thursday I received a circular, saying that (on account of matters connected with Mr & Mrs Dickens' separation, Mr Dickens was giving up Household Words, and starting a new periodical with different publishers &c. I wrote directly to Mr Wills, to ask again how much I was indebted to Household Words, & who was the real personal creditor to whom I owed the money, which I shd be very glad to repay with interest &c, as the story I was writing was unfortunately of such a length that, (as the new periodical announces 'a new story by Mr Dickens in weekly numbers',) they would not be able to publish it for a longer time than I should choose to be indebted to them. Mr Wills has not yet replied to this. I am afraid he is making some arrangement by which they *can* take my story; as Mr Dickens happens to be extremely unpopular just now,—(owing to the well-grounded feeling of dislike to the publicity he has given to his domestic affairs,) & I think they would be glad to announce my name on the list of their contributors. And I would *much* rather they did *not.* And all day yesterday we looked out for an American letter, hoping it would bring some definite proposal either from the Atlantic, or some publisher—which I cd accept before Mr Wills writes. I wish they would let me pay them, and have done with

[1] Presumably *Lois the Witch.* See Hopkins, *Gaskell,* pp. 153-4.

them. Do you understand this long and involved story? And would it be troubling you very much if I asked you—No! I don't see what can be done now. But if I try to keep my story as my own property for a month longer, will you send me word what any body will give for it in America, & how it may best be kept *out of England*—& the reach of reviews. I should like the Atlantic to have it. First (don't think me impertinent) because I don't think it is too good for the American taste, as represented by Mr Underwood,—secondly because I should really like to send it to a periodical in whh you take an interest. I have not seen the Atlantic for long, and should like much to see it. Yes! I found the American cookery books here when we got home, (Decr 20th) and many many thanks. We can't understand all the words used— because, you see, *we* speak English,—but we have made some capital brown bread and several other good things, by the help of them. I don't see the 'Minister's Wooing.'[1] I should like to do so very much; but somehow one forgets to do the right thing at the right time. Yes! we have got our drawing-room chairs & sofas covered with a new chintz. Such a pretty ones [*sic*], little rosebuds & carnations on a white ground. All the other furniture stands where it did. By little bits we pick up little bits of prettiness (such as two Black Forest carved brackets at the fair at Heidelberg,) but you'll be happy to hear we are not rich enough to make many or grand changes. Indeed I don't think I should like to do it, even if one could. The house is to be painted and papered (passages & bedrooms) in May, but we shall rather adhere to the old colours. We mean to have prettier flowers than ever this year in the conservatory. We are always full of hope and of plans in the flower-line, just about this time of the year. But the east winds, & the smoke always come; only one cannot live without hoping. We have just the same servants. Elliott (waiter) often asks after you; and is very critical about the two photographs.—Yes! thank you, much, we got the second, and like it very much, but I don't think quite so well as the other because that was Roman. The girls go on, right down well. Meta is turning out such a noble beautiful character—Her intellect and her soul, (or wherever is the part in which piety & virtue live) are keeping pace, as they should do—She works away at German & Greek—reads carefully many books,—with a fineness of perception & relish which delights me, —teaches patiently and tenderly at the Ragged school,—has poor

[1] By Harriet Beecher Stowe, 1859.

old people whom she goes to see regularly, as a friend not as a benefactor, and is ever ready with household sympathy. She has gone back a year or two into her childhood, although professing to feel 'very old' at twenty two Febry 5th, and declining to be called a '*young* woman' saying she is 'middle aged.' Marianne is as practical and humourous as ever. Her quick decision always makes me feel as if she was a kind of 'elder *son*' rather than daughter. She is going to stay at the Bright's, next Tuesday. Flossy is gone to school! Yes, our pretty Flossy, who stept into the gay world of Heidelberg, went out to two dances, and began to be a little belle, has had to don the chrysalis-shell, & go to school, at dear old Knutsford,—with some Miss Greens, (the daughters of the Unitarian Minister there,) who are like sisters to our elder girls. And Julia is sprouting up, almost as tall as Marianne. (I forgot to tell you that Meta reads with & teaches Elliott every night, & has a little orphan lad to teach French to,—among her multifarious duties. She is learning to *whip-a top* today in order to show some boys at the Ragged school.) Hearn went off yesterday into Devonshire (her native shire) for a long holiday of six weeks. Julia & I are going to see Flossy at Knutsford on Saty next[.] \March 12./ But that Saturday will be long past by the time you get this letter. Mr Gaskell has been asked to go to be Minister in Essex St London, (Mr Lindsay's place you know—) but he has declined; quite rightly,—he has made his place here, and there must be some much stronger reason than a mere increase of income before it can be right to pull up the roots of a man of his age. So his colleague Mr Ham goes ({all} and we women Gaskells are none of us sorry,—oh! for some really spiritual devotional preaching instead of controversy about doctrines,—about whh I am more & more certain *we can never be certain* in this world.) And as he goes off directly Mr Gaskell will have all the work to do for some time, whh I am very sorry for as this is the time of the year when his digestion always gets wrong. I have been trying to put in the fine edge of a wedge to get him a longer yearly holiday,—if only for once—after thirty one years of pretty hard work he should have it. The worst is that he dislikes change and travel so very much; and if he gets a holiday I am afraid he will spend it in his study, out of which room by his own free will he would never stir. Read Arthur Stanley's Three Introductory Lectures on the study of Ecclesiastical History Parker Oxford—price *perhaps* 2s-6d, not more. I do so like them and so does Meta. And Dasent's

Norse Tales,[1] which are charming, & the introduction best of all and 'Adam Bede'—(you read Scenes from Clerical Life? did you not?) I hope the Brodies will come here at Easter. Mr Ruskin called here about a fortnight ago. He was so 'nice': simple & noble. Otherwise we have been as quiet as mice and do you know your letter has made me so out of heart about my story. I *know* it is fated to go to this new Dickensy periodical,[2] & I did so hope to escape it. Don't say a word though about Meta's not having explained properly; for I have no doubt it was our fault, and she will be so sorry. And don't allude to my praise of her. My kindest regards to Mrs & Miss Nortons.

There! after all I must go on another sheet, and ruin either you or myself in postage. But I have not said a word about Thurstan. We have never seen him yet; but he keeps up a brisk correspondence with Marianne, & we sometimes hear of you by this means. He is reading law pretty hard in London. Annie Austin is married to another friend of ours, a young engineer, employed about the ocean cables; a Mr Fleeming Jenkin. It was a pretty *walking* country-wedding about a fortnight ago—and they went to Oxford for two days, & then to his *lodgings* at Birkenhead. By the bye do you know anything of a young Mr Benjamin, Fifth Avenue, New York,—whom we made acquaintance with in Heidelberg,— a very nice fellow—going to be a clergyman, (orthodox) & very full of admiration for Dr Arnold. I think you may know him, because he was very full of a certain Mr Charles Elliott,[3]—who was Professor of something (History I *think*) at the University (Harvard I *think*) at which Mr Benjamin was. He and a certain Mr Bosanquet were both learning German at Heidelberg. Mr Bosanquet Oxford, & descended from Huguenots—They were two of the most deeply religious young men I ever met with; but somehow—now don't be shocked—I am afraid they had a want to me in their composition,—a want of the sense of humour, and that Dr Arnold had too. But it *is* a *want*. Meta, Flossy and I, and a friend of Meta's, an orphan young lady who joined us, Miss Jackson, went into lodgings for nine weeks at Heidelberg, after Marianne left us. We were very stationary always meaning to travel, as soon as I found what our expenses would be,—and then

---

[1] G. W. Dasent, *Popular Tales from the Norse*, Edinburgh, 1859.
[2] *All the Year Round*.
[3] Whitehill (*Letters*, p. 128) suggests this may refer to Samuel Eliot (1821–1898), Professor of History, Trinity College, Hartford, Conn.

came the most lovely poetical *wintry* November; clear deep blue sky,—white snow not very deep, except where it had drifted into glittering heaps,—icicles, a foot long, hanging on fountain & well,—trees encased in glittering ice,—& weighed down with their own beauty,—streets—walks—clear & clean—and the high peaked house tops so beautiful. But it was not weather for travelling, being 18 degrees below something in Reaumur. Unknown cold—However we went to see Spire & Worms & Strasburg Cathedral,—& the girls worked away at German; and we 'marketted' for ourselves; and dined at one,—& walked till the early November night came on; I hired a piano & music, and laughed harder than I ever laughed before or ever shall again, the air, clear delicious dry air, put one in such health and spirits. And we knew nearly every body in Heidelberg—from the man-milliner, who offered to drive us to his 'Chasse' in the Black Forest, to Bunsen,—from Homrath the old Ferryman to the two English clergyman [*sic*] &c &c, such a good-bying as we had! What do you Americans mean to do if there is an European war? Are you going to stand by us? Now I must end. Oh, *why* did you not send me word if the Americans want my story? I could have written it twice as brightly if you had. But I know it is not your fault, so never mind. The girls still wear their old Roman cloaks. Their *two* brown silks are made into one gown for Elliott. Their bonnets are gone to the dogs. Oh! I am glad I looked over your letter. Only fancy! Mr Norris (cousin to our Heidelberg Miss Jackson,) has gone & got married—yes & has a baby too I believe by this time. After making us all so sorry for his ill health & growing bald, then he went and fell in love with Edith Lushington, a girl of 18, very beautiful (they say) daughter of Dr Lushington D.C.L., a great London belle; & she {marr} accepted him,—School inspector on 500£ a year—cottage in Staffordshire,—and went off that aft: & ordered her wedding clothes—& they have been married more than a year. Thank you much for François's letters. I like always to hear of him. And now I *have* done. Ever yours most truly

E C Gaskell

I can not get good pens. Please tell us some news of the Storys. We have written to them, but have never received any answers for months. And Mr Field & Mrs? & Mr Wilde—particularly tell us where these last are? And Mr de Vere—

₀ 419 ₀

WILLIAM FOX[1]

42 Plymouth Grove
Manchester
March 10th [1859]

My dear Mr Fox,

Our Times of today—well of yesterday—well, tomorrow it will be of some day in dream land, for I am past power of counting—

Our Times of today has taken away my breath—Who—What, Where, Wherefore, Why—oh! do be a woman, and give me all possible details—Never mind the House of Commons: it can keep—but my, our, curiosity CAN'T—

Oh! please telegraph back anything about him—how long known what is he—what *has* he (I live in Manchester city sacred to Mammon,) when did she *first* see him—Where are they going to live—Whole love story, &c., &c., &c.

Write for 26 hours consecutively, and you can't write enough.

WELL TO BE SURE

I THINK I AM

VERY

GLAD.

Yours most truly
E. C. Gaskell.

₄₀₅ 420 ₄₂₂

MARIANNE GASKELL

[After 15 March 1859]

Letter to "Herbert Grey" [2]—see his note: nice, kind, *'graceful'* civilities—beginning Dear Sir & ending Yrs truly.

As you ask me for my opinion I shall try and give it as truly as I

[1] Original MS. not seen.

[2] *The Three Paths* by H. Grey was published in 2 vols. by Hurst in 1859. See Letter 414 for Mrs Gaskell's reliance upon her daughters for help with correspondence.

can; otherwise it will be of no use; as it is I think that it may be of use, as the experience of any one who has gone before on the path you are following must always have some value in it. In the first place you say you do not call The 3 paths a novel; but the work is in the form which always assumes that name, nor do I think it is one to be quarrelled with. I suppose you mean that you used the narrative form merely to {convey}\introduce/certain opinions & thoughts. If so you had better have condensed them into the shape of an Essay. Those in Friends in Council[1] &c. are admirable examples of how much may be said on both sides of any question, without any {dogma} decision being finally arrived at, & certainly without any dogmatism. Besides if you have thought (the result of either introspection or experience,—& the latter is the best & likely to be the most healthy—) to communicate, the neatness pithiness, & conciseness of expression required by the Essay form is a capital training of style. In all conversation there is a great deal of nothing talked—and in a written conversation on thoughtful subjects these nothings come in with a jar, & cause impatience.

But I believe in spite of yr objection to the term 'novel' you do wish to 'narrate,'—and I believe you can do it if you try,—but I think you must observe what is *out* of you, instead of examining what is *in* you. It is always an unhealthy sign when we are too conscious of any of the physical processes that go on within {y} us; & I believe in like manner that we ought not to be too cognizant of our mental proceedings, only taking note of the results. But certainly—whether introspection be morbid or not,—it is not\a/ safe {for a nov} training for a novelist. It is a weakening of the art which has crept in of late years. Just read a few pages of De Foe &c—and you will see the healthy way in which he sets *objects* not *feelings* before you. I am sure the right way is this. You are an Electric telegraph something or other,—

Well! every day your life brings you into contact with live men & women,—of whom{for instance I,} yr reader, know nothing about: (and I, Mrs Gaskell for instance, do know nothing about the regular work & daily experience of people working for their bread with head-labour,—& that not professional,—in London.) Think if you can not imagine a complication of events in their life which would form a good plot. (Your plot in The Three paths is very poor; you have not thought enough about it,

[1] By Sir Arthur Helps (1817–75), 1st Series 1847, 2nd Series 1859.

—simply used it ⟨a⟩s a medium. The plot must grow, and cul-
minate in a crisis; not a character must be introduced who does
not conduce to this growth & progress of events. The plot is like
the anatomical drawing of an artist; he must have an idea of his
skeleton, before he can clothe it with muscle & flesh, much more
before he can drape it. Study hard at your plot. I have been told
that {in} those early Italian Tales from which Shakspeare took so
many of his stories are models of plots,—a regular storehouse.
See how they—how the great tragedies of all time,—how the
grandest narrations of all languages are worked together,—&
really make this sketch of your story a subject of labour &
thought. Then set to & imagine yourself a spectator & auditor of
every scene & event! Work hard at this till it become a reality to
you,—a thing you have to recollect & describe & report fully &
accurately as it struck you, in order that your reader may have it
equally before him. Don't intrude yourself into your description.
If you but think eagerly of your story till *you see it in action*,
words, good simple strong words, will come,—just as if you saw
an accident in the street\that impressed you strongly/you would
describe it forcibly.

Cut your epithets short. Find one, whenever you can, that will
do in the place of two. Of two words choose the simplest. But yr
style seemed to me good. It was the want of a plot,—& the too
great dwelling on feelings &c,—& the length of the conversations, which *did not advance the action* of the story,—& the too great
reference to books &c—which only impede the narration—that
appeared to me the prevalent faults in your book.

You see I am very frank-spoken. But I believe you are worth it.
I judge from yr letter which I like—

Please don't thank me. But try & follow my advice for I am
pretty sure it is good. You know everybody can preach better
than they can practise.

All my morning's precious time taken up in letter writing!!
Dearest Polly,

I pity the man don't you? But it is good advice after all, & I
wd not have written it for every body. Show it to Mr H A B[1]—as
a 'specimen of *reviewing*'

[1] We assume Marianne was on the visit to the Brights mentioned above, p. 537.

404 **421** 428

ELIZA BRIDELL-FOX[1]

42 Plymouth Grove
Manchester.
March 21st. [1859]

My dearest Tottie,

We first saw it in the Times, and the news flew like wildfire in the house. I wrote of it that day to Hearn (gone for a holiday into Devonshire), and dreamt about it two nights running. Could I have done more? But we knew no particulars; so I wrote off to Mr Fox, and he gave us just a few. But after that came your letter. You are a good darling, for remembering to write to me, and tell me all about it. It *does* sound very nice. Fancy your meeting your *fate* at Rome. (I dreamt of you and your husband at Albano, in the gardens of the Villa Medici—think of me if you go there) I want to know a quantity more of course. Where were you lodging at first in Rome? What were you married in? Roman scarves and cameos? Oh, and is not Rome above every place you imagined? and do you go to the Pamphile[2] Doria villa, and gather anemonies, and watch the little green lizards as we did? and whereabouts are you on the Piazza Barberini, and do you know the Storeys, and have you seen Mr Page? Oh, wretch, write! Where are you going to when Rome gets unhealthy, if you are going to stay till August in Italy. And how come the Brownings in Rome? Will you give my very kindest regards to her, and my kind regards to him. (I liked her better than him; perhaps for the reason that might be that he fell asleep while I was talking to him) and can you bring me back anything from Rome that is not very large and handsome, or will it plague you, and the unknown man, who after all will look after your luggage, and must therefore be consulted. But I like the 'sound' of him extremely, and I hope he will like me when we come to know each other, which must not be long first. I left a 'Tolla' with the Storys to be bound in Roman vellum, that is the principal thing I want. I am *very* glad you are married my dearest little Tottie, and so are we all—Mr Gaskell's love: and the girls send best love. I think you are a very fortunate person—which alludes especially to your being in Rome. I feel as if all our little family details would sound so poor and flat after your marriage, and Rome too. Only I will tell you because you

[1] Original MS. not seen.   [2] Source reads 'Pamphilby' and, below, 'Varvcrini'.

used to care for all these things. Well then—Mr Gaskell (to begin with the head of the house) is very well; very merry; and eating and drinking in a comfortable natural style, not as if he was afraid of every mouthful. His colleague Mr Ham, is going or gone to Essex St and good go with him! Mr Gaskell was asked to succeed Mr Madge,[1] and urged, and re-urged. But he declined and wisely and rightly I think. He could never get in London the influence and good he has here; and he is too old to be taken up by the roots and transplanted merely for an extra hundred or so a year. So he stays in X St and the people are very much pleased. He is to have an assistant (i.e. a young minister) instead of a colleague, a certain Mr Drummond is thought of. If he comes, Mr Gaskell will have a long summer holiday this year; for Mr Drummond is to go to Germany next winter before finally settling. So much for that. Next Marianne is at Liverpool, went last week, to stay with some friends there the Brights. She is very well and pretty jolly. *Only*, Tottie, she never reads or settles to anything—but generally does the practical and polite and elder daughter things in the house. But I wish she would take up some steady employment and settle to it. Meta on the contrary, has almost too many interests; which absorb her, and make practical duties (of some kinds) difficult to her. She is working at Greek and German; practising, drawing, teaching at the ragged school, has a little orphan boy to teach French to, reads with Elliott every night, etc: etc: and has always more books she [is] wanting to read than she can get through, being a very slow reader. She is fat and well; enjoyed Heidelberg thoroughly (we came back via Paris Dec. 20th) and I don't think she ever thinks of her year of engagement. Flossy is gone to school to the Greens at Knutsford—you know who they are don't you? Emily, Ellen, Annie—daughters of Mr Green the Unitarian minister there. Oh! now you are married and in Rome I forget what you know of petty English details, and I am afraid of boring you. Julia trots to Miss Mitchells day school every day; she is grown nearly as tall as Flossy and is very spirited and wilful, more like Meta in her naughty days than anything else. We have just the same servants. It has been a very quiet winter; only three dances for the girls. I go on much as usual; swallowed up by small household cares: never feeling well in Manchester, and always longing for the country.⟨. . .⟩

*

[1] Source reads 'Madle'.

420 **422** 429a

MARIANNE GASKELL

[?Late March 1859]

My dearest Polly,

Meta & Louy are working hard at the dining-room table, mending your pink gown; but I don't know whether they can get it done to send off before Monday, it is so much torn; & then Caroline, who is as busy as can be with other things today, will have to iron it. Where your green ribboned muslin is, no one knows. I thought you had taken it with you. However sometime or other we will look for it. Today was planned *chock*-full before your letter came; you must not send us any more work to do, old lady, for Caroline is slow, & there is a great deal to do, & Davies is very busy in the garden just now, & not up to taking boxes &c to railway, as well as his day's work. Send us word what dresses you wear;—what at Miss Yates—what at B. dinner party; & *who were there* &c &c; Our visit to Worleston was charming, & has sent me back better than I have ever felt since the day Meta & I 'kilt'[1] ourselves by going to Cheetham Hill.—We joined the Behrens, Edward & Georgina, Mr B. Emily Leon[*sic*], (whom we all like very much,) & Abby Lucas, at the Railway Station. *Somebody* paid for our tickets, I did not. Quick to Crewe; to Worleston; Mr Julius B. met us at the Station, Mr Horatio was hunting at Rugby, but came about nine,—walked to the grange,—\dressed/had tea, & every thing imaginable besides,—& went to bed pretty early in order to be up by 8 o'clock breakfast. Georgina Horatio Mr Behrens & I went in one carriage (starting at nine,) Mr Julius, Edward, Abby, Emily Louy & Meta in the other, a kind of high break, with postillions &c. Did not we go at a pace? Windy cloudy day, & *very* cold in the open carriages,—Cholomondeley a lovely place,—great old castle on rising ground above a piece of water in a park,—meet just outside the *farther* gates,—eighteen couple of hounds, not very many gentlemen, Sir Philip Egerton, Lord Grosvenor, Mr Wainwright Belhouse, a Capt Starkey (invited to dine at Worleston but 'going to a ball at Liverpool so couldn't',—half an hours hanging about, waiting for others— Then they went off to beat covers,—tried several & could not find,—coming into sight now & then,—& then being lost again,— it began to rain. (All the young Mr Behrens had sent their hunters

[1] See p. 614, n. 1.

to the meet, & mounted so our carriage party was diminished,—)
rained & blew, enough to break all our umbrellas—drove home
through a storm—lunched. I went to lie down, fell asleep, at five
got up, & made Meta come out for a walk,—Louy & old Mr
Behrens (who took very much to each other) had gone out before.
Hunters came home, & Ed. Behrens, Abby & Emily set off home
to Mrs Leo's dance. We dined at seven; turtle soup, green peas (at
½ a guinea a *quart*,) iced pudding[,] ducklings, chickens, lamb *&c
&c &c* then we worked & the gentlemen fell asleep,—to bed-*room*
(for G. came[,] talked till past 1,) breakfast at nine saw stud, &
dairy & cows,—came off at 1. Home at ½ past 2. Papa in very good
spirits; but ever since he has been too busy to be talked to,—&
today is *quite* unapproachable—found letters by the bushel. One
from Fleeming—he & Annie will 'come to dinner' on the Sunday
after next. One from Tottie, which I am sorry to say I lost as
soon as read, or you should have seen it. She describes her husband
as very charming, & seems very happy. She was nearly asking Mrs
Schwabe to the wedding, but Mrs S. had a grand ball the night
before, so Tottie thought it would not do to ask her. Mr & Mrs
Browning were there, & the Bridells dined with the Brownings
in the evening of their wedding day. Come home in August; have
rooms in the Piazza Barberini—(I've lost the number—with the
letter.) Letter from Mr Katchenowsky,—thankful & grateful &
will come\to Manchester/in April to meet the Hathertons[.]
Letter from Ly H, with some more drawings of Miss Coode's, &
some letters of the young woman's too. Long letter from Mr
Smith, which I enclose. Think how many people are coming
(possibly) in April! Mary Holland,—Flossy from school. Smiths,
—Brodies,—Katchenowsky, Uncle Sam, Hathertons—Orme—
and if Papa gets over-busy; & not talkable as today! letter from
Flamborough—stupid—They had only 3 bedrooms (one of 'em
doublebedded, & 1 a servant's) & one sitting-room,—& if that
suits, they will send terms. They *might* have sent 'em at once. I
have no time to write again. You may if you like—oh no, don't,
it's no use; we cd not pack in I think. But I wish you would
write to the principal hotel at Linton, Devon: making all similar
enquiries, as *minute as can be*. There are 2 inns; find out the best. A
letter from Hearn last night. No news; but she is very much
enjoying herself. Caroline has on an *atrocious* print today, great
stripes of crimson, blue & brown—we shall send your box to U.
John St by *luggage* train on *Monday*; & I will put money in, when I

can get it from Papa; but it is no use trying for it today. Meta & Louy are going to Mary Pillin's to see how her child is. Do please work away at the sleeves, for we are overdone with sewing—& Caroline is so slow. I was up, & at my sewing sometime before breakfast. No more news, my darling child—

Your ever affect[ionate] Mammy E C Gaskell.

310 **423** 0

ROBERT CHAMBERS

42 Plymouth Grove,
Manchester
March 28. [?1859]

Dear Sir,

Reading your Domestic Annals of Scotland,[1] warms up all my old Scottish blood,—and makes me wish heartily that our four girls could see something of Scotland, beyond the week at Glasgow and two days at Edinburgh (made so pleasant by you; one day,—) that my eldest girl had with me three years ago.[2] So your book has drawn upon you an unexpected consequence in the shape of some enquiries, whh I shall think you very good & kind if you take the trouble of answering.

We generally go to the sea about the time of the younger girls['] holidays—about June 18th for a month or so. Now is there any place like this in the neighbourhood,—(say{s} two hours' rail to) of Edinburgh?—wild sea\wanted/, & wild rocks, & bracing air, and pretty *sketchable* inland scenery,—if possible traditional & historical.—

Four bedrooms, and two (or one) sitting-rooms in a farm-house, to combine as much country as possible with sea, in order that we may not grow too Manchestery and Cockney in our views of life.

Indifferent to carpets, and such like luxuries.

Not indifferent to cleanliness and good air.

Price moderate; i.e. I should like *all* our expenses\living &

---

[1] By Robert Chambers (1802-71), published by Chambers in 3 volumes, 1859-61.
[2] Perhaps a reference to the visit in Summer 1855.

M.G.L.—T

boarding/to come to only about 8 £ a week; and we *may* be nine
persons\part of the time/, & are {[?]}\sure/to be six.

What is North Berwick like,—But we doN'T want a 'fashionable watering place'.

I beg your pardon for asking you these questions; and I shall
not be a bit surprized if you think them too impertinent to be
answered.

Yours very truly
E. C. Gaskell

145 **424** 0

ELIZABETH HOLLAND[1]

Sunday aft.
[?Early April 1859]

My dearest Lizzie,

I was very sorry indeed not to see you and very sorry indeed
for the cause: but I quite understand how you could neither have
felt doing right or being happy at leaving her. Please let me know
how she is. I had to go to London Thursday afternoon and hurried
back (My business only half done it was such a dense fog) on
Friday evening in order to be in time for your hoped for coming
on Saturday morning. They wanted me to write to put you off
but I felt as if your really coming to stay a day or two *quietly* here
was so near accomplishment I could not bear to run any risks.
Now I don't know when it will be; all our plans are in a whirl for
the next two months at least, and I would far rather not see you
than have you when we are whirling. You sound to be in your
own whirl too. It is hard work making one's idea of life dear and
I am more and more convinced that where every possible individual circumstance varies so completely all one can do is to
judge for oneself and take especial care *not* to judge other[s] or for
others. Else, I think a sewing club is an error—good for the people
whh sew, as it is self denying on their part, but not doing half or
a quarter so much good to others as might be done by the same
amount of self denial. The best mode of administering material

---

[1] Original MS. not seen. Although the source states this letter was to Eliza Fox,
its opening and the internal references to Maggie (see p. 41, n. above) and Mabel
convince us that it was written to Mrs Gaskell's sister-in-law.

charity seems to me to be by giving employment and taking thought in adapting the kind of employment and in helping to find out who can do it. If you *cut out the work, gave it to poor women to do for a moderate payment* and then either gave the ready made clothing yourselves or sold it at cost price to be given by others to the poor who needed it I should say it was far better wiser and more noiseless but I should never have given my opinion unless you had asked for it because we have a bye word in our family 'Saint Theresa' which serves (or ought to serve) to check us when we are judging of others conduct or allowing any one to speak ill without trying to put in a palliating excuse. I know nothing about Saint Theresa but that one of her titles is *'Defender of the Absent'*. But I strive more and more against deciding whether another person is doing right or wrong. Maggie has asked Meta why we did not send Flossy to Mrs Lalor's; we had several reasons one of the principal of which was that we so particularly desired her to learn that different people, equally good, might act in an entirely different manner, and yet be acting quite conscientiously and each and equally striving to do the will of God. As to Congregational tea parties, I don't precisely see the good they are to effect therefore *I* should not go to them, although I might go to *one* if it gave pleasure to those who did attend them. I don't know whether all this is any help at all to you dear Lizzie, because you write in a hurry; nor do I feel that my opinion can be of much help to any one but if you would ever care for it I would do my best to think anything you might ask one conscientously and tell you to the best of my power. But I wish you could come over—if you found you could would you write and say, but mind I won't have you to come in a whirl and a hurry just when people are coming in and out of the house and then as soon as the quiet evening comes on whirl away. It's *miserably* cold. We are all well except MA. who has got a slight cold. Flossy comes home on Tuesday. Write about Mabel[1] if only a line. ⟨. . .⟩

[1] Mabel Holland, b. 1856; youngest daughter of Mr & Mrs Charles Holland. *Holland Family*, ed. Irvine, p. 87.

_{405a} **424a** _{439a}

CHARLES BOSANQUET[1]

Plymouth Grove.
April 20. [1859]

My dear Mr Bosanquet,

Many thanks for your letter. I am going to try to answer it in brief—(a far more difficult thing to me than to answer at length because I have always to leave out so many things suggested by the subject I am writing about.) I wrote to Robert Wedgwood about Mr Lloyd Jones; he returned me many thanks *and* a campanula gracilis, (which I hope you won't think ought to be forwarded to you along with the thanks,) but had just succeeded in obtaining a curate,—to come on Trinity Sunday. Next I am commissioned to send you this letter of Miss V. d. Noddgeries, with so strongly an implied suspicion that you won't be able to read it, that I think it is only due to your kind interest in Miss v. d N. to give you the heads, as I know they will make you glad. She has *seven* pupils—(she had only *four* here,) and much employment of various kinds; very pleasant society, kindness from every body 'especially from Miss Smith and the single ladies,'—has reduced her terms[2] at Mrs Brodie's, Mrs Acland's, & Max Muller's advice, & receives sisters, I *think*, on the same terms as one girl. (But you know *I* can't read a word of the letter, so it is only recollection of what I heard.) She and her mother are generally charmed with Oxford,—of which I am as proud as if I were B.A. Oxon or M A, or Provost or Master or Dean of Ch Ch. Altogether it is a joyous grateful hopeful letter. Thank you.

Next, it would be delightful if you could come over to Ashbourne while we are there; and very nice if you cd at any time go over, & make Capt Holland's acquaintance for I am sure you wd like each other, & he has heard much of you from Mr Clarke. Arthur Duckworth is curate at Ashbourne,—and you were at Eton with him, were you not. He is brother to Russell & Herbert &c. Ashbourne is on a branch bit of the London & NW. railroad, joining it somewhere in Staffordshire,—SW. corner of Derbyshire,—to judge by the map you would have to pass through

---

[1] *Address (on envelope)* Chas B. P. Bosanquet Esq. | Rock | Alnwick | Northumberland. *Postmarks* MANCHESTER | 2X | AP 20 | 59; RUSHOLME; A | ALNWI⟨CK⟩ | AP ⟨ ⟩.

[2] See p. 613, n. 1 below.

Wirksworth in coming from Alfreton to Ashbourne. Mr Clarke *is*
coming for one day, he says, but I don't know which. Cd you
not come with him? I remember I meant to have corrected that
bit in my letter about Capt Holland's leg: it shd have been 'in
consequence of'—his knee cap slipped at that time, owing to his
long standing,—& was hastily put to rights, *not* rightly,—& was
never right again, & produced disease &c. But it was all to be
traced back to the strain at that time.

Oh Mr Bosanquet, did you see William Arnold's death in the
Times?—but you did not know him,—you remember he wrote
Oakfield,—and married somebody within a fortnight after first
seeing her,—or some such rash proceeding, I won't be quite
sure of the length of time, but the offer was made 3 days after first
seeing her; and the Arnolds were so afraid of the marriage,—& it
turned out so well[,] she being such a sweet strong character, &
having just the complementary qualities he wanted,—& how they
went back to India, sorely against his wish three or four years ago,
—poor fellow—and she died about two years ago, leaving a little
baby, as well as three other children,—& now I will copy out a
part of Fanny Arnold's letter which I am sure will interest you, &
make you feel as it does me that we must just put our lives into
God's hands, and feel that He knows best, for otherwise certain
additions to sorrow would be inexplicable,—'The peculiar circum-
'stances of his illness have added very greatly to the trial, which
'would indeed be almost too heavy to bear, if the same Wisdom
'& Love which has now ordered his lonely deathbed, had not
'promised to be the support & comfort of those who mourn, or
'try to mourn, in faith & submission. He left India on the 8th of
'Feby, hoping to meet his children, whom he had sent off round
'the Cape shortly before, in England. At Cairo he was obliged to
'stop, seriously ill, and as soon as we heard of his being there
'Walter (her youngest brother,) started in the hope of meeting
'him, and bringing him home. They passed each other in the very
'mouth of the harbour of Alexandria, each at the time uncon-
'scious of the fact. Walter followed him back to Malta, & heard
'there that the steamer in which Willie was had left five hours
'before, and that he was much better. So Walter returned home as
'quickly as he could across the continent. The next thing we
'heard, just when we were beginning to hope that we should see
'him, was by a telegram from Gibraltar (from a friend who had
'joined him at Cairo, and who, though quite a stranger to him had

'most generously given up his return home, and staid to help
'Willie—) saying that they had been obliged to land and that my
'brother was dangerously ill, and begging some one to go.
'Another of my brothers sailed immediately, but the day after he
'sailed, a telegram from Capt. Hamond reached us saying that my
'brother had died on the 9th. This is all we know as yet, and you
'may imagine with what earnest longing we look forward to
'Capt Hamond's return to hear from him all that we can ever hear
'about those last days. The four little children are daily expected
'in London, where Jane & Mr Forster' (a cousin of Chas Buxton's,
'who married Jane Arnold—they have no children) 'who have
'taken the whole charge of them, are waiting to receive them and
'bring them here first. The two eldest at 5 & 8 years old will in
'some degree perhaps be able to feel their loss. The youngest will
'not be two years old till August.' There is no need to say
another word about it.

Our plans,—in face of such mysterious sorrow we still plan,—
{but with a deeper feeling than can be expressed in words} are to
go to Ashbourne Saturday April 31 [sic], Monday May 2, or
Tuesday May 3rd. The objections to each day are as follows; The
Freds want us to go on Saturday—but Thurstan will be here, &
we can't,—Monday is the County election when Capt Holland
says all Ashbourne will be drunk & disorderly & he does not want
us to have so bad an impression of the place. If we stay here till
Tuesday we don't know where to sleep, as every bed will be
taken down on Monday.

Nextly, some of us go on,—one at a time to stay with Louy
Jackson, who, having come of age has taken the spirited step, of
engaging a great part of a furnished house in Canterbury (the
rest belonging to two old maiden ladies,) in my cousin Frank
Holland's parish of St Dunstan's, and Mrs Stanley has sent me
Arthur Stanley's 'Memorials of Canterbury'[1]—which we are all
full of,—as a delightful book,—independent of our own personal
& immediate interest in Canterbury just now. Do you know
the book?

After that we are rather at sixes & sevens,—they say we can
hardly come back, as a whole family of occupation, to this house
before the time of taking the 'little ones' Flossy & Julia to the
seaside—June 18th—. You were right about Flamborough. There
are only two bedrooms to let all through the village. We are now

---

[1] First published 1854.

enquiring about Whitby—(not the town itself,—we want some-
thing\more/primitive[,] cheaper & wilder,—) North Berwick,
Galloway sea coast,—\St Andrews, whh I should like best/& in
default of all other places, possibly Dover, as we shall so many of
us be down South, and the girls have always wanted to explore
the neighbourhood. I am *rather* against Dover, & in favour of
Scotland. I think we are certain to be in London a little after the
middle of May. Flossy comes home to-morrow, & every body is
full of plans for her. Please return Miss v. d. Noddgerie's letter
when you have read it.

Yours very truly
E C Gaskell.

399 425 0

F. J. FURNIVALL

Plymouth Grove
April the 26th. [1859]

Dear Mr Furnivall,
    Would it give you very much trouble, if you are meeting Mr
Ruskin any day soon, to find out whether a spinning wheel sent
off\from here/ten days ago has ever reached him or not?[1] Can
you be so clever as to find out without betraying your having a
commission to do so? and will you be so kind as to forgive the
liberty I am taking in giving you such a delicate task to perform?

Yours most truly
E. C. Gaskell.

411 426 581

EDWARD THURSTAN HOLLAND[2]

Wednesday—[?20 April 1859]

My dear Thurstan,
    That will be charming, only you must please to come on
Wednesday, however late, for Wednesday itself is a great deal too
late for us, for we wanted to have you for a comfortable long
time, and the painters inflexibly (landlord paints, so we are

---

[1] Cf. Waller, 'Letters Addressed to Mrs Gaskell', p. 52.
[2] *Annotation* April/59. This letter should come before 425.

obliged to submit,) come in on May 2nd, when all our beds will be taken down, & we flit to Ashbourne (in the first place). But you must please stay *till* Mon[day] and come as soon as ever you can—if before Wednesday, so much the better.

Oh the boat-race!—to have seen Minnie's face over the Times was a sight to behold! She had been so cock-a-hoop, & triumphant over Oxford (Meta's & my University,)—we should like to have triumphed over her, but the downfall was too great—one might as well have scoffed at Marius sitting among the ruins of Carthage. Now mind you come as soon as you can, & stay as long as painters & paperers will allow any of us to stay.

Your affectionate cousin
E C Gaskell.

305 **427** 458

EDWARD CHAPMAN

42 Plymouth Grove,
Manchester
Thursday, April 28th 1859

Dear Sir

I beg to acknowledge the receipt of 75£, as payment for my permission to print & publish an edition of 2,500 copies of 'North & South'.

April 28th [over stamp]

I remain dear Sir

Your [*sic*] very truly
E C Gaskell

421 **428** 0

ELIZA BRIDELL-FOX[1]

P. Grove.
May 9, 1859

My dearest Tottie,

I've not written (*not* because I wanted to give you tit for tat, and you had been an unconscionable time in writing) but because

---

[1] Original MS. not seen.

our plans have been all unsettled. At one time Paris for Whitsuntide Wm. Ma and me, then[1] *my* prudence (I have set up prudence,
just as some people set up a carriage, and am *quite* as surprised at
my new position as they are—) Well! ⟨. . .⟩ and it snows and it
blows, so merry Xmas to you my dearest Tottie. Be prepared to
see me come in before many days elapse—and till then believe
me Ever yours very affec[tionatel]y,

E. C. Gaskell.

How is Mr Forster? Alas! that he should have set up a conscience about 'Orders'!

₀ 429 ₀

UNKNOWN[2]

Ashbourne Hall,
Derbyshire.
May the 10th. [?1859]

Sir

I feel much obliged {to you} for the kind trouble you and your
son have taken in order to bring about {an} a literary-engage-
ment between me and Dr Noyes; and for your allowing me to
send my answer through you. I am sorry to say that I must
decline any such engagement at present as my time is fully
occupied.

With many thanks I remain

Yours ever very truly & gratefully
E. C. Gaskell.

₄₂₂ 429a *₄₄₃ₐ

MARIANNE GASKELL

Monday [?May 1859][3]

My dearest Polly,

I am going to plunge into dress as hard as ever I can, for we
ought to be off, on the endless route to London. Meta & Emily

---

[1] Source reads 'they'.   [2] Written in a formal hand.
[3] The references to the Boat Race (see Letter 426), the meeting with Mrs
Drummond (see Letter 421) and the arrival of Bosie seem to place this letter about
May 1859.

think that Swiss bodies of black velvet or RICH blk silk would be very pretty, *over* yr white tarlatane & Flossy's white & gold do. *But* Meta's Swiss body *does not fit*; and I am quite sure\1st/*they must be shaped to each individual figure.* 2ndly They must LACE under *the arm*, having a BONE put in {unde} by the lace-holes to keep the *stuff from wrinkling.* 3rdly. The sharpest point must be towards the neck, NOT towards the skirt. 4thly. They must be lined with *very* thin lining, or with thin silk so as to sit *close* to the figure; and the corners must not be *lumpy* as Meta's are; but sharp & neat. *The* great thing however is to make them *lace*, and to put a bone by the lace holes. Meta's is like this—[Sketch] quite narrow on one side with great thick wrinkles. Miss Davenport Bromley had one on the other night—& so had a lady at Lord Lansdowne's, which *I* thought prettier than the pointed ones: a *very* {l}low\black/ body, *only* going up to the fulness of the breast, cut *square* with shoulder straps: the white body coming above it, like a chemisette. Not such large sleeves as we have had made lately for short sleeves, but very full; *six inches* is THE measurement *to lie on* the ground behind. [Small sketch] *I* like the square cut body; but Meta does not think it so dressy. If in black velvet—remember the material is so thick it requires exquisite fitting,—& I think lining with silk, to make it sit close: a few blk velvet bows on yr under skirt, and one or two broad large bows on Flossys wd make it very pretty. As far as I can judge no one has got *new* gowns here; & pure *entire* white is mourning for girls in an evening. Mrs Willm Coltman had a white silk with black velvet {band} sash & ends, & a great blk velvet bow on the other side of her dress,—white feathers, black pansies & gold intermixed in her hair. Miss Wynne, blk lace with lilacs & blk lace in her hair—Miss Davenport Bromley white muslin, with square cut blk *silk* body as above—*I* thought of a wreath\& bouquet/of black pansies tipped with gold for Flossy,—to be worn out in some future occasion with a pale pink tarlatane dress: I was wondering about you,—for I suppose you will wear your white tarlatane & you must not look *under* dressed to F. E. But Meta & Emily don't approve of the pansies.\Meta says she *does* approve of *pansies*/—and so you must send word what ideas you two have; always regardING expense. I think it is *very* pretty of E D. sending me that book, though I suspect it is only to get a chaperone for sending it to you. Bosie called on Saturday, very full of the Boat Race (Aha!! Miss! Cambridge 100 yards behind Oxford—it is very well to *pretend* ignorance,) in the course of conversation he said 'My brother Geordie is almost as tall as I am—indeed we are all likely to be six foot'—and I was so terribly on the point of saying 'Why your father is not a tall man!' I can't think how I stopped myself & how it did *not* come out. We went to dine at the Wedgwoods— E. Will, M. & I, Mr & Mrs W Coltman, Mr Horner & Miss Susan, Mr Roget, a Miss Moore & a Mr Norris, & *heaps* of people in the evening,—Greatheds—(Miss thinks Irvin very vulgar & unrefined, & wonders how Cousin John could have had a son so the reverse of himself)—Spottiswoodes, Litchfield &c[.] Yesterday morng Meta & I went to Vere St (Mr Maurice's) & walked home;—dined, rested, & went to St Paul's Special Service in the eveng—the Dean having given us tickets. It was most striking. Mrs G. H. Holland was there, & must have thought us very clerical, as we sate with the Milman's, & waited to speak to the Provost of Queen's, who preached. Today *if we can* we are going to Ludlow's to look at wreaths\for you/—to Mr Blunts at Chelsea Rectory to lunch—to Hampstead to see Stanfields pictures—home to tea to meet Professor *Helmholz*, who is going to call this evening—tomorrow we may be going to lunch with Mr Ruskin.— *Whether* we we have time to go to Ludlow's, and from there send you a description of what wreaths there are there—or whether I suddenly close this note as it is,—(for we *must* be off soon) *answer by return*—{if} saying yr ideas—

I am glad Mrs Drummond seems so *nice*. We must have a party for her soon:—

Ever your most affec[tionate]
E C G.

Many people are wearing only lilac gowns with blk ribbons—you might wear Mrs Shadwells gown with blk—for common—& blk hand [?bred] silks are plenty—But the mourning is only to last 3 weeks beginning *last* Thursday.

413 **430** 433

GEORGE SMITH

17 Cumberland Terrace
Regts' Park, June 2 [?1859]

My dear Mr Smith,

I am going to write you rather a disagreeable letter,—disagreeable to write at any rate. Only I think you will understand what I say, if I say it frankly & openly out.

At the beginning of April Messrs Sampson Lowe & Co wrote to ask if I would let them have my next work, & on what terms? I was ill, but one of the girls wrote in my name to say I was not thinking of publishing any thing at present, much obliged to them &c.

About a week afterwards—before Easter certainly, they wrote again,—and I must say astonished me by their offer—(Mr Gaskell has got the letter in his desk at home & he is wandering about in Ireland, or you should see it—) of one thousand pounds for the MS of a 3 vol. novel. There was something the wording of which I do not quite remember—but it was to the effect that this sum was to include all American profits &c—I mean that Messrs Lowe were to have {that}\those/whatever {it}\they/might be. Now I am afraid I must own, 1,000£ does a little bit tempt me, it is such a great sum; but I do not like publishing with Messrs Lowe for one thing—and moreover *do* like publishing with you. But I know you have not the power of commanding a sale in America as they can do, and as I suppose they reckon upon doing in this instance otherwise I cannot see how they can make it pay. But I would much rather have 800£ from you than 1,000£ from them; so I have been weighing and balancing and never answering, till the other day this letter came which I enclose and I suppose I must decide. I have a story partly written. I doubt if it will reach 3 vols; and I have sometimes felt as if I should never dare to face the reviews again.[1] But I should like to work away at it this summer.

Remember I mean literally what I say. I would far rather have 800£ from you than a 1000£ from them. But should you be willing to pay me at the former rate?

---

[1] Presumably a reference back to the reception of the Life of Charlotte Brontë. The address and paper make 1859 a probable year.

I have thought that telling you the simple truth was really the most friendly & delicate-in-reality action. I hope Mrs Smith was not much tired. It was very good & kind in you both to come & call here.

Mr Coleridge has asked the girls to stop with him at Eton till Monday, so he and his wife will undertake the chaperoning.

Yours ever very truly
E C Gaskell.

₀ 431 ₄₄₉

'GEORGE ELIOT'

June 3 [1859]
17 Cumberland Terrace
Regent's Park

Dear Mr 'Gilbert Elliott',

Since I came up from Manchester to London I have had the greatest compliment paid me I ever had in my life, I have been suspected of having written 'Adam Bede'.[1] I have hitherto denied it; but really I think, that as you want to keep your real name a secret, it would be very pleasant for me to blush acquiescence. Will you give me leave?

Well! if I had written Amos Barton, Janet's Repentance & Adam Bede I should neither be to have nor to hold with pride & delight in myself—so I think it is very well I have not. And please to take notice I knew what was coming up above the horizon from the dawn of the first number of Amos Barton in Blackwood.—After all it is a pity so much hearty admiration should go unappropriated through the world. So, although to my friends I am known under the name of Mrs Gaskell, to you I will confess that I *am* the author of Adam Bede, and remain very respectfully & gratefully

Yours,
Gilbert Elliot.

---

[1] Mrs Gaskell wrote to Catherine Winkworth in early July 1859 to ask for help in confirming George Smith's opinion that 'Mr Lewes's Miss Evans' wrote *Adam Bede. Letters and Memorials*, ed. Winkworth, II, p. 277. See also Hopkins, *Gaskell*, p. 330.

₀ 432 ₀

JAMES T. FIELDS[1]

11 Kildare Terrace,
W[est?]
Tuesday Evng June 14 [1859]

Dear Sir,

Mr Gaskell has forwarded to me your note & card, and begged me to write in reply to the former. I am afraid it will be very difficult to arrange any time for meeting, in this busy town, where I dare say we are both full of engagements. I remain here until the 27th when we go into Scotland.

I am afraid that our meeting would not answer any business purpose either; for, since I heard from you & Mr Norton I have had an offer from an English publisher of 1,000£ for a three vol novel, on condition that this purchase money for the copyright shall include the American as well; and being anything but a person of business I would rather (if I do ever publish again,) have a sum down, than be uncertain how much I might receive of percentage on sale of copies. Besides I suppose my writings are more popular here than in America,—for the rate of payment is certainly very different.

Apart from business, if you ⟨. . .⟩

*

₀ 432a ₀

?MRS GEORGE SMITH

[?June 1859]

My dear Mrs Smith,

Florence brings us word of a most kind invitation from you and Mr Smith to a Greenwich\Dinner/for either the 20th or 21st, and if this good news is true, may we choose the former day? and how many of the many Miss Gaskells will you accept in my train?

Florence is brimming over with pleasant recollections of her doings at Hampstead, and makes me afraid lest this seems so very flat after it.

---

[1] This letter is in an album compiled by him. See Letter 433 also.

I was so sorry to miss your call this afternoon. Meta desires me to give you her love—and to tell you how much she hopes to see you soon—

Ever yours sincerely
E. C. Gaskell.

P.S. I hope that Brighton[1] air will do you a great deal of good— Please accept my very best thanks for your exceedingly great kindness to Marianne and Florence—you have made them so very happy.

430 433 434

GEORGE SMITH[2]

Tuesday [?21 June 1859]

My dear Mr Smith,

This is business—the girls are going to send you a round-robin of gratitude for what Flossy & Julia say was 'the pleasantest thing in all London.'—

Here is an American publisher Messrs Ticknor & Field, who wrote sometime ago wanting me to publish *first* with them in Boston, U.S. And since Mr Fields has come to England, called at Manchester, & wanted to call here with the same proposal—(a percentage of 10 cer cent on all copies sold of any work of mine *first* published in America. I did not quite understand their offer, & thought it shabby as far as I *did* understand, so I told him the truth that I had made an agreement with an English publisher &c—

And now I suppose he will come to you, as I have sent him your name. I believe him to be a very honourable man (from what Mr Sturgis, who does *not* say pretty things of the Harpers, tells me;) but to be rather a hard bargain driver. And that is all I know about him.

You have won four young hearts. What will Mrs Smith say,

---

[1] Letter 433 shows that Mrs Gaskell and her four daughters were all together in London about June 1859, which does not appear to have been the case when Mrs Smith visited Brighton in 1856 (see p. 426 above).

[2] Page 3 of this letter also contains a note from J. T. Fields, dated 20 June, asking for the name of Mrs Gaskell's publisher.

if you go on at the rate of so many a day? To be sure one had gone previously[.]

Yours very truly
E C Gaskell

433 **434** 438

GEORGE SMITH

Mr Turnbull's
Auchencairn
By (ie. 22 miles off) Dumfries
N B.
Wednesday, June 29th [1859][1]

My dear Mr Smith,

If ingratitude is virtuous I am praiseworthy! But as I am afraid it is not, I can only give as an excuse for my negligence that we were so busy, & it was so hot up to the moment of our leaving London, early on Monday morning, we never went near the Bank, our time being crammed up, & our days choke-full. But we keep our 'order' in hopes of a future day. You never no, *never* —sent a more acceptable present than Cousin Stella[2] & The Fool of Quality,[3]—and that irrespective of their several merits. But books are books here,—where potatoes have to be sent for from Castle Douglas, nine miles off—where we are uncertain what King or Queen reigns in England,—where we are far away from newspapers or railways or shops, or any sign of the world: where we go to bed by daylight, and get up because the cocks crow, & cows low to be milked, & we can't sleep any longer. Thanks many for your kind thought of us. I am sorry to say Meta lies at this present moment fast asleep with Cousin Stella in her hand; but that is the effect of bathing and an eight mile walk; not of the book itself. I know & like the Fool of Quality of old. I was brought up by old uncles & aunts, who had all old books, and very few new ones; and I used to delight in the Fool of Quality, & have hardly read it since. I mean to be so busy here; but I am, at present, continually tempted out of doors. I can hardly believe

---

[1] Address dates (see p. 581 below).
[2] By Mrs Henrietta Jenkin, Smith & Elder, 1859.
[3] By Henry Brooke, New Edition, Smith & Elder, 1859.

that we were in London two days ago. Oh! I will so try & write you a good novel; as good as a great nosegay of honeysuckle just under my nose at present, which smells not only of honeysuckle, but of very good cake into the bargain.

My girls send you all manner of pretty messages. Please write to us,—an old man whistles at the end of the field, if he has any letters for us,—and some one races down for them, holding them up in triumph, if there are many. But suppose the day should arrive when there is no whistle!

Heaven & Mr Smith avert that evil time. Besides we know nothing out here.

Yours ever most truly
E. C. Gaskell.

₀ 435 ₄₃₉

JOHN STUART MILL

July 14, 1859

Sir,

When you look at the signature of this letter you will probably be surprized at receiving it, as the only communication I ever received from you was couched in terms which I then thought impertinent unjust, and inexcusable; which I now think simply unjust.[1] For after reading the dedication of your Essay on Liberty I can understand how any word expressing a meaning only conjectured that was derogatory to your wife would wound you most deeply. And therefore I now write to express my deep regret that you received such pain through me. I still think you were unreasonable; but I like you better than if you had been reasonable under such circumstances. You used hard words towards me; I hardly expect now to be able to change your opinion of me; indeed I write now more with the intention of relieving my own mind by expressing sorrow for having given pain, than with the idea of clearing myself in your opinion. But still it would be but fair in you to listen to my view of the case. I knew nothing of the writer of the article in question; I had not even read the article. Miss Brontë knew nothing either; but the impression produced on

---

[1] Mill had objected to strictures passed by Charlotte Brontë on his future wife, then Mrs Taylor, about an article of hers in his periodical *The Westminster Review*. The letter was printed in the *Life of Charlotte Brontë*, 1st ed., II, pp. 229–30.

her mind by it made her imagine that such & such must have been the disposition & character of the person who wrote it. This imagination told as much of *her* mind & judgement,—if not more, that [*sic*] it could be held to reveal of the writer's. I do not express myself very clearly in this way. I will try & take an analogous case. I see a great picture,—the painter of which is utterly unknown to me even by name. As well as my opinion of the picture I unconsciously form some idea of the painter. His choice and treatment of a subject is either pleasing or displeasing to me, individually; and I try & discover why it is so, and to conjecture what qualities he must possess to have made it so. In speaking of these & of his character, as conjectured from his work, I believe that I should reveal as much of my own character as of his. It seemed to me that in publishing that part of Miss Brontë's letter which gave you such acute pain that no one would receive any impression of the writer of the article in question, while to some a good deal might be learnt of Miss Brontë['s] state of mind & thought on such subjects.

But I will not trouble you further with recurring to a subject which I fear still must give you pain. I will not even give you my address for I do not want you to answer this {letter.} Only please do not go on thinking so badly of me, as you must have done before you could have written that letter.

Yours respectfully & truly
E. C. Gaskell[1]

ₒ 436 ₒ

HARRIETTE —

Mr Turnbull's
Auchencairn
By Dumfries
N.B.
[c. July 1859]

My dear Harriette —

That is the right address let who will say to the contrary. I name it because letters will be so very acceptable. For as Silver-

---

[1] For Mill's draft of a reply, see E. Haldane, *Mrs Gaskell and Her Friends*, 1931, p. 269.

dale is to London, so is this place to Silverdale,—as far as being in
the world is concerned. The air is delicious, and most invigorat-
ing; butcher's meat to be had every day which is lucky, considering our appetites; but potatoes a delicacy not to be purchased
nearer than Castle Douglas, nine miles away. I will try by & bye
to unbend my mind sufficiently from household particulars to
consider a mere question of literature, but at present tomorrow's
dinner weighs on my mind, as we have eaten up all our potatoes
to-day. Eric,[1]—oh my dear Harrie I have always been meaning to
read it, & never have. You see I was out of the house, at Heidelberg in fact, when Marianne & Julia read it. But I will read it,
and send Hughie such a long criticism sometime. I wish I had it
here now, for we have a delicious length of time before us; in
whh we mean to do everything from mending stockings up to
writing novels. I must run out in the field to see—. I have been
out, & have forgotten what I went out for. The honey suckles
here smell so deliciously,—like honey suckles & like good cake
into the bargain. But we have no candles, & have to go to bed by
daylight in consequence. The Manchester & Liverpool railway
never sent on our grocery box to the Kirkcudbright steamer—so
(as 'Stick stick would not beat pig[2] &c—) the Auchencairn carrier
could not bring our things, and we can't go to bed by candlelight
tonight. So much the better—we shall go by daylight!

Write to us my dear Harrie and tell us what King of England
reigns? We are all in the dark about sophisticated life.

Yours affectionately

E C Gaskell

₀ **437** ₀

?ANN SCOTT

Plymouth Grove

Thursday [?Late July 1859][3]

My dear Mrs Scott,
    I came home last night from Scotland sooner than we expected
& heard of your kind message about the ticket to Mr Scott's

---

[1] Novel by F. W. Farrer, published by Black, 1858.

[2] A traditional story of the old lady who could not make her pig go over a stile
near home, nor a stick beat the pig, nor fire burn the stick, etc., etc.—'and I shan't
get home tonight.'   [3] Dated 1860 in another hand.

lectures; which I should be very glad to have. Much would always have more, you know,—Would it be too much to ask for another ticket for *one* of my girls? Would it be too much to ask for— No! I am afraid *that* would be too much! I write in greatest haste—

Ever yours affec[tionate]ly
E. C. Gaskell.

434 **438** 440

GEORGE SMITH

42 Plymouth Grove
Manchester—
Augt 4 [1859]

My dear Mr Smith,

At last we are at home, in a house oh! so clean, but smelling of paint to the last degree, as the workmen only went out two days before we came in. Such a contrast to our delicious Auchencairn! I am sure I was made to breathe pure air, & let my brain lie fallow in agricultural dulness; for I am come home so strong, and so ignorant, I don't even know who we are at war with, but I am sure (from the income tax) we are at war with somebody; is it with the Americans? Oh dear—and *am* I to believe in Miss Evans? I don't, and don't believe that you do, in spite of all possible evidence. I heartily agree with Mrs Smith; I am *very* sorry, IF it is true. But set against that Mr Blackwood gave a copy of Adam Bede to Dr Simpson of Edinburgh (my informant,) saying it was written by a *gentleman* whose real name was not G. Elliot. (This was when it was first published.) and the *day before yesterday*, in Edinburgh the sort of head young man in Blackwood's shop told Meta, in answer to her boldly naïve enquiry 'Do you know who wrote A B'—'No! I do not, but I know it was *not written by a lady*.' Comfort Mrs Smith with this. Do *you* really believe it? Please say. I do not think you do. It is a noble grand book, whoever wrote it, —but Miss Evans' life taken at the best construction, does so jar against the beautiful book that one cannot help hoping against hope. But two people have directly assured me they have seen the assertion of her authorship in her own handwriting. Against this Mr Quirk, the Vicar of Nuneaton told Miss C. Winkworth, who told me—that he saw the MSS of Scenes of Clerical Life *before it was published*\1856/, shown him by Mr Liggins, in Mr Liggins' writing.

And all this time I am ungrateful—but I am not. I do so like new books, & hardly ever see them but when you are so very kind. With a struggle and a fight I can see all Quarterlies 3 months after they are published; till then they lie on the Portico table, for gentlemen to see. I think I will go in for Women's Rights. I am hoping to read Shelley[1] & Cuba[2].—But preserving, re-arranging furniture—settling bills, and in the intervals of business, wondering about Miss Evans,—I have not had time yet. But I look at them as a child looks at a cake,—with glittering eyes & watering mouth, imagining the pleasure that awaits him. No! I have not read nothing—not even a review of Idylls of the King—only heard Mrs Norton's account, of Tennyson's reading it. Only think how grand we are! Meta & I *declined* joining the P. of Wales incognito party to the Trosachs—I must say absolute \home/duty prevented our being able to do it; and we were *very* sorry for it; for the whole invitation was so pretty & pleasant, & Colonel & Mrs Bruce were friends of ours to start with. But it sounds grand—as I try to comfort Meta, who won't be comforted —to have *declined*. Oh do say Miss Evans did *not* write it—and do write again, now it is cooler.—Please do. Our very kind regards to Mrs Smith,—I could draw her lovely face as it showed itself in Cumberland Terrace—

4 Miss Gaskell's affectionate remembrances—

Yours very truly
E C Gaskell

435 **439** 0

JOHN STUART MILL

42 Plymouth Grove
Manchester,
August 11th 1859

Sir,

You do me injustice, I think. And I shall try once more to set myself partially right in your opinion, because I value it; but I do not believe in any good result arising from this final attempt.

---

[1] Lady Shelley, *Shelley Memorials*, 1859.

[2] Hopkins (*Gaskell*, p. 210) suggests Michael Scott's *The Cruise of the Midge*, 1834, but gives no evidence to support the identification.

I wrote from Scotland, when I was away from books, and had no power of referring to the passage in the Life of Miss Brontë. I am now at home and have it, & your letter by me. Where\I think/you do me injustice is in saying that 'in publishing letters not written for publication you disregarded the obligation which custom founded on reason has imposed, of omitting what would be offensive to the feelings and perhaps injurious to the moral reputation of individuals.'—and the notion you seem to entertain that everything said or written by any one, which could possibly throw light on the character of the sayer or writer, may justifiably be published by a biographer, is one which the world, and those who are higher & better than the world, would, I believe, perfectly unite in condemning.'

I have expressed myself badly if you think that I intentionally disregarded the 'obligation which custom or reason has imposed &c.'—I certainly did not think that 'a foolish opinion',—a mere conjecture, obviously formed on insufficient grounds for having any weight affixed to it by the most careless reader could have been 'offensive to the feelings or injurious to the moral reputation.' That is the point on which we differ; *not* on the duty of a biographer to omit whatever can reasonably be expected to 'be offensive &c'. I acknowledge that duty; and I believe that you are the only person who has made any complaint or remonstrance to me about the publication of any part of Miss Brontë's *letters*. I tried to be very careful, and it was difficult to exactly tell where the limit (the necessity for which, let me say once again, I fully acknowledge—) was to be drawn.

Now, having endeavoured to set you right as to my recognition of the duty you seem to think I ignore,—(& some hasty expression in my last letter may have given rise to this misconception on your part,—) I will candidly say that on reading the\offensive/part over again, I believe that I *ought* to have omitted some part of what I inserted, in fulfilment of the duty which I acknowledge as much as you do. It may be that your letters, & the sense of having given pain, has awakened my conscience; it may be that in two or three years one's perception of right & wrong becomes juster, & keener,—but, if it were to be re-{written}\edited/now, I should *certainly* omit the final paragraph relating to yourself. 'In short J. S. Mill's head is, I daresay, very good, but I feel disposed to scorn his heart.' It was, I see, morally wrong to have published that. But I am not so sure about the rest.

Do you understand? I acknowledge the duty as much as you do. I have failed in this duty, as I now perceive in *one* part. As to the *other* part, that is matter of opinion. I do not yet clearly see that I have failed {in that}\in this duty with regard to that/. I do not believe that a just and reasonable person ought to have been offended by\the publication of/such a mere conjecture as to possible character. As I said[,] I\do *not*/believe that this letter will alter your opinion of me, and of the transaction which has brought us thus unpleasantly into contact. But I write for the chance.

Yours respectfully & truly
E C Gaskell—

424a **439a** 439b

CHARLES BOSANQUET[1]

42 Plymouth Grove
Monday [29 August 1859]

My dear Mr Bosanquet,

It is getting nearer to the 1st than I thought, so I hastily write down one or two things about the Lake Country. I think that if you can get hold of a portable 'Excursion' it is a capital book to have with you; also that vol (1st second, *or* third, I forget whh) of de Quincey's Miscellanies that relates to the Lakes,—places & people as they were in his day. Try for this last, if you don't get it elsewhere at Mrs Nicholson's circulating Library at Ambleside. I hope Mrs Nicholson is alive, but I don't know. She is the post mistress,—has known all the country round, for years & years; and though short & stern till she sees you are really good for something, she is true & sound at heart, & very interesting from her recollections of so much worth remembering. To go back to books. H. Martineau's is, I think, the best guide book. I should take *two* centres, *at least*,—and work round each. Keswick must be one,—with Skiddaw,—Buttermere (& over Scarf Gap to take a peep at Wastwater—a long scrambling walk, taking up quite a day *from Buttermere*, but worth the time & fatigue)—That village[—]name forgotten[—] about 2 miles from Keswick where

---

[1] *Address (on envelope)* Chas B. P. Bosanquet Esq. | The Rock | Alnwick | Northumberland. *Postmarks* MANCHESTER | X 2 | AU 29 | 59; STOCKPORT RD; A | ALNWI⟨CK⟩ | AU 30 | 59. *Octagonal seal, man's head facing left.*

there is a Druidical circle, & where the Shepherd Lord Clifford[1] was bred up by his stepfather—oh the name has come to me, *Threlkeld*,—for a short evening walk for the Shepherd Lord Clifford's sake,—\the/New Church at Keswick where Mr Myers preached so long,—and where now Mr [blank space][2] is incumbent, formerly curate to Mr Myers, & whose brother married Mary Bunsen.—Old parish Church Southey's Monument. Horse mount in Keswick St—\off/which Lord Derwentwater mounted his horse on going out in 15. Lodore of course,—and a walk past Lodore (or a row to the head of the lake,) and into Borrowdale, turning up a wild hill path about a mile to the left & over the fells till you drop down into a little picturesque primitive mountain village Wathenlath,—emphasis on '*en*',—worth seeing, & through which you pass, dropping down into the Keswick road, nearer to Keswick than Lodore.—Next centre I should like to think of your making at Skelwith; a village on the Brathay 2 miles from Ambleside,—and in Little Langdale. I think it is as—(I have been too much in a hurry to get another pen, till I found out the more haste the worse speed, and now I hope I shall be a little more legible) good a centre as Ambleside itself, and not quite so much in the beaten track of tourists. The Arnolds & Wordsworths long ago took lodgings for us at Skelwith at the house of a 'Stateswoman' a Mrs Preston of Mill Brow; to whom I give you \a/note, as she is worth knowing, as a fine true friendly sensible woman; if you liked to lodge there and she would take you in I am sure you would be comfortable, & well cared for—N.B. She would *make* you change your stockings if you got your feet wet, and such like motherly and imperative cares;—at any rate go & see her if you go to Skelwith. From Mill Brow you command the walks over Loughrigg dropping down at Fox How, the walk up the Langdales, Dungeon-Ghyll, *the walk past Red Bank, High Close farm, round to Grasmere*,—you are not beyond one of\even/my walks to Coniston,—Hawkshead,—where you would go for Wordsworth's sake, as his earliest school; you are always near enough to Ambleside &c. Wordsworth said once of the Prestons that they were a 'Homeric family'. I am sorry to say the father sometimes drinks. I say it because you perhaps ought to be told\or else when sober he is a fine simple fellow/. Mrs Preston's family

---

[1] See Wordsworth's *The White Doe of Rylstone* and 'Song at the Feast of Brougham Castle'.

[2] The name that eluded Mrs Gaskell was that of T. D. Harford Battersby.

have lived in that house and on that land for more than 200 years, as I have heard. They have no ambition but much dignity,—and look at that family of stately sons & daughters! Go to Coniston, if only to row on the Lake, & look *back* on the solemn purple Old Man. And here is a note to Miss Mary Beaver of Coniston, if you care for another introduction to a woman,—but really the residents at the Lakes *are* all women I think; and once upon a time we thought of buying land & building a house there as a future home for our girls, because there is a kind of old-fashioned chivalrous respect paid to women in all that country, which we thought would be a pleasant surrounding for brotherless women; but the damp air of the place does not agree with Mr Gaskell, who is liable to spasmodic asthma, for which, curiously enough, no air does so well as Manchester smoke. But to return to Miss Beaver. She is a sweet tempered singularly intelligent, kindhearted lady, who has lived long at Coniston—knows the dialect, the botany[,] the character of her district remarkably well; and altogether I think you might like to know her. Then again here is a letter to Mrs Davy of Ambleside,—formerly a Miss Fletcher of Edinburgh —married to a brother of Sir Humphrey Davy,—Oh—I envy you seeing Mrs Davy so soon,—only perhaps you won't get to know her well enough to care much about her. I am so sorry I am writing so untidily,—but if you knew how busy & hurried I am! It was at Mrs Davy's house in Malta Sir W. Scott stayed in his last illness & she has known, & known *well* Dr Arnold, the Wordsworths, Coleridges &c &c.—Ask her to let you see Miss Wordsworths MS. account of the two poor Greens who were lost in the snow. Wordsworth said it was the most perfect *English* narrative he ever read. And then go into Easedale & see the place \where the Greens lived/. I wonder if Mrs Davy's face will have the same kind of fascination for you that it has for me.—*How* I should like to see her again!—I am terribly afraid of Dr Davy, but that is no reason you should be; but a stiff precise *over*-gentle-manly manner always quells me till I am ashamed of myself. I don't care for Windermere; it is too cultivated & inhabited. But Mrs Davy will tell you all you ought to see far better than I can. She lost two boys—their busts are in the drawing room, in one week, of Scarlet fever, & her eyes have such a wistful searching look in them. And two years ago she lost a daughter, grown-up, —a dear dear friend of Meta's—& I have never seen her since. Patterdale I don't know. Dr Davy is a great fisher, & they know the Duddon well if you liked to go from Coniston towards Broughton Furness & Ulverston ways—(you would be close to Conishead Priory at Ulverston,—but otherwise that district is flat & dull,—) That reminds me! I have been laying traps all over England for a place for Thomas Glover this year past—and I have 'bagged' *two* places for him this last week. One agricultural, one Manchester. And he is here, staying with us for a week, in order that I may find out which will suit him best,—and I feel so grand having a *choice* when so long I have been a beggar. I have landed you in Mrs Davy's hands,—and there I leave you. She will tell you all & anything far better than I can. I have been reading White's Northumberland,[1] so I knew Carter Fell, & all your tour like old familiar names, when I met them in yr letter.

Yours ever most truly
E C Gaskell

439a 439b 446a

CHARLES BOSANQUET[2]

42 P. Grove, Manchester
Tuesday Augt 30 [1859]

My dear Mr Bosanquet,

I have remembered a *man* at the Lakes (and a clergyman[3] to boot, —for you to '*inspect*'—only, sad to say he is too great an invalid to go on with parish work, or else he was long incumbent at Bowness—) to whom I can give you a note, and whom I am *sure* you {would}\will/like.

Doves Nest is a little way (2 miles, say,) from Ambleside going past the Waterhead of Windermere, & then striking off on the left before you come to Lowood. Mrs Hemans once lived there.

I have had a note from Fanny Arnold this morng[.] She says 'I shd not like the month to come to an end without having answered your very kind letter, and assuring you in dear Mamma's name that she will be very glad to see your friend Mr Bosanquet next month, and to give him any help or advice as to seeing the Lakes,

---

[1] Walter White, *Travel in Northumberland and the Border*, 1859.

[2] *Address (on envelope)* Chas B. P. Bosanquet Esq. | Rock, | Alnwick | Northumberland. *Postmarked* MANCHES⟨TER⟩ | X 2 | AU 30 | 49; STOCKPORT RD; A | ALNWICK | AU 31 | 59.

[3] Mrs Gaskell is referring to Graves, mentioned by name after she had finished the letter. He lived at Dove's Nest.

& to show him Fox How. His being a friend of yours would of itself make us anxious to show him any attention we could, and of course his admiration for my Father must give us an additional interest in seeing him. We hope in September to be a very large family party[,] so large indeed that the old home is no longer capable of receiving all it's off-shoots, and we shall have several small colonies in Rydal and it's neighbourhood.' She goes on to say that Mrs Forster (Jane Arnold) brings William's four little orphans with her,—Mary (Mrs Hiley) brings her baby &c &c.

It rains here to-day.—I hope you won't have a wet month.

Yours ever very truly
E C Gaskell

I never know how to write introductions and I dare say I make them very formal; but I am pretty sure they will all be 'honoured'.

Mr Greaves is Ranke's (historian Ranke) brother-in-law.[1]

*

438 440 441

GEORGE SMITH

42 Plymouth Grove
Monday September 19 [1859]

My dear Mr Smith,

I have a letter from a friend, who has been living in Rome & Italy for 9 or 10 years, & who speaks Italian like a native; he is also a friend of Mr Thackeray's, a Mr W. W. Story, son and biographer of Judge Story, who was rather a famous Jurisconsult in America. Mr Story has been for some time writing a set of papers, called Roba di Roma,[2]—descriptive of the *familiar* life of the Romans,—I enclose you a list of the subjects,—some of them are full of research & study as he has had access to the grand old libraries of Greek & Latin books in the Roman palaces with a view of carrying out his scheme of tracing far into ancient times the origin of the present Roman customs, social and political,—there is a chapter on the Jews in Rome, their past & present position there, their life in the Ghetto, the price they pay for their Faith held under the Shadow of St Peters—On the Villegiatura,—it's peculiarities & *un*likeness to country life in Northern Climates

---

¹ Written on flap of cover.   ² See Letter 441.

&c &c.—Now two of these Roba di Roma papers have been already published in the Atlantic, an American Magazine; but Mr Story does not particularly want to continue them in that,—and *does* wish to contribute them, (rewriting the two first, if preferred,) to your Magazine.[1] They want me to write to Mr Thackeray, but in the first place I am not at my ease with him; & in the second place the only letter I ever did write to him was never answered, and in the third place I can't make out why the Storys did not write straight, smack away to him themselves. So I work roundabout, only I *do* think you & he *would* value these papers for your Magazine,—(& if you don't, I shall offer them to a Mr Masson, who has written to ask for things for a Mag. or something MacMillan is going to set up,—) and I should like to be the medium of Mr Story's success in his great wish of publishing in England. I am writing in such a hurry, but I hope you understand, & will you let me have an answer, please—and I am ever, with kindest regards to Mrs Smith[.]

Yours most truly

E C Gaskell

I shall send you a No of the Atlantic with R di R in, whh *please* RETURN

440 **441** 442

GEORGE SMITH

[20 September 1859]

My dear Mr Smith,

I am—we are all so *very* sorry; but I will tell you exactly how we are situated. Marianne & Meta go to pay a three-weeks, or a month's visit in Gloucestershire, tomorrow morning,—escort all waiting ready here. A friend of ours, a young man of some local distinction[2] is to be buried on Friday morning, & Mr Gaskell will have to attend his funeral; and in the afternoon I take my youngest Julia, (with the crêpé hair) to pay a visit of a few days in the country. I would gladly put this off,—I am going against my will rather, as we are much out of spirits at the sudden death of our

---

[1] The first number of the *Cornhill* came out in January 1860.

[2] This may have been John Ashton Nicholls, F.R.A.S. (b. 1823) who died on 18 September 1859. Mr Gaskell published his *Funeral Sermon and Memoir*. See *Monthly Notices of the Royal Astronomical Society*, Vol. XX, p. 131.

friend (an only child,—) but the people we are going to stay with on Friday have made such a point of our keeping to our word—(for once or twice before we have had to disappoint them,—) that I cannot give it up.

So I can only offer (I fear) a very dull & limited visit; but if you & Mrs Smith *would* come here on Thursday night; and make this into your hotel instead of the Queen's—(we know the time of the Scotch trains, & have not unusually received friends by them at ½ p. 12, P.M; I AM &c—) and then I could have the great pleasure of being with you at breakfast & lunch, and would have you to use our house as if it were your own for the rest of your stay here.—

Do, please, think of this—it is the best plan I can arrange,—& we are all so sorry we cannot do & see more of you & Mrs Smith. But we shall look forwards all the more to THE promised visit; which is to be before very long I hope, now Mrs Smith can move about. I wrote to you yesterday, to Corn Hill; a business letter about some Roman papers for your Magazine; which you will receive in time I suppose.

Do *you* know what Hawthorne's tale[1] is about? *I* do; and I think it will perplex the English public pretty considerably.

Will you please contradict *if you can*, the statement that Miss Evans is the author of Adam Bede. The girls send kindest regards, & are so sorry they will be away when you come this time. Please give my kind regards to Mrs Smith, and ever believe me yours very truly

E. C. Gaskell.

441 442 443

GEORGE SMITH

42 Plymouth Grove—Saty
[?1 October 1859]

My dear Mr Smith,

This is a private letter, please, and not to be forwarded to any Editor whatsoever please. And to make sure you won't make it public I am going first of all, and straight away to thank you very much, for thinking of my daughters four, so very kindly; only the knowledge that the box was here, smites me on my heart,

---

[1] *The Marble Faun.*

with thinking it was all owing to some bad arrangement on my part that you did not come. Yet how was I to know, oh Mr & Mrs Smith, that you were gone into Scotland,—when in June Mrs Smith was so tired with coming into London from Esher. However I won't abuse her, for I am only too glad to hear that she is so much stronger and better; and her *next* freak must be to Manchester where she shall be introduced in form to Miss (Marianne) Gaskell, Miss Meta (Margaret Emily) Gaskell, Miss Flossy (Florence Elizabeth) Gaskell, and Miss with the hair—alias Julia Bradford Gaskell. Flossy's birthday is on October 7th poor little woman, she is at school for the first birthday in her life, and so we are sending her a 'box', and her ivory shawl-broach shall be popped in. Many many thanks to you for thinking so kindly of my lassies. And now to two or three pieces of business—I will gladly await Mr Thackeray's return for the decision as you give me so much hope. He knows my dear Mr & Mrs Story as well as I do, so his *feelings* will be in their favour, but I don't mean that that will influence his judgement. I don't mean to make any complaint about his not answering my letters (Meta reminds me there were two—) but only to tell you, in your private capacity the fact. One note enclosed a letter from Mrs Story to 'Annie Thackeray'—we had been seeing Mrs Story in Paris, & she wanted Meta & Miss Thackeray to be acquainted, so gave the note of introduction which I enclosed with an explanatory note to Thackeray, asking when we might call to see Miss Thackeray? And the other was a note telling him of Miss Brontë's death, which I had just heard of—& was very much shocked & very unhappy about, & asking him if he would write a line to Mr Brontë, who, I knew had so overbalancing a measure of pride in his daughter's fame, that a letter of sympathy from T— wd do much to comfort his grief. He never replied to either of these notes of mine, *nor did he ever write to Mr Brontë.* Now please understand this is no complaint on my part, only a belief that somehow or another my *luck* is against me in any intercourse with him, & being half-Scotch I have a right to be very superstitious; & I have my lucky & unlucky days, & lucky & unlucky people,—and my only feeling about not doing any thing you ask me\for the Magazine/is because I don't think Thackeray would ever quite like it, & yet you know it would be under his supervision. Please to understand how much I admire him, & how I know that somewhere or another he has got a noble & warm self,—only *I* can't get near it. He said once something at Mr Chorley's which I shall never forget & whh makes me know this,—I mean how fine & tender he is,—somewhere. However we will put all this feeling down to foolish superstition, & your kindness has been true reality,—so I will try, and do my best—(only I know he won't like it, & we shall come to grief somehow,—) and write as well as I can,—only *need my name be put to them*,—that has been half the battle in H W. No one knew that it was *I* that was saying this or that, so I felt to have free swing. (I am going to write an article for their Xmas Number, 'All the Year Round'[1] I mean). But I shall answer Mr Masson's letter in the negative, for I can't do all, and do well. I am sorry to disoblige Mr Hughes, but I don't care 2d for Mr Masson.

So, as some American once said 'Them's my sentiments'. Now as to Miss Brontë's novel—I *wish* it were published—for it struck me as being strong & good, & characteristic; but I am afraid of Mr Nicholls, & I think *you* would be more likely to get him to grant you a favour than I; and perhaps even you more likely if you did not name my name. I am perfectly willing,—I should be *glad* once more to associate my name with hers, by writing a few introductory lines as you suggest,—but I fancy *if you asked Mr Nicholls to do this* you would have a much better chance of obtaining permission to publish it.

Would you like to see Mr Story's *second* article on 'Roba di Roma'—I could send it you or Mr Thackeray, if you liked—Just here *the* box came; I was so thankful there was only one daughter (Julia) at home; for the squeal, & scream of delight she set up, multiplied by 4, would have been perfectly deafening—as it was, it brought her Papa out of his study to see what could be the matter; and then he took to unpacking, with all due deliberation & respect to the splendid pieces of pack thread, gravely assuring Julia that he had been told when he was a little boy that if he cut a piece of string he would never have 500£ a year; & Julia did not care one atom about her future prospects of 500£ per ann, but danced about, & flew for knife & scissors,—& before they came the box was opened waiting for her busy little fingers—and she hit first upon her own beautiful bottle,—which made her Papa observe that he should wet his hair & plait it this very night, if such things came of the operation,—and so we worked on through

---

[1] 'The Ghost in the Garden Room', *All the Year Round*, Christmas Number, 1859. Reprinted as 'The Crooked Branch', 1860. See Letter 452.

the box, screaming & laughing & talking, and half checking ourselves to wish for the others. And now Julia is sitting in silent
admiration before rolling up her sister's presents in paper—I suggest that she should write her own thanks,—to which at first she
acceded with grateful alacrity—but suddenly she said 'But is he
not an author, or something of that sort'—and I think she fancies
writing to you may be like rushing into print, and rather shrinks
back. So once for all in the name of the four daughters
                    THANK YOU.
    Here is a little note enclosed from a very dear young friend of
mine, Louy Jackson;—I don't like not to do anything she asks me
to do,—but I fear there is no chance of any copying for Miss
MacFarlane is there—who was Mr MacFarlane the author? A
friend of mine has a friend a Mrs Fisher, who sate next to Mr
Liggins at dinner not a month ago; and he told her 'distinctly in
so many words' that he was the Author of Scenes of Clerical Life.
And the Bracebridges & others among his neighbours are as fully
convinced of it as ever[.] Please give my kindest regards to Mrs
Smith.
                            Ever yours very truly
                                    E C Gaskell

                        442 **443** 446

                    GEORGE SMITH

                        P Grove—October 13th [1859]
My dear Sir,
    I am very glad indeed about Mr Nicholls' note. I remember—
and so does Meta—the vivid interest of that fragment, to us at
least. Only one did so want to know the end. I am glad too Mr
Thackeray is going to write the little introduction; she would
have liked that *very* much.[1]
    Don't hurry the decision about the Roba,—I mean take full
time to think about it, sooner than decide on a 'No' too hastily.
    I am sorry about Mrs Smith; it sounds as if she were still very
delicate unless it is merely as a sort of strengthening dose of sea-
air before winter.
    I am in all the depths of perplexity at having a young artillery
officer (whom I never saw,) writing to me from Gibraltar asking

                    [1] See p. 409, n. above.

ME! to make a selection of books & periodicals to the value of 5£, for a 'soldiers reading-room' there, which he has established at his own risk, in order that they may have some place besides 'wine-shops' in which to read news, play at draughts &c &c—[1]

Now I know nothing of soldiers, but would do any thing I cd for so nice a fellow—Can you tell me if they (Government is always my '*they*') grant any money for such purposes; Don't trouble yourself with *getting* information on this point,—only *if* you know will you just say a Yes or No,—if Yes who should I apply to?

4 loves to you.

Yours very truly   E C Gaskell

*

418 **444** 453

CHARLES ELIOT NORTON

Plymouth Grove, October 25 [and 30 1859]

My dear Mr Norton,

A pamphlet has just come from you to Marianne (who is pay-ing a visit to some cousins in Worcestershire,) and it has stirred up my lazy self to do what I have been long & long intending to do,—write to you. You see I fancy—whether I am right or not—that the American mail only goes out on Saturdays,—& so all the beginning of weeks I think 'there will be plenty of time before Saturday'—and at last Saturday comes down on me like an armed man, & I play the same game next week. Otherwise, if good in-tentions were deeds, it is about five months since you ought to have heard from me. Another drawback to my letter-writing is that I cannot *mend* quill pens; & cannot write easily with *steel* pens, & never know where to get good ink, & can never find in my heart to buy good paper. Now I shall go into detail. I am sitting in the dining-room, (it is a comfort to think you know our rooms and our people,) Elliott taking away breakfast things, Meta taking Julia to school, Mr Gaskell in bed with a cold, (not very bad, thank you) and I myself in a doleful mood because some Chrysan-themums I have been nursing up into bloom this past summer were carelessly left out-of-doors this past night & have been frozen to death. One's near misfortunes always stand in the way,

<hr>

[1] See Letter 446a.

& prevent one's seeing beyond, and I really *am* so sorry about these flowers just now, that if I had time I could cry. Now there is so much ground to get over in going through the last 6 months of our lives,—if ever so rapidly that I hardly know where to begin. We had a very quiet time all last winter & spring after returning from Heidelberg until May; when our landlord volunteered to put the house into perfect repair &c &c, if we would vacate it, & give him his own time. So we dispersed. Mr Gaskell, who could not leave Manchester at first, went to stay with Miss Ewarts. I slept for a few nights at a friend's, and was here all day packing up, & generally routing and rummaging about; for things came to light quite unexpectedly, & it was almost like a little Day of Judgment for bringing forgotten circumstances clear & fresh into one's memory, through some little trifle connected with them which suddenly turned up. At last the house looked desolate enough, & I left it; Florence was at school at Miss Green's at Knutsford—(Mr Green Unitarian Minister, at Glasgow long years ago with Mr Gaskell, christened our children, his daughters great friends of our two elder girls, have set up a school at Knutsford,—) and Julia was taken in as a boarder at Miss Mitchell's, where she goes every day. Marianne & Meta made little 'giros' among their friends, I joining Meta for a week at Canterbury—(do you know how *very* beautiful that Cathedral is, & do you know Arthur Stanley's Memorials of Canterbury?) Then after a little visit at the Wedgwoods we, mother & 4 girls, (for Flossy's & Julia's holidays had begun) were for three weeks in lodgings in London; it was rather too hot for *my* full enjoyment, but the others liked it extremely. Let me think what we did worthy of record—I think we got to know Rossetti pretty well. I went three times to his studio, and met him at two evening parties—where I had a good deal of talk with him, always excepting the times when ladies with beautiful hair came in when he was like the cat turned into a lady, who jumped out of bed and ran after a mouse. It did not signify what we were talking about or how agreeable I was; if a particular kind of reddish brown, crêpe wavy hair came in, he was away in a moment struggling for an introduction to the owner of said head of hair. He is not as mad as a March hare, but hair-mad. Well! and then we saw Holman Hunt's picture, & Holman Hunt's self. I am not going to define & shape my feelings & thoughts at seeing either Rossetti's or Hunt's pictures into words; because I *did* feel them deeply, & after all words are coarse things. Long summer days are the proper times for deliberately picking out choice and careful expressions,—& then they but badly answer to one's thought. Then we dined at the Robert Macintosh's. I don't know why but I think I was more pleased at this invitation than at any we received, & would have done more to keep to my engagement. Meta & I went, & there were Mr and Mrs Macintosh, Mrs Fanny Kemble, & a very nice pretty daughter of hers, and an American, whom, begging your pardon, I did not at all like, & luckily I have forgotten his name, or else he might have turned out to be one of your intimate friends. He was tall & dark, & handsome, & pompous & well-informed & altogether disagreeable. There now! but I like Mr & Mrs Macintosh very much. Mrs Twisleton (whom we met at Sir Chas Lyell's) would not remember me; when I went straight at her, feeling that she was your cousin, & that I used to like her so much, & that your name would be a double bond now. So I came away, feeling small[.] But I must hasten on to tell you where we went to next. We made a long day-and-night's stride from London, to Auchencairn, a little village on a land-locked bay of the Solway, where we had rooms for a month in an old house, (larger than a farm-house,) that had belonged to a smuggler, in the palmy days of smuggling, close to all the scenery of Guy Mannering, and within a mile of the Maxwells of Orchardston, an ancestor of whom was the lost heir. Also it was in the Covenanter's country. I once thought of writing a paper for the Atlantic about our dear Scotch village (in Kirkcudbrightshire), but time failed me first, & now we hear that the Atlantic has failed. (N. B. Smith & Elder have offered me 1000£ for a three vol. novel, including the American rights &c, which I believe they disposed of to Mr Field, whom I never saw—Not a line of the book is written yet,—I think I have a feeling that it is not worth while\trying/to write, while there are such books as Adam Bede & Scenes from Clerical Life—I set 'Janet's Repentance' above all, still.—) Now to go back to Auchencairn. Mr Gaskell joined us for a fortnight; & when we came home he went to the Highlands to shoot & staid till the end of August. Our house at Auchencairn had a pretty field, or 'park' as the Scotch call it, between the front door and the road,—then two or three flat meadows, and then the bay, often dry alas! In this field which had a mossy bank on one side, with great beautiful trees, making armchairs of their roots, we sate & talked & lounged all through the hot summer's days, often thinking we were reading or sewing, but generally finding out at the end that it had been a mistake on our parts. Behind the house was a beautiful rocky, heathery ferny, glen, with little pools, & birch trees up which we might go to a deep inky purple mountain called Ben-Caèra. This glen unluckily was possessed by a very fierce black bull, all the day time; it was only after milking time we could venture in; and it was not every day that his lordship would condescend to accompany the cows, & {on} some evenings he remained out in the glen. About the end of the month of July we came home; and {h.} I have remained here ever since,—a good number of people having visited us meanwhile—among others Mr & Mrs Brodie from Oxford, to whom Mr Gaskell 'took' a great fancy, so we hope to persuade him to go & see them in Oxford before long. Mrs Brodie's sister, a very charming Miss Thompson is here now, keeping Meta company during Marianne's absence. Meta & Marianne went to Dumbleton in September (Thurstan Holland's home,) but only staid there about a week, going thence to the other cousins, where Marianne is now. A little word as to the authorship of 'Adam Bede'; I believe there is no doubt it is written by a Miss Mary Ann Evans; whose uncle—Evans, (Seth) married Bessy Tomlinson, a Methodist preacher, who accompanied & comforted a Mary Don, who was hung at Nottingham for child-murder about the end of the last century. Miss Evans' own father was *Adam*,—a successful builder & timber-merchant, who died a few years ago at Coventry. She kept house for him; her brother Isaac Evans, was agent to a great Warwickshire family of the name of Newdegate. This Mr Isaac Evans is very evangelical. Miss Marianne Evans translated Strauss's Life of Jesus, & then left Coventry, going to live in London where she became acquainted with Mr Lewes, author of Life of Goethe &c.—His wife left him to go and live with Thornton Hunt, (Leigh Hunt's son) & Mr Lewes went abroad (5 years ago) with Miss Evans, who now takes the name of Mrs Evans. All this is miserable enough;—but I believe there are many excuses—the worst is Mr Lewes' character & opinions were (formerly *at least*) so bad. And now it is Sunday Evening, Oct 30, & I have missed the Saturday Mail,—& Meta, Julia & I are going for a week or ten days to Whitby tomorrow. Goodnight. Write soon, & tell us all about yourself, your mother & sisters.

Your affec[tionate] friend
E. C. Gaskell

*   *

*444b **445** *451++

HARRIET MARTINEAU[1]

42, P— Grove Saturday [29 October 1859][2]

My dear Miss Martineau,

Many thanks for your most interesting letter. I am only sending
you half an answer; but I want to undo the impression which I
think both you & Miss Hennell have got, that I have been in the
least influenced by the Bracebridges. I have never (until within
this last month) seen a word of their writing, or heard a speech of
theirs on the subject. I *heard of*, but did not *see* the correspondence
in the Times (the S G O, G Eliot &c) in Spring, & then heard that
the Bracebridges were taking up Mr Liggins—But my evidence
—(I am quite convinced that it was Miss Evans who is the undis-
puted & entire author of Scenes & A. Bede, & only wish to contribute *my* evidence which it seems to me is different from any
one else's)—my evidence is this. My great admiration for Scenes
from Clerical Life made me, as I think, I told you recommend
them while yet publishing in numbers in Blackwood to the notice
of a friend, Miss Ewart, daughter of the M.P. Sometime after[,] I
should guess from collateral evidence in the autumn of 1857, the
Exhibition year,—certainly *before* Xmas 57-58 she wrote to tell
me of her cousin-in-law Mr Bacon,—clergyman at some place
near Nuneaton—name of village forgotton [*sic*], but easily ascer-
tainable through clergy list,—having written to tell her that a Mr
Liggins was the author—the son of a baker, sent to College[,]
Cambridge I think[,] by a gentleman who had noticed his talents
&c,—and associated there with people above his rank, got into
expensive (I *think* dissipated habits) had given up his intention
of going into the Church, became travelling tutor—returned
home[,] his father left him some few thousands of pounds,—on
which he lived in a queer eccentric kind of way &c. Miss Ewart
went on in her letter that Mr Bacon went on to say that either he
or Mr Quirk the clergyman at Nuneaton (I forget which,—) had
seen the MSS of Clerical Scenes in Mr Liggins hand writing \be-
fore the publication/—that the last story was decidedly the best.—
Well! I thought here was a grand new writer on the Scenes, &

[1] Printed from MS. *copy*, but substantive errors were corrected when the
original was found at a late stage.

[2] Princeton University Library has a Harriet Martineau letter, dated 30 October
1859, referring to this letter from Mrs Gaskell.

only wondered people did not 'admire' more—. I recommended Scenes from Clerical Life to one or two people among them to a Mrs Charles Sandars, the very accurate wife of a land-agent, who has long lived near Coventry, now lives near Derby. She said in reply to my information about Liggins being the author—(certainly 18 months ago,) that her husband had known him,—& had known most of the people named in Clerical Life—I remember her saying that the names were so little disguised as that Mr Dempster in 'Janet's Repentance' (the finest story yet) was a Mr Dempster-Hemming &c. That Mr Liggins lived on his property, might be called a 'gentleman-farmer' [,] was very eccentric, sometimes had a servant in the house, sometimes none, but always a great number of cats &c.

Now we will jump to the publication of Adam Bede—last March, I think. I believed all along that I knew the name of the author from all this old evidence of the authorship of Scenes of Clerical Life. (I have hunted everywhere for Miss Ewart's letters of 57 to prove dates, & first statement of facts, which are all apt to slip one's memory, but I can't find it or them, for I think there was more than one.)

I was extremely astonished to hear of the Eliot disavowal of the name of Liggins; a few days after & *not* in reply to any question Meta heard from Mary Ewart 'Don't give up the Liggins story,—though the name may not be *Joseph*, or the spelling correct, I have reason to believe that he is the author.' Miss Ewart now is convinced of Miss Evans' authorship; I merely quote from this letter to show you I heard from other than the Bracebridges, & that there may have been some strong (false) evidence laid before *them* as well as before the calm judicious Miss Ewart. I went for a couple of days to the Sandars in May; they (from the Coventry side of the Country) spoke of Mr Liggins as the undoubted author, & gave details of his eccentricity,—not for a moment of his want of honour.

Later still Kate\Winkworth/in July went to stay at Hall[1] with the Henry Bunsen's—there she met a Warwickshire Clergyman who told her that Mr Quirk of Nuneaton had seen Scenes from Clerical Life in MSS in Mr Liggins handwriting. K. W. told me the name of this intermediate clergyman, but I have forgotten it; could easily get it though, but Mr Quirk is the principal witness

---

[1] *Sc.* Lilleshall, Shropshire. The copyist left a gap originally, and wrote in 'Hall' afterwards. The original MS. reads 'Lilleshall'.

in this piece of evidence you see. Well! but now comes the most starling [*sic*] of all. A month or 6 weeks—no! less than 6 weeks ago, Mrs Charles Sandars came here. I should tell you that she is a friend of the Congreves who are recently made friends of Mr Lewes & Miss Evans—Mrs Sandars & I talked on the Evans & Liggins controversy,—she had written to Mrs Congreve, who was I think then in Switzerland,—but had received no answer. Mrs Sandars said 'I saw Mrs Fisher (a friend of hers, unknown to me) the other day, who had been sitting next to Mr Liggins at dinner' —(this dinner must have been some day *in September*) '& he told her in so many words that he was the author of Adam Bede.' I asked many questions of Mrs Sandars, but she did not seem to know more than that Mrs Fisher was in her opinion a truth-telling woman, & that she said he had *volunteered* the information & talked a good deal both about A. B. & Scenes from Clerical Life, 'quite calmly & composedly.' Mrs Sandars has since had a long letter from Mrs Congreve, quite convincing her as to the Evans authorship—But all I mean is [,] here am I admiring these books heart & soul, but sitting quiet & only catching such scraps of evidence as to their authorship as the wind brings & yet you see what a great deal has come to *me* in favour of Mr Liggins—& how much more has most likely reached the Bracebridges, especially forcible as the Sandars speak of Mr Liggins having the character of being a truthful man.—My own idea is that his eccentricity has gone into mania on this head,—& that early admiring those Scenes &c he contrived to persuade himself he wrote them—But even this leaves a great deal unaccounted for. Two more little bits,—not as to Mr Liggins,—& not worth much,—but which still weighed a *little* with me, until I had heard all the evidence on Miss Evans' side. Dr Simpson of Edinburgh told me Blackwood had from him a copy of A. B. at first—saying (Dr Simpson quite believed although not positive) that it was written by a *man*. And Meta (1st week in August, when everyone was discussing Miss Evans' claims) being in Blackwoods shop, plumped the question to the head young man 'Who wrote Adam Bede' 'I do not know. But I know it was not written by a lady—' (observe this last clause was volunteered.) Meta said 'Do you *know* it was not written by a lady?' 'Yes, I do.' All this is easily explained away; not so Mr Liggins. I have written in such a hurry but I wanted to tell you all. You are quite at liberty to pass on this letter to Miss Hennell, if you think she would care to see it. I will return her letter soon. I know you will excuse the way I have written. And you understand I am quite convinced Miss E. wrote it, only I think the Bracebridges may have had more (false) evidence to go upon than either you or I are aware of—& at any rate they had no influence over me, as until a fortnight ago I never read or heard a word of theirs on the subject. I wish—oh *how* I wish Miss Evans had never seen Mr Lewes. Yet I like his letter (quoted by Miss Hennell) to Mr Bracebridge. You see Mr Liggins' assertion of the authorship &c is of no recent date—What do you allude to of Mr Blackwoods declaration. Not at all apropos {of} to anything written above. My dear Miss Martineau I don't think you know how much I owe to you. Mr Gaskell & Meta send kindest regards.

Yours ever most truly
E C Gaskell

443 **446** 451

GEORGE SMITH

Mrs Rose's
1 Abbey Terrace
Whitby
Yorkshire, Novr 2. [1859]

My dear Mr Smith,

We rushed here for ten days on Monday; & last night your letter & Macmillan's Mag. followed us, and was received with a hearty greeting. 'We' are Meta, & Julia—for whose benefit we are come, as she has outgrown her strength—six inches in the last 12 months.—We are delighted with *our* type, & that we don't print in double columns which is so trying to the eyes; we put the page of the Virginians by a page of Macmillan last night & you can't think how much more legible *ours* was.

Well! but that's not what I am writing about; no, nor even about your kind proposal about Mr Story which I will forward to him[.] No! curiosity comes before friendship or anything else. How could you find in yr heart to be so curt about Madam Adam? Do please remember our utter isolation from all the usual sources of goss⟨ip &⟩ we don't know a creature ⟨here⟩ and the evenings are very long,—and send us PLEASE a long account of what she is like &c &c &c &c &c,—eyes nose mouth, *dress* &c for *facts*, and then—if you would—your impression of her,—which we won't tell anybody. *How came she to like Mr Lewes so much?* I know he has his good points but somehow he is so soiled for a woman like her to fancy. Oh! do please comply with this humble request. We shall be here till the 12th.

Yours ever very truly   E C Gaskell.

*

439b **446a** 491a

CHARLES BOSANQUET[1]

1 Abbey Terrace
Whitby
Novr 7th [1859]

My dear Mr Bosanquet,

Thank you very much for sending me the Missing Link,[2] and remembering my wish to know more about 'Marian'. The book came in the middle of a storm of wind & rain on Saturday Evening, and I began to read it, and pretty nearly finished it before I went to bed. It is very interesting,—and is indeed the discovery of the 'Missing Link'. Just before I left Manchester I heard of search being made for a 'Bible-woman' to work there; doubtless suggested by the success in London. But now don't think me carping if I say where I think they are in some danger. It is a little bit of sad experience of mine of late that makes me wise. Do you know I think they will find that it will destroy the simplicity and *unconscious* goodness of the women, if they encourage them to keep journals\Clause 7, page 292/of more than mere statistics? I see a little of the danger of this in the conversations recorded, whh are thrown into dramas, as it were—with a little account of looks, & gestures which seem 'touched up' as it were. For instance the blind Staly-bridge & Dukinfield man, page 209, speaks better language than he was likely to speak,—& what is more[,] nearly all the people, whose words are given, say much the same sort of things,

---

[1] *Address (on envelope)* C. P. B. Bosanquet Esq | 34 Store St | Bedford Square | London. *W.C. Postmarks* A | WHITBY | NO 8 | 59; LONDON W C | 8 E | NO 9 | 59.

[2] *The Missing Link* by L. N. R., 1859.

without distinction of individual character. I don't mean that all are willing\or unwilling/at once to subscribe for bibles,—but,— given the inclination or disinclination,—they all say much the same kind of things. I don't know whether you quite understand me,—which is my fault I dare say. I should *fear* the temptation of throwing facts into dramas; However there is so much that is beautiful in the mere facts, so much incidental deep wisdom,— wisdom which is no mere hearsay, but gained from actual experience,—& is *most* valuable that it is a most valuable as well as most interesting book. I will send it you back safe & sound in a day or two. For if I have one dazzling virtue it is that of taking care of books. (Now I hope the consequences of boasting won't come in the shape of a great blot of ink on the volume!) To return to my woman I won't tell you who,—but a *very* good man in Manchester was a few years ago brought into much notice for his philanthropy, and many people were only too glad to learn something of the peculiar methods by which he certainly *had* reclaimed the erring. So he was asked about his 'experiences', and told many *true* interesting histories. Lately I have observed that it was difficult to 'bring him to book' as it were about his cases. He would tell one of a story that made one's heart bleed,—tell it dramatically too, whh faculty is always a temptation, & when, unwilling to let emotion die without passing into action one asked for the address &c,—it always became vague,—in different ways. For some time I have suspected that he told *old* true stories, as if they were happening *now*, or had happened *yesterday*. And just lately I have found that this temptation to excite his hearers strongly, has led to *pure invention*. So do you wonder that I am afraid lest 'godly simplicity' may be injured by journal[-]keeping, & extracts from journals being printed. So ends my lecture. Julia is deep in the evenings illuminating texts & mottos. I rather think one is intended for you; and if it be, I am sure you will kindly receive it, as she is delighted at the idea of making little presents of them. I must copy you a little piece out of Pilkington Jackson's last letter 'I wish I could show you my libraries & reading rooms. I am very busy indeed, for they are assuming large proportions, and what commenced with being a single room has now expanded to a number of houses—3 different establishments. The men who subscribed to one, are allowed to go to the others. I have a man employed under me who was a sergeant in the 25th, a Sergt Smith who is secretary & lives in the Central establishment[,] collects subscriptions & superintends the sale of coffee, ginger beer &c. He is a very superior man and very much liked, & he takes a real interest in the work. We have now got within 19, of 2,000 subscribers, & they pay 1d a week, so you may fancy what an income it will bring in when the reading rooms have been long enough established to be properly appreciated. By the end of the year I fully expect to have 3,000 subscribers[.]' Now that is well done, is it not, for a young man of 23, & I *believe* it is *all* his own doing.

Tuesday Morning. Your letter is come; and I find that I may keep the Missing Link, thanks to your kindness. I am very much obliged to you. When you want the Spottiswoode introduction please apply to me. At present you seem to have your hands full. Have you seen any thing of the Buxtons yet? I hope you will call on them, though I don't quite know if they have come to town from Fox-Warren (near Weybridge) yet. Thank you too much for that list. It is just the thing. I have been in pretty close communication with Florence Nightingale lately. She sent 10£'s worth of games, & a year's subscription to several periodicals 'The Workman' among others—I wonder if it is the British Workman, Punch & the Illustrated News &c,—& has also sent me a cheque for P J. for 5£ to make the rooms comfortable, & go *towards* providing one room (to be kept for *quiet* readers & writers) with writing materials, as she says soldiers are so glad of them, & of a quiet place to write in. She advised smoking being allowed. In short she has given me no end of experience & wisdom, which Meta is copying out for P. Jackson, & which will hereafter be at the service of any of my friends, who want to establish a civilian reading-room &c. (And Mr Clarke has helped us a great deal—)[.] I am afraid Florence Nightingale is almost as ill as she can be, with heart complaint,—She lies down constantly & speaks as little as may be; is very very weak. Her soul keeps her body together. She still keeps her love of fun, & sense of the ludicrous; which I am sure is a good thing.

Ever yours very truly,
E C Gaskell.

?MARIANNE GASKELL[1]

Thursday [November 1859]

My dearest Cynthia,
    Graciously write to us my darling; we do so want to hear your ups & downs in life. Mrs Smith has written to Meta today,—looking out for a house in London where 'we hope you and your sister will be our *first* visitors', '*first*' dashed under—We are just going out. We do nothing but go out,—breakfast at ½ past 9, & Meta has breakfasted in bed these two days,—Julia & I go to Post Office; by which direction & going for them, which we do *every* day, we get our letters two hours sooner than if we wait for the delivery; so write to *Post Office*,—home about ½ past 11, Julia hungry—lunch,—go out with Hearn for a long walk, come home close upon post time\½ past 4/(so if we don't get our letters done before we go out we can't send them that day.) dine at 5,—go to sleep till ½ past 7, tea—Julia to bed at 8. Meta & I work till 10; to bed. Letters from Bosie, Mr Aidé, & Mr Steinthal, Mrs Annie Jenkin, Louy Jackson & Mrs Smith today,—all wanting answers. No news in any. I enclose two as specimens. Bosie full of having seen us at Bradford, Papa Meta & me,—in front seat of gallery; waited ever so long on staircase to see us &c &c &c,—Meta highly excited at the idea of our 'doubles' being seen. We want letters my darling of [?] with news, & not philanthropy in them. Annie Jenkins says 'You looked charming'— . . and I think that's all. Sleepiness & Hunger are the characteristics of Whitby[.] Ever your most affec[tionate] Mamy

* *

MARIANNE GASKELL

1 Abbey Terrace, Whitby
Thursday Novr 10 [1859]

My dearest Polly—
6 o'clock dinner Monday Enclosed are 5s worth of stamps, as the readiest way of furbishing you up with a little money, and Papa's

[1] Possibly to Florence Gaskell.

note, which says very little in the way of news. Mrs Roscoe asked him and me to dinner on Wednesday next,\16/to meet new Master of Grammar School, Mr Walker, & Prof: Greenwood: young ladies to come in evng—dinner ½ past 6, *punctually*, (for fear I forget.) But Meta had written, in reply to Mrs Shuttleworth the day before—to fix on next Wednesday (if it suited Mrs Shuttleworth) for us, Miss Marshall included, to dine *there*,—so I have written to Mrs Roscoe to accept for *Papa*, & decline for us; as if we go any where we must go to the Shuttleworth's—do you understand? And moreover I wonder if Cousin Charlotte would like this,—\Never mind naming this if you don't like—I dare say we can often beg tickets./to share with us in an extra Hallé, (£2 2s), ticket,—eight concerts,—Cherry would go to *three* certainly,—& that would be some where about 15 & 9d, & we could take the remainder of the time—the concerts are, you know, 10s. 6d. *each*.\separate/Meta is puzzled about a drawing-master in Manchester,—she does not know of any good one except Mr Hall (Annette Nicholls master) who, she thinks, won't give lessons except to his old pupils,—and Mr Hammersley, *School of Design*, whom *W A D* thinks well of,—but Cherry would have *to go to the* School of Design. We could enquire, if you liked, but Manchester is rather famous for NOT having a good drawing master. Julia is *very* unhappy about Cherry coming. She says you never write to her or Flossy, but are always ready to write to Dar & Fanny Wilmott\&c &c/; & that you never would have undertaken to go with *her* to lessons, & that she shall see nothing of you, now, for you will be so much occupied with Cherry. A good deal of this is morbid jealousy, I know; but there is also a little grain of truth in it, darling, about the not writing. Meta has heard from Anna Mohl today. She is still with Madame Mohl; & not coming to us. I am sorry, and yet glad, if you understand the mixture. It rains here today,—besides being desperately cold. Julia is quite well now. You can stay till Monday, love. Thank Cousin Lotte for asking you &c &c. I *think* we shall go home too on Monday.

Your very affec[tionate] Mammy.

Julia loves you *dearly*, darling. She cried sadly the night you did not come home with Meta.

431 **449** 0

GEORGE ELIOT

1 Abbey Terrace
Whitby.
Thursday, Novr 10th [1859]

My dear Madam,
Since I heard, from authority, that you were the author of
Scenes from 'Clerical Life' & 'Adam Bede', I have read them
again; and I must, once more, tell you how earnestly fully, and
humbly I admire them. I never read anything so complete, and
beautiful in fiction, in my whole life before. I said 'humbly' in
speaking of my admiration, because I remembered Dr Johnson's
words.
Perhaps you may have heard that I upheld Mr Liggins as the
author for long,—I did it on evidence, quite independent of, &
unknown to the Bracebridges. He is a regular rascal. But I never
was such a goose as to believe that such books as yours could be a
mosaic of real & ideal. I should not be quite true in my ending, if
I did not say before I concluded that I wish you *were* Mrs Lewes.
However that can't be helped, as far as I can see, and one must not
judge others. Once more, thanking you most gratefully for
having written all—Janet's Repentance perhaps most especially of
all,—(& may I tell you how I singled out the 2nd No of Amos
Barton in Blackwood, & went plodging through our Manchester
Sts to get every number, as soon as it was accessible from the
Portico\reading/table—)
                         Believe me to remain,
                              Yours respectfully
                                        E C Gaskell.

402 **450** 482

W. W. and/or EMELYN STORY[1]

[Early November 1859]

['Writing at another time that she has been for a while at
Whitby, whither she had gone for impressions preparatory to
_____
[1] From a printed source.

"Sylvia's Lovers", she mentions that Hawthorne was at the same time, on the same coast, at Redcar, ten miles off, engaged in finishing "Transformation,"[1] the subject of which she sketches as she has heard it narrated. Then touching on that outbreak of the faun nature, the animal, in the strange hero, which moves him at a given movement to the commission of a murder:'] For all of which, somehow, you like Donatello the better!

446 **451** 451a

GEORGE SMITH

42 Plymouth Grove
November 30th [1859]

My dear Sir,

This morning came the orange Charlotte Brontë for which many thanks. Only, (now I am going to be disagreeable so be prepared!) I wish you had let me know you were going to publish it, because Mr J. S. Mills & I have had a correspondence this \last 1859/August which ended in my volunteering an expression of regret for my having published an extract from one of Miss Brontë's letters in which she says something about 'scorning the heart' of the writer of the article in the W. Review (she supposed it to be J. S. M.) Now this extract—a line or two—is retained in an edition dated 1860; so, if ever he comes across it he will think my expression of regret for its previous publication a piece of hypocrisy on my part; and though he has been very savage & unreasonable in his letters to me, yet I admire him so much that I shall be sorry to lose the small scrap that I may have gained in his good opinion by my partial apology. You will explain it for me sometime, please, won't you, for I don't want to get any more hard & severe letters from him,—which I shall have, if I write even an explanation of how this happened. So much for that. All the rest is unadulterated thanks; and most especially for those brilliant lines of Father Prout's;[2] how we did delight in them, and how I should like to have written them. I think our Magazine

---

[1] Published 1861.
[2] 'Father Prout'—Francis Mahoney (1805–66), Irish humorist, contributed Inaugural Ode to the *Cornhill Magazine* (January 1860).

promises to be a famous success; and I enjoy—now you know *you* did, so you need not look moral—the Saturday's cutting up of 'Dead [?heart]¹;—oh, *how* stupid it was.—I don't think we shall ever be so stupid. We are all poorly in various ways,—we take it in turns to have breakfast in bed, & little doses of medecine & appropriate bits of biscuits & glasses of water are being delicately handed to all of us in our turn. Julia is the bright exception, and extremely merry she is. Meta has been *very* poorly. Please always call her Meta—she never was called 'Margaret' from her birth, except at her christening and during her engagement, which\is a time/we all forget as fast as we can[.] I was very much obliged to you for sending us so much about Mrs Lewes? (what do people call her,—) Do you know I can't help liking her,—*because* she wrote those books. Yes I do! I *have* tried to be moral, & dislike her & dislike her books—but it won't do. There is not a wrong word, or a wrong thought in them, I do believe,—and though I should have been more 'comfortable', for some indefinable reason, if a *man* had written them instead of a *woman*, yet I think the author must be a noble creature; and I shut my eyes to the awkward blot in her life. Did you know that a number of dissenting ministers, connected with the Eclectic Review, went to Mr Liggins, and requested him, as the author of &c to write for the{m}\ir review/, offering him his own terms. He did not *say* he was the Author, but he implied it in several ways. One of them said how much the style of A Bede reminded him of Goldsmith— Mr Liggins said it was no wonder, for Goldsmith was his favourite author, & took down a well worn copy of the Vicar,—& so on. I wonder if you would care to see a packet of H Martineau Bracebridge, & other letters about this imposture, or whether you would think them tiresome?—(They must be *in confidence* please.) I wd send them only you are so busy with your Magazine just now.

My kindest regards to Mrs Smith. Don't forget you owe us a visit,—& that the time for paying it is due. Meta coughs out a kind message to you,—no one else here. Yours most truly

E C Gaskell

¹ See p. 614 below.

*   *

451 **451a** 452

GEORGE SMITH

42 Plymouth Grove
Decr 23. [1859]

Please reply soon.

My dear Mr Smith,

Either you or I are rather blundering; I can't tell which. I don't want, & what is more I *would not take* a penny more advantageous terms than Mr C. D[1] offers. So there! and there's an end of that part of the subject. Now please clear your mind for the next branch.

I have 3 things begun. (Very bad management I know: but there are excuses for all things if you know them).

1st in order of time was begun a story, 120 pages of which are written & have been this year & a half; *not very good*, & that would not be above a 1 vol in length. *It is not good enough for the C. M.*[2] —I am the best judge of that, please,—but might be good enough for *H. W.*[3] This was the story I once thought of finishing for Mr C. D.[4] Now do you understand that far?

2nd a story of perhaps 40 (of my pages) long. Begun & I *think* good; intended *for C. M.*;[5] but delayed because of extreme dislike to writing for Mr T. & also because I do want to make it as good as I can, & so only to write at it in my best moments. (It is a great pity it was not done for Xmas time.)

3rdly The Specksioneer in 3 vols.

Published by Smith & Elder (it is to be hoped—) not far on, but very clear in my head, & what I want to write more than any thing; the only temptation otherways being that I have the $\frac{1}{4}$ of the 1st story already written. Now, tell me please goodly & truly what you would like me to do,—go straight ahead with the Specksioneer (you are not tied to the title,—) I fancy? Please remember that 1st story would not be good enough for the C. M. I know what is what as well as any one. And it is not that I want you to take *that*, on *any* terms; but to know if you would like me to work straight & hard away at the Specksioneer (after

---

[1] Charles Dickens.   [2] *Cornhill Magazine.*   [3] *Household Words.*
[4] This may be 'A Dark Night's Work' (*All the Year Round*, 24 & 31 January, 7, 14, 21 February 1863). See Letter 517.
[5] Possibly 'Curious if True', *Cornhill*, February 1860.

having done the No 2 story.—) or, if you don't care when you
have that (Specksioneer)[.] If you know the haste in which I write
you would not wonder at my explaining myself stupidly. I
extremely like & admire Framley Parsonage,—& the Idle Boy;
and the Inaugural address. I like Lovel the Widower, only (perhaps because I am stupid,) it is a little confusing on account of its
discursiveness,—and V's verses; and oh shame! I have not read the
sensible & improving articles.[1] So a merry Xmas to you & yours,

Ever yrs most truly
E C Gaskell

451a 452 454

GEORGE SMITH

42 Plymouth Grove
Tuesday Decr 27. [1859]

My dear Mr Smith,
    I will try and send you the tale for the Cornhill Magazine in a
fortnight, & the novel\3 vols/, in September next. I have written
to tell Mr Dickens I cannot do what he asks. I *should* have very
much disliked cutting up my one-vol. story into pieces: the only
temptation was that a quarter was lying by me, all ready. Or else I
had made a resolution never to write for All the Year Round again,
for several reasons. So much for that. I wrote the Garden Room
story,[2]—if people thought for a moment it was G. E's it was because of the preference for small cows over short-horns. The story
itself is *true*, more's the pity. Mr Justice Erle & Mr Tom Taylor
told it me in 1849.
    In last week's No of All the Year Round is a repudiation (by Mr
Dickens,) of having intended Leigh Hunt by Harrold Skimpole.
Please do not bring me into communication with Mr Thornton
Hunt if I tell you something. Four years ago when my friend Mr
Story returned to Europe from America he was charged by some
rich American, (name told me, but which I forget,) to see how
100£, or even 200, could be made most acceptable to Leigh Hunt.
Mr Story wrote to L. H. asking the question,—in a charming

---

[1] A. Trollope's *Framley Parsonage* and Thackeray's *Lovel the Widower* both
appeared in the first number of the *Cornhill* for Jan. 1860. See Ray, *Age of Wisdom*,
pp. 295-6.   [2] See p. 577, n. above.

frank way I am sure; and he received back such a beautiful letter
from L. Hunt,—which I am sure those interested in his memory
should see,—if not have published. Of course I can not do justice
to it, but I know he declined receiving the money in *any* shape—
statue, cash, books,—in the firmest & most graceful manner; saying that the readiness with whh he had formerly been willing to
accept from friends, what, if their circumstances had been re-
versed he should have been so glad & thankful to have rendered
them,—had been cruelly misunderstood & misrepresented; & that
he now felt it due to himself to reject material kindness, while he
was fully alive as ever to the nobleness of heart whh offered it.

Meta went to Edinburgh yesterday; & leaves us a blank in her
place. Max Müller is as full of frolic, & bright light wit as—you
are. (N.B. he is not very unlike you!) He is just married to a Miss
Pascoe-Grenfell, & funnily afraid of the expenses of a wife, I am
told.

Ever, in untidy haste
Yours most truly
E C Gaskell.

₄₄₄ **453** ₄₆₁

CHARLES ELIOT NORTON

42 Plymouth Grove
January 19th [1860]

My dear Mr Norton,
I am not going to write a word beyond this little sheet. Please
thank yourself very much for your letter, most welcome which
you wrote on Xmas Eve. And thank yourself too for the Photographs which *are to* come, & which I shall particularly like, as I
have no notion what America looks like, either in her cities, or her
country, or most of all mysterious, her forests. Sometimes I dream
I am in America, but it always looks like Rome, whh I *know* it is
not. I am so glad of François's good fortune. To be sure we will
go to the Hotel de Londres, Rue Castiglione!! I should like to be
going tomorrow, and out of this misty foggy Manchester, which
gives me a perpetual headache very hard to bear. Now all this is
not the *business* of my letter,—& the one I mean to enclose (saving

1s.) to Mr Hale. I want you *both*, as soon as you conveniently can to send me all manner of information & plans about your BLOCKS of dwellings for working-men. You know what I mean; for I don't know what you call them in America—great conglomerate sets of rooms in one vast building,—erected according to laws of health &c &c &c; in fact every experience on your side the water about lodging the working-people well, œconomically & healthily. I shall be very glad of this information as soon as possible; and very willing to pay for it's quick transmission. Marianne has just come in, 'sends her love to you, & wants to know if you have got her letter'; I give the message word for word, but I don't quite understand when she wrote. I wish you were here; I have constantly long stories I should like to tell you, but which are too long & too difficult to *write*, when one can't see the impression certain words & expressions are making. My girls, my darlings, *are* such comforts—such happiness! Every one so good & healthy & bright. I don't know what I should do if any one of them married; & yet it is constantly a wonder to me that no one ever gives them a chance. I suspect it is that here (in Manchester) the Unitarian young men are either good *and* uncultivated, or else rich *and* regardless of those higher qualities the 'spiritual' qualities as it were, which those *must* appreciate who would think of my girls. The new school of enlightened & liberal young men, of high cultivation & still higher moral and religious standard with whom we associate occasionally, are all held back by the more bigotted fathers of the last generation from too much intimacy with Unitarians. I think an unmarried life may be to the full as happy, *in process of time* but I think there is a time of trial to be gone through with *women*, who naturally yearn after children. All this it is perhaps strange to write to you; but I am so perfectly sure you understand me that I have no scruple in doing it; and you will never refer I am sure to anything in your replies, which I tell to you, as to a *brother* of my girls. Meta had rather over-worked herself in this depressing Manchester climate, which suits neither her nor me, & went on December 26th to pay a visit in Edinburgh. She returns on the 28th of this month; and on Febry 3rd when Flossy & Julia will have gone back to school, Mr Gaskell, Marianne, Meta, & I, go to Oxford; the two first never having seen it. Mr Gaskell will only be able to stay away till the 14th; we shall remain (or rather go to Portsmouth, Eton & London) till the end of the month. We have heard from the Fields in the Isle of Wight; I half wish we might be able to get to see them when we are at Portsmouth. When, WHEN are you coming to England dear Mr Norton? Mr Hale spoke as if you might be here this winter. Remember your *home* in Plymouth Grove[.] My kind regards to Mrs Norton & your sisters—

Your affect. friend
E C Gaskell

How is Miss Sedgewick? Be sure & answer this

452 454 456

GEORGE SMITH

Cowley House Oxford
('Show') Sunday
[Early February 1860]

My dear Mr Smith

I am afraid I was stupid (or *perhaps* it was you—who knows?) I ought to have told you that my dear Madame Mohl was the author of that Récamier article,[1]—stay, I'll put her letter in,—I know I can trust it to you,—and we are just off to Church. *Please* return it; it will explain that *what you have* is the National R. article as it was *first written*—twice as long as it was when printed, —*she* thinks the best part was taken out;—but you'll understand all,—I want a stronger and more practical opinion of my own (I don't mean that I shall give her yours, unless you particularly wish it,) to get her to write a book as she proposes. She would do it well—and has that sort of knowledge of *good* French & English society whh few finely-observing women possess. I mean she has —oh I don't know what I mean in this hurry. *I* think she *ought* to write it out of benevolence to her species,—but do you think it would be 'acting to empty benches'.

Yours very truly
E C G.

Such beautiful praise of Mrs Smith's *character* from Mr Munro last night[.]

[1] See p. 601, n. 3 below.

MARIANNE GASKELL[1]

[Late February 1860]

My dearest Minnie

Meta & I plan to lunch there tomorrow after which Emily will call for us to take us on to see their new house [in Kensington]. Meta goes with Louy, to revd Alfred Lyall's Harbledown, near Canterbury on *Wednesday*. I have written to Mrs Lyall (of Winchester) to say I will go there next Tuesday\week/March 7th till Friday—they\Meta & Louy/are to join me from Canterbury. There is no particular news; the only letters I have received are yours, my darling & then we came here to tea on Saturday, (after a very scanty lunch at the strong-minded Miss Nancie Smith's) talked & went to bed,—I, with my cold about as bad as it could be, but I am only in the fashion. I stayed in breakfast yesterday, & all the rest of the world went to Portland St. Then I got up, answered a note sent by a messenger from A[.] A. Jenkin to Meta, *bidding* her go there 6 Milton St to breakfast this morning, as she & Fleming were flitting down to Birkenhead this afternoon; why or for how long no one knoweth. Then I cabbed, (coughing) to Lady Coltman's; dined there with her & Willie; Mr & Mrs Clarke came in afterwards,—came home here about 5,—having heard a formidable acct of Mrs Winchester Lyall,—& that Mrs J J Tayler had had 2 epileptic attacks this last week,—and that the Euryalus had had a hole knocked in her side, & had to be mended in the Mediterranean; & that the Brodies were *charmed* with Papa, & that Ly Coltman hoped we wd not forget that he & Mr Brodie first met at {their}\her/house. Came home, quiet evening[.] *Meta* had been hearing Papa's praises from Mr Ewart. 'My *friend* Mr Gaskell' 'for I hope he will allow me to rank him as a friend'— Meta referred to Papa's walks with Mr Ewart—'Yes! he is *the* most charming companion I know' &c, so Papa's ears ought to have been burning. Ly C. had a stock of *clean, large* thick pocket

---

[1] Mrs Gaskell was using old letters. On page 1 there is an invitation to dinner dated 25 February from Mary Mackintosh of 2 Hyde Park Terrace, Kensington Gore and on page 5 another dated merely 'Sunday' from G. H. Tollet of 14 Queen Ann Street. The word 'there' in line 1 probably refers to the Mackintoshs. A Lancaster MS. copy (see p. xxv above) gives an address: 'Miss Gaskell, | 42 Plymouth Grove, | Manchester.'

handkerchiefs on her table, being, as she said, the 'kindest attention she could offer to her friends just now.' Mrs Clarke took one,
I another, & blew our noses just like two rival nightingales. Meta
[come since I began to write]¹ is gone to A A J's, & I am to meet
her at the Bridells at ½ past 3. Mr & Mrs Clarke & Ly Coltman
were all full of 'Cousin Stella'² & I had quite a reflected lustre from
the fact that I knew & could tell them all about the authoress. Mr
Clarke sent a message to her via me, Meta, Annie, to beg her to
write just such a charming novel about the North of Italy.
Madame Mohl has written that article on Madame Recamier in
the Edinburgh³—No! Nothing can be done about Mrs Dicey
except do what I did, set Mrs Rich at full liberty to say 'there was
nothing in it.' She is going to say so to Miss Smith, among other
people. I have not yet had an answer about the Derbyshire cooks
character. I am very sorry about Mrs George Melly, but her confinement *may* set her to rights. It sometimes *does*; in illnesses that
are very hopeless & mysterious. I will *try* & get M Price to come
to us; but I *think* Dan Fearon is most likely to decline Guernsey.
Still I will ask Margaret. Send on anything of our news you can
to Flossy; for I have not written to her for long, & am really
poorly with my cold, my *eyes* aching so. Certainly! we will ask
Johnnie Coates. I am *very* sorry for them all. How is Susan? Has
she got her place? We have never heard or seen anything of
E T H since Tuesday, but Will (who is rather thick with Bosie
about the model lodging house)⁴ has asked C Binns here tomorrow night. We don't know yet if he'll come or not; but if he
does, I shall 'pump' about E T H. Meta does not want to go to
Canterbury at all. If she & I have time after the Bridells, we shall
go & call on Parthe, Lady Verney, who is in town. 32 South
Street, wherever that is; vide Ly Coltman. Lady Belper called on
Ly C. to ask for my address on Saturday—I suppose for Mrs
James—Now Lady this is my word, & great is my love for you,
but I have nothing more to say. Best love to Papa & Julia from
your own old Mammy.

¹ The words within editorial brackets were written by Mrs G at the foot of
page 5 and refer to the note from Tollet which occupies most of page 5.
² See above, p. 562 and n.
³ Vol. III, No. 225 (January 1860), pp. 204–35. Cf. Letter 454, which refers to
its publication in the National Review, as does K. O'Meara in her *Madame Mohl;
Her Salon and Her Friends*, 1885, p. 156. Mme Mohl's article is a review of Mme
Lenorment's *Souvenirs et Correspondance de Madame Récamier*.
⁴ Mrs Gaskell 'managed to do Model-Lodging Houses', despite her 'wretched
cough' on 5 March 1860. *Letters and Memorials*, ed. Winkworth, II, p. 296.

454 **456** 459

GEORGE SMITH

4 Upper Belgrave St.
London
March 1st [1860]

My dear Sir,
I am very much obliged to you for your most kind *instalment* of autographs. I like Thackeray's '[?] ever at lunch' particularly. I cannot make out *two* of the signatures, and shall be much obliged to you if you will tell me what they are. One is dated from Brockbear ? Exeter, has a B under the crest, but the signature is John Romilly, or *Russell*—and is about a 'missing document'. I am very glad to hear that the Mrs Hadwen whose death was announced in the Times was no relation to Mrs Smith.
I wish Mr Trollope would go on writing Framley Parsonage[1] for ever. I don't see any reason why it should ever come to an end, and every one I know is always dreading the *last* number. I hope he will make the jilting of Griselda a long while a-doing.
On the contrary—*frosty* weather is very good for 'somebody's hair.'

Pray believe me to remain
Yours very truly
E. C. Gaskell.

455 **457** 460

MARIANNE GASKELL

The Close,
Winchester.
Friday. [March 1860]

My very dearest Polly,
Thank you *much* for writing so regularly every day[,] my darling. I am so sorry Julia's headache does not go away entirely. Hearn has some sort of a notion *against* giving her opening medicine for fear of making her constantly *require* it. But you see she *does*, as I am sure, as well as Mr Mellor, it is want of a good clear-

[1] This novel was serialised in the first issues of the *Cornhill Magazine* in 1860.

ing out that makes this head ache linger. Will you give her stewed rhubarb, and that sort of thing &c. I am very anxious to get away tomorrow, but Meta's cold is very bad now, and I am half afraid of the journey for her. However Mr Butler is coming this after-noon, so I shall ask him his opinion, which is sure to be on the safe side, as he has a great dread of my 'going North' till the warm weather has quite set in. If our present plans hold we leave here at *12* tomorrow, and get to the Ewarts 6 Cambridge Sq. by 3. But perhaps it may not suit them to receive us; and we shan't know till tomorrow. Only I think it will. Is Julia growing much? Oh! *please* ask the Tutor not to trouble himself or his friends about the press-gang affair. The Annual Register has been *care-fully* looked over *months* ago, & it is of no use going over the ground again—and so many people are now at work for me, *in Yorkshire*, that I am sure to have my information sooner or later, without troubling any one further.[1] *Please* make all this clear, with many thanks to him. I hope all tins pans & saucepans were well scoured out before the new cook came. How do you think she *cooks*? The Warden has just been to call on me; he is Mr Coleridge's friend, you know (but I can't say the liking seems mutual on the Warden's part.) He wants me to go in Mrs Lyall's bath-chair, & see the College (i.e. School) tomorrow; it is very close to here. I wish I could muster up enough of news to write a little note to Julia; but really sitting in a warm back drawing room with blinds down all the day long, and seeing no one, and no newspapers coming, and no letters except from you, my faithful darling, one has very little to say. Meta and I are *scarified* raw by mustard plaisters; and Louy almost as bad. Mr Arthur Brandreth came last night, but as he sits in another room I have seen very little of him. I don't *think* there is *any*thing between him & Louy; he is a pleasant-looking, plain *big boy*,—reddish brown hair, & do complexion, no sign of whiskers, beard or moustache, tho' he is 27; and that's all I know about him. His sister Emily B. is staying here. And now I can't write any more. Do we still go on with the same gardener. Make Sarah *keep* an account of the number of eggs brought in, & put it down *once a week* in the book. See about Tommy's dinner. How is Anne Groom. I cannot write any more—If Mr Butler alters our plans for tomorrow, I will put in a PS, otherwise they will hold, and I am your very affec[tionat]e Mammy. Do you know I've had '*bronchitis*'.

[1] A reference to Mrs Gaskell's enquiries in connexion with *Sylvia's Lovers*.

427 **458** 472

?EDWARD CHAPMAN

Wm Ewart's Esq. M.P.
6, Cambridge Square,
March the 23rd [1860]

My dear Sir,

Will you kindly send me here a copy of the best Edition of
'Mary Barton', and one also of the same of 'Ruth'; and I should
feel much obliged to you if you would enclose a bill with them.

Is it true that we are all to be struggling greedily for the 'Mill
on the Floss' *next week?*[1] You see I still consider you as a perpetual
fount of literary gossip; for which I feel rather thirsty, having had
none for a long time. Do you know by whom 'Melle Mori' is
written?

Ever yours very sincerely
E. C. Gaskell.

456 **459** 462

GEORGE SMITH

6 Cambridge Sq
Friday Evng March 23. [1860]

My dear Sir

Miss\Ellen/Nussey
Brookroyd
Birstal near
Leeds—

Your letter has been forward to me here, 6 Cambridge Sq—
where Meta and I are trying to get up our strength (after bronchitis on my part, & bad influenza on hers,) for our journey home
on Monday. It has been put off from day to day this week, on
account of our indisposition,—but we do hope to accomplish it on
Monday, & then to read the dear Cornhill.—

Thank you very much for the 'Firm's letter—I was ill in bed, &

¹ Published 4 April 1860.

unable even to read it myself when it arrived, or it should have been acknowledged sooner.

Please do you know who wrote 'Mlle Mori', published by Parker?

We are very sorry to hear Mrs Smith has been so ill; but the sorrowful shock she had in her weak state is enough to account for it.

Yours very truly
E C Gaskell

457 460 461

MARIANNE GASKELL

6 Cambridge Sq.
Monday [?26 March ?1860]

My very dearest Polly,

We are so shocked and sorry about poor Jackson. One naturally wants to know ever so much more. Did his wife *expect* him to dinner? Who first missed him, & at what time? You only say 'after tea'—was there an examination of the body at the inquest? I am so sorry; & I cannot think what will be best to be done for poor Mrs Jackson. Tommy Glover I suppose had better go & live with the Moore's, (Ruth Moore, the dress-maker to the Behrens' mother. Hannah B. knows all about them.) I want to go home on Wednesday; but there are two things in the way. Meta is very poorly with a very bad cold; saw Mr Aiken (the Ewart's doctor) yesterday, who ordered her medicine every 6 hours, no solids, keep in the house for two days &c.—she does not seem much better today, but has only just got up; and has a very bad (cold) headache. The other reason relates to Miss Smith's letter, which probably you read,—IF Miss Evanson (her young woman) came up to see Mr Shaen *early* this week, I should be sorry to miss her —but I have written this morning both to the Shaens & Miss Smith to ask them to let me know. I can't quite make out what must be done about the animals, garden &c in the interregnum there *must* be. Probably Shaw (if the case were written to him & explained,) would send out a gardener (*not* a 5s. a day one,) but they *have* them much cheaper, & you might ask him if he had a gardener who could at this pinch, help about cows, hens & pigs. Poor Mrs Jackson could not do anything at present, I fear; or else it might be a help to her to be earning a little money by attending to our pigs. (I think this is a time for seeing what Sarah is made of.)

I shall come home on Thursday, if all goes on well with Meta, —by the same train as you did, I *think*[,] but I will write again tomorrow. Williams the green-grocer would be a good person to apply to for a temporary man about the animals.

I am feeling very weak today; but have been out in the carriage —Every body,—Wedgwoods, Tollets &c &c is ill with this influenza,—Mr Aikin said yesterday it was all over the kingdom, & Katie W. sends word of it at Alderly & Wilmslow. Poor Jackson! I keep wondering if that long sorrow about his son had anything to do with it. I am so sorry. My darling what a deal of care you have had in your reign as housekeeper.—Tell me about Sarah.—I went to Portland St yesterday in & back in the carriage,—saw Duckworths, Mary Staley, Shaens[1] &c,—that's my only adventure. Pray tell Mrs Jackson how very *very* sorry I am about her loss. I shall so want your letter tomorrow. I am very glad darling Julia is better. My dear love to Papa—

Ever your very affect[ionate] Mammy.

453 461 476

CHARLES ELIOT NORTON

42 Plymouth Grove, Manchester
April 5th. [1860]

My dear Mr Norton,

I begin with the best will in the world to write you a very long letter,—whether the Fates will permit me is quite a different thing. I have so much to thank you for,—I shall take them in order of time. Photographs; some of whh I liked extremely,—but altogether I thought America would have been odder and more original; the underwood & tangle is just like England. What gave me the best idea of America, or a piece of it, was an {old} oil-painting of a Mme Bodichon, (née Barbara Leigh Smith,) and as such possibly known to you; she is illegitimate-cousin of Hilary Carter, F Nightingale,—& has their nature in her; though some of

---

[1] 'Mrs Gaskell read Emily and Will a good deal of her new story [*Sylvia's Lovers*] in London', *Letters and Memorials*, ed. Winkworth, II, p. 297.

the legitimate don't acknowledge her. She is—I think in conse-quence of her birth, a strong fighter against the established opinions of the world,—which always goes against my—what shall I call it?—*taste*—(that is not the word,) but I can't help admir-ing her noble bravery, and respecting—while I don't personally *like* her. She married two or three years ago a Dr Bodichon, of Algiers; a Breton by birth,—and they went for their honey-*year* to America,—and in some wild luxuriant terrific part of Virginia? in a gorge full of rich rank tropical vegetation,—her husband keeping watch over her with loaded pistols because of the alli-gators infesting the stream.—Well! that picture *did* look like my idea of America. Now come my thanks for your two good satis-factory-as-to-their-purpose letters about the model lodging houses.[1] Each was so clear; so useful; and the little plan made *me* even (who am very stupid about architectural plans in general,) quite understand No. 1, and No. 2. One great question still re-mains unanswered, and please you must answer it, as fully as you have done the others: it is describe an *ideal* porter? or\resident/ superintendent, or whatever you call him,—his duties? qualifica-tions? temptations? and where—in what class you find him. There now I jump away from philanthropy to my beautiful Vita Nuova,[2] which only came yesterday, but which was more identified with *you*, and Italy than anything else; & which I have so much wished to have of my own, and in print, ever since you let me read it in MS. Thank you so *very* much for it. I do so value it. (I want to send this letter off by tomorrow's mail, so I am only just touching on everything.—) Your late letters have come so quickly,—really making one feel you within call. And the other day\at/a Man-chester dinner there were 'prairie hens',—killed in your parts and eaten here! I was not at it. I only heard of them. Now I am going to rush back to Xmas & sum up our proceedings since then. Have you seen Mr Hale, because he could tell you of our Xmas which he spent with us. All during his three days visit I was suffering from one of my bad head aches; which I am afraid are produced by the air of Manchester, as I hardly ever have them—certainly not anything like so violently; anywhere else. Meta went to Edinburgh the day after Xmas day; and to our Christmas dances and gaieties I took Marianne and Flossy; who is now *seventeen*— though very young both in character and acquirements for that

---

[1] See Whitehill, *Letters*, pp. 46–7, 50–1.
[2] Norton's *New Life of Dante, an Essay with Translations*, 1859.

age. She went back to school at Knutsford after the holidays were over. And Meta came back to us, much better for the delicious northern bracing air, just in time for we 4, (Mr Gaskell, Marianne Meta & I) to go to Oxford on Friday Febry 3. Mr Gaskell and I went to the Brodie's (you remember?—Cowley House on the other side of Magdalen Bridge?) and Marianne & Meta were kindly taken in by a Mr and Miss Smith (brother & sister;) he a Balliol-man fellow, & mathematical tutor of his college, good, kind, everybody says very clever; but very measured & formal to strangers. His sister a little older, with many of his characteristics, only being a woman, I get to know her more intimately & better; and sooner to the point of thoroughly liking. Both are as good as gold; and so kind to the girls. Well! we were regularly Oxford-dissipated, dined at (Dr) Arthur Stanley's, at the Deanery at Ch. Ch. at Queen's with the provost,—with the gold College plates, —a gold Eagle in memory of the founder, John *Eagle*field,—in memory of whom they also keep up a curious old custom—on New Year's eve I think—the Dean of Hall takes a threaded needle (*aiguille—Eagle*field,) and gives it to each Scholar, saying '*Take this, and be thrifty.*' at the Vice Chancellor's (I'm returning to our engagements)—at Balliol, Mr Jowett and Mr Smith giving us the dinner,—to a debate at the Union, breakfast at Exeter, with a fellow there, who had been engaged 15 years, & could not get a living to marry upon,—lunch at Corpus with Mr Conington &c; for there really were many more things. I do like Mr Jowett; and I am so glad to feel we are really getting intimate. Oh! I have two things to send *you*; only I never can understand or make out how to get things to America; one is a photograph said to be good, of myself: and the other is two sermons preached by Arthur Stanley, in the University Ch. to the Oxford undergraduates; the last of which we heard, & which is to me, extremely striking; & moreover bears an especial reference to the circumstances of Oxford at present which will I think interest you. You know Mr Jowett is fellow of Balliol?—and tutor? and *Regius* Professor of Greek? Well! by the new regulations of the Oxford Commission there is some power conferred on the\heads of the/University, of enabling a *fellow*, who is also a *professor* to marry still holding his fellowship for a certain number of years; and also the heads of the University (congregation? convocation? whatever they call themselves—) may in each individual instance pass a law permitting each Regius professor (whose salaries average from 30 to 80£ a year, paid by government not the University,) to receive the *fees* of those who attend his lectures,—which without this permission go somewhere else—to the College I think. Now Mr Jowett would like to marry; this is well known to his friends; not anybody in particular, but to have a home, for he is a very affectionate man,—& because he thinks a fellow's life too long continued induces selfishness & a shut-up heart &c. Well! he can't marry unless these two permissions are given him by the University,—for he won't take a College living. Nearly all the other Regius-Prof⟨⟩, & Fellows *have* had their permissions grant⟨ed⟩—Max Müller is married (Fellow of All Souls & Reg. Prof. of Modern Languages,) just lately—Mr Conington, I should say only waited for some young lady to offer *to him*; having his permissions all granted—(Fellow of Corpus, & Reg. Prof. of Latin,) and being very full of matrimony, only two [*sic*] shy to ask any body,—but poor Mr Jowett is excluded from these permissions—(do you care to hear it all?— yes! I think you do.) Last December there was to be a meeting of the heads of colleges &c &c, 'a congregation' I think they call it; and Arthur Stanley, & Mr Smith and one or two others determined to try & get ⟨j⟩*ustice* for Mr Jowett in the two respects I have named. The 'congregation' was to be held on a Monday; on Sunday Evening Mr Jowett's friends were employed at Dr Stanley's writing notes &c {for} to secure votes for Mr Jowett the next day,—when he came in, ignorant, as they thought, of all that was going on. They said 'Go and talk to Mrs Stanley (Arthur's mother) we are busy but not breaking the Sabbath for it is a work of charity.' He said 'Oh! I suppose *your ass has fallen into a pit!*' The next day A. Stanley brought forward his proposal, vehemently opposed by Dr Pusey. (A S, Dr P. and Dr Jelf, (principal of King's Coll, London & who turned out Mr Fred Maurice from his professorship there on acct of his heresy about the eternal duration of punishment,) were all Canons of Ch. Ch, & as such had votes in the congregation. A. S. brought forward ⟨a⟩ letter from Dr Jelf (in London) saying it empowered him to give his (Dr J's) vote in Mr Jowett's favour. Dr Pusey jumped up with a letter of more recent date from Dr Jelf, revoking his former letter, & voting *against* Mr Jowett. Then A S in righteous indignation said he wd read the *whole* of *his* letter from Dr Jelf,—which wound up by saying 'Any one who votes *against* Mr Jowett must be either ignorant of the commonest principles of justice, or a mean coward,' or something *very* like it; which put Dr Jelf in a very awkward position, but did not give his vote for Mr Jowett; & it was carried *against* him by *one* vote. So now you are up to understanding the severe reference in Dr Stanley's sermon on labour to those, who neither working at theology themselves, do all in their power to discourage others from working. We sat amongst the Dons when the sermon was preached, and it was curious to see how many shut their eyes, as if going to sleep at that part. But it is curious also to note how Oxford *youth* is overturning everything in theory; almost as much as you Americans. For instance at a dinner party of the cleverest most distinguished young men,\several sons of noblemen/there was the most vehement unanimity as to the 'uselessness of *King-puppets*,—hereditary peerage &c—['] and one of the most striking of the debates at the Union was against Church-rates, & strongly against the 39 articles. The little quiet Prince of Wales is in the thick of all these discussions, which will, one wd think, prevent his turning out a second Chas 1st. Going {viâ} from the P. of Wales, or '*Wales of Christ Church*' as he is called there, viâ General Bruce his governor —you know\old/Lady Elgin is just dead? I got a dreadful cold with sauntering about in Oxford one bitter day with Mr Gaskell; went on {e} with Marianne & Meta to London, did not take care of it, & was laid up with bronchitis, from which I am barely recovered. So I saw nobody & did nothing for six weeks,—all the things I meant to do in London, & the people I meant to see were left *un*done, & *un*seen,—all except going to see the Streatham St lodging houses, mentioned in yr pamphlet, which was the last thing I was able to do before I took to my bed. It was very interesting. They *don't* pay as an investment,—& to judge from yr plans are not nearly as complete as your American ones. For instance there is but *one* sink &c for every *floor*; the fireplaces were the poorest kind of *parlour* grate, over or by which there was not the least oppy of cooking; there was not a peg, a shelf, or a cupboard, or even a recess in which one might *cheaply* be made. They paid 6 shillings for two bare good-sized rooms, & more in proportion for more rooms. Thurstan Holland is one of 5 young men, (all Oxford or Cambridge,) who are planning to buy a plot of ground in Holborn, & build a lodging house on it, to cost 4,000£, & to accomodate 40 families. It is for them (*not* however as represented by Thurstan, with whom I am silently & quietly much displeased,) that I am wanting this information; for it *is* a good & thoughtful thing of them to do; & I like to see that their

previous luxurious (so to speak) education has not unfitted them
for strong feeling & prompt acting in behalf of those less fortunate. We are now all at home; Flossy came yesterday; but returns
next week. Meta is going with a middle aged lady-friend, a family
connexion, to the Pyrenees on a sketching tour for two months on
the first of May; which will be very charming for her. Marianne
goes for three weeks to London in May; and during their absence,
& the comparative quiet of the house I mean to write *very* hard at
my story; which *ought* to be done by Septr but owing to my illness, & subsequent weakness it won't I fear. How is Mr *Child's*
Miss Sedgwick? How are you all? I *wish* you wd come & see us;
every now & then we hear a rumour that you are coming, but
you don't come. I—we all—*wish* you would. We shan't go into
the country this year till the end of July. Come & go with us! My
kind regards to your mother & sisters. And I think to Mr Lowell,
if he will have them please. Ever believe me to be your affectionate friend

E C Gaskell

₄₅₉ 462 ₄₇₂ₐ

GEORGE SMITH

[5 April 1860]

Oh Mr Smith! your grandfather was a brick, and your grandmother an angel; your—(how can I go higher? it is inexpressible
in the next generation)—how *very* charming you are! If I lived
near Cornhill I wd go and pay you a call of two hours & a half
long, and offer to read to you in the evening,—only think of
having the Mill on the Floss the second day of publication, & of
my very own. I think it is so kind of you, & am so greedy to read
it I can scarcely be grateful enough to write this letter; which now
shall begin all properly—My dear Sir,

Mrs Smith is very very charming & kind and sweet & pretty,—
and you are a bright warm genial witty man—but—I (privately)
don't believe that Sir J. P. K. Shuttleworth seeks your acquaintance & society for any of these {motives}\reasons/, simple & pure
—(he has generally a double set of motives for all his actions—)
but he has a novel,—partly read to Mrs Nicholls the last time she
was at Gawthrop,—partly to me,—*wholly* to many of his friends

—a novel of Lancashire society, whh is at present in MS & which he wants you to publish I have no doubt.[1] He is too vain a man to care to encounter a direct refusal of this story,—& will sound you on the subject I have no doubt before long. He is a clever painstaking man, and has really laboured hard to make this novel a good picture of country Lancashire society—manufacturers touching on the domains of squires of strong character & old family &c—but sooner or later, take my word for it, you or Mrs Smith will hear this subject gently touched upon.\Marianne begs you will watch his left eye, & provide him with Savoy biscuits./ You are so good about my 'lark' that I must send you my sonnet. There was a philanthropic concert given lately by some ladies & gentlemen—Mr Furnivall among the number,—to people in Field Lane, Holborn,—admission 2d; Thompsons, Lushingtons & other Working Men's College people went—among others our dear little friend Miss Thompson, who sings beautifully,—but who is quite proud enough to feel herself a little offended at the fulsome praise of a certain newspaper called the Bloomsbury news. Now I had a vol: of poems sent me the other day, full of sonnets to Dickens, Carlyle &c &c,—*such* bad ones; & the parcel contains this book sent to\her 'from/the author,' & my own dear precious sonnet.

> Sweet Vocalist; the Nightingale of sound!
> Singing soft music to enraptured ears,
> With heart as loving as becomes thy years,
> Winning the eyes that circled thee around,
> What matter though thine auditors were poor,
> Unwashed and ragged, the mere sons of toil,
> Wearing their lives out with perpetual moil,
> With look-out dreary as the dreariest moor,
> Thy tune-pipe blenched not at the highest notes,
> With love as well as harmony inspired;
> As little warblers strain their feathery throats
> When neighbouring nests their melodies have fired,
> Oh! mayest thou Maiden! mint thine heart of gold
> And pour its treasures in some bosom bold!

(Would you like it for the Cornhill?)

> Ever yours most very gratefully & truly
> & with kind regards to Mrs Smith,
>
> E C Gaskell

---

[1] *Scarsdale*, Smith & Elder, 1860, published anonymously.

₀ **463** ₀

UNKNOWN

42 Plymouth Grove
Ap: 16th 1860.

My dear Sir,
I was unable to write on Saturday more than the business note I sent you, and which was written rather with a view to its being showed to Mr Harper. Today I am anxious to let you hear from me on the subject of a preface or introductory chapter. A preface I object to as bringing me so personally before the public and after the quizzing in the Saturday Review on introductory Chapters as being a means of knotting unconnected stories together, I would rather not write one. I have however written the few lines which I enclose and which I hope you will like & accept instead of the preface or introductory chapter.
    Hoping you hear that you will accept the substitute
                    Believe me to remain
                        Very truly yours
                            E C Gaskell

₄₆₀ **464** ₄₆₅

MARIANNE GASKELL

[?Early May ?1860]

My dearest Polly,
Two lines to say nothing is happening. Dicky is very ill, & has been ever since Wednesday. 'Pip' & 'Roup' the Bird doctor Meta brought last night says it is, & cut open his throat, & gave him a drop of castor oil, treatment that Hearn & I repeated this morning. Meta & I went to call on Lily Robertson yesterday. She was very nice—Meta says just what she expected—'is coming on Monday,' —&c. Letters from Miss Maclean & Mrs Chas Souchay today. Miss V. d. N. asks 120£ (which she won't get.) Miss Maclean thinks there's an opening for Miss V. d N near Lichfield. Mrs Hampson[1] ill, so I've been at school this morng—Meta is there

---

[1] See p. 620 below. However, 'Miss V. d N' could be the 'Miss V. d. Noddgeries' of p. 550 above.

now.\Misses/Rankin Mitchell & Longeridge coming to tea (&
Rock Partridges—) Beautiful Hallé last night. Mr W Behrens goes
on Monday week. I am not over bright, being tired so no more
[paper torn; some words missing] dear love to Louy,—

Your very affec[tionate]

E C G.

464 **465** *465a

MARIANNE GASKELL

Sunday afternoon
[?Early May 1860]

My very dearest Polly,

It is hard work writing a novel all morning, spudding up
dandelions all afternoon, & writing again at night. Moreover I had
a *dreadful* headache on Friday; was utterly Kilt[1] & incapable—
whch came, I suppose[,] from my going with Julia to the theatre
on Thursday. I told you, didn't I, that they had asked her to go to
tea there with Lucy; well; instead about 4 Anne B came to say
she was going to take Mrs Ellis a drive, & after that wd call for us
& take us to the play ('Dead Heart',[2] Webster & Miss Woolgar,
—) so we dressed, & I wrote a bit more at my story, & a ring
(front door) came, & I rushed and it was the *post*, bringing yr
letter asking for your gown; so Hearn & I did some further
rushing, & then I left H to take it down in a cab. The letter *ought*
to have come on Thursday *morng*; and again *this* morning came
both your Friday's letter (acknowledging gown, & enclosing
Meta's,) and your Saturdays long acct of your doings. I suspect it's
at your end things go wrong, from the post marks. There is very
little to tell you my darling—your letters are my great events.
Lily Wildes [?] has got a daughter. I see nobody, my employments being as aforesaid. I am getting on with my book; 117
pages done *of* 570 *at least*; and I've broken my back over dandelions. And I have not got a cook;[3] and I don't know where we

---

[1] Wright's English Dialect Dictionary gives the meaning of this word as 'upset'.
This word is also found in Letter 422. In Mrs Gaskell's usage it appears to mean
'exhausted'.

[2] By Watts Phillips. First performance at the Adelphi on 10 November 1859.

[3] See p. 617 below.

are to go to, any more than you do, and am too squeezed-dry of energy by the time I have done my book & my dandelions to see about either one thing or another. Pilkington[1] has turned up in England *quite* suddenly; no one knows why. L V J sent me word, \at Moss Bank/having had a telegram, saying he was in England, going to the Drawing room, would come down to the North in a few days. No address nor nothing. Please write in my name to Secretary amateur Exhn and ask where Meta's Florence[2] is, and if sold, *who bought it.* I am sadly afraid Mary Broadleas Ewart did. Mrs Smith & the Ewarts live within 5 minutes of each other so you might kill both tog[e]ther. Also the W Gregs do not live very far from the Shaen's West Hill, Wandsworth so those might be killed together. Go straight up from Putney Station following yr nose till you come to Wimbledon Common, take *left* hand road & Wm Greg's house is (I *think*) *second* to the left, in a garden &c. Ida Cameron is here staying from yesterday. What do you think of *Heidelberg*[?] Julia's heart is set on fruit. There is no need to fix, only keep thinking, will you[,] love? Heidelberg *might* not be hot *on the hill* close to the Castle,—goodbye my darling. Ever your very affec[tionate] Mammy

No letter from F G today. Always describe *dress*, it amuses me, & relaxes my mind. Any Darbishire gossip?

*

*465a **466** 471

?MARIANNE GASKELL

[?Early May 1860]

⟨. . .⟩ Mrs Coleridge writes a very nice letter saying 'Helen wants {you}\MA/to go back for 4th June'; and I suppose you would like it my darling? No more letters from Meta[.] I should think it was warm down there. Send an idea for *sleeves* for Julia's silk gown. Am not I taking life coolly? I did so enjoy your letter. What about Mr Ronald C.[?] What about everything indeed. You did *not* enclose Michele's bill. This is very stupid, but I am very stupid. You can't think how hard I have worked all week. How did Meta's gown look[?] Papa goes to London about June

---

[1] Captain Pilkington Jackson.   [2] Doubtful reading.

20th, cow calves a little earlier. Julia's & F E's holidays begin about same time. Oh! I am so tired of my story. I dream about it. It is lovely hot weather[,] lovely for doing nothing I mean. Will you take into your consideration cow calving, holidays Mrs Smith; no cook &c &c &c, and then say where we are to go to? Versailles? Dieppe[,] Avranches, Bamborough, Skye, Store-away[,]¹ Heidelberg,—I am in a perplexity about Caroline too,— you would see what she said to Meta about her mother wanting her to have higher wages,—(which is a shame of the old woman, considering the expense of bringing C. over, her millinery & hairdressing lessons &c &c.) C. was very nice about it. I said I cd not give her more; that I had given her as a present 2£, towards going to see her mother at H this summer, & she might ask her mother if she would rather see her or the money,—which she has done; but no answer has been received. C. said 'I told my mother perhaps you would be going sometime to H, & wd take me'—but I said if we took any one abroad I thought it would be *Hearn* who wished so much to go'. For some reasons I would rather put off the going from home till later; on acct of my book, cow calving, great heat for travelling &c—again on the other side,—now we are without a cook and it is always pleasanter to leave as few servants as possible idle in a house, doing nothing. You are South, —Meta ditto, & those expenses may be saved. All now are speaking against the healthiness of *Jersey* at any rate in summer— Guernsey is more bleak, open & bracing, but still rather swarming with [(]*house*) insects⟨...⟩

₀ **467** ₀

HENRY SOMERSET²

Plymouth Grove
May 14 [1860].

Sir,

I am extremely obliged to you for the full particulars you have had the politeness to send me. I had received a note from Mr Rickards this afternoon, stating what he had done. I believe now that I did not date my note, as I imagine from both what you & he

¹ ? Stornoway.
² *Annotation* From Mrs Gaskell . . . to myself. H[enry] S[omerset] 1860 *and* 'A spinning wheel was given her.'

say that she has only *just* delivered it, and that in the case of emergency you name. I gave the note to her last Wednesday *fortnight* I *believe*; *week* I am certain, and I told her to take it to Mr Rickards, who I was sure would put her in the way of receiving a little out-of-doors relief to help out the scanty earnings she described herself as receiving. She has been known to me ever since her husband's death; and I have once set her up with a wheel. I name all this to show that I did not trouble you & Mr Rickards until I had tried one or two means of putting her in a way of earning a livelihood. Once more allow me to thank you, & believe me to remain yours truly E C Gaskell

Perhaps I might request you to show this note to Mr Rickards.

0 **468** 469

Mrs Fielden

42 Plymouth Grove
Manchester.
May 28th[1] [1860]

Dear Madam,
I think Mrs Pearson Langshaw has told you of my great wish to engage your cook, 'Ferguson['] and Mrs Langshaw tells me also how much you value her. I did hope to have gone to Alderley this week, from which place I thought I would try and go over to Smallwood, to see Ferguson, and make what I hope would be final arrangements. But I am quite detained at home; and instead, I wonder if you could conveniently spare Ferguson to come over here for a day, (I, of course, paying her expences,) when I could see her, and explain what her work would be &c. I am almost afraid of urging this request, as I am sorry to hear that Mr Fielden is an invalid, & it may not suit you to spare so valuable a servant even for a day. We have only a *February* Bradshaw at hand, but I enclose a list of trains from Sandbach, as it may help you to decide if you can spare her; and then perhaps you will let me know at what time she can come. I shall *prefer* a day after Thursday next. Of course I shall gladly allow her to go to Church; all our

[1] Suspect date. See p. 619, n. 3 below.

servants go there, excepting a German maid, and one who is an Independent. (We have five women-servants, and an out-of-doors-man, or gardener.) I think I need not go through the form of asking you for Ferguson's character, as the regret you express at parting with her tells me sufficiently what she is. I have no doubt she will find this a much busier place than yours, as we are a large family,—(Mr Gaskell, myself, and four daughters, not always at home, cook, housemaid, waiter[,] nurse, and sempstress.) But I shall be very glad to make arrangement with her, in consideration of this. Of course, if we suit, I shall be sorry to part with her; but I like her feeling of attachment to you so much, that if you and she ever wish to come together again, I will gladly agree to it, and try to do the best I can in other ways. Believe me to remain dear Mrs Fielden

Yours very truly
E. C. Gaskell

If I know when she comes, I will send a servant to meet her at the Station, as she may be a stranger in Manchester.

468 469 0

Mrs Fielden

42, Plymouth Grove.
Tuesday. [May 1860]

Dear Madam—

I wrote to you yesterday—& should not trouble you with another letter—but as I see your post-town is Stoke-upon-Trent & I directed Sandbach—I think you may not receive my letter. I am very much obliged to you for your kind note. I am afraid I cannot go to see Ferguson this week—as I am exceedingly busy—but I should be very glad if you could spare her to come & see me any day after Wednesday—as I should much like to see her. With many thanks for the trouble you have taken

I am—dear Madam

Sincerely your's
E. C. Gaskell—

₀ **470** ₀

UNKNOWN

Plymouth Grove
May 26th [?1860]

Dear Sir,

I find that Mrs Lyall (*The Close, Winchester*) has *never* received a copy of 'Right at Last'.[1] I am *very* much surprized at this; as you, yourself asked me to whom I should like copies to be sent, and I am sure I named Mrs Lyall. May I ask if Mr Fulcher, & Mr Russell have received their copies, as I have heard nothing from either of those gentlemen. Of course the grace & courtesy of a presentation copy is destroyed by it's not being sent *early*. I am extremely annoyed about it, and beg to remain,

Yours truly
E C Gaskell

466 **471** ◦472+

MARIANNE GASKELL[2]

Saturday morng [?26 May 1860][3]

My dearest Polly,

All is undecided—Julia & I are going to Selina's at Alderley in a very short time, to be there by dinner at 2. {Papa can} & stay till Thursday. Papa came home last night from Warrington, *very* flat, —I don't know what is the matter with him, he *says* nothing is, but he is in that silent depressed way, whh is very unusual with him when he has been from home. However I had not a pretty piece of news to greet him with,—The house was robbed on

---

[1] Published in 1860 in book form.

[2] *Address (on envelope)* Miss Gaskell | John Hawkshaw's Esq | 43 Eaton Place | Belgrave Sq | London. *Postmark* MANCHESTER | 6 X | MY 25 | 60.

[3] 25 May 1860 (postmark) is a Friday. Perhaps the envelope does not belong to this letter, a fact that would remove the difficulty that Ferguson is said to have called, although Letter 468 of 28 May is to arrange an interview. On the other hand, Catherine Winkworth in a letter of [Monday], 28 May, states that Mrs Gaskell and Julia were then at Alderley 'for a day or two'. *Letters and Memorials*, ed. Winkworth, II, p. 302.

Thursday evening,—when Julia was at home, (she knows nothing of it,) with Hearn Mary & Caroline. Luckily, they *only* took a round of beef, lying in salt, & all the towels & dirty clothes out of the wash-house,—the *back-door* must have been left open, (which annoys Papa,) & Lion did *not* bark, whh make the Police & all of us think it must have been some one in the habit of coming about the house—some of those horrid Dripping women I think, whom Sarah brought about the place. She had left (breakfast, & supper things unwashed) at 10 o'clock AM; so one can't suspect her. Such a good riddance! However though it is vexatious enough perhaps it may be a warning; as the servants were evidently terribly frightened—Mary & Hearn sitting up the greater part of the night, for they feared some one was in the house &c &c. I came back at 2 yesterday from Knutsford,—Flossy had slept with me at Cousin Mary's & was very nice,—I told her about the *possibility* of Heidelberg; & she was very nice & reasonable about it; & suggested once that we shd, if we went, ask Emily *or* Ellen G. to accompany us, she paying of course, as they were so wanting change &c, & Mrs G. had said when she heard of Meta's going 'Oh, *if* &c.' This I thought *very* nice of F E. I must go to Mrs Nicholls before I go to Alderley, so I must scutter over this note, my childie. I send on a note from Mrs Dicey, unread,—& one from H B I think, & there *is* one for you, somewhere, only I'm afraid I have lost it, from Mrs Hampson, all about her resignation &c.—though I did not read that—

Well! When I came home, I found this news of the robbery, and a note from Anna Behrens offering to take me a drive at 3, & the cook Ferguson, come over from Sandbach for a personal interview bringing the highest character from Mrs Fielden, for everything *but* temper. She is a little pleasant-looking quiet woman; she told me of her temper herself, but 'never sulks', else I had meant to ignore it. She had dined here before I came & the servants (Mary away) had liked her. *But*—how funnily things hang together!—the clergyman who is to take Mr Fielden's place, has met with a curate to take *his*, so he can come to Smallwood on June 30th, & Ferguson can leave on July 2nd & would not like to be above a fortnight at her sisters, *without* paying her something; so, after the middle of July, if we did not want her we should have to pay her 8s a week till she came; which Papa in his present frame of mind does not like. *Mary* does not want Ferguson to come till we are at home; else she might come & preserve.—

Mrs Fielden told *me* she would *not* give up the charge of their house till the middle of July & could wait till August. So that's *rather* a reason *against* going from home now; but I don't know if a sufficient one. I *asked* Emily if I might, if need were, have F E a week{s} sooner—& she hesitated, & said she wd think of it. I find fare 2nd class to Hull is 13s. 6d; from Hull to Antwerp 1£. Now fare *by excursion* to London, is 12-6, second class, (all are *return* tickets,) and 1—1, first.—Antwerp boats sail at 11, and 12 midday, —fare to A. £1-8s. Now second class *excursion* to London wd not be agreeable I think,—however we must try & wait a day or two before deciding,—& if we did fix to go viâ Hull, on the 14th? (*Wednesday* I mean) you cd come down on the Monday. Papa is, as I say, so distant & out of spirits, I don't like worrying him by consulting him. Miss A Behrens took me to call on Mrs Sam Ashton, & I improved the shining hour by setting her to work to look after the Didsbury schoolmistress & report—Then to Sophie Gaddum's, who is expecting her confinement at the *end* of this month,—is very much out of spirits, & just going to write to you to beg you to go & spend a few days with her, said her husband was so fond of you. If you were at home the week after next I promised for you, as I thought it seemed quite a piece of kindness —no day or time fixed. A letter from Mr Huth, offering all sorts of kind things through his agent at Hull about the Antwerp Steamer, —& offering to enquire about lodgings at Wiesbaden; and a scrap from Meta enclosing a letter to Effie Wedgwood; from Mentone;[1] *Palm* Sunday again, she says, & exact anniversary of the same,— next place to write to *Arona* Lago Maggiore,—though before she gets there, there are all sorts of places to be scrambled through on the Col di Tenda, Val d'Aosta &c. No news, &c. These were all the letters, except a scrap from Mrs Winkworth—saying Katie had had an attack of pleurisy,—they were going to her,—& so Julia would have to be content with Alice; whh Miss Julia does not like. This is an unsatisfactory letter as to plans &c,—but you will understand it, my darling, & 'lights' and 'advice', and your address at Brighton, thankfully received by your ever most affect[ionate]

E C G

I am glad you are going to the W Gregs,—you'd have to leave your *smart* clothes at home.

[1] See p. 630 below.

458 **472** 486

EDWARD CHAPMAN

43 Eaton Place,
Saturday, June 9th [1860]

Dear Sir,

(I came up here suddenly on Wednesday, on account of my daughter's illness.)[1] I cannot quite understand this account, which has been sent on from home. I have no doubt I had all those books in 1856, though I have now no recollection of them; and I think it is rather strange that the account against me was not sent in, when I had money in your hands from the sale of Cranford &c. The books sent on Febry 26th in this year, you yourself were so kind as to say I might have without payment if they were for me to make a present of to any private friend; and I replied to you that they were, & expressed my obligation for your kindness.

If you will kindly rectify the bill, I will at once pay you what I owe you.

Yours very truly
E. C. Gaskell

*

462 **472a** 495

GEORGE SMITH

Friday
Cowley House Oxford
[?29 June 1860][2]

My dear Mr Smith,

Now I dare say it *is* my stupidity, so I will apologize for the trouble I am giving before-hand—But where *is* the MSS—Oh! if it is lost, I shall have to hang myself! I thought it *might* be gone to Miss Shaen's

West Hill
Wandsworth

where I shall meet Marianne *to-morrow*; but this morning came my dear Cornhill, all safely *here*; so, please, where *did* I tell you to

---

[1] See p. 631 below. 6 June was on Wednesday in 1860.

[2] See below, p. 631. Marianne was, we assume, returning from Brighton to set out on the Heidelberg trip.

send the MSS? for of course it is my fault. I *am* so penitent? I shall
be at Heidelberg when the famous once-in-ten-years Miracle
Play is performed at the Ammergau,—make it worth my while,
and I'll go as your 'Special Correspondent'. Oh dear! Please
where *is* the MSS. Direct to Miss Shaen's as above.

Yours very truly
E C Gaskell.

Mr Munro has given me a Photograph of his medallion of Mrs
Smith[.]

*472+ 473 474

MARIANNE GASKELL[1]

Heidelberg as you know
Wednesday, past 12, noon
[?1 August 1860]

Really my dearest Polly, my date is all I've got to tell you since
last night. I went to bed, and Julia, like a young angel got up &
took my letters to the post at the railway Station betimes this
morning, i.e. before 8. (What time do you get my letters at,
exactly—). Then she brought {you}\F G/& me our breakfasts in
bed, for oh! I was so tired! with packing, & call{ing}s and close
air (at music at the Museum last night,—Dr Otto, Miss Kell & Mr
Schwann being our chaperones—), and then I brushed Flossy's hair
for an hour, & got clothes ready (such a heap!) for *our* Wasch
Frau, whom I have recommended to the Wheeler Smiths,—and
and [sic] then while I was writing the beginning of this note Miss
Hall came to call, & sate till dinner; and now, if we go out
directly, the chambermaid will brush our\sitting/room{s} which
it wants sorely! and I am going to telegraph to you, for I cant
bear to think of your having the fatigue of going to Bingen, & am
so afraid my letters won't reach in time to stop your setting off.
There is no great amount of news going here. I am going to take
your note to A Mohl. But I suppose she sent off the box last night
with the other dictionary. The prussian Corps is going to have a
great show on Friday—each student has subscribed *50* gulden; &
they are to have an illumination, & an affair up the river, & music,
& a procession, & no one knows what besides,—grandeur untold.

---

[1] We associate this with the next letter.

Mr Wheeler Smith Junior is setting up a small friendship with F G. J has given me such a dreadfully rare fern, I am frightened out of my life about it,—sun & rain & all the elements are to combine in happy proportion to keep it alive—& oh! the care to be taken[.] Your letters are one great pleasure—Don't be proud! Condescend to describe *your* dinners: & to all sorts of details. *Bitte.*

Your ever affect[ionate]
E C Gaskell

473 **474** 475

MARIANNE GASKELL[1]

[1 August 1860]

½ past 10, Wednesday Evening, My own dearest Polly, This note came as you see only a very little while ago, many of our things being already packed up; books, boots &c &c, and all our clothes dirty since the beginning of last week; I send it on as fast as I can to you, but I don't know when you will get it. I hope in time to prevent your having the fatigue of going to Bingen—Florence has offered to take it by the 8 o'clk post, but I don't know when you will get it. As moreover I have written to Isabella Fergusson to tell her to come to us on *Friday* I think I ought to write & tell *Mary* that she is coming, & of the change of plans; so no more at present from your very affect[ionate] mother   E C G

474 **475** *475a

MARIANNE GASKELL

Thursday morning
[Early August 1860]

My dearest Polly,

We are still here; I hardly know why, except that I do not feel comfortable in leaving you, my childie; and that I feel myself a bit languid and tired; and Julia is a good deal so; she is now resting in bed (½ p 9 o'clock). She is not *in the least* ill, no more am I. Another thing is that I keep daily & almost hourly expecting to

---

[1] This is a note on a telegraph form, from William Gaskell to his wife, bei Müller Anlagen | Heidelberg | Baden, dated from Manchester, 31 July 1860: 'Stay till you hear from me.'

hear from Meta; it seems so strange she does not write. Our last letter from her you saw, from Berne, a fortnight ago; I have written to every address she gave; and tho' in my last letter\to Paris/I said we were coming home, as planned a week ago, yet as Papa says she was to arrive at home last Saturday, she would hear both from him, Mary Ewart & housemaid Mary that at any rate we were not returning just at present, and I thought she would write directly, and perhaps say something about Papa's wishes &c. I think that whenever we come, (I suppose I *can't* have an answer from Papa to my last Saturday's letter just yet, considering he is in Scotland,—I rather reckoned on receiving a letter from Meta, *from home*, written on *Sunday*, to guide me,) I shall try and *see* Dr Engelmann, so as to hear his opinion of you, exactly; what are *causes*, and *remedies* &c. If I do *not* manage this will you ask *Hearn* to be with you sometime, when *you* do it; that we may have as much security as possible that you do, what you ought to do, Missie! I mean that you *remember* what you are to do. *What causes the indigestion.* Are you likely to be ordered to Schwalbach, I *fancy* so; because it is the great place for remedying weakness. If I could have easily left the girls here I should have come over myself to ascertain all these things on the spot. Please, my darling, don't spare money for what you really want; although you need not buy a dozen bad eggs again. You don't say anything as to how far Hearn could have time to *mend some of our clothes,* (stockings buttonless shifts, with frilling & lace torn &c.) *after* she has done yours; which were in a very dilapidated state when I sent them off? If she *would* have, I would put our *rags* into the smaller bonnet box, and you would have to buy materials (buttons, muslin &c) at K—. I think that is all the *business*. If a letter came, deciding our course, I should try and get off the next morning, telegraphing to you to meet us.\at Bingen as before/We have very fine weather here now but I think I am cowardly in shrinking from the journey to Cologne; with my no-knowledge of German: and also I *am* uneasy even here about you, and I know I should be 10 times more so in England. Now back to Monday. I went myself with the letter to you to the post; and came back literally *wet* through with 'honest sweat', though I had not hurried at all. I took off my *stays* put on petticoats, silver-grey gown, blk mantilla and just received a note from Mrs Hall, asking us to walk to coffee at Ziegelhausen (above the Stift Müller,) the next day at 4; to meet on the bridge, & then we went to the 4 o'clk train to Mannheim; meeting all the world at the station; Jamisons, Anna Mohl, Miss Hall, Adolph Udde's, Mrs Ward, King of Spain's brother-in-law, Mr Becher, Mr Schwann, Miss Kell, Baron V. Ketenbuch, Mr Furnival *&c &c*. Off we went to Mannheim. Performance did not begin till 6 so we wandered about in the Park, being bitten by gnats, at their good pleasure; they had fair play with my thin dress, & there was no need to wish them 'Bon Appetit!' for such a miserable mask as I ended by being was never seen or known before. Well! we went to see Ristori at last! and anything more magnificent I never saw. But I am not going to bore you by raptures. Miss Kell kept wishing to see her 'in repose'—'in a quieter character' &c, whh if it had come from any one less kind that [*sic*] Miss Kell has been would have enraged me extremely—as it was I did not attend to her small running commentary, so I kept my temper. It was over by $\frac{1}{4}$ past 8; and on coming out we found it raining, the streets all one puddle we in summer clothes, and no umbrellas. We managed badly. (Mr Schwann is very kind *but* 'ne scait pas vivre,' as dear Madame Mohl would say; does not know how to manage,—the Jamison party had ordered tea *before* going to the theatre, as they had learnt when the return train to Heidelberg was—not till 10; so they went comfortably to an Inn close by\the theatre/; had tea, & at the right time had a drosky,—while we, on coming out of the theatre wandered about disconsolately in the rain, looking for a carriage, which we met at last when we were wet through, close to the railway station; in the waiting room of which we had to stay for an hour & a half,—crowded, smoking &c &c. At last I got some hot coffee for the girls, as we had not ordered anything here, & I thought it possible that we should be unable to get any, as proved to be the case. Home; to bed; after I had warmed a little water, & given each of the girls a little *very* weak — and water, to try & keep off the cold which I feared they might have caught, but I think Julia's tiredness is a little the result of the wetting. It is not much; and she is very well, except for that. Tuesday morning I went leaving the girls resting in bed, & called on the V. Gagarns, A Mohl, (to get some comfortable sympathy about Ristori, & also to hear when Mme Paris Mohl is coming here,—in about a week Anna & I make out—only I half fear she is *not* coming here, but going to stay at Stuttgart, where she wants Anna & me to go over for a day to see her; but I can't leave the girls—Home, dinner; we retained our places near the bottom of the table,\We are down

again in Miss Kell's place/though the W Smiths were gone—
After dinner Mr Schwann called to settle Ristori accounts. Places
2 gulden each. Then we got ready to go to the rendez-vous on the
bridge for Mrs Hall's party. Ourselves, Mr Maltby, Mr Pennycuik,
Mr Furnivall, Col: & Mrs Fleming Mrs & Miss Hall, Mr Hermann
Jones, Mrs and the two younger Miss Fennells. At the sight of
these latter my two young ladies rebelled; & I had to read a lecture
on the duty of being *polite* to friends' friends &c. We walked
slowly along to Zeigel-hausen, hearing of a dance that was to be
given there the next day by a Mrs Rainsford (à la Stift Müller) to
which every one, save ourselves was going; poor little Julia's
heart yearned to go, especially when we saw a great beautiful
large room, opening out of the garden, with a good piano in it.
However Mrs Rainsford was already overdone with young
ladies, and was in vain search of young men most of these latter
article{s} having gone away, the Semester being ended.\The
Semester is not ended/So we contented ourselves with coffee in
the garden, & games à la your coming at/the Speyer Hof, bowing
& curtseying &c &c. Then we all came home in a boat, having the
most lovely sunset on one side over the plain & on the other a
rain-mist, all soft golden,\before the purple hills/with a great
rainbow spanning it, & falling into the dark woods: there was
a pretty sharp shower of rain which wetted us, but we did
not mind that.\I did *very* much mind the rain.[1]/We landed
near the railway Station about 8 o'clk, and separated at the end
of the Anlage—the Fennells were really very nice and kind;
Mrs F asked leave to call on us; and the girls took their wraps and
sheltered *our* girls from the rain. When we came home we found
Miss Kell was going to Baden the next day on her way into
Switzerland and she asked if we would allow her to come and sit
with us a little the next morning before starting. Then we went to
bed, being all tired and dampish. Julia for four or five mornings
past, has got up very early to give us our breakfast, & I think that
has tired her a little. Yesterday morng Miss Kell & Mr Schwann
came up. He was going to take his Aunt to Baden, & to return in
time to go to Mrs Rainsford's dance. I read them an account of the
Ammergau Play, out of the London Guardian that Mr Maltby had
lent me; & I think they will both go to one of the Septr Repre-
sentations. I like Miss Kell; she is very good & unselfish; a little
borné, à la Hampstead Unitarians, but very kind. Then we

---

[1] This insertion is not in Mrs Gaskell's hand.

began to take back all our borrowed books, and wind up our affairs as much as we could, in order to be tolerably ready for a start in case we heard from Meta or Papa, wishing us to return. Mrs Fennell called, & asked us to tea there tonight; could not accept till after the\afternoon/post had come in.—At dinner (we returned to our old places near the Pittmans) we heard rumours of a torch-procession from the English,—we went to the Harge-dorn's room to ask if it was true; and they knew no more than we did. So (I was anxious to console Julia for not going with all the English world to the Rainsford's dance) we set out on an enquiring expedition, first to yr pastry cook's, where I got a dictionary, and found my words; I received an explicit answer from a disreputable-*looking*, very polite yellow-capped student, that there was to be a torch procession from the Prussian Kreisse to the Hirsch-gasse at 9 o'clock. Then we went to Schifferdecker's and asked for leave to {stay}\be/in the shop at 9,—granted; on to buy fruit for Julia,—home, told Hargedorns, who asked to go with us, and then I went & told the Yaldwyns, (General & family) & then paid a call on the Honorable & Reverend Clements, (who had called on me, & invited the girls to drive with them to the Wolfs' brunnen—Ellinor saw the Father Clements when he was hunting about for rooms,—and to my dismay 2 out of the 6 Miss Clements also asked if they might join us,—so there was I, with two daughters, 4 Hargedorns, & 2 Clements to see after. Then we had coffee,—and then we sallied out in the dark to Schifferdeckers. No wonder people called us an 'Institut'; nine ladies.—But it was worth any amount of being laughed at. I never saw anything so picturesque as the light of the torches and the red mist ascending between the houses as we saw them coming along the Haupt Strasse, a capital band playing all the Student songs,—men on each side carrying torches flaming wildly, and the students in the dress of their respective corps, {all} walking two and two in the middle; the corps being divided by banner-carriers. The dress consisted of caps, sashes of the corps-colours, white full trowsers, stuffed into high black leather boots, coming above the knee;—after the train of 400 had passed we rushed down past Rupprechts to see them going over the bridge towards the Hirschgasse,—the reflections in the water were beautiful—all the while the Clements were *shying* the Hargedorns, (Alwina being particularly noisy & merry), & quoting their cousin the Marchioness of Londonderry to me;—they live in Durham,—& seem to be the fag-end of several noble families, Lord Leitrim, Lord Albemarle, &c &c. I was thankful when I got my party home—but they were very grateful,—the Hargedorns especially, as I had persuaded Mrs H to go. To bed,—& up again. Oh! we found Mr Becher's P.P.C. card (most of the students are off this morning.) & Mr Schwann's with a little pencil note to say that there was a torch procession to be seen off the bridge.—And so that bring me up to now,—and our present plans are to take Julia to see the Castle, Dort, interior, curiosities &c.\directly after dinner/have coffee up there, come home, go to the Fennell's,—and that's all we look forward to. ½ past 11 and no letter by *this* post. I *wonder* Meta does not write. You are a naughty girl not to warn us off the Wheeler Smiths—however we have been out ever since\they left/when they have called. Why did not *you* like 'em. You had no young men adventures with them had you? *Where* are you poorly? because *there* you can't bathe, so it would be no harm your coming to Bingen, and STOPPING ALL NIGHT *with us, there*; whh would give us a capital oppy of seeing you quietly, which I want to do in order to judge how you are. *Your* letters are *our* great pleasure; we care for all your ins & outs. When does Ellinor leave? My love to her[.] Never be surprized or alarmed at my telegraphing to say 'come &c.'—And——3 callers in succession—A. Mohl. Ellinor likes you *so much*,—she says so in her letter A M read us—Mrs Hall—oh! *so clever, & scandalously* bitter; has asked me to coffee there at 3 tomorrow to meet dear sweet Mme Benecke (I can't think how they come to know each other.) lastly Mme Benecke's own self. So we shan't {come} \leave/*tomorrow* unless indeed we went to Mannheim by the last train,—write my childie as I think we shall *most* likely now stay here till *Papa's* letter comes, which *can't* be before Monday Dinner bell—   Your most affec[tionate] E C G

*   *   *

461 **476** 480

CHARLES ELIOT NORTON

42 Plymouth Grove
Manchester
Monday, August 27 [1860]

My dear Mr Norton,
    I want a letter from you, to hear how you and yours are going on; and I know I don't deserve one till I have written myself.

Thank you *very* much for all your very valuable information about model lodging houses, the beautiful little plan, and the details. A great many of these last have been of much use in several parts of England. It is curious how the conscience of Europe seems awakening to the duty of employing the better wisdom of the educated in this direction. Niettermeyer, the old *Juris Consult* (is not that the grandly correct word?) of Heidelberg, has bought what was the old barrack for the Elector Palatine's soldiers, and is at his own sole expense in his old age turning it into what Germans consider the best style of dwelling for working people. Again there is a little town (name forgotten, but easily to be got at,) on the verge of the Black Forest, where the 'industries' lately cultivated among the Blk Foresters have taken root in the shape of the manufacture of cheap jewellery; gold with a greater\acknow-ledged/proportion of adulteration—(the name has come to me now, it is called Porchheim, or Forchheim, and the jewellery is called *P.* or Forchheim jewellery,—it is near Carlsruhe.) Well! these men who have learnt to be jewellers in the last ten years, and are thriving, and clustering together in this new little town, have been in want of dwellings, and the pastor, the physician (a Dr Otto) and one or two others, have bought land, on which they are building houses on the best & most sanatory German ideas; not great blocks, but separate dwellings, which they have the oppy of doing before Porchheim swells out into a large town. They have a remunerative fixed rent; and also a fixed weekly sum, which, if a tenant pays, in *addition* to his rent, his house becomes his, in so many years. However this letter is going to be gossipy, not philanthropic, only, you see, you led me astray, by having sent me those useful & valuable letters. I wonder when I wrote to you last? I 'guess' somewhere about last April. Well! April went over quietly; then Marianne went up to London for two or three weeks; and on the 6th of May Meta set out for Paris, Lyons, Avignon, Nice, Mentone, *over* the Col di Tenda, Turin, Val d' Aosta, Maggiore, Orta & Varallo, Lugano, Val Anzasca, over the Simplon, La Vallée, Lake of Geneva, Champèry, [*sic*] & Les Diablerets, Thun, Grindelwald, & home by Berne, Strasburg Nancy Paris. There! You can imagine her route, taken with an oldish Miss Darwin (sister of Mr Chas Darwin) in quiet respect-able luxury, stopping where they liked,—and sketching. If you want to know details about any place you must write to Meta and ask for them. *I* go on with my own self. Florence was at school at

Mr Green's Knutsford; my two eldest daughters—(I get rebuffed now if I call them by the dear old words the '*girls*') away; Julia at her day school nearly all day; and Mr Gaskell always constantly away,) so I had a charming quiet time of almost solitude. (I quite understood the wisdom of French ladies going into rétraite [*sic*],— I was so sorry to lose my girls (to *you* I must call them still the *girls*) and yet in the bustling life I too often lead, one has so little time for quiet thought—you understand, don't you.) I got on splendidly too with my new book, that-is-to-be—; I had nearly finished the first vol; and was full of it all when one morng—6th of June, I had a letter from Marianne, written in pencil & in bed from London, saying she was very ill,—supposed to be going to be small-pox. Mr Gaskell was in town, but Agnes Ewart went to ask his leave, & met me with it, at the railway Station, and off I went. Of course, with a suspicion of such a complaint I could not go to any friend's house, as I meant to see Marianne that night,— and it was Cup Day at Ascot, a thing which in my ignorance, I did not know would fill up every possible & hirable bed in London. I did not get there till $\frac{1}{2}$ p. 7, & then began my search for a bed,—at last I got a garret in a back St, & then went to Marianne; who had been left by the family, (female portion of,) to the care of the physician. It was *not* however small only *bad* chicken-pox. To cut a long story short I went after that first night to stay in the house with her; and, if it was chicken pox, she got through it in about a fortnight, & was only very weak; she then went to Brighton, to some friends with whom she was to have stayed before she was ill for sea-air before going for some weeks to a warmer climate, which her doctor ordered; and during the week she was at Brighton I was at Oxford, waiting for her summons to say she was strong enough, & to take her Florence & Julia & our dear Hearn to Heidelberg for the Midsummer holidays. We had *half* promised Julia she should go abroad, (as Silverdale was occupied) in those holidays, and when MA was ordered to have more warmth than our bitterly cold & damp English summer, we thought if we went there probably Meta could join us on her return from her tour—(however Miss Darwin did not like to part with her, so she never came; much to our disappointment and hers.) We were very happy at Heidelberg but Marianne did not get right; had uncomfortable feelings of flushing in her face, and dizziness, which made me very uneasy; so I took her to consult Dr Chelius, a wise old German physician, who ordered her to

Kreuznach; (about the ugliest dullest place in the Rhine Country. —) I took her there leaving Hearn with Florence & Julia at Heidelberg; and we found the place so full that if it had not been for Lady Charlotte Locker's kindness (she was sister to Lady Augusta Bruce) we should not have had a bed one night of our stay. At length I left Marianne there, sending Hearn to her, & Elinor Bonham-Carter, (Hilary Carter's sister,) who had to go to Kreuznach too, was there for a companion; so they two have their little ménage with Hearn for duenna. Marianne had to stay a great deal longer than we expected, and is there still, though she hopes the doctor will let her leave about Septr the 8th. After waiting for her to accompany us home, & finding it in vain, Florence Julia and I came back about 10 days ago, finding Meta returned one week; and Mr Gaskell gone into Scotland for his month's holiday. We have been very happy together, telling our adventures with as much gusto as the one eyed calenders in the Arabian Nights; and settling our home life, to be enriched by Florence's presence here; for she has 'left school', and Meta is going to take a sort of general superintendence and care lest she does not fall into 'young-lady-life'. She is to have Masters, & regular reading, and I am trying not to fall into the temptation of 'making her of use'. She is very dainty-fingered, a beautiful ready workwoman, a capital shopper &c; and *prefers* doing all these sort of little housewife things to anything presenting the least intellectual *effort* or requiring perseverance. And in a busy house such as ours often is, I know I shall swallow up too much of her time, unless I make safeguards against both her & myself in the shape of Masters &c. Meta's present perplexity is about the life of an *amateur*, and an *artist*. That does not explain what I mean, I must go into it more fully. When she was abroad, and drawing hard, she wished (for a time) to become a professional *artist*; to feel that that was to be her principal object in life. I don't know if she has *fully* given up this now; but I think she has. If she really & persistently wished it, I think, at her age, I should think it right to yield, for I believe she has great genius for it; and as, if she had married her life would have been apart & separate from mine, so I think she has a *right* to make it now; although of course it would have been a silent trial to me. But to come to the practical part. She has brought back numbers of *unfinished* drawings; *beautiful* centres, really almost like Turner's, in the middle of a blank sheet of paper,—the surrounding scenery to these centres, only *indicated* to her *memory* by a few pencil sketches. If she is to be an *artist* these careful studies will be of real use to her; an amateur thinks more of the immediate pleasure of those who see his sketches, and would *suggest to the imagination* of others what he saw, by finishing *all* up to a certain point before he began to finish only one part so highly. All the people who have yet seen these sketches are struck with the beauty of what *is* done, but complain that (by washes of colour, say;) more is not done. Meta conscientiously in her artistic conscience—disapproves of washes—is she to draw to give pleasure to others, or to improve herself? You see the complexity of the question, as to selfishness, Goethian theories of self development. I believe it to be *right* in all things to aim at the highest standard; but I can't quite work it out with my conscience, especially as I was so unlucky in the first instance, to express a wish that the whole paper had been covered &c—I wish you would send *your* opinion across the Atlantic. You see Meta yields her own opinion & wishes so immediately that one has to touch her as it were as if she were a butterfly, for fear of her leaving too much of herself in one's fingers. Do you remember our housemaid Mary?—(I have just asked Elliott if she has any message to you—She says 'Oh! Mr Norton. We (in the kitchen, understood) liked him ve⟨ry⟩ much! we wish he'd come again.') So do we in the parlour. I *always* look over the names of the American passengers, thinking you *may* have come. Well! but to go back to Mary. She has been engaged this 8 years to a young man, a very steady respectable fellow, who began a worsted mill at Huddersfield in Yorkshire, about 3 years ago; and he was doing very well, and as soon as he had repaid his borrowed capital (part of it borrowed from Elliott—) they were to have been married. Such a right, constant, prudent engagement; full of deep affection guided by principle. About a week ago Elliott came in crying—'May Mary go off for the day? Mary has heard that Shaw is dying.' I went to her directly; she was as white as a sheet, but quite tearless, making the beds with vehemence, her eyes almost fierce; & her lips clenched. 'Let me see the letter Mary while you go to get ready', and I read that in his own mill the machinery had caught him, & crushed him— some one else wrote 'a very serious accident; all his cry is for you to come to him.' We all speeded her off, and her letters are so pathetic. His right leg is crushed; & tomorrow they decide if he can bear the amputation. He has no partner; his poor little humble mill must go to rack & ruin; but as Elliott says with tears 'I should

not care for the loss of my money a bit if he can only get better.'
And so I shall leave it,—for I know no more what it will please
God to decree. This next September will be a very busy month;
so many people coming. First of all our dear Mr Field, & Mrs
Field come from Coniston next Thursday. Only fancy! they are
the first of our dear dear Roman band, except you. Shan't we
give them a welcome! Oh! I am so glad to thinking [*sic*] of seeing
them both, him especially. That naughty dear Mr Wild has made
off to America without coming near us. Scold him well, he will
mind *you*, and send him {when} to us when he comes back, oh do!
please, we were so fond of him,—his high character, his wit & fun,
& childlikeness,—don't you Americans go & cut us now. He sent
me a little note & a capital photograph of himself, which arrived
when I was at Heidelberg; will you send me his address that I may
write & thank him & scold him. What kind of pens do people
write with in America. I cannot mend quill pens, nor will steel
pens keep good long,—here is a witness thereof—in my writing[.]
So my book will never be written, & I shall end this letter now,
for want of a pen to go on with it with [*sic*]. My kind regards
to your mother, 'Jane' 'Grace', and 'Lowell', & 'Child'. Meta's
love to you—

Yours affectionately

E C Gaskell

*

₀ 477 ₀

UNKNOWN

42, Plymouth Grove,

Tuesday, Septr 4th [1860?][1]

Dear Sir,
    Which am I to thank? you; or Dr John Brown, *involuntarily* and
unconsciously doing me a kindness—? To both and each I send you
my heartiest thanks, but I think the largest share of them must be
yours. Give me an opportunity sometime{s} please, of offering
you practical proof of my gratitude. In great haste

Ever yours very truly

E. C. Gaskell.

[1] 1855 or 1860 are possible years, but on 4 September 1855 Mrs Gaskell was at
Silverdale.

MARIANNE GASKELL

Monday—[?10 September 1860]

My dearest Polly,

You wd have had a letter to greet you in England, had we been *quite* sure of yr departure from Kreuznach.[1] Yes! you would, though we've had no time to brush our hair. Scanty time to wash ourselves—(tell Hearn I've my own doubts as to Julia's *ever* having washed since we left Germany,—and as for her hair! it *looks* all very well, & I have no time to enquire farther). Mary has been away since this day 3 weeks; & ever since Thursday week *backwards* the house has been full; at least nearly so,—Mr & Mrs Field came that day; & stayed till last Wednesday—*he* CHARMING *she* very nice, but almost entirely living in her own room, & liking promiscuous teas, & odd foods, at odd times—and help in all her dressings &c. Effie came on Saturday (week backwards,) a General & Mrs Cotton, (he '*Fred*' Capt Hill's friend—*also* a friend of Mr Field's), on that same Saturday,—to lunch; a Mr MacElroy (friend of Field's) to tea, & generally all Sunday—when the Fields were on the point of going, Mary Holland wrote to offer herself for Friday night,—& Emma Shaen wrote to offer herself 'for a few days' coming to-day;—& oh dear! Papa is not well with his liver; & you can fancy *how* busy we are, & we can't get Mrs Brett & don't know who to get, & Hearn's keys can't be found—&c &c. Ellen Tollet comes on Saturday (no chance of Mary before then, & for some time after I'm afraid,) & the Shadwells (Col: Capt: & Mrs) dine with us on Monday 19. I am so afraid of your coming down into our whirl, & getting knocked up;—only you *must* keep your life tranquil & separate from ours, else all the good of Kreuznach will be thrown away. *Be sure* you do. I tell every body we don't know when you are coming home, just to keep people off from coming to see you, &c. Florence is very good & helpful, but hates her lessons like pison, & the necessary dragon who goes with her, has (*not*) a good time of it. I am going to-morrow. And it is cutting out Clothing time, so I go with her also on Thursdays—both those days are S. of Design—Tuesdays & Fridays Mr Theodores\to which Meta goes/. Tomorrow she is to

---

[1] See p. 639 below.

go ½ pt 2 to Knutsford to the Concert, respecting which we've had a row with Cousin Mary. Particulars when we meet. Susie Scott comes to one o'clk dinner today. Emma Shaen this aft: It's washing day, & Mrs Brett has never turned up; and Georgina has sent to request a private interview with me. I have never had time to write to Mrs Laurence about mutton cutlet & risolle [*sic*]. In fact we are pretty nearly all worn out with dirt & work, & being agreeable. *Mind,* when you come{s} home, take care of *yourself.* I put you under *your own and Hearn's* care. She may prowl about Regent St & pick up fashions, if she likes. I wish for all manner of things from London, but have no time to give directions. I want two *round* half-cut, half moulded glass dishes to go *inside* two of the (immense) tazzas, whh *are* come, but would hold *no end* of preserve, they are so large. And *2* half cut half-moulded oval *or* oblong glass do[.] to hold moulds of rice blancmange &c—But I dare say no one will be going near Phillips & if they do, they'll have no money, only *that* might be left unpaid. Here's G. B. (after dinner) It is such a comfort to think of you in England. Mrs Brett has never come, & the messenger, having gone for her, finds she is 'gone out to work somewhere else', which is too bad, considering that she *knew* it was washing day, & that we were without Mary, & company coming today—Oh dear! poteration[1] take the house.—Moreover we can't get a *bit* of butter;—our butter woman *won't* come, why we can't make out. *Please* bring us some butter from London—*really*, I mean it; for even Williams' make a favour of letting us have their *bad* butter. We can only make about 4lb a week at the *very* outside, & with people in the house we shall make less. Tell Hearn *all* her wits are wanted in this desolate butterless, servantless, headless, washerwomanless, company full household.

Ever your most affect[ionate]
E Gaskell—

P.S. Please tell Hearn we shall be so glad of some Devonshire cream, if she will order it for us—either from London, or by sending the cans for it as soon as she comes back here.

[1] Confusion (English Dialect Dictionary 'potterashun').

478 **479** 484

MARIANNE GASKELL

Saturday noon
[?Late 1860]

My dearest Molly [*sic*],

Nothing happens. Can you borrow Ambarvalia,[1] ditto 'Foster Brothers', & 'Bateman Household',[2] which are books one of my autographs writes, but of which I never heard in my life. Florence & I went to call on the Ed. Behrens, who were out; so we came home, & found Meta lying down. I went to the Shadwells to dinner, in a dress which scandalized my family whose opinions I laughed to scorn. Col. Marriott, Wilbraham, a very nice Capt Carpenter,—& Meta (sent for during dinner) were the party; it was pleasant. To bed; no letters for me; one from Effie to Meta; no news; Meta gone to her old woman; butter scarcer & scarcer; you *could* not bring us a little from Liverpool, could you; it is a case of such destitution that stealing is allowable. Papa has submitted with a tolerable grace to Mrs P. Ainsworth. But I am in a panic about her dulness & dinners. Any advice as to how to make it agreeable thankfully received. Col. S. will breakfast with us on Wednesday.

Your ever most affect[ionate] Mammy.

Go to bed early; bread & milk[.][3]

476 **480** 485

CHARLES ELIOT NORTON

December 10th, 1860

Monday Evng, 20 minutes to 10, sitting all by myself in the drawing room in 46 Plymouth Grove, Manchester.

[1] See p. 75 above.

[2] By James Payn. The last two were published by Hall in 1858 and 1860 respectively.

[3] Difficulties over butter (see p. 636 above), Meta's kindness to an old lady (see p. 638 below?), Mrs Gaskell's solicitude for Marianne's health and the fact that Colonel Shadwell said goodbye in May 1861 (see p. 653 below) seem to make late 1860 a probable date for this letter.

There! my dear Mr Norton, there is a date as particular as if
Dame Quickly herself had written it! When I received your long
kind letter 6 weeks ago, asking for a letter from me 'at Christmas,
if not before', I thought the 'before' so very sure & certain; and
yet now this will only reach you in time to give you my very best
& warmest good wishes on Xmas day, or there abouts. I am glad
you asked for it for *Xmas day*, instead of New Year—the one
always seems to me to be a religious, the other merely a civil,
festival. So you have my best *Xmas* good wishes, dear Mr Norton.
If you were here I should have such numbers of things to talk over
with you that scarcely seem worth putting in a letter; a letter too,
that is to cross the Atlantic, and so ought to be full of great
subjects, greatly treated. Instead of which I am first & foremost
going to tell you where every body is, and how I come to be all
alone. Mr Gaskell is dining out—i.e[.] gone to pot-luck dinner,—
with an invalid member of the congregation. Marianne is gone
across the road to tea with a Mrs Shadwell (née Coleridge, great
niece of *the* C.) wife of a Colonel Shadwell, of whom we have all
become very fond during his 4 year's [sic] residence here, as
\Assistant/Quarter Master General of the Northern Division. He
& his wife are a tolerably young childless couple. He has served in
India, China, & the Crimea, & is a great friend of Ld Clyde's, on
whose staff he was at Balaclava. We don't like *her* quite so much
as *him*. Meta is gone to tea with Mr & Mrs Nicholls the old couple,
who lost their only child John Ashton Nicholls, about a year ago,
and who are ailing, & lonely & poorly just now. Florence & Julia
have gone to bed with bad colds. The weather is damp, and warm,
and rainy, and generally unseasonable & uncomfortable. Our
housemaid Mary, only came back last Saturday week, after a 14
week's [sic] absence. She left her lover *better*; but he had never yet
been able to be moved out of the bed where he was first laid; nor
is he moved yet. But it is a great thing to have saved his life. They
fear however it will be a 'stiff-joint', and, if so, he will be a
cripple for life. Oh! we have had such a busy autumn while she
has been away[.] Almost as bad as the famous Exhibition year for
people coming & going, unexpectedly,—a sort of household 'But
men may come, & men may go, but I (i.e. bustle) go on for ever'
—especially without any housemaid. Poor Elliott, in spite of help,
which did not take off her responsibility,—got knocked up at last,
and on Saturday I packed *her* off home for Christmas, and to see
her mother, who is old & ailing. Hearn is well & bright,—she

came home with Marianne from Kreuznach, very full of foreign experience, having extremely enjoyed the life abroad. And before this you will have seen our dear Fields! I feel as if they would have told you everything about us, and as if it were of no use writing. And yet tonight I receive a little notelet from Mrs Field—Philadelphia Novr 17, so I suppose they have been moving, though I am still sitting in my accustomed place. Florence has left school—perhaps they told you that? being 18 in years, though not that in character, and hardly in looks. But she is having French German & Music lessons at home; and we are reading with her Macaulay's Biographies & Milman's Latin Xtianity and I don't think it is a bad thing for either Marianne, Meta, or myself to have an *obligation* to sit and settle to a little steady reading every day. Marianne has been very well ever since she came back from Kreuznach on September the 14th (missing the Fields to her *extreme* regret) till this last week or so, when I think the damp weather has brought a return of her indigestion[.] She is however looking very well indeed—and even now is much better than she was before she went to Kreuznach. Meta is very well; and not at all troubled—for herself at least—at hearing that Captain Hill is engaged to Miss Matilda Wilson, daughter of the Indian Mr Wilson, whose financial measures called forth the manifesto from Sir C Trevelyan. We hear that Capt Hill is coming over to be married in April, & to be 6 months in England; and Meta's great desire is to avoid any *chance* of falling in with him; consequently she is going up to London to pay a visit to the Wedgwood's in *February* instead of later on. Mr Gaskell is, we hope, going to spend his Xmas holidays at Mr Darbishire's, an old friend in North Wales. I shall probably go and spend a fortnight with some old friends in London in February,—Marianne goes to be bridesmaid to *two* friends in the Spring, at two separate places. So now you know all our probable & possible movements. I go back to the Fields's visit. You can have no notion how we enjoyed it. They were the first of 'our Romans' we had seen since we had that peep at you; and it was a sort of renewing of our youth to see them. We loved both, but very especially 'Jack' more than ever. And oh! the talking, and the jokes & the fits of laughter! Did you not hear us? Since then we have never been alone; and I find two sitting rooms are rather small accomodation [*sic*] for *doing* anything, when there are 4 daughters, and three or 4 visitors inhabiting them. So I seem to have read and written nothing, ever since we came back from Heidelberg. I *must* write though, and finish my book, about one quarter done. One piece of business—very much out of my way—only it really fell in it—I have done this autumn: helped Florence Nightingale and another friend of ours in establishing a Soldier's [*sic*] Home in Gibraltar where they can have cheap refreshments, can read, play games, write letters &c. I am still working at this, as F N. wishes above all things, before she dies, to see such Homes established on a *permanent* footing in all garrison towns. I sent you a 'Rab and his friends'[1] did I not? by the Fields. I hope you like it. Now I must go to bed.

—Wednesday, December 12. My dear Mr Norton, I certainly *have* written to you to thank you very heartily & lovingly for your book on Italy? It has been such a pleasure to read it—I keep putting it down, and fancying I hear your voice saying the different things, and every now and then I differ from you, and want to discuss them with you. How I wish we were likely to see you! There is so much in your letter to Meta, that I do so thoroughly agree with, especially all that part relating to consistency of character. But, as perhaps you can judge from the writing this letter has been taken up at all sorts of different times whenever I had 5 minutes to spare, and I find it difficult to get even an uninterrupted 5 minutes, now we have all four daughters at home; for I like to keep myself in readiness to give them sympathy or advice at any moment; and consequently I do not do as I am often tempted to do, shut myself up secure from interruption in any room. Today is the last day on which I can send off this letter with any hope of it's [*sic*] reaching you on Christmas day; and all day long people have been coming and going, in a provoking way, taking up my fragments of time. Please to give my best wishes to Mrs Norton, and your sisters, and to Mr Lowell,—and our kind love to Mr Wild. Write & tell us all about the Field's [*sic*] visit & ever believe me,

Your affectionate friend
E C Gaskell

[1] By John Brown (1810–82), 1859.

W. S. WILLIAMS[1]

46 Plymouth Grove,
December 20th, 1860.

My dear Sir,—When I was abroad this summer, I was introduced to a Miss Burnett, who asked me for an introduction to Messrs Smith, Elder & Co., with a view to the publication of an MS which she had then in hand. The other day she wrote to claim the fulfilment of my promise; and I have thought it best to perform it by writing direct to yourself, as I have been sending Mr Smith lately so many similar introductions that I have some scruples in troubling him further in that way. Besides you have always been so kind to me, however and whenever I have applied to you, that I think you will forgive me, if my bringing this MS under your notice should uselessly waste your time.

We had the pleasure of seeing Mr Lowes Dickinson last Saturday week, and a real pleasure it was to us. Mr Gaskell missed his share, however, owing to his inevitable Saturday night's sermon, but we hope that Mr Dickinson will come and see us again when he returns to Manchester, and then Mr Gaskell will make up for lost time.

About six weeks ago I paid a visit to Mr Brontë, and sat for about an hour with him. He is completely confined to bed now, but talks hopefully of leaving it again when the summer comes round. I am afraid that it will not be leaving it as he plans, poor old man! He is touchingly softened by illness; but still talks in his pompous way, and mingles moral remarks and somewhat stale sentiments with his conversation on ordinary subjects. Mr Nicholls seems to keep him rather *in terrorem*. *He* is more unpopular in the village than ever; and seems to have even a greater aversion than formerly to any strangers visiting his wife's grave; or, indeed, to any reverence paid to her memory, even by those who knew and loved her for her own sake. He refused to christen Mr Greenwood's last child when he heard that it was to be named 'Brontë' after her, and the child remained unchristened for six months in consequence, when its great delicacy coming to Mr Brontë's knowledge, he sent for it privately and christened it in his own room. When Mr Nicholls came upon its name upon the

---

[1] From a printed source.

register book, Mr Greenwood says that he stormed and stamped, and went straight home to the Parsonage to Mr Brontë to ask him for his reasons in going so directly against his wishes. Fortunately Mr Brontë had the excellent defence of saying that if the child had died unchristened Mr Nicholls' case would have been extremely awkward, and that he had thus saved him from a great scrape.— Believe me yours most sincerely,

E. C. Gaskell.

450 **482** 489

W. W. and/or EMELYN STORY

[?1860]

⟨. . .⟩ I think Rome grows almost more vivid in recollection as the time recedes. Only the other night I dreamed of a breakfast— not a past breakfast, but some mysterious breakfast which neither had been nor, alas! would be—in the Via Sant' Isidoro dining-room, with the amber sunlight streaming on the gold-grey Roman roofs and the Sabine hills on one side and the Vatican on the other. I sometimes think that I would almost rather never have been there than have this ache of yearning for the great witch who sits with you upon her seven hills.

0 **483** 0

MARK PATTISON

46 Plymouth Grove
Manchester
Janry 26th [1861]

Dear Mr Patteson [sic],

I saw in one of our Manchester papers yesterday what I am delighted to learn, that you are the Rector of Lincoln's. Mrs Brodie, whose anxiety on the subject made her fearful I dare say, had told us that you were not likely to obtain that honour, which, (may I say it?) all your friends knew you so well deserved; there-fore the little paragraph gave us the shock of a joyful surprize;— and you must let us Gaskells congratulate you on the splendid scarlet gown they hope to see you wearing with all the dignity of a Head the next time they go to St Mary's. Seriously dear Mr Patteson you must kindly accept the sincere congratulations of my daughters[,] Mr Gaskell and of

Yours most truly
E. C. Gaskell.

I am half afraid of putting 'Rector of Lincoln's' on the address of my letter, for fear it should not be true.

479 484 *484a

MARIANNE GASKELL

Mrs Lyall's. The Close.
Feb. 28th [?1861][1]

My darling Minnie, Mama has just gone to dine at the Deanery, to meet the Judges etc., who came into town today, & were received & preached to, in the Cathedral with great pomp & show. Perhaps I am going in afterwards, with Miss Lock; but I do not know whether I shall or not, as it is my last night with Louy. Yesterday we had a most successful pleasant day down at Portsmouth. Mama, Miss Lock, & I left here by the 9:54 train, & were met at P. abt an hour & a half afterwards by Capt. Xian: (is he really 'after' Sophy? If so, good luck for her)—a tall, gentlemanly, slammocky-as-to-figure man, *something* like a young slight grave Mr Rickards in face. He took us down to the docks, where his boat was waiting for him, &—Friday morning. I[2] am taking up Meta's note, while she is packing—my packing being all yet to do —I beg to give notice, and there is *vile* pen & ink in my room. We start at ½ p. 11, arriving at the Thompson's about 3. We really have very much enjoyed ourselves here; tho' until Wednesday we were perfectly quiet, and Mrs Lyall kept fearing we were dull. On Wednesday as Meta has begun to tell you, we went to Portsmouth, soon after breakfast; were met at the station by Captain Christian (who, in London had offered to show us everything—) and convoyed by him in the Royal Yacht boat—first to the Victory, the ship in which Nelson was wounded, & died at the battle

---

[1] February 28 fell on a Thursday in 1850, 1856 and 1861. The two former years are made unlikely by the fact that Florence Gaskell (b. 1842) can be asked to write and that there was, as far as we know, no visit to Silverdale in 1856.

[2] As the sense indicates, Mrs Gaskell took over from Meta at this point.

M.G.L.—Y

of Trafalgar,—places marked by a brass plate. She is now a training school for 800 boys, all going to be sailors—we went & called on the Captain & his wife, she a Miss Parry, a niece of the Dean's here, & of Sir Ed Parry, {[?]}. Then to the Fairy, the most lovely little yacht, that takes the Queen over to the Isle of Wight. We heard a great deal about the Royal family from a Mr Welsh, an old bluff sailor in command of ⟨ ⟩ her. The etiquette is to say *once* 'Yr Majesty', or your R. H., and after that to drop it & say only Sir or Madam. The day before the Queen had gone to Osborne, & she had come up to Mr Welsh & said 'Mr Welsh cannot you stop the chimney smoking, it is spoiling my new bonnet.' 'No Madam' said he 'I can't.' 'Then will you buy me a new bonnet?' 'I have no money to spare for such things, and, Madam, don't come bullying me, go and bully Captain Denman!!' But he says all things so humorously that they (R Hs) are all very fond of him. The Q. asked him if he had been sick going to Antwerp once when it was rough—'Yes.' 'Why don't you take my remedy, Mr Welsh, a few drops of Chloroform.' 'May I advise you, Madam[,] to take *my* remedy, a pipe. You would find it much more to the purpose?' From there we went to the Royal Yacht, & lunched in the Ward-room with two or 3 officers—saw Cousin Fred's photograph—Ed. & Fanny—(oh! *please* try and find out the address of Mr Henry Howson, people living in or near Manchester; she very pretty & musical,—have been at *Monte Video*. Possibly the Sterns might know.) After lunch Mrs Denman sent to beg I wd go & call on her. All these Captain's wives have drawing rooms in the ships; so we went in, & Captain & Mrs D. had expected us to lunch, which was all set out. However we sailed away in Capt Xtian's boat to the Victoria & Albert, the grand Royal yacht, that has just taken the Empress of Austria to Madeira; all the crew have fallen in love with her, she was so sweet & patient. Then to the Wellington, Sir Chas Napier's flag ship in the Baltic, then to see blocks made,—the rope walk,—over the docks &c. (we would rather have been at sea, sailing about in Captain Christian's boat than improving ourselves on land—

Then we came back here; and yesterday was pretty well filled up with returning calls, seeing the Judges come in, service in the Cathedral, dining with the Judges at the Deanery, (Martin and Willes.) I told Baron Martin of the state of siege our Manchester houses were in, & he declares it is the fault of the police; he said he wd rather have a South Lancashire jury than any; believes a person out of her mind committed the Road murder & one of the family; but that it will still be found out; as *many* people must know, & their consciences will impel one out of the number to let it out &c &c. Now I *must* go & pack.

Can you find, & *send to me* a letter of Mr Norton's, which is, I am pretty sure, in my middle dressing table drawer, *in an envelope directed* by *Mrs Brodie*. And will you send the silver (plated) coffee pot in common use to be *mended*. The *top* is loose, & in a piece of paper in one of the card-racks in the dining room. I do hope your poor eye is better. Ask F E to write if you cannot. *Do* go to Lily Robertson's wedding, darling.

Your ever most affec[tionat]e Mammy

Should we not be fixing about Silverdale[?]

*   *

430 **485** 488

CHARLES ELIOT NORTON

April 16th 1861. Plymouth Grove

My dear Mr Norton, if I could write you short letters I should write to you much oftener; but you see I can't dash off the minute Gaskell-family-detail letters I know you like all in a minute. I am sitting here by myself in the dining room by the light of one candle,—half disturbed and half-amused by the chatter of 'the children' in the next room—(Julia just come to wish me good-night, so it is 9 o'clk) where Meta Florence & Julia have been sitting till now, when Julia the chatter-box and perpetual singer having gone to bed, sudden silence succeeds. I suspect that Meta has taken up either the 5th vol. of Modern Painters,[1] or Tyndall on Glaciers,[2] both of which books she is reading now, and Florence is probably reading the 'Amber-Witch'.[3] Mr Gaskell is out, at a meeting of the Literary & Philosophical Society, making arrangements for the meeting of the British Association for the Advancement of Science, in Septr (4th to 10th) and Elliott (Elliott, Mary and Hearn are still with us) has just come in to ask me if Master would like some bread & milk when he comes home? So now you

---

[1] John Ruskin, *Modern Painters*, V, Smith & Elder, 1860.
[2] John Tyndall, *Glaciers of the Alps*, 1860.
[3] Lady Gordon, *Amber-Witch*, 1844; new ed. 1861.

know the exact state of affairs on this Tuesday Evening. Marianne has been nearly a fortnight at Buxton; first of all being bridesmaid at a friend's wedding—now having passed on to another friend's house, and enjoying the early spring in the country. She is going to be bridesmaid to another friend near London on the 2nd of July,—to Margaret Price, daughter of that Bonamy Price to whom so many of Dr Arnold's letters are addressed. About the early middle of July we all (except Mr Gaskell, who will take his holiday partly in London in June, partly in Scotland in August—) go to our dear old Silverdale on the borders of Morecambe Bay, to run wild there for the sake of Julia's health for six weeks. For the lassie is taller than either Marianne or me, & sometimes her gay spirits take the other turn into languor & weariness. We must come home however against the British Association in full health; for we are going to have our house full,—Mr and Mrs Brodie, Mr and Mrs Wedgwood and one or two others. I have taken Meta up to London this March to have her tonsils cut out,—a tickle operation but one which we hope will make both her eyes and throat stronger. We had looked forward to a day with Ruskin when she got better, and wrote to offer ourselves for any day he liked; but he never answered the letter, which rather—no, not exactly *hurt* us, because I always pride myself on my faith in my friends; but I wish he *had* answered it. More especially as Meta never had seen the Dulwich Gallery and we meant to have combined the two, and perhaps to have seduced him into going with us. We went to see Rossetti though; so prettily full of his wife[—]that Miss Syddall who was partly his pupil & partly Mr Ruskin's. He is very full also of his translations of early Italian poets; and that brings me to say how very much I enjoyed during Meta's invalid days reading again & with deliberation your Art & Study in Italy,[1]—thank you *so* much for it, and my dear Vita Nuova, which has even yet more a perfume of the happy days we were with you in Italy. I don't know that we did anything more remarkable in London. The operation was our grand event. Everybody was talking about America, & 'Essays and Reviews'.[2] If I were with you there are no end of subjects I should like to enter upon; but letters are such *earthly* ways of holding communication. By the way do you ever see Fraser's Magazine. If you do I wish

---

[1] *Notes of Travel and Study in Italy*, 1859.

[2] Controversial theological book by seven Oxford teachers, published in 1860. Contributors included two of Mrs Gaskell's friends, Jowett and Pattison.

you would look back to the number for (say either) August, Sepr, or Octr, 1860 for a short poem by 'Edward Wilberforce' the young man we all used to meet in Rome; a very odd-looking, and as *we* thought conceited person. But the poem tho' unpleasing from it's subject—which some people would say 'removes it from the province of art',—(and then where would Dante go?) is very strong & fine, so much more so than I should have expected from the author.[1] The week has stolen on to Friday, April 19th—and tomorrow is American post-day,—so I must hurry on. Marianne is still at Buxton, but Meta just asks me if I shall have room for a note to you. By and bye I expect to trouble you with a note of introduction for a young man—about whom I am much interested, simply because I think he is about the most conscientious person I know, &\that/from a deep sense of religion. But our acquaintance is in rather a peculiar state, and I shall explain to you fully how I stand with him. He is a Mr Bosanquet (descendant of Huguenots) son of a clergyman, & connected with an old established banking-firm in London of which you may have heard. We became acquainted with him when Meta, Florence & I were in Heidelberg $2\frac{1}{2}$ years ago. We had many mutual friends (Bonamy Prices, & Diceys, absent) & Bunsens then present at Heidelberg, and at whose house we constantly met him. For the first two days we stayed at the same hotel with him, and then we went into lodgings where we remained 9 weeks, he remaining the same length of time (to an hour) at the hotel. After several meetings at the Bunsens he asked me if he might spend his Sunday Aftns with us, saying that they were especially dreary in an hotel. (He was there, after being at Eton, & having taken his degree at Oxford where he was at Balliol, a pupil of Jowett's). I had seen enough of him to agree to this; for I saw that he was grave, serious, & ruling himself by Scripture law of conduct most strictly. He joined us after afternoon Church the next Sunday, & we all went a walk (the Mohls joining us), up to the Castle Gardens, in the course of which he walked part of the way with Meta, & all returned to tea at our lodgings. When we went to take off our things Meta said to me 'I wish Mr Bosanquet knew we

---

[1] 'Purgatory', published in *Fraser's Magazine* (October 1860), contained such lines as: 'And the sharp knife falls with a hiss | And the blood spurts out in a jet'. It goes on to speak of the priest's comforts to the condemned man and the latter's survey of his life, ending: 'And thus as with glazing eye | He sank into slow despair, | One look at the cheerful sky, | And he read his comfort there,— | 'Twas true that they said; and the life of the head went out in a prayer.'

were Unitarians; he speaks a great deal about religion always on
the supposition we are Church, & I feel shy of telling him we are
not.' So I said I would in the course of the evening—and I did. At
first he could hardly understand it,—he had evidently had some
unknown horror of Unitarians,—& gravely & seriously asked me
'if we believed in the Bible'—However I told him what *I* did
believe—(more I suppose what would be called Arian than
Humanitarian,)—and among other things said I had only one anti-
pathy—and that was to the Calvinistic or Low Church creed,—
to which he replied he was sorry[,] for his father & all his friends
were what was called Low or Evangelical Church,—& gave me
quite a different (& most beautiful) account of what he considered
their belief;—he said if the Bible taught him anything different
from what he believed to be the doctrines of the Church he should
immediately become a Dissenter. That 'Love & Truth' were the
two qualities that formed the Essence of the Xtian religion, & that
the *Spirit* in which actions were performed was of far higher consequence than the actions themselves. Much more was said,—he
all the time getting over the 'shock' of coming in contact for the
first time with Unitarians. We did not know if he would come
again; but he did,—& by degrees generally twice (once to bring us
his English newspaper & learn our plans &c) a day,—always talking gravely & seriously,—& by degrees (whether we ever see him
again in the old way or not) we all felt that his deep high tone, his
strictly religious mind, & his living as in the sight of God, was
doing us all good—&, to Meta, in an especial way bringing back
some of the faith in *man*kind she had at the time lost so entirely
in consequence of Capt Hill's character &c. Mind! there was no
suspicion of 'love' on either side. He seldom spoke to her:
generally to me; always gravely & on grave subjects. One week to
an hour he never came near us; which entire cessation is to this day
unaccounted for. He asked me one day if I would ever go & see
his parents at their home in Northumberland,—his own mother
was dead but his father had married again; some one whom he
seemed to love & reverence *extremely*, who had 4 sons,—he being
the only one by the first marriage,—& he spoke almost as if he
were like a young *father* to these {elder} younger brothers.—I said
if ever I was in the North I should be glad to make his parents'
acquaintance &c, & by & bye he brought me a message from his
mother, renewing the invitation in the most cordial terms & then
he began to talk to us all, (including even a young lady who was

staying with us in the places) of excursions he should like to take
us to—Holy Island, Abbotsford &c—when we went to stay at
Rock (the name of his home). Well! we left Heidelberg, & he left
it an hour after us, on {e} 6th December,—thanking me for 'the
happiest two months of his life', (in so grave & unimaginative a
person *not* mere words of course—) We stayed in Paris with Mme
Mohl,—but soon after Xmas I had a letter from him saying he was
going up to London to study law,—but might he come here for a
couple of his days on the way?—and in the letter were words like
these—'Yesterday was my birthday, & among other things I had
to thank God for, was the gift of your *friendship* as I hope I may
call it, during the past year—'—and later on in the letter he said 'we
are serving the same Master,{'} I know, although some of my
friends are not so sure as I am of this'—Well! I took this up &
wrote to him saying that 'if in any way his keeping up his acquaintance or friendship with me gave uneasiness to his friends &c I
begged he would *not* come here, but leave the continuation of our
intercourse to chance interviews {if they} which were sure to
occur,' or something of that kind, for I knew how dearly he loved
his own people, &c. However he replied that he had shown my
letter to his (step) mother, & she had consulted his father about it,
& they saw no reason why he shd not &c, only his father advised
him to have no *doctrinal* (as distinct from *religious*) conversation, so
he still persevered in offering to come, & come he did from
Wednesday to Saturday in Feb 1859. Kate (Roman) Winkworth
was here, whose Lyra Germanica he particularly admired,—& to
her he confided his pleasure in Mr Gaskell's morning prayers, his
intense wish to enlighten 'his friends' on the subject of Unitarians
&c, {his} while to me he repeatedly said that he hoped his father
& mother would be in London when we were in the following
May, & that if so might they call on me,—& he asked Mr Gaskell
to come to Rock. To all which I am thankful to say, we answered
very quietly, if not coolly.—Then he went up to London,—the
very day he got there he sought Thurstan Holland out, & on the
strength of his being our cousin, called &c.—The next thing was
his mother sending me a present of game with a pretty note
thanking me for the happy visit 'Charles' had had, & saying as I
now knew him so well, I should know how dear a child he was to
her—Then nothing particular happened till {near} May when
hearing from me that we were going on our way to London to
stay at Capt Holland's at Ashbourne in Derbyshire, he wrote to

ask if (being on his way from Northumberland to London) he might come & call at Ashbourne—Capt Holland immediately asked him to stay all night—he came, & with EXTREME pain & awkwardness said—'My father & mother will be in London at the same time that you are,{   } but, I am sorry to say *they do not wish to make any new acquaintances*; my father is very deaf, & feels unwilling to see any fresh person.' After the invitations to Rock— the holding back on our part, &c. I cd hardly believe my ears, & Marianne & Meta would *not* believe it when I repeated it,—so the next day I said 'Did I understand you rightly when I believed you said &c.'—he looked miserable, but said *Yes*. A friend of his, a clergyman, whom we knew was staying at Ashbourne at the same time, and on my saying I did not like to keep up an acquaintance evidently disapproved of by Mr B's parents, replied 'You need never fear B's doing anything he believes to be wrong, & {h   } he is old enough to judge for himself.' So since then I have gladly kept up passive intercourse with him; i.e. he once said how much he shd like to come here again 'but my father who is a man of deeds not words disapproves of my extreme enthusiasm about Fox How & Manchester.' To which I replied that we shd never ask him again, but that if he ever felt it right to come he was [']sure of a welcome.' He always calls & seeks every oppy of seeing us in London; where he has been studying law hard for 2 years & a half,—and, in his daily walks to Lincoln's Inn, he was so struck with the misery of St Giles that he has taken lodgings not far from there, established a small working man's Club, with the help of a *low* Church curate,—& he & four of his friends (law students of whom Thurstan is one,) have after much enquiry & careful consideration, set up a *small* company for buying 19 houses in the worst part of Drury Lane, getting them, & turning them into model-lodging-houses, which they mean to look after *themselves*, & so bring themselves into intercourse with the lodgers. In this way he has seen some of your letters, & read the Atlantic &c, & especially begged me for a letter of introduction to you, when he goes, in June (end of) for 6 months to America. He goes to Canada I *believe*, & then viâ *West* to the *South* before going to Boston I am afraid. If you once get over his grave Sir-Charles-Grandeson[sic] manner you are sure to like him; and as he himself once\lately/said 'I feel more & more that the so-called *Evangelicals* have a right to their name; but even more than that am I convinced that all mere doctrine is as nothing compared to that personal feeling of religion which makes a man live in the sight of God, and love Him all the dearer from the consciousness of this continual presence.' All this has been a long story, but I thought I should like you to know it, before making the acquaintance & I cannot help thinking the *friendship* of this young man. And now I must not *cross* any more. My kind regards to your Mother & sisters—Mr Lowell & Mr Child. We *thirst* for news of the dear Fields—and Mr Wild?

Your ever affectionate friend
E C Gaskell

472 **486** 0

?FREDERICK CHAPMAN

46 Plymouth Grove
Manchester
April 27th [?1861]

Dear Sir,

I should be very much obliged to you for a speedy answer to this letter; my last (from Winchester, at the end of February)[1] has remained unanswered till now, although there were several questions in it to which I should have been glad to have received early replies. Would you be so kind as to ascertain, and let me know as soon as you conveniently can, how my account with Messrs Chapman with regard to the 'Moorland Cottage', published in 1850, stands. Mr Edward Chapman gave me £50 for 1,000 copies I think, after which I was to have a share in the profits of all copies sold above that number. On this account he sent me 20£ in 1853 (I believe) and then said something about this payment (of 20£) being made *before* the requisite number of the *surplus* (above the *1,000* for which he had paid 50£ at first) was disposed of. That is the last I have heard of it, but the copy-right remains with me, and if the first edition is all disposed of I am anxious to include it with some other tales in a vol for which Messrs S Lowe & Co wish to make me an offer.[2] I conclude from your silence that you no

---

[1] Presumably to be connected with Letter 484.

[2] *My Lady Ludlow and other tales* was published by Sampson Low, Son & Co. in 1861.

longer desire to republish 'Cranford', &c—. But will you be so
kind as to give me an explicit answer.

> I remain dear Sir,
> Yours very truly,
> E. C. Gaskell.

273 and *484b 487 494[1]

MARIANNE and MARGARET EMILY GASKELL[2]

[23 May 1861]

My dearest children, I was so glad to hear from you, though my
pen does not look very like it. Julia & I walked home; going to the
Cathedral service, and arriving just *after* the anthem; then pricing
a double set of chamber-ware, 3£ the cheapest—then to look at
black shawls for you, MA & Meta, at Moore & Butterworth's—
silk barège *scarf* shawls, 35s—grenadine *shawls* ditto—(like E.
Marslands) cashmeres embroidered 3 guineas—I inclined to the
barèges much; but we left it to you to choose—came home, found
Elliott crying & faint, & had a horrid bustle to get tea ready for
Mrs Shuttleworth & Fanny Lamport; but we were ready at last,
with eggs filled with anchovy, à la Mrs Shadwell. Thought of you
two darlings, at the wrong time it seems, as you were so late
getting in. Tea, with the coffee we *ought* to have had at dinner at
the other end. Papa very agreeable. In the middle of tea Mrs
Nicholls came to spend the eveng Mr Nicholls being out; very
full of Crompton's marriage, which did very well for his cousins
Shuttleworth and Lamport. Rifle Corps attend them to Church as
a guard of honour[.] Lieutenant Rifle Corps gives a déjeuner to the
Corps on the occasion. Corps gives Mary Lalla Rookh!! Town
gives itself a public dinner. Bells ring like mad. Saddler gives Mary
a whip & bridle (ominous for the bridegroom, we think—) In
short Ludlow is in a state of delight. The Andersons give a ball on
Friday night, and a picnic to the scene of Comus (Ludlow Castle)
on Friday morning. After every body went, Julia & I dog-tired
went to bed. I think the night was unwholesome for everybody
was so dreadfully tired. Yesterday the postman told me there wd
be no afternoon delivery for the next 4 days. Julia & I did every-

[1] To Marianne; to Meta, o.

[2] A Lancaster transcript (see Appendix A) gives the address: 'Miss Gaskell | S
Kell's Esqre., | Walmer Villas | Bradford.'

thing for Elliott, washed up Breakfast things, laid dinner, waited
&c—She was *very* poorly. After dinner Mrs Shadwell came,—very
tired—very full of sorrow at not having bid goodbye to Florence,
—she had been in bed with a bad headache all Tuesday morning,
—had wanted to come here the first thing after *lunch* on Tuesday
but Col. S. had said, 'No, they'll be dining in a hurry, go into
town first, & call as you come back.' & then they had passed us &c
—she really was *very* sorry. I got her tea; & Julia & I sate doleful &
sad but trying to be cheerful[;] when Col. S. came in he was full
of kind plans for poor people,—post man *hopelessly* in a consumption, wd we see after him? would I see that a headstone was put
upon his sister's grave in N. Rode Church—would I see after
Hogan's &c—Then Papa came in, & Col. S. *kissed* me (which I'm
very proud of) & we said goodbye, & that bright bit of my life is
closed up; for what a good loving man he is,! full of thought for
others, rich & poor. He is going to take Papa to the Cosmopolitan
when Papa comes up to 'town'—Papa is very much pleased, & we
must keep them both up to it. Julia & I were so broken hearted we
could only console ourselves by going to Mrs Barber's & seeing
what we cd do for her husband—& we found her as broken-
hearted—saying all sorts of good of Col. & Mrs—& crying sadly.
I came home & wrote to Mr Beaufort\Postmaster/about Barber,
& then laid tea, & then Julia & I went to Susanna's, (who had been
in the night before, but wd not come in, finding Mrs Nicholls &c
here.) She was *deadly* tired—sleeping her last night in Nelson St,
wanting to know how long Meta could stay at Malvern—[1] till
Saturday week? I rather demurred, unless it was NECESSARY, as I
want Meta & cousin Mary to make friends,—so I *think* unless Meta
is absolutely *needed*, she'll come home next Thursday week. Then
to the Ewarts (by way of a bit of gaiety for Julia) who were just off
to the Tom Cooke's. Col. S. came in, & I was (secretly) very
much flattered by comparing the difference of his farewell to us
and to them. Home, down-hearted, & to bed. Letters from Isabel,
—not saying much,—E Shaen, only going to stay an hour here
tomorrow, going on to Christening of Selina's baby Susan
Margaret[2]—L V. J. putting off coming for a fortnight. Mary
Caroline & Amelia all off; last 2 to Belle Vue—I am deadly tired—
it is $\frac{1}{2}$ the weather I think, half down-heartedness, half (3rd half)
having done so much these too [sic] days of Elliott's work.

[1] Looking after Catherine Winkworth. *Letters and Memorials*, ed. Winkworth,
II, p. 345.   [2] On 24 May 1861. *Ibid.*, II, p. 351.

Your letters most thankfully received—Your ever affec[tionat]e Mammy, My kind love to Mrs Kell.

485 **488** 491

CHARLES ELIOT NORTON

Monday, June 10th 1861.
Dining-room in Plymouth Grove, breakfast things not as yet removed, your letter came *at* breakfast.

My dear Mr Norton,

Yesterday—a quiet Sunday, with somehow less of bustle about it than Sunday School & Ragged School usually make, Meta and I were having a long *yearning* talk about America, and our dear friends there. I am not sure that we did not shake hands upon a resolution that if we lived we *would* go over to America. I know we calculated time & expence, & knocked off Niagara, because we would rather see friends. (That is to say Meta did. I was not so clear in my own mind about giving up Niagara, so I won't pretend I was.) Then we talked over your politics, and could *not* understand them; and I half determined to do what I am doing now—take myself and Meta for average specimens of English people,—*most* kindly disposed to you, our dear cousins, hating slavery intensely, but yet thoroughly *puzzled by* what is now going on in America. I don't mind your thinking me dense or ignorant, and I think I can be sure you will give me a quiet *unmetaphorical* statement of what is the end proposed in this war. Now don't be indignant at me, (or at the English) when I tell you exactly how much I (average English) know, & how much I don't know. I understood 'the Union' to be an *expansive*, or *contractive* contract. Expansive (as being capable of including more than the original thirteen United States) it has proved itself to be. But it seems to me that the very fact of its power of expansion involved that of its *dis*solution (or contraction as I have called it above) if need were. No\over/great empire has long preserved itself in vigour. You included (by your annexations) people of different breeds, & consequently different opinions and habits of thought; the time was sure to come when you could not act together as a nation; the only wonder to me is that you have cohered so long. And yet you say in this letter 'I do not feel sure that under *any* circumstances the *right* of secession could or would have been allowed' &c[.] You will perhaps say that our great unwieldy British Empire coheres that the Roman did—yes, but we do not come in frequent contact with our colonies,—as you North & South do. People of {all} diametrically opposite opinions on many points may keep good friends on the whole if they are not brought into intimate daily communion. Doubtless a good quantity of grumbling goes on, both with just and unjust cause, at our antipodes, at our government of them; but we do not hear it 'hot and hot'.—(Besides I heartily wish our colonies would take to governing themselves, & sever the connexion with us in a comfortable friendly way.) So that altogether I (average English) cannot understand how you (American) did not look forward to 'secession' at some time not very far distant. As to the manner in which it has been done nothing it appears to me *could* have been more treacherous and base on the part of the Southerns,—and I hear no other opinion— (Moreover I have heard some letters from Southern {South} Sea Island Cotton planters—apparently kindly good old-fashioned people named Giraudet, or something like it, expressive of deep regret at the behaviour of such men as Jefferson Davis[1] &c.[)] But I should have thought (I feel as if I were dancing among eggs,) that separating yourselves from the South was like getting rid of a diseased member, (possibly there are cases where amputation is a more impatient & consequently a more cowardly thing than the slower process of trying to bring the leg back to a healthy state). We have a proverbial expression in Lancashire 'Good riddance of bad rubbish' that I think I should have applied to the Southern secessions. From what we read of the attack on Fort Sumter, 'no one killed', it sounds like a piece of bravadoing Child's play,— insolent enough, but of a piece with the sort of bullying character one always heard attributed to the South. Now comes my great puzzle. What are you going to do when you have conquered the South, as no one doubts that you will? Mr Channing says 're-assert the right of letting the U.S. flag float over the fortresses of the South, throwing out liberty to the breeze' or something like this, which just tells me nothing of what I really, & with deep interest want to know. *Conquering* the South won't turn them into friends, or pre-dispose them to listen to reason or argument, or to

[1] Davis (1808–89), President of the Confederacy during the Civil Wars, criticised for his dictatorial policies.

yield to influence instead of to force. You must *compel* them then to what you want them to do. (And what *do* you want them to do?—abolish slavery? return to their allegiance to the Union?) *Compelling* them implies the means of compulsion. You will have to hold them in subjection by force,—i.e. by military occupation. At present your army is composed of volunteers,—but can they ever leave their business &c for years & years of military occupation of a country peopled by those adverse to them? Shall you not have henceforward to keep a standing army?——If you were here I could go on multiplying questions of this kind, but I dare say you are already tired & think me very stupid. I sometimes try and compare your position to what ours in England would be if Ireland took it into her head to *secede*—but after all that is not a fair comparison.—Scotland would do better because Scotland was never *conquered*, but agreed to the Union with England in a kind of a way,—I suppose we should fight and conquer and then we should have to garrison all her forts, and keep her down—But I think I should not feel it to be *right* to do this, (& it is the nearest parallel case I can think of)—& it certainly would involve the standing army which I thought you were all so proud at being able to do without.

I have been reading your letter again——I see you speak as if the anarchical *minority* would have been able to upset the law and order of the *majority*. (They were thieves and rascals, {of} that is clear.) But I feel as if their attack on Fort Sumter was just to get rid of the little nest of Northerners in the heart of their town not to attack formally the 'majority'—. And as for the mob (in Baltimore, was it not?) attacking the Northern regiment, *that* was very bad; but your New York mobs—(nay, even your Boston mobs in abolition-meeting times) have got ahead of law and order without bringing on a national war. Now I have said out the very worst I have ever *heard* said, & you know I live in S. Lancashire where all personal & commercial intimacies are with the South. Every one looks & feels sad (—oh *so* sad) about this war; it would do Americans good to see how warm the English *heart* is towards them, although we may all be blundering in our *minds* as to the wisdom or otherwise. No! Mr Field—our dear dear Jack *never* writes to us,—which hurts us only we love him just as much as if he did. Mind, you *always* tell us about them, for it is our only way of hearing till we go to the Clam-Bake on the Shore which he promised us. Mr Wilde—where is he? You owe me a *personal* as well as a *National* letter. Put me right where I am wrong,—(you'll say I'm wrong throughout—) You would see ——I have been called off and forget what I was going to say. Your account of your lovely Sunday does sound so peaceful and charming. What is the Golden Robin? Oh! don't you long to go back to Rome. Meta & I were *so* talking about you, & Rome & America yesterday, the Pamphile Doria gardens especially, and about your face as we first saw it,—and this morning comes your letter. The reason why she & I were tête a têteing in this way was that Mr Gaskell was gone to Liverpool to preach—Marianne was visiting our friends at Knutsford and so, as the younger ones were occupied by themselves, Meta and I talked over 'old days', partly apropos of conversations she had had with Katie Winkworth at Malvern. Katie W. has been very ill again, and as her father Mr W. was also dangerously ill, & required all his family about him, Meta offered to take Katie to Malvern and nurse her there under Dr Gully's directions—so the two have been together there for the greater part of a month, quite alone, and when Katie was able to bear it, the two had long serious conversations about many things. The doctrine of Atonement on the one hand—old Roman days on the other. Besides which we have just been reading Elsie Venner[1] & we were altogether *very* American yesterday: & our love & sympathies most alive for you all. We go to Silverdale in the first week of July; I think you must address your answer there. Mrs G., S\ilverdale/; near Lancaster, will find us. And we are so glad of letters there, for not a book is to be had but what we take with us,—and we are so eager for reading of all kinds there. Marianne (did I tell you?) won't be there; she is going South to pay a series of visits, as she is not 'one of the Silverdale ones'. (Meta & Julia are *the* enthusiasts for Silverdale.) We shall all meet at home about the middle or end of August ready for the British Association here at the {en} beginning of September. Oh Mr Norton! Meta and I do *so* wish there was time for you to write to Mr Gaskell & ask him to America before the 1st *Sunday in July*,— but I am afraid there is not. Yesterday the congregation gave him an entire holiday {from} *for July and August*; and this morning one of his friends has sent him 50£ & begs him 'to put the sea between himself and England'. Now he hates the Continent; and has always fancied America; and I suppose a fortnight and two or three days would be enough for the sea-voyage both ways. And

[1] O. W. Holmes, *Elsie Venner*, 1861.

the change would be so complete!! I do *not* know all Henry
Vaughan's poems,—I know well 'They are all gone into &c,' and
parts of Silex Scintillans. I wish you would come over to see us
again. I wish you were to be with us at Silverdale,—it would be
just the place for charming long lounging talks.—Elliott has been
very poorly, and we have had to nurse her, & now she is going to
a little country inn near Bolton Abbey for a fortnight's rest before
joining us at Silverdale. Hearn has been to Paris for 10 days, as
attendant to a friend of ours who wanted a maid. But I must not
cross. Meta sends you her kind love.

Your ever affectionate friend

E C Gaskell

482 **489** 490

W. W. and EMELYN STORY

Friday Evening, June 21st

1861

My dear Mr and Mrs Story,

I have been meaning ever so long to write you a good long
letter—(which shall still come, but I have not time for it now.) I
rush to catch the post, and send this letter to Mr Sturgis to forward
to you, & ask you, (if you are at Siena or Spezzia this summer,) to
give my dear husband the welcome *there* you have so often and so
kindly offered him in Rome. The congregation have offered him
TWO months' entire holiday; and he can find no one to go with
him, but the women of his family, and he says he feels so much the
entire want of *change*, and the desirableness of having no *responsibility* that he would rather not feel that he had any one dependant
on him. And yet he would like society, if only to cheer him up a
bit,\he is *so* over-worked/—and I am so sure you would like him
—he is such a punster, & so merry when well, & so fond of
children——after trying to tempt him to do what he *ought* by
telling him of all manner of places, and planning all manner of
tours he has, within the last 5 minutes said that 'if it was not for-
cing himself on people &c &c'—and I have answered that I will
take all blame of 'forwardness' 'intrusion' &c &c,—and please, if
you would like to have him, write *directly* back here,—& also,
please, a letter post restante {Leghorn}\Genoa/; & tell him how

to get to you.—He has a holiday from *the beginning* of July,—and
—oh! I should be so much obliged to you—

Yours ever affectionately

E C. Gaskell.

₄₈₉ **490** ₄₉₈

W. W. and EMELYN STORY

46 Plymouth Grove

Manchester

Sunday, June 23rd 1861.

My dear Mr and Mrs Story,

On Friday evening I wrote to you, enclosing my letter to Mr
Sturgis, who would I thought know your summer address; but
today I hear from him that he can only forward it to Torlonias at
Rome, which will of course occasion some delay. So I am now
trying the chance of Mrs Dicey's knowing more exactly where
you are to write and tell you that 'the congregation' have given
Mr Gaskell a holiday of *two* months (not very long after 33 year's
faithful service,) and fifty pounds, to make 'a continental tour.'
Now he does not particularly care for the 'Continent', yet is tied
to go there; he cannot meet with a companion, (his own woman-
kind wd any of them, be *thankful* to go with him, but he says he
needs 'entire freedom from responsibility' which he could not
have if he had the charge of any of us, and of our luggage,—(you
need not say 'Impedimenta['] Mr Story! I can hear you!) so that
altogether he was very 'low' about where he was to go, and what
he was to do, and his feeling of loneliness on the Continent, until
Friday at dinner; when on our suggesting that he should make his
way to you in your summer retreat his face brightened immensely,
and all he said was 'Oh they would think I was intruding upon
them! I have no right to force myself on people!' So I took all the
blame, promised, that if need were, you should hate *me* & not
him for 'pushing himself in upon you',—and I sate down immediately to write the letter, which as [I] have said is travelling
round by Torlonia—But his—(Mr Gaskell's not Torlonia's) holidays begin in the first week of July, and, though I have all but
sworn you shall give him a welcome, I know he will feel more
satisfied, if he could hear from you before he starts that you *won't*

think him 'intrusive' &c. Still, as he warms up so thoroughly to the plan, (and he is just so overworked that it *is* the only thing he *has* fancied) I shall send him off viâ Marsielles [*sic*] to Genoa as soon as he will go (it *can't* be *before* the 3rd of July, *may* be a week later—) telling him to call at the Poste Restante Genoa for a letter from you, saying where you are. It is your bright charming *companionship* I want for him; so that if he has a lodging *near* you it is everything, & he is only too simple in his tastes & wants & wishes. I am so uncertain if this letter will ever reach you that I dare not put much in it; not that I have very much *to* say,—I am getting on with my book, & very much interested *in* though I can't quite make *out* American politics. Oh HOW I shall envy Mr Gaskell if he does reach you. I feel so sure you will like each other. He is very shy, but *very* merry when he is wel⟨l,⟩ delights in puns & punning, is very fond of children, playing with them all the day long, not caring for them so much when they are grown up, *used* to speak Italian pretty well, but says he can't now, 6 foot high, grey hair & whiskers & otherwise very like Marianne in looks. You'll think him stiff till his shyness wears off, as I am sure it will directly with you. Meta Florence Julia & I are all going to Silverdale, near Lancaster to live a very quiet life in the country while he is away. Oh! I wonder if my lovely plan will ever come to pass. *Where* are you? Siena? or Spezzia? if at the former place how do people get at you,—by sea from Marseilles to Leghorn—rail thence? then {you}\he/won't go to Genoa—

Your ever affectionate friend

E C Gaskell

If Mrs Dicey says you are at {Spezzia}\Siena/, and Mr Gaskell sets off *before* your answer arrives I shall ask him to enquire for a letter Poste Restante, Leghorn.

₄₈₈ **491** ₄₉₃

CHARLES ELIOT NORTON

46 Plymouth Grove
Monday Eveng, June 24th [1861]

My dear Mr Norton,

I am going to write & tell you about Mr Ruskin for I think from what I hear that letters from you, will do him great good, and cheer him very much. Do you remember my telling you, or did I?) that Meta & I wrote to him (from London) in March, offering to come over & see him any day in the next week he chose to appoint, & asking him if it wd suit him to keep his promise of taking us to the Dulwich Gallery? Moreover Meta had two very precious drawings of his to return, which she asked him some questions about? To this day we have never had an answer. But we both pique ourselves on our faith in our friends,—so we only wondered, especially as we heard\knew/he *was* at Denmark Hill. Then we heard he was engaged to deliver a lecture at the Royal Institution on April 17, & great interest was made to obtain tickets & the place was crowded; and he entirely *broke down* in his lecture. Just within this last day or two I have heard from thoroughly good authority that his father & mother have been very anxious about his low spirits & withdrawal from society all winter,—and that at his lecture—he begged to have a door either shut or open—I forget which—asked for it publicly, alleging some good reason & one of the directors, from personal spite *before* every one, refused to allow it to be done;—and that on looking up (after some arrivals had come in to the reserved seats, after he had begun his lecture,) he saw *Lady Eastlake and Mrs Millais* sitting right opposite to him, and staring at him, which finished the breaking him down.[1] All his friends are so indignant & sorry,—but they say he keeps out of the way of sympathy—still letters must reach him, & from America, where no one would be supposed to know of this nine days wonder, they wd I am sure be particularly acceptable. Do you know I believe Mr Gaskell will go and find out the Storys either in Spezzia or Siena during his two months holiday,—at least he has warmed up more to that plan that [*sic*] to any other suggested. He wants a companion, but won't take one of us, because he does not wish to have any responsibility during his holidays and the Storys have often most kindly asked him to *Rome*, so now I have written viâ Barings to say he will come to them in their summer retreat if they will have him. We tried to send him to you in America; but he thought the time too short. I am writing anyhow and with any kind of a pen, knowing you will excuse it. Next week we (Meta Florence Julia & I) go to Silverdale. The day after tomorrow Marianne sets out on a 2 months series of visits. Thank you for your kindness to Dr

---

[1] Lady Eastlake was a confidante of Mrs Millais, previously Ruskin. See Letters 195 and 211.

Thompson. Next will come (from me) Mr Bosanquet, a far more interesting person, tho' stern as an old Huguenot or Covenanter; —his interests are 'philanthropic' & social. Ever my dear Mr Norton

Yours affectionately
E C Gaskell

446a **491a** 535a

CHARLES BOSANQUET[1]

46 Plymouth Grove—
June 26th [1861]

My dear Mr Bosanquet,

Here are three notes of introduction. I *could* give you many more (tho' these are my best and most compendious,) but I fancy from the tone of what you say that you are already bored with too many. But write and tell me if you would like more. If you will *send* my note to Mr Norton as soon as you have fixed your route, & tell him what you want especially to see & to do, I think you are sure to receive *valuable* letters, & help of all kinds from him, which will serve you in good stead till you see him. He belongs to an old American family of good standing which has influential connexions with North & South; influential too in the highest sense; and in so many ways his interests are the same as yours that I am *particularly* anxious to bring you together either by correspondence, or personally, as *early* as you can manage it.

I think you know enough about him to be interested in him already, do you not? He is the\only/son of an Unitarian minister, (dead,) & started in life as a rich merchant. I don't know where his riches came from but he had them. But along with the duties of his mercantile business, he undertook others,—he devoted himself to the poor of Boston in such a way as injured his health for life,— his spine I think suffered,—or else it is slight paralysis; some days and weeks he cannot walk at all,—sometimes he is entirely confined to bed,—He is only thirty one or two, I think; but looks much older. He has been twice in Europe; first in 1850 or so— when as I have said in my note, I believe he was well acquainted

---

[1] *Annotation* 1862?

with Mrs Erskine & Miss Stirling in Paris, where he resided for
several months. I know that then a very warm intimacy began
between him & Lady Augusta Bruce, who are great friends, &
close correspondents to this day. He came afterwards to Europe to
try & recover his health in 1856,—with his mother and two sisters,
& was two years on the Continent & England.—He had lodgings
in Oxford for some time. Now he has gone back, hopeless of
bodily recovery, but, as you must have seen from his letters, as full
as can be of all his old interests. He lives with his mother and sisters
at Cambridge, which is I believe a suburb of Boston,—& is
intimate with Longfellow[,] Lowell, Agassiz, and many other men
of note. You may be quite sure of any kind of help from him,
going as you do, with an introduction from us, so don't scruple
asking for it.

Mr Hale is a nephew of Mr Everetts, & married a niece of Mrs
Stowe's. He is an Unitarian minister at Boston,—was in England
last year, when as I think I told you he saw a good deal of Dean
Alford, & was afterwards the guest of the Bp of Oxford, & Mr
Mansel at Oxford.—He wrote some of the letters you liked about
Model lodging-houses. We all like him very much indeed, tho'
we only had him here for two days. He is *such* an American-look-
ing American. Mrs Stowe is—Mrs Stowe; but I thought for
'Earthly Care's' sake you would like to know her.——Now why
did you not tell me how the Butcher's Shopman's child was going
on? Where are the Forsters living in London? How long shall you
be away? Louy Jackson comes to us to-day.

Yours very truly
E. C. Gaskell.

*39a 492 510

EDWARD HOLLAND

Silverdale, Lancaster—
Monday, July 29th [1861]

My dear Edward,

Thanks for the cheque for 20£, and the kind thought you took
about it, in writing to Mr Langshaw, to desire him to bring me
over the cash, when he pays his *friendly* visit. But you don't know
what a broken reed you trusted to in relying on the Silverdale

postman. There is a railroad from Lancaster to Silverdale, twelve miles; but there is so much respect shown for vested interests that the post continues to be managed as it has been for dozens of years for above thirty by the same man. He lives at Yealand about four miles from here, and nine from Lancaster. He rides a pony almost as old as himself over to Lancaster every morning to fetch the letters; delivers them in Yealand, walks here; *gets thirsty on the road,* drops his letters, or forgets in which of his various pockets he has put them,—but as it is his & his wife's sole dependence for a livelihood, and they have been honest hard-working people, no one likes to complain, and we submit in as much patience as we can.

I will write to our energetic friend Canon Richson about Fred; he (Canon Richson) has an admirably worked parish in the very thick of the town, & *was* wanting a curate about a month ago.[1] He employs two—sometimes three; I do not know if he gives a title,—but I will ask.

Your affectionate cousin
E C Gaskell.

491 493 497

CHARLES ELIOT NORTON

Tuesday, August 28th 1861
46 Plymouth Grove.

My dear Mr Norton,

I was going to write to you yesterday, when the post came in, & brought me three American letters—so you may fancy what 'a good time' we had of it, for we welcome American letters just now more than any others. One from you, one from Mrs Shaw, and one purely political from her son-in-law Mr Curtis, whom I have never seen. Oh! dear Mr Norton we have been *so* sorry for you all about poor Mrs Longfellow![2] It seemed to fill our minds and hearts for days; even the brief account we read in the newspapers in England; and then when we hear the details,—and sees the picture of the mother, the little girls, the pretty 'locks of hair'

---

[1] See p. 667 below.

[2] She was burned to death whilst sealing up packets containing her children's curls. See Whitehill, *Letters,* p. 88.

—the pleasant fearful occupation—and poor Mr Longfellow lying sleeping to waken up to such a dazzling flaming tragedy,—I can hardly bear to think of it. I have meant over & over again to write to poor Mrs Mackintosh (Mr Mackintosh was in America was he not?) but somehow I could not. I don't wonder at it's absorbing all your—all *people's* thoughts just like a public grief,—and then again I meant to write to you—have done for some time about your last letter (now) but one; in which you ask 'have I been too metaphorical for you?' because I believe I have said something, which was in reference to a speech Mr Channing made here, and which was published; and which I seized upon to try and *really learn* the exact state of parties in America, & it was so full of imagery, and eagles, and stars & stripes that it was impossible, hungry as I was for knowledge to get any out of it; and others said so too. Now I really do think I *do* understand your cause. I had always faith in the Northerns; but now I believe I completely understand as well as sympathize. But tell me—what *class*—as regards previous life and education were the men, who having completed their 3-months' service, left the army the morning of the Bull's Run affair. I should like to know your *account* of WHY that battle showed so cowardly & disgraceful a side of the Northern Army; if it is really *true* that the 2nd in command left the post of danger when his chief was wounded? WHY were the regiments received 'with enthusiasm in New York?' You will see we gain— 'we' the English generally, our information from The Times; and I know that Russell's writing is Panorama painting; but still these three particulars alluded to above (3-months' service men leaving,—major leaving with wounded Colonel,—New York enthusiasm), seem generally accepted as *facts* by all papers. Mr Curtis' letter seemed so just and admirable that I have taken some pains to have it printed & published in a county paper and I hope I have succeeded. Of course the *commercial* men in Manchester hear from the *commercial* men in New York; and I have seen letters from these latter in which they speak of the National Credit being so bad that your Govt cannot by any possibility, or at any rate of interest get money. Marianne, Meta & I *greedily* clutch at any bit of American news; you may trust to our full sympathy with you Northerns. Well now! for some home news. I am at any moment expecting visitors to stay in the house, who are coming today, but have not named the hour; so this letter may have to come to a rapid end. We (Mother & four daughters) all came together at home last week end. Marianne has been away for nearly three months visiting in & near London; Florence & I had gone (from Silverdale where we left Meta & Julia) for the last fortnight to see some friends in Scotland. This separation was rather against my will; I was very happy at Silverdale; but we were very much urged & Florence wished it; in some respects we were rewarded by the sight of the heather in bloom— did you ever see it?—great glorious purple sweeps like a vast sea of imperial colour; the scent of which hung about our gowns long after we came in. We were staying 7 miles beyond Dunkeld in the valley of the Tay. It was not so fine or wild as I had expected; not sufficiently in the Highlands for that; but soft beautiful scenery until we had scrambled up to the Moors. I was so sorry for the beautiful trusting wild creatures who were shot at on the 12th. Have you *heather* on any part of your Prairies[?] We saw Taymouth Castle; and one or two old Scottish castles, with Tourelles, & old half French-half Scotch architecture—(Elliott is just come in to lay lunch—I tell her I am writing to you; she bids (or asks me) to say she wishes you would come back here again,—and adds 'I liked him before ever he comed into the house—I saw he was a good gentleman of the right sort as he stood on the steps—[']) Hearn acted chaperone to Meta & Julia at Silverdale during our absence, and brought them back safe to meet us last Saturday,—we having arrived at home on the Thursday, Marianne ditto.

Mr Gaskell has been up and down in a most odd and erratic way since he left on July 3rd—Turin (viâ Mt Cenis & Chambery) Arona, Lucerne, *Baden*, Geneva, the Diablerets in the Rhone valley, where he came upon the Storys, whom he had been tracking for some time; and with whom he stayed ten days, liking Mr Story *extremely* but saying little about the rest of the family, & never naming Edie to our great surprize. Then he wrote from *Newhaven*, (in England,) last Friday to our great surprize,—extremely well & happy & enjoying English food, and English sea, and saying that he is not coming home till { August } September the 3rd; but giving us no address to which to write, as he enjoys he says being 'guided by circumstances as to where he shall go.' On September the 3rd come our visitors for the British Association of Science. We had asked months & months ago Mr and Mrs Brodie of Oxford, & Mr & Mrs Hensleigh Wedgwood; but the Wedgwoods have to go to Kissingen on account of his health, &

can't come, and Lady Brodie is dead, so the Brodies can't come. So our party consists of Fred Holland (Thurstan's younger brother, going to be a curate in Manchester) Mr Smith—Savillian Professor of Geometry in Oxford,—Mr Harcourt, Mr Brodie's assistant Chemical Student at Ch Ch,—and Mr Albert Dicey, also Oxford. I half wish the whole affair was over; not being scientific, and not feeling very strong; but this sounds inhospitable I am afraid. I think we are all settled at home for a long time now. I shall try and finish my book; it is above half-way done, & will I *think* be called 'Philip's Idol.'

Oh, *were* not you sorry about Mrs Browning's death! I wrote to Mr Story to enquire all particulars & it seems he wrote me a full account; but the letter is lost so I know little more than the bare fact. And that takes me to Florence, and you and Dante. Your photographs (apparently sent last Xmas) arrived here while we were at Silverdale. How grand and beautiful they are! Just what I care for & value; independently of the giver. Thank you so much my dear Mr Norton. I have heard *nothing* of Ruskin since I wrote last. I would do anything for him I could,—and now I must go and Meta will fill up the sheet.

Your truly affect[ionate] friend
E C G

487 494 496

MARIANNE GASKELL

[?Early November 1861]

My dearest Polly,

It is just time for the letters to go, & yours is just come. Both Papa and I agree in saying that our *feeling* is in favour of your going to the F. Ball; but alas! our judgment is against it,—Papa's more decidedly than mine, fearing the fatigue for you before so long a journey. I THINK it *might* be planned, if we had time to *think*; but I could not be *sure*, and if you were knocked up on the way to Rome[1] it would be miserable—Besides about your dress?

---

[1] We connect this with Marianne's trip with Mrs Dicey but Letters 494a and 497 give the impression that only a weekend intervened between leaving Manchester and actually going abroad.

It is none so easy getting notions about inexpensive fancy dresses.
I *wish* you could go; & so does Papa, it is so *very* kind of Mrs
Bright. [The paper is torn here, and words missing] any other time
you shd. (Joseph waits)

Your very affect[ionate]

E C G.

231 **494a** 0

LADY KAY-SHUTTLEWORTH

46 Plymouth Grove

November 18. [1861]

My dear Lady Kay Shuttleworth,

I was *very* glad indeed to receive your letter the other day, and
the report of the Institution for the Employment of Needlewomen came by the following post. Both should have been
acknowledged sooner if I had not been in considerable bustle and
some anxiety about my eldest daughter (she whom you kindly
went to see at school at Hampstead) who has not been strong for
some time, and for whom we rather feared a Manchester winter.
Last week some friends offered to take her to Rome where they
were going to winter; so we were very much engrossed with
hasty preparation; and on Saturday Afternoon she left us for five
months; which is a very long time, and seems so to all of us. I
am sure you will accept this as an apology for not replying
sooner.

I shall be very glad to make Miss Barlee's acquaintance, and,
when I next go to London—(the time very uncertain however) I
will call on her, or try to see her in any way most pleasing to her
and you. I am very much interested in her paper (or Report,)—
having seen something of the kind at work in York St Westminster, under Miss Stanley's auspices. I fancy Miss Barlee must
be well acquainted with this, as Miss Stanley also, shares part of
the Army Contract for shirts; and until very lately I have been the
means of her purchasing calico here in Manchester. Owing we
believe, to some undermining of the former Contractors, difficulties have arisen in procuring the right description of shirting,—
difficulties which possibly Miss Barlee has met with as well.

I am very sorry to think that I am not likely (at present at any rate) to help you about the Deaf and Dumb Memorial Annuities. I remember well your giving me a letter of introduction to Mr and Mrs Laing, though I believe I was never so fortunate as to see either of them; but I have always heard them spoken of with so much respect that I would gladly do anything to promote a memorial so after Mr Laing's own heart,—but this winter all our 'charity must begin at home'; for I am afraid it is likely to be a very sad one in South Lancashire: and I only hope that those who have made such large fortunes during these last two years by manufactures will give of their abundance to the work-people in their distress—however improvident these latter may have been. I never saw the book of Mr Laings ('Pastoral Visits') which you speak of; and I should much like to see it, if you have a copy to spare. We at home (father, mother and two daughters) are all well,—my youngest girl, Julia is at school with some old friends of ours, not far from here, so that some of us can often see her. Meta and Florence are the two at home; both grown up, and (the elder especially,—*as* the elder possibly but a charming mixture of woman and child, thoughtful and simple,) are great comforts and blessings to me. I should like you to see them some time. I heard of Ughtred's having to leave Harrow on account of his health, and I was sorry both for the effect and the cause. I have heard very pleasant things of the Brighton College and I hope Stewart will be happy there,—but it does seem so strange to think of that baby being a schoolboy!! Years go so strangely both quickly & slowly, don't they? Capesthorne burnt,—yes that comes in well with the lapse of time. It was there I first saw both you & Lady Hatherton, —it seems to me as vivid as yesterday—and yet how long ago!—

Pray remember me to Miss Poplawska [*sic*]; I am very sorry to hear of her finger,—it seems a very slight cause for so serious an injury, does it not? Some friends of yours have come here lately,— Col. and Mrs Greathed, and we have made their acquaintance, although their rather brilliant military line is very different from ours.

I shall be so glad to hear from you at any time, especially if I could really be of use to you; but just now I cannot be that even, if it is to try and procure any subscriptions which will go out of Lancashire. Pray believe me to remain dear Lady Kay-Shuttleworth

Yours ever very truly

E. C. Gaskell.

472a **495** 501

GEORGE SMITH

46, Plymouth Grove,
Decr 9th [?1861]

My dear Sir,

Thank you extremely for your information about Capt. Hill; and still more so for your very kind manner of communicating it.

I wonder whether you will think it is on the principle of 'better late than never', if I tell you that I am getting on pretty quickly with my novel, that two volumes are finished,[1] and that you should have the third also at any time you liked to fix, provided it was not so soon as to hurry it into incompleteness—

With my best thanks for your kindness, I am

Ever yrs very sincerely
E. C. Gaskell.

494 **496** *500a

MARIANNE GASKELL

Thursday *December 26* [1861]

My own darling, we quite meant to have written to you, all of us, yesterday,—but somehow the day got filled up in the inexplicable way days do. On Sunday we had walked to & fro chapel; Monday ditto to & from Cathedral (in a vain attempt to get in & hear the Bishop preach the Prince Consort's funeral sermon to the Volunteers,) Tuesday Meta & I wearied ourselves out for Xmas presents, {the} Xmas Day walked to & from Chapel & to Mrs Nicholls, so last night I was utterly worn out. TODAY (notice the date) came your\letter to me/last TUESDAY's (Decr 7)[2] and your letter to *Julia*, dated SATURDAY Decr 21, showing that your *Tuesday*[']s letter had not been sent on that day—And before then one of your *Saturday*[']s letters did not reach us till the Thursday *week* following. We are not anxious about you, darling, so it is only because of the delays that (we think) must take place at your end of the world in *sending* letters. Your December 7th letter had to be paid pretty heavily for at this end, although I could see you

---

[1] See p. 614 above.

[2] This is presumably an error and should be 'Decr 17'.

had paid for it at Rome. It was *2* foreign sheets and *a half,* besides
the envelope, so remember that is too much. But we are so glad
to get yr letters, you can't think; paid or unpaid,—and we don't
worry ourselves if we *don't* hear; only we like to, extremely. Meta
& I talked over the chances of *our* going to Rome today. *She*
almost wishes me to ask the Storys if they would take us in &
allow us to pay for our board; but I *distinctly* say no to this. *Could
we slip into the Monro's rooms &c?* The Trevelyans would I suspect
be monté on two [*sic*] high a scale for us. At any rate you are on
the spot and I know you will look out for the best thing you can,
& let us know *as soon as you know* of any *probable* place. So I shall
put *that* on one side. Susanna is much better—Alice is come,—has
been a week or more—Papa went to see Susanna yesterday. She
has walked (with help) into the next room, & back. Florence is
going to B⟨. . .⟩ day. Meta has writte⟨n . . .⟩ today to ask if Mr
Smith ⟨is going⟩ to Rome, as if he *were* going we were ⟨. . .⟩
you your carmelite & some more ⟨. . .⟩ ribbons. Every one here
is in *deep* mourning[.] Such sad national grief I never saw. No one
wishes each other 'a *merry* Xmas this year'—as if by one consent
every one says 'the compliments of the season, & a happy new
year.' People don't think there will be an american war. Mary
(Broadleas) Ewart heard from Mr Gladstone (W. E. G.) that the
despatch sent out to Lord Lyons[1] was *not* so positive as the papers
said; & allowed of an answer & diplomatic intervention. She had
passed through London on the Monday after P. A's death,—from
the Eastern Counties Station—all the little shops in Shoreditch
were shut up,—all blinds down—up to Buckingham Palace
where she went to leave their names, & wrote them down in a
room\hung/with black, & lighted with wax,—People could not
give their orders at Lewis' & Allonbys for crying. The poor
Queen (Lady Heytesbury told Mary) had been in terrible hysterics
at first till they could get the Dowager Dss of Sutherland to her;
but the medi⟨cal⟩ men were glad of the hysterics & tears.
⟨. . . re⟩membered young ⟨. . . c⟩aptain of the Eton ⟨. . . h⟩ad
been received by him ⟨. . .⟩ only a few days before, & ⟨. . .⟩im
a present of a Commission. I am writing in a great hurry, as I
have to take Florence to the railway. We are all very well. I want
a little *impetus* to set me off well with my writing. Julia is very
sweet & nice. Every thing here is very quiet; no engagements but
those formed before the Death. Hallé's put off their ball till the

1 On 5 December 1861.

3rd January; Reiss's on the 10th [—] those are all. We are overwhelmed by poor people; who I do think tell each other, till we
really are preyed upon. We made no great ado about presents this
year. Julia a *scarlet* Connemara Cloak. Nothing to poor Meta but
a waltz of Chopin's. Florence a remnant of silk for a gown. Are
you not sorry about poor Colonel Shadwell? Not but what they
say he enjoys it. He sailed last Saturday from Liverpool—to be
Assistant Quarter Master General in Canada; wives not allowed to
go at present,—he will be some years away. Mrs Shadwell is going
to Eton at first, & then to visit about until she may join him in
Canada. Mr & Miss Hilton went to see him off ⟨. . .⟩

493 **497** 504

CHARLES ELIOT NORTON

December 31, 1861

My dear Mr Norton,
    I have been hoping & hoping and wishing & wishing for letters
from you; and none come! I am afraid it is because I have been
so ungrateful in never thanking you for your last—and for that
beautiful noble paper of yours on the Advantages of Defeat,—a
paper which I have circulated far & wide among my friends,—
and I only wish I had more of the same kind to show,—in order to
make us English know you Americans better. However I have not
much time for writing, so I shall not enter on politics,—(only
mind you do, back again) but this year must not go out without
our good wishes going to you,—our best good wishes dear Mr
Norton for you, & yours. We are all sad here,—most people believe that we are going to war with you, because you are determined to force us into it—'*you*' meaning Mr Seward; and we are
all very sad about that,—then again our poor Queen's sorrow fills
all our hearts. We ourselves, just we Gaskells are happy (I am
thankful to say) and well. At least I trust we all are so,—but
Marianne went on November 18th to Rome for the winter; with
a Mrs Dicey a great friend of hers, who has an invalid son, for
whose sake she has had to winter in Rome for several years. We
do not expect Marianne back till April. But we have very
pleasant & happy accounts of her; which come about once a week.

She is seeing a good deal of the Storys; and describes their rooms at the Barberini as charming. She is in the Babuino. You may fancy the visions Meta & I build up of the possibility of our going to Rome to fetch her; but if we went Florence would have to go too; (Julia is at school) as she is too young & too pretty to be left, —and then comes in the great question of money. But whenever a letter comes from Marianne we go in imagination to Rome; and plan how we could inhabit (say) your, or Miss Winkworth's rooms, and what we would do, &c &c &c. Meanwhile we are very happy at home. Miss Winkworth (the eldest sister) has been very ill for the greater part of this autumn in lodgings close by here; & it so happened that no one of her own family could go and nurse her; so we have had the principal charge of her for nearly 3 months, which has occupied a great deal of our time & nearly all our thoughts, till about a week ago, when one of her sisters was sufficiently recovered from an illness of her own to come and nurse her. And Elliott (do you remember Elliott?) has had to leave us on account of her health, after seven years of service! Her friends live in the South of England, and she fancies that air & climate will suit her better. Please Mr Fields (the publisher) said I might have the Atlantic—but it is not sent to me by the English publisher—would Mr Fields be kind enough to tell him that we are on the free list. I like extremely to see it. Dr Thompson came here the other day, just after he had landed, & told us (in an hour or two) a good deal about you all. Meta & I are very faithful Northerners: literally 'faithful' for when they quote New York reports of American public speeches to show how you are determined to force us into war, our answer is something like that line of Tennyson's

'I cannot understand—I love.'

We met Mr & Mrs Adams at the Monckton Milnes, where we stayed four days in November. I liked him particularly; and I felt as if we really got to be *friends*[.] Who,—what was he in America? He seemed to know you & yours. Now I believe I must go,—only I was determined to write these few lines of best truest good wishes & love before the New Year's bells ring out—
Ever my dear Mr Norton
Your true & affectionate friend
E C. Gaskell.
Meta's love, & good wishes.

490 **498** 507

W. W. and EMELYN STORY[1]

[1861]

['After Hawthorne's romance had come out she expresses to her friends her supposition that they will have read, as every one in England had, the "Cleopatra chapter," and assures them that she is proud of being able to say to people that she had been acquainted from the first with the statue commemorated.'] I feel funnily like Quin, who, when George III. made his first speech before Parliament after his accession, said, 'I taught the boy to read!'—for I come in crowing over my having seen the thing even in the clay and describing more fully what every one is asking about. I can't say, unluckily, 'I taught the boy to imagine beauty.' ['And in relation to a collection of tales, promised to her publishers, but with which, for the time, she is disinclined to proceed—'] I could *tell* the stories quite easily. How I should like to do it to you and Mr Story and Edith, sitting over a wood-fire and knowing that the Vatican was in sight of the windows behind! . . . You don't know how a scrap of paper from Rome is valued in this house. ['And then at the last:'] Please don't forget you have my 'Tolla'[2] with you somewhere—left to be bound in the pretty Roman vellum binding. But if it is lost never mind it; only if you come upon an old shabby copy remember it is mine. I am very loth to shut up this letter—it somehow seems like closing up Rome for ever.

481 **499** *499a

?W. S. WILLIAMS[3]

46, Plymouth Grove
February 1st [?1862]

My Dear Sir,
    You must please consider this letter as *private* for I want to consult you about one or two things. In the first place, have you read

---

[1] From a printed source.
[2] Edmond About's 'first, and truly beautiful, little novel' (Henry James).
[3] Original MS. not seen. '1850' and '[c. 1860]' have been added to the typescript, but the references to Mme de Sévigné make us associate this letter with Letter 502 below.

my two vols of my new novel?[1] If you have I am afraid you do not like them because you say nothing about them. If you *have* I should like to send you a sketch of the third vol: to make you see how everything in the first two 'works up' to the events and crisis in that. But if you have *not* read it I should be very glad if you would tell me so, as I cannot help feeling a little disheartened by the ambiguous sentence in your note to-day, which I cannot interpret either one way or another as to your having read it or not. If somebody (out of my own family) would be truly interested in my poor story it would give me just the fillip of encouragement I want. I am sure you will understand this feeling, though you may think I ought to be too strong to have it. Mr Smith who has had it (the MSS. of the first two vols) for a month has never said a word about it; which has made me fear he does not like it; and though I do not imagine him to be any great judge of it from an artistic point of view, yet as our bargain was made beforehand I should be so sorry if he felt himself bound to take it whether he liked it or no. I cannot help liking it myself, but that may be because firstly I have taken great pains with it, and secondly I know the end; and I cannot help thinking that if you *have* read it, and don't like it at present, you *will* when it is finished and you see how all works up to the crisis. But then authors are so easily deceived about their own things! Mind, I *dont* want you to read it, only to tell me whether you have or not. In the next place I want to tell you why I asked about Miss Kavanagh's books (I cannot get the last of her's in Manchester anywhere, unless by purchase.)

I began a series of articles for 'All the Year Round', while I was waiting for someone to like my novel; and also because at this time of the year I have so many interruptions that it is difficult to abstract oneself sufficiently from the day's business to write anything *entirely* out of one's head. So as I said, I began to write some articles which I intended to send to 'All the Year Round' as pictures of French Society in Paris and the provinces in the 19th century. (I think what gave me the start was the meeting with a supposed-to-be well-educated young lady who knew nothing about Madame de Sévigné, who had been like a well-known friend to me all my life.) But I think my MSS. promises to be very interesting, and I am rather unwilling to send it to 'All the Year Round' to be broken up into bits, unless it were to be published as a whole afterwards, indeed I am not sure if I should not

[1] *Sylvia's Lovers.* See Letter 495.

prefer it's being published altogether in a vol: at first. But knowing that Miss Kavanagh wrote on those subjects I wanted to know how far she had forestalled me, or how far I should interfere with her.[1] And I *should* be very much obliged to you if you *would* kindly lend me her book, allowing me of course to pay the carriage. I have not yet been able to get her first book, but I think I know from you what period it embraces, the 18th century, while mine is the 19th. My book is rather Memoirs elucidatory of the Life and Times of Madame de Sévigné.[2] The sort of subjects are, 'Who was Madame de Sévigné?' 'Her friends in Paris and the Hotel Rambouillet,' 'Her Two Cousins, (Bussy-Rabutin and Emmanuel de Coulanges,) with the history of Madame de Miramion,' 'Her widowed life and her children,' 'Her old age,—debts, and death.' (Then as to society in the Provinces I should take that rather rare book Fléchier's 'Grands jours d'Auvergne, or de Clermont, I forget which.) Fléchier was contemporary with Madame de Sévigné both at the Hotel de Rambouillet and in the later days which she spent with Madame de Grignan in Provence, and his account of his expedition with the de Caumartins when the Président de Caumartin went to hold the Grand Assize at Clermont, and called up all classes of society in Auvergne to account for their misbehaviour and their crimes is very curious and interesting.

Now may I ask how far this ground has been preoccupied by Miss Kavanagh? or how far, supposing it has not been occupied by her, you think Mr Smith would care to publish such a one volume work? Do not tell him, if you please; as it would be a pain to me to have him troubled about a thing he might reject; and I should only regard your opinion *as* an opinion, and not as a verdict. If I sent it to 'All the Year Round['] they would publish it *in bits*, I know; and I think their publishers, Chapman & Hall, would take it afterwards; but I should not like to publish anything with any other publisher than Mr Smith, till my novel was completed, unless how it came to pass. I hope you understand this rather confused letter, and will allow me to consult you as a friend on all these points. I am sure you will consider this letter as confidential and believe me to remain, dear Sir,

Yours ever most truly,
E. C. Gaskell.

*

[1] Miss Kavanagh published *French Women of Letters; Biographical Sketches*, 2 vols., 1862.   [2] Never materialised.

₀ **500** ₀

UNKNOWN

46, Plymouth Grove.
Feb. 7. 62.

Dear Sir,

I am extremely sorry that I must decline your offer of writing a set of papers such as you name for the Daily News, for my hands are already overfull with literary engagements. Had I the leisure, however, requisite for such an undertaking, I shld hesitate before undertaking it. The statistical view of the question, I am not competent to deal with, and as to the new phases of life and character, which, doubtless, this sad crisis does call out, they are so varied, so indistinct, & so difficult to appreciate truly, that I, living here in Manchester, with the best opportunities, should shrink from the attempt to define them.

The statistical and commercial view is really, at present, by far the most interesting and important one. The attitude of the working-class is so very passive that there seems little to say about it, further than commendation of their patient spirit of endurance.[1]

Revd Charles Beard,
care of Crompton Potter Esqre,
16, Charlotte Street,
Mosley Street,
Manchr

and   Travis [sic] Madge Esq,
14, Bath Street,
Boston Str.
Hulme,
Manchr

are the only two people whom I cd recommend as at all likely to undertake the task successfully.

The former is author of 'Port-Royal' published by Longmans last Spring; extremely able, & living in the thickly populated manufacturing districts fifteen miles S. of Manchr. The latter is a zealous amateur missionary amongst the Manchr poor; perhaps too depressed by constant sight of their misery to write anything *brilliant*.   Yrs in gt haste,
very sincerely
E. C. Gaskell.

*

[1] 'Great distress prevailed' in January, *Annals*, ed. Axon, p. 286.

GEORGE SMITH

46 Plymouth Grove
March 18th [?1862]

My dear Sir,

Mr Gaskell says if you will come and pay him a visit of a week
he will undertake to teach you how to pronounce 'Specksioneer'
before the end of that time.

What do you think of 'Philip's Idol';—then again you may say
people will call it 'Philip's idle',—

I don't think I care about the title much. 'Philip's *darling*' does
not quite express the same thing as *idol*,—but perhaps sounds
better. Only I would rather have it 'idol' if you don't mind.
'Monkshaven' might do, might it not?\very stupid/though—
'Sylvia's lovers,'—but then there is a 'Nanette & her lovers', is
there not? and published by you, too. About the length of the
vols: I suspect the third will be longer than either; and I shall be
very glad to move a little of the second into the first, so as to leave
myself scope for adding to the second volume if necessary.

Would you mind sending proofs,[1]—for the postage of which I
will pay,—to *Frau von Schmidt*

T. O. for end of name

Zalíerov, 206 Neu Wien, Vienna

If the postage is likely to come to very much I could, I think
send them through the Ambassador's bag as Frau von Schmidt &c
knows Mr Robert Lytton attaché at her end, & I know Lady
Augustus Loftus' sisters & people at this. But if, as we believe,
proofs can go for a very small payment I will gladly pay it. Frau
v. Schmidt is a friend of mine, a German young lady, speaking
& writing English almost as well as a native,—who made a love-
marriage—(not so common abroad as here—) and her husband,—
(formerly employed in Hungary as a Government surveyor,—
and known to Dr Arthur Stanley & many English friends who
have been hospitably received by them at Pesth, has fallen into
disgrace with the Austrian Government, for his Hungarian sympathies,—& has consequently been deprived of his employment,

[1] *Sylvia's Lovers* was published in February 1863.

and at present they are very poor, and she thinks that if she had the power of translating one of my books *early*, she might gain a little money; and if she is willing to take the trouble I shall be only too glad to do what I can to help her.

Please only send *one* proof till I know the price; & if it gets safe past the Censor Office. I have not a scrap of anything written by me but the beginning\first chapter/of a sort of Memoir of Mme de Sévigné and her Times,[1]—but I will write you as good a short story as I can if it will be of any help to you, & you will let me know *soon* against what time you want it. For the April number I suppose?

Yours very truly
E C Gaskell

501 **502** 512[2]

GEORGE SMITH

46 Plymouth Grove
March 28th [?1862][3]

My dear Sir,

It seems to me that you must have been thinking me very ungrateful inasmuch as all this time I have never thanked you for Mr Aidé's book.[4] But at first I was ill (whh made the gift all the more valuable;) and then I thought I would read it first: and very pleasant it was to be carried out of murky smoky Manchester into something so purely Italian as the beginning is,—it is a regular atmosphere of Italy; I like the story much the best of any of his, don't you?

Next, thank Mrs Smith for her kindness in calling on Florence, —(who was, I can assure *you*, dee[p]ly impressed with the beauty of her visitor) I hope from the fact of her calling that you & Mrs Smith's anxiety about your little girl,—(who is *not* 'Dolly' but I don't know what she *is*—) is over.

Next—I don't think you a bit 'greedy' about Mme de Sévigné, —but I think you may be 'reckoning without your host' i.e. without your editor, whoever he is to be.

---

[1] See p. 675 above.   [2] To Smith & Elder.   [3] Watermark dated 1861.
[4] *Carr of Carrlyon*, published in March 1862.

Lastly *please*—who wrote the 'Fit of Jealousy?'—It gives one the idea of great & *varied* power.

Yours very truly
E. C. Gaskell

278b **502a** 0

HENRY MORLEY

46, Plymouth Grove,
April 1st [1862]

My dear Mr Morley,

Thank you extremely for your 'true kindness' in sending me that critique on my last work. It is very gratifying to be identified with an authoress whose works I have always shunned after one dreary experience, with almost illnatured prejudice.

But thank you still—*much*—more for your kind remembrance of Mr Gaskell & myself. I can assure you that we feel the same for you; & that nothing would give us greater pleasure than to renew our acquaintance {with you}, and to add to our store of pleasant associations, with you.

I am glad you like 'Garibaldi',[1] but I have no right to yr thanks, as the task of editing the book was imposed on me by force, not adopted of my own free will.

Ever very sincerely yrs
E. C. Gaskell.

0 **503** 0

GODFREY LUSHINGTON

Friday April 18. [?1862]

Dear Mr Lushington,

Now you know full well we should be most ungrateful people if we did *not* thank you; so you must submit quietly. In the first place I am so glad to have the two engravings. Death the Avenger

[1] *Garibaldi at Caprera* by Col. Vecchj. Translated by L. & M. Ellis, with preface by Mrs Gaskell, Macmillan, 1862.

is, to me, almost repulsively terrific; but it enhances the perfect peace and sweet restfulness of the other. I have not read the criticism upon them as yet, as all morning long we have been cutting shirts out of your calico,—to give work to some of them who are so craving for it; but I am going to do so this rainy afternoon. I have dipped into Mr Harrison;[1] in fact almost read it, here & there in bits—I feel as if in one or two places I could have told him more, or set him to rights; but there is an immense deal of truth in the whole, especially considering that it was gathered by one man in the short space of 3 weeks. What a beautiful acct that is of Mr Jackson of Leeds, whom I never heard of before!—I mean to make out Charles Hadfield, if I can do so without impertinence, as he lives very near us.—Another thing is that having employment for *unmarried* women is a really good thing—as many a one in Liverpool can tell\by the want of it there/,—and I don't\think/ he shd say we have the 'garbage of Lpool', because they have a worse set there\than even we have here/. What he says of Mr Forster is true to the letter. And then he contradicts himself—he praises the Free Library here, & says the 'Men' (of Manchester) 'are worthy of it'; and the next page abuses our people as hard as he can. But the pure-bred Lancashire man is a right down fine fellow,—it is the admixture with Irish\&c/ that pulls them down. However I can not write sensibly for I am listening with both my ears, & half my heart to something so exquisite of Seb. Bach's that you must hear sometime. {Meta} Oh, it is so exquisite now —like the music of heaven,—I keep forgetting what I wanted to say.—I believe it was the separate messages of thanks[.] Marianne is charmed with the Abend Lied which she has been singing to me; & bids me tell you it is a most beautiful thing, but that she has changed it into E. flat, as she thinks a flat key would suit it much better. Meta is very much obliged to you for the Minuet, which she hopes soon to have the oppy of playing to you[;]\she did not know it/; & Florence says she will give you a message when you come; but I may say 'Thank you' now for her[.]

Our week has been very quiet and eventless. Not even Fred

[1] Frederic Harrison lent Mrs Gaskell the MS. account of his impressions of a tour of the manufacturing districts of Lancashire and Yorkshire in the autumn of 1861 (*Autobiographic Memoirs*, 1911, I, p. 257). Harrison's letter to Mrs Hadwen (see Letter 456) tells of a visit to Jackson of Leeds (*ibid.*, I, pp. 258–9), commenting: 'Men like that confirm me in my intention to remain in the Church of England until someone turns me out'. For this information we are indebted to Professor Martha S. Vogeler of Long Island University, U.S.A.

has been near us; but we have been busy enough in different ways. Marianne goes next week to her concert at Worcester; and I suppose sometime the week after—but I fear not *before* the 1st of May, we shall go to Oxford. Next Tuesday is our Easter Assembly to which we should have tried to tempt you if you had been in these Northern regions, as it [is] always a very good bright pretty ball. That is our only piece of prospective gaiety.

Yours very truly
E. C. Gaskell

497 504 526

CHARLES ELIOT NORTON

46 Plymouth Grove
April 22nd [1862]

My dearest Mr Norton,

We are all so glad to hear of your happiness; of that you are sure, & may be sure. We mean to love her dearly; but please tell us a little more about her: I mean her personal appearance &c; for I think I can make a mental outline of her character from what you say of her. But we want all and any particulars you will tell us about her; where you first met, *when*, &c &c &c—so please write us the longest letter you can find time for. I am so particularly glad to think of your being married; almost as if you were my own son,—for I have often thought that of all the men I ever knew you were not only the one to best appreciate woman; but also, (which is very probably) the other side of what I have just said the one to require along with your masculine friendships, the sympathetic companionship of a good gracious woman. So give my love to 'Susan' and thank her from me, for making you happy; and God bless you both. About Marianne; I know her letter goes in the same sheet as this but I do not know what she has said in it; all I know is that—firstly Dr Manning strongly impressed her in Rome; but I hope that evil influence is done away with now. She says she never has been a Unitarian in belief; but she has never inquired; nor has she a logical mind; so that now that she is reading with her Papa very carefully,—she only seems to feel that all that he says 'is very *clear*', without being convinced,

—i.e. seeing the force of the Unitarian arguments. Nor yet can she define her own belief, nor speak about it, nor give her reasons for it. All this is stating the very worst side for her, if you understand what I mean by 'worst side'. *Arguments* never did seem to have much force for her in *abstract* things. She is one of the clearest people I know about *practical* things; in consequence of this intellectual—what shall I call it? of her's, it becomes very difficult either for herself or others to exactly understand where she stands with regard to doctrine. However she is really *trying*; and she is also trying to be so good and humble that I feel as if the grace of God would be given her to perceive what to her may be saving truth. This, I am afraid, is a perplexing account; but it is no more perplexing than she is to herself on such subjects, I fear, poor child. Set against that *great* unselfishness & sweetness, & meekness. But I must catch this mail

Your ever affect[ionate] friend
E C Gaskell

I shall be so *thankful* if you can help about MA.

*500a 505 506

MARIANNE GASKELL[1]

You wd hear about LVJ's *apparently not* wanting FE? saying it would be so dull. FE. however clings to going to *W.* if not inconvenient to Mrs Lyall, so we have written to ask[.]

Cowley House
{Wednesda}\Thurs/
[1 and 2 May 1862]

My dearest Polly, My story is found! and is going to bring me in a good price!\150£ only *don't tell any one*/Where it wandered to I can't tell; but, after being sent off from Manchester\by PASSENGER train/on the Wednesday it did not reach London till Monday.[2] However they make me a good *bid* for it today; only I don't know when they will pay me. Mr Smith has never done

[1] *Address (on envelope)* Miss Gaskell | Edward Holland's Esq M.P. | Dumbleton Hall | Evesham. *Postmarks* K | OXFORD | MY 4 | 62 *and* ⟨ST CLEMENTS | May 4th | 1862⟩ *and* ⟨EVESHAM | May 5th | 1862⟩.
[2] 'Six Weeks at Heppenheim', *Cornhill*, May 1862? Or, possibly, 'Cousin Phillis', *Cornhill*, November 1863—February 1864.

yet for my C. Hill story.[1] Don't mention that C H M. story to any one please. Florence says you told the Greens about it; but I wd rather not have it spoken about, please; because Papa knows nothing of it, & then I don't like other people to know, when he does not. Did anyone tell you that Alice Winkworth came for a bit on Monday mg. (She & Mrs W are at Alderley for packing up the things, & came over to Stephen's on Saturday—) She is going to Susanna as soon as she can, from Alderley; & from what she said they\the parents/want to move Susanna to Malvern; but I doubt if she *can* be moved; or even if she will consent to give up her Dr Goodman with whom she seems to be much pleased. Anyhow Alice is going—say sometime at the beginning of next week,— how long she can be spared to stay is another thing but I am sure there is no need for yr giving up Boughton; as you see darling, Susanna is provided for for sometime certain. You might write to Alice (care of Stephen, for I don't know their new Southport address,—) asking how Susanna is &c—towards the *end* of next week, or beginning of week after; & then you would most likely hear their plans. *Also*, will you write a long Dumbleton letter to Papa, *telling him all they say of their gratitude about Fred*; & Papa would, I know, like to hear from you, too, now he is alone. The Reiss party went off very well Meta did not go;\stopped with A. J./there were two little plays, & then some dancing. Friday morng before breakfast. When I got to this point yesterday I was called down to Mr & Mrs Matt. Arnold; & that and other company took me up till past 6, which is the time for sending letters out. Yours has just come, darling. I wrote to Isabel a week ago to ask her to take the ticket for Meta; I shd have liked very much to go but there seemed to be so many reasons against it,—one, what was to become of Florence, another my MSS lost, & with it I feared all chance of going to London, whereas I knew that the Wedgwoods would always be glad to have Meta: for a day or two: I think I never told you that Fleeming at Annie's suggestion, went on Saturday to see all the lodgings we have thought of,—& he is decidedly *against* Mrs Hare's, Sloane St; small rooms drawing-room (*the largest*) being—but I'll copy the whole set for you *from Fleeming's memoranda*. Mrs Marshall (where they were,) 32 Belgrave Road, Warwick Sq. (not a healthy situation A. says but a *very* nice landlady.) Double dining-room with two bed-rooms on the 3rd floor 3 guineas a week. Drawing-room 32 feet

[1] 'Curious if True', *Cornhill*, February 1860.

by 16 with two bed-rooms on 2nd floor 5 guineas a week. Annie *thinks* we *might have the whole for 7 guineas.* Mrs Soeber (the Ewart's place) 31 Westbourne Place Eaton Sq. Outskirts of grandeur. House has nice outside. Drawing room 16 feet by 22, (South aspect so wd be very hot in Summer,) with a bedroom & dressing-room with bed in it, & bedroom on the 3rd floor 6 guineas; with dining-room as well 8 guineas, respectable land-lady.—Both prices & accomodation are rather different to what she told us,—you see here are but 3 bedrooms, even including the Dg room. Mrs Hare 92 Sloane St out of the question: cunning dirty old woman for landlady; rooms meanly & dirtily furnished *largest sitting room 13 by 11 feet.* 8 Gloucester Road—rooms let at present, seem rather small; situation *very* pleasant, close to the Exhibition & fresh & country-like, rooms sitting & bedroom on the first floor with back parlour as bedroom; respectable landlady. This again gives much less accomodation than Hilary offered. Meta & I are puzzled. Belgrave Road sounds far the best, *but for* the situation not being healthy. All this time I don't feel as if I had thanked you half enough my darling for having thought so very sweetly & kindly about Elijah & me. I shall be very glad to go, if it can be managed,—and Meta is also so very much obliged to you for thinking of her. We went to see Miss Smith yesterday. She seems better, though she was lying down; only she looked brighter & altogether happier. Excepting her (Mrs Dicey comes home on May 10th) we have seen no one; *literally.* For Oxford is quite empty & shut up. Today & tomorrow they come back however. Now I shall put away my letter for the present. ⟨. . .⟩

505 **506** *506a

Marianne Gaskell

Wednesday [?7 May 1862]

My very dearest Polly,

I have ever so much to say to you; but Meta & Florence are up in their own room, and if Philo comes in I want to stop writing and talk to her. Thank you so *very* much my darling for your Elijah ticket. I shall so enjoy it; and thank you for thinking of it. I will enclose you Julia's letter & Cousin Mary's; I think\hope/

you will see from both of them that Julia is only yearning to be with us all; enjoying ourselves as she thinks, poor lassie. You see Mary speaks *twice* of her looking so *very* well. However I think your plan of going to Knutsford on your way home a very good one. *Have you written to Alice* (care of Stephen, for I do not know Susanna's Southport address,) to learn their plans? If not I wish you would *at once*; & let me know the answer. For if you went there I would send you a 5£ note (*in two halves*{)} so I should know in time) for your expences, so that you should not have to ask Papa for any money. Do you weigh probabilities, & let me know. If you have not *already* written to Alice I fear there will be no time to do so now, & get the answer, & let me know, before we go abroad; and if you have *not* written, write *to me* at once, & I will send you the 1st half note; & if you *don't* go to Southport you can pay me back when we meet in London. The Thompsons are strongly urging Putney as a place for us; only they name a *house* which would require servants of our own. Else I would be very generous in cabs, and if it is high pure air it wd be very good for Meta & Julia. Meta however I can see does not fancy being so far away from the Exn. We made up our plans yesterday after *much* consultation. We leave here on Monday at 9-30 a.m. I go with Meta & Florence as far as Reading. There they branch off to Basingstoke & Winchester; Meta & I agreed that she *ought* to stay a night with L V J, so she remains with her till Tuesday 3 30, & then comes to me in London[.] I meanwhile have accepted G. Behrens' offer of a bed at 8? Bentinck St (we are not sure of the number, having lost her note) Here's Philo—Meta says she tore up Cousin Mary's letter,—but in one part she said speaking of Julia *last* Saty 'She is looking so well; fat and strong-looking'—and again 'You can't think how handsome Julia is growing.' So I do hope it was only a little contrasting *her* life with ours, that made her doleful, & feeling not well. Still it will be a *great* comfort to me, as well as to her, poor darling if you go & see her on your road home. If I could see you I could tell you a great deal that was very amusing about 'Cousins' V. & G. on Saty & Sunday. Mr Brodie told Mrs he thought 'Cousin V's' attentions to F E were 'very morbid'. Neither Meta nor I noticed them however: nor can we even recall *what* can have given Mr B. this notion. Cousin V. has collected a good sum of money for Travers Madge's poor people; which is very good of him. Both Meta & I like him better than Mr G. L. Now to go back to our plans for I have not time to tell you everything in detail as I should like to do. On Tuesday I mean to look out lodgings every where; & to go at [sic] meet Meta at 5-50 at the Waterloo Station, and on our return to call in Belgrave Road to see those. On Wednesday she & I will again go up & down every where; & we hope to *fix* that day; as on Thursday we hope to set out for Paris,—(tell us your hotel; and about the Castiglione; and tell me *where* the Panthe—oh I can't spell the word, —is*exactly*/for we must leave our large boxes *somewhere*.[1]

*

498 **507** 535

W. W. STORY

Cowley House,
Oxford, May 9th [1862]

My dear Mr Story,

I think you have mistaken my last letter—Please read it again, & see if I say a word about not valuing, or thanking you for, your frankness as I ought. I know I wrote warmly about Meta; *not* angrily but only wishing to disabuse you of the notion that *she* had 'proclivities' towards R. C.ism. As long as I hoped & thought it was only that MA had frightened Mrs Dicey without cause, I was anxious to keep it from Mr Gaskell. When I learnt from your letter how serious it was, I was thankful to you for telling us, and for telling it to him, sorry as I was (*of course*) to have the *extreme* pain of learning such things. I think you are misjudging me, *a little*, dear Mr Story; but I don't mind—for *I* can love *you* all the same; I think you have been a true kind friend. Why Meta named Mr Norton Mr Martineau & Mr Kingsley is this. (I write in *great* haste, so I may not measure my words *fully*.) Marianne has all her life been influenced by people, *out of her own family*—& seldom by the members of it, in anything like the same degree, in all matters of opinion. She is now reading with her father; but I fear his *extreme* dislike & abhorrence of R. C-ism; & thinking all the arguments adduced by its professors 'utterly absurd', makes *her* more inclined to take up it's defence thinking it unjustly treated. I hope

[1] There follows a letter from Meta, from which it appears that Marianne was staying at Dumbleton.

you received the scrap out of the Times of May 3rd praising the Cleopatra[1] &c. I have no time for more. Dear love to you all.

Your affectionate friend

E C Gaskell

₀ **508** ₀

UNKNOWN

Cowley House
Oxford, May 10th 1862

In compliance with a request from Messrs Ticknor and Fields, I beg to state that they are publishers authorized by me to publish an American edition of my novel entitled 'Sylvia's Lovers'; they having made an arrangement with my publishers in London, Messrs. Smith Elder & Co, for that purpose.

Elizabeth C. Gaskell

*506a **509** *509

?MARIANNE GASKELL[2]

[?16 May 1862]

⟨. . .⟩
P.S.
Friday *Evening*. We have been about all day—and have *fixed* on *32 Belgrave Road Pimlico*, Mrs Marshall's, where A J lodged. We are to have double dining rooms (folding-doors) both drawing-rooms, making a very pretty room 32 feet long,—4 bedrooms, & one if not two attics. We cannot have *all* this at first; because an Irish M P. has the drawing room floor till June 8th., & then they wd need a day or two to clean. But we engage {them}\one set 2 bedrooms & attic/from *June 3rd*; and I told her that probably you & Hearn (who is to have the attic) wd come on that day; if

---

[1] Story's statue 'Cleopatra' is mentioned as having been sent to the London Exhibition in a letter to Norton, 3 May 1862 (James, *Story*, II, p. 72—see also I, p. 33).

[2] A full version of this letter will be found in Appendix A.

we (including F E.) do *not* come on that day; you could sleep there, (writing beforehand to order meat bread &c.) If we come, \on the 3rd/you & F E. would have to go on to the Smith's,— anyhow you would have to go on the 4th[.]

None of the houses at Putney suited us; all were too small or could only be let for several months. We had a long rainy miserable day, Isabel going with us. *She* said how much she should like to go abroad with us,—& this morning writes to say she will be at the London Bridge Station tomorrow at 10-25, & we shall get into Paris viâ F. & Boulogne at 8.30. Direct

Aux Soins de

Mme Lamy

Rue de la Paix

I forget the No & it is not down in the book—11—12—13—14— I don't know whh. We shall be there till the next *Wednesday* at any rate.

Your *very* most affect[ionate] E C G.

₀ **509a** ₀[1]

WILLIAM SHAEN

32, Belgrave Road,

S.W.

June 16. 1862—

My dear Mr Shaen,

Am I right in believing that you are acquainted with Mr Mudie?—And if so, would it be much trouble for you to enquire from him whether he has any Branch-Library in Paris, or any intention of establishing one\there/? I am enquiring about this for the advantage of Melle Marie Souvestre, (daughter of the celebrated author) who is anxious to find some means of seeing new English books as soon as possible after their publication, that she may have the opportunity of selecting some for translation. Since her father's death, Melle Souvestre, who is a most charming and unusual girl, has added to her mother's small 'vente' very considerably, by some extremely good translations from English authors—but she cannot afford to buy all likely English books, for the chance of some being suitable for translation, and is therefore

[1] See p. 783, n. 2 below.

very anxious to hear of some first-rate lending-library in Paris
where she might meet with them.

Ever most truly yrs
E. C. Gaskell.

*

492 **510** 0

EDWARD HOLLAND

46 Plymouth Grove
Manchester—
August 14, 1862

My dear Edward,

Mr Gaskell is away on his annual wanderings,—a holiday much
needed by him but which he takes without any plan, so I neither
know where to find him, nor when he will return. I always open,
&, if possible, answer his letters during these absences of his; and
today your letter was an answer to mine of yesterday. I am sure
Mr Gaskell will most gladly contribute the 5 per cent requested to
the distress around us, as desired by the Manchester, Sheffield, &
Lincolnshire railway Cy and thank you for signing the letter all
ready.

I have a great 'spite' at the Catherine Dock Shares, which is not
diminished by their diminishing dividend, but I quite agree with
you that this is not the time for selling out.

I think I know all ⟨. . .⟩¹ has won the respect & love of all who
know her. I suppose I had better give you a receipt for the dividend &c. Received for the revd William Gaskell, the sums of
£11 5s od & £53-2-6 being the dividends on the Kath. Dock
Shares, & Manchester, Sheffield & Lincolnshire Railway. Augt 14
E. C. Gaskell 1862 Manchester We are all well. Marianne with
the Wilmots, in Derbyshire, Florence at Judge Crompton's in
Hampshire.

Your affec[tionat]e cousin
E C Gaskell

Would you be so kind as to make the enclosed check payable to
me? Elizabeth Cleghorn Gaskell.

¹ The middle portion of the letter is missing.

*499a **511** *511a

W. S. WILLIAMS[1]

46 Plymouth Grove,
Manchester
August 20th 1862

Dear Sir,

I have received your letter, written on behalf of Messrs Smith
and Elder, enquiring when the\MSS of the/third volume of
Sylvia's Lovers would be placed in the hands of the {publishers}
\printers/. I am sorry to say that my engagements are such that I
do not like to promise that the MSS shall be completed before the
end of January; by which time, if all goes on as well as I now hope,
the completed MSS shall be sent to you; *if not sooner*. I sent to you
the corrected proofs of the end of the *2nd* volume by yesterday's
post; and by today's I will send you the few lines which I wish to
have inserted instead of those at present printed on page 63,
vol 1st.

I remain dear Sir

Yours very truly
E. C. Gaskell

*

502 **512** 517[2]

SMITH and ELDER[3]

46 Plymouth Grove
Septr 4th [1862]

Gentlemen,

I can only repeat what I have said before; that you shall have
the conclusion of my story as soon as I can finish it. But from local

[1] *In folder marked* PUBLICATION DEPARTMENT No 2/3412 Mrs Gaskell Manchester Date 20th August 1862 Answd same date Mr Williams.

[2] To George Smith.

[3] *Address (on envelope)* Messrs Smith & Elder | 65 Corn-Hill | London E.C.
Postmark I | SP 4 | MANCHESTER | 1862 | z. *In folder marked* PUBLICATION DEPART-
MENT No 2/3611 Mrs Gaskell Manchester Date 4th September 1862
Answd 3 October 1862 in private note from G S Mr Williams. [The words 'in
private note from G S' appear to be in George Smith's hand.]

causes my time is so much occupied that I am unwilling to have any specified time. I can only say that if from this delay of mine Messrs Ticknor and Fields choose to 'recede' from their bargain, I shall be content to have the sum thus lost deducted from what Mr Smith agreed to pay me. Still I should like to remind you that *I* never named any positive time for the completion of the book, and only yielded to Mr Smith's request that the printing might be commenced because I believed it to be convenient to him, and also because he stated that this beginning to print need not hurry me. I remain, gentlemen,

Yours faithfully

E. C. Gaskell

₀ **513** ₀

Uɴᴋɴᴏᴡɴ[1]

Plymouth Grove,
Manchester.
Sep. 12—[?1862]

My dear Sir,

I hope that you will not measure my gratitude to you for so kindly sending the Cleopatra-poem, by my promptitude in writing to thank you for it. Please accept now my best thanks for it. I admired it as a whole quite as much as I had expected to do from the extracts that I had seen in the reviews. Cleopatra seems to be the special means of inspiration for Mr Story, for I think he has never in sculpture equalled his marble Cleopatra; and certainly this poem is by far the finest that he has ever written.[2]

Thanking you again for the pleasure I had in reading it, I remain,

Very sincerely yours

E. C. Gaskell.

---

[1] Written in a formal hand. The paper associates this letter with 575 (late information), but the latter is not dated with certainty.

[2] See James, *Story*, II, p. 217. The poem can be found in Story's *Graffiti D'Italia* (Edinburgh & London, 1868, pp. 147–54), presumably reprinted from a periodical.

*511a 514 0

?W. S. WILLIAMS[1]

46 Plymouth Grove
September 14th [1862]

Dear Sir
I have received your letter of the 11th and am very much puzzled by this passage—
'If at your convenience you would oblige us with sheet 16 Vol 1 to the end & sheets 1 to 15 of Vol 2 for press the printers would be able to work them off at once'[.] Neither Mr Gaskell nor I can make it out as *all* the revises of the proofs have been returned, and we think there must have been some mistake in the post. Will you direct to me
Care of
William Shaen Esq—
6 Cornfield Terrace
Eastbourne

Believe me to remain

Yours truly
E. C. Gaskell

0 515 0

UNKNOWN[2]

Sept 25, [?1862] Eastbourne,
Sussex

My dear Madam,
I have received your letter at this out of the way place, (where I shall not remain much longer, so *Plymouth Grove, Manchester* will be your best address, if you have to write again.) Your MSS has not been forwarded to me along with your letter; so at present

[1] Perhaps a dictated letter. *In folder marked* PUBLICATION DEPARTMENT No 2/4048 Mrs Gaskell Manchester Date 14th September 1862 Answd 15th September 1862 Mr Williams.   [2] *Annotation* [1862].

I have no opportunity of judging of it's merits; when I have read it I will give you the best & truest opinion I can. I feel very sorry for you, for I think I can see that, at present, at least you are rather overwhelmed with all you have to do; and I think it possible that the birth of two children,—one so close upon another may have weakened you bodily, and made you more unfit to cope with your many household duties. Try—even while waiting for my next letter, to strengthen yourself by every means in your power; by being very careful as to your diet; by cold-bathing, by resolute dwelling on the cheerful side of everything; and by learning to œconomize strength as much as possible in all your household labours; for I dare say you already know how much time may be saved, by beginning any kind of work in good time, and not driving all in a hurry to the last moment. I hope (for instance,) you soap & soak your dirty clothes well for some hours before beginning to wash; and that you understand the comfort of pre-paring a dinner & putting it on to cook *slowly*, early in the morn-ing, as well as having *always* some kind of sewing ready arranged to your hand, so that you can take it up at any odd minute and do a few stitches. I dare say at present it might be difficult for you to procure the sum that {may} is necessary to purchase a sewing machine; and indeed, unless you are a good workwoman to begin with, you will find a machine difficult to manage. But *try*, my dear, to conquer your 'clumsiness' in sewing; there are thousand little bits of work, which no sempstress ever does so well as the wife or mother who knows how the comfort of those she loves depends on little pecularities which no one but she cares enough for the wearers to attend to. My first piece of advice to you would be *Get strong*—I am almost sure you are out of bodily health and that, if I were you, I would make it my first object to attain. Did you ever try a tea-cup full of *hop-tea* the first thing in the morning? It is a very simple tonic, and could do no harm. Then again try *hard* to arrange your work well. That is a regular piece of head-work and taxes a woman's powers of organization; but the reward is immediate and great. I have known well what it is to be both wanting money, & feeling weak in body and entirely dis-heartened. I do not think I ever cared for literary fame; nor do I think it *is* a thing that ought to be cared for. It comes and it goes. The exercise of a talent or power *is* always a great pleasure; but one should weigh well whether this pleasure may not be obtained by the sacrifice of some duty. When I had *little* children I do not think I could have written stories, because I should have become too much absorbed in my *fictitious* people to attend to my *real* ones. I think you would be sorry if you began to feel that your desire to earn money, even for so laudable an object as to help your husband, made you unable to give your tender sympathy to your little ones in their small joys & sorrows; and yet, don't you know how you,—how every one, who tries to write stories *must* become absorbed in them, (fictitious though they be,) if they are to interest their readers in them. Besides viewing the subject from a solely artistic point of view a good writer of fiction must have *lived* an active & sympathetic life if she wishes her books to have strength & vitality in them. When you are forty, and if you have a gift for being an authoress you will write ten times as good a novel as you could do now, just because you will have gone through so much more of the interests of a wife and a mother.

All this does not help you over present difficulties, does it? Well then let us try what will—How much have you in your own power? How much must you submit to because it is God's appointment? You have it in your own power to arrange your day's work to the very best of your ability[,] making the various household arts into real studies (& there is plenty of poetry and association about them—remember how the Greek princesses in Homer washed the clothes &c &c &c &c.) You would perhaps find a little book called The Finchley Manual of Needlework of real use to you in sewing; it gives patterns and directions &c. Your want of strength may be remedied *possibly* by care & attention; if not, you must submit to what is God's ordinance; only remember that the very hardest day's bodily work I have ever done has never produced anything like the intense exhaustion I have felt after writing the 'best' parts of my books.

All this letter is I fear disheartening enough: you must remember I have not seen your MSS as yet; & I can only judge of it from such a number of MSS sent me from time to time; and only *one* of these writers has ever succeeded in getting her writings published, though in several instances I have used my best endeavours on their behalf.

Have you no sister or relation who could come & help you for a little while till you get stronger,—no older friend at hand who would help you to plan your work so that it should oppress you as little as possible? If this letter has been of *any* use to you, do not scruple to write to me again, if I can give you help. I may not always be able to answer you as soon as I do now, for at home my life is very very much occupied, but I will always *try* & do so. And do my dear, always remember to ask God for light and help —for with Him all things are possible—and it almost astonishes one sometimes to find how He sends down answers to one's prayers in new bright thoughts, or in even more bright & lovely peace.

Your sincere though unknown friend
E. C. Gaskell

509 516 *523a

MARIANNE GASKELL

Thursday Morning
35 Marine Parade
Eastbourne.
[September 1862]

My dearest Polly,

Here is Mrs Story's letter forwarded to me by you this morning;—you may fancy what a flutter it has put us into. I have written to give them their choice, of coming *here*, or going to P. Grove on Monday,—they are to *telegraph* their decision to *us*; *write* it to *you*; so that by *Saturday Morng*, I reckon, that *you* will hear. If they decide to come to P. Grove, we shall return on Monday\all thro'/, with our return tickets, getting in latish at night, say 8 or 9. You had better (in case they decide on this) write to Mrs E. Wilkinson, & offer to give up yr place to Mrs Story & ask for Mr Story to go as an extra person; you may depend upon it she will make them very welcome. She knows them; they are lions & Northerners &c. Ask Hearn to secure lodgings (she knows all about them) for Clarke & boys. Order meat, consulting with Mary. Secure any help that Mary or Hearn think is needed. You see they *want* quiet; so I *doubt* if our proposed PARTIES will do; but about this I will consult Meta & let you know. I think you had better *not* tell Papa of this hurry until their decision comes; it *may* be to come *here*. Or they *may* come round by Manchester *here*; in which case send a hamper *by them*; with *cooked* round of Beef (better be got ready any how) more tea, soap, candles *&c &c &c &c*, as we shall *try* to take them in to our lodgings,—taking others with a view to accomodate them; so we shall need all possible provisions.

Our letters are all underpaid, so we have to repay. *Is* it not a case of Harcourt over again—no time for a word more to catch the morning post. *If you hear they are coming* engage any help you like[;] don't spare[.]

E G

512¹ **517** 532

GEORGE SMITH

[?Late September 1862]

⟨. . .⟩ it as soon as possible for {many}\one or two/reasons, although, for my own part, I should be glad for it not to be published before February. The particular reason which I have for wishing to send you the MSS as soon as ever I can is this. I think I have told you of a MSS which I have had lying by me for 4 years, half-finished, of a (probably) one volume story. This spring I sent it\incomplete as it was/to 'All the Year Round,[']² who paid me for it at once, saying that they should not require the conclusion, in all probability, until the story they were in treaty for, to *succeed* 'No Name' had been published. But now they write to say it is most desirable for them to have the end\of my story/by the end of this month, which makes me very anxious first to finish 'Sylvia's Lovers'. I should be so much obliged to you if you could *soon* tell me how many of *my* pages would be required for the 3rd vol.

It has been a great comfort having both the rest here, & the quiet time for writing; but I believe we ought to be going back to Manchester, (& very hard work, I fear, which exhausts one both bodily & mentally with depressing atmosphere of both kinds.) There are just one or two things which make the exact day of our leaving here uncertain, but we shall not in any case, leave *before* Saturday; so if you could write by return I should be sure to receive your letter here. After that Manchester will be the safest address.

¹ To Smith & Elder.
² Probably 'A Dark Night's Work'. See Letter 451*a*.

Will you kindly send proof sheets to Messrs Williams and Norgate,—for Tauchnitz? I wish North & South would make friends,
& let us have cotton, & then our poor people would get work,[1]
and then you should have as many novels as you liked to take, and
we should[2] not be killed with 'Poor on the Brain', as I expect we
shall before the winter is over. We were really glad before leaving
home to check each other in talking of the one absorbing topic,
which was literally haunting us in our sleep, as well as being the
first thoughts on wakening and the last at night. ⟨. . .⟩

₀ **518** ₀

UNKNOWN[3]

46 Plymouth Grove
Manchester.
September 30th [1862]

Sir,
I am going to publish a one-volume story in 'All the Year
Round', where I suppose it will occupy from ten to twelve
numbers. The title of it is 'A Night's Work',[4]—and they offer me
early proof-sheets in order to have it republished in America.
After it is completed in All the Year Round I have the right to
have it republished here in one volume.
Are you inclined to make any offer to me for the power of
republishing it in America? If so, perhaps you will be so kind as to
write by return steamer, and if your proposal is satisfactory I will
make prompt arrangements for sending you out proof-sheets ('All
the Round' [sic] type) of the whole story.
I remain, Sir

Yours respectfully
E. C. Gaskell

[1] Reference to the Cotton Famine in Lancashire as a result of the American Civil
War.
[2] From this point to the end the text is taken from the Knutsford Edition of
Mrs Gaskell's Works, ed. A. W. Ward, I, p. xxxviii.
[3] *Annotation* Sepr 30/62.
[4] 'A Dark Night's Work', *All the Year Round*, 24 Jan.–21 March 1863.

₀ **519** ₀

UNKNOWN

Plymouth Grove
Manchester.
Decr 11. 1862

Sir,

I beg to decline your proposal of writing for a new weekly periodical. I am not in the habit of writing for periodicals, except occasionaly [*sic*] (as a personal mark of respect & regard to Mr Dickens) in Household Words. I never fixed any price on what I did then, nor do I know at what rate he pays me. I choose my own subjects when I write, and treat them in the style that I myself prefer. But half a dozen papers in H. W. are all I ever wrote for any periodical as I dislike & disapprove of such writing\for my-self/as a general thing.

Yours &c
E. C. Gaskell.

*

₀ **520** ₀

UNKNOWN

Saturday Evening
February 7. [1863][1]

My dear Sir,

We have paid for the passage of a Mrs Regan[2] & child in the 'Merrie England', lying in the East India Docks bound for Sydney; and, by the enclosed note you will see that Mr Walcott says she is to sail on the *11th*; the same date, with the addition of WEDNESDAY is repeated in the emigration paper.

But in the Manchester Guardian she is advertized to sail on the *10th*, & it is of *great* consequence to us to know on *what* day she (Mrs Regan) must be in London, *as soon as possible*, as we have

[1] Several years are possible, but the *Manchester Guardian* of 7 February 1863 contains the relevant advertisement.
[2] This name might be Ryan.

some more preparations as to her outfit &c to make. Could you
tell us *by telegraph,*—

AT WHAT TIME*? ON WHAT DAY? the Merrie England will sail?

Yours very truly

E. C. Gaskell

*At what time must the passengers be on board?

₀ 521 ₀

UNKNOWN

[*c.* February 1863]¹

⟨. . .⟩ There is only one thing [in *Sylvia's Lovers*] I should like to
alter. Some one—Judge Coleridge—as far as I can make out, from
arms, &c., and from Judge Crompton's testimony as to the handwriting—has sent me an anonymous letter 'from an old lawyer,'
saying I had made a mistake in old Daniel's trial, in representing
the counsel for the *defence* as making a *speech* for the prisoner.
Whereas, at that time, they were not allowed to do so; only to
watch the case and examine witnesses.

*

₀ 522 ₀

MISS BLAGDEN

Casa Sandelli

Wednesday [?May 1863]²

My dear Miss Blagden

I have sent to ask Ly Charlotte Locker to come here to tea
tomorrow night,—will you\& Miss Stebbin if she is with you,/
kindly return with Meta & me tomorrow evening³ from Mr
Kirkup's & spend the evening here?

Yours most truly

E C Gaskell

¹ From a printed source, which dates 'just after the appearance of the first
edition'.

² Dated from passport information. Mrs Gaskell was also in Florence in April
1857, but see Letter 527, which appears to refer to a recent visit, and Letter 523.

³ Alteration; doubtful reading.

0 **523** 53ᵤ

THOMAS A. TROLLOPE

Casa Sandelli
Florence.
Thursday [?May 1863]

My dear Mr Trollope—

It will give us, such great pleasure, if you will come, and drink tea with us this evening;

We are hoping to see Lady Charlotte Locker and Miss Blagden, this evening at half past eight—

With kind regards to Mrs Trollope—

Believe me
Sincerely yours
E. C. Gaskell.

*

*523a **524** 540

MARIANNE GASKELL

Hotel Barbesi, Venice
Monday Evening
[1 June 1863]

My dearest Polly,

Your Florence letter came yesterday,—your letter to Venice (dated May 27, telling of your plans, Edith Greg's marriage, M A Siltzer's engagement &c) came {yesterday} just now. I do hope you are gone to Mapledurham; only I thought you were going to the Aidés *from* WINCHESTER, or *before* you went there. You asked me if it would not be a good plan to go & see L V Jackson *between* the Cromptons & Smiths, & I said yes; & if you go to Mrs Lyall's, go to the Aidés for a day or two before they go up to town in June,—& then I thought you would be at Winchester & cd easily come over to Paris viâ Newhaven; and now it does seem rather backwards & forwards work; but still if it is using the money to give you pleasure, my darling never mind. Only *why don't you go to Winchester* as you *planned?*—Perhaps you have told

me in some letter that has missed. I only got one to the Casa
Barbesi; but several\from you/were waiting for me at the Poste
Restante, when we got to Florence. Why did Mrs Lyall not have
you? I only suggested the Aidé's as *being* NEAR Winchester. However I dare say you have explained her reason for declining your
visit and are wondering why I am so ignorant; and I am glad even
at some cost that you, or some of us should go to the Aidé's and I
hope you will have gone to Mapledurham; only as I don't know
where you will be I direct this to Mr C C—'s care. Your visit there
sounds to have been very pleasant. I confess I dread mine extremely. I feel sure I shall never get on,—and I can never play
proper I am afraid. & Florence is very shy of my going, I can see,—
I think she thinks we shan't suit. However I shall do my best.
About your coming darling—I did think of your coming by
Newhaven, & taking a return ticket,—but poor Julia dreads the
sea so much, it is perhaps as well for you to come with Mr
Crompton, only PLEASE *come by Folkestone & Boulogne*, as the
cheapest—we shall have I suspect to return—I was going to say
2nd class—but I remember our new belongings[1] wd not like to
send to meet 2nd classers. Only do come by *F & B*; as we shall all
return together[.] I do want to get Florence's dresses '*set agait*'
before the Monday if I can. I always planned your coming on
Thursday, & our meeting you,—& on Friday our having all our
Lamy business set on foot, and as much more shopping done as
we could., & resting Saturday & Sunday;\& having Mr C. C./
trying on Monday or Tuesday &c.. But now I suppose we must
manage it differently. I think we shall leave here on Saturday
aft 6; for Verona; & Sunday, *June 7* for Milan. (Julia wants us to
stay till Sunday morng & make a long day day of it to Milan;) at
any rate Milan {Monday} *Sunday* night; Bellinzona *Monday*
night, Inn at the top of St Gothard, *Tuesday* night. Lucerne,
(direct there aux soins de M. le propriétaire du

Schweizer-Hof
Lucerne
Switzerland,

if you write again,) WEDNESDAY night, June 10th, and the next
day, viâ Bâle, as far as we can get on our road to Paris. It is about
$18\frac{1}{2}$ hours from Paris to Lucerne; vice versa I mean; but that
would be too long a day for any of us. But we shall try and get as
far as we can on the Thursday; so as to, *if we can*, see & fix with

[1] Florence Gaskell had become engaged to Charles Crompton.

Mme Lamy a little on the *Friday afternoon*. But if we could get a few patterns, you could help us to choose on the Saturday, & perhaps things might be got on with. I wish I knew of some place in Paris where you could be waiting for us. Mme Lamy would receive & *wash* you,—& at the Hotel Brighton (3 old ladies keep it,)—but after all we *may* not (as you are uncertain) arrive at Paris in time to do anything on Friday. I have written to the Hotel du Reservoir at Versailles to reservoir[—] ask their terms as it is in by far the pleasantest situation; but I have not heard as yet. I shall write to *Mr Crompton* when I do hear, as being more certain of his address. I am afraid we *must* do some shopping on Saturday if we don't do it on Friday, as I can't afford to stay TOO long (so large a party), at what may be an expensive hotel—So prepare Mr Crompton's mind for a probable little giro into Paris that\Saturday/afternoon. I tell you nothing of ourselves; we are all very well, & enjoying Venice very much; only wishing you were with us my darling. I am sorry that MSS has gone to Mr Froude, as I don't like his having to take Mr Smith's refuse for old friendship's sake.[1] But I have done my best to remedy this by writing to Mr Froude to bid him send the MSS back to Mr Smith, & to desire {him}\the latter/to seal it up *at once*, & send it to me, care of W[.] Shaen. At any rate, dear[,] you did your best, but I am *very* angry with Mr Smith[.] *Don't you have anything more to do with it*, love. Mr Smith did *quite* right to refuse it, as it's one probable great merit was it's *novelty*, and as there had been previous articles on the subject it had no longer the recommendation of novelty—but then he should never have presumed to settle to whom I would like to have it sent. I said when I saw that he had gone right against my distinct desire, & called a night's work a *dark* night[']s work, that I wd never publish with him again; & this confirms me. I do not think he ought to have done it. Write *at any rate* to me, *care of Mme Lamy*[.] We will call for the letter there after and I will direct to Mapledurham. Your own

E G

---

[1] See p. 712 below.

₀ **525** ₀

Mr Proby

Plymouth Grove,
Manchester. July 7 [?1863]

Dear Mr Proby,

Strangely enough the cause of my writing to you, is our having
—by accident—left a small debt at Venice unpaid. When we
remembered our negligence in London, we wrote to Signor
Barbesi asking him what the amount had been, and how we could
best transmit it to him. He replied in a very pretty note that he
should not allow us to re-fund the sum he had paid on our behalf;
but that if we wanted to put ourselves out of his debt, he should
consider the best way of our doing so would be for us to write to
you, and tell you that we had found you fully justified in your
recommendation of his hotel.

This I gladly do; having been very much pleased indeed with
the hotel, and with Signor Barbesi's kindness and attention, and I
am really glad on my own account to have this opportunity of
thanking you for sending us to him.

He *is* the Signor Barbesi of the Palazzo Zucchelli, after all the
contradictory advertisements in Bradshaw—

We remember your kindness with sincere gratitude, and hope
that if ever you are near us, you will let us help you in any local
difficulty should any occur, and at any rate give us the pleasure of
seeing you.

Very truly yrs
E. C Gaskell.

₅₀₄ **526** ₅₂₈

Charles Eliot Norton

July 13, 1863
46 Plymouth Grove

My dear Mr Norton, Don't you know the way in which, if you
have not written for a long time to any friend you find it so very
difficult to begin? Well, but I am going to begin, only what shall I

tell you? if I had but been writing to you as I ought to have done all this past year I should have said no end of things, which even now I am sorry to let go into oblivion. First and foremost I feel as if I had behaved so disagreeably and ungratefully to Grace, in never even acknowledging her charming long letter about Susan, and your acquaintance, friendship, love, and your close approaching marriage. It was just exactly what I wanted to know, and at the time I was full of pleased gratification and passive gratitude. I believe I was too busy and too anxious just then to write a *long* letter; & foolishly thought a *short* letter in reply to such a one was ungracious, when I had so much to say,—and the time for writing a *long* letter did not come till I was too much ashamed of my long silence to make use of it. And now I have so much to say that I must shake it all out as if it was coming out of a bag, helter, skelter. In the first place thank you & Susan so *very* much for my dear little American pencil. I do so like it and value it—*please what sort of wood? is it?* I almost thought it was marble or agate, it was so cool and hard; but somebody told me it was *wood*. Thank you so much dear friends—it seems as if it was so far away for any one to be thinking about me,—almost as if it had been sent out of Heaven. Florence too is so much pleased with her fan; and she & the new son Charlie talk of writing to you themselves. You may be sure that what gives *them* pleasure makes me happy too. But I have had to take a good while to reconcile myself to the parting from this dear child, who still seems so much a child, & to want 'mother's shelter' so much. She knew Mr Crompton pretty well from having stayed in his father's house last autumn for six weeks or so,—but *we* did not—we had just been introduced to him,—and knew the pleasant straightforward look on his face—(some people call him handsome)[.] When she engaged herself to him—(in passing through London to join me in Paris before going to Italy, as I think Meta must have told you.—) I wrote to ask him,—her—& Mr Gaskell if we should still go on to Italy; and all three said yes,—so we went, and our little lassie was very happy & peaceful; and enjoyed everything very much; and was not anxious about letters or anything. He came to meet us at Versailles, (where we stayed a week to choose dresses &c in Paris,) & since then we stayed a fortnight in London at his father's house, in order to make general family acquaintance & friendship. He is the eldest of 7 children, father & mother both alive. He is 30, (Florence 20) and his father & mother both say he has*not*/given them a moment's uneasiness since his birth in any way. He has almost perfect health, & perfect temper; *I* should have said *not* clever; but he was 4th wrangler at Cambridge and is a Fellow of Trinity, and is getting on very fast in his profession; so I suppose he has those solid intellectual qualities which tell in *action*, though not in *conversation*[.] But his goodness is what gives me the thankfullest feeling of confidence in him. They will have to live in London—(probably Harewood Sq, off the New Road, Regent's-Park-wards) and will have to begin œconomically—(one of his nice feelings is his thorough hearty approval of his father's plan of dividing his property among his 7 children equally, instead of making an eldest son, à la mode Anglaise—) Florence is very œconomical and managing. We tell her she will *starve* her husband she is so full of œconomical plans. Mr Crompton's eldest sister (a year younger than he) is married to Mr Llewellyn Davis, a clergyman whose writings in Macmillan &c.—he is one of Mr Maurice's school, are very likely known to you—he signs J. Ll. D. He has also published {works} sermons on the Atonement—true meaning of Sacrifice &c. Mr Crompton is not exactly a Unitarian, nor exactly broad Church,—but perhaps rather more of the latter than the former. He is so good-principled he may be called a religious man; for I am sure the root of his life is in religion. But he has not imagination enough to be what one calls *spiritual*. It is just the same want that makes him not care for music or painting, —nor much for poetry. In these tastes Florence is his superior, although *she* is not 'artistic'. Then he cares for science,—in which she is at present ignorant. His strong good, *un*sensitive character is just what will, I trust, prove very grateful to her anxious, con-scientious little heart. They are to be married *here*—(the Cromp-tons all wished for a *country* wedding,—and he had a particular friend, a clergyman, who he particularly wished to marry them—) but, after some discussion it is settled that they are to be married in Brook Street Chapel—where Mr John James Tayler used to preach,—by Mr Gaskell. No one but the two families are to be at the wedding,—and it is to take place some day in the first week of September,—*day* not fixed yet. They go into Scotland; return here to pay us a little visit before settling down for the lawyer's year in London,—about Octr 20. He will come the Northern Circuit, and bring her here to stay with us, as often as he can dur-ing those times. So much for *that*. I was touched by what you said in one of your letters to Meta,—about her being weighed down into care by the pressure of the sorrow around her. I am always so afraid it is so. Last autumn & winter was *such* hard work—we were often off at nine,—not to come home till 7, or 1/2 past, too worn out to eat or do anything but go to bed. The one thought ran thro' all our talk almost like a disease. Marianne worked quite as hard, if not harder than Meta,—(tho' we all gave our lives to 'the Distress'—) but Marianne did not think so deeply about it all as Meta,—nothing like it. She decided quicker in individual cases; and shook them off sooner,—out of her mind I mean,—but Meta laboured day and night in weighing and planning and thinking,—and going out again, after a hard hard day if she thought one little scrap of duty or kindness or enquiry had been omitted. And oh! I was so sorry to see her fade away under it all—the over-pressure on the brain telling on the spine, & necessitating rest, while yet the very brain made her refuse by it's activity. I cannot tell you what a nightmare last winter was—and at the last we seemed to have done more harm than good—not 'we['] alone—perhaps 'we' less than most; but the imposition, the deterioration in character &c &c were so great. It is of no use dwelling on it now—i.e going into details,—but if you were here I should so have liked to consult you about what *really does good* among the poor. We fear next winter will be as bad; but at present there is a great lull. To go back to the kind of disheartening things—people who were good & hardworking before, & at the beginning of the 'relief', people we knew & had respected, were found paying a man 6d a week to answer to their name, & claim relief for them in different districts[.] Our charwoman,—a widow, who had brought up her children well & without help from the parish,—declined coming to wash here (which she had done for 7 years,) because she could get more by *not* working, & applying to the Relief Board. One *local* Relief committee—consisting of small shop-keepers, were found to have supplied themselves with great-coats out of the Funds intrusted to them &c &c &c &c. I must go now,—I will write again soon—especially if you will write to me. Thank you so much for sending us those loose sheets of newspaper extracts. Who wrote *Two Summers*, a poem in the September No of the Atlantic, 1862.[1]

> Your ever affec[tionate] friend
> E C Gaskell

[1] Vol. X, p. 311, by 'Florence Percy', *i.e.* Elizabeth C. Akers (1832–1911). It probably reminded Mrs Gaskell of her son's death.

I have not told you a word about Italy—How *often* & OFTEN we
thought of & talked about you—how we took yr book to Orvieto
&c &c[.] My kind love to Susan—& to your mother & Jane &
Grace.

₀ 527 ₀

?CATHERINE NORTH

46 Plymouth Grove.
July 16. [?1863][1]

My dear Miss North,
    I enclose you the promised note to Mr Trollope, which I can
only hope will lead to as pleasant an acquaintance between him
and you, as ours was. Both he and his wife completely won possession of our hearts in Florence, and I am so glad to think of any
friends of mine succeeding to the pleasure of our intercourse at the
Villino Trollope.
    I have such a charming remembrance of my afternoon tea with
you, dear Miss North—

Ever yours very truly
E. C. Gaskell

₅₂₆ 528 ₅₄₆

CHARLES ELIOT NORTON

46 Plymouth Grove
July 28th [1863]

My dear Mr Norton,
    We are all so very glad to hear of your & Susan's happiness in
your little boy; whom we never expected, though I suppose you
did. I do hope your anxiety about Susan was not very serious, and
I shall be anxious to hear again, although I trust from what you
say that she is sure to complete her recovery without further
draw-back. Is not your Mother pleased? But I forget—he is not
her first grandchild, though he is *your* first child.

[1] See the title of the article in Letter 556.

It is so impossible to learn the truth here about any thing in America,—one telegram seems hopeful—the next bad again—Is not this violent resistance to the conscription in New York very bad? Yet if I make out rightly you must have written hopefully at the very time when the riots were going on; and to judge by the newspaper accounts they must have been a very serious demonstration of the popular feeling being against the continuation of the war, at any rate in New York; and in the very moment of success on the Mississippi too! Please write us a political letter; but most of all write to us about your wife & boy,—and tell her I think she has passed the acme of her life,—when all is over and the little first born darling lies nuzzling and cooing by one's side. I do rejoice with you dear friend on your new title of Father. Our love to you all. In haste.

Your affectionate friend
E C Gaskell

ₒ 529 ₒ

Mr Wilbraham

46 Plymouth Grove
August 26th [?1863]

Dear Mr Wilbraham,
I think you are one of the Secretaries for the Emigration Society of Factory Operatives,[1]—although I dare say I have not got the right title. Could you tell me how an operative of the name of Shapcott, who has worked for ten years in Clarke's Mill Ancoats, and has an *excellent* character can take his family out to one of the Colonies, and to *which* Colony it would be desirable for a man, aged between 30 & 40, with a wife and four children under 8, to go to? His wife has been known to us for a long time as a good striving patient woman, willing to turn her hand to either cleaning, washing or needlework; and Shapcott himself is equally willing; can read and write & 'do sums' *pretty* well. Three of their four children are girls;

---

[1] The Emigration Aid Society was established in April 1863 and 1000 operatives left Lancashire for New Zealand, so we date this letter in this year, although 1865 is not impossible. (On 22 August 1864, Mrs Gaskell was in Pontresina. See Chadwick, *Mrs Gaskell*, p. 298.)

I am afraid you are not at home, as Mr Vernon Lushington called on you last Sunday, & found you out; but I shall be very glad of any answer or information as soon as you return[.]

Yours very truly
E C. Gaskell

₀ **530** ₀

MRS SHAW[1]

Plymouth Grove,

Manchester, Aug. 29 [1863]

My Dear, Dear Mrs Shaw:

You cannot think how our hearts bled for you, when we had the sad news we had only guessed at in the papers, confirmed to us, by a letter from Mrs Sturgis. I know as well as any one that he died nobly doing his duty, 'laying down his life for others,' thus showing the greatest love possible; but O! dear friend, I know what it is to lose a child, and I do feel for you. Some one has sent us the lines on Colonel Shaw,[2] signed 'E. S., Boston.' Reading them, and thinking of you and of him, *where he is buried,* I say that I would rather be the mother of your dead son, than the mother of any living man I know. I wish I had ever seen him, if only for five minutes,—noble hero, true Christian. What does the poor insult signify? Will not God raise him up to His own right hand, from any depth of earth? Yes, and those whom he died for will rise with him, and bear their solemn witness of blessing to him before the throne.

I cannot write more. Dear Mrs Shaw, good bye! God be with you, as he was when he strengthened you to give up your child to His service!

Your true and affectionate friend,
E. C. Gaskell.

[1] Original MS. not seen.
[2] Mrs Gaskell wrote a short appreciation of Robert Gould Shaw in *Macmillan's Magazine,* December 1863, IX, pp. 113–17.

₀ **531** ₅₃₃

JOHN RELLY BEARD

46 Plymouth Grove
Septr [1863]

My dear Dr Beard,

I want you to enter into a conspiracy against Mr Gaskell; and like all conspirators you must be so kind as to do your work quietly & silently.

The case is this. For years past Mr & Mrs Story (the American sculptor & his wife, he the son of Judge Story) who live at Rome have been urging Mr Gaskell to pay them a visit there. Two years ago he met them in Switzerland,[1] & he & Mr Story became real friends. This year (in August) Mr Story wrote to beg him to go to them at Siena,—saying (all that was very true,) that Mr Gaskell would work the longer for having a\complete/holiday & change of scene. That was out of the question owing to our daughter's approaching marriage. Then came the question 'Could not Mr Gaskell go to them in Rome in the winter?' This, we, his family[,] are exceedingly anxious that he should do. The congregation (as far as we can learn) are most willing. Six weeks would allow him *nearly* 5 weeks there. The Storys entreat him to come. He says 'It is too far off to plan for, but he does not see how he could go, because of the Home Mission.' Now could he not start *directly* after the January Examination; and would there not be some means, under the circumstances of prolonging his annual holiday from Home Mission work so as to allow him six weeks clear? He will (as you know) take no steps that can cause the slightest inconvenience to others, least of all to the Students; nor do I know what could be done. I do not even remember exactly how long that annual holiday is. Is there no teacher in Manchester who could do something to keeping up the Students to their work, although probably not so well as Mr Gaskell. I would willingly pay whatever might be required to secure the services of such a one.\Mr Poynting? but *I* don't know./You know how Mr Gaskell will dislike any 'fuss'—or asking any favour; but it does

---

[1] See Letter 493.

seem to me a pity he should miss this opportunity; for you know Rome is not visitable after May, or before November.

Pray help us.

Yours very truly
E. C. Gaskell

517 **532** 539

GEORGE SMITH

46 Plymouth Grove
Septr 20th [1863]

My dear Sir,

Firstly I gladly accept your offer of 50£ for the copyright of Lizzie Leigh[1] &c—.

Secondly—I have ever so many things begun. 'Life and Times of Madame de Sévigné' more in my head than out of it; but I think it will be good. 'Notes of a wanderer'[2]—all sorts of odd bits, scenes, conversations\with rather famous people in Paris/, small adventures, descriptions &c &c met with during our two last journeys abroad in Brittany Paris, Rome, Florence—50 pages written—\I thought of sending this to Mr Froude to make up for the 'Camorra'—that unlucky piece of work/

'Two Mothers' in my head very clear—A story begun for the Xmas number of Household Words; not promised to them, or even spoken about to them,—but I thought that if I wrote another for H W, (and they always want me to do so,) I could make up a vol: with the former stories in H W, of which I retain the copyright—about 20 pages written,—might be 100, I think. Now I should like to help you much as you are at pinch—(only I should still more like to have the fun of criticizing *your* first story, & you say you shall try your hand, all others failing,—) but then I don't know if Cousin Phillis[3] (this last story) would not be too short for your purpose; & secondly if you had it it wd not help me to fill

---

[1] A receipt is extant, dated Manchester, 24 September 1863 (Mrs E. V. Gordon's collection).

[2] 'French Life', *Fraser's Magazine*, April–June 1864.

[3] *Cornhill*, November 1863–February 1864.

up & sell the copyright of a volume. So I don't exactly know what to do.

Our bride & bridegroom[1] write as if they were very happy reading law, novels, driving fishing & boating—(Llanberis) We look to yr coming again soon. Till then I shall not forgive myself, —yet my blunder was made with the best intentions[.]

Yours most truly

E C Gaskell

531 **533** 534

JOHN RELLY BEARD

Saturday Morg

[?September 1863]

Dear Dr Beard,

Your letter *about the Chapel* just received. What about the *Home Mission*? please reply, for I am afraid of one piece of my plot exploding (in a letter from the trustees, before the other is concluded. The greatest haste & with no end of thanks, dear Famulus,

Yours most truly

E C Gaskell

533 **534** 542

JOHN RELLY BEARD

46, Plymouth Grove.

Septr 24th Thursday [1863]

Dear Dr Beard,

Thank you *most truly* and heartily. With your help I feel confident that I shall win; and if I do, I shall not forget that {I owe half}\I more than half owe/my victory to you.

But whether I win or lose, I shall always be most gratefully and truly yrs

E. C. Gaskell.

---

[1] Florence and Charles Crompton.

507 **535** 0

W. W. STORY

46, Plymouth Grove,
Octr 2nd [1863]

My dear Mr Story,

I got your kind letter yesterday, which must have crossed mine to you on the road. About this other please take no further notice; as I cannot help thinking that it must seem to you\very/ inconsiderate of me to have proposed ourselves to you for a visit in the middle of what, as your letter reminds me, is in every way such a full, busy time for you. I remember how many claims dear Mrs Story had on her time when we were staying with you in the Via Sant'Isidoro; and your acquaintance must almost have doubled itself since then, and this winter you will have your brother-in-law and his wife to take everywhere and introduce to all the contrasted phases of Roman life. So that altogether I feel as if I ought to be very penitent for ever having offered ourselves to you: but you see it was the great magnet that was to draw Mr Gaskell to Rome, the hope of seeing you and Mrs Story there, and though I do not mean to despair at all, yet I think that he will consider it rather like Hamlet without the part of Hamlet if Rome does not yield him a good deal of your company. I have gone so far in arranging with different people to facilitate his holiday for the month of February & a week of March, that I think he will still go to Rome; but I shall send him en garçon, for I dare say that he would feel more independent in an hotel without me, and with no tie to bring him back from his Forums, or the old book-stalls of the Piazza Navona, until the pangs of hunger remind him that there is such a thing as dinner.

Now, dear Mr Story and dear Mrs Story, please forgive me for my having offered ourselves to you at a time when I might have known the strain of hurry that would be wearing on you. I know so well myself what it is to have a great many people coming en masse, dependent on you for a certain amount of amusement and help, and coming\in/& going\out,/and talking, and requiring an amount of civility and exertion that almost breaks you down: for Manchester has several times lately been the centre of a sight-see-ing crowd (at the time of the Arts Treasures, of the British

Association's meeting here &c. &c.) and I have always felt that I would be the last person to add the straw to the back of any camel who might be in the same over-burdened state:—and yet here I go and offer to pay you a visit in the very thick of a time that I dare say seems to you already far too full and busy, as you look forward to it.

You must not even consider Mr Gaskell a charge when he is in Rome—when you can walk out with him, it will be his rarest treat, and if you will ever fire a piece at him as you go or come from your studio it will brighten his\whole/day for him: but you must never feel bound to do more than you are inclined for.

I should like to know how long beforehand I ought to engage a room for him, as last year we heard of people, whose rooms had been engaged six weeks before they came finding them given to others their arrival. *Is the new hotel opened yet? or is the Angleterre still the best?*

I am sure that you will not think me very troublesome to beg for an answer to these two questions.

Ever, with best love to Mrs Story,

Yours aff[ectionate]ly & truly
E. C. Gaskell.

491a **535a** 540a

CHARLES BOSANQUET[1]

46 Plymouth Grove
Manchester.
Octr 10th [1863]

My dear Mr Bosanquet,

Although I feel very much ashamed of my long silence I do not intend our correspondence to cease for want of an acknowledgement of apparent neglect on my part. I have to thank you much for a letter received in February when we were almost worn-out with the busy work of the winter; most of our days being spent from 9 A M to 7-30 P.M. in the Sewing-Schools. We were all so knocked up by this fulfilment of extra duty that, as soon as the great strain of the Distress was lessened by the organization in the

[1] *Annotation 1863.*

distribution of Relief, and by the increased amount of mill-work for our girls, we resolved to have some entire change before this next winter, by going abroad for a time. But on our passage through London in March, Florence,—you remember the little Flossy of Heidelberg days,—became engaged to the eldest son of Judge Crompton, a distant relation of ours. This did not however prevent our going abroad; as for many reasons it was almost necessary, & Mr Crompton, (a barrister,) knew that it was very unlikely that Florence could have the advantage of going to Italy after she was married. During those few days in London, Meta, visiting a friend in Russell Sq: saw you in the distance, and ran after you for some way, hoping to overtake you; but in vain. All summer we have naturally been much occupied about Florence; we were only a very few days in London on our return; but I then asked Thurstan Holland for your address, hoping to find time to call on Mrs Bosanquet. He told me she had just got a little daughter; so I felt it was not a suitable time for a stranger to try and make her acquaintance. Now Florence is married; and she would be so very glad to see you if you are ever passing 89 Oxford Terrace; as she says she has never seen you since the old Heidelberg days. We are settled down to another winter, without many events, and with the prospect of much less hardship I am thankful to say; but still with a good deal to be done. We have a dear and most valuable cousin established in Manchester as a curate; he was very much interested in the account published in the Times some time ago, date unknown, of a Bloomsbury flower-show, the rules and details of which he thought might be made available in his parish. If you should be acquainted with these (TOWN) rules for a cottage flower-show, I should be very much obliged to you if you would send them to us. And all this time I have not congratulated you on the birth of your little girl! And Mrs Bosanquet too!—and the grandfather and grandmother! and uncles. But I do most sincerely and earnestly hope that your little daughter may be a great comfort and blessing to you. Pray let me hear from you before a great lapse of time; and ever believe me (whether a good or a bad *correspondent*)

Yours most truly

E. C. Gaskell[1]

1 See p. 477, n. 2 above.

523 **536** 0

THOMAS A. TROLLOPE

46, Plymouth Grove—
Novr 4. [1863]

My dear Mr Trollope,

Will you allow me to introduce to you Mr Albert Rutsen, who is very anxious to add the pleasure of your acquaintance to the other delights of Florence. Mr Rutsen is travelling in company with a Mr Symonds, who is very intimate with some very dear friends of mine, and whom therefore I consider almost as an acquaintance; but not actually knowing him myself, I hardly like to trouble you with giving him also an introduction to you—You may have heard of him as the successful candidate for the Newdigate prize at Oxford a year to two ago.[1] I am plunging myself, you see, still more deeply in debt[2] to you, dear Mr Trollope; and you give me no opportunity of repayment! When will you?

Yours, with kindest remembrance to Mrs Trollope, most truly
E. C. Gaskell.

0 **537** 0

JAMES DIXON

46 Plymouth Grove
Manchester
November 14 [1863]

Thank you very much for your corrections, which will be really useful to me in a fresh edition of Sylvia's lovers which is to appear very soon.[3] At least I hope they will be in time as I shall forward them to the publisher by the same post as that which takes this letter. You are quite right in supposing that Whitby was the place I meant by Monkshaven; but I was only there once for a fortnight, about four years ago, in such cloudy November weather that I might very easily be ignorant of the points of the compass if I did not look at a map; and I am afraid that I did not

---

[1] *The Escorial*, 1860.   [2] Perhaps a reference to Letter 527.
[3] Illustrated by Du Maurier.

test my accuracy by so doing. I did not intend Haytersbank for any particular place, or if I had some faint recollection of a farm house like it, it must have been a place near Sunderland where I once stayed for a couple of nights. I had forgotten that there was such a town as Kirby Moorside until you named it. I am afraid that several of the mistakes you are so kind as to point out appear very careless; but I lead a busy life in many ways, and I have sometimes to put aside my MSS for weeks and even months; at others, just when I have begun to write some interruption comes, and I hastily finish off a sentence before leaving off writing.

Thank you once more—you will see I am only really obliged to you for your friendly helpful letter.

E. C. Gaskell.

₀ 538 ₀

MADAME WEIGERMANN

46, Plymouth Grove,
Monday, Novr 23 [1863][1]

My dear Madame Weigermann,

Would Tuesday, the 1st of { September }\December/, suit you for us to come to you? I am afraid that this is the only evening in next week that we have disengaged, and we hope so very much that it will be convenient to you, as we are looking forward to a quiet long evening with you as a real treat.

Marianne will be away; but Mr Gaskell, Meta and myself { (}and (if you will allow us to bring\her/) Miss Thompson will make up our number. Would you kindly let me have one line just to say whether this day will suit you, and at what hour you have tea—and whether you will let me bring Miss Thompson.

Ever yours affectionately,
E. C. Gaskell.

[1] November 23rd fell on a Monday in 1857 and 1863. The watermark is dated 1862.

?GEORGE SMITH

46 Plymouth Grove
Monday morng
[?Late 1863]

My dear Sir,

I suppose it would not be possible for either you or me to ask for a sight of the letters in which Mr F. Chapman says 'the substance of the agreement is contained'? I did not write at once because I wanted to hear Harry Crompton's opinion,—he, being aware of all the previous transactions & letters. I send you his letter just received—(to be burnt when read—). I have not written to Mr F. Chapman I was in such a rage;—but do you think I had better,—asking to see *letters* &c.—or ask Charlie Crompton to go, on my part &c.—I cannot remember ever having said a word of the kind,—indeed I firmly believe I never heard of the 'three month's notice' in any way. But one *may* forget; and I shd be so sorry either to do anything dishonourable, or to injure you & get you into any turmoil. There are '*queer*'\safe?/things about Mr F Chapman's behaviour about 'North & South', but that will keep.[1]

Yours most truly
E C Gaskell

?MARIANNE GASKELL

[December ?1863]

My dearest child, Cranford is worth gold, being out of print & the present row between Fred: Chapman, Mr Smith & I,[2] likely

---

[1] Amongst receipts given by Mrs Gaskell to Smith & Elder is a note which may be connected with the subject of this letter. It reads: 'This cheque\for £28.17.0/is for royalty paid to Mrs Gaskell's Solicitor by Mess⟨rs⟩ Chapman & Hall on copies of "Cranford" & "Lizzie Leigh" published by them under an old agreement (which they alleged remained in force) after we had purchased the copyrights. It should be credited to each book in equal proportions. GS Jany 3/65'. Mrs Gaskell received from Smith & Elder £50 in full payment for the copyright of *Cranford* on 6 March 1863 (she dated the receipt from Paris on 16 March 1863) and the same amount for *Lizzie Leigh and other Tales* on 24 September 1863. (Collection of Mrs E. M. Gordon.)   [2] See Letter 545.

to prolong it's being out of print. The only copy in the house is Hearn's. *Don't give any presents*; that is cousin Mary's & my most *strenuous* advice. Would you like some *tracts*? to hang on the tree (Isabel's suggestion.) Yes! we are going to the assembly. Alice is ill—scarlet fever I *fear*,—& has not been here since Wednesday last. So *I am going* in the same dress I wore at the B. Ball, brown moirè, & new head-dress, for my *blue* is much too small for me, & the *grey* pelerine is not done. I find Isabel is writing to you & will tell you all the news, which is not much. Mrs Pender had 10,000£ worth of diamonds on at the B. B. & 400£ worth of lace. I went to see Mrs Shuttleworth yesterday—I am afraid Mr S. is sinking. He was in bed, had been since last Wednesday; & taking little besides champagne. Meta & Isabel went to Mrs Pender's at the same time to look at drawings &c, but we all turned up home to dinner at 6; & then Meta went to the St Cecilia. Harry C. comes tomorrow. I THOUGHT (from Florence's letter *enclosed*) you were going to *her* from Dumbleton; but I don't understand my family's movements. I *think* she & Charlie come here 26th; we dine at the Pender's on Xmas day; Schuncks to meet the Taylers on the 30th Emil Beiss's ball on the 31st, Grundy's on the 6th; on which day Herbert J's child is to be christened.

No more news—Mr
Green—Mrs Sydney
Potter been   E G.

535a 540a 0

CHARLES BOSANQUET[1]

December 5th [1863]
46 Plymouth Grove

My dear Mr Bosanquet,

I have been waiting and waiting for my cousin Mr Holland to bring me in his list of subscriptions to Mr Parkes' 'booklet' on window-plants; at least they were subscriptions he hoped to obtain. But as they do not come in I enclose my own half-crown's worth of stamps; and I will forward any more that may arrive.

[1] *Annotation 1863.*

Your, and your friend's subscription (1£) bought\grey/linsey enough for 6 good comfortable *shirts*,—which have been distributed & caused great thankfulness. Thank you once more for the help.

Have you seen Dr Stanley's farewell sermon at Ch. Ch.\ preached Novr 29,/& the beautiful reference to Mr Leeke's character? Do read it if it comes in your way. It is published by Parker, of the Strand, the Oxford publishers.

Yours always very truly

E. C. Gaskell

539 **541** 545

?GEORGE SMITH

46 Plymouth Grove

Tuesday, Decr 8th [?1863]

My dear Sir,

I am so *very* sorry; but Mr Gaskell in cleaning out his desk, (full of letters & papers) has found this *signed* agreement,—so we have been wronging Mr Chapman after all! I am very sorry. What can I do? *please* let me pay for the horrid old stereotypes, or whatever they are.—I enclose your cheque for 50£, for you to take the money off for the stereotypes. I am trying to catch the morning post. *I will not write to Mr F Chapman till I hear from you.*

Yours most truly

E C Gaskell.

*

534 **542** 543

JOHN RELLY BEARD

Monday, Decr 14 [1863]

46 Plymouth Grove

My dear Sir,

I should not have allowed your most kind letter to have remained unanswered so long, had not a little 'hitch' occurred in the possibility of the Storys being able to receive Mr Gaskell this

winter as they wrote to tell me with what extreme pleasure they
should have renewed their invitation &c, but that they expected a
large family of relations\from America/to stay with them, & fill
up their house. For the same reason I have forborne to press Mr
Gaskell on the subject. But I have just received a letter from Mrs
Story saying she has secured a sleeping-room in the neighbourhood for Mr Gaskell; that he must entirely *live* with them; that
she had delayed writing because she had expected a final decision
from their American relations, which had not arrived. So I set to
work with renewed vigour; seeing moreover the extreme fatigue
of his work telling on my husband; for probably you know he has
had to take Mr Scott's work at Owen's College. May I therefore
ask you to fix a time & place in town—Herald Office, Chapel-
room,—Home Mission—Boardroom—when I can see you & ask
your advice how to proceed. I do not believe that Mr Gaskell *will*
make any requests for himself; but I believe he will gladly? accede to
any arrangements *made for him*, to have a six week's holiday after
the H. M. B Examination is over[.]

    With very sincere gratitude,

I remain
Yours very truly
E. C. Gaskell

542 **543** 544

JOHN RELLY BEARD

46, Plymouth Grove,
Decr 18th [?1863][1]

My dear Dr Beard,

    Meta went to Mrs Gloyn's today; and she spoke very kindly
and generously about Miss Cooper and her wish to help such
girls by taking them into her school.

    But at present, she says, she has not, she fears, a cranny into
which she could stow an additional boarder—She has already
more than her full number, and is likely to have for some time.

    She said, however, that she must think over the matter for a
week, and that then she would let me know her decision—

[1] Other letters to Dr Beard belong to 1863, and this paper has the same watermark as one of them, though not the same format.

I am afraid, however, that unless Miss Cooper could live as an
outsider—a day-boarder—and lodge elsewhere, that there wd be
no chance for her.

Yours most truly,
dear Dr Beard,
E. C. Gaskell.

543 **544** 0

JOHN RELLY BEARD

Wednesday Evening
30th [December 1863]
46 Plymouth Grove

My dear Dr Beard,
Neither the Chapel trustees, nor the Home Mission Board make
any sign!
Could you write me a note that I might show to Mr Gaskell,
which would *assure him* {as fully as possible of the willingness}
\that they consider/it as *settled* that he may take the 6 weeks
holiday after the (say) 21st of January.

I am already armed with a note from Mr Greenwood 'dis-
missing' him from Owen's College for that time; but until I have
some distinct proof to show him that all is arranged with the
Chapel & H M. B (Unitarian Herald\permission/necessary?) I
dare not open my parra—where do the double consonants come—
parallels—

Yours ever a faithful plotter.

541 **545** 550

GEORGE SMITH

Plymouth Grove,
Jan. 1st [1864]

My dear Sir,
Thank you extremely for your kind present of Doyle's clever
'Bird's-eye Views of Society',[1] which have already been highly

[1] Richard Doyle: *Bird's-eye Views of Society*. Smith & Elder, 1863. Contributed
to the *Cornhill*, 1861–63.

approved of in this their new form by my daughters, who have been spending their time over it ever since its arrival.

We were so glad to hear a word or two of the poor Miss Thackerays from your note to-day. How sadly desolate they must be? What are their plans? or have they any yet?

Would you kindly let me know by return of post (unless inconvenient to you) by what date you must have the end of 'Cousin Phillis' to begin printing from?[1] Will you give Mrs Smith our united love and best wishes for many Happy New Years, and with the same wishes for yourself I am

Yrs very sincerely
E. C. Gaskell.

P.S. Has Mr Frederick Chapman been really silenced, do you think? or has he only drawn back to make a fiercer spring?

528 546 551

CHARLES ELIOT NORTON

at Dr Allman's, (The Professor of Natural History)
21 Manor Place
Edinburgh
February 1st [1864]

My dear Mr Norton, You will see by the above address that we are staying away from home—'we' being Meta and me. Mrs Allman was a dear friend of mine before her marriage (her brother married a Miss Winkworth;) and Dr Allman is the most charmingly wise and simple man I ever met with. I mean he is full of deep thought & wisdom & knowledge and also like a child for unselfconsciousness, and sweet humility. *You* would so like & value him. They have no children; but their happiness seems perfect, even without. How is your darling? I am fond of babies from the very beginning; but your little fellow must now be getting to what is popularly called *the* interesting age; when the pretty intelligence and affection that is in these little ones comes out to public view; to fathers & mothers they have made their appearance long before. When I think how long it is since I have written to you I am vexed & ashamed; but one always fancies one

[1] *Cornhill*, November 1863–February 1864. See also p. 439 n. above.

ought to put on one's best clothes & one's diamond ring (like Addison, is it not?) before writing to America. The little daily notes, almost without beginning and without end, that one talks out on paper seem impossibilities when they have to go across the Atlantic to that other country which is (justly to one's imagination) called the *New*—(other)—*World*. I should so often have written to you had it not been for this; for I have had many questions to ask you and many things to say. I don't quite like to ask the question but *have* I ever written to you since Florence was married? Sept. 8th. It was a very quiet wedding; a very serious one to me; for it was the first breaking up of a home; and the whole affair had appeared to me so very sudden; only I believe it was not; and that it really was for my child's happiness. I trust so. She had no doubts or fears; and she was in general an undecided person. They went a quiet little journey in Wales; down to Llanstinan, the judge's house in Pembrokeshire. Then they came up North back again to us for a fortnight; and then I got to know & like my new relation better than I had done[.] He is so truly humble; & so exquisitely sweet-tempered; so desirous of being a *son* to us; and a brother to the girls! My only fear is literally that he should spoil Florence; he is pretty strict & self-denying towards himself but if he could dress her in diamonds and feed her on gold, and give her the moon to play with, and *she wished for them* I don't think he would question the wisdom of indulging her. I hope by and bye he will lift her up into the standard of high goodness of which she is thoroughly capable. But she is very young for her age, & as yet requires the daily elevation of her thoughts & aims. But again she is so loving & generous,—her new affluence of money makes her remember all the little wishes we have ever expressed & she is like a fairy godmother to us. He is prospering exceedingly as a special pleader; & only wants us all to come & make his house our home. I have not been as yet; no more has Mr Gaskell; no more has Meta. The reasons why have been these,—first—they came to *us* in Octr & stayed till nearly November; then Marianne was far from well, & had to go from home to less foggy air than Manchester; & Julia was at school; and friends came to see us,—a sister of Mrs (now Lady) Brodie's stayed with us six weeks. And at Christmas Florence came again, & took back Julia with her; and Hearn— you remember Hearn?—her old nurse; & Marianne went to her from Gloucestershire; so her house was full. Then Meta fell ill,— bad influenza almost passing into low fever; & was ordered bracing air; so last Monday (this day week) I brought her here on an invalid bed; and the change has done wonders. Another piece of family news is this; Mr Gaskell is going to Rome on February 22 for six weeks or two months!! The Storys asked him to go to them in Siena last summer; and when he refused because of Florence's marriage Meta & I determined that if we could plan it or arrange it he should go & see Rome this winter. So after no end of small arrangements we got all the difficulties smoothed away; and now, as I said, he is going; by himself, because he prefers it. Now I think I have rapidly gone through our family history up to this point. We go home some day next week; so when you get this you may think of us at home. Thank you so very much for the little parcel of books, that came one eveng when we were obliged to go out, leaving Meta alone just recovering from the worst of her illness. She was so touched & pleased to find she could have your companionship while we were away. How *very* interesting that report of the Sanitary Commission is? it tells one so very much one wanted to know. I want you please to write me a *war*-letter (as well as a Peace-Shady-Hill[1] one). I want you to give me an accurate idea of what *proportion* of territory has now returned to it's allegiance, as compared to what now remains rebel. I want you to tell me what Genl Butler really is—whether an 'Our Hero' as a paper in the Atlantic called him; or an *over*-stern & violent man? I think the feeling for the North is strengthening very much in England; & Lord Houghton, (R M. Milnes) who came to call on us in December thought so too, & he has more opportunities of knowing. I was so sorry to see that Dr Wendell Holmes called England 'The Lost Leader.'—I went & read the poem to Meta, who did not know it;—& we did so grieve! I have not half said my say, yet here am I at the end. Can you get *for me*, *Vol. 1*, of Elliott's Proceedings,[2]—a Charleston book of Science Dr Allman wants *very* much, to refer to in finishing some work of his own,—& Trubner cannot get it. Dr Allman is known to Agassiz, who would perhaps help in the search. And will you if you can get it, send it straight to Professor Allman & let me know how much I owe you? Meta's dear love to you & to our unknown friend Susan

Yours ever affectionately

E C G.[3]

[1] Norton lived at Shady Hill, Cambridge, Mass.
[2] Daniel G. Eliot (1835–1915) published various folios of birds.
[3] Recovered from the shipwreck of the 'Bohemian' C. E. N. [Note by Norton.]

₀ **547** ₀

UNKNOWN

21 Manor Place
Edinburgh.
Saturday, Feb. 6 [1864]

Dear Sir,

Your letter has been forwarded to me here, where I am on a visit; and I hasten to say how gladly I shall consent to your request that a friend of yours may translate into German my little notice of Colonel Shaw in Macmillan.[1] He was so good & noble that it is well for as many to hear of his self-sacrificing life as may be. Thank you for what you tell me of the kind appreciation of your countrymen for my writings.

In great haste

Yours very truly
E C Gaskell

₅₄₀ **548** *₅₅₀ₐ

?MARIANNE GASKELL

[?26 February 1864]

30 Q. Anne St also before breakfast, on Friday.[2] So you see I am an early bird too[.]

My own darling, I perfectly understand your letter, and I quite agree with you that BANNING can & shall wait[.] We always paid him immediately when he was a poor struggling man, & now that he is rich, a month or two evidently can make very little difference; especially as we can never get our bills in, when we ask for them & do want to pay 'em.—After breakfast &c. Charlie has called & left at the door a note from Papa to Florence; dated MARSEILLES WEDNESDAY, 3 o'ck.[3] He sounds as if he might have been a *week* in Marseilles, he has done so much there in the way of being at his bankers[,] changed his money at a money changers,

---

[1] See Letter 530.
[2] 'Read to yourself first' inserted in another hand.
[3] We assume that this is William Gaskell's trip to Rome after Charles Crompton had married his daughter in the previous September.

taken his berth &c.—which considering it was *3* PM on *Wednesday* & that he did not leave London till 7-40 AM *Tues*day is pretty quick work. It is very short, & is going on to Julia, so of course you will see it. He has 'left snow & rain behind him' & finds Marseilles warm,—tho' at Arles there was snow. But I shan't tell you any more—not that there is much to tell, because you will see it so soon. *I* had no letters this morng. So now to go back to yours. I hope I am right in expecting another dividend from Cousin Edward! but I feel sure that I am. Papa *meant* to have left you 20£, but 5£ to Ned, & 5£ to Meta (both '*unforeseen*' he said) took away half. Hearn would let us have her wages for a week or two, I am sure: if needed. But the Kath: Dock must pay soon I *think*; & I *hope* it IS 50£. However I will put all that on one side. I do trust you got paid your 4£ 18-6d poor money dear?? If not I shall add *that* to the cheque CERTAINLY. You are quite right to put your sick kitchen money in the BANK.

I hope you know more of Mrs Walker than I do before writing any testimonial. I thought her charming at first,—& I do think her management of the girls, *as far as I saw* it in two or three times very good & pleasant. But after that ugly suspicion & her apparent incorrectness in two or three cases,—which I never had time to enquire about before going to Rome I should have been terribly puzzled. *Did the Guardians* GIVE HER ANY TESTIMONIAL? About your sick kitchen dear,—I don't think any but *Manchester* people are likely to subscribe; nor do I think those unconnected ⟨. . .⟩

₀ **549** ₀

UNKNOWN

89 Oxford Terrace
Hyde Park
March 9. [1864][1]

Dear Sir,
    Will you allow me to write to you in the *first* person, as it will be easier to me to say what I want in that manner? I enclose two

---

[1] So dated by A. S. Whitfield (*Mrs Gaskell, Her Life and Work*, 1929, p. 80), who was the first to print it.

letters for you to deliver in Manchester. I only wish I had been at home there to do anything in my power for a nephew of my dear friend Madame Mohl. Our house is *46 Plymouth Grove*; and if you will call there, and ask for my daughter Miss Gaskell, she will, I am sure, do anything in her power, which is pretty great, to forward any views you may entertain after your arrival in Manchester. Of course she may be from home; at any rate will you please to call at the above address, & ask for a letter, which will be sent there for you, of introduction to a Mr Byers,—{Pea} Byers & Peacock is the firm,—which will, I hope, be given in such terms as to be more than a mere common introduction. Mr Byers is a German; a very benevolent, eccentric old bachelor; but the head of engineering works, which now hold the first place in Manchester.

You must know Mr Fairbairn well by reputation. He has withdrawn from any active share in business, but it is something to see him, & get his advice—he is often from home, but it is worth trying often to see him. The other note is to a connexion of ours a boy of eighteen or so, son of Judge Cromptons, who has lately come, as an articled apprentice I believe, to Peacock & Byers.—His father took counsel with most of the principal engineers of the country, & followed their advice in sending him for a year, at least, to these works. He will give you his opinion of the work he has to go through in a very sensible way, I am sure. He is at home every *evening* (except Wednesdays & Fridays—) at work all day. I also enclose some of my cards. If you have time they will enable you to see the things best worth in Manchester; viz

'*Murray's* FINE spinning—mills', in *Union* St (I think) just off Ancoats Lane, every body there knows 'Murrays'. You would there see the whole process of preparing & spinning cotton, with the *latest* improvements in the machinery required: the more questions you ask the better they will be pleased, as they will evince interest.

'*Hoyle's*' print-works, Buxton St (Ardwick) off the London Road,— may be taken in conjunction with 'Murray's', Mr Fairbairn &c,—as they are all in the same direction. You would there see the process of printing cotton goods,—very well explained too by the person who takes you about.

'*Whitworth's*' Machine{ry} Works, *Canal St, Brook St* or very near there. (The rifle works which have made Mr Whitworth so famous, are out of Manchester, and not easily shown). But these works are very interesting, if you do not get a stupid *fine* young man to show you over—try rather for one of the *working* men.

Sharp & Roberts, Bridgewater Foundry. Good to see in the Railway-Engine line.

LOCKETTS. *Very* clever *small* machinery. For instance they engrave the copper rollers used in calico-printing; made a machine for making (adul*terated* of course,) raw coffee? berries, when people began doubting *ground* coffee. These works are *well* worth seeing but you would have to look up the address in a *directory*— (it is in Salford,—a suburb of Manchester.—

These arrangements are all supposing that I am *not* at home when you come to Manchester: but I need hardly say what a pleasure it would be to me if I should have returned home before you reached it, when I should have the pleasure of meeting you, and of giving you a little more personal help. If there is anything further that I can do by writing, pray ask me.

                Yrs truly,   E. C. Gaskell.

347a **549a** 0

REV. R. S. OLDHAM[1]

                Plymouth Grove
                March 13. [?1864]

My dear Mr Oldham,

My second girl in[*sic*] in London staying with some of Mr Maurice's friends; and she sends us word that you are appointed head Master of Salisbury. This she hears either through the Hamiltons (Dean of Salisbury) or through the Maurice's; she does not say which; but either way is pretty good authority, and I do hope it may be true, as if I suppose rightly that it is the Head Mastership of a *School*, I think that you are almost more qualified than any man I know to influence young people to high and holy aims. This sounds like the impertinence of direct praise; but if you'll only forgive me the impertinence, I think with Keble that great praise only makes one feel more deeply humiliated in our

---

[1] Dated in pencil, '1864'. Other letters of 1864 are written on similar paper.

inner souls. Well! I *am* glad of it. I hope it is true. Now suppose it is not!

And then do you know Salisbury; & Salisbury Cathedral? and the New Forest? and Bemerton, George Herbert's parish, almost a suburb of Salisbury—and the Nightingales live very near Salisbury,—and altogether, begging dear smoky old Glasgow's pardon, & not forgetting lovely Kelvin Park[,] I think the change to Salisbury will be very charming.[1] So give my kind regards to Mrs Oldham, and congratulate her from

Yours most truly
E C Gaskell.

You'll return the Kaiserworth pamphlet some time, please.

545 550 553

GEORGE SMITH

46 Plymouth Grove
May 3rd [1864]

My dear Mr Smith, I have been at home nearly a week; but, owing to some sorrow among my friends & one or two other causes I have been unable to answer your letter before. And indeed I don't know what to say now. I threw overboard the story of the 'Two Mothers['] because I thought you did not seem to like it fully—and I have made up a story in my mind,—of country-town life 40 years ago,—a widowed doctor has one daughter Molly,—when she is about 16 he marries again—a widow with one girl Cynthia,—and these two girls—contrasted characters,—not sisters but living as sisters in the same house are unconscious rivals for the love of a young man, Roger Newton, the second son of a neighbouring squire or rather yeoman. He is taken by Cynthia, who does *not* care for him—while Molly does. His elder brother has formed a clandestine marriage at Cambridge—he was supposed to be clever before he went there—but was morally weak—& disappointed his father so much that the old

---

[1] Marianne Gaskell wrote a similar letter, now in the possession of Mr J. G. Sharps, which mentions that she and her mother had visited Salisbury for a day three years before.

gentleman refuses to send{his}Roger, & almost denies him education—the eldest son lives at home, out of health, in debt, & not daring to acknowledge his marriage to his angry father; but Roger is his confidant, & gives him all the money he can for the support of his inferior (if not disreputable) wife & child. No one but Roger knows of this marriage—Roger is rough, & unpolished—but works out for himself a certain name in Natural Science,—is tempted by a large offer to go round the world (like Charles Darwin) as naturalist,—but stipulates to be paid *half* before he goes away for 3 years in order to help his brother. He goes off with a sort of fast & loose engagement to Cynthia,—while he is away his brother breaks a blood vessel, & dies—Cynthia's mother immediately makes fast the engagement & speaks about it to every one, but Cynthia has taken a fancy for some one else & makes Molly her confidant.—You can see the kind of story and—I must say—you may find a title for yourself for *I* can not. I have tried all this time in vain. I think it will be in 3 volumes,—but I never can tell before hand—Please how much of *my* writing is 24 pages of the Cornhill? And by what day of the month *must* you have the next months MSS to print, in case I am driven very hard?[1]

I have not a moment of time to spare; only I must say how *very* sorry I am about this further trouble about Cranford.[2]

Yours most truly
E C Gaskell

*

546 551 560

CHARLES ELIOT NORTON

July 4th 1864
Cowley House, Oxford
(the Brodies—do you remember it?)

My dear Mr Norton, Meta has *just* sent me on your letter and somehow I want to write on the rebound; if one puts it off for a minute, an hour or a day—the time is apt to defer itself indefinitely to a week, a month, a year, & the sort of *good* effervescence of love & gratitude goes off,—not the reality to be sure. It is not

---

[1] *Wives and Daughters* ran in the *Cornhill*, August 1864–January 1866.
[2] Smith & Elder published it for the first time, in an illustrated edition, in 1864.

five minutes since I read it, 2 P.M—by time, a cool, cloudy, pretty *autumnal* kind of day; with pretty bursts of sunshine in the distance, not near enough to warm us. The carriage is at the door to take us to Stanton Harcourt, (which I have never seen,—) & my things are on while I write, & I may be called away any moment. You remember Stanton Harcourt—in Pope's Letters—and later still, they say, in 'the Old Home'—Well we are going there—& coming back to tea at 7, when Goldwin Smith comes to tea,—so you may fancy how apropos your letter is. And tomorrow I go to see some newly discovered old pictures in the Bodleian. Sir K. Digby by V. Dyke &c—and at 1 P.M. I go home; I shall be there tomorrow night, after a 10 days,—or rather 9 days' absence,—a week in London,—& I came here on Saturday. Meta & Julia (who left school 'for good' a fortnight ago, & is full of promise,—the merriest grig, the most unselfish girl by *nature*, that I ever knew; with a deep sense of religion in her unusual, I think, at so early an age),—Meta & Julia are alone—such happy friends, keeping house for Mr Gaskell; who has been to Rome & come back, and is a different creature in consequence, showing the advantage of change & travel. Marianne is in London, seeing her friend's with Florence's for her home house. Dear little Florence is curiously unchanged by marriage in many ways; takes her place as *third* daughter at home, runs errands &c. but is a little bit tyrannical over her sweet-tempered husband in her own house. Meta is not strong; but then the doctor said she would not be for a year or so, after her low fever in the winter, and I think she has made as much progress as we could expect. 'Bracing air, & a high situation' is ordered for her; and we *talk* of Switzerland,—going to a high Alpine pension, & living there for a month or six weeks quietly— carriage come, every one in; goodbye—

Friday Eveng—July 9th 46 Plymouth Grove. Mr Goldwin Smith did *not* come to tea at the Brodie's, nor did I see him but I left\part of/your letter for him to see how pleasantly you speak of him. He is going to America in August, meaning to stay till nearly Xmas, & thus throwing his next year's work till late on in the Summer. All this time I have never thanked Susan for her '*nice*' long letter—I mean her *charming* long letter, received by me in March last; and giving such a pleasant pretty account of you all & particularly of dear little Eliot[.] I like particularly to hear of him[.] Indeed I enjoy *domestic* letters about you all; only at Oxford on Monday Evng, when Mr G. Smith was *not* there two people—I won't say *who*, attacked me, saying your letter was ASSERTION, but no *facts* I tell you plain out, because I always do want to have the FACTS if I can, on which your opinions are based. *I* fully believe you, because I know you; but what *facts* am I to give in answer to such {things}\speeches/as this. 'It is a war forced by the Government on the people, the {conscription} orders for enlistment are not readily or willingly responded to, and the army is principally composed of mercenaries—German for the most part. 2ndly It is a war for territory; the pretext of slavery is *only* a *pretext* with a large majority; a few more enlightened have it really at heart['], and then they refer to the Emancipation proclamation only setting the slaves of *rebels* free,—Again the reports of the luxury of New York, & the great extravagance of living there, make many say the *Nation* does not suffer,\but riots while the hired army is slain by thousands./{Again} Again they ask me by what force— standing army, or military government—the rebel provinces if once reconquered, are to be held? I know that all these questions arise out of the wicked mistatements [*sic*] of the 'Times'— but they are difficult to answer, unless I simply reassert my faith in what *will* be, sooner or later. And then very very good people say no great evil was ever put down by violence,—that they even doubt if the abolition of slavery is worth the immense blood & sacrifice of this war, as by the spread of opinion it was almost sure to have been put an end to, before 50 years were over by the slaveholders themselves,—to which I reply by the annexation &c. I feel that I may be hurting you by even naming all this; but you do not know what *very* good conscientious people urge all this, especially after the account of one of these bloody terrible battles. Numbers of English people have *faith* in the North; but cannot tell how to reply to questions based upon the week-day bible as the Times is sometimes called. Dr Mackay was as perhaps you know considered an out & out liberal here, and this old repute of his makes some people say Here is a republican! look at *his* reports! I am sure with many & many of these people it is with no unfriendly feeling to Americans that they ask these questions. They own that in the beginning the South was rebellious, & treacherous, but they say that those who *hesitated* once as to the Xan lawfulness of holding slaves, must now have assumed that it is a part of patriotism to uphold slavery, & that in fact it is a war of extermination. They say this *really* in sorrow—I have one person in particular in my mind, who holds these opinions & uses these arguments—such a good noble conscientious man, though he is so wrongheaded,—he joined the Southern Association as soon as the Emancipation proclamation was published,—for the reason I have given above—it's *only* including the slaves of *rebels*. I don't think you will be vexed with me,—Saturday\July 15/—I only want to have good arguments & facts for good people,—who attack me when I am away from such books as Mr Goldwin Smith [*sic*]— which at the same time they will not read. You will say this does not prove them to be *good* people; but you don't know how the Times is almost the *only* reading of many who are *very* busy and have but little leisure, & that perhaps wd listen to me *talking*[.] This letter has been so much interrupted and is not nearly so 'NICE' as I meant it to have been. Remember me to your mother & sister. My kind love to Susan, a kiss for Eliot. Meta's dear love,— she wants to write—

Your affect[ionate] friend
E C Gaskell,

₀ 552 ₀

ABIGAIL B. ADAMS

Manchester
July 7th 1864

My dear Mrs Adams,

Here comes another note, to beg you to accept the accompanying autographs, to be sold for the benefit of the Sanitary Commission. I give them with all my heart,—and I trust they will do some of the good anticipated.

They are

A letter from *Florence Nightingale*

A note from Mr *Thackeray* to his publisher, Mr Smith; signed *only* with his initials—(W M T.) as he was in the habit of doing.

Letter from *John Forster* Author of the 'Lives of the Statesmen of the Commonwealth', 'Life of Oliver Goldsmith'—'Life of Sir John Eliot' &c, and formerly Editor of the 'Examiner Newspaper'.

Letter from *Wm Howitt.*

Letter from *R. M. Milnes*

Letter from *Miss Brontë* (this is, & ought to be very valuable,—it is a very rare autograph.

Letter from *Harriet Martineau*.
Letter from\the Honble/*Mrs Caroline Norton*
Letter from *Charles Dickens*.

Yours ever most truly
E. C. Gaskell

550 **553** 554

GEORGE SMITH

Monday, July 25th [1864]
46 Plymouth Grove

My dear Mr Smith,

I am ashamed to have kept this bill unpaid so long, but I have had much to occupy me during the past week; and today & to-morrow Florence & Mr Crompton come; so in my hurry I am afraid I have taken up a very bad pen wherewith to write a letter to one who writes so exquisitely neatly himself. There! we will try this, which is a shade better! because I want to propitiate you before I make a request, which I may as well plunge into at once. Will you advance me 100£ of the payment of 'Wives & Daughters'. I want it to take Meta (& the others too) into Switzer-land; but it is on *Meta's* especial account that we go. She has been having the old headaches, and tendency to fainting,—whh is called by the doctors 'nervous exhaustion', and 'utter want of bracing',—and her own and unvarying instinct leads her to wish, almost with yearning, for 'glacier-air'[.] She was once in that air with Miss Darwin, & was so much the better for it, that though she would quite *agree* to Scotland, yet Minnie & I came to the resolution yesterday,—when Meta was ill all day long—that we would go to Switzerland, 'coute qui coute' pretty literally. Minnie's contrast of character works so admirably on Meta;—and the Sisters are so fond of each other that I quite turn my back on Minnie's proposal to stop at home,—and of course the dear little 'widow' must come too. Mr Gaskell goes into Scotland directly after the 12th, on that day if he can—& then, if not sooner, *we* intend to start. Are you and Mrs Smith going soon on your travels? & if so shall you pass through *Bâle*? I have a particular reason for enquiring if it is not impertinent. Thank you very much for your congratulations. It has been a good deal of a worry; which we, not being in love, have felt a good deal more than the parties concerned. His father objects strongly—has forbidden both me & Minnie to reply to his letters; & I fear will with draw his present allowance to his son when he marries,—which is far enough off, (though WE none of us\here/object to long engagements,) as Thurstan's 'professional income' on which his father says he is to rely, is at present less than nothing. The *only* objections are the relationship\Edward constantly speaks of Minnie with great affection/*second* cousins—& Minnie's being older.—However we are in the middle of a pretty little family 'tiff',—; which will, I suppose, die out in time, but is unpleasant in the interval.[1] I don't know what business I have to tell you all this; only you and Mrs Smith have been so very kind to me, and my daughter, that one can't always help thinking one's own interests worth telling. I am sure you will not mention this,—not even please, in your reply.

Yours very truly
E C Gaskell.

Thank you very much for sending Cousin Phillis to Madame Mohl. Our present plan is to go to Pontresina, beyond a cheap, unknown-*ish* place—and to live there quietly en pension,— Thurstan would I think join us,—& I should write hard.

553 554 556

GEORGE SMITH

46 Plymouth Grove
July 30th. [?1864]

My dear Mr Smith,

You may have 20 good marks added to the number already gained for this lovely paper. It is a regular embarras de richesse all the colours. The blue and the red\& chocolate/divide my affections equally so whichever you like best I like best. I don't think the G. one bit too big and I do think the monogram quite as perfect as Mr George Smith & Mr Harrington Balfour; what higher praise can it have?

As I am to command and have owing to your kindness, I like the monogram both on paper & envelopes, but if I may, I should like a very small quantity with 46 P. Grove, but not much please

<hr>

[1] See p. 744 below.

as the principal amount of my correspondence is carried on from home. Don't insult my powers of cooking. You always believe I can do nothing useful. If you will come won't I make you lobster sauce with Brodignagian [sic] pieces in it, and melted butter for you to wash your hands in like the little boy in the storybook, to say nothing of a Mayonnaise like one I made the other day, and which met with universal cudos. I am obliged to praise myself because you give me credit for not being able to do a thing. For our sakes I hope you will both be too ill to cross the channel and so will have to end your travels by coming to us. But for your sakes I hope you will get to Switzerland.[1] When am I to have a G. S. monogram for a cigar-case?

Yours very sincerely
E. C. G.[2]

₀ 555 ₀

SAMUEL LAWRENCE

Plymouth Grove
Tuesday Evening.
Septr 12th. [1864]

My dear Mr Lawrence,

I am afraid that you will have thought me very negligent in not answering your note before—I have been very busy since its arrival; and although I do not mean to say that I have never had time to write a line in reply, yet I think that I have had such a weight of writing on my hands that I have been almost justified in putting it off from day to day in hopes of more leisure.

I should have not the least objection to Mr Smith's becoming the possessor of your likeness of me; indeed it would be pleasant to feel that I was hanging on the walls of so kind a friend—

When next I am in London, I hope that I (and my cap) may be able to give you another sitting[3]—

With my kind remembrances,

I am yours very truly
E. C. Gaskell.

[1] Associated, we assume, with trip mentioned above (p. 736).
[2] Signature as monogram.
[3] The portrait, now in the possession of Mrs E. M. Gordon of Biddlesden Park, Brackley, Northants, is reproduced in Hopkins, *Gaskell*, facing p. 320.

554 **556** 557

GEORGE SMITH

Tuesday, Decr 6th [1864]

My dear Mr Smith,

Do you know two VERY clever people just made one? i.e. John Addington Symonds, (only son of Dr Symonds of Clifton, whom some people know) who took no end of honours at Oxford,—is witty, clever *really* brilliant,—and Catherine North, daughter of the MP for Hastings even more full of genius,——well—on their wedding journey they have been writing a paper on Christmas,[1]— which looks to me *very* clever, & Mr Symonds wants to know if it can go into the Cornhill for January (he is a writer in the Saturday by the way,—a *regular* writer.) I have only got it by this *morning's* post, & will send it on by this *evening's*; only I knew it was the time for 'making up' the next months Cornhill,—& that not one hour was to be lost, so I write anyhow to catch the morning's post; and will write again on my *own* business in a day or two.

Yours most truly E C Gaskell

'Thoughts on Xmas. In Florence, 1863.'
by John Addington Symonds
110 words in a page
32 pages
3520 words in the whole paper

Mr Symonds took the Newdegate, & a double first. But he *might* be very dull for all that; only he *is* not.

556 **557** 561

GEORGE SMITH

46 Plymouth Grove
Manchester
December 6th [1864]

My dear Mr Smith,

I accept the offer of 100£ for the copyright of North and South *with thanks*. Only please I don't want the money now;[2]

[1] Married 10 November 1864. The article appeared in January 1866.
[2] Receipt dated 46 Plymouth Grove, 20 May 1865. (Collection of Mrs E. M. Gordon.)

only to know how much I may reckon upon, for the purchase of the (impossible) house. Oh! What a fool I was to let the East Grinstead house slip through my fingers! This is a soliloquy. You see I have not the knack of getting interest for my money. Mr Shaen has 600£ towards the nest egg for the house; but as I *may* want it any day he says it is not worth investing. So will you please keep the 100£ for me? Next I did not know I asked for any more copies of Wives & Daughters—and I think you must have misunderstood,—or I must have expressed myself badly when I said—or meant to say—I should like one more printed copy of all I had written, as I had not one either in MSS or print, and had forgotten all the names. You sent me this copy; and I do not want any other for myself; only if you would be so good as to send a copy of the Cornhills containing 'Wives & Daughters' to Madame Mohl

    120 Rue du Bac
       Paris

I should be very much obliged to you. The Germans are such a sensible people that they like my words, and are ready to read,—& the publishers to publish German translations of Cousin Phillis, & Wives & Daughters,—and Monsieur Mohl's neices [*sic*],—who translated Sylvia's Lovers, will translate Wives & Daughters,[1] after Madame Mohl has read it.

I long, shall long, have longed, and will ever long till I get it, for a whiff of Brighton air. But our house has been full, & I have had to play chaperone, and now Meta is leaving Brighton, and Florence & Mr Crompton come here on Saturday—so alas!

Yours most truly
E. C. Gaskell

414 558 570

ANNE ROBSON [2]

Jany 2 1865.
Eardiston.

My dearest Nancy,
    Meta has forwarded me your kind letter of good wishes which I have sent back to William (who shares it with me) by this day's

---

[1] See Whitfield, *Gaskell*, p. 228.   [2] Original MS. not seen.

post. Eardiston is an old house in Worcestershire that Judge Crompton has taken for 2 years; to which place Florence, Marianne and I came on Saturday to keep New Year. They wanted us all to come but Wm did not fancy a journey in cold weather and for so short a time. Julia had some dances etc. on hand and Meta stayed with her. Charlie and Florence were with us for three weeks before coming here; that is to say Charlie was at the *Liverpool* Assizes and came over on Saturdays till Mondays; Florence being with us all the time. The Cromptons have asked Thurston Holland to come next Saturday till Monday as he will be down at the Worcester Sessions; we all disperse on Monday on which day the C.s return to London and we to Manchester. William is, as usual at this time of the year, dining out almost every day and is besides engaged in preparing a set of lectures on the Lancashire dialect to be delivered at the Royal Institution. He is, I think, very well, at least he was when I left him on Saturday before this frost began; but frost which suits me never suits him, so much for us two heads of the family. Marianne comes next. She is very well and very happy and the prospect of a long engage- ment does not seem to 'tell' upon her at all. She is looking very well and very handsome; and altogether as young as her intended 18 months younger Thurstan. Meta is very far from as strong as we could wish. She is bodily strong excepting for the violent pain in two places in her spine, which the least worry still brings on; and it is almost impossible to keep her from worry. For instance the other day, when I was unable to be with her; three people came in unexpectedly to lunch; we have a new cook and Meta did(n't) think we had enough meat for lunch etc. *so* her pain in her back came on and then, unless she exercises very great self-control crying that is almost hysterical succeeds. She does not like to have all this spoken about, so don't allude to it, as she has a horror of being thought hysterical but I think these fits of crying are of that nature, though accompanied with this pain in the spine. Mr Erichsen is still prescribing for her—a great deal of open air, 6 hours a day—but no fatigue early hours, a *great deal of meat* to eat, bitter beer, a little society, but not large assemblies, as much change as possible and tonics. He has already greatly improved her health; which had never been strong since the sewing days. When she was in London for a couple of days at the Wedg- woods on coming from Brighton, she tried in vain to find you— 57—75 a *hundred &* 57 and 75 (she had got these two numbers in her head—in a variety of *Morningtons*. We make out she got to a public house that must be very near you. Florence is blooming and bright and I hope won't get so many invitations this year as she did last but they have already begun and I don't think perpetually dining out is good for her. I almost wish they had not such an enormous circle of acquaintance. Certainly no girl was ever more kindly received by her husband's family or more doated on by her husband. She is thoroughly happy and we have her with us for nearly 3 months a year. Last autumn as I dare say you know, she and Charlie and Thurstan too for that matter, went with us to Pontresina in Switzerland. We had but very little money to spend so our object was to go to cheap healthy places and live there without moving about, and for me to settle to my writing whilst there. We found our two places, Pontresina and Glion (up above the Lake of Geneva) where we lived for 3-4 a day and I think never did such a party go to Switzerland and travel about less. We never saw Mt Blanc nor the Jung frau nor Monte Rosa nor the Matterhorn nor Vevay (4 miles from us at Glion) nor Lausanne, Geneva, Interlacken, [?] Lauterbrunnen, etc., etc. Here is a long screed about us all dear Nancy.

From your ever affec[tionate] sister

E. C. Gaskell.

0 **559** 562

JOHN RUSKIN[1]

Monday, Febry [?1865]
46 Plymouth Grove
Manchester

My dear Mr Ruskin

I must begin at once upon my subject, if I am to catch today's post. I have just seen our good and dear friend, Mr Alfred Water-house, the architect of our Assize Courts. (I think you know him, and I know you have seen his work.) He is in dismay because he has just learnt that his name is not likely to be among the *six*? who are to be appointed by Mr Wm Cowper ('Woods & Forests') to compete for the new Law Courts in London. He hears that 'the affair is to be pushed on', and is going up to London this afternoon

[1] See p. 746 below.

to see, if by any fair and delicate means Mr W. Cowper can be induced to *allow* him to compete. I say '*delicate* means' because although Mr Gladstone has spoken out unreservedly his admiration of the Courts, Mr Waterhouse said he should not like to apply to him, because he did not think it would be quite right to ask one Minister to apply any pressure on another. I am afraid I am not 'delicate', for I mean to write right and left by this post to any one who can, I think, help Mr Waterhouse to obtain the liberty of competition he has so set his heart on. But so often a woman's meddling does harm! My first letter is to you—is it asking too much to ask you to interest yourself in this. I fancy an expression of your opinion as to Mr Waterhouse's capability would at once secure him a place among the limited number of competitors,—and after that it rests with his good sword! Will you, *please*, do it dear Mr Ruskin⟨?⟩ But, at any rate, if you see well to refuse, remember Mr Waterhouse knows *nothing* of my request. I purposely kept silence as to what I inten⟨ded⟩ to do for fear of being forbidden.

Yours ever *most* truly (though you don't come & see us,)
E. C. Gaskell

No more would you let Meta & me come & lunch with you at Denmark Hill—but I am very proud of being one of those who can regard others, irrespective of '*mutual* esteem'.

₅₅₁ **560** ₅₆₉

CHARLES ELIOT NORTON

Sunday Evening
February 5th 1865
46 Plymouth Grove
Manchester

My dear Mr Norton, To think you will really touch this bit of paper! It has suddenly struck me as so odd & strange. I am so glad about your little daughter's[1] birth! If I had been in time I should so like her to have been called after me; and though perhaps Elizabeth is not the prettiest of names yet it has very pretty abbreviations, and pet names. Now I am going to tell you just how the

---

[1] Sara Norton. The Nortons' next daughter was named after Mrs Gaskell.

family are situated. *I* am in the dining-room, by myself. It is after
our usual early Sunday Evening tea; Mr Gaskell is preaching at
X St Chapel,—all just as usual. In the drawing-room Marianne
and Thurstan Holland are sitting. They have been engaged to each
other for six months now, after an attachment of as many years;
opposed 1stly because they are cousins (*second*), and 2ndly because
she is 18 months older than he—& also because he, though the son
of a rich man, has *eleven* brothers & sisters, and has to make his
way in that most tedious of all professions *chancery* law. He is a
barrister now of 3 years standing, & makes nearly 100£ a year;
but this is swallowed up by necessary expenses, chambers & the
like. Still they are in very good heart and have been very constant
to each other; and *we* don't mind a long engagement for we shall
keep our child that much the longer. I only hope it won't tell on
her health; but at present she is gay and bright and happy; and
he comes down to see her as often as he can[.] Meta's health is, I
am sorry to say, not satisfactory; though we hope better than it
was. For more than a year she has been suffering from extreme
nervous debility & pain in the spine; brought on by any worry or
distress[.] I think this was originally brought on by her anxiety
about Marianne, during the last visit of the latter to Rome when
she became so intimate with Dr Manning; and partly it came from
her devotion to the sewing-schools in that first winter of the
Cotton Famine; the air in the rooms was so terribly bad, & the
stories of individual distress which she heard preyed so much
upon her. She fought against feelings of languor, headache, &
backache as long as she could, when she had much better have
yielded to them; and has had to pay a long penalty for this. We
took her,—did I tell you [?—] to Switzerland as a bracing place
this last autumn[.] I, my 4 daughters, Charlie Crompton and
Thurstan Holland went to Pontresina in the Grisons, 6,000 feet
above the level of the sea—primitive, cheap & bracing; There she
had a very bad attack of headache,—(bewildering whirling headache is the kind—) and a Mr Erichsen a great famous London
surgeon was staying in the hotel, & prescribed for her with such
good effect that she has continued under his care; & by his advice
she went to Brighton in November, & stayed there till Xmas,
living out of doors, and having warm seawater douches on her
spine with very good effect. But he says it will be a year or more
yet before she will have regained her usual health—and all that
time, & probably longer she is to follow a certain régime, of

frequent change of air, very good living, early hours,—to be perpetually in the open air &c &c &c. She is *not* to read deep books, she is *not* to visit the poor, she is *not* to be worried &c. So she, to whom we all went for sympathy and advice leads a life as apart from ours as we can make it; but the old habit of going to her still survives and we have continually to check ourselves to keep her in peace. And this she knows & grieves over. But just now she seems very much better.

Florence's marriage has turned out such a happy one. Her husband is really like a son & brother to all of us; so unselfish, sweet-tempered and good; and he lets her come down to us whenever she likes; and when he can come, he is just as pleased as if this were his home. He goes the Northern circuit; so we often have them here. Julia is now 18, and the life of the house; she is more like Meta than any of the others, though not so fond of reading as Meta was at her age. Hearn is still with us. Of course she is,—after 22 years of service she is as much one of the family as any one of us. I wish we could see you again dear Mr Norton; we never thought it would be so long, did we, when we parted? Those were very happy Roman days—I have loved America ever since. Every now and then I send batches of autographs over to America,—through Mrs Adams (the minister's wife) and once Mrs Field wrote for some *just* after I had sent all I could lay my hands on, through Mrs Adams for the same purpose—the Sanitary Bazaar. Will you please tell Mrs Field so for I should not like her to think I neglected any request of hers. Thank you too for *the* most interesting packet of books you sent me about 2 months ago. I have lent them well about since. Mr Goldwin Smith was in Manchester; but he never came to see us, and I was too ill to go and make [*sic*] him out. Yes! for three months in the autumn I was almost confined to the house; and I almost began to despair of ever getting out again, I was so very {weak}\weak/for so long. But now, thank God! I am a great deal better; nearly quite strong again, I shall be when *light* comes back. I am always in-fluenced so much by darkness, or cloudy skies[.]

I really *am*; it is not fancy. Now I think I have given you a long bulletin of home-news as you ask for; and I mean in this letter, to confine myself to it. I always mean,—when I write *one* letter, to follow it up close with another picking up all my dropped stitches. Do you ever hear anything of Mr Ruskin? Perhaps you will wonder how I got to him! Through Meta's great faith in her friends. I thought that sometimes you must have to practise faith towards me, when I am a long time in writing. Mr Ruskin has been twice in Manchester lately—& never called to see us; and I was sorry & vexed, but Meta said nothing wd shake her faith in him; & some chance *obliging* us to write to him there came back such a nice affectionate explanatory letter as fully justified Meta. Oh! (again you won[']t see the connecting link—it is the Storys—) Will you ask Mr Lowell if he would *give* me his Fireside Travels, with his writing inside? I was so entirely delighted with that book, and should *so* like to have it *from him*. Do you mind? Sometimes I dream I go over to Boston & see you and Susan and the little ones. But l always pass into such a cold thick damp fog, on leaving the river at Liverpool that I never get over to you. But my heart does; and I send you my dear dear love. To you & Susan & your little ones, & your mother & Grace and Jane, and some very nice message to Mr Lowell. We did so rejoice in Mr Lincoln's re[-]election I must tell you that,—although I have resolved that this shall be a purely domestic letter. Meta sends her dear love to you,—& the lovers would, I doubt not, send some kindly message if they knew I was writing.

Your very affectionate friend
E. C. Gaskell

557 **561** 563

GEORGE SMITH

Monday, Febry 20 [1865]
46 Plymouth Grove

My dear Mr Smith,

I *believe* about 870 pages of my writing; but it is very difficult to tell. I could make it longer I have so much to say yet; but oh! I am so tired of spinning my brain, when I am feeling so far from strong! However my brains are as nothing to yours! How do you manage! I hate intellect, and literature, and fine arts, and mathematics! I begin to think Heaven will be a place where all books\& newspapers/will be prohibited by St Peter: and the amusement will be driving in an open carriage to Harrow, and eating strawberries & cream for ever. I must say I expect to have that Roman

Emperor with the very long throat (that he wished for on earth) for my companion.

I have beguiled myself into forgetfulness of my own story by reading 'Tony Butler'[1]—it is so clear!—and Lowells 'Fireside Travels'.

Why don't you ask Miss (Maggie) Elliott to write you a novel? 6 Grosvenor Crescent—daughter of the Dean of Bristol—author of 'Jem' (something)—'the Dale Boy, in the Febry or March No of 1864 Fraser's Magazine—She would do it well.

Yours very truly
E C Gaskell

559 562 0

JOHN RUSKIN[2]

[?Late February 1865]

My dear Mr Ruskin—

⟨. . .⟩ and then again—about 'Cranford' I am so much pleased you like it. It is the only one of my own books that I can read again;—but whenever I am ailing or ill, I take 'Cranford' and—I was going to say, *enjoy* it! (but that would not be pretty!) laugh over it afresh! And it is true too, for I have seen the cow that wore the grey flannel jacket—and I know the cat that swallowed the lace, that belonged to the lady that sent for the doctor, that gave the emetic &c!!!

I am so glad your mother likes it too! I will tell her a bit more of Cranford that I did not dare to put in, because I thought people would say it was ridiculous, and yet, which really happened in Knutsford! Two good old ladies—friends of mine in my girlhood, had a niece who made a grand marriage, as grand marriages went in those days & that place! (to Sir Edward Cust)[3] The bride & bridegroom came to stay with the two Aunts, who had bought a new dining room carpet, as a sort of wedding welcome to the

---

[1] Charles Lever, *Tony Butler*, Blackwood, 1865.

[2] Original MS. not seen. Ward (ed. *Works*, II, p. xxiv) quotes from a Ruskin letter of 21 February 1865 to which this is the reply.

[3] Sir Edward Cust (1794–1878), general, M.P. for Grantham (1818–26) and Lostwithiel (1826–32), master of ceremonies to Queen Victoria (1847–76). Married Mary Anne Boode of Peover Hall, Knutsford, 11 January 1821.

young people—but I am afraid it was rather lost upon them, for the first time they found it out, was after dinner, the day after they came. All dinner time they had noticed that the neat maid servant had performed a sort of 'pas-de-basque', hopping & sliding[1] with more grace than security to the dishes she held. When she had left the room, one lady said to the other: 'Sister! I think she'll do!' 'Yes', said the other, 'she managed very nicely!'

And then they began to explain that she was a fresh servant, and they had just had laid down a new carpet with white spots or spaces on it, and they had been teaching this girl to vault or jump gracefully over these white places, lest her feet might dirty them! The beginning of 'Cranford' was *one* paper in 'Household Words'; and I never meant to write more, so killed Capt Brown very much against my will: See what you have drawn down upon yourself, by gratifying me so much! I'll stop now however,

Yours gratefully & truly,
E. C. Gaskell.

561 563 565

GEORGE SMITH

Cambridge,
March 5—[1865]

My dear Mr Smith,

I am going to Paris about Friday in this week—10th—*not later*. Would you be so kind as to let me have a *printed* copy of the MS last sent to you—as I shall write there;\at Paris,/and where I hope to have a great deal of time[.] I want the *catch-word* of what I wrote last. Please send it to 89 Oxford Terrace

Hyde Park—

Also—in the last piece sent (April or May part[;] I *think* the latter —) there is a word omitted in describing the band at the Ball;—I did not know what instrument to put in; and wise people tell me 'CLARIONET' Also—please *entirely* take out the words 'HE IS A PRINCE AMONG MEN'—also I think in the same *May* part; but it is in a speech of *Cynthia's* (and *extremely* out of character) to her mother after the latter has been rude to Roger.

---

[1] Ward has 'striding'; likewise a typescript in the Brotherton Library, Leeds. Both these versions are slightly shorter than our copy text.

I left home rather hurriedly on Monday, or would have altered these things myself; but I don't think I am often troublesome to you, so please excuse it this time. My address in Paris will be *Chez* M Mohl

>   (Membre de l'Institut)
>   120 Rue du Bac[.]

Yours ever most truly
E. C. Gaskell

308 **564** 0

EMILY SHAEN[1]

Paris, 27 March,/63. [?1865]
120 Rue du Bac.

I think you will like to hear how I am going on in Paris. It is a very amusing life; and I'll try and describe a day to you. Mme Mohl lives on the fourth and fifth stories of a great large hotel built about 150 years ago, entre cour et jardin, 'cour' opening into the narrow busy rue du Bac, 'jardin' has a very large (10 acres) plot of ground given by Cardinal Richelieu to the Missions Etrangères—and so not built upon, but surrounded by great houses like this. It is as stiffly laid out in kitchen garden, square walks, etc., as possible; but there are great trees in it, and altogether it is really very pretty. That's at the back of the house and some of the rooms look on to it. On the fourth story are four lowish sitting rooms and Mme Mohl's bedroom. On the fifth slopes in the roof, kitchen, grénier, servants' bedrooms, my bedroom, work-room, etc.; all brick floors, which is cold to the feet. My bedroom is very pretty and picturesque. I like sloping roofs and plenty of windows stuffed into their roof anyhow; and in every corner of this room (and it's the same all over this house) French and English books are *crammed*. I have no watch, there is no clock in the house, and so I have to guess the time by the monks' singing and bells ringing (all night long but) especially in the morning. So I get up and come down into the smallest and shabbiest of the sitting-rooms, in which we live and eat all day long, and find that M. Mohl has had his breakfast of chocolate in

---

[1] From a printed source. Mrs Gaskell was in Rome on 27 March 1863 (Passport, but see also the ending of her 'French Life'.)

his room (library) at $\frac{1}{2}$ past 6, and Mme Mohl hers of tea at 7, and I am late having not come down (to coffee) till a little past 8. However I take it coolly and M. and Mme come in and talk to me; she in dressing gown and curlpapers, very, very amusing, he very sensible and agreeable, and full of humour too. I'll give you one or two specimens of Mme Mohl's witty expressions. Speaking of *men* cooks in great families she calls them '*tom*-cooks.' Another day 'Let me see what year it was when M. Mohl *worried the baker.*' 'What do you mean?' 'Oh, you know we stayed with Hilary Carter at Kensington and a baker kept the post office, and he never had any foreign stamps, and M. Mohl wanted them every day, and was always going for them, till at last the baker said, "Sir, Sir, you will worry me to death—"' and he did die soon after (M. Mohl the most good-natured of men stands by and smiles)!⟨. . .⟩

Then, after my breakfast, which lingers long because of all this talk, I get my writing 'Wives and Daughters' and write, as well as I can for Mme Mohl's talking, till 'second breakfast' about 11. Cold meat, bread, wine and water and sometimes an omelette— what we should call lunch, in fact, only it comes too soon after my breakfast, and too long before dinner for my English habits. After breakfast no 2 I try to write again; and very often callers come; *always* on Wednesdays on which day Mme Mohl receives. I go out a walk by myself in the afternoons; and when we dine at home it is at six sharp. No dressing required. Soup, meat, one dish of vegetables and roasted apples are what we have in general. After dinner M. and Mme Mohl go to sleep: and I have fallen into this habit; and at eight exactly M. Mohl wakes up and makes a cup of very weak tea for Mme Mohl and me, nothing to eat after dinner; not even if we have been to the play. Then Mme Mohl rouses herself up and is very amusing and brilliant; stops up till one, and would stop up later if encouraged by listeners. She has not been well, but for all that she has seen a good number of people since I came; she has generally a dinner-party of 10 or 12 every Friday, when we spread out into all the rooms (and I am so glad, for continual living and eating in this room and no open windows makes it very stuffy) and 'receive' in the evening.

Guizot has dined here and Mignet and Montalembert since I came; and many other notabilities of less fame. But everybody stays up the first half of the night, as I should call it. When we go out for the evening we go to dress directly after our dinner nap and tea; and just cross the court-yards even in snow, or step to the

Porter's Lodge opening into the Rue du Bac, and send him for a coach. We 'jigget' to some very smart houses (for all Mme Mohl's friends are very smart people and live in very grand houses) curtsey as low as we can to the Master of the house, and shake hands with the Mistress, sit down and in general have a great deal of very beautiful music from the masters of the Conservatoire, quartettes and quintettes; make a buzz of talk, look at fine dresses, and I come home hungry as a hawk about one a.m. *I am going out a great deal to dinner:* last night I dined at a Russian house, a real Russian dinner. First soup made of mutton, and sour kraut; very nasty and horrible to smell. Then balls and rissolles very good; fish, rice, eggs and *cabbage*, all chopped up together, and cased in bread. Then caviare and smoked fish handed round with bread and butter. Then sweetbreads done in some extraordinary fashion, then eels, chopped up with mushrooms, lemon juice and mustard. Then rôti of some common sort; then gelinottes or Russian partridge, which feed on the young sprouts of the pine trees, and taste strong of turpentine. Then a sweet soup, ball of raisins and currants like plum-pudding, boiled in orange-flower water. I think that was all—it was all I took at any rate. The gentlemen hand the ladies back to the drawing-room, just as they have handed them *in* to dinner. The other night M. Guizot and M. de Montalembert dined here; the latter speaks English as easily as he does French; and was very eager about the American war; abusing the English for their conduct towards the Northerners and professing the warmest interest in the North. We never see any newspaper here so we don't know what is going on. Guizot (who is 78) looks *much* older since I saw him last. Good bye my dearest Emily for I am suddenly called off.

Your own affec[tionate] friend E. C. G.

₅₆₃ **565** ₅₇₆

GEORGE SMITH

[London]
[?April 1865]

My dear Mr Smith,
    I broke down in Paris, & for the last fortnight could not leave the house till the day I came here. I am not strong and not able

to see any one. I tried to get the Rive Gauche; but (all the advertisement on the first page about regularity of time of publication,
& place to 'abonner' &c is a sham—) the paper has *vanished* for the
time; tho' through one of the occasional writers I offered 5 fr
a copy; there is only one, picked out by M Mohl out of a set
of old papers sold by an old woman in the open\air/Place de St
Sulpice—He got specimens of all the other papers she had—I send
them,—one he wrote on 'Underhand Bonapartist—) The story
goes—Rogeard refused to leave Paris saying he would stand his
trial for Labienus[1]—4 friends gave him a dinner on it's success,
drugged the wine, & carried him off to express train for Brussels.

There is one page missing 581 (or 2)[;] it is at home, & you
shall have it in a day or two.

Don't either you or Mrs Smith take the trouble to call. I am not
strong enough to see any one just yet.—Oh for a house in the
country.

Yours most truly
E C Gaskell

*550a **566** 567

MARIANNE GASKELL[2]

89 O. T.
Monday morning
[24 April 1865]

My dearest Polly,

Pray let Jane go as soon as you can get rid of her; even if there
is no one to take her place. About Lizzie—I am vexed, for it does
not seem as if she had given the true reason. Don't THINK of getting her a silk gown. I had thought of it when I fancied she had
injured her health in our service—i.e. in our bad air—. Something
from 5s to 10shillings\—for a present for her: *not more./*I think
your jackets *are* dear; especially as braiding is so out of fashion. But
pray see that they *fit*; the brown Holland ones last year were *not*

---

[1] *Le Propos de Labiénus*, a publication seized by the French authorities. Mrs
Gaskell was asked to obtain a copy for Smith. See L. Huxley, *The House of Smith,
Elder*, London (for private circulation), 1923, p. 77.

[2] *Address (on envelope)* Miss Gaskell | 46, Plymouth Grove | Manchester.
Postmarks LONDON ⟨W⟩ | 6 | AP 24 | 65 *and* MANCHESTER | AP 25 | 1865.

well cut—too low in the neck and too tight across shoulders [Here there is an illustrative diagram] &c. Emily C. has got a jacket *made* for her at Sewells, with the right bead trimming sent for from Paris,—where *bead* trimming is de rigueur,—(steel or black brad-steel most expensive—) for 3£-3s. However if these *fit* well & look well, you all ought to have nice looking things this year. Mme Lamys were 4£ with *blk* bead 6£ with *beautiful* steel trimmings. We all like Jane Jones from your account. I think Lizzie is leaving for *wages*, whh I would have increased. Florence does *not* admire her Lamy trimming. *No* morning gowns are trimmed at the bottom in Paris. The *only* kind I saw was like a spiked VV *petticoat* of darker silk below; which was done (*I think*) with *lined* RIBBON—(& got dirty directly I should fancy.) Mme Lamy said she was not trimming any *morning* gowns\skirts/; and all the *walking* gowns here strike me as *very* long after Paris; tho' their *evening* gowns are {far} longer than English. Florence says the cord wears out directly. *Pray* don't have your skirt trimmed, unless you put the ribbon vandykes—(a good way up—) *not* at the bottom so as to look *loose like a petticoat* do you understand?—*Pray* be careful about Lizzie's making. I did say she should never make a *new* dress again; her seams & sewing are so bad & careless; make her *almost* backstitch the seams, & iron them out flat. I am so sorry she is making your gowns. I am so afraid she will spoil them. The green sounds *lovely*. But oh! *don't* let Lizzie spoil them!

I am not strong. I *was* so well that first 3 cold weeks in Paris; but the close overpowering heat, & the real want of food, & lowness of diet have made me so weak, I almost get out of spirits about ever being fit for anything again; whh is I know nonsense, especially remembering how well I was 3 weeks or a month ago. I want to see as much as I can about houses while here. Please ask E T H to send me the admission to the Wallingford House, *if it is still* unsold. But I have but little hope; I don't know why. Meta comes today at 2 P.M. She has heard from Mr Spencer, (proprietor of the Arundel House—) *only* the gardens ('walled & well-stocked with fruit trees'—) are to be had for the 2,000£; the rest of the meadows orchards &c, are 20 acres, & will cost *altogether*, 6,300£, being 'very good ground & surrounded by the Duke of Norfolk's estates.' ⟨. . .⟩ Send the advertisemt of the Arundel house.[1]

---

[1] Written on flap of envelope. (This information, together with some details of the envelope above, was taken from a typed transcript.)

MARIANNE GASKELL

Tuesday, mg
[?25 April 1865]

My dearest Polly, I am so sorry you have all this trouble, darling,
—and I *am* so puzzled about the *right* thing to be done. I confess
I am inclined to do *nothing*; for one thing one ought to hear *both*
sides, before doing such a thing as writing to Mr Andrews; and
that would involve bringing Hearn\or Lizzie/face to face with the
cook. Jane *might* (very *unlikely*) have some explanation to give.
(I remember once it was *proved* that the last cook went out after
supper for some bread wanted the next mg for breakfast,—very
careless &c—& wrong to go without leave.) One wishes to do
right both by Mr A. & Jane. It seems to me it wd not be right to
write to Mr A, without making enquiries &c,—which would be
getting Hearn &c—into a row; & it might be difficult to prove
so long after the time or date. *Do get rid of her on Thursday.* Please
love; She has copies (& so have I, in the pocket of the dining-room
portfolio, *or* in my chiffonier drawer, *or* (unlikely) in the 'My
book' box, *or* some other box in the *dining*-room,—) of the *kitchen
linen in her charge,* which should be {well} looked over: and ask
her, if she is aware of anything being broken, which ought to be
replaced[.] (New cooks *always* want their own peculiar little odds
& ends for cookery &c: so unless things are *wanted* for {cookery
&} cleanliness I would not get them, till the new cook comes.—
I think what I would do the most about is Sarah. *After* one Jane is
gone, and before the other comes, will you speak to Sarah,\before
Jessie/and tell her I wish her to mind what *Jessie* says to her,
about *personal cleanliness, and tidiness in her bedroom,* & that I feel
sure from what I know of Jessie that she will always speak
kindly to her (*mind you say this* BEFORE JESSIE;) of course she is to
receive all directions *about her work* DOWNSTAIRS from the cook;
but she is to be willing & grateful for instructions about her *up*-
stairs work, (study schoolroom steps passage &c) from either
Hearn, or Jessie. I hear *Sarah wants new &* LONGER *gowns.* Her large
legs seem to have made a great impression; & her *rough manners,*
on Florence. Please see after her always being respectful, and nice-
mannered. *Her mother is*; & you might tell her how much I was

struck with her mother's pretty ways, and gentle voice. And will
you ask Hearn to see about her having longer *petticoats*, & *new*
dark print gowns, *with frills round the neck*, and tidy sleeves &c;
as well as some new *lighter* prints—(say lilacs) for Sundays. Will
you say *at the very first* to the new Jane, that she is not to go out
without letting us know & asking leave of the head of the house
at home. That she is NEVER to send Sarah out *after* dark. I am so
glad you are sending Amelia to Knutsford on May 1st. I mean (*at
present*) to come home at the end of next week (May 6th) or beginning of week after. I always meant to be at home by the time
of the change of cooks. But I am thankful never to see Jane again;
& I am vexed with Lizzie too. I am so much better today—(owing
to a good night, owing to Meta's b—y bottle!!) I am afraid I
wrote a grumbling letter yesterday my darling,—I *was* so weak.
I had to keep lying down in the midst, & I don't know what I
said. I hope your jackets will be very pretty my darling. *Meta likes
braiding*, better than beads, so I am very glad they are to be
braided; & if she but makes them to fit they will look handsome
to the end of the Chapter; a good thing always does. Mrs Smith
called yesterday, leaving flowers. I was really not well enough to
see her, or any one. I think Hearn must send up some of the mysterious fluid I took last night in a parcel, to replace Meta's store.
Thurstan came, & Florence asked him to dinner. He stayed, & had
work to do, which took him away early. Meta is going to Putney
Park with Carry & Emily in the open carriage; to come back to
dinner. She says Dumbleton is so healthy: & she looks so well.
Lady Augusta wrote last night to ask me to dine with them on
the 2nd, & C. & F E to come in the evening. I asked if Meta
might come too (as I know she may,—) & now F E & I think they
may be having *the* bride & bridgroom *V Ls*. I am so pleased to be
feeling better & stronger. I am taking Mr Mellor's tonics. Yesterday I did not go out at all,—I was so bad, with 3 bad nights. I
hope I shall come back quite strong now. Only I *should* like some
good sea this year. The Ewarts want me to go there—& the
Brodies there (i.e. Malvern—for Sir B's health) on my way home.
Now I'm going to end & go to F E, who is I think a little tired
today, and Meta going off to Putney Park, so she'll be alone.
What did Lizzie mean about asking her father to let her come
back again &c,—when all the time she was applying for another
situation? I suspect she never meant to stay with us *beyond* a year.
Please see she does not spoil your gowns. My dear love to Juliet

& thank her for her letter. I think I shall write to her next. Thank you for all the trouble you are taking for me, darling. I don't want to come home *till* Cousin Mary is gone. She did so snub me that day at Knutsford!

Your own affec[tionate]
Mammy

₀ 568 ₀

(46, Plymouth Grove
Manchester)
London.
April 27. [?1865][1]

Dear Madam,
    I have received a letter from Miss Parkes this morning in which she tells me of your kind wish that I should contribute to the Magazine that you propose to start. I am, however, unable to promise this, as my time will be very fully occupied during the next year or so—
    With much regret

I am yours truly
E. C. Gaskell.

₅₆₀ 569 ₅₈₃

CHARLES ELIOT NORTON

89 Oxford Terrace
Hyde Park
April 28 1865

My dear Mr Norton,
    Meta & I have met here, under the Crompton's roof: I from Paris, where I had been staying with Mme Mohl, who had been ill, she from Dumbleton. We were both so glad for you, and

---

[1] The only other dated example of the watermark is found later this year and Mrs Gaskell was in London on 27 April 1865.

yours & the North,—on Wednesday last (day before yesterday) we came home from paying calls; & found to our surprize that the Daily News had come by post—'What can Charlie have sent this paper for?' said Florence {?} and she opened it,—& read out 'Assassination of President Lincoln' My heart burnt within me with indignation & grief,—we could think of nothing else,—but we *could* hardly talk of *that*,—and all night long we had only snatches of sleep, wakening up perpetually to the sense of a great shock & grief. *Every* one is feeling the same. I never knew so universal a feeling. I hope you will hear of the deep national sympathy by this mail. *I* missed the speech which Meta has been so much struck by, by being in Paris; but one has long seen & felt the character growing, & the underlying strength in the firm religious feelings. And today Julia forwards us (from home) Susan's letter, claiming our sympathy in your *rejoicing*—We are so anxious for the next mail? We do so want to know what Johnson is really like. I liked the report of his speech—'I accept the duties, trusting in God's help,' is what is given in the papers—But he is *said* to have been drunk &c &c. *Do* write soon, one of you; please do. Mr Mason says the assassins are not Southerners—of course this is only conjecture on his part. Oh! I am so grieved—Tomorrow we may hear more,—but we must ease our minds by writing *tonight*. Goldwin Smith has written a letter asking people not to prejudge Johnson—even though the story &c may be true of his drinking. Poor Mrs Lincoln—it adds to the depth of the crime that it should be done in her presence. I hope you Americans will see all our true & universal sympathy,—it has been to *all* like the shock attending the death of a distant friend[.] We *all* respected him so, even those who sympathized with the South. Where is Butler? Has not he great administrative abilities? But how President Lincoln has worked up to the last,—and now he has peace. One of you do write to us—*home* the address. Our dear love to you both, & the babies too. God bless you & them dear dear friends.

Yours ever truly & affec[tionate]ly

E C Gaskell

₅₅₈ **570** ₀

ANNE ROBSON[1]

Wednesday, 46, P. G
[?10 May 1865]

My dearest Nancy, Thank you so much for your letter I am always so glad to have one from you, and to hear all the family news. I really think you & I are the only two (from this house) who keep up direct communication *'on family affairs'*. At least *we* seldom hear anything of *you*, except straight from your own letters. Wm, I, Marianne & Julia are at home now but MA & Julia are going to London on (or about) the 27th of this month;[2] Julia to Florence's, Marianne up & down to a variety of places, the George Holland's, (Wimbledon) Smiths, (Hampstead,) Florences the Cromptons &c. I have given Wm a Handel-Festival ticket in hopes of inducing him to stay a *second* week in London. He goes up to his University Examinations on the 18th or 19th, and has been very much inclined to declare that he will & *must* come back at the end of that week; but I think now he is beginning to find out he can stay a little longer, and wait in & about London till after the Handel Festival, going home on Saturday July 1st. Mind, it is not *quite* fixed, but I *think* he is relenting. Everybody *here* wants him to take more holidays, and every body *there* (away from home) wants him to come to them; but it is almost impossible to push, pull, or stir him from home. I never know what makes him so busy; as if we any of us ask him he always says 'it's only so much extra fatigue going over all I have got to do.' I *fancy* a great many people refer to him on business or family difficulties; and besides the necessary thinking this requires, he writes letters *very* slowly and very neatly and correctly, so that replying to these letters takes up a great deal of time. He has his 3 days (of 4 hours each,) at the Home Mission-Board,—and that is in a very close room which (*I* should say) added to the fatigue. However the Memorial Hall will be opened in August, where he will have a good-sized, and well-ventilated room. Once a week he goes down to lecture at the Owens' College—{and that is} (for the six *winter* & *bad-weather* months of the year. That takes up two long hours; and on a Monday too which is often a hard day with committees &c, but you might as well ask St Pauls to tumble

[1] *Annotation* May 10—65.   [2] 27 May (see p. 774 below).

down, as entreat him to give up this piece of work; which *does* interest him very much, & which no one could do so well certainly; only it comes at such an unlucky time. Then, there is the plaguing Unitarian Herald; which takes up six or seven hours a week, (*at the office*) & a great deal of odd time at home; and which we, his family, *wish* he would draw out of, & leave to be conducted by younger men. I think he really *likes* all these things; he meets with people he likes; and all the subjects he is engaged upon interest him very much. And when he *is* at home, we only see him at meal-times; so that it is not the giving-up of the *family* life to him, that it would be to many men. He seems very well, & very happy; and says he is never so well as in Manchester; but one wishes that at his age he could have a little more repose of mind. He does not like any of us to go with him when he goes from home, saying it does not give him so much change; & with us he does not make so many acquaintances certainly, as he did at Rome for instance, where he made so many pleasant friends. I had got money enough (from my writing) both to pay for *his* going, & for Meta's *or* mine, *or* both of us, *with him* but he quite declined it, giving the reason as above,—'being more independent, & getting more complete change.' I wish he was not so thin; but that he has been for years now. For these last few winters he has always had a cold *during the cold weather*; but it goes off in the warm weather. He has a capital appetite, & generally sleeps like a top at nights. He keeps his study *terribly* hot; but then he likes it; and I sometimes fancy it is because he can't regulate the warmth of *other* houses that he dislikes so much leaving home. He *always* goes to the Edmund Potters in his holidays; wherever they take a house, generally in Scotland; this year I believe it will be in Wales. Mrs Potter says she has often asked me (in her letters to him,) to accompany him; but if she has, he has never told me of it; preferring the entire change, & independence. In East wind, or *very* cold weather his liver gets out of order, & then he is depressed & generally uncomfortable & easily annoyed; but in general I should say he is *much* more cheerful & happy in his mind, than he used to be, when younger. He is *very* fond of Charlie Crompton[,] & his & Florence's 'coming circuit' 3 times a year is a great pleasure to us all. But Wm trots off to his study, whoever is here all the same. Marianne's prospects of marriage are still very distant we believe. Thurstan *is* getting on at the Bar; but it must be very slowly; and the 100£ a year we could allow (*at first* at any rate) and the 300£, a year his father allows will not keep house in London, and pay law-expenses too. But they are very cheerful, correspond daily; and contrive to see each other very often; he is coming down here next Tuesday, & will very likely take Julia & MA back with him; as if so, & all 3 go, they will travel 2nd class. You have seen Meta & Florence for yourself, and later than I have. Meta is not yet *strong*, though she looks so well. She dare not go out visiting at night, or into crowds; or write many letters &c as all that still brings on a bad pain at the back of her head, & top of her spine; but she is MUCH better; & in another year or two I hope she will be as well as she was before the sewing-school winter. Julia is a great darling; very merry, and a greater reader than any except Meta; very useful, very sweet-tempered, and a great favourite with everybody, particularly with Florence & Charlie, who would like her to *live* with them. I think Maggie & Edith are coming here on Saturday to stay till Monday, all the time they could give us, I am sorry to say; as they stay at the Hollins's till Saty morng. Julia seemed to like them very much indeed when she stayed there at Xmas; and I want to keep up the cousinliness. Hearn is not well at all just now, as much depression of spirits as anything, I think.—She wants some change of thought and scene, & we have a variety of plans for giving her it, as she has no home to go to, now-a-days. She is a dear good valuable *friend*. We want some very retired, *yet* very near a doctor,—place to go to in the autumn,—*by the sea* yet with pretty *in*land country—in fact Silverdale (with a rather larger house), as it used to be. Now all the *good* houses there are taken by the year. *I* should like an *inn* where we could *board* at so much a week. Charlie & Florence & Thurstan will be with us for part of the time. Do *you* know any place that would be suitable *sea*-ry, clean & cheap? We should take Hearn with us? Charles Herford (Mrs Robberds son-in-law has just been having the small-pox, and is sadly marked as yet. Mrs Robberds looks as well, and almost, just the same, as ever. The Miss Marslands ditto. Mrs Shuttleworth is getting to the state of 'cheerful' widowhood; though she is five miles off, we see a good deal of her, as she has a carriage, & often comes over her[e]. I have been to ask Wm if he has any message—'Tell Nancy I shall be writing in a day or two', was all he said. *I* think your account of Sam sounds anxious; but I don't think Wm does. But then he does rather hate *facing* anxiety; he is so *very* anxious when he *is* anxious, that I think he always dislikes being made to acknowledge there

is cause. Mrs Watts need not write to me—for I HATE photographs
& moreover disapprove of biographies of *living* people. I always
let people *invent* mine, & have often learnt some curious particulars about myself from what they choose to say. I wish Wives
& Daughters were done.—It is to last till after the December No;
and I have WRITTEN August No, and have four more numbers to
write, & *such* a quantity of story to get in. I must set to and write
hard at it; & I shan't do anything else for the next 6 weeks, except
house-keep, & nursing & cheering up Hearn. So don't expect any
more endless letters for a long time. Have you heard of the sad
death of Annie (Green) Falcon's little boy of 17 months old, who
got into his bath, full of hot boiling water, while his nurse was
away fetching cold water,—was scalded, poor little fellow! and
just when they thought he was getting over it, he sank quite suddenly last Sunday week—She is expecting another in autumn—
but it can never be like the one she has lost. Goodbye my dearest
Nancy[.] Love to the two Williams

Your ever affect[ionate] sister
E. C. Gaskell.

₀ **571** ₀

U<small>NKNOWN</small>

42 Plymouth Grove
Manchester

June 4th [?1865]

Sir,

I disapprove so entirely of the plan of writing 'notices' or
'memoirs' of living people, that I must send you on the answer I
have already sent to many others; namely an entire refusal to
sanction what is to me so objectionable & indelicate a practice, by
furnishing a single fact with regard to myself. I do not see why
the public have any more to do with me than to buy\or reject/
the wares I supply to them.

I am sorry to seem uncourteous to a friend of Dr Morell's and
Professor Nichol's; but it is not *you*, but the impertinent custom,
of which I want to show my disapprobation.

I never had anything to do with 'any public works of usefulness'—but suppose I had? What respect cd you have had for a

person who distinctly flew in the face of the precept 'Let not thy left hand' &c,—.

I would gladly give you any information or help of any kind that I thought justifiable, even at the cost of a good deal of trouble to myself. But I will not, in the present instance, because I consider it *un*justifiable, and I may add that *every* printed account of myself that I have seen have [*sic*] been laughably inaccurate. Pray leave me out altogether.

Yours truly

E C Gaskell

567 **572** 573

MARIANNE GASKELL[1]

[? June 1865]

My dearest Polly,

You will be early down, so here is a letter to beguile your time. Don't you think you & Isabella had better go turn & turn about out with Florence? I think 2 young ladies are too many for her to take every where. If I were you I would say so to Florence, before Isabella. Thank you so *very* much for going & seeing MA Mostyn, love. I am afraid you had a very tiring day: and I am so sorry you missed seeing the Blunts. *Mind, if they ask you, I wish you to go.* Where *is* Meta's hat? I have no news to tell you. I am writing away, but I hate my story, because I am not to have more money for it, I believe. Fred has not yet turned up—(he may come to tea,—) but I won't forget to thank him for his kindness to you at Cambridge[.] I am so very very sorry for dear little Flossy's troubles; & so disappointed in Margaret. She must have done something *very* bad to be turned off at a moment's notice. I hope Florence will be very careful what {[?]} sort of a character she gives her. It ought to be quite *true*, but on the *kind* side of truth. Hearn is gone home today—she went yesterday indeed— *so* smart. ALL the painting inside & out is put off till August, I dare say I told you this before. The men have been off drinking, & are dismissed. I have got a man from [?Bannings] to paint all

[1] This and the following letter appear to relate to Mrs Gaskell's house-hunting in 1865.

the furniture in Julia's room, so that will be ready; but I have got no bed; so she'll have to go into the green room. Lion has been ill; & the newly calved cow has been ill; both better now, thank you. You see I have nothing else to tell you. We are living the quietest of quiet lives. *Do* go & see the Ewarts as much as you can. They were so good to me. And I do feel *grateful* to my children if they will pay attention to those whom I love, or who have been kind to me. How is Emily Crompton? Have you been to the Tollets? I fear not; I am very glad you got so pretty a bonnet. Really I have nothing to say. Mrs Eustace Greg & Mary Harvey lunched here yesterday[.] M. Harvey was full of the good Switzerland (Zermatt) had done her 5 years ago, when she went with the Enoch Harveys; & another time she went in a boat from L'pool to Nantes, & up the Loire,—she was very agreeable. The E. Gregs hope to see you in London. Francis Greg is puzzled about his toilette covers. No letters come for any one. *Yours are such pleasures.*

Your own most affect[ionate]

E C G

No news of Great Bookham? When does F E come here.

572 **573** 574

MARIANNE GASKELL

Tuesday. [?June 1865]

My dearest Polly,

We are not dining till 7 while Papa is away; so in spite of Meta's having already written I shall scribble a line or two to you. Thank you *so* much, darling—thank both you & dear Florence for going over to Bookham for me. Your account of the house was *admirable*. What did Florence think of it, *comparing it to the* house, we 4 went to see at Sunning-Hill, that Sunday we went to Windsor? However I don't think at all that it wd do,—unless indeed we could pull it down, (keeping the pretty garden as it is;) and re-build it. So *that* job's jobbed. I send you another advertisement, *which* PLEASE TAKE CARE OF. I hope Isabella went on smoothly to the last. I hear she was *charmed* with Charlie. Did she go off with flying colours? paying all her calls, at the houses to which she had been—*Hyde Park Sq*, & the rest of them? Did the Cromptons think her pretty &c &c—we have never heard\enough/details about *her*.

Julia is come home a little tired with packing, and not very hungry, in spite of the splendid lunch I had provided,—& that Meta & I had fasted for till she arrived—at 20 m. to 3. We are thinking of you on the river all this time. We have a *lovely* day here. Julia brings word that Cousin Mary is most likely coming to us *next* week,—in which case I shan't be able to go to the Smiths— (& Elder's) which this morng I wrote to say I would. But I have sent Hearn to the Fairbairns, to know if *they* will be at home, as *if they are* THEY will take Cousin Mary. Your own very affect[ionate]

E C Gaskell

573 574 •575a

MARIANNE GASKELL

Friday [?August 1865]

My dearest MA, Here is the acknowledgment all in due form to Cousin Edward.[1] It came quite safely. I am going to try to get out a little[,] otherwise I don't know how to bear the journey,[2] & the 'being agreeable' tomorrow—when I've done nothing but lie on a sofa & be X this last 3 weeks. I don't sleep, that's the worst. Fryston is as muggy and damp as this, in a low flat country all intersected with dykes. No news of Mr Tyndall—(tenant) who has I'm afraid slipped thro our fingers. No letters but yours. Pray *pray* write often to Julia, who is low at our going away; *please* do.

Your very affec[tionate] Mammy

---

[1] See Letter 581.

[2] We assume this is the visit to Fryston in the West Riding. In Letter 576 Mrs Gaskell refers to bad headaches before she went to Fryston.

₀ 575 ₀

LADY HOUGHTON[1]

Plymouth Grove.
Tuesday. [22 August 1865]

My dear Lady Houghton,

I do not know how to thank you enough for the very great pleasure of our visit to you;—I can only say that we enjoyed it even more than our former one to Fryston, (which we had always quoted as the very happiest we ever had), and beg you to believe in our deep gratitude for all your kindness to us.

We are full of 'sunny memories' of our visit, and we feel as if we could hardly help thinking and talking too much about it, instead of keeping to the work {in hand} waiting for our return. Meta begs to add her thanks to mine and to send her love to you and the dear children. And will Miss Newton and Mrs Blackburne and her daughter accept our kind remembranes [sic].

Ever yours aff[ectionate]ly
E. C. Gaskell

*

₅₆₅ 576 ₅₈₆

GEORGE SMITH

Wednesday Morng
46 P. G.
[?23 August 1865][2]

My dear Mr Smith,

After much cogitation, Meta & Hearn go up to London, (89 Oxford Terrace,—that empty but hospitable house,) this afternoon; & down to Alton[3] tomorrow. (They hope Mr Smith won't think they are colloguing with the valuer.) They will take all requisite measurements for choosing furniture,—and as far as they can—for matching the (already hideous) furniture. This they reckon will take them until Friday Aft:, when they return to

---

[1] See p. 692, n. 1 above.
[2] This, and the date of Letter 580, depends on the presumed date of Letter 581.
[3] In Hampshire, where Mrs Gaskell had bought a house called 'The Lawn'.

London, & that good dear Meta has undertaken to order the required furniture so as to have it ready to be sent down as soon as Mr White vacates the house,—which he wishes not to do *before* Sept 29. Then it will require a thorough cleaning, & a very little paint,—& then—Ho for a tenant. I answer advertisers in the Times, H H[1] Farnham, & refer them to Mr Enoch which I feel to be taking a great liberty. I have had such bad head aches, (before I went to Fryston),—that I am behindhand with Wives & Daughters,—wherefore I let Meta go,—I hope it is not selfish, & I hope she won't be knocked up.—I have answered about Rick of Hay—Mr White says incoming tenant ought to pay something for standing crops,—apples, potatoes onions??

I never heard Mrs Smith was ill—I am so sorry. Julia is poorly too—Mr Gaskell in Scotland.

Yours most truly
E C Gaskell

o **577** 579

MR LOWE[2]

46 Plymouth Grove
August 24 [1865]

My dear Sir,
Are you in a generous humour, and will you give me 'the Gayworthys'[3]—I am so delighted with all the specimens I see in reviews. If you will, & will send it to me at

Charles Crompton's Esq
89 Oxford Terrace
Hyde Park

it will be forwarded to me directly. I have already recommended it to several people, Ld Houghton among the number, who ordered it directly.

Yours very truly
E. C. Gaskell.

---

[1] *Hampshire Herald.*

[2] *Annotation* this copy has been sent & you may like to write to her direct. See Letter 579 for recipient's name.

[3] By Mrs A. D. T. Whitney (1824–1906), Boston, Massachusetts, 1865.

₀ **578** ₀

UNKNOWN

46 Plymouth Grove
Manchester.
August 24 [?1865]

My dear Sir,

Your letter & the beautiful monogram were sent on here from Fryston;—thank you very much for all the trouble you must have taken. But it is a great success.

I sent you the French book (4 vols, F. Jeune on the outside— the present Bp of Peterborough, who gave it me—) by todays post.

Meta desires me to give you her very kind regards.

Yours very truly
E. C. Gaskell

₅₇₇ **579** ₀

MR LOWE

46 Plymouth Grove
Manchester
Augt 29 [1865]

Dear Mr Lowe,

Thank you very much for your letter, and for so kindly, and promptly sending me 'The Gayworthys'. *The* daughter who had the pleasure of receiving you here, during the year of the Manchester Exhibition, received the book quite safely, at her sister's Mrs Crompton's, 89 Oxford Terrace, and is I expect, bringing it down to me today, when I shall be delighted to read it. I do not know 'Faith Gartney's Girlhood' but from what I have seen quoted from the Gayworthys I should *think* all that the authoress writes, would be sure of a welcome. Have you heard from Mrs Stowe lately. I always like to hear news of her. I am glad to think of your having some relaxation, & hope you may be having as fine weather in Cornwall, as we have, even in dirty Manchester.

Yours very truly
E. C. Gaskell

*575a **580** 582

MARIANNE GASKELL

89, Oxford Terrace
Hyde Park
Thursday Evng—9 P M
[31 August 1865]

My dearest Polly,
   From Meta's letter (which I sent Oakes to meet,) I found she
quite wanted my help for a day or two in London; & so (though
very unwilling to leave Julia who is *very* far from strong & very
much out of spirits in consequence,) I came off by the ½ p. 9 train,
\yesterday/taking a return excursion 2 class ticket 1-17-6, by
which I must go home tomorrow Friday,—I was so uneasy at
leaving without having heard from you,—but Julia promised to
send on letters directly & I have got yours & Thurstan's tonight[.]
Meta & Hearn met me at the Euston Sq Station—{Hearn}\Julia/
having telegraphed to them to do so, & we went to Heals directly,
& staid there as long as it was light—bought all the bed-room
things—(Meta having wants & measurements &c) except carpets.
Then came here, & dined. Meta has been kept in suspense all week
by the Alton agent (Mr Williams) knowing of a lady-tenant who
had commissioned him to find her a house,—& *had furniture*; but
in spite of 2 letters from Meta; *one* telegraph from Meta; 2 letters
from Mr Enoch, he has never answered one word,—though he
told Meta he would see the lady the day after Meta saw him
(Friday)[.] Every morng Meta has been to Pall Mall to hear if
they had had a letter,—as we did not like to furnish, till we heard.
But today no time was to be lost,—and we have been all day at
Shoolbreds, in the City (after carpets,—a failure—) Shoolbreds
again, Heals, Copelands in {Rus} Bond St (for China & glass—
Mr Smith get us 22½ per cent discount there,—& did not come
home till 8 to dinner, *dead-beat*, & *sadly* disappointed at no letter
from Manchester. However it came,—& it was *such* a relief. Do
stay & REST for another week at Dumbleton[1] if they will have you
for Thurstan says you are not as strong as before you went to
Alton,—and *you* say you were not well before you went; so I
don't expect you are very well now, 'working it by the rule of

---

[1] She returned to Plymouth Grove on 7 September 1865 (Letter 583).

three['] as Miss Marslands say. I hope\cleaning out/the drains—
ugh—may make a difference but certainly Manchester is not a place
to *regain* health in. About Howarth & Hale's bill,—can you tell me
where to find your receipts? I dare say the Album was that book
of mine.—But please write to F Langshaw to pay her bill *straight*—
Thank you for sending the Alton bills. I will put by the money for
them. I do hope you will sometime learn to understand how a
mother may crave to have a line or two, twice a week or so. You
really can't tell how anxious I have been. Julia promised to telegraph to Cousin Fanny if no letter arrived at P. G. this morning
But I am so thankful to get your & Thurstan's acct though not as
good as I could wish. I certainly received no letter *after* the one in
which you said your head & back were aching, *and* that you would
write the next day. And about the going to Alton, I wish you &
Thurstan would read *my* & *Meta's* letters of August 10th *over*
again. In *mine* I said I would make a copy of the list before I sent
it,—but I was not able to sit up so long,—and Meta, writing *after*
me, but by the same post,—told Thurstan so, & that I should be
extremely obliged to him or to you, if you, either of you, would
make a copy for me? Just do read those two letters of August 10
over again, & tell me if I am not repeating correctly,—for of course
I took no copies of my letter, or of Meta's, so I may be mistaken.
However that is spilt milk—and my great regret is that you
should now be suffering from what you did, *quite rightly*, as you
& Thurstan understood my letter. Only *do* read those two,
(August 10 letters) again.—I am quite worn out tonight,—I go
home tomorrow to go with Julia to tea at Miss Marsland's; as,
besides the return ticket, only lasting so long,—I don't want {my}
to be missed. Papa comes home end of next week. He is at
E. Potters Invereishy

> Boat of Insh
> Kingussie
> Inverness-shire.

I am very glad I came, tho' for we have done an immense deal,—
only kitchen things now, left undone. I mean general *house* things
&c: Valuer made list (excluding rejected articles 156£—which is
I believe already paid.

I must end now. Do write again if only 2 lines to say how you
are, darling. I am feeling very much dispirited about *every* body's
health,—[1]

---

[1] There follows a contribution from Meta.

EDWARD THURSTAN HOLLAND[1]

46 Plymouth Grove
Oh no I mean
89 Oxford Terrace
Thursday night
[?31 August 1865]

My dear Thurstan,

Thank you very much for your very nice & kind letter. I am so tired & worn out I must refer you to Minnie for all particulars. Do you think that fall backwards out of the rocking chair on the Hall-floor she told me of when I was at Fryston has had anything to do with 'the looking ill & feeling ill' you speak of as *before* she went to Alton, I was so hoping she would come back brilliantly well from the care-free life, & good air of Dumbleton. I am so tired I hardly know what I say. I go home tomorrow after a morning's final shopping. We have got *all* the things at 3 or 4 shops; not to be sent to Alton *till* 29th Sept—bills to go in to, & references to be made to, Messrs Smith & Elder.

Thank you about Kath. Dock,—& thank yr father. There *may* be some good cause for the Shares going up—I missed annual report. *If* trustees are necessary I shd like none better than you & Charlie, but I wd rather do *without* trustees, IF possible. Mr Shaen I *fancy* suggested some way in whh they might be done without —Meta is writing to ask him to tell *you* what he said to us. *Also* C. C. suggested '4 daughters' instead of 'next of kin';\Vide Sheet 2nd[2]/{& also if the 4 daughters die, without children,\after/before Mr Gaskell & me, that it (Lawn) shd go to their respective husbands—You know I want it to go to unmarried ones,} or one —But I am too stupid to do more than refer to Mr Shaen who took down notes of what I said, only I want my daughters childless widowers to have it, sooner than its' going off to collateral relations of Mr Gaskell's[.] I dare say I shall plague you enough when you get back to London—although at present we *do* feel as if we had done everything—except find a tenant.—

[1] *Annotation* [by recipient?] 1 Sepr/65. [A Friday.]
[2] This sheet may be missing. The sheet beginning with the words 'or one' immediately following the long deletion is headed '3'.

The Miss Cherringtons have written to Debenham & Tewson, to be informed if it is again in market.

Your very affect[ionate]

E C Gaskell

*

580 **582** *582a

MARIANNE GASKELL[1]

Saturday Mg—
P. Grove.
[2 September 1865]

My dearest Polly I *could* not help the disappointment I was afraid you would feel, at not hearing from me *yesterday*. If my letter was not even *more* stupid than I am afraid it was, I think you must have understood from it, that after a letter from Meta received on Wednesday *mg*—I went to London *by the* $\frac{1}{2}$ PAST *9* train that means taking a second class return ticket for 3 days; She & Hearn met me at Euston Sq Station, and we shopped till past 7,—Meta having made out a capital 'tabular statement' (as Mr Smith calls it,) of everything wanted thro' the house, size of space into which every thing had to fit, & colours it had to go with. (She had waited & waited for a letter or answer to telegram from Mr Williams as see accompanying letters, which *please both you & Thurstan read attentively*, looking at dates & making yrselves fully masters of contents. I shd be *much* obliged to E T H if he could take this trouble.) Thursday, after *Meta* had had no letter, she went to Pall Mall,—*they* had had none, & advised us to continue the furnishing by way of having *every* thing made & ready as soon after Sep 29 as *possible*. So again a long *crazing* day of furnishing; going into the City,—far beyond St Paul's out of duty, being told carpets were cheaper there,—but they were coarse common things, not really cheaper[,] so we came back to Shoolbreds, Meta being rescued (in Wood St Cheapside,) from getting crushed between two immense lorries by a very kind man[.] Home at 8—{forw} yr letter forwarded by Julia came soon after, —*also* one from Mr Smith (forwarded) to ask for another letter-article for Pall Mall Gaz. *by return* of post—simply impossible—

---

[1] A Lancaster transcript (see Appendix A) gives the address: 'Miss Gaskell | Ed. Holland Esq., M.P., | Dumbleton Hall, | Evesham.'

but has to be written *today*, *before* we go to James Reiss's, $\frac{1}{2}$ p 3—
Oh dear! I *am* nearly killed, but the *stress* of every thing is nearly
over. Yesterday Friday mg—I planned to come home in time to
go to $\frac{1}{2}$ p. 6 tea at Miss Marslands with Julia, as engaged; & Meta
& Hearn were to follow at night, doing kitchen things at Burton's
&c first—when, just as I was starting came a note from Mr Enoch
to Meta. He had heard from Mr Williams; anonymous ladies had
been over the house, liked it, appointed to call on Mr Williams
at 3 P M yesterday. I left Meta writing to Mr Enoch to ask
whether (to save time, Mr Williams being so dilatory in writing)
she had not better go down to Alton to be there *by 3*[,] see the
lady at Mr Wms & get list of *her* furniture if she tho[ugh]t of
taking house. You will see from the last letter (which I have just
received along with yrs) what Mr Enoch said when he called.
Mr Smith can get us 22$\frac{1}{2}$ discount on the things\—furniture/we
get off *his* shops,—he ships off so much. I am the less scrupulous
since I heard of Wilkie Collins' 5000£.[1] I *must* go & write for the
P. M. G. tho' Meta forgets we dine at the James Reiss—we are
going that *she* (Meta) may see his unique collection of engravings;
one of the rarest in England, that she did so want to see; & what
I'm to say I don't know. *Take care of Meta's letters please.* I only
want you & Thurstan to be au courant of every thing. I came
home $\frac{1}{2}$ p. 5, had a cup of tea, & hurried with Julia to Miss
Marslands—who luckily had 2 roast chickens for tea; for I was
nearly dead for want of food & rest. I found a letter from Miss
Marshall asking Julia to an Archery Meeting at which her nephew
is president, on Thursday & Julia has no clothes—Hearn away, ditto
Hughes (which last is naughty & provoking,—) so I have got a
new gown[,] ribbons & hat to see after, for I find the darling wd
like it. *If* the house gets let, & the work cleared off, I think we
may go (with a Cook's Excursion ticket 6£-6s) there & back for
a month to Switzerland, Geneva Berne Frebourg Neufchatel the
week after next. It wd be cheaper than Scotland,—where Papa
could not get a bed one night. Remember this has been our
busiest week—this over, & I fancy there will be much less to be
done; don't *hurry* home, darling. Do get strong in the quiet &
good air of Dumbleton.—I *think* we cd spend 3 weeks *stationary*
in Switzerland for 60£ ?? I must however write a great deal more
at Wives & Daughters first—My illness (3 weeks from bed to

[1] Smith gave Wilkie Collins 5000 guineas in 1863 for a novel for the *Cornhill Magazine*. This turned out to be *Armadale*, 1866.

sofa & vice versa—caused by drains I do believe—) threw me
terribly behind hand. *Do* take care of yrself[.] My lo⟨v⟩e to
E T H—oh *how* dead I feel!—

E G

Both Hearn & Meta (*in the dusk*) thought the garden *out of order*,
& carelessly kept outhouses very untidy.

*   *

₅₆₉ **583** ₀

CHARLES ELIOT NORTON

September 8, 1865, 46 Plymouth Grove
Manchester

My dear Mr Norton, and also
My dear Susan, for I have both of you to thank very much for
your letters,—I am not going to lose time for apologizing as I dare
say I ought to do,—for the length of time I have been in writing;
but I shall plunge at once into the middle of things. It is at the
close of a very hot sultry day; for we have been having unusually
hot weather here; I am sitting in the drawing-room, Meta playing
to herself consciously,—and to me unconsciously; Marianne &
Julia have gone for a walk,—though it is getting very dark; and
we are waiting tea for them. Mr Gaskell has been a month in
Scotland,—with friends; and we are expecting him home tomorrow after his holiday; Florence and Charlie have today been
married two years, & are in London, setting out tomorrow for
Geneva, Baveno, Lugano, and the Italian Lakes. Marianne only
came back yesterday from Dumbleton—(Thurstan's home,)
where she has been spending the greater part of his legal holiday.
So now we are all '*placed*' like the men at chess, I will go on to
something else. And first let me thank you, my dear Susan very
much for your photograph of Lincoln,—and *you*, Mr Norton for
this larger one which has come lately; in this past week in fact;
with the delicious book on the portraits of Dante which it is a
pleasure even to open,—it,—& the faces themselves seem to carry
one so *up* into a [']purer æther, a diviner air.' I am so *very* much
obliged to you for thinking of sending it to me. It only came this
past week,—along with 'Fireside Travels', for which I am writing
to thank Mr Lowell. I want very much to hear that you are not
feeling the reaction after a great long time of latent thought and

anxiety. I tried to hear something special of you from two (separate) Americans—at least one was a ci-devant Yorkshire blacksmith from Chicago,—who turned up unexpectedly—the one on Monday, the other on Tuesday—but they neither of them could say anything very particular about you. The American Yorkshireman was a Mr Collier Unitarian Minister at Chicago,— who had been nurse and Captain of nurses under the Sanitary Commission; the Tuesday man was introduced by our dear Mr Field; a Mr Phillips Brooks, Episcopalian clergyman of Phila-delphia and formerly a student at Cambridge. He had been among the freed negroes. Indeed *both* told us *most* interesting things. I don't know which was the most interesting. We hope they were the fore-runners of you all in your turns. But life never flows back, —we shall never again have the old happy days in Rome, shall we? Mr Brooks said you had the Storys with you this Spring in America[.] We never seem to hear or see any them [*sic*] of them now; but we love them all the same, tho' they have passed out of our orbit. We have been having rather a quiet summer; though I dare say it won't sound so in a letter. I went to Madame Mohls in Paris, rather unexpectedly in March—(oh I believe I told you all this,—) and with a visit to Florence I staid away 2 months— hearing of Mr Lincoln's death when I was in London, with Meta; and seeing the *most* universal national sympathy. Did I tell you a friend of ours was asked by the workmen of Staley Bridge,— (Meta has taken to playing Chopin's Funeral March, unknowing what I am writing about,) to preach a funeral sermon for Presi-dent Lincoln—He went; and to his surprize found about 30,000 men,—each with a *bit of mourning* crape on sleeve, or hat—and he had to preach out of doors—all Lancashire workmen. Then Meta & I came home, & Julia & Marianne went up to London— (May 27, and Marianne only returned yesterday,—) and Mr Gaskell followed for a fortnight's holiday in June. And then I did a terribly grand thing! and a secret thing too! only you are in America and can't tell. I bought a house and 4 acres of land in Hampshire,—near Alton,—for Mr Gaskell to retire to & for a home for my unmarried daughters. That's to say I had not money enough to pay the whole 2,600£; but my publisher (*Smith* & Elder) advanced the 1,000£ on an 'equitable mortgage.' And I hope to pay him off by degrees. Mr Gaskell is *not to know till then*, unless his health breaks down before. He *is* very well and very strong thank God; but he is sixty, & has to work very hard here, his work *increasing* with his years, and his experience; & in the winters he feels this. The house is large—(not quite so large as this;[)] in a very pretty garden (kitchen flower-gardens & paddock between 3 & 4 acres,) and in the middle of a pretty rural village, so that it won't be a lonely place for the unmarried daughters who will inherit. In the mean time we are furnishing it (500£ more) & hoping to let it for 3 years; after which we hope to induce Mr Gaskell to take possession himself. By that time I HOPE to have paid off the mortgage 1,200£,—his two daughters will be most likely married in London; & in London every one says he will be welcomed as a co-labourer with many of his friends; so that he will not leave off work, tho' he will *lessen* it by the change. 1 3/4 hours will take him to London where his brothers and sister & Florence already are, & where we hope Marianne will be by that time. Till then it is a secret from Mr Gaskell[.] When I have got it *free* we plan many ways of telling him of the pretty home awaiting him[.] Meta claims my paper; so with dear love to you all believe me ever your true and affect[ionate[friend

E. C. Gaskell

Now Meta! begin.

0 584 0

JAMES R. LOWELL

46 Plymouth Grove
Manchester—
September 8th [1865]

My dear Mr Lowell,

You can't think how much I shall value Fireside Travels,[1] (which only reached me during this past week,) now that I have got it of my 'very very own' (as the children say,) and with that charming little bit of writing from you at the beginning. I don't mean that I did not delight in the book from the very first time I read a page in it; but the sense of property in it gives it a double value, and the feeling of successful beggary is very charming, though perhaps I ought to be ashamed. Only I am *not*, because I *am* successful. I have known you so long! I knew serious poems of yours long ago,—twenty years or so; but my personal knowledge

[1] Published 1864.

of you began in Rome 1857,—when (did you know it?) you and one other went about with the dear Storys, and me and mine up and down Rome. 'Here James and Anna lodged'—'Here we had such a happy day with the Lowells' &c &c &c. And our well-loved and highly-prized Mr Norton used to say 'I only know she came and went' to us in the happy evenings in the Piazza de Spagna. I fancy it was not in print then; and we used to try and catch it from him,—and did catch (for very love of nine,) the exact accent in which he said 'onn-ly'. Well then the Bigelow papers[1]—I think I could stand a Civil Service Examination in them; and we had three copies of our own, till a little daughter married, and carried off one. So don't I know you? and are not we friends, and dear to [one] another as well as 'dear to those who are dear to us[']? We have had two Americans here this week. A Mr Collier (a Yorkshire American) of Chicago, nurse under the Sanitary Commission,—and a Mr Phillips Brooks, a Cambridge \U.S./student, *and* an Episcopalian minister in Philadelphia. We tried hard to squeeze them dry about America; but though we talked five or six hours consecutively we could not do it,—But we were glad to see them, as the swallows who are to make our summer. Now, said we the Americans will be coming over, and travelling about again, & perhaps we may see some of our own people. 'Our own people' being the Nortons, the Fields Mr Hamilton Wilde—(where is he? oh where?) dear Romans of old, —Mr Hale, and one or two others known more slightly,—and *you* dear Mr Lowell, if you will be one of 'our own people'— our 'dear Americans'—[']whose very step has music in't when they come up the Stair.'

Yours very much obliged, and with most true regard

E. C. Gaskell

•582b 585 587

?MARIANNE GASKELL

Dieppe, Friday, October 6th [?1865][2]

My own darling—We have just got your letter (*over-charge 1 franc 20c from not being sufficiently affranchie*—), I *am* so sorry about *the*

---

[1] *The Biglow Papers*, ed. H. Wilbur, 1848.
[2] Dating depends on Letters 582 and 586.

smell. I enclose a piece for you to *read* to, or *give* Papa, as you see best, at the right time. And now I will tell you my *theory* by whh I account for the pestiferous smell. You see *the* contents of WC &c go into a cess-pool at the corner of the yard near the coal-cellar & stable, & going under both. A drain goes under the house out into the garden & into a cess-pool in the field. *Adjoining* both drain & cess-pool is the cistern *under the pantry*, from which the water goes (or *ought* to go) to the *scullery tap*. Now this tap has been dry ever since July. Rowlands said at first that it was owing to the dry summer, but after filling it with *town's* water (it is usually filled with *rain*,) the scullery tap was still dry, showing that it *leaked* somewhere. Now where it leaked *out* the smells must come in, especially when the water gets low so as not to fill up the hole. The smell is sure to *come in* from the cess pool or drain adjoining if the cistern is not *quite* sound. When it IS quite sound {it}\the flag with the ring in it/ought to be CEMENTED *down*. As it has been all summer it has been a gully-hole inside the house[.] I am sure it is most seriously injuring our health. I had done all I could before I left, with Mr Coates & Rowlands; but still the scullery tap *did not run*; & until it does that smell will go on. The whole system of drainage is bad. It was so in the Micholls' time; & they left in consequence—I always thought until this last summer, that it had been remedied—Both Charlie & Georgina have perceived the smell *in the drawing room* & spoken about it. However one does not expect to write about *drains* from Dieppe, does one? My dear darling, we have heard from Florence this mg—So provoking! our letters to Harry from Crewe, on first hearing of the Judge's illness[1] have never reached! That & your letter missing makes me strongly suspect the tipsy Crewe butler. Three times we sent to Crewe about yr missing letter; once by Ellen Tollets maid,—once by Mr de Bunsen, & once by the usual servant. Mr de B. looked over the letters. Poor dear Julia's heart so yearns after Switzerland that she can't enjoy this place—(which I think is charming)—we have had a talk this morning (*very* tantalizing to my dear girls,) about going there; but we have settled that the *wisest* thing is to stay near the sea. Now to go back to when I wrote last. From the Grosvenor. Our bill was not much there, owing to various contrivances but I did feel *so* ill, I begged them suddenly to come off to Newhaven, feeling as if I must get a breath of sea-air, after a *wretched* sleepless night. We got to

---

[1] See Letter 588 and n.

Newhaven about 4, but found the inn very rough and dirty, 170 passengers arriving by mg boat, not *so* many departing, but still more than a *hundred*;—we had a very comfortable dinner (after a walk on the ugly sea-shore), & then went to bed. I slept like a top; going to bed at 8 (feeling worn out) and wakening at 8. We had no breakfast so to speak, but 2 mutton chops a piece, & bitter beer. We met Mrs Milner-Gibson, just arrived from Dieppe on the stairs. She advised us to come to this hotel—(not named in Murray, but very clean & civil people.) For 10 years she has come to Dieppe, & could not say enough in its praise. She goes herself to a much grander hotel (the Bristol) but when she has left her children here she has left them in charge of Mme Guibon (the landlady here to whom she gave us a letter of introduction). Mrs *Crowe* is here,—lives here regularly; Mme Gosch, wife of the Danish Envoy in London,—friend of Mary Ewart of Broadleas, to whom also Mrs M Gibson gave us a note; but the Gaskell hatred of society prevails, & we have not delivered it. We have a pleasant sitting room au premier, *two* double-bedded rooms, (one opening out of the sitting room,—) breakfast (coffee bread & butter in our room—) lunch any time we like—chocolate, cold meat, bread & butter Neufchatel Cheese & grapes—in the Salle à manger at a little table, & dinner at the table d'hote (10 persons only 1 gentleman which Julia finds dull—) soup, fish, 2 meats, pudding & desert—) for 9 francs a piece, *service* included. Bougies, wine & fire extras. We are 2 minutes from the sea, & the house is as sweet as a nut. For ½ a franc we can go into the Establissement close at hand, hear a (shocking) out {of}\in/air band) & read the news. Everything is shutting up for the winter—but the air & sky are splendid, & I feel like a different creature. Our passage here was as smooth as smooth cd be. I shall write to Papa next,—about the drains. No room in this letter.

Yr own dearly loving Mammy.

Such a delightful crossing. I was so sorry when it was over—'like a lake'[.]

576 **586** 0

GEORGE SMITH

Hotel de Paris
Dieppe
Thursday, Oct 12—[1865]

Thank you my dear Mr Smith, the P. M. Gs[1] came all safe, &
right, and are such a pleasure! They come *through* Paris, and *are*
opened; but not considered objectionable I suppose. This place
gets more and more charming as the weather becomes rougher &
wilder, & the people (smart ones I mean,) disappear. We are becoming highly *authorial* (if there is such a word), in this hotel.
Mrs Crowe; and a M. Alfred de Bréhat who has sent me his
romans, as a compliment to the author of Ruth (pronounced
Roit,). I never heard of him before in my life,—but he says you
are a great éditeur & a 'brave homme' so I suppose you know him,
& I shall consider you responsible for the morality of his works,
which now lie on the table close by Meta & Julia. Please we shall
be leaving Dieppe at the beginning of next week,—arriving at
Alton about the 23—& pray don't send me any more P M Gs[.]
Meta & Julia say they too are authors. They rest their claim on
THE Index. Hearn sends word one of the tops to a sauce tureen &
one of the chairs is broken in carriage; *all else right.*

Yours most truly, E C Gaskell

581 **587** 0

EDWARD THURSTAN HOLLAND

Hotel des Bains
Boulogne
Wednesday, Octr 25. [1865]

My dear Thurstan,

Please we are quite hoping to see you on the 28th\at '*The
Lawn*'/—you won't mind everything being rough. We can give
you bread & cheese & cold meat, and 'Alton Ale' & tea & bread

[1] *Pall Mall Gazettes.*

& butter & 'excellent milk' (Hearn says,) & a hearty welcome.
Come sooner if you can. I want all sorts of advice about the garden
&c &c— No time for more from your ever affec[tionat]e cousin

E. C. Gaskell

585 **588** 0

MARIANNE GASKELL

Tuesday afternoon
[?31 October 1865]

My own darling, we sent letters\to the Cromptons/to Alton to
catch the 12 o'clock post to London, so we told the boy to wait
to see if any letters came by the *mid*day post, & he brought back
yours, my darling. To answer your questions first. Hearn thought
that onions[,] apples & potatoes could be sent to Manchester in
sacks, (if Oakes had any) instead of our having to *buy* hampers.
About the boots,—she is 'very much obliged to you, & very
'sorry you shd have had all that trouble and now she supposes
'they must wait till she comes back. She *did* carry them away her-
'self, when she bought them; but they were too narrow for her, so
'she {sent} took them herself down again to Holmes; could not
'see Mr Holmes, but saw 2 of the shopgirls, who both came to
'look at them and told her how they might be widened; by open-
'ing down the front. But you are not to give yourself any more
'trouble about them.' I have written by this morning's post to
Papa to tell him we had 'crossed the channel'—(I did not say
where from or to where) and were now spending the remainder
of our time & money at a little village on the borders of Hampshire ⟨. . .⟩[1] cut down near the house so as to make the dining
room lighter. That is all we are going to do to the garden at
present. The house wants numbers of little bits of joinering, &
painting the *wood*work of the window frames, & other *wood*
work, so as just to keep it all together until *the* future painting of
the whole house. And the wet weather is *so* against all this. The
upholstering woman, who engaged to come & help E. has never

[1] This letter consists of 4 leaves, the last pair being conjugate. This lacuna indicates a gap in the sense between the first two, but the hand, colour of paper and ink
are similar in all leaves.

turned up yet; & Meta & Julia are gone in the rain down to Alton
to try & find her & bring her up by main force. *And* Heal's list
is sadly wanted from home, along with *any* mem*s* about Burtons.
Neither are quite complete as far as we can {tell} guess, and until
we have the things *complete* it is no use making our dear '*lists*'.
Copeland, also, has not sent all yet; but *he* says they are not sent
because they are not ready. Until the carpets are cut out we can't
tell how much we shall have to return to Shoolbreds, & the
carpets can't be cut out till the upholstering woman comes to help
E. So you see we seem at a stand still, which is *very* provoking.
We are rather puzzled about Mrs Moray—She sent up (through
Mr Williams) today {s} to offer 170 for house, without {land}
C. Miller's land; 190 *with* it (the rent of it, to *me* will be 22£—*10s*)
I sent word I would see her on Thursday or Friday at any time
she would appoint, but gave no answer about the terms offered,
thinking I might as well have all the masculine advice I could before then. It is a *great* drop from 210£; and will *not* leave me
100£, after paying interest to Mr Smith[,] income & property
tax. She is *said* to be 'sure pay' tho'. Shall I run the chance of a
better tenant or not? The house & garden seem to me *alone* worth
170, *without* furniture. But we don't know who to leave in charge
of the house when we go? &c &c &c, and you know I'm an old
fidget, and if we *don't* let it!—It will be so nice, & so complete.
We long for you to see it so much. Every day we like it better &
better even in the midst of all the *half* furnished state, painters, &
charwomen—Tomorrow, & not till then, these latter will have
finished their 5 weeks' cleaning—& then I have engaged a very
nice servant (out of place) to come in & cook & clean the rooms
we live in. Oh I must tell you something. Last night the ringers
rang the 3 church bells, and then came to say they had been ringing for our arival [*sic*] (we had never heard the bells) & I had to
give them 2s–6d. Hearn liked it tho'. She seems very well now;
I am giving her sherry every day, twice; Oh dear—Mrs Moray, I
wonder what I ought to do? I had such a charming note from
C[harles] C[rompton] this morning, which I have sent on to
Papa. I do think her being of such help to Lady C. just now may
draw them together very nicely. I am so sorry to think that we
shall never see the dear kind judge again.[1] Charlie proposes that
F should come down here for a little time, as he says she is quite
knocked up; but of course she could not come just yet. I am

[1] Judge Crompton died on 30 October 1865.

going to finish my story while here if I can—but I am constantly called off just now. Only I may as well make use of this waiting time. We have seen none of our neighbours as yet. I am going to sell all the apples we can't give away or eat at 1s–6d a bushel. We like the gardener & his wife very much. They have 7 children & each works very hard, and are very civil. Your most loving mother in the dark[.]

₀ **589** ₀

UNKNOWN

November 9th 1865
Holybourne

Dear Sir

I return you Mr Priest's bill, which is quite right. We have retained his mats for gardening purposes, as they are as cheap as what we can get here.

We are *returning* all the packing-materials used by *Heal, Burton,* and *Copeland.* We are re*taining* those used by *Shoolbred,* in packing.

I am extremely obliged to you for all the kindness {to the} which you take this trouble; everything that has passed through your hands has been so entirely satisfactory. I am sure the advertisements will be all right; but I can't help wishing that the tenant would turn up. Mr White made upwards of nine tons of hay off the land last year, besides the 3£ rent paid to him for the aftermath. Hay is now selling here at 6£ 10s the ton. Nine or ten women made the hay in 3 days.

(That is for the information of the tenant.)

I remain dear Sir,
Yours very truly,
E. C. Gaskell.

₀ **590** ₀

UNKNOWN

[?1865]

My dear Madam,
   I received your fortnightly subscription of 6s. (in stamps), duly in course of post, and beg to return you my best thanks for your kind & continued subscription towards our poor operatives. At the same time I hope I may say that work has now a good deal increased; and, (though many fear that this improvement is only temporary,) that just at present no further contributions are required, as we hope the funds in hand will prove sufficient for some time.[1] If the worst anticipations are realized, and work again becomes scarce, and the funds fall low, I will take the liberty of reminding you of the fact, that if you then like to recommence your kind subscription you may do so. Pray believe me to remain
                    Yours gratefully & truly
                                   E C Gaskell[2]

[1] The final meeting of the Council of the Cotton Relief Fund was held on 4 December 1865; no grants had been made since 19 June. *Annals*, ed. Axon, p. 297.
   [2] William Shaen told Catherine Winkworth on 15 November 1865 that the very last letter Mrs Gaskell wrote was one to him on Saturday evening [11 November], 'full of life and spirits, and ending "it is so nice to think we shall see you on Wednesday".' *Letters and Memorials*, ed. Winkworth, II, p. 428.

591

GEORGINA ?BEHRENS

Ardtornish   *by Bonawe*
Morvern.
N.B.

That is Mrs Octavius Smith's address, dearest Georgina—does it not read Ossianic—'Morvern'—Meta & I have read this 1st vol of Rachel Gray[1]—I think it very interesting—In haste yrs ever affec[tionate]ly

E C Gaskell

I hope dear little Nettie keeps better

592

GEORGINA ?BEHRENS

My dearest Georgina,

Isaac Greenbury
Jet
Ornament Manufacturer
St Hilda Hall
Baxter Gate
Whitby.

References to Mrs Rose,\1/Abbey Terrace[2] or to Mrs Broderick Sneaton Rectory. In greatest haste[.]

Your very affec[tionat]e

E C Gaskell

593

?JOHN BRIGHT

My dear Mr Bright,

I *did* 'feel like reading' your article, and like it very much, as I knew I should from what you told me of it. But then you know I

---

[1] By Julia Kavanagh, 1856.
[2] Mrs Gaskell stayed here on her visit in November 1859.

am not (*Unitarianly*) orthodox! So you may be 'anile' and 'senile' and all the rest of it in spite of my opinion to the contrary. However if you are ever so mischievous we shall be glad to see you here. Harriet says our dear ugly bleak Silverdale would please you. You can hear from her *what* it—and\what/our life is.—And if you would like to come to us on Friday or Saturday\next/,—(*do*, if you can, & especially if you will promise to like Silverdale, and stay over Sunday as long as you like,) we have Harriet's room at liberty, & a warm welcome ready for you. Mind! I won't talk theology—Unitarian or otherwise,—and you are to be carnal & *hungry* not spiritual and regardless of food. We never talk sense— but we are very happy. Now write & say you will come.

Yours very truly
E C Gaskell

594

?James Bryce[1]

46 Plymouth Grove
May 17.

My dear Sir,

Here are the two promised notes of introduction. Mr Winkworth's is to his *house*; so it will be better to call there in the evenings; Mr Neeld's is to his *works*—so about 11 AM will be the best time to attack him, unless you like to go out to his house at Bowden, 8 miles off by rail.

Mr Winkworth says Bolton is a town wanting a *very* liberal MP. You can ask him all about it.

Yours very truly
E. C. Gaskell

[1] In Bryce Collection, Bodleian Library. *Annotation.* If to Bryce himself most likely 1864 or 1865.

595

G. J. Chester[1]

> 46 Plymouth Grove
> Manchester
> April 10th

Mrs Gaskell presents her compliments to Mr Chester, and, in compliance with a suggestion of Mrs Vaughan's, of Doncaster, ventures to enquire from him if he knows whether an admission to the 'Duke of Norfolk's Almshouses', Shrewsbury Road, opposite to the Cholera Monument, can be procured for a very deserving old woman, Mary Leatham—widow, aged 71, living at 13 Canning St, attendant on the services at St Mary's Church. Her husband for several years farmed 270 acres of land at Stone near Gainsborough,—but he was unfortunate, and died some years ago, leaving her with three children, two daughters and a son, Wm Leatham, Shear-Striker, in Messrs Greaves employment. Mrs Leatham & a little grandson, (child of one of the daughters, who married, and went to America,) live with this son; but he has lately become a great invalid, and as Mrs Leatham from age and infirmity is unable to work, her friends fear she may have to go to the workhouse; unless something can be done for her. She is a highly respectable & has been a very active woman, who, at one time was in a different position in life.

Mrs Gaskell understands that the Clergy of Sheffield have the presentation to *half* the number of these Almshouses.

596

Eliza Fox[2]

> Friday morning.

My dearest Tottie,

It seems funny to be sending you round word of Smith's daughter, but it just strikes me you may'nt hear that the young

---

[1] Amongst Autographs of Rev. Greville J. Chester, Bodleian Library.
[2] Original MS. not seen.

lady came on Wednesday evening at $\frac{1}{2}$ past 9.⟨. . .⟩ so much for that I am so glad!⟨. . .⟩ I send you a note from Chappy I am pleased with the man; he has really learned to take an interest in poultry, and shows a sense of fun. I have written to ask him whether he minds being called my dear Chloe?⟨ . . .⟩ *Do* send me word about pearl necklace, and if there is a lovely young Lavinia in the shape of Mrs Forster?

Yrs. very affec[tionately]
E. C. G.

597

?F. J. FURNIVALL[1]

Tuesday:

My dear Sir,
Thank you very much. I know well what to do with them,[2] both according to the author's & the giver's wish. This is about as disagreeably short a note as I ever wrote; but I am 'dazed' with business of all kinds.

Yours very truly
E C Gaskell

I've not forgotten about the sermons.

598

F. J. FURNIVALL[3]

46 Plymouth Grove
Sunday night

Dear Mr Furnivall
(Thank you for the Zulu[4]—it is capital,—) please send post haste, any information about Co-operative *Stores* to George Melly Esq.

90 Chatham St
Liverpool

[1] Other Brit. Mus. letters are to Furnivall.
[2] A pencil note over this word in MS. reads: '12 copies of Ruskin's tract'.
[3] Watermark dated 1862.   [4] A conical straw hat once worn by children?

He has got to lecture on the subject on the 12 (next Wednesday!) in S. George's Hall—and wants information terribly.

Yours very truly

E C Gaskell.

599

F. J. FURNIVALL[1]

46 Plymouth Grove

Manchester

July 8th

Dear Mr Furnivall,

I think poor Miss Watts a most deserving case from the statements in the paper—and I am very much obliged to you for giving me an oppy of signing it.

Yours very truly E C Gaskell

600

MARIANNE GASKELL

Saturday *Plymouth Grove*

My dearest Polly,

I am *not* gone for a good many reasons, & I was so glad to get your letter, (the only one I did receive) this morning, for I had been fidgetting myself terribly about the boat expedition yesterday. Not that I object to your going in boats &c. Susanna & Mary E. came in to tea yesterday—Susanna in a fidget to get me off; because poor dear Emily had been getting a *fresh* spare-room in the very highest story ready for me. But I did up my accounts, & they've come to a great deal; no expense that I could help; none personal, but I must have a new cloak if I went to London, besides travelling expenses &c &c. Besides I want to appear at Chapel tomorrow, (Mr Davies of Lancaster to preach,) & at a 'Congregational tea-party' at Hayward's Hotel on Monday Evng—for Papa's sake. So write again here[,] my darling. I've no news. I am going to call on the Healds to wish them goodbye, & Mary

A E. is going in back seat. I am tired & good for nothing. But I send you newspapers to make up. I shall probably write again to-morrow—but it must be to one of the children. I am *dead* tired.

Yours very affec[tionate]ly

E C Gaskell

601

MARIANNE GASKELL

Stationer's Shop, Reading
2 o'clock, P.M. Wednesday

My dearest Polly,

I have missed one of the two *new broad* leather straps which I use for my boxes. It was not in the luggage van; so one of three things must have happened to it. Either you or Meta have got it on\one of/your boxes. *Look & see* & get Hearn to look & see if all the straps but one are returned right. If you have not brought it home, it must either be left at Broad Leas, or be in the Chippenham coach. Either way ask Agnes to ask Sommer to look for it, if he can, & return it by her. Miss Emily Taylor got out at Reading,—picked me up, as I was hunting for my strap (price 5s) & told me she was going to stay with two old Norwich friends, now living in Reading, Glover by name, very musical people. Had been a month in North Devon; never saw any place so beautiful to her fancy in her life. Bideford, Cloveley, Westward Ho & all the rest of it. Then I've been to see the Abbey;\not much left but walls/& now I've told you all my news. I've eaten my peach & one sand-wich[.] Write & tell me you're safe at home. Yours very affect[ionate]ly mother

E C Gaskell

602

MARIANNE GASKELL[1]

12 o'clock Wednesday

My dearest Polly,

I've got to write to Papa, as well as you, & get the children ready by 1, & take 'em to dancing, & when we come back the post

[1] A small sketch of a gown is on the last page of this letter.

will be gone, so I can only write in the greatest hurry. But I
know you will like to hear. I could *not* take {Meta} Julia back
because the instant I got out of the booking-room, the door was
shut upon me, & no one was allowed to go in. Julia was however
very jolly. We went on to Satterfields; I left Julia to try on boots
with Miss Winssory, while I 'rowed' about my gowns at Miss
Daniels'. When I came back I found Julia great friends with Miss
Winssory, & the last pair of brown boots, which *we* could not get
on, fitting admirably. Julia had picked out 'Guard's bouquet' &
wanted me to buy it, but it was 5s[.] When we came home I sent
to ask Fleeming to tea. (What was the message he gave you? I
forgot to ask you.) He came; & talked incessantly & very cleverly
to Selina. Stephen too came in. Yesterday there seemed to be
every possible interruption & obstruction to our plan of going to
Dinting, *but* we set off about 20 m to 11, & got there in 2 hours; *so*
Mrs Potter hopes we will often come, in a similar way. Of course
Flossie had cried about going, & Lucy was not there; but Clara
was very kind, & they had the poney out, & Flossy rode, & just
when Julia was to have ridden (Will leading,) it began to rain &
they had to come in, & we to give up our drive. Mr Potter came
to dinner, Crompton soon after. No news but very kind. About
20 to 7 we set out home, got here by ½ p. 8, found a fire—(oh!
how cold I was, not having had wraps enough over those hills!)
in the schoolroom, & tea; all Sarah's providing, for Elliott had
gone to wait at Susanna's. Annie & Selina gone there too. Barbara
put the children to bed, for I was deadly tired. A. & S. did not
come back till past 11, & we weren't in bed, what with telling
day's adventures, till near 1. Consequence Selina has a headache,
& A. S. stopped in bed to breakfast, & I am very good for nothing.
Elliott went to Liverpool before we were down to breakfast this
morning. The children are *very* good, but (tell Meta) I really
don't think they will have time for drawing for I'm obliged to
make them of household use, what with a servant away, & 2
spare-rooms, & myself not feeling over strong, & oh! people calling
& wanting me right & left. Now I've no time for more. Next
letter to Meta. No letters but the enclosed today. None from Papa.

Your ever affect[ionate] E C Gaskell

Bring back enclosed letters be sure. Meta's gown came, looked
beautiful, *but* neither A. nor Selina could get the berthe lower
down than half way through the neck.

603

?MARIANNE GASKELL

Sunday. Meta better. Mr Mellor speaks hopefully of Knutsford for Tuesday for her. Oh Cousin Mary does write so often about those patterns. I will never borrow anything for you again, unless you will take the responsibility of returning it. I enclose a nice note from Mrs James. But as she did not write I fixed to go to Emily Shaen's, where I shall arrive on Wednesday. I suppose now this nasty warm thaw is come, you are *up* & I'm *down*. At any rate I think you'll be warm enough with the provision of wraps I've made for you. Hannah Tayler is staying here. In haste ever your very affect[ionate]

E C Gaskell.

We're rather disappointed not to hear from you today.

604

MARIANNE GASKELL

Friday Evening

My dearest Polly,

Just received your second letter, Thursday—it is all quite right if you are *sure* they want you to stay,—so never mind the other letter—I thought you might be in the way, and yet that Mrs Dicey would think herself bound to ask you. I send you a likeness of Papa—(*or* Enoch Harvey!) whh Meta sends me, instead of a letter,—Papa says the flies round his hat are exact likenesses—but that it was unfair of Meta to take him, when he was half asleep, sitting out of doors after dinner & the sun blinding him. It looks very weak—does not it? Come home on Friday. My love to the Prices, especially Nancy,—poor child—I am quite glad to have some one to send my love to

Yours most aff[ectionate]ly
E G.

Yes, Miss Giffard is sister to Charlotte—George—The paralytic Ly G is Charlotte George's mother at any rate—

605

MARIANNE GASKELL

My darling Polly.

So many thanks for your letter or notelet my childie. I am so sorry you were so very tired, (take steel & bitter beer; or if you prefer it get a small barrel of *stout* such as A Jenkin got for her wet nurse\at Mackie's/And I am afraid you would be in too great discomfort to enjoy the rest of yesterday—when the rain kept us in doors all day, & Meta & I got *wonderfully* freshened up, &\we/ seem to be recovering our strength in this land of clover & good food. Please get yourself paid out of the Slate if it (i.e. the Slate) is rich with 6s. from the calf. We could not find out to whom you had consigned our luggage ticket to the last,—every one declaring their ignorance of it. But we had plenty of time, & Thurstan came to help, and by signing a paper we got our luggage which had been in sight all the time. We had no adventures in our 2nd class journey here; only Mr & Mrs Greaves\were here/, but we are momentarily expecting Uncle Charles & Aunt Lizzie. We did not stir out yesterday, and ached all over; today we have *done* Warwick & Kenilworth Castles; first walking[,] 2nd in the carriage. I don't *think*, (unless *in the least* wanted, & we should have *plenty* of time to pack up & come off *after* Saturday's post which comes in before 8—) we shall come home on Saturday, but stop till Monday; it is so resting & refreshing. But then I keep thinking of you all bustling at home,—(I want to know about the Penitentiary washing? Altogether Meta & I are in the usual pleasant state of indecision as to Saturday & Monday, & the post just going out.

Your ever most affect[ionate]

E C G.

606

?MARIANNE GASKELL

My darling,

Here's your gown & sash & white body. I have written 10 pages today & *can't* be sensible. How is dear Mr Shuttleworth? No other letters—

Your own

E Gaskell

607

MARIANNE GASKELL

My dearest Polly, It is just before dinner & not a pen to be found—
Meta is very low & poorly *but perhaps that may be accounted for. She*
has not been off the sofa today hardly—Julia is going to be met at
4-20 tomorrow. I thought of you all yesterday—& today as I went
to my lodgings in the rain I thought of you again poor dear lassie[.] I
want you *to write by return*, if you wish for any dresses &c to be
sent you, for Hearn is going home on *Thursday* aft. & could pack
them up & take the{m} box to the Station. Such a sad letter from
Mab W. yesterday, as summons came & they all went up to see
Minnie Bridgeman on *Sunday* not sure if they should find her
alive—but today I hear she is better. Meta!—& I are to dine at the
S. Winkworth's on Wednesday next, and we all go to *tea* at the
Waterhouses on Friday 20—Next Week is Unitarian Carnival—&
Mr Green comes here—I think I shall ask *Mrs G* tho' Papa objects
& does not think she can come. I'm glad I came home because of
Meta—she says the Gaddums & the Concert quite upset her, &
brought on the *numb*ness. Julia is so bright though she has got a
cold. *Do* write to *Meta*.   E C G

608

MARIANNE GASKELL[1]

Dearest Polly,
   Don't let Emma Gallagher go till I have come back. Ask Margaret to set her to rub up the plate (instead of getting a man from
Ollivants.) I should like it done *before* Elliot comes. Tell Margaret
to see that she washes it *thoroughly*—(every bit of it) in *cold* water
& *soap*; she had better take it bit by bit; having green baize bags
made for it. And to get the *white* plate powder from Ollivants and
to have her leather free from grease; & to *warm* it before she rubs
with it—*warm the leather* I mean. Ask Margaret to look after her
doing this; and ask Hearn to see after the bags. I should like to have
it done before Elliott comes. But she is to come on Saturday next:
& *to be met by some train that* passes through Tring and Leighton
about *8* & gets into Manchester about 2-20[.] I have lost Mrs
Ouvry's note. Your own affect[ionate] Mammy   E C G.

[1] *Address (on envelope)* Miss Gaskell.

I am sorry to give you this trouble, love, but if we *save* Ollivant, we can keep E. G. a week longer; *here* I've no chance of meeting with anything for her. Explain to Margaret, & she will see about it. Don't forget meeting Elliott[.][1]

609

?DAVID GRUNDY

42 Plymouth Grove.
Decr 4th.

My dear Mr Grundy,
    I wonder if you would be so kind as to give us a little help in this matter,—my two elder girls wanted to visit at the workhouse, & I applied to Mr Rickards[2] who did not think it desirable; but made out a list of 10 old women, receiving parish relief, whom they might visit, &c,—and Mr Somerset the relieving officer called here and told me all these old women had borne a good character,—and they are all above 70. Now both Marianne & Meta are so sorry to see the thin poor clothing they go out in, to receive the parish money, (2s. *in* money, 2s. *worth* in food, so you see they cannot *save* to buy clothing,) & we think if you would kindly let us have a few fents & scraps of cloth we could manage a cape or cloak apiece for Xmas day. You perhaps are aware of that 'wisdom of the ancients', that says 'Much would have more', and 'Give them an inch & they'll take an ell', so doubtless you will see the applicability of the argument that you *once* gave us a grand and beautiful bundle of woollen shag, and *therefore* we ask you to give us some more. But I know two or three poor women to whom I should be glad to give the employment of making up even such small scraps of woollen stuff,—and poor old women shivering to the Union in a worn bombazine petticoat, & calico gown & shawl equally worn, won't be particular if they have a covering of many colours, so that it is warm.
    Believe me to remain ever
                                            Yours very truly
                                            E. C. Gaskell.

[1] Written on flap of cover.
[2] C. H. Rickards laid the foundation stone of a new Workhouse on 5 September 1855. *Annals,* ed. Axon, p. 268.

610

CHARLES HALLÉ

My dear Mr Hallé

Thank you much for your *autograph* letter. I had no idea you could write—I thought you left that art to baser clumsier fingers. So I shall cherish up the rare & valuable production, and be very proud of my treasure. Has any one in Manchester a similar rarity? I am so pleased—I really never heard of your writing to any one before. Florence shall be at the London Road Station at 4-5 P.M. on Saturday the 8th and trust to your further kindness to convey her to 1 Cumberland Place.

Yours most truly—I should like to say affectionately

E. C. Gaskell

611

JAMES B. HARRISON[1]

46, Plymouth Grove,
Sunday Afternoon.

My dear Sir,

Alice and Ellen Larghe are spending the day with us today, and I have just heard from the former that she is getting rather uneasy about her sister's health, as she suffers from headache and irregularity of various kinds. I have told them that I will write and beg you to call on them tomorrow at Mr Phillip's; so perhaps, unless inconvenient to you, you will have the great kindness to do so, and to cross-examine Ellen very minutely, as I think she rather underrates the importance of her own health, and is inclined to shirk any care on the subject.

With united kind regards,

I remain yrs very truly
E. C. Gaskell.

[1] *Annotation* Dr J. Bowyer Harrison.

612

MRS HEALD

Plymouth Grove,
Sunday

My dear Mrs Heald,

We shall be very glad indeed to come to you on Tuesday, and spend a long day with you. I hope you won't all think it a *very* long day, if we do what Meta and I have just planned; go to Stockport by the 12 train (arrives 12-*15*) in the morning, & return by the 8-38 train, which stops near us at Longsight in the evening.

Believe me, dear Mrs Heald,

Ever yours very truly
E. C. Gaskell

613

MRS HEYWOOD[1]

My dear Mrs Heywood,

Shall you think me very unreasonable if I ask you to allow Mary Olga to spend Monday evening the 26th with Florence & Julia who are going to have a few friends.

Believe me to remain

Yours very sincerely
E C Gaskell

614

GEORGE HOPE[2]

121 Upper Rumford Street,
Manchester, 13*th February.*

I will not let an hour pass, my dear sir, without acknowledging your kindness in sending me my dear mother's letters, the only relics of her that I have, and of more value to me than I can express, for I have so often longed for some little thing that had once

---

[1] Probably a dictated letter.

[2] From a printed source. We accidentally missed the date [1849].

been hers or touched by her. I think no one but one so unfortunate as to be early motherless can enter into the craving one has after the lost mother.⟨. . .⟩ It never entered my head to imagine you wished to see me for any other reason than as the daughter of old friends. You cannot think how it gratified one to be sought out for their sakes,—a gratification I should certainly have been very far from feeling if I had for a moment suspected you of coming from mere curiosity. I have been brought up away from all those who knew my parents, and therefore those who come to me with a remembrance of them as an introduction seem to have a holy claim on my regard. ⟨. . .⟩ If either you or Mr Miller come again to Manchester you must come to us and see if we cannot give you such accommodation as you require, without going to an hotel. ⟨. . .⟩—Ever yours very truly,

Elizabeth Cleghorn Gaskell.

615

LADY HOUGHTON[1]

6, Cambridge Square.
Wednesday.

My dear Lady Houghton,
I am afraid that I must decline your most kind and tempting invitation for Saturday, as I am leaving for Manchester tomorrow; and must not prolong my absence beyond that day, even for the pleasure of seeing you {again} and Lord Houghton.

Ever very truly yours
E. C. Gaskell.

616

?MARY HOWITT[2]

['On another occasion':] Long ago I lived in Chelsea occasionally with my father and stepmother, and *very*, *very* unhappy I used to be; and if it had not been for the beautiful, grand river, which was an inexplicable comfort to me, and a family of the

---

[1] R. Monckton Milnes became Lord Houghton in August 1863.
[2] From a printed source.

name of Kennett, I think my child's heart would have broken. The sole remaining member of the family, Fanny Kennett, is now probably an old lady; the last thing I heard of her was her being dreadfully shocked that I had married a *Unitarian* minister.

617

MARY HOWITT[1]

⟨. . .⟩ Your letter made my mouth water with 'the primrose-bordered lanes,' &c. Living in Manchester, all round about being a clayey soil, one sees little or nothing of spring flowers. It is always a festival when we first find the little celandine, but as for cowslips, my children don't know them even by sight.

618

MISS JAMES

April 21st

My dear Miss James,

I write with more regret than I can well express to you to say that circumstances have just lately arisen which make it impossible for us to receive the pleasure of your visit when you propose. My eldest daughter (*not* the one you saw) writes me word that she received a note from you a day or two ago, & that she has answered it—but as I am sure that she could not tell you sufficiently how *very* sorry I am about this change of circumstances, I am sending this note as a kind of postscript.

It is not my absence in London that hinders our having what otherwise would have been such a real pleasure to us, as I am going to Manchester on Monday; but it is just one of those cases where one must throw oneself on one's friend's mercy begging them to believe that for once though there *is* the will, there is *not* the way—

I hope that you will consider your visit as only postponed till your next sojourn in the North—Ever yrs most truly (though treacherously)

E. C. Gaskell

[1] Original MS. not seen.

619

Miss Leo

My dear Miss Leo

The bearer of this note is Anne Daly (an Irish girl very delicate poor thing, with a bad cough,) who has come over to be with her sister, Rebecca Daly, well known to me. They are orphans; very nice girls,—Anne Daly has been brought up in an Irish Sewing School, & can 'flower' i.e. embroider, *very* well; she can crotchet a little.

Yours most truly
E. C. Gaskell

'Jane Ormond' is coming too—

620

Mrs Loudon

⟨. . .⟩ afternoon we heard from Mrs Greaves, who had agreed to allow us to remain for this one more play; today there is another letter from Mrs Greaves, which, as Miss Holland is not at home, I have not dared to open; but which may again disarrange our plans, whh quite depend on her convenience, and which we *only* departed from in order to go to the theatre, which we have been repeatedly prevented from doing by evening engagements. The dinner engagement is simply that we all meet at Mr Forster's to a five o'clock dinner, before going to the Play.

I have explained every thing at some length my dear Mrs Loudon, that you may see exactly how we are situated; we only remain that one evening to have the pleasure of going to the Theatre; but as you seem to wish us to come, if only for a short time, I will come after the Play is over, if you do not think that too late; I am afraid it will be 12 o'clock. With Miss Holland's compliments, I remain dear Mrs Loudon,

Yours very truly
E. C. Gaskell

621

ROSA ?MITCHELL

My dear Rosa,
 Please would you come & drink tea & sup with us next Sunday *but one*, instead of *next* Sunday? It would suit us better I believe—

Yours very affec[tionate]ly

E C Gaskell.

622

MRS NASMYTH

Plymouth Grove

Thursday

My dear Mrs Nasmyth,
 We are so very much obliged to you & Mr Nasmyth for your kind thought of us, in sending us the Concert tickets—I wish you could have heard the exclamations of joy on receiving them! for it is sometimes hard work to make 2 tickets do duty for 4, especially when the said 4 people are all equally fond of music, & equally desirous of giving up their own pleasure. Thank you again very much indeed. I am very much obliged to you for your kindness in liking the evening here. It could only have been your kindness, for we kept regretting and regretting that, owing to the failure of some friends whom I think you & Mr Nasmyth would like to have met—you had come so far for what we feared you would find so dull an evening. But we'll hope for 'better luck next time', & trust us you have only to hold up your little finger, & you will have us over at Patricroft, With our united kind regards,—the girls almost beg to send a separate message of love to you & Mr Nasmyth,

Believe me to remain

Yours very truly

E. C. Gaskell

(I only came home today[)]

623

?PARTHENOPE NIGHTINGALE[1]

⟨. . .⟩ly poor comfort,—but it is meant most earnestly to just be a little drop of balm, if it can. Yes! it *does* seem long since our 'walk in the dim & golden twilight,'—To-day is much such a day, a pale, mellow watery light over all,—just a touch more colourless, as beseems the wan season of the year; & altogether the recollection of that walk is so fresh in my mind, that it seems to me as if it might be some distant anniversary of some eventful day of youth that came up, as Bettina[2] says all the small doings of Madame V. Goethe as a girl, recurred to her on her deathbed. Yes! and we too in our little ways have been doing & seeing a great deal,—since then. Every day has seemed chock-full, rammed down with business; but none of it of the grand or picturesque kind. The funniest little event of late has been the arrival of a letter directed to

Madame Gaskell
l'illustre auteur
Angleterre

which had been two months travelling about England in search of my illustriousness; the mocking commentary on which was an envelope *covered* with '*Not Knowns*'; a sight to be seen! And Miss Tollet, (Ellen), has been here; and we enjoyed having her uncommonly; & I think she was gracious back again in enjoying us a little. And (tell Mr Nightingale[)] The tears of old May day, are by one Loveybond;[3] and if he asks me who he is, I can't tell him; but they were first published in No 82 of the 'World'. And here are the Roman letters on a slip of paper. And '*powse*' (Mrs Siddons at Sheffield,) is dirt thrown out in a heap; from the Welsh *pws, refuse*—I send you this letter for the sake of the P.S. which is ⟨. . .⟩

[1] Other letters in this Collection are to Parthenope Nightingale.

[2] See p. 61 above.

[3] Edward Lovibond (1724–75) contributed five papers to Edward Moore's periodical *The World*. No. 82 appeared on 25 July 1754. The poem is a lament by 'old May-Day' at her supersession by a younger rival as a result of the reform of the calendar in 1752.

624

ELLEN NUSSEY[1]

⟨. . .⟩ Edinburgh, compared to London, is like a vivid page of history compared to a dull lecture on political economy.

625

MR OLLIVANT

Plymouth Grove,
Jan. 10th

Dear Mr Ollivant,
   Your letter was long in reaching me, owing to Miss Smith's absence from Oxford. It followed me thence to Worthing, from which we are distant more than a day's post. It is this delay that has prevented my sooner thanking you for your great kindness in directing some more old clothes to be sent to me for distribution. 'Old clothes' however, considering one's associations with that term, is a very disrespectful way of speaking of them, if they are at all equal to what we already owe to your kind help and thought.
   May I beg you to add yet one further favour to what you have already done, and thank Mrs Jones on my behalf?
                                    Ever yours very truly
                                         E. C. Gaskell.

626

MRS OUVRY

My dear Mrs Ouvry,
   I *have* tried, indeed I have; and I will try; but this letter is all the shadow of a chance I have got at present. Still I am on the look-out. The Miss Banks, who writes this letter, is a charming & good person, who keeps a girls' school at Hampstead, along with her

[1] From a printed source.

sister Mrs Lalor, (equally good, though not equally charming.) My daughter was at school there, and I can answer for the safe, though it might be a busy, place, if she did apply. There are about twelve pupils, and there are four women-servants I believe. I don't stop even to mend my pen, for if I did, some one wd be sure to come in, & interrupt me, our household is so busy a one just now.

We are so fond of our Elliott (I forget her Xtian name, but she's not the L. Buzzard Elliott, but *your* Elliott, you know—) She is good, willing and *very* truthful & conscientious[.] Besides she is so affectionate that one can't help being affectionate back again. Thank you for her. Dear Mrs Ouvry, I should like to see you again. Does it not seem curious to think I only saw you just that little one evening? Elliott desires me to say she hopes you are better. *I* hope you can read illegible writing but it must be that, or none at all—

Yours most truly
E C Gaskell.

627

ANNE ROBSON

Plymouth Grove
Friday

My dearest Nancy,

We have suddenly bethought ourselves how pleasant it would be to go & see you, for a day. We. i.e. Meta (whom you have not seen for I don't know how long,) Julia, who has never seen her little cousins & I. We have had a very long consultation with our nice man Will; the result of which is this. If all goes on well, we mean to set out in our little poney-carriage tomorrow morning at 8; rest a little ½ way—and be with you between 11 & 12,—*if we don't come by 12*; you may be pretty sure we are not coming; and set off home at 6, AT THE LATEST; earlier I think, but that will depend on the time we take in coming. We shall go to the Nag's Head to put our poney up, & perhaps you would give Will a dinner. Only don't mind what you give us; & if inconvenient, park 2 of the 4 off to White cross.

M.G.L.—DD

I wish I could have given you longer notice, but that, as it happens is impossible. I want Julia who is a bit languid to have a good long day out of doors: and I think we shall avoid the heat in this way for her. Ever your affec[tionat]e sister   E. C. Gaskell

William is at Mrs Schwabe's in Wales.

628

ANN SCOTT[1]

Plymouth Grove—

My dear Mrs Scott,
It would give both Mr Gaskell & me great pleasure if you & Mr Scott could spend next Friday Evening with us quite quietly. We shall drink tea at half past seven, & I hope you will be able to join us—
Believe me yours most sincerely

E. C. Gaskell.

629

?GEORGE SMITH[2]

⟨. . .⟩ Don't hurry or put yourself or anybody else to the least inconvenience about either [About threequarters of leaf cut away]
I think your boy is a noble fellow; and your & Mrs Smith's complaints of his 'roughness & shyness &c'—are just a hypocrital[sic] veiling of parental vanity,—a 'pride that apes humility.' He is a little darling—and if I could have had half an hour with him we should have become great friends.

Ever yours very truly
E C Gaskell—

(I'm trying to write like Mr Aidé.)

[1] A. J. Scott was appointed first principal of the Owen's College on 22 October 1850.
[2] Other letters in this Collection are to George Smith. Mrs Gaskell probably met Aidé about 1857.

630

SAMUEL A. STEINTHAL

42 Plymouth Grove
Thursday Morg

My dear Mr Steinthal,

I have got a much clearer idea of what Miss Hibberd wants, and her reasons for wanting it\from your letter just received/; perhaps I was stupid before. But it is difficult to give help in such a case. A *great* deal must depend on Miss Hibberd herself. I will tell you how. I can give her one or two introductions (for instance,) to people who can give good information, if, in the one case the questioner has the art of *extracting*,—in the other if she has the art of *rejecting* rubbish. I am not choosing my words, but I consider that I am writing in confidence. Miss Jane Alcock to whom I am enclosing a note, has visited for years & years; and has really valuable information to give; but she does not talk much, or express herself easily, and is very shy and reserved; would almost be frightened at the notion of any thing she said being of value, or that it would be re-produced in speech or action. I should however rely very much both on her *facts* and on her *opinions*, (two very different things, & to be kept carefully separate in an enquiry of this sort.) Then there is Agnes Ewart to whom I will also enclose a note; she talks a *great deal*[,] she does really know a great deal, and her facts would be good & accurate; her opinions (I think) crude & unformed, but expressed without the least shyness or reserve. I think these two are the best women I can think of. Stay! there is Miss Winkworth, who comes to Manchester tomorrow; but who is ill & out of health, so I don't know if she could see any one. Or else at {[?]} one time, & for years she visited very constantly & has an enlarged enough mind to form just opinions & to classify them into theories, fit to be worked upon. All these people however can but bring a grain of corn each to form the loaf of bread. A person *must* live in Manchester to make this loaf. Does—but she is sure to —Miss Hibberd know Mary Merryweather,—(M. M. as she is often called); because her management of Mr Courtauld's girls is *the* most successful I ever heard of—& she had just that feeling of *independence* (for want of a better word, writing in a great hurry,) to encounter; a feeling, call it what you will, stronger in Lancashire & Yorkshire, (from race perhaps,) than any where else in

England. Who wrote that paper on the factory system that Ld Brougham read? Mr Thomas Wright, beautiful as he is in many ways, is not to be *quite* relied on for his facts,—and not at all for his opinions,—which he generalizes into two great theories,—one that good mothers are all important—true,—and another that we are going to the dogs because 'people think so much about recreation now a days.' I do admire a person who has failed, and perseveres. I am afraid myself that the plan of a house for factory girls can not be carried out, unless indeed in one small place, where most of the employment, comes from *one* manufacturer, who can bring all the force of his wishes & opinions to bear on the success of the scheme.

It requires that the factory girls themselves should be conscious of wants of a high kind,—(such as of wise advice, of strengthening help in cases of temptation or trial,—of the outward safe-guard of rules & regulations, & a hundred other things),—*before* they consent to enter the place where these advantages are offered, but where {other} certain liberties & licenses are denied them, {of}\liberties & licenses/which they {recognize the}\set above the/higher privileges offered to them\in a 'home'/. You cannot *compel* them to enter; and it takes education to make them aware of what *induces* American factory girls,—of a higher standing socially, morally & mentally,—to go into the homes provided for them at Lowell &c. Besides I think that in the few places where the scheme has had even a partial success the girls have been brought from a distance, the 'supply (of girls) not being equal to the demand' at the place itself. This is the case I know at Mary Merryweather's in many instances. But here & in large towns generally, the girls are daughters of factory workers, or begin to work in the mills while they live at home. They leave home (in general) because some home regulation is distasteful to them; or (often) because their meals are not what they like,—or because their parents expect too large a share of their earnings. With the exception of the last reason for going into lodgings, the other causes for such a step would *un*fit them for being inmates of a 'Home',—where they would have to conform to rules, & probably have little choice in the way of eating (beyond natural wholesome variety—) I am writing a long letter but I have gone on putting down thoughts as they arose, & I don't know that they are worth much. Only remember that I have warned ⟨. . .⟩

631

EMELYN STORY

My dear Mrs Story,
I am going to introduce some friends of ours (the Miss Wilkinsons) to you—I am sure you will like them and that in making them known to you, and you known to them I am doing a mutual service. They mean to spend the winter in Rome.

Yours very affec[tiona]tely
E C Gaskell.

632

EMELYN STORY

Plymouth Grove,
Manchester.
Decr 8. [?1863][1]

My dear Mrs Story,
I very seldom like to give any of my friends who may be going to Rome letters of introduction to either you or Mr Story, out of consideration to the endless claims upon your time and hospitality; but I am making an exception in favour of Mr William H. Langton, who will be the bearer of this note. I have not the pleasure of knowing him myself, although for many years I have had the privilege of his father's acquaintance, and as I know that in this case the proverb of 'Like father, like son' is fortunately justified, I have no hesitation in introducing him to you as one whom you will like to receive, and who will value the opportunity of learning to know you and Mr Story. He is travelling with two companions, Mr Henry H. Coddington (a Cambridge graduate), and Mr Addison Birley; and if you will allow this introduction to include them, I shall consider it an additional kindness.
Ever, with our united true love to you all,

Yours very affectionately,
E. C. Gaskell.

[1] See Letter *541a below.

633

?CATHERINE WINKWORTH[1]

⟨...⟩ I wish I could help taking to men so much more than to women (always excepting the present company, my dear!) and I wish I could help men taking to me; but I believe we've a mutual attraction of which Satan is the originator.

634

ALICE —[2]

October 2.
Plymouth Grove—

My dear Alice,
Will you come & dine here on Sunday next,—I hope before that time to have learnt all particulars from Satterfield's & Mrs Johnson's & we can talk it over together.
Yours very truly
E C Gaskell

635

UNKNOWN

121, Upper Rumford St[3]
Tuesday morng

Allow me, Sir, to return you my best thanks for your Lyrical ballad, 'The Triumph for Salamis', which I have just received. It *looks* most tempting, and I mean to take it with me to Bolton Abbey, whither I am on the point of going. But independently of the intrinsic value of the poem, there is the great pleasure of receiving marks of approbation and sympathy from distant and unknown friends; (and such I may call you, may I not?) especially from one, first known to me through 'Baby May' two or three

---

[1] From a printed source ('to Miss Winkworth').
[2] Larghe, Winkworth?
[3] This house was vacated in early 1850.

years ago, but every poem of whose has made me feel to know and like him better and better. I remain

Sir, yours truly
E. C. Gaskell

My love to 'Baby May'.

636

UNKNOWN[1]

Benlaw, Peebles
Wednesday evening.

Dear Sir,

I am afraid we shall not be with you until ½ past 11 to-morrow morning, as Mr Thomson wishes to take us to see Donaldson's Hospital. We go into Edinburgh by the earliest train which arrives soon after 9, and we shall come to you as soon as possible.

Yours truly,
E. C. Gaskell

We will be at 339, High Street at ½ 11.

*

637

?WILLIAM CHAMBERS[2]

Plymouth Grove,
Manchester.
February 29th

My dear Sir,

Mrs Jenkin's christian name is Henrietta in case Mr Ritchie[3] should think of paying her by a P.O. Order and her address, which I remember I omitted to give you the other day is

8, Blackheath Terrace,
Greenwich,
near London.

[1] Original MS. not seen.

[2] Original MS. not seen. For identification of correspondent see Letter *636a in Appendix A.

[3] Possibly Leitch Richie (d. 1865), editor of *Chambers' Journal* and occasional publisher of books of a popular character.

I am very glad to learn that her paper has met with your approbation.

My daughter joins me in kind remembrances, and believe me ever yours very truly,

E. C. Gaskell

638

UNKNOWN[1]

Plymouth Grove
Manchester
Saturday.

Sir,

There was not the slightest occasion to make any apology for writing to me. I take great interest in what you tell me of your scheme, and I think if you can indeed set up such a Magazine as Fraser's, bringing an earnest spirit of godliness (Unitarian instead of High Church) to bear upon all the aspects of Life you will do a right-down good work. But I am sure you must not expect immediate success,—not for a long time. Remember the Athenaeum which now seems to fill an absolute want in literature, and to be universally read in all circles (whereas, a magazine imbued with a religious spirit of any description would be sure to be eschewed by some.) And yet 14,000£ was absolutely sunk by Mr Dilke, before it began to pay; and it was a losing concern all the time that Mr Fredk Maurice & Stirling had it. There are{so} many publishing arts of bringing a periodical into notice; and I do not fancy Mr John Chapman is 'up' to them; which may be very much to his credit as a man, but disadvantageous to any periodical which he {conducts.} publishes. I know that it was a very long time before Fraser was brought up to a paying point,—much was sacrificed; and that, in a time, when there were not half the periodicals there are now. I could go on giving instances of the really large sums which have to be sunk, on the risk of hope of obtaining a wide & extensive circulation. I name all this because of late years I have heard a good many particulars of this sort, of which I was quite ignorant before, and of which I think it possible, that you may be unaware now, and I do not believe from what I

---

[1] *Annotation* By G. Melly.

have heard & seen of Mr J Chapman, that he is quite practical & keen enough to tell you all you ought to know before you embark in this undertaking. Only, *if you do* begin, allow a large margin for probable loss & disappointment at first, and work steadily on through it all. If you have capital & patience enough to persevere I believe it will answer at length. You must excuse[1] my plain-speaking on all this. If I did not really think your plan a good one, I would not take the trouble of saying this; and if I had a little more time I would try & put it all a little less abruptly; but I am very busy in many ways just now; which brings me to the second part of your letter—namely whether I cd contribute to such a magazine. I doubt if I could. I certainly could make no promise. I do not care about the terms of remuneration, and, if I had time at any time I would send you a paper as a little proof of good-will 'for nothing' as the children say. And very likely I might; but I cannot promise. I have more promises unfulfilled than I like to feel the responsibility of just now; and I must work them off; and they take up\and *will* take up/all my spare time.

I hope you will understand my most hurried letter. First I warn you of the difficulty & expense. Secondly, if you do begin, I wish you good-speed. Thirdly I will not promise, nor pledge myself to anything. I cannot—but I think that for all that I may turn out like Cordelia.

Yours very truly
E. C. Gaskell

639

UNKNOWN

42 Plymouth Grove
Novr 26.

Dear Sir,

The copyright of Mary Barton belongs, I believe, to Mess[rs] Chapman & Hall; at any rate I have nothing to do with it.

Yours truly
E. C. Gaskell

[1] Princeton University Library fragment ends here & is continued by a Yale University Library fragment.

640

Unknown

42 Plymouth Grove
Manchester—
March 4

Sir,

I have great pleasure in complying with your request for my autograph; and I only wish that I could think of something suitable to say. But nothing either wise or witty will come into my head.

I am ashamed to say I do not know where 'Camelford' is,—but I conclude from the sound of 'Lante Glos' it is somewhere on the borders of Wales.

Yours truly,
Elizabeth Cleghorn Gaskell

641

Unknown[1]

46, Plymouth Grove
Saturday Evening.

⟨. . .⟩ thoughts, and we could not have a pleasanter one than you will supply.

In gt haste,
Yours most truly
E. C. Gaskell.

642

Unknown[2]

⟨. . .⟩ You were rather provoking with your impatience about that d——d book.

[1] An associated note indicates that F. P. B. Martin sent this as an autograph to a friend.

[2] From a printed source, which states it was signed 'Shrew' and concerned Charlotte Brontë's *Shirley*, 1849.

643

Unknown[1]

['In the early days in the old home,'] Miss Jewsbury lay on the floor and read half through the Essays of Elia and called our drawing room 'such an ugly room in which we should always be unhappy'.

644

Unknown[2]

⟨. . .⟩ the years of one's life are slipping away fast and every year seems to get busier and busier.

[1] From a printed source.
[2] From a printed source.

APPENDIX A

Additional Letters

This Appendix contains letters that became available after our edition had reached the page-proof stage, and the majority of them are from the Lancaster Collection of transcripts. We find that forty-two new texts in this Collection exist in both typed and handwritten copies, while forty-four survive in typescript only. The manuscript copies are homogeneous, the work of a single copyist; the typed transcripts are very diverse, seemingly made and corrected in ink or pencil on various occasions, so that it is impossible to generalise about their textual characteristics. Fortunately, this situation does not present insuperable difficulties to an editor, since a full collation of letters existing in more than one version reveals a high degree of substantive agreement with significant common errors in the transcription of proper names especially. In practice, then, we have been able to treat the new material in our usual way (see page xxvi of the Introduction) and record the relatively few substantive variants in the footnotes.

It would be natural to suppose that the manuscript copies were made before the typescripts with which they are so evidently connected, but the typescripts provide the fuller text: whole clauses can be found in them that are missing from the corresponding manuscripts. The latter supply single words or brief phrases at most. We assume that at least some kinds of typescript have more textual authority than the manuscript copies and we call attention below where we think that there is supporting evidence for our opinion. (See notes to 91b, 118a, 484b and 500a in particular.) Even where the evidence is inconclusive and we cannot tell which version is closer to what Mrs Gaskell actually wrote, it is quite easy to glance over the occasional variants printed at the foot of the page.

645

EDMUND EVANS

46 Plymouth Grove
Dec. 3rd

Dear Sir,
I regret very much that we are engaged on Wednesday,
Thursday, and Friday evening, and therefore I cannot have the
pleasure of asking you to spend either of those evenings with us,
but if you stay over Saturday and could give us the pleasure of
your company at 8 o'clock we should be very glad. If you do not
stay beyond the end of the week, perhaps you could make it convenient to come here some time in the afternoon of either of the
days, and I promise you a cup of tea to refresh you after the
exertion of coming so far.

Believe me to remain
very truly yours
E. C. Gaskell.

646

UNKNOWN[1]

Plymouth Grove
Saturday Evng—

My dear Mary,
You did not tell me what kind of autographs Miss Jones wished
for,—so I can only guess. Some people fancy painters, some statesmen,—some are content with M.Ps.
The best plan will be for Miss Jones to ask me for any *particular*
autograph she wishes for,—and if I have a duplicate I will send her
one. I enclose a note from Dickens, Holman Hunt, Lord Wrottesley, late P. R. S.[2] and one of a very few scraps I have left of Miss
Brontë's handwriting on an envelope. I am sorry it has not her
signature; but here is *mine*.

Yours affectionately
E. C. Gaskell.

[1] Original MS. not seen. Source describes it as 3¼ pp., 8vo.
[2] Source reads 'Wriothsley, late P. K. S.'.

647

? WILMOT[1]

⟨. . .⟩ her bright wits to work. I should like to send my kindest good wishes to Miss Wilmot—but in truth I am afraid of you all, and until you extend the golden sceptre, & forgive me for not having hatched your precious eggs into prize black Spanish, I dare say no more than that I am yours tremblingly

E. C. Gaskell

648

MISS WATKINS[2]

Dear Miss Watkins,
    Thank you very much for the use of the Pinking Machine. May you live long to lend it to me (and I live long to use it).

[E. C. Gaskell]

649

MARIANNE GASKELL[3]

My dearest Polly,
    I so fully expected you to-day that I did not write yesterday, and can't much to-day I have so much to do; and one of my bad headaches. I ought to go into town before dinner but here is the man come to put down carpets and I can't leave. Lucy has done most abominably. I am in a fright about your gowns and the children's. However she is gone not to be recalled, and has left me with two spoilt gowns on my hands. Margaret came back on Saturday night; the children are enjoying themselves exceedingly.

---

[1] Original MS. not seen. Source describes it as a fragment of ¾ p., 8vo.
[2] 'A.L.s. 1 p. 8vo, N.D.' (Cutting from unknown bookseller's catalogue, owned by Mr W. P. Telfer of Knutsford.)
[3] Original MS. not seen.

Poor Pussy is dying we fear. Meta's bonnet must await your return. I don't want to go to the Concert to-night at all, at all,

Your very affec[tionate] mother

E. C. Gaskell

I did not quite like your last letter. There were some very careless mistakes, 'we' for 'were' and no stops, and Mr Hepworth on whom you passed the judgment of 'having no consolation' is a very sensible man for all his Yorkshire accent. It is only to get him on his own subjects which perhaps may not be yours; but I have exceedingly enjoyed one or two talks with him. Don't get either flippant or judgmatical my darling. I don't mind your calling anything dull because that is only an account of the impression made on yourself; but it is not like you, love, I think and hope, to show such a want of humility in passing opinions. My own dear little girl, I know you will take this in good part.

650

MARIANNE GASKELL[1]

Sunday

My dearest Polly,

Don't be *surprized* if we *don't* turn up to-morrow. We may or we mayn't. It will be late if we do: keep your own hours & engagements separate my dear. It is *the* most lovely house & gardens I ever saw.

Violet: 'Have you brought any music down Miss Gaskell?'
Meta: 'No'
Violet: 'Oh—but I've brought *Op. 7* down with me.'

I like the ⟨   ⟩[2] and am your and Florence's very affec[tionate]

Mother

We could have done with Hearn very well & she was expected.

---

[1] Original MS. not seen.
[2] Gap of about half a line in typescript source.

651

MARIANNE GASKELL[1]

[11 September]

My dearest Polly,

Very many happy returns. Mrs Shadwell's girls come, which under the circumstances we are sorry for.

I enclose all letters worth having, & they are our only events. Nothing pretty for Meta's dress at Scotts so we are writing to Marshall & Snelgrove. Hearn & I are deep in house linen, t'others at Ragged School. Last night's whist party a great success. More than mine. Oh! I am so tired to-day.

Your ever affec[tionate]
E C G.[2]

[1] Original MS. not seen.
[2] Sources read 'Elz', silently emended henceforth.

The undated letters in Appendix A end here. The letters that follow are dated, and numbered as if they were in the main sequence (see page xxix above). An asterisk with one of the smaller letter numbers indicates that the previous or following letter to the same person is also printed in Appendix A.

15 [*continued from p. 45 above*]¹

⟨. . .⟩ lovely evening² about 7 we went, and on alighting found
ourselves in the middle of 180 gay people who were promenading
about on the terraces. Fancy the picturesqueness of this, with the
setting sun lighting up the noble views in the background. No
one had hat, bonnet or shawl on. I must first tell you of the
etiquette about dress. No one under 40 in summer wears anything
but muslin, white of course in general—Artificial flowers too are
quite out of the question, yet if you mean to dance, flowers in
your hair is the signal, so every German girl knows how to weave
the prettiest natural garlands—Mine was geranium—Thekla wove
it,—but the prevalent & fashionable flower was the intensely
scarlet pomegranate blossom with its deep green leaves—Matilda
had ivy & looked like a Bacchante. Orange blossom & myrtle are
never worn except the former by a betrothed, the latter by a
bride. After parading about & being introduced to gentlemen,
Mrs Howitt came up & said I must follow her without question-
ing. I did so & after winding about we got into the wood past the
waterfall, down some old mysterious stone steps, & into the banks
where the nuns lay buried—each (for they were all noble) with
her escutcheon carved over her, & a sculptured figure (some very
fine) as large as life of the abbesses. These banks were 'still as
death', & lighted by long casement windows coming out in the
terrace side, all hid by vines from the gay crowd outside. Was it
not a picturesque contrast between the dead & the living? When
we ascended to 'upper day' every body had gone in, & the stars
were coming out all bright & beautiful.

     We heard the excellent band playing the merriest waltzes of
Strauss & Chopin, & went in through a gallery all window on
one³ side, & all orange-trees (in tubs) on the other. I forget to
say the fountains in the grounds had the gayest garlands of rich
dahlias of all colours round them, such garlands, as they have
everywhere in Germany, & nowhere in the ⟨ ⟩ world else. The
chandeliers were garlanded in like manner, & with more refined
flowers—And now I must tell you the order of a German ball—A
card is hung up in a conspicuous place with the order of the

----

¹ Original MS. not seen. The copyist gives an address and date: Mrs Charles
Holland | Chas Hollands Esqre | Exchange Alley | Liverpool. | Aug. 41.
     ² Sources read 'coming'.
     ³ MS. source reads '{the}'.

dances on it. All nonsense, for the order is well known before
hand. 1 a waltz, 2 a galoppe waltz, 3 a francaise (alias quadrille),
4 a waltz, 5 a galloppade, 6 a cotillion—supper (such as it is), the
tisch-waltze (are you German enough to take? *table* waltz) galoppe
waltz francaise cotillion. But every body goes engaged to the ball
—Thekla was engaged for the whole evening before going—& so
are most of the belles. So every now & then the master of the
house privately orders the band to play a trumpet call which
sounds everywhere—& that is the signal for a 'free-waltz', when
every one is free of her engagements & bound to dance with the
first asker.—Such hurrying to the belles as there was! The call was
always some martial call—& the trumpets were never played on
at any other time. The waltzes always began with a most pathetic
march—slow, mournful & solemn, when every gentn went up to
his partner—handed her by the tips of the fingers into the circle,
& presently the air changed into the quickest possible waltz—just
our waltz step but like flying in its airiness—Everyone takes
2 turns round the room—I was desperate dizzy after my two
turns, & was on the point of taking my partner's (a Baron, my
dear, only Barons are not more than any other *von*, in that country
of Barons &c.) arm, when Thekla touched me 'Don't be offended
with me, Mrs G.—but I forgot to tell you no one takes a gentn's
arm & I have heard English ladies so much remarked upon for this',
so I very properly stood holding & being held by the tips of my
fingers in the most decorous manner, thinking of the funniness of
morality which in one place makes it immoral to be taken by the
waist, in another to be taken by the arm. I had a glorious share of
dancing every dance till I was worn out & when the end of the
evening came I had danced every dance but one, the great mistake of the eveng. William said I was sadly tired & very dizzy,
when a very ugly man asked me to dance—I told him I was too
much tired when lo & behold he turned out to be Wolfgang von
Goethe, grandson to the illustrious Wolfgang—and Wm said I
shd have danced with the *name*—numbers of illustrious names
were in the room. The von Berlichingens, descendants of the good
bright & true Gotz von Berlichingen, Luther's friend & Goethe's
hero—the fraulein a lovely creature, soft, sweet, & with a skin like
lilies & round her brother the little Count, a little gentlemanly
laddikin waltzed like mad, but most beautifully—about 14. The
von Herders, grand daughters of the illustrious von Herder, *the*
great German writer of the last century—One of the Miss von

Hs was a rival beauty to Miss von Berlichingen—very different, not so much flesh & blood beauty, but more like a Madonna in the style of face—like one of Corregio's they say. To show you how much importance they attach to the *von*, this girl all young & simple as she seems has refused offer after offer of the most unexceptionable kind because they were not noble & is now engaged to an oldish, ugliesh, very poor man because he is a Mr *von* Beaulieu. They were so strange in their goings on, they are betrothed—a solemn ceremony taking place sometime before marriage but they made nothing of a kiss 'before folk', and he took her hand to stroke his face [MS. torn][1] with his arm round her waist—yet *they* did not [MS. torn][1] of arms. Everybody however cried shame on them [MS. torn][1] especially—she was too young to know better.

I said Thekla was engaged all evening—but there were 2 Princes, von Furstenberg, the nephews of the Grand Duke, & if *they* asked a young lady she was bound to give up previous engagements & dance with them—They were *very* handsome & rather agreeable, speaking English admirably—& are moreover immensely rich (at least the Hereditary Prince) so people did not dislike the rule—but it might be very[2] disagreeable. One of them was very attentive to Thekla (a great belle she is) & she had to give up engagement after engagement for him. The cotillion was so pretty—such amusing & graceful *tours*, one where the lady sat down with a mirror in her hand & her partner—Oh dear I must go, I have been writing with my things on—If you care to hear more, & I have not told you half, write to me Missie—I go home *tomorrow*. Aunt Ab says I shall be too late, so goodbye. She thanks for nasturtium seed which has behaved well in some way or other.

Your very affect[ionat]e sister
E. C. Gaskell.

[1] Note in sources.
[2] Typescript source omits 'very'.

15 **16***a* 145

ELIZABETH HOLLAND[1]

Sunday morning
Willie asleep everyone else out.
[Summer 1845]

My dearest Lizzie,

I have just received your letter & if one does not answer a letter directly when the impulse is on one there is no knowing how long one may wait for 'a convenient season'. So here goes though I've nothing to say very particular except that I want your mother to come & wonder I don't hear; could make her so comfortable & children long for her & William's holidays begin end of next week & I am so glad you like the Androwitch & is it not well translated? using old fashioned plain spoken words in all simplicity *And* I am so sorry to hear about Alice feeling responsible as I ought to do; & she does sound proudly without order. She would *so* fidget here [;] all the Holland fidgetiness would blaze out in crossness. I am so busy & so happy. My laddie is grunting so I must make haste. I can't make out what you do with *five* ponies. Such a great number. You say 'at present I can see after her' (i.e. Alice). Can't you nine months hence my lady? Are things in *that* state? Where do you get your pretty gowns from? tell me? You said they were all taken up by the Robsons? Was that a tally diddle? I wish I had been inside of home (articles & pronouns very useless part of speech to mothers with large families aren't they?) I have Florence & Willie in my room which is also nursery, call Hearn at six, ½ p 6 she is dressed, comes in, dresses Flora, gives her breakfast the first; ½ p. 7 I get up, 8 Flora goes down to her sisters & Daddy, & Hearn to her breakfast. While I in my dressing gown dress Willie. ½ p. 8 I go to breakfast with parlour people, Florence being with us & Willie (ought to be) in his cot; Hearn makes beds etc in nursery only. 9 she takes F. & I read chapter & have prayers first with household & then with children, ½ p. 9 Florence & Willie come in drawing room for an hour while bedroom & nursery windows are open; ½ p. 10 go in kitchen, cellars & order dinner. Write letters; ¼ p. 11 put on things; ½ p. 11 take Florence out. 1 come in, nurse W. & get ready for dinner; ½ p. 1 dinner;

[1] Original MS. not seen.

½ p. 2 children, two little ones, come down during servants' dinner half hour open windows upstairs; 3 p.m. go up again & I have two hours to kick my heels in (to be elegant & explicit). 5 Marianne & Meta from lessons & Florence from upstairs & Papa when he can comes in drawing room to 'Lilly a hornpipe', i.e. dance while Mama plays, & make all the noise they can. Daddy[1] reads, writes or does what she[2] likes in dining room. ½ p. 5 Margaret (nursemaid) brings Florence's supper, which Marianne gives her, being answerable for slops, dirty pinafores & untidy misbehaviours while Meta goes up stairs to get ready & fold up Willie's basket of clothes while he is undressed (this by way of feminine & family duties). Meta is so neat & so knowing, only, handles wet napkins very gingerly. 6 I carry Florence upstairs, nurse Willie; while she is tubbed & put to bed. ½ past 6 I come down dressed leaving (hitherto) both asleep & Will & Meta dressed (between 6 and ½ p.) & Miss F. with tea quite ready. After tea read to M. A. & Meta till bedtime while they sew, knit or worsted work. From 8 till 10 gape. We are so desperately punctual that now you may know what we are doing every hour.

Willie comes on grandly & so does his red hair. He has dimples just[3] like *your* Willie—is very good & *very* hungry. About Marianne & Meta I must consult William. Miss ⟨   ⟩ —you don't say when it would be most convenient to you. All the directions about them I have to give are please let Meta's feet be warm in bed (a hot bottle she has here by Dr H' direction) & *please* (though not likely at all) don't let them ever come in contact with Martineau children. You need not ask why but please *don't*. I hope they will give no trouble or anxiety & I am sure they intend not to do so and ought not. This visit is *such* a pleasure in store & the *not* going such a Damocles' sword. You *must* come & see us. I have expected you every fine day this fortnight. I think you *do* want just such a servant as you describe—a bonne I should call her & she such a boon[4] in families. I heard Mr Carver's niece was wanting *just* such a situation applied to Mrs J. L. Taylor[5] only did not like taking her meals in kitchen especially with men servants. Is she worth seeing after? I will 'hearken out' for you. Don't

---

[1] A 'u' has been typed above the 'a' in this word.

[2] ? he.

[3] MS. source and typescript (before pencil correction) read 'put'.

[4] Sources read 'about'.

[5] ? J. J. Tayler. MS. source reads 'J. T. Taylor', and typescript 'J' could equally be a 'T', two keys having been struck.

'kill your children with lessons', as dear Julia Bradford used to say to me. Only a little lessoning does give a relish to the rest of the day in winter only don't *over* do it 'specially with Charlie. No news here—somebody is going to be married to somebody I heard yesterday but forget who they both are. So Robinson is still 'shoving it into them'—this I conclude only from your saying he waits for your letter. I am glad I can keep up with your doings & goings on in the children way & domestic ditto with having seen. Is A. Holland coming to you & when? It would have been much more sensible if you had told me *when* you *wanted* children. Goodbye. I have many more oddments to say but W. wakes.

Ever yours most affec[tionately]
E. C. G.

₁₇ **17*a*** ₁₈

MARIANNE AND MARGARET EMILY GASKELL[1]

Wednesday
[1846]

My dearest Girls,

I wish I could write to you so as to make my letters as agreeable to you as yours are to me. Thank *you* Meta for yours received on Sunday, and *you* Marianne for yours received yesterday. It is ungrateful to '*look a gift horse in the mouth*' (Aunt Lizzy will tell you what this means) but my Dear Miss Meta do you know your epistle was *rather* of the untidiest. You *can* write nicely & tidily, & do try love, to do so *habitually*. I had such a pretty basketful of things given me yesterday by Mrs Dukinfield Darbishire. In the first place it was a pretty basket but that was to be returned. At the top were beautiful flowers, then came cool green vine leaves, & underneath such beautiful bunches of purple & white grapes— the first they had cut. I kept them till after dinner for a surprise for Papa & Flossy who were delighted with their goodness as well as their prettiness. Mrs D. D. says they are so glad to be at home again & she made me laugh by telling me what she had had to bring from London. 10 children, six servants, three horses, *one cow* & 27 hundred weight of luggage. Miss Ferguson has been over

---

[1] Original MS. not seen.

here to see me, but she had notes in her hand for you, so I dare say she told you all the Pendlebury messes.[1] Mr Turner[2] & Mr William Turner went on Monday, in his dog cart full of dogs & driving tandem with a bugle for his groom to blow as soon as they were fairly away. The dogs yelped so at being shut up. Daddy said it was a noisy enough turn out even for you Meta. Miss Maunsol has been up to the Great St Bernard so when you come back we must[3] ask her in to tea & get her to tell us all about our friends the Monks & the dogs. Flossy was not quite well yesterday; and wanted you back again sadly. I have promised her to have Maggie & Agatha when you come home. Mr Newman called to wish us good bye the other day. He left his love for you. I am very sorry to think we shall not be likely to see him again. Mrs Alcock has called since I began this note; she is going a tour in Wales & called to know our dear Mrs Hughes' address at Port Madoc as she said she should like to see a person who had shewn us such kindness & besides she thought Mrs Hughes would like to hear all particulars about us. Tell Meta *Mr Honest Netherlands* is at Knutsford with Cor.[4] & Gertrude her old friends. Mrs Shuttleworth is going to Paris & better still is going to have such a pretty riding horse. Flossy says I am to give her love & Papa has made her two kites. The first went up into some trees where it stuck but the last is still to be seen & flown when the wind bears. She & Papa are very happy together flying it sometimes. I ask Flossy what message I am to send & she says 'Sunday and Monday' so you may make head or tail out of that as you can, for I can't interpret. 'I got grapes yesterday & to-day did you?' 'Monday and Tuesday'. Oh! nonsense Flossy, I shan't write any more so I am your very affec[tionate] mother

E. C. Gaskell.

o **39a** 492

EDWARD HOLLAND[5]

Southport. January 13th 1849

My dear Edward,
   I have been spending a week here; & your letter of the 10th has

---

[1] ? news.   [2] 'Twiner' in sources.   [3] 'much' in typescript source.
[4] Sources read 'Coo'.   [5] Original MS. not seen.

had to be forwarded. Your proposal about the Cath. Dock Shares seems to both my husband & me a very kind & advantageous one; & we gladly consent to having the £1500 so invested put into the general fund at its present value; and in the division to form part of the moiety which is to be invested for me—to be considered as an investment already made in my behalf in short. I don't know if I have expressed myself sufficiently clearly to shew you that I fully sanction what you propose; but I *do*.

My poor Mary Barton is stirring up all sorts of angry feelings against me in Manchester; but those best acquainted with the way of thinking & feeling among the poor acknowledge its *truth*; which is the acknowledgment I most of all desire, because evils being once recognized are half way on towards their remedy. I am ever dear Edward

Your affec[tionate] cousin
E. C. Gaskell.

I return to Manchester on Monday next. Thank you for all your trouble.

₀ 45a ₀

ANNE GREEN[1]

Sunday morning.
27, Woburn Sq.
[13 May 1849]

My dear Annie,

I must try hard to write you a few lines, for I should like to tell you about yesterday, and I think my dear old friend (who *could* make puddings, but never *did*, do you remember, Annie?) will like to hear about. Must I begin at the beginning? Well! we got up; that was the first thing; and we dressed[;] that was the second; and then we cabbed it to Mr Monckton Milnes', meeting Mr Procter, (Barry Cornwall,) at the door: he had promised to meet us the day before; Mrs and Miss Procter were already there. There were the House of Lords there, Miss Holland says; but independently of the Lords, there was Guizot, and Whewell, and

---

[1] *Annotation* Received in Spring 1849 *and* 13.5.1849. See p. 79 above for the date and the name of the recipient.

{Ar}\arch/deacon Hare. I did not know who Whewell was, as he came in too late to be introduced; but he began to talk about Silverdale & all our dear old places in the North, and we got on famously. He sent me a book of his in the course of the afternoon, with such a nice note. We were very merry, and it was a very short two hours which every one had said was the proper number of hours to stay at breakfast. Then we went to the Exhibition; and thence to Stafford House[,] the Duke of Sutherlands. We saw the most beautiful picture-gallery, statues, and furniture & flowers I ever could have fancied, and in the most perfect taste. But I found it very tiring, looking up at the pictures, gilding, &c, and was very glad to come out, and proceed leisurely home. We dressed and went to dine at Mr Dickens', making (with our morning's breakfast,) what Anne calls, 'a rich day'. We were shown into Mr Dickens' study; this is the part, dear Annie, I thought you would like to hear about.

It is the study where he writes all his works; and has a bow-window, \is/ about the size of Uncle Holland's drawing room[.] There are books all round, up to the ceiling, and down to the ground; a standing-desk at which he writes; and all manner of comfortable easy chairs. There were numbers of people in the room. Mr Rogers (the old poet, who is 86, and looked very unfit to be in such a large party,) Douglas Jerrold, Mr & Mrs Carlyle, Hablot Browne, who illustrated Dickens' works, Mr Forster, Mr and Mrs Tagart, a Mr Kenyon. We waited dinner a long time for Lady Dufferin; (*the* Hon. Mrs Blackwood who wrote the Irish Emigrant's lament,) but she did not come till after dinner. Anne sat between Carlyle & Rogers,—I between Dickens & Douglas Jerrold. Anne heard the most sense, and I the most wit; I never heard any one so witty as Douglas Jerrold, who is a very little almost deformed man with grey flowing hair, and very fine eyes. He made so many bon-mots, that at the time I thought I could remember; but which now have quite slipped out of my head. After dinner when we went upstairs I sat next to Mrs Carlyle, who amused me very much with her account of their only servant who comes from Annandale in Scotland, and had never been accustomed to announce titles; so when Count Pepoli called she announced him as Mr Compilloly; Lord Jeffrey as Lorcherfield; and simply repeated it louder & louder each time; till at last Mrs Carlyle said 'What is it—man, woman {and}\or/beast?' to which the servant answered 'a little wee gentleman, Ma'am.' Miss Fanny

Kemble called in a hat & a habit, and when Mrs C. spoke to the servant about bringing Miss K. in, unannounced, the servant said 'I did not know if *it* was a Mr or Mrs.'—

In the evening quantities of other people came in. We were by this time up in the drawing-room, which is not nearly so pretty or so home-like as the study. Frank Stone the artist, Leech & his wife, Benedict the great piano-forte player, Sims Reeves the singer, Thackeray, Lord Dudley Stuart, Lord Headfort, Lady Yonge, Lady Lovelace, Lady Dufferin, and a quantity of others whose names I did not hear. We heard some beautiful music. Mr Tom Taylor was there too, who writes those comical ballads in Punch; and Anne said we had the whole Punch-bowl, which I believe we had. I kept trying to learn people's faces off by heart, that I might remember them; but it was rather confusing there were so *very* many. There were some nice little Dickens' children in the room,—who were so polite, and well-trained. We came away at last feeling we had seen so many people and things that day that we were quite confused; only that we should be glad to remember we had *done* it. I have written this letter dearest Annie, in the midst of talking and conversation, but I hope it will be intelligible, and amuse you a little, my dear. Give my dearest love to my girls and Mrs Green & your sisters, and ever believe me

Your very affect[ionate] friend
E. C. Gaskell

₀ 72+ ₀

UNKNOWN[1]

June 15th, 1850

Thank you for the autographs, I liked Bryants & Leigh Hunts— and kept George Dawsons just because Wm was so indignant at anybody thinking 'that mans' worth keeping, & now it's Saturday & I'm in raptures with Mr Forster who has got me £30 for a poor authoress from the Literary Fund;—a *lady* whom I picked up in Knutsford aged 72, grand-daughter of a baronet *and* an earl, living on 10£ a year—formerly wrote words [*sic*] for A. K. Newman—& had to fill up a form with a list of her works—& fancy my dismay when the first I had to ⟨. . .⟩

<hr>

1 Original MS. not seen.

_{72a} **74a** ₈₁

LADY KAY-SHUTTLEWORTH[1]

Plymouth Grove,
Manchester
August 19 Monday. [1850]

My dear Lady,

Your letter has been forwarded *here*: which has occasioned a little delay in its delivery. Thank you very much for it. It is so tempting an invitation and so kind of you to propose my making an acquaintance I have wished for so much, that my husband has helped me to overcome all difficulties and to accept it. I am very sorry (and so is he) to say that he has particular engagements this week, which will prevent his accompanying me. Some future time I hope to make him known to you.

I am half afraid I shall not give you an opportunity of sending me word if any circumstances has occurred to make my visit inconvenient if I fix tomorrow (Tuesday) as the day on which I hope to be with you; and yet as I must be at home again on Saturday I do not like to put if off until Wednesday. My husband, who will take this note into town, will make some inquiry as to the most desirable train for me to go by, and put it in as a P.S. to this note. I, too, am very full of public nurseries just now; that is to say, I am rather hearing of objections to them; but very much interested about them. Have you seen Mrs Hobhouse's pamphlet.

In great haste Yours very truly,
E. C. Gaskell

₉₀ **91a** _{*91b}

MARIANNE GASKELL[2]

Sunday afternoon. [10 March 1851]

My dearest Polly,

To-morrow morning Meta & I are going to Capesthorne to stay there till Wednesday morning so I must try & get in a line or two here, but the Sunday School girls are coming in ¼ of an

---

[1] Original MS. not seen.   [2] Original MS. not seen.

hour so I don't know if I shall have very much time. Mrs Davenport asked us & Papa too to go on Thursday & stay till Wednesday but we could not go there for many reasons so I put it off
until to-morrow & Miss Meta is rather put out at having to go at
all. Sir James & Lady Kay Shuttleworth are there which makes me
wish to go as it is a good while since I saw her. Tottie went to see
some friends in Liverpool yesterday & is to stay till Wednesday;
when we come back on Wednesday Meta goes to Mrs Austin's
to spend a few days with Annie, & Tottie, the two little ones & I
go to Mrs Mason's to tea; that is to say if Tottie really does come
home on Wednesday.

Now for this past week. I was not tired with writing to you
love, I was 'knocked up by going out for the first time'. Oh this
gold pen! it *will* blot & nobody shall help it. I have been a good
deal in the garden this past week. We have got peas, Jerusalem
Artichokes, cabbages, mignonette etc down, pinks, carnations,
campions, canterbury bells & the hot bed is just 'set agait' (vide
Frank) for cutting for the borders etc. On Friday (Thursdays
Annie Austin always comes) & this last Thursday Papa went to
dine at the Langton's. We all (Papa Tottie Meta & I) went to drink
tea at Mr Satterfields, *my* first tea drinking out of our own house,
since I came home. There were only ourselves & of course Mr S.
showed Tottie the pictures while we sat & worked & talked over
Mrs Bellhouse's death; nothing very particular happened anyway.
Mrs Shuttleworth has I think been our only caller this week, a
thing which as you know, I do not much regret. Mr D. Darbishire
has been here two evenings (Monday & Tuesday) for Tottie to
finish her drawing of him which she has done I think very well
but I think he was disappointed in it. I have written many letters
this week & have many more to write which I think I shall keep
for the leisure of Capesthorne.

Did I tell you that Captain & Mrs Holland are going for 2
months to Rome leaving their children in charge of the Isaacs?
I am glad you were firm about Easter with Helen Tagart.[1] It is
very kind of them to ask you. After Papa has done his lectures
next Thursday week I shall write & ask Miss Brontë to come here
& Dr Wm Carpenter is coming on the 27. Mrs Hodgetts & Emily
too will I think come too for a little time till they have arranged
their plans & sometime this Spring Snow Wedgwood will come

[1] Sources read 'Jaqart'. Other variant forms of this name have been silently
emended below.

I hope. Tell us when you know when your holidays will be. I like you to take an interest in politics because I like you to have many & wide interests but I want you to give *good* reasons for all your opinions or else you become a mere partizan. We hope too for a longer letter next Sunday. I think you have been very good hitherto in writing long letters but you must never cut the *home* letters short again. How are the shoulders [diagram][1] that way? or this [diagram][1] Let me know. How is the singing going on? & what chance have you of Mr Bennett? Mr Gunton was very glad to hear that you were likely to learn from him. Flossy is learning Trab Trab etc. Papa often wants to know about your singing. He says he thinks Mr Lalor's lessons must be something like his— are they? The Austins go on or about the 1st of April to visit friends in Sussex first. I am afraid poor Meta will miss Annie sadly but I mean to ask Emmy & Maggie in April. Flossy & Meta were at the Austins last night; they acted Debut-day—But (very bad) & pass-port & played at the ⟨. . .⟩

*91a **91b** 92

MARIANNE GASKELL[2]

Nursery
Sunday afternoon.
[17 March 1851]

My dearest Polly,
    I don't know that I have very much to say only I was very much obliged to you for your long letter this morning love & I dare say you would like a return in kind. Meta is still at the Austin's whither she went on Wednesday, very soon after Mr Gunton's lesson, for which we came back from Capesthorne. Meta however comes back tomorrow & so does Tottie & as Emily & Mrs Hodgetts make this a home house, & a dining place for a centre of calls & Papa goes to Mr Meyers to dinner I expect we shall have plenty of coming & going all day. After Meta went on Wednes-day Papa, the two little ones & I went to tea at Mrs Mason's, an evening much as usual; a most hospitable tea to which Florence just come from dancing did ample justice, that lame sister of Mrs Mason's very pleasant & agreeable & Mrs Mason herself rather

---

[1] Copyist's insertion.   [2] Original MS. not seen.

poorly which she has continued to be ever since; she did not go to chapel this morning on that account. Thursday being fine & frosty I went a-calling. Mrs Shuttleworth's (out at the Introductory lectures at Owen's College) Mrs Robberds—only Mary, Miss Pilkington & Anne Pilkington in. Anne Pilkington lame so obliged to lie down on a sofa—a bad account of Travers Madge who 'feels very well' but the doctors say the disease is making progress. Then on to Miss Marslands.[1] They too were at the lecture but I left a message asking them to tea; then to Mrs Sydney Potters. Out too, so did not I do well in the calling line? Miss Marslands came to tea. On Friday I went & called again on Mrs Shuttleworth's & thence to Mrs Leislers.[2] Laddie Leisler has been *very* ill with the croup. He was bled twice on Thursday, once in the jugular vein, but was better on Friday. After dinner to the Fairbairns. They were at Knutsford at Uncle Hollands. After tea to Miss Mitchell's to read to old Mr Turner which I mean to try & do very often both for his sake & Miss Mitchell's; as it sets her at liberty. I was well tired at night. Yesterday I was very busy in the garden where I mean to be tomorrow too. Papa has bought a new frame at a sale, & we are going to have it for a cold frame to harden out the plants from the hot bed; & we are sowing Thunbergias & planting gladioli etc. for the greenhouse in which by the[3] way a pair of robins are building a nest between two flower pots on the top shelf near the dining room window. Flossy & Baby enjoy watching them fly backwards & forwards with the dead leaves which they bring from out of doors.

Who do you think has got your *this* morning's letter to read? Miss Fergusson. We met her as we were going down to chapel this morning & she asked a great deal after you so I gave her your letter & told her she *must* bring it back soon which will I hope ensure us a visit from her. She looked very well but said that Johnnie was not much better. There is no one in Dundas Place yet, but I hope there will be by about the 27th when I expect we shall have the house full. Dr William Carpenter, Mrs Davenport (don't you think I'm bold to ask *her*?) Miss Brontë etc. & perhaps Mrs Hodgetts & Emily. The latter wants to go out as a daily governess. Mrs James Darbishire is better but still in a very precarious state, at Stanleys. I hope Lady Kay Shuttleworth will come

[1] Sources read 'Marksland'.

[2] Sources read 'Leishers' and 'Leisher' in next sentence. Later variants of this name have been silently emended.

[3] MS. source reads 'they'.

to us in April in her way to or from Gawthrop at Easter. *If* she
should ask you to play or sing, play or sing *good* music; and what
you can do *quite correctly* if ever so slowly;[1] for she has an admirable ear & is quite distressed by incorrect or slatternly playing.
How does your singing get on? You have not named it in either
of these two last letters. Perhaps your cold has prevented your
having your lessons, but don't lose more than you can help; for
as Papa says it is a famous opp[ortunit]y for you & such as can
never occur again. I am glad to hear you are liking your harmony
lessons. Emily Winkworth said the Concert Stück was nothing
without an orchestra but it is good practice I dare say. Thank you
for your advice about the children's dress. I read it all to Hearn &
we mean to profit by a great deal of it, though *I don't know* if we
shall get the silk frocks. Frederick & Annie Holland are gone to
Rome only to stay 2 months however; & the Charles Buxton's
are gone to Sicily which is, they say, carpeted & fragrant with
flowers. The Ben Shaens have taken a small house in Burlington
Street. Papa dines out to-morrow at the Meyers as I think I said
before, & on Wednesday it is the Ministers' meeting at Mr
Taylers. What must the little ones wear out of doors over their
every day prints? Meta is going to have the Warburton's garden
for her own; but at present it is very empty. Flossy continues very
faithful to you. I have got the 'Guesses at Truth',[2] & thank you for
them darling. And Papa has given me a new writing case, a *little*
larger & much better made than the old one, which is regularly
defunct having come all to pieces all on a sudden. We have sown
our first crop of peas. We are giving up beans as they did not
answer; we have sown mustard, cress, radishes, lettuces, cauli-
flowers, mignonette, etc. Can you tell who wrote the Review of
Miss Martineau's letters in the (this week's) Inquirer signed I. R.
You have never given your reasons for being glad a Protectionist
government[3] has not come in: & both Papa & I want to know
them; & to have them straight from yourself without your asking
any one. Admire Flossy's envelope—it is one Ellen Green gave
her which she thinks you will like.

Your very affec[tionate] mother
E. C. Gaskell.

[1] The words, 'and what . . . slowly', are not in the MS. source, though they
seem authentic. Other similar cases occur below.

[2] By Julius and Augustus Hare.

[3] Sources read 'Protestant forerunner', but cp. p. 148 above.

₉₆ **96a** ₉₇

MARIANNE GASKELL[1]

Nursery. Saturday.
[May or June 1851]

My dearest Minnie,

Meta is *sadly* disappointed at your not having written to her. I am sure if you knew how much out of spirits she is from weakness you would write to her pretty often. She is better than when you left but cried a good deal when she found you had gone away without wishing her goodbye. Indeed my dear Polly, you *must* write her a good *long* & very full letter. She will be interested in all sorts of little details. Yesterday she was in the drawing room but her eyes are so painful she can not read, & Mr Partington thought it would amuse her to be in the nursery & watch the little ones. I went to see Miss Mitchell yesterday; she is now quite well again. The Winkworths, Mr W. Shaen, & Travers Madge are coming to tea to-night. Our lodgings in London are quite secure which is very pleasant. I am to take you & Meta to Warrington next Saturday & go on, picking up Cousin Anne at Hartford. I will send you some stamps in this letter & pray write often to Meta. You know we shall want to hear about everything love; tell us what you have done each day. *Do you want your pills?* You quite forgot them. The children at Liscard like their lessons with Mr Morley very much. Florence is writing to you. I hope you will answer *her* letter too. Meta says again 'Please ask Marianne to write'.

Ever my dearest girl
Your affec[tionate] mother
E. C. Gaskell.

₉₇ **97+** ₉₇ₐ

MARIANNE GASKELL[2]

Spare Dressing Room
Sunday. [May 1851]

Every one is gone to chapel or church dearest Polly. Every one at home I mean; for Hearn Meta Flossie & Baby went to Bowden

---

[1] Original MS. not seen.   [2] Original MS. not seen.

yesterday. Mary took them as I was too weak & Papa too busy to go; & returned last night. Flossy was dreadfully tired when she got there. You have no idea how weak & ill she looks, & how *very* weak she is. But I am glad to hear her appetite seems better. Mary says she enjoyed the farm house bread & eat an egg which she has not been able to do for a long time before & planned to have milk put by for breakfast à la Silverdale. She is nursed on the knee just like a baby & does not want to be spoken to or disturbed. Only to put up her head against our[1] shoulders & lie still. Papa has given her $\frac{1}{2}$ a glass of port wine at 11 o'clock for some days past which is a good deal for a little girl of her age. Poor darling! She is so gentle & good. We have not yet heard from Canobie but I have written again with a new address & we hope to hear to-morrow or the next day. Papa laughs readily at the notion of your getting frocks *here* where most girls have got them made in London & sent down here. Miss Daniels has not yet sent your Carmelite home like Caroline Holland's material. Do you want a grey barège *as well*? I dare say you do, you know, only I should like to know if you really want it or only fancy it would be pretty & *if* you *want* it, do you want it now? at the holidays or when? Be sure you see about your[2] shifts etc. Helen Tagart knows of some dress maker in Hampstead who is a nice maker she said, but do with fewer & plainer gowns only have them well made. Do you want a bonnet before the holidays? I dare say you *do*. I only want to know which are *wants* & which are fancies. I should think you need not bring all your clothes home, if Mrs Lalor will allow a box to be left. Your green merino might be peppered or camphored to keep out moths; & your books, slate, desk etc. might be left, might they not?

I quite agree with Miss Banks in fearing that you may be too fond of gaiety; only I hope you will let gaiety take its due place as a thing to be enjoyed & not to be ravenous after. About influence I fancy Miss Banks & I should differ. I do not think any influence acts *permanently* well but what is *unconsciously* exercised by its possessor, but I dare say after all it is only differing from what you make Miss Banks say in your note, not from what she really says. I hope I shall know her some day; for she sounds very nice & kind. I am very much pleased to find my plan has answered & that you are pretty nearly in rags; if you had not had a very small stock of gowns you would have never worn your old ones

---

[1] Typescript source reads 'out'.   [2] Word in MS. source only.

my little lady. I crawled out into the garden yesterday & watched Frank pot out. We have far too many *red* flowers. We want *whites* & *blue*, try to suggest some. We are putting a dozen calceolarias for yellow lights. Meta's garden is so pretty & she works in it morning noon & night. I can hardly get her out of it at all. She is staying at Bowden till to-morrow. Maria comes back to-morrow. I have engaged Mrs Henry Long's[1] under nurse as waiter & now I hear she is so *very* little I am afraid she & Maria don't match. The Strawberry blossom is very thick indeed. I am glad to hear about the holidays.

I never see the Household Words, do you? Tell me if my dear old sailor's narrative is appearing yet. You'll know it by the old spelling if by nothing else. The poor Nortons I don't wonder at your feeling very sorry for them, dearest Polly. How old are they? I think I have heard Annie Austin speak of them. I have had no letters for several days from any one—partly because I have not written to any one. Papa is remarkably well & very busy as Mr Robberds is from home, gone to Cleator in Cumberland. I wonder if Mr Lalor sees anything of Mr Fred. Maurices History of England for the working classes. Mr Ludlow has sent me some numbers, but I have lent them so widely about I have lost them I am afraid. Did I tell you of some of the Sunday School girls wanting to go to Germany? & how we got the Hamburgh Consul to give them papers etc. & how they are not going because of the *diet*; such a funny & yet not a bad reason, for Marianne Warburton is very delicate you know. Meta thinks you are '*very gay*' & so do I when I remember I was five years at Miss Byerley's & never drank tea out of the house *once* let alone going to plays etc. etc. etc. etc. The house is so strange without a child in it; so *very* quiet. We are going to have a cat, a *travelled* cat for it is the Austin's kitten, born in Manchester & gone up to London (like you) to finish its education. You are to bring it down. I think everything is *shaping* for Meta going up to town just before your[2] holidays begin. Papa does not wish it talked about for many reasons so we don't talk of it. He does not want to have any engagements or *to have it known he is in London* but I *think* (now keep a secret) it is likely he & Meta & I (if I am strong enough) will go up to the old Panton Sq. lodgings—somewhere about the last day of June & stay a week & take you back. But *Papa won't go if any one knows he is there* so if you name it you may prevent

[1] Sources read 'Lond's'.   [2] MS. source reads 'the'.

him going by so doing. He would have to call & be civil on a dozen people & he wants to have all the time for the Exhibition etc. He is uncertain about Ipswich. But we only got your note just before he went to chapel so I have had no talk with him. He laughed so much at your having gowns sent from here that I don't know if I shall get leave to send it, but if I do I will put in that tin box (bring it back) (which is *not* our's I am afraid) with a nosegay for Miss Banks if you like to give it her. The greenhouse is very full of flowers & indeed we have a double stock for Mrs Shuttleworth has begged we will have all hers that are in flower while she is in London. Bring your fragments of green silk from home. They'll patch up Meta. Papa says I'm to tell you Botanic is spelt with only one 'N'. Oh you goosey gander! I *know* you knew that. The Leislers are in London with the D. D's. I do hope Miss Mitchell may be able to go. Cousin Anne was here the other day. She told Papa there was a case of wax flowers of wonderful beauty (& some wonderful price too) in the Exhibition, a spray of mignonette 40 guineas! Something else £1500!!!!! Meta has turned up her nose at the Exhibition ever since & *is* the Koh-i-noor no larger than *that*! Dear-ah-me!

Now is not this a handsome letter, all written lying down; but I thought my little woman should hear soon as she seemed anxious about home. Meta has taken crotchet, Mr W. Scott's poems & her sketch book to Bowden. It is a small old fashioned farm (like Wood's at Green Heys) at the *foot* of the hill. More's the pity; & they have a double bedded room & a sitting room. I long to go over & see them. They will stay a fortnight I think. But much will depend on Flossy. Papa intends to go over on Tuesday & see if she is gaining[1] strength. Sophie Gaddum is come home. I have not seen her, but they say she is as fat as you. Miss Brontë is going up to London. She always asks after you & how you like school. She offers to come to us the end of June just when we can't take her in again; for we shall only have two servants, Hearn & Maria (the waiter does not come till we have returned from I-don't-know-where, where we are going to spend the holidays & Mary has asked leave to go home that week to her sister's marriage etc.)

Your very affec[tionate] mother,

E. C. Gaskell.

---

[1] MS. source reads 'getting'.

97a **97b** 100

MARIANNE GASKELL[1]

[?Summer 1851]

⟨...⟩ (it is the cheapest & best by far in the long run) & then take care of them. We all want *very* much to know when the holidays begin. Have you *no* idea? and supposing for variety's sake, you put in a few stops into your next letter. Old Wm is rather bitter today. The little ones & he are going to have a *boiled* sole for dinner. And now goodbye, old child; & believe me your very affect[ionat]e

Mammy E C G.

0 **97c** 98

MRS BOOTH

11 Panton Sq.
Wednesday Morning.
[?Early July ?1851]

My dear Mrs Booth,

I am so much ashamed of my apparent carelessness in not sooner having acknowledged your very kind invitation to dinner on Tuesday next; but to tell the truth, until I took up your card just now to ascertain the exact address before setting off to return your call, I never saw the writing; and now, although I am most anxious to have the great pleasure of seeing you again, I believe I must beg you to allow me to ask some friends with whom we go to stay on Monday, if they have made any engagement for us\on Tuesday/; I will write immediately to you on receiving their answer; and I only hope it will allow us to accept an invitation which it would give us so much pleasure to avail ourselves of. Believe me dear Mrs Booth

Yours truly
E. C. Gaskell.

[1] Original MS. not seen.

MARIANNE GASKELL[1]

Thursday [28 August 1851] 9 o'clock.

My dearest Polly,

I am sitting in the schoolroom while Meta is having her music lesson so I shall write to you as we have been so busy for many days that I have not had time & I dare say you will want to know about the wedding just as much as I want to know about your lesson with Mr Bennett & what he said & what Pergetti said about your voice & how *hard you are working* to practice well etc. When did I write last? I'm sure I've forgotten, but I shall conclude it was before last Wednesday week, when we went (Annie S. Papa & I) to Mr Leislers to a sociable tea; met the Richard Birleys, Ewarts, De Merys & a sprinkling of Germans. It was very dull all the beginning of the evening & at 11 o'clock when we were to go away we found it was raining cats & dogs so Papa said he would go & send a cab & Annie & I were left alone with Mr & Mrs Leisler— & we waited & waited & it struck 12 & it struck 1 & it struck 2 & no cab came & it poured on. At last & at length a cab came and we came home & found all the servants up & 'Master out hunting for the Missis'—it seemed Papa had sent cab upon cab & returned home 3 times expecting to find us there but the cabs had been snatched up & none had come.[2] We had coffee for *breakfast* & then went to bed; we were all famously knocked up the[3] next day; quite tired out. Friday we (Meta & all) went to the Satterfields to tea. Pleasant quiet evening, made pleasant by the kind unpretending tone of the conversation. *No* ill natured remarks but everything gentle & good. No one there but Susanna & Stephen. Saturday there seemed to be the beginning of the wedding commotion. Mr Winkworth called to arrange about our being sent for on the Tuesday; but unluckily they were so late in announcing this arrangement that Papa & I after a sufficient quantity of wondering had resolved to write & ask Mrs Hervey to take us in on *Monday* to be in readiness for going to Dean[4] Row Chapel on

---

[1] Original MS. not seen.

[2] MS. source omits 'and we came home' and 'expecting . . . snatched up' in this sentence.

[3] MS. source omits 'the'.

[4] Sources read 'Bean', though the typescript 'B' is not clear.

Tuesday; &[1] as we were making her into a convenience & had not
received her answer we could not fall in to Mr Winkworth's plan,
which we were sorry for, on many accounts; as I did not want to
be absent from home for a night. However the Lea Hall[2] plan
was decided upon. On Saturday morning the Ben Shaens, Louy
Allman (just arrived) & Mr Sam Shaen (ditto) came to tea. Emily
had come to Dundas Place to make final arrangements & Will
had come down with Louy & Sam & gone to Dundas Place but
before the end of the evening he came in here & looked over the
marriage service with Papa. On Sunday he & Emily came in after
morning chapel. 6 Shaens had been at Brook St. You may make
out who they were at your leisure. Poor Emily was very tearful.
She walked round the garden & the little ones stripped their
flower beds for her. In the evening we went to the Shuttleworths
& met John & Hannah Tayler; they were going with Mr and
Mrs T. into Scotland the next day & Meta & I have promised to
take Hannah's class at the Sunday School during her absence (Oh!
I went with Agnes Ewart to the public nursery on Friday. I found
2 babies therein). Monday I wrote letters to nearly everybody
except you, Tottie & Miss Brontë, to all of whom I ought to
write; & I *received* a letter from your Aunt Anne. They (the
Robsons) are going to remove to a larger house in Bewsey Place
if you know where that is. The two little boys are coming on
famously & so is the little Ashfield girl. ⟨...⟩

*100*a* **101*a*** 102

MARIANNE GASKELL[3]

[Thursday 4 September 1851]

⟨...⟩ given them the same hand book for that plan. They will be
privately home at 8 Bedford Row on next Tuesday week (16th or
17th) & I mean to write & welcome them, & I think you'll like
to do so too. Emily was *very* much pleased by your Sunday note.
She took away her bouquet (the flowers came from Covent

---

[1] Followed by 'so' in MS. source.
[2] MS. source reads 'Hole', as did the typescript source before a later pencil
alteration to 'Hall'.
[3] Original MS. not seen.

Garden market and were beautiful) & the rose which lay on the altar. After they were gone we sauntered round the garden & then Selina took me in one of the carriages to Lea Hall & Papa staid at Alderley to come back here on Tuesday night. I staid at Lea Hall till early yesterday morning when I came home to be in time for Julia's birthday. I found Papa had[1] Mr Sam Shaen & Louy with him. It was a dismal morning & we doubted if it would clear off; & indeed we gave up the thought of going to spend the day at Bowden as had been planned & in the midst of that disappointment came your note & the comical creatures which delighted Julia extremely, & Papa no less I think. Then it cleared up so I sent Hearn & the three girls off with a dinner in a basket & tea & sugar to drink tea at Miss Walkers (where they lodge you know). I meant to go with them myself but could not, callers kept pouring in so. Agnes & Eliza, Miss Jewsbury to ask us to drink tea with the Carlyles etc. etc. but I got away after a lunch–dinner, rushed to Bowden & called on Mrs Haughton. Drank tea with the children, came home at six dressed, went to Miss Jewsbury's and here I sit this morning. The Satterfields[2] are all coming tomorrow night (Agnes, Eliz. Mr & Miss) with Susanna & Selina. On Saturday Miss Jewsbury & Mrs Carlyle dine here; to–day Annie comes back from Alderley & Louy comes here to join her for two days. Monday we all go to Dinting to spend the day at the E. Potters so it all sounds very busy does not it? & I'm terribly afraid of being knocked up in the middle, I am so tired to–day. Flossy's love & 'what a nice present that was'. Baby's dear love. I *believe* dearest we shan't send you a box on your birthday. I am not quite sure; but we find we must be so very careful about money & your jacket is not even begun & it would make two sendings.

Ever Your very affect[ionate]

E. C. Gaskell.

[1] MS. source reads '&'.
[2] Typescript source reads 'Tatterfields'.

102 **102***a* 103

MARIANNE GASKELL[1]

Uncle Holland's
Knutsford
Friday.
[17 October 1851]

My dearest Polly,

Papa gave me this note yesterday just when I was coming off for you so I shall add a line or two to tell you all our funny misdoings yesterday in coming here. In the first place we were to have come by the 11 o'clock train via *Altringham*, which fare was 2*s*. but just as we were ready Helen & Emily Tagart came from Norcliffe & then Mrs Robert Worthington came to tell me of a housemaid, so we had to plan to come by *Chelford*, price 3*s*. 6*d*. and Frank was told to take the luggage to the London Road Station. Instead of which when Meta & I arrived at the Station (*walking*) we found no Frank & no luggage; but we thought we had better come on as it was already past the time when Cousin Mary expected us. Were not we bold? We came off however trusting in Frank's taking them back again, & Hearn sending him back (after a good scolding) with them to follow us by the next train. Accordingly they came about 9. So now we and our boxes are comfortably here. We ourselves got here in dinner time; had dinner & then went to see Cousin Susan & her charming baby— for it *is* charming, a sweet little coaxing creature who curls up into the neck and clasps tight, half hiding its face, half smiling at you—reddish hair, blue eyes & a bright dazzling fair complexion. But it is in its ways it is so pretty & loving. Then we came home; & then we would have dressed if we could, but we could not. Then Cousin Susan & Emmy & Maggie came to tea—& then my box came & so we settled for a quiet casino evening.

The Charles Buxtons have asked Miss Bremer to occupy their house in Grosvenor Crescent while they are in Norfolk; whether she will do it or not I do not know, as I thought she was going before. We met Harry Holland an evening or two ago in Manchester; he is engaged as you know, don't you, to the Miss Hibbert Signor Pergetti's pupil, Lizzie by name, who sings so

---

[1] Original MS. not seen.

well. But they are not to be married for two years. I want very much to know how your toothache is, & I am looking forward to your Sunday letter *here* with great pleasure. I fancy we shall stay at this house until Tuesday then go to Mrs Green's to the next Monday (Oct. 27th) when we shall go home. Of course this plan may be modified or not. Cousin Fanny is at Liscard with Aunt Lizzie etc. She *talks* of staying in her small house in Portmadoc all through the winter & in the Spring fixing on some permanent abode. Bowden I almost fancy it will be; as there the Collins live—the old Mrs Holland & Miss Harriet who used to live in Grosvenor Street & she would be between Manchester & Knutsford at both which[1] places she had friends. Mrs Carlyle sends me word she asked to see you, but you were busy with your music lesson. *Tell us what songs you are learning with S. Pergetti.* Have you got to anything of Mozart yet. Caroline Holland had only ten lessons from him & yet they say whatever she tries to learn she sings in that good style & with that taste & correctness which makes it such a pleasure to listen. Do you think Miss Banks *could* come to us after Xmas? We are going to try to wash at home, as this new housemaid Mrs R. W. told me of is a very good washer.

Goodbye my darling.

Your very affect[ionate] Mother

E. C. Gaskell.

₀ **108*b*** ₀

UNKNOWN[2]

Dec: 8th 1851

⟨. . .⟩ I was sorry to find dear from your letter that you were just a little out of spirits; I can quite understand the feeling of being transferred from the interests & sympathies of two such different parents, each of whom look to you for sympathy. I wish you well through your 'two shirts'. I never made one in my life; I think I shall take to it for winter work. We are turning regular farmers. We have a cow.—and we're going to have two pigs, for we're having a pig-stye built, & we churn, & we wash, & we mangle at home. It makes us a busy house.

---

[1] Word not in MS. source.   [2] Original MS. not seen.

114 **114a** 116

S<small>MALL CAPS</small>

M<small>ARIANNE</small> G<small>ASKELL</small>[1]

Wednesday morng [18 February 1852]

My dearest Polly,

I miss Mr Gunton's day which always reminded me to write
to you & I also get 'moidered'—as to whatever I wrote last to you
or Meta. Papa & I congratulate you on your beautiful wrap which
Meta & Annie are almost as full of as you are. Meta has sent me
a long merry account of your doings on Saturday. We were disappointed not [to] have your letter on Thursday; we always are,
darling, when we don't hear on that day. My dearest lassie, I wish
you *could* have gone to the Austin's, but I think it is quite right
you did not. *Whose* history of the F. Revolution are you reading?
Has Signor Pergetti never come all this half year till now? I am very
sorry if so, for it is losing your opportunities sadly. I hope you are
making as much of them as Meta seems to be doing with her
drawing-lessons, working away 5 or 6 hours a day: & remember
how Papa looks to your singing. I see it constantly in many of his
little speeches; he looks forward to it as such a pleasure. I am very[2]
sorry Miss Banks is poorly. I wish I cd do anything for her. The
children who like Bessy's Troubles[3] are great geese, & no judges
at all, which children generally are, for it is complete rubbish I
am sorry to say. I am very stupid altogether with writing up &
down the kingdom on behalf of our dear Mr Wright, for whom
we want to get subscriptions enough to purchase him an annuity,
as his health is failing, very much. Meta would tell you Mrs
Davenport is Lady Hatherton now. I had a very nice merry letter
giving an account of the wedding from Lord Hatherton, after I
had heard of it from Mr Crackenthorpe. Agnes Sanders[4] address is
Mrs S.
Charles Saunders[4] Esq.
Edgwick near
Coventry.
& they would be very glad I am sure to have a *newsy* letter from
you to her, but I will copy what Eliza says. 'I am afraid poor
Nessy will feel the disappointment more every day; the very
slightest allusion to a child, A ⟨. . .⟩

---

[1] Original MS. not seen.   [2] Word omitted in MS. source.
[3] By Mrs Gaskell.   [4] ? Sandars.

116 **116a** 117

MARIANNE GASKELL[1]

Thursday [26 February 1852]

My dearest Polly,

Meta keeps my pen so busy that[2] I hardly know when to write. But I was so glad to get your letter (which I did on *Sunday*). This week has been unusually busy. In the first place I've had writing to do *without end*, till my wrist actually swelled with it—for the subscription to Mr Wright in the first place (ask Mr Lalor if he thinks the Inquirer would lend it a helping hand to making the fact of there being a subscription known). Monday—I can't remember anything about Monday except that I conclude I was keeping myself a prisoner for a bad sore throat I have had; mustard plaister etc. etc. being required. It came on quite suddenly last Thursday & I was very ill with it for two days & very anxious to get better because we had asked Selina & Emily Green here for Tuesday & Wednesday in this week to go to the Johnson's in Lime Grove & the Schwabes last night. However they came; & to the Johnsons we went. I muffled up to my ears to spend a very dull evening. Not knowing or wishing to know any one[3] there. Last night it was better because I did know people; but we staid up till 2 o'clock & I am terribly tired to-day. I have had a good piece of writing to do for the Athenaeum as well. Selina & Emily gone back to Alderley. Katie is staying with Susanna in Dundas Place but coming to dine with us to-day. It is the weekly lecture at the Chapel. Mr Thorn[4] preaches & the S.S. girls are to come on Saturday fortnight *as well* as (not *instead* of) Sunday Months. Meta sent[5] me word she saw you at Bennett's concerts. She is very busy with her drawing & I am delighted to think of her profiting so well by the opp[ortunit]y as she seems to be doing. Mrs Wedgwood sends word she is going to take me to call on Mrs Carlyle next week. I hardly know how long she will stay in London. Tottie wants her to go there & that would be where she could have lessons from Mr Wl. I.[6]

Flossy & Julia have got the delectable Annie's[7] to-day, so are

---

[1] Original MS. not seen.   [2] Word omitted in MS. source.
[3] MS. source reads 'know who was'.   [4] ? Thom.
[5] Typescript source reads 'send'.
[6] MS. source reads 'Mr WI. I', the 'W' having been squeezed in.
[7] ? Annis [Smith]. See p. 211 above for the adjective.

very quiet & busy & happy. Sophie Gaddum asked after you last night. The party consisted almost entirely of Germans, it being Ash Wednesday when many English don't like to visit. There were several Hungarians. Vernon Darbishire goes to study agriculture. He is in high spirits about it[,][1] liking it much[2] better than law. Robert was there last night, apparently quite well; & very nice & kind & pleasant. Theodore Schwabe is come home. To-morrow I go to a 'ladies party' at Mrs Sydney Potters. Tuesday to[3] a ditto ditto at Mrs Shuttleworth's all in honour of Miss Marslands, & their guests the two Miss Humphreys. The little robin is in the greenhouse again this year. I do hope it will build there. We have plenty of crocuses out in the greenhouse but no where else. The pigs live & flourish. I almost think we shall have another cow as well as this; our butter answers so well. Mrs Mason is going to live at Mr Hampton's house at Bowden. Tell me about Mr Bennett's concert. How funny for you & Meta to be meeting in a London concert room! It is *so* cold. *How is your headache?* be sure you tell me also what Pergetti says & what he gives you to learn. In fact dearest tell me everything you can in every way. I do so like to hear of it all. Meta & you seem to have taken a fit of admiring each other. Oh dear! love this is a stupid letter, but what can you expect from a mother who has sat up till past 2 two nights running in close rooms & with a sore throat? Besides I've written very close & I am your ever affec[tionate] mother

E. C. Gaskell.

47 118a 177

MARGARET EMILY GASKELL[4]

Sunday afternoon.
[28 March 1852]

My dearest Meta,
    Its such a lovely day I can't help popping in & out of the garden & never settling to my writing though I've been into town and back again. First & foremost Uncle Sam wants to know if you

---

[1] MS. source omits 'it'.   [2] Typescript source reads 'must'.
[3] MS. source reads 'is'.   [4] Original MS. not seen.

have a *gooa box of colours* as he wants to give you one if you haven't. Now I *think* you have—but you know best your wants in this line. Thanks for your letter. *Be sure you answer about the colour box to me.* I am so glad now you & Polly are so near, it will save me some writing trouble. Why did not you tell Mrs Lalor you always wore that frock in the afternoon & why did you let yourself be *choked up* near the fire? I am so glad you are seeing so much of M. A. I was quite startled last night by finding out it wanted *3 weeks* (instead of a *fortnight* as I had fancied) to the end of Easter week. Yes! Mrs Paul Fearon *is* very lovely. I saw her once upon a time. I am so glad about you & M. A. *You want some money* don't you. Tell me in time what you do. I have given Papa your message. We gave up going to breakfast at the Schwabes on Friday it is such a distance. Then they asked us for yesterday, which was worse so we declined that. However I have done the gracious thing & offered myself for to-morrow for I am very fond of Mrs S. and don't like her to think we *won't* come. Friday evening we took Hannah to the Park dance. A large house with *very* small rooms but any number of them. There were nearly 300 there. Rathebones,[1] Caton & Norcliffe[2] Gregs, Murrays, Mellys, Altringham Worthingtons, Potters (the fat Sir John), Wm Woods, *Fairbairns*, Batemans, Fosters, a quantity of officers in plain clothes, one Captain Heywood, danced so badly every one was laughing at him; he did *very* slow waltz to the deux temps & was out of time in what he did. There was a crush &[3] crowd into supper. Mrs Schwabe & I tried 3 times before we got in; it was such a little room. The hosts were two Mr Philips—very kind & good natured not very gentlemanly—we came home about 3, found Hearn up, had tea & went very fresh to bed to get up with an awful headache yesterday.

Papa said however that I must go to the Fairbairns to dinner & by dint of wet cloths & tea I got myself up. 2 Mr Philips came again, & Sir[4] John Potter again. Mr and Mrs Wm Fairbairn, *George Fairbairn* (tell M. A.) Mr & Mrs Leonard Horner;[5] & Miss Horner, Batemans, Schwabes, & Ld & Ly Murray were to have been there but were all knocked up by the night before so did not come. Mr Mark[6] Philips took me in to dinner. It was a very yea nay kind of affair, rather flat because there were too many of the *Fairbairn*

---

[1] Sources read 'Rallebones'.   [2] Comma in sources deleted.
[3] MS. source reads '& a'.   [4] Typescript source reads 'Philips again, Sir'.
[5] 'Homer' in sources, silently emended henceforth.   [6] 'Mack' in sources.

family.[1] I always like Miss Horner & she & I had good long talks after dinner. I had a long letter from Lord & Ly Hatherton yesterday. They came back from Paris on Monday & want me to go & see them this week. Papa urges me to go & thinks the change will do me good; but it is 60 miles off & I could[2] only stay a very few days (the Hathertons are going to spend the Easter holidays with the D. & Duchess of Sutherland!) I leave Teddesley on the 6th. However I've not answered the note yet; partly too I have not a gown to go in (Ly Hatherton says 'whether material jackets & waistcoats of the same *for morning*')[3] besides which we are engaged every evening this week. Taylers to-morrow, Susanna W. (her book is coming to a second edition) on Tuesday, Lee's[4] (alas!) Wednesday, Schwabes (to meet the Bunsen's) Thursday etc etc etc. If I go to the Hatherton's I go on *Tuesday* & my address will be

Mrs G.
The Lord Hatherton's
Teddesley Park
Staffordshire

Don't forget the 'The' (it is as significant as Papa's Revd). Flossy is very well. Only still plaistered up about the chin. I have had a charming long letter from Katie in Edin; I don't know when they come home. Papa is going into North Devon for a few days at Easter & he & I talk of going up to London at Whitsuntide. Ly Hatherton sends me £5 for Mr Wright. She says her likeness is good & very like. I don't think I ever sent you Ld H's account of their wedding because I know it would be greater charity to send it to A. Patterson Sandars.[5] Well I shall close this so goodbye darling.

Ever your very affec[tionate] mother
E. C. Gaskell

Keep this account of Mrs D's marriage.

---

[1] Both the MS. and the typescript source have '½' at this point, and the latter omits the full stop. It would seem that the MS. copyist followed a mechanical error of the typist.

[2] MS. source reads 'can'.

[3] Sense not clear; perhaps 'woollen material'.

[4] Sources read 'Ler's'.

[5] Sources read 'A. Pallerson Sanders'.

₁₂₀ **122*a*** ₁₂₃

MARIANNE GASKELL[1]

Tuesday
[4 May 1852]

My dearest Polly,

We have fixed to go to the Tower house at Silverdale 3 windows being made to open wide viz., two little bedrooms and
staircase. I am so sorry dearest to say that I believe we cannot ask
Miss Banks. There are one or two reasons. All that relate to myself
I can get over, i.e. packing close etc. but I find Papa does not like
the idea of having a *stranger* in the house in holiday time when
you know he likes to play pranks, go cockling etc. etc. and feel at
liberty to say or do what he likes. I told him I did not think Miss
Banks *was* so very particular, but he says it would make him uncomfortable, and so it must be given up darling. *But any time
when we are at home* that you can think of to ask Miss Banks *do
darling* or ask me to write to her which would I think be the
proper thing. She could not come from the 23rd of June to the 29
(when we go to Silverdale) on her way anywhere could she? or
next Christmas? Any time *at home* we shall be glad to see her, but
I think you may fancy how Papa would feel constrained and
obliged to be 'proper'. We have asked Tottie but I am afraid there
is some hitch at home about *her* coming; and we have asked Miss
Mitchell. I had a letter from Mrs Schwabe to-day saying she had
seen you and Meta on Sunday; and that you were looking well
and happy. I must write her *to-day* before she goes to Paris to
thank her; and that will I fear oblige me to cut short my letter to
you darling a little; as all morning James[2] has been off in the old
say way[3] and it has thrown a good deal of work into the house of
one kind or another. I have also to write to Mme Avril and
enclose her Mrs Schwabes[4] and Mr Edmund Potters letters; both
declining her designs as 'impracticable'. I can do no more so must
return them. Do you remember Mrs Sam Marsland? She is dead
in Germany! We have just heard of it and Papa is going there to
see them. Papa seems very well and bright and likes the notion of
Silverdale evidently. I have sold my[5] stock of Libbie Marsh's

---

[1] Original MS. not seen.   [2] Source reads 'games', but cp. p. 187 above.
[3] Perhaps 'sad way'.
[4] Source reads 'Schwarbes', which will be silently emended henceforth.
[5] Source reads 'by'.

Three Eras to Chapman for £12. I shall be so glad of your help to take care of the fowls. The hens lay eggs apiece though. We have a nice water place made for the ducks under the acacia in what was the children's garden. I like your account of your songs. I am glad you are getting to rather more lively ones—and I am glad that you are going to the Opera soon. Miss Mitchell was here last night and the night before. Mr Wright too last night. He is a 'gentleman at large' now. Meta comes home as you very probably know this day week with Mr Taylor (who will be in the morning at the Tagarts) by the 5 o'clock express train getting in at 11 at night. The little ones are to sit up to meet her. Baby *was* brave about her teeth. They are both with Annie[1] Smith to-day. Best love my darling

Yours very affect[ionate]ly
E. C. Gaskell

126 130a 131

MARIANNE GASKELL[2]

Gunton-time
Saturday
[28 August 1852]

My dearest Polly,

Don't expect a long letter from me for I have had a blister on my back, and that and the hot weather make me be in no good writing cue. *What did Dr Holland say?* Saba, Cor and Gertrude are at Knutsford, whither Mr Henry Holland and his bride are coming to-day. You will have heard how very poorly darling Baby was on Saturday and Monday, both which nights we had to sit up with her. She is quite well now, though easily tired and feeble owing to the hot weather; but well enough to go to Bowden yesterday with Papa and me and stronger than I was in the walking way. Flossy rather wants you to put her to rights being in that frame of mind when everything is wrong. Mrs Schwabes come to Crumpsall and I meant to have gone to see her to-day but am too tired with yesterday, and not up to both it and the girls in the evening. Emily and Agnes Darbishire called yesterday and are

---

[1] ? Annis.   [2] Original MS. not seen.

coming here with the two Leislers on Monday. I hope Meta will make an hospitable hostess. We should have called on the Robert Darbishires this week but I was ill etc so we only sent cards. I have not heard of a cook yet. Jane Burton is stopping on in her place at Mrs Gibson's at Grasmere. Maggie Cannon is come home from the Tyrol and drank tea here one night with Rosa Mitchell. Yesterday Meta spent with Eliza Patterson. Agnes comes back from Scotland on Monday and comes to us the week after. Selina comes into Manchester next week to Dundas Place. I had a letter from Susanna giving a good account of Emily who had however only on that day (Monday) been able to speak or to hear the letters. She expressed great pleasure at the receipt of yours and said she should like you to be told how much she had enjoyed it and thanked you for the kindness expressed. ⟨. . .⟩

134 **134*a*** 135

MARIANNE GASKELL[1]

Friday [1 October 1852]

My dearest Polly,
    That comes of a pen too full of ink which dropped on my only sheet of paper. Consider the conduct of your Mother as a warning & not as an example! Papa is in a great fidget lest you should give up your lessons with Pergetti just when he thinks you are going to benefit by them; but I tell him you won't for that I have especially told you (vide my last letter[2] but one or two I forget which) that *that* you *must* not do. I am writing after dinner; we are going to have a tournification[3] as soon as the servants have had their dinner: (*very* cold). Annie & Ellen have gone to dine at their cousin's the Green's; that's that! My right arm is very bad & Mr Mellor[4] comes to see it & caustics it so you must excuse bad writing for it ought to be in a sling & was all yesterday. You must *buy* yourself an apron you goose! The carriage of yours would cost 2 shillings or more. Moreover carmelites (embroidered or not embroidered) wash like prints. They are all laughing at me for telling you buy a new one, saying are you to buy a new muslin

---

[1] Original MS. not seen.   [2] Sources read 'lesson'.
[3] Sources read 'tomnification'.   [4] Sources read 'Wellor'.

gown every time it gets dirty. The Greens are wearing carmelites just like yours, (three times washed) I think they said by the common washerwoman. I'll send Mrs Lalor a report to-morrow. The Ewarts are now thinking of a house in Nelson St near S. Winkworths.[1] That baby of Major Ewart's is a charming one. I went to Thackeray's lecture last night & Papa on Tuesday; our only events except the *want* of an event viz., the hens laying eggs. Don't tell me it's bitterly cold because I know it. Also that you are going to the Austin's to-morrow. *You* had better be getting a new gown or two I think, but not a third carmelite against this gets dirty. You can (I fancy) do without a new winter cloak—or do you want one. Thackeray sent me word he was coming here to-day but as he has not come I shan't stay in any longer. We are dining at the Schuncks[2] to meet Juliet Gallenga[3] on Wednesday. That is our only engagement. Meanwhile I am very busy making flannels going to the School twice a week etc. I really can't write more my arm aches so. Thank Mrs Lalor for the Inquirer. Flossie was delighted with her letters & books more especially as she was the only one in the house who had letters that morning. Get your apron child & don't be a goose. Remember the carriage of those two petticoat bodices that did *not* fit cost 2 shillings.

Your[s] very affect[ionate]ly
E. C. Gaskell.

144 144*a* *144b*

MARIANNE GASKELL[4]

Plymouth Grove,
Tuesday. [December 1852]

Papa says you may stay my dearest Polly. Perhaps I shan't have time to write more than this as I am very poorly & unequal to much writing. I see Papa is a little vexed at your not being more anxious to come home but I can quite understand it. No we've not heard from G. Shaen nor nobody but business letters etc. M E[5] is in very good spirits about going to school & rather amused

---

[1] Sources read 'Wiedrookler'.   [2] Sources read 'Selwicks'.
[3] Sources read 'Gallenza'. Henceforth, all these forms will be silently emended.
[4] Original MS. not seen.   [5] Sources read 'She'.

at your fancying she won't like it. However I dare say she *will* meet with more troubles than she expects & she & I too feel your letter as very kind darling. She has been very busy at work. We wonder if you bought the piano? if your gowns? if your bonnet? yet you imply you did etc. etc. etc. No one tells one anything nowadays. Mrs Jameson has been here, gone now—engagements every night but I am not well enough to go,—'little-go' here on Friday to which we thought you'd be back. Maggie Leisler, St & Alice W. & one or two others. Miss Carpenter comes on Saturday—a dance at Mr Henry's[1] (Woodlands) the 30th for children to which you are to act chaperone—27 Mr & J. Taylers. Mrs Schwabes 29 ——— oh! my head aches to think of it all. Mr Gunton is engaged for Florence. Rosa & Mary Ewart both thought you ought to be spared that worry—only I shall trust the superintendence of practising to you. I can't write more to-day. Snow is still ill at the Scotts. Mr Wedgwood and Rich still there —I have presents of books to acknowledge & thank for 'Francis Croft'[2] and a poem of Robert Montgomery's 'from author' & I can hardly see what I write but I am ever my darling

Yours affect[ionate]ly
E. C. G.

I must write to Mr Sandars about your getting to Agnes & coming home.

*144a 144b 147

MARIANNE GASKELL[3]

[?December 1852]

My dearest Polly,

No! you must *certainly* come home for the Boyce & Beauty party. Papa says its 'an engagement' & is very decided about it & I myself don't think Meta will be strong enough to go; so on every account you must come home on Wednesday, without fail; I should *like* by the *morning* omnibus but yet I am not sure if you

---

[1] Sources read 'Hurry's'.
[2] *The Fortunes of Francis Croft*, by Bayle Saint-John, 1852.
[3] Original MS. not seen.

can manage this. I doubt if we shall let Meta go to the Green's love. She is very far from strong & Papa has objected to her going to Knutsford for 'one night only' on account of fatigue. But I should be so very sorry to hurt them that we shall see about this to-morrow. She has been to the Sunday School today but was too tired to go out yesterday & has been in bed by *ten*; she is grievously disappointed & so am I at your non-account of the Deane's dance; she says 'you *might* have sent it her as a make up for not going'. The *last* report in Manchester is *you* my lady & Beauty. Miss Marslands are strong on the subject—the wag tongues. We were not out yesterday till Papa & I went to the Ewarts, Scotts, Leislers, Susanna & Selina. No particular letters this morning. You must be decided about Woodlands. We let you go from home as much as ever we can.

Your very affec[tionate]
E. Gaskell.

147 147a *147b

MARIANNE GASKELL[1]

Saturday morning.
[?1852][2]

My dearest Polly,

I send you Meta's letter which is very satisfactory I think—and here's a *beautifully* written letter from Florence is it not? I mean if I can to write to her to-day as well as to Papa—well! *and* when I got home here yesterday (after you scuttled into the 'bus & never looked out at me) I found a note sent by Lady Coltman[3] asking you & me to a family dinner at 7 yesterday—only Arthur & Russell Duckworth, or if we could not come to that, to lunch there at one on Tuesday. Now could you manage *this last* do you think? I would meet you at Portland Street Chapel & would go to Lady C's & then I must be back to go to Mr Maurice's at 3 & Emily wishes you'd stop here all night & 'bus it back. Now turn

---

[1] Original MS. not seen.

[2] Mrs Gaskell was apparently staying with William and Emily Shaen who married on 2 September 1851, and it seems possible that Marianne was still at school at Hampstead.

[3] Sources read 'Coltmore'.

this over in your mind dear; you can't send an answer but I think it sounds very feasible & at any rate you'll find me moving about Portland St Chapel vestry 'at the close of the present service'. Here also is a letter from Annie Shaen[1]—asking you to go there to-day at 3 with Mr Sam Shaen[1] which of course you can't do & so goodbye

Ever your own affec[tionate] mother
E. C. Gaskell.

*147a 147b *156a

MARIANNE GASKELL[2]

Friday. [?January 1853]

My dearest Polly,

Thanks manifold for your satisfactory letter relating to bureau. I have written for it; yesterday was so busy cutting out all morning—Exhibition of pictures, servants party evening, that I could not write about anything. Only asked Meta to write a message or two for me. About Rachel, all I have to go upon is that little speech of Miss Green's & you knowing her etc will be best able to tell how far it should be acted upon or not. Only if anything can be done I should[3] like to have it done quickly as I would rather have her than any one else; but must decide some way soon. Also have you any money left out of £10 besides what you will want? Tell me dear if you can, though it does not much signify. About going to the Tagarts next week I am afraid both Meta & I behaved shabbily towards them, so for that reason I would like you darling to have made yourself a small victim & have gone; for they are *really* kind; were very kind to Papa last spring & I should be sorry to hurt them. On the other side, for the children's sake you are wanted at home—only I should consider it a yet *more positive* duty, considering your relation to Miss Banks, for you to stay at Holly Hill if owing to illness or sorrow you could be of use there. So that's that.

Flossy is practising steadily & well for Mr Gunton ½ an hour with Meta, who says she knows her piece; half an hour per se.

---

[1] Sources read 'Shaw'.   [2] Original MS. not seen.
[3] MS. source omits 'be acted ... I should'.

As soon as shoes etc. are made she & Julia are going to dancing, very much to Julia's wrath—And I have broken Miss Birchel[1] to Flossy with rather good effect. When Meta is at home she is to dragonize & prepare French lessons; so you will have that much more time for English. Flossy is *very* good; mind, I don't know how she will take lessons; but I see many little struggles with temper which almost always end in victories. Julia is occasionally vicious but very funny & a great darling. Papa is in Liverpool. Katie & Sleeky here; go home to S. School & District to-morrow & return on Monday till the Elders come home some day next week probably. Papa comes home to-morrow, Mrs Jameson writes to-day to put off her coming till the 27, which will make me have to alter my small engagements of various kinds, such as Mr Satterfield & Mr Ryan on Tuesday etc. etc. Meta probably told you about the Davy invitation. I shall be glad for her to go. It's a *wholesome* house for her to stay at; & an acquaintance I value for her; & she has not been strong or in spirits lately. But the state invitation from Mrs Davy has not come yet. The boots sound very nice. Jane Taylor & her mother—is in a mess with her & ⟨ ⟩ 'fiasco' if you like it better, but Mr Rustone & I are laying our heads together. Mary Lievesley[2] & her child leave to-morrow; there is early dinner to-day & Margaret, Hearn, children, etc. etc. Mary & me are going to Bowden. Yesterday we had early dinner & cooked our own tea in this dining room last night amidst no end of laughing. Selina & I fried ham & eggs better than any you ever tasted. (We set the fat on fire & had to run out of doors out of the window blazing pan in hand, amidst screams of children— but we set it down on the steps & it went out at last. But *never* pour water on *blazing* fat. That's my experience.) The toast was not so first rate. We were like thorough cooks & only did the best dish well. I believe we attempted too much for one fire. But the tea was uproarious & then we played at dumb crambo with the children till late bed time & then I whipped them into a hot bath by way of washing made easy. And where Julia's hair is to-day is better imagined than described. Meanwhile the party downstairs went on as joyously. Wm host, Margaret hostess, Hearn heroine, 2 whist tables (great difficulty in finding cards!) I thought it my duty to stay up till company had departed; so it was $\frac{1}{2}$ p. 11 before I went to bed & what with cutting out in Chapel room, going to Picture Exhibition with Katie cooking etc. I *was* tired; I am today

---

[1] ? Mitchell.   [2] Sources read 'Lievisley'.

too. I believe the Ewarts came home last night. But I have not
seen them. Meta is going soon over but I don't suppose there'll
be any news you'll not have heard. Oh I am so tired.

Your affect[ionate] mother

E. C. G.

I wonder how it would do for me to tell Twinings to send our
tea (year's stock) to *you* at Hampstead. It would save carriage.
I've got a new winter gown, & am rather smart.

*147b **156a** 158

MARIANNE GASKELL[1]

8 Hyde Park Gardens,
Thursday. [26 May 1853]

My dearest Polly,

It's not that I have much news; and darling, you must send on
my letters to Meta and write with them yourself. Oh! how hot it
is. I keep thinking if I had but my muslin gown. I have a good
mind to ask you to tell Hearn to send it in a brown paper parcel
(if the Daniels' one, the new one—is much the better, but only
one.) I don't think it wd crush much, and the carriage would save
me many a headache. Direct it *here.* Then I rather want to get the
little girls hats; and I want the measure of their heads. I don't
know that I can fit them so you had better not say much about it.
How does Elizabeth go on, love? I hope Margaret is going to
Mary's next week. Coax Papa to give you drives in Tommy. It is
just the weather for it and will do both you and him good, and
the little ones too. He says what a comfortable tea you had got
ready for him. Elizabeth's fare must be repaid to her. I think I
have told Papa *up* to today but I have not told him any more.
Ly Coltman is out, and I am sitting in a great large quiet airy bedroom, high up in the house; as large as our drawing room. It is
before lunch,—at 4 we are to go with the Dean of Hereford, and
the Dean of Salisbury (for a good Unitarian Ly Coltman knows a
mighty number of Deans) to see Mr Nashs reformatory schools,
in Westminster. Mr Nash was a clerk and has given up his life

<hr>

[1] Original MS. not seen.

and his time to reforming criminals for some years past. Sending out as many as 100 every year to the Colonies. When they come in —— Mrs Price has been calling and lunching here; and we are to have her to join us in our expedition to Mr Nash's at ¼ to 4. It is two now, and I want to rest and to get my dress ready for tonight when we are to dine at the Duckworths, and afterwards perhaps to go to the James Boothes. Tomorrow 17 people dine here[—]Mr and Lady Coltman and myself, the Dean of St Pauls, Mrs Milman and their son, Sir Charles and Lady Trevelyan—those are all I know who are coming. Ly Trevelyan is cousin to Mrs Price and sister to Macaulay. Tell Papa here is a note just come in (via Bloomsbury Sq.) from Mrs Milman, inviting him and me to breakfast at the Deanery *today*; and Lady Coltman has just also popped in to say Mr Hallam has been to meet us there at breakfast. On Saturday I go to Crix with a return ticket for Monday. Monday there is a dinner party here. Tuesday at the Monckton Milnes—and Ly Coltman plans to take me to the Zoological Gardens which I have never seen and Kensal Green Cemetery some day. I wish I could hit on some little article of dress, not *very* ⟨. . .⟩

193 **198*a*** *1986

MARIANNE GASKELL[1]

[May-June 1854]

My dearest Polly,

I must write to you and try to get in a note to Julia too, as I promised her one yesterday; only I was so glad to get your letter, love. About my coming to Poulton, I don't think it's at all likely I shall come. I think it is rather more likely I shall go to London: though that's not very likely; but if I came to Poulton I should like you to be there; because I am sure sea is good for you, and you'll have no other sea-chance this year: I am as thankful as can be to have you there, because I do hope it will set up your health; and you must mind and take care of yourself. I am glad to hear of the beer. Take it regularly, and get your medecine regularly, and don't take too long walks; and don't go out much alone, except on roads you know, and in the middle of the day. But *if you*

[1] Original MS. not seen.

ask Hearn at one end and your Uncle Langshawe at the other you can't be wrong. But be sure not to over-tire yourself. Be out of doors as much as possible. I don't think that money spent last week much. If the little Langshawe's come over, get buns, &c.—*what won't give Miss Robinson trouble*—ginger-bread or something. I *do* think Mr & Mrs Langshawe are charming and as you say he is so thoroughly good and true and kind, the source of his charming-ness lies in his out and out goodness, and that in his quiet deep religion. I shan't forget how that was brought to bear long ago on my shirking Miss Noble.

I have been thinking about Church. I quite agree with you in feeling more devotional in Church than in Chapel; and I wish our Puritan ancestors had not left out so much that they might have kept in of the beautiful and impressive Church service. But I always *do* feel as if the Litany—the beginning of it I mean,—and one or two other parts did so completely go against my belief that it would be wrong to deaden my sense of it's serious error by hearing it too often. It seems to me so distinctly to go against some of the clearest of our Saviour's words in which he so expressly tells us to pray to God alone. My own wish would be that you should go to Chapel in the morning, and to Church in the even-ing, when there is nothing except the Doxology to offend one's sense of *truth*. I am sure this would be *right* for me; although I am so fond of the Church service and prayers as a whole that I should feel tempted as you do. With our feelings and preference for the Church-service I think it is a temptation *not* to have a fixed belief; but I know it is wrong not to clear our minds as much as possible as to the nature of that God, and tender Saviour, whom we can not love properly unless we try and define them clearly to our-selves. Do you understand me my darling! I have often wished to talk to you about this. Then the one thing I *am* clear and sure about is this that Jesus Christ was not equal to His father; that, however divine a being he was *not* God; and that worship as God addressed to Him is therefore wrong in me; and that it is my duty to deny myself the gratification of constantly attending a service (like the morning service) in a part of which I thoroughly dis-agree, I like exceedingly going to afternoon service. But I must leave this subject now.

Pray don't take too long walks. I am afraid I never told you that I did not mind your reading Jane Eyre. I am reminded of it by Susy Gully's note. What is it about the ring? Yesterday I thought I should go to Emily Shaen's. Today is heaped up with its own little dilemmas and work. I am going out a round (tomorrow) of calls with Mrs Shuttleworth, and it is 11 now, and there is a School Committee tonight. I have written to Mme Mohl begging them to come here when they are in England. Poor Susy! I think it sounds very uncomfortable for her, poor girl! And I don't think you must go there love, I think you had better not show me her letters. You may be able to be a kind helping friend to her if she tells you all, and yet evidently there are things that should be told as little out of the house as possible. Everybody has their home-troubles; but the best way in general is hardly to acknowledge them even to oneself, much less make them the subject of conversation with others, out of the house especially. But Susy's are peculiar, and really seem to need confiding to some one, as she has no mother. Only, dear! I think you had better not show them to me for the reason I have named above. Your bonnet sounds beautiful and makes my mouth water! How pretty it will be with your green gown and lilac? Had not I good instinct. I fancy that Miss Kate Bond is very nice. I should like you to stay with the Langshawes, I am *very* fond of them indeed. But don't jump too easily at a kind speech, which might be made without much *household* consideration. Only if they really ask you *go*; ditto Mrs MacBreth. No! nobody can manage my worries, but myself. Some of them are clearing off a little; but I don't think the damp weather suits me, it makes me feel depressed and anxious about trifles. Chas Herford came about supplies; and Stephen W. to sit a bit last night,—just after I had come back from finding my woman in Oldham Road. Study being cleaned today.

Your own affect[ionat]e. El. Gaskell.

*198a 198*b* 202

MARIANNE GASKELL[1]

[?May–June 1854]

⟨. . .⟩ Only I hope you understand everything. I should be very glad if you could read the Psalms a little with the children on a

[1] Original MS. not seen.

Sunday. I want to go on with Joseph's history myself. I felt sorry
I had said what I did just at *last* dearest, before you went; only it is
true that I think there are some temptations to concealment etc.
in your friendship with Mr Ewart which have always made me
very uneasy; & do take care love against this. I wish you would
write & speak openly to me; if not of your thoughts & feelings at
all times at any rate of your wishes & troubles. But I must end.
The 'worry' relates to the congregation & I must try & arrange
matters without passing the 'worry' on to Papa; so I see no chance
of leaving home at present though I long to accept the invitation
renewed & *re*-renewed from E. Shaen.

Your own affec[tionate] mother
E. C. G.

205 **205+** 209

MARIANNE GASKELL[1]

Betley Hall
Newcastle Staffordshire
[15 June 1854]

My dearest Polly,

Newcastle is *seven* miles off alas! Thank you much for your
letters though they contain annoying news. I do not think either
of the sisters have behaved well. I warned Anne especially of the
heavy washes; and I cannot help fancying they must have heard
of some other places. But I must hear from you and from Margaret how far it would be desirable to make some different washing arrangement. It might be done; if it was very desirable to
keep Anne. Only if as you say, they neither of them seem inclined
to settle, they had better go. I am so sorry Caroline had to go. If
you write to Lancaster will you name our want? Servants seem
so very scarce anywhere that I do not know to whom to apply. I
wrote to Papa to Warrington yesterday. I was very nearly directing it to Manchester but it was quite as well I did not as he went
yesterday. I can't as yet fix my train, but I will before the end of
this letter and then *Will had better meet me with Tommy* as Katie is
bringing my large box and I have only a portmanteau and carpet
bag. I was *very* sorry love for your disappointment about the

<hr>

[1] Original MS. not seen.

Langshaws. It was very disappointing just at the last moment. Don't encourage any Brewster engagements for me; simply because I shall be more busy than I can well tell you and have no time for anything not necessary. This is a charming place after London, 4 miles from Crewe, not a pretty house but very large clean and old-fashioned, and, as it were in the depths of the country. On one side (it is in a park) an old fashioned flower garden full of flowers; on another a lawn with flower beds on it sloping down to a 'mere' beyond which is a rockery and a heronry. Such numbers of birds I never heard! I opened my[1] bedroom window at 3 this morning it was so delicious to hear them. Then a great last [*sic*] quiet bedroom is a luxury. The family consists of Mr Tollet, a year younger than Uncle Holland and 4 daughters, the *youngest* older than I am, quiet stately ladies very kind and good. Then there is a charming little grand daughter (mother dead) of 13. Minnie Clive; who is the darling of every body. Oh! will you copy Kebles' Evening Hymn for her some time. We are going a drive after 2 o'clock lunch and out in a boat on the mere after dinner in the evening. Leighton Buzzard was a great bustle; a great number of small rooms, each very full. Mr Stevenson good and conscientious but I don't like Mrs Stevenson, she is fussy and under-bred. Nice girls. Oh! I am so sleepy with this hot day! I will go home to-morrow *Friday* by the train that arrives in Manchester at 4-45 so will you send Will dear. Till then goodbye for I must go and be civil.

My dear love to the little ones
Yours most affect[ionate]ly
E. C. G.

209 209a 210

MARIANNE GASKELL[2]

Wednesday morning.
[13 September 1854]

My darling Minnie

We are so full of sad news—poor dear little Mimi[3] is dead! We did not know it till we came home; everybody in the house was so grieved about her. Everything in the way of care was taken of

---

[1] Source reads 'by'.   [2] Original MS. not seen.
[3] Source reads 'Minie', altered to 'Minnie'.

her darling. She was seen last one Saturday evening (the Saturday after you left) about $\frac{1}{2}$ p 7 playing happily with the black cat in the garden. Hearn missed her at $\frac{1}{2}$ past 9 and she and Margaret looked every where till $\frac{1}{2}$ past 11, garden house, coach house etc. In the morning she was found dead but with no marks of pain on her. Papa was sadly grieved and Jane and Hearn both cried in telling me. Darling I am so sorry! I am half ashamed of being so *very* sorry for the little pretty gentle playful animal when we think of the poor Duckworths. All we know as yet is from the TIMES, speaking of deaths from cholera in 5th reg. 'Senior Capt Duckworth dead'. 'Poor Capt Duckworth much lamented both by officers and men'. That is all we know at present. But I enclose you a note from Mimea[1] (which please consider *private* and burn *directly*) that came this morning from Ramsey; forwarded thence by post master. Then again Sarah Taylor (Miss Boyce's niece) is so ill I fear Meta (who is gone to enquire) will bring word of her death from brain fever at Leamington. Mrs Allen has been telegraphed for home from Venice. Poor Harriet and Marianne are at home—waiting for telegraph messages all by themselves! Meta is sadly out of spirits. I constantly come upon her and find her crying. We are all well thank God.

Mary Ewart comes home on Saturday. The Majors leave Nelson St to-morrow and Agnes goes to Humberstone in the afternoon to return with Mary. I enclose you a P.O. for £2 payable at Hampstead to pay Mrs Knight's bill (which I can't find anywhere) but which was somewhere about 35s for Meta's blue m.d. laine. Mrs Knight *ought* to deduct the mistaken carriage of the wrong box 3s4d but I don't know if she will. But if Miss Banks thinks you had better not go into London don't on any account. Papa was there a fortnight ago and says the smells were awful. *If* you go don't tire yourself and don't miss any regular meal by going; better go at ⟨   ⟩ *very if*. I owe a Good morrow Phillippian to Wm Shaen and I wanted to get him an ivory set of pocket tablets; nice and good. But I could easily get them here, anything better than risk your health my darling. Jane is leaving; gave me notice on Monday, to return to Mrs Gibsons, she had engaged herself there before I came back and is very anxious to go soon before Miss Lilla's marriage. Rather shabby I think and so does Margaret who is very indignant. A worse acct of Sarah Taylor—she is still alive. Both doctors have given up all

[1] ? Minna.

hope. Miss Boyce still *hopes*. Poor girls! Do write to Meta soon love. She is so very *quietly* sad and so good and silent about her own feelings in trying to make the little ones happy. We are going to keep Julia's birthday on Saty; Hallé's,[1] Leislers and a cake. Jane Stuart is going to Paris for the winter. Meta will like to hear about Festival. Miss Noble is very ill; many people think she won't recover. Mr Stevenson wrote to tell me to break to Sarah Elliott that her father and brother both died in one night of Cholera. She is in terrible grief. I *rather* think of taking her in Jane's place. But just now I don't feel as if I could fix on anything. Mr Chorley is not going to Norwich. My darling write to us, if only to tell us you are well. Meta is making a strong pull for Maggie Holland to go to Mrs Lalor's. My kind love to Miss Banks. Ask her and Eveleen here at Xmas. I never saw Meta so depressed. I went to her last night (papa wanted me to go with him to drink tea at Miss Marslands or I would not have left her) when I came home. It was in the dark and I kissed her and her cheeks were wet with tears and she said 'oh poor Mimi' and then she talked of Mimi[2] and then of the Taylors and I had nothing cheerful to tell her and to-night Papa and I are going to the Ewarts and they've no room for her. And Agnes keeps dwelling on the misery of the D's and the pain poor people must have suffered to Meta. And Mrs Ewart is terribly out of spirits. We *don't* expect you home in the least dear. Only write to Meta and take care of your own health.

Your very affec[tionate]
E. C. G.

The only smile I have got up on Meta's face was by telling her you were between 20 and 30 yesterday.

234*a* 242*a* 246

MARIANNE GASKELL[3]

Tuesday morning
[?5 June 1855]

My dearest Polly,
    I promise to answer every letter you write to Meta, but I don't

---

[1] Source reads 'Halli's'.
[2] Source reads 'Minnie' and 'Minie' in this sentence.
[3] Original MS. not seen.

know if I can always write long letters. Your letter to-day had all
the interest of a novel. We quaked about your gown, we were in
despair. What will our heroine do in such a dilemma? When lo
and behold the good fairy steps in and makes your fate end happier than *my* heroines generally do. But oh what heat to dance in!
and who is Mrs Douglas Halford? Don't do anything that annoys
Mrs James while you are staying with her. You will very likely
find ways and means of seeing and doing people and things if you
wait a little patiently, my darling. I do so long and pray for more
patience myself. This hot weather over-does me a good deal. But
however I am going on right ahead only sometimes wishing a
little for Hearn. Let me see, I wrote last on Tuesday. In the evening Miss Mitchell came to supper. She was very full of Mr Coates'
sale (Pendleton) where she is going to buy one or two things for
her new house. Meta had been to Birch Church in the afternoon
with Katie and the S. School in the morning so she was sadly
tired. I went to bed early. Yesterday we planned to go and call on
Mrs Errington and I was puzzled how to do it wisely and well.
Meta and I walked some distance took a cab the rest of the way,
found the regt on parade and all the officers busy, Mrs Errington
too ill to see any one (she caught a bad cold the night of the ball)
left a sheaf of 5 cards, 2 Mrs Gaskell's and three Mr's and drove
off to the Square without seeing anyone. Then we met Katie and
I bought another gown; not very pretty, a kind of barège, tolerably cheap. I went meaning to buy it and *was not* tempted. Then
we went some errand of Katie's and then[1] suddenly I bethought me
in a fit of goodness that (like all *my* goodness only works me evil
—very immoral I know!) that I would give Meta some piece of
music, with 3 shillings I had, to practise while you were away so
we wended our way to Hime & Beales when lo! there were Mrs
Birley and Mrs Genbryer; very gracious and sweet almost affectionate; giving a message from 'Sir Henry' to Meta, something
about cutting or not cutting her one Sunday in the fields near
Birch *and* then she asked Meta to go with her to the Theatre on
Thursday, urging her and me very very much till one did not
know how to refuse her. Mrs Birley joined, 'no gentlemen of the
party except the Capt and Heming'. Meta evidently wanted extremely to go and all I could gain was a respite to 'consult Papa'.
He left it to me; and I thought and thought and I hope I have
done right in letting her go. She was *very* good, begged to give

[1] Source repeats 'then'.

it up if it made me uncomfortable etc. but owned she should regret it much—and I thought it *possible* that the reality might be so dull and not [*sic*] that it would be better to let her have that than to be feeling much regret for something which she imagined would be very pleasant. But anxiety as to do right for her made me very tired the rest of the evening.

When we got here—Katie was coming to tea—I found Papa had just answered the enclosed note from Mr Potter in the negative saying his feelings were in favor of accepting, his judgment against it, on account of lessons. On the whole I am not sorry as I mean somehow to give the children a holiday when Meta goes with me to Betley—sometime before the end of this month, as Emily comes to us at the beginning of next. Flossy, contrary to all expectation is *so* good. *Did A. Shaen say*[1] *anything to you on the journey about Crix for F. E.*[2] *and Julia. Of course you won't shew my notes or tell their contents as regards Meta to anyone. Mary Ewart or Mrs James not excepted.* Susanna came to tea so handsomely dressed. Stephen later on, bringing a suddenly very bad account of Mrs Winkworth[3] who had been so ill on Saturday night that he had had to take a coach and come over to Manchester for Mr Dunville. Katie and Susy were very much vexed with him that he had not come for them. Very bad spasms of a very serious kind. Katie has been to see Mr Dunville before returning to Alderley this morning and brings word he will order her to Malvern, and then it makes Emily's coming down at all till late autumn uncertain. I never knew such an *un*certain year. Such an impossibility of getting anything fixed! I have written a private note to Bristol Mr James begging him to urge Papa to join him. No more news or letters. F. E.[2] and Julia went to Mrs Shuttleworth's yesterday to meet the Philipses but brought back no news but that Miss Noble was better.

Ever thine own dear Mammy.

[1] Source reads 'saying'.   [2] Source reads 'F. G.'.
[3] Source reads 'Winbrook'.

257 **259*a*** *264a*

ELLEN NUSSEY[1]

Plymouth Grove,
Manchester
July 27th 1855

Dear Miss Nussey.

I am extremely obliged to you for your kind answer to my almost illegible note. I wrote it with Inn pen & ink at Skipton, where we were detained that Monday night after our visit to Haworth. I am sure you can be of more service to me than any one else, because you have been her dear friend for so many years, and must have known her through all the progress of her character. From what I can judge from the letters Mr Nicholls has entrusted me with, her very earliest way of expressing her-self must have been different to common; and I look forward with deep personal interest, (independent of the value of any materials they may furnish me with for my difficult & terribly interesting task) to the reading of any of them which you may think it right to entrust me with. I am sorry Miss Wooler shrank from the idea of my coming to see you at Ilkley as you thought of. As you say it would have been better to talk about her on the hills, and in the free open air than in a room, and moreover I should much like to see Miss Wooler. You must not think of returning home a day sooner on my account. But I am afraid that all that August 6th to August 11th week, I am fully occupied. May I come over for a day at the beginning of the following week, *not* Monday. If you do not object to this time may I take silence for consent, I write a little nearer to the time and fix the exact day.

Yours very truly
E. C. Gaskell

[1] Original MS. not seen.

*259*a* **264*a*** *264*b*

ELLEN NUSSEY[1]

Lindeth Tower,
Silverdale,
Nr Lancaster.
[*c.* 7–10 August 1855]

Dear Miss Nussey,

I am going to Manchester on Monday next—the thirteenth—
and if it would suit you for me to come over to Birstal on
Tuesday the fourteenth by the train that leaves Manchester at 8.50
and arrives at Birstal at 10.55 I should be very glad indeed to do
so. I should leave at 4.5 that afternoon, and perhaps I could contrive to see Miss Wooler before then, what do you think? Would
she allow me to see her? I should particularly wish to do so, but
as I don't know distances, and as I fear Miss Wooler may dislike
seeing me, I must ask if you think she would allow me to call. If
Tuesday did not suit you, would Wednesday be better? I am sure
you will kindly tell me the truth if possible by return of post. I
am here with my children by the sea, but I am obliged to go to
Manchester on business on Monday next.

Believe me to remain, Dear Miss Nussey,
Yours very truly,
E. C. Gaskell.

*264*a* **264*b*** *267*

ELLEN NUSSEY[2]

Lindeth Tower,
Silverdale,
Saturday Aug. 11th [1855]

My Dear Miss Nussey,

It is my full intention to come to Birstall on Tuesday morning
next: but if anything *should* happen to make this inconvenient to
you, will you write to me at Plymouth Grove, Manchester,

---

[1] Original MS. not seen.   [2] Original MS. not seen.

whither I go on Monday next. I should so very much like to see Miss Wooler that it is my present plan to be able to *cram* a journey on to Ilkley into Tuesday: but I am entirely ignorant of distances, and the length of time it takes to get from one place to another, so that I think I must be guided by your kind advice when I get to Birstal, especially as I agree with you that it would be better to take Miss Wooler by surprise. I am very much obliged to you for asking me to stay all night: I should much prefer getting back to Manchester on Tuesday night: but if it is decided that I go on to Ilkley, and *if* that makes me too late for the last return train to Manchester, I shall very thankfully avail myself of your kindness. I write in great haste to catch the post in this out-of-the-way place.

Yours very truly,
E. C. Gaskell.

264b **267** *267a*

ELLEN NUSSEY[1]

Lindeth Tower,
Silverdale,
Thursday Sept. 6th [1855]

My Dear Miss Nussey,

    Your letter has been forwarded to me here where my family and I are staying: I have been here ever since I saw you with the exception of a little journey to see 'Cowan's Bridge.' We (Marianne and I) go on to Glasgow tomorrow and shall remain there about three weeks, after which we go home and are stationary. Will the end of this month be too late for me to avail myself of the opportunity you offer me of seeing Miss Wooler? My Glasgow address is Charles Wilson's Esq., 286, Battle[2] Crescent, Glasgow. I have not been very well or strong since I saw you, but still nothing to complain of. A large family (and we had friends staying with us) in the country where there were literally no shops, makes rather a busy life for a housekeeper. I have been too busy to write a line beyond necessary letters, and not always even them. I have read *once* over all the letters you so kindly

---

[1] Original MS. not seen.   [2] This is given as 'Bath' in the next letter.

entrusted me with, and I don't think even you, her most cherished friend could wish the impression on me to be different from what it is, that she was one to study the path of duty well, and having ascertained what it was right to do, to follow out her idea strictly. They give one a very beautiful idea of her character. I like the one you send today much. I shall be glad to see any others you will allow me to see. I am sure the more fully she, Charlotte Brontë—the *friend* the *daughter* the *sister* the *wife* is known—and known where need be in her own words—the more highly will she be appreciated. I had a letter from Mr Brontë about a week ago, but he does not give any definite particulars (I have so bad a headache I think I should not have written to anyone but you, but I am anxious to reply to your letter, although I am in such pain that I seem hardly to know if I am writing sense).

Believe me to remain, Dear Miss Nussey, With very kind regards to Mrs Clapham.

*267 **267a** *268a

ELLEN NUSSEY[1]

Dunoon,
Argyleshire
Sept. 25th 1855.

My dear Miss Nussey,

I am staying here with my unknown half sister, whom it is 24 years, as I think I told you, since I met: and who of course is almost unknown to me. Marianne is with me, and I believe we shall remain among our relations in Scotland until somewhere about the end of next week; i.e. about Sept. [*sic*] 5 or 6th. If it suited you for me to come over to you on Monday following, October 8th and remain all night under your kindly roof-tree, or if the Thursday following would suit better—on either day I should be most glad to avail myself of your kind proposal that I should meet Miss Wooler. On the 10th (the Wednesday in that week) a servant, who has been with us for sometime, leaves us to set up dress-making, and I must be at home to instal another in her place. Marianne is very much obliged to you for including

---

[1] Original MS. not seen.

her in your kind invitation, but she will have a good deal to do at home after her long absence, and desires me to say that she should not like to leave so soon again. We both, however, hope that when I see you, I can fix a time with you, when you can come over and make acquaintance with our home. Marianne was touched even to tears (and she is not a demonstrative person) when I told her how you cared for her from what Miss Brontë had said about her.

We met Dr Scoresby the other day at Sir John Maxwell's: to my surprise he told me that he had been vicar of Bradford for some years and knew Mr Brontë well in those days. He told me many curious anecdotes about the extraordinary character of the people round Haworth.

With kind regards to your sister

Believe me to remain, Dear Miss Nussey,
Yours most truly,
E. C. Gaskell

286, Bath Crescent, Glasgow, is the safest address, if you will kindly reply.

*267a **268a** *270a

ELLEN NUSSEY[1]

Plymouth Grove,
Thursday
Oct. 4th '55

My dear Miss Nussey,

I came home last night and this morning I have received your letter forwarded to me from Glasgow. I shall be very glad indeed to come to you on Monday next by the train that leaves Manchester at 11.45, and arrives at Birstall[2] at 1.50. I plan leaving on Tuesday by the 12.40 train, and so I think that *probably* Monday will be the best day for me to try and see Roe[3] Head, but a good deal would depend upon the time which would enable me to see the most of Miss Wooler, and if, from any cause Tuesday suited you better, I could put off my return till the 4.10 train; only, as our servant will leave early the next day, I might be wanted at

[1] Original MS. not seen.　　[2] Source reads 'Bristol'.　　[3] Source reads 'Row'.

home to see after a few final things before her departure. I have got a successor who promised well, for all but two things, gifts in reality, but exposing one[1] to temptation I fear in a place like this, beauty and youth.

With kind regards to your sister—Thank you

Yours most truly,

E. C. Gaskell

268a **270*a*** *271a*

ELLEN NUSSEY[2]

[*c.* 20 October 1855]

Dear Miss Nussey,

I am overwhelmed with business and I believe this is the *second* letter only I have had time to write since I saw you—The first was to Mr Smith, to whom I wrote the day after I returned to Brookroyd,—I was very urgent asking for any papers, letters, &c.—and quoting his own words as 'any materials he had being at my service,' &c.—but, although more than ten days since I wrote I have received no answer, which vexes, annoys and disappoints me.

Thank you much for your enclosures. I wish I had more leisure, but it is my busiest time of the year just now, and our house has been and is, almost fuller than it will hold of company, for whose amusement and entertainment I have to plan each day. I think with much pleasure on my two half-days with you. Though I did not gain much *direct* information from Miss Wooler, I made her personal acquaintance and that is a great satisfaction for now I can apply to her by letter in a far easier and more confidential way, when I want, as I know I shall, to ask direct questions, at certain points of my narrative. I am glad I saw Oakwell Hall too,—*very* glad. I think I dare not ask Mr Brontë for those letters unless I go over and see him, and I must go soon, and make a final attempt on Mr Nicholls to see if he will allow me to see any of her papers. What would you advise me to do about Mr Smith? Thank you for your kind message to my home circle—They send kind regards to you, and sincerely hope to make your acquaintance before long. Dear Miss Nussey I am so glad we have begun to know

---

[1] Source reads 'me'.

[2] Original MS. not seen. Typescript dates this letter 'Jan./56.'

each other! Remember me most kindly to your sister, and ever
believe me,

Yours most truly,

E. C. Gaskell.

---

*270a **271a** *275+

ELLEN NUSSEY[1]

November 3rd '55.[2]

My Dear Miss Nussey,

At last—and by dint of a very cross letter, I have heard from
Mr Smith apologising &c., and enclosing about 20 letters, some
of them only fragments of dear Miss Brontë's. The remainder, he
says contain matter of too purely personal a nature to be generally
interesting, but with these he says I may do as I like if I will only
take care to return them to him. He is very civil, more civil than
satisfactory. However, when I have time—(Oh! precious com-
modity! where are you hiding yourself?) I shall follow your
advice and present myself at Cornhill some fine morning and see
what conversation may do. For I am sure I have not got half of
what Mr Williams and he together *might* give: and what they
shall give, or I'll know the reason why. And I am more than half
tempted, being in London, to go on to Brussels and have a look
at M. & Madame Heger. At present all the cousins and friends I
have seen on the wing, and are volunteering visits, visits that
would be most charming and acceptable at any other time, but I
so want to get on with my writing just now and I do so want to
see Messrs Smith & Williams—and yet I am not and shall not be
able all this month at any rate. The letters Mr Smith does send,
principally relate to the other Brontë's transactions with Newby,
or else they are (very clever) criticism on Thackeray, man and
writings. I had my second cross letter before I received your last,
so I still retain the arguments you suggest as weapons against the
refractory Dr John. I have had so bad a pain in my side all week
that I have been good for nothing, or I would have written
sooner. My kind love to your sister. Your help and sympathy do

[1] Original MS. not seen.   [2] Source reads '56'.

me a great deal of good in my perplexing search for materials. How is Miss Wooler?

Yours most truly,
E. C. Gaskell.

Any chance of borrowing Scatcherd's History of Birstall &c? Are not *you* Caroline Helstone?

*271a 275+ *275a

ELLEN NUSSEY[1]

Plymouth Grove
Decr 17th, 1855.

My Dear Miss Nussey,

Mama is so terribly busy that she really cannot find time to write to you, but she has asked me to do so for her, as she cannot bear that you should remain any longer unthanked for your most interesting account of Miss Anne Brontë's death at Scarborough, which she has had much pleasure in reading, and which she hopes you will allow her to make use of in the Memoir. She is sadly afraid that you will think her ungrateful for not having written sooner to acknowledge it, but she hopes you will understand that it is want of time which has prevented her doing so, and I am sure I can testify to the many calls which there have been upon her time for these last few weeks. First of all one of the servants was taken suddenly ill, and from her perpetual ravings the medical man feared typhus fever, so of course Mama had to pay her the greatest care—Happily it turned out to be nothing worse than a very severe attack of influenza. Ever since that there has been a succession of visitors staying in the house, which has quite prevented her from writing any but the merest business letters. She has received several letters of Mrs Nicholls' from Mr Smith, and she hopes to learn from them many particulars about their intercourse when she goes to London this next spring, as she thinks she shall have to do. She has also received a packet of letters from Mr Williams, (another London publisher, I believe), which she says are almost more beautiful than any others of Miss Brontë's that she has seen.

[1] Original MS. not seen.

She is out at this present moment; if she were at home I am sure she would desire her love to you, but instead will you kindly accept my best wishes for a Merry Christmas and happy New Year, and believe me, My Dear Miss Nussey,

Yours most truly,

Meta E. Gaskell.

*275+ 275a *276a

ELLEN NUSSEY[1]

[*c.* 20 December 1855]

My Dear Miss Nussey,

(This is me and not my daughter). I *do* want you to come, I should be very glad indeed to see you as soon as you could come after the 11th of January (till when our spare room is occupied) but it will be but fair to tell you that this would be entirely for my own *pleasure* (and I hope a little for yours also) in making you acquainted with my home people, as I have not yet written a line of the Memoir. I literally have had no time; all the very little leisure I possess (not taken up beforehand by positive family duties and engagements) has been taken up in writing such letters as to Mr Smith, to old schoolfellows of Miss Brontë's at Cowan's Bridge &c. I hoped to have got at any rate ¼ written before the New Year; but as I said before, I have not had time to write a word of the actual biography. I have no idea *who* put in that little paragraph, I once thought it must have been Mr Smith; but he seems too indifferent to have taken even that much trouble. I have never heard from Haworth since the end of August; I hope still to go over there before Spring, as I feel that I can do so much more by *seeing* people than by writing. Of course this takes me a much longer time, but I think the result will be all the more satisfactory. The very first hours of leisure I have shall be given to this precious work. Thank you, I tried several places (you see even such a thing as that takes a good amount of letter writing) and at last I have succeeded in procuring a copy. Yes! it was our new maid, but I think her illness has endeared her to us, she bore it so patiently and well. Miss Brontë's letters to Mr Williams *are* very

<hr>

[1] Original MS. not seen.

fine and genial. She seems heartily at her ease with him; which I
don't think she does in those I have seen to Mr Smith. I feel so
sorry to think that my hope and expectation of having a portion
of my work done by this time, has been the means of delaying
your visit to the South. Will you and can you come here on the
way South. I shall *extremely* like to have you for our visitor, but
it would not be right to conceal from you the actual state of
nothingness in which the Memoir is at present. About your
account of Anne Brontë's death we will talk when I see you, it
seems to me very desirable to have it from an eye-witness. My
girls desire to be very kindly remembered to you. Will you give
my kindest regards to Mrs Clapham and believe me ever most
truly yours,

E. C. Gaskell.

A Merry Christmas and a happy New Year to you and yours.

*275a 276a *276b

ELLEN NUSSEY[1]

January 7th '56.

My dear Miss Nussey,
    I have been trying to get off an engagement of rather long
standing by which I promised to go and see a friend when sent
for. She begs me to come to her on the 14th, (next Monday) and
remain the week: and I believe no time will suit her so well: so
I can only hope that *that* would not have been the time at which
you would have fixed to come, but pray let me know as soon as
ever you ⟨. . .⟩[2] I should be so sorry if any of them interfered
with the great pleasure of seeing you under this roof.

---

[1] Original MS. not seen.
[2] About three and a half lines left blank in typescript source.

*276a **276b** *280a

ELLEN NUSSEY[1]

Plymouth Grove
January 9th [1856]

My dear Miss Nussey,
 I was very sorry to receive your letter this morning: for we had
all begun to look forward to your visit with great pleasure, and
yet from what you say I see it *will* be better to postpone it till you
return from the South. It would be only (I will hope) for *mutual*
pleasure now: then I really do hope that you may find me with a
good stretch of work done, when probably a good talk over with
you may do me a great deal of service. I believe now my engagements are clearing away, and that I shall soon be able to set to
work in real earnest. I do not feel however as if this delay has been
lost time, as I have got the form of the work pretty well arranged
in my head. I am going to write for Miss Brontë's letters (if I
dare!) Thank you for paving the way so nicely and kindly. My
love to your sister—and my girls send you theirs.
                              Yours most truly,
                                  E. C. Gaskell

*276b **280a** 294

ELLEN NUSSEY[2]

Plymouth Grove,
Friday Feb. 22nd, [1856]

Dear Miss Nussey,
 I am writing at Mama's request as she is too busy now to do
any writing, to say that she is quite unable to give you the information respecting the memoirs that your letter seems to desire.
She has begun it and written about 20 pages, but of course interruptions will come and come unexpectedly, therefore she begs
me to say that it is quite impossible to give you any idea of when
it will be finished. There are two seasons in the year when it is

---

[1] Original MS. not seen.   [2] Original MS. not seen.

best to publish, Easter and November. *Certainly* it will not be completed by this Autumn and it is hardly likely to be ready for the Easter after, so that the Autumn following is the more probable time, though she cannot at all tell whether it will be finished then. She thinks the interest of the public will not have subsided. The two great biographies that have come out lately 'Arthur Stanley's Life of Dr. Arnold' and 'Lady Holland's Life of Sydney Smith' have both been written eight or ten years after the death of the subjects of the memoirs and yet the interest has not been wanting for them in the eyes of the public.

Mama sends her kindest regards, and believe me to remain,

Yours sincerely,

Marianne Gaskell.

₀ **285a** ₀

UNKNOWN[1]

Parham Place, Wednesday Eveng
[?30 April ?1856]

Dear Madam,

I am extremely obliged to you for the two letters of introduction which you have kindly sent me through Mr Greg. They *exactly* meet my wants; and I feel very grateful to you. I shall certainly try to go to Malines to see Madame de Brouwer, and thank you for your minute directions where to find her.

Believe me to remain

Yours truly

E. C. Gaskell

[1] Original MS. not seen. Typescript source describes it as 2 pp., 8vo. It was presented to a Mrs Edgerley of Menston.

MARIANNE GASKELL[1]

> Victoria Hotel
> Euston Square.
> Tuesday morning (Eliza's room)
> [?6 May 1856]

My own dearest Polly,

I must not leave England without a line or two to you darling child. We go to-night by the route you planned via Dover & Ostend. Eliza is here all safe & right; so far so good! But so many other things have gone wrong[2] that I am in despair & can hardly keep from perpetually crying which is partly being so overtired. Ldy C. begged for the children (on Tuesday) to stay *over Monday* to see the Academy Exhibition; & by her directions I wrote *one* letter (& I had before posted 2 by the butler's directions) all to tell Papa by Monday evening's post that the children will not be coming till to-day. Well he never got them! Lady C. heard the Exhibition was *not* open on Monday so the children never went; while all the time it *was* open & they might have gone & to-day came 2 letters from Papa; one posted on Sunday desiring an immediate acknowledgment of enclosure, & another last night, miserable about children. Oh! I am *so* sorry. Moreover—oh I have forgotten what I have got to say. The children went to a child's party at Sir James Clark's last night, & met Gertrude Holland. Write to me

> Chez Mme Haydon
> 47 Avenue Soison d'Or,
> Porte Louise,
> Bruxelles.

Dearest love to Jennie

> Your very affect[ionate]
> E. C. G.

> Lady Matilda Maxwell
> 21 Dover Street
> (Brown's Hotel)

is leaving very soon.
Call on Mrs James be here.
Your white muslin gown is (with Meta's) at E. in a packing box

---

[1] Original MS. not seen.   [2] MS. source omits 'have gone wrong'.

ELLEN NUSSEY[1]

Plymouth Grove,
Tuesday July 15th, 1856.

My Dear [Miss] Nussey,

As I have come I am taking some of the writing off Mama's hands, and therefore you are receiving a letter from me instead of from her. She begs me to thank you very much for your letter which contained some very wise and kind advice. There are so many questions she wants to ask you and that is the reason you are so soon again to be troubled with another letter.

Miss Brontë in one of her letters to you (Mama *thinks* written in the year 1835,) gives you some advice as to what books to read. Mama wants to know how Miss Brontë can have become acquainted with the books that she mentions to you. From Keighley Mama knows she could get novels but where such standard works as Miss Brontë refers to in her letters were obtained is a puzzle to Mama. At Haworth Mama says she did not see many books except quite new ones that had been given to Miss Brontë since she became famous. If you would kindly let her know all you know.

Mama also wants to know if you think before her visit to Haworth she had better let Mr Brontë know that she is coming or take them unawares? She wants to go either this week or next, after that time she will not be able to go for some weeks. She is afraid it seems making too great a fuss if she writes beforehand and yet not knowing what their engagements are, if she goes without letting them know, she is afraid it might be inconvenient. So if you would tell her what you think would be the best she will be very much obliged to you. She wants to know if the aunt made favourites? What were Emily's religious opinions? Did she ever make friends? How did they spend their time at home between leaving Roehead and going out as governesses? Whether Charlotte ever *wrote* stories at Miss Wooler's? Mama is afraid she is very troublesome, but things occur to her often when she is writing, that she wants to know, often more to fill up the picture in her own mind, than for any publishing purposes, for instance she wants to know whether the aunt ill treated the children,

[1] Original MS. not seen.

as she fancies Miss Brontë once told her that Mrs Reid's treatment of Jane Eyre was very similar to what they experienced from their aunt. Mama desires me to give you her love and

> Believe me to remain,
> Yours very truly,
> Marianne Gaskell.

*294a 297a *310a

Ellen Nussey[1]

> Plymouth Grove,
> Friday July 25th, 1856.

My dear Miss Nussey,

Mama went to Haworth yesterday with Sir James Kay Shuttleworth. Mr Brontë was ill with rheumatism, but he got up to receive her. Martha was away from home so they had only a little girl to do for them. However, Mama lunched at the Inn, so they were in no way disturbed by their coming. Mr Nicholls gave Mama the Professor, and all that was written of Miss Brontë's new novel. Altogether, the visit was very satisfactory and Mama has come back in very good spirits about the result of the visit.

> Yours (in great haste) sincerely & truly,
> Marianne Gaskell.

*297a 310a *322a

Ellen Nussey[2]

> Plymouth Grove,
> Thursday Sept. 11th, 1856.

My Dear Miss Nussey,

Mama has just got in the Memoir to the year 1846, and that is the year the Poems by Ellis, Acton and Currer Bell were published. Mama did not find any allusion to their publication in the letters and she wants to know can and will you be so kind as to

---

[1] Original MS. not seen.   [2] Original MS. not seen.

tell any facts connected with their publication that you can remember. She is working away most indefatigably, but so many things have to be woven in about '46 that it makes it very difficult.

Believe me to remain,
Most sincerely yours,
Marianne Gaskell.

274 **314a** 315

W. S. WILLIAMS[1]

Tuesday, Plymouth Grove
[October 1856]

My Dear Sir,

I have been ill, and since both weak and lazy, otherwise I should have thanked you for your most interesting letter before now. I received it when I was not allowed to write any letters, or indeed to read any. It was particularly interesting as being the *other side* of an account I had already received. I will enclose you the letter to which I refer, for I am sure you will be interested in reading it, and you deserve some better regard for your kindness than I can give you myself. It is a copy of a letter Miss Brontë wrote to Miss Taylor (Rose Yorke)[2] her friend in New Zealand. Don't hurry yourself to return the letter. I shall know it is safe, I shall like to have it back again sometime, but I shan't want it for a month or two yet.

Yours ever very truly,
E. C. Gaskell

[1] Original MS. not seen.   [2] Source reads 'Yorks'.

*310*a* **322***a* *322*b*

ELLEN NUSSEY[1]

Plymouth Grove
Thursday December 11th. [1856]

My dear Miss Nussey,

I am again going to ask you a question for Mama. She has a most decided impression almost amounting to certainty that Miss Brontë told her that at the time of the publication of Jane Eyre, Bramwell Brontë was in such a state that they never told him either of its being written or of the great success it met with. Mama is as sure as she can be that Miss Brontë told[2] her that. It is a question she does not like to ask Mr Brontë but if you can give her an answer she will be very much obliged to you indeed. She is working very hard at the Memoir and she wants to know if you can come about January 12th and let her read it[3] to you. Independently of any reading we shall be so very glad to have you here so I hope you will be able to come.

With love from Mama
Believe me to remain,
Yours truly,
Marianne Gaskell

*322*a* **322***b* *326*a*

ELLEN NUSSEY[4]

Dec. 18th 1856.

My dear Miss Nussey,

I don't know if you received a letter I wrote about a week ago, asking you how Bramwell Brontë received the news of the publication of 'Jane Eyre' or whether he was even told. Mama has an impression that Miss Brontë told her[5] he had never been told. Also Mama wants to know if you can come and stay here on January 10th or thereabouts, and then Mama hopes to be able to

---

[1] Original MS. not seen.   [2] Source reads 'hold'.
[3] Source reads 'if'.   [4] Original MS. not seen.
[5] Source reads 'here'.

read you the Memoir. Mama is working away desperately hard at present. As soon as you can send us an answer as to whether you can come to us we shall be glad as some other plans are depending upon it. I hope, and so does Mama, very much that you will be able to come.

I am writing in great haste so excuse more.

Yours very sincerely,

Marianne Gaskell.

*322*b* **326a** *327*

ELLEN NUSSEY[1]

42, Plymouth Grove

Dec. 26th [1856]

My dear Miss Nussey,

I believe the other day when I wrote to you I stupidly mentioned the 10th as the day on which we hoped to have the pleasure of seeing you, but the 12th was the day I ought to have said. Monday was the day I had in my mind but I had got the date wrong. Monday January 12th is the day when we hope to see you here. Mama joins me in Christmas wishes and

Believe me to remain

Yours sincerely,

Marianne Gaskell

352 **353a** *360a*

ELLEN NUSSEY[2]

Plymouth Grove

Friday Morning

[19 June 1857]

Dearest Miss Nussey,

Mama wants me to write to you and tell you how glad we shall all be to see you on Tuesday evening, or Wednesday morning, for as long as ever you can stay.

---

[1] Original MS. not seen.   [2] Original MS. not seen.

We have seen nothing of Mrs Dugdale since we came back, but I so often think of that lovely face and long for another sight of it.

We shall be so glad to see you again, dear Miss Nussey, for we did so enjoy your last stay here.

Ever yours affectionately,

Meta Gaskell

*353a **360a** *362a

ELLEN NUSSEY[1]

Plymouth Grove

Friday. [?10 July 1857]

My Dear Miss Nussey,

Mama's love and she begs me to tell you that she has been advised by many friends to put the revision of the third edition into other hands, so if you will write her a *formal* note, such a one that she can pass on to her publisher, telling all the corrections you, Miss Wooler and any of your friends wish made. She finds it really will be quite impossible for her to do it herself. We are all pretty much as you left us. Mr Norton has come and is now going to the Exhibition with Mama. Dear Miss Nussey, I really cannot write more. If you were here I could talk but writing I cannot manage.

Yours ever very affectionately,

Marianne Gaskell

*360a **362a** *381a

ELLEN NUSSEY[2]

July 23rd, '57.

My Dear Miss Nussey,

I have only time for two words. There is to be *no* preface,—*no* mark, foot-note or appendix of any kind. This enclosed sentence is to be inserted at page 12. More than that the publishers, lawyers

---

[1] Original MS. not seen.   [2] Original MS. not seen.

&c., say would not interest the 'public,' nor be read by them. I am going (utterly knocked up and ill) to Skelwith on Saturday next for four or five days. Mrs G, Mrs Preston's, Mill-Brow, Skelwith Bridge, Ambleside.

Write and say if you approve. Wedding put off till next November, December or January *12 months*—to take place in Egypt, whither Capt Hill comes to meet her. He sails Sept. 4.

Yours ever affect[ionately]
E. C. G.

372 376*a* *404a*

MARIANNE GASKELL[1]

Sea Scale
near Whitehaven.
Friday
[?9 October 1857][2]

My dearest Polly,

Here we are very merry but very disconsolate if you understand what that means. Our spirits are good but our prospect is dull; our bedroom is large & (oh so) airy but very boisterous & cold. This morning (we got here in the dark last night) I said to Meta—'Look out at that window & tell me what you can see'. The sea & rain quoth she—'Look out at the other' (at right angles) '& tell me what you can see'. 'The sea & rain' again. Since then & directly after breakfast we have been out on the shore (we can throw a stone into the sea at high tide out of our windows) & there is a very fine sea certainly & flat sand hills all round & far away 8 miles off mountains. Our inn is a very dreary respectable place—where they give us 2 bedrooms, sitting room, 4 meals a

---

[1] Original MS. not seen. Sources give address and date as follows: Miss Gaskell | Plymouth Grove | Manchester. | Oct. 19. 1877 [*sic*].

[2] The date given with the address of this letter is obviously impossible. The sense suggests a date between Marianne's returning home from and Florence's going away to school, i.e. between 1853 and 1858. The only year in this period on which 19 October fell on a Friday was in 1855, but from knowledge of Mrs Gaskell's whereabouts in October this date, and likewise those of 1854 and 1858, are most unlikely. Of the remaining years 1857 is more probable than 1856, and in addition would fit better with the date actually given. If the date was originally read from a postmark, it may have been 9 October 1857, which was a Friday.

day, fire & light for 4s 6d, but half an hour after we got here we were tired of the place, not but what we are very well. Meta a *great* deal better than when we left—in spite of fatigue & being on our legs a great deal. She is writing & telling Papa our adventures —which were briefly these. On the way down to the Station, I tried to persuade her that Southport was very charming—but I found she would only be *resigned* to go there; so we determined to follow your plan; & went to Lancaster; arrived there $\frac{1}{2}$ an hour too late, & so too late for the train to Morecambe. We might have taken a carriage but thought the expense too great; so we wandered into the town speculating whether we would call on any of our friends. There was a great bustle, a confirmation going on, so we did not like going to the Langshawes, & were thinking of Richard & Eliza when Meta was suddenly taken with the[1] pangs of hunger (very luckily as it turned out) so we went & got cold beef, bread & beer in a 'pot house' (i.e. Kings Arms Hotel) & had just time to hurry back & go to Silverdale. We got there at $\frac{1}{2}$ p. 4, left our luggage at the Station & tramped to Mrs Thornton's, got a gentleman for the winter—to the P.O. when we met Mr Jackson & he & Miss Rawlinson joined in saying we should get no lodgings, inn full with 6 ladies. Miss R. never offered her rooms, indeed they have a 3rd person living with them, either friend or servant, a family at the Blacksmiths going to stay a fortnight longer. Down we went to Pratts, which was dirty & damp. Mrs Bate apologized 'it had never had its summer clearing—& they were all busy in the potatoes harvest—never took in anyone without a servant as she had her own little family, cows etc.'—on learning who we were she said well if we could get no where else she would ask her husband when he came in & if he gave leave & she could have a couple of days for cleaning she would see if she could manage with us—but then again when she heard it was only for a week or 10 days or a fortnight at most, she gave it up.

Then we went to Mrs Glom who said Arnside town Farm was full & repeated what she had sent word through Tommy about every place being engaged. However we thought Papa would be better pleased if we tried for ourselves & we went back to Miss Rawlinson & asked if she would not take us in, to which she reluctantly agreed if her rooms would do, but oh they are so small, sitting & bedrooms would leave a great space in Caroline's room if they were both put in it & *so* close—Miss Rawlinson & her sister

---

[1] Word not in MS. source.

& Meta & I all agreed that it might do for one (Susanna found it close for her you know) yet that two could never squeeze in; they could not let us have 2 rooms so off we went to Richmond's but they were in their house & had given up letting it—to the *old* Yew Tree butcher's. No! she would not have us without a servant & if we sent for one she would not be ready for two days & did not think she should like lodgers there; & she & her husband have the character of drinking. By this time it was dark & we had been on our feet coaxing people to have us all the time & now we had to walk back to the station disheartened & only glad we had got some food at Lancaster.

At the station we asked about Grange. The Station master said it was full but (for love) telegraphed while we waited for the train to ask if certain lodgings he recommended were to let—answer 'full'. Miss Wallers of Cart Lane were also full—so we took our tickets for Furness asking guards & porters. The inn at Grange where we went with A. A. *is* the one that turned out Mrs Rodick. There is *no* inn at Kents'[1] Bank now; it is divided into lodging houses. You have to bring your own servants as the places are empty. The Grange Inn is kept by two rough disreputable girls & their father. They warned us against it at Silverdale. The Commercial Inn, that one close to the station, *on the sea shore* was recommended to us as we came along the line. Oh! how tired we were when we got to Furness. We had tea & went straight to bed. The Steampackets have stopped going from Piel to Fleetwood. Next morning it poured with storms of rain & we were tired. But we planned to leave at 12 spite of storms & rain & either to go back to Lancaster (which I wish we had done) but we heard that Mrs Arnold & Fanny were coming the next train & we thought we would wait & see them & gather information. They had heard of this place so we came on here. It is the *dreeest* place I ever was at. Holborn Hill had that beautiful inland walk. Here there are none —to be sure there is famous sea rolling & roaring right close to us & the house is blown through at every corner. We got *two* great bottles & slept together & heaped shawls on us to get warm as the waitress says 'it is a blustrous place'. Of the family we two are certainly *the* two to come to it. The Arnolds want us to go to Fox How end of next week. (We have had to wear a pair of drawers for a dressing gown, owing to Hearn's queer packing up—we thrust our arms through the legs). The sea makes so much noise

---

[1] MS. source reads 'Keats' '.

we can't hear the trains that go within 10 yards of the house. These Hillses (mother & daughter) lived 13 years at Siena, daughter sings, is engaged to a Mr Curwen (studying at St Bees), are acquaintances of the Arnolds who gave us a note to them which we have not delivered; but we are sure Fanny A. will write & tell them we're here. But I don't believe we shall be here long. We do so hate the place. *In a great hurry*—just come for letters before we expected. *Write me by return here* as we *cannot* stay beyond *Monday* at our present feelings. My dear love to the children.

Your ever affec[tionate] E. C. G.

*362a **381a** *385a

ELLEN NUSSEY[1]

Plymouth Grove,
Wednesday. [?November 1857]

My Dear Miss Nussey,

I am writing to you partly on Mama's behalf, partly on my own, and to begin with my own affairs first—I am quite *grieved* about the knife—I have not that I know of got it in my possession, nor do I remember your lending it to me, but as you did so, it must be safe *somewhere* in the house, which I promise you shall be hunted through till I have found it. Will you kindly let me have one line to say, whether, when found it shall be sent by post to you or not—Dear Miss Nussey, if it should be lost I *shall* be so sorry!

Now to Mama's business. First and foremost she is so sorry not to have been able to send you a copy of the 3rd edition—of which, however, she has actually not had one herself! Messrs Smith & E. felt it very risky to publish a third edition, as from the check given to the second—they suffered some loss, for tho' they could not sell what remained to them of the second, yet Mudie's 1500 copies were thrown into the market for the public. Mama has been very sorry about Miss Martineau correspondence, with which I believe she has been totally unconcerned.

We have been so terribly busy all the year—even now, as you may see, I am writing in a desperate hurry—but not too great to

[1] Original MS. not seen.

send you all our loves in—and very much from me to yourself
and many hopes that all your family are well.

Ever yours affectionately,

Meta Gaskell

*381a 385*a* *421a

ELLEN NUSSEY[1]

Plymouth Grove

Decr 30, '57.

My dear Miss Nussey,

Thank you very much indeed for your letter, sad as its contents
were. I do indeed condole with you most sincerely on the loss of
your mother. I never knew what it was to have one, but from
what I feel for my children I feel sure that love for them lives as
long as the mother lives, whatever failures of nature and mind
come on in extreme old age. And oh! dear Miss Nussey faithful
love is, I do think, the greatest of earthly goods! Besides you will
love the object of daily thought and care, and that alone is enough
to make a terrible blank in your life. I am sorry you are to leave
Brookroyd, and it was so very 'homey' looking a place. You must
come to us before you settle down any where, and see Meta
again. No I don't think it is the quiet and repose that tries me, on
the contrary I am almost afraid of liking them too well, for I am
inclined, either from laziness or depression, to refuse all invitations, and even to go out of the house as little as possible. I believe,
however, this is reaction after all this last terrible summer. I kept
thinking during that latter time of the Exhibition—Oh, in three
weeks, in 3 days, in 3 hours I may give way to sorrowful thinking,
the deadly feelings of fatigue. *Now* I must exert myself and live in
the present, and I lashed my self up to being active, and talkative
&c., when I really *could* hardly do it. Of course I must 'pay' for
this, and it is well I have such a quiet time to 'right' myself in.

Mr Gaskell is in London, with his brother, for a week or ten
days. Marianne is quite well, though not so strong as she was before the influenza, she has gone to stay at Knutsford for 4 or
5 days. Meta *either* fainted *and* sprained her ancle, or sprained her

[1] Original MS. not seen.

ancle *and* fainted (one, the cause and the other the consequence), a week ago, in getting up from a table where she had been writing for sometime, she has been laid up on the sofa ever since, but is otherwise pretty well. I don't know whether she has heard from India (Dowlaisheram, near the mouth of the Godavery) since I wrote last, but Capt. Hill is appointed to the command of his Regiment Sappers and Miners, and is stationed at Dowlaisheram and getting 800 rupees (£80) a month, *besides* his military pay, so as far as money goes their affairs are prospering. Mr Gaskell never names his name! Marianne has turned round ever since *your* talk with her, dear Miss Nussey—for which thank you truly, and is as unselfish a sister, and generous sensible and prudent an adviser as need be. Julia and Flossy are going on New Year's day with Hearn[1] to stay 3 weeks with cousins in Worcestershire. Yes! Miss Ewarts lost their brother Lt. Col. Ewart, his wife, and their little child in that frightful massacre at Cawnpore (I dare say I have told you all this news before.) Haworth *is* queer. How strange their not writing to you! My kind regards to Mrs Clapham. Write soon and tell me how you are. Meta's kind love.

Yours truly and affectionately,
E. C. Gaskell

*376a 404a 405

MARIANNE GASKELL[2]

94 Haupt[3] Strasse,
Heidelberg.
Friday, Morning Oct. 1. [1858]

My dearest Polly,

(Notice & tell me when you receive this letter, as I want to know how long letters take in getting home.) We received your Wiesbaden letter yesterday noon & were very glad to receive it as you may be sure, my darling. I am so glad to think you have

---

[1] Source reads 'Ham'.

[2] Original MS. not seen. The sources give the following address and date: Via France. | Miss Gaskell, | 42 Plymouth Grove, | Manchester, | England. | Affranchied. | Oct. 3. '58.

[3] Sources read 'Hausst' and other forms, all of which we have changed to 'Haupt'.

seen our messages for I can write to you & think more satisfactorily. I shall journalize since Tuesday. We called up the Post after
we had left you at your Railway carriage, but there were no
letters. Then we came here & engaged these rooms for the next
day & then returned to the dear Prinz Carl where I began to calculate up our expenses & found that *without any extras of any* kind
our coming here *must* come to 53 florins a week instead of 45 as
you & I had reckoned. This dispirits me, for extras *will* be required let alone washing etc. etc. Then Ida came to take Meta up
Hietelung to the Castle & Flossie & I were left in our bedroom
counting up our money and doing our accounts; when loe &
behold Mr Mohl was shewn in in a swallow tail coat & primrose
coloured gloves. Flossie made a rush for the next room when she
was caught by the German washerwoman, & sent back to have
the bill paid. Mr Mohl had been calling on Sir Harry & Lady
Verney on the floor below. He offered to get me any books out
of the University library or to lend me any of his own—told me
he was a Master of Arts of Cambridge when Prince Albert was
appointed Chancellor. He named six German ⟨   ⟩ for degrees among whom Mr Mohl was one. *Our* Paris M. Mohl is
coming here in a week or two. Then he went & I took Flossie out
for a walk on the bridge & on to the right side, in the opposite
direction to the Bunsens house. All the world was on the bridge
admiring the sunset—back to Prinz Carl & met Meta desperately
tired with a long clamber Ida had taken her after her Hietelung
tea (in the Prinz Carl breakfast room) quite alone. Mr Bosanquet
gone to the Odenwald for some days & his book left in our hands.

The next morning we thought of you dear old lassie starting at
six. Meta began to sketch the view from our bedroom window &
Flossie & I began to carry books etc. in bags & baskets here; I left
Flossie here & went backwards & forwards between the two places
finding Lady Verney sitting with Meta one time. She stayed a
long time with us. Sir Harry had gone to 'the Camp'. He was in
the army once, & is anxious to know how the men are managed
in tents in Germany, with a view of forwarding Florence Nightingale's schemes. Dine at the 1 o'clock table d'hote for the last time.
Only a few old German couples there. The host as polite & attentive as ever. $\frac{1}{2}$ past 3 moved here; Flossy made busily most useful
in unpacking, & arranging. Meta has the back room to herself,
Flossy & I the front one. It is scrupulously clean, washed out every
day, & *all premises* sweet & clean. The noise in the street is very

great, that is the worst. Dr Zimmer (the old man) was travelling physician & companion for 15 years to Count de Sales, Lady de Tabley's father & knows Tabley &c. &c. The Diceys lodged here last year; & Mrs Chapman & her two daughters—(American Mrs Chapman). Altogether it is highly respectable & rather *scrumpy*. After our hard work in removing, repacking, unpacking & arranging we were tired & faint & hungry, & thought we should *never* get tea. We went out & bought 2½d. worth of grapes for a birthday treat. Such beauties! When tea came there was a very small allowance of butter, & 6 of those *littlest* rolls; poor Flossy looked dismayed & asked if we might not have some more bread so I asked & we got three more rolls, all of which were finished the last *butterless* we were so hungry. I was dreadfully tired & went to bed directly after tea.

I stopped in bed to breakfast yesterday morning. After breakfast Meta & I went and saw M. Plarr[1] about Meta & Flossy having German lessons, which they are to have every other morning at 10 o'clock. They are gone there now for their first. I like Madame Plarr *extremely*, & only wish theirs was a healthy situation for I would far rather be there than here, where altogether we pay pretty well for our meals—everything seems grudged. I mean mille bread & butter—both tea & the coffee are *excellent*. When Meta & I came home we found our dinner arrived from Sulzers. An immense quantity of soup, which we none of us liked, a large dish of potatoes in their jackets, perhaps from 20 to 30, of which we ate six, but which would have been delicious with butter, a dish of cabbage (untouched), 4 excellent & rather large sausages, all eaten. Flossy 1, I one & Meta 2, a great piece of coarse looking ribs of roast beef, which Meta tasted, & said was not good, so it went away almost untouched, a very good large pudding—rice with egg. We kept some of that *for tea*. Altogether we had a great deal too much, so we are going to ask for only one portion, at a higher price today, & reserve part of our money, for some meat at tea, a time when we all seem to want our food the most.

After Flossy & I went to the post, & got yr letter, came home & presently Mr Mohl & Ida called (Madame & Ida had called in the morning—also a note from Lady Verney saying the Bunsens wanted us to go there,—only we could not—) & we all went a long scrambling walk up to the coffee house above the Castle where M. Mohl treated us to coffee & kuchen, & we had a lovely

[1] Sources read 'Plazz', silently emended henceforth.

view. Nothing can exceed the kindness of the Mohls. They brought us back here, when it was quite dark; & we then had our tea; but it did not seem to do us good, & we felt very low & weak *in body*, not in mind. I read the first chapter of Lord Mahon's History (Mr Mohl had lent it to us—) aloud—and then Meta & I had some wine, & a roll we had kidnapped from tea (in order that they might not judge of our appetites by that night's consumption when we had had an interlude of coffee & kuchen—) & we[1] went to bed. As I said Meta & Flossy are gone to their lesson at M. Plarr's; & then they come back here to deposit their books—(Meta is to read Ranke's History of the Popes with M. Plarr,) & go to the Mohl's to have a *cooking* lesson, in the *Pralinee* line. Don't you wish you were here? After our 1 o'clock dinner we mean to go & call on Lady Verney & the Bunsens. We *hope* for letters but I am afraid none will come. We have left our address 94 Haupt Strasse, at the post office.

Oh darling, I opened a note yesterday to you from Mrs Dicey,[2] she had seen *our* name in the strangers list & wrote to ask whether we are coming back through Wiesbaden & if you could go & stay with her & if I would make any use of her house in Binns Terrace if I were returning through London, as she fears with the exception of a short visit to England on business she will have to remain abroad all winter as Frank's cough has returned & Edward is far from well & will most likely be ordered to winter somewhere abroad. That is all she says as it was only a note. I wrote to her telling her I had opened it thanking her &c. & asking for all Dresden intelligence. Flossy is brilliantly well, as hungry as a hawk & very sweet tempered. I am well, only so very weak. I mean I feel well but every exertion is a trouble to me. But I daresay this will go off. I do so look forward to your letters from home. I wish we could see an English newspaper. I do so want to hear how Julia is. Little darling child! be sure you take care of her! Meta & Flossy gave me a very pretty stag's horn brooch for my birthday present. The piano was tuned yesterday. Now I must end my letter unless indeed we hear from you before the English post goes out, a chance for which it is worth while keeping my letter open till afternoon.

Friday evening. When Flossy & I came in from our walk just after dinner we found a letter from Papa dated Tuesday & yours from Cologne. Papa's has made us all very sad & anxious about

---

[1] Word in MS. source only.   [2] Sources read 'Diny'.

darling Julia. *Pray* love write a *minute* & *true* account of her. All
evening that I have been reading Lord Mahon aloud I have been
thinking how I could rush home via Strasbourg & Paris to see her
for myself. Remember *telegraphs*—I calculate we shan't have your
letter till *Wednesday* next & it seems a long time to wait. Do thank
Hearn *very much indeed* for her letter but I mean to answer it
myself. Flossy is learning her German '& crying for the first time
since you left' & Meta is beginning a letter to Julia. We went to
the Mohls for a walk before dinner '1 o'clock' & then had *one*
portion—no soup, macaroni, three pork chops & a piece of very
tenderly cooked meat which we kept for tea & some little sponge
cakey puddings. After dinner Meta & Flossy did their German;
& I read French & had a letter from the proprietor of the Victoria
Hotel, Dresden, *90 thalers* for two bedrooms & a sittingroom for
a month & five francs a day for everything else except light &
fire. We make out it would be 30£ a month *at least*. We went out
then for a walk & being umbrellaless were caught in a shower &
wet; came home & changed & then Flossy & I went out again for
a longer walk. She likes Heidelberg very much. Meta is going to
finish her sketch from the Prinz Carl windows tomorrow morning & Flossy & I plan a pretty long walk. We are so sleepy we go
to bed between 8 & 9. The Mohls want us to go there but we
think we would rather not go out in the evenings. At least not till
we hear a better account of Julia. It has just become very cold
since the rain & I am thinking of you & your night voyage on
board your Antwerp packet. My poor old poppet. Thank Papa
very much for his letters. I shall write to him next only I thought
you would like to hear how our ménage went on. I am very much
obliged to him for writing so often. Give my dear love to Hearn,
& thank her *very* much for her note. Tell her how much I value
her letters, & beg her to write. I dare say, under the circumstances
it is better for her not to go into Devonshire but to keep it for long
days & next May. Oh how I do want your next letter, my[1] child!
I cannot think how I am to get over the days till Wednesday. And
now I shall put this away for tonight.

　Saturday morning. Meta & Flossy have been so sleepy, they
have breakfasted in bed; & Sir Harry & Lady Verney have been
to wish good bye as they are going home today, or rather to
Mayence today & then home as fast as they can go. They were at
the Bunsens last night to tea, & say that the Chevalier seemed very

　　　　　　　[1] Word omitted in MS. source.

well. Will you tell this to Susanna, as I think she was anxious about him. We have had a very nice letter from Schmidt of the Rose Hotel this morning, saying that the umbrellas are not to be heard of anywhere; and[1] saying that you had slept there, & gone on &c. We are now writing to Coblenz. Flossy wants to write to Julia, but I beg her to put it off for a day or two, as Meta is writing today. Give our very dearest love to the darling. Oh do write & give both *your impressions*, & the *real facts* about her. Tell me how Papa is too—Are there *two* letters from India? or only *one*? The maneuvres are finished, but there is an 'Exposition of Industry' in the Black Forest which has charmed Sir Harry. The country people make clocks & watches &c.—And now good-bye my dear child. I shall write to Papa & Julia very soon. I do so want to hear from you, how you think everything is going on. Give my dearest love to Papa & thank him very much for having written so often. Go & *call on the Diggles*. Have you got the van Houtte seeds all safe? Meta has got *both* your Louisa Sandars studs quite safe & is taking great care of your hat & is giving your studs occasional airings & has got a collar of yours. Ever your very affectionate Mother

E. C. Gaskell.

*385*a* **421*a*** 0

ELLEN NUSSEY[2]

Plymouth Grove,
March 21st '59.

My Dear Miss Nussey,

I have so much to tell you that I believe it is the reason I have not written. Do you understand this? If I could have dashed you off with a short rapidly written note, I could have found plenty of time for that; but I wanted to tell you at length of the end of that affair of which you saw the beginning. We were abroad (Meta Marianne Flossy and I altogether for the first month; then Marianne returned home with some friends from Wiesbaden) from the middle of September until December 20th and on

---

[1] MS. source lacks 'saying that . . . anywhere; and'.
[2] Original MS. not seen.

coming home I found your letter among others awaiting me, as they had not been forwarded to me in Germany (on account of the expense). We went abroad because Meta had had a great deal of anxiety during the last few months which had ended in her breaking off her engagement with Capt. Hill. She heard something (a thing *not of itself* of much consequence) while she was staying[1] with Mrs Mackinnon, about this time last year, which was in direct contradiction to a statement of his, made when he was in England. I can not tell you what this thing was, being bound in honour to secrecy, nor does it signify much, as it was the apparent falsehood which it revealed which made it of consequence. Meta wrote to him on April 20th telling him how she had become aware of a fact which he had denied, saying that unless he could give some explanation which would show that she was mistaken she should feel that her confidence had been most painfully shaken, and begging him to write as soon as he could and relieve her of this anxiety, as an explanation of the seemingly contradictory circumstances was quite possible. I did not see her letter, of course, but I am sure from what she said of it, it was quite a nice and affectionate letter. She could have had an answer to it by the 3rd of July; but none came. Until then he had written weekly; but from that time she had no letter *at all* up to our going from home, on Sepr 8th; nor had I, though I had written (quite separately) to ask him to make some arrangement as to where Meta was to meet him, in October, and to tell me all the details of the arrangements for the journey &c. he wished to have made. At the beginning of August Meta wrote to his sisters to enquire about him; fearing he might not be well, the reply was that they had heard regularly by each mail, that he was quite well, only that he complained of Meta's want of confidence in him, and said no marriage could be happy where the wife did not implicitly trust the husband. Meta determined after hearing this from his sisters to wait two mails longer, and then if she did not hear, to break off her engagement, and write and explain all the details and send copies of the letters to his brother (Captain Dudley Hill,—a man a good deal older, and as far as we can judge a very nice person[)]. This she did; and Captain Dudley Hill said 'she was more than justified in breaking off her engagement,' in which I think that you, dear Miss Nussey, will agree. When all was over,—although I think her mind had been tending that way ever since her discovery of his

---

[1] Source reads 'stating'.

apparent falsehood in March,—she became very listless and languid and Mr Gaskell thought that complete and entire change of
scene would be the best for her—so, as I said, we four set out up
the Rhine to Heidelberg, where we took lodgings in a German
family, and hired a piano, and Meta and Flossy, after Marianne
left, set themselves to German lessons &c, and we lived a pretty
regular quiet life there; breakfasting at 8, dining at one, and drinking tea about 7. There was nothing to write about, as one day
was just like another; but we were very happy, and very busy
with reading, German, music, and as long as the fine weather
lasted, Meta sketched the beautiful old Castle, and we took long
walks every afternoon after the German master had been.

Since we came back we have been very quiet; the girls and I
have been to three dances this winter, one at Mrs Dugdale's. All
the girls are well; Meta very bright and merry again, and we
never talk of former days or allude to them. Marianne is just now
staying at West Derby, Liverpool, with some friends. Flossy is at
school at Knutsford, and Julia rather misses her; but we can go and
see her in two hours, and she will come home at Easter for a few
days holiday. Miss Winkworth is in London, lodging near her
married sister Mrs Shaen; she has been there for three months,
and is to remain a month longer; she is gone to study in the
British Museum for a translation of one of Baron Bunsen's books
on which she is engaged. I have not seen her since we came back
from Heidelberg. Miss Ewarts are both at home; taking great
charge of and care for the little orphan boy,—the child of Col.
and Mrs Ewart, killed at Cawnpore. I know you will like to hear
a pretty thing about this boy. Old Mr Ewart, his grandfather,
Agnes and Mary's and Colonel Ewart's father, was in business,
was unfortunate, and was privately helped by friends to keep him
from failure. This was in 1830: he died about 1837. One of his
sons, Mr Peter Ewart has been very prosperous in the Indian
trade: and three years ago he paid off the six friends who had
helped his father, and who had never expected to see their money
again, so they gave him a silver tea-urn. Just before Christmas last
he paid them all the interest of this borrowed money. They remonstrated, said they would not take it,—and on his insisting
settled it (3000£) on Harry; who had only his little pension of
40£ previously.

Since I began Mrs Fairbairn has been here and interrupted me
so long that it is just post time. But I daresay you are glad to be

spared a longer letter. Do write soon, and say you are better,—
you speak of 'bad pain'—what was it?

Meta sends her kind love to you. Mr[1] Gaskell's kindest regards

Yours affectionately,

E. C. G.

You'll get a book from me.

₀ 432+ ₀

DUCHESS OF SUTHERLAND

11 Kildare Terrace
June 18. [?1859] W.

Dear Duchess,

I must apologize for not sooner acknowledging your note, and
the permission you so kindly sent me to see Stafford House; but
we have been at the Crystal palace all day, and I only found your
Grace's letter on our return at nine this evening.

May I beg you to accept my best thanks for the pleasure we
expect to receive through your kind courtesy? Believe me to
remain, dear Duchess,

Yours respectfully

E. C. Gaskell

₀ 439*c* ₀

MARY BEAVER[2]

42 Plymouth Grove
Tuesday. Aug 30 [1859]

My dear Miss Beaver,

I have been taking a great liberty—giving a young friend of
ours a letter of introduction to you.—Will you please not disgrace
me, by saying you have quite forgotten all about me, & can't

---

[1] Source reads 'Mrs'.

[2] Original MS. not seen. The typescript source describes it as 4 pp., 8vo. It was
presented to the Rev. G. A. Payne.

think what right etc. etc,—For I should like you and him to know each other a little. He is a Mr Bosanquet, son of a clergyman in Northumberland, studying law in London: going on Sept. 1st to walk all about the Lakes for the first time,—having a great true admiration for Dr Arnold,—whose character I think he somewhat resembles; being very grave, and religiously earnest in his thoughts, and his life. I wish this letter of mine would *provoke* you to write and tell me something about yourself. It seems now as if our Manchester tie was broken: and we so seldom go to the Lakes—of late years: and yet I am always craving a little after the dear old places and people, whenever I hear of any one going Amblesidewards. We went into Scotland this year, on the borders of the Solway; which was not so much sea as we wanted; but still in many ways a very pleasant place; Auchencairn by name. The quiet peacefulness of the place was delicious; we sate out of doors from morning till night; it was too hot to walk very much, besides the fact that our pleasantest walk was guarded by a very vicious bull. Ever yours most truly

E. C. Gaskell

429a 443a •444a

?MARIANNE GASKELL[1]

[Mid-October 1859]

⟨. . .⟩ is going to Heidelberg in July so most likely she will go with her. The cloak does for Julia now she is petticoated. I will gladly do the carpet for Mrs Shadwell. How old is the Captain, older or younger than the Colonel? How is the Tutor? Mrs Nicholls has sent us an oval framed likeness of poor Sam which is hung up where the centre vase was over the drawing room chiffonier vase in the[2] dining room chimney piece. I went to call & thank yesterday, meeting Miss E. Watkins then, & I believe she is the only person I have seen since you left & I recd no letters yesterday so I can't be agreeable. It is very cold too & my eternal throat is sore. So I feel X. Oh Stephen came in last night again for my note to Miss Thompson.[3] My courage had rather oozed out

---

[1] Original MS. not seen.   [2] Word supplied from MS. source.
[3] Sources read 'Thomason', but see p. 582 above.

about asking her as I know I shall never be wise enough in a tete
a tete with a girl who does not read poetry & novels but Adam
Smith, Niall etc. & has 'no sense of humour but takes everything
literally'. I have asked her to stay as late as she can on *Tuesday* but
oh! I *know* I shall never be either wise or good enough & I am all
in a tremble at the thought thereof. I had a very nice letter from
Thos[1] Darwin before yesterday—his opinions on prize fighting &
the ring combined with a little literature. Meta has heard no
further from Miss Darwin so *Tuesday* must be our latest day for
writing to Paris. Miss Williamsons go on much as usual; Miss
Sarah a little better but not much. Your two little Baxters are
poking about greenhouse etc. ⟨. . .⟩

*443a **444a** 447

MARIANNE GASKELL[2]

Tuesday.
[25 October 1859]

My dearest Polly,
   I am writing you a line or two though we are really overwhelmed with business. Elliott out for the day to spend wages &
buy winter gown, Susanna & Katie coming to tea, Papa ill with a
cold & not 'showing', Isabel ditto & having mustard plasters etc.
on her throat & unable to go to-morrow. Miss Bessy R. Parkes
coming any moment to 'want my judgment' on something or
other—& probably to tea as well. Meta carried off just in the acme
of business by Mr Wright to see a poor family in Water Street
with a view to getting a boy to the Ragged School, Papa wanting
me to go to Porters & Mrs Nicholls' & I unable to go out because
of awaiting Miss Bessy P—that's our house to-day! & here am I
sitting with my things on and moaning & groaning because my[3]
Bessy does not come. I am very sorry you have got a cold but you
are no worse than everyone else if that's any comfort. I should
have one if I had time & nearly every one else in the *house* has
one & all the crysanthemums are killed & the new man who
ought to come instead of Dixon has not been this fortnight. We
did think of trying Whitby for to-morrow after Isabel went; but

---

[1] ? Chas.   [2] Original MS. not seen.   [3] Typescript source reads 'by'.

she is too poorly to go, & of course everything gets more & more put off. Mr Coleridge sends me an autograph of Mr Robert Walpole's & wants your address to see if you would not pay him a visit at Eton. I am writing any way with all my hot shawls etc. on & waiting for B. R. P.. A pamphlet from Mr Norton N. S. came for you to-day. I should trample my pheasant's wing under my feet instead of wearing it in my hat if I were you. I am so tired & do so want a breath of fresh air. Callers swallow up all my days & I never get out nowadays. There is no news whatever. Send word about Henrietta Bright's lunch & mutual impressions. Both Papa & Isabel have had their breakfasts in bed for several days.

Ever your very affec[tionate] & very dull mother

E. C. Gaskell.

379 444b 445

?HARRIET MARTINEAU

[?Late October 1859]

⟨. . . under⟩stand?—and agree with me I am sure.[1]

And after all one gets into a desponding state of mind about writing at all, after 'Adam Bede', and 'Janet's Repentance' choose (as the Lancashire people say,) whoever wrote them. You heard truly that I have stuck out that I believed that a *man* wrote them. I am shaken now, and should like much to receive your evidence. I would rather they had not been written by Miss Evans, it is true; but justice should be done to all; & after all the writing such a book should raise her in every one's opinion, because no dramatic power would, I think enable her to think & say such *noble*/ things, unless her own character—\perhaps/ somewhere hidden away from our sight at present,—has such possibilities of greatness & goodness in it. I never can express myself metaphysically; and I have been interrupted many times while trying to make this sentence clear. I saw a letter from Mrs Bracebridge last week saying after recapitulating the evidence in favour of Miss Evans 'But we remain convinced that Mr Liggins has had a great deal to do with the writing these books especially with "Clerical Scenes".' And just after the appearance of the *second* number of 'Clerical

---

[1] Crossed out by another hand, which also inserted 'I' at the top of this sheet.

Scenes', in Blackwood—now something like 2 years & a half ago
—I was expressing my great admiration of it to a friend,—and a
week or ten days afterwards she wrote to me to say that her
cousin Mr Bacon, a clergyman\at some parish she named/near
Nuneaton, knew the author of Clerical Scenes\a Mr Liggins, a
gentleman farmer/, & had seen the MSS of the whole series, &
said that one of the stories to come, far exceeded in merit the one
then publishing (Amos Barton.) Now I think that very few people
had found out the merit of Clerical Scenes so early as that; and it
was two years before all the world exclaimed at Adam Bede's
appearance; so that circumstance (of seeing the whole MSS in Mr
Liggins' hands,) is still a puzzle.

I must end this letter, though I have not half said my say on
numerous points. I hope you are really tolerably well, although
you speak of being much affected by cold. Yours ever most truly
E C Gaskell

381 **446**+ *451+

MARIA MARTINEAU

Mrs Rose's
Abbey Terrace
Whitby
Novr 4th [1859]

My dear Miss Martineau,
We came off here rather suddenly in a little interval of leisure,
in order to get a taste of sea air before winter. We left, not knowing where we should lodge, or to what address our letters were to
be forwarded; arriving here on Tuesday morning, after a night
passed at York in order to show Meta & Julia, my companions,
the Minster &c, and to arrive here early in the morning with a
view to having plenty of time for lodging-hunting. We stay here
till the 12th. I name all this to account for my seeming neglect in
not bo⟨th⟩ acknowledging your own, and ⟨[?]returning⟩ Mr
Bracebridge's and Miss H⟨?owell's⟩ letters sooner. How interesting & ⟨curious⟩ the whole affair is! interesting ⟨I⟩ mean in the
poor sense of tra⟨cking⟩ out a rogue; and such a goose ⟨of a⟩
short-sighted one too! for he mu⟨st⟩ almost be hooted out of the

n⟨eigh⟩bourhood now, one would thin⟨k⟩ unless indeed the temptation ⟨to⟩ laugh at those parsons in his ⟨sleeve⟩ was too strong for him! But th⟨en⟩ you say he has taken money, ⟨&⟩ that alters & blackens the case, ⟨thou⟩gh one had quite got to the bottom ⟨or M⟩r Quirk's *seeing* the MSS of Clerical ⟨Scen⟩es so long ago in Liggins' hand⟨wri⟩ting & in Liggins' possession. There ⟨is a⟩ story going about which if not ⟨true⟩ is 'ben trovato' touching the clergy⟨ma⟩n—(was it Mr Quirk?—I never ⟨see⟩ any London paper, & only get ⟨dri⟩blets of information as to their ⟨con⟩tents,) who wrote to the Times. ⟨A⟩ clergy-man wrote to Mr Black⟨woo⟩d, saying that he would only ⟨be⟩ convinced that Liggins was ⟨*no*⟩*t* the author by seeing some ⟨of⟩ the real author's handwriting. ⟨By⟩ the same post Mr Blackwood ⟨rec⟩eived a letter from Miss Evans, ⟨say⟩ing she did not know whether ⟨Lig⟩gins or the clergyman who ⟨wrote⟩ in the Times was the greater ASS. Mr Blackwood immediat⟨ely⟩ enclosed this note to the clergy⟨man.⟩ Still this does not refute the alle⟨ged⟩ fact, of Mr Quirk having seen the ⟨MSS⟩ &c &c. How-ever there is no doubt ⟨that⟩ Liggins has both admitted pass-⟨ively⟩ & asserted actively, (to Mrs Fisher, ⟨who⟩ was a Miss Drury 'of a famil⟨y⟩ well-known in the neighbourh⟨ood⟩ of Coventry,') that he was the a⟨u⟩thor.

I shall like very much inde⟨ed⟩ to hear from you if you hear anything more about it. You⟨r⟩ letters are always a great pleas⟨ure⟩ & about this imposture I am par⟨ti⟩cularly curious. It seems strange that no one has hitherto seemed to doubt Mr Liggins honour,—however much they spoke against his drinking habits &c. And I remember seeing a very nice letter in one of the Athenæums of last May or June, speaking in honest & respectful terms of Mr Liggins' character,—by a nephew of his, I think.

Ever yours most truly
E C Gaskell.

Meta sends her best & kindest regards, (she did say 'love'.)

MARIANNE GASKELL[1]

1 Abbey Terrace,
Monday.
[7 November 1859]

My dearest Polly,

We are all just going out, & I have only time for a line or two.
I have sent your letter on to Papa about Cherry. I should like *ex-tremely* to have her; not merely on her own account but because
they have been so very kind to you; but Papa *did* say he hoped
that after Miss Marshall we should be free from visitors for a time
—& as Meta had then written to ask Anna Mohl who is at Paris
to come to us, we even rather hoped that she might decline it.
We have not heard from her, A. M., yet in answer to 2 letters
written to her & asking for a speedy reply to our invitation. However I am sending the (your) letter on to Papa & we shall see what
he says. I will ask him to write straight to you, that there may be
no loss of time; for *don't mention it please* we have had a fright about
Julia which has thrown me back with my letters & writing generally & now it is Monday evening & neither this nor my letter to
Papa will go out till to-morrow. Yesterday, Sunday, I was down
first & in very good time & I was settling to some writing letters
before breakfast when Hearn came down in a great fright asking
me to go up to Julia, she was very ill, & Hearn could not tell what
was the matter with her—she was moaning & would not speak. I
went up, found her lying across the bed, half dressed, very white,
her eyes half closed, I wanted her to go to bed again but she kept
saying 'not to bed, not to bed please' so Hearn carried her down in
shawls & laid her here on the best sofa we could make up by the
fire, & there she lay, looking *so* ill. Meta says she could quite[2]
have fancied her in a fit, & I thought of scarlet fever directly. She
kept moaning & very white so I sent Meta off for a doctor &
Hearn for some hot tea (we are having coffee for breakfast) Meta
picked up a young doctor almost directly—he said she was very
feverish etc & should be free from visitors for a time, ordered *two*
of her & my usual pills & a fever draught to be taken every three
hours & said he would call again. We gave her some hot tea &

---

[1] Original MS. not seen.					[2] MS. source omits 'quite'.

wrapped her feet in hot flannel & she fell asleep and we watched by her for two or three hours. She wakened & was *very* sick; & from that time got better; was very indifferent when dinner came & she had nothing but biscuit & tea; lay on the sofa half dressed till just before tea when she went up, dressed, pills did their duty & she was as merry as a grig by the time the doctor came again. He was very stern however about my having given her a lightly boiled egg at tea (she *was* so hungry) & said she was too feverish for anything of the kind. However she had a good night, was down to breakfast first of all & has been a walk, not a long one, to-day. I was so frightened because Papa had prophesied evil from taking her from home; but indeed Meta says how frightened *she* was too, at her extraordinary look. *Don't name it please*, for I don't think we need have sent for a doctor or been so much alarmed. All yesterday we were very noiseless & quiet because of her dosey state on the sofa. That is our principal event. Nothing else for Sunday has of course made an interruption in our letters & we don't seem to have received the right number for some time. Flossy wants to ask Ada Long at Xmas & I have said she may. Katie & Susanna are at Malvern & would be passing through from Manchester to Worcester just about the time on Monday when you were going through. Kate was to stay 3 weeks there so per-haps *she* on her return might be an escort for Cherry if that affair was arranged. You understand love that we were a great deal *over* frightened about Julia. Something must have disagreed with her or those ticklish b-w-ls of hers got wrong.

Ever your very affec[tionate]
Mammy

*447a 447b 448

?MARIANNE GASKELL[1]

Tuesday morning.
[8 November 1859]

My dearest Cynthia,

Here is your letter come this morning and as it seems so much wished for about Cherry I am going to take it upon myself

[1] Original MS. not seen.

(though with a little fear and trembling) and consequently enclose a note to Cousin Charlotte asking for Cherry to pay us a visit etc. I am sending both your letters on to Papa. We must now hope that Anna Mohl can't come just yet; but I wish she would answer. Meta has written to her, twice, once at Dumbleton, and once from P. Grove to which I added a P.S. Julia is *quite* well. We have got Louisa Hutchins' cards sent on this morning—very pretty of her to remember us was it not? Meta is going to sketch out of a house in the East Terrace to-day, where she fancies she shall have a pretty view—said house belonging to a friend of Mrs Rose's. I have had a letter from Bosie[1] this morning. He owes a debt of gratitude to Whitby for having set up his father in health. 'I bear it special good will for the good looks it gave my father; I left him hardly recovered from a sharp attack of illness and when he break-fasted with me the other day on his way to Essex after ten days or so at Whitby he was more than himself again'. It is raining to-day but after lunch we are going out, I will enclose you pretty nearly all—I was going to say the stamps I have—but on second thoughts, let me know if you want money and I will send you a P.O. order payable to *Mr John Whitmore Isaac* for what you want and he will give you the money. I write to-day you reply to-morrow—I get your letter and send off P.O. order on Thursday—so you see it will be in time.

Your *very* affect[ionate]
Mammy

*446+ 451+ 0

Maria Martineau

Plymouth Grove.
Decr 6. 1859.

My dear Miss Martineau

　I return you the letters, and please thank your Aunt very much for allowing me to see them. I don't think I have so 'severe' an opinion of Mr Bracebridge as Mr Reeve has[.] I, perhaps, have come more in contact with people who have heard Liggins' assumptions, direct or indirect, of authorship; and who have,

---

[1] Source reads 'Rosie', silently emended henceforth.

until now, believed that whatever might be his faults, he was *truth*ful, can better understand how Mr Bracebridge, having two conflicting statements brought before him, was inclined, as long as the evidence de⟨. . .⟩

₄₄₅ **451**++ ₀

HARRIET MARTINEAU

42 Plymouth Grove
Wedy Decr 7th [1859]

My dear Miss Martineau
    Thank you much for letting me see Mr Bracebridge's letter; which is so imperturbable in it's good-temper, and so inconsequential in it's reasoning as to be a small marvel in it's way. I did not see the date of the Bracebridge letter; indeed it was only a *copy* that I saw, shown me by my cousin Captain Holland, in the 2nd week of Octr. He & his wife came here\& to Knutsford/from Lord Belper's; and this letter from Mrs Bracebridge had, (as I understood,) been received by one of the party (Lady Sitwell I *think*) *during their stay there*\their visit having been for less than a week/[.] I should not affix the slightest importance to Mr Liggins saying anything; but I fancy it would be very easy to obtain Mr Lewes' direct denial or confirmation of the statement Liggins made, as to having lodged in the same house with Mr Lewes; though I don't know what importance that would be of in deciding the authorship of Adam Bede, &c. because, as you have several times said, we have every reason for respecting *her* word, & nothing can be clearer than her declaration that she, & she alone wrote every word, & thought every thought. I have over & over again heard (what Mr Reeve alluded to) that Diss was Deerbrook, and this that & the other person Mrs Rowlands &c; and have been myself complimented or reproached, as the case might be, with having used such or such an incident, or described such & such a person, & never seem able to understand how one acquires one's materials unconsciously as it were. I am very glad of the success of 'once a week'. Please thank Miss Hennell for all her kind expressions towards me. I hope your '*tic*' is better. To-day, *here* is clear

& bracing[.] With kindest regards to your niece Maria, ever believe me to be[,] dear Miss Martineau

Yours affectionately

E C Gaskell

₄₆₅ 465*a* ₄₆₆

MARIANNE GASKELL[1]

Wednesday. [?Early May 1860]

My dearest Polly,

I am so glad to receive your letters,—for I'm sadly worried in small ways, & your letters are a great relief, & very few people write to me, & Papa is so busy, (Mr Drummond off for his holiday,) & what Mrs Nichols said is *true* about Sarah, & I *shall* be so glad to get her out of the house next Thursday week,—though I have not a scrap of a cook to fall back upon, & Mary's mother is ill & Mary has asked to go home & see her next week: so eggs & bread & cheese seem likely to be our fare. It's well my family is away; for Julia does get *some* kind of a dinner at Miss Mitchell's, & Papa says he'll dine out & Alice Taylor wants another situation *and* 10s., & Miss Hall is away, & I have to see about a successor to Mrs Hampson,—(that Miss Taylor from Didsbury) & I'm *afraid* John won't do; not from any *moral* faults which is a comfort, but because he has no head or method in any way,—fetches spade at one errand, rake at another,—forgets to sow seeds, forgets to order food for pigs, &c., & I think that at present at least he would be better *under* another gardener, who cd & would direct his daily work; all whh he would do willingly & good temperedly. And my book is really killing me,—i.e. I can't sleep at nights for thinking of my story (*Have you written to Secretary Amateur Exhibition* in my name, about Meta's Florence; if sold, to whom?) I am glad you snubbed Sophy. My book is getting *on* famously,—¼ done of the whole; & only begun 8th of April. Tell me your plans. When do you go to Holly Hill? On the Saturday June 2nd to Eton I suppose. But don't stay there beyond the 5th or *6th for the outside*, I *beg*. Papa I *know* would dislike it. Then have you any further plans or invitations? Do try & not make yr letters 2d

[1] Original MS. not seen.

weight. You can not think how we are trying to economize, because it is quite clear we must give more to next cook, & probably to the gardener. I know how difficult it is to write when one
is from home,—but I *am* so glad of your letters—none from Meta.
I enclose scrap from L. V. J. & am your affect[ionate] Mammy.

Did I tell you? L. V. J. came here for a few minutes on Monday,
while Mrs A & Emily went to call on the Watkins. She had had a
telegram Thursday, & another Friday from P.[1] both of whh I saw.
He only says in the first. 'In England. Don't come up. I will come
to you'. In the second 'Don't come will be in the North in a few
days going to Drawing room'. She had written *begging* for letters
& reasons & had got none in answer; so she did not know if she
shd go to Lupset on Tuesday or not; but as you may see by other
side, she *is* going.[2]

471 **472**+ 473

MARIANNE GASKELL[3]

3–45   Cowley House
                                          Oxford, Thursday.
                                          [?28 June 1860]

My dearest Polly,

I am *sure* that under the circumstances you had better get *quite*
over your weakness and consequent headache before starting so,
as Philo would tell you I have put off going till Wednesday *on*
Saturday next. So (to get my *business* done) will you come to
London *on Saturday* so as to be at the *Waterloo* Station in time to
start for *Wandsworth* by the train that leaves at *3–45* I, coming
from Reading *to Vauxhall*, shall take my place in that same train
back to Wandsworth from Vauxhall (the train does *not* stop at
Wandsworth going *up* so I must return that bit of the road). At
Wandsworth I have asked Annie S. to send a cab to meet us; and
we go on there to see what they (Shaens) would prefer to do with

[1] Pilkington Jackson.
[2] To Lupset Hall, Wakefield, according to the copy of the 'scrap' mentioned
above.
[3] Original MS. not seen.

us. I have offered us to stay there till Monday; but as there was no
time to hear how this putting off would suit them, I have enclosed
two notes to Annie, out of which she is to *choose* which she will
send on to Mrs Greg—one says we will go to the Gregs on
Saturday and one says we will go there on *Monday*; The Greg's
answer is to be sent to the Shaens—so we must call there for *that*
at any rate. Do get well, my darling! My great regret at stopping
at the Shaen's (which I should prefer for all other things to the
Gregs) is that you won't have *wine* as I am sure you ought to
have, unless the air has made you much stronger and now to tell
you why I did not write yesterday.

Amabel, Isabel and I were at the Ch. Ch. Ball till 4 in the *morning*, then I put my weary self to bed, went to sleep, and was
wakened by the intelligence that it was ½ p. 8 and that we were
to be at Queens by ½ p. 9 *punctually* to go with them to the theatre.
I hurried on my clothes, had no time to put on *your* gown though
it was *the* day of all days—took your letter all but unread in my
pocket, and had only time hastily to decide that you had better
wait a few days and to *direct* envelopes to you and Hearn which
Mrs Brodie said she would fill up—for I found to my surprize the
day was all *mapped out completely* and there would be no coming
home there till the evening. I had got *our* passports off to be vised
the day before; but there will have to be one got for Hearn.
Adams (the passport man) says about this I have done nothing. I
sadly want to consult you my darling about many things. Where
are we to sleep—Bruges (½ an hour from Ostend—curious old
town) or *Ghent* (2 hours from) where we were very comfortable
before. Are we to sleep at an hotel (J. P. Green recommends
Radleys Black Friars) or on board the Ostend packet, supposing
we start on Wednesday—when it leaves at 7 a.m. (10 hour's
passage). Don't *forget to remind me to write to Mrs Nicholls*. Do
you understand that I am stopping here till Saturday morning
11 o'clock and I shall be *very* glad of a letter *here* on Saturday
morning which I can receive if you write to-morrow. The
thunder yesterday gave me a dreadful headache so I had to come
home in the middle of the festivities lie down, wet draperies, have
my prussic acid medicine made up etc. Mrs Brodie's letter had
gone to you by that time; but I could not write a line.

Please answer Hearn's enquiries. Do you hear of any one going
to Harrow. Papa comes to Oxford next Thursday evening to be
Mr Smith's guest at Balliol. Vevay Switzerland is Meta's address

if you send off your letter this week. *Please* write to her. What do you think of Bosie's conversion?

Ever your most affect[ionate] Mammy

Write to Hearn about her questions.

475 **475a** 475c

MARIANNE GASKELL[1]

Miss Gaskell
Heidelburg
Thursday
[Early August 1860]

My dearest Polly,

Events don't live here in full force; here is a letter for you, which I opened *verily* by mistake at first. One came for Florence at the same time which I snatched up and I could not believe I should be equally unfortunate with the second, but when I saw yours it was irresistible to read it; quite by way of chaperonage of course, and not a bit for gossipry. However there is not much news of any kind in it, as you will find. I went and called the Maltbys yesterday as soon as I had written to you. They are so true. He had been to *Dover*, not meeting his friend at Brussels since he quitted Ellinor at Bingen, left here at $\frac{1}{2}$ past[2] 2 on the Thursday and returned on Tuesday morning all he had 'seen of England being a thunder storm, lamb and fried soles'. He had slept at Bingen on Monday night and had had a great mind to go over to Kreuznach to see you and Ellinor and bring me a report. Mr Maltby had borrowed a book from Mrs Fane for me (her own writing—that's all I can tell you about it alas! as you shall hear) and after some conversation it turned out he had known Cousin Carlotte well as a young man and often danced with her and Cousin Louisa. Knew the Diffells, knew 'Richard Croft' very well. 'Mrs Maltby's sister is married to one of the Conduits (whatever that may be) of Eton of the name of Eyre.' I had named to Mrs Maltby that Julia had bought some pomegranate flowers for Flossy that had been thrown away in our flitting upstairs and how

---

[1] Original MS. not seen.　　　　[2] Source reads 'part'.

sorry we were etc. and yesterday it seems that Mrs Maltby had been sending all over H— to get some to replace their loss, but with no success. Then the girls joined me and to call on A. Mohl.[1] (I called on Mme Benecke—out) we encountered the Flemings— he is titular Earl of Wigton and likely soon to have the estates, when he will be something more than *titular* Earl. A Mohl was rather at a loose end and charmed at my proposal that she should go out with us; firstly to Rupprechts (I am trying to put myself in mourning—blk ribbons and gloves are all I can manage but with my checked silk gown that does very well) and then we had ⟨...⟩

335 **475b** *476a

W. S. WILLIAMS[2]

42, Plymouth Grove,
Manchester.
Aug. 25th [1860]

My Dear Sir,
    Would you be so kind as to send me down all the five volumes of 'Modern Painters' with the bill. I want to make a present of them to my daughter Meta; and fancy I may obtain discount by getting them straight from the Publishers.
                                    Yours very truly,
                                        E. C. Gaskell

*475a **475c** 478

MARIANNE GASKELL[3]

411 [*sic*] P. Grove.
[? August 1860]

Darling Mima,
    Yes, you are a good girl. I am so much obliged to you for find-ing out about that man. Miss Jane did stay for such a long time

---

[1] Source reads 'Molh', silently emended henceforth.
[2] Original MS. not seen.   [3] Original MS. not seen.

the other day, though she did not tell us any news. She says one finds it very dull & lonely. Nothing much has happened. We went this morning to the washerwoman & to call on Emma but she was out. There was a letter from Hearn this morning, she had been to see Dar. Yesterday was the Judge's birthday. I remember last year so well. I went to wish him many happy returns. I do so hope K. does you good. Its after dinner & I am drunk. Thank you so much about writing & asking about the man. How interesting all the accounts of May are. It is quite right about the biscuits. M. E. sends her dear love. The dinner went wrong & she's rather low. Its very interesting about C. Wedgwood. She is not a sister of Mrs Bowen's though I believe. I am writing in gt haste.

ARE THE HOLLANDS COMING HERE TO DINNER OR NOT? whatever you like only M. E. wants to know on account of Mrs Richards.

Yr loving
E. C. G.[1]

I've never heard from Ida.
Love to Coz. Mary do tell her how it was I did not come to see her.

•475b 476a 481

W. S. WILLIAMS[2]

42, Plymouth Grove,
Manchester.
Aug. 29th [1860]

My Dear Sir,

I am very much obliged to you indeed for so kindly and so speedily sending me the books I asked for, and which gave great delight to my daughter, when they arrived yesterday morning. I beg to enclose a Post Office Order for the amount.

I am sorry to say my book does not get on at all, with the best wishes on my part to go on writing. First one domestic occupation or event claims my attention then another. My eldest daughter has been very far from well all summer, and this has taken up

[1] Sources read 'T. R. G.', which *could* be a misreading of J. B. G. Our dating depends upon identifying 'K' as 'Kreuznach'.
[2] Original MS. not seen.

much of my time and thought. She, writing from Kreuznach, begs me to thank Mr Smith for his kind thoughtfulness in sending her the September Cornhill. She is so lonely and dull, that independently of the pleasure reading the Magazine will be, she seems very much touched and gratified by the remembrance. Please tell Mr Smith all this.

I do so want to know the names of the authors. Is J. R. Mr Ruskin; and if so, *where is he*, my daughter Meta wants to send him her drawings. Who wrote 'Stranger than Fiction?' But though I ask these questions please don't think yourself bound to answer them.

> Believe me to remain, My Dear Sir,
> Ever yours very truly,
> E. C. Gaskell

484 484a •484b

MARIANNE GASKELL[1]

> The Close, [Winchester]
> Saturday
> [?2 March 1861]

My dearest Polly,

This is a business letter in a great measure but Meta tells me if I get it in to the post before 11 you will get it to-morrow when Caroline might write to Sophie. But read that part of Anna Mohl's letter relating to Sophie *carefully* over to Caroline. It does so entirely *contradict* the whole *tone* as well as the words of Sophie's behaviour that I can't help wondering how far Dr Meyer's brusque manner may have led to his receiving that impression from her. *But has she ever written* to C. to say she was *well* now? So much depends on what her feeling of *willingness* to come is. It seemed to me to be positive longing to come to England. Consult Hearn about it too. I am very sorry to give you such a piece of work to do on a Sunday when you are naturally so busy. *And what do you and Hearn think* of Amelia? Has Caroline heard from her mother? about Sophie. Please *be sure* and *send back* (with any advice you can about the water proof cloak) A. Mohl's letter,

---

[1] Original MS. not seen.

which is a very true one I think. *Meta is* writing to ask her to go
up to the Speyer Hof: to see Sophie; but as she is in love etc. etc.
it is as well to get Caroline also to work to ascertain Miss Sophie's
real wishes. As for news my darling there is none here. I came on
Thursday as appointed in a storm of wind and rain; dined at
½ p. 6, got very sleepy, went to bed at 10—and yesterday breakfasted at 9 *sharp*, went for a walk in the town with the L. V. J.
before lunch. Lunch at one. Slept afterwards on the sofa in my
room, had a cup of tea at 5, dined at ½ past 6; the old Dean and
Mrs Garnier (his daughter in law) and Miss Garnier his grand
daughter, came in to tea. He is 84 and told me about his descent
from the Huguenots etc but nothing worth repeating; though
rather interesting as coming from so old a man. I ought to have
written to Julia to-day and my next letter shall be to her. And now
I must stop in order to get a scrabble in to Papa for his Sunday
letter before the 11 o'clock post. L. V. J. is *much* altered 'selon
moi' (as A. M. says) so quiet and indifferent about life in general
and Gaskell's in particular. Report about Amelia.

Ever your most affec[tionate] Mammy

*484a 484b 487

MARIANNE GASKELL[1]

1 Cumberland Place
Regents Park
FRIDAY. [March 1861]

My dearest Marianne,
      It is just after breakfast & we are all sitting in this great large
immense drawing room (which I don't like half as well as the old
one with the balcony) Effie & Meta playing the Fingal duet so
there's my time & place. We left the Thompson's on Wednesday
evening (5 o'c) & your letter enclosing Harriett's was directed
there so only arrived here last night too late to reply to. The only
possible objection darling is about the loneliness of Flossy, & I do
not see that this is an insuperable objection. I am afraid Fanny
Wilmot might find it dull staying with her alone or else I should
be only too glad to cement that friendship (I don't know if I told

---

[1] Original MS. not seen.

you that we asked Mrs Lyall to ask Dar to dinner one day & I kept Dr Moberley's note in reply to send to Mrs Wilmot, as though it says little that little is so nice). Mrs Lyall says she will try & ask him again pretty often to her usual 2 o'clock dinner as that gives the boys the liberty of going out of bounds which they enjoy, but to return to Fanny. I should be extremely glad if she might come & you might perhaps think of something that could be done by F. E. & her by way of 'seeing Manchester'; the worst is they are too young to go about sight seeing by themselves. I am so very anxious you should go my darling & stay as long as you can; the more so as I don't quite see my way clear to your coming to London (proper) this year. The Prices keep asking 'when is Marianne coming up to town' but one can't say 'when any one asks her' & the Wedgwoods have done ditto. We called on the Price's on Sunday & Bertha told us that they had had a house offered them in Hertfordshire or Berkshire for three months & that she thought they should go there in April & stay there till after Margarets wedding. I fancy all the Thompsons plans are upset by Mrs Thompson's illness which I believe will end fatally in a very short time. I want to scrape up with Mr Greg (who tho' he knows I am in town through the Price's has taken no notice of me by note or call) in order to secure a visit for you if you do come up to town.

So to return to your plans my darling. Do arrange to stay as long as you can at Liverpool & make as many happy plans for F. E. that you can—get her books from the Portico 'Manse of Mastland, or Maskland', *very* highly spoken of, everybody speaking of it, translated from the Dutch by Keightley[1] & ask F. Wilmot & 'recommend' Flossy to Shadwell's Georgina, Ewarts etc. And one thing more, I have now written to Silverdale—for one thing I wanted to know about Sophie (who has I think behaved very badly) & another I & Meta have been wondering how far you ought to go to Kreuznach[2] again *this* year. The Ernest Bunsens say 2 years together—does so *very* much more than a year here & a year there. They are going again & are *most* civil & kind about you in every way. Meta & I are wondering if this would be really desirable for you—in which case we would not

[1] *Manse of Mastland*, 1860.
[2] A case where the MS. reading ('Crenznach') is the same as the typescript one before subsequent correction of the latter in pencil. Also, the MS. source has a superfluous '&', which presumably follows a typescript 'and', although it had been lightly cancelled with hyphens.

go anywhere unless health required it, but stay & enjoy the summer & the cow calving at home & write my story as hard as might be. I wish you would tell us your *real opinion* on this head *regardless* of expense—which could easily be managed—& would be as nothing in comparison with making you into a strong woman. How does Amelia go on? What hopes have you & Hearn of her doing? How does Mary go on? How is Shaw? You never told me. Please tell her I asked.

To-night we are going to Lady Lyell's, to-morrow *morning* to Lambeth Palace with Mr V. Lushington to hear the decision about All Souls College (whether the Fellowships there shall be decided by *merit alone* or by birth & other circumstances). *Godfrey L.* is on the 'merit alone' side along with two other 'fellows', the Warden & other authorities on the opposite. Archbishop of Canterbury to give the decision. In the evening there is a dinner party here. On Monday at $\frac{1}{2}$ p. 1. Mr Bowman is going to perform Meta's 'little operation' on her tonsils. I have a note from him this morning recommending that 'Miss Gaskell should have a glass of sherry at one o'clock on Monday'. I think Mrs Gaskell will have one too. After that she is to be quiet indoors for a few days, & then to see him again for him to see that it is healing properly. Towards the end of next week I expect we shall go to the Shaen's but a good deal depends on Meta's throat. Effie is laying in a stock of music & of novels for Meta's amusement next week as she is not to talk much till her throat is all right. Mr Bowman says it will do her eyes good, as it is the living membrane that gets inflamed & relaxed. Meta says it will be like a new life to her if she gets her throat & eyes seen about & put to rights. Miss Darwin has had another tussle to get her to go to the Pyrenees, Pampeluna etc 2 months from the 20th of April. But I have been the stern mother. It is the opinion here that E. T. H. is making up to Miss Darwin & that Dumbleton would not dislike it as he must 'marry money'. But if there is anything in this we shall hear if[1] the Pyrenean scheme will be given up for the present at least. Don't name this however. Yesterday we lunched at the Ewarts. Only Mary at home, she drove us to the Hogarth Club pictures & thence we went to Rossetti's where we got a great welcome & a strong wish that his wife was at home. He has taken one or two more rooms on the same floor as his studio. I shall write to F. E. to-morrow. Give my dearest love to her & Julia. We are going to

[1] Sources read 'of'.

try & call on Mrs Fane to-day so as to give her an account of it. Will you try Florence's voice? She is very anxious (or was when I left) to learn to sing & I think she would be grateful to you for helping her in the preliminary steps. Remind Hearn about the Italian seeds that are to be given to the gardener & please speak to him yourself about them—greenhouse heat from 60 to 65, & will you see that he is sowing seeds generally for a good supply of flowers for *next* winter, primulas, cinerarias etc. etc. & altogether brush him up with a little interest. My dearest love to Julia & Papa. Write a long letter telling all details of home news & the Wilds[1] dinner & *date* your letter.

Your own most affect[ionate]
Mamy.

499 499a 511

W. S. WILLIAMS[2]

46, Plymouth Grove
Feb. 6th [1862]

My Dear Sir,

I am truly obliged to you for your frank kind note, a note which I know gave you both more pain and more trouble to write than if your verdict had been more favourable. I am indifferent about the title, as I have another in reserve 'Philip's Idol'— which would perhaps answer the purpose better if the book is ever completed.

I am very much obliged to you for letting me see Miss Kavanagh's new work. I will take great care of it and return it before long. Once more, please accept my best thanks for giving your opinion of my MSS so candidly and kindly. Of course I don't *quite* agree with you but I know too well with what a partial eye an author looks on his books to urge my opinion against yours. I do not think you have read the second volume, have you, though even that in the development of the story only leads up to the third.

Ever my Dear Sir,
Yours very truly and gratefully,
E. C. Gaskell

[1] Sources both read 'Wilda', which looks like a *typing* slip. The Gaskells' friends are elsewhere called 'Wildes'.

[2] Original MS. not seen.

496 **500*a*** 505

MARIANNE GASKELL[1]

[Early 1862]

⟨. . .⟩ back straight, when I was taken ill that Tuesday & now I am glad the letter did not go, as the quieter all is done & the less that is said the better. I leave all at your end to the decision of *you and Mrs Dicey*[2] whatever you two think best had better be done; only do avoid Dr Manning. I concentrate all my wish on that for the present, till I know more, I *wish* your letter would come, tho' it would only be a letter after the telegrams; not after the letters Meta wrote. I have not been out yet. I come down before lunch & go up to bed early (last night between 6 & 7) & am very good for nothing—but oh! if I do but hear good accounts of you my child—good accounts in every way—that you are pretty strong, that you are not led off by excitement to go a few steps (as you think *only*) on a wrong & terrible way—that you are avoiding temptation & referring doubtful cases to Mrs Dicey who, you know love, is at present in the place of a parent to you, I shall get all right. Only tell me the truth. There is no news—or there seems to me none, compared with what I want to hear from you. *Don't go to the Storys' Friday afternoons* if it is there you meet Dr Manning because it will be awkward to have to so change your manner to him as to provoke questions & explanations. Oh! I am so sorry I ever let you go to Rome—we have so missed you at home & if it is all to end in this way, but I know it won't. Only you see I am not well & am so stupid & do so want your letter. Louy Jackson is coming (did I tell you?), at least she offered & Meta accepted when I was ill & we have not heard from her & think she must be coming. Godfrey Wedgwood is engaged to Mary Jane Hawkshaw[3] & they are to be married in June. Mr Bosanquet is engaged to a Miss Eliza Carr of Northumberland & they are to be married in August. God bless you & *have you in His holy keeping* my dearest darling.

Your ever most affec[tionate] mother

E. C. Gaskell.

[1] Original MS. not seen.
[2] Sources read 'Diny', silently emended henceforth.
[3] Sources both read 'Hawksgaw', another very possible typing error.

506 **506*a*** •509

MARIANNE GASKELL[1]

Thursday
[8 May 1862]

My dearest Polly.
   Did I tell you all our plans yesterday—
                Miss Behrens
                23 Bentinck Street
                Manchester Sq.
receives us from Monday till Thursday—*we shall stay to receive
morning post on that day* before going to Paris. Wednesday is to be
our *especial looking out* and deciding on lodging day. Hilarys are
in the ascendant just now—only we should want another servant
and there are *only at the outside* 6 *single* beds. Would you like to go
to Mrs George Smiths, Hampstead? She writes to beg some of us
will go—only one spare room to offer etc—we *thought* of you and
Florence as you would get more *general* London gaiety; and you
neither of you care too much for the Exhibition, *pure*. About the
Hallé's. I think it must depend (*exact* time I mean) on Alice's
answer etc. I don't think Minni sounds to have written on *purpose*
to ask you to *fix* exact day and you might say 'beginning of June'
as an 'approximation' (as Mrs G. Smith would say). Meta (in my
name) writes to Mrs G. S. to say that I and one of my daughters
or two of them will come for 3 or 4 days beginning of June. If
we have H. B. C's lodgings we can't have them *just* at the beginning of June, but I shan't know *when* for a day or two. *Does
Dumbleton really think of asking Julia?* Please answer this; as if it
did it would make a gt difference in our various plans. You would
go to E. B. Carter's while *she* spent 1st part of her holidays at
Dumbleton; *but* we shd not *then* ask the little Brodies the beginning of July as we half thought we had better do. Mr H Smith
was here last night. Mr Story and Dr M. have had a great quarrel
and are no longer friends. Mrs Dicey comes to England on the
10th inst. Mind you *write to her.* You see if we cd not get the
lodgings *quite* at the beginning of June and Florence was 'de trop'
by that time at Winchester (one does not *know* about Mrs Lyall's
engagements) you might come up to town and either fetch her
from W. or meet her and you two go to the Smiths while Meta

[1] Original MS. not seen.

and I might linger on two or three days abroad, after that you might go to the Hallé's. Direct to Mrs Smith thro *Smith & Elder* as they are changing their house, 45 Pall Mall W, or 65 Corn Hill E.C. only allow a day or two *extra* for this going round. Mind I shall send you some money if you go to S. Port as *I* wish to give Susanna the comfort of your society if you go. If you go to the Smiths I think Papa will give you enough to get you to London etc. and after you get there I will furnish you with what you want. This is very dull my darling and I could tell you heaps of bits amusement but Philo[1] has called me twice and I must go.

> Your own very affec[tionate]
> Mamy.

I hope you will understand it all? If not ask and fully understand before we go abroad for we *may* be difficult to catch by post afterwards. K.[2] Greaves says Mr Commissioner Gaskell is looking out for suburban lodgings or house for the Liscardites which I *think* makes one afraid of Putney.

*506a **509** 516

MARIANNE GASKELL[3]

> Friday morning,
> 23 Bentinck St
> [?16 May 1862]

My dearest Polly,

You are a sweet good child in every way & I cannot tell you how much I am loving you for your humility & sweetness. I *quite* trust you love to go to the Hallés only be sure you tell Papa about it in *time* that *if* he has any objection you can arrange your plans in accordance with his wishes. I am pretty sure, & so I think, is Meta that he *has* heard about it—was told before we left home; but still you know things so often go in at one ear with him & out at another that it will be as well to be quite sure. We have not yet fixed on our house etc; but as we *finally* go to-morrow we must fix to-day & before I close this letter. Meta had a letter this morning from L. V. J. In it she says Mrs Lyall wants Meta & me to

---

[1] Source reads 'Phili'.   [2] ? R.   [3] Original MS. not seen.

come to Winchester on our way back from France to pick up
Florence; & *that her large spare room will be at liberty for us till the
4th June*. I *think* we shall do this; but why I name it now is to show
you that I *think* Florence is *sure* to stop till the 3rd or 4th. We must
be in town by the 4th because of the Elijah. My darling (When I
went to Wimbledon yesterday I offered to pay etc. & found you
had done it—thank you *very* much love, for the pleasure) so as far
as I can see at present this will be the plan. For us to come via
St Malo Jersey Southampton Winchester, getting here on the
3 or 4th when I shall hope to find you & Hearn, who might come
up together in the lodgings (which however if we take those that
seem most likely *at present*—namely 32 Belgrave Road, won't
hold us *all* till after the 8th) & then, after a good talk together, I
think you & Florence had better go for your 4 or 5 days to Mrs
Smith's; & then for her to come to us & you to go to the Hallés
for a week or 10 days, *not longer* either for their sakes or ours for
we shall want to have you. I think it can be well arranged for
Julia to come up with Emily Aspland (as she & Florence did before) being carefully met here etc. so that I see no need for your
waiting for her. Papa too is coming that week; only earlier than
the 13th. I am afraid I don't know if the Greens will like to spare
her before the holidays begin.

And now about lodgings. We have been most persevering in
devoting our whole days to the research. (N.B. I *almost* think you
might write to Mrs Smith naming the 3rd or 4th as the *probable*
days of going to her; as she might like to know before long).
Back to lodgings. Hilary's are engaged till June 15th & are *very*
bare; & with cook etc. would be dear—advantages, airiness &
nearness to the Xn. But however the time they are occupied for[1]
puts *them* out of the question. Mrs Soebers are—detestable dear &
dirty *very* small rooms, *very* close, only 3 bedrooms, 9 guineas.
She did not know who we were; & we were so thankful *not* to
have engaged that pig in a poke! Mrs Marshall's (Annie Jenkins)
2 dining rooms, 2 *very* pretty drawing rooms, 4 good well furnished bedrooms & one or two attics, 6 guineas a week. At present
occupied by *two* parties; one of whom leaves June 1st (when we
could have dining rooms, 2 upper bedrooms & 1 attic for
3 guineas) the other, (a M.P's party) leaves on the 8th when we
should have the whole house which is incomparably the best,
cheapest, best furnished & pleasantest landlady & cleanest servants

---

[1] Word omitted in MS. source.

we have seen. The *only* doubt is as to the healthiness of the situation. About 400 yards nearer the river than the[1] Thompson's, about 200 from the Victoria Station. Yesterday spite of the rain we went to Putney & Wimbledon but could find *nothing* there, we saw *2 houses* 1 lodgings.[2]

223 **509*b*** 0

?CATHERINE WINKWORTH

46 Plymouth Grove
July 23 1861 [1862]
no end[3]

⟨. . .⟩ Paris altogether was abominable; noisy, hot, close, smelling of drains—*and*—perpetual cooking &c; and we were none of us well there. I however laid a good foundation for future work at Mme de Sévigné, saw M. Hachette about it, got all manner of introductions to\the private part of/public collections of MSS, books[,] portraits &c; went to every old house in Paris that she lived in, & got a list of books 'pour servir', & a splendid collection of all the portraits of herself, family & contemporaries. I could have done much more if I had not found that Meta was becoming absolutely *ill* with unappetizing food, noisy nights, close air. We spent one *charming* day—entirely out of doors at S. Germain, Meta & Isabel sketching in the Park & I, prowling about, & getting them food &c &c. Then on Saturday aft: we left going to Chartres that eveng. Chartres Cathedral is *so* beautiful do you know it. Sunday afternoon we went on to Vitré, just in Brittany the town near which les Rochers is. It is a *most* picturesque half inhabited town; we went to the Hotel de Sévigné, her old town house, which in her days was called La Tour de Sévigné,—an

---

[1] Word omitted in MS. source.

[2] There follows a note from Meta and then the postscript printed as Letter 509 on pp. 688–9 above. Meta's note mentions that Mrs Gaskell had met Holman Hunt at the Shaens the evening before.

[3] In another hand. *Address* (*on envelope*) Miss C. Winkworth | Miss Shaen's | West Hill | Wandsworth | London | *SW*. *Postmarks* MANCHESTER | OC 11 | 61 | and LONDON SW | E7 | OC 12 | 61. We prefer the date 1862 as fitting better with the movements of Florence and Marianne. In 1862 June 4 (the day of the Eton celebrations) fell on a Wednesday. Mrs Gaskell presumably wrote 'June 5' in error.

immense barrack of an old half-fortified house; only half furnished, & never cleaned since her days; a more filthy place I never
saw; but the people were very civil, & the town extremely sketchable, with old walls covered with snap dragon, valerian, wall-
flowers &c,—with wooden colonnades supporting the first floors
of the houses; and tourelles here, there & everywhere. Monday we
took a little market cart, & drove, shaking & laughing to Les
Rochers. No one has ever said half enough of its beauty—you go
up rising ground, through grassy high hedged lanes,—suddenly
turn to yr left into a sort of park-like field, up thro' a field very
like a Silverdale field near Arnside Tower, with little rocks crop-
ping out, & all sorts of delicate flowers {cropping ov} carpeting
the ground[,] see a vast picturesque pile before you with 13, (that
I *counted*) towers, of all sorts of sizes & shapes, a great walled in
garden,—walled, & pillared and balled with grey stone, whh is half
tumbling down, showing old avenues, & heaps of roses, and sparkling fountains within,—a long range of grey, ric⟨h⟩-coloured
farm buildings at a little distance from the house with a space like
a village green between, with cocks & hens, & donkeys, and
turkeys &c all flourishing about, and here and there a blazing peacock, cows in the farm yard beyond,—opposite (you have the
house itself at the farthest part of the left hand, the old garden
coming from it towards you,—the farm-buildings on yr right [&]
the green right before you & *opposite*,) a great grove of high dark-
coloured old trees—older than Mme de S. by a great deal,—then
we dismissed our market cart to the stables & turned round & lo
& behold we were high up on a plateau of ground with 30 miles
of sunny champaign country lying below us [here a sketch is
inserted] that sort of way, only not *such* a steep descent. It was a
most charming day.

The next we went on at early dawn to Fougères, a curious
old town where we staid all day at an inn—where we entered
straight from the street into the kitchen, & thence went out into
a square court with 4 tiers of wooden galleries, out of whh the
bedrooms opened,—very curious & very filthy. On the next
morng by a carriage of the country to Pont Orson, where we
breakfasted & thence to Mt St Michel,—that night to Avranches;
where we staid 2 days, kept by the rain & a laudable desire to wash
our clothes. We went & called on the Healds there, who were
leaving the next day, heartily tired of their stay there. And now I
must put this letter away for today. Thursday morning[.] I sent

off the first 3 sheets of this letter yesterday, as I hope you are aware before now.[1]

Friday morning. To go back to our French journey. We went viâ coupé of diligence (which we shared with a regiment of fleas[)] to St Lo, where Meta & Isabel went to see the Cathedral, (but they turned up their noses at all Cathedrals after Chartres whh *was* superbly beautiful,) & on by rail to Caen, where we stopped all night in a clean hotel, kept by a very cockney ci-devant London butler, of the name of Humby—('Umby's 'Otel) recommended by the Healds, who had stayed there for 4 months last winter. It is not down in Murray, but ought to be for its cleanliness, civility, and moderate charges; but it was funnily cockney: and one felt how English people might live abroad without coming in contact with the picturesqueness & variety of foreign life. The poor Heald girls were utterly weary of their foreign life, & so was Mrs Heald I think. Of course they had to go abroad to œconomize. They went in Novemb⟨er⟩ & took rooms (en pension) at Hu⟨m⟩by's. The Hotel looks on to a grea⟨t⟩ common stretching down to th⟨e⟩ narrow river,—no distant view (Saturday morng) and the Healds lived there at a foggy time of the year in 3 small clean roo⟨ms,⟩ knowing no one, and *very* dis⟨mal⟩, the sea (*flat* part of coast of Normandy,) 8 or 9 miles off, to which, along sandy fields, wi⟨th⟩ sandy turf banks for fence⟨s⟩ all flat and foggy the Healds used to walk, 'by way of an object.' They got dingy nove⟨ls⟩ from the Caen\Circg/Library, & ha⟨d⟩ no other books, I fancy. No wonder they 'hate living abroad!' From Caen we went to Rouen via sea to Havre, & by rail, and stayed there 2 days in all the luxury of a well-managed hotel. Thence straight to London (Dieppe & Newhaven,) in time for our Elijah on June 4th.

We three arrived at the new Victoria Station, not 10 minutes walk from our lodgings in Belgrave Road, on the evening of Tuesday, June 3, and there we parted, Isabel to return to Wimbledon, Meta & I to our lodgings where we found Marianne & Florence, who, with Hearn had come up the day before; (No! *Florence* had been at Winchester with Louy Jackson & Mrs Lyall during our absence, M A & Hearn had met her the day before at the Waterloo Station.) Fred Holland (2nd son at Dumbleton, curate here under Canon Richson,) was in town for a week, staying at a Colonel Knox's in Belgrave Square, (curious contrast to his life in Ancoats,) and he came every morng to help us & arrange

[1] The first page of this fragmentary letter is headed '*3 sheet*'.

plans during our stay, & was evidently most anxious to heal the
old Thurstan breach; and you know Marianne *had* just been staying at Dumbleton! Well on Wednesday June 5, M A & Florence
were fetched by Mr Smith (my publisher) to pay him\& Mrs S/a
visit at Hampstead for a week. In the eveng Isabel, Amabel & Mr
Fred Thompson called for Meta & me to take us to Exeter Hall
to hear the Elijah. It was the Derby day; and London *awfully* full,
—so, at the conclusion of the concert, no cabs were to be had. In
the waiting-room Mr V. L. came up, & introduced me to his
aunt (his mother died in 1837, his Aunt, Miss Carr, well known to
my Aunts in other days, when Hollands & Carrs were near neighbours.) Miss Carr said something about being so much obliged for
our kindness to her nephew &c, & hoping to see us at Ockham
(Ockham is near\5 miles from/Weybridge,[)] belongs to Lord
Lovelace, but Dr L rents it, & the family have it for a country
house; town house 18 Eaton Place. (G. & V. L living at an
official house of Dr L's in Doctor's Commons; & having their
chambers in Lincoln's Inn & the Temple.[1]) Then Mr F Thompson &
Amabel & Isabel were *obliged* to go off, *walking* to the Waterloo
St—in order to catch the last train to Wimbledon; so Meta & I
were left forlorn, all the ladies of the L-party having gone, but
M⟨r⟩ V. L. having offered to find u⟨s⟩ a cab. He was more than
an hour away; & meanwhile we *almost* alone in the waiting room,
fell over head & ears in love with Mr Otto Goldsmidt, w⟨ho⟩ was
waiting for his wife to cha⟨nge⟩ her dress, and meanwhile tal⟨ked⟩
to the only other people in the waiting-room; so pleasantly, &
goodly, and gentlemanly. Then *they* went, and he looked rat⟨her⟩
pityingly & half-inclined to speak at *us*, and then *he* was called, &
off *he* went, and the men began to put out the lights, & it was
past 12, and then V L came back with a cab, having been to Haymarket and Temple & I don't know where. When we came back
I found Thurstan had called (our first time of *possible* meeting
since the old row,) and left a request for us to go to Eton the next
day, it being the annual day for boat-races, fire-works &c, and
he had sent his boat down there, to be ready to row us on the
river.

Before breakfast the next morng, Fred (his brother, you know)
came, & re-urged the plan. We were engaged to Emily's that
night to a great party, but Fred said we could go straight from the
Paddington Station (on our return from Eton, at $\frac{1}{2}$ p 8) to

---

[1] 'G.L' has been inserted over 'Lincoln's' and 'VL' over 'Temple'.

Emily's; so we sent Hearn & our dresses there; and set off ourselves for Eton at 3. Thurstan Fred & Scott Holland,—a young cousin still at Eton, for our squires. We had no dinner, but lunched at the boys' old tutors, lounged in the lovely 'playing-fields' meeting no end of friends (for every one in the least connected with the place goes to it on that day—) and then went with all the rest of the world to the river and embarked in Thurstan's boat, & rowed a great way up the river, & then walked to the field, where the different Eton boat crews were having their supper, under tents, band playing &c. Then it began to rain, so we ran back thro' the long wet grass to our boats, muffled ourselves in cloaks & plaids, & were rowed back to the island in the river to be illuminated by the fireworks. We sate in our boat among a thick crowd of other boats in pelting rain till the pretty Eton racing-boats came down the river from their supper; every minute the rain coming on more & more steadily, which delayed the boats. Then they came with shout & song & music down the dark river, into the bright coloured gleam of the fire works & coloured light {going}\coming/smoothly down with the current out of the darkness into the shining water,—into the darkness again,—all the crews standing up motion⟨less⟩ as they passed the brilliant illuminated 'Floreat Etona'. The thing reminded *me* of the Saxon Kings comparison of human life to the swallows flying thro' the tent, out of darkness coming,—into darkness going. Meta said s⟨he⟩ thought of the verse in the Ancient Mariner 'A Sera⟨ph⟩ band' &c,—for each figure ⟨was⟩ motionless and bright, & the smooth current bore them past so noiselessly & still. The fireworks were of course a failure in the pouring rain. Drenched & miserable ⟨. . .⟩

511 **511a** 514

W. S. WILLIAMS[1]

46, Plymouth Grove
August 22nd [?1862]

My Dear Sir,

I send you the revise—I am afraid there are still many corrections to make. I also send you another chapter to *add to the*

[1] Original MS. not seen.

2nd volume please; I think the printer is quite right in wanting some more to add to it. Shall I send the MSS to you in *chapters* which can be printed off straight away? That might expedite matters—and I will write it as fast as I can.

Yours very truly,
E. C. Gaskell

₀ **519*a*** ₀

UNKNOWN[1]

46 Plymouth Grove
Manchester
Janry 7 [?1863]

Sir,

I have received your letter asking me to contribute to your volume of stories[2] published for the Lancashire Relief Fund. I am so much occupied with Sewing Schools etc.—that I really hardly know if I can find time to write anything, as it takes an unfatigued *body*, as well as a willing *mind*, to write even a short story.

—You do not say when you expect to have your book published? and the time at which you would require my story would have a great deal to do with my decision. If I am able to write anything, I should never think of taking any remuneration; I should like to show my sympathy with your effort,—which is the only reason I do not at once refuse.

Yours truly
E. C. Gaskell.

[1] From a MS. transcript made by Mrs Jane Whitehill, headed 'Copy of A.L. in the Knutsford Library'.

[2] No likely volume was identified in a preliminary check made by a most helpful member of the Local History Staff of Manchester Central Library.

₀ **521a** •₅₄₁ₐ

MR PERKINS[1]

Hotel d'Allemagne
Sunday
[?May ?1863][2]

Dear Sir,

Mrs Sargent told me yesterday what a kind offer of help you made me through her in our difficulties about our Florence route; and I am writing in a rather unceremonial way to claim the fulfilment of it. I should have much preferred coming to call myself; but as I cannot unfortunately do so this morning, and as we are rather in a hurry to settle our plans, I am taking the great liberty of sending my courier to you in hopes that you will most kindly give him 'renseignements' on one or two points, on which many people have told me that you are the best authority—

But before naming them, will you let me explain to you why I have never yielded to my wish of calling on Mrs Perkins. She was so well known to me by name, and I had heard so much of both you and her from my daughter, that I had quite hoped to share her pleasure in your acquaintance; but I believed that I must expect a visit from you, if this wish was mutual, and it was only from Mrs Sargent last night that I learnt that the etiquette was for me to have called on you—I am sufficiently punished for having been the slave of (a mistaken) etiquette!

We want very much to go to Perugia, to see it and Assisi, and then to go to Orvieto. Would our best plan be to go to Perugia *through* Orvieto, and take Assisi in a day *from* Perugia; or would it be better to go by the regular Perugia route, and return to Orvieto? And if we go by the regular road to Perugia, must we sleep at Assisi, or can we take that in the middle of a long day between Foligno and Perugia? Must we sleep two nights between Rome and Foligno? and can we sleep at *Narmi*? Then if our best plan is to return from Perugia to Orvieto, must we sleep at Citta della Pieve, or is there a cross road in which one can come in one day from Perugia to Orvieto? From Orvieto, in case we returned to it *from* Perugia, could we join the railway to Siena in one day?

---

[1] Original MS. not seen. Source describes it as 8 pp., 8vo.
[2] Mrs Gaskell also went to Florence in April 1857 (Passport information).

M.G·L.—HH

and if not where had we better break the journey between Orvieto and the last point of the railway?

Do please forgive my thus asking you to do duty as Murray, in this troublesome way; but everyone from whom I have asked advice, has told me 'Why don't you go to Mr Perkins? he knows better than any one,' so please look upon this trouble as the penalty of your reputation for wisdom and experience!

If you will enlighten my cousin (who brings you this,) I should feel really grateful; and I shall hope to thank you 'de vive voix' when I am meaning to call on Mrs Perkins—at length!

Yours truly
E. C. Gaskell

P.S. In thinking it over, I feel that I am asking you so much that perhaps you will send me an answer to my questions at your leisure in writing: but my cousin will tell you our wishes & possibilities.

516 523a 524

MARIANNE GASKELL[1]

Florence. Wednesday.
20 [May 1863]

My dearest Polly,

I am in a fidget about your dress; please get yourself what is necessary to look as nice as possible. Marshall & Snelgrove have ready made gowns (for full dress) & if needed you can get yourself some flowers. I meant to get you some at Nattiers (Paris) but if you want them, & do look nice & ladylike my darling, please get them in London, Only get good & becoming ones. We have been trying to think what dresses you have, & are puzzled—it seems so very long since we have seen you. Please tell Amabel we accept her (family) invitation for June 24 is it not? (I privately do so want your letter to see if you will come to Versailles my darling, *but don't name it to anyone.* If you have not enough of money have it put down to me (giving Plymouth Grove address) at Marshall & Snelgrove's etc—only do be well dressed clean &

---

[1] Original MS. not seen.

fresh. We are still delighted with our lodgings, although we have a $\frac{1}{4}$ of a plan for leaving them on Monday next & going for a week to Venice, chiefly at Julia's most earnest desire. But to-day Francois is ill in bed with Eastern fever caught in the Holy Land last night [sic] & returning (as Col. Shadwell's did) & is so poorly we doubt whether even if we determined to go on Monday to Venice he would be fit to travel. So Poste Restante Florence till the end of this month will be our safest address. All the world is here; Lockers, Dillys, Miss Cushman, etc. etc. all the Roman people beside the Trollopes etc. etc. who are naturally here.

Mrs Charles Stanley (widow of the Bishop's son) is in this house on the same floor & we see a great deal of her; Meta rides out with her etc. But she goes to-morrow. We do so delight in Lady Charlotte. She is so funny & ⟨   ⟩ and good natured & witty, & between her & the Stanleys we hear no end about the Prince of Wales' ménage. But I have not time to tell you. Hearn in Francois' illness takes this letter to the post. Does not know enough Italian to pay for it, so you will have to pay double which serves you right for not writing, you little monkey. We are all well. Meta perhaps the least so, i.e. the most easily knocked up; but then she gobbles down pictures etc. all day long. We are over done with loads of books all of which we want to read but have no time for since our friends have forced us out. Please apologize to Mr Crompton for the accompanying notes being so stupid & confused—I wrote it [sic] in the midst of chatter, dinner & knocking over an ink bottle. The Jane[1] Gregs are here; Mr & Mrs Amy & Bertha, they came here last night. I went to call on the Bright's yesterday at the Hotel de Grande Bretagne[2]—& found them all in. The Blacketts are here & we have had to call & ⟨   ⟩ we neglected them in Rome. It is fearfully hot & we envy the (Sainted!!!) Bishop of Siena who made a gift to the Virgin of all his clothes but I think I must tell Lady Crompton that I have made a gift of all my gowns if we stay there & *to-day Florence says she should like to stay at Hyde P. Sq. on her return.* So I shall stay. *Is Julia expected?* She would delight in it only is shy about not being asked—only our dress will be on its last legs & I shall have no money to refit *my poor old self* with in Paris. By the way *if* there is an article on *La Camorra* in the June Cornhill & *if* you come to Versailles would you ask Mr Smith for the money therefor & *bring it with you, but don't breathe to anyone* that the said

---

[1] ? Sam. [2] Sources read 'Britaque'.

article is mine. Now I must end. Please entreat Isabel to write to me; a long lovely gossipy letter including Oxford as well as London.

Your own Mammy.

*521a 541a 0

MR PERKINS[1]

Manchester
Decr 9 [?1863]

Dear Sir,

I feel as if the first thing that I ought to do in writing to you, was to tell you how capitally our Perugian journey answered, as the last time I saw you was when you so very kindly smoothed all the difficulties of our route for us: but I must only just thank you for your great help and the consequent success of our journey en passant,—for the object of my writing to you is to beg that you will allow me to introduce to you the son of a friend of mine, Mr William H. Langton, and his two travelling companions, Mr Addison Birley, and Mr Henry Coddington. You know that last spring we used quite to laugh at Mr Dicey for his perpetual refrain of 'Go and ask Mr Perkins,' whenever we appealed to him for any information about Rome, art, and or music; so that I looked upon you as a very wise and useful person, before my own experience of your great kindness and invaluable help in the case of the Perugia route. I feel therefore that if you will let these three gentlemen have the pleasure of making your acquaintance, I shall have secured for them a great advantage, and I am sure that they will rightly appreciate it— They are, I believe, extremely musical—

I have had some very interesting letters from Mr Norton since my return home full of the same brave, hopeful feeling about the prospects of his country. I remain, with kind regards to Mrs Perkins,

Yours very truly
E. C. Gaskell

---

[1] Original MS. not seen. Source describes it as 4 pp., 8vo.

MARIANNE GASKELL[1]

> Sunday pouring rain, before church.
>
> [3 July 1864]

My dearest Polly,

All my news is in these letters. *Please take care of Hearn's & return it to Meta. Is* it not provoking that Charlie should have sent his note to *Manchester*, if he had sent it to Hampstead you & I must have gone to *one* (at least) of the places yesterday morning? I am so sorry I could cry about it. Would there be a *chance* of *your* going! I am so sorry about it. As *my* dress is to Mrs Smiths so is Philo's to mine. I *can* not[2] get shabby enough to take my proper place below my dear lady. I am so fond of her though. Margaret seems to me *much* improved although of course I have seen very little of her as yet. The house will be very singular, but with some beautiful rooms in it. The schoolroom is superb, large with 5 windows all commanding separate views. Wayland—the sculptor at the Assize Courts is here, carving cornices etc etc. Sir B. & Philo want us *exceptionally to go with them* or *be* with them in the autumn. A Sir R. Vaughan has offered them his house up above Dolgelle—& could not we be there with them? 5 sitting rooms bracing air etc. or the Tyrol—or the Pyrenees—to which place the [?Silver][3] Smith & Mr Grant Duff would also go. In short they are fuller & more vague about their plans than we are—which is saying a great deal. The new drawing room will be beautiful & is to absorb the present dining room merely as a *recep.* for private reading or quietness.[4] Mr Harcourt is here (Oxford) Max Muller, Goldwin Smith & the Silvery one. To-morrow we all go to Stanton-Harcourt & on Tuesday home, via Bletchley. No time for more before church my darling. Send on letters *here* till after post time 8 a.m. on *Tuesday.*

> Your own most affec[tionate]
>
> E. C. G.

---

[1] Original MS. not seen.   [2] MS. source omits 'not'.

[3] Sources read 'Silon' with superscript 'Silver (?)'.

[4] Sources read 'quickness'.

MARIANNE GASKELL[1]

Tuesday. [22 August 1865] 46 P. G.

My dearest Polly,

I am so very[2] sorry you had all the useless trouble & fatigue of going over to Alton yesterday. I was very ill when I wrote to you 3 weeks ago so I cannot remember if I said positively you were *to go on the 21st* but I *quite* agree that it is better in general to *keep blindly to the words of an agreement.* I am so behindhand with my writing W & D's that I had to write as hard as I could at Fryston[3] (before breakfast & late at night) but I *fancied as I had distinctly said to Thurstan that I wished the Valuer to go down about the White's furniture & settle about that before I went down* & as he *repeated* that in his answer to me as 'most desirable' I suppose I thought that you would understand that as the lists were not forthcoming either to the Whites or to me—the whole thing was delayed *until the valuer had been.* I am sorry enough about it, as it makes me be every day in a state of uncertainty very unfavourable to my powers of writing. I wrote to Thurstan on the *10th* & fancied that all would have been arranged by the 21st. but you know as well as I do the delays which have arisen; first the lists, then Mr White away in York & Mrs White declining to act until his return. I am sick of the whole thing & very much regret that it has all to be settled just now, when I *must* save all my health & strength for writing & have no one to whom I can delegate the acting. I am very sorry indeed for your day yesterday & terribly disappointed that you have seen the house without me. I was *very* much disappointed at there not being a line from you with the lists; for which thank you dear. I wish you had just asked the question in the envelope about whether—the element of valuation having been introduced into the concern, *after* I had planned to go down on the 21st—it did not make some difference. However it is spilt milk, spilt fatigue & disappointment & money. (By the way are the Kath. Dock dividends due yet? I want them sadly; & *you must want some more money I am afraid?*)

Julia is not well, overdone by heat & responsibility I fancy while we were away. The ear rings came quite safely, *registered* letters

[1] Original MS. not seen.　　　　　　[2] MS. source reads 'am ever so'.
[3] Sources read 'Frystore'.

always do; I think, at least I fancied they never required acknowledgment. Meta has had bad headaches for some time & I wanted
her to have no more than necessary letters & to Julia to write at
Fryston (& there has been a great deal more of odd pieces of
business to be done for other people than we have ever told you
of dear). No use worrying you at a distance, & I *am* so badly
behindhand in Wives & Daughters. All these worries about Alton
do so incapacitate me from writing. Now I must do it all myself—
I mean about Alton etc. Indeed I see Thurstan grudged me the
time you could have given me & you would have had to return
before much of the *work* was done. We have never heard from
Papa. We stayed till yesterday at Fryston hoping till yesterday's
morning post to hear that the valuer had been, as it would have
saved me a good deal of money for me & Hearn to have gone
straight up to London from Tonybridge & we planned telegraphing to you to meet us the next day. But no letters ever came.
To-day we have telegraphed to Mr Ewart to ask if Mr White has
ever sent for the valuer; as the days are passing on & Papa may
come home next week. It is very hot & distressing here. My old
sleepless nights have begun again & Julia seems very much out of
order; does not touch her breakfast & has constant feeling of sick-
ness & headache. We are going to have the drains up in the yard
& see if anything is wrong there. Julia won't hear of going from
home but I think she must not be left alone again. She has worried
her sweet little self about servants, Papa's letters etc. *As soon as ever*
I hear that the valuer has been I shall go. *I shall want the list in
Mr White's handwriting* sent to Thurstan because on it *I made my
pencil memoranda of what furniture would be wanted.* Florence would
come & help me any day & Charlie is only too anxious she should,
but I feel that I ought not to take her away from Lady Crompton
who has no *woman* but her just now, only all the boys. Meta &
Julia are lunching with Emily Greg. They made the engagement
a fortnight ago & neither of them felt quite up to a hot game of
croquet; but I thought it was better for them to go; but it is
broiling hot.

There was a constant procession of people thro' the house at
Fryston—Judges, Marshals, Mr FitzStephen, Mrs Borter & Edith,
Mr & Mrs Lowe, Mr Cholmondeley, Sir John Lowther, Mr
Kitson (brother to your old schoolfellow) Mr Wickham, Mr &
Mrs Parker, Mr Swinburne ('Atalanta in Calydon') Mrs Black-
burn & Miss Blackburn, Miss Newton (a cousin of my lords)

Mr & Mrs Maurice (rev. F. D) & all their men[1] & maids. Oh! & School inspectors & three or four clergymen, Dr and Mrs Vaughan etc. I keep thinking of your disappointment yesterday at not finding us there—*its an unlucky* house & I believe I was a fool to set my heart on the place at all. For it will be a perpetual worry, finding tenants & replacing furniture & worry tells on my writing power. Yet writing will be the only way to pay[2] off the debt which the necessary purchase of furniture will largely increase. Mr Enoch's telegram came 'White accedes to alterations in the list. Valuer goes to Alton Thursday'. That is very awkward. One may be pretty sure the decision won't be made (with so dilatory a person as Mr White) before the end of the week & then next week Papa may come home any day. I am quite sure having a valuer is the right step for I am no judge of old furniture but certainly this fortnight's delay—from Aug 10th to next Thursday is just a fortnight—is most unlucky. I am writing to Mr Enoch to send him the lists you copied out; to fully empower him to [letter torn][3] me after receiving the valuer's report only to get the thing arranged & settled so that I can go down soon. I *must* have 2 days for travelling, 1 day for measurement & getting patterns of paper & colours at Alton, 2 days in London for buying carpets etc. etc. 5 days in all, work as hard as I can. Mr White has not yet got a house for himself. Mr Drummond has been calling with his brother from Edin; & his wife. They have come back from Mrs Eustace Gregs but brought no news. I fancy everybody is away from Manchester.

When are you coming home? Give us some idea please, you need not be tied to it you know, if any reason turns up etc. *And don't forget the Kath. Docks dividend.* I shall never write up the money for the house I'm afraid. However I'm going to take a tonic (by Meta's & Hearn's compulsion) & see what I can do. I am so sorry to think of your fatigue yesterday love. But *do* write & ask questions when you are not sure. You are doing nothing you know while I am writing hard at my book, & Meta doing the letters etc. of the family. Goodbye darling.

Your own affect[ionate] Mammy

[1] Typescript source reads 'mens'.   [2] MS. source reads 'way of paying'.
[3] Insertion by copyist.

₀ **581a** ₀

UNKNOWN

46 Plymouth Grove
Sep. 2d [?1865]

Dear Sir

I copy an extract from a letter from Mr Bache to my husband. 'I have sent to Mr John Phillips an article for insertion in your "Unitarian Herald" in which I have written "Holy Ghost" [—] pray alter it if you can to "Holy *Spirit*" [—] *not* however in *italics*' —As my husband is away in Scotland, I thought it better to send you the extract, that you may correct the mistake Mr Bache has made.

I am truly yours,
E. C. Gaskell.

₅₈₂ **582a** *582b

MARIANNE GASKELL[1]

Sunday. [3 September 1865]

My dearest Polly,

When we came home from a dinner at the James Reiss last night we found Meta & Hearn. Meta had seen Mr Enoch in the morning who had brought her a letter from Mr Williams (at last).

Alton. Sept 1. 1865. 'The Lawn, Holybourne' 'Sir, I am requested by my client to ask for full particulars relative to the above. The rent she thinks much too high, considering there is no land, & that there will be great expense in keeping the grounds & walks in order without any return. She would like to know whether there would be a power to sub-let. Two sisters live together & should either die the place would be too large for the survivor. She would like wise like to know the quantity of land, number & size of rooms, etc. The furniture to be left in the Drawing room would be sufficient (curtains excepted). The bed-rooms would require to be fully furnished, she has some easy chairs etc'.

[1] Original MS. not seen.

That's an exact copy. Mr Enoch had written to give dimensions of rooms & quantity of land. (Mr Smith advises the leasing of Sir C. Miller's land any how—whether *house* tenant wants it or not; with power of subletting). Mr Enoch had stuck to 2 or guineas (£2. 10.) minus Sir C. Miller's land, only told Meta he thought the £10 might be knocked off in consideration of 2 ladies without children being likely to be good tenants. That he should say that the garden *did* bring in a 'return' & that they should have a fuller answer on Tuesday. I have told Meta to write & ratify what Mr E. said; only *insisting* on knowing more in detail & accurately *what furniture they will require*—if earthenware china and[1] glass? If kitchen requisites etc. You see we are so worn out—what with these horrid drains etc. that we do want a holiday, quite away if we can, from care about the house for 3 weeks or a month. I wish you could *hurry on all enquiries about Mr Christian. What family has he? What children? Would he keep up garden etc. pretty well?* Hearn says it is sadly out of order now; & Meta says 'quite a different place to what it was in June'. If we could but get off next week (Sunday) though I don't see how—*All* the furniture (& *very nice*) is chosen if not positively ordered. This note is to E. T. H.

Your E. G.

582a **582b** 585

MARIANNE GASKELL[2]

Sept. 5. 1865
Tuesday, 46 P. G.

My dearest Polly,

Florence sends me a copy of her letter to you about Switzerland, &, after a good deal of thinking I do believe it would be such a nice place for you to go (N.B. I will send you *up* any thing you want to London, & you can send *down* from there—*luggage* train—what you don't want—or leave it at Oxford Terrace till you come back. *That* can all be easily managed). You see I don't think *I* shall be comfortable leaving England with this house on

---

[1] MS. source reads 'or'.

[2] Original MS. not seen. The typescript source was misdated '1895', as was the MS. one before later correction. Address given as follows: Miss Gaskell | Edward Holland's Esq. M.P. | Dumbleton Hall, | Evesham.

my back (though I think it is all going on beautifully—no letter from Mr Enoch as yet—so things remain in Status quo as when I last wrote) & Julia is very persistent in saying *she* does not want to go from home at all; & I can't help fancying that if the drains are (ever) put to rights this house will be better air. They are a great way on; not quite finished. Marion Thurstan speaks of your 'well'ness at Pontresina & I do think a little Swiss air *might quite set you up*. We might get change from the numbers of invitations that come showering in. For this week alone I have refused 1st Georgina's for us *all*; Miss Marshall's (Archery meeting & Ball) for *Julia & me*. The Nightingales again (and this I *did* regret) for *Julia* and *me*.[1] The Kennedys (Mrs at length) for us *all* to Knock Malling. So if people have once got into the cycle of invitations they will most likely go on; & we can go from home for bits as we see fit. I wish I could *telegraph* all this to you, for I think you may be wondering what to do. Thank Thurstan so very much for his letter. *I* don't understand (have not taken the trouble—as I've heaps of writing etc. to do) the *law* part. Meta does. By the way ASK THURSTAN IF THE TENANT OR LANDLORD REPAIRS ALL OUT-SIDE DRAINS? Mr Coates[2] says *in*side drains are the landlord's affair; *out*side tenants which seems to me reversing the natural order of things (Mr Coates by inside means inside the *house*). I wonder if you would telegraph from *Evesham* to-morrow what your decision is about Switzerland. Don't be scrupulous about *money*—I shall pay all easily if you go. We could not have gone till Papa comes home because of no money—& we never hear. Only I *think* he *must* come home this week. Yesterday morning Selina Collie came;[3] about 11 & presently afterwards came a very nice American (Yorkshire man) & the two staid till 5 o'clk. This was pleasant but sadly interrupted my writing. To-day another American turns up (yesterday we'd a letter from Mr Hale) with a letter from Mr Field & being refused admission before is coming between 4 & 5. Cousin Mary & Miss Wedgwood to-morrow. I am very weary of it all, but one's duty is to be hospitable I suppose, only no one else seems to have anything to do.

E G.

[1] Sentence lacking in MS. source.   [2] Sources read 'Bates'.
[3] 'Collins' in MS. source.

₀ **636*a*** ₆₃₇

WILLIAM CHAMBERS[1]

42 Plymouth Grove.
Manchester

My dear Sir,
    As all the obligation in our acquaintance lies on my side, & as I have already much to thank you for, I feel rather reluctant in making to you a request, which from that circumstance alone may seem presumptuous, that you will look at the accompanying Manuscript which is written by a friend of mine who is desirous of having it admitted into your Journal. You will be able to judge better perhaps, than I can—of its merits & suitability, but if you will kindly look through it, it will be conferring a great favour on me.

Yours truly.
E. C. Gaskell.

[1] Original MS. not seen.

APPENDIX B

Sources

In the following list of sources we have given each owner or location a reference number and have also indicated (in the column on the right) the number of letters taken from each source, making no distinction between complete and fragmentary letters. An asterisk is used to distinguish copies.

Ref. no.		Quantity
1	Mrs Helen H. Arnold	1
2	Mr P. Bayliss	1
3	Mrs Joyce Buckley	1
4	Mr G. Fielding	1*
4a	Mr Alan Gill	1
5	Mrs E. M. Gordon	7
6	Miss Elspeth Holland	4
7	Lord Hatherton [In Staffs Record Office, D260.M.F.5.27, 24 and 30]	3
8	Mrs Trevor Jones	51
8a	Mr J. T. Lancaster [Now owned by Mr J. G. Sharps]	86*
9	The Honourable Mrs C. B. Leaf [Now in the possession of Mrs Douglas Walker]	3
10	Sir John Murray	93
11	Miss M. S. Oldham [See nos. 18 and 27 below]	2
12	Mrs Mary Preston	9
13	Mr Peter Rhodes	1
14	Mr Samuel Roscoe	1
15	Miss P. L. Ruddock	1
16	Mrs A. R. Rush [See no. 53 below]	1
17	Mr John H. Samuels	1
18	Mr J. G. Sharps [Now also owns one letter listed under no. 11 above and letters listed under 8a above]	5
19	Lord Shuttleworth [Originals replacing transcripts formerly lent by the Honourable Mrs B. James]	9
20	Miss Edith S. Spence	1
21	Sir Harry Verney	12
22	Professor A. S. Whitfield	4
23	Birmingham University Library [Reproduced by courtesy of Sir Wilfred Martineau]	8
24	Bodleian Library, Oxford	3
25	Boston (Mass.) Public Library [Reproduced by courtesy of the Trustees]	2
26	The British Museum	13
27	The Brontë Museum, Haworth [Now also owns one letter listed under no. 11 above]	2

Ref.		*Quantity*
no.		
28	Brown University Library	I
29	California University Library, Los Angeles	11
30	Cambridge University Library	I
31	Cornell University Library	2
32	Curtis Museum, Alton, Hants	3
33	Dickens House, London [Reproduced by courtesy of Mr Henry C. Dickens]	3
34	Fitzwilliam Museum, Cambridge	2
35	Harvard University Library, The Houghton Library	36
36	Henry E. Huntington Library and Art Gallery, San Marino, Cal. [Reproduced by permission of the Library; ref. HM 1888]	10
37	The University of Iowa Libraries, Iowa City	I
38	Illinois University Library	3
39	John Rylands Library, Manchester	2
40	Knutsford Unitarian Chapel	3
41	Leeds University, The Brotherton Collection	85
	(b) Eliza Fox transcripts (typed)	36*
	(c) Jane Coolidge biography of Mrs Gaskell (typed)	12*
	(d) Miscellaneous transcripts (typed)	13*
42	Library of Congress	I
43	Liverpool University Library	I
44	McGill University Library	I
45	Manchester Central Library	13
46	Manchester Literary Club	I
47	Manchester University Library	13
	(b) Copies in MS. Life of Charlotte Brontë	2*
48	National Library of Scotland [Reproduced by courtesy of the Trustees]	10
49	The New York Public Library, Henry W. and Albert A. Berg Collection	15
50	New York University Libraries	12
51	The Historical Society of Pennsylvania	4
52	The Pierpont Morgan Library, New York	18
53	Princeton University Library, Morris L. Parish Collection [Now also owns one letter listed under 16 above]	37
54	Rutgers University Library	5
55	University of Texas, Humanities Research Center Library	6
56	Trinity College, Cambridge, The Houghton Collection	10
57	Unitarian College, Manchester	9
58	The Victoria and Albert Museum	2
58a	Mrs Jane Whitehill	1*
59	Yale University Library	22
60	*The Brontës. Life and Letters*, ed. C. Shorter, 1908, II, pp. 292, n. 1; 396-9	2*
	(b) *Letters on Charlotte Brontë*, pr. pr. for C. Shorter, 1915	1*
61	*The Brontës. Their Lives, Friendships and Correspondence*, ed. T. J. Wise and J. A. Symington, 1932, IV, p. 136 [Basil Blackwell]	1*

Ref.		*Quantity*
no.		
62	*The Life of Sir William Fairbairn, Bart.*, ed. W. Pole, 1877, pp. 460–2	2*
63	Margaret Howitt, 'Stray Notes from Mrs Gaskell', *Good Words*, XXXVI, 1895, pp. 606–11	3*
64	Elizabeth Haldane, *Mrs Gaskell and Her Friends*, [1930], pp. 25, 68, 90–7, 118, 119–20, 120, 141–8, 239–40, 242–3, 251–2, 285, 287, 288, 296 [Hodder & Stoughton]	15*
65	*George Hope of Fenton Barns: A Sketch of His Life Compiled by his Daughter* [C. Hope], Edinburgh, 1881, pp. 177–8	1*
66	*Anna Jameson. Letters and Friendships*, ed. Mrs Steuart Erskine, [1915], pp. 293–4	2*
67	William Knight, 'Whitwell Elwin', *Retrospects*, 1st series, 1904, pp. 271–2	1*
68	T. Wemyss Reid, *The Life, Letters and Friendships of Richard Monckton Milnes*, 1890, I, p. 481	1*
69	Sir Edward Cook, *The Life of Florence Nightingale*, 1914, I, p. 347	1*
70	Anonymous, 'A Few Words About "Jane Eyre"', *Sharpe's London Magazine*, n.s. VI, 1855, p. 342	1*
71	Henry James, *William Wetmore Story and His Friends*, 1903, I, pp. 353, 355–9	8*
72	Anonymous, Cutting [See Letter 648, note]	1*
73	*The Works of Mrs Gaskell*, with introductions by A. W. Ward, 1906, I, pp. xxxviii, lxii–lxiv; VI, pp. xxvi–xxvii	3*
74	*Letters of Mrs Gaskell and Charles Eliot Norton*, ed. Jane Whitehill, 1932, pp. xviii–xix [Oxford University Press]	1*
75	*Letters and Memorials of Catherine Winkworth*, ed. [S. Winkworth], pr. pr., Clifton, 1883, I, pp. 160–2, 165, 166–7, 197–9, 480–81; II, 1886, p. 428	6*

APPENDIX C

WATERMARKS

Each watermark described below has been given a reference number. More scientific methods of examining paper would undoubtedly have increased the number of descriptions and our list even ignores some distinctions made and recorded on our cards in actual practice. We did not feel, however, that the more elaborate approach was necessary for the purposes of this edition or for dealing with original letters that may turn up in future years.

Unless otherwise indicated, paper is white laid. We have transcribed small capital letters as if they were capitals and confess to some uncertainty about our readings of intertwined, decorative script letters.

Ref. no.	Description
1	Crown *over* Britannia; *also* 'J MANGNALL' | '1835'
2	Prince of Wales feathers | *script* 'JRJ' | '1836'
3	*Open capitals and figures* 'J GREEN & SON' | '1837'
4	*Open capitals and figures* 'G & R TURNER' | '1831'
5	Posthorn *in* crowned shield | *script* 'CH' [Centre of design falls between chainlines, which are approx. 27 mm. apart]
6	*As 5, but centre of design coincides with chainline* | *script* 'H'
7	*As 5, but chainlines approx. 33 mm. apart*
8	*As 5, but cipher not visible and chainlines approx. 24 mm. apart*
9	*As 5, but cipher not visible*
10	*As 5, but cipher not visible and centre of design coincides with chainline*
11	*As 5, but centre of design coincides with chainline* | *script* 'WP'
12	*As 5, but* | *script* 'H'
13	*As 5, but centre of design coincides with chainline* | *script* 'P'
13a	*As 5, but centre of design coincides with chainline* | *script* 'J'
14	*As 5, but centre of design coincides with chainline* | *script* 'APS'
15	*As 5, but chainlines approx. 32 mm. apart* | *script* 'CA'
16	*As 5, but* | *script* 'AP & S'
17	*Open capitals* 'IM⟨ ⟩'
18	*Open capitals* 'BUSBRIDGE'S' | 'EXTRA SUPER'
19	*Open figures* '1853'
20	*Open figures* '1854'
21	*Open figures* '1856'
22	*Open figures* '1857'
23	*Open figures* '1858'
24	*Open figures* '1860' [Blue-monogrammed paper]
25	*Open capitals* '⟨ R⟩NER' | '⟨ R⟩D MILLS'
26	*Open capitals* 'A PIRIE & SONS'
27	*Open capitals and figures* 'A PIRI⟨E & SONS⟩' | '18⟨ ⟩'
28	*Open capitals and figures* 'A PIRIE & SONS' | '1853'
29	*As 28, but blue wove paper*
30	*As 28, but* | '1856'

Ref.   *Description*
no.

31   *As 28, but* | '1858'
32   *As 28, but* | '1859'
32a *As 28, but* | '1860'
33   *As 28, but* | '1861'
34   *As 28, but* | '1862'
35   *As 28, but* | '1863'
36   *As 28, but* | '1864'
37   *Script* 'A Pirie & Sons' [Tail stroke of 'S' touches chainline]
38   *As 37, but tail stroke of 'S' does not touch chainline*
39   *Script* 'AH' | *open capitals* 'SUPERFINE'
40   *Script* 'T & JH' | *open figures* '1860' [Wove paper]
40a *As 40, but* | '1862'
41   *Script* 'T & JH'
42   *Script* 'T & JH' | *open figures* '1859'
43   *As 42, but* | '1862'
44   *As 42, but* | '1863'
45   '⟨   ⟩SON' [Blue paper]
46   *Oval shape,* 'REG' *visible in one quarter* [Chevron wirelines]
47   *Inkstand* [Very faint]
48   *Script* 'Joynson's' | 'Improved Extra' | '1854'
49   *Script* 'De La Rue & Co'
50   *Open capitals* 'J WHATMAN' | '⟨   ⟩'
50a *As 50, but wove paper* | *open figures* '1849'
51   *As 50, but wove paper* | *open figures* '1836'
52   *As 50, but wove paper* | *open figures* '1851'
53   *Open capitals* 'JOYNSON'
54   *Open capitals and figures* 'JOYNSON' | '1850'
55   *As 54, but* | '1851'
56   *As 54, but* | '1852'
56a *As 54, but* | '1854'
57   *As 54, but* | '1856'
58   *As 54, but* | '1859'
58a *As 54, but* | '1860'
59   *As 54, but* | '1863'
60   *Script* 'AP & S' | *open capitals* 'SUPERFINE'
61   *As 60, but open cap.* 'S' *cut by chainline*
62   *Script* '⟨?T&J⟩H' | *open capitals* '⟨?TURKEY⟩MILL'
63   *Script* 'B & Co' | *open capitals* 'EAST MALLING' | 'KENT'
64   *Open capitals* 'JOYNSON'S' | 'IMPROVED EXTRA'
65   *Open capitals and figures* 'EXTRA SUPER' | '1854'
66   *Open capitals* '⟨   ⟩' | 'EXTRA SUPER'
66a *Open capitals* 'JOYNSON'S' | 'EXTRA SUPER' | *open figures* '1850'
67   *Open capitals* 'C ANSELL'
68   *Open capitals and figures* 'TOWGOOD' | '1850' [Wove paper]
69   *Open capitals* '[?] DEWDNEY' | '[?]EXTRA SUPER'
70   *Open capitals and figures* 'GO⟨   ⟩' | '18⟨ ⟩'
71   *Open capitals and figures* 'A COWAN & SONS' | '1862'

Ref. no.	Description
71a	*As 71, but*	'1854'
72	*As 71, but no date*
73	*Open capitals* 'CHAFFORD MILL'
74	*Script* 'T & JH'	*open capitals* 'TURKEY MILL'	*open figures* '1858'
75	*Script* 'IM'	Fleur de Lis
76	*Script* 'A' *and* Fleur de Lis
77	[?Design]	*script* 'B'
78	*Script* 'T & [?] GB'
79	*Open capitals* (?*and figures*) 'R TURNER'	'⟨ ⟩'
80	*Oval, possibly rampant lion with shield*
81	*Open capitals* 'T DE LA RUE & CO'	'EXTRA'
82	*Open capitals* 'C HARRIS'

APPENDIX D

EMBOSSED DESIGNS

These embossed designs, usually found in the top left-hand corner of a page, have been described in the same way as the watermarks. We also give the over-all shapes of the designs and their measurements in millimetres, the vertical coming before the horizontal unless a simple diameter is all that is needed.

Ref. no.	Description of design and lettering	Shape and approx. size in millimetres	
1	'LONDON' *over* crown *over* 'SUPERFINE'	*tablet*	15 × 20
2	Crown *and* [?]	*circle*	15
3	Rose *and* foliage [Cf. 18]	*shield*	11 × 11
4	Lion *over* crown	*circle*	13
4a	*As 4*	*circle*	10
5	Prince of Wales feathers *in* coronet [Cf. 7]	*circle*	11
5a	*As 5*	*circle*	9
6	'DELARUE' | '& Co' | 'LONDON'	*tablet*	10 × 12
7	Prince of Wales feathers *in* coronet *over* label	*circle*	12
7a	*As 7*	*circle*	11
8	'LONDON' *over* crown *over* 'SUPERFINE'	*circle*	14
8a	*As 8, but smaller crown*	*circle*	12
9	Crown	*circle*	10
9a	Crown	*circle*	12
9b	Crown	*circle*	15
10	*Upper half of* lion rampant, *facing left*	*circle*	11
11	'[?]SUPER' | 'SATIN'	*oval*	11 × 14
12	*Design not clear*	*oval*	12 × 15
13	'SUPER' | 'SATIN'	*circle*	11
14	Crown *and* [?]wreath	*circle*	12
15	'INDIA OFFICE' *over* Royal Arms	*oval*	20 × 24
16	Crown *over* 'SUPERFINE'	*circle*	12
17	*Triptich of gothic letters* 'ECG'		19 × 24
17a	*As 17*		18 × 21
17b	*Triptich of gothic letters* 'JBG'		18 × 21
18	Rose, etc. [Cf. 3]	*shield*	13 × 12
19	*Gothic letters* 'Ivory'	*plate*	11 × 15
20	'SUPER' *over* crown *over* 'LONDON'	*circle*	11
21	Lion, *moving left*	*circular*	12
22	'LONDON SUPERFINE' *around* quartered shield	*oval*	11 × 13
23	[?]Prince of Wales feathers	*shield*	14 × 12
24	Rose *and* foliage	*circle*	11
24a	[?]Rose *and* foliage	*oval*	14 × 12
25	Prince of Wales feathers *in* coronet	*shield*	11 × 11
26	'DEIGHTON' | 'WORCESTER'	*tablet*	11 × 13
27	'SUPERFINE' *over* dove	*circle*	12

Ref. no.	Description of design and lettering	Shape and approx. size in millimetres	
28	'BRINE' | 'MAIDSTONE'	tablet	11 × 14
29	[?]Fleur de lis	[No border]	12 × 9
30	'EXTRA' | 'SATIN' | 'LONDON'	tablet	10 × 12
31	*Small* crown *on* [?]Garter badge	shield	13 × 12
32	'DOBBS' | 'LONDON'	crowned sign	13 × 14
33	Crown *over* 'DOBBS'	circle	10
34	*Gothic letters* 'CREAM' | 'LAID'	oblong	11 × 18
35	'EXTRA' | 'CREAM LAID'	tablet	11 × 14
36	Crown	shield	11 × 9
37	'Super' *over* Prince of Wales feathers *over* scroll *over* 'Bath'	circle	11
38	Two flowers *and* foliage	circle	9
39	'[?]SENDER' | 'CANTERBURY'	shield	9 × 9
40	'LONDON' *over* crown *over* 'EXTRA SATIN'	circle	12
41	Star	circle	12
42	'FINE STRAW NOTE'	oval	15 × 20
42a	'FINE STRAW' *over gothic letters* 'Note'	oval	10 × 14
43	Prince of Wales feathers *in* coronet *over* 'Simpson'	circle	13
44	Rose	circle	9
45	[?]Prince of Wales feathers	oval	10 × 8
46	'J ALLOM' | 'YORK'	tablet	12 × 14
47	'G J' | 'PALMER' | '27, LAMBS' | 'CONDUIT' | 'STREET'	shield	13 × 12

APPENDIX E

Table of Descriptions

We have recorded information about individual letters in eight columns below, which should be read in conjunction with Appendices B, C and D.

COLUMN

(i) The reference numbers assigned to each letter in the main text.
(ii) Sources. See Appendix B for identifying numbers.
(iii) Abbreviations as follows: M [Manuscript], MC [Manuscript Copy], PC [Printed Copy], TC [Typescript Copy], M★ [Manuscript seen in Photographic Copy].
(iv) Number of pages on which there is writing. A figure after a plus sign indicates the number of pages on which there is crossed writing. The figure 0 in this and other columns indicates that the particular information was not thought to be worth recording (e.g. the number of pages of *copies*, their watermarks, etc.).
(v) Format. Standard abbreviations have been used.
(vi) Abbreviations as follows: L [Laid Paper], W [Wove Paper], M [Mourning Paper], B [Blue or Blue Grey].
(vii) Watermarks. See Appendix C for identifying numbers. A cross indicates either that the watermark does not exist or that we were not able to see enough to make it worth recording.
(viii) Embossed Designs. See Appendix D for identifying numbers. A cross indicates either no design or one that is illegible.

Note A blank space in any column means that we lack information, *not* that it is necessarily non-existent.

(i)	(ii)	(iii)	(iv)	(v)	(vi)	(vii)	(viii)
1	41*c*	TC	0	0	0	0	0
2	41	M	4+3	4to	W	×	×
3	8	M	4+2	4to	W	×	1
4	8	M	4+2	4to	W	4	2
5	41	M	4+3	4to	W	51	×
6	15	M	2+1	4to		×	×
7	41	M	4+3	8vo	W	×	×
8	63	PC	0	0	0	0	0
9	41	M	4+2	F	L	2	×
10	8	M	2+1	4to	W	3	2
11	8	M	4+1	F	L	2	×
12	63	PC	0	0	0	0	0
13	8	M	4	F	L	1	×
14	8	M	4+1	4to	W	×	×
15	41	M	4	4to	W	×	×
16	41	M	4	4to	W	×	×
17	41	M	4	8vo	WB	×	×
18	8	M	4+1	8vo	W	×	×
19	41*c*	TC	0	0	0	0	0

(i)	(ii)	(iii)	(iv)	(v)	(vi)	(vii)	(viii)
20	29	M★	4	8vo	L	?10	40
21	41	M	6	8vo	?W	×	×
22	52	M★	4	8vo	L	×	×
23	52	M★	4+1	16mo	W	×	9a
24	52	M★	4	8vo	L	×	×
25	52	M★	2	8vo	W	×	22
25a	64	PC	o	o	o	o	o
26	52	M★	3	?16mo	L	?10	7
27	41	M	4	?8vo	L	×	8
28	52	M★	3	?16mo	L	×	×
29	75	PC	o	o	o	o	o
30	75	PC	o	o	o	o	o
31	52	M★	2	8vo	L	×	×
32	75	PC	o	o	o	o	o
33	52	M★	4	8vo	L	79	×
34	52	M★	4	8vo	W	×	×
35	75	PC	o	o	o	o	o
36	41c	TC	o	o	o	o	o
37	52	M★	4	?12mo	W	×	9
38	52	M★	6	?12mo	W	×	9
39	53	M★	8	?12mo	W	×	9
40	35	M★	6	?12mo	L	?5	×
41	52	M★	4	?16mo	L	?7	×
42	73	PC	o	o	o	o	o
43	25	M★	4	8vo	L	67	×
44	29	M★	1	frag.	L	76	×
44a	37	M★	4+2	?16mo	L	×	36
45	66	PC	o	o	o	o	o
46	41b	TC	o	o	o	o	o
47	8	M	4	8vo	W	×	14
48	41b	TC	o	o	o	o	o
49	75	PC	o	o	o	o	o
50	41	M	4 1	8vo 4to	L	×	×
51	41b	TC	o	o	o	o	o
52	41b	TC	o	o	o	o	o
53	41b	TC	o	o	o	o	o
54	41b	TC	o	o	o	o	o
55	41b	TC	o	o	o	o	o
56	41	M	4	8vo	L	×	6
57	64	PC	o	o	o	o	o
58	53	M★	2	8vo	L	×	×
59	49	M★	8	12mo			
60	41	M	2 4	8vo 4to	L	×	×
61	52	M★	6	8vo	L	77 & ?10	×
62	52	M★	4	8vo	L	78	?7
63	41b	TC	o	o	o	o	o
64	41b	TC	o	o	o	o	o
65	45	M	4	8vo	LM	50	6
66	18	M	2	8vo	LM	53	6
67	53	M★	4 2	?16mo 8vo	L	× ×	× ×

(i)	(ii)	(iii)	(iv)	(v)	(vi)	(vii)	(viii)
68	41b	TC	0	0	0	0	0
69	41b	TC	0	0	0	0	0
70	41b	TC	0	0	0	0	0
71	31	M★	4	8vo	WM	×	×
72	19	M	8	8vo	L	×	6
72a	19	M	12+1	8vo	L	×	×
73	41b	TC	0	0	0	0	0
74	41	M	4	8vo	L	×	×
75	41	M	12	8vo	L	×	×
76	47b	MC	0	0	0	0	0
77	70	PC	0	0	0	0	0
78	49	M★	4+1	12mo			
79	41b	TC	0	0	0	0	0
80	40	M	3	8vo	L	×	6
81	19	M	4+frag.	8vo	L	66a	6
82	48	M★	4	?8vo	L	8	5
82a	19	M	4	8vo	L	?11	32
83	19	M	7	8vo	L	13a & ?13a	46
84	64	PC	0	0	0	0	0
85	41b	TC	0	0	0	0	0
86	19	M	12+1	8vo	L	×	×
87	52	M★	4+1	?16mo	W	×	×
88	57	M	3	8vo	L	15	×
89	52	M★	2	8vo	L	?66	×
90	41	M	4	4to	L	69	×
91	18	M	2	8vo	L	×	7
92	8	M	4	8vo	L	×	4
93	41	M	4	8vo	L	× & 9	× & 8
94	8	M	8	8vo	L	13	9
95	8	M	5	8vo	L	46 & ×	6 & ×
96	41	M	4	8vo	W	68	?7
97	41	M	4	8vo	L	10	6
97a	41	M	4	8vo	L	54	6
98	53	M★	3	?8vo	L	×	6
99	41b	TC	0	0	0	0	0
100	41c	TC	0	0	0	0	0
101	41	M	8	8vo	W	×	?7
102	41	M	4	8vo	W	×	?7
103	59	M★	3	8vo	L	73	×
104	8	M	4	8vo	W	×	×
105	49	M★	7	12mo			
106	64	PC	0	0	0	0	0
107	41	M	4	8vo	L	×	4
108	53	M★	2	8vo	L	×	32
108a	41b	TC	0	0	0	0	0
109	41	M	4	8vo	W	×	×
110	41b	TC	0	0	0	0	0
111	53	M★	7	8vo	L	×	5a & 5
112	41b	TC	0	0	0	0	0
113	55	M★	4	8vo	L	×	×
114	41	M	4	8vo	LM	?10	6
115	22	M	3	?8vo	WM	50a	×
116	41	M	4	?16mo	W	×	×

(i)	(ii)	(iii)	(iv)	(v)	(vi)	(vii)	(viii)
117	41	M	4	8vo	L	×	×
118	50	M★	3	?8vo			
119	50	M★	4+1	8vo			
120	8	M	4	8vo	L	18	6
121	45	M	4	8vo	L	18	6
122	45	M	6	8vo	L	10	6
123	8	M	4	8vo	L	18	6
124	41b	TC	0	0	0	0	0
125	7	M	4	?12mo	L	53	6
126	41	M	4	8vo	L	?66	6
127	41	M	8	8vo	L	× & 55	×
128	45	M	3	8vo	L	18	6
129	16	M	3	8vo	L	18	6
130	45	M	5	8vo	L	×	3
131	8	M	4	8vo	L	×	7
132	8	M	4	8vo	L	×	3
133	41	M	2	8vo	W	52	×
134	59	M★	3	8vo	L	56	6
135	8	M	4	8vo	L	×	6
136	8	M	4	8vo	L	10	6
137	41b	TC	0	0	0	0	0
138	49	M★	4	12mo			
139	67	PC	0	0	0	0	0
140	49	M★	8	?8vo			
141	8	M	8	?16mo	L?	×	7 & × & 7
142	41	M	4	8vo	L	70	×
143	41	M	2	?12mo	L	×	×
144	26	M	4	8vo	L	×	4
145	8	M	4	8vo	L	×	16
146	41b	TC	0	0	0	0	0
147	41	M	4	8vo	L	×	16
148	8 & 41c	M+TC	4	8vo	L	8	5
149	64	PC	0	0	0	0	0
150	41b	TC	0	0	0	0	0
151	41b	TC	0	0	0	0	0
152	68	PC	0	0	0	0	0
153	41c	TC	0	0	0	0	0
154	19	M	16	8vo	L	6 & 41	9 & 8
155	48	M★	4	?12mo	L	×	8
156	56	M	2	8vo	L	55	×
157	64	PC	0	0	0	0	0
158	8	M	4	8vo	L	10	×
159	26	M	2	8vo	L	×	×
160	41	M	4	8vo	L	×	×
161	49	M★	2	?16mo			
162	45	M	8	8vo	L	41	8
163	8	M	6	8vo	L	12 & 17	8
164	26	M	4	16mo	L	×	×
			3	8vo		12	8a
165	41	M	4	8vo	L	×	×
166	64	PC	0	0	0	0	0
167	47b	MC	0	0	0	0	0
167a	38	M★	6	?12mo	L	×	×

(i)	(ii)	(iii)	(iv)	(v)	(vi)	(vii)	(viii)
167b	38	M★	8	?12mo	L	×	×
168	56	M	4	8vo	L	12	8a
169	41b	TC	0	0	0	0	0
170	26	M	4	8vo	L	12	8a
171	36	M★	6	8vo	L	?9	9
172	36	M★	8+1	8vo	L	?9	8
173	8	M	3	4to	W	×	4
174	8	M	4	8vo	L	8	5
175	41	M	3	8vo	L	×	8
176	36	M★	6	8vo	L	11	17
177	59	M★	3	8vo	L	5	×
178	45	M	4	8vo	W	×	?12
179	40	M	2	8vo	W	×	42a
180	45	M	7	8vo	L	49	6
181	19	M	8+1	8vo	L	19	31
182	9	M	6	8vo	L	× & 19	17 & 31
183	59	M★	4	8vo	L	×	×
184	9	M	6	8vo	L	×	9a
185	41	M	2	4to	L	×	×
186	53	M★	4+1	8vo	L	×	×
187	41	M	2	8vo	W	×	×
188	26	M	3	8vo	L	×	9a
189	56	M	3	8vo	L	×	×
190	50	M★	2	8vo			
191	26	M	8	8vo	L	×	9a
192	26	M	4	?12mo	L	×	×
192 cont.	48	M★	2	?12mo		×	×
193	41	M	3	8vo	L	×	9a
194	41	M	3	8vo	L	×	?18
195	48	M★	14	?12mo		×	×
196	58	M	1	8vo	L	×	9a
197	58	M	7	8vo	L	×	9a
198	26	M	1	8vo	WB	29	×
199	8	M	4	8vo	WB	29	×
200	64	PC	0	0	0	0	0
201	41	M	4	8vo	L	×	9a
202	41	M	5	8vo	L	×	9a
203	41	M	4	8vo	L	×	?9a
204	56	M	3	?8vo	L	×	×
205	8	M	2	8vo	L	×	×
205a	47	M	4	8vo	L	×	22
206	18	M	3	4to	WB	29	×
207	61	PC	0	0	0	0	0
208	8	M	4	8vo	L	×	12
209	41	M	1	8vo	L	×	×
210	41	M	3	8vo	L	×	×
211	41	M	14	8vo	L	×	×
212	8	M	4	8vo	L	×	4
213	6	M	4	8vo	WB	×	×
214	21	M	4+3	8vo	L	×	?12
215	21	M	4+1	8vo	L	×	4
216	6	M	4	8vo	WB	29	×
217	64	PC	0	0	0	0	0

(i)	(ii)	(iii)	(iv)	(v)	(vi)	(vii)	(viii)
218	21	M	4	8vo	LB	10	×
219	53	M★	3	8vo	L	×	?24
220	29	M★	4	8vo	L	×	×
221	6	M	4	8vo	L	48	7
222	41b	TC	o	o	o	o	o
223	75	PC	o	o	o	o	o
224	6	M	4	8vo	L	×	4
225	59	M★	7	8vo	L	5	×
226	8	M	4	8vo	L	5	×
227	49	M★	4	?8vo			
228	21	M	1	Card	o	o	o
229	8	M	4	8vo	L	5	×
230	59	M★	2	8vo	L	?5	×
231	9	M	4	8vo	L	×	30
232	12	M	4	8vo	L	×	47
233	12	M	5	8vo	L	×	?47
234	66	PC	o	o	o	o	o
234a	41	M	4	8vo	L	×	?18
235	52	M★	4	8vo	L	×	×
236	21	M	1	8vo	L	9	×
237	26	M	3	8vo	L	9	×
238	12	M	8	8vo	L	9	×
239	12	M	5	8vo	L	82	×
240	41b	TC	o	o	o	o	o
241	10	M	4	?12mo	L	?18	6
242	10	M	13	8vo	L	×	4
243	10	M	4	8vo	L	×	4
244	10	M	4+1	?12mo	L	×	×
245	10	M	4	8vo	L	×	4
246	8	M	3	8vo	L	×	4
247	41	M	3	8vo	L	20	×
248	41	M	1	8vo	L	×	?22
249	62	PC	o	o	o	o	o
250	41b	TC	o	o	o	o	o
251	41	M	4	8vo	L	×	×
252	8	M	4	8vo	L	20	×
252a	41	M	1	8vo	L	20	×
253	59	M★	2	8vo	L	×	×
254	14	M	4	8vo	L	?20	×
255	21	M	5	?12mo	L	18	6
256	10	M	7	8vo	L	×	4
257	45	M	4	8vo	L	10	20
258	12	M	4	8vo	L	71a	?16
259	41	M	6	8vo	W	×	×
260	49	M★	3	?12mo			
261	10	M	3	12mo	L	18	6
262	21	M	2	8vo	L	×	18
263	21	M	1	8vo	L	48	7
264	12	M	4	8vo	L	81	6
265	53	M★	4	8vo	L	×	6
266	49	M★	4	?12mo			
267	41c	TC	o	o	o	o	o
268	21	M	3	8vo	L	×	4

(i)	(ii)	(iii)	(iv)	(v)	(vi)	(vii)	(viii)
269	10	M	2	8vo	L	×	4
270	10	M	2	8vo	L	×	4
271	10	M	4	8vo	?L	×	4
272	34	M	4	8vo	L	×	4
273	41	M	6	8vo	L	×	4
274	41d	TC	0	0	0	0	0
275	56	M	10	8vo	L	×	17
275a	41c 41d	TC	0	0	0	0	0
276	41b	TC	0	0	0	0	0
277	41c	TC	0	0	0	0	0
278	56	M	6	8vo	L	47	17
278a	41	M	2	8vo	L	×	×
278b	47	M	4	8vo	L	×	?4
279	21	M	6	8vo	L	47 & ×	17 & 4
280	50	M★	6	8vo			
281	42	M★	4+1	8vo	L	×	?22
282	35	M★	2	8vo	L	×	22
283	59	M★	5	8vo	L	57 & ×	6 & 22
284	10	M	8	8vo	L	×	22
285	49	M★	3	?8vo			
286	10	M	2	8vo	L	×	22
287	56	M	2	8vo	L	×	?18
288	22	M	3	12mo	L	?56a	21
289	10	M	2	8vo	L	×	22
290	29	M★	3	8vo	L	×	22
291	12	M	3	8vo	L	×	8a
292	59	M★	2	8vo	L	×	×
293	10	M	4	8vo	L	×	8a
294	60	PC	0	0	0	0	0
295	53	M★	2	8vo	L	×	×
296	59	M★	4+1	8vo	L	×	4
297	10	M	8+1	8vo	L	×	4
298	10	M	4	8vo	L	×	26
299	10	M	7	8vo	L	×	8
300	21	M	4	8vo	L	×	8
301	10	M	4	8vo	LB	10	3
302	10	M	2	8vo	L	×	8
303	10	M	6	8vo	L	×	8
304	41	M	4	8vo			
305	53	M★	4	8vo	L	×	7
306	28	M★	3	8vo	WB	×	×
307	36	M★	1	8vo	L	×	?8
308	41	M	12	8vo	L & WB	× & ×	?8 & ×
309	10	M	4	8vo	L	×	8
310	41d	TC	0	0	0	0	0
311	10	M	7	8vo	WB	×	×
312	10	M	4+1	8vo	WB	×	×
313	71	PC	0	0	0	0	0
314	10	M	9	8vo	WB	×	×
315	41d	TC	0	0	0	0	0
316	60b	PC	0	0	0	0	0
317	10	M	4	8vo	L	×	4

(i)	(ii)	(iii)	(iv)	(v)	(vi)	(vii)	(viii)
318	10	M	8	8vo	L	65	4
319	10	M	4	8vo	L	×	-4a
320	10	M	7	8vo	L	×	8
321	3	M	3	8vo	?L	×	×
322	10	M	8	8vo	L	× & ×	8 & 7
323	10	M	2	8vo	L	×	?8
324	10	M	8	8vo	L	× & ×	× & 8
325	10	M	7	8vo	L	×	?8
326	10	M	21	8vo	L	×	7a
327	49	M★	1	?8vo			
328	10	M	12	8vo	L	×	7a
329	71	PC	0	0	0	0	0
330	41	M	7	8vo	L	×	?7a
331	10	M	3	8vo	L	×	7a
332	10	M	4	8vo	L	×	7a
333	10	M	3	8vo	L	×	7a
334	10	M	4	8vo	L	×	7a
335	41d	TC	0	0	0	0	0
336	10	M	13	8vo	L	×	7a
337	50	M★	4	8vo			
338	10	M	6	8vo	L	×	8
339	10	M	3	8vo	L	×	7a
340	41	M	3	8vo			
341	10	M	5	8vo	L	×	16
342	74	PC	0	0	0	0	0
343	10	M	4	8vo	L	×	16
344	10	M	4	8vo	L	×	16
345	71	PC	0	0	0	0	0
346	35	M★	1	8vo	L	×	×
347	35	M★	2	8vo	W	×	×
347a	11	M	4+1	8vo	L	×	?8
348	10	M	4	8vo	L	×	8
349	35	M★	4+1	8vo	L	×	×
350	10	M	8	8vo	L	×	×
351	47	M	4	8vo	L	×	8a
352	49	M★	7	12mo			
353	10	M	4	8vo	L	×	8
354	35	M★	6	8vo	L	×	×
355	53	M★	2	8vo	L	×	×
356	12	M	1	8vo	L	×	8
357	33	M	2	8vo	L	×	?8
358	62	PC	0	0	0	0	0
359	31	M★	2	8vo	L	×	9a
360	35	M★	4	8vo	W	×	6
361	27	M	1	8vo	L	×	×
362	12	M	2	8vo	L	×	×
363	10	M	6	8vo	L	64	25
364	10	M	2+1	8vo	L	×	8
365	10	M	8	8vo	L	×	8
366	10	M	4	8vo	L	×	25
367	10	M	9	8vo	L	64	25
368	23	M★	8	8vo	L	×	×
369	10	M	4+1	8vo	L	×	8

(i)	(ii)	(iii)	(iv)	(v)	(vi)	(vii)	(viii)
370	10	M	6	8vo	L	×	8
370a	41b	TC	0	0	0	0	0
371	27	M	3	8vo	L	×	?8
372	8	M	8+1	8vo	L	×	10
373	53	M*	2	8vo	L	×	8a
374	35	M*	8+1	8vo	L	×	×
375	71	PC	0	0	0	0	0
376	50	M*	4	?12mo			
377	44	M*	2	?8vo	L	?43	×
378	53	M*	3	8vo	L	×	43
379	23	M*	7	8vo	W	×	32
380	7	M	12	8vo	L	×	4
381	23	M*	3	8vo	L	×	×
382	10	M	12	8vo	L	×	8
383	7	M	12+1	8vo	L	×	8
384	35	M*	18	8vo	W & L	×	×
385	35	M*	2	8vo	L	×	×
386	36	M*	4	8vo	L	?10	16
387	10	M	9	8vo	L	× & 30	3 & 22
388	56	M	8+1	8vo	L	×	3
389	35	M*	5	8vo	L	×	×
390	18	M	4	8vo	L	×	3
391	56	M	8	8vo	L	×	3
392	20	M	3	?16mo			
393	2	M	6	8vo	?L	×	6
394	35	M*	12	8vo	W	×	×
395	45	M	4	8vo	L	×	18
396	1	M*	2	8vo	L	×	?18
397	50	M*	3	8vo			
398	36	M*	4	8vo	L	×	?6
399	36	M*	4	8vo	LM	?14	×
400	51	M*			L	×	9b
401	35	M*	8	8vo	W	×	×
402	71	PC	0	0	0	0	0
403	35	M*	6	8vo	L	×	×
404	41b	TC	0	0	0	0	0
405	41	M	8	8vo	?L	×	×
405a	47	M	4+2	8vo	L	×	8a
406	69	PC	0	0	0	0	0
407	10	M	4+1	8vo	L	22	22
408	53	M*	2	8vo	L	×	×
409	8	M	8	8vo	L	×	8
410	10	M	6	8vo	L	26	22
411	54	M*	4+2	8vo	W	×	37
412	10	M	8	8vo	L	×	8
413	10	M	8	8vo	L	26	22
414	59	M*	5	8vo	W	×	?37
415	48	M*	8	?8vo	L	26	22
416	48	M*	1	?8vo	L	26	×
417	48	M*	6	?8vo	L	26	×
418	35	M*	16+1	8vo	L	26	×
419	41b	TC	0	0	0	0	0
420	50	M*	12	8vo			

(i)	(ii)	(iii)	(iv)	(v)	(vi)	(vii)	(viii)
421	41b	TC	0	0	0	0	0
422	41	M	6	8vo	L	26	22
423	51	M★	4	8vo	L	26	×
424	41b	TC	0	0	0	0	0
424a	47	M	7	8vo	L	×	?8a
425	36	M★	1	8vo	L	×	25
426	8	M	3	8vo	L	×	8
427	52	M★	1	8vo	L	×	25
428	41b	TC	0	0	0	0	0
429	51	M★	1	?8vo	WB	×	×
429a	59	M★	6	8vo	L	?9 & ×	×
430	10	M	7	8vo	L	32	×
431	59	M★	4	8vo	L	32	×
432	35	M★	4	8vo	L	×	39
432a	5	M	4	8vo	W	×	6
433	10	M	3	8vo	L	58	×
434	10	M	7	8vo	L	32	×
435	54	M★	5	8vo	L	32	×
436	53	M★	4+3	8vo	L	80	×
437	39	M	3	8vo	L	×	?4
438	10	M	8	8vo	L	32	×
439	54	M★	5+1	8vo	L	42	×
439a	47	M	10	8vo	L	16 & ?42	×
439b	47	M	4+1	?8vo	LB	74	×
440	10	M	8	?8vo	LB	62	9
441	10	M	6	8vo	L	31	×
442	10	M	10	8vo	L	×	28
443	10	M	4+1	?12mo	L	×	23
444	35	M★	8+1	8vo	L	×	8
445	53[23]	MC★[M]	[16]	[8vo]	[L]	[×]	[8a]
446	10	M	3	8vo	L	×	8
446a	47	M	8	8vo	L	16	×
447	8	M	2	8vo	L	×	×
448	41	M	4	8vo	L	23	×
449	53	M★	5	?8vo	L	?74	33
450	71	PC	0	0	0	0	0
451	10	M	10	8vo	L	16	×
451a	10	M	8	8vo	L	31	×
452	10	M	8	8vo	L	23 & 26	× & 22
453	35	M★	4+1	?8vo	L	?74	×
454	10	M	4	8vo	L	×	×
455	8	M	7	16mo	L	0	0
456	10	M	4	8vo	L	×	24
457	59	M★	4	8vo	L	×	19
458	53	M★	2	8vo	W	?41	25
459	10	M	3	8vo	L	×	19
460	59	M★	4	8vo	L	×	19
461	35	M★	8+1	8vo	L	×	×
462	10	M	4	8vo	L	?32	×
463	45	M	3	8vo	L	×	19
464	41	M	4	8vo	L	×	8
465	8	M	4+1	8vo	L	×	8
466	8	M	4	8vo	L	×	8

(i)	(ii)	(iii)	(iv)	(v)	(vi)	(vii)	(viii)
467	46	M	4	8vo	L	×	4
468	45	M	4	8vo	L	×	×
469	53	M*	2	8vo	L	×	×
470	36	M*	2	8vo	L	×	8
471	41	M	6	8vo & 16mo	L	× & ?58	×
472	53	M*	3	8vo	L	×	?2
472a	10	M	3	8vo	L	×	×
473	8	M	2	8vo	L	×	?8
474	41	M	1	0	0	0	0
475	41	M	8	4to	L	×	×
476	35	M*	8	8vo	W	×	×
477	53	M*	2	8vo	L	×	?2
478	41	M	8	8vo	L	×	×
479	41	M	3	8vo	L	×	8
480	35	M*	8	8vo	W	×	×
481	60	PC	0	0	0	0	0
482	71	PC	0	0	0	0	0
483	24	M	3	8vo	L	32a	×
484	8	M	8	8vo	L & LB & L	× & 45 & ×	× & × & 15
485	35	M*	10+1	8vo	L	×	×
486	13	MC	[4]	[8vo]	0	0	0
487	8	M	6	8vo	L & W	39 & ?40	×
488	35	M*	8+1	8vo	W	×	×
489	49	M*	4	8vo			
490	55	M*	4	8vo	WB	×	×
491	35	M*	4+1	8vo	L	×	×
491a	47	M	8	12mo	L	58a	?6
492	8	M	5	8vo	L	×	8
493	35	M*	7	8vo	W	×	×
494	41	M	3	8vo	L	28	17b
494a	19	M	9	8vo	L	×	8
495	10	M	3	?8vo	L	×	29
496	8	M	4	8vo	L	×	×
497	35	M*	5	8vo	W	×	×
498	71	PC	0	0	0	0	0
499	41d	TC	0	0	0	0	0
500	17	M*	5	?12mo			
501	10	M	7	8vo	L	×	24
502	10	M	4	8vo	L	33	×
502a	47	M	4	8vo	L	33	×
503	53	M*	8	8vo	L	26 & ×	× & 25
504	35	M*	4	8vo	W	×	×
505	41	M	8	8vo	L	× & ?58	× & ?17a
506	41	M	8	8vo	W	×	×
507	55	M*	4	8vo	W	×	×
508	53	M*	1	8vo	L	×	×
509	41	M	3	8vo	W	×	×
509a	38	M*	4	?12mo	WB	×	×
510	8	M	8	8vo	L	38	×
511	5	M	4	8vo	W	×	×
512	5	M	5	8vo	W	×	11
513	48	M*	3	?8vo	L	71	13

(i)	(ii)	(iii)	(iv)	(v)	(vi)	(vii)	(viii)
514	5	M	3	8vo	L	34	×
515	53	M★	15	8vo	W & L	× & 39	×
516	41	M	5	8vo	L	?33	×
517	10 & 73	M & PC	4 & o	8vo & o	L & o	60 & o	× & o
518	53	M★	3	?16mo	L	×	5
519	53	M★	3	8vo	L	×	5
520	53	M★	4	8vo	L	34	22
521	73	PC	o	o	o	o	o
522	53	M★	1	8vo	L	×	6
523	53	M★	1	8vo	L	×	6
524	8	M	8+1	8vo	W	×	11
525	54	M★	3	8vo	L	×	×
526	35	M★	8+1	8vo	W	×	×
527	53	M★	2	8vo	L	34	22
528	35	M★	4	8vo	L	×	×
529	29	M★	4	8vo	L	×	42
530	41c	TC	o	o	o	o	o
531	57	M	4	8vo	L	59	×
532	10	M	4+1	8vo	L	35	×
533	57	M	2	8vo	L	60	22
534	57	M	2	8vo	L	35	×
535	55	M★	8+1	8vo	L & W	×	× & ?11
535a	47	M	8+1	8vo	L	×	45
536	53	M★	4	8vo	W	×	×
537	30	M	6	8vo	L	59	32
538	29	M★	3	8vo	L	43	×
539	5	M	4	8vo	L	44	×
540	41	M	3	8vo	L	×	×
540a	47	M	4	8vo	L	43	×
541	5	M	3	8vo	L	59	32
542	57	M	6	8vo	L	×	?45
543	57	M	3	12mo	L	59	6
544	57	M	3	8vo	L	60	22
545	10	M	4	8vo	L	35	22
546	35	M★	6+1	8vo	W	×	×
547	34	M	3	8vo	L	50	17a
548	8	M	4	8vo	L	×	×
549	40	M	8	8vo	L	×	×
549a	11	M	4	8vo	L	×	22
550	10	M	7	8vo	L	60	×
551	35	M★	8+1	8vo	L	60	×
552	35	M★	4	8vo	L	60	22
553	10	M	8	8vo	L	35	×
554	10	M	4	8vo	L	24	×
555	29	M★	4	8vo	L	×	3
556	10	M	3	8vo	L	61	22
557	10	M	4	8vo	L	60	22
558	41c	TC	o	o	o	o	o
559	25	M★	4+1	8vo	L	?60	22
560	35	M★	11	8vo	L	×	38
561	10	M	3	8vo	L	60	22
562	4	MC	o	o	o	o	o
563	10	M	3	8vo	LM	36	×

(i)	(ii)	(iii)	(iv)	(v)	(vi)	(vii)	(viii)
564	64	PC	0	0	0	0	0
565	10	M	4	8vo	L	63	×
566	41	M	4	8vo	L	×	×
567	59	M★	7	8vo	L	63	×
568	18	M	2	8vo	L	37	?2
569	35	M★	4+1	8vo	W	×	×
570	41	M	12	8vo	L & W	×	× & 27
571	39	M	4	8vo	L	×	8
572	41	M	4	8vo	WB	×	×
573	41	M	4	8vo	WB	×	×
574	41	M	2	8vo	L	?14	13
575	56	M	4	8vo	L	71	13
576	10	M	5	8vo	W	×	27
577	49	M★	2	?12mo			
578	32	M	2	8vo	L	?14	13
579	53	M★	4	8vo	L	72	×
580	41	M	10	8vo	W	×	×
581	59	M★	6	8vo	L	×	?3
582	8	M	10	8vo	L	14	13
583	35	M★	7	8vo	L	×	×
584	35	M★	7	8vo	L	?14	13
585	59	M★	4+1	8vo	?W	×	×
586	10	M	4+1	8vo	LB	×	6
587	54	M★	3	?12mo	L	×	×
588	8	M	8	8vo	L	37	8
589	53	M★	4	?16mo	L	×	44
590	49	M★	3	8vo			
591	53	M★	2	8vo	L	53	×
592	29	M★	2	?8vo	L	21	×
593	59	M★	2+1	8vo	L	×	×
594	24	M	3	8vo	L	×	4
595	24	M	4	8vo	L	60	22
596	41b	TC	0	0	0	0	0
597	26	M	1	8vo	L	×	?7
598	26	M	2	8vo	L	34	22
599	26	M	1	8vo	L	34	×
600	26	M	2	8vo	L	×	×
601	41	M	4	8vo	L	10	35
602	41	M	8	8vo	L	×	×
603	41	M	2	8vo	L	×	×
604	41	M	4+1	8vo	L	×	8
605	41	M	4	8vo	WB	×	×
606	41	M	1	8vo	L	37	×
607	8	M	4	8vo & ?	L & W	25 & ×	×
608	59	M★	2	24mo	L	×	×
609	32	M	5	8vo	L	×	?8
610	50	M★	3	8vo			
611	45	M	3	8vo	W	×	?11
612	47	M	2	8vo	L	×	6
613	22	M	1	?16mo	L	×	9
614	65	PC	0	0	0	0	0
615	51	M★	2	8vo	L	×	×
616	63	PC	0	0	0	0	0

(i)	(ii)	(iii)	(iv)	(v)	(vi)	(vii)	(viii)
617	41*d*	TC	0	0	0	0	0
618	50	M★	4	8vo			
619	32	M	3	8vo	W	×	42*a*
620	48	M★	4	?8vo	L	×	32
621	53	M★	1	8vo	L	×	×
622	22	M	5	8vo	L	×	9
623	21	M	4	8vo	L	?47	7
624	64	PC	0	0	0	0	0
625	50	M★	4	?12mo			
626	59	M★	4	8vo	L	×	×
627	29	M★	3	8vo	L	×	41
628	41	M	1	8vo	?L	×	×
629	5	M	3	8vo	L	27	×
630	57	M	8	8vo	L	×	8
631	55	M★	1	8vo	L	×	×
632	55	M★	3+1	8vo	L	×	×
633	64	PC	0	0	0	0	0
634	43	M	1	8vo	L	×	8
635	53	M★	4	?16mo	L	×	×
636	41*c*	TC	0	0	0	0	0
637	41*c*	TC	0	0	0	0	0
638	53 & 59	M★	4 & 3	8vo	L	5 & 12	5 & ×
639	29	M★	1	8vo	L	75	17
640	33	M	2	8vo	L	53	6
641	50	M★	1	?24mo			
642	64	PC	0	0	0	0	0
643	64	PC	0	0	0	0	0
644	64	PC	0	0	0	0	0

Appendix A

Additional Letters

(i)	(ii)	(iii)	(iv)	(v)	(vi)	(vii)	(viii)
645	29	M★	2	8vo	L	×	?14
646	41*d*	TC	0	0	0	0	0
647	41*d*	TC	0	0	0	0	0
648	72	PC	0	0	0	0	0
649	8*a*	TC	0	0	0	0	0
650	8*a*	T & MC	0	0	0	0	0
651	8*a*	T & MC	0	0	0	0	0
15 [*cont.*]	8*a*	T & MC	0	0	0	0	0
16*a*	8*a*	T & MC	0	0	0	0	0
17*a*	8*a*	T & MC	0	0	0	0	0
39*a*	8*a*	T & MC					
45*a*	33	M	4	4to	L	50*a*	×
72+	8*a*	T & MC	0	0	0	0	0
74*a*	8*a*	TC	0	0	0	0	0
91*a*	8*a*	T & MC	0	0	0	0	0
91*b*	8*a*	T & MC	0	0	0	0	0
96*a*	8*a*	T & MC	0	0	0	0	0
97+	8*a*	T & MC	0	0	0	0	0

(i)	(ii)	(iii)	(iv)	(v)	(vi)	(vii)	(viii)
97*b*	8*a*	T & MC	o	o	o	o	o
97*c*	36	M★	3	8vo			?6
100*a*	8*a*	T & MC	o	o	o	o	o
101*a*	8*a*	T & MC	o	o	o	o	o
102*a*	8*a*	T & MC	o	o	o	o	o
108*b*	8*a*	T & MC	o	o	o	o	o
114*a*	8*a*	T & MC	o	o	o	o	o
116*a*	8*a*	T & MC	o	o	o	o	o
118*a*	8*a*	T & MC	o	o	o	o	o
122*a*	8*a*	TC	o	o	o	o	o
130*a*	8*a*	TC	o	o	o	o	o
134*a*	8*a*	T & MC	o	o	o	o	o
144*a*	8*a*	T & MC	o	o	o	o	o
144*b*	8*a*	T & MC	o	o	o	o	o
147*a*	8*a*	T & MC	o	o	o	o	o
147*b*	8*a*	T & MC	o	o	o	o	o
156*a*	8*a*	TC	o	o	o	o	o
198*a*	8*a*	TC	o	o	o	o	o
198*b*	8*a*	T & MC	o	o	o	o	o
205+	8*a*	TC	o	o	o	o	o
209*a*	8*a*	TC	o	o	o	o	o
242*a*	8*a*	TC	o	o	o	o	o
259*a*	8*a*	TC	o	o	o	o	o
264*a*	8*a*	TC	o	o	o	o	o
264*b*	8*a*	TC	o	o	o	o	o
267	8*a*	TC	o	o	o	o	o
267*a*	8*a*	TC	o	o	o	o	o
268*a*	8*a*	TC	o	o	o	o	o
270*a*	8*a*	TC	o	o	o	o	o
271*a*	8*a*	TC	o	o	o	o	o
275+	8*a*	TC	o	o	o	o	o
275*a*	8*a*	TC	o	o	o	o	o
276*a*	8*a*	TC	o	o	o	o	o
276*b*	8*a*	TC	o	o	o	o	o
280*a*	8*a*	TC	o	o	o	o	o
285*a*	41*d*	TC	o	o	o	o	o
286*a*	8*a*	T & MC	o	o	o	o	o
294*a*	8*a*	TC	o	o	o	o	o
297*a*	8*a*	TC	o	o	o	9	o
310*a*	8*a*	TC	o	o	o	o	o
314*a*	8*a*	TC	o	o	o	o	o
322*a*	8*a*	TC	o	o	o	o	o
322*b*	8*a*	TC	o	o	o	o	o
326*a*	8*a*	TC	o	o	o	o	o
353*a*	8*a*	TC	o	o	o	o	o
360*a*	8*a*	TC	o	o	o	o	o
362*a*	8*a*	TC	o	o	o	o	o
376*a*	8*a*	T & MC	o	o	o	o	?6
381*a*	8*a*	TC	o	o	o	o	o
385*a*	8*a*	TC	o	o	o	o	o
404*a*	8*a*	T & MC	o	o	o	o	o
421*a*	8*a*	TC	o	o	o	o	o
432+	4*a*	M	3	?8vo	L	×	×

(i)	(ii)	(iii)	(iv)	(v)	(vi)	(vii)	(viii)
439c	41d	TC	o	o	o	o	o
443a	8a	T & MC	o	o	o	o	o
444a	8a	T & MC	o	o	o	o	o
444b	23	M★	4	?8vo	L	×	×
446+	23	M★	7	8vo	L	×	×
447a	8a	T & MC	o	o	o	o	o
447b	8a	TC	o	o	o	o	o
451+	23	M★	3	16mo	L	×	×
451++	23	M★	6	8vo	L	?37	×
465a	8a	T & MC	o	o	o	o	o
472+	8a	TC	o	o	o	o	o
475a	8a	TC	o	o	o	o	o
475b	8a	TC	o	o	o	o	o
475c	8a	T & MC	o	o	o	o	o
476a	8a	TC	o	o	o	o	o
484a	8a	TC	o	o	o	o	o
484b	8a	T & MC	o	o	o	o	o
499a	8a	TC	o	o	o	o	o
500a	8a	T & MC	o	o	o	o	o
506a	8a	TC	o	o	o	o	o
509	8a	T & MC	o	o	o	o	o
509b	48	M★	16	?12mo			
511a	8a	TC	o	o	o	o	o
519a	58a	MC	o	o	o	o	o
521a	41d	TC	o	o	o	o	o
523a	8a	T & MC	o	o	o	o	o
541a	41d	TC	o	o	o	o	o
550a	8a	T & MC	o	o	o	o	o
575a	8a	T & MC	o	o	o	o	o
581a	57	M	2	8vo	L	35	×
582a	8a	T & MC	o	o	o	o	o
582b	8a	T & MC	o	o	o	o	o
636a	8a	T & MC	o	o	o	o	o

APPENDIX F

Miscellaneous

Receipts for copyrights, etc.

Receipts in the possession of the Pierpont Morgan Library:

1	11 December 1848	£100	'copyright' of *Mary Barton*
2	14 January 1851	£50	'manuscript' of *The Moorland Cottage* [see p. 142, n. 1 above]
3	24 January 1853	£500	'copyright' of *Ruth*

[An associated 'memorandum of an agreement' is dated 23 August 1852]

4	18 June 1853	£100	'fifteen hundred copies' of *Cranford*
5	17 April 1855	£250	'First Edition' of *North and South* 'in two vols post 8vo'
6	26 February 1856	£71.17.6	'Royalty on 3250 copies of Cranford and 2500 copies of "LL and Other Tales"'

[Two associated memoranda, one a condensed version of the other, of an agreement for publication in a cheap form (at two shillings) of *Cranford* and 'a volume of selected Tales'. Chapman and Hall were to pay a royalty of threepence on each copy sold for two years from the date of publication, the accounts to be made up at Midsummer and Christmas. They further undertook to print some of the tales such as *Libbie Marsh* in a separate form 'and give Mr Gaskell one half of whatever profit may arise'. 8 May 1855.]

Receipts in the possession of Mrs E. M. Gordon:

1	31 December 1862	£1,000	'entire copyright' of *Sylvia's Lovers*
2	6 March 1863	£50	'entire copyright' of *Cranford* [see p. 719, n. 1 above]
3	6 March 1863	£200	'entire copyright' of *A Night's Work*
4	24 September 1863	£50	'copyright' of *Lizzie Leigh and Other Tales* [see p. 719, n. 1 above]
5	4 November 1863	£250	'entire copyright' of *The Grey Woman, Curious if True, Six Weeks at Heppenheim* and *Cousin Phillis*
6	19 May 1865	£100	'copyright' of *North and South*

Night Fancies

(Poem in the collection of Mrs Trevor Jones. It is annotated by an unknown hand: 'I think this is by Elzth Cleghorn Stevenson', i.e. Mrs Wm Gaskell.)

> The ever rushing winds
> Chasing each other o'er the trembling earth
> (Like children at their games
> Wild hurrying in their mirth)

The winds come hastening by
  Shaking my desolate room
And bring with them strange sounds
  Dead voices from the tomb.

They call me by a name,
In the deep and still midnight,
The name I heard in childhood
When heart and hope were bright.

Those voices often shouted
  In the fields behind our home,—
And to our mother murmured low,
  When the hour of prayer {had} was come.

And the name they utter now
With a clear, unearthly tone
Hath passed away,—'tis heard no more
From me, with the dead 'tis gone.—

My Mother spoke it fondly
  To the child upon her knee,
My Father in a solemn tone
  Named it, when blessing me.

And in my dreams I hear it
  In a gentle loving voice
That like a gleam of sunshine
  Once made my heart rejoice.

The voice of her I loved
  When first I loved the flowers
Whom I loved through the shine & shade
  Of many anxious hours—

With whom the blessed words
  In the old old Church were spoken
And we were bound by a tie more strong
  Than the awful grave has broken

She comes with a look of gentleness
  In the quiet hours of sleep
And I know she loves me still
  Yet I cannot choose but weep

When I hear my childhood's name again
  'Twill be the greeting of the Blest
Welcoming the lonely one
  To their Eternal Rest

                          E G.

Precepts for the guidance of a Daughter
(in the collection of Mrs Trevor Jones)

1: Remember Evelyn was *not* the first Norman King of England.
2: Wash your hands.
3: *When* you have washed them, hold a book in them.
4: Diminish your calves.
5: Pluck your arms.
6: Don't have the same thing said of you that was said of Master Philip.
7: Get up early, but not *too* early.
8: Talk German so fast that no one can ascertain whether you speak grammatically or no.
9: Don't gobble; it turns maidens and turkey-cocks purple.
10: Remember John Still.
11: Don't talk like Scott & Adsheads' about young men's dress.
12: Forget ties and studs for one *little* week.
13: Don't swear.
14: Assume the power of reading, if you have it not.
15: Hold your book right way up. N.B. you may know which is the right way by examining at what end of a page the numbers occur. Where the numbers are that is the top; to be held *away* from you.
16: Not to make a sequence.
17: Not to leave your room like a hay-field, of which the grass *is* gowns & brushes.
18: Not to take pocket-handkerchiefs for articles of virtue.

    Altogether to conduct herself as becomes the daughter of E. C. Gaskell & sister of M. E. Gaskell.[1]

Fragment

(The following fragment from the Yale University MSS. is, we think, in Meta Gaskell's hand and may be of her own composition. On the other hand, it could have been written from her mother's dictation.)

⟨. . .⟩ and I think that about half is occupied by Ld and Ly Amhurst. She was the daughter of the last Duke (but one) of Dorset. When her brother died, she & her sister succeeded to the estates; but not to the title, wch is extinct. Ly Amhurst has Knole for her lifetime, & her sister, Ly Delaware, after her death. The last Duke, (their brother), while still quite a young man, was out hunting hares near Dublin one day, when in leaping a wall {he fel} his horse fell on him on the other side. He rose from under it, tried to seize the reins, staggered, & fell down dead. Ly A. looks as if she had never got over this shock; her face is very sad though very pleasant. The first room we went into was called the Brown Gallery: the floor, the frettings on the ceiling, & the furniture were all of dark old oak, wch gives\it/its name, I suppose. All along one side there are casement windows painted with armorial bearings, & all along the other side there are portraits. The whole effect of the room was oppressively gloomy &

---

[1] This line is, of course, in Meta's hand.

dark—& there was a smell of dust &c—There were portraits of everybody one had ever heard of. Francis, duke of Guise, Montmorency, Queen Elizabeth, with such a ruff, & such a pinched, crabbed face, Henry 8th with a cap & feather & jolly face, Philip XVI, whoever he may be, who had a very beautiful but wild face, & who was painted in a grey, cold, colour, & many, many other people. There was Dudley of Leicester. I can't think however Queen Elizabeth fell in love with such an ugly man! He had a great red forehead, & pointed chin. There was another of Milton. The face struck me before I knew whose it was. It was rather Mr. Hallé-ish. The next room was 'Lady Betty Germaine's bed-room': the next was her dressing-room, in wch there hung a portrait of her by Sir Joshua. She was in a sort of white dress, (like a shift) sitting by the sea, with her arm over a lyre. In one of the next rooms there was a picture of a Lady—a Miss Stewart. Charles II had her likeness,\in the character of Minerva,/put on the reverse of a coin bearing his own face:—And it is this figure, now called Brittania, that we have on our pennies &c. There was a picture in the same room of Abraham entertaining the angels. It was so queer:—they were having dinner off a table and out of things very much like ours, & Abraham seemed so unconscious of their being angels, though he was brushing up against one of their wings. In one room there was\a/picture of a middle-aged officer (I thought) in uniform & short hair; but to my surprise I found out that it was one of the Empresses of Russia, in the dress she wore when she rode out to review her soldiers. In one room there was a little recess occupied seemingly by a very pretty cottage-girl, in a red stuff dress & apron, spinning: when you came closer you saw all at once that it was a\flat/figure cut out of something & then painted. ⟨. . .⟩

Letter concerning Mrs Gaskell's death

(The following letter is taken from a copy in Princeton University Library. Its account of Mrs Gaskell's death is not, we think, generally known. (Cf. Hopkins, *Gaskell*, p. 319, and *Letters and Memorials*, ed. Winkworth, II, pp. 428–9.) The cuts were made by the copyist.)

E. T. HOLLAND to C. E. NORTON

6 Old Sqre. Lincoln's Inn
18 Novr 1865

My dear Norton,

I have to break my silence to you by sad news which will call out all your sympathies and regrets, for I know that you held Mrs Gaskell one of your dearest friends & loved her as she did you. The mail will carry out to you in the newspapers the announcement of her death but I must not let it go without also carrying to so dear a friend of hers a letter to tell you of that sad event a little more fully and to let you know how her family bear her loss: & I am writing for them at Minnie's request.

She died at the little village of Holybourne near Alton in Hampshire on Sunday afternoon last the 12th inst & her death was terribly sudden & quite un-expected. She was sitting in the drawing room after an early tea about a quarter to six in the afternoon with all her daughters but Minnie round her and was telling them and Charley Crompton of a conversation which she had not long before with Mr Justice Crompton who died 12 days ago when suddenly she fell forward and died at once in a moment without any pain or any struggle: until a medical man came the poor girls half thought that she was merely in a fainting fit, so that the shock was not quite so great to them as it might have been, but of course it was a most terrible shock. Mr Gaskell & Minnie were at Manchester & C. Crompton went there to bring them down on Monday whilst I went down to the poor girls at Holybourne: the Doctor gave disease of heart as the cause of death. She had always wished & often spoken of her wish to die a sudden painless death like this and we all believe that her end was particularly happy. Up to the very last moment she was feeling as well as could be, as she had said over and over again in the last few days before her death she felt better than she had done for years, & years younger than she had been doing a few weeks before, & she was more than ordinarily happy & full of spirits for she had just realised a plan of which for the last year she had been full, wh. was to buy a house in the country out of her own money and hand it over as a present to Mr Gaskell, and it was in this her own house that she died. She had been there for the previous fortnight busily engaged in arranging the furniture & planning how she could best please him & she had just got everything into order and readiness & was rejoicing in the carrying out of her wish when she was suddenly taken away. Her end was peaceful and happy and painless & came as she had wished it to come: & all this is a great comfort to those who loved her.

We buried her at the little town of Knutsford in Cheshire yesterday afternoon, whither I had taken her coffin on Thursday. Knutsford I do not doubt you know is her 'Cranford'. Was it not fit that she should be buried there? Mr Gaskell and the girls are all bearing their loss well. He is calm and peaceful and quite gently resigned to God's Will. Minnie has behaved like her own noble self. Meta too, tho' overwhelmed at first, is bearing her loss very well indeed & has regained her calmness & has not broken down physically as much as might have been expected. Florence and Julia too are bearing up as well as could be expected. Poor girls it is a heavy blow to all of them. They all went home on Thursday to Manchester.

⟨. . .⟩ I feel her loss very deeply for all who knew her well must have loved that kind sympathetic heart which shared every one's joys or griefs, that fresh intellect, that powerful imagination, that kindly interest that she took in every one about her.

⟨. . .⟩ I have been obliged to write hurriedly—⟨. . .⟩

Yours most truly
E. Thurstan Holland

INDEXES

References have been classified as follows:

   I. Select Family Index
      For Mrs Gaskell, her husband and children—arranged in mainly chrono-
      logical order, but not containing references to literature or to other people.

   II. Literary Index
      Containing references to Mrs Gaskell's writings and to other literary
      works mentioned in the letters.

   III. General Biographical Index
      Contains all but the very minimal references.

Reference is by the number of the letter given in Arabic numerals (and not of page,
except for those to the Introduction which are indicated by lower-case Roman
numerals). If a letter is not found in the main sequence, the reader should consult
Appendix A. In general, a number out of sequence at the end of a list will mean
that the letter referred to is in this appendix.

References in heavy type indicate that letters so numbered are addressed to the
person under whose name they are indexed.

In the General Biographical Index brief details and dates are given wherever
possible. In some cases it has not been possible to determine whether more than
one person or family is referred to in different places. Entries for persons referred
to at any length are subdivided under a series of headings for each person. Lists
of numbers occurring after the last semi-colon in such entries indicate miscellaneous
unclassified references.

The following abbreviations are employed: G—Mrs Gaskell; WG—William
Gaskell; MA—Marianne Gaskell; ME—Meta Gaskell; FE—Florence Gaskell;
JB—Julia B. Gaskell; M/c—Manchester; *LCB—Life of Charlotte Brontë*; *MB*—
Mary Barton.

I. SELECT FAMILY INDEX

GASKELL, ELIZABETH CLEGHORN (1810–65)—School 97+.
   1832—Courtship 1; marriage xiv, 2.
   1836—Sandlebridge 4; working on poets 4.
   1838—Bazaar 7; and WG 13; Cheshire countryside 8; Seedley, Pendleton, M/c
      (Bradfords') 14.
   1841—Heidelberg 15.
   1843—Daily regime 16a.
   1847—London (Howitts') 18; Crix 19; Bollington 21.
   1848—Southport 27; Plas Penrhyn 28, 29; political views 29.
   1849—London 44, 44a, 45, 45a, 47; Stratford 48; Lake District 49; Sewing 'Bee'
      49; search for new house 55, 60.
   1850—New house at Plymouth Grove 69, 70, 101; work for prisoners 55, 61, 62;
      Christian Socialism 67; death of 3 young cousins 63, 64; picture for Wright
      (q.v.) 63, 65, 70; children's nursery 83; Silverdale 72a; Briery Close, Win-
      dermere (Kay Shuttleworths') 75–8; Poulton 81; Warwick, after illness 83;
      Boughton (Whitmore Isaacs') 86; London 87; offer to visit C. Brontë 86.

*Indicates letters addressed jointly to Marianne and Meta Gaskell.

1863—On G & the Cromptons 524; engagement 526; marriage 526, 532, 535*a* (and 546, 551, 560); Italy with G (q.v.); visits to G 546, 553, 557, 558.

1865—Health & position 558; trouble with servants 572; Switzerland & Italy 583. Letter to: **201**.

GASKELL, WILLIAM ('Willie') (1844–5)—25*a*, 70, 16*a*.

GASKELL, JULIA BRADFORD (1846–1908)—xiv, xv.

1850—At Plymouth Grove 70.

1851—Described 101; birthday 101*a*; first letter to MA 107; ill 109.

1852—Birthday party 131; ill 130*a*.

1853—Behaviour 147*b*.

1854—Birthday party 208.

1855—Possible visit to Crix 242*a*.

1856—London with G 284; difficulties with FE 292.

1857—Lake District with FE 354.

1858—Ill 404*a*.

1859—Worcestershire 385*a*; growing up 414, 418, 421; school 421, 494*a*; delight at George Smith's present 442; Whitby with G 444, 446, 447, 447*a*; jealousy 448.

1860—Heidelberg with G (q.v.) & FE 473.

1861—Growing up 485; love of Silverdale 488, 490.

1863—Italy with G 524, 523*a*; London (FE) 546.

1864—Leaves school 551; character & attitude 551, 560.

1865—London 570; ill 576, 580, 575*a*; Dieppe with G & ME 585, 586. Letters to: **194, 199, 203, 208**.

II. LITERARY INDEX

(a) MRS GASKELL

Views on various literary topics (see asterisked items in Select Family Index above under 'Gaskell, Elizabeth Cleghorn, *Comments*' etc.)

'Bessy's Troubles at Home' 112n, 260, 114*a*

Cousin Phillis 505n, 532, 545, 553, 557, Appx. F

Cranford xx; for *Household Words* 110; G's purpose and delight in 562; cheap edition 235; copyright troubles 382, 486, 540, 550; receipts 305, 539n, Appx. F copy to Williams & Norgate 179; Cranfordism 195

'Crooked Branch, The' (see 'Ghost in the Garden Room, The')

'Curious if True' 451*a* n, Appx. F

'Dark Night's Work, A' 451*a* n. 4, 517, 518, 524, Appx. F

'Disappearances' 418

'Doom of the Griffiths, The' 384n, 403

'French Life' 532

'Ghost in the Garden Room, The' 442, 452

'Grey Woman, The' Appx. F

Hale, Margaret and Hale, Mr (see *North and South*)

'Hand and Heart' 260

Haytersbank (see *Sylvia's Lovers*)

Legh, Job (see *Mary Barton*)

'Libbie Marsh's Three Eras' 74, 80, 108, 235, 260, 122*a*

(b) Other Literary References

III. General Biographical Index